America's Experiment
with
Capital Punishment

America's Experiment
with
Capital Punishment

*Reflections on the Past, Present, and Future
of the Ultimate Penal Sanction*

Second Edition

EDITED BY
**James R. Acker
Robert M. Bohm
Charles S. Lanier**

CAROLINA ACADEMIC PRESS
Durham, North Carolina

ISBN 0-89089-064-1
LCCN 2003106095

CAROLINA ACADEMIC PRESS
700 Kent Street
Durham, North Carolina 27701
Telephone (919) 489-7486
Fax (919) 493-5668
www.cap-press.com

Dedications

To my parents, Roy and Dell, and to Jenny, Elizabeth, and Anna.

—JRA

To my brothers and sisters, Rick, Lori, Lorie, and Will.

—RMB

To Adriana, our son Trevor Charles, his grandmother, Dorothy, and his grandfather, Henry.

—CSL

And, to our students—past, present, and future—whose death-penalty opinions, whatever they may be, might be informed ones.

In Memoriam

Henry Schwarzschild passed away on June 1, 1996. Henry was a spokesperson extraordinaire on capital punishment issues. The strength of Henry's convictions, and the inspiring and inimitable way in which he expressed them, were universally respected and admired, regardless of listeners' viewpoints or ideology. We miss him sorely.

Contents

Acknowledgments

First and foremost, we wish to express our gratitude to the individuals who contributed chapters to this book. The role of editor is not supposed to be so trouble free, let alone so exhilarating. Now, more than ever, we are convinced that it is a special and dedicated group of people whose scholarship and life works focus on the death penalty. It has been a unique learning experience and a real pleasure to work with the authors of the chapters that appear in the following pages, and we thank them all for the experience and their work products. Specific thanks go to Bill Bowers for coming up with the title for this volume, *America's Experiment with Capital Punishment*, and for encouraging us to go forward with the book when we began to have doubts that we could make a go of it. Jo Anne DeSilva spent countless hours on word processing, photocopying, mailings, and other thankless tasks for which we now do extend our thanks.

Part I

Introduction

Introduction

America's Experiment with Capital Punishment

James R. Acker
Robert M. Bohm
Charles S. Lanier

Capital punishment has been a part of American culture since long before the United States was founded. Nearly four centuries have passed, and more than 19,000 people have been executed by lawful authority in the territorial U.S. since the earliest confirmed death sentence was carried out in 1608, in colonial Virginia (Bohm 1999:2; Coyne and Entzeroth 2001:5). Debate about the death penalty—including its morality, effectiveness, and legality—has been as persistent as the punishment itself (Banner 2002; Mackey 1976; Masur 1989). The most recent generation of Americans has witnessed a tumultuous sequence of events—both social and legal—that has significantly transformed the landscape of capital punishment in this country. Much has ensued even in the five years since the publication of the first edition of this book.

Among the most dramatic recent developments was Illinois Governor George Ryan's decision in January 2000 to impose a statewide moratorium on executions. Three years later, immediately before leaving office, with his doubts about capital punishment having grown even stronger, Ryan pardoned four condemned convicts and commuted to life imprisonment without parole the death sentences of the remaining 167 who were awaiting state execution. The moratorium decision was prompted most immediately by the exoneration of 13 individuals in little over a decade who had been wrongly convicted of capital murder in Illinois courts and sentenced to death (*Report of the Governor's Commission on Capital Punishment* 2002:4). One among that group, Anthony Porter, came within two days of his scheduled execution and was cleared only after journalism students managed to secure the real murderer's confession (at 1). When he later issued his blanket commutation of the men and women on Illinois' death row, Ryan declared, "Our capital system is haunted by the demon of error, error in determining guilt, and error in determining who among the guilty deserves to die."

If the system was making so many errors in determining whether someone was guilty in the first place, how fairly and accurately was

3

it determining which guilty defendants deserved to live and which deserved to die? What effect was race having? What effect was poverty having?

And in almost every one of the exonerated 17, we not only have breakdowns in the system with police, prosecutors and judges, we have terrible cases of shabby defense lawyers....

...Because our three year study has found only more questions about the fairness of the sentencing; because of the spectacular failure to reform the system; because we have seen justice delayed for countless death row inmates with potentially meritorious claims; because the Illinois death penalty system is arbitrary and capricious—and therefore immoral—I no longer shall tinker with the machinery of death (Death Penalty Information Center 2003).

The Illinois moratorium of 2000 was followed by another in May 2002, when Governor Parris Glendening ordered a halt to executions in Maryland pending completion of a study which, in January 2003, produced evidence of racial and geographical disparities in that state's death-penalty system (Baldus and Woodworth 2003; Lanier and Acker, forthcoming; Paternoster and Brame 2003). Notwithstanding that evidence, incoming Governor Robert Ehrlich Jr. lifted the moratorium, over the opposition of Maryland Attorney General J. Joseph Curran Jr., who called for outright abolition of the capital sanction (Liptak 2003). Meanwhile, the Nebraska Legislature voted in 1999 to stay executions throughout the state and commission a study of the death penalty's administration. Governor Mike Johanns' veto prevented the moratorium from taking effect, although the contemplated study subsequently was carried out (Baldus and Woodworth 2003; Kirchmeier 2002:43). New Hampshire lawmakers went farther still, and in 2000 passed a bill repealing the state's death penalty. Governor Jeanne Sheehan vetoed the measure, thus thwarting the abolition effort (Kirchmeier 2002:47). On the local level, scores of municipalities, including city councils in Atlanta, Baltimore, New York City, Philadelphia, and San Francisco, passed resolutions in the late 1990s and early 2000s advocating statewide execution moratoria (American Bar Association 2001:99; Kirchmeier 2002:46–47). Several states have commissioned studies of the operation of their death-penalty laws (Lanier and Acker, forthcoming), and substantial bipartisan support emerged in Congress during summer 2002 for the Innocence Protection Act (2002) (Justice Project 2002), a bill providing for DNA testing and establishing standards for court-appointed counsel in state capital cases.

The Supreme Court announced two major rulings in 2002 placing new constitutional constraints on capital-punishment laws. Those decisions were especially noteworthy because each overturned precedent of relatively recent vintage. In *Ring v. Arizona* (2002), the justices departed from *Walton v. Arizona* (1990) and announced that the Sixth Amendment requires juries to find all facts essential to a capital-punishment decision, including the aggravating circumstances on which a death sentence rests. This ruling calls into question hundreds of death sentences and the statutory procedures followed in the nine states that had placed capital-sentencing authority in the hands of judges (Acker and Lanier 2003). In *Atkins v. Virginia* (2002), the Court overruled *Penry v. Lynaugh* (1989) and held that executing mentally retarded offenders violates the Eighth Amendment (Streib 2003). Just four months after this decision, Justice Stevens, joined by Justices Breyer, Ginsburg, and Souter, dissented from the denial of a petition for writ of habeas corpus filed on behalf of an offender convicted of committing murder at age 17. They argued that the Court should consider the implications of *Atkins* for juvenile offenders (*In re Stanford* 2002; see also *Patterson v. Texas* 2002). Deadly sniper attacks concentrated in Maryland, Virginia, and Washington D.C. later led to the arrest of a 17-year old suspect, Lee Malvo, who along with an older companion is almost certain to face capital prosecution. Despite their initial expression of interest in reviewing the issue, the justices have since declined to intervene in cases involving juvenile offenders confronting execution (Greenhouse 2003).

Summer 2002 also saw a lower court boldly declare the federal death penalty unconstitutional. Judge Jed Rakoff of the United States District Court for the Southern District of New York ruled that the risk of erroneous convictions and executions was so grave that carrying out capital sentences under federal death-penalty law would violate due process (*United States v. Quinones* 2002). Although quickly overturned on appeal, this ruling reflects a remarkable degree of judicial skepticism about capital punishment that would have been almost unthinkable even a few years ago. A second federal district court decision, presently on appeal, invalidated the federal death penalty law on narrower grounds, citing procedural deficiencies involving the admission of evidence at the sentencing hearing (*United States v. Fell* 2002).

The documented commission of error in capital cases has played a major role in fueling distrust of the death-penalty process. In 2000, Professor James Liebman and colleagues reported the results of their study of the error rate in over 4,500 state capital cases decided between 1973 and 1995. Among their findings:

- "[T]he overall rate of prejudicial error in the American capital punishment system was 68%. In other words, courts found serious, reversible error in nearly 7 of every 10 of the thousands of capital sentences that were fully reviewed during the period" (Liebman *et al.* 2000a:i).
- "After state courts threw out 47% of death sentences due to serious flaws, a later federal review found 'serious error'—error undermining the reliability of the outcome—in 40% of the *remaining* sentences" (at i–ii).
- "High error rates put many individuals at the risk of wrongful execution: 82% of the people whose capital judgments were overturned by state post-conviction courts due to serious error were found to deserve a sentence

less than death when the errors were cured on retrial; *7% were found to be innocent of the capital crime*" (at ii).

- "High error rates exist across the country. Over 90% of American death-sentencing states have overall error rates of 52% or higher. 85% have error rates of 60% or higher. Three-fifths have error rates of 70% or higher" (at iii; *see also* Liebman *et al.* 2002; Liebman 2000; Liebman *et al.* 2000b).

As noted by Professor Liebman and his colleagues, the procedural errors confounding capital cases sometimes ensnare the innocent. More than 100 death-sentenced prisoners have been released from death rows around the country over the past 30 years based on doubts about their guilt (Death Penalty Information Center 2002). Although it is disputable whether all of those freed were factually innocent, DNA and other incontrovertible evidence has made it clear that innocent people have been convicted of capital murder and sentenced to death under modern death-penalty systems. Some have come perilously close to execution, if not executed (Radelet and Bedau 2003; Scheck *et al.* 2000; Westervelt and Humphrey 2001).

Even though public doubts about the death penalty appear to be intensifying (Bohm 2003), support for capital punishment remains generally robust (Acker 2002). Punishment by death has deep roots in this country, with a particular stronghold in the South (Banner 2002:112–143). In early 2003, capital-punishment laws remain in force in 38 states, in the federal jurisdiction, and in the United States Military. More than 3,700 Americans are under sentence of death. Executions have occurred at least on a weekly basis for the past several years and more than 800 have been carried out since 1977 (NAACP Legal Defense and Educational Fund, Inc. 2002:1, 9). Notwithstanding recent court decisions favorable to capital defendants, the Supreme Court regularly denies death-sentenced prisoners' claims and allows executions to go forward, narrowing potential future avenues for relief in the process (*e.g., Mickens v. Taylor* 2002; *Ramdass v. Angelone* 2000; *Sattazahn v. Pennsylvania* 2003; *Weeks v. Angelone* 2000; *Williams v. Taylor* 2000a, 2000b). These recent decisions are a part of the Court's three decades-long refinement of modern death-penalty doctrine.

The death penalty came to an abrupt but temporary halt in 1972, when the Supreme Court ruled that its arbitrary application violated the United States Constitution. Many states quickly enacted new death-penalty statutes designed to correct the identified constitutional deficiencies. Thirty years later, a host of fundamental questions involving law, social policy, and morality remain unanswered about America's renewed commitment to capital punishment. The chapters in this book critically evaluate this dramatic period of change in the death penalty and its administration. Collectively, they assess the history, the present status, and the likely future of capital punishment in this country.

Furman v. Georgia,[1] a landmark Supreme Court case under any definition of that term, was decided on June 29, 1972. The justices' nine separate opinions, which sprawl over more than 230 pages in the *United States Reports,* comprise a remarkable jurisprudential treatise on the death penalty that encompasses issues of law, history, government, penology, social science, and philosophy. The Court expressed its 5–4 holding in a brief, per curiam opinion. It simply announced that "the imposition and carrying out of the death penalty in these cases [one involving murder, and the other two involving rape] constitutes cruel and unusual punishment in violation of the Eighth and Fourteenth Amendments" (*Furman v. Georgia* 1972:239–240). The consequences of the Court's action were immediate and profound.

In *Furman's* aftermath, the death sentences of all 631 men and 2 women who inhabited the nation's death rows in 1972 were invalidated, and all state and federal death-penalty laws then on the books were scuttled (Meltsner 1973:292–293). A frenzy of legislative activity ensued to reinstitute capital punishment consistent with the justices' ambiguous ruling (Zimring and Hawkins 1986:38–45). *Furman* naturally inspired elation among the condemned and their lawyers, most notably in the offices of the NAACP Legal Defense and Education Fund (Legal Defense Fund), whose attorneys had orchestrated the legal assault on capital punishment (Meltsner 1973:290). On the other hand, Georgia's Lieutenant Governor, Lester Maddox, branded the *Furman* decision "[a] license for anarchy, rape [and] murder" (quoted in Meltsner at 290). Other politicians vowed that the Court would not have the last word on capital punishment, and some promoted a constitutional amendment to nullify its ruling (Zimring and Hawkins 1986:38).

The full ramifications of *Furman* were not immediately apparent. One Legal Defense Fund lawyer boldly predicted that "[t]here will no longer be any more capital punishment in the United States" (Meltsner 1973:291). Another contemporary observer ventured that "the capital-punishment story has ended for either the present or forever" (Wolfe 1973:415). Others speculated that legislatures were still at liberty to enact changes that would satisfy enough of the justices to allow the death penalty to survive future constitutional challenges (Note 1974; Polsby 1973). The latter forecasts, of course, proved to be accurate. The United States had not forever seen the end of capital punishment.

In retrospect, *Furman* marked the end of one era of the death penalty in America, and the dawning of a new one. The Court's decision wiped death-

---

1. *Furman* involved a murder conviction and death sentence from Georgia. It was joined for decision by the United States Supreme Court with two rape cases—one from Georgia (*Jackson v. Georgia*) and one from Texas (*Branch v. Texas*)—that also had resulted in death sentences. The justices had planned to review another capital sentence imposed in a murder case (*Aikens v. California*) when they agreed to decide *Furman* and its companion cases, but a California Supreme Court ruling based on state constitutional grounds vacated the offender's sentence of death before the Supreme Court had an opportunity to render a decision (Acker 1993:13, n. 44).

penalty laws from the statute books, temporarily closed the country's execution chambers, and redefined the constitutional parameters of capital punishment. It also occasioned a wholesale re-examination of the capital-punishment enterprise. Beginning in late 1972, state legislatures hurriedly passed replacement death-penalty statutes.

The justices first reviewed the new legislative handiwork just four years after *Furman* was decided. They approved capital-punishment laws from three states that varied considerably in their particulars, but shared certain important characteristics. For example, the new laws all provided for separate guilt and penalty hearings and thus allowed information relevant to a capital-sentencing decision to be introduced independently of the guilt trial, where it may have been prejudicial or irrelevant. The approved laws also incorporated specific criteria designed to narrow or channel sentencing discretion, and each authorized appellate review of death-penalty decisions (*Gregg v. Georgia* 1976; *Jurek v. Texas* 1976; *Proffitt v. Florida* 1976). At the same time, the Court rejected laws that automatically mandated the death penalty following conviction for a capital crime (*Roberts v. Louisiana* 1976; *Woodson v. North Carolina* 1976).

Furman's legacy embraces contemporary death-penalty laws. The predominant purpose of this book is to provide a critical examination of this legacy, and to ponder the continuing evolution of capital-punishment statutes and their implementation. *Furman* set the stage for a grisly natural experiment[2] involving capital punishment in this country, allowing the authors who have contributed to this book to reflect on death-penalty practices of a different day, to assess the present status of capital punishment, and to speculate about what the future holds for the death penalty in the United States.

Just months before his retirement from 24 years of service on the Supreme Court, Justice Harry Blackmun engaged in an analogous exercise in a remarkable dissenting opinion in *Callins v. Collins* (1994), an otherwise obscure death-penalty case from Texas that the Court had declined to review on certiorari. In this opinion, Justice Blackmun voiced a sober assessment of the nation's death-penalty practices. He announced his belief that "the death penalty, as currently administered, is unconstitutional" (*Callins v. Collins* 1994:1159), and declared that he would thereafter "no longer tinker with the machinery of death" (at 1145).

Those sentiments were all the more remarkable because Blackmun had voted in *Furman* against invalidating death-penalty laws (*Furman v. Georgia*

---

2. We do not mean to imply the use of scientific procedures or the controlled manipulation of variables. Rather, we use the term "experiment" in recognition of the fact that the nation's death-penalty laws irretrievably were altered in *Furman's* aftermath, and the American people and their elected officials were forced to consider anew whether and in what specific form replacement legislation should be enacted. The significance of *Furman's* intervention can be examined by assessing the changes in death-penalty laws and practice that followed the Court's decision.

1972:405–414); had joined with the Court in 1976 to uphold "guided-discretion" capital-sentencing statutes, including the same Texas law under which Callins had been sentenced to death (*Jurek v. Texas* 1976); and even had dissented from the Court's conclusion in 1976 that mandatory death-penalty laws are unconstitutional (*Roberts v. Louisiana* 1976; *Woodson v. North Carolina* 1976). Yet, in 1994, Justice Blackmun confessed:

> For more than 20 years I have endeavored—indeed, I have struggled—along with a majority of this Court, to develop procedural and substantive rules that would lend more than the mere appearance of fairness to the death penalty endeavor. Rather than continue to coddle the Court's delusion that the desired level of fairness has been achieved and the need for regulation eviscerated, *I feel morally and intellectually obligated simply to concede that the death penalty experiment has failed.* It is virtually self-evident to me now that no combination of procedural rules or substantive regulations ever can save the death penalty from its inherent constitutional deficiencies. The basic question—does the system accurately and consistently determine which defendants "deserve" to die?—cannot be answered in the affirmative.... The problem is that the inevitability of factual, legal, and moral error gives us a system that fails to deliver the fair, consistent, and reliable sentences of death required by the Constitution (*Callins v. Collins* 1994:1145, emphasis added).

In the ensuing chapters of this book, Justice Blackmun's premise that America's post-*Furman* "death penalty experiment has failed" is explored from a cross-section of disciplines, including law, psychology, sociology, philosophy, and criminal justice. The selections analyze issues vitally important to capital punishment, and offer intriguingly different perspectives on the past, present, and future of this country's ultimate penal sanction. In the process, they scrutinize the legal, philosophical, and empirical foundations of the American institution of capital punishment.

The first five chapters of this book deal with public opinion, law, politics, and capital punishment.

Robert M. Bohm surveys "American Death Penalty Opinion: Past, Present, and Future" in Chapter One. He opens with an historical overview of attempts to gauge death-penalty opinion in America—which began in 1936 when the first scientific poll on capital punishment was conducted—and then explores contemporary death-penalty opinion polling. Here, Bohm focuses on several empirical investigations designed to assess the "Marshall Hypotheses" (i.e., that the American public knows little about the death penalty and its administration and that an informed and knowledgeable populous would not support the death penalty), derived from Justice Thurgood Marshall's opinion in *Furman v. Georgia* (1972). Bohm concludes by speculating about death-penalty opinion in the future, and its possible effect on the practice of capital punishment in America.

Carol S. Steiker and Jordan M. Steiker next examine the last 30 years of "Judicial Developments in Capital Punishment Law," which were generated by the Court's decision in *Furman*. The Steikers begin by reviewing concerns about the administration of the death penalty that led up to the Court's three decades of "continuing constitutional regulation of capital punishment." They explain their assertion that the practical effect of the Court's complex jurisprudential regulation has been negligible. This jurisprudence is comprised of several tenets, including narrowing the class of death-eligible defendants, channeling sentencer discretion, individualized sentencing, and "death is different" (i.e., the need for heightened reliability in capital cases). The Steikers contend that "current death penalty law acts to legitimate capital punishment." They conclude with an assessment of likely future judicial developments in this area.

James R. Acker and Charles S. Lanier explore "Beyond Human Ability? The Rise and Fall of Death-Penalty Legislation" in Chapter Three. The authors begin by considering death-penalty legislation in effect when the Court decided *McGautha v. California* (1971), and essentially conceded the impossibility of statutes capable of guiding sentencers in capital cases. The justices' abrupt repudiation of the "impossibility" doctrine in *Furman* precipitated the contemporary "guided discretion" death-penalty laws. Acker and Lanier examine specific differences among contemporary death-penalty laws (e.g., definitions of capital murder, determinations of death-eligibility, the sentencing process, etc.), and conclude that "post-*Furman* statutory reforms have failed to eliminate significant problems in the administration of capital punishment." As such, they posit that current death-penalty statutes—which have not eliminated problems of race discrimination, erroneous convictions, and unequal justice—are destined to be the "beginning of the end of capital-punishment" in America.

Stephen B. Bright discusses the growing commitment to expediency at the expense of fairness in his chapter entitled "The Politics of Capital Punishment: The Sacrifice of Fairness for Executions." Bright begins with a look at the invidious role played by the death penalty in shaping elections and otherwise influencing the political process. He explains the impact on courts generated by the pressure politics of death, and ponders the ultimate effect of death-penalty cases on the "independence, integrity, and impartiality of the judiciary." Bright also raises the specter of denying legal representation and access to the courts as a strategy to speed executions, and concludes that a system committed to expediency produces convictions and sentences of death, rather than justice.

Richard Wilson's chapter on "The Influence of International Law and Practice on the Death Penalty in the United States" contributes an important perspective on legal developments outside of the United States and their potential influence on domestic capital-punishment law. He describes how a majority of countries in the world have abolished the death penalty in law or practice, thus relegating the United States to the company of odd national bedfellows—China, Iran, and Saudi Arabia—in being a world leader in carrying out executions. Wilson reviews relevant treaties and decisions of international courts and considers their implications for United States law as this country increasingly diverges from international human rights norms pertaining to capital punishment. He speculates that international law may be of particular relevance to constitutional developments in the United States regarding the execution of juvenile offenders.

Selections in the next section of the book examine a series of issues related to the justice and utility of the capital sanction. Chapters explore the philosophical and Biblical foundations of the death penalty, the morality of capital punishment, deterrence, future dangerousness, the execution of women, juvenile offenders, and the mentally retarded, and how the issue of innocence figures into the discourse of capital punishment.

In Chapter Six, Robert Blecker embarks on an impressive historical and philosophical review tracing the "Roots" of capital punishment, invoking Biblical admonitions, the ancient Greeks, and other sources. He weaves the recurring themes from this ambitious inquiry into a tapestry that encompasses contemporary death-penalty laws and practices. He argues that the death penalty is morally justified on retributive grounds for "the worst of the worst" murderers, and then critically examines the challenges confronted in attempting to limit the reach of the modern death penalty to those worst offenders and no others. He suggests that "[w]hether we end up limiting death appropriately or eliminating it entirely, seems far from settled," although he forcefully maintains that capital punishment in principle is defensible, if not compelled, for especially opprobrious killings.

Relinquishing empiricism and legal analysis for morality, Ernest van den Haag examines "Justice, Deterrence, and the Death Penalty" in Chapter Seven. Van den Haag considers both the moral and non-moral (i.e., instrumental) purposes of punishment, relying on the shockingly graphic description of a murder committed by a death-sentenced offender in Georgia to bolster his argument that society does, indeed, have a moral right to impose the death penalty. He is not convinced that the death penalty has a proven "brutalization" effect, nor is he persuaded that unequal application of the capital sanction undermines its legitimacy: "the moral quality of capital punishment is no more affected by its unfair distribution than an unfair distribution of cookies affects their quality." Although van den Haag allows that "if an innocent is executed the miscarriage of justice is irreparable," he nevertheless believes that abolishing the death penalty would be "unwise as well as immoral."

Ruth D. Peterson and William C. Bailey present a thorough review of deterrence studies in "Is Capital Punishment an Effective Deterrent for Murder? An Examination of Social Science Research." They first summarize deterrence theory and its application to the death penalty. They examine deterrence research by discussing various methodologies used (e.g., simple comparisons, aggregate studies, multivariate, and time-series analyses), jurisdictions investigated and/or compared (e.g., abolitionist, retentionist), and type of capital offense examined (e.g., first-degree murder, felony murder). They conclude that "most criminologists seem convinced that capital punishment is not a more effective deterrent for murder than imprisonment," and reflect on the future role of deterrence research in the debate about capital punishment.

Chapter Nine finds Jon Sorensen and James Marquart questioning the use of "Future Dangerousness and Incapacitation" as a goal in capital sentencing. Sorensen and Marquart discuss the importance of future dangerousness in the post-*Furman* era in terms of sentencing goals or purposes (i.e., retribution, deterrence, and incapacitation), and conclude that "it is unfair to sentence someone to death on the basis of a prediction about what they may do at some point in the future." They next address the futility of predicting future dangerousness by examining the three types of behavioral predictions (clinical, actuarial, and anamnestic), and their associated problems. They emphasize that jury deliberations in Oregon and Texas center "almost entirely on the issue of future dangerousness," resulting in a "process [that] becomes more mechanical than moral." To Sorensen and Marquart, such unwarranted focus results "in the same sort of standardless sentencing denounced by the Court in *Furman*."

Victor L. Streib next writes about the death penalty's application against special subgroups of the population in his chapter entitled "Executing Women, Children, and the Retarded: Second Class Citizens in Capital Punishment." Streib concentrates on the period of death sentencing beginning with *Furman* and continuing until the present. He begins his exposition with a discussion of death-sentencing rates for women; he concludes that "women are unlikely to be arrested for murder, extremely unlikely to be sentenced to death, and almost never executed." He next examines the historical background and legal context for executing both juveniles and the mentally retarded, focusing on *Thompson v. Oklahoma* (1988) and *Stanford v. Kentucky* (1989) [juveniles], and *Penry v. Lynaugh* (1989) and *Atkins v. Virginia* (2002) [the mentally retarded]. Streib concludes his chapter by comparing the three groups in terms of basic culpability for criminal punishment, evolving standards of decency, and the rationale for capital punishment.

Engaging in "The Execution of the Innocent" is the topic of Chapter Eleven, written by Michael L. Radelet and Hugo Adam Bedau. The authors, who are renowned for their seminal study identifying "Miscarriages of Justice in Potentially Capital Cases" (Bedau and Radelet 1987), present their work in three stages. They first define the term "innocence," which is construed narrowly and conservatively, and note how it legitimately could be expanded to become more inclusive. Next, they review research utilized in previous studies to identify innocent persons who were convicted and, in some cases, sentenced to die and even executed. The authors point out that even defenders of capital punishment "now concede the inevitability of executing the innocent," and conclude their chapter by exploring the importance of this reality for appellate courts, clemency boards, legislatures, and the general public.

The next seven chapters focus on the administration of the death penalty in the United States. They confront issues of legal representation, capital juries, mitigation, race discrimination, federal habeas corpus, and the financial costs of capital punishment.

Michael Mello and Paul Perkins offer a pessimistic assessment of the likelihood that competent and effective defense counsel regularly will represent the accused in capital cases in "Closing the Circle: The Illusion of Lawyers for People Litigating for Their Lives at the *Fin de Siècle*." The authors reflect on the lengthy saga of the right to effective, court-appointed counsel, reviewing cases from *Powell v. Alabama* (1932) through *Gideon v. Wainwright* (1963). Mello and Perkins also discuss legal representation in capital habeas corpus—a procedural vehicle through which state prisoners can challenge legal errors in federal courts—noting there is no constitutional right to counsel in this process. After questioning the adequacy of the Court's standard for judging the effectiveness of capital counsel (*Strickland v. Washington* 1984), the authors discuss provisions of the *Anti-Drug Abuse Act of 1988* (1997) (*see also McFarland v. Scott* 1994) and the *Antiterrorism and Effective Death Penalty Act of 1996* (1997) (AEDPA). Through the former legislation, Congress provided a right to counsel in federal capital habeas cases. In the AEDPA, federal lawmakers set requirements for the appointment of counsel in state capital post-conviction proceedings that states must satisfy to benefit from that Act's other procedural provisions. In conclusion, the authors caution that the Court will "recognize a formalistic 'right to counsel,' but allow the states to administer that 'right' however they like, with virtually no federal judicial oversight of how meaningful the 'right' is in the real world, day-to-day reality of capital post-conviction litigation."

Marla Sandys and Scott McClelland write about "Stacking the Deck for Guilt and Death: The Failure of Death Qualification to Ensure Impartiality" in the next chapter. Sandys and McClelland initiate their essay by noting that capital juries are unique because they make life and death sentencing decisions as well as decisions involving guilt and innocence. They next explore "death qualification," and the evolving standard for disqualifying potential capital jurors as set by Supreme Court mandate (i.e., pre-*Witherspoon*; *Witherspoon v. Illinois* 1968; and *Wainwright v. Witt* 1985). Sandys and McClelland continue their essay by revisiting "conviction-proneness" studies (i.e., social science research suggesting that death-qualified juries are more likely than nondeath-qualified juries to find accused offenders guilty). They focus on the courts' reception of such studies in two cases: *Hovey v. Superior Court of Alameda County* (1980) and *Lockhart v. McCree* (1986). They also examine "life qualifying" (i.e., "reverse-*Witherspooning*") prospective jurors as addressed by the Court in *Morgan v. Illinois* (1992) and discuss findings from the Capital Jury Project regarding how capital jurors consider and act on mitigation evidence, as well as the legal implications of those findings. In closing, Sandys and McClelland summarize research conclusions suggesting that: "death-qualified jurors, regardless of the standard, are more conviction-prone, less concerned with due process, and they are more inclined to believe the prosecution than are excludable jurors."

In a second chapter on capital juries, William J. Bowers, Benjamin D. Fleury-Steiner, and Michael E. Antonio illuminate the decision-making process of jurors in "The Capital Sentencing Decision: Guided Discretion, Reasoned Moral Judgment, or Legal Fiction?" Bowers, Fleury-Steiner, and Antonio begin by reviewing theoretical and social science research on the decision-making process of jurors. The authors next delve into the world of capital jurors by examining research dealing with the influence of statutory guidelines and jurors' understanding of sentencing instructions. Bowers, Fleury-Steiner, and Antonio then detail some of the findings of the ongoing national Capital Jury Project, and introduce some accounts ("in their own words") of sentencing decisions offered by actual jurors in capital cases. The authors' presentation suggests that juries' capital-sentencing judgments are largely unregulated by legal standards, and thus remain arbitrary and capricious—or undeniably similar to the sentencing practices the justices found unconstitutional in *Furman v. Georgia* in 1972.

In Chapter Fifteen, Craig Haney addresses "Mitigation and the Study of Lives: The Roots of Criminality and the Nature of Capital Juries." Haney begins by noting two aspects that make mitigation evidence "elusive" at sentencing— the miseducation of American jurors via media reports, and incomprehensible jury instructions. The way to overcome these failings, according to Haney, is through a "painstakingly researched, thoughtfully assembled, and carefully and comprehensively presented chronicle" of a capital defendant's life. Haney thus summarizes literature on multiple risk factors—poverty, childhood abandonment and neglect, child abuse and maltreatment, and institutional failure— and notes their effect on children and young adults. He also examines literature regarding various responses to childhood trauma including alcohol and drug use, and gang membership. Haney concludes that "[s]tudy after study has confirmed the cycles of desperation, hopelessness, and violence; cycles in which many capital defendants have become enmeshed."

David C. Baldus and George Woodworth examine the controversial issue of "Race Discrimination and the Death Penalty—An Empirical and Legal Overview" in Chapter Sixteen. Beginning with the link between discretion and discrimination, the authors discuss early forms of overt discrimination and later, more subtle forms of discrimination. They next address ethical ("The core ethical concern is fairness"), moral, and legal concerns ("At a strictly doctrinal level, the law is less conflicted than is ethical and moral opinion on the question"), before contemplating actual evidence of race discrimination in the administration of the death penalty. In the final section, the authors describe judicial—both Supreme Court, e.g., *McCleskey v. Kemp* (1987), and state court claims—as well as legislative responses to charges of race discrimination.

In closing, Baldus and Woodworth observe that "the problems of discrimination in the use of the death penalty are as susceptible to identification, adjudication, and correction as are the practices of discrimination in other areas of American life."

Eric M. Freedman next addresses "Federal Habeas Corpus in Capital Cases." Freedman's treatment of habeas corpus (the "Great Writ of Liberty") begins with the historical origins of habeas corpus, and its application in the Civil War and postbellum era in America (including the case of Leo Frank in Georgia, in 1915). Freedman next illuminates contemporary habeas corpus practice by listing numerous instances where such review prevented grave injustices in capital cases. He then explores issues surrounding the "retroactivity doctrine" announced in *Teague v. Lane* (1989). Drawing on his historical and contemporary discussion of habeas corpus, Freedman ends by cautioning that: "defending injustice on the basis of federalism disserves both federalism and justice."

In the final chapter of this section, Robert M. Bohm examines "The Economic Costs of Capital Punishment: Past, Present, and Future." The purpose of this chapter, Bohm notes at the outset, is "to compare the costs of capital punishment with the costs of alternative punishments." He attributes the generally greater costs of capital punishment to the more rigorous protections required by the Court's "death is different" doctrine (e.g., bifurcated trials, guided-discretion statutes, automatic appellate review, etc.). Providing specific dollar figures, Bohm analyzes costs by meticulously examining five stages of the capital punishment process: pretrial, trial, posttrial, imprisonment, and execution. He also examines future costs in four areas: streamlining the appellate and post-conviction process, the costs of mistakes, "start-up" costs, and the LWOP alternative (Life Without Parole). Bohm concludes that "the evidence clearly shows that capital punishment systems in the United States are always more expensive than punishment systems without capital punishment."

The last group of chapters deals with terminal stages of the penalty of death, and includes essays on physician involvement, families, life on death row, clemency, and executions.

In Chapter Nineteen, Charles Patrick Ewing reflects on the involvement of health care professionals with the death penalty in "'Above All, Do No Harm': The Role of Health and Mental Health Professionals in the Capital Punishment Process." Ewing sets out to examine "the clash between professional ethics and the law when health care professionals actively participate in the death penalty process." He explores this rift by looking, first, at the involvement of health care professionals in securing a sentence of death (i.e., in assessing and/or restoring competency to stand trial, and in helping to determine aggravating and mitigating circumstances). Ewing turns next to the role of health care professionals in assessing—and in some cases restoring—the competency of prisoners to be executed. He rounds out his treatment of this issue by examining the involvement of health care professionals in the execution process itself (i.e., in "certifying" and "determining" death, and in assisting in the actual execution).

Margaret Vandiver discusses the death penalty's impact on "The Families of Homicide Victims and of Condemned Prisoners" in Chapter Twenty. Vandiver first summarizes the literature dealing with the experiences and needs of those families ("There is even less research on the experiences of families of condemned and executed prisoners than on families of homicide victims"). She next confronts the disparate roles of the families in the legal context, most particularly at sentencing. Vandiver writes of family input in terms of both mitigation and victim impact testimony; she further illuminates those roles with accounts of Supreme Court rulings in *Booth v. Maryland* (1987) and *Payne v. Tennessee* (1991). In the final section, Vandiver not only explores ways to help families, including victim assistance and crime prevention programs, but offers directions for future research as well.

Robert Johnson writes movingly about living conditions for the condemned in "Life Under Sentence of Death: Historical and Contemporary Perspectives" in Chapter Twenty One. Johnson begins with a brief historical treatment of the conditions of confinement for condemned prisoners before considering life on modern death rows, current conditions on death rows, and some illusory death row reforms. He observes that "close custody has been and remains the central characteristic of life under sentence of death." He illustrates the continuing viability of this premise by describing conditions on a particular "high tech" modern death row, which originally was conceived as a "reform institution." He characterizes Oklahoma's H-Unit as "a solitary and sterile, a cold, oppressive human wasteland in which prisoners are interred—confined underground—in utterly self-contained cell blocks replete with dimly lit and sparsely furnished concrete cages." A "postscript" to the chapter examines life for women on death row.

The waning use of Executive power to commute death sentences is the focus of Daniel T. Kobil's chapter on "The Evolving Role of Clemency in Capital Cases." Kobil begins by noting the "symbiotic relationship between capital punishment and clemency." He emphasizes that the Supreme Court has invested great faith in clemency as a safeguard against executing the innocent, yet his careful analysis questions whether this reliance is justified. After defining "clemency" and its various forms, including reprieves, commutations, and pardons, Kobil tenders a short historical overview of the development of clemency power under both state and federal governments. He next explores recent uses of clemency, including former Illinois Governor George Ryan's decision as he left office in January 2003 to spare the lives of all prisoners then under sentence of death in that state. After discussing the future of clemency in capital cases, he addresses the need for due process protections in clemency proceedings. He identifies several procedural protections that would enhance the reliability of clemency decisions, and also offers substantive criteria for guiding those decisions.

Deborah W. Denno examines "Execution and the Forgotten Eighth Amendment" in the concluding chapter. She launches her exposition with distressing accounts of the botched executions of William Kemmler (1890), Jesse Joseph Tafero (1990), and Pedro Medina (1997), after which she notes, "The United States Supreme Court has never reviewed evidence concerning whether any method of execution violates the Eighth Amendment's Cruel and Unusual Punishments Clause." Denno thus sets the stage for a discussion of Eighth Amendment execution claims, beginning with a review of the "early execution methods jurisprudence," to provide a framework for analyzing later execution methods. She then evaluates the constitutionality of electrocution and of lethal injection—which is the most widely used contemporary method of carrying out death sentences—in light of principles derived from Eighth Amendment case law. She also scrutinizes the penological justifications advanced by states for either changing or retaining particular execution methods. An Appendix to her chapter documents the frequency of "botched executions" that have occurred in a number of states in the post-*Furman* era.

The chapters presented in this book thus provide a comprehensive examination of death-penalty law and practice. They nevertheless do not exhaust the virtually limitless number of issues relevant to the death penalty in the United States. We highlight below a few topics not squarely covered within these pages that nevertheless are important to capital punishment and its administration. Several of those topics raise issues meriting further study.

Prosecuting attorneys occupy a crucial role in death-penalty systems. In most jurisdictions, they have vast and essentially unregulated discretion to decide whether to seek a death sentence in capital murder trials (*McCleskey v. Kemp* 1987). As Baldus and Woodworth report in this volume, and as other researchers have documented (Bowers and Pierce 1980; Paternoster 1984; Paternoster and Brame 2003; Sorensen *et al.* 2001:402–404; Sorensen and Marquart 1990–1991), charging decisions can be a major source of arbitrariness in the administration of capital-punishment statutes. Although a few jurisdictions require centralized review and approval of prosecutors' decisions to pursue a capital sentence, or have adopted charging guidelines for potentially capital cases, such procedures do not appear to have eliminated uneven charging patterns (Acker 1996:81–88; Little 2000:553–563). The entire process leading up to prosecutors' decisions to seek the death penalty merits continued scrutiny, not only by researchers but also by the officials directly responsible for making and monitoring those decisions.

In that vein, the commission appointed to study Illinois' death penalty following Governor Ryan's moratorium on executions made two crucial recommendations to help cabin prosecutorial charging discretion in potential capital cases:

- "The Illinois Attorney General and the Illinois State's Attorneys Association should adopt recommendations as to the procedures State's Attorneys should follow in deciding whether or not to seek the death penalty, but these recommendations should not have the force of law, or be imposed by court rule or legislation" (*Report of the Governor's Commission on Capital Punishment* 2002:82).

- "The death penalty sentencing statute should be revised to include a mandatory review of death eligibility undertaken by a state-wide review committee.... The state-wide review committee would be composed of five members, four of whom would be prosecutors. The committee would develop standards to implement the legislative intent of the General Assembly with respect to death eligible cases..." (at 84).

Issues relating to the appointment, performance, and compensation of defense counsel in capital cases—which are considered by Stephen Bright, and Michael Mello and Paul Perkins in this volume, and which have been reviewed by Bright (1994) and others (Coyle, Strasser, and Lavelle 1990; Kreitzberg 1995) in greater detail elsewhere—also are critically important. Minimal qualifications and adequate funding for defense attorneys are essential if individuals accused of capital crimes are to receive able representation (Friedman and Stevenson 1992; Vick 1995; White 1993). Shockingly, many death-row prisoners have no legal representation at all (Mello 1988). The American Bar Association has called for a moratorium on executions until legal counsel are universally available to condemned prisoners, the general quality of defense representation in capital cases is improved, and other administrative deficiencies are corrected in death-penalty systems (*American Bar Association Resolution and Report* 1997; Coyne and Entzeroth 1996).

Several important issues also surround appeals in capital cases. For example, should death-sentenced offenders be permitted to waive appellate review of their convictions or sentences? Should state courts be required by statute to undertake "comparative proportionality review" of death sentences? Through such proportionality review, cases resulting in death sentences are compared to other, potentially similar cases in which murder is punished only by imprisonment. Appellate courts then attempt to identify arbitrary and "excessive" capital sentences. The Supreme Court has ruled that the Constitution does not mandate such review (*Pulley v. Harris* 1984). Important questions concerning this process include how effective the courts have been in detecting comparatively excessive and arbitrary death sentences, and what procedures are apt to produce more reliable comparative proportionality review decisions (Bienen 1996). Related issues involve the impact that death-penalty appeals have on state supreme courts' dockets, and how other cases are affected when capital appeals consume a large share of those dockets. As demanding as capital trials are, difficult issues related to the appeal of capital cases resonate throughout the entire judicial system (Acker and Lanier 1995).

Another area ripe for exploration transcends the more usual research involving the economic costs of the death penalty, although it still deals with budgetary considerations. Particularly in states where the death penalty has recently been introduced, it could be revealing to explore whether other programs have been scaled back or even eliminated because funds have been reappropriated to implement capital punishment. State and federal budgets are finite. Money used to build a death row and death chamber, to purchase execution apparatuses, to train attorneys and judges, and to finance other facets of capital punishment systems must come from new revenues or from other previously-funded programs. Of course, no budget report will particularize funds previously allocated for education, medical research, or feeding and caring for the elderly as being reappropriated to construct a lethal injection chamber. Research could help illuminate where money previously was being spent in comparison to current allocations. Budget analysts certainly could be instrumental in exploring this area of study.

The short- and long-term effects of local moratorium efforts, and of official commissions charged with studying the death penalty's administration in several states remain to be evaluated. Monitoring what influence former Illinois Governor Ryan's actions—first, in ordering a statewide moratorium on executions, and then in commuting all death sentences imposed in the state—ultimately will have in other death-penalty jurisdictions, as well as assessing their future impact in Illinois, also promises to be of interest. America's war against terrorism and changing international opinion about capital punishment additionally may be important in helping give shape to this country's future death-penalty practices and policies.

In sum, three decades after the modern era of capital punishment began in this country, there is no shortage of issues that remain open for research, analysis, and discussion. Nor is there any doubt that death-penalty issues will continue to be debated for the foreseeable future. Although it is impossible to forecast the precise contours of that debate, it is our hope that the chapters in this book will make a positive contribution to it as they contemplate the past, present, and future of America's ultimate penal sanction.

References

Acker, J.R. (2002) "The Death Penalty: Down But Not Out in the Summer of '02." *Contemporary Justice Review* 5:381–387.

Acker, J.R. (1996) "When the Cheering Stopped: An Overview and Analysis of New York's Death Penalty Legislation." *Pace Law Review* 17:41–227.

Acker, J.R. (1993) "Mortal Friends and Enemies: Amici Curiae in Supreme Court Death Penalty Cases." *New England Journal on Criminal and Civil Confinement* 19:1–59.

Acker, J.R. and C.S. Lanier (2003) "Beyond Human Ability? The Rise and Fall of Death Penalty Legislation." (This volume.)

Acker, J.R. and C.S. Lanier (1995) "Statutory Measures for More Effective Appellate Review of Capital Cases." *Criminal Law Bulletin* 31:211–258.

American Bar Association (2001, August) *Toward Greater Awareness: The American Bar Association Call for a Moratorium on Executions Gains Ground*. Chicago: American Bar Association.

American Bar Association Resolution and Report (1997) *reprinted in* Appendix (1998) *Law and Contemporary Problems* 61(4):219–231.

Anti-Drug Abuse Act of 1988 (1997) 21 U.S.C.A. §848(q)(4)(B).

Antiterrorism and Effective Death Penalty Act of 1996 (1997) 28 U.S.C.A. §2261.

Atkins v. Virginia (2002) 122 S.Ct. 2242.

Baldus, D.C. and G. Woodworth (2003). "Race Discrimination and the Death Penalty: An Empirical and Legal Overview." (This volume.)

Banner, S. (2002) *The Death Penalty: An American History*. Cambridge, MA: Harvard University Press.

Bedau, H.M. and M.L. Radelet (1987) "Miscarriages of Justice in Potentially Capital Cases." *Stanford Law Review* 40:21–179.

Bienen, L.B. (1996) "The Proportionality Review of Capital Cases by State High Courts After *Gregg*: Only 'The Appearance of Fairness'?" *Journal of Criminal Law and Criminology* 87:130–314.

Bohm, R.M. (2003) "American Death Penalty Opinion: Past, Present, and Future." (This volume.)

Bohm, R.M. (1999) *Deathquest: An Introduction to the Theory and Practice of Capital Punishment in the United States*. Cincinnati, OH: Anderson.

Booth v. Maryland (1987) 482 U.S. 496.

Bowers, W.J. and G.L. Pierce (1980) "Arbitrariness and Discrimination under Post-*Furman* Capital Statutes." *Crime & Delinquency* 26:563–635.

Bright, S.B. (1994) "Counsel for the Poor: The Death Sentence Not for the Worst Crime but for the Worst Lawyer." *Yale Law Journal* 103:1835–1883.

Callins v. Collins (1994) 510 U.S. 1141.

Coyle, M., F. Strasser and M. Lavelle (1990) "Fatal Defense: Trial and Error in the Nation's Death Belt." *The National Law Journal* 12:30–44 (no. 40, June 11).

Coyne, R. and L. Entzeroth, eds. (2001) *Capital Punishment and the American Agenda*. 2d edition. Durham, NC: Carolina Academic Press.

Coyne, R. and L. Entzeroth (1996) "Report Regarding Implementation of the American Bar Association's Recommendations and Resolutions Concerning the Death Penalty and Calling for a Moratorium on Executions." *Georgetown Journal on Fighting Poverty* 4:3–73.

Death Penalty Information Center (2003) "In Ryan's Words: 'I Must Act.'" Available on-line at http://www.deathpenaltyinfo.org/RyanCommuteSpeech.html.

Death Penalty Information Center (2002) *Innocence: Freed from Death Row*. Available on-line at http://www.deathpenaltyinfo.org/Innocentlist.html.

Friedman, R.E. and B.A. Stevenson (1992) "Solving Alabama's Capital Defense Problems: It's a Dollars and Sense Thing." *Alabama Law Review* 44:1–60.

Furman v. Georgia (1972) 408 U.S. 238.

Gideon v. Wainwright (1963) 372 U.S. 335.

Greenhouse, L. (2003) "Justices Deny Inmate Appeal in Execution of Juveniles." *New York Times* (Jan. 28) at A18.

Gregg v. Georgia (1976) 428 U.S. 153.

Hovey v. Superior Court of Alameda County (1980) 616 P.2d 1301 (Cal.).

In re Stanford (2002) 123 S.Ct. 472.

Innocence Protection Act (2002) H.R. 912, S. 486.

Jurek v. Texas (1976) 428 U.S. 262.

Justice Project (2002) *Death Penalty Reform Legislation Takes Next Step Toward Passage.* Available on-line at http://www.justice.policy.net/ipa/.

Kirchmeier, J.L. (2002) "Another Place Beyond Here: The Death Penalty Moratorium Movement in the United States." *University of Colorado Law Review* 73:1–116.

Kreitzberg, E. (1995) "Death Without Justice." *Santa Clara Law Review* 35:485–518.

Lanier, C.S. and J.R. Acker (forthcoming) "Capital Punishment, the Moratorium Movement, and Empirical Questions: Looking Beyond Innocence, Race, and Bad Lawyering in Death Penalty Cases." *Psychology, Public Policy and Law* ___:___–___.

Liebman, J.S. (2000) "The Overproduction of Death." *Columbia Law Review* 100:2030–2156.

Liebman, J.S., J. Fagan, A. Gelman, V. West, G. Davies and A. Kiss (2002, Feb. 11) *A Broken System, Part II: Why There is So Much Error in Capital Cases and What Can Be Done About It.* Available on-line at http://www.law.columbia.edu/brokensystem2/.

Liebman, J.S., J. Fagan and V. West (2000a) *A Broken System: Error Rates in Capital Cases, 1973–1995.* Available on-line at http://justice.policy.net/jpreport/index.html.

Liebman, J.S., J. Fagan, V. West and J. Lloyd (2000b) "Capital Attrition: Error Rates in Capital Cases, 1973–1995." *Texas Law Review* 70:1839–1863.

Liptak, A. (2003) "Top Lawyer in Maryland Calls for End to Executions." *New York Times* (Jan. 31) at A19.

Little, R.K. (2000) "The Future of the Federal Death Penalty." *Ohio Northern University Law Review* 26:529–580.

Lockhart v. McCree (1986) 476 U.S. 162.

Mackey, P.E. (Ed.) (1976) *Voices Against Death: American Opposition to Capital Punishment, 1787–1975.* New York: Burt Franklin & Co.

Masur, L.P. (1989) *Rites of Execution: Capital Punishment and the Transformation of American Culture, 1771–1865.* New York: Oxford University Press.

McCleskey v. Kemp (1987) 481 U.S. 279.

McGautha v. California (1971) 402 U.S. 183.

McFarland v. Scott (1994) 512 U.S. 849.

Mello, M. (1988) "Facing Death Alone: The Post-Conviction Attorney Crisis on Death Row." *American University Law Review* 37:513–607.

Meltsner, M. (1973) *Cruel and Unusual: The Supreme Court and Capital Punishment.* New York: Random House.

Mickens v. Taylor (2002) 122 S.Ct. 1237.

Morgan v. Illinois (1992) 504 U.S. 719.

NAACP Legal Defense and Educational Fund, Inc. (2002, Summer) *Death Row U.S.A.* New York: Criminal Justice Project, NAACP Legal Defense and Educational Fund, Inc.

Note (1974) "Discretion and the Constitutionality of the New Death Penalty Statutes." *Harvard Law Review* 87:1690–1719.

Paternoster, R. (1984) "Prosecutorial Discretion in Requesting the Death Penalty: A Case of Victim-Based Racial Discrimination." *Law & Society Review* 18:437–478.

Paternoster, R. and Brame, R. (2003) "An Empirical Analysis of Maryland's Death Sentencing System with Respect to the Influence of Race and Legal Jurisdiction: Final Report." Available on-line at http://www.urhome.umd.edu/newsdesk/pdf/finalrep.pdf.

Patterson v. Texas (2002) 123 S.Ct. 24.

Payne v. Tennessee (1991) 501 U.S. 808.

Penry v. Lynaugh (1989) 492 U.S. 302.

Polsby, D.D. (1973) "The Death of Capital Punishment? Furman v. Georgia." Pp. 1–40, in P. Kurland (ed.), *The Supreme Court Review* 1972. Chicago: University of Chicago Press.

Powell v. Alabama (1932) 287 U.S. 45.

Proffitt v. Florida (1976) 428 U.S. 242.

Pulley v. Harris (1984) 465 U.S. 37.

Radelet, M.L. and H.A. Bedau (2003) "The Execution of the Innocent." (This volume.)

Ramdass v. Angelone (2000) 530 U.S. 156.

Report of the Governor's Commission on Capital Punishment (2002, April) Springfield, IL: State of Illinois. Available on-line at http://www.idoc.state.il.us/ccp/ccp/reports/index.html.

Ring v. Arizona (2002) 122 S.Ct. 2428.

Roberts v. Louisiana (1976) 428 U.S. 325.

Sattazahn v. Pennsylvania (2003) 123 S.Ct. 732.

Scheck, B., P. Neufeld and J. Dwyer (2000) *Actual Innocence: Five Days to Execution and Other Dispatches from the Wrongly Convicted.* New York: Doubleday.

Sorensen, J., D. Wallace and R.L. Pilgrim (2001) "Empirical Studies on Race and Death Penalty Sentencing: A Decade After the GAO Report." *Criminal Law Bulletin* 37:395–408.

Sorensen, J.R. and J.W. Marquart (1990–1991) "Prosecutorial and Jury Decision-Making in Post-*Furman* Texas Capital Cases." *New York University Review of Law & Social Change* 18:743–776.

Stanford v. Kentucky (1989) 492 U.S. 361.

Streib, V.L. (2003) "Executing Women, Juveniles, and the Mentally Retarded: Second Class Citizens in Capital Punishment." (This volume.)

Strickland v. Washington (1984) 466 U.S. 668.

Teague v. Lane (1989) 489 U.S. 288.

Thompson v. Oklahoma (1988) 487 U.S. 815.

United States v. Fell (2002) 217 F.Supp.2d 469 (D. Vt.), *appeal pending.*

United States v. Quinones (2002) 205 F.Supp.2d 256 (S.D.N.Y.), *reversed,* 313 F.3d 49 (2d Cir.).

Vick, D.W. (1995) "Poorhouse Justice: Underfunded Indigent Defense Services and Arbitrary Death Sentences." *Buffalo Law Review* 43:329–460.

Wainwright v. Witt (1985) 469 U.S. 412.

Walton v. Arizona (1990) 497 U.S. 639.

Weeks v. Angelone (2000) 528 U.S. 225.

Westervelt, S.D. and J.A. Humphrey (Eds.) (2001) *Wrongly Convicted: Perspectives on Failed Justice.* New Brunswick, NJ: Rutgers University Press.

White, W.S. (1993) "Effective Assistance of Counsel in Capital Cases: The Evolving Standard of Care." *University of Illinois Law Review* 1993:323–378.

Williams v. Taylor (2000a) 529 U.S. 362.

Williams v. Taylor (2000b) 529 U.S. 420.

Witherspoon v. Illinois (1968) 391 U.S. 510.

Wolfe, B.H. (1973) *Pileup on Death Row.* Garden City, NY: Doubleday & Company.

Woodson v. North Carolina (1976) 428 U.S. 280.

Zimring, F.E. and G. Hawkins (1986) *Capital Punishment and the American Agenda.* New York: Cambridge University Press.

Part II

Capital Punishment: Public Opinion, Law, and Politics

Chapter 1

American Death Penalty Opinion: Past, Present, and Future

Robert M. Bohm

Thirty years after the Supreme Court's decision in *Furman v. Georgia* (1972)—the ruling that temporarily halted capital punishment in the United States—about seventy percent of adult Americans indicated that they favor the death penalty for persons convicted of murder. This level of support is substantially lower than the eighty percent that favored the death penalty in a 1994 poll, which was the highest level of support for the death penalty in more than sixty-five years of scientific opinion polling.[1] However, it is considerably higher than in 1966—the year that death penalty support fell to 42 percent, its lowest level ever.[2] In no year for which polls are available has a majority of Americans opposed capital punishment.

American death penalty opinion is important because such opinion, perhaps more than any other factor, probably accounts for the continued use of capital punishment in many jurisdictions in the United States. If most citizens in death penalty jurisdictions opposed capital punishment, it is unlikely the

---

1. See Jones (2002) for the most recent poll data. Unless indicated otherwise, figures reported in this chapter are from the Gallup polls, which are the oldest and most sustained effort to measure American death penalty opinion (see Bohm 1991). However, see the Appendix to Ellsworth and Gross (1994) for a list of 90 death penalty opinion surveys conducted in the United States between 1936 and July 1993, the text of the questions asked, and the proportions of respondents providing each recorded answer. For more recent polls, see the Death Penalty Information Center web site. Although some of those polls measure opinions about the death penalty for certain other categories of persons, such as juveniles and the mentally retarded, for certain other types of crimes, such as rape or kidnaping, and for certain kinds of death sentences, such as mandatory versus discretionary, this chapter focuses primarily on death penalty opinions for capital or aggravated murder. All post-*Furman* executions have involved capital or aggravated murderers.

2. Erskine (1970:295) cites a Harris Survey released on July 3, 1966, that showed that only 38 percent of respondents favored the death penalty, 47 percent were against, and 15 percent had no opinion.

penalty would be employed. Strong public support may contribute to the continued use of capital punishment in at least five ways. First, it probably sways legislators to vote in favor of death penalty statutes (and against their repeal).[3] Few politicians are willing to ignore the preferences of most of their constituents.[4] Currently, support of capital punishment is also a rather easy way for politicians to signal and demonstrate their more conservative "law and order" credentials.

Second, strong public support likely influences some prosecutors to seek the death penalty for political rather than legal purposes in cases they might ordinarily plea bargain. As White (1987:17; also see Dieter 1996; Callahan et al. 2000) relates from his interviews with defense attorneys:

> some prosecutors are more reluctant to plea bargain now than they were a few years ago, because they feel that in today's climate failure to seek the death penalty in certain types of cases could have a devastating effect on their political careers.

Third, to retain their positions, some trial-court judges feel public pressure to impose death sentences in cases in which such is inappropriate, and some appellate-court judges may uphold death sentences on appeal when they should not (see Bright 2003; Dieter 1996; Bright and Keenan 1995). Among judges recently removed from office following their unpopular death penalty decisions were: Chief Justice Rose Bird and two other justices of the California Supreme Court, Tennessee Supreme Court Justice Penny White, Mississippi Supreme Court Justice James Robertson, Justice Charles Campbell of the Texas Court of Criminal Appeals, Texas district court judge Norman Lanford, and Washington Supreme Court Justice Robert Utter (Bright 2003; Dieter 1996:2–4).

Fourth, some governors may be dissuaded from vetoing death penalty legislation and commuting death sentences because of strong public support for the penalty (but see fn. 4). With regard to commutations, it is instructive to note that prior to 1970, governors in death penalty states "routinely commuted up to a third of the death sentences that they reviewed.... Today, however, commutations of death sentences by governors [and review boards] are rare events" (Baldus and Woodworth 2003; also see Kobil 2003; Burnett 2002; Dieter 1996). Like other politicians today, few governors are willing to ignore

---

3. On Tennessee legislators, see Whitehead (1998); on Indiana legislators see McGarrell and Sandys (1996); but see Sandys and McGarrell (1994). Evidence indicates that public opinion has affected policymaking in the United States in other areas, such as civil rights (Oskamp 1977:241; also cf. Page et al. 1987; Page and Shapiro 1983; Monroe 1979; Erikson 1976; Weissberg 1976).

4. See Dieter (1996). With regard to the death penalty, former New York Governors Hugh Carey and Mario Cuomo and former California Governor Jerry Brown are three notable exceptions. Each governor vetoed death penalty legislation despite strong public support for the penalty.

what they perceive are their constituents' preferences. Also, as is the case with other politicians today, support of capital punishment generally defines for his or her constituents much of a governor's political agenda—at least the part that concerns crime.

Fifth, and arguably most important, strong public support might be used, at least indirectly, by justices of both state supreme courts and the United States Supreme Court as a measure of "evolving standards of decency" regarding what constitutes "cruel and unusual punishment" in state constitutions and under the Eighth Amendment of the United States Constitution.[5] In the *Furman* decision, decline in public support was cited as such a measure (p. 329).

The chapter is divided into three major sections. First is the history of American death penalty opinion. This section describes what is called here "the too simple and, therefore, misleading death penalty opinion question period." The second section surveys the present period and chronicles what is called "the more complex and revealing death penalty opinion question period." This section begins with a description of research that tested the hypothesis that death penalty support is largely a product of ignorance about the way capital punishment is actually administered. The final section addresses the future of American death penalty opinion and the effect it may have on the practice of capital punishment in the United States.

The Too Simple and, Therefore, Misleading Death Penalty Opinion Question Period: The Past

Interviews for the first scientific death penalty opinion poll in the United States were conducted in December, 1936, by the American Institute of Public Opinion, producers of the Gallup polls (Bohm 1991). The poll gauged public sentiment about the death penalty in light of the unprecedented media attention given to the execution of Bruno Hauptman, the alleged Lindbergh-baby kidnaper and murderer. The poll showed that 61 percent of the 2,201 adults interviewed "believe[d] in the death penalty for murder" and 39 percent did

---

5. On state constitutions, see Bedau (1987, Chap. 8); on the Eighth Amendment, see Marshall in *Furman v. Georgia* 1972:329; also in *Furman*: Douglas (p. 242), Brennan (pp. 269–70); Burger (p. 383), and Powell (p. 409); *Trop v. Dulles* 1958:101; *Weems v. United States* 1910:349, 373; *Robinson v. California* 1962:666; also cf. *Estelle v. Gamble* 1976:102; *Roberts v. Louisiana* 1976:336, 352; *Woodson v. North Carolina* 1976:301; *Gregg v. Georgia* 1976:173, 227. But see Rehnquist's dissent in *Atkins v. Virginia* 2002, where he is highly critical of using public opinion as a measure of evolving standards of decency.

not (Bohm 1991:115). The category of "no opinion" or "don't know" was not included as an option. Since that first poll in 1936, dozens of surveys of American death penalty opinion have been conducted (see fn. 1).

The most recent Gallup poll on death penalty opinion in the United States, conducted in 2002, found that 72 percent of Americans were in favor of the death penalty for a person convicted of murder, 25 percent were opposed, and 3 percent had no opinion (Jones 2002). Note the slight difference in the wording of the questions in the 1936 and 2002 polls. In the 1936 poll, respondents were asked, "Do you *believe* in the *death penalty* for murder?" (In the 1937 and later Gallup polls, respondents were asked, "Do you *favor or oppose capital punishment* for murder?") In the 2002 poll, respondents were asked, "Are you *in favor* of the death penalty for a person *convicted* of murder?" Although it is doubtful that the subtle differences in question wording significantly altered the resulting death penalty opinions, the wording of death penalty opinion questions and the response categories that are provided, as will be discussed in more detail later, can make a significant difference in the distribution of opinions (McGarrell and Sandys 1996; Sandys and McGarrell 1995; Jones 1994; Bowers 1993; Bohm et al. 1991; Williams et al. 1988; Harris 1986; Ellsworth and Ross 1983; Sarat and Vidmar 1976).

Over the past sixty-five years or so, support of and opposition to capital punishment have varied substantially.[6] However, when the increases and decreases are plotted over time, a v-shape can be observed. Thus, viewing the "v" from left to right, in 1936, 61 percent of respondents favored the death penalty; in 1966, only 42 percent of respondents favored it; but, by 2002, 72 percent of respondents supported it. Put differently, between 1936 and 2002, there has been an overall 11 percentage point increase in support and 14 percentage point decrease in opposition to the death penalty. The three percentage point difference between overall support and opposition is a function of the 3 percent of respondents with "no opinion" in the 2002 poll (the "no opinion" category was not included in the 1936 poll). When the sixty-six year period is divided into the 1936 to 1966 and the 1966 to 2002 periods, the relatively precipitous decrease then increase in support (or increase then decrease in opposition) for the penalty is readily apparent. Between 1936 and 1966, support of capital punishment decreased 19 percentage points, while opposition increased

---

6. The five most volatile short-term periods between 1936 and 1994 were: (1) 1953–1957 (23% decrease in support, 5% increase in opposition, and 17% increase in "no opinions" or "don't knows"); (2) 1960–1966 (11% decrease in support and 11% increase in opposition); (3) 1966–1967 (11% increase in support and 8% decrease in opposition); (4) 1971–1976 (16% increase in support and 12% decrease in opposition); and (5) 1978–1994 (18% increase in support, 11% decrease in opposition, and 7% decrease in "no opinions") (see Bohm 1991). With the exception of an analysis of the 1966–1967 period (see Bohm 1992a), there have been no attempts of which this author is aware to explain the volatile periods.

8 percentage points (the difference is due to the 11 percent of "no opinion" responses in the 1966 poll). Between 1966 and 2002, on the other hand, support of the death penalty increased 30 percentage points, while opposition decreased 22 percentage points (again, the difference is attributable to changes in "no opinion" responses). Note that the increase in death penalty support between 1966 and 2002 was nearly a third greater than the decline in death penalty support between 1936 and 1966.

A detailed analysis of the 71 percent increase in death penalty support since 1966 has yet to be written. However, it appears that the *Furman* decision, itself, played an important part. As noted, 1966 marked the nadir in death penalty support in the United States. Yet, by 1967, support for the penalty had risen to 53 percent and opposition had decreased to 39 percent—an 11 percentage point increase in support and an eight percentage point decrease in opposition (see Bohm 1991:116).[7] The increase in support was relatively short-lived because by the end of 1971, death penalty support had fallen to 49 percent (see Bohm 1991:116). The Court's decision in *Furman v. Georgia* was announced on June 29, 1972. In 1972 Gallup conducted two polls that asked about death penalty opinions, one before the *Furman* announcement (interviews from March 3–5) and one after it (interviews from November 10–13) (see Bohm 1991:116). In the pre-*Furman* poll, 50 percent of respondents favored the death penalty, 42 percent opposed it, and nine percent had no opinion. The poll conducted post-*Furman* showed that 57 percent of respondents supported capital punishment, only 32 percent opposed it, while 11 percent had no opinion (see Bohm 1991:116). In short, between March and November, 1972, approximately four months before and four months after the announcement of the *Furman* decision, support for the death penalty increased 7 percentage points and opposition dropped 10 percentage points. Although other factors may have had an effect, it appears that significant public discontent with the *Furman* decision was decisive. With few exceptions, death penalty support has been increasing steadily ever since.

Death penalty support in the United States for persons convicted of murder probably peaked at 80 percent (at least according to the Gallup polls) in 1994 (Moore 1994). With the exception of a short period of time between February 2000 and October 2001, death penalty support has remained at more than 70 percent since 1994. During that short window eight national public opinion polls found that only 62–68 percent of adults or registered voters nationwide were in favor of the death penalty for a person convicted of murder.[8] This was

---

7. For an analysis of the historical circumstances, i.e., the social events and economic trends, that contributed to the dramatic reversal in death penalty support and opposition between 1966 and 1967, see Bohm (1992a).

8. In a Gallup poll conducted in October 2001, only 68 percent of adults nationwide were in favor of the death penalty for a person convicted of murder; in Gallup polls conducted in

the lowest level of support recorded in a national poll in more than twenty years, and likely the first time the level of support had fallen below 70 percent during that period. The drop in support was probably a function of the media attention given to people convicted of capital crimes and sentenced to die who were actually innocent and the resulting nascent death penalty moratorium movement.

Demographic Characteristics of Respondents

Although more recent polls have included a greater variety of questions about death penalty opinions, earlier polls focused primarily on the percentage distribution of opinions themselves (as described previously) and the percentage distribution of opinions by demographic characteristics of respondents.[9] For most of the Gallup polls, information is available on the following ten demographic characteristics: (1) gender, (2) race, (3) age, (4) politics, (5) education, (6) income or SES, (7) occupation, (8) religion, (9) city size, and (10) region of the country (Bohm 1991).

During the first half century of Gallup polling, between 1936 and 1986, five of the demographic characteristics varied substantially and five of them did

---

August 2000, and February 2001, 67 percent of adults nationwide favored the death penalty for a person convicted of murder; in a Gallup poll conducted in February 2000, and a *USA Today*/Gallup poll conducted in June 2000, only 66 percent of adults nationwide were in favor of the death penalty for a person convicted of murder; in a Gallup poll conducted in May 2001, 65 percent of adults nationwide were in favor of the death penalty for a person convicted of murder; in a Harris poll conducted in July 2000, only 64 percent of adults nationwide "believed" in capital punishment; in an ABC News.com poll conducted in June 2000, only 63 percent of adults nationwide favored the death penalty for persons convicted of murder; and in an NBC News/*Wall Street Journal* poll conducted in May/June 2000, only 62 percent of registered voters nationwide favored the death penalty for a person convicted of murder (www.pollingreport.com/crime.htm#Death; Jones 2002).

9. Death penalty opinion research published prior to 1975, when death penalty support was more moderate than it is today, frequently attributed support of capital punishment to some rather unflattering social psychological characteristics such as dogmatism, authoritarianism, and racism. Proponents of capital punishment were less likely than opponents to approve of gun registration laws or to favor open housing legislation and more likely to favor restrictive abortion laws, approve of the John Birch Society, move if blacks moved into their neighborhoods, and support such things as restrictions on civil liberties, discrimination against minority groups, and violence for achieving social goals (Vidmar and Ellsworth 1974; also see Bohm 1987). However, in light of the dramatic increase in death penalty support in recent years, one might hope that such a distinctive personality profile of death penalty proponents no longer applies. Unfortunately, recent evidence suggests otherwise. Support of capital punishment by many whites continues to be associated with prejudice against blacks (see Barkan and Cohn 1994; Bohm 1994; United States General Accounting Office 1990).

not (see Bohm 1991). Characteristics showing greatest variation, in order of the magnitude of that variation, were race, income or SES, gender, politics, and region of the country. In other words, between 1936 and 1986, whites, wealthier people, males, Republicans, and Westerners tended to support the death penalty more than blacks, poorer people, females, Democrats, and Southerners. The characteristics showing much less variation over the fifty years were age, education, occupation, religion, and city size.

Although a majority of people in all demographic categories, *except race,* supported the death penalty in the 1986 poll, there was substantial variation within categories for all of the demographic characteristics except religion. City size was not a category in the 1986 poll. Thus, blacks, females, people under 30, Democrats, college graduates, people in the bottom income or SES category, manual laborers, and Easterners and Southerners were less likely to support or more likely to oppose the death penalty than were whites, males, Republicans, high school graduates, people in the top income category, clerical and sales workers, and Westerners and Midwesterners (Bohm 1991).

In the 2002 poll (the most recent one available), support is great in every social category examined with at least 64 percent of the respondents in every demographic category, *including race,* favoring the death penalty for convicted murderers.[10] Although data for blacks were not reported in the 2002 poll because of small sample size, nearly 60 percent of blacks supported the penalty in recent years (67 percent of non-whites favored the death penalty in the 2002 poll). Black support in the past, as noted previously, has been much lower. A recent study found that black proponents are hardly distinguishable in other characteristics from their white counterparts. Black proponents tend to be male, married, politically conservative, have high incomes, come from middle- and upper-class backgrounds, live in urban areas and the South, are afraid of crime, have never been arrested, and perceive that the courts are too lenient with criminals (Arthur 1998).[11]

The 2002 poll reported information about seven of the ten demographic characteristics reported in the earlier polls plus four additional ones. Not enough reliable information was available for income or SES in the 2002 poll, and the categories of occupation and city size were omitted. Characteristics showing the greatest variation, in order of the magnitude of that variation, were sex, ideology, region of the country, race, type of community, politics, employment status, religion, age, and marital status. In other words, in 2002, males, conservatives, Westerners, whites, rural and suburban residents, Re-

---

10. Demographic data from the 2002 death penalty poll were obtained directly from The Gallup Organization. My thanks to Maura A. Strausberg, Data Librarian, for her help.

11. For one interesting and detailed position on the death penalty offered by a black man, see Jackson (1996).

publicans and Independents, the employed, Protestants, those between 30 and 49 years of age, and married people favored the death penalty more than females, liberals, Easterners, Midwesterners, and Southerners, nonwhites, urban residents, Democrats, the unemployed, Catholics, those 50 years of age and older, and people who are not married. The characteristics with insignificant variation were education and having children under 18.[12] Note that the characteristics (for which there are comparable data) that distinguished death penalty opinions in the 1936 through 1986 polls are the same ones that distinguished death penalty opinions in the 2002 poll. In other words, the same sorts of people continue to favor the death penalty the most strongly. Based on findings from the most recent Gallup poll, then, it is not much of an exaggeration to state that most Americans favor the death penalty—or so it seems.

The More Complex and Revealing Death Penalty Opinion Question Period: The Present

Prior to the *Furman* decision in 1972, little critical scrutiny of the figures reported in various death penalty opinion polls existed. The reported percentages of support and opposition were generally accepted as accurate indicators of public sentiment. One of the first people to question the validity of death penalty opinion poll results, albeit indirectly, while at the same time emphasizing their importance, was former Supreme Court Justice Thurgood Marshall.

The Marshall Hypotheses

In his opinion in *Furman v. Georgia*, Justice Marshall stressed the importance of public opinion with respect to the constitutionality of the death penalty. In the opinion, he identified several standards by which to judge whether a punishment is cruel and unusual. One such standard was: "where a punishment is not excessive and serves a valid legislative purpose, it still may be invalid if popular sentiment abhors it" (at 332). Thus, wrote Marshall, "It is imperative for constitutional purposes to attempt to discern the probable opinion of an informed electorate" (at 362 fn. 145). He stressed that the public's choice about the death penalty must be "a knowledgeable choice" (at 362 fn. 145).[13]

---

12. See note 10.

13. Elaborating on this point, Marshall wrote that "the question with which we must deal is not whether a substantial proportion of American citizens would today, if polled, opine that capital punishment is barbarously cruel, but whether they would find it to be so in the light of

Like many death penalty opponents, Marshall believed that, given information about the death penalty, "the great mass of citizens would conclude...that the death penalty is immoral and therefore unconstitutional" (at 363).[14] He assumed that support of the death penalty is a function of a lack of knowledge about it, and that opinions are responsive to reasoned persuasion. The one exception to the assumption, recognized by Marshall, was that if the underlying basis of support for the death penalty were retribution, then knowledge would have little effect on opinions. Though some of his colleagues on the Court disagreed with him, Marshall maintained that retribution "is a goal that the legislature cannot constitutionally pursue as its sole justification for capital punishment" (at 363).[15] He added, "I cannot believe that at this stage in our history, the American people would ever knowingly support purposeless vengeance" (at 363).[16]

Social scientists did not take long before they subjected Marshall's assertions to empirical investigation. Two of the first three studies that systematically tested all or part of what have become known as "Marshall's hypotheses" were conducted in the United States; the third was conducted in Canada. A fourth study employing Stanford University undergraduates as subjects, although not a direct test of Marshall's hypotheses, is nevertheless relevant and will be discussed shortly. In one of the American studies, subjects were from the San Francisco Bay area and the data were collected in 1974 (Ellsworth and Ross 1983). In the other American study, subjects were from Amherst, Massachusetts and data were collected in 1975 (Sarat and Vidmar 1976). The Canadian

---

all information presently available" (*Furman v. Georgia* 1972:362). For Marshall, however, "this is not to suggest that with respect to this test of unconstitutionality people are required to act rationally; they are not [and often do not—author's addition]. With respect to this judgment, a violation of the Eighth Amendment is totally dependent on the predictable subjective, emotional reactions of informed citizens" (at 362). Even if the American people were adequately informed about the death penalty and its effects, Radin (1978) is but one scholar who believes that public opinion polls should not be relied on in constitutional adjudication. She argues that public opinion polls should not be used because they (1) "show that the majority of the public favors few of the protections embodied in the Bill of Rights"...[and] "the purpose of the Bill of Rights is to protect certain rights of individuals from an overreaching majority"; (2) "are subject to methodological errors"; and (3) "may record frivolous or ill-considered answers, or answers influenced by intrinsic factors" (1978:1035–6).

14. In his dissent in *Furman*, Justice Powell disagreed with Marshall and argued that the public would not oppose the death penalty if it were informed about its administration (1972:430–46).

15. In *Furman*, Justice Stewart, who voted with the majority, opined that retribution was psychologically necessary for maintaining social stability (1972:308).

16. Disagreement over the legitimacy of retribution as a purpose of capital punishment may be the product of confusion over what retribution actually means. For discussions of the different meanings of retribution, see Cottingham (1979); Radin (1980); Bohm (1992b).

study (Vidmar and Dittenhoffer 1981) does not indicate when data were collected. Although three of the four studies support all or part of the Marshall hypotheses,[17] possible problems relating to social conditions at the times data were collected and to methodology render the findings potentially inapplicable to current experience and generally invalid.

Regarding social conditions at the times data were collected, following the *Furman* decision in 1972, there was a flurry of activity as 35 states moved quickly to adopt new death penalty statutes designed to meet the Supreme Court's objections. Thus, in 1974 and 1975, the issue of the death penalty was receiving much media and public attention. But at the time the aforementioned studies were conducted no one had been executed in the United States since 1967. No one had been executed in Canada since 1962. (Canada abolished the death penalty in 1976 and has not reinstated it.) A problem is that at the times data were collected for the American studies, the issue of the death penalty was "abstract," as no one was being executed. As will be indicated later, public opinion about the death penalty is sometimes dramatically different when people consider the death penalty in "concrete" situations (e.g., at times when people are being executed) rather than in the abstract.

A methodological dilemma for all studies of this type is operationalizing the concept of "informed" or "knowledgeable about the death penalty." According to Justice Marshall (*Furman v. Georgia* 1972:362–3), for "the average citizen," except those who base their opinion on retribution, knowledge of some of the information listed below is "critical" to an informed opinion and "would almost surely convince [the average citizen] that the death penalty was unwise." Without evaluating or debating the veracity of Marshall's claims or information, an informed citizen, for Marshall, would know some of the following:

> that the death penalty is no more effective a deterrent than life imprisonment, that convicted murderers are rarely executed, but are usually sentenced to a term in prison; that convicted murderers usually are model prisoners, and that they almost always become law-abiding citizens upon their release from prison; that the costs of executing a capital offender exceed the costs of imprisoning him for life; that while in prison, a convict under sentence of death performs none of the useful functions that life prisoners perform; that no attempt is made in the sentencing process to ferret out likely recidivists for execution; and that the death penalty may actually stimulate criminal activity...capital punishment is imposed dis-

---

17. The study by Ellsworth and Ross (1983) only examined opinions and knowledge about the death penalty. It did not examine whether knowledge about the death penalty would change opinions. Also see Longmire (1996), for the effects of knowledge about the death penalty on death penalty opinions.

criminatorily against certain identifiable classes of people; there is evidence that innocent people have been executed before their innocence can be proved; and the death penalty wreaks havoc with our entire criminal justice system (at 362–4).

What Marshall fails to stipulate is how much of the information listed above a citizen must know to be informed about the death penalty. Must a citizen know all of the information to be considered informed or does knowing fifty to sixty percent of it suffice? Without setting a standard Marshall leaves unanswered the key question of what it means to be informed or knowledgeable about the death penalty.

Results of the fourth study, the one using Stanford University undergraduates as subjects (the authors did not indicate when their data were collected), differed dramatically from the results of the other three studies. The authors of the fourth study (Lord et al. 1979) discovered that knowledge or information can have an entirely different effect on death penalty opinions than the one supposed by Marshall. Lord et al. found that information about the death penalty polarized opinions, instead of changing them from in favor to opposed or vice versa.[18] In other words, subjects who initially favored the death penalty tended to favor it more strongly after receiving information about it, while subjects who initially opposed the death penalty tended to oppose it even more after becoming informed. The researchers attributed polarization to biased assimilation, that is, subjects interpreted evidence so as to maintain their initial beliefs:

> Data relevant to a belief are not processed impartially. Instead judgments about the validity, reliability, relevance, and sometimes even the meaning of proffered evidence are biased by the apparent consistency of that evidence with the perceiver's theories and expectations. Thus individuals will dismiss and discount empirical evidence that contradicts their initial views and will derive support from evidence, of no greater probativeness, that seems consistent with their views (Lord et al. 1979:2099).

Ellsworth and Ross (1983) believe that "biased assimilation" is a probable explanation for the effect of knowledge on opinions in their study. According to Ellsworth and Ross (1983:152):

---

18. Lord et al. (1979: 2100) presented 24 proponents and 24 opponents of the death penalty (all subjects were undergraduate students) "first with the results and then with procedural details, critiques, and rebuttals for two studies dealing with the deterrent efficacy of the death penalty—one study confirming their initial beliefs and one study disconfirming their initial beliefs" (for more detail, see Lord et al. 1979: 2100–2101).

> [We] are tempted to infer that the attitude [opinion] comes first
> and the reasons second.... It looks very much as though our re-
> spondents simply went down the list of reasons, checking whatever
> side of the scale was compatible with their general attitude [opin-
> ion] toward capital punishment. The picture that emerges is one of
> an emotionally based attitude [opinion], tempered by a sense of
> social desirability (also see Roberts 1984; Tyler and Weber 1982).[19]

In short, contrary to expectations held by Justice Marshall and many other
death penalty opponents, information about the death penalty may not significantly reduce the overwhelming public support that currently exists for capital
punishment. Notwithstanding the support for Marshall's hypotheses presented
above, if the results of the Lord et al. study are reliable, the effect of exposing people to information about the death penalty may be to polarize them on the issue.

Two other methodological problems with the aforementioned studies, and
to a lesser extent with more recent ones, are related to the validity of the experimental stimulus and the experimental manipulation. The first problem involves the form that "knowledge" takes, and the second has to do with the way
"knowledge" is imparted to subjects. In the study by Sarat and Vidmar (1976),
the experimental conditions involved reading two 1500 word essays that described "scientific and other information" about the death penalty. The experimental manipulation was preceded by a pretest and followed by a posttest. The
entire operation took only one hour. Sarat and Vidmar (1976:183 fn. 59) are
candid about the inadequacies of the manipulation:

> Without question our information manipulations had limited po-
> tential for developing truly informed opinion about the death
> penalty—the issues are intricate and complex while the essays are
> short and simple; furthermore, exposure to the information took
> place in a brief interview session without time for reflection, dis-
> cussion, or clarification.

Nevertheless, as alluded to previously, the experimental manipulation
proved somewhat successful. On the pretest, 62 percent of the (181 randomly
selected adult) experimental subjects favored the death penalty, 27 percent opposed it, and 10 percent were undecided. On the posttest, 42 percent favored
the death penalty, 38 percent opposed it, and 21 percent were undecided. Although the experimental stimulus did not produce a majority of subjects op-

---

19. The concepts "attitudes" and "opinions" are often used synonymously, especially when
discussing the death penalty. However, according to at least one authority (Oskamp 1977),
opinions should be equated with beliefs, which are primarily cognitive, while attitudes are more
emotion-laden. That distinction is ignored in this chapter which employs the concepts "opinion" or "opinions" except in direct quotes (in which case the concepts are bracketed).

posed to the death penalty, it did decrease support and increase opposition and indecision.

The study by Vidmar and Dittenhoffer (1981) improved the validity of the experimental manipulation in Sarat and Vidmar (1976) by increasing the opportunity for subjects to assimilate information about the death penalty. In the study by Vidmar and Dittenhoffer (1981), subjects were asked to read a 3500 word essay on the death penalty (emphasizing the Canadian experience), and a series of eight articles. The articles contained representative material on the death penalty intended to augment the essay. The subjects also had the option of reading two books—Sellin's *Capital Punishment* (1967) and Bedau's *The Death Penalty in America* (1967)—and were invited to pursue any other related reading. After two weeks, and presumably after having read the assigned materials, subjects met in small (apparently unsupervised) discussion groups of three or four persons to "freely discuss the facts and issues involved in the capital punishment debate and to try to reach a final decision within an hour" (Vidmar and Dittenhoffer 1981:49). Again, the experimental manipulation was preceded by a pretest and was followed by a posttest.

Like the results reported by Sarat and Vidmar, the results of the Vidmar and Dittenhoffer study indicate that the experimental manipulation was effective. On the pretest, 48 percent of the experimental subjects favored the death penalty, 33 percent were opposed to it, and 19 percent were undecided. On the posttest, 24 percent were in favor, 71 percent were opposed, and 5 percent were undecided. Vidmar and Dittenhoffer's experimental stimulus, unlike the one used by Sarat and Vidmar, did produce a majority of subjects opposed to the death penalty.

Despite the improvement of Vidmar and Dittenhoffer's experimental manipulation over the one utilized by Sarat and Vidmar, the Vidmar and Dittenhoffer study still had serious deficiencies. First, the experimental group consisted of only 21 nonrandomly selected students (18 in the control group). Second, the experimenters had to assume that the subjects did indeed read the assigned material. Third, even if subjects did read the material, it was not possible to determine how much of the material was comprehended. As to the discussion groups, Vidmar and Dittenhoffer (1981:45–46) are probably correct that discussion should enhance conditions for opinion change, because active learning is presumed to be more conducive to opinion change than passive learning. However, without supervision, the experimenters could not be sure of what happened in the discussion groups. Was the death penalty in fact discussed? Did one member of the group dominate discussion? Were some of the group members intimidated or angered by others? Furthermore, a discussion of only one hour was probably not long enough for such an "intricate and complex" topic. Subjects were not given sufficient opportunity to reflect upon contradictory beliefs or to research information about which they disagreed. A discussion of only one hour also allowed a persuasive speaker to have extraordinary influence. In short, a discussion period of only one hour was probably not long enough to produce the intended effects of the experimental manipulation.

For those and other reasons, Bohm and his colleagues, beginning in the mid-1980s, conducted a series of studies that used an experimental manipulation which provided subjects with more information, provided greater control over the circumstances in which the information was acquired, and allowed subjects more time to evaluate and integrate the information into their own systems of beliefs. Specifically, the experimental stimulus employed by Bohm and his colleagues was a college class on the death penalty.[20]

Although there was minor variation in the experimental stimulus in different classes (between 1985 and 1989), a death penalty class generally met a total of 40 hours a semester. Bedau's *The Death Penalty in America*, Third Edition (1982) was the assigned text for the course. In addition to the text, coursework included lectures by the instructor, presentations by guest speakers, videos, and discussion. Topics discussed were the history of the death penalty in the United States, with special emphasis on relevant Supreme Court cases; public opinion; evidence about general deterrence and incapacitation; religious and retribution arguments; and information on the administration of the death penalty (e.g, sources of arbitrariness and discrimination, executions of innocent persons, costs, etc.).

In most of the experiments, subjects completed questionnaires at the beginning and the end of the semester. Although their content varied somewhat

---

20. There are at least two potential problems with Bohm and his colleague's experimental design. First is the use of student subjects. Whether students are representative of the general public with regard to death penalty opinion is questionable. However, in the 2002 Gallup poll, there is not much variation in death penalty support based on education: 73 percent of respondents with a high school education or less, 70 percent of respondents with some college, and 71 percent of respondents with a college education supported the death penalty, see note 10. Variation in other years, however, has been greater (see Bohm 1991:131–32). In any case, the reason for using student subjects was that it was one of the only ways to employ a prolonged stimulus experimentally. Brevity of exposure to the experimental stimulus was a weakness of previous research (cf. Sarat and Vidmar 1976; Lord et al. 1979; Vidmar and Dittenhoffer 1981). A second potential problem with Bohm and his colleague's experimental design is the influence of the instructor. A charismatic teacher could have a significant influence over his or her students' opinions. The instructor in the death penalty classes was always forthright about his strong opposition to the death penalty, but emphasized that his opinion should not influence the opinion of anyone else. Despite his personal opinion, both sides of all issues were presented, and no preference was shown intentionally for either side. Also, the instructor played "devil's advocate" to the positions taken by students to provoke thoughtful consideration of the issues. Students were fully aware from the outset that their grade in the class was independent of their views. Informal feedback from all the classes and results of two to three year and more than ten year follow-up studies of the 1988 and 1989 classes indicate that "demand characteristics" had negligible effects (Bohm et al. 1993:42; Bohm and Vogel 2002).

from semester-to-semester, the questionnaires, at minimum, generally sought information about the three principal variables in Marshall's hypotheses: opinions toward the death penalty, knowledge about the death penalty, and desire for retribution. The questionnaires also asked for demographic information about the subjects.

Bohm and his colleagues measured death penalty opinions with four questions, because they believed that the general death penalty opinion question asked in the Gallup and other polls did not accurately reflect the complexity of public sentiment about the penalty. Each of the questions represented a different type of support or nonsupport for the death penalty. The first question was: "Which of the following statements best describes your position toward the death penalty for *all* persons convicted of first-degree murder?"[21] Only 28.3 percent of less informed subjects opposed the death penalty for *all* persons convicted of first-degree murder (24.7 percent of males; 31.1 percent of females; 18.3 percent of whites; 37.6 percent of blacks), but 46.6 percent of more informed subjects were opposed to it (41.2 percent of males; 51.1 percent of females; 32.3 percent of whites; 60 percent of blacks) (Bohm et al. 1991:373–75, Tables 2, 3 & 4).

A second question asked subjects whether they favored the death penalty for "*some* people convicted of first-degree murder." This question is the one that is most similar to the general death penalty opinion question asked in the Gallup and other polls. Results for this question are similar to those for the previous one: 28 percent of less informed subjects opposed the death penalty (24.7 percent of males; 30 percent of females; 22.6 percent of whites; 30.6 percent of blacks), but 49.5 percent of more informed subjects opposed it (49.5 percent of males; 50 percent of females; 40.9 percent of whites; 56.6 percent of blacks) (Bohm et al. 1991:373–75, Tables 2, 3 & 4).

The third and fourth questions were asked because prior research (Ellsworth and Ross 1983; Jurow 1971) has found that support for the death penalty is greatly attenuated when a distinction is made between support in the abstract and support in concrete situations.[22] The first "concrete" question was:

---

21. Although, in 1976, in the cases of *Woodson v. North Carolina* and *Roberts v. Louisiana*, the Supreme Court rejected mandatory statutes that automatically imposed death sentences for defined capital offenses, a question about the death penalty for all persons convicted of first-degree murder remains instructive. Not only does it give an indication of people's opinions in light of the Supreme Court decisions, but it also serves as a basis of comparison for other questions about the death penalty considered in this research.

22. The distinction made between "abstract" questions and questions involving "concrete" situations is somewhat artificial. As is well known, what people say and what people do are often very different. Research indicates that correlations between people's attitudes [opinions] and their behavior are "rarely above .30, and often are near zero" (Wicker 1969). The largest correlations are typically found when the researcher focuses on a specific attitude [opinion] toward a well-defined situation. Conversely, when the attitude [opinion] is a very general one that is pre-

"If you served on a jury in a trial where the defendant, if found guilty, would automatically be sentenced to death, could you convict that defendant?" Only 22.5 percent of less informed subjects could not convict (14.4 percent of males; 30 percent of females; 5.4 percent of whites; 23.5 percent of blacks), while 34.4 percent of more informed subjects could not convict (30 percent of males; 38 percent of females; 21.5 percent of whites; 47.1 percent of blacks) (Bohm et al. 1991:373–75, Tables 2, 3 & 4).

Finally, the second concrete question was: "If asked to do it, could you pull the lever that would result in the death of an individual convicted of first-degree murder?" On this question, 47.2 percent of less informed subjects (45.4 percent of males; 55.5 percent of females; 37.6 percent of whites; 64.7 percent of blacks) and 49.6 percent of more informed subjects could not pull the lever (50.5 percent of males; 62.2 percent of females; 40.9 percent of whites; 72.9 percent of blacks) (Bohm et al. 1991:373–75, Tables 2, 3 & 4).

Another reason for asking subjects four different death penalty questions was to ascertain whether subjects had a "coherent moral position" toward capital punishment. As Radin (1978:1041) explains:

> The reason it is often suggested that one ought to look to what people do rather than what they say, or even more pointedly, that those who favor the death penalty should be asked whether they would be willing to pull the switch themselves, is that a person is more likely to have reached a coherent moral position if she is going to be required to transform her beliefs into action.

Although Bohm and his colleagues wondered how people could have a coherent moral position toward the death penalty when they were ignorant about the subject, they nevertheless examined whether responses to the four questions formed a Guttman scale and thus were indicative of a coherent moral position. To their surprise, their findings suggested that their subjects did indeed hold coherent moral positions toward the death penalty, whether they were informed or not (Bohm et al. 1991:368–69). When they used subjects' Guttman scale coefficients as measures of opposition to capital punishment, Bohm et al. (1991:375) found that while only 34.7 percent of less informed subjects opposed capital punishment, 56.3 percent of more informed subjects opposed it. This was the only measure that produced a majority of all subjects opposed to the penalty.

---

sumed to influence a variety of different situations, much less consistency between attitude [opinion] and behavior is found (Crespi 1971). Thus, what people say about the death penalty in general, and what they would do as jurors in a capital murder trial, for example, probably are not the same. For that matter, what people say they would do if they served as jurors in a capital murder trial, and what they would do if they actually served may not be the same. This, of course, is a problem with all survey research.

In sum, results of this research provided at least qualified support for all three of Marshall's hypotheses (cf. Bohm et al. 1991; also see Bohm 1989; Bohm 1990; Bohm et al. 1990; Bohm and Vogel 1994). Subjects generally lacked knowledge about the death penalty and its administration prior to exposure to the experimental stimulus, but were more informed following it. To the degree that retribution provided the basis for support of the death penalty, knowledge had little effect on opinions. The hypothesis that an informed public would generally oppose the death penalty was supported in one test but not in others. (In some tests, a majority of black males and a majority of black and white females opposed the death penalty.) Thus, even though support for the death penalty might decline after subjects have been informed, the reduction may not be great enough to create a majority opposed to the death penalty (Bohm 1989; Bohm et al. 1991; Bohm and Vogel 1994). This may hold true even when subjects are asked diverse death penalty opinion questions, such as "personal involvement" questions (Bohm et al. 1991; Bohm et al. 1993).

Other findings of this research include the following: (1) exposure to death penalty information may result in the polarization of opinions (favoring or opposing more strongly) (Bohm et al. 1990; Bohm 1990); (2) it may be more difficult for subjects to change their positions if they have to publicly announce their death penalty opinions (Bohm 1990); (3) initial beliefs about the death penalty and such issues as deterrence, revenge, and incapacitation generally are not affected by giving people information about those issues (Bohm et al. 1993; Bohm and Vogel 1994); and (4) when opinions about the death penalty do change, it is most likely because of administrative reasons such as racial discrimination or executing innocent people (Bohm 1989; Bohm and Vogel 1994; Bohm et al. 1991; Bohm et al. 1993; Sandys 1995; Clarke et al. 2000–2001).

However, when the death penalty opinions of subjects in the 1988 and 1989 classes were examined two to three years later, it was discovered that opinions on the two abstract death penalty opinion questions (that is, "Do you favor or oppose the death penalty for *all* and for *some* people convicted of first-degree murder?") had rebounded to near their initial pretest positions (Bohm et al. 1993). Opinions on the two "concrete" death penalty opinion questions (that is, could you convict? and could you pull the lever?) did not change significantly for the 1988 and 1989 classes at any of the three points in time (pretest, posttest, or follow-up) (Bohm et al. 1993).[23] Another follow-up study of the 1988 and 1989 death penalty classes more than ten years after students completed the class (Bohm and Vogel 2002) revealed small increases in support of the death penalty

---

23. There was some significant change in opinions on the concrete questions in some of the tests.

from the first follow-up period on the abstract opinion measures. However, as was the case in the first follow-up study, the personal involvement measures did not change significantly in the second follow-up study (Bohm and Vogel 2002). Furthermore, results of the follow-up studies do not appear to be a function of a loss of knowledge, the irrelevancy of the death penalty class, or the influence of the instructor (Bohm et al. 1993:42; Bohm and Vogel 2002). Why, then, did opinions rebound? Perhaps it was because death penalty opinions are based primarily on emotion rather than on cognition and that, in the long run, cognitive influences on death penalty opinions give way to emotional factors.

In any event, results of the follow-up studies suggest that most death penalty opinions may not be significantly influenced by increased knowledge about the penalty or may be influenced only temporarily, at least if that knowledge is obtained in a college classroom.[24] If Justice Marshall had in mind a stimulus like the one employed in the research by Bohm and his colleagues, then Marshall's belief that death penalty opinions can be changed substantially (by increasing knowledge about the subject) may be wrong. This does not mean that death penalty opinions are intransigent. Opinions do change, as evidenced by the more than sixty-five year history of public opinion polls on the death penalty in the United States. It only means that classroom knowledge may not be an effective way of changing those opinions.

Asking about Alternatives to the Death Penalty

Perhaps more important than the amount of accurate knowledge a person has about the death penalty is the way in which the death penalty opinion question is asked. As mentioned previously, a critical problem with the general death penalty opinion question (e.g., Do you favor or oppose the death penalty for murder?) is that there is either no context to the question or the context of the question is left ambiguous. That is, when people are asked whether they favor or oppose the death penalty, or, for that matter, whether they favor or oppose the death penalty for *all* people or for *some* people convicted of first-degree murder, it is left to the imagination of each individual as to whether that means (1) the death penalty or no penalty at all, (2) the death penalty or a too lenient alternative penalty such as five or ten years in prison, (3) the death penalty or a severe penalty such as a lengthy prison sentence but with opportunity for parole, (4) the death penalty or an alternative severe penalty such as life imprisonment with no possibility of parole, or, perhaps, the death penalty and some other alternative. With the exception of their latest studies (see Wright et al. 1995; Bohm and Vogel 2002), Bohm and his colleagues did not fully anticipate this possibility.

---

24. Also see Patenaude (2001), but see Sandys (1995), for different results.

Yet, it appears that many people support the death penalty because they fear an alternative penalty will not be punitive enough or that it may be inappropriate given the severity of the crime. For example, several studies show that 25–40 percent of the public (depending on the sample) believes that "the average prison term served by someone sentenced to life imprisonment is less than 10 years," even though the statement is false (Bohm et al. 1991:371; Ellsworth and Ross 1983; Wright et al. 1995; also see Bowers 1993; McGarrell and Sandys 1996; Bowers et al. 2003).

However, when the death penalty question is asked, and a harsh and meaningful alternative is provided, support of capital punishment drops, sometimes precipitously. In a 2002 Gallup poll (Jones 2002), when respondents were given a choice of the death penalty or life imprisonment as the better penalty for murder, a slim majority, 52 percent, preferred the death penalty, 43 percent favored life imprisonment, and five percent had no opinion. These findings were consistent with the results of recent polls. In many polls, when given the option between the death penalty and life imprisonment with absolutely no possibility of parole, less than one-half of the public supports the death penalty (see, for example, Gallup and Newport 1991:44; also see Jones 2002; Bowers et al. 1994; Ellsworth and Gross 1994; Bowers 1993). When given the option between the death penalty and life imprisonment with absolutely no possibility of parole *and* the payment of restitution by the offender (who would work in prison industry) to the victim's family or the community (LWOP+), only 19 to 43 percent of the public (depending on the sample) prefers the death penalty over the alternative (see Bowers 1993; Sandys and McGarrell 1995; McGarrell and Sandys 1996).[25] Thus, on the surface, a majority of the public appears receptive to replacing capital punishment with a harsh and meaningful alternative such as LWOP+. This is especially true of non-whites, people 65 years of age or older or women 50 years of age or older, Easterners, people with a post-graduate education, Democrats, and the unemployed (Jones 2002).

A problem is that the public is also very skeptical about the ability of correctional authorities to keep capital murderers imprisoned for life. For example, in a recent national survey, only eleven percent of registered voters believed that an offender sentenced to life imprisonment without possibility of parole would never be released from prison (cited in McGarrell and Sandys 1996:509). Thus, although the public may say that it prefers the alternative of LWOP or LWOP+ over capital punishment, in practice, it may not want to make the

---

25. Bowers (1993:168) notes that there is evidence suggesting that "a majority of the public would also be willing to accept parole after a fixed term of at least 25 years in preference to the death penalty on the condition that it was coupled with a restitution requirement and that the defendant had fully met the restitution requirement."

substitution because it fears that the alternative may not adequately protect it from the future actions of convicted capital murderers.

Asking about Different Types of Death-Eligible Murders

Another ambiguity with general death penalty opinion questions is the type of murder, or first-degree murder, the pollsters have in mind. Not all death-eligible murders are the same. In a recent study, Durham and his colleagues (1996) presented people with 34 different murder scenarios, which varied by aggravating and mitigating circumstances. Murders in some scenarios were death-eligible, and murders in others were not. Respondents were asked what they thought was the appropriate punishment.

The researchers found that people's willingness to impose the death penalty may be greater than public opinion polls indicate. Only 13 percent of respondents would sentence all of the murderers to death, but about 95 percent would sentence at least one to death (Durham et al. 1996:726). There was also a huge variation in the willingness of people to impose the death penalty on different types of murderers. For one scenario, more than 90 percent of respondents thought death was the appropriate punishment, while for another, fewer than 25 percent of respondents so believed (Durham et al. 1996:727). Even people in groups historically most opposed to the death penalty were likely to believe the death penalty was appropriate for at least some types of murderers. Although people's willingness to impose the death penalty was generally greatest for first-degree and felony murders, an unexpected finding was that several felony murders drew little death penalty support (Durham et al. 1996:727). Durham and his colleagues also discovered that aggravating circumstances were more influential on sentencing decisions than were mitigating circumstances (1996:727). Finally, when the researchers compared their data with information obtained from the prosecutor's office, they found that the people they surveyed were more willing to impose the death penalty than was the prosecutor or than the law would have allowed (Durham et al. 1996:727). These data suggest that death penalty support in the United States, for at least some types of murders, may be every bit as strong as recent public opinion polls suggest, and it may be even stronger for specific types of death-eligible murders.

Other Death Penalty Opinion Questions

As noted previously, recent polls have included a greater variety of questions about the death penalty than did earlier polls. In fact, much more information is available about annual death penalty opinions today than at any time in the history of death penalty opinion polling. Besides questions about the death penalty versus LWOP and different types of death-eligible murders, recent polls have included questions about the administration of the death penalty, such as whether it is applied fairly,[26] whether an innocent person has been executed and what to do about it,[27] and whether poor people are more likely to receive the death penalty than people of average or above average income. Questions have been asked about the frequency with which the death penalty is imposed (too often, not enough, right amount)[28] and whether the death penalty should be imposed on certain categories of offenders, such as the mentally retarded,[29] the

---

26. An NBC News/*Wall Street Journal* poll conducted in July 2000 found that 42 percent of registered voters nationwide thought that the death penalty is not applied fairly (42% believe it is applied fairly, 8% responded that it depends, and 8% are not sure). In a *USA Today*/Gallup poll conducted in June 2000, 41 percent of adults nationwide believed the death penalty is applied unfairly (51% believed it was applied fairly, and 8% had no opinion). Sixty-three percent of the respondents to that poll favor the suspension of the death penalty until questions about its fairness can be studied (www.pollingreport.com/crime.htm#Death).

27. A Harris poll conducted in July 2000 revealed that 94 percent of adults nationwide think that innocent people are sometimes convicted of murder. Perhaps even more telling, according to a CNN/*USA Today*/Gallup poll conducted in June 2000, 80 percent of adults nationwide think that in the past five years a person has been executed who was, in fact, innocent of the crime with which he or she was charged. A *Newsweek* poll conducted in June 2000 also found that more than 80 percent of adults nationwide think that at least some innocent people have been wrongly executed since the death penalty was reinstated in the 1970s: 8 percent think that "many" innocent people have been wrongly executed; 33 percent think that only "some" innocent people have been wrongly executed; and 41 percent think that only a "very few" innocent people have been wrongly executed. That same poll discovered that 82 percent of adults nationwide think that states should make it easier for death row inmates to introduce new evidence that might prove their innocence, even if that might result in delays in the death penalty process. Ninety-five percent of adults nationwide think that states should permit DNA testing in all cases where it might prove a person's guilt or innocence (currently only Illinois and New York give inmates the right to have their DNA tested), and 88 percent of adults nationwide think that the federal government should require states to permit DNA testing under those circumstances (www.pollingreport.com/crime.htm#Death).

28. Twenty-two percent of respondents replied "too often," 24 percent replied "about the right amount," 47 percent replied "not enough," and 7 percent had no opinion (Jones 2002).

29. In June 2002, in *Atkins v. Virginia*, the Supreme Court ruled 6–3 that it is cruel and unusual punishment to execute the mentally retarded. Results of a recent Gallup poll indicate that a national consensus against the execution of the mentally retarded appears to have emerged since the Court last considered the issue in *Penry v. Lynaugh* (1989). According to the poll, only 13 percent of respondents favored the death penalty for the mentally retarded who are convicted of capital crimes, 82 percent opposed it, and 5 percent didn't know or refused to answer. Among subgroups, only 18 percent of males, 9 percent of females, 13 percent of whites, and 14 percent of nonwhites favored the death penalty for mentally retarded capital offenders (Jones 2002).

mentally ill,[30] juveniles,[31] and women.[32] Additional questions address whether the death penalty is morally acceptable, whether it acts as a deterrent,[33] and whether there should be a moratorium on it. Reasons for favoring the death penalty also have been sought.[34] Poll questions have asked about George W. Bush's handling of death penalty cases as governor of Texas and how that would affect whether a person would vote for him as president. Finally, recent death penalty polls have included questions about the appropriateness of the death penalty for specific offenders, such as Timothy McVeigh, Terry Nichols, Juan Raul Garza, Andrea Yates, and Osama bin Laden.

Another recent development in death penalty opinion polling is the Gallup organization's decision to conduct three death penalty opinion polls a year. This was done for the first time in 2000 and again in 2001. Also, the Gallup organization began conducting consecutive annual death penalty opinion polls for the first time beginning in 1999. We will have to see whether these two trends continue.

---

30. According to a Gallup poll conducted in 2002, only 19 percent of respondents favored the death penalty for capital offenders who were mentally ill, 75 percent opposed it, and 6 percent didn't know or refused to answer. Among subgroups, only 22 percent of males, 16 percent of females, 20 percent of whites, and 16 percent of nonwhites favored the death penalty for mentally ill capital offenders (Jones 2002).

31. A Gallup poll conducted in 2002 found that only 26 percent of respondents favored the death penalty for juveniles, 69 percent opposed it, and 5 percent didn't know or refused to answer. Among subgroups, only 31 percent of males, 21 percent of females, 25 percent of whites, and 29 percent of nonwhites favored the death penalty for juveniles. (Jones 2002) The level of support (or lack thereof) of the death penalty for juveniles in 2002 represents a dramatic change from the results of a Gallup poll conducted in 1994. In the 1994 poll, 60 percent of Americans thought that when a teenager (note the change from "juvenile" to "teenager") commits a murder and is found guilty by a jury, he (the survey item did not address female teenage killers) should get the death penalty (compared with 80 percent who favored the death penalty for adults), 30 percent opposed the death penalty for teenagers, and 10 percent had no opinion (Moore 1994). Seventy-two percent of those who favored the death penalty for adults also favored it for teenage killers.

32. According to a recent Gallup poll, 68 percent of Americans favor the death penalty for women convicted of murder, 29 percent oppose it, and 3 percent don't know or refused to answer. In the same poll, 72 percent of Americans favored the death penalty in general, 25 percent opposed it, and 3 percent didn't know or refused to answer. Among subgroups, however, 72 percent of males but only 63 percent of females favored the death penalty for women, and 72 percent of whites but only 51 percent of nonwhites favored the death penalty for women (Jones 2002).

33. According to a recent Gallup poll, when asked their reasons for supporting the death penalty, only 10 percent of respondents chose "Deterrent for potential crimes/Set an example" (Jones 2001).

34. When asked why they favored the death penalty for persons convicted of murder, 48 percent of respondents mentioned "an eye for an eye/they took a life/fits the crime," 20 percent mentioned "save taxpayers money/cost associated with prison," and 10 percent mentioned "deterrent for potential crimes/set an example." No other reason was mentioned by at least 10 percent of respondents (Jones 2001).

The Future of American Death Penalty Opinion

One of the more ambitious attempts to explain death penalty opinion in the United States was based on the results of a twenty-year longitudinal study of the development of moral judgment in American males. From that study, Kohlberg and Elfenbein (1975:617) concluded that "nonfactual cognitive components of attitudes [opinions] toward capital punishment are determined by developing moral standards," as opposed to "irrational, purely emotional factors." Since the American public generally is not well-informed about the death penalty, then one might assume, following Kohlberg and Elfenbein, that death penalty opinions are primarily the product of "developing moral standards." Kohlberg and Elfenbein posited six moral stages and explained that as society progressed "through the universal, invariant sequence of moral stages," there is "a radical decline in support for capital punishment" (1975:637–638). At stage 6, to which society had yet to "progress," no person could support capital punishment (1975:637).

In the process of conducting their research, Kohlberg and Elfenbein (1975:638) observed that:

> A gradual socio-moral evolution is evidently taking place in the United States that can be described and theoretically explained as moral stage development across social institutions and individuals over time. In large part, this evolution takes the form of a movement from Stage 4 to Stage 5.

According to Kohlberg and Elfenbein, then, society is morally developing to a stage where the public will not support the death penalty. This observation, however, was published in 1975 during the hiatus on capital punishment in the United States and after a period of decline in support. Subsequent developments, such as increasing public support for the death penalty and an increase in the number of death sentences and executions, indicate either that Kohlberg and Elfenbein relied on a faulty theory, that they were wrong in their assessment of the moral evolution of American society, or that the American public is regressing in its moral development.

Public opinion about capital punishment, or at least public support, may prove to be irrelevant if and when the penalty is ever abolished in the United States. As Zimring and Hawkins (1986:12) have observed, "Successful and sustained abolition [of capital punishment] has never been a result of great popular demand." In most countries that have abolished the death penalty, a majority of citizens continued to support retention at the time of abolition and shortly thereafter. Only after some time did death penalty support generally decline until opposition dominated public opinion (Zimring and Hawkins, 1986). In short, abolition of capital punishment, where it has occurred, generally has been achieved despite relatively strong public support for retention. For this reason, surmise Zimring and Hawkins, politicians and other opinion-makers probably will have to lead the public on this issue if capital punishment is ever to be abolished in the United States.

Based on my own analysis of the dramatic reversal in death penalty opinion in the United States beginning in the 1966–1967 period (Bohm 1992a), I have concluded that "the key to understanding temporal variations in death penalty opinions probably lies in the fear and anxiety engendered by the social events of an era" (p. 539). The strength of death penalty support and opposition appears to be both a psychological barometer of the level of dread and angst in a society and a symbolic marker of the social landscape. In particular, levels of support and opposition seem to demarcate the threshold level of people's tolerance of media-reported crime, and, at the same time, serve as an indicator of people's threshold tolerance of social change. Based on the findings of the study, it seems reasonable to assume "that historical changes, such as a political shift away from the conservative social policies of the last two decades, are apt to either produce a dramatic shift in future death penalty opinions or to be marked by changed death penalty opinions as the political shift passes a certain threshold level" (p. 539). Either way, it is unlikely that the practice of capital punishment could be sustained if a majority of American citizens were to oppose it.

References

Arthur, J. (1998) "Proximate Correlates of Black's Support for Capital Punishment." *Journal of Crime and Justice* 21:159–72.

Atkins v. Virginia (2002) 122 S. Ct. 2242.

Baldus, D. C. and G. Woodworth (2003) "Racial Discrimination and the Death Penalty: An Empirical and Legal Overview." (This volume.)

Barkan, S. E. and S. F. Cohn (1994) "Racial Prejudice and Support for the Death Penalty by Whites." *Journal of Research in Crime and Delinquency* 31:202–209.

Bedau, H. A. (1987) *Death is Different: Studies in the Morality, Law, and Politics of Capital Punishment.* Boston: Northeastern University Press.

Bedau, H. A. (1982) *The Death Penalty in America,* Third Edition. New York: Oxford University Press.

Bedau, H. A. (Ed.) (1967) *The Death Penalty in America: An Anthology,* Rev. ed. Chicago: Aldine.

Bohm, R. M. (1994) "Capital Punishment in Two Judicial Circuits in Georgia: A Description of the Key Actors and the Decision-Making Process." *Law and Human Behavior* 18:319–338.

Bohm, R. M. (1992a) "Toward an Understanding of Death Penalty Opinion Change in the United States: The Pivotal Years, 1966 and 1967." *Humanity and Society* 16:524–542.

Bohm, R. M. (1992b) "Retribution and Capital Punishment: Toward a Better Under-standing of Death Penalty Opinion." *Journal of Criminal Justice* 20:227–236.

Bohm, R. M. (1991) "American Death Penalty Opinion, 1936–1986: A Critical Ex-amination of the Gallup Polls." Pp. 113–145 in R. M. Bohm (Ed.) *The Death Penalty in America: Current Research.* Cincinnati: Anderson.

Bohm, R. M. (1990) "Death Penalty Opinions: Effects of a Classroom Experience and Public Commitment." *Sociological Inquiry* 60:285–297.

Bohm, R. M. (1989) "The Effects of Classroom Instruction and Discussion on Death Penalty Opinions: A Teaching Note." *Journal of Criminal Justice* 17:123–131.

Bohm, R. M. (1987) "American Death Penalty Attitudes: A Critical Examination of Recent Evidence." *Criminal Justice and Behavior* 14:380–396.

Bohm, R. M. and B. L. Vogel (2002) "More Than Ten Years After: The Long-Term Stability of Informed Death Penalty Opinions." Paper presented at the annual meeting of the Academy of Criminal Justice Sciences, Los Angeles, CA.

Bohm, R. M. and R. E. Vogel (1994) "A Comparison of Factors Associated With Un-informed and Informed Death Penalty Opinions." *Journal of Criminal Justice* 22:125–143.

Bohm, R. M., L. J. Clark, and A. F. Aveni (1991) "Knowledge and Death Penalty Opinion: A Test of the Marshall Hypotheses." *Journal of Research in Crime and Delinquency* 28:360–387.

Bohm, R. M., L. J. Clark, and A. F. Aveni (1990) "The Influence of Knowledge on Death Penalty Opinions: An Experimental Test." *Justice Quarterly* 7:175–188.

Bohm, R. M., R. E. Vogel, and A. A. Maisto (1993) "Knowledge and Death Penalty Opinion: A Panel Study." *Journal of Criminal Justice* 21:29–45.

Bowers, W. J. (1993) "Capital Punishment and Contemporary Values: People's Mis-givings and the Court's Misperceptions." *Law and Society Review* 27:157–175.

Bowers, W. J., B. D. Fleury-Steiner, and M. E. Antonio (2003) "The Capital Sentenc-ing Decision: Guided Discretion, Reasoned Moral Judgment, or Legal Fiction?" (This volume.)

Bowers, W. J., M. Vandiver, and P. H. Dugan (1994) "A New Look at Public Opinion on Capital Punishment: What Citizens and Legislators Prefer." *American Journal of Criminal Law* 22:77–150.

Bright, S. B. (2003) "The Politics of Capital Punishment: The Sacrifice of Fairness for Executions." (This volume.)

Bright, S. B. and P. J. Keenan (1995) "Judges and the Politics of Death: Deciding Be-tween the Bill of Rights and the Next Election in Capital Cases." *Boston Univer-sity Law Review* 75:759–835.

Burnett, Cathleen (2002) *Justice Denied: Clemency Appeals in Death Penalty Cases.* Boston: Northeastern University Press.

Callahan, L., J. R. Acker, and C. Cerulli (2000) "Accommodating Death Penalty Leg-islation: Personal and Professional Views of Assistant District Attorneys Toward Capital Punishment." *American Journal of Criminal Justice* 25:15–29.

Clarke, A. W., E. Lambert, and L. A. Whitt (2000–2001) "Executing the Innocent: The Next Step in the Marshall Hypotheses." *Review of Law & Social Change* 26:309–345.

Cottingham, J. (1979) "Varieties of Retributivism." *Philosophical Quarterly* 29:238–46.

Crespi, I. (1971) "What Kinds of Attitude Measures Are Predictive of Behavior?" *Public Opinion Quarterly* 35:327–334.

Death Penalty Information Center, www.deathpenaltyinfo.org

Dieter, R. C. (1996) "Killing for Votes: The Dangers of Politicizing the Death Penalty Process." Washington, DC: The Death Penalty Information Center, www.deathpenaltyinfo.org.

Durham, A. M., H. P. Elrod, and P. T. Kinkade (1996) "Public Support for the Death Penalty: Beyond Gallup." *Justice Quarterly* 13:705–736.

Ellsworth, P. C. and S. R. Gross (1994) "Hardening of the Attitudes: Americans' Views on the Death Penalty." *Journal of Social Issues* 50:19–52.

Ellsworth, P. C. and L. Ross (1983) "Public Opinion and Capital Punishment: A Close Examination of the Views of Abolitionists and Retentionists." *Crime and Delinquency* 29:111–169.

Erikson, R. S. (1976) "The Relationship between Public Opinion and State Policy: A New Look at Some Forgotten Data." *American Journal of Political Science* 20:25–36.

Erskine, H. (1970) "The Polls: Capital Punishment." *Public Opinion Quarterly* 34:290–307.

Estelle v. Gamble (1976) 429 U.S. 97.

Furman v. Georgia (1972) 408 U.S. 238.

Gallup, A. and F. Newport (1991) "Death Penalty Support Remains Strong." *The Gallup Poll Monthly* (June).

Gregg v. Georgia (1976) 428 U.S. 153.

Jackson, Rev. J. with J. Jackson, Jr. (1996) *Legal Lynching: Racism, Injustice and the Death Penalty*. New York: Marlowe.

Jones, J. M. (2002) "Slim Majority of Americans Say Death Penalty Applied Fairly." The Gallup Organization, www.gallup.com/poll/releases/pr020520.asp.

Jones, J. M. (2001) "Two-Thirds of Americans Support the Death Penalty." The Gallup Organization. www.gallup.com/poll/releases/pr010302.asp.

Jones, P. R. (1994) "It's Not What You Ask, It's the Way that You Ask It: Question Form and Public Opinion on the Death Penalty." *The Prison Journal* 74:32–50.

Jurow, G. L. (1971) "New Data on the Effect of a 'Death Qualified' Jury on the Guilt Determination Process." *Harvard Law Review* 84:567–611.

Kobil, D. T. (2003) "The Evolving Role of Clemency in Capital Cases." (This volume.)

Kohlberg, L. and D. Elfenbein (1975) "The Development of Moral Judgments Concerning Capital Punishment." *American Journal of Orthopsychiatry* 45:614–640.

Longmire, D. R. (1996) "Americans' Attitudes About the Ultimate Sanction Capital Punishment," pp. 93–108 in T. J. Flanagan and D. R. Longmire (eds.) *Americans View Crime and Justice: A National Public Opinion Survey*. Thousand Oaks, CA: Sage.

Lord, C. G., L. Ross, and M. R. Lepper (1979) "Biased Assimilation and Attitude Polarization: The Effects of Prior Theories on Subsequently Considered Evidence." *Journal of Personality and Social Psychology* 37:2098–2109.

McGarrell, E. F. and M. Sandys (1996) "The Misperception of Public Opinion Toward Capital Punishment: Examining the Spuriousness Explanation of Death Penalty Support." *American Behavioral Scientist* 39:500–513.

Monroe, A. D. (1979) "Consistency between Public Preferences and National Policy Decisions." *American Politics Quarterly* 7:3–19.

Moore, D. W. (1994) "Majority Advocate Death Penalty for Teenage Killers." *The Gallup Poll Monthly,* September 2–5.

Oskamp, S. (1977) *Attitudes and Opinions.* Englewood Cliffs, NJ: Prentice-Hall.

Page, B. I. and R. Y. Shapiro (1983) "Effects of Public Opinion on Policy." *American Political Science Review* 77:175–190.

Page, B. I., R. Y. Shapiro, and G. R. Dempsey (1987) "What Moves Public Opinion?" *American Political Science Review* 81:23–43.

Patenaude, A. L. (2001) "May God Have Mercy on Your Soul! Exploring and Teaching a Course on the Death Penalty." *Journal of Criminal Justice Education* 12:405–425.

Penry v. Lynaugh (1989) 492 U.S. 302.

Radin, M. J. (1980) "Cruel Punishment and Respect for Persons: Super Due Process for Death." *Southern California Law Review* 53:1143–1185.

Radin, M. J. (1978) "The Jurisprudence of Death: Evolving Standards for the Cruel and Unusual Punishment Clause." *University of Pennsylvania Law Review* 126:989–1064.

Roberts, J. V. (1984) "Public Opinion and Capital Punishment: The Effects of Attitudes Upon Memory." *Canadian Journal of Criminology* 26:283–291.

Roberts v. Louisiana (1976) 428 U.S. 325.

Robinson v. California (1962) 370 U.S. 660.

Sandys, M. (1995) "Attitudinal Change Among Students in a Capital Punishment Class: It May Be Possible." *American Journal of Criminal Justice* 20:37–55.

Sandys, M. and E. F. McGarrell (1995) "Attitudes Toward Capital Punishment: Preferences for the Penalty or Mere Acceptance?" *Journal of Research in Crime and Delinquency* 32:191–213.

Sarat, A. and N. Vidmar (1976) "Public Opinion, the Death Penalty, and the Eighth Amendment: Testing the Marshall Hypothesis." *Wisconsin Law Review* 17:171–206.

Sellin, T. (1967) *Capital Punishment.* New York: Harper & Row.

Trop v. Dulles (1958) 356 U.S. 86.

Tyler, T. R. and R. Weber (1982) "Support for the Death Penalty: Instrumental Response to Crime, or Symbolic Attitude?" *Law and Society Review* 17:21–45.

United States General Accounting Office (1990) *Death Penalty Sentencing: Research Indicates Pattern of Racial Disparities.* Gaithersburg, MD: U.S. General Accounting Office.

Vidmar, N. and T. Dittenhoffer (1981) "Informed Public Opinion and Death Penalty Attitudes." *Canadian Journal of Criminology* 23:43–56.

Vidmar, N. and P. Ellsworth (1974) "Public Opinion and the Death Penalty." *Stanford Law Review* 26:1245–1270.

Weems v. United States (1910) 217 U.S. 349.

Weissberg, R. (1976) *Public Opinion and Popular Government.* Englewood Cliffs, NJ: Prentice-Hall.

White, W. S. (1987) *The Death Penalty in the Eighties: An Examination of the Modern System of Capital Punishment.* Ann Arbor, MI: University of Michigan Press.

Whitehead, J. T. (1998) "Good Ol' Boys and the Chair: Death Penalty Attitudes of Policy Makers in Tennessee." *Crime and Delinquency* 44:245–256.

Wicker, A. W. (1969) "Attitudes Versus Actions: The Relationship of Verbal and Overt Behavioral Responses to Attitude Objects." *Journal of Social Issues* 25:41–78.

Williams, F. P., D. R. Longmire, and D. B. Gulick (1988) "The Public and the Death Penalty: Opinion as an Artifact of Question Type." *Criminal Justice Research Bulletin* 3:1–5.

Woodson v. North Carolina (1976) 428 U.S. 280.

Wright Jr., H. O., R. M. Bohm, and K. M. Jamieson (1995) "A Comparison of Uninformed and Informed Death Penalty Opinions: A Replication and Expansion." *American Journal of Criminal Justice* 20:57–87.

Zimring, F. E. and G. Hawkins (1986) *Capital Punishment and the American Agenda.* Cambridge: Cambridge University Press.

Chapter 2

Judicial Developments in Capital Punishment Law

Carol S. Steiker
Jordan M. Steiker

Introduction

Three decades ago, the Supreme Court in *Furman v. Georgia* (1972) abolished the death penalty as it was then administered in the United States. Four years later, the Court in *Gregg v. Georgia* (1976) and its quartet of accompanying cases sustained some new death penalty statutes that appeared to address many of the concerns voiced in *Furman*. In doing so, the Court embarked on a course of continuing constitutional regulation of capital punishment in America.

Virtually no one thinks that the constitutional regulation of capital punishment has been a success. But oddly, and we think significantly, critics of the Court's death penalty jurisprudence fall in two diametrically opposed camps. On the one hand, some critics claim that the Court has created an overly complex, absurdly arcane, and minutely detailed body of constitutional law that imposes an unacceptable burden on states' attempts to administer their capital punishment schemes. This set of critics notes the sheer volume of death penalty litigation, the labyrinthine nature of the doctrines that such litigation has spawned, the frequency with which federal courts overturn state-imposed death sentences, and the lengthy delays that occur between the imposition of death sentences and their execution. On the other hand, a different set of critics claims that the Supreme Court has in fact turned its back on regulating the death penalty and no longer even attempts to meet the concerns about the arbitrary and discriminatory imposition of death that animated its "constitutionalization" of capital punishment in *Furman*. These critics note that the Court's intervention has done little or nothing to remedy the vast over-representation on death row of the young, poor, and mentally impaired or the continuing influence of race on the capital sentencing decision. Under this view, in the anguished words of Justice Harry Blackmun, who twenty years after his dissent in

Furman radically changed course and argued for the constitutional abolition of the death penalty, the Court has done no more than "tinker with the machinery of death" (*Callins v. Collins* 1994:1145).

A sustained examination of the past quarter century of constitutional regulation of capital punishment reveals, surprisingly, that both sets of critics are substantially correct. The death penalty is, perversely, both over- and under-regulated. The body of doctrine produced by the Court is enormously complex and its applicability to specific cases difficult to discern; yet, it remains unresponsive to the central animating concerns that inspired the Court to embark on its regulatory regime in the first place. Indeed, most surprisingly, the overall effect of the Supreme Court's quarter century of doctrinal development has been largely to reproduce the pre-*Furman* world of capital sentencing.

In this chapter, we explore the concerns about the administration of capital punishment that led the Court to begin its regime of constitutional regulation. Using those concerns as a guide, we explain how the Court's death penalty doctrine, despite its complexity, has failed to engender much positive change. Moreover, the very complexity of the Court's doctrine may now pose an obstacle to future change by generating a false impression that the Supreme Court's highly visible involvement in the administration of capital punishment insures—perhaps even *over*-insures—against arbitrary or unjust executions. We conclude with some predictions about the future of judicial regulation of capital punishment in America.

Furman and *Gregg*:
The Commencement of Constitutional
Regulation of Capital Punishment

Until the Supreme Court's decision in *Furman v. Georgia* in 1972, the administration of capital punishment was simply not a subject about which the federal Constitution was thought to have much to say (Bedau 1968). Before the end of World War II, there was little litigation raising constitutional issues regarding capital punishment in the state or federal courts. The Supreme Court made no constitutionally significant rulings regarding the death penalty except that states were required to provide indigent defendants with court-appointed counsel in capital cases, a requirement it later extended to all non-petty criminal cases resulting in a sentence of incarceration. In the 1950s and 1960s, there was a marked increase in constitutional litigation regarding capital punishment and the entire criminal justice system. Still the Supreme Court declined or evaded numerous opportunities to rule on various procedural and substantive challenges to the death penalty, even as it began to interpret the "due process" clause of the Fourteenth Amendment to mandate certain procedures in state civil and criminal proceedings generally. This consistent policy of avoiding constitutional rulings on issues surrounding capital punishment led legal scholar Alexander Bickel to predict that "barring spectacular extraneous events, the moment of judgment" regarding the death penalty was "a generation or more away" (Bickel 1962:242).

Bickel's quite reasonable prediction, however, turned out to be wrong. Within ten years of his assessment, opponents of capital punishment, buoyed by the "revolution" in criminal procedure advanced by the Warren Court, had successfully drawn the Court into the constitutional fray. The NAACP Legal Defense Fund led the effort to halt executions through a "moratorium" strategy by raising a myriad of procedural and substantive challenges to state death penalty schemes in cases in which execution dates were set (Meltsner 1973). After their much-heralded success in limiting the practice of excluding from capital cases all jurors with conscientious scruples against the death penalty (*Witherspoon v. Illinois* 1968), the abolitionist and reformist forces appeared to lose decisively in *McGautha v. California* (1971). In *McGautha*, the Court upheld, against a challenge brought under the Fourteenth Amendment's "due process" clause, the existence of unguided discretion in capital sentencing. The very next year, however, the Supreme Court granted review in *Furman*, a case raising the same sweeping challenge as *McGautha*, but this time under the Eighth Amendment's proscription of "cruel and unusual punishments."

Both the arguments of the litigants and the ensuing opinions of the deeply divided Court reveal that *Furman v. Georgia* did not present merely a minor or technical challenge to particular aspects of state death penalty practices, but rather required an encompassing assessment of the moral, political, and practical dimensions of the American system of capital punishment. The immediate effect of *Furman*'s rejection of unguided jury discretion in capital sentencing was to invalidate the death penalty not only in Georgia, but in 38 other states, the District of Columbia, and the federal government. Although *Furman* remains the longest decision ever rendered by the Supreme Court, the majority "opinion" in the case was a terse one-paragraph invalidating under the Eighth Amendment the death sentences imposed on the three petitioners in the case. Each of the five Justices in the majority then appended his own opinion, none of which was joined by any other Justice. Each of the four dissenters wrote his own opinion as well, although some of them joined in each other's dissents. The opinions presented a staggering array of arguments for and against the death penalty, leaving lower courts, state legislators, and legal observers at a loss to know which arguments would dominate in the decision of any future cases.

Indeed, the main question left in the wake of *Furman* was whether there would *be* any future cases. Only Justices William Brennan and Thurgood Marshall argued in *Furman* that the death penalty was per se cruel and unusual punishment. Justices William Douglas, Potter Stewart, and Byron White expressly left open the question whether a more structured capital sentencing regime might someday pass constitutional muster. While many observers at the time believed that *Furman* signaled the end of capital punishment in America, in the weeks and months immediately following the decision, state and federal lawmakers across the country geared up to revamp and revitalize the death penalty.

The extent to which *Furman* was a beginning and not an end to constitutional regulation of the death penalty became clear in 1976, when the Supreme Court considered five new state statutory schemes in light of its decision in *Furman*, upholding three (*Gregg v. Georgia*; *Jurek v. Texas*; *Proffitt v. Florida*) and striking down two of the schemes (*Woodson v. North Carolina*; *Roberts v. Louisiana*). *Gregg v. Georgia* and its quartet of accompanying cases clarified that the death penalty was not per se invalid under the Eighth Amendment and that the Court would now be involved in the ongoing business of determining which state schemes could pass constitutional muster. In the three opinions upholding statutes in Georgia, Florida, and Texas, the Court did not attempt to list in any definitive fashion the prerequisites for a valid capital punishment scheme; rather, it simply upheld each particular scheme presented on the basis of its own peculiar mix of procedural protections. Hence, the 1976 cases established the essentially provisional nature of the Supreme Court's capital punishment jurisprudence and marked the clear commencement of the Court's ongoing regulatory role.

The roots of all of the rest of the Supreme Court's capital jurisprudence can be traced to the themes that the Court sounded in 1972 and 1976. Since 1976, the Supreme Court's pronouncements on capital punishment have been essentially backward-looking; majority and dissenting Justices alike have cast their positions in terms of what *Furman* and *Gregg* et al. command and permit. This is not to deny that the morass of *Furman* and the tentative, provisional tone of the 1976 opinions left future Justices a wide margin of deniability. Nonetheless, it seems likely that the Court itself would think it fair to measure the success of its capital punishment jurisprudence against the concerns articulated in *Furman* and *Gregg* et al. These concerns can be grouped around four ideas: desert, fairness, individualization and heightened procedural reliability.

Desert

At the time of the Court's decision in *Furman*, many jurisdictions in the United States authorized the death penalty not only for murder, but also for crimes such as rape, kidnaping, armed robbery, and even some assaults. Moreover, virtually every death penalty jurisdiction afforded sentencers absolute discretion to impose either death or life imprisonment (or sometimes merely a term of years) in capital cases. The Georgia statute reviewed in *Furman* itself was exemplary: it afforded the jury full discretion to sentence a defendant convicted of forcible rape to death, life imprisonment, or imprisonment for not less than one nor more than 20 years. The rape law of Texas, also reviewed in *Furman*, was similar, allowing the jury to impose death, life imprisonment, or imprisonment for any term of years not less than five. Juries were typically given very little guidance about how to choose among such different sentences. Florida's sentencing instructions were representative: juries were told that the decision to impose death or a lesser punishment for murder was to be "determined purely by the dictates of the consciences of the individual jurors" (*Baugus v. State* 1962:266).

One primary problem with such broad and discretionary schemes identified by the *Furman* and *Gregg* Courts was that the state and federal legislatures that drafted such statutes were never required to articulate a theory about the most death-worthy crimes or defendants. The Justices in *Furman* repeatedly noted that the number of those actually sentenced to death represented only a tiny fraction of those eligible to be executed by the broad net cast by the state statutes at issue in the case. The death penalty appeared, in Justice Stewart's evocative image, to strike like "lightning" (*Furman v. Georgia* 1972:309). Such sentencing systems provided no guarantee that each imposition of the death penalty reflected the larger community's considered judgment—as articulated through its elected representatives—about who deserved to die. What was missing, in Justice White's words, was a clear indication of "legislative will" (at 311). This failure can be described as a problem of overinclusion: without narrower statutory mandates, individual sentencers might return sentences of death in otherwise ordinary cases and thus perhaps run afoul of the larger community's moral standards.

This fear was clearly a subtext in *Furman* itself. Of the three petitioners, two had been sentenced to death for rape, which raised the possibility that the penalty was being applied when a community consensus was lacking. Indeed, four years later in *Gregg*, one reason given by all of the Justices in the majority for upholding the revised Georgia statute was that the Georgia Supreme Court had used its new power of broad appellate review to strike down the imposition of the death penalty for armed robbery as disproportionate to the crime. In both *Furman* and *Gregg*, then, the Court's concern about overinclusion—its fear that unbridled sentencing discretion might lead to the execution of those who did not deserve it—was paramount.

Fairness

Distinct from the concern about desert in capital sentencing is the concern about fairness. Even if every defendant sentenced to death under a capital sentencing scheme "deserved" to die according to the larger community's considered judgment, the scheme could still be subject to challenge on the basis that it treated others, just as "deserving" as the condemned defendant, more leniently for no reason, or for invidious reasons. In other words, a person sentenced to death could make one of two distinct complaints. He might say simply, "I don't deserve the death penalty." But he also might intelligibly say, "Whether or not I deserve the death penalty, there are other people who also deserve it and who are not getting it." Thus, a sentencing scheme could avoid the problem of overinclusion (the failure to distinguish the deserving from the undeserving), but still present the problem of underinclusion (the failure to treat equally deserving cases alike).

These two distinct concerns implicate different institutions within the criminal justice system. The task of ascribing desert, and thus avoiding overinclusion, falls largely within the realm of the legislature, which speaks as the voice of the larger community. The *Furman* Court fueled its concerns about desert by observing the sheer infrequency with which sentencers imposed the death penalty: such rarity of imposition, the Court observed, suggested that the death penalty was not serving any useful function in society and that it no longer reflected any considered community judgment or "legislative will." But even if death penalty statutes on the books could be said to reflect community judgment and legislative will, the problem of translating that will into practice would still remain. In this process of translation arises the inevitable possibility of arbitrary or even discriminatory enforcement of community norms by the sentencer (usually a jury) in whom resides the ultimate power to pronounce life or death. Unlike its concerns about desert, the *Furman* Court's concerns about fairness were fueled not by the infrequency of the imposition of the death penalty, but rather by the *patterns* of its imposition.

Justice Douglas' concurring opinion in *Furman* presents the clearest expression of the fairness concern—what he himself called the "equal protection" theme "implicit" in the Eighth Amendment's proscription of cruel and unusual punishment (at 249). In sounding this theme, Douglas used anecdotal and statistical evidence to demonstrate that the death penalty in the United States was visited disproportionately upon the "poor, young, and ignorant" and upon "the Negro, and the members of unpopular groups" (at 250). He noted explicitly what was largely a subtext for the other concurring Justices: in each of the three cases before the Court in *Furman*, the defendant was black, and in the two rape cases the victims were white. Douglas decried what he evocatively termed the "caste" aspect of the imposition of the death penalty and argued that the discretionary capital sentencing schemes at issue were "pregnant with discrimination" (at 255, 257). At no point did Douglas attempt to argue that the defendants before the Court (or the largely poor, young, ignorant, black, or unpopular defendants who had previously been executed) did not "deserve" the death penalty, by reference either to internal community norms or to some external, Court-imposed notion of proportionality. Rather, Douglas' concern was quite clearly with those who got away: "A law that stated that anyone making more than $50,000 would be exempt from the death penalty would plainly fall…. A law which in the overall view reaches that result in practice has no more sanctity than a law which in terms provides the same" (at 256).

This focus on fairness, as distinct from desert, was apparent again four years later in *Gregg v. Georgia* (1976): a plurality of the Court upheld Georgia's new capital sentencing scheme partly on the basis that the new statute provided "clear and objective standards" that would control sentencer discretion "so as to produce non-discriminatory application" (*Gregg v. Georgia* 1976:198). The *Gregg* plurality went on to praise the "important additional safeguard against arbitrariness and caprice" (at 198) afforded by Georgia's automatic appellate review and comparative proportionality determination. The latter procedure required the Georgia Supreme Court to compare each sentence of death with sentences imposed in similar cases and permitted it to reference those cases in which the death penalty had not been imposed (at 204–205 and n.56). Indeed, the new Georgia statute most explicitly addressed the *Furman* Court's concerns about discrimination by calling upon the state's highest court to determine in each capital case "[w]hether the sentence of death was imposed under the influence of passion, prejudice, or any other arbitrary factor," based partly on a questionnaire filled out by the trial judge that disclosed whether race played a role in the case (at 211–212, White, J., concurring).

Individualization

One possible response to the *Furman* Court's concerns about desert and fairness was to attempt to control sentencer discretion. This approach, apparent in Georgia's revised statute and also in the new statutes of Florida and Texas, was upheld by the *Gregg* Court in 1976. A second plausible approach, however, was to enact *mandatory* capital sentencing schemes, in which the death penalty was automatically imposed for certain types of crimes. Such schemes would necessarily contain the crucial ingredient of legislative will because they would compel legislatures to agree on circumstances that would require, not merely permit, the imposition of the death penalty. Additionally, such schemes would allow no possibility of discrimination by the sentencer (although the prosecutor, with charging discretion, would clearly have room to maneuver). Indeed, three of the five judges in the *Furman* majority—Douglas, Stewart, and White—expressly hinted that mandatory death penalties might withstand constitutional scrutiny, even as they struck down the discretionary statutes then in existence. Not surprisingly, a number of states responded to *Furman* by rewriting their capital sentencing schemes as mandatory death penalty statutes.

In 1976, however, the Supreme Court considered and rejected the mandatory approach, striking down capital statutes from Louisiana and North Carolina, and implicitly dooming all such laws elsewhere. The Court saw mandatory penalties in opposition to rather than in service of the goals of desert and fairness. Those two goals are each different facets of the basic norm of equal treatment, the idea that like cases should be treated alike. In the Court's view, mandatory death penalty statutes ran afoul of this basic norm because they erroneously relied on the flawed belief that "every offense in a like legal category calls for an identical punishment without regard to the past life and habits of a particular offender" (*Roberts v. Louisiana* 1976:333). In other words, in order to treat like cases alike, sentencers must have access to information about relevant likenesses and differences.

In the 1976 cases rejecting mandatory death penalties, the Court located the source of the constitutional standard for relevant capital sentencing information in the "evolving standards of decency that mark the progress of a maturing society" (*Trop v. Dulles* 1958:101). In applying such "evolving standards of decency" to the context of capital punishment, the Justices explained that they detected an overwhelming societal consensus against the imposition of mandatory death sentences. They also noted that the fundamental respect for humanity underlying the Eighth Amendment required consideration of "the character and record of the individual offender and the circumstances of the particular offense as a constitutionally indispensable part of the process of inflicting the penalty of death" (*Woodson v. North Carolina* 1976:304).

This latter "respect for humanity" argument built on Justice Brennan's opinion in *Furman* four years earlier, in which he tried to construct an argument against the death penalty based on the idea that "[t]he State, even as it punishes, must treat its members with respect for their intrinsic worth as human beings" (*Furman v. Georgia* 1972:270). Ultimately, Justice Brennan failed to convince his brethren that respect for humanity required the abolition of capital punishment altogether. However, his lengthy *Furman* concurrence did begin to develop a notion of human dignity that formed the basis of the Court's requirement of individualized sentencing.

What no one foresaw at the time, but which by now has become apparent, is the inherent tension between, on the one hand, controlling sentencer discretion so as to promote desert and fairness in the application of the death penalty, and, on the other hand, requiring individualized consideration by the sentencer of all relevant distinguishing traits among defendants. The best means of controlling discretion tend to undermine individualized consideration, and the process of individualized consideration creates opportunities for the free play of the very discretion that needs to be controlled. The 1976 cases, taken together, thus planted the seeds of one of the fundamental instabilities in current death penalty doctrine.

Heightened Procedural Reliability

Like its commitment to individualized capital sentencing, the Supreme Court's concern for heightened procedural reliability in capital cases built on Justice Brennan's solo concurrence in *Furman*. Just as Justice Brennan elaborated the notion of "human dignity" implicit in the Court's "evolving standards of decency" formulation of the Eighth Amendment, he also singlehandedly constructed the now-familiar "death is different" argument. Arguing that death as a punishment differs in kind, and not merely in degree, from all other punishments, Justice Brennan attempted to demonstrate that its uniqueness as a punishment, both in severity and finality, rendered it cruel and unusual in all circumstances. No other Justices in *Furman* joined in that conclusion (although, arguably, Justice Marshall agreed).

Four years later, however, a plurality of the Court echoed Brennan's *Furman* concurrence by noting, in language that would be repeated many times in future cases:

> Death, in its finality, differs more from life imprisonment than a 100-year prison term differs from one of only a year or two. Because of that qualitative difference, there is a corresponding difference in the need for reliability in the determination that death is the appropriate punishment in a specific case (*Woodson v. North Carolina* 1976:305).

The Court thus concluded that although the practice of individualized sentencing "generally reflects simply enlightened policy rather than a constitutional imperative," the Eighth Amendment requires individualized sentencing in capital cases (at 304).

The 1976 Court's willingness to require a special decision-making process in capital cases that clearly is not necessary in non-capital proceedings was generated by its concern about the "reliability" of death verdicts. What did the Court mean by "reliability"? Accuracy, perhaps? But what does accuracy mean in the context of capital sentencing? By referencing "the fundamental respect for humanity underlying the Eighth Amendment" (*Woodson* at 304), the Court seemed to suggest that reliability in capital sentencing has something to do with respecting and confronting the humanity of the individual defendant. And by speaking of the "appropriate[ness]" of death as punishment (at 305), the Court implied that reliability is tied to strong notions of desert and fairness among defendants. Hence, one can view the Court's commitment to heightened procedural reliability as its *manner* of making good on its three substantive commitments—to desert, fairness, and individualization in capital sentencing.

A Quarter Century Later: The Failure of Constitutional Regulation of Capital Punishment

Over the past twenty-five years, the Court has essentially reaffirmed its basic conclusion of the 1976 cases: that state death penalty practices are subject to constitutional scrutiny but that such scrutiny need not be fatal to the death penalty. Given the number of capital cases litigated in federal court (including the U.S. Supreme Court), the voluminous opinions issued by federal judges, and the scores of death sentences stayed or reversed over that period, one might be tempted to conclude that federal constitutional scrutiny is extraordinarily searching. Close examination of the litigation that has emerged over the past quarter century reveals, however, that contemporary death penalty doctrine is in fact remarkably undemanding. It is undeniably true, as many critics have claimed, that the Court's death penalty doctrine is complex, arcane, and minutely detailed. But this complexity does not translate, as the critics seem to assume, into significant impediments to states' efforts to impose the ultimate sanction. Instead, much of the recent capital litigation in the federal courts concerns statutory provisions that state legislatures could readily remedy or that in fact have already been repealed. Indeed, if a state sought to design a capital statute from scratch today, it could easily avoid federal constitutional difficulties and, perhaps more tellingly, could do so without departing significantly from the statutory schemes struck down in *Furman*.

The Court's death penalty jurisprudence can be evaluated in terms of several doctrines that correspond to the concerns of *Furman* and *Gregg* outlined previously. The Court's efforts to ensure that the death penalty is reserved for the most deserving defendants—its concerns about "desert" from a retributive perspective—are reflected in the Court's decisions requiring state schemes to "narrow" the class of death-eligible defendants as well as its decisions assessing the "proportionality" of the death penalty for certain offenses and offenders. The equality and fairness concerns of *Furman* are addressed by doctrines focusing on the related effort to "channel" sentencer discretion at all stages of the decision-making process. The Court's insistence on "individualized" sentencing is captured in its decisions concerning a defendant's right to present and have considered mitigating evidence that may call for a sentence less than death. The remainder of the Court's death penalty decisions collectively define the requirement of "heightened reliability" in capital proceedings.

Narrowing the Class of the Death-Eligible

Given the observed rarity of death sentences in relation to serious violent crimes, including murder, the Court insisted in *Furman* and the 1976 cases that death penalty jurisdictions, speaking through their legislatures, designate in advance those offenders most deserving of death. By forcing states to articulate their theories of the "worst" offenders, the narrowing doctrine purportedly guards against "overinclusion"—that is, the application of the death penalty in circumstances in which, notwithstanding the sentencer's decision, the sentence is not deserved according to wider community standards.

As the Court has elaborated this idea, states can narrow the class of the death-eligible by requiring the prosecution to prove the existence of some "aggravating factor" beyond what is required for conviction of murder itself. Courts can further narrow the class of the death-eligible through some sort of post-sentencing proportionality review in which courts determine whether particular sentences are actually deserved in light of prevailing sentencing practices and attitudes.

Despite the promise that the narrowing doctrine would significantly reduce the problem of overinclusion, the doctrine as elaborated by the Court has done no such thing. Death-eligibility remains remarkably broad; indeed, nearly as broad as under the expansive statutes characteristic of the pre-*Furman* era (Givelber 1994). States have adopted, and the Court has sustained, aggravating circumstances that arguably encompass every murder, such as Arizona's circumstance that asks whether the defendant committed the offense in an "especially heinous, cruel or depraved manner" (*Walton v. Arizona* 1990), and Idaho's circumstance that asks whether "[b]y the murder, or circumstances surrounding its commission, the defendant exhibited utter disregard for human life" (*Arave v. Creech* 1993). Far from ensuring that the class of the death-eligible is meaningfully narrowed, factors that focus on whether an intentional murder was "especially heinous" or manifested an "utter disregard for human life" invite an affirmative answer in every case.

Moreover, many states have adopted numerous aggravating circumstances. Thus, even in state schemes that rely primarily on objective, non-vague aggravating factors, such as committing murder in the course of a felony, or killing a police officer, the factors collectively suffer from the same defect as individual factors that are impermissibly vague. Instead of guiding sentencers toward a particular "theory" of the worst murders, they seem to indiscriminately describe the circumstances surrounding most murders. Empirical work reflects this dynamic, as virtually all persons sentenced to death in Georgia before *Furman* would have been deemed death eligible under Georgia's post-*Furman* statute (Baldus, Woodworth and Pulaski, Jr. 1990:102).

At the same time, the Court generally has exhibited reluctance to use proportionality analysis as a separate means of narrowing the class of death-eligible offenders. Though the Court ruled the year after *Gregg* that the death penalty is disproportionate for the crime of raping an adult woman (*Coker v. Georgia* 1977), it has carved few categorical exemptions from the death penalty for other classes of defendants who are unlikely to be among the truly "worst" offenders. For example, after initially concluding that the death penalty was disproportionate as applied to a perpetrator who had not killed, attempted to kill, or intended to kill (*Enmund v. Florida* 1982), the Court subsequently retracted that standard and sustained the imposition of the death penalty for persons convicted of felony murder regardless of whether they intended to commit, attempted to commit, or actually committed murder (*Tison v. Arizona* 1987). More significantly, the Court later declined to conclude that the death penalty is disproportionate as applied to juvenile offenders (*Stanford v. Kentucky* 1989). This decision has allowed the United States to occupy the position of the world's leader in executions of juvenile offenders since 1990, with more than all of the rest of the countries reporting such executions combined. The same year that it upheld the execution of juvenile offenders, the Court also concluded that the death penalty was not inherently disproportionate for offenders with mental retardation (*Penry v. Lynaugh* 1989), a decision it recently reversed (*Atkins v. Virginia* 2002) on the grounds that a growing legislative consensus and the Court's own independent evaluation together suggested that executing offenders with mental retardation violates the "evolving standards of decency that mark the progress of a maturing society" from which the Eighth Amendment draws its meaning (*Trop v. Dulles* 1958:100–101). Whether the Court's decision in *Atkins* will lead to more categorical exemptions, such as for juvenile offenders or for offenders with other forms of mental illness or impairment, is still an open question. On the one hand, *Atkins* explicitly contrasted the recent legislative momentum against executing persons with mental retardation with the relative legislative stasis concerning the execution of juvenile offenders (*Atkins v. Virginia* 2002:2249 n.18). On the other hand, advocates of further categorical exemptions from the death penalty are encouraged by what appears to be a significant shift in the Court's proportionality methodology. In noting the existence of a national consensus, the Court referenced (albeit in a footnote) professional positions, religious opinions, practices within the world community, and polling data (*Atkins v. Virginia* 2002:2249 n.21).

Those decisions on categorical exemptions, taken together, suggest that the narrowing of the class of offenders and offenses subject to the death penalty should be accomplished primarily, as in the pre-*Furman* regime, by sentencer discretion guided by statutory criteria rather than court mandate. Because the statutory criteria (generally in the form of aggravating circumstances) do not themselves accomplish any significant narrowing, this approach is essentially indistinguishable from the standardless discretion embodied in the pre-1972 statutes. Relatively minor participants in felonies that lead to death, juvenile offenders, offenders with mental impairments or illness not classified as mental retardation, and other defendants who may appear less deserving of the death penalty must rely on the discretionary decision-making of prosecutors and sentencers to protect them from a punishment that the broader community might deem excessive as applied to them. In this respect, the fear of over-inclusive application of the death penalty that accounted in part for the Court's decision to enter the constitutional thicket remains quite justified.

Channeling Sentencer Discretion

Furman and the 1976 decisions sought not merely to ensure that the death penalty was imposed only on deserving offenders, but also to ensure that similarly situated offenders would be treated equally. Overinclusion, of course, constitutes one kind of inequality (because it subjects some offenders to the death penalty who are by definition not as deserving as others), but it is not the only kind. Inequality also results if some, but not all, deserving offenders receive the death penalty, especially if there is no principled basis for distinguishing between those who receive the penalty and those who do not.

The 1976 decisions appeared to suggest that the most promising means of avoiding this sort of inequality was to focus or "channel" the sentencer's discretion on the relevant decision-making criteria. In this respect, the 1976 decisions seemed to reject Justice Harlan's insistence in *McGautha* that efforts to channel discretion are doomed to fail because of both the difficulty of cataloguing the appropriate considerations and the uselessness, in terms of channeling, that a truly exhaustive list would represent. Notwithstanding the 1976 decisions' seeming endorsement of channeling as a separate constitutional requirement, current doctrine has veered sharply in the direction of Justice Harlan. The Supreme Court has emphatically disclaimed any separate requirement to channel discretion apart from the requirement that states narrow the class of death-eligible offenders (*Zant v. Stephens* 1983). Accordingly, under current doctrine, once a state has limited the death penalty to some sub-class or subclasses of murderers, the state can give the sentencer absolute and unguided discretion to decide between death and some lesser punishment. Indeed, a state could constitutionally achieve the "narrowing" function at the guilt phase of a capital trial and ask one simple question at punishment: life or death?

The collapsing of the channeling requirement into the narrowing function fundamentally ignores a crucial concern of *Furman*. Narrowing the class of the death eligible in no way addresses the problem of underinclusion, because open-ended discretion after death-eligibility permits, even invites, the jury to act according to its own unaccountable whims. Without guiding the sentencer at all points of its decision-making, there simply is no guarantee that the "equal protection" concerns highlighted in *Furman* will be meaningfully addressed. If we are worried that the failure to provide precise guidance to capital sentencers may lead them to use irrelevant characteristics (such as physical attractiveness) or impermissible ones (such as race or class) to determine who should live and who should die from among the equally eligible, this problem is not resolved merely by narrowing the range of persons among whom the sentencer can discriminate (Steiker and Steiker 1992:863).

The abandonment of channeling as a distinct constitutional requirement is unsurprising because genuine channeling cannot be achieved by focusing solely on aggravating factors. One of the fundamental conclusions of the 1976 decisions was that capital sentencing proceedings must be "individualized" so as to permit a capital defendant to present mitigating evidence about his background, his character, or circumstances of the crime that might offer a basis for a sentence less than death (*Woodson v. North Carolina* 1976). As a matter of doctrine, this individualization requirement ultimately evolved into a capital defendant's virtually unconstrained right to present any conceivable mitigating evidence that might influence the sentencer's punishment decision. Thus, state efforts to channel consideration of mitigating evidence, far from being constitutionally required, became constitutionally impermissible.

Once channeling the sentencer's consideration of mitigating evidence becomes impermissible, it is difficult to see a basis for insisting on channeling the sentencer's consideration of aggravating evidence. If the sentencer may refuse to impose a death sentence for any or no reason at all (and nothing guides the sentencer in that decision), there is no effective means of preventing underinclusion. In such circumstances, guiding the sentencer in its consideration of aggravating evidence will not meaningfully contribute to "equality" in sentencing, because the absolute discretion afforded the sentencer at the critical moment of decision will render insignificant whatever guidance has been achieved on the aggravating side.

The Court's focus on narrowing as the sole constitutionally required means of addressing arbitrariness in capital sentencing—to the exclusion both of channeling and proportionality review—has yielded a significant consequence for death penalty doctrine. Because states need not channel sentencing discretion, the punishment decision need not have any structure at all. Under current doctrine, a state could choose to limit death-eligibility through its definition of capital murder (as many states have), and then simply ask the sentencer to decide punishment in light of any aggravating or mitigating factors that the sentencer deems significant. Although no state has yet chosen to leave the punishment phase unstructured to this degree, such a scheme would clearly withstand constitutional scrutiny given current doctrine. Indeed, such a scheme would also avoid much of the complicated litigation that has arisen as a result of states' decisions to design more elaborate sentencing proceedings.

The constitutional permissibility of such a scheme seems odd given the Court's strong emphasis in the 1976 decisions on the creation of a separate structured punishment phase in the post-*Furman* statutes it sustained. In those decisions, the Court did not explicitly indicate that a bifurcated proceeding with a carefully designed punishment phase was constitutionally indispensable. Nonetheless, a casual (and even a careful) observer of the interaction between the Court's decisions and statutory developments following *Furman* would likely have regarded such a proceeding as the new hallmark of permissible death penalty schemes. That current doctrine would permit a state to enact a statute defining nineteen or so categories of capital murder and to provide for a punishment phase structured around one general question—life or death—reveals the extent to which the Court has retreated from the more ambitious regulatory efforts that its 1976 decisions seemed to embrace and indeed to require.

If the Court now demands so little of states in terms of guiding sentencer discretion, what accounts for the extensive and complex litigation surrounding states' use of aggravating circumstances? Over the past twenty years, the Supreme Court has heard over a dozen cases involving constitutional challenges to states' efforts to guide sentencing discretion. Notwithstanding our claim that compliance with current doctrine is relatively simple, many inmates have prevailed in such challenges, and litigation concerning states' efforts to guide sentencer discretion remains substantial.

Some of this litigation is based on the minimal requirement that states narrow the class of the death-eligible through some non-vague factor or aggravating circumstance (*Godfrey v. Georgia* 1980). In such cases, if the challenged circumstance is impermissibly vague, the sentence must be reversed. Invalidation of the vague aggravating circumstance leaves nothing to support the death verdict other than the defendant's conviction for murder. Many of the remaining cases involve verdicts in which the sentencer relied on both permissible and impermissible aggravating circumstances. The sentencer's reliance on an impermissibly vague aggravating circumstance in a scheme which affords the sentencer absolute discretion once the defendant has become death-eligible (based on the sentencer's identifying at least one satisfactory aggravating circumstance) does not mandate reversal of the sentence (see *Zant v. Stephens* 1983).

The doctrine has become more intricate, though, in cases involving schemes in which the state has structured its punishment phase so that the sentencer is required to weigh aggravating and mitigating factors against each other to determine the appropriate sentence. Under such schemes, the Court has held that the sentencer's reliance on an invalid aggravating circumstance requires the state courts either to reweigh aggravating and mitigating factors (excluding the improper aggravating factor) or to determine whether the sentencer's consideration of the improper factor was "harmless" beyond a reasonable doubt if the sentence is to be sustained (*Clemons v. Mississippi* 1990). Thus, even though states can entirely forgo "structured" sentencing phases that involve the explicit weighing of aggravating and mitigating factors, the Court has insisted that once a state has adopted such a scheme, it may not ignore the sentencer's reliance on an improper factor in that structured decision-making process. This wrinkle generates substantial, highly technical litigation, because it requires courts to assess whether a given scheme is "weighing" or "non-weighing," and, if "weighing," whether the state courts have appropriately reweighed the relevant factors or adequately applied harmless error analysis.

Two significant observations about these developments emerge. First, the extensive litigation concerning the adequacy of particular aggravating circumstances continues only because many states have failed to purge dubious aggravating factors from their statutes. The Court has made clear that aggravating factors that are evaluative as opposed to objective are vulnerable to constitutional attack. The vast majority of aggravating circumstances have not and will not encounter this sort of challenge. States can, for example, fully satisfy the narrowing requirement through aggravating circumstances that focus on the presence of a separate felony, the killing of more than one person, the killing of a peace officer, or the commission of the crime while in prison. The requirement that states limit their aggravating circumstances to objective factors does not significantly inhibit a state's ability to render virtually all murderers death-eligible; rather it simply obligates states to establish the breadth of their statutes in unmistakably clear terms.

The second observation relates to the first. Even if a state chooses to persist in its use of a potentially vague aggravating circumstance, it could avoid a substantial amount of litigation by restructuring its punishment phase. Accordingly, much of the intricate litigation concerning whether a state's scheme is weighing or non-weighing, whether a state court has appropriately reweighed aggravating and mitigating factors, and whether a state court limiting construction "genuinely" narrows the class of the death-eligible, is entirely avoidable.

Individualized Sentencing

In its rejection of mandatory sentencing in the 1976 decisions, most notably in *Woodson v. North Carolina*, the Court made clear that a defendant is entitled to an "individualized" proceeding that facilitates the sentencer's consideration of mitigating evidence. Those opinions did not, however, answer two crucial questions concerning the scope of that right. First, the opinions did not specify what kinds of evidence could be regarded as "mitigating" so as to trigger the defendant's right to offer the evidence as a basis for a sentence less than death. Second, the opinions did not define the extent to which states are permitted to structure the sentencer's consideration of mitigating evidence. Current doctrine has rendered both of those uncertainties moot, because all death-penalty schemes presently permit unconstrained consideration of mitigating evidence. Accordingly, virtually all of the current litigation concerning the individualization requirement is backward-looking, gauging the constitutionality of statutory provisions and state practices that are no longer in force. Ironically, then, the past twenty-five years of intricate litigation over states' fulfillment of the individualization requirement is coming to an end only because states have voluntarily reproduced the open-ended consideration of mitigating factors that was a central feature of the pre-*Furman* statutes.

In a series of post-*Woodson* decisions, the Court sustained challenges to virtually all state-imposed limitations on the presentation of mitigating evidence. The Court's all-inclusive approach to individualization simplifies the doctrine by discouraging piecemeal evaluation of the relevance of particular kinds of mitigating evidence. More significantly, the Court's approach exacerbates the tension between the individualization doctrine and the Court's concern in other decisions for focused death-penalty decision-making. By making constitutionally relevant any and all traits or experiences that distinguish one individual from another, the Court invites arbitrary and even invidious decision-making.

As *Furman* recognized, the greater the discretion afforded the decision-maker, the less accountable the decision-maker will be to public values. If standardless discretion is problematic because it gives those with a mind to discriminate the opportunity to discriminate, unconstrained consideration of any kind of mitigating evidence is problematic precisely for the same reason. Although such discretion cannot be used to render a defendant death-eligible contrary to community standards, it can be used to exempt favored defendants from the death penalty or to withhold severe punishment for crimes against despised victims. And if, as we have argued, *Furman*'s equal protection concerns relate to both overinclusion and underinclusion, the Court's insistence that the individualization requirement encompasses all conceivably mitigating evidence undermines its efforts to achieve equality in the administration of the death penalty. The NAACP Legal Defense Fund understood and expressed this idea early on in its brief to the Court in *McGautha*, the 1971 case in which the Court upheld standardless discretion against a due process challenge: " 'Kill him if you want' and 'Kill him, but you may spare him if you want' mean the same thing in any man's language" (Brief Amici Curiae of the NAACP Legal Defense and Educ. Fund, Inc., and the National Office for the Rights of the Indigent 1971:69).

Although compliance with the individualization requirement has become straightforward in that the Court requires states to allow defendants to introduce any potentially mitigating evidence, litigation over the scope of the requirement has been substantial. Many states, remembering the critique of open-ended discretion in *Furman*, did not read the 1976 cases to require such a complete return to unfettered sentencer consideration of mitigating factors. Eleven years passed before the Court revisited the Florida statute that it had provisionally approved in the 1976 decisions and ruled that the statute's refusal to permit consideration of unenumerated mitigating factors (i.e., mitigating factors not specified in advance by the legislature) violated the Eighth Amendment (*Hitchcock v. Dugger* 1987). Accordingly, the perception that the death penalty is extensively regulated in this area stems not from intricate or stringent regulation so much as from a miscommunication between the Court and the states regarding the near completeness of the return to pre-*Furman* discretion with respect to mitigating factors.

Death Is Different

One of the central themes of the 1976 cases concerned the need for heightened reliability in capital cases. According to the Court, the qualitative difference between death and all other punishments justifies a corresponding difference in the procedures appropriate to capital versus non-capital proceedings

(Radin 1980). The Court echoed the "death is different" principle in a number of subsequent cases, but close examination of the Court's decisions over the past twenty-five years reveals that the procedural safeguards in death cases are not as different as one might suspect. Although the Court has carved out a series of protections applicable only to capital trials, it has done so in an entirely ad hoc fashion and left untouched a substantial body of doctrine that relegates capital defendants to the same level of protection as non-capital defendants.

The Court has invoked the notion of heightened reliability to allow questioning of jurors concerning racial prejudice in cases involving interracial murders (*Turner v. Murray* 1986); to invalidate a death sentence based in part on information in a pre-sentence report that was not made available to defense counsel (*Gardner v. Florida* 1977); to prevent prosecutors from deliberately misleading jurors about the consequences of their decision by overstating the extent of appellate review (*Caldwell v. Mississippi* 1985); to require the inclusion of a lesser-included offense instruction in cases which the evidence would support a guilty verdict for a non-capital offense (*Beck v. Alabama* 1980); and to permit the defendant to inform the jury of the real consequences of a "life" sentence when the state argues that the defendant would be dangerous in the future and "life" means life without possibility of parole as a matter of state law (*Simmons v. South Carolina* 1994). The Court also has invoked the "death is different" doctrine in post-trial proceedings to overturn a sentence based in part on a prior conviction that was later invalidated (*Johnson v. Mississippi* 1988), and to suggest that some post-trial judicial consideration of newly-discovered evidence of innocence may be mandated when the inmate makes a "truly persuasive" showing of actual (as opposed to legal) innocence (*Herrera v. Collins* 1993).

The decisions described above, taken together with the cases elaborating the requirement of individualized sentencing, represent the sum total of the Court's applications of the death-is-different doctrine. It should be apparent from the brief summary of those decisions that the doctrine does not reflect a systematic effort to regulate the death penalty process so much as a series of responses to particular circumstances in which the Court deemed a state rule or practice manifestly unreliable or unfair. Although certain themes unite some of the decisions, such as "truth" in sentencing and the need for collateral procedures in extraordinary cases, the Court has not explained precisely how death is different from all other punishments other than to reassert that death is final and severe. As a result, the Court appears to invoke the death-is-different principle on a case-by-case basis without a more general theory of the fundamental prerequisites to a fair and principled death penalty scheme.

More importantly, that those decisions exhaustively account for the Court's death-is-different doctrine reveals the extent to which the death penalty is not in fact different. There are numerous contexts in which capital defendants receive no special safeguards. For example, courts judge counsel in capital cases according to the same, highly deferential, standard applicable to all criminal cases (*Strickland v. Washington* 1984). Partly as a result of this deferential standard, representation in capital trials remains notoriously poor, especially for indigent defendants (Bright 1994). Capital defendants also lack any distinctive protections in the availability of state and federal review of their convictions. Under current doctrine, states need not provide any postconviction proceedings in criminal cases, including capital cases. On the federal side, the Court has not mandated any particular federal review of state convictions, and has in fact imposed substantial procedural barriers to such review for both capital and non-capital petitioners.

Perhaps the most promising gauge of "heightened reliability" in capital sentencing can be found in the actual sentencing patterns of the various states that provide for capital punishment. Although evaluating the fairness and reliability of state schemes is concededly difficult, several researchers have sought to examine the role of race in post-*Furman* sentencing practices. The leading study in this area, conducted by the Baldus group, concluded that continued sentencing disparities in Georgia in the post-*Furman* period are likely attributable to racial discrimination (Baldus, Woodworth and Pulaski, Jr. 1990:185). Similar studies have uncovered race-based sentencing disparities in Florida, Illinois, and many other states (Gross and Mauro 1989:69).

Confronted with a constitutional challenge based on the Baldus study, the Court seemed to disavow any authority to recognize one rule in the death penalty context and another for all other punishments. According to the Court, taking the race-discrimination claim based on the Baldus study "to its logical conclusion [would throw] into serious question the principles that underlie our entire criminal justice system" (*McCleskey v. Kemp* 1987:314–15). Given that "[t]he Eighth Amendment is not limited in application to capital punishment, but applies to all penalties," the Court worried that "if [it] accepted McCleskey's claim that racial bias has impermissibly tainted the capital sentencing decision, [it] could soon be faced with similar claims as to other types of penalty" (at 315).

The Court's answer to the Baldus challenge, in perhaps the most provocative test of the reach of its death-is-different principle, was thus to deny that the Constitution permits a distinctive set of rules in the capital context. In this respect, the decision confirms that the Court's death-is-different doctrine does not authorize any far-reaching challenges to states' ability to administer the death penalty. In evaluating potential attacks on the death penalty, the Court simply will not construe the Constitution to place "totally unrealistic conditions on its use" (*McCleskey v. Kemp* 1987:319). Despite protestations that the Court has embarked on an elaborate scheme of death-penalty regulation, the Court's death-is-different doctrine is nothing more than a modest, ad hoc series of limitations on particular state practices. As with the Court's other death penalty doctrines, the seemingly intricate and demanding constraints appear quite marginal upon closer inspection.

The Court's recent, highly-publicized decision requiring juries—not judges—to make the factual determinations necessary to expose a defendant to death eligibility illustrates this same dynamic (*Ring v. Arizona* 2002). The decision clearly invalidates the practices of five states and potentially affects the sentences obtained in many others with "hybrid" sentencing schemes involving both judge and jury. But the dislocation in terms of litigation and reversals is not attributable to any heightened protection in capital cases. In fact, prior Court decisions had embraced judicial factfinding in capital cases (*Walton v. Arizona* 1990) and the sole question in *Ring* was whether capital defendants would receive the same protection the Sixth Amendment affords non-capital defendants. After initially suggesting that capital defendants might be entitled to different (and less) protection in this regard (*Apprendi v. New Jersey* 2000), the Court ultimately held otherwise two years later in *Ring*. A casual observer of the Court might be tempted to view *Ring* as yet another significant obstacle to states' implementation of the death penalty in light of its potential impact on the sentences of hundreds of death-row inmates. In fact, the case involves another quite minimal requirement imposed by the Court, and its potentially large impact is the result of the Court's longstanding acceptance in *Walton* and *Apprendi* of judicial factfinding in capital cases.

Virtually all of the complexity in death penalty law over the past twenty-five years stems from a failure in translation rather than an insistence on fulfilling the ambitious goals of *Furman* and the 1976 decisions. This communication gap, in which the Court rarely identified in clear and unanimous terms the minimal obligations of states in the post-*Furman* era, and in which states failed to respond quickly (or in some cases at all) to obvious correctable defects in their state statutes in light of those minimal obligations, has left us with the worst of all possible regulatory worlds. The resulting complexity conveys the impression that the current system errs, if at all, on the side of heightened reliability and fairness. And the fact of minimal regulation, which invites if not guarantees the same kinds of inequality as the pre-*Furman* regime, is filtered through time-consuming, expensive proceedings that ultimately do little to satisfy the concerns that led the Court to take a sober second look at the country's death-penalty practices in the first place. In short, the last twenty-five years have produced a complicated regulatory apparatus that achieves extremely modest goals with a maximum amount of political and legal discomfort.

Hidden Costs of the Court's Failure

The existence of a complex and burdensome system of constitutional regulation that, paradoxically, does little or nothing to rationalize the administration of capital punishment carries with it another, less apparent cost. When the regulatory apparatus is so massive and seemingly oppressive, we worry that its very existence might convince people, both within and outside of the criminal justice system, that the imposition of the death penalty is highly regulated and carefully monitored, even when it is not. This impression of stringent regulation may well render participants in the criminal justice system and the public at large more comfortable with the death penalty than they otherwise might be.

In short, we worry that the Supreme Court's complex body of constitutional law relating to capital punishment has the effect of "legitimating" the use of the death penalty in the United States. Here, we use the verb "to legitimate" not in the formal sense of "to authorize," nor in the normative sense of "to justify," but rather in a sense derived from the works of theorists Max Weber and Antonio Gramsci: to legitimate is to induce a false or exaggerated belief in the normative justifiability of something in the social world; that is, to induce belief in the absence of or in contradiction to evidence of what the phenomenon is "really" like (Steiker and Steiker 1995:429–432).

Two separate compelling arguments support the claim that the Court's death penalty law has a legitimating effect on actors within the criminal justice system. First, the Court's focus on controlling the discretion of capital sentencers creates a false aura of rationality, even science, around the necessarily moral task of deciding life or death. Legal scholar Robert Weisberg has argued convincingly that the Court's attempt to tame the "existential moment" of decision in the capital sentencing process has had the effect of reducing the anxiety that judges and juries feel about exercising their sentencing power (Weisberg 1983:353). The Court's current capital punishment law thus permits such institutional actors "to reassure themselves that the sanctions they inflict follow inevitably from the demands of neutral, disinterested legal principles, rather than from their own choice and power" (at 385). Weisberg powerfully, if anecdotally, illustrates this point by comparing jury instructions and closing arguments in capital sentencing hearings before and after the innovations of *Furman* and *Gregg*. Whereas pre-*Furman* jury instructions "aggressively reinforced the notion that the jury could not look to the law for any relief from the moral question of the death sentence," post-*Furman* instructions and prosecutorial arguments urge capital jurors to "realize that their apparently painful choice is no choice at all—that the law is making it for them" through a form of "legal arithmetic" that tallies aggravating and mitigating circumstances (Weisberg at 371–377). Weisberg's impressionist account is bolstered by the empirical work of the Baldus group, whose study of sentencing patterns in Georgia reveals a higher per capita sentencing rate after the Supreme Court's "reform" of capital sentencing schemes (Baldus, Woodworth and Pulaski, Jr. 1990:102–103).

The second argument for legitimation within the criminal justice system focuses on how the Court's constitutionalization of capital punishment has diluted sentencing judges' and juries' sense of ultimate responsibility for imposing the death penalty. The Supreme Court's Eighth Amendment jurisprudence has itself recognized the ways in which knowledge of a lack of final responsibility for imposing the death sentence can impermissibly bias a sentencing jury's decision. In *Caldwell v. Mississippi* (1985), the Court reversed a death sentence imposed after the prosecutor was permitted to argue to the sentencing jury that its decision to impose the death sentence would be reviewed by the state supreme court. Such an argument, opined the Court, impermissibly denigrated the jury's sense of "awesome responsibility" for imposing the death penalty, especially because it was simply not true that appellate courts could redo the moral calculus assigned to the sentencing jury (at 329). Yet, what the Court's Eighth Amendment law forbids the prosecutor or judge to tell a seated sentencing jury is exactly what the law itself "tells" every potential juror. The Court's constitutionalization of capital punishment under the Eighth Amendment has necessarily entailed systematic federal review of all capital cases and has prompted much greater state appellate review to preempt further constitutional challenges. Given the wide coverage of such review in the popular press and the number of capital cases that come to juries as retrials of earlier convictions or sentences, capital sentencing juries (and, of course, judges) must know that their imposition of a death sentence is not the end of the matter, but rather the beginning of a lengthy chain of review. Yet, this "fact," of which we presume a large number of jurors are aware, is no more "true" than is the prosecutor's argument in *Caldwell*; appellate courts do not generally review the moral appropriateness of the imposition of the death penalty. Rather, as we have demonstrated, the vast majority of the Court's decisions regulating state death penalty practices touch peripheral, rather than core issues. The Court's death penalty law thus leaves sentencing judges and juries with a false sense that their power is safely circumscribed.

Each of these two arguments about sentencing judges and juries can fairly be extended to other actors within the criminal justice system. Just as sentencers may be comforted by the apparent mathematical precision of the new capital sentencing regimes (Bowers 1995), prosecutors may feel emboldened in seeking the imposition of the death penalty. And just as sentencers may be reassured by the existence of layers of review between their sentence and the moment of execution (if it ever comes), state appellate courts may be reassured by the existence of federal habeas review, and governors may feel that any sentence that survives both state and federal review is not an appropriate vehicle for exercising the power of clemency. Two death penalty scholars have made this type of argument in attempting to account for the drastic post-*Furman* decline in the use of the clemency power. Hugo Bedau has argued that the decline in clemency resulted from "the perception...that death sentences are now meted out by trial courts with all the fairness that is humanly possible, even if in the dark, pre-*Furman* past they were not" (Bedau 1990–1991:268). Franklin

Zimring has made a similar argument, observing that in the post-*Furman* world of capital punishment, executions are regarded "as the moral responsibility of Supreme Court justices" rather than of state governors (Zimring 1992:17). The diffusion of moral responsibility that occurs when a decision is perceived (correctly or not) to be divided among a number of decision-makers—the aptly described "problem of many hands"—affects all participants in the decision-making process, which in the capital context may include everyone from law enforcement agents to the actual executioner.

Many of the arguments we have made about legitimation of the death penalty within the criminal justice system also suggest a legitimation effect in the public-at-large. Robert Weisberg, whom we cite approvingly above, parts company with us here, doubting this broader legitimating effect on the grounds that "[m]ost Americans are probably only barely aware how capital punishment operates or fails to operate, much less how the law of capital punishment has developed" (Weisberg 1983:384). Legal scholar Alan Hyde has generalized this objection to broad legal legitimation arguments of all sorts: "If legal decisions and rules are largely unknown to the population, not well-regarded when known, and cannot be shown to influence belief or behavior in the absence of sanction, how could they, by projecting particular values, legitimate an order?" (Hyde 1983:414). Although Weisberg and Hyde are probably correct that members of the general public do not know much about the intricacies of the Court's death penalty doctrine, our guess is that they *think* they know a great deal. We have already argued that they know about the existence of extensive review of capital sentences and that their ignorance about the precise nature of such review actually enhances the legitimating effect of such "knowledge." Similarly, the delays that occur between death sentence and execution are matters of common popular knowledge. Indeed, the past decade has seen increasingly strident attempts by state and federal legislators to address exactly this issue, in response, no doubt, to perceived popular pressure. Public perceptions about the nature of death penalty regulation legitimate *not* because such regulation is "well-regarded" (in Hyde's parlance), but rather because the elaborateness of the Court's death penalty jurisprudence fuels the public's impression that any death sentences that are imposed and finally upheld are the product of a rigorous—indeed *too* rigorous—system of constraints.

The public's vague and incomplete knowledge about an intricate scheme of constitutional regulation of the death penalty thus acts as a society-wide *Caldwell* argument. The public develops a strong but false sense that many levels of safeguards protect against unjust or arbitrary executions. They are thus likely to accept any executions that finally make it through the system as being more than fair enough. The Supreme Court's death penalty law, by creating an impression of enormous regulatory effort, while achieving negligible regulatory effects, effectively obscures the true nature of our capital sentencing system. The pre-*Furman* world of unreviewable sentencer discretion lives on, with much the same consequences in terms of arbitrary and discriminatory sentencing patterns.

This is the hidden cost and the deep irony of the Supreme Court's capital punishment jurisprudence. The abolitionist lawyers who pushed for the very reforms that the Supreme Court has endorsed believed that those reforms would end or at least rationalize the death penalty as a social institution. They would no doubt be surprised to observe the extent to which current death penalty law acts to legitimate capital punishment—by denying contradictions between individualized consideration and fairness over a range of cases, by masking the moral choice and wide discretion of capital sentencers, and by promoting the appearance of intensive regulation despite its virtual absence. Thus, the impulse to abolish or reform the death penalty has produced a body of law that may contribute substantially to the stabilization and perpetuation of capital punishment as a continuing social practice.

The Path to Come

For reasons that should be apparent in light of the history of constitutional regulation of the death penalty, predictions about the future are particularly hazardous. Just a few years ago, in the mid-1990s, like Alexander Bickel (1962) a quarter century before, we faced a political and legal landscape in which significant reform seemed far in the future. The death penalty was spreading to jurisdictions that had not actively sought or applied the punishment in many decades. In the wake of the Oklahoma City bombing, Congress had enacted substantial limitations on the availability of federal review of capital sentences, and the Supreme Court rejected some initial constitutional challenges to the statutory reform. Popular support for the death penalty appeared unusually strong.

But the past three years have begun to see some dramatic changes both in popular and political attitudes toward the death penalty. Most observers trace the heightened critical appraisal of our death penalty practices to events in Illinois. After the exoneration of more than a dozen death-row inmates in that state, Republican Governor George Ryan declared a moratorium on executions beginning in early 2000—a moratorium that remains in place. Many other municipalities subsequently adopted resolutions in favor of suspending executions and Maryland's Governor Parris Glendening has recently declared a moratorium pending a study of racial bias within the state. In addition, numerous jurisdictions, including the federal government, have considered or implemented various reforms, including mandatory DNA preservation and testing, higher standards of proof in capital cases, and the initiation of new "self-studies" of death penalty practices. Polling data from May 2001 likewise revealed that public support for the death penalty had fallen to its lowest level in nineteen years, down from a high of 80% in 1994 to a level of 65% only seven years later. At the same time, international pressure against American death penalty practices, particularly from Europe, is increasing. Indeed, the amicus brief of the European Union was cited in the Court's 2002 decision in *Atkins* banning execution of persons with mental retardation. It is uncertain whether the current momentum of critical appraisal is, like the moment immediately preceding *Furman*, a fleeting episode, or whether domestic and international events will pull the United States down a new road of reform or even abolition. The uncertain legacy of the events of September 11 complicate the picture, as recent habeas reforms reflect Congress's interest in combating terrorism in part through an "effective death penalty."

Perhaps supporters of the death penalty have become victims of their own success. Political efforts to hasten the pace of executions and limit the grounds for appeal might well have invited the sort of scrutiny, both internal and external, that the present regime until recently had managed to avoid. As the most visible signs of contemporary regulation are withdrawn, actors within the criminal justice system are no longer able to indulge the comforting presumption that their decisions and actions are rendered less significant or meaningful by "extensive" checks elsewhere established. So as the numbers of those sentenced to death and executed began to climb in the late 1990s, the general public seems to have revisited the fairness and reliability issues surrounding state death penalty practices that first surfaced three decades ago. Indeed, Congress's decision to curtail federal habeas for death-row inmates was responsible in part for the American Bar Association's recent decision to call for a nationwide moratorium on executions pending restoration and enhancement of federal courts' authority to review the constitutional claims of state prisoners. Just as there is irony in the stabilization of the death penalty by its reformers, so is there irony that the success of death penalty proponents seems to be fueling a new generation's re-examination of the justice of the death penalty.

If future reform is forthcoming, we hope that it is framed in light of the lessons of the post-*Furman* era. Meaningful equality in the distribution of the death penalty cannot be secured simply by finding new and intricate ways of instructing the decision-maker. Indeed, Justice Harlan could find nothing but vindication in the post-*Furman* experiment with guided discretion schemes. As Justice Harlan argued, it is simply impossible to capture in words the myriad considerations related to the death penalty decision. Moreover, the necessity of affording capital decision-makers wide discretion to consider mitigating factors essentially ensures that some offenders will benefit from the arbitrary or discriminatory exercise of that discretionary power.

Accordingly, the most promising avenues for reform must focus primarily on significant aspects of state death penalty schemes apart from the sentencer's moment of decision. For example, the Court could insist on more meaningful narrowing of the class of death-eligible offenders by compelling states to limit both the number and breadth of their aggravating circumstances (as well as their encompassing definitions of capital murder). At the same time, the Court could expand its categorical exclusions to death eligibility, as it recently did for persons with mental retardation (*Atkins v. Virginia* 2002), so as to exempt defendants such as juveniles or offenders with mental impairments or mental illness not classified as mental retardation, who are unlikely to fall within the class of the "worst" offenders. These reforms together would substantially decrease the likelihood of disproportionate verdicts and address in a more cogent way than current doctrine the "freakish" administration of the death penalty decried in *Furman*.

The Court could also police more vigorously the outcomes of state death penalty schemes by precluding, for example, the imposition of the death penalty in jurisdictions whose sentencing disparities exceed some threshold of acceptability. As with Court-imposed proportionality limits on the death penalty, Court-imposed limits on arbitrariness create difficult line-drawing problems. The answer to such problems ultimately must rest upon an account of the "difference" of death. If, as *Furman* and the 1976 decisions suggest, the death penalty must be administered fairly if at all, the Court could insist that tolerable inequalities in non-capital sentencing become intolerable when life is at stake. If we take seriously the sentiment in *Furman* that a caste system of capital punishment renders the punishment "cruel and unusual," litigation over the bottom-line of states' efforts to administer the death penalty seems preferable to tolerating a caste system solely because we cannot precisely identify how the system operates (Kennedy 1997).

An alternative type of reform would involve a greater focus on procedural aspects of death penalty systems that contribute significantly to arbitrariness. As discussed above, the "heightened reliability" decisions issued by the Court thus far do not target the most obvious sources of inequality. Rather, the Court's death-is-different doctrine seems to demand only that states *refrain* from certain objectionable practices, such as engaging in prosecutorial misconduct or promulgating misleading sentencing instructions. These types of painless intervention may well be justified, but they do not represent a comprehensive effort to ensure that defendants are treated equally in state death-penalty proceedings.

Perhaps the most significant source of inequality in the administration of the death penalty is the unevenness of representation. The Court has sought to address the representation issue solely by providing for post-trial, extraordinarily deferential review of counsel's performance. The obvious alternative to policing counsel in this manner is to establish firm guidelines for representation in capital cases that would include, among other things, minimum standards for appointment, adequate compensation for both counsel and experts, and presumptions about certain fundamental aspects of death-penalty preparation and presentation. Such presumptions might include investigation of both guilt-innocence and punishment phase defenses, consultation with appropriate experts regarding physical evidence and psychiatric issues, thorough cross-examination of state witnesses, and research and advocacy regarding potential inadequacies of the state capital scheme, including on appeal.

As it stands, it is commonplace in many states for trial counsel to fail to present any evidence or argument during the punishment phase of a capital trial. Attorneys on direct appeal also routinely fail to attend oral argument at the one post-trial hearing in which all state law issues are subject to review. Notwithstanding these sorts of practices, federal and state courts have consistently rejected ineffectiveness of counsel claims.

Another sort of procedural reform would focus on post-trial review of capital verdicts. Although it is commonly assumed that death-row inmates have numerous postconviction opportunities in both federal and state courts to challenge the legality of their convictions and sentences, the availability of such opportunities is in fact quite limited in many circumstances. As for post-trial proceedings in state court, the Court has firmly rejected the proposition that states must provide any collateral mechanism for challenging criminal convictions, capital or otherwise. At least one death-penalty state (Arkansas) has recently abolished state collateral review of most federal claims, and many other states have tightened or are tightening procedural rules regarding the filing of state postconviction petitions.

Federal review is likewise collapsing. Under current doctrine and the new Anti-Terrorism statute, death-row inmates are afforded no special exemption from the elaborate array of procedural hurdles that substantially restrict petitioners' efforts to vindicate constitutional rights. As a result, an enormous number of federal postconviction claims are rejected without ever reaching the underlying constitutional claim of the state prisoner. Although concern for finality of state judgments and timely litigation of constitutional issues counsels against wholesale repudiation of procedural rules in capital cases, it seems odd for a system that espouses a commitment to heightened reliability to maintain extraordinary limitations on capital defendants' ability to correct errors that concededly undermine such reliability.

Our enthusiasm for these particular reforms is tempered by our more general ambivalence and doubts about the likely value of extensive constitutional regulation of capital punishment. We certainly believe that courts could do more to rationalize and equalize states' administration of the death penalty by focusing on the "core" issues of proportionality, representation, and postconviction review rather than by regulating the minutiae of state sentencing instruction. But even "productive" constitutional regulation focused at the core might not be enough. The troubling dynamic we have identified, in which court regulation tends to lessen internal and external accountability for the death penalty, will no doubt remain as long as the courts are viewed as a significant part of our death penalty system. And though these suggested reforms might reduce arbitrariness, we simply cannot predict how much arbitrariness would remain. The ultimate question, which we do not attempt to answer here, requires a constitutional and moral judgment about the consequences of the "difference" of death: do its severity, finality, and symbolic significance require a level of fairness and accuracy in its administration beyond human capacity? Our hope is that future generations will not avoid answering this question by presuming that the present set of largely unhelpful doctrines has cured the ills identified in *Furman* and later cases.

References

Antiterrorism and Effective Death Penalty Act of 1996, Pub. L. 104-132, 110 Stat. 1214.

Apprendi v. New Jersey (2000) 530 U.S. 466.

Arave v. Creech (1993) 507 U.S. 463.

Atkins v. Virginia (2002) 122 S.Ct. 2242.

Baldus, D.C., G.G. Woodworth and C.A. Pulaski, Jr. (1990) *Equal Justice and the Death Penalty.* Boston: Northeastern University Press.

Baugus v. State (1962) 141 So.2d 264 (Fla.), *cert. denied*, 371 U.S. 879 (1962).

Beck v. Alabama (1980) 447 U.S. 625.

Bedau, H.A. (1968) "The Courts, the Constitution, and Capital Punishment." *Utah Law Review* 1968:201–39.

Bedau, H.A. (1990–1991) "The Decline of Executive Clemency in Capital Cases." *New York University Review of Law & Social Change* 18:255–72.

Bickel, A.M. (1962) *The Least Dangerous Branch: The Supreme Court at the Bar of Politics.* Indianapolis: Bobbs-Merrill Company, Inc.

Bowers, W.J. (1995) "The Capital Jury Project: Rationale, Design, and Preview of Early Findings." *Indiana Law Journal* 70:1043–1102.

Brief Amici Curiae of the NAACP Legal Defense and Educational Fund, Inc., and the National Office for the Rights of the Indigent (1971), filed in *McGautha v. California*, 402 U.S. 183 (1971), No. 71-203.

Bright, S. (1994) "Counsel for the Poor: The Death Sentence Not for the Worst Crime but for the Worst Lawyer." *Yale Law Journal* 103:1835–1883.

Caldwell v. Mississippi (1985) 472 U.S. 320.

Callins v. Collins (1994) 510 U.S. 1141.

Clemons v. Mississippi (1990) 494 U.S. 738.

Coker v. Georgia (1977) 433 U.S. 584.

Enmund v. Florida (1982) 458 U.S. 782.

Furman v. Georgia (1972) 408 U.S. 238.

Gardner v. Florida (1977) 430 U.S. 349.

Givelber, D. (1994) "The New Law of Murder." *Indiana Law Review* 69:375–422.

Godfrey v. Georgia (1980) 446 U.S. 420.

Gregg v. Georgia (1976) 428 U.S. 153.

Gross, S. and R. Mauro (1989) *Death and Discrimination: Racial Disparities in Capital Sentencing.* Boston: Northeastern University Press.

Herrera v. Collins (1993) 506 U.S. 390.

Hitchcock v. Dugger (1987) 481 U.S. 393.

Hyde, A. (1983) "The Concept of Legitimation in the Sociology of Law." *Wisconsin Law Review* 1983:379–426.

Johnson v. Mississippi (1988) 486 U.S. 578.

Jurek v. Texas (1976) 428 U.S. 262.

Kennedy, R. (1997) *Race, Crime, and the Law.* New York: Pantheon Books.

McCleskey v. Kemp (1987) 481 U.S. 279.

McGautha v. California (1971) 402 U.S. 183.

Meltsner, M. (1971) *Cruel and Unusual: The Supreme Court and Capital Punishment.* New York: Random House.

Penry v. Lynaugh (1989) 492 U.S. 302.

Proffitt v. Florida (1976) 428 U.S. 242.

Radin, M.J. (1980) "Cruel Punishment and Respect for Persons: Super Due Process for Death." *Southern California Law Review* 53:1143–85.

Ring v. Arizona (2002) 122 S.Ct. 2428.

Roberts v. Louisiana (1976) 428 U.S. 325.

Simmons v. South Carolina (1994) 512 U.S. 154.

Stanford v. Kentucky (1989) 492 U.S. 361.

Steiker, C. and J. Steiker (1992) "Let God Sort Them Out? Refining the Individualization Requirement in Capital Sentencing." *Yale Law Journal* 102:835–70.

Steiker, C. and J. Steiker (2002) "Should Abolitionists Support Legislative 'Reform' of the Death Penalty?" *Ohio State Law Journal* 63:417–32.

Steiker, C. and J. Steiker (1995) "Sober Second Thoughts: Reflections on Two Decades of Constitutional Regulation of Capital Punishment." *Harvard Law Review* 109:355–438.

Strickland v. Washington (1984) 466 U.S. 668.

Tison v. Arizona (1987) 481 U.S. 137.

Trop v. Dulles (1958) 356 U.S. 101.

Turner v. Murray (1986) 476 U.S. 28.

Walton v. Arizona (1990) 497 U.S. 639.

Weisberg, R. (1983) "Deregulating Death." *Supreme Court Review* 1983:305–395.

Witherspoon v. Illinois (1968) 391 U.S. 510.

Woodson v. North Carolina (1976) 428 U.S. 280.

Zant v. Stephens (1983) 462 U.S. 862.

Zimring, F. (1992) "Inheriting the Wind: The Supreme Court and Capital Punishment in the 1990s." *Florida State University Law Review* 20:7–19.

Chapter 3

Beyond Human Ability? The Rise and Fall of Death Penalty Legislation

James R. Acker
Charles S. Lanier

Introduction:
The Different Faces of Capital Punishment

Discourse about capital punishment often digresses rapidly into polarized "pro" and "con" positions regarding whether government can ever legitimately exact life in punishment of crime. This focus is understandable, but a number of compelling secondary issues are ignored when debate does not advance beyond the fundamental question of whether the death penalty can ever be justly imposed. For example, if a jurisdiction enacts capital-punishment laws, how should the death penalty be distributed? For which offenses and offenders should it be reserved? What procedures should govern its imposition? The essential question, "should the state ever be authorized to kill?," too often overshadows and preempts consideration of a host of other issues that are of great theoretical and practical importance to the death penalty's justifiability and continued existence.

Capital punishment is a legislative creation. Shorthand references to "the death penalty" can obscure the profoundly significant differences in capital-punishment statutes that have existed historically and that continue to exist today. Death-penalty statutes define who is eligible for the capital sanction, designate the crimes that qualify as capital offenses, create the criteria and procedures used to select offenders who are sentenced to death, and regulate many other important administrative issues ranging from the qualifications of capital jurors, to the processing of appeals, through establishing the method of carrying out executions. Secondary issues of this nature are important in their own right and, at least for the foreseeable future, are more likely to be the subject of meaningful reassessment than is the fundamental question of whether capital punishment ever should be authorized.

We begin this chapter by briefly reviewing the history and evolution of death-penalty statutes in the United States. We next examine specific provisions of contemporary capital-punishment legislation, focusing on some of the important differences reflected in existing statutes. We conclude with speculation about future legislative trends, and explain why we believe that the present reform era in death-penalty statutes is an important way station leading toward the eventual demise of the capital sanction.

An Abbreviated History
of Death-Penalty Legislation

The Season of *McGautha*

Just over three decades ago, or little more than the blink of an eye in the long history of the death penalty, *McGautha v. California* (1971) was the law of the land. When *McGautha* was decided in May of 1971, more than 600 prisoners awaited execution under state and federal authority (U.S. Department of Justice 1982:18). The great majority of those death sentences had been imposed for murder, and a significant number for rape. Among the many other crimes punishable by death throughout the country were kidnaping, burglary, robbery, treason, arson, train wrecking, bombing, assault by life-term prisoners, espionage, and aircraft piracy (Bowers 1974:43–56; Savitz 1955; Sellin 1967).

McGautha joined challenges brought by two prisoners convicted of murder and sentenced to death under different state procedures. Dennis McGautha, whose prior record included four felony convictions, was sentenced to death by a California jury for first-degree murder committed during an armed robbery (*People v. McGautha* 1969). James Crampton was sentenced to death after an Ohio jury rejected his plea of not guilty by reason of insanity and convicted him of the first-degree murder of his wife (*State v. Crampton* 1969). At the time of McGautha's trial, California was one of six states where capital trials were bifurcated. This procedure allowed evidence that specifically related to sentencing issues to be presented at a separate hearing, conducted after the conclusion of the trial on guilt or innocence (*McGautha v. California* 1971:208). Ohio followed the more common practice of having the jury determine both guilt and punishment during a single set of deliberations following the capital murder trial.

Capital sentences in California, Ohio, and elsewhere throughout the country were imposed at the unfettered discretion of trial juries. The law not only authorized the exercise of such discretion, it required it as well. The trial judge's instructions to the jury prior to the penalty-phase deliberations in Mc-Gautha's case are illustrative:

[I]n this part of the trial the law does not forbid you from being influenced by pity for the defendants and you may be governed by mere sentiment and sympathy for the defendants in arriving at a proper penalty in this case; however, the law does forbid you from being governed by mere conjecture, prejudice, public opinion or public feeling.

... Notwithstanding facts, if any, proved in mitigation or aggravation, in determining which punishment shall be inflicted, you are entirely free to act according to your own judgment, conscience, and absolute discretion....

Now, beyond prescribing the two alternative penalties, the law itself provides no standard for the guidance of the jury in the selection of the penalty, but, rather, commits the whole matter of determining which of the two penalties shall be fixed to the judgment, conscience, and absolute discretion of the jury.... (*McGautha v. California* 1971:189–190).

McGautha argued that the jury's decision to sentence him to death after receiving these instructions was wholly unguided, standardless, and in violation of his right not to be deprived of life without due process of law. Crampton echoed this claim,[1] and additionally contended that Ohio's single-verdict procedure for determining guilt and punishment violated his right against compelled self-incrimination. He objected that he only could be heard on matters that the jury might consider relevant to sentencing if he offered testimony during the guilt phase of his trial.

The Supreme Court upheld the sentencing procedures in both *McGautha* and *Crampton* by a decisive 6–3 vote.[2] Justice Harlan's majority opinion

---

1. The Ohio jury charged with determining Crampton's guilt and sentence was instructed that the punishment for first-degree murder was death unless the jury recommended mercy, in which case the punishment was life imprisonment. The trial judge charged the jury that:

> You must not be influenced by any consideration of sympathy or prejudice. It is your duty to carefully weigh the evidence, to decide all disputed questions of fact, to apply the instructions of the court to your findings and to render your verdict accordingly. In fulfilling your duty, your efforts must be to arrive at a just verdict. Consider all the evidence and make your finding with intelligence and impartiality, and without bias, sympathy, or prejudice, so that the State of Ohio and the defendant will feel that their case was fairly and impartially tried (*McGautha v. California/Crampton v. Ohio* 1971:194–195).

For examples of sentencing instructions administered to juries in other capital cases during this general era, and accompanying argument from prosecutors and defense attorneys, *see* Weisberg 1984:363–383.

2. Five justices joined the majority opinion in *McGautha*. Justice Black concurred "in the Court's judgments and substantially all of its opinion" (*McGautha v. California* 1971:225). Justices Douglas, Brennan, and Marshall dissented.

sounded two basic themes in approving unregulated sentencing discretion in capital cases. First was the belief that it would be impossible to create and enforce statutory standards that could effectively guide capital-sentencing discretion. Second was an expression of faith that such standards were unnecessary because juries could be trusted to make life and death sentencing decisions responsibly. The impossibility theme was summarized in the following, famous language:

> Those who have come to grips with the hard task of actually attempting to draft means of channeling capital sentencing discretion have confirmed the lesson taught by…history.… To identify before the fact those characteristics of criminal homicides and their perpetrators which call for the death penalty, and to express these characteristics in language which can be fairly understood and applied by the sentencing authority, appear to be tasks which are beyond present human ability.
> …The infinite variety of cases and facets to each case would make general standards either meaningless "boiler-plate" or a statement of the obvious that no jury would need (*McGautha v. California* 1971:204, 208).

The Court's fundamental faith that juries could be trusted to exercise their capital-sentencing discretion responsibly was asserted no less equivocally:

> In light of history, experience, and the present limitations of human knowledge, we find it quite impossible to say that committing to the untrammeled discretion of the jury the power to pronounce life or death in capital cases is offensive to anything in the Constitution. The states are entitled to assume that jurors confronted with the truly awesome responsibility of decreeing death for a fellow human being will act with due regard for the consequences of their decision and will consider a variety of factors.… (*McGautha v. California* 1971:207–208).

The About-Face in *Furman*

The assumptions animating death-penalty legislation in this country in 1971 were consistent with the Court's premises in *McGautha*: capital-punishment decisions defy jurisprudential guidance, but juries nevertheless could be trusted to divine and act on unarticulated principles of justice to produce fair sentences in individual cases. Today, these premises sound foreign and unacceptable, following the Court's abrupt reversal and condemnation of unguided capital-sentencing discretion in *Furman v. Georgia* (1972). Individual justices in *Furman* were distinctly distrustful of the sentencing outcomes in capital cases. They respectively characterized death-penalty laws as being "pregnant with discrimination" (*Furman v. Georgia* 1972:257, opinion of Douglas, J.); as being imposed on "a capriciously selected random handful" of offenders (at 309–310, opinion of Stewart, J.); as supporting "no meaningful basis for distinguishing the few cases in which [the death penalty] is imposed from the many cases in which it is not" (at 313, opinion of White, J.); and as being "inflicted arbitrarily" and "smack[ing] of little more than a lottery system" (at 293, opinion of Brennan, J.). The *McGautha* Court's approval of untrammeled capital-sentencing discretion was branded by one justice as "an open invitation to discrimination" (at 365, opinion of Marshall, J.).

Furman invalidated wholly discretionary capital-sentencing statutes on Eighth Amendment grounds, and precipitated immediate and sweeping reforms in the states' death-penalty laws (Zimring and Hawkins 1986a:38–45). The *Furman* Court's repudiation of the capital-punishment statutes that had been approved so unflinchingly and unapologetically in *McGautha* took many contemporary court-watchers by surprise (Meltsner 1973:281–289). It also may have mystified those with a longer perspective on history, who would have recognized that the death-penalty statutes at issue in both *McGautha* and *Furman* were generations removed from legislative schemes that could much more readily be classified as oppressive and atavistic. Indeed, the discretionary sentencing systems that were upheld in *McGautha* and then invalidated in *Furman* culminated from a series of reforms in the nation's capital-punishment laws that had been evolving since the early days of statehood.

The Longer Course of History: From Mandatory Death to the Post-*Furman* Statutes

Early Statehood through the 1960s

The legislation ruled unconstitutional in *Furman*, which gave juries complete discretion to sentence convicted capital offenders to either death or imprisonment, was unquestionably progressive when measured against the longer backdrop of history. At the time of the American Revolution, all of the colonies except Rhode Island had 10 or more capital crimes on their books, and these laws carried over into the early states. Thus, by 1790, the death penalty commonly was promised for crimes including murder, treason, arson, burglary, robbery, rape, buggery, and counterfeiting, and was provided less frequently for offenses such as mayhem, horse theft, forgery, and stealing from a church (Mackey 1976:xii–xiv). Death sentences were mandatory (Tushnet 1994:21; *Woodson v. North Carolina* 1976:289). In other words, capital punishment was automatic after a defendant was found guilty under those laws—in radical contrast to the death-penalty legislation prevailing at the time of *Furman*.

However, throughout history, mandatory capital-punishment laws existed more in name than in practice. Owing to their inability to accommodate unique case circumstances, they proved to be unjust, and thus unenforceable. A number of formal and informal devices helped ameliorate the unyielding nature of mandatory death-penalty laws.

For example, the common law doctrine of "benefit of clergy" spared many a miscreant the gallows (Banner 2002:62–64). Under this rule, the fiction was maintained that offenders who could read (or even could feign reading) were members of the clerical order and thus were subject only to the jurisdiction of ecclesiastical courts, which did not recognize the death penalty (Bedau 1982:7; Hobson 1996:502–503; Langbein 1983:37–41). Executive pardoning power also was used liberally to ensure that many death sentences were never carried out (Acker 1990:563–566; Acker and Lanier 2000:211–215; Hay 1975:43–49; Radzinowicz 1948:91–97). Jurors as well rebelled at the inflexible application of a sanction as harsh as death. Grand juries sometimes stubbornly refused to return true bills of indictment in capital cases (Acker 1989:92–93), and it was not uncommon for petit juries to refuse to convict obviously guilty offenders, knowing that a guilty verdict would result in a sentence of death (Mackey 1974).

Legislatures moved to modify mandatory capital-sentencing policies when evidence mounted that these laws were unjust and unworkable. In 1794, Pennsylvania reserved automatic punishment by death for the newly-created crime of first-degree murder, defined as murder "perpetrated by means of poison, or by lying in wait, or by any other kind of willful, deliberate and premeditated killing, or which shall be committed in the perpetration or attempt to perpetrate any arson, rape, robbery, or burglary" (Keedy 1949:773). All other murder was classified as second-degree, and was punishable only by imprisonment. These changes reflected a growing movement for penal reforms in Pennsylvania toward the end of the 18th century, including revision of the death-penalty laws (Filler 1952:124–126; Mackey 1976:xiv–xvi). The preamble to the Commonwealth's 1794 Act provided that:

> Whereas the design of punishment is to prevent the commission of crimes, and repair the injury that hath been done thereby to society or the individual, and it hath been found by experience that these objects are better obtained by moderate but certain penalties, than by severe and excessive punishments: And whereas it is the duty of every government to endeavor to reform, rather than exterminate offenders, and the punishment of death ought never be inflicted, where it is not absolutely necessary to the public safety... (Wechsler and Michael 1937:703, n. 10).

The creation of degrees of murder, and the consequent limitation of the death penalty to the most heinous kinds of cold-blooded killings and felony-murders, spread quickly beyond Pennsylvania to a number of other states

(American Law Institute 1980:123). Several jurisdictions substituted prison sentences for crimes previously punishable by death. Thus, by 1797 Vermont retained only three capital crimes; Maryland had but four by 1810; and New Hampshire (1812) and Ohio (1815) soon limited the death penalty to just two offenses (Mackey 1976:xvii).

The practice of mandatory capital punishment itself yielded next. This action was propelled by the reformist spirit that the death penalty should be reserved only for cases with the most compelling circumstances. Also underpinning this movement was the practical consideration that juries continued to nullify mandatory capital-punishment laws by refusing to convict offenders—notwithstanding clear evidence of guilt. Accordingly, the death penalty was made optional for treason, rape, and arson in Maryland in 1809. In 1838, Tennessee became the first state to implement discretionary capital sentencing for murder; Alabama followed suit three years later (Bedau 1982:10). No fewer than 20 additional jurisdictions converted from mandatory to discretionary death-sentencing laws between the Civil War and the end of the 19th century (Bowers 1984:10). This trend continued into the 20th century (Bye 1926:231–239), and by 1963 mandatory capital punishment had all but vanished from the American landscape (Bowers 1984:10–11).[3]

Laws governing executions also evolved in ways designed to minimize the cruelty and incivility of the death penalty. Once great spectacles that attracted thousands of raucous on-lookers (Madow 1995:471–478; Masur 1989:95–96), hangings were moved inside jailhouse walls to be secluded from public view (Banner 2002:144–168). Pennsylvania was the first state to eliminate public executions in 1834, followed by New Jersey, New York, and Massachusetts the next year. To avoid the ribaldry and shocking lack of decorum that often surrounded public hangings (Bye 1926:234–235; Davis 1957:33–34), private executions quickly were instituted elsewhere as well (Bessler 1997:41–44; Bowers 1984:8; Madow 1995:94). Nevertheless, more than 20,000 people gathered in Owensboro, Kentucky as recently as 1936 to watch Rainey Bethea, a black man, hang as punishment for raping and murdering a white woman. Although roughly 1500 spectators witnessed a hanging the following year in Galena, Missouri, all were admitted by special passes into a stockade that enclosed the gallows. Thus, Bethea's is considered "[t]he last truly public execution in America" (Bessler 1997:32; *see also* Bedau 1982:13).

---

3. Mandatory capital punishment persisted beyond 1963 only for exceptional crimes and only in a few jurisdictions. For example, Rhode Island provided for automatic death for life-term prisoners convicted of murder, Massachusetts retained a mandatory death penalty for murder committed during forcible rape, and Ohio law mandated capital punishment for assassinating the President of the United States or the Governor of a state (*Furman v. Georgia* 1972:307, opinion of Stewart, J.).

Attempts to identify progressively more humane methods of execution also followed. Although burning, boiling, quartering, and other forms of torturous executions were not unknown in colonial times (Banner 2002:70–86; Bye 1926:235; Mackey 1982:2–3, 22–25), the savagely horrific execution practices that were employed more commonly in England never took firm hold in America (Bedau 1982:14–15). When the New York Legislature introduced the electric chair to carry out death sentences in 1888, its announced goal was to provide a more humane means of causing death than hanging (Denno 1994:561–573). Although electrocution was far from always a swift and efficient method of execution (Denno 1994:598–607; *Louisiana ex rel. Francis v. Resweber* 1947), over half the country's death-penalty jurisdictions utilized the electric chair by 1920 (Bowers 1984:12). Other states adopted lethal gas or execution by firing squad (Bowers 1984:12–13; Bye 1926:235–236).

As methods of execution changed, the final act of carrying out death sentences gradually became the business of the states, instead of local communities. This transfer of responsibility began in 1864 in Vermont and Maine. All states except Delaware and Montana had centralized the execution process by the 1960s, so executions routinely occurred within state penitentiaries rather than in local jails (Bowers 1984:13–14, 41–47).

Beginning with Michigan in 1847, Rhode Island in 1852, and Wisconsin in 1853, a number of states abolished (or essentially abolished) capital punishment (Davis 1957:43; Filler 1952:130). The abolition movement peaked, primarily in northern states, in the three decades before the Civil War (Banner 2002:131–143), and had another brief resurgence just before World War I (Bowers 1984:8–10; Filler 1952). Still, some states eliminated capital punishment only to restore it a few years later. The last state for nearly half a century to abolish the death penalty without reinstating it was North Dakota, in 1915. Alaska and Hawaii entered the union in 1960, after repealing their death-penalty statutes while still territories. In the mid-1960s, Oregon, Iowa, and West Virginia repealed their death-penalty laws. Vermont, New York, and New Mexico, on the other hand, so limited the reach of their capital-murder statutes that they virtually achieved abolitionist status. By 1969, 14 states were or nearly were abolitionist jurisdictions (Bowers 1984:9–10).

Legislative Responses to Furman and the Court's Subsequent Reaction

By the late 1960s, the courts rather than state legislatures became the focus of the abolitionist movement (Haines 1996:11–14). The judicial assault on the death penalty followed on the heels of nearly two centuries of legislative activity. Statutory reforms had produced a notable reduction in the crimes punishable by death; replaced mandatory sentencing with sentencing discretion; produced less barbaric executions which were removed from public display and conducted under state, rather than local authority; and occasionally even re-sulted in the repeal or *de facto* elimination of the capital sanction. Ironically, the introduction of unfettered sentencing discretion into the capital-sentencing process, which was declared unconstitutional in *Furman*, represented one of the principal reforms in the nation's death-penalty laws during this extended era. Legislatures consequently were challenged to redesign capital-sentencing statutes in response to *Furman's* fractured and uncertain mandate.

However, several states faltered when rewriting their laws. Reasoning that wholly eliminating discretion was the remedy for unbridled sentencing dis-cretion, almost one-third of the 35 state legislatures that reenacted capital-punishment laws between 1972 and 1976 restored mandatory death on con-viction for specified crimes (Acker 1996a:145; *Gregg v. Georgia* 1976:179–180; *Woodson v. North Carolina* 1976:313, dissenting opinion of Rehnquist, J.). By a vote of 5–4, the justices declared mandatory death penalties unconstitutional (*Roberts v. Louisiana* 1976; *Woodson v. North Carolina* 1976).[4]

This judgment relied in part on the country's historical rejection of manda-tory capital punishment (*Woodson v. North Carolina* 1976:288–301). The jus-tices further concluded that the problem of unguided sentencing discretion was not cured by compulsory death-sentencing laws, and might even be exac-erbated because of juries' nullification propensities (at 302–303). The Court additionally held that the core Eighth Amendment value of protecting human dignity required that individualized consideration be given to offense and of-fender circumstances prior to the imposition of a death sentence (at 303–305).

On the other hand, with only Justices Brennan and Marshall dissenting, the Court gave its approval to replacement legislation that sought to channel or regulate—but not eliminate—the exercise of capital-sentencing discretion. On the same day in 1976 that it invalidated the mandatory capital-punishment statutes, the Court used cases from Georgia, Florida, and Texas to uphold three forms of "guided discretion" death-penalty laws (*Gregg v. Georgia* 1976; *Jurek v. Texas* 1976; *Proffitt v. Florida* 1976). The approved statutes shared cer-tain characteristics. For example, only specified classes of aggravated murder were punishable by death; thus, capital-sentencing discretion could be exer-cised only in a relatively narrow, legislatively-defined category of cases. Addi-

---

4. A three-justice plurality, consisting of Justices Stewart, Powell, and Stevens, joined in the lead opinions in *Woodson v. North Carolina* (1976) and *Roberts v. Louisiana* (1976). Justices Brennan and Marshall, who were of the opinion that capital punishment *per se* violated the Eighth Amendment's prohibition against cruel and unusual punishments, concurred in the judgment in these cases. In following years, the Court invalidated mandatory death-penalty statutes applying to the narrow crime categories of murdering a police officer (*Roberts v. Louisiana* 1977), and murder committed by a prisoner serving a life sentence (*Sumner v. Shu-man* 1987).

tionally, trials were bifurcated, so that a separate penalty hearing was conducted following an offender's conviction for capital murder. At this penalty trial, both the prosecution and the defense were authorized to introduce evidence specifically focusing on issues relevant to sentencing. This process allowed the sentencer to give individualized consideration to the circumstances surrounding the offense, as well as to the offender's prior record, character, condition at the time of the crime, and other potentially relevant information before deciding the appropriateness of death or life imprisonment. All of the statutes also required appellate review of capital convictions and sentences.

The revised death-sentencing statutes from Georgia, Florida, and Texas still differed in several important respects. Both Georgia's and Florida's laws incorporated basic features of the Model Penal Code's death-penalty provisions (American Law Institute 1980:§210.6),[5] by identifying aggravating and (in Florida's statute) mitigating features related to a crime or an offender, and then requiring those factors to be considered in the sentencing process. For example, Georgia and Florida law enumerated 10 and 8 statutory aggravating circumstances, respectively, at least one of which had to be proven at the penalty trial before a convicted murderer became eligible for a death sentence (*Gregg v. Georgia* 1976; *Proffitt v. Florida* 1976).

Juries in Georgia were instructed to consider mitigating evidence before deciding on a sentence. However, the statute not only failed to itemize relevant mitigating factors, it also did not explicitly require that aggravating and mitigating circumstances be balanced against each other (or weighed) as part of the sentencing process. Florida's statute included a list of seven mitigating factors, and the jury was "directed to consider '[w]hether sufficient mitigating circumstances exist...which outweigh the aggravating factors found to exist; and... based on these considerations, whether the defendant should be sentenced to life [imprisonment] or death'" (*Proffitt v. Florida* 1976:248). Furthermore, unlike capital juries in Georgia, which had final sentencing authority, juries under Florida law only recommended imposition of either death or a prison

---

5. The Model Penal Code (MPC) was prepared by the American Law Institute, a collection of accomplished lawyers and academic legal scholars, to provide a model set of criminal laws that could be considered for adoption, in whole or in part, by appropriate political bodies. The MPC proved to be highly influential in shaping many areas of the criminal law (Symposium 1988), including capital-punishment law (Zimring and Hawkins 1986b). The death-penalty provisions of the MPC were adopted in tentative form in 1959, and were approved by the American Law Institute in 1962 (Givelber 1994:377, n. 13). As such, they preceded the Supreme Court's significant constitutional rulings regarding the death penalty by several years. Although the Advisory Committee recommended by a vote of 18–2 that the American Law Institute endorse abolition of the death penalty, the Institute accepted the view that its recommendation would not be influential, "and the Model Code therefore does not take a position on whether the sentence of death should be retained or abolished" (American Law Institute 1980:111).

sentence. Thus, trial judges remained at liberty to depart from the jury's advisory verdict in making the ultimate sentencing decision.[6]

The Texas statute approved by the Supreme Court, on the other hand, was markedly different. Capital murder was defined restrictively to include only five types of intentional, aggravated killings. The class of offenses punishable by death thus was narrowed prior to the penalty phase and the statute, unlike the Georgia and Florida laws, did not rely on proof of aggravating sentencing factors. Cases resulting in a conviction for capital murder advanced to a penalty trial, where the jury considered three sentencing issues: whether the killing was committed deliberately, "whether there is a probability that the defendant would commit criminal acts of violence that would constitute a continuing threat to society," and whether the defendant acted unreasonably in response to any provocation by the homicide victim (*Jurek v. Texas* 1976:269). The prosecution was required to prove each sentencing issue beyond a reasonable doubt. The defendant also was given the opportunity to introduce evidence, including mitigation evidence, at the sentencing hearing. If the jury unanimously answered the three penalty-phase issues affirmatively, the trial judge sentenced the offender to death; otherwise, the defendant received a sentence of life imprisonment.

Georgia's statute required the state supreme court to perform three discrete functions: to determine whether individual death penalties were "imposed under the influence of passion, prejudice, or any other arbitrary factor"; to ensure that sufficient evidence existed to support the jury's finding of one or more statutory aggravating factors; and to determine "[w]hether the sentence of death is excessive or disproportionate to the penalty imposed in similar cases, considering both the crime and the defendant..." (*Gregg v. Georgia* 1976:212). Although not specifically required by statute, the Florida Supreme Court announced its commitment to perform the latter function undertaken by the Georgia Supreme Court, or to conduct "comparative proportionality review" of capital sentences (*Proffitt v. Florida* 1976:250–251). Appeals to the Texas Court of Criminal Appeals were automatic in cases resulting in sentences of death, but Texas law did not require, and the appellate courts did not engage in comparative proportionality review of capital sentences (*Jurek v. Texas* 1976:269; *Pulley v. Harris* 1984:48–50). Although the Supreme Court considered appellate review to be "an important additional safeguard against arbitrariness and caprice" (*Gregg v. Georgia* 1976:198), it attributed no constitutional significance to the different appeals provisions in the three state statutes.

---

6. Florida trial judges were allowed to impose a death sentence over a jury's recommendation of life imprisonment only when "'the facts suggesting a sentence of death [are] so clear and convincing that virtually no reasonable person could differ'" (*Proffitt v. Florida* 1976:249, quoting *Tedder v. State* 1975:910).

Two broad legal principles emerged from the Supreme Court's 1976 capital-punishment decisions. First, mandatory death-penalty laws were constitutionally infirm.[7] Second, legislatures would be given considerable leeway in crafting guided-discretion laws that passed constitutional muster—as long as they met minimal requirements. Statutes would be required to narrow the category of cases punishable by death, and would further have to allow the sentencer to give individualized consideration to offense circumstances and offender characteristics at a separate penalty hearing. Laws also had to provide for appellate review of capital sentences. Beyond these prescriptions, the threshold for constitutionally sufficient death-penalty legislation remained decidedly permissive (Steiker and Steiker 2003, 1995; Weisberg 1984).

A Closer Look at Contemporary Death-Penalty Statutes

Compared to the mandatory death-penalty laws universally in effect at the end of the 18th century, and the wholly discretionary capital-sentencing laws that were equally widespread thirty years ago when *McGautha* and *Furman* were decided, contemporary death-penalty statutes are numbingly complex. It is futile in the post-*Furman* era to embark on a discussion of "the death penalty" from a procedural standpoint, for there are almost as many variations on capital-sentencing laws as there are capital-punishment jurisdictions. The devil truly is in the details in these statutes. In this section we review, with a broad brush, different provisions of contemporary death-penalty legislation. We examine similarities and differences among capital-punishment statutes, focusing on substantive and procedural provisions that are most likely to influence the administration of these laws.

Capital Murder

Supreme Court rulings that the death penalty is constitutionally excessive for rape (*Coker v. Georgia* 1977) and kidnaping (*Eberheart v. Georgia* 1977) have created uncertainty about whether death is legally appropriate for crimes that do not directly result in the loss of life. Nevertheless, espionage (18 U.S.C.A. §794, 2002), treason (*e.g.*, 18 U.S.C.A. §2381, 2002; Miss. Code Ann. §97-7-67, 2002), trafficking in large quantities of drugs (18 U.S.C.A. §3591(b)(l), 2002), conduct by drug kingpins that consists of directing, advising, authorizing, or assisting another person who attempts to kill a public offi-

---

7. See note 4 above.

cer, juror, or witness, even if such a killing does not occur (18 U.S.C.A. §3591(b)(2), 2002), and a sprinkling of other offenses that do not involve homicide (Acker and Lanier 1993c:292, n. 2) endure under some laws as capital crimes. Even if the death penalty is constitutionally permissible for crimes other than murder, virtually all capital prosecutions will certainly continue to involve that single offense. In all jurisdictions, capital murder—or killings punishable by death—constitutes a discrete subclass of the crime of murder. The precise definition of capital murder is important substantively, because it helps determine the potential reach of the death penalty. How capital murder is defined can have important procedural implications, as well.

Aggravating Circumstances: Elements of the Crime or Sentencing Factors— Procedural Implications

"[S]tatutory aggravating circumstances play a constitutionally necessary function at the stage of legislative definition: they circumscribe the class of persons eligible for the death penalty" (*Zant v. Stephens* 1983:878). In defining the minimum requirements for death-penalty eligibility, "the State must establish rational criteria that narrow the decision-maker's judgment as to whether the circumstances of a particular defendant's case meet the threshold" (*McCleskey v. Kemp* 1987:305). The aggravating circumstances that define the threshold of death-penalty eligibility can be included either as elements of capital murder, or as sentencing factors that must be proven at the penalty phase of a trial (*Lowenfield v. Phelps* 1988). Most states follow the lead of the Model Penal Code by defining murder broadly, and then relying on proof of aggravating circumstances at the penalty trial to accomplish the constitutionally required narrowing of the class of death-penalty eligible offenses.

For example, Georgia's capital-punishment laws conform to the latter model. Murder is defined in Georgia simply as unlawfully causing the death of a human being "with malice aforethought, either express or implied," including during the commission of a felony (Ga. Code Ann. §16-5-1, 2002). A convicted murderer becomes eligible for the death penalty if and only if the prosecution subsequently establishes the existence of one or more of 10 statutory aggravating circumstances at the penalty-phase trial (Ga. Code Ann. §17-10-30(b), 2002).

These provisions stand in contrast to laws that exist in states such as New York (N.Y. Penal Law §125.27, 2002) and Texas (Tex. Penal Code Ann. §19.03, 2002), where aggravating circumstances are defined as elements of capital murder. As crime elements, aggravating factors must be proven during the guilt phase of a capital trial. The same elements supporting a first-degree murder conviction are deemed to be aggravating factors for sentencing purposes under New York's statute,[8] and are balanced against mitigating circumstances for the determination of the sentence (N.Y. Crim. Proc. Law §§400.27(3), (11), 2002). In Texas, juries consider special sentencing issues during penalty-phase proceedings, with the principal consideration being the offender's likely future dangerousness (Texas Code Crim. Proc. Ann. art. 37.071(2)(b)(l), 2002). If the jury decides that the defendant may constitute a continuing threat to society, it then considers whether there are sufficient mitigating circumstances to warrant a sentence of life imprisonment rather than death (at art. 37.071(2)(e)).

Significant procedural consequences thus hinge on whether aggravating factors are defined independently of the crime of murder and are sentencing considerations only, or whether they constitute elements of capital murder. For example, where aggravating circumstances are not crime elements (e.g., Georgia), grand juries will not review the sufficiency of the evidence supporting them, leaving prosecutors with virtually unchecked authority to initiate capital prosecutions even in jurisdictions where indictments are used as charging instruments (Acker 1989; Acker and Lanier 1993c:303–306). Until recently, the existence of aggravating sentencing factors could wholly elude jury review in states that rely on judges as the final sentencing authority in capital cases. The Supreme Court put a stop to that practice in *Ring v. Arizona* (2002), when it ruled that the Sixth Amendment guarantees that "[c]apital defendants, no less than non-capital defendants,... are entitled to a jury determination of any fact on which the legislature conditions an increase in their maximum punishment" (at 2432; *see also Apprendi v. New Jersey* 2000).

Rules of evidence and constitutional exclusionary rules may not be recognized when aggravating factors are proven during penalty-phase proceedings, although such rules clearly apply when aggravating circumstances are defined as elements of capital murder (Acker and Lanier 1993c:310–312). Furthermore, when murder is defined broadly and proof of aggravating factors is delayed until the penalty trial, significantly more murder trials are likely to be conducted before death-qualified juries, even if the likelihood is remote that the prosecutor actually will seek a death sentence (at 301–307; *Lockhart v. McCree* 1986:188, n. 4, Marshall, J., dissenting). The death-qualification process can significantly disadvantage capital defendants by altering the trial jury's composition and making the resulting jury more conviction-prone than a jury that has not been death-qualified (Sandys and McClelland 2003).

For these and other reasons (Acker and Lanier 1993c:312–315), trials in which statutory aggravating factors must be proven as elements of capital mur-

---

8. If proven at the penalty-phase trial, two statutory aggravating factors in addition to those defined as elements of first-degree murder also may be considered under New York law (N.Y. Crim. Proc. Law §400.27(7), 2002).

der are more apt to be procedurally rigorous, and thus more protective of the accused's interests, than capital murder trials in which proof of aggravating circumstances is delayed until the penalty phase. Nevertheless, statutes in nearly two-thirds of the country's death-penalty jurisdictions follow the model proposed by the Model Penal Code and adopted in Georgia. They define murder broadly, and then make aggravating factors relevant only to the issue of sentencing (at 298–302).

The Scope of Death-Eligible Offenses

The subclass of criminal homicides punishable by death must be defined legislatively. Whether they serve as crime elements or exclusively as sentencing considerations, the aggravating factors that help perform this function "must genuinely narrow the class of persons eligible for the death penalty and must reasonably justify the imposition of a more severe sentence on the defendant compared to others found guilty of murder" (*Zant v. Stephens* 1983:877). The relative size of the category of potentially capital crimes depends on the number and scope of the legislatively-defined aggravating circumstances, as well as on factors such as mens rea requirements, and felony murder and accomplice liability.

Statutory Aggravating Factors

The number of aggravating circumstances that define a killing as a capital offense varies widely. For example, Connecticut law recognizes only eight aggravating factors (Conn. Gen. Stat. Ann. §53a-46a(i), 2002), while California (Cal. Penal Code §190.2, 2002) and Delaware (Del. Code Ann. tit. 11 §4209(e), 2002) each list 22. Most statutes include roughly 10 to 12 aggravating factors (Acker and Lanier 1993a:492–493; U.S. Department of Justice 2001). Because some of these factors are more significant than others, their specification is more important than how many there are in determining the size of the category of offenses punishable by death.

Some aggravating factors focus on *offender characteristics*. The defendant's prior criminal history is a common aggravating circumstance, although there are important differences in what is made relevant among the laws. Only prior convictions may be considered under some statutes, while the greater range of an offender's previous criminal "activity" is significant under others. Several jurisdictions limit the types of prior offenses that can be taken into account, typically to felonies that involve the use or threat of violence to other persons. Some laws are narrower still, and only make the previous commission of another murder or other felonious homicide relevant (Acker and Lanier 1994b:111–116; Acker and Lanier 1993a:487–488).

Imprisonment is another typical offender-related aggravating factor. The most restrictive statutes are limited to murders committed by prisoners serving life-term sentences. More commonly, aggravating circumstances of this type apply to all prisoners, and occasionally to escapees, jail inmates, and even parolees and probationers (Acker and Lanier 1994b:111–118; Acker and Lanier 1993b:398–399). The defendant's future dangerousness, another offender-based aggravating factor recognized in many states, is variously considered as a traditional sentencing circumstance, or as a threshold factor absent which the offender cannot be sentenced to death (Acker and Lanier 1994b:118–121; Acker and Lanier 1993a:488).

A second general category of aggravating factors focuses on the *manner in which the murder was committed*, including the motive for the killing. The most practically significant aggravator among this class is the contemporaneous felony circumstance. It is not unusual for 70 to 80 percent of the death sentences imposed within a jurisdiction to involve murder committed during a contemporaneous felony (Baldus, Pulaski, and Woodworth 1986:138–139; Givelber 1994:413–414).[9] Most such killings occur during armed robberies (Rosen 1990:1132–1133, n. 76). Additional contemporaneous felonies typically enumerated in statutes include rape, burglary, arson, kidnaping, and sometimes drug and other offenses. The single most crucial issue relating to the contemporaneous felony circumstance is whether the prosecution must prove that the offender killed intentionally. In a majority of jurisdictions even an unintentional killing committed in the course or furtherance of one of the enumerated crimes renders the offender death-eligible (Acker and Lanier 1994b:123–124; Acker and Lanier 1993b:391–393).

Another particularly significant offense-related aggravating circumstance, which is included in roughly three-fourths of death-penalty statutes, involves some variation of the Model Penal Code's provision that the murder "was especially heinous, atrocious or cruel, manifesting exceptional depravity" (American Law Institute 1980:§210.6(3)(h)). The most common, related statement of the "heinous, atrocious or cruel" (HAC) factor refers to murders that are "outrageously or wantonly vile, horrible or inhuman, in that [they] involved torture, depravity of mind, or an aggravated battery to the victim" (*e.g.*, Ga. Code Ann. §17-10-30(b)(7), 2002; Acker and Lanier 1994b:128). Circumstances of

---

9. The commission convened to study Illinois' death penalty following Governor George Ryan's announced moratorium on executions, effective January 31, 2000, recommended eliminating the state's contemporaneous felony aggravating factor. "Since so many first degree murders are potentially death eligible under this factor, it lends itself to disparate application throughout the state. This eligibility factor is the one most likely subject to interpretation and discretionary decision-making. On balance, it was the view of the Commission members supporting this recommendation that this eligibility factor swept too broadly and included too many different types of murders within its scope to serve the interests capital punishment is thought best to serve" (*Report of the Governor's Commission on Capital Punishment* 2002:73–74).

this type are considered necessary to address "the special case of a style of killing so indicative of utter depravity that imposition of the ultimate sanction should be considered" (American Law Institute 1980:137). These circumstances are widely utilized: between 60 and 80 percent of murders resulting in death sentences in some jurisdictions involve HAC or related factors (Baldus, Pulaski, and Woodworth 1986:138–139, n. 14).

A major problem plaguing HAC factors is their unavoidable vagueness: "A person of ordinary sensibility could fairly characterize almost every murder as 'outrageously or wantonly vile, horrible and inhuman'" (*Godfrey v. Georgia* 1980:428–429). As drafted, HAC factors provide no meaningful basis for distinguishing between killings, and thus do not effectively channel capital-sentencing discretion (*Godfrey v. Georgia* 1980; *Maynard v. Cartwright* 1988). These circumstances generally survive constitutional challenge after the courts give them a narrowing construction (*Arave v. Creech* 1993; *Walton v. Arizona* 1990). Still, their imprecision invites such broad discretion that the risk of arbitrary and capricious sentencing decisions remains high (Rosen 1986).

HAC factors are deficient both conceptually and linguistically. Achieving consensus about the attributes of a unique class of "heinous, atrocious or cruel" murders seems dubious; even more unlikely is finding language that can adequately describe this type of killing. Nevertheless, HAC factors remain prevalent in statutes and are applied frequently. Their continued use cannot help but raise questions about the effectiveness of post-*Furman* legislative reforms.

Several other statutory aggravating circumstances involve the manner in which a murder was committed or the offender's motive, although none rival contemporaneous felony and HAC factors in practical significance. Other common circumstances of this ilk include killings for pecuniary gain and for hire, killings committed to avoid arrest or to escape custody, knowingly creating a great risk of death to others in addition to the murder victim, or killing more than one person, either during a single transaction (mass murder) or in separate transactions pursuant to a common scheme or course of conduct (serial murder). Killings committed after substantial premeditation and planning, by lying in wait, by poison, or by explosives or other destructive devices are punishable by death in some jurisdictions, as are killings committed to disrupt or hinder any governmental function or the enforcement of laws. In a few jurisdictions, killings motivated by a victim's race, nationality, religion, or the victim's exercise of constitutional rights are capital crimes (Acker and Lanier 1994b:130–140; Acker and Lanier 1993b:399–402).

A third category of statutory aggravating circumstances makes *victim* characteristics relevant. The murder of law enforcement officials and others who formulate or administer the law or protect public safety is a capital homicide in all death-penalty jurisdictions. Police officers, correction officers, firefighters, judges and prosecutors, and various elected and appointed public officials are the murder victims most commonly recognized under these provisions. A related capital offense under many statutes involves killing crime witnesses to prevent or retaliate for their testimony. Other provisions make killing children punishable by death, and less commonly the murder of elderly persons, pregnant women, or peculiarly vulnerable victims (Acker and Lanier 1994b:140–151; Acker and Lanier 1993a:491–492; Acker and Lanier 1993b:402–406).

Mens Rea Requirements

Another factor significantly affecting the range of homicides punishable by death is the mens rea requirement imposed by law. The crucial issues are whether an intent to kill is both (a) necessary and (b) sufficient to support a capital sentence.

In light of the close relationship between the purposefulness of conduct and culpability, it may be surprising that an offender can be convicted of murder and sentenced to death absent proof of an intent to kill in a majority of capital-punishment jurisdictions. These cases frequently arise through application of the felony-murder rule which, as discussed more fully below, traditionally makes even accidental killings committed during the perpetration of dangerous felonies a form of capital murder. However, in some states "depraved heart" killings— i.e., unintentional killings committed recklessly, under circumstances manifesting extreme indifference to the value of life—also are punishable by death (Acker and Lanier 1993b:385–387). In a few jurisdictions, on the other hand, a capital sentence cannot rest on intent to kill alone. Something more, such as premeditation or deliberation, also must be established under this minority rule (at 383).

Both the deterrent and retributive objectives of capital punishment become more defensible, logically, as the mens rea requirement for murder is more demanding. The death penalty presumably should be most effective to discourage intentional killings, especially those preceded by planning (premeditation) and cool reflection (deliberation). Nonpurposeful homicides, and even spontaneously committed intentional killings, would seem largely immune to influence by threatened sanctions. The opportunity for advanced contemplation is especially important, logically, because the hypothesized marginal deterrent value of the death penalty over life imprisonment implicitly requires some weighing or assessment of the comparative disadvantages of these two kinds of punishment (Zeisel 1977).

Additionally, most people would agree that killings committed in cold blood, following premeditation, indicate a greater depravity than do hot-blooded and essentially spontaneous, albeit intentional killings.[10] Intentional killings *prima facie* reflect greater culpability than unintentional killings. This

---

10. As applied by the courts, the requirements of "premeditation" and "deliberation" often lack the meaning that their literal definition suggests. In practice, these requirements of first-

premise clearly holds true with respect to accidental killings, although some have argued that "depraved heart" murderers, who essentially are indifferent about whether their conduct results in the loss of life, are at least as blameworthy as offenders who purposely kill (Fletcher 1978:264–265, 447–448; Givelber 1994:382–384; Stephen 1883:94).

Felony Murder and Accessorial Liability

The Eighth Amendment neither limits the death penalty to murderers who intentionally kill their victims, nor restricts it to offenders who personally cause their victims' deaths. Felons who are vicariously liable for murder committed by a cofelon also can be sentenced to death. These doctrines have important implications for capital punishment in the context of the felony-murder rule. The Supreme Court has ruled that "major participation" in the underlying felony, coupled with the mens rea of "reckless indifference to human life," can justify the capital punishment of an offender convicted of felony murder, even if the felon did not personally kill the homicide victim and did not intend that anyone be killed (*Tison v. Arizona* 1987:158). Many statutes authorize the death penalty under such circumstances (Acker and Lanier 1993b:391–396; *Tison v. Arizona* 1987).

The scope of a jurisdiction's felony-murder rule and attendant capital-punishment provisions can significantly affect the breadth of the class of crimes punishable by death. Under classic felony-murder doctrine, the offender's decision to commit a dangerous felony supplies the "malice" required to support a murder conviction. Thus, when a killing takes place during the perpetration of a felony, or the immediate flight therefrom, it is defined as murder even if committed accidentally or negligently. The felony-murder rule is often criticized because offenders who unintentionally kill or kill during the heat of the moment while committing robbery, burglary, rape, kidnaping, arson, or another designated felony, are considered equally blameworthy as murderers who make the purposeful, deliberate decision to kill (Finkel 1990:819–821; Rosen 1990:1115–1117). The United States "remains virtually the only western country still recognizing a rule which makes it possible 'that the most serious sanctions known to law might be imposed for accidental homicide'" (Roth and Sundby 1985:447–448, *quoting* Jeffries and Stephan 1979:1383).

Because of its tenuous link to culpability, the felony-murder rule has been abandoned in a few jurisdictions (Roth and Sundby 1985:446, n. 6), and restricted by several limiting principles in the overwhelming majority of jurisdictions where it continues to be recognized (LaFave and Scott 1986:622–641). Even where this rule is operative, an offender convicted of felony murder is not

---

degree murder have not always distinguished carefully planned murders committed after calm reflection from more impassioned, spontaneous, hot-blooded killings (Keedy 1949).

invariably exposed to the risk of capital punishment. Several jurisdictions limit the death penalty to intentional killings, or to the actual killer (Acker and Lanier 1993b:391–396; *Enmund v. Florida* 1982:790). Legislative limitations on the scope of capital-punishment eligibility should be welcome in light of the "moral obtuseness of felony murder" (Givelber 1994:385), the doctrine's inability to discriminate effectively among murderers on grounds of relative culpability (Myers 1994), and the vast charging and sentencing discretion that the felony-murder rule invites, with the corresponding potential for abuses (Rosen 1990:1124–1137).

Exclusions from Death-Penalty Eligibility

Legislatures not only define the class of offenses punishable by death, but they can exempt classes of offenders from death-penalty eligibility as well. Such exclusions presumably reflect the categorical judgment that the death penalty is not a morally appropriate sanction under certain circumstances. Most commonly affected are youthful offenders. For example, although the federal Constitution permits the capital punishment of murderers at least as young as age 16 (*Stanford v. Kentucky* 1989),[11] several jurisdictions set a higher minimum age by statute. Approximately 16 states and the federal government have legislation prohibiting the death penalty for offenders younger than 18. Five additional states require murderers to be at least 17 to be eligible for capital punishment (Streib 2003).

Statutory enactments were instrumental in persuading a majority of the Supreme Court to make a constitutional about-face regarding the execution of mentally retarded offenders. In 1989, when the justices first considered—and rejected—the argument that the Eighth Amendment prohibits the capital punishment of mentally retarded murderers, only federal law and two death-penalty states legislatively disallowed such a practice (*Penry v. Lynaugh* 1989). By 2002, 16 additional states had enacted legislation exempting the mentally retarded from death-penalty eligibility. Both "the number of" jurisdictions adopting statutory prohibitions and "the consistency of direction of change" helped convince a 6–3 majority of the Court in *Atkins v. Virginia* (2002) that

---

11. In *Thompson v. Oklahoma* (1988), a four-member plurality of the Court agreed that the Eighth Amendment prohibited the execution of an offender who was only 15-years old at the time of his crime. However, Justice O'Connor concurred only in the result, and reserved judgment about whether offenders younger than 16 could be punished by death consistent with the Eighth Amendment if legislation specifically authorized that practice (at 852). The Oklahoma statute at issue in *Thompson* failed to specify a minimum age for death-penalty eligibility. Following the Court's decision in *Atkins v. Virginia* (2002), barring the execution of mentally retarded offenders, Justices Breyer, Ginsburg, and Stevens joined in calling for a reconsideration of the ruling in *Stanford v. Kentucky* (1989) that permits the execution of 16- and 17-year old murderers (*Patterson v. Texas* 2002, dissenting from denial of stay of execution).

executing mentally retarded offenders would violate contemporary standards of decency (at 2249; *see also* Streib 2003): "The practice...has become truly unusual, and it is fair to say that a national consensus has developed against it" (*Atkins v. Virginia* 2002:2249). Although some additionally have advocated for legislative and constitutional exemptions of seriously mentally ill offenders from death-penalty eligibility (Ellis 1993; Emanuel 1989), there has been little movement to date in this direction.

The Model Penal Code proposed ruling out capital punishment for an additional class of cases, even where a defendant is properly convicted of capital murder. The prohibition would apply to cases where, "although the evidence suffices to sustain the verdict, it does not foreclose all doubt respecting the defendant's guilt" (American Law Institute 1980:§210.6(l)(f)). Despite the substantial influence of the MPC in other areas of death-penalty law, this provision of the Code has been uniformly ignored (Acker and Lanier 1993b:414–416). Such legislative indifference has been exhibited even though "lingering doubt" about an offender's guilt is a practically important sentencing consideration in capital trials (Geimer and Amsterdam 1988:28–34),[12] and notwithstanding the distressing incidence of miscarriages of justice based on erroneous convictions in capital cases (Radelet and Bedau 2003). A statutory exclusion along the lines of the MPC proposal obviously would not be a cure-all for the problem of erroneous convictions (Gross 1996), but it could figure in to an occasional case. The irrevocability of the capital sanction provides a principled justification for this additional safeguard.

The Sentencing Process

The legislative changes most immediately demanded by *Furman* involved capital-sentencing procedures. It quickly became clear, as the Supreme Court upheld three different forms of "guided discretion" statutes in *Gregg* and its companion cases, that no fixed capital-sentencing formula was constitutionally mandated. Although the sentencing provisions in contemporary death-penalty statutes share many attributes, they remain remarkably diverse in their details, including such key features as the identity of the decision-maker, available sentencing alternatives, and the criteria and procedures that structure sentencing decisions.

The Sentencer

As the 2001–02 Supreme Court Term drew to a close, death-penalty jurisdictions relied on different decision-makers to impose sentence in capital cases.

---

12. Research involving jurors who have served in capital cases suggests that "'[r]esidual doubt' over the defendant's guilt is the most powerful 'mitigating' fact" considered during penalty-phase deliberations (Garvey 1998:1563; *see also* Koosed 2001; Pignatelli 2001; Reid 1999).

Juries had final sentencing authority in 29 states and under federal law. In four additional states (Alabama, Delaware, Florida, and Indiana), trial judges chose between a sentence of life imprisonment and death, but only after considering a recommendation, or advisory sentencing verdict, from a jury. Five states—Arizona, Colorado, Idaho, Montana, and Nebraska—gave judges the exclusive authority to impose sentence, without any input from juries (Acker and Lanier 1996:138). The Supreme Court then decided *Ring v. Arizona* (2002).

Ring does not expressly outlaw continuing reliance on judicial sentencing in capital cases, but it is likely to produce changes in sentencing procedures, if not in the identity of the decision-maker, in the nine states that did not give juries ultimate sentencing authority. Reversing course from earlier rulings (*Spaziano v. Florida* 1984; *Walton v. Arizona* 1990), the justices held in *Ring* that juries—not judges—must find the aggravating factors on which a capital sentence is predicated. The ruling was rooted in the Sixth Amendment right of trial by jury. Relying on *Apprendi v. New Jersey* (2000), the *Ring* Court held that "[i]f a State makes an increase in a defendant's authorized punishment contingent on the finding of a fact, that fact—no matter how the State labels it—must be found by a jury beyond a reasonable doubt" (*Ring v. Arizona* 2002:2449).

The ruling thus appears to allow states to continue to use judge sentencing in capital cases, as long as juries first find the essential facts—*e.g.*, statutory aggravating factors—that support the punishment decision. *Ring* further makes clear that essential sentencing facts must be established under the heightened "proof beyond a reasonable doubt" standard; reliance on less demanding proof does not suffice. The full implications of *Ring* have yet to be determined, either for the death-penalty statutes in the jurisdictions that did not rely on jury sentencing, or for the hundreds of prisoners condemned to death by judges in those states (*Ring v. Arizona* 2002:2449–2450, O'Connor, J., dissenting).

Historically, juries have been widely utilized to make capital-sentencing decisions because they serve as "a link between contemporary community values and the penal system—a link without which the determination of punishment could hardly reflect 'the evolving standards of decency that mark the progress of a maturing society'" (*Witherspoon v. Illinois* 1968:520, n. 15, *quoting Trop v. Dulles* 1958:101). Nevertheless, statutes and/or case decisions prevent jurors from serving in capital trials unless they are willing to exercise the sentencing discretion authorized by law. Prospective jurors are disqualified by operation of law if their views either in favor of or against capital punishment are so strong that they would substantially impair their ability to consider imposing the full range of statutory sentencing options (*Morgan v. Illinois* 1992; *Wainwright v. Witt* 1985).

Empirical research suggests that the process of "death qualifying" and "life qualifying" jurors threatens the impartiality of the guilt-phase jury. It also undermines the jury's representativeness by disproportionately excluding African-

Americans and women (Sandys and McClelland 2003). The parties' exercise of peremptory challenges, which typically are especially plentiful in capital trials, can further skew the composition of the jury (Acker and Lanier 1996:160–168; Winick 1982). Ironically, statutes that provide for jury sentencing in death-penalty cases, in order to give the community a direct voice in this important process, are significantly undercut by other laws that operate to selectively exclude certain community members from participating. For instance, there are no statutes that limit death- and life-qualification procedures to the penalty phase of capital trials, a practice that would facilitate the more complete participation of all segments of the community during the guilt-phase trial (*cf.*, *Lockhart v. McCree* 1986).

Sentencing Alternatives

The sentencer's task in a capital trial is somewhat more complicated than deciding whether a convicted offender should be sentenced to death. The judge or jury is confronted with choosing death or an alternative sentence, either life imprisonment with parole eligibility ("life") or life without parole (LWOP). Statutes offer one of three types of sentencing options: (1) death-LWOP; (2) death-LWOP-"life"; or (3) death-"life." The nation's death-penalty laws are a mixture of these three types of schemes (Acker and Lanier 1995b:55–56).

Research suggests that it is important for juries to understand the full implications of their sentencing options. People often underestimate the length of time an offender actually will serve in prison if given a "life" sentence. Survey respondents frequently assume that a "life" sentence results in release on parole in less than 15 years (Bowers 1993:167–171; Bowers and Steiner 1999:645–652). Jurors consequently may choose death over "life" in order to negate the chance that a murderer may return to the community in such a relatively short period of time (Bowers and Steiner 1999:652–660; Eisenberg and Wells 1993:4–9; Lane 1993: 334–343).

Indeed, the Supreme Court has recognized that, at least when the prosecution has put a defendant's future dangerousness at issue, and when a "life" sentence means life without parole, due process requires that the sentencing jury be instructed about the offender's ineligibility for parole (*Kelly v. South Carolina* 2002; *Shafer v. South Carolina* 2001; *Simmons v. South Carolina* 1994). An instruction explaining the true duration of a life sentence is not constitutionally required, however, if the offender may some day be released on parole (*Ramdass v. Angelone* 2000). It is now clear that the meaning jurors ascribe to "life imprisonment" may profoundly influence their sentencing decisions in all capital cases, even when a prosecutor has not raised the prospect of an offender's future dangerousness (Blume, Garvey, and Johnson 2001; Sorensen and Marquart 2003). Still, only a few death-penalty statutes require that parole eligibility and minimum sentence requirements associated with the "life imprisonment" sentencing option be explained to juries (Acker and Lanier 1995b:57). Providing such information routinely would only seem to enhance the reliability of the sentencing process.

More fundamentally, statutes presenting both LWOP and "life" imprisonment as alternatives to a capital sentence have advantages over schemes where the only sentencing options are either death-LWOP or death-"life." Where a "life" sentence is the exclusive noncapital sentencing choice, offenders might be sentenced to death for lack of an alternative (LWOP) that is perceived either as more commensurate with justice, or as a more effective community safeguard (Acker and Lanier 1995b:57–58; Lane 1993). By the same token, some capital murders may be sufficiently mitigated that a "life" sentence is more appropriate than either LWOP or death. However, in only a minority of jurisdictions do statutes permit the sentencing authority to choose between death, life without parole, and a "life" sentence (Acker and Lanier 1995b:55–56).

Guiding the Sentencing Decision

Post-*Furman* death-penalty laws commonly are known as "guided-discretion" statutes, although the aptness of this description is debatable (Steiker and Steiker 2003). The degree to which contemporary legislation actually helps structure the capital sentencing decision has been challenged openly even by several of the justices (*Lockett v. Ohio* 1978:622–624, White, J., dissenting in part; at 629–633, Rehnquist, J., dissenting in part; *Walton v. Arizona* 1990:657–673, Scalia, J., concurring in the judgment; *Graham v. Collins* 1993:478–500, Thomas, J., concurring; *Callins v. Collins* 1994:1141–1159, Blackmun, J., dissenting from denial of certiorari). These post-*Furman* capital-punishment statutes essentially create a somewhat narrower class of offenses punishable by death, and then provide that within that class of cases the sentencer must not be constrained from considering mitigating factors that might justify a sentence of less than death (*McCleskey v. Kemp* 1987:303–306). The ultimate sentencing decision must be individualized; at this stage "the State cannot channel the sentencer's discretion" (at 306; *see also* Gillers 1980). Consequently, the antithesis of "guided discretion" is demanded. The Court generally seeks to enforce the much more modest constitutional imperative that "a capital sentencing scheme must 'suitably direc[t] and limi[t]' the sentencer's discretion 'so as to minimize the risk of wholly arbitrary and capricious action'" (*Arave v. Creech* 1993:470).

That legislatures have wide latitude in crafting capital-sentencing guidelines is something of an understatement. One commentator has suggested that "the Court has reduced the law of the penalty trial to almost a bare aesthetic exhortation that the states just do something—anything—to give the penalty trial a legal appearance" (Weisberg 1984:306). In this section, we briefly review the different statutory sentencing models engendered under this permissive jurisprudence.

Balancing Schemes

The most widely used sentencing model requires the judge or jury to identify the aggravating and mitigating factors associated with the offense and offender, to balance or weigh those factors against one another, and to make a punishment decision based on this comparative assessment. There are significant variations among statutes that rely on this balancing approach.

For example, some schemes limit the sentencer to consider only aggravating factors enumerated in the statute. Others provide that after finding at least one statutory aggravating circumstance, any other aggravating evidence — even if not linked to a sentencing factor included in the statute — may be considered in the sentencing process (Acker and Lanier 1993a:491–498). Consideration of mitigating circumstances, though, is not symmetrical. The Constitution requires that all relevant mitigating evidence be admissible in a capital trial, so proof cannot be limited only to statutory mitigating factors (*Hitchcock v. Dugger* 1987; *Lockett v. Ohio* 1978). Nevertheless, several death-penalty laws include nonexhaustive lists of mitigating circumstances identified by legislatures as meriting the sentencer's consideration. Other statutes list no mitigating factors (Acker and Lanier 1994a:310–341).

One form of evidence that may be considered in some jurisdictions is so potentially significant to the sentencing process that it is almost *sui generis*. Testimony from relatives of the murder victim describing the victim's personal qualities and their own sense of loss as a result of the killing — so-called "victim impact evidence" — is admissible in capital penalty trials in several states (Acker and Lanier 1993a:498). The emotional impact of such testimony can be tremendous (Berger 1992; Levy 1993:1046; Vandiver 2003). Whether victim-impact testimony is relevant to a capital-sentencing decision, and in particular to the measure of the harm caused by the offender and the offender's culpability, is disputable (Sarat 2001:33–59).[13] After twice ruling that such evidence was constitutionally irrelevant to a capital-sentencing decision, the Supreme Court abruptly reversed course and authorized victim-impact evidence to be

---

13. Also in some dispute is the type or scope of victim impact testimony that should be allowed at capital penalty hearings. For example, some assert that witnesses, such as the victim's surviving family members, should be able to provide "reverse" impact testimony to the sentencer — i.e., testimony that "bring[s] to the attention of the jury that those most adversely affected by the crime are comfortable with a life sentence and the jury should be comfortable with imposing such a sentence" (Barnes 2002:245–246). Not surprisingly, perhaps, prosecutors have challenged the admissibility of such testimony (Perkins 2001). Others note the possibility of testimony from the defendant's family that might counter more traditional victim impact evidence that focuses on how the loss of the deceased affects survivors (King and Norgard 1999; *see also* Blumenthal 2001).

admitted during penalty-phase proceedings (*Payne v. Tennessee* 1991, *overruling Booth v. Maryland* 1987 and *South Carolina v. Gathers* 1989).

Following the admission of aggravating and mitigating evidence, sentencers are given various instructions about how to use such evidence under different balancing formulas. The most fundamental division is between *permissive* and *"quasi-mandatory"* balancing approaches. Under permissive schemes, the sentencer is not obligated to impose the death penalty, even if aggravating factors outweigh mitigating circumstances. Instead, a "life option" exists. That is, notwithstanding the relative weight of the aggravating and mitigating factors, a life sentence may be imposed if the sentencer considers it appropriate. Under quasi-mandatory balancing provisions, no judgment is made about the propriety of a death sentence independent of the weighing of aggravating and mitigating circumstances. Thus, the sentencer is directed to impose a death sentence if (a) one or more aggravating factors have been proven, but no mitigating circumstances exist, or (b) the weight of the aggravating evidence exceeds that of the mitigating evidence (Acker and Lanier 1995b:27–33, 42–47).

Quasi-mandatory balancing provisions risk camouflaging the moral nature of the sentencer's task behind the more formulaic exercise of tabulating and comparing aggravating and mitigating circumstances. For example, if the prosecution proves *any* aggravating factor (the specific aggravator established is irrelevant) under such a statute, and if either the defendant presents no mitigation evidence or the sentencer concludes that no mitigating factors have been established, the law mandates that a sentence of death be imposed (*Blystone v. Pennsylvania* 1990). In short, no explicit deliberation is required about whether death is a deserved punishment under the quasi-mandatory approach. Ostensible gains in consistency of sentencing under these provisions would appear to be more than offset by their troublesome features. For example, the sentencer has no opportunity to assess the moral significance of the aggravating factor(s) at issue, nor to consider directly whether the offender's conduct is so condemnable that capital punishment is appropriate under the facts of a particular case (Acker and Lanier 1995b:29–30).

Balancing schemes have additional nuances. To justify a sentence of death, some require the prosecution to prove that aggravating factors outweigh mitigating factors. Under others, the defendant must show that sufficient mitigating circumstances exist to make a death sentence unwarranted. When the prosecution is assigned the burden of persuasion concerning this ultimate balance, "proof beyond a reasonable doubt" is required under some statutes, but not all, and for some sentencing issues, but not others. When the defendant bears the burden of persuasion, either to establish the existence of mitigating factors or to show that the mitigation evidence is sufficiently substantial to call for leniency, the "preponderance of the evidence" standard typically prevails, although many statutes are nonspecific (Acker and Lanier 1995b:34–40).

Threshold Schemes

Under "threshold" sentencing systems, a conviction for capital murder and proof of at least one statutory aggravating factor makes the offender eligible for death. The judge or jury then typically is instructed to "consider" other relevant aggravating circumstances, as well as mitigating factors, before making a sentencing decision. The sentencer is not explicitly directed to weigh or balance aggravating and mitigating factors in this process (Acker and Lanier 1995b:47–49; Bowers 1995:1041–1047).

For example, Georgia's statute, which was approved by the Supreme Court in *Gregg*, instructs the sentencing jury to "consider, any mitigating or aggravating circumstances otherwise authorized by law, and any…statutory aggravating circumstances which may be supported by the evidence" (Ga. Code Ann. §17-10-30(b), 2002). How the jury makes the leap from "consider[ing]" the aggravating and mitigating circumstances to arriving at a sentencing decision remains undefined. The statute offers no additional guidance. It simply provides that:

> A sentence of death shall not be imposed unless the jury verdict includes a finding of at least one statutory aggravating circumstance and a recommendation that such sentence be imposed. Where a statutory aggravating circumstance is found and a recommendation of death is made, the court shall sentence the defendant to death (Ga. Code Ann. §17-10-31, 2002).

"Threshold" sentencing laws are eerily reminiscent of pre-*Furman* statutes. In fact, they almost literally are throwbacks to that era (Steiker and Steiker 2003). The essential difference lies only in the requirement for bifurcated guilt and penalty trials, and the provision that the jury find at least one statutory aggravating circumstance before it considers whether death is the appropriate punishment (Weisberg 1984:353–354). Otherwise, the resemblance is striking, especially for laws like Georgia's which do not even list mitigating factors for the sentencer's consideration. These statutes make little pretense of attempting to guide or structure the final sentencing decision.

Special Sentencing Issues

Balancing or considering aggravating and mitigating circumstances are of secondary importance to the capital-sentencing process under a third type of statute. Instead, these measures organize penalty-phase deliberations around one or more special sentencing issues. Notwithstanding the fact that laws of this type are in effect only in Oregon, Texas, and Virginia, they are of great practical significance. Texas (with 278 executions through late August 2002) and Virginia (with 86) rank first and second in the number of executions conducted under post-*Furman* statutes. Together, they account for over 45 percent of this country's executions since 1977 (Death Penalty Information Center 2002). Oregon had recorded just two executions during that time (*Id.*).

The Texas statute approved by the Supreme Court in *Jurek v. Texas* (1976) was partially revised in 1991 in response to the Court's later ruling (*Penry v. Lynaugh* 1989) that the law did not allow the sentencing jury to consider mitigating evidence effectively in all cases. The Texas law focuses on the offender's predicted future dangerousness. At the conclusion of the penalty trial, the jury is directed to answer "yes" or "no" to the special issue: "whether there is a probability that the defendant would commit criminal acts of violence that would constitute a continuing threat to society" (Tex. Code Crim. Proc. Ann. art. 37.071(2)(b)(l), 2002). If a unanimous jury responds affirmatively, it then considers whether sufficient mitigating circumstances exist "to warrant that a sentence of life imprisonment rather than a death sentence be imposed" (at art. 37.071(2)(e)). A unanimous negative response requires that a death sentence be imposed. Oregon's statute is essentially the same as the Texas law (Or. Rev. Stat. §163.150, 2002).

Virginia's sentencing provisions operate somewhat differently. The jury is authorized to consider two sentencing issues—one focusing on the defendant's future dangerousness and the other asking whether the offender's "conduct in committing the offense was outrageously or wantonly vile, horrible or inhuman, in that it involved torture, depravity of mind or aggravated battery to the victim" (Va. Code Ann. §19.2-264.4(C), 2002). If the jury makes an affirmative finding on either issue, it next considers relevant statutory and nonstatutory mitigating factors before rendering a sentencing decision (at §19.2-264.4(B), 2002).

Death-penalty statutes like those in Texas, Oregon, and Virginia largely attempt to distill the complex judgment concerning an offender's continued fitness to live to a simpler "yes-no" answer, given in response to discrete, ostensibly fact-dependent special sentencing issues. Schemes like these can be successful only to the extent that the special issues capture the moral essence of the sentencing decision, and, concomitantly, that the sentencer is capable of providing reliable answers to them. If the questions are deficient conceptually, or if the answers are unreliable, then such sentencing statutes are fatally flawed. Special sentencing issue schemes predicated on predictions of future dangerousness are suspect on both of these grounds.

The first issue is whether it is morally and legally defensible to focus not on an offender's adjudicated past conduct when making a life or death sentencing decision, but to speculate about what the offender *might* do in the *future*. One observer, a native Texan, has concluded that this sentencing philosophy alone "is really enough to stamp this section as outside the bounds of civilized law" (Black 1974:63).

The form of the issue presented to the jury also requires scrutiny. The jury is not asked to decide whether the offender *will* commit "criminal acts of violence" (which remain undefined) that would constitute "a continuing threat to society" (which also remains undefined), but rather "whether there is a *probability*" of this eventuality. The equivocal nature of the question thus completely deflates any significance that otherwise might have attached to the required "proof beyond a reasonable doubt" standard. An affirmative answer to the sentencing issue translates into nothing more than a "definite maybe" regarding the offender's propensity to engage in future violent criminal conduct (Wexler 1981:63; *cf.*, Black 1974:63).

Finally, even if the issue the jury considers has merit, the sentencing framework collapses if the question cannot be answered reliably. Predictions of future dangerousness, even by mental health professionals, are roughly as accurate as predictions based on the flip of a coin (*Barefoot v. Estelle* 1983:920–923, Blackmun, J., dissenting; Marquart, Ekland-Olson, and Sorensen 1989; Sorensen and Marquart 2003). It thus seems apparent that capital-punishment statutes that rely on special sentencing issues are highly problematic, both as conceived and as applied.

The Sentencing Statutes in Application

In their various permutations, the post-*Furman* sentencing statutes are geometrically more complex than the laws they replaced. An important inquiry is whether changes in the written laws have translated into corresponding reforms in the administration of the death penalty. A number of studies have examined the application of the new capital-sentencing statutes. Even though a comparative assessment of pre- and post-*Furman* laws is difficult, the results, by and large, are not encouraging.

One consequence of the increased complexity of modern death-penalty statutes is the difficulty jurors experience in applying such laws. Even jurors with the best intentions cannot faithfully apply laws they do not understand. For instance, jurors appear to misapprehend judges' instructions in the capital-sentencing process with some regularity (Diamond 1993; Luginbuhl and Howe 1995).

More fundamentally, jurors may believe they are not fully responsible for the death-penalty decisions they render. Consciously or subconsciously, some may take refuge behind the elaborate verbiage of sentencing statutes, and reason that it is "the law" rather than they who determine the offender's entitlement to life (Bowers 1995:1093–1098). Others may believe that the sentence they impose is not truly final; that if it is excessively harsh it will be reduced by judges who later review it on appeal. This impression may diminish jurors' sense of responsibility for their sentencing decisions, thus undermining the reliability of the process (Hoffmann 1995).

Most discouraging, perhaps, is that there is mounting evidence that the elaborate sentencing criteria and procedures mandated by statute are largely irrelevant to the actual deliberations and verdicts of juries. Life and death sentencing decisions in practice often continue to be made independently of balancing, threshold, or other statutory formulas (Bowers 1995; Bowers, Fleury-Steiner, and Antonio 2003; Hans 1995). Many jurors also appear to make up their minds about the appropriate sentence prematurely, during or immediately after the guilt phase of the trial, without even considering evidence offered during penalty-phase proceedings (Bentele and Bowers 2001; Bowers, Sandys, and Steiner 1998).

If the deliberative process has not been channeled effectively by the new capital-sentencing statutes, then what results have the post-*Furman* laws produced? It is apparent that even highly objective sentencing decisions could not fully compensate for arbitrary decisions made at other discretionary junctures of the criminal justice process, most notably prosecutorial charging decisions. Nor could they eradicate the influence of other potentially biasing factors, such as ineffective defense counsel, inadequate resources for the defense, unrepresentative juries, incomplete or ineffective appellate review, and a host of other considerations.

We attempt no detailed review of these issues because many other researchers, including several in this volume, have already explored and reported on these topics. Several profound problems continue to plague the death penalty's administration, notwithstanding post-*Furman* statutory reforms. The pernicious influence of race, for example, persists in capital charging and sentencing decisions (Baldus and Woodworth 2003). Rural-urban and other geographical differences within states result in divergent prosecutorial and sentencing decisions in similar cases (Paternoster 1991:175–180). The poor quality of defense counsel, as well as the inadequacy of resources for the defense of capital cases, portend potentially devastating consequences for the accused (Bright 2003, 1994). Death-qualification and life-qualification procedures also can significantly compromise both the representativeness and the impartiality of capital juries (Sandys and McClelland 2003), and peremptory challenges exacerbate these problems (Acker and Lanier 1996:160–168). Either because statutes do not require them to engage in comparative proportionality review, or because such review is performed haphazardly, appellate courts largely have been an ineffective safeguard against arbitrary and aberrational capital-sentencing decisions (Acker and Lanier 1995a:237–248; Bienen 1996; Sprenger 1988). However sophisticated, though, no statutes are capable of ensuring that innocent people will not be convicted of capital crimes, sentenced to death, and executed (Gross 1996; Radelet and Bedau 2003). In short, post-*Furman* statutory reforms have failed to eliminate significant problems in the administration of capital punishment.

The Future of Capital-Punishment Legislation

Death-penalty statutes are concrete representations of abstract support for capital punishment. They are the literal, written prescriptions for government-sponsored executions. Despite the imperfect correspondence between law on the books and the law in practice, their specifics help establish many vital attributes of capital-punishment systems. They define the domain of crimes and the class of offenders that are punishable by death, and detail the legal procedures that are to be observed from the earliest stages following the commission of a crime through execution. The formidable task of legislating death has evolved significantly over America's history, and we fully expect this process will continue over the ensuing years. However, we believe that death-penalty statutes ultimately are destined for extinction.

Although contemporary post-*Furman* statutes represent a wholesale revision of earlier capital-punishment laws, the new legislation in practice has delivered little more than a series of empty promises. Serious and perhaps inexorable problems linger in the administration of modern death-penalty statutes. These problems strike at the heart of procedural fairness. Among them are issues such as race discrimination, the risk that innocent people will be convicted of capital crimes and executed, unharnessed charging and sentencing discretion that result in the arbitrary distribution of death sentences, a lack of commitment to provide high quality defense counsel, insufficient resources to level the playing field for poor people charged with capital crimes, procedural obstacles to securing judicial review of substantively meritorious claims of error, and others.

There is evidence that these problems are beginning to command attention outside of the ranks of abolitionists, the criminal defense community, and a small segment of the American public. We are reluctant to ascribe too much significance to recent events because historically, reforms in capital-punishment laws have waxed and waned over extended cycles. Changes in death-penalty policies are driven not only by deliberate policy decisions, but also by unpredictable events such as highly publicized horrific crimes, social upheaval, and particularly visible miscarriages of justice (Banner 2002). Nevertheless, we think it noteworthy that the devastating events of September 11, 2001 caused little more than a ripple in death-penalty laws, producing just a scattering of legislative revisions to include killings associated with "terrorism" among aggravating sentencing factors or capital crimes (*e.g.*, N.Y. Penal Law sec. 125.27 (1) (a) (xiii), 2002; N.J. Stat. Ann. sec. 2C:11-3(c)), 2002). Significantly, other developments reflecting skepticism about capital punishment laws have not degenerated in the wake of September 11. There are indications that Americans' support for capital punishment is beginning to ebb.

For example, the New Hampshire legislature voted in 2000 to repeal the state death-penalty statute, the first such action taken by a legislative body in decades, only to have Governor Jeanne Sheehan veto the measure. Nebraska legislators passed a bill in 1999 ordering a moratorium on future executions and commissioning a study to investigate possible race discrimination in the state capital-punishment law. These provisions failed to become law when Governor Mike Johanns declined to sign the bill, although the legislature thereafter did manage to appropriate money for the study and have it carried out. On the federal level, bills were introduced calling alternatively for abolition of capital punishment and a moratorium on executions, although neither commanded significant support. However, the proposed Innocence Protection Act, which provides for DNA testing and requires the appointment of qualified counsel in capital cases, had garnered considerable bipartisan support in Congress by summer 2002 (Lanier and Acker, forthcoming).

Elsewhere, spurred by emergent problems with capital punishment, government-appointed commissions were studying death-penalty laws and their administration in several states. Illinois set a prominent example. Three years after the Chicago-based American Bar Association's 1997 call for a national moratorium on executions[14], Illinois Governor George Ryan ordered a statewide halt to carrying out further death sentences (Kirchmeier 2002). He then appointed a blue-ribbon commission to study the state's death-penalty law and its operation. The moratorium and study were prompted by Illinois' having witnessed the exoneration of 13 death-sentenced individuals in little more than a decade (*Report of the Governor's Commission on Capital Punishment* 2002:4), many of whom spent several years on death row and were released only following investigations conducted by journalism students and volunteer attorneys. The commission issued its report in April, 2002. Among its 85 recommendations were calls for extensive narrowing of the death-penalty's reach and also for significant procedural reforms throughout the investigation, charging, trial, and post-conviction stages of cases. In May, 2002, Maryland Governor Parris Glendening took similar action, imposing a moratorium on executions in that state pending completion and review of a study examining apparent racial and geographic disparities in the death-penalty's administration (Lanier and Acker, forthcoming).

With renewed attention focused on defects in capital-punishment systems, and on the costs of administering the death penalty, the growth rates of the na-

---

14. The American Bar Association promoted a national moratorium on executions based on several concerns about the death-penalty's administration, including the quality of representation provided by defense counsel in capital cases, evidence of race discrimination, the continuing subjection of juveniles and (at that time) mentally retarded offenders to the death penalty, and the erosion of judicial review and the accompanying risk of exposing innocent people to conviction and execution (Coleman 1998).

tion's death rows have recently begun to decline. In 1996, 299 newly sentenced prisoners joined state and federal death row populations. Five years later, in 2000, the number of new entries to prisons' death houses had dipped to 214 (U.S. Department of Justice 2001:9; U.S. Department of Justice 1997:9). Executions also have experienced a recent modest decline. After peaking at 98 in 1999 during the post-*Furman* years, executions dropped off the following year to 85, and then to a five-year low of 66 in 2001 (NAACP Legal Defense and Educational Fund, Inc. 2002:9). These developments would have been unlikely without at least tacit public approval and, in fact, recent Gallup polls reflect a slight but significant downturn in support for the death penalty. Roughly 7 in 10 Americans reported backing the death penalty for murder in 2002, down from the 80 percent support measured in 1994. These figures drop dramatically when pollsters rephrase their questions by asking whether respondents prefer the death penalty to an alternative punishment such as life imprisonment without the possibility of parole (Bohm 2003a).

It would be naïve to base a prediction about the eventual demise of death-penalty legislation on trends of such short duration. The death penalty has been a part of a substantial majority of American jurisdictions since earliest statehood. Within the last decade, capital punishment has been reinstated in two states—Kansas, in 1994 (McAllister 1995) and New York, in 1995 (Acker 1996b)—and legislatures in several abolition jurisdictions including Alaska, Iowa, Maine, Massachusetts, Michigan, Rhode Island, Wisconsin, and the District of Columbia have heard calls for its reenactment. The thousands of prisoners presently inhabiting death rows, the hundreds of new ones that join them annually, and the scores each year who are executed, speak undeniably to the death-penalty's continuing presence in this country in the early 21st century.

At the same time, Americans increasingly are forced to confront the many shortcomings and failures of contemporary death-penalty statutes. Recent experience and the results of empirical research have dramatically begun to strip the public, elected officials, and the courts of the secure comfort of maintaining the death penalty as an abstract symbol of justice or as an effective crime-fighting tool. As the United States becomes increasingly out of step with Western European and other North American countries in its capital-punishment policies (Wilson 2003), the death-penalty's political, legal, moral, and social costs can be expected to grow increasingly unaffordable. Its siphoning of scarce economic and judicial resources will be more difficult to defend in a society with pressing needs for education, health care, housing, care for the elderly, and meaningful criminal justice reforms. Its perceived necessity also will diminish as the alternative sanction of life imprisonment without parole becomes increasingly accepted as a societal safeguard, which can accomplish the death penalty's other essential objectives with far fewer costs.

In the not-too-distant future, we anticipate that a definitive backlash must inevitably occur regarding capital punishment in the post-*Furman* years, as the public tires of and becomes increasingly unwilling to endure laws whose singular objective is to take offenders' lives. These attitudes are likely initially to lead to a narrowing of death-penalty statutes to encompass a relatively small category of extremely heinous crimes—such as assassinating public officials, or murdering police officers or multiple victims—much as already has been proposed by the Governor's Commission in Illinois (*Report of the Governor's Commission on Capital Punishment* 2002). Heightened procedural safeguards almost certainly will be adopted to accompany these substantive reforms. Such incremental steps toward abolition would be consistent with long-term historical trends. They also should prove to be politically feasible because the symbolic safety net represented by the death penalty can be preserved at the same time that several of the liabilities of carrying out capital sentences are minimized.

Eventually, we believe, the public and government officials will come to appreciate and accept that the remaining vestiges of capital punishment are both unnecessary and ill-advised. In time, we predict, the death penalty and its authorizing legislation will wither, die, and disappear from the American legal landscape. The continued administration of capital-punishment laws is destined to expose more problems than are put to rest by using this ultimate sanction.[15] We forecast that, ironically, the post-*Furman* era of death-penalty statutes one day will be recognized as the beginning of the end of capital-punishment legislation.

References

Acker, J.R. (1996a) "The Death Penalty: A 25-Year Retrospective and a Perspective on the Future." *Criminal Justice Review* 21:139–160.

Acker, J.R. (1996b) "When the Cheering Stopped: An Overview and Analysis of New York's Death Penalty Legislation." *Pace Law Review* 17:41–227.

Acker, J.R. (1990) "New York's Proposed Death Penalty Legislation: Constitutional and Policy Perspectives." *Albany Law Review* 54:515–616.

Acker, J.R. (1989) "The Grand Jury and Capital Punishment: Rethinking the Role of an Ancient Institution Under the Modern Jurisprudence of Death." *Pacific Law Journal* 21:31–118.

Acker, J.R. and C.S. Lanier (2000) "May God—Or the Governor—Have Mercy: Executive Clemency and Executions in Modern Death-Penalty Systems." *Criminal Law Bulletin* 36:200–237.

---

15. After an extensive review of empirical research on the administration of capital punishment in America, we note elsewhere that: "Our plea is a simple one—to assemble and make available trustworthy data about the full range of empirical issues implicated by a jurisdiction's capital-punishment system. It is our belief that when the true facts are marshaled and fully penetrate the public conscience, they cannot help but tip the scales radically against capital punishment" (Lanier and Acker, forthcoming).

Acker, J.R. and C.S. Lanier (1996) "Law, Discretion, and the Capital Jury: Death Penalty Statutes and Proposals for Reform." *Criminal Law Bulletin* 32:134–180.

Acker, J.R. and C.S. Lanier (1995a) "Statutory Measures for More Effective Appellate Review of Capital Cases." *Criminal Law Bulletin* 31:211–258.

Acker, J.R. and C.S. Lanier (1995b) "Matters of Life or Death: The Sentencing Provisions in Capital Punishment Statutes." *Criminal Law Bulletin* 31:19–60.

Acker, J.R. and C.S. Lanier (1994a) "In Fairness and Mercy: Statutory Mitigating Factors in Capital Punishment Laws." *Criminal Law Bulletin* 30:299–345.

Acker, J.R. and C.S. Lanier (1994b) "'Parsing This Lexicon of Death': Aggravating Factors in Capital Sentencing Statutes." *Criminal Law Bulletin* 30:107–152.

Acker, J.R. and C.S. Lanier (1993a) "Aggravating Circumstances and Capital Punishment Law: Rhetoric or Real Reforms?" *Criminal Law Bulletin* 29:467–501.

Acker, J.R. and C.S. Lanier (1993b) "The Dimensions of Capital Murder." *Criminal Law Bulletin* 29:379–417.

Acker, J.R. and C.S. Lanier (1993c) "Capital Murder from Benefit of Clergy to Bifurcated Trials: Narrowing the Class of Offenses Punishable by Death." *Criminal Law Bulletin* 29:291–316.

American Law Institute (1980) *Model Penal Code and Commentaries: Part II Definition of Specific Crimes*, §§210.0 to 213.6 (Official Draft and Revised Comments) Philadelphia: American Law Institute.

Apprendi v. New Jersey (2000) 530 U.S. 466.

Arave v. Creech (1993) 507 U.S. 463.

Atkins v. Virginia (2002) 122 S.Ct. 2242.

Baldus, D.C., C.A. Pulaski, Jr., and G. Woodworth (1986) "Arbitrariness and Discrimination in the Administration of the Death Penalty: A Challenge to State Supreme Courts." *Stetson Law Review* 15:133–261.

Baldus, D.C. and G. Woodworth (2003) "Race Discrimination and the Death Penalty: An Empirical and Legal Overview." (This volume.)

Banner, S. (2002) *The Death Penalty: An American History*. Cambridge, MA: Harvard University Press.

Barefoot v. Estelle (1983) 463 U.S. 880.

Barnes, A.N. (2002) "Reverse Impact Testimony: A New and Improved Victim Impact Statement." *Capital Defense Journal* 14:245–264.

Bedau, H.A. (1982) "Background and Developments." Pp. 3–28 in H.A. Bedau (ed.), *The Death Penalty in America*, 3d ed. New York: Oxford University Press.

Bentele, U. and W.J. Bowers (2001) "How Jurors Decide on Death: Guilt is Overwhelming; Aggravation Requires Death; and Mitigation is No Excuse." *Brooklyn Law Review* 66:1011–1080.

Berger, V. (1992) "*Payne* and Suffering—A Personal Reflection and a Victim-Centered Critique." *Florida State Law Review* 20:21–65.

Bessler, J.D. (1997) *Death in the Dark: Midnight Executions in America*. Boston: Northeastern University Press.

Bienen, L.B. (1996) "The Proportionality Review of Capital Cases by State High Courts After *Gregg*: Only 'The Appearance of Justice'?" *Journal of Criminal Law and Criminology* 87:130–314.

Black, C.L., Jr. (1974) *Capital Punishment: The Inevitability of Caprice and Mistake.* New York: W.W. Norton & Company.

Blume, J.H., S.P. Garvey, and S.L. Johnson (2001) "Future Dangerousness in Capital Cases: Always 'At Issue.'" *Cornell Law Review* 86:397–410.

Blumenthal, J.A. (2001) "The Admissibility of Victim Impact Statements at Capital Sentencing: Traditional and Nontraditional Perspectives." *Drake Law Review* 50:67–91.

Blystone v. Pennsylvania (1990) 494 U.S. 299.

Bohm, R.M. (2003) "American Death Penalty Opinion: Past, Present, and Future." (This volume.)

Booth v. Maryland (1987) 482 U.S. 496.

Bowers, W.J. (1995) "The Capital Jury Project: Rationale, Design, and Preview of Early Findings." *Indiana Law Journal* 70:1043–1102.

Bowers, W. (1993) "Capital Punishment and Contemporary Values: People's Misgivings and the Court's Misperceptions." *Law & Society Review* 27:157–175.

Bowers, W.J. (1984) *Legal Homicide: Death as Punishment in America, 1864–1982.* Boston: Northeastern University Press.

Bowers, W.J. (1974) *Executions in America.* Lexington, MA: Lexington Books.

Bowers, W.J., B.D. Fleury-Steiner, and M.E. Antonio (2003) "The Capital Sentencing Decision: Guided Discretion, Reasoned Moral Judgment, or Legal Fiction?" (This volume.)

Bowers, W.J., M. Sandys, and B.D. Steiner (1998) "Foreclosed Impartiality in Capital Sentencing: Jurors' Predispositions, Guilt-Trial Experience, and Premature Decision Making." *Cornell Law Review* 83:1476–1556.

Bowers, W.J. and B.D. Steiner (1999) "Death by Default: An Empirical Demonstration of False and Forced Choices in Capital Sentencing." *Texas Law Review* 77:605–717.

Bright, S.B. (2003) "The Politics of Capital Punishment: The Sacrifice of Fairness for Executions." (This volume).

Bright, S.B. (1994) "Counsel for the Poor: The Death Sentence Not for the Worst Crime but For the Worst Lawyer." *Yale Law Journal* 103:1835–1883.

Bye, R.T. (1926) "Recent History and Present Status of Capital Punishment in the United States." *Journal of Criminal Law and Criminology* 17:234–245.

California Penal Code (*Westlaw* 2002) §190.2.

Callins v. Collins (1994) 510 U.S. 1141.

Coker v. Georgia (1977) 433 U.S. 584.

Coleman, Jr., J.E. (1998) "Foreword." *Law and Contemporary Problems* 61(4):1–4.

Connecticut General Statute Annotated (*Westlaw* 2002) §53a–46a(i).

Davis, D.B. (1957) "The Movement to Abolish Capital Punishment in America, 1787–1861." *American Historical Review* 63 (October):23–46.

Death Penalty Information Center (2002) "Number of Executions by State Since 1976" (Available electronically on World Wide Web at URL: "http://www.essential.org/dpic/").

Delaware Code Annotated (*Westlaw* 2002) title 11 §4209(e).

Denno, D.W. (1994) "Is Electrocution an Unconstitutional Method of Execution? The Engineering of Death Over the Century." *William and Mary Law Review* 35:551–692.

Diamond, S.S. (1993) "Instructing on Death: Psychologists, Juries, and Judges." *American Psychologist* 48:423–434.

Eberheart v. Georgia (1977) 433 U.S. 917.

Eisenberg, T. and M.T. Wells (1993) "Deadly Confusion: Juror Instructions in Capital Cases." *Cornell Law Review* 79:1–17.

Ellis, V.W. (1993) "Guilty But Mentally Ill and the Death Penalty: Punishment Full of Sound and Fury, Signifying Nothing." *Duke Law Journal* 43:87–112.

Emanuel, A.S. (1989) "Guilty But Mentally Ill Verdicts and the Death Penalty: An Eighth Amendment Analysis." *North Carolina Law Review* 68:37–66.

Enmund v. Florida (1982) 458 U.S. 782.

Filler, J. (1952) "Movements to Abolish the Death Penalty in the United States." *The Annals of the American Academy of Political and Social Science* 284 (November):124–136.

Finkel, N.J. (1990) "Capital Felony-Murder, Objective Indicia, and Community Sentiment." *Arizona Law Review* 32:819–913.

Fletcher, G.P. (1978) *Rethinking Criminal Law*. Boston: Little, Brown & Co.

Furman v. Georgia (1972) 408 U.S. 238.

Garvey, S.P. (1998) "Aggravation and Mitigation in Capital Cases: What do Jurors Think?" *Columbia Law Review* 98:1538–1575.

Geimer, W.S. and J. Amsterdam (1988) "Why Jurors Vote Life or Death: Operative Factors in Ten Florida Death Penalty Cases." *American Journal of Criminal Law* 15:1–54.

Georgia Code Annotated (*Westlaw* 2002) §16-5-l.

Georgia Code Annotated (*Westlaw* 2002) §17-10-30(b).

Georgia Code Annotated (*Westlaw* 2002) §17-10-31.

Gillers, S. (1980) "Deciding Who Dies." *University of Pennsylvania Law Review* 129:1–124.

Givelber, D. (1994) "The New Law of Murder." *Indiana Law Journal* 69:375–423.

Godfrey v. Georgia (1980) 446 U.S. 420.

Graham v. Collins (1993) 506 U.S. 461.

Gregg v. Georgia (1976) 428 U.S. 153.

Gross, S.R. (1996) "The Risks of Death: Why Erroneous Convictions are Common in Capital Cases." *Buffalo Law Review* 44:469–500.

Haines, H.H. (1996) *Against Capital Punishment: The Anti-Death Penalty Movement in America, 1972–1994*. New York: Oxford University Press.

Hans, V.P. (1995) "How Juries Decide Death: The Contributions of the Capital Jury Project." *Indiana Law Journal* 70:1233–1240.

Hay, D. (1975) "Property, Authority and the Criminal Law." Pp. 17–64 in D. Hay, P. Linebaugh, J.G. Rule, E.P. Thompson, and C. Winslow (eds.), *Albion's Fatal Tree: Crime and Society in Eighteenth-Century England*. New York: Pantheon Books.

Hitchcock v. Dugger (1987) 481 U.S. 393.

Hobson, C.L. (1996) "Reforming California's Homicide Law." *Pepperdine Law Review* 23:495–563.

Hoffmann, J.L. (1995) "Where's the Buck?—Juror Misperception of Sentencing Responsibility in Death Penalty Cases." *Indiana Law Journal* 70:1137–1160.

Jeffries, J.C., Jr. and P.B. Stephan III (1979) "Defenses, Presumptions, and Burden of Proof in the Criminal Law." *Yale Law Journal* 88:1325–1407.

Jurek v. Texas (1976) 428 U.S. 262.

Keedy, E.R. (1949) "History of the Pennsylvania Statute Creating Degrees of Murder." *University of Pennsylvania Law Review* 97:759–777.

Kelly v. South Carolina (2002) 122 S.Ct. 726.

King, R. and K. Norgard (1999) "What About Our Families? Using the Impact on Death Row Defendants' Family members as a Mitigating Factor in Death Penalty Sentencing Hearings." *Florida State University Law Review* 26:1119–1173.

Kirchmeier, J.L. (2002) "Another Place Beyond Here: The Death Penalty Moratorium Movement in the United States." *Colorado Law Review* 73:1–116.

Koosed, M.M. (2001) "Averting Mistaken Executions by Adopting the Model Penal Code's Exclusion of Death in the Presence of Lingering Doubt." *Northern Illinois University Law Review* 21:41–129.

LaFave, W.R. and A.W. Scott, Jr. (1986) *Criminal Law*, 2d ed. St. Paul, MN: West Publishing Co.

Lane, J.M. (1993) " 'Is There Life Without Parole?': A Capital Defendant's Right to a Meaningful Alternative Sentence." *Loyola (Los Angeles) Law Review* 26:327–393.

Langbein, J.H. (1983) "Shaping the Eighteenth-Century Criminal Trial: A View from the Ryder Sources." *University of Chicago Law Review* 50:1–136.

Lanier, C.S. and J.R. Acker (forthcoming) "Capital Punishment, the Moratorium Movement, and Empirical Questions: Looking Beyond Innocence, Race, and Bad Lawyering in Death-Penalty Cases." *Psychology, Public Policy and Law* ___:___–___.

Levy, J.H. (1993) "Limiting Victim Impact Evidence and Argument After *Payne v. Tennessee*." *Stanford Law Review* 45:1027–1060.

Lockett v. Ohio (1978) 438 U.S. 586.

Lockhart v. McCree (1986) 476 U.S. 162.

Louisiana ex rel. Francis v. Resweber (1947) 329 U.S. 459.

Lowenfield v. Phelps (1988) 484 U.S. 231.

Luginbuhl, J. and J. Howe (1995) "Discretion in Capital Sentencing Instructions: Guided or Misguided?" *Indiana Law Journal* 70:1161–1181.

Mackey, P.E. (1982) *Hanging in the Balance: The Anti-Capital Punishment Movement in New York State, 1771–1861*. New York: Garland Publishing, Inc.

Mackey, P.E. (1976) "Introduction: An Historical Perspective." Pp. xi–liii in P. E. Mackey (ed.), *Voices Against Death: American Opposition to Capital Punishment, 1787–1975*. New York: Burt Franklin & Co.

Mackey, P.E. (1974) "The Inutility of Mandatory Capital Punishment: An Historical Note." *Boston University Law Review* 54:32–35.

Madow, M. (1995) "Forbidden Spectacle: Executions, the Public and the Press in Nineteenth Century New York." *Buffalo Law Review* 43:461–562.

Marquart, J.W., S. Ekland-Olson, and J. Sorensen (1989)"Gazing Into the Crystal Ball: Can Jurors Accurately Predict Future Dangerousness in Capital Cases?" *Law & Society Review* 23:449–468.

Masur, L.P. (1989) *Rites of Execution: Capital Punishment and the Transformation of American Culture, 1771–1865*. New York: Oxford University Press.

Maynard v. Cartwright (1988) 486 U.S. 356.

McAllister, S. (1995) "Federal Constitutional Requirements Governing Trial, Sentencing and Direct Review in Capital Cases." *Journal of the Kansas Bar Association* 64:20–34.

McCleskey v. Kemp (1987) 481 U.S. 279.

McGautha v. California (1971) 402 U.S. 183.

Meltsner, M. (1973) *Cruel and Unusual: The Supreme Court and Capital Punishment*. New York: Random House.

Mississippi Code Annotated (*Westlaw* 2002) §97-7-67.

Morgan v. Illinois (1992) 504 U.S. 719.

Myers, M. (1994) "Felony Killings and Prosecutions for Murder: Exploring the Tension Between Culpability and Consequences in the Criminal Law." *Social and Legal Studies* 3:149–179.

NAACP Legal Defense and Educational Fund, Inc. (2002, Summer) *Death Row, U.S.A.* (published and distributed by the NAACP Legal Defense and Educational Fund, Inc., New York).

New Jersey Statutes Annotated (*Westlaw* 2002) §2C:11-3(c)).

New York Criminal Procedure Law (*Westlaw* 2002) §400.27.

New York Penal Law (*Westlaw* 2002) §125.27.

Oregon Revised Statute (*Westlaw* 2002) §163.150.

Paternoster, R. (1991) *Capital Punishment in America*. New York: Lexington Books.

Patterson v. Texas (2002) 536 U.S. ___, 2002 WL 1986618.

Payne v. Tennessee (1991) 501 U.S. 808.

Penry v. Lynaugh (1989) 492 U.S. 302.

People v. McGautha (1969) 70 Cal.2d 770, 452 P.2d 650, 76 Cal. Rptr. 434, *death sentence affirmed, McGautha v. California*, 402 U.S. 183 (1971).

Perkins, L.M. (2001) "Court of Common Pleas Criminal Division Rules on Sentencing Testimony: Victim's Mother May Address Court on Behalf of Defendant." *Lawyers Journal* 3:3–4.

Pignatelli, C.S. (2001) "Residual Doubt: It's a Life Saver." *Capital Defense Journal* 13:307–322.

Proffitt v. Florida (1976) 428 U.S. 242.

Pulley v. Harris (1984) 465 U.S. 37.

Radelet, M.L. and H.A. Bedau (2003) "The Execution of the Innocent." (This volume.)

Radzinowicz, L. (1948) *A History of English Criminal Law and Its Administration from 1750*, vol. l. London: Stevens.

Ramdass v. Angelone (2000) 530 U.S. 156.

Reid, L.T. (1999) "Blind Justice: Excluding Relevant Mitigating Evidence During Capital Sentencing." *Journal of Gender, Race and Justice* 3:343–371.

Report of the Governor's Commission on Capital Punishment (2002, April) Springfield, IL: State of Illinois.

Ring v. Arizona (2002) 122 S.Ct. 2428.

Roberts v. Louisiana (1977) 431 U.S. 633.

Roberts v. Louisiana (1976) 428 U.S. 325.

Rosen, R.A. (1990) "Felony Murder and the Eighth Amendment Jurisprudence of Death." *Boston College Law Review* 31:1103–1170.

Rosen, R.A. (1986) "The 'Especially Heinous' Aggravating Circumstance in Capital Cases—the Standardless Standard." *North Carolina Law Review* 64:941–992.

Roth, N.E. and S.E. Sundby (1985) "The Felony-Murder Rule: A Doctrine at Constitutional Crossroads." *Cornell Law Review* 70:441–492.

Sandys, M. and S. McClelland (2003) "Stacking the Deck for Guilt and Death: The Failure of Death Qualification to Ensure Impartiality." (This volume.)

Sarat, A. (2001) *When the State Kills: Capital Punishment and the American Condition*. Princeton, NJ: Princeton University Press.

Savitz, L.D. (1955) "Capital Crimes as Defined in American Statutory Law." *Journal of Criminal Law, Criminology and Police Science* 46:355–363.

Sellin, T. (1967) "Executions in the United States." In T. Sellin (ed.), *Capital Punishment*. New York: Harper & Row.

Shafer v. South Carolina (2001) 532 U.S. 36.

Simmons v. South Carolina (1994) 512 U.S. 154.

Sorensen, J. and J.W. Marquart (2003) "Future Dangerousness and Incapacitation." (This volume.)

South Carolina v. Gathers (1989) 490 U.S. 805.

Spaziano v. Florida (1984) 468 U.S. 447.

Sprenger, S.M. (1988) "A Critical Evaluation of State Supreme Court Proportionality Review in Death Sentence Cases." *Iowa Law Review* 73:719–741.

Stanford v. Kentucky (1989) 492 U.S. 361.

State v. Crampton (1969) 18 Ohio St.2d 182, 248 N.E.2d 614, *death sentence affirmed sub nom.*, *McGautha v. California*, 402 U.S. 183 (1971).

Steiker, C.S. and J.M. Steiker (2003) "Judicial Developments in Capital Punishment Law." (This volume.)

Steiker, C.S. and J.M. Steiker (1995) "Sober Second Thoughts: Reflections on Two Decades of Constitutional Regulation of Capital Punishment." *Harvard Law Review* 109:355–438.

Stephen, J.F. (1883) *A History of the Criminal Law*, vol.3. New York: Burt Franklin.

Streib, V.L. (2003) "Executing Women, Children, and the Retarded: Second Class Citizens in Capital Punishment." (This volume.)

Sumner v. Shuman (1987) 483 U.S. 66.

Symposium (1988) "The 25th Anniversary of the Model Penal Code." *Rutgers Law Journal* 19:519–954.

Tedder v. State (1975) 322 So.2d 908 (Fla.).

Texas Code of Criminal Procedure Annotated (*Westlaw* 2002) article 37.071(2)(b)(l).

Texas Code of Criminal Procedure Annotated (*Westlaw* 2002) article 37.071(2)(e).

Texas Penal Code Annotated (*Westlaw* 2002) §19.03.

Thompson v. Oklahoma (1988) 487 U.S. 815.

Tison v. Arizona (1987) 481 U.S. 137.

Trop v. Dulles (1958) 356 U.S. 101.

Tushnet, M. (1994) *The Death Penalty*. New York: Facts on File, Inc.

United States Code Annotated (*Westlaw* 2002) tit. 18 §794.

United States Code Annotated (*Westlaw* 2002) tit. 18 §2381.

United States Code Annotated (*Westlaw* 2002) tit. 18 §3591(b)(1).

United States Code Annotated (*Westlaw* 2002) tit. 18 §3591(b)(2).

U.S. Department of Justice (2001) *Capital Punishment 2000*. Washington, D.C.: Bureau of Justice Statistics, United States Department of Justice.

U.S. Department of Justice (1997) *Capital Punishment 1996*. Washington, D.C.: Bureau of Justice Statistics, United States Department of Justice.

U.S. Department of Justice (1982) *Capital Punishment 1981*. Washington, D.C.: Bureau of Justice Statistics, United States Department of Justice.

Vandiver, M. (2003) "The Impact of the Death Penalty on the Families of Homicide Victims and Of Condemned Prisoners." (This volume.)

Virginia Code Annotated (*Westlaw* 2002) §19.2-264.4.

Wainwright v. Witt (1985) 469 U.S. 412.

Walton v. Arizona (1990) 497 U.S. 639, *overruled in part, Ring v. Arizona*, 122 S.Ct. 2428 (2002).

Wechsler, H. and J. Michael (1937) "A Rationale of the Law of Homicide: I." *Columbia Law Review* 37:701–761.

Weisberg, R. (1984) "Deregulating Death." Pp. 305–395 in P.B. Kurland, G. Casper and J. Hutchinson (eds.), *The Supreme Court Review* 1983. Chicago: University of Chicago Press.

Wexler, D.B. (1981) *Mental Health Law: Major Issues*. New York: Plenum Press.

Wilson, R.J. (2003) "The Influence of International Law and Practice on the Death Penalty in the United States." (This volume.)

Winick, B.J. (1982) "Prosecutorial Peremptory Challenges in Capital Cases: An Empirical Study and a Constitutional Analysis." *Michigan Law Review* 81:1–98.

Witherspoon v. Illinois (1968) 391 U.S. 510.

Woodson v. North Carolina (1976) 428 U.S. 280.

Zant v. Stephens (1983) 462 U.S. 862.

Zeisel, H. (1977) "The Deterrent Effect of the Death Penalty: Facts v. Faith." Pp. 317–343 in P.B. Kurland (ed.), *The Supreme Court Review* 1976. Chicago: University of Chicago Press.

Zimring, F.E. and G. Hawkins (1986a) *Capital Punishment and the American Agenda*. New York: Cambridge University Press.

Zimring, F.E. and G. Hawkins (1986b) "A Punishment in Search of a Crime: Standards for Capital Punishment in the Law of Crime and Homicide." *Maryland Law Review* 46:115–132.

Chapter 4

The Politics of Capital Punishment: The Sacrifice of Fairness for Executions

Stephen B. Bright

The issue of crime has dominated political campaigns at all levels of government in the United States since 1968, and the death penalty has dominated the discussion of crime. Unfortunately, politicians have not engaged in a thoughtful or constructive exploration about how best to prevent crime, but have competed to show who is the toughest on those who have committed violent crimes. They have argued over who is most in favor of longer prison terms, harsher conditions of imprisonment, greater use of the death penalty, less due process and less judicial review.

And they have delivered on their promises to "get tough." The United States now incarcerates a greater percentage of its population than any country in the world. New sentencing laws require long periods of imprisonment and give judges little discretion in deciding the length of prison sentences. Thirty-eight states provide for the death penalty. Over 50 federal crimes are punishable by death. Congress has severely restricted the review of capital cases by federal courts to make way for more and speedier executions. Children are increasingly being prosecuted as adults. The United States is one of only five countries in the world that has executed children in the last six years and is the leader among those five.

One casualty of this war against crime—this war the United States is fighting against its own people—is a commitment to fairness. In the quest to obtain more convictions, longer prison terms, more death sentences and speedier executions, legislators, executives and even judges are showing less and less concern for the possibility of mistake—the conviction of an innocent person—or the importance of fair and equal treatment of all people accused of crimes.

As described elsewhere in this book, it is well established that the lawyers appointed to defend poor persons facing the death penalty are often woefully inadequate and, as a result, juries are often deprived of critical information needed for an accurate determination of guilt or sentence (Mello and Perkins 2003); that imposition of the death penalty is often influenced by the race of the victim of the crime and the race of the accused (Baldus and Woodworth

2003); and that a disturbing number of people sentenced to death have later been found to be innocent (Radelet and Bedau 2003).

The influences of poverty and race on the outcome of cases are long standing deficiencies of the criminal justice systems of the United States. They are inconsistent with fundamental notions of justice, enshrined in the Bill of Rights of the United States Constitution, which include fair and equal justice for all, a competent lawyer for the person accused of a crime, and an adversarial trial at which the best evidence and arguments are presented on both sides of an issue in the hope of obtaining just verdicts and sentences.

There has always been a substantial gap between the promises of the Bill of Rights and the actual quality of justice dispensed in the courts. For example, the right to a lawyer has been celebrated as fundamental to the American justice system, but poor people accused of crimes frequently are assigned court-appointed lawyers who lack the ability, resources and inclination to handle a serious case. Although the Supreme Court held in 1963 that a poor person accused of a felony has a right to a lawyer *(Gideon v. Wainwright* 1963), most state legislatures have been unwilling to provide the funding needed to establish public defender programs with reasonable caseloads and sufficient resources to provide quality representation. Similarly, although courts have repeatedly declared their commitment to removing the influence of race from criminal cases, gross racial disparities in sentencing and other indications of the influence of racial bias in the criminal justice system are routinely ignored by courts. Nevertheless, the commitment to counsel, to eliminating racial bias, and to other elements of fairness served as important aspirations for how the criminal justice system *should* work, even if the goals were seldom recognized in practice.

But even a commitment to achieving fairness has mostly been abandoned as crime has become the dominant political issue. Politicians have denigrated the Bill of Rights as nothing more than a collection of "technicalities," suggesting that the most precious rights of citizens are nothing more than inconvenient impediments to ridding society of murderers, rapists, robbers and other criminals. They have promised results — getting criminals off the streets, more and faster executions — and increasingly the goal of fairness is being sacrificed to obtain those results.

Those who compete to establish their anti-crime credentials often express impatience with a fair process. Fairness takes time and costs money. For example, fairness requires paying the cost of a lawyer for the poor person who cannot afford one. Fairness requires the cost and delay involved in preparing a transcript of a trial so that a higher court may review the proceedings. When the process required by the Constitution has been violated — such as when a court finds that a jury has been deprived of important evidence or given the wrong explanation of the law — fairness requires a new trial, which involves additional time and expense.

On occasion, the time and costs required for this process produce frustration. When a particularly notorious case is reversed due to a constitutional violation, some may attack courts as delaying or preventing executions. Politicians promise to speed up executions. To make good on those promises, some politicians have called for the removal of judges from office who do not do their bidding, passed laws restricting the power of courts to correct constitutional violations, and even denied lawyers in crucial proceedings to people who cannot afford them.

However, when a fair process is sacrificed to produce desired results, injustices are more likely to occur and go uncorrected, and courts lose their legitimacy and credibility. This chapter examines the source of these developments in the political arena and their influence on the legal system.

The Politics of Crime

The competition among politicians to establish who is toughest on crime is similar to the competition among politicians during the Cold War to show who was toughest on Communism. In that era, politicians announced that they were against Communism and accused their opponents of being "soft on Communism," just as today's politicians accuse one another of being "soft on crime."

The one-sided nature of the discussions makes them susceptible to demagoguery. After all, no one is in favor of violent crime, just as very few people supported Communism. The anti-Communist crusaders of the 1950s argued that much should be sacrificed—resources, personal reputations, civil liberties and even basic notions of due process—in the pursuit of those fostering Communism. Today, similar sacrifices are called for in the pursuit of those who commit violent crime.

Richard Nixon, who rose to prominence as a young Congressman by exploiting the fear of Communism, was also one of the first politicians to exploit the crime issue. Crime was a major issue in Nixon's successful campaign for President in 1968, in which he promised a new attorney general in place of Ramsey Clark, a defender of civil liberties and procedural safeguards (Nolan 1992).

In 1988, Lee Atwater urged Republicans to concentrate on the crime issue because "[a]lmost every candidate running out there as a Democrat is opposed to the death penalty" (Harwood 1989:1A). George Bush was elected President that year with the help of advertisements criticizing his opponent for allowing the furlough of Willie Horton, who committed a rape in Maryland while on a weekend furlough from a Massachusetts prison (Anderson 1995; Engelberg 1988; Martz et al. 1988).

Candidates for governor of Texas in 1990 argued about which of them was responsible for the most executions and who could execute the most people

(Oreskes 1990). One candidate ran television advertisements in which he walked in front of photographs of the men executed during his tenure as governor and boasted that he had "made sure they received the ultimate penalty: death" (Cohen 1990:A19). Another candidate ran advertisements taking credit for thirty-two executions (Cohen 1990). In Florida, Governor Bob Martinez ran television advertisements in his campaign for reelection in 1990 showing the face of serial killer Ted Bundy, who was executed during his tenure, and informing voters that Martinez had signed over ninety death warrants in his four years in office (Cohen 1990).

Martinez was following the lead of a previous Florida governor, Bob Graham, who, after being initially derided as "Governor Jello," reinvented himself as tough by signing death warrants (Von Drehle 1995:268). Graham demonstrated in two terms as governor and a successful race for the United States Senate that, as one observer noted, "nothing [sells] on the campaign trail like promises to speed up the death penalty" (Von Drehle 1995:325). He increased the number of warrants signed each month during his campaigns for reelection as governor in 1982 and for the Senate in 1986 (Von Drehle 1995:200–201, 293). One assistant attorney general responsible for representing the state in capital cases had to work so hard as a result of Graham's warrant-issuing spree during his Senate campaign that the prosecutor commented, "Nine months of Bob Graham running for the Senate nearly killed me" (Von Drehle 1995:293).

The ultimate use of the death penalty to get votes came in Bill Clinton's successful campaign for the presidency in 1992. Determined not to be painted "soft on crime" as the previous Democratic candidate had been by the Willie Horton advertisements, Clinton scheduled the execution of Rickey Ray Rector, a brain-damaged, African-American who had been sentenced to death by an all-white jury, so it would occur shortly before the New Hampshire primary (Frady 1993). Rector had destroyed part of his brain when he turned his gun on himself after killing the police officer for whose murder he received the death sentence.

Clinton returned from New Hampshire to preside over the execution of Rector. Logs at the prison show that in the days leading to his execution, Rector was howling and barking like a dog, dancing, singing, laughing inappropriately, and saying that he was going to vote for Clinton (Frady 1993:105). After the execution, guards found that Rector had put aside his pie thinking that he was going to come back and eat it after the execution.

By 1994, crime had so eclipsed other issues that an official of the National Governor's Association commented that the "top three issues in gubernatorial campaigns this year are crime, crime, and crime" (Phillips 1994:11A). One observer noted that "[f]rom California to Texas to Florida, candidates for governor sound as if they're running to be executioner" (Minzesheimer 1994:9A). One Democratic media consultant expressed frustration, saying, "No matter how far to the right we get, Republicans get righter. We say 'Hang 'em.' They say, 'Gas 'em'" (Phillips 1994:11A).

Although Texas carried out forty-five executions during Democrat Ann Richards's four years as governor, her opponent in her bid for reelection, George W. Bush, attacked her, arguing that Texas should execute even more people, even more quickly (*Arizona Republic* 1994). Incumbent Republican governors in California, Illinois, and Iowa attacked their opponents' personal opposition to the death penalty in winning reelection in 1994. One of them, Pete Wilson of California, recovered from "abysmal" approval ratings to win reelection by following the advice of the old master, Richard Nixon, who told him to hit his opponent hard on crime (Fineman 1995).

New York Governor Mario Cuomo was defeated the same year after a campaign in which he was attacked for his vetoes of death-penalty legislation during twelve years in office and for his refusal to return a New York prisoner to Oklahoma for execution. His opponent, George Pataki, promised to reinstate capital punishment and to send the prisoner back to Oklahoma for execution. Upon election, Pataki supported and signed into law legislation providing for the death penalty in New York and returned the prisoner, Thomas Grasso, to Oklahoma where he was promptly executed (Kifner 1995).

Promises were being kept on the federal level as well. President Clinton signed into law the Violent Crime Control and Law Enforcement Act of 1994, which provides for the death penalty for over 50 federal crimes. Two years later, he signed into law the Antiterrorism and Effective Death Penalty Act of 1996, which placed new, unprecedented restrictions on the review of state criminal convictions by the federal courts. A year and a half before the 1996 presidential election, President Clinton ran his first three television advertisements in his bid for reelection; all three focused on crime and Clinton's support for expansion of the death penalty (Purdom 1995).

Senators who voted to confirm judges labeled "soft on crime" were attacked for their votes. Bill Frist, in his successful campaign to unseat Tennessee Senator Jim Sasser in 1994, attacked Sasser for having recommended the nomination of a federal district judge who, two months before the election, had set aside a death sentence. Frist appeared at a news conference with the sister of the victim in the case. After the victim's sister criticized Sasser for recommending the judge for the federal bench, Frist said that Sasser's vote to confirm one of President Clinton's nominees showed that he "still hasn't learned his lesson" (*Commercial Appeal* 1994:3B).

Despite growing concerns about the fairness of the process and the risk of executing innocent people, most politicians have continued to support the death penalty. As one observer noted, "Supporting the death penalty—saying so in public—is a way for an otherwise liberal and progressive-thinking man or woman to flash tough-on-crime bona fides. Personally, they might think capital punishment to be barbaric; they might believe in their hearts that no society that puts criminals to death can consider itself civilized. But they flash support for the ultimate penalty anyway" (Rodricks 2002). One of the "leading

Democrats" in Maryland, the president of the state senate, bragged, "I have been for [capital punishment] all my life. If there's a gallows, I'll pull the lever. If there's a gas chamber, I'll turn the valve. If it's lethal injection, I'll insert the needle" (Rodricks 2002).

The death penalty has become the ultimate litmus test for demonstrating that one is not "soft on crime." Mere support for the death penalty is not enough; one must also be for applying the death penalty to more crimes, curtailing judicial review, and selecting tough judges who will impose and uphold death sentences. However, the one-sided nature of the crime debate is undermining the impartiality of judges and the rule of law. It has become more important to carry out executions than to adhere to the requirement of the Bill of Rights.

The Impact on the Courts and the Rule of Law

Unlike legislatures or executives, judges are not expected to gauge public opinion by resort to focus groups or public opinion polls before making their decisions, but are to decide issues based on the Constitution and laws "undisturbed by the clamor of the multitude" (Warren 1926:vol.1, p.303). Courts are expected to uphold the law, including the procedural protections of the Bill of Rights, which include such concepts as a fair trial, an impartial jury, and counsel for the defense. Indeed, one of the highest responsibilities of a court is to protect the rights of various minorities—political, racial, ethnic—from the majority. Judges take an oath to enforce the law, whether it be the First Amendment right of a newspaper to publish unpopular opinions or the right of a suspected murderer to a fair and impartial trial. As the United States Supreme Court once said:

> The very purpose of a Bill of Rights was to withdraw certain subjects from the vicissitudes of political controversy, to place them beyond the reach of majorities and officials and to establish them as legal principles to be applied by the courts. One's right to life, liberty, and property, to free speech, a free press, freedom of worship and assembly, and other fundamental rights may not be submitted to vote; they depend on the outcome of no elections (*West Virginia State Board of Education v. Barnette* 1943:638).

The Bill of Rights cannot be enforced when a judge can be removed from office for an unpopular decision. Judges in most states are elected, unlike federal judges who hold their offices for life tenure once confirmed by the United States Senate. Most state court judges either face an opponent periodically in either partisan or non-partisan elections, or, in some states, the judges are placed on the ballots in "retention" elections in which citizens vote whether to keep them in office.

In 1986, the Governor of California, George Deukmejian, publicly warned two justices of the state's supreme court that he would oppose them in their retention elections unless they voted to uphold more death sentences (Wiegand 1986). Obviously, the governor did not know what legal issues might be presented by those cases; all he was interested in was results. He had already announced his opposition to the retention of Chief Justice Rose Bird because of her votes in capital cases (Wolinsky 1986). Apparently unsatisfied with the subsequent votes of the other two justices, the governor carried out his threat. He opposed the retention of all three justices and all lost their seats after a campaign dominated by the death penalty (Clifford 1986). Deukmejian appointed their replacements in 1987.

After a decision by the Texas Court of Criminal Appeals, reversing the conviction in a particularly notorious capital case, a former chairman of the state Republican Party called for Republicans to take over the court in the 1994 election (Elliott and Connelly 1994). The voters responded to the call. Republicans won every position they sought on the court that year (Williams 1994).

One of the Republican candidates, Stephen W. Mansfield, campaigned on promises of greater use of the death penalty, greater use of the harmless-error doctrine, and sanctions for attorneys who file "frivolous appeals especially in death penalty cases" (Elliott and Connelly 1994:32). Before the election it came to light that Mansfield had misrepresented his prior background, experience, and record, that he had been fined for practicing law without a license in Florida, and that—contrary to his assertions that he had experience in criminal cases and had "written extensively on criminal and civil justice issues"—he had virtually no experience in criminal law (Elliott and Connelly 1994; Elliott 1994; Williams 1994).

Nevertheless, Mansfield received 54 percent of the votes in the general election, defeating the incumbent judge, a conservative former prosecutor who had served twelve years on the court and had been supported by both sides of the criminal bar (Elliott 1994). After his election, the *Texas Lawyer* declared Mansfield an "unqualified success" (Elliott 1994).

Justice James Robertson was voted off the Mississippi Supreme Court in 1992. His opponent in the Democratic primary ran as a "law and order candidate" with the support of the Mississippi Prosecutors Association (Case 1992:15–20). The resolution of the prosecutors association asserted that Robertson's opponent "best represents the views of the law abiding citizens" and "will give the crime victims and the good, honest and law abiding people of this state a hearing that is at least as fair as that of the criminal in child abuse, death penalty, and other serious criminal cases" (Case 1992:16 n.108).

Robertson was attacked for a concurring opinion he had written expressing the view that the Constitution did not permit the death penalty for rape where there was no loss of life. Robertson and his fellow justices who had taken an oath to uphold the Constitution of the United States had no choice. The United States Supreme Court had held ten years earlier that the Eighth Amendment did not permit the death penalty in such cases (*Coker v. Georgia* 1977). Robertson's defeat was attributable in part to the fact that he followed his oath and upheld the law.

Justice Penny White was voted off the Tennessee Supreme Court after a decision by that court in a death penalty case led the Republican Party and other groups to oppose her retention. Justice White's opponents succeeded in turning her retention election into a referendum on the death penalty. In doing so, they also distorted Justice White's record on the court.

The Republican Party mailed a brochure to voters titled, "Just Say NO!" with the slogan, "Vote for Capital Punishment by Voting NO on August 1 for Supreme Court Justice Penny White." Inside, the brochure described three cases to demonstrate that Justice White "puts the rights of criminals before the rights of victims." It described one case as follows: "Richard Odom was convicted of repeatedly raping and stabbing to death a 78 year old Memphis woman. However, Penny White felt the crime wasn't heinous enough for the death penalty—so she struck it down" (Bright 1997:331–336).

The mailing did not disclose that, in fact, Odom's case was reversed because *all five* members of the Tennessee Supreme Court had agreed that there was at least one legal error which required a new sentencing hearing (*State v. Odom* 1996). Neither Penny White nor any other member of the court expressed the view that the crime was not heinous enough to warrant the death penalty. Indeed, the court sent the case back to the trial court for a new sentencing hearing, making it quite clear that the Court did not find the death penalty inappropriate for Odom. Justice White did not write the opinion in the case. Yet, Tennessee voters were led to believe that she had personally struck down Odom's death penalty because she did not think the crime was "heinous enough." Justice White's opponents also blamed her for the fact that Tennessee has not carried out any executions in the last 36 years. But the Odom case was the only capital case which came before the Court during White's 19 months on the Court and, thus, the only case on which Justice White could have had any impact.

There have been several other instances in which judges have been attacked and removed from the bench for their votes in capital cases (Bright and Keenan 1995). Such attacks and removals of judges from office make it unlikely that the judges who remain in office will be free to enforce the law. For example, immediately after Justice White was removed from office, the Governor of Tennessee, Don Sundquist, said: "Should a judge look over his shoulder [in making decisions] about whether they're going to be thrown out of office? I hope so" (Wade 1996:A1). This contrasts sharply with a statement made by Supreme Court Justice John Paul Stevens at the American Bar Association meeting in Orlando the same month: "It was never contemplated that the individual who has to protect our individual rights would have to consider what decision would produce the most votes" (Stevens 1996:12).

The threat that a judge can be removed from office because of an unpopular decision—even though the decision is legally correct—undermines the independence, integrity, and impartiality of the judiciary. A grievance similar to the one made against King George III in the Declaration of Independence could be leveled against those politicians who have made support for the death penalty the litmus test for judges: "He has made judges dependent on his Will alone, for the tenure of their offices...."

Judges who remain on courts but refuse to enforce the law in instances where an unpopular outcome could jeopardize their careers violate their oaths to uphold and enforce the law. They compromise their own integrity and the integrity of their courts. In addition, the credibility of the courts suffers when judges are perceived as giving in to political pressures.

Furthermore, the overall quality of justice is affected when courts are composed of judges who are there to produce certain results. Since the removal of three of its justices in 1986, the California Supreme Court, which was once one of the most distinguished state supreme courts in the country, has become an undistinguished death mill. Today, the court is known mostly for the lengths it will go to find any constitutional violation "harmless," the legal doctrine that allows a court to uphold a conviction on the theory that the violation did not make much of a difference in the outcome of the case. One scholar has pointed out that the California Supreme Court's harmless error decisions reflect "jurisprudential theory" less than a "desire to carry out the death penalty" (Kessler 1991:85, 89).

The vulnerability of state court judges also discourages the most responsible and conscientious lawyers from becoming judges. No lawyer wants to give up his or her practice to become a judge if upholding the law could result in removal from office. When judges must depend upon majority approval, courts are unable to perform one of their most important constitutional roles, described by U.S. Supreme Court Justice Black as serving as "havens of refuge for those who might otherwise suffer because they are helpless, weak, outnumbered, or because they are...victims of prejudice and public excitement" (*Chambers v. Florida* 1940:241). Because as Supreme Court Justice John Paul Stevens has observed, "the emotional impact of [capital] cases gives rise to a special risk of error" (Stevens 1996:13), there is a particularly urgent need for independent courts which will enforce the rule of law.

The Denial of Competent Lawyers and Limits on Review by the Courts

Representation of the accused by competent lawyers is as important as an independent judiciary in assuring fair and reliable results in any kind of case, but particularly capital cases. Juries receive only the evidence presented by the lawyers. If a lawyer fails to investigate thoroughly and to secure the presence of witnesses at trial, the jurors may be deprived of critical information. The professional knowledge and skills of a lawyer are also needed to ensure that the trial is a fair one, carried out in accordance with established procedures. Otherwise, those fundamental protections, designed to ensure a fair trial and a reliable result, mean nothing. A lawyer who is ignorant of important legal principles may not know what evidence can be presented, how the jury is to be instructed, whether there are limits on what the police and prosecution can do, and other fundamental matters. Despite the complexity of capital cases and the enormous stakes involved, legislators in many states have failed to provide programs and resources needed for competent representation to those facing the death penalty. Many states have no public defender offices or specialized capital defender offices to represent those facing death.

A stark example of the results of lack of public defender offices, inadequate funding, and the indifference of elected judges is provided by an account of a capital trial in Houston, Texas:

> Seated beside his client—a convicted capital murderer—defense attorney John Benn spent much of Thursday afternoon's trial in apparent deep sleep.
>
> His mouth kept falling open and his head lolled back on his shoulders, and then he awakened just long enough to catch himself and sit upright. Then it happened again. And again. And again.
>
> Every time he opened his eyes, a different prosecution witness was on the stand describing another aspect of the Nov. 19, 1991, arrest of George McFarland in the robbery-killing of grocer Kenneth Kwan.
>
> When state District Judge Doug Shaver finally called a recess, Benn was asked if he truly had fallen asleep during a capital murder trial.
>
> "It's boring," the 72-year old longtime Houston lawyer explained (Makeig 1992:A35).

This does not offend the right to counsel guaranteed by the United States Constitution, the trial judge explained, because, "[t]he Constitution doesn't say the lawyer has to be awake." The Texas Court of Criminal Appeals apparently agreed. It rejected McFarland's claim that his constitutional right to counsel had been denied (*McFarland v. State* 1996).

George McFarland is not the only person condemned to die in Houston at a trial where his lawyer slept. Calvin Burdine and Carl Johnson both had the misfortune to have attorney Joe Frank Cannon assigned by Harris County judges to defend them. Cannon was appointed by judges in Houston to numerous criminal cases in 45 years despite his tendency in the later stages of his career to doze off during trial. Burdine and Johnson were among ten clients of Cannon who were sentenced to death.

The Texas Court of Criminal Appeals upheld Burdine's death sentence (*Ex parte Burdine* 1995), but a federal court, by a vote of 9–5, set aside Burdine's conviction. (*Burdine v. Johnson* 2001). The dissenting judges argued that Burdine's conviction and death sentence should be upheld because he could not show that anything significant had happened during the time his lawyer was sleeping.

Both the Texas Court of Criminal Appeals and the United States Court of Appeals for the Fifth Circuit held that Cannon's sleeping during Carl Johnson's trial did not violate the right to a fair trial and to counsel (Dow 1996). Carl Johnson was executed by Texas on September 19, 1995.

Harris County, which includes Houston, sentences more people to death and is responsible for more executions than any other jurisdiction in the country (Willing 1999; Tolson 2001). During the administration of the prosecutor who left office there in 2001, 61 people sentenced to death in Harris County were executed—more executions than were carried out by any *state* during this period except Texas and Virginia (Tolson 2001). Harris County had 150 people on death row at the end of 2001, more people than most states have under sentence of death. When one city—the capital of capital punishment—has three cases involving sleeping lawyers, all allowed by the presiding trial judges and upheld by the state's highest criminal court, it speaks volumes about the lack of commitment to fairness by the courts.

Representation by competent lawyers is essential to ensure juries are as well informed as humanly possible before deciding whether to convict a person or sentence that person to death. Yet Supreme Court Justice Ruth Bader Ginsburg has said that she has "yet to see a death case, among the dozens coming to the Supreme Court on eve of execution petitions, in which the defendant was well represented at trial" and that "[p]eople who are well represented at trial do not get the death penalty" (Ginsburg 2001).

A person condemned to death at trial may appeal to a higher court. The U.S. Supreme Court has held that lawyers must be provided for those who cannot afford them at the trial and on one appeal. However, there are two other important stages of review. The U.S. Supreme Court has held there is no right to a lawyer at those stages, even in capital cases (*Murray v. Giarratano* 1989). The first stage is state post-conviction review. At this stage, the condemned may raise issues that were not apparent at the time of trial, such as the withholding of evidence favorable to the defense or, as in the case of Calvin Burdine, the denial of a competent lawyer at trial.

The second stage is federal habeas corpus review—the legal procedure by which a person may petition the federal courts for review of a conviction or sentence on the grounds that it was obtained in violation of the U.S. Constitution. As the United States Supreme Court once observed:

> Over the centuries [the Writ of Habeas Corpus] has been the common law world's "freedom writ" by whose orderly processes the production of a prisoner in court may be required and the legality of the grounds for his incarceration inquired into, failing which the prisoner is set free. We repeat what has been so truly said of the federal writ: "there is no higher duty than to maintain it unimpaired," and unsuspended, save only in the cases specified in our Constitution (*Smith v. Bennett* 1961:712–713; *Bowen v. Johnson* 1939:26).

There is no question that the vindication of constitutional rights through the common law world's great "freedom writ" has carried a price: executions have not been carried out where the conviction or sentence was obtained in violation of the Constitution; a second trial is required where the first was marred with constitutional errors; and delays are inevitable while courts review the records of trials. The political goal of swifter executions could not be achieved in cases where the conviction or sentence was obtained in violation of the Constitution. As a result, some have attacked habeas corpus review as delaying executions, disrupting the administration of criminal justice by the states, causing friction between federal and state courts, and frustrating the war against crime.

In response to this frustration, Congress eliminated two key elements of fairness in order to increase the number and speed of executions. In the fall of 1995, Congress made it more difficult for those under death sentence to obtain competent lawyers to represent them in state post-conviction proceedings by eliminating federal funding for the programs that provided lawyers to the condemned. The following spring Congress stripped the federal courts of much of their power of habeas corpus review by enacting the Antiterrorism and Effective Death Penalty Act.

The programs which provided representation—called "resource centers" or "post-conviction defender organizations"—were established in 1987 because many inmates were without counsel. These small programs had the enormous responsibility of providing lawyers to the condemned in habeas corpus proceedings. They had about 200 lawyers to deal with the post-conviction representation of over 3,000 men, women and children condemned to death. When the resource centers were created, it was envisioned that they would be jointly funded by state and federal governments to recruit volunteer lawyers to provide free representation to the condemned in both state and federal review. But many states with the largest death rows—such as Texas, Alabama, and Nevada—refused to fund the resource centers in their states.

As a result, many of the centers were understaffed. They handled many complex cases which often were litigated under immense pressure without adequate time or resources. Nevertheless, the lawyers at these programs made a substantial contribution to justice by building an expertise and working long hours to provide representation in cases when no volunteer lawyer stepped forward to represent the condemned inmate.

For example, Walter McMillian, an African American man sent to death row in Alabama, was set free after six years on Alabama's death row, because Bryan Stevenson and other lawyers at the Alabama Resource Center proved that he was innocent of the murder for which he had been condemned to die (Earley 1995). Lawyers at the resource center in Missouri developed evidence of the innocence of Lloyd Schlup and won a new hearing for him from the United States Supreme Court (*Schlup v. Delo* 1995). Lawyers at the resource center in Louisiana persuaded the U.S. Supreme Court that Curtis Lee Kyles was entitled to a new trial because the prosecution had failed to disclose critical exculpatory evidence (*Kyles v. Whitley* 1995). Executions of other wrongfully convicted inmates were prevented because of the work of the resource centers or lawyers recruited by them. Apparently, because of their success in the courts, the resource centers came under attack by the National Association of Attorneys General and their funding was eliminated by Congress.

Denying lawyers to those on death rows, many of whom are mentally retarded, mentally ill, illiterate or semi-literate, for complex legal proceedings constitutes an extraordinary sacrifice of fairness in the quest to obtain executions. An inmate under death sentence must first seek post-conviction relief in the state courts before applying for federal relief. Although federal courts have the power to appoint lawyers for death-sentenced inmates in federal habeas corpus cases, some states either do not provide counsel in state post-conviction proceedings or provide only token payment to lawyer assigned to handle such matters. Georgia, a state with a large death row, does not provide lawyers for state post-conviction proceedings. Alabama, another state which condemns many to death, provides compensation of only $1,000 to a lawyer for representing a person under sentence of death in post-conviction proceedings. Other states, like Texas, provide more in compensation, but the lawyers appointed often lack the specialization needed to handle such complex cases. Some lawyers have missed deadlines for obtaining court review or were not even aware of what issues could be raised at the post-conviction stage. The resource centers provided specialization, but now that specialization is missing in many states.

Condemned inmates have had an even greater need for lawyers since President Clinton signed into law the Antiterrorism and Effective Death Penalty Act in April, 1996. The Act placed new, unprecedented restrictions on habeas corpus review. It imposes a one-year time limit for the filing of any habeas corpus actions and even provides for a six-month deadline for capital cases in states where certain conditions have been met. This is the first time in the nation's history that Congress has imposed a statute of limitations on habeas corpus actions. The Act also places a number of other new restrictions on the power of federal courts to review convictions and sentences.

Thus, with passage of the Act, poor people who have been wrongfully imprisoned or sentenced to death suddenly face a new, complex set of barriers to vindication of their constitutional rights. Yet, many do not even have lawyers to help them understand the Act or comply with its provisions. Some condemned persons may even be denied a chance to present their claims to a federal court because, without lawyers, they will be unable to comply with the one-year statute of limitations.

The Resulting Lack of Fairness in the Courts

The lessened commitment to fairness seriously undermines the reliability of the results reached in many cases. It also undermines respect for the courts by the community. No one will respect a system where the kind of justice a person receives depends upon how much money he or she has. Although the public may want a particular result in one case, ultimately citizens will have little respect for courts that bend with the political winds or refuse to enforce fundamental constitutional protections in order to bring about desired results.

By far the most disturbing consequences of a lack of fairness is the risk of executing an innocent person. Supreme Court Justice John Paul Stevens has observed that the "recent development of reliable scientific evidentiary methods has made it possible to establish conclusively that a disturbing number of persons who had been sentenced to death were actually innocent" (Stevens 1996:13). Justice Sandra Day O'Connor has echoed this concern, saying, "If statistics are any indication, the system may well be allowing some innocent defendants to be executed" (O'Connor 2001). Both justices attributed the risk of executing the innocent in large part to the failure to provide competent lawyer to poor people facing the death penalty (Stevens 1996:12).

Since the Supreme Court upheld the resumption of capital punishment in 1976, over 100 people sentenced to death were freed after their innocence was established (Weinstein 2002a, 2002b; Radelet and Bedau 2003). Over 100 people have been exonerated by DNA evidence since it has been used to identify the perpetrators of crimes. Questions of innocence in many other cases cannot be conclusively resolved by scientific or other evidence.

Anthony Porter, sentenced to death in Illinois, had a particularly close call. He was to be executed after his case had been affirmed on appeal by the Illinois Supreme Court, and upheld in the state and federal post-conviction review processes. The only reason he was not put to death was because there was a question as to whether Porter, a person of limited intellectual functioning and mental impairments, was mentally competent to be executed; that is, whether he understood that he was being put to death as punishment for the crime of which he had been convicted. A person who lacks the mental ability to understand this relationship cannot be executed, but is instead treated until he is "restored to competency." When he has improved to the point that he can understand why he is being executed, he is put to death. Because there was a question about whether he could understand why he was being executed, a court stayed his execution in order to determine his competency to be executed (Belluck 1999).

After the stay was granted, a journalism class at Northwestern University and a private investigator examined the case and proved that Anthony Porter was innocent. They obtained a confession from the person who committed the crime. Porter was released from death row (Belluck 1999). He was the third person released from Illinois's death row after being proven innocent by a journalism class at Northwestern (Terry 1996). His case—and the fact that thirteen people sentenced to death in Illinois had been exonerated and twelve have been executed between 1977 and 2000—resulted in Illinois Governor George Ryan declaring a moratorium on capital punishment in early 2000 (Mills and Armstrong 2000).

Other factors besides the quality of legal representation contribute to the risk of executing the innocent. Eyewitness identifications are not always accurate, important evidence is not always disclosed to the defense and the court, informants trade testimony of dubious credibility for leniency, false confessions are sometimes obtained from people with mental impairments or limitations or other vulnerabilities, and other flaws in the process may contribute to the conviction of an innocent person (Scheck, Neufeld and Dwyer 2000). Yet most jurisdictions are unwilling to adopt identification procedures that are more reliable, provide for full disclosure of all evidence before trial, restrict testimony from informants, require the videotaping of questioning of suspects and take other measures to improve the fairness and reliability of the process from collection of evidence by police through trial.

And other decisions besides guilt are affected by poor legal representation and the lack of fair procedures. A finding of guilt raises a second question of how the offender is to be punished. The punishment is supposed to fit both the crime and the offender with the ultimate sanction—death—reserved for only the most heinous crimes and the most incorrigible offenders. The U.S. Supreme Court has said that a jury's sentence in a capital case is to be "a reasoned *moral* response to the defendant's background, character and crime" (*Penry v. Lynaugh* 1989:319; *California v. Brown* 1987:545). But many of those sentenced to death are distinguished not by the heinousness of their crimes or their criminal records, but by the poor quality of legal representation they received, their race or the race of their victim, their mental limitations, or other factors that in a fair and just system would have no influence on the sentence imposed.

Those who cannot afford attorneys are often assigned lawyers who lack the knowledge and resources to present evidence at the penalty phase that could persuade a jury to impose a sentence other than death. The death penalty is never mandatory for any crime; juries always have discretion to accept it or reject it. But juries can make that decision only on the basis of evidence presented by the lawyers. For example, Alabama executed a mentally retarded man, Horace Dunkins, in 1989. (The Supreme Court has since held that execution of the mentally retarded violates the Constitution.) Before the execution, after reading in a newspaper that Dunkins was mentally retarded, a person who had been on the jury in the case said she would not have voted for the death sentence if she had known of his mental limitations (Applebome 1989). But because of the poor legal representation that Dunkins had received from his court-appointed lawyer, the jury did not learn during the trial that he was mentally retarded. The sentencing trial of a man put to death by Georgia in 2002, Wallace Fugate, lasted only 27 minutes. The jury learned almost nothing about Fugate, who had no record when he was arrested at age 42, and had been a hard worker, good neighbor and reliable and trusted friend to many throughout his life.

The lack of commitment to fairness is also evident in the failure of courts to keep improper influences, such as racial prejudice, from influencing the outcome of cases. Racial disparities are found throughout the criminal justice system. Virtually every report that has examined the operation of the death penalty has found racial discrimination in its infliction. The U.S. General Accounting Office reported that a synthesis of 28 studies shows a pattern of racial disparities in charging, sentencing and imposition of the death penalty in the statutes adopted since 1972 (U.S. General Accounting Office 1990). The International Commission of Jurists, a highly regarded organization made up of jurists from around the world, after a visit to the United States in 1996, also found racial discrimination and arbitrariness in the infliction of the death penalty (International Commission of Jurists 1996).

Yet, courts tolerate racial discrimination and often refuse even to examine issues of racial prejudice. Even after a thorough and well-respected study showed significant racial disparities in the infliction of the death penalty in Georgia, the Supreme Court allowed Georgia to continue carrying out death sentences (*McCleskey v. Kemp* 1987).

Instances of racial discrimination in cases in which the death penalty was imposed are ignored by courts. For example, two African American men sentenced to death by an all-white jury in Utah were executed even though jurors received a note which contained the words "Hang the Nigger's" [sic] and a drawing of a figure hanging on a gallows (*Andrews v. Shulsen* 1988). No court, state or federal, ever had a hearing on such questions as who wrote the note, what influence it had on the jurors, and how widely it was discussed by the jurors. William Henry Hance was executed in Georgia without any court holding a hearing on the use of racial slurs by jurors who decided his fate (Herbert 1994a; 1994b). Other courts have refused to look behind gross racial disparities for discrimination (Bright 1995). The tolerance of racial discrimination and the refusal of courts even to deal with these issues reveals a lack of commitment to fairness.

The failure to provide lawyers during state post-conviction review and legislation narrowing post-conviction review reveals that many legislators and judges prefer to hide violations of the Bill of Rights to exposing and correcting them. The failure of courts to reverse cases despite racial discrimination, sleeping lawyers, and other constitutional violations sends a message that constitutional violations are inconsequential. It tells judges, prosecutors, law enforcement officials and the public that departures from constitutional standards in the quest for convictions and death sentences are acceptable and will be tolerated. It confirms the notion voiced so often by politicians that the Bill of Rights is nothing more than a collection of "technicalities" that get in the way of convicting the accused and carrying out their sentences. The underlying assumption is that because those accused are guilty, the denial of a competent lawyer or other basic elements of fairness does not matter.

The provisions of the Antiterrorism and Effective Death Penalty Act restricting the power of federal courts to correct constitutional error in criminal cases represent a decision that results are more important than a fair process; that finality is more important than fairness; that it is more important to get on with executions than to determine whether convictions and sentences were fairly and reliably obtained.

The price paid for such expediency is enormous. Such a system produces results—convictions and death sentences—but it does not produce justice. Such a system may be popular in the short run, but courts that bend to the political winds or that have been rendered powerless to correct fundamental injustices will ultimately not be seen as legitimate by citizens, nor their judgments regarded as credible. Most importantly, the protections provided to all citizens are being significantly lessened. In Robert Bolt's play, *A Man for All Seasons*, a young man argues that laws that are inconvenient or unpopular should not be followed; indeed, he would "cut down every law in England [to pursue the Devil]" (Bolt 1962:66). Thomas More responds: "[a]nd when the last law was down, and the Devil turned round on you—where would you hide...all the laws being flat? This country's planted thick with laws...[do you] really think you could stand upright in the winds that would blow then?" (*Id.* at 66). The same question needs to be asked today of those who would cut down constitutional protections in pursuit of terrorists or death sentences.

References

Anderson, D.C. (1995) *Crime and the Politics of Hysteria.* New York: Random House.
Andrews v. Shulsen (1988) 485 U.S. 919.

Antiterrorism and Effective Death Penalty Act of 1996, Pub. L. 104-132, 110 Stat. 1214, *amending* 28 U.S.C. § 153.

Applebome, P. (1989) "Two Electric Jolts in Alabama Execution." *New York Times* (July 15):A6.

Arizona Republic (1994) "Bush Brothers Cast Foes as 'Soft' for Not Killing Enough." *Arizona Republic* (November 3):B5.

Belluck, P. (1999) "Class of Sleuths to Rescue on Death Row." *New York Times* (February 5):A14.

Bolt, R. (1962) *A Man for All Seasons.* New York: Random House.

Bowen v. Johnson (1939) 306 U.S. 19.

Bright, S.B. (1997) "Political Attacks on the Judiciary: Can Justice Be Done Amid Efforts to Intimidate and Remove Judges From Office for Unpopular Decisions?" *New York University Law Review.* 72:308–338.

Bright, S.B. (1995) "Discrimination, Death and Denial: The Tolerance of Racial Discrimination in the Infliction of the Death Penalty." *Santa Clara Law Review.* 35:433–483.

Bright, S.B. and P.J. Keenan (1995) "Judges and the Politics of Death: Deciding Between the Bill of Rights and the Next Election in Capital Cases." *Boston University Law Review.* 75:759–835.

Burdine v. Johnson (2001) 262 F.3d 336 (5th Cir.).

California v. Brown (1987) 479 U.S. 538.

Case, D.W. (1992) "In Search of an Independent Judiciary: Alternatives to Judicial Elections in Mississippi." *Mississippi College Law Review.* 13:1–36.

Chambers v. Florida (1940) 309 U.S. 227.

Clifford, F. (1986) "Voters Repudiate 3 of Court's Liberal Justices." *Los Angeles Times* (Nov. 5): p. 1:1.

Cohen, R. (1990) "Playing Politics with the Death Penalty." *Washington Post* (March 20): A19.

Coker v. Georgia (1977) 433 U.S. 584.

Coleman v. Thompson (1991) 501 U.S. 722.

Commercial Appeal (1994) "Political Notebook." *Commercial Appeal* (Memphis) (October 8):3B.

Dow, D.R. (1996) "The State, the Death Penalty, and Carl Johnson." *Boston College Law Review.* 37:691–711.

Earley, P. (1995) *Circumstantial Evidence: Death, Life and Justice in a Southern Town.* New York: Bantam Books.

Elliott, J. (1994) "Unqualified Success: Mansfield's Mandate: Vote Makes a Case for Merit Selection." *Texas Lawyer* (November 14):1.

Elliott, J. and R. Connelly (1994) "Mansfield: The Stealth Candidate; His Past Isn't What It Seems." *Texas Lawyer* (October 3):1, 32.

Engelberg, S. (1988) "Bush, His Disavowed Backers and a Very Potent Attack Ad." *New York Times* (November 3):A1.

Ex parte Burdine (1995) 901 S.W.2d 456 (Tex. Ct. Crim. App.).

Fineman, H. (1995) "Riding the Wave." *Newsweek* (May 22):19.

Frady, M. (1993) "Annals of Law and Politics: Death in Arkansas." *New Yorker* (February 22):105–133.

Gideon v. Wainwright (1963) 372 U.S. 355.

Ginsburg, R.B. (2001) *In Pursuit of the Public Good: Lawyers Who Care, Joseph L. Rauh Lecture at the David A. Clarke School of Law of the University of the District of Columbia* (April 9) available at http://www.supremecourts.gov/publicinfo/speeches/sp_04-09-01a.html.

Harwood, J. (1989) "Approving Atwater: GOP Committee Backs Its Chairman." *St. Petersburg Times* (June 17):1A.

Herbert, B. (1994a) "Jury Room Injustice." *New York Times* (March 30):A15.

Herbert, B. (1994b) "Mr. Hance's 'Perfect Punishment.'" *New York Times* (March 27):D17.

Holland v. Illinois (1990) 493 U.S. 474.

International Commission of Jurists (1996) *Administration of the Death Penalty in the United States* (Geneva, Switzerland).

Kessler, C.E. (1991) "Death and Harmlessness: Application of the Harmless Error Rule by the Bird and Lucas Courts in Death Penalty Cases — A Comparison and Critique." *University of San Francisco Law Review* 26:41–91.

Kifner, J. (1995) "Inmate is Executed in Oklahoma, Ending N.Y. Death Penalty Fight." *New York Times* (March 20):A1.

Kyles v. Whitley (1995) 514 U.S. 419.

McCleskey v. Kemp (1987) 481 U.S. 279.

McFarland v. State (1996) 928 S.W.2d 482 (Tex. Ct. Crim. App.).

Makeig, J. (1992) "Asleep on the Job; Slay Trial Boring, Lawyer Said." *Houston Chronicle* (August 14):A35.

Martz, L., et al. (1986) "The Smear Campaign." *Newsweek* (October 31):16.

Mills, S. and K. Armstrong (2000) "Governor to Halt Executions." *Chicago Tribune* (January 30):1.

Minzesheimer, B. (1994) "Executioner's Song Heard in Governor Races." *U.S.A. Today* (October 27):9A.

Murray v. Giarratano (1989) 492 U.S. 1.

Nolan, J.F. (1992) "In Riots' Political Fallout, Right May Gain Might." *Boston Globe* (May 3):24.

O'Connor, S.D. (2001) *Remarks at the Meeting of the Minnesota Women Lawyers* (July 2).

Oreskes, M. (1990) "Death Penalty Politics: Candidates Rush to Embrace Execution." *Courier-Journal* (Louisville, KY) (April 8):D1, D4.

Penry v. Lynaugh (1989) 492 U.S. 302.

Phillips, L. (1994) "Crime Pays as a Political Issue." *USA Today* (October 10):11A.

Purdum, T.S. (1995) "Clinton Gets Early Start on Ad Campaign Trail." *New York Times* (June 27):A12.

Radelet, M.L. and H.A. Bedau (2003) "The Execution of the Innocent." (This volume.)

Rodricks, D. (2002) "Death penalty support looks tough but does no good." *Baltimore Sun* (May 13):1B.

Scheck, B., P. Neufeld, and J. Dwyer (2000). *Actual Innocence: Five Days to Execution and Other Dispatches from the Wrongly Convicted.* New York: Doubleday.

Schlup v. Bowersox (1996) No. 4:92CV433-JCH, Memorandum Opinion and Order of May 2 (D. Mo.).

Schlup v. Delo (1995) 513 U.S. 298.

Smith v. Bennett (1961) 365 U.S. 708.

State v. Odom (1996) 928 S.W.2d 18 (Tenn.).

Stevens, J.P. (1996) "Opening Assembly Address, American Bar Association Annual Meeting." (August 3) (copy available from United States Supreme Court Press Office, Washington, D.C.).

Terry, D. (1996) "DNA Tests and a Confession Set Three on a Path to Freedom in 1978 Murders." *New York Times* (June 15):A6.

Tolson, M. (2001) "A Deadly Distinction." *Houston Chronicle* (February 23):1A.

United States General Accounting Office (1990) *Death Penalty Sentencing: Research Indicates Pattern of Racial Disparities*. Washington, D.C.: U.S. General Accounting Office.

Von Drehle, D. (1995) *Among the Lowest of the Dead: The Culture of Death Row*. New York: Times Books.

Violent Crime Control and Law Enforcement Act of 1994, Pub. L. 103-322, 105 Stat. 1796.

Wade, P. (1996) "White's Defeat Poses a Legal Dilemma: How is a Replacement Justice Picked?" *Memphis Commercial Appeal* (August 3):A1.

Warren, C. (1926) *The Supreme Court in United States History*. Boston: Little, Brown, and Co.

Weinstein, H. (2002a) "The Nation's Death Penalty Foes Mark a Milestone Crime: Arizona Convict Freed on DNA Tests is Said to be the 100th Known Condemned U.S. Prisoner to be Exonerated Since Executions Resumed." *Los Angeles Times* (April 10):A16.

Weinstein, H. (2002b) "Pa. Death Row Inmate Acquitted at Retrial, Freed." *Los Angeles Times* (May 7):A21.

West Virginia State Board of Education v. Barnette (1943) 319 U.S. 624.

Wiegand, S. (1986) "Governor's Warning to 2 Justices." *San Francisco Chronicle* (March 14):1.

Wilgoren, J. (2002) "Confession Had His Signature; DNA Did Not." *New York Times* (August 26):A1.

Williams, J. (1994) "Election '94: GOP Gains Majority in State Supreme Court." *Houston Chronicle* (November 10):A29.

Willing, R. (1999) "Geography of the Death Penalty." *USA Today* (December 20, 1999):A1.

Wolinsky, L.C. (1986) "Governor's Support for 2 Justices Tied to Death Penalty Votes." *Los Angeles Times* (March 14d):3.

Woods, J. (1996) "Public Outrage Nails a Judge." *Nashville Banner* (August 2):1A, 2A.

Chapter 5

The Influence of International Law and Practice on the Death Penalty in the United States

Richard J. Wilson

In August of 1996, Daryl Renard Atkins and William Jones robbed Eric Nesbitt, drove him to an automated teller machine in his pickup truck where cameras recorded their withdrawal of additional cash, then took him to an isolated location in Virginia where he was shot eight times and killed. Jones avoided the potential death penalty by pleading guilty and agreeing to testify against Atkins, who was convicted of murder.

At the penalty phase of his trial, where the jury decided whether a death sentence should be imposed, Dr. Evan Nelson, a forensic psychologist, testified that Daryl Atkins had an IQ of 59, a score that puts him in the lowest 1 to 3% of the population. Any score below 70, the doctor testified, defines the person as mentally retarded. The jury sentenced Atkins to death. After a successful appeal in Virginia and resentence to death, Atkins appealed again. The Supreme Court of Virginia upheld the imposition of the death sentence over two strong dissents, which argued that "the imposition of the sentence of death upon a criminal defendant who has the mental age of a child between the ages of 9 and 12 is excessive." (*Atkins* v. *Commonwealth* 2000:324).

Atkins' case went to the United States Supreme Court, and on June 20, 2002, six of the nine Justices held that the execution of mentally retarded persons is a violation of the Eighth Amendment to the U.S. Constitution, which forbids excessive as well as "cruel and unusual" punishments. The majority's reasoning was noteworthy in many respects, but a single phrase in the court's opinion is crucial to the issues raised in this chapter. Justice Stevens, writing for the majority, reviewed the practice of the States and noted "the consistency in the direction of change" toward abolition of capital punishment for the mentally retarded. He concluded that the "practice, therefore, has become truly unusual, and it is fair to say that a national consensus has developed against it." In a footnote to support that conclusion, the majority developed the basis for what it called the "broader social and professional consensus" to support the direction of State legislatures. International practice is a factor, the Justices concluded, in Eighth Amendment considerations. "Within the world community," they noted, "the imposition of the death penalty for crimes committed by mentally retarded offenders is overwhelmingly disapproved" (*Atkins v. Virginia* 2002:2249, n. 21).

The issue decided by the Court was not whether it was *bound to follow* international law, but whether international law and practice was *relevant at all* in reaching its decisions in capital cases. It did consider international practice in this instance, in part because of the pressure put on the Court by some of our closest allies and by a significant number of our own diplomats. Both the majority and the dissents referred to a friend-of-court brief filed by the 15 countries of the European Union supporting the majority's conclusion, the first such brief filed by the Union in a capital case in the United States (*McCarver v. North Carolina* 2001).[1] Another powerful and influential friend-of-court brief was that of nine former U.S. diplomats, who argued that the death penalty in the United States impairs U.S. foreign policy interests and strains relationships with our closest allies (Koh 2002:1119–1120).

The Court's reluctance to apply international law directly, as well as its conclusion that international practice is only one of the many factors in consideration of the constitutionality of the death penalty, are evidence of the current antipathy and resistance to the use of international norms by our courts. However, that antipathy was not always so. This chapter will trace, in very broad outline, the general historical trajectory on the use of international law in deciding constitutional issues involving the death penalty. It will document increasing U.S. exceptionalism and isolation in the world community on death penalty practice and will examine the increasing external pressures on the United States to abolish capital punishment. Finally, the chapter will examine the growing body of domestic court cases that incorporate international norms into their consideration of the legality of the death penalty.

An Historical Perspective on International Law in the U.S. Supreme Court

In its reliance on international perspectives in *Atkins*, the strong Supreme Court majority hearkened back to principles which are part of the founding roots of America, when international law and practice were essential to our

---

1. The friend-of-court briefs originally filed in *McCarver v. North Carolina*, a case from earlier in the term on the same issue, were all accepted for filing in the *Atkins* case when *McCarver* was dropped from the court's docket.

understanding and application of domestic law. The Declaration of Independence itself starts with familiar language, but what follows is not so familiar to many:

> When in the Course of human events, it becomes necessary for one people to dissolve the political bonds which have connected them with another, and to assume among the Powers of the Earth, the separate and equal Station to which the Laws of Nature and of Nature's God entitle them, *a decent respect to the opinions of mankind* requires that they should declare the causes which impel them to the separation.

Professor Harold Koh notes that in 1776, the fledgling United States had no law of its own, and the Framers of the Constitution looked to what was then called the Law of Nations, or international law, which was necessarily applied in the courts of the American colonies. The newly independent United States had no choice but to display a "decent respect" for the opinions of mankind. (Koh 2002:1087) In fact, Professor Koh notes a deep and long pattern of reliance by our Supreme Court on international law in all areas, not just in the interpretation of the Eighth Amendment (Koh 2002:1091–1096).

The U.S. Constitution, too, recognizes the legitimate authority of international law. Article VI, clause 2, states: "This Constitution, and all the Laws of the United States which shall be made in Pursuance thereof; *and all Treaties made, or which shall be made under the Authority of the United States, shall be the supreme Law of the Land*; and the Judges of every State shall be bound thereby, any Thing in the Constitution or Laws of any State to the Contrary notwithstanding." (Emphasis added) Treaties, the most formal expression of international law, thus are given a central role in the governance of the nation by the Constitution itself. The last part of the clause is of particular importance because most death sentences are handed down in the States, and the federal constitution gives clear supremacy to treaties over State law.

Up to and through the 1970s and '80s, the Court referred to international norms in death penalty cases interpreting the scope of the Eighth Amendment. In *Coker v. Georgia*, for example, the Court found that international practice regarding the death penalty for rape was relevant to the Eighth Amendment's interpretation through "evolving standards" of "dignity, civilized standards, humanity and decency" (*Coker v. Georgia* 1977:596 n.10). In *Enmund v. Florida*, the justices made reference to comparative international practice in interpreting the doctrine of felony murder (*Enmund v. Florida* 1982:797 n. 22). In *Ford v. Wainwright*, the Court again invoked the practice of "civilized societies" in the capital punishment context (*Ford* v. *Wainright* 1986: 409). And in 1988, a majority in *Thompson v. Oklahoma* found that international practice was relevant in determining that the death penalty was unconstitutional as applied to a fifteen-year-old (*Thompson v. Oklahoma* 1988:830).

In 1989, however, a narrow five to four majority broke with deep national tradition of the inclusion of international norms and practice in Eighth Amendment analysis. In *Stanford v. Kentucky*, the Court ruled that the Eighth Amendment does not prohibit the execution of juveniles who commit their crimes at age sixteen, whatever international opinion may be. Justice Scalia's opinion for the Court asserted, in a footnote, that juvenile sentencing practices in other countries are irrelevant because "it is *American* conceptions of decency that are dispositive" (*Stanford v. Kentucky* 1989:369 n.1). That view, however, held sway for only thirteen years in our constitutional history before swinging back to the view expressed by the majority in *Atkins*. Moreover, Professor Koh points out that Justice Scalia's view on international law's relevance to the determination of evolving standards of humanity is inconsistent not only with long historical tradition but with the justice's own views in non-capital cases. In the anti-trust context, for example, Justice Scalia argues that U.S. law should not be interpreted inconsistently with international norms (Koh 2002:1085).

As the sole superpower in the post-Cold War world, the U.S. government struggles with the relevancy of international law or world opinion to its foreign policy as well as its domestic law, particularly to advance its objectives in the war on terrorism after September 11, 2001. Many U.S. judges today continue to be skeptical or reluctant to apply international norms in their decisions. Both Chief Justice Rehnquist and Justice Scalia, for example, wrote stinging dissents in *Atkins*, explicitly rejecting the majority's reliance on international opinion or practice. Justice Scalia calls the practices of "the so-called 'world community'" irrelevant, asserting that its "notions of justice are (thankfully) not always those of our people" (at 2264). While suspicion of the application of international norms may lie, at least in part, in those same deep roots of American rebellion against foreign authority, the United States risks bitter resentment and legitimate claims of hypocrisy by the community of nations if it continues to aggressively apply the death penalty while asserting a commitment to human rights at home and abroad.

Global Perspectives on the Death Penalty

World law and practice is moving steadily towards abolition of the death penalty. Within only the last fifty years, the world has developed a system of treaties and other international norms, all of which see abolition of the death penalty as a legitimate end of international human rights law (Schabas 2002:1). The most significant international treaties on human rights all contain a provision protecting the right to life. While all of those treaties include limited exceptions permitting the death penalty in a narrow set of circumstances, a systematic review of all international norms on the death penalty "shows an inexorable progress towards abolition" (Schabas 2002:19). Moreover, there are three treaties by which countries explicitly commit to peacetime abolition of the death penalty. As of March 2002, the Second Optional Protocol to the International Covenant on Civil and Political Rights had been ratified by 44 countries, with seven more states having signed the treaty, which indicates their intention to become parties to it at a later date. Eight states in the Americas have ratified the Protocol to the American Convention on Human Rights to Abolish the Death Penalty. The United States has neither signed nor ratified either protocol. Thirty-nine countries have ratified Protocol No. 6 to the European Convention on Human Rights (Amnesty International 2002b:3), which bans the peacetime use of the death penalty. Another new protocol to the European Convention, Protocol 13, bans the death penalty in all circumstances, including for crimes committed in times of war or imminent danger of war. It was adopted by the Council of Europe in February of 2002, and it has not yet entered into force. The new Protocol brings Europe "a step closer to a creating a death penalty-free zone" (Amnesty International 2002a).

A total of 110 countries, a clear majority of the world, have abolished the death penalty in law or practice. Seventy-six countries and territories have abolished it for all crimes, another 14 have abolished it for all but exceptional crimes such as those committed in wartime, while another 20 countries are abolitionist in practice because they have not carried out executions for the past ten years or more. Eighty-five countries retain the death penalty, but the trend is away from retention. More than 30 countries and territories have abolished the death penalty for all crimes since 1990, an average of more than three per year (Amnesty International 2002b:1). Moreover, not all retentionist countries execute those they have sentenced to death. In 2001, for example, only 31 countries accounted for the more than 3,048 executions. Four countries— China, Iran, Saudi Arabia and the United States—conducted 90% of all known executions (Amnesty International 2002c).

New international criminal tribunals created within the UN system all prohibit capital punishment, even where their jurisdiction includes the vilest and most serious of crimes known in the world: genocide, war crimes and crimes against humanity. The temporary international criminal tribunals for the former Yugoslavia and for Rwanda, sitting in The Hague and Arusha, Tanzania, respectively, both bar the death penalty, as does the newly created International Criminal Court (ICC). Hostility of the Bush administration to the ICC, which will also begin operations in The Hague as early as 2003, is open and aggressive. The United States has not only "unsigned" the ICC treaty (an unprecedented action of questionable legality in international law), but has taken steps to obtain bilateral agreements with individual countries not to submit Americans to the Court's jurisdiction if they are arrested in those countries (Human Rights Watch 2002b). It has also signed into law the American Servicemembers Protection Act of 2002, which authorizes the use of military force to liberate an American held by the ICC, which will sit in the Netherlands. Critics sarcastically dubbed the provision the "Hague invasion clause" (Human Rights Watch 2002a).

U.S. Divergence from International Human Rights Norms on the Death Penalty

The United States was a leader in the creation of the United Nations, which came into being in the wake of the horrors of World War II and the Holocaust. The U.S. also took a leading role in the drafting and adoption by the UN of the Universal Declaration of Human Rights, the first modern statement of individual protection against abuses of state power. Our government also took a leading role in the creation of the Organization of American States (OAS) and another lesser-known regional document on human rights in the Western Hemisphere, the American Declaration of the Rights and Duties of Man. The American Declaration was actually adopted some months before its global counterpart in 1948. At the time of their adoption, these two human rights documents did not have the force of law. They expressed the human rights principles and aspirations for the region and the world, but governments, then as now, were reluctant to guarantee personal freedoms as legally binding obligations. The two declarations were, in short, what their names imply—statements of goals for governments and not "treaties," one of the names given to international agreements that are legally binding.

Over the next two decades, the UN and the OAS became more assertive in their articulation of human rights norms. Both organizations adopted several human rights treaties that set out human rights more fully than the declarations of the 1940s. In the UN system, the most important of these treaties for our purposes were the International Convention on the Elimination of All Forms of Racial Discrimination (Race Convention), adopted by the UN in 1966, the International Covenant on Civil and Political Rights (ICCPR), also adopted in 1966, and the Convention Against Torture and Other Cruel, Inhuman or Degrading Treatment or Punishment (Torture Convention), adopted in 1987. The ICCPR is one of the most important and widely ratified human rights treaties in the world, with 148 states as parties, as of September 2002. The OAS adopted the American Convention on Human Rights in 1969. The American Convention, along with several other human rights treaties in the Inter-American human rights system, serve as regional compliments to the global treaties. There are now 25 parties to the American Convention.

Governments agree to be bound by treaties through a process of ratification, which is a government's expression of willingness to be bound by the treaty's provisions with all other ratifying nations. Procedures for treaty signature, which is the first formal step toward treaty ratification, and for ratification itself vary from country to country. Ratification of a treaty makes a country a party to the obligations assumed under the treaty, and even after signature of a treaty, a country is expected not to violate the core purposes of the document. Once a country becomes a party to a treaty by ratification, it often assumes additional obligations for treaty enforcement that often include a mechanism for that purpose under the treaty itself. In the ICCPR, for example, the relevant enforcement mechanism is the Human Rights Committee, a body of 18 human rights experts sitting in Geneva, Switzerland and New York City who review periodic state reports on treaty compliance. The Committee can also hear individual complaints against countries that are parties to the ICCPR if the country against which the complaint is filed has agreed to allow such complaints by ratifying a special, additional set of treaty rules called a "protocol" to the ICCPR.

The Inter-American system for the protection of human rights was set up to monitor compliance with the American Declaration and Convention. The Inter-American Commission on Human Rights, a group of 7 independent experts on human rights sitting in Washington, DC, reviews human rights complaints arising in the Americas. Cases decided by the Commission can go on to the Inter-American Court of Human Rights in San Jose, Costa Rica, so long as the relevant country has ratified the Convention and agreed to submit to the Court's jurisdiction. The Court, with 7 members appointed in their individual capacity by the OAS General Assembly, issues binding decisions, while both the Human Rights Committee and the Inter-American Commission issue recommendations to governments that arguably have binding legal effects as well.

The United States has been resistant to accountability in both the global and regional systems for human rights protection. When it finally ratified the ICCPR in 1992, and both the Torture and Race Conventions in 1994, the government attached to the treaties numerous exceptions to their provisions, generally called "reservations." The U.S. took a reservation, for example, to those portions of Article 6 of the ICCPR which prohibit the execution of juveniles as part of the broad protections of the right to life. That particular reservation provoked an irate response from eleven countries of the European Union and the Human Rights Committee, all of which expressed their view that the reservation was invalid because it is incompatible with the objectives and purposes of ratification of the treaty (Bedau 1997:246–247).

When it ratified both the ICCPR and the Torture Convention, the U.S. also filed reservations that limit its obligations to protect against "cruel, inhuman or degrading treatment or punishment," as expressed in both treaties. The U.S. asserts that the clause "means the cruel and unusual punishment" prohibited by the U.S. Constitution. Thus, by its reservation, the government means to assume no new obligations under the treaty other than those already existing due to Supreme Court interpretations of cruel and unusual punishment. The broader treaty language might well limit the application of the death penalty

(Schabas 1996). As yet, there have been no definitive decisions by our courts as to the legal effect of these and other treaty reservations.

The Human Rights Committee, after reviewing the first periodic report of the United States government on its compliance with the ICCPR in 1995, was critical of U.S. law and practice on the death penalty. While it used the language of diplomacy, the Committee's conclusions were pointed (Human Rights Committee 1995:¶281):

> The Committee is concerned about the excessive number of offences punishable by the death penalty in a number of states, the number of death sentences handed down by courts, and the long stay on death row which, in specific instances, may amount to a breach of article 7 of the Covenant [protecting against cruel, inhuman or degrading treatment or punishment]. It deplores the recent expansion of the death penalty under federal law and the re-establishment of the death penalty in certain states. It also deplores provisions in the legislation of a number of states which allow the death penalty to be pronounced for crimes committed by persons under 18 and the actual instances where such sentences have been pronounced and executed.

Another global body for the protection of human rights is the UN Commission on Human Rights, a group of governmental representatives from 53 countries sitting annually in Geneva to review human rights situations around the world. That body, since 1997, has called for the progressive abolition of the death penalty. Its 2002 resolution reaffirmed its opposition to the death penalty for those under 18 at the time of their offenses, and it called on all parties to the ICCPR to consider ratification of the protocol to that treaty which aims at abolition of the death penalty (UN Commission on Human Rights 2002). The Commission has also appointed a Special Rapporteur on Extrajudicial, Summary or Arbitrary Executions, whose annual report, since 1991, has made specific references to abuses by the United States in its application of the death penalty. After a special mission to the United States in 1998, the Special Rapporteur called on the United States to adopt a moratorium on executions and to discontinue the practice of execution of mentally retarded persons and juveniles, among other reform measures (UN Commission on Human Rights 1998:¶156).

At the regional level, the United States signed but has not ratified the American Convention on Human Rights, which means it is not subject to the jurisdiction of the Inter-American Court of Human Rights. This does not, however, mean that it can completely avoid scrutiny in that system for its own human rights violations. The Inter-American Commission on Human Rights can still hear individual complaints against the United States. In fact, over time, several decisions by international bodies have found that the human rights recognized in the American Declaration, and in the OAS Charter, a treaty to which the U.S. is a party, together create binding legal human rights obligations. The Inter-American Commission applies that law to the United States. The United States government, however, "categorically" rejects any assertion that the American Declaration has acquired binding legal force and refuses to comply with Commission recommendations (Wilson 2002:1160).

The Inter-American Commission on Human Rights has heard and decided an increasing number of cases against the United States alleging wrongdoing in capital cases. In all of the decided cases but one, the Commission has found serious violations of human rights. In its 1998 decision in *William Andrews v. United States*, for example, the Commission found that Mr. Andrews, an African-American, had been denied equality and a fair trial. The jury at his trial with another African-American co-defendant in Utah had produced a note from the jury room with a hand-printed message saying "Hang the nigger's [sic]." Domestic courts had never held a hearing on who wrote the note or where it came from, nor had they passed on its potential prejudicial impact on the jury. In the domestic legal system, Andrews' case caused Justice Thurgood Marshall to file a written dissent from denial of review by the U.S. Supreme Court, referring to the jury's note as "a vulgar incident of lynch-mob racism reminiscent of Reconstruction days" (Wilson 2002:1178–1179).

More recently, in *Raul Garza v. United States*, the Commission reviewed its first federal death penalty case. In 2001, the Commission held that Mr. Garza had been denied a fair trial and due process of law when the sentencing jury in his case was allowed to hear evidence of four unadjudicated murders in Mexico with which Mr. Garza was connected. The Commission called for commutation of Garza's death sentence. Attempts to enforce the Commission's decision in the U.S. Courts failed, and on June 19, 2001, Mr. Garza was executed, about a week after the execution of Timothy McVeigh for his role in the Oklahoma City federal building bombing (Wilson 2002:1180–1182).

In both *Andrews* and *Garza*, despite the fact that the U.S. government appeared and aggressively opposed the petitions before the Commission, it ultimately refused to take any action to comply with recommendations of the Commission at any stage in the proceedings. The State Department's Office of the Legal Adviser, which represents our government in this litigation, takes no action to support the Commission's decisions in our courts, as it might have in *Garza*. In both *Andrews* and *Garza*, the petitioners had sought a request from the Commission to the U.S. government for what are called "precautionary measures." The measures are sought at the time the complaint is filed to prevent an execution while the case is still pending full review by the Commission. The request for precautionary measures does not prejudge the final outcome of the case and asks only that the domestic legal system take steps to protect the life of the petitioner during the Commission's review.

While most countries in Latin America comply with such measures from the Commission or the Inter-American Court of Human Rights, the United States refuses to comply with requests for precautionary measures in any death penalty case. William Andrews was executed in Utah in 1992, long before the decision by the Commission in his case, when the U.S. refused to act to even temporarily spare his life at the Commission's request (Wilson 2002:1176, 1185–1186). Despite complete rejection by the U.S. government of the authority of the Commission's rulings here, however, the Commission is likely to decide many more capital cases involving the United States. Staff sources there estimate that 60–70% of all new filings against the U.S. in 1999 and 2000, some 130 cases, involve the death penalty (Wilson 2002:1174–1175).

Pressure from Outside of the United States: Barring Extradition to Face Capital Punishment

In 1989, the European Court of Human Rights decided the case of Jens Soering, a young German citizen whose extradition was sought from England to the United States. Soering faced capital murder charges in the Commonwealth of Virginia. His lawyers challenged his extradition on several grounds in Britain, and after full review there, the case went to the European Court in Strasbourg, France, where the arguments continued.

The European Court found a violation of Article 3 of the European Convention on Human Rights, which prohibits "inhuman or degrading treatment or punishment" (*Soering v. United Kingdom* 1989:¶ 111). The Court concluded that if he were to be extradited to the United States, Soering would face what the Court called "the death row phenomenon." The death row phenomenon was made up of a number of factors, some of which are shared by all inmates on death row in the U.S., and some of which were unique to Mr. Soering. The Court found that the average time a condemned prisoner can expect to stay on death row in Virginia, at the time, was six to eight years. During that time, the Court noted, inmates await their executions with growing anguish, often under repeated warrants for execution which are ultimately suspended. Conditions on death row are also extremely harsh for all who are under sentence of death. The Court noted the risk of physical and homosexual attack, as well as the stringency of custody in general. Finally, the Court noted that Soering himself was only 18 at the time of his alleged offense, and reports showed strong evidence that he suffered from a mental disturbance that might mitigate his culpability. Taken together, the Court concluded that it could not condone the virtually inevitable mistreatment of Mr. Soering on death row in Virginia, and that to send him there to face a possible capital sentence would constitute inhuman or degrading treatment (*Soering v. United Kingdom* 1989:¶¶ 105–109). As a result of the Court's ruling, England sought and obtained assurances from Virginia that Soering would not be subjected to the possibility of a death sentence, and he was extradited, tried and sentenced to two life terms (Lillich 1991:141).

More recent decisions by international and domestic tribunals also seek to prevent the execution of individuals whose extradition is sought to the United States. In 1994, for example, the Human Rights Committee reviewed the case of Charles Ng, whose extradition from Canada was sought by California officials, where he faced capital charges. The Canadian authorities ignored a request from the Committee to prevent Ng's extradition pending their review of the case. The Committee concluded that Ng's potential execution by gas asphyxiation constituted cruel and inhuman treatment under article 7 of the ICCPR (*Ng v. Canada* 1994:¶ 16.4). As a result of the Committee's requests to it, the Canadian government sent a note to the United States asking for information on the method of execution to be used in Ng's case. The United States informed Canada that it was now possible for a condemned person in California to choose between execution by gas chamber and execution by lethal injection. Canada also told the Committee that it would take into account its views in *Ng* in future extradition decisions (Schabas 1997:139).

The Canadian Supreme Court looked to both the "death row phenomenon" and its previous treatment of Charles Ng when it decided *United States v. Burns* in 2001. In that case, two persons, Glen Sebastian Burns and Atif Ahmad Rafay, sought the protection of the Canadian courts against a decision to permit their extradition to the State of Washington, where they faced capital murder charges. Both were Canadian citizens and 18 years old at the time of their alleged crime. The Minister of Justice of Canada had decided not to invoke a seemingly discretionary procedure under the US-Canada extradition treaty that allowed the ministry to seek assurances against the death penalty as a condition of extradition.

The Court found that the Justice Minister's failure to seek assurances against the death penalty was a violation of Section 7 of the Canadian Charter of Rights and Freedoms, the Canadian equivalent to our federal Bill of Rights. Section 7 protects the right to life, liberty and security "and the right not to be deprived thereof except in accordance with the principles of fundamental justice" (*United States v. Burns* 2001:¶ 58). The Court had ruled against the same argument ten years earlier. However, it found that there were now many factors that mandate the seeking of assurances, including "the evolution of international extradition standards, the worldwide trend toward abolition, growing concerns over the adequacy of US capital procedures and the inherent risk of wrongful conviction and execution" (Amnesty International 2001). Burns and

Rafay were returned to Washington State for trial with a guarantee that they would not face the death penalty.

In May of 2001, the Constitutional Court of South Africa ruled that South African government officials had violated constitutional and statutory obligations by refusing to seek assurances against the death penalty for Khalfan Khamis Mohamed, whose extradition was sought by the United States in connection with the bombing of our embassy in Tanzania. Mohamed was summarily deported directly into the hands of waiting U.S. officials. Drawing from many international and comparative sources, including its own 1995 decision finding that the death penalty in South Africa violated fundamental human rights and the constitution, the Court found that the government had violated Mohamed's right to life and dignity, and his right to be protected from cruel, inhuman or degrading punishment (*Mohamed and another v. President of South Africa and others* 2001). It also took the highly unusual step of sending its judgment directly to the U.S. federal judge presiding over Mohamed's capital murder trial. The judge instructed the jury about the decision, and after three days of deliberation, the jury announced that it could not reach unanimity on the death penalty. Mohamed was sentenced to life imprisonment without possibility of parole (Amnesty International 2001).

The life sentence imposed on Khalfan Mohamed took place some months before the attacks on the World Trade Center and the Pentagon on September 11, 2001. Since that time, the U.S. Justice Department has put enormous pressure on foreign governments to extradite suspected terrorists to the United States without binding the U.S. not to seek the death penalty. In general, those pleas have not been successful. In fact, some governments have responded with a harder line out of concern with the potential threats of vindictive punishment and the weakening of due process and fair trial protections here, all in the name of national security. Mexico, for example, has extended protections under its extradition treaty with the United States by refusing to send accused persons here who face either the death penalty or a potential life sentence, due to their constitutional commitment to the potential for rehabilitation (Thompson 2002). European Union members have stated that they will not extradite suspected terrorists to the United States without assurances against the death penalty, but Spain and France have indicated additional concerns about the extradition of suspects who might face trials by special military tribunals here (Dembart 2002). Amnesty International has noted that impediments to extradition may cause the United States government to expand the practice of forcibly taking suspects from other countries without resort to the courts, called "irregular rendition," to guarantee the option of imposing the death penalty here (Amnesty International 2001). The United States Supreme Court approved that practice in a case involving the kidnapping of a Mexican national by U.S. officials to the United States for trial (*United States v. Alvarez-Machain* 1992).

Denial of Consular Access to Foreign Nationals on Death Row in the United States

On May 1, 2002, the Oklahoma Court of Criminal Appeals, the highest court of that state in criminal appeals, vacated the death sentence of Gerardo Valdez, a Mexican citizen who had been convicted of a murder that occurred in 1989. Among the claims raised in his appeal was an argument that the State of Oklahoma did not comply with the terms of the Vienna Convention on Consular Relations (Vienna Convention). That treaty, ratified by the United States, requires that local authorities notify a detained foreign national, without delay, of his right to communicate with the consulate of his home country. If the detainee requests access to his consulate, Article 36 of that treaty requires that the local authorities must notify consular officials of the detention, also without delay. State officials conceded that Mr. Valdez had not been notified of his consular rights at the time of his detention, and the Mexican government did not become aware of his arrest, conviction and sentence until April of 2001. Oklahoma prosecutors agreed with the defense that the government had not complied with the Vienna Convention, but they argued that non-compliance with the treaty should have no effect on Valdez's conviction or sentence.

Mexican officials took a strong role in assisting Mr. Valdez as soon as they learned of his detention in Oklahoma. In addition to filing a friend-of-court brief on his behalf in the Court of Criminal Appeals, consular officials assisted in the representation of Mr. Valdez at his clemency hearing before the Oklahoma Board of Pardons and Paroles. Through expert testimony, they established that Mr. Valdez suffered from severe organic brain damage as a result of head injuries sustained in his youth. His brain damage was exacerbated by alcohol abuse in the family, and these factors contributed to and altered his behavior. Mr. Valdez's appointed lawyer, for whom this was his first capital murder case, had not investigated for or found the evidence in question.

The Parole Board heard the new evidence and recommended to the governor that the death sentence be commuted to life without parole. Governor Frank Keating, however, ultimately denied clemency and the case went back to the courts. When presented with his subsequent appeal arguing the Vienna Convention issues, the Court seemed to go to great pains to hold that the conviction should not be overturned because of a violation of the treaty or due to ineffective representation by the trial lawyer. The Court reversed the conviction, however, holding that it "cannot have confidence in the jury's sentencing determination and affirm its assessment of a death sentence where the jury was not presented with very significant and important evidence bearing on [Valdez's] mental status and psyche at the time of the crime" (*Valdez v. State* 2002:710).

Gerardo Valdez is one of over 120 identified foreign nationals on death row in the United States as of August of 2002, and like some 55 of those individuals, he is a Mexican national (Death Penalty Information Center 2002). National attention first came to this issue when Angel Breard, a Paraguayan national under sentence of death in Virginia, raised the claim in the United States Supreme Court. Mr. Breard had been convicted in 1993 of capital murder, and as in *Valdez*, the Paraguayan government did not become aware of his situation until well after his conviction, death sentence and initial appeals. While both Paraguay and the defense lawyers attempted to gain consideration by the courts of the Vienna Convention issue, review was denied in both federal appeals and the United States Supreme Court (*Breard v. Greene* 1998).

Paraguay, in a last-minute effort to prevent Breard's execution, took a dramatic step. It filed a complaint with the International Court of Justice (ICJ), sometimes called the "World Court." The ICJ sits in The Hague, the Netherlands, and its jurisdiction is limited to disputes by one nation against another. In this case, the personal claims of Angel Breard were raised on his behalf by his government, Paraguay, which argued that the Vienna Convention dispute resolution provisions permitted the ICJ to resolve the conflict on treaty obligations between it and the United States. The ICJ accepted the filing and issued a request for provisional measures to the United States government asking it to ensure that Breard was not executed during the pending proceedings before the Court (*Case* 1998). While its order was issued before the execution and judgment in the U.S. Supreme Court, the Supreme Court declined to honor the order of the ICJ for provisional measures, and the execution proceeded as scheduled. The *Breard* decision thus represents yet another instance in which decisions by international tribunals on the death penalty are not honored by our government.

There would be one more important occasion to consider the Vienna Convention issue, however. Germany filed a claim with the ICJ in 1999 in much the same circumstances as Paraguay had a year earlier (Paraguay had withdrawn its claims from the ICJ docket in the interim). Like the other cases before it, German consular officials were not notified of the arrest or death sentence of Walter LaGrand, a German national on death row with his brother, Karl, in Arizona. As in *Breard*, the ICJ issued a request for provisional measures on March 3, 1999, after which the German government sought to file an original action to enforce the ICJ ruling in the U.S. Supreme Court. The Court refused to exercise its original jurisdiction, and Walter LaGrand was executed in Arizona's gas chamber.

Despite Walter LaGrand's execution, the case in the ICJ continued. In June of 2001, the ICJ issued a stinging rebuke to the United States, rejecting virtually all of the arguments raised by our government to defend its actions. First, the ICJ held that its provisional measures were binding, concluding that "the various competent United States authorities failed to take all the steps they could have taken to give effect to the court's order" and stop the execution. Second, on the merits, it held that the Vienna Convention provided protection of the individual human rights of Walter LaGrand, and that the United States had violated both LaGrand's and Germany's rights under the treaty as well. Third, it held that procedural rules invoked by the United States—technical rules in capital cases to prevent the hearing of the merits of a claim—wrongly prevented the full benefit of treaty protection to LaGrand. Fourth, and most important, the ICJ held that an apology by the United States for its admitted violation of the treaty was simply not enough. If the United States failed to provide notification to other German nationals under severe sentences, "it would be incumbent upon the United States to allow the review and reconsideration of the conviction and sentence by taking account of the violation of the rights set forth in the Convention" (*LaGrand Case* 2001).

The full effects of the *LaGrand* decision are still unfolding in the courts of the United States. The decision was invoked as a key part of the arguments in the *Valdez* case. Although the Oklahoma Court of Criminal Appeals formally rejected it as binding precedent for procedural reasons, there is little doubt but that the decision had indirect persuasive effect in the resulting resentencing decision. There are numerous cases raising issues involving violations of the Vienna Convention still in the courts, and no defendant has sought review by the U.S. Supreme Court or the ICJ on the issue since the *LaGrand* decision.

The Next Frontier?
Abolition of the Execution of Juveniles

As noted above, there are many issues on which international law and practice may influence limitations and eventual abolition of the death penalty in the U.S. The short-term future is likely to provide our courts opportunities to honor decisions by the Inter-American Commission on Human Rights in capital cases involving the United States. Another short term issue is likely to be whether countries will extradite alleged terrorists to the United States to face trials before civilian or military courts in which the death penalty will apply. Some courts are still grappling with the question of the "death row phenomenon" argument, although no decision on that issue has been favorably decided by our courts, and the U.S. Supreme Court has rejected review of the question on several occasions. Still another issue is the question of the way in which the courts are likely to interpret the benefits of the Vienna Convention on Consular Relations for the more than 120 foreign nationals on death row in the U.S., particularly in light of the *LaGrand* decision by the International Court of Justice. In the long term, there is little doubt that the world-wide momentum toward abolition will leave the United States increasingly isolated, both diplomatically and legally. Even the most resistant politicians and judges are likely to realize that the detriments of the death penalty far outweigh its advantages, and it will go the way of the guillotine and the rack.

The abolition of the death penalty for juveniles, however, is the most significant issue in which international law and practice is likely to play a significant role in the near future. There are several reasons why that is so. First, the *Atkins* decision by the United States Supreme Court, discussed at the outset of this chapter, struck down the death penalty for the mentally retarded. One reporter called the decision "the closest thing to a road map the court has ever provided to abolitionists" (Von Drehle 2002). The decision opens the door to challenge the use of capital punishment against other categories of persons for whom criminal responsibility is limited by cognitive or developmental abilities. When a person is retarded, he or she thinks and acts like a child, and children are not generally punished as severely as adults, even for the most serious of crimes. If a person with mental retardation cannot be sentenced to death because neither retributive nor deterrence goals are served, a child (or a person with serious mental illness) stands in the same legal posture before the law.

Moreover, international law and practice on the death penalty for those under 18 stands in very nearly the same posture with juveniles as it does with mentally retarded persons. International law, as noted in several places in this chapter, uniformly condemns the execution of juveniles in treaties, other decisions and statements by international bodies and deep international custom. In practice, only seven nations reportedly have carried out executions of juveniles since 1990: Iran (6), Saudi Arabia (1), Nigeria (1), the Democratic Republic of Congo (DRC) (1), Yemen (1), Pakistan (2), and the United States (14) (Amnesty International 2000). Moreover, due to changes in the laws of those countries, today only the United States and Iran, one of the countries designated by George W. Bush as part of the "Axis of Evil," are known to carry out the execution of juveniles (Koh 2002:1104).

The constitutionality of the execution of juveniles has come very close to adjudication in the United States Supreme Court twice in recent years, and on both occasions the cases raised issues of international law. In 1999, the Court denied review in *Domingues v. Nevada*, a case in which the Nevada Supreme Court had narrowly upheld a challenge to Domingues' conviction based on the ICCPR (*Domingues v. Nevada* 1999). Domingues had been convicted and sentenced to death for a crime committed when he was 16 years old. He argued to the Nevada courts that the ICCPR contains an explicit prohibition on the execution of juveniles in article 6(5). Three of the judges of the Nevada Supreme Court held that the specific reservation by the U.S. to that article in the treaty "negated" the claim of an illegal sentence. The two dissenters were blunt in their criticism of the majority. One of the judges believed that there were good arguments as to why the treaty reservation was invalid, thus requiring the lower court to determine the validity of the entire treaty. The other dissenting judge simply did not want to be in the same camp "with such countries as Iran,

Iraq, Bangladesh, Nigeria and Pakistan in approving death sentences for children" (*Domingues v. State* 1998). The U.S. Supreme Court invited the Solicitor General to submit its views on the petition for review, but ultimately declined to pass on the merits of the case.

In late August of 2002, another case before the U.S. Supreme Court raised the issue of the legality of the execution of juveniles under international law. In the case of Toronto Patterson, three justices of the Supreme Court dissented from denial of review of the case by the high court. Because four votes are needed for review, Patterson's execution went ahead. Justice Stevens, writing for the three justices in an unusual published order, asserted that there was an "apparent consensus…among the states *and in the international community* against the execution of a capital sentence imposed on a juvenile offender." He called for the Court to take up the issue "at the earliest opportunity" (*Patterson v. Texas* 2002:24).

If and when a case comes before the Supreme Court for review, it will present more complicated legal questions under international law than that of the validity of the execution of the mentally retarded. The international dimension of the mental retardation issue was a relatively straightforward presentation of the practice of nations combined with a body of international custom. The validity of the execution of juveniles under international law, while potentially addressed as an issue of custom, is likely to raise thorny questions as to the validity of reservations to a human rights treaty and the courts' role in review of the validity of those reservations. These procedural hurdles notwithstanding, the juvenile death penalty is rapidly becoming a thing of the past throughout the world, and the U.S. will eventually fall into line with the world community in abolishing its use.

References

Amnesty International (2000) *Children and the Death Penalty: Executions Worldwide Since 1990.*

Amnesty International (2001) *United States of America: No Return to Execution—the US Death Penalty as a Barrier to Extradition.* (November 29).

Amnesty International (2002a) Press Release, "Council of Europe: A step closer to a death penalty-free zone." (February 22).

Amnesty International (2002b) *Facts and Figures on the Death Penalty.* (March).

Amnesty International (2002c) Press Release, "Worldwide executions doubled in 2001." (April 9).

Atkins v. Commonwealth (2000) 534 S.E.2d 312 (Va.).

Atkins v. Virginia (2002) 122 S. Ct. 2242.

Bedau, H. A. (1997) "International Human Rights Law and the Death Penalty in America," Pp. 246–248, in R. Hood (ed.), *The Death Penalty in America: Current Controversies.* New York City: Oxford University Press.

Breard v. Greene (1998) 523 U.S. 371.

Case Concerning the Vienna Convention on Consular Relations (Paraguay v. United States of America) (9 April 1998) Request for the Indication of Provisional Measures: Order, General List No. 99 (International Court of Justice).

Coker v. Georgia (1977) 433 U.S. 584.

Death Penalty Information Center (2002) *Foreign Nationals and the Death Penalty in the United States* (August 15), at http://www.deathpenatlyinfo.org/foreignnatl.html.

Dembart, L. (2001) "Death Penalty? Issue May Split Allies," *International Herald Tribune* (Dec. 13).

Domingues v. Nevada (1999) 528 U.S. 963.

Domingues v. State (1998) 961 P. 2d 1279 (Nev.).

Enmund v. Florida (1982) 458 U.S. 782.

Ford v. Wainwright (1986) 477 U.S. 399.

Human Rights Committee (1995) *Summary record of the 1405th meeting: United States of America*, CCPR/C/SR.1405. (April 24).

Human Rights Watch (2002a) Press Release: "U.S.: 'Hague Invasion Act' Becomes Law." (August 3).

Human Rights Watch (2002b) Press Release: "Opposition Mounting to U.S. Arm-Twisting on ICC." (August 13).

Koh, H. H. (2002) "Paying 'Decent Respect' to World Opinion on the Death Penalty." *U.C. Davis Law Review* 35:1087–1131.

LaGrand Case (Germany v. United States of America) (21 June 2001) Judgment, General List No. 104 (International Court of Justice).

Lillich, R. (1991) "The *Soering* Case." *American Journal of International Law* 85:128–149.

McCarver v. North Carolina (2001) United States Supreme Court, No. 00-8727, Brief of *Amicus Curiae* the European Union in Support of the Petitioner, filed 8 June.

Mohamed and another v. President of the Republic of South Africa and others (2001) CCT 17/01 (Constitutional Court of South Africa).

Ng v. Canada (1994) Human Rights Committee, Communication No. 469/1991, CCPR/C/49/D/469/1991.

Patterson v. Texas (2002) 123 S.Ct. 24.

Schabas, W. A. (1996) *The Death Penalty as Cruel Treatment and Torture: Capital Punishment Challenged in the World's Courts.* Boston: Northeastern University Press.

Schabas, W. A. (2002) *The Abolition of the Death Penalty in International Law* (3rd ed.). Cambridge University Press.

Soering v. United Kingdom (1989) 161 European Court of Human Rights (Ser. A).

Stanford v. Kentucky (1989) 492 U.S. 302.

Thompson v. Oklahoma (1988) 487 U.S. 815.

Thompson, G. (2002) "Mexico: Extradition to U.S. Blocked," *New York Times* (May 23).

UN Commission on Human Rights (1998) *Report by the Special Rapporteur on Extrajudicial, Summary or Arbitrary Executions on a Mission to the United States of America*, E/CN.4/1998/68/Add.3.

UN Commission on Human Rights (2002) *The question of the death penalty*, E/CN.4/2002/L.104. (April 19).

United States v. Alvarez-Machain (1992) 504 U.S. 655.

United States v. Burns (2001) 1 Supreme Court Reports 283 (Canada).

Valdez v. State (2002) 46 P.3d 703 (Okla. Crim. App.).

Von Drehle, D. (2002) "Does Ruling Signal Shift in Thinking?" *Washington Post* (June 25).

Wilson, R. (2002) "The United States' Position on the Death Penalty in the Inter-American Human Rights System," *Santa Clara Law Review* 42:1159–1190.

Part III

The Justice and Utility of the Capital Sanction

Chapter 6

Roots

Robert Blecker

Controversy swirls about the death penalty, like fallen leaves blown by every passing breeze. Depending on the day's news and editorial slant, with each new brutal crime or last minute legal escape from death row, public opinion shifts—haphazardly it sometimes seems, to those trying to engage in the current debate.

Step back a half-century: In 1953, the Royal Commission declares no formula possible to determine who lives or dies. Six years later the Model Penal Code proposes what the United States Supreme Court has constitutionally demanded since 1972 when *Furman* began this modern era: Structured death penalty laws dictating that a jury first find guilt or innocence and then in a separate sentencing proceeding guiding its discretion as to whether the aggravated murderer deserves to die. Can we ensure equal protection and due process without race or class bias? Must the differences between those who do and do not die be explained, predicted, applied rationally and without emotion? Can a "maturing" society discern its own "evolving standards of decency," as the U.S. Supreme Court has required since 1958 (*Trop v. Dulles*)? Even as seasons change from abolition to moratorium to reinstatement; from legislation to judicial decision; from academic studies and commissions to media and political campaigns, where long dormant arguments spring again to life, and like autumn's canopy, burst into color and are shed, America's experiment with the death penalty continues, developing, reforming along better established lines. Looking back these past fifty years, random swirl now seems more like controlled swaying.

Now square that distance, and step back 2500 years or so, when the first five books of the Old Testament were finally assembled, and genius flowered in ancient Greece. Trace the death penalty debate in the U.S. today from its branches to its main limbs, down the trunk and underground to ancient roots in common soil from which Western culture has been generating....

"A man's character is his fate," Heraclitus declared in the 6th century B.C., with one of his slippery claims that still tantalizes us. A jury deliberates whether a convicted killer lives or dies: Was his homicidal act aberrant—was it essentially in or out of character? Mostly he will do what has been done to him; must we do to him as he has done? Who has he become and what will become of him? The jury's assessment of the defendant's character determines his fate.

Society's character, too, determines its fate. In the aggregate, our choices display—are—our character. Mostly we do what we do because of who we are. But character—traits and dispositions that make up each person or society's unique identity—is formed fatefully, sometimes fatally—largely without conscious choice or awareness.

It's a strange tree, this death penalty. The long view shows it growing smaller, limited to fewer crimes, imposed more and more rarely—morally compacting, progressively refined. Today, from all sides, states are pressed either to reform the death penalty or reject it—and soon. Whether we end up limiting death appropriately or eliminating it entirely seems far from settled. Meanwhile, sampling the soil—examining and interpreting some of the main roots of Western culture—the Old Testament and ancient Greece[1]—even cursorily and eccentrically in the dappled light of today's debate, would seem to nourish both past and present. And if it cannot enable us to predict precisely our future shape, it may at least help guide us in pruning well to grow better.

The Good Book

"In the Beginning…"

The first sin—or crime (in the Beginning there was no distinction)—was capital. The Sovereign had warned Adam not to eat the apple lest he *"surely die on that day"* (Genesis III:3). Found guilty, Adam and Eve were condemned to hard labor and permanently denied access to immortality. Adam would toil the fields, Eve would suffer in childbirth and perpetual subordination. And someday, both would die. By the time they did die, however, hundreds of years later, it seemed as if their original sin had been forgotten, if not forgiven. With long procedural delays, while the condemned live out their lives in prison, it still seems that way today.

What took the Sovereign so long to execute this first death sentence?

Perhaps on reflection, God accepted some responsibility for the conditions that produced the capital crime, having placed the tree smack in the middle of

---

1. Although I have attempted here to map the Ancients onto today's death penalty debate, I am not a Biblical or Classical scholar, and have relied on others' translations, picking and choosing as seems elucidating. Conversations with Rabbis Lee Friedlander, Philip Schechter, David Sperling, and Michael Stressfeld, and Professors Alyssa Gray and Murray Lichtenstein helped inform my perspective. Our current death penalty, however, mostly drives this Biblical exegesis—easily, it turns out, because the Bible and Ancient Greek philosophy drive today's penalty. My challenge has been to extract the values and lessons from the Ancients neutrally, honestly, and with balance, while I feel and know to a moral certainty that death is sometimes rightful punishment.

the garden and making it tempting. Arguably, too, Adam and Eve were induced, perhaps entrapped by the serpent, the Lord's own agent. They each had raised a defense of sorts: Confronted by the Accuser, Adam instantly flipped the script, implicating Eve—*"the woman thou gavest to be with me, she gave it to me..."* (Genesis III:12). Eve pinned it on the snake. Still, both were condemned.

Looking back, this first capital crime—theft and possessing contraband—arguably seems trivial and the punishment extreme, even vindictive. Perhaps being mortal was the cost of knowing the difference between Good and Evil. If so, death is a stiff price to pay for our change in character. We were expelled from the Garden to prevent access to the Tree of Life and have rebelled through medical science ever since. In any case, so long delayed, disproportionate, and with no deterrent effect, from the beginning the death penalty seems to have failed miserably.

"More Than I Can Bear..."

When Cain killed his brother Abel, God not only spared but protected him. Abolitionists embrace this story: Just as God declined the death penalty, even for this intentional premeditated killing, so too humankind, made in the image of God, should show mercy and spare intentional murderers.

But *why* had Cain killed Abel? God had graciously accepted shepherd Abel's prized animal, but rejected farmer Cain's fruits. Cain must have felt humiliated and resentful toward his brother when God "did not respect Cain and his offering." Cain was *"very angry"* Scripture tells us, and depressed—*"his countenance fell"*—but he did not snap. He and his brother had a conversation to which we are not privy. Thereafter, out in the field Cain "arose" and intentionally slew him.

What was the nature of this killing? We cannot know for sure. Feeling 'dissed' by God, Cain must have stewed on it. It may have been premeditated, but perhaps also provoked and passionate. We can imagine an anguished Cain crying as he killed Abel. What legal fate awaits a person today whose intentional[2] killing was an outrageously unwarranted response to a minor slight that hurt him deeply or, as in this case, a provocation from the action of another—namely God's rejection? Life, or death for Cain? In traditional common law such brooding would not mitigate murder, unless the deadly act was a sudden reaction in the "heat of passion." Today, however, many states permit the defendant's slow burn to mitigate the murder to manslaughter. Such a killing probably would not be capital—statutes often specifically exempt from the

---

2. Buber questions whether it was at all intentional: "Cain does not yet know what death and killing are," he insists. "He does not murder, he has murdered" (Buber:89).

death penalty even an *inadequately* provoked passion killing, although an aggressive prosecutor might characterize the homicide as cold blooded and try to
convince a jury that Cain had lured Abel to the field in order to kill him.

Looked at in this light, the story of Cain hardly stands for categorically rejecting capital punishment, even for premeditated murder. As the Hebrew text
suggests, Cain did not "murder" Abel; he "killed" him. God spared Cain because Cain was not the worst of the worst. The real lesson from the story of
Cain and Abel is that not all killers deserve to die.

The incident can teach us more. Cain initially attempted to obstruct justice
by answering evasively, if not outright lying to Authority: *"Am I my brother's
keeper?"* He refused to cooperate or confess, disavowing any responsibility to
care for the brother he had just killed. *"What hath thou done?"* an angry God
demanded. *"The voice of your brother's blood is crying to me from the ground.
And now you are cursed from the ground"* (Genesis IV:10–11).

The past counts. The earth does not belong only to the living. Bloodshed cries
out to be avenged: Emotively, the blood of the dead victim compels us to act.

God spared Cain, the killer, but sentenced him to life as a fugitive, rootless,
to "wander forever." When rejecting the death penalty today, we confine intentional murderers for life, also removing them from hearth and home.

It is *"more than I can bear,"* protested Cain. A perpetual stranger in a strange
land, he would always feel vulnerable to attack. When Cain cried out in agony,
God comforted and protected him: *"If any one slays Cain, vengeance shall be
taken on him sevenfold. And the LORD put a mark on Cain, lest any who came
upon him should kill him"* (Genesis IV:13–15).

Cain's relief shows that he, and God believed that the threat of death, and
sometimes only the threat of a ferocious kind of death—in this case
"vengeance sevenfold"—could deter murder. Ironically then, the first murderer heard the first death penalty pronounced not as *punishment for,* but as
protection from the consequences of his own conduct.[3] As God protected Cain
against lethal violence during his lifetime banishment, so today, even while
they confine them, states seek to protect convicted murderers by specifically
threatening with death those who kill a fellow prisoner.

When Cain spoke in his own defense at sentencing, he never protested lack
of notice. Though his parents, Adam and Eve, had been warned that eating the
fruit was a capital offense, the Lord never explicitly forbade killing. Eating
from the tree in the middle of the garden became evil only because it was positively prohibited. But killing a brother from jealousy was *malum in se*—self-
evidently and objectively wrong, and thus no explicit notice was necessary.
Without protest then, the trial of Cain had relied on the unarticulated natural

---

3. Dershowitz points to this, but offhandedly characterizes Cain as a "cold-blooded" murderer (Dershowitz 2000:204, 214).

law, the moral fact implicit in humanity, that murder is evil. The outcry of Abel's blood was the proof; the earth's pollution its consequence.

Today too, more than the killer's violation of previously announced law, the victim's lingering cry moves retributivist advocates of the death penalty. For them, deterrence is secondary. The story of Cain is less about a death penalty threatened for others, than it is about that punishment *not* visited upon him.

As a lesser substitute punishment, even lifetime banishment for Cain was not to be unbearable. But the past does count. There must be a reckoning. Unless we heed the anguish of the victim and inflict deserved punishment, we too shall suffer and "be cursed from the ground." From the beginning, however, at least with homicide, God seems discriminating: Although he may have murdered Abel, Cain was not the "worst of the worst" and thus did not deserve to die.

God's Covenant with Noah: "By the Hand of Man…"

Things got worse. The "earth" generally was "corrupt" and "*filled with violence.*" Disgusted, and regretting the whole Creation, the Lord decided to "blot out" all life, except for Noah and his family and one pair of each living thing. After the Flood, the Sovereign seems to have regretted this indiscriminate mass execution, and promises "*never again*" to repeat it. Blessing them, God tells Noah and his family to "*be fruitful and multiply, and fill the earth*" (Genesis IX:7).

"*I give you everything,*" God continues, in this purely life-affirming moment. But the blessing comes with restrictions. "*For your lifeblood I will surely require a reckoning; of every beast I will require it and of man; of every man's brother I will require the life of man*" (Genesis IX:5). This reckoning with the past will not be God's domain alone. Scripture famously continues: "*He who sheds the blood of man, by man shall his blood be shed*"(Genesis IX:6).

This line from *Genesis* challenges Bible literalists who would be death penalty abolitionists.[4] Their best counter is to suggest that God's statement is merely a prediction: Humans will retaliate for homicide. God does not command the death penalty, the argument goes. God embeds retaliation in human nature, to be expected with certainty. Scholars say that although the original Hebrew text permits this future tense interpretation, it is most strained in light of repeated unambiguous commands for the death penalty elsewhere in the Old Testament. Why would God in this passage alone merely predict what elsewhere is repeatedly mandated, and refined?

---

4. Some Christian fundamentalists deny that non-Jews are bound by Mosaic law, thus making Genesis uniquely significant.

"By the hand of man shall his blood be shed," Scripture commanded, *"for God made man in his own image"* (Genesis IX:6). When a human made in the image of God has been murdered, other humans acting in the image of God will execute the person responsible for the lifeblood. "The guilt of the murderer is infinite because the murdered life is invaluable" (Greenberg 1970:26). But the image of God is not God, suggesting a state of perfection to which humans can only aspire, but never attain.

Unqualified, a command to humans to kill "whoever sheds the blood of man" would be grotesquely overbroad. Both *Leviticus* and *Numbers* refine that command and distinguish types of homicides, well beyond the example of Cain. But near the Beginning—destroying almost all life in the Flood and commanding Noah immediately afterwards—God appears to administer and ordain the death penalty without much concern for individual desert.

At the other extreme, abolitionists today cling to *"thou shalt not kill"* as if God's great commandment delivered to Moses from Sinai was a blanket prohibition covering the death penalty. But the Hebrew refutes this, scholars agree. "Thou shalt not murder," it more literally enjoins, and not "Thou shalt not kill."[5] Thus to insist that the death penalty itself *is* murder begs the question and butchers the text. Semantically, Scripture does not, and logically could not prohibit the death penalty, for which it calls throughout the Law. Abolitionists would do better to stop perverting this famous Commandment for rhetorical effect.[6]

"To Slay the Righteous with the Wicked..."

"Be blameless and I will make my covenant between me and you," the Lord had instructed Abraham (Genesis XVII:2). The implication was clear: The righteous would prosper; and the wicked would be struck down. *"Wilt thou indeed destroy the righteous with the wicked?"* (Genesis XVIII:23) Abraham later challenged God, who was about to obliterate Sodom with all its inhabitants. *"Will you destroy the innocent with the guilty?"* (Genesis, XVIII:23) Abraham protests in another translation. But today, the "guilty" are not always "wicked,"[7]

---

5. A categorical note accompanies the Oxford Bible translation, "you shall not kill": "This commandment forbids murder (see Gen. IX:5) not the forms of killing authorized,...e.g. war or capital punishment."

6. Worse, when abolitionists divert the Commandment from the killer to society broadly, "Thou shalt not kill" has no chance to stand emphatically for what it should: To each person individually, "Do not commit murder!" And to the People, the Community derivatively, "Do not knowingly execute the innocent or those who do not deserve to die."

7. Exodus XXIII:7 commands: *"The guiltless and the righteous slay thou not."* From this dual mention, the rabbis inferred that in capital cases, after the defendant had been condemned, a witness might step forward with exculpatory evidence and force a retrial, lest the guiltless be

nor are the "innocent" always "righteous." In contemporary bifurcated death penalty trials, the fact-finder first determines legal guilt or innocence. Then during the "penalty phase," the focus shifts from factual guilt to the moral plane of desert. No longer "did s/he do it?"—the separate question now becomes "does s/he *deserve to die* for it?"

Jesus' challenge to those who would execute the prostitute—"Let him who is without sin cast the first stone"—implies not that she is innocent, but either that there are no righteous people or that every righteous person is guilty of something. Today, many street criminals stand convicted of crimes they did not commit. But because they committed so many other crimes for which they were never apprehended[8], there is a prison saying: "Maybe you serve time not for what you've done all the time, but all the time you serve, you serve for what you've done" (Blecker1990:1166). The scales of justice balance out for the un-righteous-but-legally-innocent. In the furor over capital punishment today, as evidence mounts that "innocent" people are being released from death rows, the public officially concentrates on "legal" innocence, but more easily tolerates individual "legal error" as long as the mistake attaches to criminals already seen as unrighteous.[9]

"Far be it from thee to do such a thing, to slay the righteous with the wicked," Abraham's challenge continues, *"so that the righteous fare as the wicked"* (Genesis XVIII:25). Far wrong, indeed, to execute the innocent in order to slay the deserving. God is presumed to stay clear from working such injustice. And today we go to great lengths to ensure that the innocent shall not be put to death. But it tears at us when righteous victims suffer while their wicked killers thrive. Retributivists need to exact punishment so the wicked, too, shall suffer along with their righteous victims. Nor can retributivists tolerate sheer arbitrariness, where the wicked and righteous seem to be punished indifferently.

Abraham gets God to promise to spare Sodom if fifty righteous persons can be found dwelling within. Then Abraham has the guts to lead God down the slippery slope. Suppose there are forty-five, forty, thirty, twenty...? Abraham

---

slain. An acquittal, however, was final. Because, the rabbis reasoned, the accused had been found righteous, and newly discovered evidence against him might establish only that this righteous defendant was not innocent (*Babylonian Talmud Sanhedrin*1935:33b).

8. "Though he had not smitten him yet—he was termed a wicked man" (*Babylonian Talmud Sanhedrin*1935:54b).

9. When I witnessed the execution of Benny Demps in Florida, I was acutely aware but untroubled that the evidence left some doubt about whether Demps had murdered a fellow prisoner for which he was ostensibly being put to death. Years earlier, Demps brutally murdered two innocent passersby who happened to come upon him in an orange grove while he was trying to open a safe from an earlier robbery. He had been sentenced to die and only escaped execution when the Supreme Court emptied death rows across the U.S. in *Furman v. Georgia* (1972), a completely unrelated case.

bargains God down one last time and then he quits. And God concedes: *"For the sake of ten I shall not destroy it"* (Genesis XVIII:22–32).

Abraham's challenge to the Judge of Judges is justly celebrated as brave: Defense counsel acting on behalf of others (Adam, Eve, and Cain had all defended themselves)—denying the Supreme Authority's moral right to risk executing the innocent. God and man must spare many guilty persons who deserve to die rather than execute the innocent. Humans are, after all, made *"in the image of God."*

But Abraham had stopped at ten. He did not suggest that God spare all the wicked of Sodom for the sake of a single righteous soul, at least one of whom—Lot—he knew resided there. In the end, Lot's sons-in-law thought Lot was jesting when he warned them to flee; they, although not wicked, died along with the rest of Sodom and Gomorrah. It seems by destroying whole cities as punishment, the Judge of all Earth risked killing persons who did not deserve to die for the certainty of killing larger numbers of guilty who did. The lesson here—justice systems have limits. We must *greatly* favor sparing the guilty lest we execute the innocent. But there are limits: Some error is inevitable and unfortunately must be tolerated.[10]

When Lot and his family fled, God commanded them not to look back. Lot's wife almost instinctively stared at the rightful destruction of the wicked—and was instantly turned into a pillar of salt. Does this passage warn that the public generally should not witness death sentences carried out? Lot's family were innocents who happened to dwell among the wicked. There was no need to witness this mass destruction, done neither in their name nor as an object lesson for them.

On several occasions in the Old Testament God will punish entire populations, innocents along with the guilty.[11] But humans, although made in the image of God, are not God and must not slay the righteous indiscriminately with the wicked. Human life is special. Unlike all other contemporary Near Eastern cultures[12] (Greenberg1970:29–30), the Bible embraces individual culpability, rejecting collective or vicarious punishment: *"Parents shall not be put to death for children, nor children for parents; each shall be put to death for his own crime,"* Deuteronomy XXIV:16 famously declares. And lest they slay the righteous with the wicked, humans are to uphold a presumption of innocence. *"Keep far from a false charge,"* God commands in Exodus XXIII:7, *"and do not*

---

10. *The Genesis of Justice* (pp. 86–89) independently makes the same point.

11. In the book of *Joshua*, God aids the Hebrews to slay whole cities. This divinely produced wholesale destruction of innocents defies contemporary humanistic justification, as does today's terrorist bombers, indiscriminately targeting innocent civilians.

12. For example, according to the Babylonian Code of Hammurabi (Laws:209–210), "if a man strike a [pregnant] woman" and caused her to die, his daughter was to be put to death.

slay the innocent, for I will not acquit the wicked." God guarantees it: Although acquitted by human judgment, the wicked shall be divinely punished.[13]

In today's secular society whose Constitution guarantees the separation of church and state, many citizens are skeptical that punishment somewhere else necessarily follows otherwise unpunished crime in this world. Government must overcome our natural resentment that wicked persons walk free and prosper. The People demand justice from their government in this world. We must rest our commitment to a presumption of innocence on a satisfaction that comes from believing that the righteous, although they have acted wickedly, will not die at the hands of the State. How better to "keep far" from a false charge, and thus "not slay the innocent and righteous," than to indulge all real doubts for a defendant's benefit?

"You Shall Inquire Diligently... and if It Be True and Certain"

"If there is found among you...a man or woman who has done evil...and it is told to you and you hear of it then you shall inquire diligently, and if it is true and certain that such an abominable thing has been done...you shall stone that man or woman to death" (Deuteronomy XVII:2–5).

No subtle message here: We are obliged to investigate, prosecute, and punish with death the worst of all crimes. But prosecution and punishment demand diligent inquiry. Reports and rumors may not be true. There is a dual fervor here: The Bible commands us to punish the wicked, but only if *it is true and certain* that an abominable thing has been done.

This demand was for *factual* certainty only—and what else could be required? For a people whose very meaning of "moral" was to strictly apply God's command, a moral certainty that a defendant deserved to die flowed automatically from a finding of factual guilt, with no prerogative to commute the sentence. In Biblical days, eyewitness testimony was probably the most reliable of all evidence. Yet even the testimony of a witness of sound mind with no motive to lie, who swore to being absolutely certain that the defendant committed the capital crime, was not enough to sentence a person to die, even if corroborated by circumstantial evidence.

"Presumption of innocence," and "proof beyond a reasonable doubt" are modern terms with ancient roots: "Keep far" from a false charge, and only after "diligent inquiry" demonstrates the fact as "true and certain" shall the defendant be put to death; and even then, only if two witnesses swear to the same events. This ancient imperative, "super due process," is as pulsing as the de-

---

13. The Old Testament does not explicitly mention an afterlife, but Divine Justice outside the human sphere is clearly implied.

mand for punishment: *"And you shall stone that man or woman to death. On the evidence of two witnesses or of three witnesses he that is to die shall be put to death; a person shall not be put to death on the evidence of one witness"* (Deuteronomy XVII:5–7).

"Then You Shall Do to Him As He Had Meant to Do..."

What if witnesses were lying? Suppose two people conspired to have the defendant wrongly executed by the State? *"If a malicious witness rises against any man to accuse him of wrongdoing, then both parties to the dispute shall appear before the...judges [who] shall inquire diligently, and if the witness is a false witness and has accused his brother falsely, then you shall do to him as he had meant to do to his brother so you shall purge the evil from the midst of you. And the rest shall hear, and fear, and shall never again commit any such evil among you"* (Deuteronomy XIX:16–19).

Like kind punishment: We do to the false witness what he would have had done to the innocent defendant. This ancient retributive measure feels right; it is poetically just, retributively just, emotionally just. By it we restore a balance and satisfy the retributive impulse to purge, or to "put away the evil." We gratify a deeply felt need rooted in the past. Then Scripture immediately returns attention to the living and the future: *"And those that remain shall hear and fear and never again commit..."* (Deuteronomy XIX:20). Punishment then becomes forward-looking, its purpose to prevent other people from committing similar crimes. But deterrence, more frequently found throughout the text, is ultimately peripheral. The need to restore the balance, to strike down the one who destroyed the life force, drives the Biblical death penalty (Bailey 1987:37).

Retribution and deterrence, thus paired in the Old Testament, are still coupled today. The United States Supreme Court has repeatedly held that in order to be constitutional, the death penalty must serve either a retributive or a deterrent purpose (*Coker v. Georgia* 1977; *Enmund v. Florida* 1982; *Lockett v. Ohio* 1978; *Tison v. Arizona* 1987). Capital punishment may never rest solely on convenience or its efficiency in incapacitating those we catch. The individual must deserve it uniquely, and/or others must change as a result.

Scripture seems to make this same point: "Purge the evil" and "the rest shall hear." Much more often than it justifies punishment, the Old Testament explains its purpose. It speaks principally in terms of deterrence, focusing on the good punishment will do in keeping the congregation law-abiding.

However, independent of deterrence, a witness who would send a man to his death falsely, deserved to die: *"Your eye shall not pity; it shall be life for life, eye for eye, tooth for tooth..."* (Deuteronomy XIX:21). Scripture here demands *attitude*: It exudes righteous indignation that one person would lie and scheme to use the community's justice process as a murder weapon. Inflict like-kind punishment; let him experience what he would have his victim experience. Show no pity.

Only a hardened heart can be emotionally distanced enough to rightly punish this defendant. As Adam Smith explored brilliantly 250 years ago in his *Theory of Moral Sentiments* (1759), we can have no pity for the defendant only if we have complete sympathy for the victim. If the victim is dead, we can remember, imagine, and stay angry at his suffering and tragic end.

What if the perjurer's scheme is detected before an innocent person is put to death? The putative victim, relieved to be alive, and recognized as an innocent person nearly executed unjustly, might want to put the incident to rest. The crime may seem less heinous because no one died. But, as measured by his intent, the deserts of the perjurer are the same. What would be gross injustice to an innocent person becomes appropriate punishment for the guilty—homeopathically giving him a taste of his own medicine. Do to him exactly what he *would have* had done. "Moral luck"—the good fortune that his victim escaped harm—counts for nothing here. The judges must imagine what would have happened and punish the intent fully.

The passage instructs that an attempt that fails or is nipped in the bud should sometimes bring the death penalty. Thus far, however, the states and federal government have rejected this. Many urged the death penalty for Richard Reid, the Al Qaeda trained "shoe bomber" who would have blown up a plane full of people but for the timely restraint of alert passengers and crew, moments before the bomb was to have gone off. "You shall do to him as he had meant to do." The U.S. Supreme Court, however, would probably hold the death penalty disproportionately "cruel and unusual" for attempted murder where nobody died.

But whether or not the scheme succeeds, Scripture demands that judges keep outrage fresh and cut off all sympathy. And witnesses, both lying and truthful, assume responsibility for the executions their testimony produced. Thus, *"the hand of the witnesses shall be first against him to put him to death, and afterward the hand of all the people. So you shall purge the evil from the midst of you"* (Deuteronomy XIX:18–19). The whole community participates in the punishment, with the witnesses casting the first stones. Today the citizenry participates by sending representatives to witness the execution. If contemporary practice were to preserve the spirit of Scripture, perhaps jurors, the sentencing judge, and/or the prosecutor would more actively participate, at least by witnessing the execution they had partly produced.

Biblical commands foreshadow today's "super due process" before we condemn a person to death. States have long since discarded the two-witness rule, but by making witness-killing capital, legislatures do attempt to protect witnesses from others who would slay them to prevent their truthful testimony.

On the other hand, the law inadequately protects innocent defendants against lying snitches, or "jail house informants" as they are more politely called. Today, we have nearly come full circle; commissions charged with reforming the death penalty recommend that the "two witness" requirement be restored, and executions be prohibited based solely on an informant's uncorroborated testimony.[14] At trial, of course "a State may not entrust the determination of whether a man should live or die to a tribunal organized to return a verdict of death" (*Lowenfield v. Phelps*1988:258, Marshall, J., dissenting, quoting *Witherspoon v. Illinois*1968:521). What else does a special commitment to a presumption of innocence and super due process require in the context of capital cases?

A storm rages.

"You Shall Accept No Ransom…"

From earliest times, the victim's family responded to homicide. They would retaliate if they could; blood feuds would develop, or the killer might flee. Or a "blood price" could be paid as a settlement, buying the killer peace and the victim's survivors some measure of satisfaction. It has stayed that way in the streets.[15]

All other pre-Biblical Near Eastern cultures allowed the victim's family or the community to settle up and be compensated for their loss[16] (Greenberg1970:26–27). Seemingly, moral guilt was irrelevant. The slayer was simply worth more alive, perhaps as a slave. (Or today as a lifer inside.) For utilitarians it has always been about costs and benefits. The blood price worked: No one complains, and anyway, "Don't cry over spilt blood"—just put it behind you and move on.

As defendant-friendly as the Bible was when it came to *proving* capital murder, however, it did not allow murderers to live who deserved to die: *"And these things shall be a statute and ordinance to you throughout your generations,"* declared the Lord, emphatically laying down the law: *"The murderer shall be put to death…but no person shall be put to death on the testimony of one witness.[17] Moreover, you shall accept no ransom for the life of a murderer, who is guilty, but he shall be put to death"* (Numbers XXXV:29–31).

The ancient Hebrews recognized that money can never truly compensate for murder, and they also embraced its moral corollary—that no property crime

---

14. See the Illinois Governor's Commission on Capital Punishment (2002).

15. Today's no-fault insurance and civil negligence lawsuits also help settle the dispute.

16. Hittite Law provided: "Whoever commits murder, whatever the heir himself of the murdered man says (will be done). If he says, 'Let him die,' he shall die, but if he says 'Let him make compensation,' he shall make compensation. The King shall have no role"(Roth1997:225).

17. Defense attorney Martin McClain insists that New York prosecutors often exclude Orthodox Jews as jurors because of their commitment to this biblical requirement.

should be capital. Theft was one thing—but death was different. Successful prosecution for burglary brought double your money back. But murder brings only death. By refusing to allow the killer to buy his way out, the Old Testament taught that individual human life is incommensurably valuable (Greenberg1970:26–27). Human life has no price: No amount of money given could ever equal the value of an innocent life taken. Life was neither expressible nor dischargeable in monetary terms, as humans are made in God's image. Justice shall not be bought; the victim's family shall not be bought off.

"*Accept no ransom,*" in lieu of the death penalty, "*for blood pollutes the land, and no expiation can be made…for the blood that is shed in it, except by the blood of him who shed it*" (Numbers XXXV:33). No longer were close relatives competent to decide what was adequate compensation for the victim. Only the murderer's death could demonstrate the infinite value of human life.

Also repulsed by blood pollution and compelled to reject the blood price, while the Old Testament was being assembled, the ancient Greeks, too, expressed the ultimate value of human life concretely: The convicted murderer must die. As with the ancient Israelites, the ancient Athenians decreed that when it came to murder—powerful and weak, rich and poor—all were equal before the law. In the spirit of equal protection, nobody bought his way out of homicide.[18] The core moral correlate equally demanded that no one could be condemned to die because he was too poor to show why he should live. No ransom was allowed, but executions were prohibited until diligent inquiry showed the murder was true and certain. When it came to death as crime and death as punishment, there was a single standard of justice, based upon anger and mercy, but never money.

Abolishing the blood price, and thus *extending* the death penalty to the wealthy who deserve it, advanced Western Civilization. Many deep-seated values combined to produce this great advance. The Hebrews recognized that the dignity of the individual victim demands the death of the killer. What can be said for those abolitionists today who claim "human dignity" as exclusively their own concern,[19] while they also claim public support for what they call the "better" option of "life without parole *plus* some monetary restitution to the victim's family"? To retributivists, this seeming embrace feels retrograde and wrong.[20]

Abraham had argued against "sweeping" away the righteous with the wicked. God had swept away all except Noah and his family, but regretted it af-

---

18. Today, however, Sen. Edward Kennedy and O.J. Simpson cast their shadows.

19. Retributivists would expropriate anger as theirs exclusively; in this they are too often aided by abolitionists, although a growing minority insist on their share of emotion (see Bandes 1999).

20. The European Union today coerces all candidates to accept the great economic benefits of membership as the blood price in lieu of the death penalty that they are required to abolish as a price of entry.

terwards. Any true retributivist today must be committed to equal justice. While retributive death penalty supporters are coming to grips with their responsibility to ensure due *process* and equal protection, they seem less aware of *substantive* changes they must also make in the law.

For neither by application nor *by definition* are the rich to be favored over the poor. Today, most state statutes declare that a pecuniary motive aggravates an intentional killing. And society applies that aggravator to professional assassins, as it should. But the pecuniary motive is also applied routinely to robbery felony-murderers, who almost always are poor and rob from a pecuniary motive, but often do not kill from one. And at the same time that states extend the death penalty indiscriminately to poor people who robbed when somebody else did the killing, callous corporate executives who knowingly kill and maim scores of unsuspecting employees or hundreds of unsuspecting consumers, strictly from a pecuniary motive, not only are exempted from the death penalty, they are very rarely prosecuted at all.[21]

Justice must not be polluted by class bias. The poor must never be "swept along" to execution because they cannot pay.

"Thou Shalt Not Forget…"

A retributivist who maps the Old Testament onto the death penalty debate today is likely to emphasize an independent obligation to the past, when by and large the law looks forward, emphasizing deterrence far more than desert as the primary purpose of punishment. But "*remember what Amalek did unto thee*," God specifically commands the Israelites. "*As ye came forth out of Egypt, how he met thee by the way, and smote the hindmost of thee, all that were enfeebled in the rear, when thou was faint and weary.*" A person who attacks and kills society's most vulnerable members is never to be forgotten or forgiven. Even if God were to give the Jews "*rest from all thine enemies*," they must forever kill Amalek on sight, "*that thou shalt blot out the[ir] remembrance under heaven; thou shalt not forget*" (Deuteronomy XXV:17).

Those who prey on children, the elderly, the weak and infirm—today's "vulnerable victim" aggravated killers should never be forgotten nor forgiven.[22]

---

21. See, for example *People v. Warner Lambert* (1980) and the infuriating saga of the Ford Motor executives who balanced settlement and trial costs from highway deaths, against the costs of modifying the Pinto's exploding gas tanks. Because it was cheaper, they left that deadly machine unmodified, to immolate victims of rear end collisions. Although hundreds of unsuspecting passengers were killed and thousands badly burned, not one corporate executive was even indicted.

22. Thus, retributivists today strongly oppose releasing imprisoned Nazi war criminals, however aged and infirm they may have become.

Rich or poor, the victims' "blood pollutes the land.... The voice of your brother's blood cries out." The past counts.

"Since He Had Not Hated His Neighbor in Time Past..."

It was one thing to declare *"the murderer he shall die,"* and quite another to kill him. Commanded not to be satisfied with a blood price, the victim's family instead designated a "blood avenger"[23] to hunt down the killer of their kin. But not all killers deserve to die. Accidents happen. For thousands of years cultures have marked this basic moral fact, deeply embedded in human nature: Different homicides call for different punishments. Intention counts.

"Whoever strikes a man so that he dies, shall be put to death," declares Exodus categorically, indiscriminately. *"But if he did not lie in wait for him,"* the passage continues, *"then I will appoint for you a place to which he may flee"* (Exodus XXI:12). *"You shall set apart three cities...you shall prepare the roads...so that any manslayer...may flee to one of these cities and save his life.... But if a man willfully attacks another to kill him treacherously, you shall take him from my altar, that he may die"* (Deuteronomy XIX:2–12). Today instead of roads in good repair, the airwaves are kept clear and secure telephone lines maintained to the death chamber, for the Governor and the courts to issue last moment stays, so an execution can be reconsidered.

By statute 3000 years ago, premeditation made a killing capital, as it still does by statute today, in most death penalty states. But then and now, *"Whoever kills his neighbor unintentionally, not having hated him in time past—as when a man goes into the forest with his neighbor to cut wood, and his hand swings the axe to cut down a tree, and the head slips from the handle and strikes his neighbor so that he dies, he may flee to one of these cities and save his life; lest the avenger of blood in hot anger pursue the manslayer and overtake him...and wound him mortally, though the man did not deserve to die, since he had not hated his neighbor in time past"* (Deuteronomy XIX:4–7).

This compound retributive command at once excuses the avenger who in the heat of passion adequately provoked, intentionally slays the accidental killer of his kin before he can reach the city of refuge, while at the same time, explicitly resting just deserts on the initial killer's intent and attitude. Deuteronomy XIX displays an equally clear commitment not to execute those who do not deserve to die. The U.S. Supreme Court now recognizes in its death penalty jurisprudence that retribution, perhaps *the* principal justification for punishment, *limits* even as it supports punitive measures. A true retribu-

---

23. Today, of course, the State divides the role among police, prosecutors, judges, and corrections.

tivist, drawing an essential lesson from Scripture, must feel at least as constrained to ensure that those who do not deserve to die are not killed, as to ensure that those who do are put to death.

If the roads were good and the manslayer reached the city of refuge, the congregation assembled and two or more witnesses were examined. How were the factfinders to decide the killer's mental state, especially without a confession, to determine whether he deserved to die? Deuteronomy declares, and contemporary juries agree, that a killer who hated his victim most likely intended to kill him. Numbers XXXV also lays out the process by which intentional (and therefore capital) murder is inferred from the manner of the killing: *"If he struck him down with an instrument of iron, so that he died, he is a murderer; the murderer shall be put to death. And if he struck him down with a stone, in the hand, by which a man may die, and he died, he is a murderer; the murderer shall be put to death. The avenger of blood shall himself put the murderer to death"* (16–19). Numbers continues by inferring the motive of the killer from the manner of the killing: *"And if he stabbed him in hatred, or hurled at him lying in wait, so that he died, or in enmity struck him down with his hand, so that he died, then he who struck the blow shall be put to death; he is a murderer"* (XXXV:22).

A particular defendant may not have acted pursuant to his apparent motive. Because motives often cannot be established directly with certainty, the power of inference must supplement the limitations of the evidence. As long as the factfinder has made *"diligent inquiry"* so that by best efforts the motive appears *"true and certain,"* we cannot be frozen by fear of possible error or that a future technology we cannot now envision will reveal a different truth. Absolute certainty is simply impossible. Every age has its own standards of certainty, its own fineness of reality, its advancing means of being convinced.[24]

"Accustomed to Gore...and Its Owner Has Been Warned"

"When an ox gores a man or a woman to death, the ox shall be stoned...but the owner of the ox shall be clear. But if the ox has been accustomed to gore in the past, and its owner has been warned but has not kept it in, and it kills a man or a woman, the ox shall be stoned, and its owner also shall be put to death" (Exodus XXI:28).

We can presume this was no trained killer ox. Although it was the ox that gored, a human omission, failing to keep the animal confined, was a proximate cause of death. But the defendant-owner of the ox had not killed intentionally.

---

24. But see the district court opinion in *United States v. Quinones* (2002), declaring the entire federal death penalty unconstitutional on the possibility of error not yet discoverable by known means.

There was no past hatred of the victim, no malice at all. The owner simply did not care enough about other people's lives. He put human lives at risk, for convenience or profit. But once "warned" that he did have a goring ox—a beast out of control—like many drunk drivers, robbers high on crack, or callous corporate executives today, the owner consciously disregarded a deadly risk of danger.

Many killings are neither clearly premeditated nor as freakishly accidental as an ax head flying off its handle at an odd angle. Perhaps when the woodsman swung the ax he was negligent: He never noticed, but should have, that its head was loose and that the victim was standing close by in harm's way. Or he might have chosen not to repair the loose ax head, or give warning, thus knowingly putting his unsuspecting neighbor at risk. The recklessness may have been real, but the risk too remote for the killer to deserve to die.

Today many states identify a culpable mental state between negligence and intent by relying on the Model Penal Code's definition of "recklessly," *i.e.* being "aware of and consciously disregarding a substantial risk" of death. Most states recognize a more culpable recklessness that comes from subjecting others to a "grave" risk of death rather than the lesser "substantial" risk. Reckless homicide also may become murder when a number of people are placed at risk. Whatever risk the goring ox presented at the time, it seems grave looking back upon it after the victim has been gored. Back then and today, however, what morally makes the killing murder was not the risk as much as the *attitude* of the risk taker. Taking grave risks and ignoring a "prior warning" support the inference that the actor was indifferent to the lives of others. Although it need not involve anger or hate, scheming or plotting, a "depraved indifference to human life"—unintentional but wanton and abandoned—can be every bit as heinous as a premeditated intent to kill.

Although the Goring Ox illustrates how non-intentional killings may sometimes deserve death, unlike the premeditated murderer or capital perjurer, the Old Testament did allow a depraved indifference reckless killer to settle up. Despite being death-eligible, the owner might escape with his life, if the court or victim's family were willing to accept a blood price. Only for this reckless and indirectly caused homicide does Biblical law permit ransom. How much? The sky was the limit: *"He shall give for the redemption of his life whatever is laid on him"* (Exodus XXI:30). As an alternative to death, no penalty was too great; whatever was demanded of the reckless killer, whether by the court or the victim's family, he was to give in return for his life. The greater power to execute included the lesser power to strip the offender of everything he owned, consigning him to poverty and misery.

Today too, states generally punish a depraved indifference reckless murder as the moral equivalent of intentional murder. Although the U.S. Supreme Court ruled in *Tison v. Arizona* (1987) that a State *may* execute a person who does not intend to kill as long as the actor's reckless indifference was a primary cause of the victim's death, many states reject that option, reserving the death penalty and its temporary substitute, life without parole, exclusively for intentional killers.

Alive or dead, an ox was valuable. But the command was clear: *"It shall be stoned and its flesh shall not be eaten"* (Exodus XXI:28). Do not profit from the killer's death. The incalculable non-utilitarian value of human life demanded that any future benefits be sacrificed to the past. The instrument of death, a living being, was to be treated as responsible and not made an object of gain.[25] Usefulness must be shunned, lest the past and the humanity of the slain—the reason for the punishment—be forgotten. Although they often travel together, even in the same sentence, utilitarianism and retribution ultimately clash.

In Biblical times as now, the vast majority of unintentional killings did not deserve punishment by death. *"If he stabbed him suddenly without enmity,"* continues Numbers XXXV in its detailed gradations of homicide, *"or hurled anything on him without lying in wait, or used a stone, by which a man may die, and without seeing him cast it upon him, so that he died, though he was not his enemy, and did not seek his harm, then the congregation shall judge between the manslayer and the avenger of blood, in accordance with these ordinances"* (16–24).

If diligent inquiry determined the killing was accidental, negligent, or even ordinarily reckless, but not intentional, again, there must be *"cities of refuge for you, that the manslayer who kills any person without intent, through error or unawares—may flee there"* (Numbers XXXV:11). The negligent or reckless killer must live therein, until the high priest died. If the unintentional killer prematurely ventured from his place of refuge, the avenger of blood was authorized to kill him on the spot. Inside the city of refuge, however, the unintentional killer was free to live. Refuge and confinement were merged, oddly, it may seem, although today too, young convicted killers often consider their sentences in prison to be refuge from the mean streets.

Ancient Greece

"If I Order You to Set Me Free… You Must Tie Me Tighter"

Whereas the Israelites saw a transcendent God ruling the universe with humans created in His image and struggling to comprehend His ways, the ancient

---

25. This ripens into the Kantian retributive prohibition against using other people as a means to our ends.

Greeks saw a "world ruled by…gods human in their passions, a world ruled by caprice" (Guthrie 1962: Vol.I, at 44).[26]

Homer recounts that when the goddess Circe reluctantly released her beloved Odysseus to continue his progress home, she warned of several deadly perils awaiting him, especially the Sirens, whose song he must at all costs ignore. Odysseus prepared to withstand temptation by limiting his own power to lead his men to their mutual destruction. Thus, before they reached the Sirens, as their leader had commanded, his men put wax in their ears and bound him to the mast. "If I implore you and order you to set me free, you must tie me up tighter than ever," Odysseus demanded.

When Odysseus heard "sounds sweet as honey," the Sirens' call—"Come this way and listen to our voice!"—he was aroused: "I longed to listen and I ordered the men to set me free" (Homer:132). Now they were all in a bind: Did the later command take precedence? Then was then; now is now. Had Odysseus the right to change his mind?

The men rejected their leader's attempt to countermand his earlier command, and kept on rowing until the danger passed. Only because a rational Odysseus at an earlier time had provided procedures for keeping his own passion in check, and only because his men could subordinate the present and keep covenants with the past, did they all survive this trial.

The lesson should be clear to a society where the People are sovereign: We must limit our own power to act on our passions of the moment, or face self-destruction. In a republic, public passion is filtered through the People's elected representatives. And when legislatures or administrations are tempted summarily to execute society's outlaws, their passions too must be restrained, by their constitutions and judges sworn to uphold them. Appropriate punishment, morally commanded, becomes possible in the face of public outrage and the urge to act immediately only if we find a way to restrain passion long enough to investigate and deliberate. To be reliably and fairly administered, the death penalty must operate as a deliberate product of a deliberative process. Popular opinion counts, but only for so much.

And so it is today, roughly 3000 years after Odysseus ordered himself bound to the mast, that constitutional rights operate to check the passions of the People and their elected representatives. In the end, the constitutional guarantee of Due Process together with the Eighth Amendment's prohibition against "cruel and unusual punishments," operate, as Justice Thurgood Marshall de-

---

26. Overwhelmingly here, Guthrie's (1962) multivolume history brings alive the world of the Presocratics, Socrates and the Sophists, and much of Plato. Except for some later sections interpreting Plato's *Laws* and *Statesman*, and Aristotle's *Ethics* and *Politics*, this essay relies on Guthrie throughout, sometimes without quotes, in essential though fragmentary phrasing. Guthrie should not be held responsible, however, for mapping the death penalty.

clared, concurring in *Furman v. Georgia* (1972), as "our insulation from our baser selves" (at 345).

"If All Agree…"

Human beings feel a primal urge to retaliate when a member of their family is slain. In Homer's time, the Heroic Age, roughly 1200–800 B.C., homicide was strictly personal. The killer escaped, the victim's family caught and killed him, or the blood price settled it monetarily with the victim's family (Bonner and Smith 2000: Vol.II, at 192).[27]

Killers who escaped the family's initial wrath could go into exile and, as with Cain, were safe from retaliation, as long as they stayed away. The blood price acted only partly as compensation to the family for its loss. It also helped defray sacrifices "to appease the spirit of the dead" (Bonner and Smith 2000: Vol. I, at 21). Homer reveals no distinctions among homicides, except special horror at killing one's own kin. But early human beings must have known intuitively that some killings were worse than others. Recognizing that accidents do happen brings a feeling of restraint, nearly as primal as the urge for revenge.

Draco's gift to Athens, its first written Constitution, was so indiscriminately bloody, with death as the standard punishment for a host of crimes, that even now "draconian" means "harsh, severe, barbarously cruel." The Old Testament also looks like a bloody code. Of course, today it is a crime against humanity for any government to exterminate homosexuals as such, or put people to death for worshiping the wrong gods. Today, we know *better*.

Except for homicide. We have refined but not rejected Scripture's substantive distinctions. Biblical homicide law's commanded process and presumption of innocence continue as basic mandates in the United States. We have grown but kept connected to those roots. So too, when Solon rid Athens of Draco's bloody code and substituted a whole new Constitution, a whole new set of laws designed to last unchanged for at least another hundred years, the great lawgiver kept virtually intact Draco's law of homicide, which was largely a codification of earlier practice (Bonner and Smith 2000: Vol. I, at 133).

But one great change had taken place in the culture since the time of Homer: The community had become consciously and emotionally involved. As with the ancient Hebrews, for the ancient Greeks the decisive change was the idea—really a *feeling*—that "*blood pollutes the land*" (Numbers XXXV:33).

Because he was polluted, the manslayer himself posed a public menace. While at large in public places, the guilty killer would contaminate society. In

---

27. Robert Bonner and Gertrude Smith's two-volume *The Administration of Justice from Homer to Aristotle* (2000) is the principal source here for homicide jurisprudence in ancient Greece.

Athens, the victim's family initiated the homicide prosecution, and once they publicly accused the killer, pollution immediately attached, and an interdiction automatically issued. During preliminary investigation the accused, now polluting, was strictly prohibited from appearing in public places. If he violated that interdiction, anybody could legally kill him on the spot (Bonner and Smith 2000: Vol. II, at 193).

Although the government had taken over homicide trials, the victim's family prosecuted. They might prefer a monetary settlement, but blood pollution complicated that remedy. A money settlement with the family would leave a contaminating killer at large. The response to homicide had become more than merely personal pay back: Only punishment sufficient to cancel the pollution would end the public threat. And only the community would determine which punishment was sufficient. But in a code where death is the casual and indiscriminate punishment for petty crimes, why not play it safe and make death the punishment for all homicide? Because all killings are not alike. Animating the Old Testament, this moral fact also animated the Ancient Greeks. There seems a basic impulse in Western culture to mark off officially—specially denounce and distinguish from all others—the worst killings. Today in the U.S. many states execute no one, yet cling to their capital statutes as a way to distinguish and denounce. Bonner and Smith (2000: Vol. I, at 103) suggest that homicide became a public concern less to assure prosecution, than to *limit* punishment by distinguishing different killings correctly.

This feeling that the victim's blood morally pollutes us until the killer is dealt with adequately—this felt need to sort out homicides and punish killers only as deserved—this deep-seeded retributive urge primarily moves death penalty advocates.

"Death is different" has become cliché in today's capital jurisprudence. But a host of crimes in ancient times brought the death penalty. As punishment, death may have been common, but as crime, killing has been treated specially. Even a lawgiver like Draco, who used death indiscriminately as a penalty, still carefully distinguished among homicides. Although execution has not always been a special punishment, murder since the beginning has been a special sort of crime.

The aristocratic Aeropagus, the highest court of legal guardians which descended from the Homeric Council of Elders, sat *en masse* to try premeditated murderers and would-be tyrants.[28] The Athenians so cared about distinguish-

---

28. Every society is most angry at "treason"—the direct attack on the core of the collective identity: For the Israelites the worst treason was to worship false gods or engage others in the attempt. For ancient Athenians and most Americans today, the worst treason is the attempt to establish a tyranny (Bonner and Smith 2000: Vol. I, at 108). Just as anyone could kill the killer who returned to pollute, anyone could kill the traitor. Faced with cumbersome legal process and sometimes a family not inclined to prosecute for homicide, Athenians found ways to prosecute

ing homicides that they established separate courts to try separate types of killings. One court of fifty-one tried unpremeditated killings; another dealt with justifiable killings. A special court was established for one who killed again while in exile for a prior killing. (Many states in the U.S. also single out prisoners serving life sentences and repeat killers.) Aristotle tells us that these recidivist killers, already banished and now facing another charge of homicide, conducted their defense from a boat lest they contaminate the court assembled on the shore (Aristotle 1974:135). Finally, there was a special denunciatory court for unidentified killers, with jurisdiction also over animals and inanimate objects that had caused the death of human beings (Bonner and Smith 2000: Vol. I, at 110).

After preliminary investigation,[29] at any time prior to trial the accused could voluntarily go into exile, thereby implicitly confessing his guilt, and be banished forever. Or he could stand trial and after hearing the prosecution's opening, still choose to go into exile. This also amounted to a guilty plea, and again the exile would be for life (Bonner and Smith 2000: Vol. I, at 108; 118). Forever banished from his homeland, forever contaminated, there could never be a pardon. Even after factional wars and coups were settled with general amnesties and wholesale pardons, in Ancient Greece homicide was always exempt from pardon. EWOP—exile without pardon—meant that. No hope of seeing home, ever. Today, there is no statute of limitations for murder, and so far in the United States although no longer in Europe, LWOP truly means life without parole or pardon.[30]

If a killer who had fled before trial found life without his native Attica unbearable without hope of parole, and snuck back home, anybody could legally kill him or alert the authorities—"hale him into court" (Bonner and Smith 2000: Vol. I, at 121). Like today's prison escapee, or lifer who kills again, he who violated exile would generally be considered incorrigible, undeterrable, permanently polluting—a continuing danger to the community—and deserving death. "Haling him into Court" was the innovation; killing him on sight (Bonner and Smith 2000: Vol. II, at 193) was the ancient option. "It shall be permitted to slay [illegally returning] homicides...but not to abuse them or to extort blackmail," the Athenian Code declared. No torture, even of the con-

---

some homicides as political offenses. Today too, the federal government sometimes pursues local homicide cases as Civil Rights violations.

29. As homicide procedure developed, successive investigations were conducted for three months, with trial on the last three days of the fourth month. During that time, the killer was free from harm: "Anyone [who] slays a homicide while he keeps away from markets and games," was to be tried as an ordinary murderer (Bonner and Smith 2000: Vol. I, at 116;114).

30. Today of course, LWOP holds out only the slimmest hope of executive clemency. Should the death penalty be eliminated tomorrow however, undoubtedly as in Europe, LWOP would be next under attack.

demned who had returned to pollute the community. And no blackmail—life could not be bought: No blood price—for blood pollutes the land.

Witnesses were always sworn in homicide cases, whereas in other cases they testified under oath only at the demand of the other side (Bonner and Smith 2000: Vol. I, at 108). An accused killer who stood trial and was convicted of *unpremeditated* homicide was banished for a year or two, or until he received a pardon from the victim's family, which paid the debt and thereby ended the pollution. But the family had to be unanimous: "If there is a father or a brother or sons let them grant pardon to the homicide if all agree. Otherwise the one who opposes it shall prevent pardon" (Bonner and Smith 2000: Vol. I, at 113). One holdout's simmering anger, a desire to continue punishing overrode the collective will to end it reasonably.[31]

"Like Members of the Same Body…"

Athough an accused who had gone into exile before the verdict could never receive a pardon from the family or the court, if he did stand trial and was found justified, he would be released without punishment or debt. But if convicted of premeditated murder, as in the Bible, he was put to death (Bonner and Smith 2000: Vol. II, at 194–195). Today too, many States continue to make a premeditated killer death-eligible, while other capital statutes reject planning *per se* as morally irrelevant.

But now as then, premeditated murder was worse than involuntary manslaughter, which was worse than justified or accidental killing. Passion killings have always been a problem: "If anyone kills *without* premeditation… he shall be exiled," the Athenian Code declared. "If one slays another who is the aggressor (*i.e.*, in a quarrel)…the kings shall decide the nature of the homicide…. The same procedure shall be followed whether a slave is killed or a free man" (Bonner and Smith 2000: Vol. I, at 114). And under the Athenian penal code, as today: "If a man while defending himself kills another on the spot who is unjustly and forcibly carrying off his property there shall be no punishment for the slaying"[32] (at 114). Although Draco reputedly was the first in Athens to distinguish premeditated, unpremeditated, and justified or accidental killing, 2500 years later these distinctions: intentional—provoked—reckless—accidental—justifiable—seem permanently part of human nature—deeply embedded, and real.

---

31. Today prosecutors routinely consult the victim's family on whether to seek death; judges before sentencing hear victim impact statements, but the family may not recommend a specific punishment.

32. Scholars have disagreed among themselves but where the killing was justified, the killer was probably not considered polluting, and definitely did not owe payback to the victim's family.

And then there was felony murder. In ancient Athens, where the homicide was connected with some other crime such as robbery or burglary or kidnapping, anyone with knowledge of the killing could initiate prosecution—there need be no interdict. The accused was imprisoned until trial, before a stripped-down court of eleven (Bonner and Smith 2000: Vol. II, at 214). Death was the penalty. So among homicides, only premeditated murder and felony murder got the death penalty. Twenty-three hundred years later in 1794, Pennsylvania became the first State again to reach this advanced stage by enacting a new statute that restricted the death penalty to "murder in the *1st degree*," which comprised premeditated homicide and felony murder. More than two centuries later in many states, today these two aggravating circumstances account for the bulk of the condemned.

Although the victim's family generally initiated homicide prosecutions, and could commute sentences, trial and punishment were in the name of the People. "If a man obtain a conviction for murder," Demosthenes informs us, "even then he gets no power over the condemned, who for punishment is given up to the laws and to persons charged with that office." The victim's family, however, was guaranteed the right to "behold the condemned suffering the penalty which the law imposes, but nothing further" (Bonner and Smith 2000: Vol. II, at 193). When Timothy McVeigh, the Oklahoma City bomber, was put to death, opinion was split over whether the public generally, or only the families of the 168 victims, should be allowed to witness the execution. The U.S. Attorney General ultimately ordered the execution broadcast on closed-circuit TV, but only to the victims' families.

Whether they went into exile before trial, or went to trial and were convicted and condemned, premeditated killers were allowed no pardon (Bonner and Smith 2000: Vol. II, at 194). Like Odysseus at the mast, the ancient lawgivers put it out of their own power to reconsider. No matter how old and infirm the killer, how distant the memory of the victim, how diminished the cost to the family, the pollution never ended—*"the voice of your brother's blood"* cried out permanently. The past counted, forever.

With one exception: Regardless of the community's or family's wishes, when a dying victim forgave his attacker, no pollution attached, even for premeditated murder. There would be no trial; the family could exact no penalty, nothing was owed. On the other hand, a dying victim could beg his surviving relatives to avenge his death, which then became their solemn moral obligation (Bonner and Smith 2000: Vol. II, at 195–196). Emphasizing forgiveness by the slain, some abolitionists today press for a legally binding "living will"—formally declaring in advance that, "Should I be murdered, no matter how heinously, I wish my killer's life to be spared." Retributivist advocates also should give such declarations great weight, short of making them absolutely binding on prosecutors. The past counts, and in life as in death, we should, if we can, give victims a voice, if not a veto.

With the idea of "blood pollution" in the Old Testament and Ancient Greece, humanity had taken a giant step. Blood pollution binds the community to the slain. The victim's next of kin initiated prosecution, accepted payment and granted pardon, or witnessed the execution, but there surfaced a communal urge to execute cold-blooded killers. In "the best governed State… those who were not wronged were no less diligent in prosecuting wrongdoers than those who had personally suffered," declared Solon. And not merely from abstract duty. "Citizens like members of the same body should feel and resent one another's injuries" (Bonner 1927:60). Ancient utilitarians must have urged execution to prevent a bad harvest, the surest proof of contamination. But blood pollution—the voice of the dead crying out in anger and anguish as his killer, living free, pollutes the land—calls to us in a manner not strictly empirical, moves us to act from motives not strictly rational. Nevertheless, to those who feel morally obliged, the urge to punish is real.

These last 30 years during the death penalty's modern era, in a society deeply split over how to punish murder, and with a Supreme Court forced to regulate its every aspect, changes in death penalty jurisprudence appear to be fast and furious. It seems as though we are in the midst of one of those rare spurts of feverish activity and perhaps are experiencing a radical paradigm shift where the whole world will take on new meaning. Taking the long view, however, homicide substance and procedure continue to remain the most conservative aspect of law in Western culture. Although homicide law seems relatively unchanged in general, and remained virtually unchanged during the three centuries between Draco and Aristotle, seemingly stagnant, unselfconscious, and stuck in quasi-religious ancient ruts, beneath the surface Western culture was germinating core philosophical and scientific foundations on which modern death penalty jurisprudence rests.

Thales

Twenty-five centuries ago, science in the West began with Thales, Solon's contemporary, who faithfully sought the simpler order underlying this apparently complex and haphazard world in terms of the basic *stuff*—the substance that composed it. Western mathematics, too, begins with Thales, who discovered (or invented) an abstract *process* of proof by which we can all arrive at the same truth. Today's death penalty jurisprudence, concerned with substance and process, draws essentially from both.

As a scientist, Thales suggested that water was the simple stuff underlying the apparent diversity of the world (Guthrie 1962: Vol. I, at 68), a decidedly primitive explanation by today's standards. The Old Testament and Draco too gave us simple categories of killings such as by poison and premeditation, that are also rather primitive in comparison to today's death penalty statutes. Scientific legislators continually search for regularity and distinctions among the great variety of killers and killings. They probe human nature and the reality of the streets to determine what "really" makes one murder worse than another. In June 2002, the United States Supreme Court weighed in substantively in *Atkins v. Virginia,* by holding that states may not execute the mentally retarded. Just two months later, when Texas executed a man for a murder committed when he was 17, three U.S. Supreme Court Justices publicly protested (*Patterson v. Texas* 2002). But as the fall term opened, the Court declined to decide whether a killer younger than 18 could ever constitutionally deserve to die (*In re Stanford* 2002), seemingly biding their time until they could declare a national consensus against it. Then the Sniper hit, terrorizing cities from Baltimore to Richmond. When the Sniper turned out to be a pair of multiple killers, the younger only 17, all hope for a national consensus against executing juveniles was dashed.

Is it worse to kill two people than one, or if the victim is a child, or if the killing is felony murder? Can depraved recklessness be as bad as intent? The substance of contemporary death penalty jurisprudence and debate goes to "aggravators" and "mitigators"—the killer's mental state, his character and background, the methods of the killing, the number and suffering of the victims—all of which set apart some murders and murderers as worse—and within that group, the worst of the worst. We seek simple death penalty statutes that reflect substantial differences. Who, if anybody, deserves to die, and why?

Thales, like Solon, traveled to Egypt and observed royal revenue agents trying to determine tax abatements due to farmers whose once rectangular plots had shrunk after the Nile flooded. A practical people, the Egyptians had developed rules of thumb for measuring the earth. Thales alone apparently felt the need to prove their truth (Kline 1953:16–17). Thus was the state of geometry—earth measure—when reason in the West leaped from taxes calculated on changing land masses to the permanently important abstraction, mathematics. Thales' great contribution was *truth by proof,* through methods that were repeatable, demonstrable, and permanent. Mathematics is an abstract *process* separate from concrete reality—the stuff to which it usefully applies. A proposition was true by virtue of a universally shared process of proof applied to basic axioms (Kline 1953:24; Cornford 1957:5; Guthrie 1975:23). Once the rules were given, the conclusions necessarily followed by pure analysis.

Mathematics became law's ideal. In a society with a rule of law, something deeply worth having, general rules classify situations and specify penalties. Given the substance—what counts, what features matter, what criteria the rules use in classifying—specific situations call for certain responses. Regardless of whether powerful people actually do get away with it, as a matter of analysis they have "broken the law." Capital murder can be said to have been committed even if it goes unpunished.

Capital jurisprudence today is largely about process: How do we *establish* substantial truth—who has the burden of persuasion and by what weight; who decides who lives or dies, and how? From ancient times until now, death penalty process has involved diligent inquiry to achieve a necessary measure of certainty before we risk executing the innocent. Today we dispute whether proof beyond a reasonable doubt is a standard sufficient to support a sentence of death. Within a few centuries after the Old Testament was stitched together, Talmudic rabbis resisted literally applying death penalty law to a host of substantive crimes that they sensed did not deserve capital punishment. Ever since, feeling constitutionally constrained to keep the punishment in principle, abolitionist jurists have attempted covertly to abolish an inhumane substantive law by making it impossible to apply in practice. "Proof to an absolute certainty,"[33] for example, is an absurd standard, simply unattainable in the real world.

Only since the 19th century have we become painfully aware that mathematics is not necessarily about the real world at all. It is devoid of content; pure process, and fit for all possible and impossible worlds. In today's death penalty debate, urging an impossible process for *this* world is disingenuous. Abolitionists would serve scientific traditions better if they were more forthright and did not mask substantive disagreement as "reformed" process.

Impossible process aside, before imposing death as punishment for murder, special, super due process remains a basic cultural norm: The Old Testament's two witness rule; deeply discounting snitch testimony; insisting on diligent inquiry; accepting proof only if it is true and certain; staying far from slaying the innocent with the guilty. Today's emphasis on DNA testing, competent counsel, diligent investigation, and proof beyond a reasonable doubt, is all about constitutionally guaranteed process for determining the truth. Whatever the content of the axioms or aggravators—whatever the stuff that makes a person deserve life in prison or death—equal protection requires assigning guilt and applying punishment *equally* across race and class.

Process—questions of who decides and how to decide who deserves to die— can, of course, directly influence who lives or dies. Solon redistributed power and wealth to the lower classes by giving them juries. In 2002, the U.S. Supreme Court held in *Ring v. Arizona* that juries and not judges must find the facts on which the death penalty is based. *Who* decides may determine *what* is decided: Substance and process do affect each other. Due process requires clear categories. Otherwise they will be held void for vagueness, for giving inadequate notice to the sentencer of what counts as the worst of the worst. Because we are unable to apply the category consistently, "especially, heinous, atrocious and cruel"—however real—as of now cannot by itself, be the stuff which distinguishes who lives and dies.

---

33. I have no absolute certainty that my computer will not attack and kill me this instant, yet I bravely write on.

Thus, with Thales, the first philosopher of the West, was born the great jurisprudential divide between substance—the real stuff—and the process for proving that stuff.

Anaximander, Thales' student, rejected his teacher's scientific theory that water was the single basic stuff, in favor of pairs of successively encroaching opposites such as hot-cold, moist-dry. Drawing upon more ancient retributive metaphor, Anaximander explained the essential dynamic, the changing seasons, as injustice followed by reparation. This explanatory metaphor of injustice and reparation, like the basic function of punishment in the Old Testament, drew on the most elemental feeling: A like-kind response can restore a prior balance thrown out of equilibrium (Guthrie 1962: Vol. I, at 84). When the United States was founded, this same metaphor of encroachment—power encroaching on liberty—saturated the debate. Leading opponents of the death penalty today embrace that metaphor, basing their opposition not so much on a conviction that no one deserves to die, but that government with the power to kill inevitably encroaches on liberty (see Bedau 1997).

Anaximenes, Anaximander's student, returned to Thales' credo of a single stuff underlying reality. The difference between earth, water, wind and fire was simply how much of that stuff was in any given space (Guthrie 1962: Vol. I, at140). Anaximenes had secured a basic foundation for death penalty jurisprudence: Differences of kind—substantial differences—were really at bottom differences of degree.

In the Old Testament as today, recklessness permits of more or less—more or less risky, more or less unconcerned with others' fate. Beyond a certain degree, a "substantial risk" becomes "grave," indifference becomes depraved, and reckless manslaughter becomes murder. Intent can be formed less and less suddenly until it becomes premeditated. Today, in many states, the killer's indifference to or positive enjoyment of the victim's suffering reaches a point where it becomes "callous" or "cruel," thereby making the killing death-eligible. And moral blameworthiness diminishes with youth or mental impairment until it becomes an absolute bar to the death penalty. "The word 'unusual,'" declared the first Justice White almost a century ago, "primarily restrains the courts... from inflicting lawful modes of punishment to so unusual a degree as to cause the punishment to be illegal" (*Weems v. United States* 1910:409).

Differences in degree become differences in kind; too much discretion becomes unconstitutional caprice.

"Imposing Limits on the Unlimited to Make the Limited..."

The formal impulse leapt forward with Pythagoras: The universe was a *kosmos*—a well-ordered whole—proportional, measurable, rational. From the beginning, Good—the limited and ordered—was set against Evil—chaotic and unlimited. The *kosmos* was maintained by imposing measures or limits on the unlimited to make the limited (Guthrie 1962: Vol. I, at 206–207).

So too, the moral *kosmos* of the death penalty.

Moved by a conviction that lesser crimes deserve proportionately lesser punishment, retributivist advocates today would punish with death all but only those who deserve it—the worst of the worst. Dividing the continuum of musical notes into discrete ratios, Pythagoras found that harmonics confirmed his world view of rational proportionality (Guthrie 1962: Vol. I, at 205). Today we do justice by dividing the continuum of killings into different types of homicide. Punishment must be proportional to the crime and the criminal.

"If the guilty man deserves to be beaten," declares Deuteronomy, *"the judge shall cause him to lie down and be beaten in his presence with a number of stripes in proportion to his offense."* Another translation has it, *"according to the measure of his wickedness, by number"* (XXV:1). This is thoroughly Pythagorean. Numbers not only explained the physical world, they were moral qualities[34] (Guthrie 1962: Vol. I, at 212). The Magna Carta shared this commitment to proportionality almost a thousand years ago when it declared, *"A free man shall be amerced for a small fault only according to the measure thereof, and for a great crime according to its magnitude"* (Eng. Magna Carta 1215: Sec. 20).

In 1892, dissenting in *O'Neill v. Vermont*—one of the Supreme Court's first forays into the meaning of "cruel and unusual"—Justice Field would have invalidated a punishment of 54 years at hard labor for selling liquor without a license. True, there was no physical torture, but the potential punishment was disproportional—"exceeding in severity considering the offense" (at 338). The Eighth Amendment was "directed against all punishments which by their excessive length or severity are *greatly disproportioned* to the offenses charged" (at 340, emph. added).

During the modern era of death penalty jurisprudence, the Supreme Court has embraced Justice Field's standard, consistently demanding proportionality when evaluating the constitutionality of the death penalty: In *Coker v. Georgia* (1977), the Court held that death is disproportionate for the rape of an adult woman; in *Thompson v. Oklahoma* (1988), for a killing committed when the defendant was less than sixteen; and in *Atkins v. Virginia* (2002), for the mentally retarded defendant. In each case, death was "cruel and unusual" precisely because it was disproportionate to the heinousness of the crime or criminal. In the tradition of Pythagoras, many states today require a "proportionality review," where an appellate court measures the death sentence in the particular

---

34. The essence of justice was equality—or requital. Thus, justice for the Pythagoreans was the first square number, 4.

case against other similar murders and murderers to determine whether it is comparatively disproportionate.

Committed to proportional punishment, today's retributivist death penalty advocates embrace a Pythagorean program, seeking to impose limits, to moderate unlimited anger at each particular murder and measure it instead against the worst possible. The retributivist resists the "kill them all" set, so bent on revenge they would indulge in limitless and formless rage. For the retributivist death penalty advocate, unlimited and unrestrained punishment is evil. The retributivist advocate also disagrees with abolitionists for whom death is *always* disproportionate, no matter how heinous the murderer. The retributivist embraces Pythagoras' faith that society can limit punishment without eliminating the legitimate impulse to hurt—yes *hurt*—those who injure us. Like Odysseus, we would impose categories and procedures in advance to keep in check human nature's passion for revenge. When it comes to homicide, restraints can be imposed on unlimited rage to ensure limited and proportional punishment.

Those who celebrate only reason and ratio, and allow only "objective" determinate measures, will disparage or discount non-rational factors that are not amenable to precise measurement. How much should count "the voice of your brother's blood," or the intensity of the victim's suffering, or "especially cruel" when it is so much easier, and more "objective" to count the number of bodies or a defendant's prior convictions?[35] Yet we know intuitively gradations that are real, but neither strictly rational nor discretely measurable.

Most of us painfully remember from high school that with his own theorem, Pythagoras destroyed his whole rational philosophy, when he proved the diagonal of a square was "incommensurable" with its sides. So too, the circumference and diameter of a circle had no measurable ratio. Pythagoras had discovered irrational numbers—real, but not rational.

Similarly today, for many of us death penalty advocates:[36] Utilitarian rationality, a future-oriented calculus of costs and benefits, is inadequate. No strictly rational death penalty law can be constructed and applied exhaustively to achieve justice. We need a richer language that includes non-rational, informed emotion. Moral desert can never be reduced strictly to reason, nor measured adequately by rational criteria: Forgiveness, love, anger, resentment are part of justice. The past counts. Not rationally, but really.[37]

---

35. Professor Laurence Tribe has noted this tendency of quantifiable measures to "dwarf soft variables" (1971:1361).

36. *I.e.,* non-Kantian retributivists—for Kant it is strictly duty, strictly rational, logical and ideological.

37. "Ancient Hebrew law discovering the principle of the sanctity of life, contrasting the severity with which it treats homicide (applying the *lex talion*), with its leniency towards crimes against property. In this view, too, exact retaliation is an advance over compensation, making as

"You Cannot Step in the Same River Twice..."

Heraclitus rejected Pythagoras' ideal of a stable, rational, peaceful and harmonious world. The basic fact was strife; everything was in continuous motion and change, all flux and flow. "You cannot step in the same river twice," he famously summed up, "for fresh waters flow on." Thus, he also rebelled against the Pythagoreans' clear-cut distinctions between good and evil. "To God, all things are good and fair and just"; it was all relative (Guthrie 1962: Vol. I, at 450; 448). A contemporary Heraclitean denies we can meaningfully categorize homicides in advance, by relying on real differences among types of killings. Since everything is in flux, no two situations ever repeat, therefore no two killings are alike. General rules can never deal adequately with non-repeating concrete specific situations. Every killing and killer is unique. And as Heraclitus declared, beneath all apparent calm and stability lies an unceasing struggle and the clash of contrary tensions. In order to reach a "just" result, a jury's verdict of guilt and its sentence of life—or death—must be the product of vigorous contention between active defense counsel and state prosecutor.

Extreme Heracliteans, today's moral anarchists, see the death penalty as the product of strife rather than consensus, where those in power arbitrarily and capriciously kill whom they choose and then call it justice. As Heraclitus insisted, everything was relative; opposites were identical (Guthrie 1962: Vol. I, at 452). One person's "martyr" was another person's "mass murderer." One murder committed by the defendant might be followed by another murder committed by the State. The difference between the worst of the worst and the thoroughly justified was *ad hoc*, depending on who had the power to make the label stick.

For Heraclitus, a river was nothing more than the constantly changing stuff that flowed through it. Any identity must be found in its form (Guthrie 1962: Vol. I, at 467). People, too, were constantly changing. Biologists inform us that all the cells in our bodies periodically are replaced, yet still we are the same persons we were. Or are we? In 1998, over a storm of protest, Texas executed Karla Faye Tucker, who had found Christ in prison. True, this beautiful woman had brutally murdered her two victims with a pick-ax, but by the time the State executed her, her supporters worldwide claimed that Karla Faye had morphed into someone different. Is this metaphor too much of a stretch? Plato used it in the *Symposium*: "Even during the period for which any living being lives and retains his identity—as a man is called the same man from boyhood to old age—he does not in fact retain the same attributes, although he is called the same person," says the wise Diotima to Socrates. "And not only his body, but his soul as well. No man's character, habits, opinions, desires, pleasures,

---

it does the important moral insight that life and property are incommensurable" (Henberg 1990:6).

pains and fears remain always the same: new ones come into existence and old ones disappear" (Guthrie 1962: Vol. I, at 467).

Oddly, those who believe that permanent rehabilitation or redemption is possible must also confront the Heraclitean challenge. Retributivist advocates of a proportional death penalty may acknowledge that while time marks a body, and personality does change, essential character remains constant. "A man's character is his fate." Retributivist advocates must also meet Heraclitus head on and insist that killings do resemble each other in relevant ways. They can be distinguished as more or less deserving of punishment, by criteria specified in advance and applied in an adversary setting.

In the end, even Heraclitus backed away from his extreme moral nihilism, embracing a mysterious concept of a "rational fire" which took physical form and operated as a standard against which all other stuff was measured and evaluated (Guthrie 1962: Vol. I, at 462). Retributivist death penalty supporters today might see this "rational fire" as "informed emotion"—at once subjective, particular, and evanescent—yet an intuitive standard whose heat, when felt, can be applied.

"Man Is the Measure..."

After Parmenides insisted that the entire world of the senses, including movement itself, was all an illusion, and his disciple Zeno backed up these claims with paradoxes that could not be refuted, the Greeks, in disgust at obviously absurd scientific theories, turned their attention inward, away from the universe and onto humankind. "Man is the measure of all things; of the things that are, *that* they are," proclaimed Protagoras, the first and greatest Sophist, "of the things that are not, that they are not" (Guthrie 1962: Vol. II, at 4; Plato 1957:152). A new age of humanism had dawned.

Professional teachers traveled from city to city, publicly competing for big fees, paid by anxious parents eager for their children to master the art of rhetoric so they could entertain at the Assembly and convince at the law courts. Wanting no problems from the local authorities, these Sophists proclaimed that whatever seemed right to an individual or a State, was right. They preached situational ethics: Good was whatever worked; truth whatever people found pleasing and could be persuaded to act upon; reality was appearance; everything was relative, subjective, arbitrary. We live today, and for tomorrow.

Man is the measure—the measured and the measurer.

In the other corner, looking like a boxer with a crushed nose, weighing in tenaciously against this relativist, individualist, empiricist outlook, Socrates battled the Sophists, insisting on "absolute standards, permanent and unvarying truths existing above." And for Plato, Socrates' disciple, good and evil— "concepts such as justice...and equality exist apart from the human mind." They are independent and constant standards "to which human perceptions and human actions can and must be referred" (Guthrie 1962: Vol. II, at 4).

Whether death penalty abolitionist or advocate, this commitment to the transcendence of moral facts such as "human dignity"—or not—still fractures the debate.

To the Sophists the solution was clear: If you convince people and entertain them, they will shower you with money and power. Live in the present; look forward to the future, learn how to manipulate the world to your advantage. A skilled rhetorician can convince anyone of anything. Appearances are deceptive but can be manipulated. Every question has two sides. Argue effectively—there is no truth. Appearance is reality. Whatever a person thinks is good, is good as long as he thinks it. If he thinks stealing from us or killing us is good, we merely have to change his mind.

"In punishing wrongdoers," Protagoras declared, "no one concentrates on the fact that a man has done wrong in the past, or punishes him on that account, unless taking blind vengeance like a beast. No, punishment is not inflicted by a rational man for the sake of the crime that has been committed (after all one cannot undo what is past) but for the sake of the future, to prevent either the same man or, by the spectacle of his punishment, someone else, from doing wrong again" (Plato 1956:324b).

When it came to justifying punishment, Plato also looked forward, insisting in *The Laws*, his last and least idealistic dialogue and the only one where Socrates is absent, that almost every criminal could be rehabilitated through education. Plato did, however, anticipate some "hard shell"—today we call them "hard core"—recidivists who could not be softened to society. Even for these villains, Plato never expressed satisfaction at punishment as retributively deserved for past bad acts. "For truly judgment by sentence of law is never inflicted for harm's sake. Its normal effect is one of two: It makes him that suffers it a better man, or, failing this, less of a wretch." The worst of the worst were simply better off dead: "Longer life is no boon to the sinner himself in such a case, and that his decease will bring a double blessing to his neighbors; it will be a lesson to them to keep themselves from wrong, and will rid society of an evil man. These are the reasons for which a legislator is bound to ordain the chastisement of death for such desperate villainies, and for them alone" (Plato 1978:862e–863).

However they divided on other issues, Plato and Protagoras wanted the death penalty reserved only for incorrigibles, and justified capital punishment by its future benefit to society, especially its deterrent effect. "The ayme of punishment is not a revenge but terrour," concurred Hobbes, the first modern Sophist (Hobbes 1651:355).[38]

---

38. How and why would we punish today's suicide terrorists who are not terrified by death? They believe they are martyrs and will be rewarded, by death. They are coerced into committing suicide. The Model Penal Code mitigates the murder if the defendant believed his killing was

For today's Sophists—who for centuries have been calling themselves utilitarians—no less than for Protagoras, the past has passed. Retribution is "irrational," beastly. The rational person—a rational policy maker—looks only to the future, comparing costs and benefits. Punishment rehabilitates if possible, incapacitates when necessary, but in any case primarily deters. Utilitarians today continue to make capital punishment a question of cost and benefit. And they consult public opinion exclusively for what is just. Does the majority support the death penalty? If so, let's have it—if not, let's not. Man is the measure.

Disparaging polls as beside the point, many abolitionists and all retributive advocates maintain that there are moral facts. The death penalty is humane or inhumane—just or unjust—whether or not it is popular, or most effectively deters murder. There *is* a moral fact of the matter—transcendent, real, and divorced from present practice. Most abolitionists know—not merely believe, but know—that the death penalty is undeserved and inhumane, even if ninety percent of the people support it. Most proponents, both in the United States and Europe, know—also independently of public opinion—that capital punishment is necessary and just. Ironically, retributive advocates and many abolitionists can never ultimately reconcile, precisely because they share this anti-Sophistic commitment to moral facts, which can never be verified by polling.

Today's death penalty debate divides along original fault lines that separated the Sophists from Socrates and Plato. Some opponents seize on the increasing unpopularity of certain practices such as the electric chair, or executing juveniles and the mentally retarded, as grounds to find them unconstitutional. However, when confronted with overwhelming public support for a punishment he considered a basic violation of human dignity, Justice Marshall in *Furman* appealed not to public opinion, but rather to "informed public opinion"—an unwritten, transcendent Platonic ideal if ever there was one.

Less blatant than Protagoras, other justices have used actual public opinion to measure the death penalty's constitutionality. For example, the majority in *Atkins* purported to identify a discernable consensus against executing mentally retarded offenders by relying in part on the momentum of public opinion. Ostensibly reporting events, but in reality trying to effect abolition by changing attitudes, pollsters and leading media like the *New York Times* readily cooperate sophistically by consciously selecting and spinning their coverage, and then report the new "consensus" they so labor to create.

Homicide law Platonists, whatever their opinion about the death penalty, share a conviction that real moral differences exist among killings. The modern consensus that a planned torture murder is worse than an accidental killing

---

morally justified. Gorgias, the Sophist who extolled the art of persuasion above all others, insists that if Helen was persuaded into adultery, she was as guiltless as if she had been abducted by force. This reasoning ripens into today's "domination by another" metaphor.

feels like it must have been true forever. To Demosthenes 2500 years ago, it felt that way too. Punishing deliberate crime but not accidents? "Not only will this be found in the (positive) laws, but nature herself has decreed it in the unwritten laws and in the hearts of men" (Guthrie 1962: Vol. III, at 118).

These objectively different types of killings deserve different responses not because society says so: Society says so because the types really are different. A Platonist perpetually searches further for the real distinctions among homicides that make them more or less deserving of punishment. As did Demosthenes, we look in the unwritten law and the hearts of men.

Sophists scoff. Herodotus showed that customs long accepted as absolute, universal and divine, were in fact local and relative. Many Sophists were atheists or agnostics, their disbelief in the gods based on the prosperity of the wicked and the sufferings of the just. For the Sophist Critias, religious practice and even the gods themselves were human inventions to keep people in check through their fear of punishment. Whereas the Hebrews and the Greeks during the Homeric age regarded law as immutable because divinely inspired, the Sophists saw written law as arbitrary, man-made and shifting.

Denying that moral facts existed apart from popular opinion, Sophists denounced the "unwritten law" (Guthrie 1962: Vol. III, at 70). Long denoting basic moral principles, universally valid, which overruled the positive laws, "unwritten law" now seemed sinister and menacing in a new democratic environment. Democrats saw the written law as the bulwark against tyranny, preventing an exercise of power essentially arbitrary and capricious. Written codes ensured *isonomia*—equal protection of the law—a watchword of the Age. There were "two sides to every question"; everybody's opinion at the Assembly and law courts counted. The People were sovereign; their consensus showed up as law.

When the Supreme Court struck down all state capital punishment regimes as arbitrarily and capriciously administered, a plurality identified the juries' unguided discretion to choose life or death as the fundamental constitutional flaw. Scrambling to meet *Furman's* constitutional objection, many states enacted detailed, written death penalty codes to guide the jury and limit caprice. Some states fully embraced the mathematical ideal of Thales and Pythagoras, enacting mandatory death penalty statutes which specified in writing all and only those factors which, once found, would result in automatic punishment by death.

The Court nevertheless invalidated those mandatory death penalty laws. States now must codify aggravating criteria to ensure equal protection and application of the law. Yet they must always leave possible mitigations *unwritten*. Justice requires mercy, when appropriate to the human heart. And mercy, a key component of the death penalty, requires the unwritten law. On the other hand, abolitionists denounce "non-statutory aggravators"—unwritten law that may tip the scale in favor of death. As Pythagoras discovered that accounting for what is real requires a language richer than the rational, so too we have re-discovered that real justice is much richer than written law.

"Evolving Standards of Decency..."

Today, almost everybody on all sides of the death penalty debate embraces another sophistic article of faith: Progress. Protagoras especially embraced a progressive view of human history. In his myth of creation, Zeus sent Hermes to bring humans two indispensable moral virtues—*dike* and *aidos*. *Dike* is a sense of justice. *Aidos*, more complicated, is most like conscience—combining shame, modesty, and respect for others. Although they were not innate, all people must have these virtues for a community to survive (Guthrie 1962: Vol. III, at 66). Thus, Zeus decreed that anyone incapable of acquiring these virtues must be put to death, "for he is a plague of the state" (Plato 1956:322d). Nothing was objective, but certain feelings and attitudes so polluted the community they mandated death.

Mores may differ in different societies, and people might change their views, but in the long run, human history was progress. All practices and opinions may be equally true, but they were not equally sound. The Sophists were justified in charging people money to help substitute views that, once adopted, seemed and therefore were better. All standards may be variable and changing, but overall they were changing for the better.

This paradoxical faith in real progress while objective values are denied, commands the allegiance of the Court today. "Time works changes," a majority declared in 1910 in *Weems*. The cruel and unusual punishment "clause of the Constitution may be therefore progressive, and is not fastened to the obsolete, but may acquire meaning as public opinion becomes enlightened by a humane justice" (at 378). The Eighth "Amendment must draw its meaning from the evolving standards of decency that mark the progress of a maturing society," Chief Justice Warren declared famously in *Trop* in 1958 (at 101). For the past half century and especially since *Furman*, the entire Court has been thoroughly Protagorean. Public opinion may shift suddenly and wildly after a particularly egregious killing, or after a particularly sympathetic convicted killer is finally executed, but in the long term, society can and does progress. The justices unanimously agree that the constitutional meaning of "cruel and unusual" must cause and reflect that progress.

Abolitionists, such as Justice Brennan in *Furman*, tend to see human progress in the grand scheme as the progressive limitation and eventual elimination of the death penalty. As a matter of history, advocates find it undeniable that over millennia, punishment has become more and more limited. Retributivist advocates also believe in progress. Certain truths may be transcendent and timeless, but our understanding of these moral facts, and practices that reflect this awareness, do evolve and improve. Platonists, motivated by a belief in the possibility of progress and an obligation to achieve it, thus continue to search for moral categories that more nearly result in homicides being classified correctly and killers more nearly getting what they deserve.

Even American constitutional fundamentalists—strict constructionists who embrace the Founders' original intent—concede that some crimes which brought the death penalty in 1788 may not constitutionally do so today.[39] And they also concede that some methods of punishment such as ear cropping, standard at the birth of our Nation, have simply *become* cruel and unusual when measured against modern evolving standards of decency.

However starkly Protagoras and Socrates disagreed about whether justice and truth were entirely subjective, they both believed in progress and the social compact. Having shared in its formation, citizens must submit to the law, even as they struggle to enlighten the ignorant to change it. They must obey that product of an evolving, imperfect but progressing consensus. Thus it was, that facing his own execution based upon wrongful conviction and sentencing, Socrates refused to escape, blaming his unjust fate not on the laws themselves, but on their faulty administration.

Using the same distinction today, many abolitionists ground their opposition to capital punishment on government's inability to administer the penalty fairly, regardless of whether anybody can be said to deserve to die. These opponents, and even some supporters, back a moratorium on executions for as long as it takes to improve the death penalty's administration. Yet, those who would strictly abide by the social compact, having sworn an oath to uphold the Constitution and the law, including public officers personally opposed to the death penalty and private citizens sitting as jurors, ought to subordinate their individual opinions to the public consensus as reflected in the law. Through acting or restraining themselves, they should play their part in moving a killer toward State-sanctioned death. At the same time, motivated by a faith in progress—whether toward some transcendent pre-existent justice or toward practices popularly regarded as humane—like Socrates, they should remonstrate in the courts and the assemblies, and dedicate themselves to improving the regime by eliminating the death penalty.

Other abolitionists, however, like the Sophist Antiphon, deny all obligation flowing from the social compact. Since positive law is arbitrary and capricious, the plaything of the more powerful and persuasive, a person may violate the law when he can get away with it. Some abolitionist judges and jurors share this view, and would nullify the law while pretending to apply it.[40] Abolitionist

---

39. *E.g.*, The First Congress made forgery of federal currency a capital crime.

40. After *Ring*, the first federal court judge to declare the federal death penalty unconstitutional obscured his own personal antipathy in false history and highly questionable doctrine, and his decision was promptly reversed on appeal (*United States v. Quinones* 2002). In *United*

prosecutors do the same. For example, a Manhattan district attorney may declare that he will seek the death penalty according to the New York Penal Law in the "appropriate circumstances." Nevertheless, however heinous a murder or murderer may be, the appropriate circumstances never arise. Such covert disobedience violates the oath of office and the lesson of Socrates. The greater obligation is to submit to the law, all the while openly attempting to persuade the authorities of their mistake. The responsible capital defense counsel, too, adopts that model. But those who proclaim a faith in democracy, while they undermine it by substituting their own personal convictions for the consensus of the moment, may appeal to a consensus in a larger world. Whether world public opinion should inform the Eighth Amendment bitterly divides the U.S. Supreme Court.[41] A majority in the United States may support the death penalty today, abolitionists insist, but a united European Union and Canada have abolished it, in every instance in the teeth of overwhelming public support for its retention.[42]

Individuals thus can justify civil disobedience, as Antiphon himself did, by disparaging local convention in favor of a cosmopolitan, universal human dignity. The Greeks debated whether slavery should be abolished as inhumane, and many abolitionists believe that their campaign is a continuation of a crusade against slavery. The belief that universal laws of nature override local conventions can fuel a death penalty advocate's or abolitionist's genuine commitment to transcendent human dignity. But it had a brutal form historically, and still does today.

Surrounded by the Athenians and desperately trying to stay free and neutral in the war between Athens and Sparta, the inhabitants of the small island of Melos pled for justice with the Athenian representatives sent to convince them to submit. "Justice depends upon the equality of power to compel," Thucydides reports the Athenian representatives as warning. "In fact, the strong do what they can; the weak accept what they must." Forget justice: "What is looked for

---

States v. Fell (2002), however, a second federal judge more plausibly found unconstitutional the statute's relaxed evidentiary standards at sentencing. The stories are legion of single jurors promising during *voir dire* honestly to apply the law, yet at sentencing stubbornly rejecting the death penalty, although under current standards capital punishment is clearly warranted.

41. See *Atkins v. Virginia* (2002: 2249, n. 21) *citing* international opinion, and Chief Justice Rehnquist's dissent attacking that same opinion as irrelevant.

42. Cf., Steiker (2002). European abolitionists use a Protagorean defense that while all opinions are equally true, some are better than others. Elitists, claiming to be democrats, and their American disciples, insist that society does better without a death penalty. Thus, these "representatives" take it upon themselves to shape public opinion, confident that the People will eventually embrace the abolition forced upon them. Following the events of September 11, with rape-murders of children making headlines, European voices called anew for a death penalty, based, however, solely on grounds of deterrence.

is a preponderance of power in action" (Thucydides 1954:358–365). Callicles, the Sophist, scorns Socrates, insisting on the natural right of the strong to dominate the weak. This most selfish view, that the powerful rightfully dominate whenever they can, animates many murderers today, who see their own crimes and society's punishment as equal proof that the only real law is "the law of the jungle." Everyone does what they can get away with, or else dies in the attempt.

Cynics—they called themselves Realists then, and now—see the death penalty regimes as more proof of this philosophy. Legislatures, the People's representatives, supposedly have enacted neutral death penalty statutes to be applied by prosecutors and judges, equally to all. In his famous funeral oration, Pericles declared that in Athens, "Everybody is equal before the law." The United States claims a commitment to world leadership in continuing that humanistic tradition of equal protection of the law: Social status must be divorced from legal rights.

Sure.

Any class-based death penalty, any racist death penalty violates not only human dignity, but also our commitment to equality before the law. In the United States, many capital defendants still do not have competent investigatory, trial and appellate counsel, although more and more leading law firms supply topnotch abolitionist counsel *pro bono* in capital cases. But the core commitment to equality before the law must go deeper than improved counsel and increased funding for the process. *Isonomia* also attaches to how we *define* capital murder—its substance also can be infected with race or class bias.[43]

Our roots, Biblical and secular, demand an emphatic commitment to equality under law, from the definition of capital murder to its punishment by death. Whether from the command of Leviticus to *"love thy neighbor as thyself,"* or the rejection of a blood price, or injunctions in homicide law to treat slave and freeman equally, the message is clear: Like cases must be treated alike; and different cases treated differently. All persons must be treated equally. Equal treatment—*isonomia*—is an ideal at the very core of western humanism. If we fail to reflect this essential egalitarianism in the definition, detection,

---

43. Robbery felony-murder, the aggravator that may have put more people on death row today than all others combined, has a definite race/class bias and effect regardless of the legislature's intent. If the killer's monetary motive correctly aggravates the killing, what are we to say for society's tolerance and respect shown to ranking corporate executives who consciously maintain deadly workplaces, or manufacture unnecessarily lethal products from the best of motives—the profit motive. These "red collar killers" are morally indistinguishable from other mass murderers who, with a depraved indifference, kill unsuspecting innocents. Not only are these pillars of the community never executed; they are rarely indicted, much less imprisoned. Unless we are to confirm the cynicism of Callicles and street killers, we must respond to hired killers *as* hired killers, across class and race.

prosecution, and punishment of murder, we only will have confirmed Thrasymachus' definition of justice as "the interest of the stronger." Transcendent or progressing, our death penalty must never arbitrarily divide homicide into more or less egregious types that reflect only the desires of the dominant, with power and money to impose on the rest.

"On the Impulse of the Moment"

Socrates squared off against the Sophists. Whereas the Sophists saw a world where all was arbitrary, relative, and subjective, Socrates insisted on absolute objective values capable of being known, but very difficult to put into practice. As Guthrie observes, Socrates "lived and went to his death in the conviction that the moral problem: 'What am I to do?' cannot be adequately answered without an antecedent knowledge of objective standards of value" (Guthrie 1962: Vol. III, at 328, n.2).

Today, informed death penalty reformists who pursue moral refinements in substance and process while they administer the ultimate punishment in a deeply flawed system, embrace Socrates' amalgam of humility about substance and also his confidence in the method. Like Socrates, we first collect instances that almost all would agree are the worst of the worst. Next, we examine these cases to find common qualities, or the essential characteristics they share. Socrates, with Plato and Aristotle, maintained that after examining enough particular instances, the human mind had an innate, intuitive ability inductively to divine their common essence (Guthrie 1962: Vol. III, at 429). This common quality or nexus of common qualities—"the one thing said of them all, running through them all, in them all, that by which they are all the same"—was their nature, essence, form, idea (Guthrie 1962: Vol. III, at 432).

The Supreme Court has upheld this methodology in *Furman* and its progeny, and repeatedly demanded that state legislatures guide jury discretion over life and death by "objective" categories—aggravators distinguished and defined in advance—capable in practice of being applied so as to ensure punishment proportionally correlated to desert or deterrence.

Rejecting the retributive assertion that "especially heinous, atrocious, and cruel" captures a real idea, a real essence of the most vicious and contemptible killings, the Court thus far has disqualified this aggravator (but not "torture"), as unconstitutional because it is essentially ill-defined, vague, subjective, and prone to be misapplied. Other aggravating circumstances, such as "in the course of and furtherance of robbery," "killing more than one victim," "endangering several other persons at the time of the killing," and "serving a life sentence" may be precise and provable by objective facts. But mental states or attitudes which can deservedly make a killer death-eligible, such as "extreme recklessness with a depraved indifference to human life," "cold, calculated, premeditated," and "especially heinous, atrocious, and cruel," are equally real and morally more relevant, despite their fuzzy boundaries. Just because we can list and define an aggravator objectively and distinctly—because we can apply it consistently—hardly means it justifies making a killer death-eligible. Furthermore, as Aristotle emphasized repeatedly, we cannot discover nor should we demand the same precision in ethics as in science.

Although Plato proposed a homicide code which in substance went well beyond the traditional distinctions of intentional, negligent, accidental, and justifiable killings, he would have continued ancient and traditional practices, such as the dying victim's prerogative to pardon the killer (Plato 1978:868), and most emphatically, blood pollution, which he saw attaching automatically at the moment of the slaying with no need for a public pronouncement. Secular and rational, Plato nevertheless insisted on modern respect for the "venerable and ancient myth" that a victim who had died by violence "has his wrath kindled against the author of his death while the deed is still fresh. How he is likewise filled with fear and horror by his own bloody fate, how he is aghast to see his murderer haunting walks that were once familiar and his own." Because of the victim's "distract[ed] soul," Plato would continue to deny parole forever to any killer who fled before trial. If the alleged killer stayed, anybody could prosecute, and if found guilty, "the convicted offender shall be put to death, and shall not receive burial in the land of his victim" (Plato 1978:865d–e, 871d).

Parricide was the most "purely wicked homicide" imaginable to Plato, "for which it is a grim and repulsive task even to provide in a legislation." Any son otherwise tempted to commit such an act should be terrified by that "tale—or doctrine—call it what you please, on the authority of the priests of ancient days," that "tells us expressly that there is a justice watching to avenge a kinsman's blood, and…that he who has dealt in such guilt shall infallibly be done by as he has done" (Plato 1978:872c–e). Thus, in this mythological form of divine retribution, the gods would ensure that:

> If any man have slain his father, there shall come a time when he shall have to suffer the same violent end at the hands of a child; if his mother, his certain doom in later days is to be born himself a female creature, and in the end, to have his life taken by those whom he borne. When pollution has been brought on the common blood, there is no other way of purification but this; the stain refuses to be effaced until the guilty soul have paid life for life, like for like, and this atonement lulled the wrath of the whole lineage to sleep (Plato 1978:872e–873a).

This stern warning was remarkably similar to the Old Testament—as it was done, so shall it be done, in this world or the next. For Plato, this was "truth… firmly believed by those who occupy themselves with such matters…that vengeance is taken on such crimes beyond the grave, and when the sinner has returned to our own world once more, he must infallibly pay nature's penalty—must be done by as he did—and end the life he is now living by the like violence at another's hand" (Plato 1978:870d–e).

Even as they witness a brutal murderer continue to enjoy and live a long life while the memory of the suffering victim decays, many abolitionists, especially religious Christians today, maintain their moral equilibrium through faith that justice will be done in the hereafter. However, ours is a society that separates church and state, and commits itself to human justice in this world.

What should we do to that worst of all non-believers—undeterred by "the dread of vengeance from heaven"—a son who contrives and deliberately slays his own father to inherit more quickly? The "magistrates shall put him to death," urges Plato, then "cast him out naked, outside the city at an appointed place," where "all the magistrates, in the name of the State, shall take each man his stone and cast it on the head of the corpse as in expiation for the State" (Plato 1978:873a–b). The body was not to be buried. This most extreme punishment, this collective ritual expression of extreme disgust, was inflicted on the killer's body only after execution, much like the Old Testament's hanging after death. Even here, however, there must be no torture. Certain punishments were simply too cruel and unusual, however heinous the crime.

The same penalty the Lord rejected for Cain as too painful in Genesis—being exiled at the perpetual mercy of hostile forces—Plato too, rejected: "For no offense whatsoever shall any man be made a hopeless outlaw, not even though he have fled beyond our borders. Death, prison, stripes, ignominious postures of sitting or standing…fines—these shall be our punishments" (Plato 1978:855c).

Essentially continuing traditional practices and punishments, Plato greatly refined homicide law substantively, by classifying killers according to their psychology. Anticipating today's aggravator, "killing from a pecuniary motive," Plato identified greed as "the chief source of the most aggravated charges of willful homicide." Also noting "the spirit of rivalry with its brood of jealousies and dangerous company," Plato anticipated today's "gang related" and "drug related" capital murders. His classification of killing committed from "craven and guilty terrors," especially motivated by fear that another person will expose past, private misdeeds, presaged today's "killing a witness" aggravator. A person who ordered a killing was, for Plato, nearly as guilty as the assassin; he was to be executed, but allowed to be buried in his native land. Plato's proposed homicide code was designed not for an ideal world but for this one—not for heroes, but for "slips of humanity" (1978:853c).

The Laws became most nuanced when Plato distinguished two types of intentional but passion-driven homicides: "It is an act of passion when a man is done away with on the impulse of the moment, by blows or the like, suddenly and without any previous purpose to kill, and remorse instantly follows on the act. It is also an act of passion when a man is roused by insult in words or dishonoring gestures, pursues his revenge, and ends by taking a life with purpose to slay and without subsequent remorse for the deed" (Plato 1978:866d–e).

Was a spur of the moment killing where the actor "lost it" for a moment and instantly regretted it, as bad as the "slow burn" or passion boiling and bubbling from insult or injury which ripened into a plan to kill? Are these distinctions with or without a moral difference? Did the killings differ only in degree or were they different in kind? Is the distinction relevant to judgments about which killers should live or die?

The Old Testament made the defendant's anger a basis for inferring premeditated intent and thus death-eligibility. This was refined in 1727 in *King v. Oneby*, and for the next 250 years in Anglo-American common law an intentional killing committed in "the heat of passion," but only on a "sudden quarrel," was manslaughter and therefore not death-eligible. If the defendant's passion "cooled" even for an instant, if he showed he could calculate or "deliberate" about anything, the killing was no longer passionate and the crime no longer manslaughter, but murder and deserving of death (*Oneby* 1727:465).

But Plato had not been so sure: "I take it we cannot treat these as two distinct forms of homicide; both may fairly be said to be due to passion and to be partially voluntary, partially involuntary." On the other hand:

> The man who nurses his passion and takes his revenge not at the moment and on the spot, but afterward and of set purpose, resembles the deliberate murderer. He who does not bottle up his wrath but expends it all at once, on the spot, without premeditation, is like the involuntary homicide; still we cannot say that even he is altogether an involuntary agent, though he is like one. Hence the difficulty of deciding whether homicides of passion should be treated in law as intentional or, in some sense, unintentional (Plato 1978:866e–867b).

Not until 1980 did the New York Court of Appeals catch up with Plato, holding that "simmering" emotional disturbance, no less than explosive rage, could mitigate murder to manslaughter. (*People v. Casassa* 1980).

Plato had pressed on. "The best and soundest procedure," the Athenian declared,

> is to class each sort with that which it resembles, discriminating the one from the other by the presence or absence of premeditation and legally visiting the slaughter where there is premeditation as well as angry feeling with a severer sentence while that which is committed on the spur of the moment and without purpose aforethought with a milder sentence. That which is like the graver crime should receive the graver punishment, that which resembles the lighter, a lighter (Plato 1978:867b–c).

Plato's psychology became more subtle when he allowed emotion to mitigate the killing, but less completely where emotion drives planning. Plato ultimately made it a matter of degree, providing a longer banishment for passionate but premeditated killing than for sudden passionate killing—but in neither
circumstance was death deserved. Like Plato, modern statutes distinguish two
types of passion killings: Adequately provoked passion mitigates murder to
manslaughter; inadequately provoked passion is still murder, but may, although it need not, tip the balance from death to life.

For Aristotle, every moral question, including the justice of death as punishment, necessarily involved emotions. "It is easy to get angry—anyone can
do that...but to feel or act towards the right person to the right extent at the
right time for the right reason in the right way—that is not easy, and not
everyone can do it" (Aristotle 1953:1109a). The killer's feelings count, but so
too, do society's when we decide whether to kill in return.

Aristotle repeatedly warned that precision is impossible: "It is not easy to
determine what is the right way to be angry, and with whom, and on what
grounds, and for how long" (Aristotle 1953:1126a). Should society be angry at
rapists who murder and mutilate children? How angry? Why? For how long?
And most important, "What is the right way to be angry?" These challenges
confront legislatures in establishing punishments, and also juries in deciding
between life and death in particular cases.

At the penalty phase of a capital trial, the defense typically argues that the
killing is not reflective of the defendant's character. Aristotle saw passion
killings as a particularly unreliable basis on which to judge character: "All acts
due to temper or any other of the unavoidable and natural feelings to which
human beings are liable...are injuries; but this does not of itself make them
unjust or wicked men, because the harm that they did was not due to malice; it
is when a man does a wrong on purpose that he is unjust and wicked" (Aristotle 1953:1135). "A man may lie with a married woman...under the influence of
passion. Then although his conduct is unjust, he is not an unjust man; I mean
that the act of stealing does not make a man a thief, nor the act of adultery
make him an adulterer; and similarly in *all* other cases" (Aristotle 1953:1134a,
emph. added). A person who has killed another does not thereby become "a
killer." His conduct—an act and its accompanying mental state—was murder;
yet his character may not be that of a murderer. What a person does is not necessarily who he is. Deliberate "choice," observes Aristotle wisely, "seems...a
more reliable criterion for judging character than actions are" (Aristotle
1953:1111b).

The actor's intent and motive counted heavily in deciding his moral blameworthiness. But outcomes do not always match intentions. What if the would-
be murderer failed in his purpose, and his victim, although wounded, fortunately survived? Plato wrestled with the perennial challenge of balancing intent
and harm, including how to respond to offenses such as attempted murder and

assault with the intent to kill. "If anyone intend and purpose the death of a person with whom he is on friendly terms, he who wounds but fails to kill with such intent deserves no mercy, and shall be made to stand his trial for homicide with as little scruple as though he had killed" (Plato 1978:876e–877a).

Do we do to him as he has done, or as he would have done? Is attempted murder as bad as murder? Was Kant correct that the only purely evil thing is an evil will? Or should the would-be murderer get the benefit of the victim's good luck? These questions continue to plague us. The Supreme Court would almost certainly find the death penalty disproportionate for attempted murder, even for a would-be mass-murdering terrorist like the recent shoe-bomber who was only prevented from blowing up an airplane full of people by the last moment interference of alert passengers and crew.

Uncharacteristically irrational, Plato, too, would credit the lucky: "The law will show its reverence for his…propitious fortune…which has, in mercy to both wounder and wounded, preserved the one from a fatal hurt and the other from incurring a curse and disaster. It will show its gratitude and submission…by sparing the criminal's life and dooming him to lifelong banishment to the nearest state, where he shall enjoy his revenues in full" (Plato 1978:877a–b).

Attitude counts, but so does luck. Death is different.

"If We Know Anything We Know This…"

"The most indisputable of all beliefs," Aristotle called it: "Contradictory statements are not at the same time true." The law of non-contradiction is the most elementary law of logic. A thing cannot be and not be in the same sense at the same time (Aristotle 1941:1005b). "Our jurisprudence and logic have long since parted ways," Justice Scalia bemoaned. The law cannot require and prohibit the same practice at the same time. "The practice *Furman* pronounced Constitutionally prohibited, *Woodson* and *Lockett* pronounced Constitutionally required" (*Walton v. Arizona* 1990:657, 663).

Is the Supreme Court's whole modern death penalty jurisprudence self-contradictory? Consider its well known outlines through the prism of ancient antagonism.

"You are entirely free to act according to your own judgment, conscience and absolute discretion," McGautha's jury had been instructed. Beyond life or death, "the law itself provides no standard for [your] guidance" (*McGautha v. California* 1971:183). The Supreme Court held in *McGautha* that it did not violate due process for states to give juries "absolute discretion" to decide life or death. There was no real alternative to standardless discretion, the majority declared: "No formula is possible that would provide a reasonable criterion for the infinite variety of circumstances that may affect the gravity of murder" (*citing* Royal Commission on Capital Punishment § 595). It was simply, "beyond present human ability...to identify before the fact characteristics of homicides and their perpetrators which call for the death penalty." The flux and flow of different circumstances, their infinite complexity made every killing different. Situations do not repeat; every person is unique. Because we cannot step in the same river twice, the *McGautha* majority permitted absolute discretion. "The very antithesis of due process," the dissent called this same standardless discretion; "nothing more than government by whim" (at 250).

The next year, *Furman v. Georgia* reversed course and ushered in the modern age of capital punishment by striking down as "cruel and unusual" the death penalties haphazardly administered across the United States. Absolute discretion allowed for race and class bias, and produced arbitrariness resulting in the execution of a "capriciously selected random handful" (*Furman v. Georgia* 1972:248, opinion of Douglas, J.). In *Furman*, the Supreme Court demanded of death penalty law in the United States what Pythagoras had demanded of the *kosmos:* that it impose limits on the unlimited to make the limited. That there be proportional punishment based on rational criteria.

Reacting to *Furman*, the states adopted structured death penalty statutes, based largely on the Model Penal Code. Four years later, the first post-*Furman* death sentences reached the Supreme Court: "The Georgia legislature has plainly made an effort to guide the jury's discretion, while at the same time permitting the jury to dispense mercy on the basis of factors too intangible to write into a statute, and [we] cannot accept...that the effort is bound to fail," three justices concurred, upholding the new state statute (*Gregg v. Georgia* 1976:221). "Furman mandates...discretion must be suitably directed and limited," Justice Stewart said for the plurality (at 189). Georgia, Florida, Texas had satisfied that requirement. A state could have it both ways—limited aggravation with unlimited mercy.

At the same time it upheld states' "guided discretion" legislation, the Court struck down mandatory death penalties. Death could not be imposed automatically, even for aggravated murder (*Woodson v. North Carolina* 1976). The Constitution prohibited standardless capital sentencing discretion and required guided discretion. Mandatory death penalties, however, gave sentencers no discretion at all. *Lockett v. Ohio* (1978) built upon *Woodson's* constitutional demand for "particularized consideration," holding that a jury "may not be precluded from considering as a mitigating factor any aspect of a defendant's character" (at 304). Lest mercy be prevented, "respect due to the uniqueness of the individual" (at 304) forbade defining mitigating circumstances exhaustively in advance.

"The Court has now completed its about-face since *Furman*," complained Justice White, dissenting in *Lockett* (at 631). "Today's opinion undercuts *Furman*," Justice Rehnquist agreed (at 631). Allowing the defendant to offer "any fact, however bizarre...will not eliminate arbitrariness but codify and institutionalize it." In short, "it can scarcely be maintained that today's decision is the logical application of a coherent doctrine" (at 629).

Two streams of cases flowed from *Furman*. *Gregg* and its progeny required consistency, based on aggravators clearly defined by the legislature and regularly applied in practice. The other line of cases, based on *Woodson* and *Lockett*, required that each offender be considered individually, as a concrete but complex, unique human being. Together, these doctrines seemed simultaneously to prohibit and require a jury's absolute discretion. As a matter of basic logic, "at least one of these judicially announced irreconcilable commands must be wrong," Scalia insisted (*Walton v. Arizona* 1990:673). Was the jury's discretion to decide life or death limited, or not? Surely it could not be both. Aristotle had laid our logical foundations: "The same attribute cannot at the same time belong and not belong to the same subject and in the same respect." This was "the most certain of all principles. If we know anything, we know this" (Aristotle 1941:1005b).

Purportedly then, the Court's modern Eighth Amendment jurisprudence has been built on two core values—consistency and fairness. However, consistency—essentially treating like cases alike and ensuring equality before the law—clashed directly with fairness—treating every human being as a unique individual and recognizing that the measure of a person is more than a single act. Heraclitus may have delighted in contradiction and the simultaneous truth of opposites, but Heraclitean "logic" was to Aristotle what the Supreme Court's jurisprudence is to Justice Scalia and like-minded critics—simply "absurd" (*Walton v. Arizona* 1990:667).

The Court "has completely exploded whatever coherence the notion of 'guided discretion' once had," Justice Scalia complained (*Walton v. Arizona* 1990:661). The basic doctrine of the whole post-*Furman* era rested on illogic—a "simultaneous pursuit of contradictory objectives" (at 667). The entire show was nothing more than a "jurisprudence containing the contradictory commands that discretion to impose the death penalty must be limited but discretion not to impose it must be unconstrained" (at 668).

"This Court's Eighth Amendment jurisprudence is *not so patently irrational* that it should be abruptly discarded," Justice Blackmun countered weakly, for four dissenting Justices in *Walton*, damning death penalty logic with faint praise (at 680). Four years later in 1994, near the end of his career, Blackmun himself was finally driven over the edge (*Callins v. Collins* 1994).

Accumulating evidence from the modern era finally convinced him that a death penalty could never be "at once consistent and principled but also humane and sensible to the uniqueness of the individual," as the Court previously had demanded (*Eddings v. Oklahoma* 1982:110). The Court's modern jurisprudential contradiction could never be reconciled in practice.[44] To chase the problem "down one hole"—whether fairness or consistency—was to force it

---

44. "Experience has taught us that the Constitutional goal of eliminating arbitrariness and discrimination from the administration of death can never be achieved without compromising

out the other. This irrationality released Justice Blackmun's long-standing deep-seated personal revulsion at the death penalty. Now at long last, when his understanding had finally caught up to his feelings, the Justice could famously proclaim: "From this day forward I no longer shall tinker with the machinery of death" (*Callins v. Collins* 1994:1130). Justice Scalia publicly welcomed his new ally into the logical fold, joining "those of us who have acknowledged the incompatibility of the Court's *Furman* and *Lockett-Eddings* lines of jurisprudence" (at 1128).

If the whole modern death penalty jurisprudence did rest on self-contradictory logical foundations and therefore was impossible in practice, the jurisprudence if not the death penalty itself must be discarded. Rather than continuing to "coddle the Court's delusion," Justice Blackmun would have abolished the death penalty as unconstitutional *(Callins v. Collins* 1994:1130). Justice Scalia, on the other hand, would abandon the entire *"Woodson-Lockett"* line of reasoning. Fairness would no longer be constitutionally guaranteed; mandatory death penalty schemes without individualized attention to the murderer's character would be permitted. For Scalia, even "cruel" punishment was permissible, as long as it was regularly applied. A constitutional fundamentalist, Justice Scalia would rest a jurisprudence of death on consistent if non-humane, solid logical foundations: "If it is not [unusual] then the Eighth Amendment does not prohibit it, no matter how cruel" (*Walton v. Arizona* 1990:670).

The assault on the logical "machinery of death," begun by Justices Marshall and Brennan, now championed by Scalia and Blackmun, demanded rebuttal. More than any other member of the Supreme Court in the modern era, Justice Stevens has upheld the logic of states' death penalty machinery, even as he has helped construct a capital jurisprudence founded on fairness and consistency. Upholding Georgia's death penalty regime as a model in *Zant v. Stephens* (1983), Stevens adopted the state supreme court's analysis of its own statute: Georgia law was a pyramid which contained "all cases of homicide of every category." The punishment became more severe as one moved "from the base to the apex, with the death penalty applying only to those few cases which are contained in the space just beneath the apex. To reach that category a case must pass through three planes of division" (at 871).

The first plane separated the murderers from lesser homicides such as reckless manslaughter, accidental killings, and self-defense. Here "the function of the trier of facts is limited to finding facts. The plane remains fixed unless moved by legislative act." The second plane separated out the death-eligibles. Again, a jury as factfinder must find aggravating factors previously defined by statute. And "the third plane separates from all cases in which...death *may be*

---

an equally essential component of fundamental fairness—individualized sentencing" (*Callins v. Collins* 1994:1129, Blackmun, J., dissenting).

imposed, those cases in which it *shall be* imposed. There is an *absolute discretion* in the factfinder to place any given case below the plane and not impose death" (*Walton v. Arizona* 1990:717, citing *Zant v. Stephens* 1983:871, emphasis added).

In short, consistency could be demanded at the stage of death-eligibility; fairness, however, required absolute discretion in the selection of who lives or dies. The scheme involved one "final limitation." The Georgia Supreme Court trumpeted itself as the last great backstop against arbitrariness. Reviewing the jury's exercise of discretion in the automatic appeal, the state's high court would decide whether the death penalty was "imposed under the influence of passion, prejudice, or any other arbitrary factor; whether the statutory aggravating circumstances are supported by the evidence; and whether the sentence of death is excessive or disproportionate to the penalty imposed in similar cases" (*Zant v. Stephens* 1983:872).

Justice Marshall, in dissent, had scoffed at this notion. "Under today's decision all the State has to do is require the jury to make some threshold finding. Once that finding is made, the jurors can be left completely at large, with nothing to guide them but their whims and prejudices" (*Zant v. Stephens* 1983:910, dissenting opinion). Georgia's death penalty structure made "an absolute mockery" of *Furman* (at 910).

"Two themes have been reiterated in our opinions," Stevens countered (*Zant v. Stephens* 1983:884). "There can be no perfect procedure," as Chief Justice Rehnquist had declared (at 904). But because death was qualitatively different from all other punishment, "It is of vital importance to the defendant and to the community that any decision to impose the death sentence be and appear to be, based on reason rather than caprice or emotion" (at 885).

Although sharply disagreeing on the constitutionality of the death penalty and the coherence of the logic which supported it in *Zant*, Justice Marshall, Justice Stevens, and the Georgia Supreme Court all rejected emotion as irrational and thoroughly inappropriate for deciding life or death. That decision, all sides agreed, must be entirely rational—the product of rational categories clearly defined and accurately applied. Otherwise, said Marshall, it was "mere prejudice and whim" (*Zant v. Stephens* 1983:910).

Furman outlawed caprice and demanded "guided discretion," thus requiring every state with a death penalty to impose limits on the unlimited to make the limited. By insisting that individual persons are unique and forbidding an exhaustive list of mitigating factors, the *Lockett-Eddings* line of decisions effectively outlawed Socrates' program of collecting instances, then finding the common essence, and categorizing exhaustively in advance all and only those who deserve to die. We could not step in the same situation twice for new characters and fresh facts flow on. Pythagoras or Heraclitus? Justice Scalia demanded in effect: One or the other (and possibly neither)— but not both.

In a world where logic is strictly limited to non-emotional rationality, Scalia's scathing attack seems persuasive. Choosing between life and death, after all, involves only a single decision. The Court cannot logically command *unlimited* discretion *not to* impose death *and* at the same time insist on *limited* discretion *to* impose the death penalty. X—limited discretion—cannot be both true and false, commanded and prohibited, in the same sense at the same time. Like Heraclitus' tightly strung bow apparently resting in a corner, underlying the modern era's seemingly stable reconciliation of fairness with consistency is a tension of irreconcilable warring opposites. If examined through a strictly limited rational lens, death penalty jurisprudence—at once demanding fairness and consistency—does appear internally incoherent.

Rejecting emotion as irrational and unlawful, defenders of the Court's current death penalty jurisprudence are hamstrung: "The size of the class may be narrowed to reduce sufficiently that risk of arbitrariness," declared Justice Stevens valiantly, "even if a jury is then given complete discretion to show mercy when evaluating the individual characteristics of the few individuals who have been found death-eligible" (*Walton v. Arizona* 1990:716). But could "showing mercy" and "evaluating" a person's character be accomplished strictly rationally by applying general criteria?

The "final stage" or penalty phase of a capital trial is "significantly different" from the guilt phase, concurred Justice Rehnquist in *Zant*. The jury at sentencing "makes a unique individualized judgment regarding the punishment that a particular person deserves" (*Zant v. Stephens* 1983:900).

All supporters of the Supreme Court's jurisprudence in this modern era demand fairness and consistency. Retributivist supporters of the death penalty especially need to show how both core values can be respected simultaneously—how we can generally treat like cases alike and at the same time act on the uniqueness of each particular case. We need a special kind of justice that can give us fairness *and* consistency, and we need a language rich enough to meet that challenge.

Heraclitus and Pythagoras, Plato and Aristotle show us the way.

Pythagoras' proof of incommensurability had exploded his own philosophy that rationality, discreteness, and proportionality underlay the *kosmos*, and formed a well-ordered whole. Real numbers are not all rational. The guilt phase narrows the class of death-eligible offenders rationally, factually, according to general criteria. The sentencing phase, however, assesses more than guilt—more than conduct, it measures character. In deciding between life and death, we need an incommensurably richer language to express, and a particular non-rational human faculty of moral intuition to measure, character and desert.

Because the debate during the modern era of the death penalty has taken place almost exclusively on a rational plane, it has failed to use real but non-rational language to explain the particular justice of desert. Without emotion we are trapped in "Flatland."[45] It may sound mystical, new age, and eccentric to insist that rationality, reason, proportionality, and issues of fact do not, and cannot exhaust the inquiry. Although the discovery of a real language "unutterably" richer than the rational was startling for Pythagoras, the need for a concept of justice that transcends general consistency to reconcile it with the defendant's particular humanity was neither new age nor mystical to Aristotle, the rationalist, nor to Plato, his teacher.

"Law can never issue an injunction binding on all which really embodies what is best for each," Plato declared in the *Statesman*; "it cannot prescribe with accuracy what is best and just for each member of the community at any one time. The differences of human personality, the variety of men's activities, and the restless inconstancy of all human affairs make it impossible [to] issue unqualified rules holding good on all questions at all times" (Plato 1957:294b).

Death "is the one punishment that cannot be prescribed by a rule of law," Justice Stevens declared (without citing Plato), arguing unsuccessfully at the time that only juries and not judges in capital trials could be constitutionally entrusted with the decision of life or death (*Spaziano v. Florida* 1984:469). The death penalty, Stevens insisted, was "ultimately understood only as an expression of the community's outrage—its sense that an individual has lost his moral entitlement to live" (at 469). A community's "outrage"—its "moral sense"—must be more than a strictly rational measurement, but this was as close as Justice Stevens came to explicitly acknowledging the richer realm of real informed emotion necessary for capital justice.

The Court has by and large united to imprison itself on a rational plane. Distrusting the citizenry, fearing that hatred cannot be bridled and once admitted must inevitably burst into uncontrollable prejudice and blind rage, the Court has sought to suppress emotion entirely. The dead victim's family are allowed their grief and public sound bites of fury. A grim detached rationality is expected of the rest of us, including the jury that decides the killer's fate.

In *McGautha*, where the majority affirmed "standardless discretion," the trial judge had instructed the jury that "[you] may be influenced by pity...and

---

45. Edwin Abbott, a mathematician, wrote the charming parable *Flatland*, in which the characters—circles, squares, and triangles all live on a plane, disparaging the points who live in only one dimension. A sphere visits from Spaceland and lifts up a circle from the plane to get a sense of "up". Returning to Flatland, the circle preaches a third dimension, insisting on a language rich enough to include—"up". Proclaiming a richer reality lands the circle in prison (Abbott 1884). While the Georgia Supreme Court did use the three-dimensional pyramid to explain its jurisprudence, it could have done so with no loss of meaning by using triangles with bases and apexes. Perhaps the more apt analogy from plane geometry, for Georgia, would be concentric circles moving toward the center of evil.

you may be governed by mere sentiment and sympathy" (*McGautha v. California* 1971:189). *Absolute* discretion might include anything. Yet, McGautha's jury was warned, the "law does forbid you from being governed by mere conjecture, prejudice, public opinion or public feeling" (at 189). But that was pre-*Furman*. Post-*Furman*, there was no place for emotion in the law. So in *California v. Brown* (1987), the Supreme Court allowed a jury, when deciding life or death, to be strictly prohibited from being "swayed by mere sentiment... sympathy, or passion" (at 538). Justice O'Connor, attempting to resolve the conflict between fairness and consistency, issued the Court's new watchword: The death sentence must be "a reasoned moral response" to the evidence (at 545, concurring opinion). Sentencing was "a moral inquiry into the culpability of the defendant, and not an emotional response to the mitigating evidence" she insisted (at 545), as if it could ever be moral if it were not also partly emotional.

"It is impossible, then, for something invariable and unqualified to deal satisfactorily with what is never uniform and constant," Plato had declared (1957:294c). Thus, a "legislator... in matters of right... will never be able in the laws he prescribes for the whole group to give every individual his due with absolute accuracy" (at 294e–295). Aristotle agreed. Like Plato, he revered the law as a rational, consistent application of general rules. Yet he too wrestled with its limitations in particular cases of human conduct: "It is obvious that to rule by the letter of the law or out of a book is not the best method.... On the other hand, rulers cannot do without a general principle to guide them; it provides something which, being without personal feelings is better than that which by its nature does feel. A human being must have feelings; a law has none. Against that one might say that a man will give sounder counsel than law in individual cases. It seems clear then that... laws must be laid down, which shall be binding in all cases, *except those in which they fail to meet the situation*" (Aristotle 1962:139, emphasis added).

Who could know, and how, when rational criteria strictly applied failed to do justice? Could rationality alone demonstrate the limits of rationality alone? And when the law failed, how could people "deal with these undetermined matters to the very best of their just judgement?" Setting the tone for modern jurisprudence, Aristotle struggled to deny emotion: "He who asks Law to rule is asking God and Intelligence and no others to rule; while he who asks for the rule of a human being is bringing in a wild beast; for human passions are like a wild beast and strong feelings lead astray rulers and the very best of men. In law you have the intellect without the passions" (Aristotle 1962:143).

But in the end, there was nowhere else to turn but to human beings—passionate and unregulated—for that necessary supplement to "reasonable consistency" which makes true moral justice possible. "The advocates of the rule of law do not deny this," Aristotle conceded, "do not suggest that the intervention of a human being in such decisions is unnecessary; they merely say that there should be not one person only but many" (Aristotle 1962:145). Thus, "when the law either will not work at all or will only work badly" in singular instances, the power to correct it should not rest with a single person. "As a larger amount of water is less easily polluted, so a larger number of people is less easily corrupted than a few," Aristotle observed, reluctantly admitting an *ad hoc* decision-making based upon collective human deliberation inevitably guided by informed emotion. "The judgement of one man is bound to be warped if he is in a bad temper or has very strong feelings about something. But...it would take a lot of doing to arrange for all simultaneously to lose their tempers and warp their judgements" (Aristotle 1962:140). "A capital sentencing jury representative of a criminal defendant's community assures a *'diffused impartiality,'*" Justice Powell agreed. (emph. added) (*McCleskey v. Kemp* 1987:310, quoting *Witherspoon v Illinois* 1968:519).

Can we conceive, much less put into practice, an equitable death penalty regime that provides "fairness and consistency"? Plato embraced the written law as "the fruit of long experience," and yet imagined "the true Statesman," who would know when to "allow his activities to be dictated by his *art* and pay no regard to written prescriptions. He will do this whenever he is convinced that there are other measures which are better" (Plato 1957:300b–c). The jury at the guilt phase are like all other citizens, bound strictly by the written law. Once they decide guilt, however, at the sentencing phase, the jury become a "*true statesman*." With the code to guide but not bind them, they are bound to do their best in this particular case.

Aristotle, ever practical, saw little chance of a true statesman ever emerging in this world, but rested his faith on the jury to approach the ideal as nearly as possible. The jurors would be empowered to do justice. But justice must transcend the universalism of the strictly legal and encompass the infinitely more complex particular human dimension. And thus, in the *Ethics*, Aristotle gave the West "equity" — "*neither absolutely identical nor generically different*" from legal justice (Aristotle 1962:1137a). "Although both are morally good, the equitable is better of the two" (at 1137b).

Thus, fairness did limit consistency: "What causes the problem," said Aristotle, "is that the equitable is not just in the legal sense of 'just' but as a corrective of what is legally just. The reason is that all law is universal, but there are some things about which it is not possible to speak correctly in universal terms. Now, in situations where it is necessary to speak in universal terms but impossible to do so correctly," we need equity. "So in such a situation in which the law speaks universally, but the case at issue happens to fall outside the universal formula, it is correct to rectify the shortcoming," Aristotle explained. "Such a rectification corresponds to what the lawgiver himself would have said if he were present, and what he would have enacted if he had known of this particular case" (Aristotle 1962:1137b). In a democracy the People are the lawgiver. Their legislatures enact general statutes. And later in court, with a particular capital case before them, their juries further shape the law.[46]

Modern death penalty jurisprudence—both equitable and legal—demands and supplies fairness and consistency. "That is why the equitable is both just and also better than the just in one sense," Aristotle explained. "This is also the reason why not all things are determined by law.... For where a thing is indefinite, the rule by which it is measured is also indefinite [and] shifts with the contour." It is, in short, "adapted to a given situation" (Aristotle 1962:1137b).

"If this is not a scheme based on 'standardless jury discretion,' what is?" Justice Marshall had demanded in *Zant* (at 906). But at the sentencing phase, has the jury really been "left completely at large, with nothing to guide them but their whims and prejudices" (at 910)? Because it will be emotional must it thereby be pernicious and uninformed?

"In the final analysis, capital punishment rests on not a legal but an ethical judgment—an assessment of what we called in *Enmund* the 'moral guilt' of the defendant," Justice Stevens had insisted, dissenting in *Spaziano*. "And if the decision that capital punishment is the appropriate sanction in extreme cases is justified because it expresses the community's moral sensibility—its demand that a given affront to humanity requires retribution—it follows I believe... that the life or death decision depends upon its link to community values for its moral and constitutional legitimacy" (*Spaziano v. Florida* 1984:483).[47] Eighteen years later, in *Ring v. Arizona* (2002), he finally became part of a majority which recognized that retributively, only a jury could reliably make this moral and emotional decision.[48]

Abolitionists and advocates during our modern era who have fought valiantly to maintain consistency and fairness must understand—must *feel*—that in that final stage where the jury goes with its gut—moral intuition must be partly emotional. Every moral question is essentially emotional. Aristotle

---

46. Thus, according to Chief Justice Rehnquist and Justices Scalia and Thomas dissenting, legislation and jury verdicts should be "the sole indicators...of decency for the purposes of the Eighth Amendment" (*Atkins v. Virginia* 2002:2253).

47. If we are fully to incorporate Aristotle's wisdom and acknowledge that a collective jury is better able than a single judge to reflect the moral sense of the community, and through its greater numbers to defeat the unjust effects of extreme, eccentric, and uninformed passion—then after successive filtrations, when we do reach that final penalty stage, perhaps a vote of eleven-to-one for death should suffice.

48. Formally, *Ring* requires only that a jury decide "any fact on which the legislature conditions an increase in punishment" (*Ring v. Arizona* 2002:2432), and does not specifically require that the jury make the final sentencing decision. But if a judge were to decide whether jury-determined aggravating circumstances substantially outweighed mitigating factors, would that moral "fact" not thereby also be covered by *Ring*? Responding to *Ring*, states have generally allocated the life or death decision to juries.

and Adam Smith, and increasingly in our own times moral philosophers—both for and against the death penalty—realize this.[49] We should acknowledge the inevitable, and declare legitimate the inescapable role of emotion. Mercy and justice require it.

By its tone, if not by definition, the very measure of desert is partly emotional. Juries will err, morally, and condemn to death factually guilty death-eligibles who do not deserve to die. As Aristotle reiterated, we cannot expect the same degree of accuracy in moral as in scientific questions. But the categories can be narrowed, and the jury can be made to *feel* its responsibility to separate the legal question—is this murder death-eligible?—from the moral question—does this murderer deserve to die? Once law and equity are brought together, once we explicitly allow informed emotion—moral intuition, that innately human sense—our jurisprudence on which that condemnation rests becomes explicable and coherent. A thing cannot both be and not be *in the same sense at the same time.*

Discretion is at once limitless and limited—but in different senses at different times.

Dissenting in *Callins v. Collins,* Justice Blackmun went right to the edge of this separate dimension: "Prohibiting a sentencer from exercising its discretion to dispense mercy on the basis of factors too intangible to write into a statute is offensive to our sense of fundamental fairness and respect for the uniqueness of the individual" *(Callins v. Collins* 1994:1133). But ultimately, he shied away: "The basic question—does the system accurately and consistently determine which defendants 'deserve' to die?—cannot be answered in the affirmative" (at 1130).

Without intuition and emotion, it cannot be answered at all.

Dissenting in *Walton,* Justice Brennan (joined by Marshall) did acknowledge separate dimensions, but also failed to acknowledge the emotional and intuitive implications: "*Lockett* and *Furman* principles speak to different concerns…the *Lockett* rule flows primarily from the Amendment's core concern for human dignity, whereas the *Furman* principle reflects an understanding that the Amendment commands that punishment not be meted out in a wholly arbitrary and irrational manner" *(Walton v. Arizona* 1990:676). Applying these cases together leads the Court to "insist that capital punishment be imposed fairly, and with reasonable consistency, or not at all"[50] *(Walton v. Arizona* 1990:676, quoting *Eddings v. Oklahoma* 1982:112).

---

49. *Cf.,* Pillsbury (1989) and the collection of essays in Bandes (1999).

50. Scalia in *Walton* also comes close—again without acknowledging the emotional basis for moral decision-making: "Since the individualized determination is a unitary one (does this defendant deserve death for this crime?), once one says each sentencer must be able to answer 'no' for whatever reason it deems *morally* sufficient (and indeed for whatever reason any one of 12 jurors deems morally sufficient), it becomes impossible to claim that the Constitution

Legal justice—rule-bound consistency—is what we demand of the jury at the guilt phase of a capital trial. Legal discretion must be limited and guided at this stage by well-defined homicide distinctions, based on *mens rea*, defenses, affirmative defenses, and other factors that can be applied rationally and consistently. But when it comes to the penalty phase, where character and not conduct is the issue, each defendant's unique personality and background assume center stage. There, we seek fairness: "Equity"—the moral truth, based in the jury's intuition—that mysterious rich mix of reason *and* emotion that combines to determine whether a person *really*—not merely rationally—deserves to die.

To Root in a Flowing Stream: Conclusion

We navigate in a leaking boat, repairing as we sail.[51] We drag behind us what sailors call a "sea anchor"—an ancient core that slows our progress but keeps us steadier, staying our course, even in the midst of emotional storms. The Sophists called these essential standards of decency, *nomos in physis*—deep-seated customs that characterize a culture. "Trials for homicide," Aristotle informs us, "were to be conducted according to the ancestral custom"[52] (Aristotle 1974:111).

Ancestral custom—the past counts: Blood pollutes the land. Many abolitionists may feel this, but they have learned to suppress the sentiment as shameful. Because the past counts and blood pollutes the land, the malevolent killer must suffer.[53] The victim's family shall have a voice greater than strangers—the victim greater still—but, in the end, the killer's fate deeply concerns the community.

The essential human punitive impulse cannot be denied, but to do justice it must be limited. "*Imposing limits on the unlimited to make the limited*," Pythagoras teaches. We limit the *measure* of punishment: "Like for like" feels appropriate for starters. We shall do to the scheming snitch as he would have done to his victim. "*He who sheds the blood of man by man shall his blood be shed*," God declares. "The extraordinary and symmetrical syntax of this great command—(shed-blood-man/man-blood-shed) mirrors the situation. Action demands an equal and apposite reaction."[54] The Pythagoreans defined justice,

---

requires consistency and rationality among sentencing determinations to be preserved by strictly limiting the reasons for which each sentencer can say 'yes'" (*Walton v. Arizona* 1990:656).

51. The author of this metaphor escapes me.

52. Magna Carta guaranteed London its "ancient liberties" without ever specifying what they were.

53. Today more retributivists might oppose the death penalty as unnecessarily cruel if the alternative—LWOP—were made more necessarily cruel.

54. Prof. Murray Lichtenstein in conversation.

Aristotle tells us, as "suffering that which one has done to another" (Aristotle 1962:1132b). Although "Eye for an eye" began as the great *limit* on punishment —*only* an eye for an eye—it "has been perverted, in common understanding, into an act of cruelty. Properly understood, it intends to limit the excesses which codes in the ancient Near East allowed" (Bailey 1987:50). In the same spirit *Deuteronomy* demands strictly measured corporal punishment only as deserved, lest the person punished be degraded. This sense of "appropriate" as like-kind limited punishment, becomes "proportional punishment" under the Eighth Amendment.

Imposing limits on the unlimited, channeled discretion is the central demand of Pythagoras and *Furman*. Like Socrates, we collect instances and find essences. We discover and clearly mark off the continuum of homicide into different degrees of blameworthiness. We guide the jury's discretion by announcing and applying these aggravators, so that punishment will be proportional and only the worst of the worst shall be put to death.

Substantively, the decision—life or death—*must* be morally just. Formally, law aspires to become a calculus of categories applied objectively. Life or death would follow demonstrably from a set of rules applied to a particular act under any given set of circumstances. Ideally, Western homicide law, like mathematics, would be perfectly cumulative—once established, true for always. Over time, capital crimes and procedures would only be refined by being made more limited and precise. In fact, however, homicide and death penalty jurisprudence have developed more like science or chess. Progressively, they have acquired new lines, embraced new understandings and fashions, and occasionally have rejected conventional wisdom as error and returned to ancient roots, which take on new meaning. Over millennia, even as we have jettisoned morally primitive and cultish practices and penalties, we continue to draw from our ancient homicide law as cultural wellspring.

But Socrates and Jesus were executed. Both prosecutions, however, were political. And neither defendant was tried for murder. Although each was unjustly put to death, neither condemned the death penalty *per se*. Jesus refused to put up a defense at trial. And Socrates virtually "volunteered" for death. After being convicted by a bare majority of a 500-person jury, in a separate penalty phase to determine his fate, after the prosecutor weakly called for his death, rather than propose a brief exile, Socrates submitted to that same jury as their only alternative his own "just deserts"—a lifetime of free meals in the hall reserved for the most honored Olympic athletes.

Those who followed Socrates sought to give content to the "good" that he had urged we seek, but had left undetermined. We adopted the Socratic program, as well as the Biblical goal of separating the righteous from the wicked by attempting to give more precise content to "evil": Capital killings essentially included the coldly calculated and planned, and excluded accidents, negligent and justified killings, and homicides by children and the insane. At the extreme, the *scheming* who kill even their own kin for money should be destroyed.[55] Also at the extreme are coldly calloused and depraved killings, such as the goring ox in the Bible, and before that in the Code of Hammurabi the collapsing house badly built. In the 19th century, allowing a horse to run in a crowd exhibited a special depravity. Spray shooting into a crowd is the contemporary analogue. Perhaps the most callous of all, a wealthy pharmacist dilutes chemotherapy for extra profit, not caring about the agonies he causes hundreds of trusting cancer patients who rely on his medicine to treat their disease. Even absent a specific intent to kill, a wanton recklessness with a depraved indifference to human life can be sufficiently heinous to deserve death.

Before convicting and condemning, we must make most diligent inquiry, as the Bible commands, never presuming guilt from accusation, nor accepting its first, superficial appearances. Homicide *is* special. The victim's death is a special injury; the killer's death is a special punishment. We commit ourselves to careful, thorough investigation. A presumption of innocence attaches from the beginning. Resolving reasonable doubts for the defendant, we demand corroboration. Snitch testimony alone is never enough. Super due process is owed throughout: *We must be certain before we kill a person.* Even after conviction and sentence we will entertain new evidence, and be willing to reconsider.

When it comes to punishing murder, both the Bible and the Ancient Greeks teach us that rich and poor shall be treated alike. The wealthy may not buy their way out. All stand *equal before the law.* There must be no class or race bias, but we must be discriminating. Today, as in Exodus XXIII:1, while a homeowner may slay a nighttime burglar, burglary itself is not a capital crime. The ancients teach us to limit our confidence in these measures—to limit our faith that we can achieve proportional punishment through classifying crimes and attaching punishments as deserved.

Humbled and tentative as we declare and apply our death penalty, we must limit our rage. There is a time for anger, the Bible tells us—*"your eye shall not pity him"*—even *"a time to hate and kill"* (Ecclesiastes III:3). But all emotion, especially anger, must be kept in check, warned Aristotle, preaching the Golden Mean throughout, and specially praising "gentleness"—moderation in anger. "Being gentle means to be unruffled and not to be driven by emotion, but to be angry only under such circumstances and for as long a time as reason may bid." Aristotle warned against "excessive" anger, "shown against the wrong persons, under the wrong circumstances, to an improper degree, too quickly, and for an unduly long time.... Short tempered people are quick to be angered at the wrong people, under the wrong circumstances, and more than is right,

---

55. "The law of homicide demanded forfeiture of 'the psyche which did or planned the deed' combining (in the word) the senses of life and the power of thought and deliberation" (Guthrie 1962: Vol. III, at 468).

but they get over it quickly, and that is their best quality." But "bad tempered" people "cannot be reconciled without exacting their revenge" (Aristotle 1962:1125b).

"A gentle person is forgiving rather than vindictive" (Aristotle 1962:1126a). But even gentleness was not perfectly moderate. The "gentle" person was likely to "be more prone" to too little anger—"a kind of apathy or whatever else it may be," Aristotle criticized. "For those who do not show anger at things that ought to arouse anger are regarded as fools.... Such people seem to have no feelings, not even for pain" (at 1126a).

"It is morally right to hate criminals," declared Fitzjames Stephen, the great 19th century English judge and historian, and emotive retributivists' patron saint (Stephen 1883: Vol. II, at 81–82). Capital murderers especially should be hated. Abolitionists sometimes seem abstractly ideological in rejecting all hatred or anger, except at the government or the social conditions they hold responsible for the brutal murder. Often they seem emotionally one-sided, reserving pity mostly for the condemned, and dislike for those who would execute them. Reflexively they favor the underdog, regardless of why the condemned has been rendered powerless to stop those who would execute him. They show their true gentle spirit by emphasizing restoration and rehabilitation.[56]

At the opposite extreme, carried away by an indiscriminate thirst for revenge, many death penalty proponents issue their inhumane battle cry, urging us to "Kill them all; let God sort it out later." For Aristotle, rage was more dangerous than apathy—it was "much more common for it is more human to seek revenge" (Aristotle 1962:1126a). For the last 150 years apathy and rage have been in closer balance.

"We must watch the errors which have the greatest attraction for us personally," Aristotle warned (Aristotle 1962:1109b). The true retributivist who calls for punishment—pain and suffering because it is deserved—especially despises sadists. In fact, feeling satisfied at deserved punishment, the retributivist hates sadists more deeply for subjecting vulnerable victims to their selfish whims.

From the Bible we learn that the victim's human dignity is paramount. From Aristotle we explicitly learn that "*righteous indignation*" is the right attitude here—"the mean between envy and spite."[57] That old Hellenic virtue of *aidos*—an "inner feeling of respect for what deserves respect and revulsion from wrongdoing as such and not from fear of punishment" still animates us (Guthrie 1962: Vol. II, at 494).

---

56. In this respect Plato was a kindred spirit.

57. "The righteously indignant man feels pain when someone prospers undeservedly; an envious man exceeds him in that he is pained when he sees anyone prosper; and a spiteful man is so deficient in feeling pain that he even rejoices when someone suffers undeservedly" (Aristotle 1962:1108b).

And when we do slay the condemned, even as we seek "solace in the face of suffering" (Henberg 1990:6) by the execution, we should feel pain mixed with satisfaction. "These severe penalties are at once supremely right and superlatively shameful," says Plato (1978:860b).

From the ancient Hebrews in their Torah and Talmud and the Ancient Greeks in their philosophy and practice, our humility in identifying those who deserve to die calls for continuous study, and at trial, skilled champions on both sides. But in academic writing and public discussion, we should model ourselves less on Protagoras, for whom debate was a "verbal battle," and more on Socrates, who engaged in dialectic: Minds not bent on winning an argument antagonistically but commonly searching, "One helping the other that both may come nearer the truth" (Guthrie 1962: Vol. III, at 43; 449).

To arrive at true desert, however, we need more than a Socratic catalogue. We need a jurisprudence of informed emotion, expressed in a language richer than the strictly rational, employing a grammar that allows for reason *and* emotion, deep enough to cover law and equity, and embracing both consistency *and* fairness. Discrete legal categories can never be sufficient, for reality flows, as Heraclitus was insisting 2500 years ago. "There are not two classes of murder but an infinite variety, which shade off by degrees from the most atrocious to the most excusable," declared the Royal Commission on Capital Punishment Report 50 years ago, implicitly siding with Heraclitus against Pythagoras, and with *McGautha* against *Furman*. Factors making death appropriate in particular cases "are too complex to be compressed within the limits of a simple formula" (§498). Where law leaves off, equity enters: Real justice can never be compressed fully into a rational design. "Infinite" factors "affect the gravity" of the murder. Ultimately the life or death decision is real, and as such, infinitely finer than a strictly legal decision. "Motives of the offense and the character...of the offender can never be inferred from the legal quality of his criminal act" (Royal Commission §595). The Greeks generally believed that humans had an intuitive faculty that allowed them immediately to apprehend the true nature of a situation (Guthrie 1962: Vol. II, at 19). Some moral intuition, although non-rational, is indispensable.

For 3000 years, and especially these last 50, we have been building upon stable homicide law, refining categories of those who deserve to die, occasionally shedding former beliefs, sometimes severing roots such as capital punishment for religious or morals offenses—progressively shrinking the class of death-eligibles. We draw up and apply our codes, approaching the substance and process with Socratic humility and great caution.

"The Gods did not reveal to men all things in the beginning," declared Xenophanes a century before Protagoras, "but in course of time, by searching, they find out better" (Guthrie 1962: Vol. I, at 399). Must this search inevitably culminate in abolition? The ancient Greeks were aware of an asymptote—a curve that progressively approaches but never quite reaches another. Trusting that "over time the types of murder for which the death penalty may be imposed would become more narrowly defined and would be limited to those which are particularly serious or for which the death penalty is particularly appropriate," (*Zant v. Stephens* 1983:877, *quoting* Justice White in *Gregg v. Georgia* 1976:222), we, too, might be moving toward a morally more refined death penalty where *we execute virtually all and only those very, very few who truly deserve to die.*

We have far from reached that point. Meanwhile, fallible human beings "made in the image of God," we stumble along, erring but doing our best at justice. "*Justice, justice, shall you pursue*"—literally "*chase after*" (Deuteronomy, XVI:20). We can all envision more perfect worlds. But in the end, said Plato, "We must take things as they are…and gather together to work out written codes, chasing to catch the tracks of the true constitution" (Plato 1957:301d–e), dragging behind us, however chipped away and crusted, our common core of deeply rooted values.

We can only and we must do our best chasing justice, striving to do better. We know there is "no perfect procedure," nor perfectly defined set of substantive aggravators. "Who lives or dies?" ultimately is an ethical question, whose correct answer necessarily must be partly emotional. We cannot demand the same precision in ethics as in physics. Each sphere, each age has its own measure of progress and error, tuned to its developing technical skill and moral sensibility. When it comes to the death penalty, some truth is eternal, some out of reach. Evolution is inevitable and progress possible.

References

Abbott, E. (1884) *Flatland*. London: Seeley & Co., Ltd.

Aristotle (1974) *Constitution of Athens and Related Texts*. Von Fritz, K. and E. Kapp (trans.). New York: Hafner Press.

Aristotle (1962) *Nicomachean Ethics*. Ostwald, M. (trans.). Englewood Cliffs: Prentice Hall.

Aristotle (1962) *The Politics*. Sinclair, J.A. (trans.). Baltimore: Penguin Books.

Aristotle (1953) *Ethics*. Thomson, J.A.K. (trans.). London: George Allen Ltd.

Aristotle (1941) *Metaphysics*. Ross, W.D. (trans.), in R. McKeon (ed.), *The Basic Works of Aristotle*. New York: Random House.

Atkins v. Virginia (2002) 122 S.Ct. 2242.

Babylonian Talmud Sanhedrin (1935). London: Soncino Press.

Bailey, L.R. (1987) *Capital Punishment: What the Bible Says*. Nashville: Abingdon Press.

Bandes, S. (1999) *The Passions of Law*. New York: New York University Press.

Bedau, H.A. (1997) "Why the Death Penalty is a Cruel and Unusual Punishment." Pp. 232–237 in H.A. Bedau (ed.), *The Death Penalty in America*. New York: Oxford University Press.

Blecker, R. (1990) "Haven or Hell? Inside Lorton Central Prison: Experience of Punishment Justified." *Stanford Law Review* 42:1149–1249.

Bonner, R.J. (1927) *Lawyers and Litigants in Ancient Athens*. Chicago: The University of Chicago Press.

Bonner, R.J. and G. Smith, (2000) *The Administration of Justice from Homer to Aristotle, Volumes I and II*. New Jersey: The Lawbook Exchange, LTD.

Buber, M. (1952) *Good and Evil*. New York: Charles Scribners & Sons.

California v. Brown (1987) 479 U.S. 538.

Callins v. Collins (1994) 510 U.S. 1141.

Coker v. Georgia (1977) 433 U.S. 584.

Dershowitz, A. (2000) *The Genesis of Justice*. New York: Warner Books, Inc.

Eddings v. Oklahoma (1982) 455 U.S. 104.

Enmund v. Florida (1982) 458 U.S. 782.

Furman v. Georgia (1972) 408 U.S. 238.

Greenberg, M. (1970) "Some Postulates of Biblical and Criminal Law." Pp. 18–37 in J. Goldin (ed.), *The Jewish Expression*. New York: Bantam Press.

Gregg v. Georgia (1976) 428 U.S. 153.

Guthrie, W.K.C. (1975) *The Greek Philosophers From Thales to Aristotle*. New York: Harper and Rowe Publishers.

Guthrie, W.K.C. (1962) *A History of Greek Philosophy, Volumes I, II, and III*. Cambridge: University Press.

Henberg, M. (1990) *Retribution: Evil for Evil in Ethics, Law and Literature*. Philadelphia: Temple University Press.

Hobbes, T. (1651/1968) *Leviathan*. C.B. MacPherson (ed.). Baltimore: Penguin Books.

Homer: The Odyssey (1937) Rouse, W.H.D. (trans.). New York: Mentor Press.

Illinois Governor's Commission on Capital Punishment (2002). Springfield, IL.

In re Stanford (2002) 123 S.Ct. 472.

King v. Oneby (1727) 92 Eng. Rep. 465.

Kline, M. (1953) *Mathematics in Western Culture*. London: Oxford University Press.

Lockett v. Ohio (1978) 438 U.S. 586.

Lowenfield v. Phelps (1988) 484 U.S. 231.

McCleskey v. Kemp (1987) 481 U.S. 279.

McGautha v. California (1971) 402 U.S. 183.

New King James Bible (1990) New York: American Bible Society.

The Oxford Annotated Bible with the Apocrypha (1965) Revised Standard Version, H. May and B.Metzger (eds.). New York: Oxford University Press.

O'Neill v. Vermont (1892) 144 U.S. 323.

Patterson v. Texas (2002) 536 U.S. 984.

The Pentatuch and Haftorahs (1960) Hertz, J.H. (ed.). London: Soncino Press.

People v. Casassa (1980) 404 N.E.2d 1310 (N.Y.), *cert. denied*, 449 U.S. 842 (1980).

People v. Warner-Lambert (1980) 414 N.E.2d 660 (N.Y.).

Pillsbury, S.H. (1989) "Emotional Justice: Moralizing the Passions of Criminal Punishment." *Cornell Law Review* 74:655–710.

Plato (1978) *Laws*. A.E. Taylor (trans.), in E. Hamilton and H. Cairns (eds.) *The Collected Dialogues of Plato*. Princeton, New Jersey: Princeton University Press.

Plato (1957) *Statesman*. Ostwald, M. (ed.) and J.B.S. Kemp (trans.). Indianapolis: Bobbs-Merrill Educational Publishing.

Plato (1957) *Theaetetus*. Cornford, F. (trans.), in *Plato's Theory of Knowledge*. New York: The Liberal Arts Press.

Plato (1956) *Protagoras.* Ostwald, M. and B. Jowett (trans.). New York: The Liberal Arts Press.

Ring v. Arizona (2002) 122 S.Ct. 2428.

Roth, M. (1997) *Law Collections from Mesopotamia and Asia Minor* (2nd ed.). Atlanta: Scholars Press.

Royal Commission on Capital Punishment (1949–1953).

Smith, A. (1759/2000) *Theory of Moral Sentiments.* New York: Prometheus Books.

Spaziano v. Florida (1984) 468 U.S. 447.

State v. Walton (1989) 769 P.2d 1017 (Ariz.).

Steiker, C. (2002) "Capital Punishment and American Exceptionalism." *Oregon Law Review* 81:97–130.

Thompson v. Oklahoma (1988) 487 U.S. 815.

Thucydides: The Peloponnasian War (1954) R. Warner (trans.). Baltimore: Penguin Books.

Tison v. Arizona (1987) 481 U.S. 137.

Tribe, L. (1971) "Trial by Mathematics." *Harvard Law Review* 84:1329–1393.

Trop v. Dulles (1958) 356 U.S. 86.

United States v. Fell (2002) 217 F.Supp.2d 469 (D.Vt.).

United States v. Quinones (2002) 205 F.Supp.2d 256 (S.D.N.Y.),*reversed,* 313 F.3d 49 (2d Cir.).

Walton v. Arizona (1990) 497 U.S. 639.

Weems v. United States (1910) 217 U.S. 349.

Witherspoon v. Illinois (1968) 391 U.S. 510.

Woodson v. North Carolina (1976) 428 U.S. 280.

Zant v. Stephens (1983) 462 U.S. 862.

Chapter 7

Justice, Deterrence and the Death Penalty

Ernest van den Haag

I

Suum cuique tribue[1] (to give to everyone what he deserves) is to do justice. What is deserved?[2] In penal justice this depends on the gravity of the crime and the culpability of the criminal, both hard to determine. There is no objective measure of the cardinal gravity of a crime; or of the cardinal severity of a punishment; nor, finally, do we have an objective indication of what punishment is deserved per se by each degree of gravity.

However, ordinal ranking is possible. Crimes of a similar kind can be arrayed according to comparative gravity; and punishments according to comparative severity. Although ultimately it depends on subjective evaluations too, ordinal ranking is helpful, e.g., by telling us that murder with torture, or with premeditation, (or multiple murder), is more grave (and deserves more punishment) than murder without—even if we cannot determine how much more. We can conjecture also that manslaughter deserves more punishment than assault, or theft, and menacing less. But we cannot determine how much more or less, nor whether execution is more severe than life in prison (most convicts think so).

Physical punishments, such as mutilations, are more readily coordinated with the crimes they punish. Thus, the ancient *lex talionis* required fewer decisions on the comparative gravity of harms and punishments. But the *lex talionis* is irrelevant to criminal justice. It treated crimes as torts, which entitled victims to retaliation or compensation according to the harm inflicted, whereas we consider crimes mainly as harms to society, which entitle it (and only it) to retribution (van den Haag 1992). Retribution, as deserved by the

---

1. Domitianus Ulpianus. See also Thomas Aquinas: jus suum unicuique tribue...est justitia.
2. A discussion of desert is found in van den Haag (1994).

crime, is the paramount moral purpose of punishment. It is an end in itself, a categorical imperative. Doing justice by retribution is an expressive, rather than an instrumental act, retrospective by definition. The very notion of "punishment" is retrospective.

Still, retributive punishment may yield legitimate, instrumental, non-moral (though not immoral) benefits. Being instrumental, these benefits are prospective. Thus, incapacitation of the convict by imprisonment, while it lasts, obviously protects society.[3] Rehabilitation (sometimes called specific deterrence) may help to protect society by discouraging crimes by the released convict. Deterrence, finally, restrains others than the convict from doing in the future what he did in the past. It is the most important instrumental benefit of punishment.

Although a desirable effect consistent with it, deterrence is not part of the moral aim of justice.[4] Deterrence can be justified, however, as an important instrumental purpose of punishment, if not as an independent one. It would be unjust to punish any person, guilty or innocent, merely to deter others. However, the deterrent effect of just (deserved) punishment, intended or not, is morally justifiable, since the convict volunteered for risking the punishment which has deterrent effects. He is not punished merely to deter others, which would be inconsistent with justice, even if he is guilty. However, if his deserved punishment deters others, it helps to repay for the harm the crime did to the social order—to pay his "debt to society."

Many abolitionists insist that the death penalty is no more deterrent than life in prison. This empirical question is, in principle, answerable by experiments, which, however, are seldom practical, feasible, or conclusive.[5] But the justice of a punishment, such as the death penalty, as distinguished from deterrent effects, cannot be proved or disproved by any experiment. I must quarrel therefore with the title of the present collection of essays, *America's Experiment With Capital Punishment*. The title misleads, by suggesting that the justice of the death penalty can be treated as a hypothesis confirmed or disconfirmed by an experiment.[6] Alternatively, the title implies that justice does not matter, compared to deterrence—which would not improve matters.

Deterrence is the only purpose of the threats of the criminal law. Punishment of those who were not deterred carries out these threats and 1) retributes, and 2) keeps the promise of the law (a threat is a negative promise and prom-

---

3. Incapacitation may be independent of punishment, which in turn need not be incapacitative. We incapacitate some of the insane non-punitively and punish some convicts without incapacitation, e.g., by fines.

4. Some philosophers think deterrence is not consistent with the moral purpose of punishment.

5. See Section III of this chapter.

6. The only function of experiments is to confirm or disprove hypotheses.

ises must be kept—*pacta sunt servanda*).[7] So much for the moral purposes of punishment.

There are two non-moral (instrumental) purposes of punishment as well: 1) Legal threats of punishment would become incredible and lose their deterrent effectiveness if not carried out by actual punishment; and 2) the conditional threat of punishment addressed to prospective criminals is also a positive promise to the law abiding, which may help to keep them law abiding. If threats were not carried out against those not deterred by them, the law abiding, who took the threats seriously and formed the habit of abiding by the law, would have been fooled. At least some of them may have foregone crimes in part because they believed that they would be punished if they committed them. If those who were not deterred are not punished, the legal threats which helped restrain the law abiding would be revealed as bluffs. Criminals would have gained an advantage by breaking the law, while the law abiding would have been placed at a disadvantage by trusting the law. The social order which depends on the formation of law abiding habits would be undermined.

II

Traditionally murder has been thought the most grave of crimes, deserving the most severe punishment. Other crimes, such as theft, or even rape, leave the victim capable of recovering. Murder does not. It is final. So is the death penalty, which, therefore, traditionally has been thought fitting.

Can any crime be horrible enough to forfeit the life of the criminal? Can death ever be a deserved punishment? Some abolitionists do not think so. Others even believe, for unintelligible reasons, that no society has a moral right to impose the death penalty.[8] I am confident that the following excerpt may help answer this question. (*Res ipsa loquitur.*)

> …The appellant, after telling Donna how pretty she was, raised his fist and hit her across the face. When she stood up, he grabbed her by her blouse, ripping it off. He then proceeded to remove her bra and tied her hands behind her back with a nylon stocking. Mc-Corquodale then removed his belt, which was fastened with a rather large buckle, and repeatedly struck Donna across the back

---

7. Threats differ from positive promises because they can be legitimately canceled without the consent of the threatened, whereas positive promises can be legitimately canceled only with the consent of those to whom they were made.

8. Opposition to capital punishment is intelligible. The idea that society has no moral right to impose it is not. Who, or what could grant that right to society, which is the source of rights, however inspired? Does "has no moral right" mean more than "shouldn't"?

with the buckle end of the belt. He then took off all her clothing and then bound her mouth with tape and a washcloth. Leroy then kicked Donna and she fell to the floor. McCorquodale took his cigarette and burned the victim on the breasts, the thigh, and the navel. He then bit one of Donna's nipples and she began to bleed. He asked for a razorblade and then sliced the other nipple. He then called for a box of salt and poured it into the wounds he had made on her breasts. At this point Linda, who was eight months pregnant, became ill and went into the bedroom and closed the door. McCorquodale then lit a candle and proceeded to drip hot wax over Donna's body. He held the candle about 1/2 inch from Donna's vagina and dripped the hot wax into this part of her body. He then used a pair of surgical scissors to cut around the victim's clitoris.

While bleeding from her nose and vagina, Leroy forced the victim to perform oral sex on him while McCorquodale had intercourse with her. Then Leroy had intercourse with the victim while McCorquodale forced his penis into the victim's mouth. McCorquodale then found a hard plastic bottle which was about 5 inches in height and placed an antiseptic solution within it, forcing this bottle into Donna's vagina and squirted the solution into her. The victim was then permitted to go to the bathroom to "get cleaned up." While she was in the bathroom, McCorquodale secured a piece of nylon rope and told Bonnie and her roommate that he was going "to kill the girl." He hid in a closet across the hall from the bathroom and when Donna came out of the bathroom he wrapped the nylon cord around her neck. Donna screamed, "My God, you're killing me." As McCorquodale tried to strangle her, the cord cut into his hands and Donna fell to the floor. He fell on top of her and began to strangle her with his bare hands. He removed his hands and the victim began to have convulsions. He again strangled her and then pulled her head up and forward to break her neck. He covered her lifeless body with a sheet and departed the apartment to search for a means of transporting her body from the scene. By this time, it was approximately 6:00 a.m. on the morning of January 17.

McCorquodale soon returned to the apartment and asked Bonnie for her trunk and Leroy and McCorquodale tried to place Donna's body in the trunk. Finding that the body was too large for the trunk McCorquodale proceeded to break Donna's arms and legs by holding them upright while he stomped on them with his foot. Donna's body was then placed in the trunk and the trunk was placed in the closet behind the curtains. McCorquodale and

Leroy then went to sleep on the couch in the living room for the greater portion of the day, leaving the apartment sometime during the afternoon.

Because a strong odor began to emanate from the body, and her efforts to mask the smell with deodorant spray had been unsuccessful, Linda called Bonnie to request that McCorquodale remove the trunk from the apartment. Shortly after 8:00 p.m. McCorquodale arrived at the apartment with a person named Larry. As they attempted to move the trunk from the closet, blood began spilling from the trunk onto the living room floor. McCorquodale placed a towel under the trunk to absorb the blood as they carried the trunk to Larry's car. When McCorquodale and Larry returned to the apartment they told Linda that the body had been dumped out of the trunk into a road and that the trunk was placed under some boxes in a "Dempsey Dumpster." Donna's body was found about half a mile off Highway No. 42 in Clayton County (*McCorquodale v. State* 1974:579–580).

Justice William Brennan thought the death penalty inconsistent with "the sanctity of life" (*Furman v. Georgia* 1972:286). His unargued notion may derive from the ancient *homo homini res sacra* (man is a sacred object to man). But the Romans, who coined the phrase, believed the sanctity of life best safeguarded by executing murderers who had not respected it. Brennan may also have based his view on the Constitution. However, it does not grant an imprescriptible right to life which murderers would be as entitled to as their victims.[9] He also held that execution is a "denial of the executed person's humanity" (at 290). Yet, philosophers, such as Immanuel Kant and G.W.F. Hegel, thought that punishments, including the death penalty, recognize and asseverate the humanity of the convict, even though he himself may have repudiated it by his crime.

We protect ourselves from ferocious beasts, but we do not punish them, because, unlike criminals, they cannot tell right from wrong or restrain themselves accordingly. Animals therefore are not, but criminals are responsible for their actions because they are human. Their punishment acknowledges rather than denies their responsibility and, thereby, their humanity. Brennan finally asserts that "the deliberate extinguishment of human life by the state is uniquely degrading to human dignity" (*Furman v. Georgia* 1972:291). He does not tell whether the criminal or the executioner is degraded, nor wherein the degradation lies, or whether any crime could degrade humanity and call for a degrading punishment.

Capital punishment, a deliberate expulsion from human society, is meant to add deserved moral ignominy to death. This irks some abolitionists, who feel that nobody should be blamed for whatever he does. But murder deserves

---

9. Christian theology, as does the U.S. Constitution, protects only innocent life and heretofore authorized the death penalty (see Section IX of this chapter).

blame. Death may well be less punishment than what some criminals deserve. Even torture may be. But, although they may deserve it, we no longer torture criminals. Unlike death, torture is avoidable. It is now repulsive to most people, and no longer thought entertaining, as it was in the past (van den Haag 1975).

However much deserved, the death penalty should not be imposed if, by not threatening it, we can save innocent lives.[10] If (unlike the Supreme Court) we believe that rape deserves capital punishment, we nevertheless should not impose it because the threat would be an incentive to the rapist to murder his victim and make apprehension and conviction less likely without increasing the severity of his punishment if convicted. Indeed, capital punishment should be threatened rarely, because it would give threatened criminals—e.g., burglars—an incentive to kill victims, witnesses and arresting officers. However, the importance of trying to deter a first murder by the threat of capital punishment outweighs the usefulness of not encouraging additional murders by not threatening capital punishment for the first. Therefore, the threat of capital punishment for murder is not counter-productive, whereas it might be for most other crimes.[11]

Nature has sentenced us all to death. Execution hastens, but does not create the unavoidable end of human life. What makes execution different is that it brands the executed as morally unworthy to belong to human society. The phrase "death is different," darkly intoned by abolitionists, is impressive and rings true, although it applies to execution more than to death. What follows from it? More capital punishment, or less? Or just caution in inflicting it?

III

The paramount moral purpose of punishment is retributive justice. But there are important non-moral purposes as well, such as protection of life and property. They are achieved mainly by deterrence. It seems obvious that more severe and certain punishments deter more than less severe and certain ones.[12] Yet, abolitionists contend that the death penalty is no more deterrent than life

---

10. We cannot impose capital punishment, or any punishment, without first threatening it. As the Romans taught us *nulla poena sine lege* (no punishment [can be imposed] unless first threatened by law).

11. This calculation also justifies making the death penalty possible for violent crimes, but not mandatory.

12. Rationally it should make little difference whether severity or certainty is increased. A burglar after a hundred burglaries in fifteen years may be convicted twice, serving five years each time, or a total of ten years. Or, he may be convicted ten times, serving one year each time, again for a total of ten years. There is no material difference, although the more frequently convicted burglar may spend more time in jail waiting for trial. Yet, the more frequent convictions may produce more deterrence. Most criminologists believe so although the matter has not been

in prison, or, alternatively, that the additional deterrence is redundant. As mentioned, this empirical question could be decided by experiment. We could threaten capital punishment for murders committed on Mondays, Wednesdays, and Fridays (MWF) and life imprisonment on the other days. If fewer murders are committed on MWF, the death penalty would be likely to be more deterrent than life in prison. However, the MWF murders do not deserve more punishment than the others. It would be morally capricious to impose the death penalty just on MWF murderers. We will have to rely on observation and statistical analysis, rather than experiment, to establish degrees of deterrence. Preponderantly, though not conclusively, the data tend to show the death penalty to be the most deterrent punishment available. Possibly, people fear the death penalty irrationally, despite low probability (executions are rare), just as they are irrationally attracted to lotteries with high prizes despite the low probability of winning.

Apart from less deterrence, life imprisonment, the alternative to capital punishment, also protects society less than capital punishment does. The convict may escape, he may be granted a furlough,[13] or his sentence may be commuted by governors who, unavoidably, retain the right to pardon. Not least, the lifer may endanger guards and fellow prisoners, since without the death penalty there is no further punishment to deter him.[14]

To proponents of capital punishment, deterrence, though important, is not decisive. Justice is. Still, most believe that the threat of execution does deter more than life imprisonment. In contrast, abolitionists believe that capital punishment not only is morally unjustifiable, but also has no more deterrent effect than life imprisonment. However, they would continue to advocate abolition, even if the death penalty were shown to deter more than life imprisonment. In effect, abolitionists appear to believe that the non-execution of murderers is morally more important than saving the innocent lives execution would save if it deters more than imprisonment. Asked whether they would execute murderers if each execution were to deter ten murders, thereby saving ten innocent lives, all abolitionists I have questioned answer in the negative.[15]

---

well explored. Note that more frequent apprehensions are more costly, as are the more frequent trials. In practice, additional severity is more readily attained than additionally certainty.

13. It is not clear why furloughs are granted, but unfortunately they are.

14. One could permanently chain prisoners serving life sentences. But we will not do so for moral and constitutional reasons. When Cesare Bonesana, Marchese di Beccaria, in his *Dei Delitti e delle Pene* (1764), preferred life imprisonment to execution, he thought the former to be more painful. It would be, if prisoners were held in the cruel conditions usual in his time. They will not be.

15. Thus, the abolitionist argument alleging lack of deterrence is not decisive for abolitionists, and perhaps not quite serious. The same may be said about the argument based on alleged racial discrimination. Asked whether they would oppose the death penalty where there is no

IV

The vulgar argument that holds execution to be wrong, because it does to the murderer what he did to his victim, neglects to note that many punishments do to the criminal what he did to his victim. In the past this was thought to be the essence of justice.[16] The difference between a crime and a punishment is social, not physical. There is no need for physical dissimilarity. A crime is an unlawful act, legal punishment is a lawful act. Taking a person from his family and confining him against his will in a small cell may be an unlawful kidnaping, or a lawful arrest. The difference is not physical. Neither is the difference between murder and execution, or being fined and being robbed.

There is no evidence for brutalization caused by the death penalty (Phillips 1982; Phillips and Bollen 1985; Stack 1984). The idea that legal killing will lead to imitation by illegal killing, or to any increase in violent crime, is unsubstantiated. And proponents do not explain why legal imprisonment does not lead to kidnappings, or why violent crime in Singapore and Saudi Arabia, both renowned for executions and physical punishments, is so infrequent.

The brutalization argument might be somewhat more valid against televising executions, although there are more salient arguments against televising. The executions would be sandwiched between sitcoms, sports, advertisements, contests and popular songs. The effect would be not so much to brutalize as to trivialize executions. Until two hundred years ago they served as popular entertainment. *Tempora mutantur et nos mutamur in illis*—we should not go back to using punishments as entertainment. Moreover, TV could show how the murderer is deprived of his life, but not what he did to his victim. The uninformed would be unduly stirred to pity for the criminal rather than the victim.

V

If an innocent is executed the miscarriage of justice is irreparable. Since judges and juries are human and therefore fallible, we can minimize, but not

---

racial discrimination—in China, Africa, or Scandinavia—they answer affirmatively. Thus, the argument from discrimination also is less than decisive, and possibly not quite serious.

16. Thus, in his 1779 "Bill for proportioning Crime and Punishments," Thomas Jefferson proposed: "Whosoever shall be guilty of rape, polygamy, or sodomy with man or woman, shall be punished, if a man, by castration, if a woman by cutting through the cartilage of her nose a hole of one half inch in diameter at the least. [And w]hosoever…shall maim another, or shall disfigure him…shall be maimed, or disfigured in like sort: or if that cannot be, for want of the same part, then as nearly as may be, in some other part of at least equal value…" (quoted in Kaufman 1973:42).

altogether avoid such miscarriages. There is a trade-off in minimizing them. To avoid convicting innocents we require so much evidence for conviction that many guilty persons escape punishment—which is no less unjust than convicting the innocent.[17] Guilt must be shown "beyond a reasonable doubt" and jurors must be unanimous. Courts exclude evidence and testimony if obtained unlawfully, e.g., by a search without a warrant, or without probable cause. This exclusion does not help in determining a defendant's guilt or innocence. There are many such exclusionary rules. They prevent courts from admitting much of the available evidence.[18] They are meant to restrain the police. They may. But the exclusionary rules also help the guilty, when proof of their guilt cannot be admitted. Yet these rules do not protect the innocent who cannot benefit from the exclusion of evidence for guilt.

We have more than 20,000 homicides annually, but only about 300 death sentences (and less than 50 executions). At this rate most of the about 3,000 murderers now on death row are far more likely to die of old age than by execution. On the average convicts spend more than eight years appealing their convictions. This seems a long time. Many appeals are repetitious as well as frivolous. Despite elaborate precautions, nothing short of abolishing punishment can avoid miscarriages altogether. The salient question about the death penalty is not: Could innocents be executed by mistake? (The answer is yes—courts are fallible) but: Does the death penalty save more innocent lives than it takes? Is there a net gain or loss?

Many desirable social practices cannot avoid killing innocents by accident. For instance, ambulances save many lives, but also run over some pedestrians. We do not abolish ambulances, because they save more innocents than they kill. So does the death penalty, if it deters some murders, as is likely, and if the miscarriages are few, as is likely too. It seems safer then, to rely on executions, which through deterrence, may save innocent lives, than it would be not to execute and risk not saving an indefinite number of innocents who could have been saved. If we execute a convicted murderer and his execution does not produce additional deterrence, his execution, though just, would not have been useful. But if his execution deters prospective murderers, not executing him would sacrifice innocent people who would have been spared had he been executed.

In all criminal cases, the prosecution must show guilt beyond a reasonable doubt to convict. Capital cases require more. There is first a trial to determine

---

17. Here I differ from Blackstone. The matter is discussed in Reiman and van den Haag (1990).

18. The ostensible purpose of these bizarre rules is to restrain the police from trying to obtain evidence by illegal means. However desirable this purpose, pursuing it by excluding evidence does not help courts in determining guilt. It obviously is a hindrance. Police can be more directly punished when acting unlawfully. The purpose of trials is to determine whether the defendant is guilty. For that purpose it does not matter how the evidence was obtained.

guilt. If the defendant is found guilty, a second proceeding determines whether he should be sentenced to death.[19] This second hearing considers mitigating and aggravating circumstances and leads to the death penalty only if the weight of the aggravating circumstances exceeds that of the mitigating ones.[20] These sentencing hearings have tended to develop into minitrials. It might be a good idea to limit them. After all, many of the facts relevant to the sentence have already been presented to the jury during the guilt trial. Two days, one for the defense, one for the prosecution, to present evidence and testimony should be sufficient, unless the judge feels that special circumstances require additional time.

Although the Constitution clearly authorizes the death penalty in the Fifth and Fourteenth Amendments, in the past some judges found it unconstitutional. That objection was put to rest. But many judges continue to delay carrying out death sentences, often with factitious reasoning.

Until about two hundred years ago the death penalty was the punishment for all serious crimes, and many we regard as trivial today. Prison for punitive, as distinguished from investigative purposes is a fairly recent innovation. The American colonies meted out the death penalty freely and the practice continued after independence. When capital punishment is mentioned in the Constitution's Fifth and Fourteenth Amendments it is to require that it (and all other punishments) be imposed by "due process." The states were left to decide on punishments. This constitutional interpretation was questioned after the Second World War. The Eighth Amendment prohibition of "cruel and unusual punishments" was used by some justices to question the constitutionality of the death penalty despite the fact that the Eighth Amendment had been passed at the same time as the Fifth, which explicitly authorized deprivation of "life, liberty and property" by "due process."

Dissenting from previous interpretations, Justices Brennan and Marshall claimed that capital punishment was unconstitutional because cruel, and also because irrational inasmuch as it did not achieve the instrumental purpose of deterrence. Both justices appear to have discounted the moral (retributive) purpose of capital punishment. However, punishments need not be deterrent to be constitutional. They need only be just, i.e., deserved and proportional to the gravity of crimes. No serious effort was made to show that the death penalty is perceived to be cruel in the light of "evolving standards of decency." That last phrase was used by then Chief Justice Warren in *Trop v. Dulles* (1958) to overturn an expatriation decision. Yet Warren, in *Trop*, also stated that the death penalty "cannot be said to violate the constitutional standard of cruelty" (p. 99).

---

19. The threat of the death penalty leads many murderers to agree to life imprisonment to avoid the death penalty and persuades others to testify against accomplices.

20. The aggravating and mitigating circumstances are listed in the law. The jury determines which preponderate.

Even if cruel the death penalty would not be unconstitutional unless shown to be "unusual" as well. It would have to be uncustomary. The "and" in "cruel and unusual" is conjunctive. But the penalty was and is quite customary in the United States. Clearly, in prohibiting "cruel and unusual" punishments, the framers meant to prevent judges from inventing new (unusual) punishments which were cruel. They did not mean to prohibit customary punishments.

Constitutional objections to the death penalty have been put to rest. They never had any basis in fact or logic. However, politically the death penalty remains controversial owing to moral and religious objections. The Second World War was fought against the Nazi regime that had abused the death penalty, killing numerous persons whether charged with a crime or not. (This was done by our ally the Soviet Union, as well.) In reaction to the abuses, the death penalty was abolished in most of Europe. It is still used in most of Asia and Africa, as well as the United States. The elite both in Europe and in the United States oppose the death penalty. They are likely to continue to prevail in Europe, where elite sentiment tends to be influential. It is less influential in the United States, where popular sentiment is more likely to prevail. Popular sentiment is staunchly in favor of the death penalty, which is therefore likely to be retained in the United States in the foreseeable future.

According to polls, while the great majority of Americans support capital punishment most lawyers, judges, ministers, professors and Hollywood celebrities oppose it. Is it coincidental that comparatively few members of these elite groups are likely to be murdered? The burden of crime, particularly violent crime, is borne mainly by common folk. It is taxi drivers, convenience or liquor store clerks, young Blacks, people in housing developments or slums, who are primarily endangered by crime, including murder. It is the cultural elite of college graduates that finds excuses for crime.

Perhaps college education helps explain opposition to the death penalty. Students are taught, accurately, that the great majority of criminals, including murderers, were mistreated and abused as children. Students infer, incorrectly, that mistreatment is the cause, or "root", of criminality. Unfortunately, they are not taught that the majority of mistreated and abused children do not become criminals, let alone murderers. Mistreatment and abuse are neither necessary nor sufficient causes of murder. To be sure, poverty, lack of education, childhood abuse, and, more important perhaps, the absence of a law-abiding family, may dispose to crime more than affluence and suburban living. But the former circumstances do not make it impossible to avoid crime. The responsibility for it remains with the individual who volunteers for crime.

The threat of punishment is meant precisely to deter persons who, for whatever reason, are disposed to crime. The legal threat is not needed for others. The so called causes of crime are, at best, explanations, but neither justifications nor excuses, let alone exculpations. Causes are exculpatory only if they compel crime and thus eliminate responsibility. It is reasonable to assume that there are some exceptional factors in the background of murderers, since murder is an exceptional action. Such factors may help explain criminal acts. They cannot exculpate.

Anatole France sarcastically remarked "the law in its majestic equality prohibits rich and poor alike to steal bread or to sleep under bridges," implying that the rich are hardly tempted to commit the crimes that may be nearly, but not quite, irresistible to the poor. No one any longer arrests the homeless who sleep under bridges, nor a hungry person who steals bread. Still, the law is meant to prohibit stealing by those tempted by their circumstances as well as by those who are not.[21] For the latter the prohibition is academic, for the former burdensome. Is this unjust, as Anatole France suggests? Hardly. Although its prohibitions apply to everyone, the criminal law necessarily burdens mainly those who by their circumstances are tempted to do what it prohibits. They are the ones that need to be deterred. There would be no need for criminal laws if no one were tempted to break them. And, surely, the most disadvantaged groups are most tempted to engage in unlawful acts, since they have the fewest legitimate resources to fulfill their desires. The prohibition of stealing imposes a greater burden on the poor than on the rich. But the greater temptation does not justify yielding to it.[22]

Education tends to influence most those who get most of it, the professional classes. In modern times education may induce students to regard nothing as final and to feel that no decision ever should be. Since showing that the earth is not flat science has undermined many certainties and sewn many doubts. Thus the uneasiness about certainty among the educated. Death is and remains final. However, inflicting death as a final punishment which cuts off the future and any possibility of change seems psychologically in conflict with the spirit of the times imbued as it is by doubtfulness. Death is certain and we cannot abolish it. However, we can abolish the death penalty. The spirit which prevails among the educated elite pushes us to do so. The finality of the death penalty makes us uncomfortable. Never mind that the death penalty does not create death but merely hastens it. People like to ignore death—which the penalty makes hard to do. Moreover, extreme moral blame attaches to capital punishment—and we like even our courts and judges to be non-judgmental. It follows that, if present trends continue, the death penalty is likely to become more rare. Yet, history does not allow any trend to continue forever. Prediction is chancy. Still it seems likely currently that the death penalty will continue in America, Asia

---

21. The latter include those who steal for the sake of luxury; the former those who steal because of pressing poverty.

22. If criminal acts arise from internal or external compulsions so that they cannot be avoided the law does not regard these acts as crimes. Only acts the actor volunteered for, acts he could have avoided, can be crimes.

and Africa but is unlikely to be reinstituted in most of Europe where it has been abolished.

VI

Many abolitionists contend that the death penalty is distributed unfairly, that Blacks and the poor are likely to be executed for murders which are punished less severely when committed by whites. This was quite true at one time but recent data indicate it no longer is.[23]

An unfair distribution of punishments (or rewards) is objectionable qua unfair. But it does not affect the moral quality of what is distributed. No objection to distribution does. Thus, if capital punishment is immoral per se even an impeccably fair distribution among the guilty would not justify it morally. On the other hand, if capital punishment is morally justified, no distribution, fair or unfair, could make it immoral.

Consider two kinds of discrimination. The death penalty (or any other punishment) may be distributed capriciously, e.g., by a lottery, among those equally guilty. The capriciousness cannot be avoided altogether. Criminal justice systems can minimize but not eliminate chance: one murderer may be found "not guilty" for lack of evidence. Another may be less lucky—even though both are equally guilty. Or, the discrimination may be intentional: the death penalty is deliberately imposed only, or mainly, on guilty Black murderers, never on legitimately guilty white ones. Such a distribution would be unfair and inconsistent with equal justice under law. But an unfair distribution does not affect the moral quality of what it distributes—unless the unfair distribution somehow inheres in the penalty and cannot be separated from it. Otherwise the moral quality of capital punishment is not more affected by its distribution than an unfair distribution of cookies affects their quality.[24]

Although often conflated and confused, equality and justice are different concepts. Equal justice certainly does not mean equal equality. Rather, it means justice distributed according only to factors the law recognizes as relevant, i.e., independently of irrelevant factors such as wealth, race, or religion and independently of how the available evidence has been obtained.

We can have equal injustice. A tyrant may impose the death penalty on all his opponents, or on all Jews, bachelors, Bosnians or homosexuals. The distri-

---

23. In 1986 about 2 percent of all persons convicted of murder were sentenced to death. About 12 Blacks were sent to death row for every thousand arrested for murder, vs. 16 whites.

24. To be sure, unequal distribution could violate the "equal protection of the laws" mandated by the Fourteenth Amendment. But the unequal distribution would have to be deliberate to be in violation.

bution would be equal but the law, including the penalty, would be unjust. Equal injustice of this sort has occurred throughout history. So has unequal justice. No society has found a way to avoid inequality altogether though much progress has been made in avoiding deliberate inequality and discrimination. Still, accidental inequality, luck and chance play a greater role than we like. One guilty criminal will be convicted and executed while another gets away with murder. He was never caught, or the evidence left the court doubtful. Courts seek truth; but, at best, they find evidence. Yet, unequal justice is justice still and the best we can do. If Smith gets way with murder and Jones, guilty, but no more guilty than Smith, is executed Jones's guilt was not diminished. Guilt is personal. No murderer's guilt is diminished because other murderers escape punishment. It is objectionable that some murderers get away with impunity, but their impunity does not reduce the guilt of others. Justice demands that those deserving it suffer the death penalty, even if others, who deserve it no less, escape because of discrimination, prosecutorial incompetence, insufficient evidence or for any other reason.

VII

David Baldus has investigated death sentences in Georgia to find that, if the victim of a Black murderer is white, the murderer is much more likely to be sentenced to death than if his victim had been Black. This practice clearly discriminates against Black victims whose life is valued less than that of white victims. The practice does not, however, discriminate against Black murderers. Indeed Black murderers are favored: murder tends to be intraracial; most black murderers murder black victims. Usually they are spared the death penalty, while white murderers, who murder white victims, are not.

VIII

Punishments retribute for the harm, the disruption of peace and security, that crime imposes on society as well as for the harm done to individual victims. These victims may feel that retribution does (or does not) satisfy their wish for revenge. But retribution is independent of revenge even if often confused with it. Abolitionists, by identifying retribution with revenge, expect to benefit from the bad reputation revenge has acquired, which may go back to dubious interpretations of the Bible. In Romans XII:19 the apostle Paul writes: "Avenge not yourselves for…vengeance is mine. I will repay sayeth the Lord." The Apostle continues (Romans 13:4): "The ruler…beareth not the sword in vain for he is…a revenger to execute wrath on him that doeth evil." (Elsewhere the Gospels favor turning the other cheek.) Paul clearly opposed individual revenge, but endorsed retribution by the ruler who "beareth not the sword in vain." Even if revenge motivated the retributive punishment of murderers, it would be irrelevant to the justice, or validity, of the punishment. Motives are irrelevant to the justice (deservedness) of what they motivate and retribution is independent of the motive of revenge.

IX

Many criminologists believe deterrence requires that prospective criminals calculate the advantages of crime and compare them with the disadvantages, including punishment. Criminals usually do not do that. Nor does deterrence theory require that they calculate. To be sure, criminals volunteer for the risk of punishment because they expect a net advantage from crime. But they calculate no more than law abiding persons calculate to remain law abiding. Society offers disincentives to law breakers and incentives to law abiding persons. These incentives and disincentives powerfully contribute to the formation of law abiding or law breaking habits. But few people calculate. Law abiding people habitually ignore criminal opportunities. Law breakers habitually discount the risk of punishment. Neither calculates. Both follow habits largely produced by the incentives and disincentives society offers, which have different effects on different individuals in different circumstances. Once these habits are ingrained they are followed almost independently of new incentives and disincentives. The major impact of criminal justice is on habit formation, not on habits already formed. Most of our behavior arises from habits which are seldom explicitly calculated. One must be careful, then, not to confuse the rational reconstruction of one's behavior with the processes that actually lead to it.[25]

X

Turn now to sundry arguments for abolition, some more popular than valid. The French writer Albert Camus insists that "a man is undone by waiting for capital punishment well before he dies. Two deaths are inflicted on him, the first being worse than the second, whereas he killed but once" (1961:205). (Would it follow that, had he murdered two persons, capital punishment would have been just?) The mistake Camus makes is in his belief, shared by

---

25. One may base the prediction of behavior on simple observation rather than attempting to understand the processes that lead to it. One could predict behavior the way one predicts the trajectory of a bullet, without assuming that the bullet calculates. The calculation of the observer should never be attributed to the observed, be it a bullet or a person.

many abolitionists, that the pain inflicted on the murderer should not exceed that of his victim. This limit derives from the limit the lex talionis set for retaliation or compensation. But the lex talionis regarded as torts acts we consider crimes. Camus' reasoning might govern tort rules for compensation. But criminal law must not be confused with tort law. Punishment for a crime is neither compensation nor retaliation, but retribution, as threatened by law, for the harm inflicted on the social order. Retribution need not be limited to, or be equal to the suffering of crime victims.[26]

A somewhat frivolous argument alleges that life imprisonment without parole would cost less than execution. The argument is of doubtful relevance and accuracy. If one correctly calculates the cost of life imprisonment for murderers, who must be held in expensive high security prisons, it seems no less than the cost of execution. (Most murderers are young and likely to spend a long time in prison.) On the other hand, the cost of execution has been greatly inflated by the very persons who complain about it. They insist on lengthy procedures which add far more to cost than to justice. Frivolous appeals could be reduced with considerable savings. The cost of execution is currently estimated at about $2.5 million. If one assumes a cost of $30,000–40,000 for a year in high security prison and adds the cost of legal appeals (lifers keep their attorneys busy) and further assumes an average of forty years in prison, the cost is about the same whether we execute or incarcerate for life. But, as mentioned, the cost of execution is far higher than required by justice.

Some technical advantages of the death penalty should not be overlooked. By threatening it, prosecutors may persuade accomplices to testify against murderers, or persuade the murderers themselves to plead guilty in exchange for a life sentence. Also, in a hostage situation police can promise the criminal that the prosecution will not ask for the death penalty if he releases his hostages. Without the death penalty the criminal can threaten to kill his victims, while police can only threaten incarceration.

Religious objections to the death penalty reflect the Zeitgeist more than theology. In his Summa Theologica Thomas Aquinas writes: "a man shall be sentenced to death for crimes of irreparable harm." In his Summa Contra Gentiles Thomas points out that "[murderers] may be justly executed.... [T]hey also have, at the critical point of death, the opportunity to be converted to God through repentance." (They did not give this opportunity to their victims.)

Trendy abolitionists often conflate two different virtues, justice and charity. They must be distinguished. Justice tries to mete out what is deserved. Charity impels us to love and help regardless of desert. Religion enjoins compassion and forgiveness, even of murderers, but does not suggest that justice should be

---

26. There is no way, in any case, of measuring the suffering of a person awaiting execution and comparing it to the suffering of a murder victim.

replaced by compassion. Scripture presents God as legislator and judge who imparts *Justitia Misericordiae Dulcore Temperata*: Justice tempered by mercy, but not replaced by it.

Abolition of the death penalty would promise prospective murderers that we will never do to them what they will do to their victims. Such a promise seems unwise as well as immoral.

References

Beccaria, C. (1764) *Dei Delittie dell e Pene.* Firenze: Felice Le Monnier. (English trans., *On Crimes and Punishments* (1963) New York: Bobbs-Merrill Co.)

Camus, A. (196l) *Resistance, Rebellion, and Death.* (J. O'Brien trans.) New York: Alfred A. Knopf.

Furman v. Georgia (1972) 408 U.S. 238.

Kaufmann, W. (1973) *Without Guilt and Justice: From Decidophobia to Autonomy.* New York: P.H. Wyden.

McCorquodale v. State (1974) 211 S.E.2d 577 (Ga.).

Phillips, D.P. (1982) "The Fluctuation of Homicide After Publicized Executions: Reply to Kobbervig, Inverarity, and Lauderdale." *American Journal of Sociology* 88:165–167.

Phillips, D.P. and K. Bollen (1985) "Same Time Last Year: Selective Data Dredging for Negative Findings." *American Sociological Review* 50:101–116.

Reiman, J. and E. van den Haag (1990) "On the Common Saying that it is Better that Ten Guilty Persons Escape than that One Innocent Suffer: *Pro* and *Con.*" *Social Philosophy & Policy* 7:221–248.

Stack, S. (1987) "Publicized Executions and Homicides, 1950–1980." *American Sociological Review* 52:532–540.

Trop v. Dulles (1958) 356 U.S. 86.

van den Haag, E. (1994) "How Is Entitlement Deserved." *Public Affairs Quarterly* 8:395–402.

van den Haag, E. (1992) "The Lex Talionis Before and After Criminal Law." *Criminal Justice Ethics* 11:2, 62.

van den Haag, E. (1975) *Punishing Criminals: Concerning a Very Old and Painful Question.* New York: Basic Books. (*Reprinted* (1991) Lanham, MD: University Press of America.)

Chapter 8

Is Capital Punishment an Effective Deterrent for Murder? An Examination of Social Science Research

Ruth D. Peterson
William C. Bailey

Does the provision for capital punishment afford citizens an added measure of protection against being murdered? Are homicide rates lower in jurisdictions where executions are more common? Does delaying capital punishment rob this penalty of its deterrent effectiveness? Would greater media coverage of executions make capital punishment more effective in deterring murder? Academics and citizens alike have long debated these questions.

In this chapter we attempt to contribute to an understanding of deterrence and the death penalty by: (1) summarizing the major tenets of deterrence theory and how it applies to the death penalty; (2) briefly examining early comparative investigations of homicide rates for death penalty and abolitionist jurisdictions; (3) illustrating the comparative methodology with recent homicide data; (4) examining more recent time-series and cross-sectional multivariate studies of deterrence and capital punishment which became popular during the1970s; (5) assessing the adequacy of recent multivariate studies; and (6) suggesting further research to examine remaining questions about deterrence and capital punishment.

In our review and assessment of the literature, we will be concerned solely with the "general" deterrent effect of capital punishment—how the threat and application of the death penalty discourages would-be killers. We will not examine works on special deterrence—how effective capital punishment is compared to life in prison, or long term incarceration, in discouraging repeat offending. Capital punishment is, of course, 100 percent effective in preventing recidivism. Our analysis is also restricted to studies that have appeared in academic volumes and refereed journal articles. We do not consider opinion pieces that have appeared in popular magazines or newspapers. Nor do we consider unpublished analyses which have yet to receive appropriate professional scrutiny.

Deterrence Theory and
Capital Punishment

Deterrence theory rests upon the premise that individuals weigh the costs and rewards associated with alternative actions, and choose behaviors that yield the greatest gain at the least cost. Thus, crime occurs when illegal actions are perceived either as more profitable (rewarding) or less costly (painful) than conventional alternatives. From a deterrence viewpoint, crime prevention is achieved through providing a system of sanctions that (1) convinces would-be criminals that crime does not pay or law-abiding behaviors pay more (general deterrence); and (2) prevents recidivism by teaching a direct lesson to those who have already engaged in crime (special deterrence). To achieve maximum deterrence, sanctions must be severe enough to outweigh the benefits derived from crime, administered with certainty, administered promptly, and made known to would-be-offenders. The hypothesized effects of these dimensions of punishment on crime are contingent rather than additive. For example, regardless of their degree of severity, sanctions cannot deter if their level of certainty is zero.

Deterrence proponents view murder as rational behavior, and assume that in calculating the gains and losses from killing, potential offenders are aware of the death penalty and regard it as a more *severe* sanction than imprisonment. Here, murder is discouraged because the threat of one's own death presumably outweighs the rewards gained from killing another. In addition, some contend that capital punishment provides an important educative function in society by validating the sanctity of human life (Berns 1979; van den Haag 1975, van den Haag and Conrad 1983).

Despite this logic, many criminologists have challenged the applicability of deterrence theory to murder. These scholars contend that most murders are not premeditated; rather they are emotionally charged and spontaneous events—"acts of passion" (Bowers and Pierce 1980; Chambliss 1967; Luckenbill 1977). Under such conditions, it is unlikely that would-be-offenders ("killers") give serious, if any, thought to the death penalty.

Critics of deterrence also have questioned whether the message conveyed by executions underscores the sanctity of life. Proponents of what has become known as the brutalization thesis contend that the message communicated by executions is lethal vengeance and a disrespect for human life:

> Executions demonstrate that it is correct and appropriate to kill those who have gravely offended us. The fact that such killings are to be performed only by duly appointed officials on duly convicted offenders is a detail that may get obscured by the message that such offenders deserve to die (Bowers and Pierce 1980:456).

Indeed, some of the most important founders of the general deterrence doctrine were opposed to the death penalty because they were convinced that capital punishment communicates to the general public that it is proper to kill those who have wronged them. In so doing, reliance on the death penalty puts the lives of citizens at greater risk (Beccaria 1764/1963; Bentham 1843/1962).

The Empirical Research

Studies considering the deterrence/brutalization issue span many decades. They can be divided into three general categories based upon chronology, methodology, and substantive concerns: early comparative studies, multivariate analyses of general homicide for states and the nation, and analyses of capital homicides.

The Past: Early Comparative Studies

Early examinations of capital punishment and deterrence in the U.S. and abroad involved several types of comparative investigations. Some studies compared mean homicide rates for states with capital punishment (retentionist states) to rates for non-retentionist or abolitionist jurisdictions. Others compared homicide rates for capital punishment states with rates for neighboring non-death penalty states (Schuessler 1952; Sellin 1967; Sutherland 1925). And still others compared homicide rates for the same states before and after the abolition and/or reinstatement of the death penalty (Bedau 1967; Schuessler 1952; Sellin 1955, 1959, 1967). By examining contiguous states and making before/after comparisons for the same states, investigators hoped to control for factors other than punishment that influence homicide rates.

None of the early comparative analyses provided support for the deterrence argument. Rather, in study after study during the first six decades of this century, scholars documented that murder rates were often higher in death penalty than in abolitionist jurisdictions, and that abolition and/or reintroduction of capital punishment was sometimes followed by an increase in murders and sometimes not. Based on this evidence, most criminologists came to agree with Sellin (1967:138) that: "the presence of the death penalty in law and practice has no discernible effect as a deterrent to murder."

Murder Rates for Death Penalty versus Abolitionist States

Below (Table 1) we examine homicide data for U.S. states for the period 1980–2000. The purpose of this analysis is to illustrate the aggregate compara-

Table 1
Mean Rates of Murder and Non-Negligent Manslaughter
for Death Penalty and Abolitionist States

Year	Abolitionist States	Death Penalty States
1980	5.2	9.4
1981	5.3	9.2
1982	5.2	8.5
1983	4.8	7.3
1984	4.4	6.9
1985	4.6	7.0
1986	4.7	7.6
1987	4.9	7.1
1988	4.5	7.2
1989	5.1	7.1
1990	5.0	7.9
1991	5.1	8.2
1992	4.9	7.8
1993	5.3	8.1
1994	4.4	8.0
1995	4.1	7.6
1996	3.6	7.1
1997	3.5	6.6
1998	3.2	6.2
1999	3.6	5.5
2000	2.8	5.2

tive methodology, and to assess whether average and yearly murder rates are still lower for abolitionist jurisdictions.

For the period 1980–2000, Table 1 presents mean rates of homicide by year for death penalty and non-death penalty states. If capital punishment affords citizens an added measure of protection against being a victim of homicide, then the murder rate per 100,000 population should be lower for death penalty than abolitionist jurisdictions. The results show that year-by-year murder rates for abolitionist and retentionist states were quite stable over the 1980–2000 period. Contrary to the deterrence hypothesis, for each of the 21 years, the average rate is higher for states that prescribe capital punishment for murder. Indeed, murder rates ranged from 1.4 (1989) to 2.0 (1996) times higher for retentionist jurisdictions over the period.

This pattern is consistent with that observed in the early comparative analyses, but it does not prove that capital punishment is not a deterrent to murder. Nor does it prove that capital punishment produces higher homicide rates (brutalization). It is possible that death penalty and abolitionist jurisdictions in the U.S. differ in other significant respects which influence lethal violence. For example, research has documented that murder rates are significantly higher in jurisdictions with large urban, black, youthful, and poor populations. If these socio-demographic conditions are found more commonly in death penalty than abolitionist jurisdictions, then they could account for the lower average murder rate for states without capital punishment, and any actual deterrent effect taking place would be masked in the type of analysis presented in Table 1.

Early investigators explored this possibility in two ways. First, by conducting simple before-after studies of murder rates for individual jurisdictions which initiated the death penalty for murder after a period without capital punishment, abolished the death penalty after a period of prescribing capital punishment, or abolished capital punishment for a short period and then returned to the death penalty. If capital punishment protects citizens against murder, then offense rates for a jurisdiction should rise if the death penalty is abolished, and decline when the death penalty is introduced. Because changes in socio-demographic conditions generally are not subject to immediate change, before-after analyses of murder rates for states provide an important "control" advantage over aggregate comparisons of average homicide rates for death penalty versus abolitionist jurisdictions.

The results of before-after analyses have not been consistent with deterrence expectations. Instead, the abolition of capital punishment has sometimes been followed by an increase in killings, and sometimes not. Similarly, the reinstatement of the death penalty has sometimes been followed by a decline in murder, and sometimes by an increase in lethal violence. Typically, however, the abolition and/or reinstatement of the death penalty has *not* been followed by an unusual increase or decrease in killings. Moreover, observed changes have paralleled closely those for neighboring states which have experienced no change in the provision for capital punishment.

Comparison of Neighboring Death Penalty and Abolitionist States

On the assumption that neighboring states typically are similar with respect to other factors influencing levels of homicide, a second strategy that has been used to isolate the possible deterrent effect of capital punishment has been to compare murder rates for *neighboring* death penalty and abolitionist states. These comparisons have also yielded negligible results for the deterrence hypothesis.

In Table 2 we illustrate the contiguous state strategy with murder rate data for the 1980–2000 period for six groupings of retentionist and abolitionist states that commonly were considered in earlier studies. Abolitionist states are indicated with an asterisk (*). Due to space constraints, we have rounded murder rates to whole numbers (per 100,000 population).

For most of the six groupings, the evidence is contrary to the deterrence hypothesis. For New England states, New Hampshire is the only state that prescribes the death penalty for murder. Rates are consistently lower for New

Table 2
Rates of Murder and Nonnegligent Manslaughter for Neighboring Death Penalty and Abolitionist States 1980–1990

State	Period	1980	1981	1982	1983	1984	1985	1986	1987	1988	1989	1990
*Maine	1980–2000	3	3	2	2	2	2	2	3	3	3	2
*Vermont	1980–2000	2	4	2	4	2	3	2	2	2	2	2
New Hampshire		3	3	2	2	1	2	2	3	2	3	2
*Rhode Island	1980–2000	4	4	4	3	3	4	4	4	4	5	5
*Massachusetts	1980–82 1984–2000	4	4	4	4	4	4	4	3	4	4	4
*Michigan	1980–2000	10	9	9	10	10	11	11	12	11	11	10
*Ohio	1980	8	7	6	6	5	5	6	6	5	6	6
Indiana		9	7	7	5	6	6	6	6	6	6	6
*Wisconsin	1980–2000	3	3	3	3	3	3	3	4	3	4	5
*Iowa	1980–2000	2	3	2	2	2	2	2	2	2	2	2
Illinois		11	11	9	10	9	8	9	8	9	8	8
*North Dakota	1980–2000	1	2	1	2	1	1	1	2	2	1	1
South Dakota		1	2	3	2	2	2	4	2	3	1	2
Montana		4	3	4	2	2	6	3	4	3	4	5
Wyoming		6	6	9	6	3	4	5	2	3	4	5
*West Virginia	1980–2000	7	6	5	5	4	4	6	5	5	7	6
Virginia		9	9	7	7	8	7	7	7	8	8	9
*Oregon	1981–83	5	4	5	4	5	5	7	6	5	5	4
Washington		6	5	4	5	5	5	5	6	6	4	5
Idaho		3	4	3	4	3	2	3	3	4	3	3

* States without capital punishment for the periods indicated. Death penalty status determined as of December 31st of the years indicated.

Table 2, continued
Rates of Murder and Nonnegligent Manslaughter for Neighboring
Death Penalty and Abolitionist States 1991–2000

State	Period	1991	1992	1993	1994	1995	1996	1997	1998	1999	2000
*Maine	1980–2000	1	2	2	2	2	2	2	2	2	1
*Vermont	1980–2000	2	2	4	1	5	2	2	2	3	2
New Hampshire		4	2	2	1	2	2	1	2	2	2
*Rhode Island	1980–2000	4	4	4	4	3	3	3	2	4	4
*Massachusetts	1980–82	4	4	4	4	4	3	2	2	2	2
	1984–2000										
*Michigan	1980–2000	11	10	10	10	9	8	8	7	7	7
*Ohio	1980	7	7	6	6	5	5	5	4	4	4
Indiana		8	8	8	8	8	7	7	8	7	6
*Wisconsin	1980–2000	5	4	4	5	4	4	4	4	3	3
*Iowa	1980–2000	2	2	2	2	2	2	2	2	2	2
Illinois		11	11	11	12	10	10	9	8	8	7
*North Dakota	1980–2000	1	2	2	0	1	2	1	1	2	1
South Dakota		2	1	3	1	2	1	1	1	3	1
Montana		3	4	3	3	2	4	5	2	3	2
Wyoming		3	4	3	3	2	3	4	5	2	2
*West Virginia	1980–2000	6	6	7	5	5	4	4	4	4	3
Virginia		9	9	8	9	8	8	7	6	6	6
*Oregon	1981–83	5	5	5	5	4	4	3	4	3	2
Washington		4	4	5	6	5	5	4	4	3	3
Idaho		2	4	3	4	4	4	3	3	2	1

* States without capital punishment for the periods indicated. Death penalty status determined as of December 31st of the years indicated.

Hampshire than for abolitionist Rhode Island and Massachusetts over the 1980–2000 period. However, the pattern for New Hampshire is very similar to that for Maine and Vermont, neither of which is a death penalty jurisdiction. For some years rates are higher for New Hampshire than for Maine and/or Vermont, and for other years the pattern is in the opposite direction. However, for most years, the rates are the same for these three states. Also of note, Massachusetts provided for capital punishment in 1983, but the murder rate remained at 4.0 throughout the early 1980s.

Turning to other jurisdictions, in the West rates are lower for abolitionist North Dakota compared with retentionist South Dakota, Montana, and Wyoming. And in the South, murder rates are lower each year for abolitionist West Virginia compared to Virginia, a death penalty state during the period. For the three Northwest states, the period where rates for death penalty and an abolitionist state (Oregon 1981–1983) can be compared is quite short. Still, there is no indication of a deterrent effect for capital punishment. Note also that the murder rate did not decline with Oregon's return to capital punishment in 1984.

The two groupings of mid-western states provide mixed results. Compared to Indiana and Ohio (which was without the death penalty from 1978–1980), homicide rates are consistently higher for abolitionist Michigan. This, on the surface, is consistent with the deterrence argument. In the opposite direction, however, murder rates are consistently higher in Illinois than in neighboring Wisconsin and Iowa which were abolitionist states throughout the period. Unfortunately, these opposing patterns can lead to misleading conclusions. It is well-recognized that Illinois's high homicide rate is very largely a function of killings in one city—Chicago. There is no counterpart to Chicago in Wisconsin and Iowa. Accordingly, Illinois and its abolitionist neighbors are ill-suited to address the deterrence and death penalty question using a simple comparative methodology.

The case is similar for contiguous Michigan, Indiana, and Ohio. Throughout the period the homicide rate in abolitionist Michigan was dominated by killings in a single city—Detroit. When Detroit's killings are excluded in calculating the Michigan homicide rate, there is no indication of an added measure of protection afforded by the death penalty in neighboring Ohio or Indiana. However, excluding a high homicide community from one type of state (Detroit in Michigan), but ignoring the effect of similar atypical communities in neighboring retentionist states (Cleveland in Ohio, and Indianapolis in Indiana, for example) is to betray the intent of contiguous state comparisons—to control for those "other" factors influencing homicides.

In sum, although more enlightening than simple aggregate comparisons of states, the contiguous state methodology has some important limitations. As the above findings illustrate, in some, but not all, cases neighboring death penalty and abolitionist states are not similar enough to draw reasonable conclusions. In addition, relying on contiguous state comparisons means that we ignore the death penalty question for some jurisdictions. Notably, except for West Virginia, there are no abolitionist states in the southern or border regions of the country. Finally, the contiguous state approach does not differentiate properly between neighboring death penalty jurisdictions which vary in their actual *use* of capital punishment.

The Certainty of Capital Punishment

Based on the deterrence perspective, criminal sanctions must be administered with a high degree of certainty if they are to be effective in preventing crime. Yet, neither aggregate nor contiguous state comparisons of murder rates provides a means of addressing the certainty hypothesis. To assess this issue requires examining the correspondence between murder rates and *actual* levels of use of capital punishment. Investigators did not give systematic attention to the certainty of capital punishment until 1952 when Schuessler examined average execution rates for the period 1937–1941 for 41 death penalty states. Schuessler divided states into four groups according to their homicide rate, and computed the mean execution rate (number of executions per 1,000 homicides) for each group of states. He noted the following pattern:

Homicide Rate by Quartile	Average Homicide Rate	Average Execution Rate
Highest	15	21
Upper Middle	8	18
Lower Middle	4	19
Lowest	2	25

These data showed that homicide rates do not decline consistently as the certainty of execution increases, leading Schuessler (1952) to conclude that the death penalty has little if anything to do with the relative occurrence of murder.

Importantly, Schuessler's simple bivariate comparison of murder and execution rates does not permit one to rule out the possibility that murder rates may be higher or lower for high execution or low execution states due to the influence of various social, demographic and economic factors. In other words, retentionist states that make varying use of capital punishment may differ in other important respects which *contaminate* simple bivariate comparisons that were the central focus of research through the 1960s. The mid-1970s saw growing recognition of this possible limitation, and this recognition ushered in a new round of death penalty research.

Contemporary Death Penalty Studies

In the mid-1970s, Isaac Ehrlich (1973, 1975) correctly pointed out that previous comparative analyses largely ignored the certainty of capital punishment, failed to consider additional deterrence variables such as the certainty of imprisonment for murder, and did not introduce important socio-demographic control variables associated with murder rates formally in a statistical analysis. In response to these concerns, Ehrlich designed a study to examine how such shortcomings may have influenced the results of earlier studies. His analysis considered several measures of the certainty of capital punishment, including the ratio of executions to prison admissions for murder. He also used complicated statistical techniques to control for a variety of socio-demographic factors. The required data were aggregated on an annual basis for the U.S., 1933–1969.

Holding constant the influence of other contributors to homicide through statistical techniques, Ehrlich found that over the period there was a significant national decline in the level of execution and a significant rise in the murder rate. In contrast to previous analyses, Ehrlich concluded that capital punishment is a significant deterrent to murder; most notably, he suggested that on average each execution over the 1933–1969 period may have prevented seven to eight murders.

Despite its apparent strengths, Ehrlich's study came into serious question due to various data quality and procedural problems that became apparent when researchers attempted to replicate his analysis (Bowers and Pierce 1975; Klein, Forst and Filatov 1978; Passell and Taylor 1975; Yunker 1976). Here we note just a few of the most serious limitations. First is the problem of aggregation error/bias stemming from Ehrlich's examination of the nation as a whole rather than individual states. To illustrate, over the 1933–1969 period, yearly homicide rates on average were higher for death penalty than abolitionist states, and execution rates obviously were higher for retentionist than abolitionist jurisdictions (where executions legally were not permitted). Unfortunately, by computing annual rates of homicides and executions without distinguishing between the two types of states, Ehrlich's findings do not reflect the reality for either death penalty or non-death penalty jurisdictions.

Second, Ehrlich emphasized the certainty of execution and ignored whether jurisdictions provide for capital punishment (see Baldus and Cole 1975). This oversight is ironic in light of Ehrlich's criticisms of other researchers for taking into account only the severity (presence of) dimension of capital punishment. Most importantly, because of his failure to take into account the percent of the population living in abolitionist jurisdictions, it is not possible to determine from Ehrlich's study whether citizens who resided in death penalty states were afforded an added measure of protection by the provision for capital punishment.

Finally, subsequent studies showed that any suggestion of deterrence in Ehrlich's analysis was tied directly to which specific years during the

1933–1969 period were examined. For 1933 through the mid-1960s, no evidence of deterrence was observed. Only when the time-series was extended to 1969 did there appear to be a deterrent effect. This "flip-flop" in findings combined with the other limitations led most scholars to disregard Ehrlich's study.

The Aftermath of Ehrlich

Although Ehrlich's study soon lost credibility, his work is important because he paid direct attention to the certainty hypothesis by examining the deterrent effect of executions versus imprisonment for murder. He also introduced a new statistical approach—multivariate regression analysis—as a means for isolating the effect of capital punishment from the effects of various socio-demographic factors on homicide. Despite the failure of researchers to replicate his findings, the multivariate approach pioneered by Ehrlich has become a standard in death penalty research.

Since Ehrlich, there have been dozens of multivariate longitudinal time-series studies of the U.S. and individual states, and cross-sectional state analyses of murder rates and death penalty practices. Because of their large number and the fact that the findings have been highly uniform, we review here only a sampling of post-Ehrlich studies which make an important contribution to death penalty research in terms of the: (1) geographic units or time periods being examined, (2) type of deterrence variable under consideration, or (3) type of murder examined.

State Level Time-Series Studies

As noted, national time-series capital punishment studies are subject to serious problems of aggregation bias. To address this problem, some researchers have examined homicide and execution time-series data for individual death penalty jurisdictions for periods dating back to the early part of this century. California (Bailey 1979c), Illinois (Decker and Kohfeld 1984), New York (Bowers and Pierce 1980), North Carolina (Bailey 1979a), Ohio (Bailey 1979d), Oregon (Bailey 1979b), Utah (Bailey 1978), and Washington, D.C. (Bailey 1984b) are among the jurisdictions examined. None of these analyses produced evidence of a deterrent effect for the certainty of capital punishment. This is true despite the fact that these studies consider periods in U.S. history when levels of execution, and the ratio of executions to homicides, were much higher than found over the last few decades. Thus, state-level time series analyses suggest that the deterrent effect of capital punishment might be negligible even if there were more extensive use of capital punishment.

Further support for this conclusion comes from a recent monthly time-series analysis of homicide and execution patterns for Texas for the 1984–1997 period (Sorensen, Wrinkle, Brewer and Marquart 1999). During 1984–1997,

Texas conducted more executions than any other state. For example, in 1997, 37 (50%) of the nation's 74 executions took place in Texas. However, the level of execution was not constant over the period. The number of executions was flat from 1984 (n=3) through 1991 (n=5), but then rose dramatically from 1992 (n=12) through 1997 (n=37). To test the certainty hypothesis, Sorensen and colleagues formed a monthly time-series (n=168) for (1) the general murder rate, (2) the rate of felony murders—burglary-, robbery- and sexual assault-related killings, (3) the number of executions, and (4) a number of control variables: percent metropolitan population, the unemployment rate, percent AFDC population, percent persons 18–34 years of age, the homicide conviction rate, and the incarceration rate for felons.

Using standard time-series multiple regression techniques, Sorensen et al. found a very slight positive relationship between monthly executions and the general murder rate, and a very slight negative association between executions and rates of felony murder. In neither case was the tradeoff between executions and killings statistically significant. Sorensen et al. conclude that for the most active execution state in the nation, there is no evidence that capital punishment deters murder in general, or felony murders, which are death eligible crimes in Texas and in other retentionist states.

Cross-State Analyses

Some researchers have conducted cross-sectional analyses of the relationship between state executions and murder rates while controlling for various sociodemographic factors. In some analyses, measures of the certainty of imprisonment for murder and the length of prison sentences for murder were incorporated as additional deterrence variables (Bailey 1975, 1977, 1980b, 1983; Ehrlich 1977; Forst 1977; Passell 1975; Peterson and Bailey 1988). Ehrlich (1977) was the only researcher to report evidence of a deterrent effect for executions. Because no other investigations observed a deterrence pattern, Ehrlich's work was once again subject to scrutiny. And once again scholars found serious theoretical and methodological difficulties with his analysis (Barnett 1981; Beyleveld 1982; Brier and Feinberg 1980; Friedman 1979; McGahey 1980).

The Celerity Issue

Proponents of deterrence argue that for legal sanctions to be effective, they must be administered *swiftly* (with celerity). Jeffery (1965:299), for example, has emphasized the importance of the celerity (and certainty) of sanctions in accounting for the negative evidence for the death penalty:

> The *uncertainty* of capital punishment is one major factor in the system. Another factor is the *time* element. A consequence [the death penalty] must be applied immediately if it is to be effec-

tive.... The lesson to be learned from capital punishment is not that punishment does not deter, but that the improper and sloppy use of punishment does not deter.

Despite this emphasis, with one exception (Bailey 1980a) the celerity of executions has been a neglected issue in deterrence research. Bailey conducted a cross-state analysis for 1951–1960 examining the relationship between homicide rates for death penalty states and (1) the certainty of execution for homicide, (2) the certainty and severity of imprisonment for homicide, and (3) the celerity of the death penalty—the elapsed time between the sentencing and execution of convicted murderers. Controlling for various socio-demographic factors to avoid spurious results for the sanction variables, Bailey found no evidence that speedy executions discourage murder. At the bivariate level the correlation between 1960 murder rates and the average elapsed time (1951–1960) between sentencing and executions was near zero r = -.01). This pattern persisted in the multivariate analysis.

Analyses of Execution Publicity

Another fundamental premise of deterrence theory is that to prevent crime, the threat and application of the law must be communicated to the public. Some deterrence theorists contend that the publicity surrounding punishment serves important educative, moralizing, and normative validation functions (Andenaes 1974; Gibbs 1975, 1986). Applied to capital punishment, high levels of execution publicity should result in lower homicide rates.

Most research examining the deterrent impact of execution publicity has focused on more recent periods (since 1977). After a 10-year moratorium on capital punishment (1968–1976), executions resumed in the U.S. in January, 1977. The first few executions after the moratorium received considerable print and electronic media coverage. For example, the execution of Gary Gilmore in Utah on January 17, 1977 was front page news across the country, and was the lead story for the evening news for the three major television networks.

McFarland (1983) examined whether the tremendous amount of news coverage given the first four executions to follow the moratorium (Gary Gilmore in Utah, 1977, John Spinkelink in Florida, 1979, Jesse Bishop in Nevada, 1979, and Steven Judy in Indiana, 1981) produced a significant decline in U.S. homicides. Examining weekly health statistics for homicide for various periods leading up to and following each of the four "celebrated" executions, McFarland did not find evidence of a significant downward (or upward) shift in weekly killings. The Gilmore execution was followed by a decline in the level of U.S. weekly homicides for two weeks following the execution, but homicides during the next few weeks seemed to be unaffected. The dip in killings immediately following Gilmore's execution suggests a possible short-term deterrent effect, but McFarland rejects this interpretation. Rather, he demonstrates that the significant decline in killings following the Gilmore execution was confined to parts of the country that experienced abnormally severe winter conditions during that period. Following the Gilmore execution in Utah weather conditions were normal for the western states. For those jurisdictions there was not a notable decline in homicides.

Stack (1987) took a different approach in examining the deterrent effect of media coverage of executions. For the 1950–1980 period, he conducted a monthly time-series analysis of the relationship between murder rates and the *amount* of newspaper coverage devoted to executions (high, medium or low), while statistically controlling for the level of unemployment and the percent of the population aged 16 to 34 years. Executions recorded in *Facts on File* (a comprehensive national index of major news stories) and appearing in the *New York Times* were classified as receiving high levels of publicity. Those appearing in the *New York Times*, but not in *Facts*, were classified as receiving moderate media attention. And executions not receiving coverage in either source were considered as low-publicity cases. Stack found a significant decline in homicide rates for months with highly publicized executions, but not for moderate or low execution publicity months. Over the three decades, he estimated that "16 [highly] publicized executions may have saved as many as 480 lives," for an average of 30 persons saved per execution (Stack 1987:538).

Bailey and Peterson (1989) replicated Stack's investigation for the years Stack considered (1950–1980) and for a more extended period (1940–1986). In doing so, they corrected for a number of problems of the earlier investigation including several coding errors for the execution publicity variables. Stack had classified 23 executions (occurring during 16 different months) as receiving high levels of publicity. However, using his classification scheme,

Bailey and Peterson document 26 high publicity executions spread over 19 months. After correcting the coding errors for the media data, Bailey and Peterson found merely a chance association between execution publicity and homicide rates. This non-deterrence pattern persisted when the analysis was extended from 1940 through 1986.

Television News Coverage of Executions

For the periods considered by Stack (1950–1980) and Bailey and Peterson (1940–1986), newspapers provided an important source of daily news. However, the percent of homes with television sets grew dramatically from less than 10 percent in 1950 to over 98 percent by the early 1980s, with surveys showing that television had become the most "popular," "complete," intelligent," and "unbiased" source of news for the American public (Bower 1985:17).

Because of the growing importance of television news, Bailey (1990) examined the relationship between monthly murder rates and evening television news coverage devoted to executions in the U.S. for the 1976–1987 period.

Figures for murder and nonnegligent manslaughter came from the FBI, and news coverage data from the Vanderbilt Television News Archives. He found only a chance association between homicide rates and the *amount* of television news coverage devoted to executions. Similarly, he did not observe consistent evidence of deterrence when different *types* of coverage were aired, e.g., very graphic versus a matter-of-fact presentation of the execution, or murderers presented as fully deserving of executions versus those where there was serious concern about the fairness of the death sentences (as in cases where youth or retarded persons were executed). In sum, researchers have given attention to the possible deterrent effect of execution publicity. However, this body of work has produced no credible evidence that the level or type of print or electronic media attention devoted to executions significantly discourages murder.

Deterrence and Different Types of Murder

While support for the deterrence argument has been negligible, most death penalty researchers have made use of either police data for murder and nonnegligent manslaughter, or public health figures for homicide derived from coroners and medical examiners. The FBI homicide category of murder and nonnegligent manslaughter is defined as "the willful nonnegligent killing of one human being by another" (Federal Bureau of Investigation 1995:13). Observing the World Health Organization's *International Classification of Diseases*, the National Center for Health Statistics defines homicide as "a death resulting from an injury purposely inflicted by another person" (National Center for Health Statistics 1967:9). The use of homicide data defined in such broad terms is problematic because the death penalty is not aimed at deterring all types of homicide (van den Haag 1969, 1975, 1978; van den Haag and Conrad 1983). Rather, only certain types of killing are capital crimes. Specifically, most death penalty jurisdictions restrict capital punishment to (1) planned, intentional killings, i.e., premeditated murder, first degree murder, or aggravated murder, and/or (2) killings that result from the commission of another felony, i.e., felony murders. It is these "capital" murders, not the overall rate of homicide, that should be examined in deterrence investigations. Unfortunately, the data sources noted above do not differentiate capital from non-capital killings.

In deterrence investigations, the use of a broad category of homicides would be acceptable if it could be assumed that the proportion of capital to total homicides is a constant over time and across jurisdictions. Most death penalty investigators have been willing to accept this assumption, but no one has succeeded in accurately identifying and counting capital offenses hidden in the available FBI and Public Health homicide figures.

Studies of Capital Murder—First Degree Killings

Despite this difficulty, there have been a few attempts to examine directly the impact of capital punishment on death-eligible killings. Bailey (1975) examined for 1967 and 1968 *first degree murder* rates and execution rates for states, controlling for a variety of sociodemographic factors associated with homicides. Figures for first-degree murder (the number of prison admissions for first-degree murder) came from a survey of state correctional authorities. Consistent with studies of general homicides, this analysis of "capital killings" provided no indication of deterrence. Average rates of first-degree murder were not higher for abolitionist (1967 = .18, 1968 = .21) than death penalty (1967 = .47, 1968 = .58) jurisdictions, and there was only a slight non-significant inverse correlation between levels of execution and rates of first-degree murder (1967, r = -.137, 1968, r = -.194.

Bailey (1984a) also conducted a monthly time-series analysis of executions and first-degree murders in Chicago, Illinois for the period 1915–1921. First-degree murder figures were taken from Chicago Police Department reports, and Cook County execution data were drawn from the records of the Cook County Prison. Contrary to deterrence expectations, Bailey found a slight and non-significant positive relationship r = .158) between rates of first-degree murder and monthly executions, controlling for important social and demographic factors that contribute to homicides.

Felony Murder

A recent analysis by Peterson and Bailey (1991) calls into question the possibility of deterrence for felony murder—the most common type of capital homicide. Felony murders and suspected felony murders constitute a quarter to a third of homicides annually, and they also account for a majority of executions. For the period Peterson and Bailey examined (1971–1987), there were 93 executions in the U.S. Of these, 67 (72%) were for murders associated with robbery, rape, burglary, and kidnaping. In view of these figures Peterson and Bailey argued that for recent years, an analysis of felony murders would provide the most direct test of the possible deterrent effect of capital punishment for *capital murder*. Thus, using unpublished FBI felony murder data, they examined the relationship between the *amount* and *type* of television news coverage of executions and overall monthly felony murder rates, as well as rates for killings resulting from rape, robbery, burglary, larceny, vehicle theft, narcotics crimes and arson. Their analysis also took into account selected law enforcement and socio-demographic control variables. Only rates of narcotics-related murders were found to be significantly lower during months when there was television news coverage of "questionable" executions—those where the person who was put to death was very young or retarded. Peterson and Bailey were not able to offer a plausible explanation for this unique pattern.

Killings Involving Strangers vs. Non-Strangers

Cochran, Chamlin, and Seth (1994) conducted a weekly time-series analysis of felony murder to examine the possible deterrent effect of Oklahoma's return to capital punishment after a 25 year moratorium. On September 10, 1990 Charles Coleman was executed at the Oklahoma State Penitentiary. Examining the 1989–1991 period (n = 156 weeks), Cochran et al. did not find a statistically significant decline in total felony murder following the Coleman execution. However, they did observe what they termed a strong brutalization effect for the Coleman execution for killings involving strangers. The mean number of weekly killings involving persons not known to one another was .42 for the pre-execution period compared to an average of .76 for the post-execution period. This significant increase in stranger killings (+.34) is not due to any non-execution factor that Cochran and his associates could detect.

In a follow-up investigation Bailey (1998) extended the Cochran, Chamlin and Seth Oklahoma analysis by incorporating into the 1989–1991 weekly time series selected sociodemographic control variables (population, percent age 15–34 years, the unemployment rate, percent AFDC population), the number of executions carried out in other states, and the amount of newspaper coverage executions received in the *Oklahoman*, which is the largest daily newspaper in the state. This analysis was facilitated by Cochran sharing the data that had been gathered for a number of types of homicide, not all of which had been examined in their article. These include: (1) total killings, (2) capital homicides, (3) total felony murders, (4) felony murders involving strangers, (5) felony murders involving non-strangers, (6) total robbery-related killings, (7) robbery-related killings involving strangers, (8) robbery-related killings involving non-strangers, (9) total killings involving strangers, (10) argument-related killings involving strangers, (11) non-felony murders involving strangers and (12) total non-stranger homicides.

A series of multiple regression analyses revealed that Oklahoma's return to capital punishment was followed by a significant increase in total killings involving strangers and non-felony homicides involving strangers. However, even a greater level of support for the brutalization argument came from the execution frequency and newspaper coverage variables. Both of these death penalty factors proved to be associated positively and significantly with eight of the twelve types of homicide. The four types of murder giving no evidence of brutalization (or deterrence) are: (1) total felony murders, (2) felony murders involving strangers, (3) robbery-related killings involving strangers and (4) robbery-related homicides involving non-strangers. No prior study had provided such extensive evidence of the possible brutalization effect for capital punishment.

To determine if the evidence of brutalization found for Oklahoma killings involving strangers is unique to that jurisdiction, Cochran and Chamlin (2000) replicated their 1994 analysis by examining weekly homicide patterns in California for the 1989–1995 period. After a 25-year moratorium, California returned to capital punishment with the highly publicized executions of Robert Alton Harris on April 21, 1992, and David Edwin Mason on August 24, 1993. Cochran and Chamlin assess whether California's return to capital punishment with these two celebrated executions resulted in a significant upward shift (i.e., brutalization effect) in killings involving strangers, as was the case following the September, 1990 Coleman execution in Oklahoma. In addition, they examine the possible contingent (stranger/non-stranger) effects of highly publicized executions.

To elaborate, Cochran and Chamlin propose that highly publicized executions may have either deterrence or brutalization effects depending upon the types of killing and the degree of informal control found in the victim-offender relationships. They hold that highly publicized executions will tend to *deter* felony-murders (a form of instrumental homicide where the assumption of rationality inherent in deterrence perspectives may hold), while such executions will tend to *spark* (brutalize) argument-based killings (an expressive form of homicide where victims may be viewed as deserving of death). Cochran and Chamlin further argue that the deterrent or brutalization potential of highly publicized executions may depend upon the "operation of informal sanctioning systems" (2000:691). Thus, they propose that the deterrent effect of executions should be stronger in felony murders involving non-strangers than those involving strangers. This argument is based on the premise that legal sanctions activate informal control systems; thus, in affronts involving family, friends, and acquaintances, the prior association serves as a form of informal control that further reduces (deters) the likelihood that a killing will occur. In contrast, Cochran and Chamlin argue that *brutalization* is more likely in transactions where inhibitions against the use of violence are already absent or considerably reduced, such as for affronts involving strangers. In short, Cochran and Chamlin propose that for instrumental homicides such as felony murder, capital punishment combines with the informal social controls that result from social ties between persons known to one another to discourage such killings. On the other hand, in expressive argument situations involving strangers, the lack of social ties between the parties means that no informal social control mechanism is in place to counteract the brutalization effect of capital punishment, resulting in the production rather than reduction of this form of lethal violence.

To explore these notions, Cochran and Chamlin examined weekly (n=364) homicide counts for the 1989–1995 period for: (1) total homicides, (2) total felony murders, (3) felony murders involving strangers, (4) felony murders involving non-strangers, (5) killings involving arguments, (6) argument-related killings involving strangers, and (7) argument related killings involving non-strangers. Their primary research strategy involved applying a multi-intervention autoregressive statistical analysis (ARIMA) to determine if the Harris and Mason executions produced a downward (deterrence) or upward (brutalization) shift in killings.

The results of this analysis revealed that most types of homicide were unaffected by California's return to capital punishment. However, the Harris execution in April 1992, was followed by a significant increase in argument-related killings involving strangers. This type of killing increased by an average of 1.1 per week during the post-Harris execution period. Cochran and Chamlin present this result as evidence of a significant brutalization effect. In contrast, the level of felony murders involving non-strangers declined significantly following the Mason execution in August 1993. The post-Mason execution period was associated with a decline of -.932 such killings per week. Cochran and Chamlin present this finding as evidence of deterrence for non-stranger felony murders. Based on these contrasting patterns, they conclude that California's return to capital punishment had both a deterrent and brutalization effect that is consistent with their hypotheses. However, they also report that these dual effects tend to cancel one another out statistically, with the net impact of California's return to capital punishment for the 1989–1995 period being essentially zero.

Cochran and Chamlin should be commended for taking seriously the possible contingent nature of social ties, informal social control, and capital punishment in encouraging or discouraging different types of murder. However, their findings must be viewed as quite tentative. For example, a number of very serious questions can be raised about the reliability of their analysis. As one example, Cochran and Chamlin's study is basically an extended before-after analysis of weekly homicide counts in California surrounding the Harris and Mason executions. As such, the study ignores important deterrence and capital punishment variables such as residents' exposure to publicity about executions occurring in other jurisdictions, and television news coverage of execution events in and outside of California during 1989–1995.

To illustrate, the Harris and Mason executions did receive considerable media attention, but these were not the only execution events to which California residents were exposed. Between 1989 and 1995 there were 209 executions performed in the U.S., and most received coverage in major California newspapers, including the *Los Angeles Times*, the *San Francisco Chronicle*, the *San Diego Union Tribune* and the *Sacramento Bee*. In addition, during the 1989–1995 period some executions (n=26) received television evening news coverage by the major networks—ABC, CBS and NBC. Such coverage could not be included in the ARIMA statistical models used by Cochran and Chamlin. Indeed, in light of the ARIMA strategy, it has to be assumed that the significant amount of newspaper and television news coverage of other executions that took place during 1989–1995 did not influence (increase or decrease) homicides in California. If this assumption is correct, then Cochran and Chamlin's before-after analysis is not biased due to omitting these publicity variables.

However, the accuracy of this assumption is called into question by an auxiliary analysis that the investigators conduct. Specifically, Cochran and Chamlin conduct a regression analysis where the number of weekly killings for each of the seven types of homicide is regressed against (1) a 0/1 dummy Harris execution variable, (2) a 0/1 Mason execution variable, (3) the weekly count of executions that took place in other states, and (4) the number of seconds of ABC, CBS, and NBC evening television new coverage of executions. Cochran and Chamlin report the results of this alternative regression analysis in footnote 7 as follows:

> In all seven of the models tested, the Harris execution was associated with a significant increase in homicides; the effect of the Mason execution was insignificant. Similarly, the parameter estimate for the out-of-state execution series failed to attain statistical significance in all seven models. The effects of execution publicity, however, were significant and negative in five of the seven models.

Unfortunately, this limited discussion is not sufficient to assess how well the regression results comport with Cochran and Chamlin's hypotheses (or their ARIMA analysis). For example, readers are not told which types of homicide appear to be deterred by television news coverage of executions. However, Cochran and Chamlin generously shared their computer printout with us so that we could report their results more clearly for this chapter. In Table 3, we have transcribed from the printout the regression results for the four death penalty variables that Cochran and Chamlin examine. For each of the seven offense categories, unstandardized regression coefficients and associated t-statistics are reported.

We note first that it is not clear how much credence should be lent to this regression analysis since Cochran and Chamlin do not include important non-death penalty control variables such as those used in the Sorensen et al. Texas 1984–1997 analysis (e.g., sociodemographic and law enforcement control variables found to be associated with homicide). But even taking the findings at face value, they do not comport well with the authors' ARIMA analysis or their argument that the deterrence or brutalization effect of capital punishment depends upon the nature of the relationship between combatants. To illustrate, Table 3 indicates that most types of killings, not just argument related killings involving strangers increased significantly following the Harris execution. And, while the Harris execution was followed by a significant *increase* in felony murders involving strangers, the amount of television news coverage of executions is associated with a significant *decrease* in these type of killings. These patterns and the result showing that Mason's execution was not associated negatively or positively with any of the seven offense categories call into question the argument that "stranger status" makes a difference in whether capital punishment promotes or prevents felony murders. Also contrary to Cochran and Chamlin's hypothesis, the results in Table 3 suggest that the hypothesized brutalization ef-

Table 3
Summary of Results for the Cochran and Chamlin Multiple
Regression Analysis for Death Penalty Factors for
California Weekly Homicides, 1989–1995

Death Penalty Variables	Statistic	Total Murders	Type of Homicide					
			Total Felony Murders	Felony Murders (Strangers)	Felony Murders (Non-Strangers)	Total Argument Killings	Argument Killings (Strangers)	Argument Killings (Non-Strangers)
Harris Execution (April, 1992)	b	22.16	15.56	6.16	5.33	11.17	5.65	11.09
	t	1.62	4.27*	4.49*	4.44*	2.03*	5.24*	2.81*
Mason Execution (August, 1993)	t	2.08	-2.80	-.19	-1.19	5.05	.28	.80
	b	.16	-.65	-.11	-.80	.86	.21	.18
Out-of-State Executions	b	.44	.27	.19	.07	-.01	-.08	.24
	t	.69	.93	1.01	.43	-.03	-.49	.10
Execution Television News Coverage	b	-.02	-.01	-.01	-.00	-.01	-.00	-.01
	t	-2.61*	-2.77*	-2.37	-.47	-1.49	-.53	-2.43*
	R^2	0.96	0.87	0.74	0.7	0.92	0.74	0.88
	N	24,980	5,690	2,288	1,815	8,269	1,986	5,605

*$p < .05$ for a two-tailed test of statistical significance

fect of capital punishment is more (not less) pronounced for argument-related killings involving persons known to one another (non-strangers). This too raises questions about the proposed claims regarding the linkages among pre-existing social relationships, informal social control, and the impact of the death penalty on homicide.

In brief, then, Cochran and Chamlin's hypothesis that the impact of formal social control efforts (the death penalty) may interact with certain relationship patterns to further discourage (deterrence) or promote (brutalization) homicides has intuitive appeal. However, their analysis does not provide a basis for either accepting or rejecting the proposed conditional nature of the relationship between capital punishment and different types of homicide. Their ARIMA analysis ignores important deterrence and death penalty variables, such as print and electronic media attention devoted to executions. Their multivariate regression analysis takes into account these deterrence variables but excludes important sociodemographic, emergency medical service, and law enforcement variables such as the arrest rate for murder and the general incarceration rate, which were not constant in California during the 1989–1995 period. And, even ignoring the model specification problems, Cochran and Chamlin's results do not comport well with their arguments. Because of these serious problems, it is our view that the Cochran and Chamlin study does not provide convincing evidence that capital punishment deters or encourages (brutalizes) killings.

Capital Punishment and Police Killings: A Special Population

Apprehending criminals is dangerous business. Each year thousands of police officers are assaulted and some are killed in the line of duty (Federal Bureau of Investigation 1994). Some law enforcement spokespersons have argued that the death penalty affords the police an added measure of protection against being slain in the line of duty.

A few investigations have attempted to assess whether capital punishment deters lethal assaults against police. In 1982, Bailey examined for U.S. states (1961–1971), the relationship between annual police homicide rates per 1,000 *police officers,* and the certainty of execution for murder. For each year (1961–1971), his models of police killing rates included the ratio of total executions to total criminal homicides, a dummy variable differentiating death penalty from abolitionist states, and four control variables—proportions urban and black population, and rates of poverty and unemployment. Bailey found no indication that policing is less hazardous in death penalty states; nor in jurisdictions where executions are at higher levels. An extension of this analysis for the 1973–1984 period produced the same non-deterrence findings (Bailey and Peterson 1987).

Most recently, Bailey and Peterson (1994) conducted a national, time-series analysis of police killings. Certainty was operationalized as the ratio of police killings to the number of monthly executions of "cop killers." They considered a general police killing rate (the number of officers killed per 100,000 police personnel) *and* rates for killings involving (1) on-duty and (2) off-duty police, and killings of (3) general jurisdiction and (4) special function police. The monthly time-series spanned 1976 through 1989. Over this period, 1,204 law enforcement officers were killed feloniously (FBI 1987–1989), and there were 120 executions in the U.S., 12 of which involved "cop killers." Bailey and Peterson found no evidence that overall and specific types of police killings were responsive to the provision for capital punishment, execution rates, or television news coverage devoted to executions.

Summary of the Status of Research on Types of Murder

Taking the evidence on specific types of murder as a whole, then, only a single investigation (Cochran and Chamlin 2000) has found any suggestion that capital punishment may deter first-degree murders or felony murders. Since most capital homicides are felony murders the contrary findings for these types of killing have to be taken as strong evidence against the death penalty and deterrence argument. Similarly, if the killing of a police officer means a higher risk of receiving a death sentence and being executed, as is the case in the U.S. in recent years (compared to citizen killings), then the death penalty should be noticeably effective in deterring police killings. But here, too, the evidence is negative. Capital punishment does not appear to provide police officers with an added measure of protection against being murdered.

Future Research on Capital Punishment and Deterrence

Implications of Past and Contemporary Research

To summarize, there is a long history of deterrence research regarding capital punishment. Early comparative analyses were numerous, spanned many years, and have been conducted throughout the world. More recent analyses have focused primarily on the U.S. Though they lack temporal and global breadth, recent studies complement comparative research in their added theoretical and methodological sophistication. Overall, they have given detailed attention to important data quality issues, extended the range of theoretically important deterrence variables examined, and relied on very powerful statistical techniques to control for other contributors to homicides. They also have isolated the possible deterrent effect for murder (including capital killings) of the provision for capital punishment (severity), levels of execution (certainty), promptness of executions (celerity), and publicity surrounding executions.

On balance, deterrence hypotheses for capital punishment have fared quite poorly. Considering severity, comparative studies consistently showed a pattern of higher or similar levels of homicide in death penalty compared to abolitionist jurisdictions. Regarding certainty, one noted investigator (Ehrlich) has reported that higher execution rates are associated significantly with lower rates of general homicide. However, Ehrlich's (1975, 1977) research has been seriously challenged and is largely discredited. Third, researchers have examined the impact of both print and electronic media attention devoted to executions on overall homicides. In addition, the possible deterrent effect of television news coverage of executions for felony murder has been considered. Among those studies, only Stack has found support for deterrence, but mistakes in his analysis call his findings into question. Celerity is the most neglected issue in empirical examinations of murder and capital punishment. Still, the one study considering this issue for U.S. states (1951–1960) produced no evidence that prompt executions deter homicides (Bailey 1980a). Because the celerity question has received so little attention, we are not able to conclude, "with confidence," that prompt executions are or are not effective in preventing murder. We can only say that the evidence to date is not supportive of deterrence. No evidence of deterrence has come from studies examining the deterrent effect of death sentences and executions on capital murder (Bailey 1984a; Cochran et al. 1994; Dann 1935; Savitz 1958). Studies examining the impact of executions and execution publicity on rates of felony murder—the most common type of capital homicide—have shown little support for the deterrence hypothesis (e.g., Peterson and Bailey 1991). As detailed above, one recent study (Cochran and Chamlin) found evidence that capital punishment may deter felony murders. However, because of serious theoretical and methodological problems, we are unable to have confidence in this latest evidence.

Based upon the research summarized above and similar types of studies, most criminologists seem convinced that capital punishment is not a more effective deterrent for murder than imprisonment. In fact, the American Society of Criminology, the largest professional association of criminologists in the U.S., passed a resolution in 1989 condemning the death penalty for a variety of reasons, including its lack of utility as a deterrent to murder (Petersilia 1990). This consensus may in part account for the fact that only a few capital punishment and deterrence analyses have appeared in the professional literature in the last few years. In short, for many criminologists the capital punishment and deterrence question is a dead issue.

We are in general agreement with our colleagues that the evidence against capital punishment as an effective deterrent is extensive and cannot be dismissed as resulting from theoretical or methodological weaknesses. Of course, we could be wrong in drawing this negative conclusion. Some death penalty proponents claim that deterrence is taking place all around us, but is not recognized as such. If so, proponents could better serve their cause by schooling death penalty researchers on how they are systematically missing the mark in detecting such widespread deterrence. For example, for more than two decades, Professor Ernest van den Haag (1969, 1978, 1990; van den Haag and Conrad 1983) has complained that extant studies simply are not good enough to prove that capital punishment is not an effective deterrent to murder. The one exception that he cites is Ehrlich's 1975 analysis. However, van den Haag does not address why he views Ehrlich's findings as valid and "mountains" of contrary evidence (including reanalyses of Ehrlich's own data) as unworthy. Moreover, van den Haag has not made any concrete suggestions about steps that could be taken to help us resolve on empirical grounds the deterrence and death penalty issue.

We are certain that social science researchers would also welcome the advice and recommendations of legislators and the judiciary regarding further study of deterrence and capital punishment. During the past 25 years a number of justices of the United States Supreme Court have emphasized the fundamental importance of the deterrence question to the constitutionality of capital punishment. For example, Haney and Logan (1994:87–90) note the following points made by Supreme Court justices:

> [T]he most hotly contested issue regarding capital punishment is whether it is better than life imprisonment as a deterrent to crime (Justice Marshall wrote in *Furman v. Georgia* 1972:345).
> [Deterrence is] one of the two principal social purposes of the death penalty—the other [is] retribution (Justice Stewart in *Gregg v. Georgia* 1976:173).
> Deterrence [is] the "principal battleground" on which the war over the constitutionality of the death penalty [is] to be fought (Justice White in *Roberts v. Louisiana* 1976:354).
> Capital punishment can serve as a deterrent only when murder is the result of premeditation and deliberation (Justice White in *Enmund v. Florida* 1982:798–99).
> A majority of the Court has concluded that the general deterrence rationale adequately justifies the imposition of capital punishment at least for certain classes of offenses for which the legislature may reasonably conclude that the death penalty has a deterrent effect (Justice White in *Spaziano v. Florida* 1984:478).
> When a mad man is executed...[it] can be no example to others (Justice Marshall in *Ford v. Wainwright* 1986:407).

> Society's important interest in deterrence...is diluted when defen-
> dants are allowed to escape execution based on factors that have
> nothing to do with their criminal responsibility (Justice Powell in
> *Skipper v. South Carolina* 1986:13).
>
> For many types of murders, the death penalty undoubtedly is a signif-
> icant deterrent (Justice Powell in *Skipper v. South Carolina* 1986:13).
>
> The potential deterrent value of the death sentence [is] "insignificant"
> [for juveniles] because it [is] unlikely that teenage defendants would
> make the necessary cost-benefit analysis. If one posits such a cold-
> blooded calculation by a 15 year old, it is fanciful to believe that he
> would be deterred because so few persons this age have ever actually
> been executed (Justice Stevens in *Thompson v. Oklahoma* 1988:837).

Either explicitly or by implication, the above statements make it clear that
many Supreme Court justices are believers in deterrence. It is as if the Court
has considered, but simply "overruled," the empirical evidence (Haney and
Logan 1994:89). Of significance here, the High Court has not pointed to the
specific studies, or types of studies, that have been successful in demonstrating
that capital punishment is more effective than imprisonment in deterring murder, nor why the contrary evidence is not trustworthy. Are the justices simply
placing confidence in the Ehrlich study of overall homicide rates? This was the
only analysis suggesting deterrence during the period when the above cases
were decided. However, none of the justices has noted a single study conducted in the U.S. or abroad that informs their opinions on the deterrence
issue. As a result, it is impossible to know the factual basis of the Court's repeated assertions that capital punishment is an effective deterrent.

Also, the justices do not make it clear for which types of murder capital
punishment is an effective deterrent. In *Gregg v. Georgia* (1976) and a decade
later in *Skipper v. South Carolina* (1986) Justices Stewart and Powell, respectively, indicated that *many* types of murder are subject to deterrence. Yet, neither of those justices provided even a partial list of the many types of de-
terrable murder. And as the evidence reported in this chapter indicates, studies
do not support this claim. Similarly, the justices fail to document the bases of
assertions that certain types of offenders (sane persons, older persons) are de-
terrable. And, there is also no research to support such propositions.

In sum, like Professor van den Haag, a number of the justices of the U.S.
Supreme Court ignore the implications of the research on deterrence and capital punishment. This is a tragic "abuse of the empirical record" (Haney and
Logan 1994:89–90) for all concerned, including social scientists who would
welcome the insights of the Court on this important academic and policy issue.

There are also those who seem to long for the "good old days" regarding
capital punishment. They, too, have provided little assistance in suggesting
more informative and possibly conclusive deterrence and death penalty stud-

ies. For example, Jeffery (1965) complained that our system of capital punishment has been robbed of its possible deterrent effectiveness because (a) the ratio of executions to homicides is very slight, so capital punishment is far from a certain sanction in this society, and (b) when executions do occur, they typically take place only many years after the offense and the conviction of the killer. The assumption is that returning to the "good old days," when we executed killers more frequently and more promptly, would restore capital punishment as an effective deterrent to murder.

Jeffery's observations on the matter of the certainty and celerity of executions in recent years are correct. To illustrate, in 1930 there were 147 executions of convicted murderers, and 11,077 reported murders, for a rate of 13.3 executions per 1,000 homicides. The execution rates for 1940 (14.9), 1950 (11.7), 1960 (4.9), and 2001 (4.1) show a clear trend of capital punishment being a much less commonly used sanction over the last six plus decades. Although data are not available from the U.S. Federal Bureau of Prisons prior to 1956, the pattern is similar for the celerity of executions. For the 1951–1960 period, the average elapsed time between receiving a death sentence and being executed was 14.4 months, with the range being from 4.6 to 46.1 months. In striking contrast, for persons put to death in 2000, the average elapsed time between being sentenced to death and execution was 11 years and five months (or 122 months).

Thus, compared to earlier periods, under our current system of capital punishment, executions are neither certain nor prompt. But have our current practices robbed the death penalty of its effectiveness in preventing murder? The answer appears to be no. As noted throughout this chapter, not a single comparative study conducted in the U.S. dating back to the turn of the century has produced any evidence of a marginal deterrent effect for capital punishment. And no reliable multivariate time-series or cross-sectional analysis of the U.S. or individual states dating back to the early part of the century has produced any evidence of a significant deterrent effect for capital punishment.

In short, the empirical evidence does not support the belief that capital punishment was an effective deterrent for murder in years past. Nor is there any indication that returning to our past execution practices would have any deterrent impact on the current homicide problem. For some, executing more killers and doing so more promptly may be important goals, but a greater level of societal protection against murder should not be the expected payoff.

Future Deterrence Research

So, where do we go from here to gain a better empirically-based understanding of the marginal deterrent effectiveness of capital punishment? What are the remaining issues and crucial studies that need to be conducted to put the deterrence and death penalty question to rest? Unfortunately, we have no satisfying answer to this question. For more than 20 years we have been consumers of countless deterrence and death penalty studies, and in our own work we have attempted to move the deterrence and death penalty issue towards closure by taking on a series of theoretical and methodological issues using a variety of contemporary and archival data. As social scientists, we hold the general opinion that for any particular question, more data are better than less data. However, we are less certain that this is true regarding deterrence and capital punishment.

On the one hand, we see no indication based upon past efforts that additional national or state-level time series or cross-sectional analyses of overall murder rates and capital punishment practices will add anything of significance to a better understanding of this issue. Rather, short of conducting a series of highly randomized, but controlled, experiments with capital punishment whereby the luck of the draw determines for jurisdictions levels of the (a) certainty of execution, (b) celerity of execution, and (c)) where the media publicity surrounding executions is purposefully manipulated by some authority, we have no confidence that studies will reveal anything other than more non-deterrence findings. Obviously, for legal and ethical reasons, we cannot conduct those types of controlled experiments to help resolve the deterrence and death penalty question. That being the case, it may not be helpful for death penalty investigators to continue to turn out studies of the variety described in this chapter.

Nonetheless, we think that it is important to continue to monitor the impact of capital punishment on homicides. First, deterrence apparently will continue to be an important policy issue. Thus, even if most social scientists perceive the death penalty and deterrence issue as settled, it is important to provide citizens, legislators, and members of the judiciary with recent versus dated research. In doing so, researchers may make minor inroads (or at least round out the death penalty and deterrence picture) by making an effort to assess whether murder rates for different types of populations (e.g., minorities versus non-minorities, the poor versus more affluent groups, younger versus older persons, populations close to execution or murder sites, and the like) are more or less responsive to capital punishment. In addition, it is important for social scientists to keep abreast of and to examine carefully published studies that appear in the professional literature. Ehrlich's (1975), Stack's (1987), and Cochran and Chamlin's (2000) research provide critical lessons in this regard.

References

Andenaes, J. (1974) *Punishment and Deterrence*. Ann Arbor: The University of Michigan Press.

Bailey, W.C. (1975) "Murder and Capital Punishment: Some Further Evidence." *American Journal of Orthopsychiatry* 45:669–88.

Bailey, W.C. (1977) "Imprisonment vs. The Death Penalty as a Deterrent to Murder." *Law and Human Behavior* 1:239–60.

Bailey, W.C. (1978) "Deterrence and the Death Penalty for Murder in Utah: A Time-Series Analysis." *Journal of Contemporary Law* 5:1–0.

Bailey, W.C. (1979a) "An Analysis of the Deterrence Effect of the Death Penalty in North Carolina." *North Carolina Central Law Journal* 10:29–1.

Bailey, W.C. (1979b) "Deterrence and the Death Penalty for Murder in Oregon." *Williamette Law Review* 6:67–5.

Bailey, W. C. (1979c) The Deterrent Effect of the Death Penalty for Murder in California. *Southern California Law Review* 52:743–64.

Bailey, W.C. (1979d) "The Deterrent Effect of the Death Penalty for Murder in Ohio." *Cleveland State Law Review* 28:51–81.

Bailey, W.C. (1980a) "Deterrence and the Celerity of the Death Penalty: A Neglected Question in Deterrence Research." *Social Forces* 58:1308–1333.

Bailey, W.C. (1980b) "A Multivariate Cross-Sectional Analysis of the Deterrent Effect of the Death Penalty." *Sociology and Social Research* 64:183–207.

Bailey, W.C. (1982) "Capital Punishment and Lethal Assaults Against Police." *Criminology* 19:608–625.

Bailey, W.C. (1983) "The Deterrent Effect of Capital Punishment During the 1950's." *Suicide* 13:95–107.

Bailey, W.C. (1984a) "Disaggregation in Deterrence and Death Penalty Research. The Case of Murder in Chicago." *Journal of Criminal Law and Criminology* 74:827–859.

Bailey, W.C. (1984b) "Murder and Capital Punishment in the Nation's Capitol." *Justice Quarterly* 1:211–233.

Bailey, W.C. (1989) "Deterrence, Brutalization, and the Death Penalty: Another Examination of Oklahoma's Return to Capital Punishment." *Criminology* 36: 711–733.

Bailey, W.C. (1990) "Murder and Capital Punishment: An Analysis of Television Execution Publicity." *American Sociological Review* 55:1308–1333.

Bailey, W.C. (1998) "Deterrence, Brutalization, and the Death Penalty: Another Examination of Oklahoma's Return to Capital Punishment." *Criminology* 36:711–733.

Bailey, W.C. and R.D. Peterson (1987) "Police Killings and Capital Punishment: The post-*Furman* Period." *Criminology* 25:1–25.

Bailey, W.C. and R.D. Peterson (1989) "Murder and Capital Punishment: A Monthly Time-Series Analysis of Execution Publicity." *American Sociological Review* 54:722–743.

Bailey W.C. and R.D. Peterson. (1994) "Murder, Capital Punishment and Deterrence: A Review of the Evidence and an Examination of Police Killings." *Journal of Social Issues* 50:53–74.

Baldus, D. and J. Cole (1975) "A Comparison of the Work of Thorsten Sellin and Isaac Ehrlich on the Deterrent Effect of Capital Punishment." *Yale Law Journal*. 18:170–186.

Barnett, A. (1981) "The Deterrent Effect of Capital Punishment: A Test of Some Recent Studies." *Operations Research* 29:341–370.

Beccaria, C. (1764/1963) *On Crimes and Punishment* (translation by H. Paolucci). Indianapolis: Bobbs-Merrill.

Bedau, H. A. (1967) *The Death Penalty in America* (rev. ed.). New York: Doubleday.

Bentham, J. (1843/1962) "The Rationale of Punishment." Pp. 338–525 in J. Browning (Ed.), *Works of Jeremy Bentham*. New York: Russell and Russell.

Berns, W. (1979) *For Capital Punishment*. New York: Basic Books.

Beyleveld, D. (1982) "Ehrlich's Analysis of Deterrence." *British Journal of Criminology*. 22:101–123.

Bower, R.T. (1985) *The Changing Television Audience in America*. New York: Columbia University Press.

Bowers, W.J. and G. Pierce (1975) "The Illusion of Deterrence in Isaac Ehrlich's Research on Capital Punishment." *Yale Law Journal* 85:187–208.

Bowers, W.J. and G. Pierce (1980) "Deterrence or Brutalization: What is the Effect of Executions?" *Crime and Delinquency* 26:453–484.

Brier, S. and S. Feinberg (1980) "Recent Econometric Modeling of Crime and Punishment: Support for the Deterrence Hypothesis?" *Evaluation Review* 4:147–191.

Chambliss, W.J. (1967) "Types of Deviance and the Effectiveness of Legal Sanctions." *Wisconsin Law Review* 1967:703–719.

Cochran, J. and Chamlin, M. (2000) "Deterrence and Brutalization: The Dual Effects of Executions." *Justice Quarterly* 17: 685–706.

Cochran, J.K., M.B. Chamlin, and M. Seth (1994) "Deterrence or Brutalization? An Impact Assessment of Oklahoma's Return to Capital Punishment." *Criminology* 32:107–134.

Dann, R. (1935) *The Deterrent Effect of Capital Punishment*. The Committee of Philanthropic Labor of Philadelphia Yearly Meeting of Friends.

Decker, S.H. and C.W. Kohfeld (1984) "A Deterrence Study of the Death Penalty in Illinois, 1933–1980." *Journal of Criminal Justice* 12:367–377.

Ehrlich, I. (1973) *The Deterrent Effect of Capital Punishment*. National Bureau of Economic Research. Working Paper Series No. 18.

Ehrlich, I. (1975) "The Deterrent Effect of Capital Punishment: A Question of Life or Death." *The American Economic Review* 65:397–417.

Ehrlich, I. (1977) "Capital Punishment and Deterrence: Some Further Thoughts and Additional Evidence." *Journal of Political Economy* 85:741–788.

Enmund v. Florida (1982) 458 U.S. 782.

Federal Bureau of Investigation (1992) *Crime in the United States: Uniform Crime Reports*. Washington DC: U.S. Government Printing Office.

Federal Bureau of Investigation. 1995. *Law Enforcement Officers Killed and Assaulted: Uniform Crime Reports*. Washington D.C.: U.S. Government Printing Office.

Ford v. Wainwright (1986) 477 U.S. 399.

Forst, B. (1977) "The Deterrent Effect of Capital Punishment: A Cross-state Analysis of the 1960's." *Minnesota Law Review* 61:743–767.

Friedman, L. (1979) "The Use of Multiple Regression Analysis to Test for a Deterrent Effect of Capital Punishment: Prospects and Problems." Pp. in 61–87 in S. Messinger and E. Bittner (Eds.), *Criminology Review Yearbook*. Beverly Hills: Sage.

Furman v. Georgia (1972) 408 U.S. 238.

Gibbs, J.P. (1975) *Crime, Punishment and Deterrence*. New York: Elsevier.

Gibbs, J.P. (1986) "Deterrence Theory and Research." Pp. 87–130 in G.B. Melton (Ed.), *Nebraska Symposium on Motivation-1985: The Law as a Behavioral Instrument*. Lincoln, NE: University of Nebraska Press.

Gregg v. Georgia (1976) 428 U.S. 153.

Haney, C. and D.D. Logan (1994) "Broken Promise: The Supreme Court's Response to Social Science Research on Capital Punishment." *Journal of Social Issues* 50: 75–100.

Jeffery, C.R. (1965) "Criminal Behavior and Learning Theory." *Journal of Criminal Law, Criminology, and Police Science* 56:294–300.

Klein, L., B. Forst, and V. Filatov (1978) "The Deterrent Effect of Capital Punishment: An Assessment of the Estimates." Pp. 331–360 in A. Blumstein, J. Cohen, and D. Nagin (Eds.), *Deterrence and Incapacitation: Estimating the Effects of Criminal Sanctions on Crime Rates.* National Academy of Sciences.

Luckenbill, D. (1977) "Criminal Homicide as a Situated Transaction." *Social Problems* 25:171–186.

McFarland, S.G. (1983) "Is Capital Punishment a Short-term Deterrent to Homicide?: A Study of the Effects of Four Recent American Executions." *Journal of Criminal Law and Criminology* 74:1014–1030.

McGahey, R.M. (1980) "Dr. Ehrlich's Magic Bullet: Economic Theory, Econometrics, and the Death Penalty." *Crime and Delinquency.* October 1980.

National Center for Health Statistics (1967) "Homicide in the United States 1950–1964." *Vital Health and Statistics* 20:9.

Passell, P. (1975) "The Deterrent Effect of the Death Penalty: A Statistical Test." *Stanford Law Review* 28:61–80.

Passell, P. and J. Taylor (1975) "The Deterrent Effect of Capital Punishment: Another View." Discussion Paper 74-7509. Columbia University.

Petersilia, J. (1990) "Death Penalty Resolution Debated and Endorsed." *The Criminologist* 15:1.

Peterson, R.D. and W.C. Bailey (1988) "Murder and Capital Punishment in the Evolving Context of the post-*Furman* Era." *Social Forces* 66:774-807.

Peterson, R.D. and W.C. Bailey (1991) "Felony Murder and Capital Punishment: An Examination of the Deterrence Question." *Criminology* 29:367–395.

Roberts v. Louisiana (1976) 428 U.S. 325.

Savitz, L. (1958) "A Study of Capital Punishment." *Journal of Criminal Law, Criminology and Police Science* 49:338–341.

Schuessler, K. (1952) "The Deterrent Effect of the Death Penalty." *Annals* 284:54–62.

Sellin, T. (1955) "The Royal Commission on Capital Punishment, 1949–1953." Report of the Great Britain Parliament. (Papers by Command 8932) (Pp. 17–24). London: H. M. Stationery Office.

Sellin, T. (1959) *The Death Penalty.* Philadelphia: American Law Institute.

Sellin, T. (1967) *Capital Punishment.* New York: Harper and Row.

Skipper v. South Carolina (1986) 476 U.S. 1.

Sorensen, J., Wrinkle, R., Brewer, V. and Marquart, J. (1999) "Capital Punishment and Deterrence: Examining the Effect of Executions on Murder in Texas." *Crime & Delinquency* 45:481–493.

Spaziano v. Florida (1984) 468 U.S. 447.

Stack, S. (1987) "Publicized Executions and Homicide, 1950–1980." *American Sociological Review* 52:532–540.

Sutherland, E. (1925) "Murder and the Death Penalty." *Journal of the American Institute of Criminal Law Criminology* 51:522–529.

Thompson v. Oklahoma (1988) 487 U.S. 815.

van den Haag, E. (1969) "On Deterrence and the Death Penalty." *Journal of Criminal Law, Criminology, and Political Science* 60:141–147.

van den Haag, E. (1975) *Punishing Criminals: Concerning a Very Old and Painful Question*. New York: Basic Books.

van den Haag, E. (1978) "In Defense of the Death Penalty: A Legal-Practical-Moral Analysis." *Criminal Law Bulletin* 14:51–68.

van den Haag, E. (1990) "Why Capital Punishment?" *Albany Law Review* 54:501–514.

van den Haag, E. and J. Conrad (1983) *The Death Penalty: A Debate*. New York: Plenum.

Yunker, J. (1976) "Is the Death Penalty a Deterrent to Homicide?: Some Time Series Evidence." *Journal of Behavioral Economics* 5:1–32.

Chapter 9

Future Dangerousness and Incapacitation

Jon Sorensen
James Marquart

Criminal sanctions are justified by the purposes they are intended to serve. Proponents of the death penalty typically tout its ability to meet retributive or utilitarian goals. The central focus of the Court's inquiry in *Furman v. Georgia* (1972) was whether death sentences were imposed in a uniform and fair manner, an essential requirement of retributive justice. On the discourse related to utilitarian goals, general deterrence has been prominent (Peterson and Bailey 2003), while less often discussed has been the goal of incapacitation. Nonetheless, utilizing capital punishment for the purpose of incapacitation has become very common in the post-*Furman* era. A few reenacted statutes explicitly rely on incapacitation in the sentencing of capital defendants, and many others do so implicitly. Further, studies have found that concerns about future dangerousness influence the degree of support for the death penalty in attitudinal surveys and weigh heavily in jury deliberations.

Many issues are raised when the death penalty is utilized for its incapacitative value. First, in states where jurors have an explicit obligation to consider the future conduct of the defendant, they tend to give less thought to retributive concerns in their deliberations. Second, jurors seldom have accurate information available to assist them in making predictions about a defendant's long-term potential to commit future acts of violence. Third, in the absence of accurate information, jurors are forced to rely on the testimony of, often unscrupulous, expert witnesses or their own preconceived notions about a murderer's propensity to commit future acts of violence. Statutes which demand, as well as those which allow death penalty decisions to be based on future dangerousness result in the same sort of standardless sentencing denounced by the Court in *Furman*.

The Importance of Dangerousness in the Post-*Furman* Era

Following *Furman*, state legislatures enacted different types of statutes that were designed either to eliminate or reduce the discretion of sentencing authorities. Under mandatory statutes, once a person was found guilty of capital murder (e.g., murder of a police officer, murder during the course of a robbery), the death sentence automatically was imposed. The Court invalidated mandatory statutes in 1976. The justices reasoned that statutes which totally eliminated sentencing discretion did not allow juries and judges to consider mitigating evidence, which may make a particular defendant less deserving of the death penalty than others (*Roberts v. Louisiana* 1976; *Woodson v. North Carolina* 1976). In the same session, the Court upheld statutes which guided the discretion of jurors by providing a list of aggravating circumstances, one of which had to be certified before the convicted murderer could be sentenced to death (*Gregg v. Georgia* 1976; *Proffitt v. Florida* 1976). Under the guided discretion statutes, juries also had to consider any mitigating circumstances that might make a case deserving of a sentence less than death.

Most of the post-*Furman* statutes, case law, and legal rhetoric tend to focus on the retributive aspects of capital punishment. In order to serve the retributivist goal, laws governing capital punishment must be fair and sentences proportionate to the crime. If laws are to allot defendants their just deserts, the process must consistently mete out the death penalty to the most culpable offenders who have committed the most egregious offenses. The new procedures also were designed to spare those offenders whose character and background, personal moral culpability, or circumstances of the offense suggested that they were not deserving of a death sentence. Most newly implemented capital punishment statutes included a provision for proportionality review, in which state supreme courts were charged with determining whether each death sentence imposed was disproportionate compared to sentences imposed in similar cases (Baldus, Woodworth, and Pulaski 1990). Again the concern was that "equal justice," a necessary prerequisite for any rational retributive system of punishment, would be served.

The justices also addressed the goal of general deterrence in *Furman*. Mandatory capital-sentencing statutes enacted after *Furman* often were aimed at deterring particular crimes. The death sentence is often seen as unique in its ability to deter calculated and extremely reprehensible sorts of murder, such as the killing of a police officer, or when no other severe alternative appears to serve as a threat to those contemplating murder, such as murder committed by an inmate already serving a life sentence. Guided discretion statutes often enumerate the same sorts of categories of murder as aggravating circumstances in the hopes of preventing those types of murders by assigning them the status of capital offenses.

The goal of incapacitation also is implicit in many of the aggravating circumstances of post-*Furman* guided discretion statutes. Offenders committing certain types of murder (e.g., murder for hire, murder of a potential witness to avoid prosecution) are often considered to present a continuing threat to the community. Some aggravating circumstances are directly related to the goal of incapacitation, such as when killings are committed by offenders with previous convictions for murder or other serious or assaultive crimes. Similarly, when mitigating circumstances are listed, most statutes include an instruction for those defendants with no significant history of prior criminal behavior. The presence or lack of prior criminal record has an explicitly teleological dimension. Rather than simply being concerned with just deserts for the current offense, these circumstances provide sentencing authorities the opportunity to determine punishment on the basis of the likelihood that the defendant will commit another assaultive offense, possibly a homicide, in the future.

An even more explicit indication than the defendant's prior criminal record, although even less objective, demonstrates that some of those reimplementing statutes in the wake of *Furman* were thinking primarily in terms of incapacitation. Some state statutes refer to the potential threat, or lack of threat, posed by the defendant in the future. Even if not explicitly listed in a statute, evidence of nondangerousness, which tends to negate potential future dangerousness, must be allowed as a mitigating factor in the punishment phase of capital trials in all states (Sicola and Shreves 1988; *Skipper v. South Carolina* 1986).

Texas and Oregon, however, are the only states using a "special issues" format in which a question regarding the future dangerousness of the defendant must be answered in each case (Costanzo and Costanzo 1994). The statutes in both of these states define first-degree murders narrowly (e.g., murder of a peace officer, felony murders, murders for hire, prison murders). Under early versions of these laws, three questions were posed to jurors during the punishment phase of capital trials. The first and third questions concerned whether the killing was deliberate and, if raised by the evidence, whether it was unreasonable in response to any provocation. Empirical studies have shown that both of those questions tend to be given little thought by jurors (Costanzo and Costanzo 1994; Haney, Sontag, and Costanzo 1994) and are nearly always answered in the affirmative (Marquart, Ekland-Olson, and Sorensen 1989). Indeed, the fact that a defendant has been convicted of first-degree murder typically warrants an affirmative answer to those questions (Black 1976). Had deliberateness been lacking or sufficient provocation present, the jury most likely would have convicted the defendant of a lesser degree of homicide.

The other special issue in the two states concerns the incapacitation of the defendant. In each state jurors are asked if there is "a probability that the defendant would commit criminal acts of violence that would constitute a continuing threat to society" (Texas Code of Criminal Procedure, art. 37.071,

1985). In Oregon the following statement is added to the special issue to assist in the deliberation: "Consider any mitigating circumstances offered in evidence, including, but not limited to, the defendant's age, the extent of the mental and emotional pressure under which the defendant was acting at the time the offense was committed" (Oregon Rev. Stat., sec. 163.150, 1988). Effective September, 1991, because of the U.S. Supreme Court ruling in *Penry v. Lynaugh* (1989), the Texas statute was modified, leaving the special issue concerning future dangerousness as the only remaining original question. In cases of accomplice liability, jurors must now answer a question about the extent of the defendant's participation in the victim's death. Jurors also must now answer a question concerning whether sufficient mitigating evidence is present to warrant a life sentence. Nonetheless, in Texas and Oregon jurors are called upon to make what is essentially an unguided determination regarding the future conduct of the defendant. This unguided speculation influences whether the defendant receives a life or death sentence.

Studies completed in Texas and Oregon have found that jurors' beliefs regarding a defendant's potential for violence is often the decisive factor in sentencing. Among the 126 capital cases resulting in life sentences in Texas during 1974–1988, juries answered the special issues of deliberateness affirmatively in 76 percent of the cases, and lack of provocation affirmatively in 91 percent of the cases when raised (Marquart et al. 1989). The future dangerousness special issue, on the other hand, was answered affirmatively in only 15 percent of the life-sentence cases. Thus, in 85 percent (107 of 126) of the cases in which jurors returned a life sentence in the penalty phase of a capital trial in Texas during 1974–1988, a prediction about the future dangerousness of the individual resulted in this leniency. A recent study, completed after the 1991 restructuring of the statute, found that while jurors sometimes agree that mitigating evidence warrants a life sentence, the level of future dangerousness posed by defendants remains the primary determinant of their sentencing decisions (Brock, Sorensen, and Marquart 2000).

A survey of 27 jurors who sat on 9 capital cases in Oregon illuminates the nature of deliberations on the issue of future dangerousness (Costanzo and Costanzo 1994). Jurors unanimously agreed on the issue of provocation and disagreed on deliberateness in only two of the nine trials, one involving an extremely intoxicated defendant and the other possible coercion by a codefendant. Most of the jurors believed that those two special issues had already been answered during the guilt phase of the trial. In each case resulting in a life verdict in the study, jurors had failed to reach agreement on the issue of future dangerousness. The authors concluded that under the Oregon statute, "the issue of future dangerousness plays a prominent, if not central, role. Virtually all disagreements and prolonged discussion concerned only the second question of future dangerousness. Jurors clearly perceived the penalty decision as hinging on this issue" (Costanzo and Costanzo 1994:168).

While the goals of incapacitation and general deterrence are implicit in guided discretion statutes, nowhere but in Oregon and Texas is the explicit concern of the statute a utilitarian goal—incapacitation. The fundamental problem with such a utilitarian approach is obvious: it is unfair to sentence someone to death on the basis of a prediction about what he or she may do at some point in the future, rather than on what is deserved for the current offense committed. Even though the Texas statute has explicitly adopted this utilitarian position, the U.S. Supreme Court still evaluates the statute on the retributive basis of its ability to distinguish between those who are more or less deserving of a death sentence (*Barefoot v. Estelle* 1983; *Jurek v. Texas* 1976; *Penry v. Lynaugh* 1989). In fact, the changes in the Texas statute wrought by *Penry* resulted from the premise that sentencers must be allowed to consider as mitigating evidence any factors that may make the person less deserving of a death sentence even if that evidence suggests the offender will be a greater threat to the community in the future. Nevertheless, the "future dangerousness" provision has remained intact.

The Futility of Predicting Future Dangerousness

Even if incapacitation is accepted as a rationale for capital punishment in the post-*Furman* years, the process of determining who may pose a future threat renders the ideal of incapacitation meaningless unless those who will kill or commit serious assaultive acts in the future can be accurately predicted. In order to make an accurate assessment of the probability that an individual will commit additional acts of criminal violence, the availability of particular information is critical.

One crucial piece of information required by jurors in assessing the likelihood that a defendant not sentenced to death would present a future threat to society is how long the defendant will be incarcerated while serving the alternative sentence. Research has shown that jurors underestimate the amount of time to be served by those given a life sentence (Bowers and Steiner 1999). This is often with good reason. In the 1970s, a sentence of "life" in many states carried a relatively short term of imprisonment prior to parole eligibility. Upon the enactment of the post-*Furman* death penalty statute in Texas, a capital murderer sentenced to life imprisonment could be released on parole after serving 20 years in prison (S.B. 145, 60th Leg., Reg. Sess., Ch. 659, Tex. 1965). Jurors have often heard anecdotes about those given life sentences serving very short terms of imprisonment, as they did in many places during the 1970s, or more recently about non-capital murderers serving relatively short terms, and so are still prone to underestimate the minimum length of time to be served by capital defendants if given a life sentence.

Currently, however, most states offer life without the possibility of parole as an alternative to the death penalty. In Texas, the amount of time capital murderers are required to serve has been increased several times during the past three decades so that capital murderers sentenced to life must now serve 40 years before being eligible for parole release (Texas Govt. Code, section 508.145(b), 2002). When jurors are asked to make a determination about whether a defendant "would commit criminal acts that would constitute a continuing threat to society," it is imperative that they know earliest date on which the defendant could possibly be released back into society.

Historically, in order to protect defendants, states have not allowed juries to be informed of parole eligibility dates. Recently, however, the U.S. Supreme Court has recognized the importance of supplying this information to jurors when they are asked to assess the likelihood of future dangerousness posed by a defendant. In *Simmons v. South Carolina* (1994), the Court held that if the only alternative to the death penalty is life without the possibility of parole and the future dangerousness is at issue, then defendants must be allowed "to inform the jury of [his] parole ineligibility, either by a juror instruction or in arguments by counsel" (*Ramdass v. Angelone* 2000:165). In *Shafer v. South Carolina* (2001:39–40), the Court held that it was not enough for a judge to instruct a jury that "life imprisonment [meant] until death of the offender" and that "parole eligibility or ineligibility [was] not for [their] consideration." In a dissent from denial of certiorari in *Brown v. Texas* (1997), Justice Stevens noted the inconsistency in Texas' practice of instructing jurors as to parole eligibility in all but capital cases, and the obvious tension between that practice and their ruling in Simmons, given that Brown, at that time, would have to serve 35 years without the possibility of parole. The Texas legislature capitulated, providing for a jury instruction on parole eligibility when requested in capital cases (S.B. 39, 76th Leg., Reg. Sess., Tex. 1999). Currently, then, at least when future dangerousness is at issue, jurors are typically given an instruction as to the meaning of a "life sentence" to assist them in their deliberations.

Some issues remain to be resolved. For instance, should jurors be informed of the possibility that a defendant may gain freedom through other official avenues, such as a pardon? In California, juries have been informed that the "Governor may in the future commute or modify a sentence of life imprisonment without the possibility of parole to a lesser sentence that would include the possibility of parole" (*Calderon v. Coleman* 1999:142). Jurors were then instructed that "the matter of a Governor's commutation power is not to be considered by you in determining the punishment for this defendant." While the Ninth Circuit found this to be unconstitutional, the U.S. Supreme Court remanded the case without deciding its constitutionality because, in the Court's view, the Ninth Circuit had failed to perform the correct harmless-error analysis.

Another area of concern to jurors is the chance of an inmate escaping from a penal institution, a possibility often alluded to by prosecutors. It is the responsibility of defense counsel to make sure that, if the issue is raised, jurors are supplied with accurate information concerning the likelihood of a convict, especially a capital murderer escaping in their jurisdiction. A dramatic anecdote concerning an escape can inflate jurors' estimation of the likelihood of such an occurrence. Actual figures show that successful escapes are extremely uncommon. Among the 40 jurisdictions responding to a survey conducted by the American Correctional Association, 577 inmates escaped from custody during the year 2000. Considering that these jurisdictions housed over 1 million prisoner in that year, the actual likelihood of an inmate escaping was less than 6 in 10,000 (American Correctional Association 2002:19). Furthermore, over 87% of these inmates were successfully returned to custody. The damage caused by anecdotal accounts, however, may be irreparable.

If defense counsel are successful in convincing jurors that the defendant will actually be incarcerated for the rest of their life or a sentence that will keep them behind prison walls for a long enough period to keep the citizenry safe, then jurors' concerns rightfully shift to the prison community. Again, jurors are likely to have many misconceptions regarding the actual level of violence within the prison system. Modern prisons are uniquely equipped to reduce the violence potential among its charges. Respondents to the aforementioned survey reported only 42 inmate deaths at the hands of other inmates in the year 2000 (American Correctional Association 2002:7). This translates into a homicide rate in prison of 4.2 per 100,000 inmates, compared to the homicide rate in the outside community of 5.5 per 100,000 members of the general public (Federal Bureau of Investigation 2001). Even more rare than the killing of an inmate is the killing of a correctional officer. No correctional officers were killed in any of the jurisdictions reporting during the year 2000. In comparison, 51 police officers were feloniously slain in the line of duty during that year (Federal Bureau of Investigation 2001).

Even among capital murderers, research has shown that the levels of homicide and other assaultive behaviors are surprisingly low in the prison setting. Studies have shown the rate at which convicted murderers commit homicides in prison to be about 2 per 1,000 inmates per year or less, regardless of whether they are murderers serving a term of imprisonment (Wolfson 1982:168), capital murderers serving life without parole (Sorensen and Wrinkle 1996:548), or capital murderers commuted from a death sentence (Marquart and Sorensen 1989:19–21; Reidy, Cunningham, and Sorensen 2001:70). The rate of violent behavior among these same inmates was found to be less than 6 per 100 inmates per year (Marquart and Sorensen 1989:21; Sorensen and Wrinkle 1996:548).

Reliance on those studies, however, would likely result in an overestimate of the violence potential among current capital defendants for two reasons. First, they included data from previous decades when overall rates of violence in prison were higher; recent advances in classification along with the proliferation of lock-down units have resulted in a reduction in overall rates of prison violence in recent years. Second, the data used to calculate rates in those studies were drawn disproportionately from the initial stages of the inmates' terms of incarceration; rates of violence in prison decrease with the length of time served (Reidy et al. 2001:73; Sorensen, Wrinkle, and Gutierrez 1998:228–229). Taking these factors into account, a recent study, based on the records of 6,390 murderers serving time in Texas prisons during the 1990s, estimated the probability of a capital defendant committing an act of violence during a 40-year period of incarceration to be 16.4% and the probability of committing murder to be 0.2%, or about 2 in 1000 (Sorensen and Pilgrim 2000:1264).

The daunting task of determining which capital defendants will be the few that present a future danger to the prison society is facilitated only slightly by having additional information available. In making their determinations, jurors could rely on three types of predictions: anamnestic, actuarial, and clininical. Anamnestic predictions, those based on an individual's previous pattern of offending, are the best means of forecasting future dangerousness. The drawback to this method is that it is dependent on context. As noted earlier, most capital defendants, while perhaps a threat to the outside community, are not likely to commit violent acts in prison. The defendant's behavior during a previous incarceration or while in jail awaiting trial are the most telling indicators of violence potential in the prison environment.

An actuarial prediction (or risk assessment) is derived from a formula based on membership in a group for which a consistent and tested pattern of conduct has been shown. Perhaps the best known type of actuarial prediction is the life-expectancy table extensively employed in the insurance industry. Specific variables such as smoking history, alcohol history, drug-taking history, exercise pattern, and diet are entered into a straightforward and mathematically predictive formula. Actuarial tables have long been used in prisoner classification and parole decision-making. Actuarial predictions are most useful in providing jurors with a relative likelihood of violence occurring as opposed to a simple "yes" or "no" on the question of future dangerousness. This is because of the low base rate of violent recidivism. Even if a particular factor is identified that makes the defendant twice as likely to commit a violent act in prison, the odds will still favor a prediction of nondangerousness. Actuarial predictions are best suited, then, to predict nondangerousness in cases in which a defendant shares none or very few of the characteristics with those who in the past have repeated their offense (Radelet and Marquart 1990).

Clinical predictions made by mental health professionals in homicide cases are primarily intuitive and subjective. Hypotheses about the structure and dynamics of the particular individual's personality are derived from clinical impressions of personality factors and their interaction, both of which are evaluated on the basis of the offender's personal history, psychometric tests, and the clinician's past experience and expertise. Any evidence consistent with previous observations of violent behavior among other individuals can be used to support a prediction of future dangerousness. As such, clinicians are prone to overpredict dangerousness, resulting in an extremely high number of false positives (Monahan 1981). The extent to which clinicians are able to provide accurate assessments of future dangerousness coincide with their use of base rates and actuarial data, still a rarity among clinicians on the death penalty circuit (Cunningham and Reidy 1999).

The main problem with making long-term predictions of future violence is the complex nature of dangerousness. Most jurors, when weighing the evidence, view the defendant as a threat to society (especially in the future society) based on the current offense. The "hysteria of the moment" is used to forecast the future. The image of the offender is one of a permanent threat. In reality, capital murderers, like other murderers, are good risks in the prison setting and could be incapacitated in that manner. Regardless, jurors cannot predict with any degree of accuracy that a particular offender will be a future threat. The task of making accurate predictions of future dangerousness is fraught with speculation; yet, jurors routinely overpredict and opt for death.

Doctors of Death

Although clinical assessment is the least accurate basis for prediction, it is commonly used in capital trials in the post-*Furman* era. Also, the doctors or other mental health professionals who make the assessment and predictions are afforded a great deal of status by jurors. Hence their testimony often carries great weight in jury deliberations. Before discussing the testimony of psychiatrists in modern capital trials, a brief historical overview of the role of doctors in capital trials is instructive.

Clinical assessment of defendants in capital trials is not a new phenomenon. In Europe and the American colonies through the eighteenth century, a common practice in witchcraft trials was to rely on the testimony of medical doctors who claimed expertise in determining if the accused were witches, and whether the events in question were the result of witchcraft. A contemporary account of the role of Dr. Thomas Browne in the trial of two young women accused of witchcraft in an English assize illustrates this process. Amy Denny and Rose Cullender were accused of witchcraft after having muttered threats to a local merchant that supposedly resulted in the "death of a child, overturned carts, bedeviled cattle, infestations of 'lice of extraordinary bigness,' and similar awful and awesome matters" (Geis and Bunn 1981:2). In this case, Dr. Browne, a self-proclaimed expert, was called to assess whether the acts were the result of witchcraft, and whether the accused were witches. Dr. Browne consulted the famous physician-philosopher's classic book, *Religio Medici*

(1642), which outlined many of the manifestations of witchcraft. He concluded that both girls were witches. The two girls were sentenced to death and burned at the stake. Geis and Bunn (1981) surmised that Dr. Browne played an instrumental role in the trial and its outcome. The jury undoubtedly was swayed by his medical standing, his testimony about similar events in Denmark caused by sorcery, and his condemnation of the accused.

In the nineteenth century, the Italian physician and later, university professor, Cesare Lombroso testified as to whether certain defendants were born criminals (Gould 1981:138). According to Lombroso, the born criminal's biological inferiority could be detected by his atavistic features (e.g., low sloping forehead, protruding lips)—indicators that the person was a throwback to a prior evolutionary state. Lombroso's categorization of a person as a born criminal meant that there was no hope of rehabilitation, for in his typology born criminals were naturally evil and immune to the effects of punishment. Because Lombroso believed that born criminals were immune to efforts to prevent their further criminality, either through rehabilitation or deterrence, he supported the death penalty for dangerous offenders whom he believed would continue to commit criminal acts.

In America during the early twentieth century, the growth of the human sciences greatly affected thought and practices regarding crime. Investigations into family histories found that crime and other sorts of deviance tended to run in families. Studies, such as those of the Jukes (Dugdale 1877) and the Kallikaks (Goddard 1912), suggested that criminality or feeblemindedness was hereditary. An aggressive eugenics movement during the first half of this century resulted in the sterilization of over 70,000 persons thought to be mentally or morally unfit. Earnest Albert Hooton, an American anthropologist from Harvard writing in the 1930s, believed that criminals were physically different from noncriminals. He concluded that the extirpation of genetically inferior organisms was the only means of eradicating crime (1939:309).

Along with the rise of the sciences in explaining human behavior in the early twentieth century, concerns about rehabilitating offenders arose within the context of civil and criminal law. Because it was believed that the human sciences would soon be able to predict human behavior, their role under the law and within the courtroom was broadened. As was the case with the work of Lombroso, the necessary counterpart of rehabilitation is incapacitation. If certain persons are unsalvageable from the standpoint of rehabilitation, then society must be protected through incapacitation. While the older rationales of retribution and deterrence were concerned mainly with the gravity of the offense, the rationale of social defense through rehabilitation and incapacitation encouraged the examination of the traits of individual criminal offenders.

The dual roles of social defense and the medical model of corrections led to the promulgation of indeterminate sentencing laws. One of these types of law called for singling out "dangerous offenders," either for very specialized intensive treatment or incapacitation. Special sentencing for dangerous offenders, particularly violent, sexual, and recidivist offenders, was enacted by most states by the 1960s. Under those laws a prediction often had to be made about whether particular offenders presented a continuing threat to society because of the likelihood of repeating their offenses. The courts often looked to psychiatrists and other clinicians to help them make this determination.

Why the courts relied on these medical professionals to make such predictions about the future dangerousness of individuals could be due to several factors. Mental health experts were convenient. They already made civil decisions in the courtroom concerning whether to involuntarily commit persons to mental institutions, at least partially on the basis of their potential for criminal behavior (Steadman 1983). Additionally, those with titles of authority and a professional status simply are assumed to have such abilities (Petrunik 1982). Faced with the need to make a decision, reliance on psychiatrists in these situations is pragmatic. Their medical credentials and reliance on the canons of science give the appearance of infallible authority (Steadman 1983). Although psychiatric predictions frequently are inaccurate, and seldom based on scientific principles, they reassure jurors whose predictions about a defendant's future behavior determine whether he or she lives or dies.

Just as Sir Thomas Browne was considered qualified to judge whether certain acts were caused by witches, modern-day psychiatrists are considered qualified to make decisions regarding the future behavior of offenders who have committed violent acts. The involvement of psychiatrists in adjudicating these offenders serves a definite political agenda. Their involvement in predicting future dangerousness in the courtroom relieves lawyers of the responsibility to prove such, and judges or jurors of making the determination. As Sir Thomas Browne himself once wrote, "[T]is as dangerous to be sentenced by a Physician as a Judge" (Geis and Bunn 1981:9).

Social scientists have recently become aware of the role of psychiatrists as agents of social control in the administration of justice. Thomas Szasz (1972), for example, elaborates on the role of psychiatrists in labeling as "mental illness" behaviors that powerful factions desire to have suppressed. He cites the publication of Dr. Samuel Cartwright in the *New Orleans Medical and Surgical Journal* of 1851 on the "Diseases and Peculiarities of the Negro Race." In the article, Dr. Cartwright wrote of the natural biological inferiority of Negroes and the medical need for slavery which he considered a "therapeutic necessity of slaves and a medical responsibility for their masters" (Szasz 1972:337). In his article, Dr. Cartwright identified or labeled as mental illness two diseases peculiar to Negroes: "drapetomania," or running away from the master; and "dysaethesia aethiopis," or neglect of work. Both of those mental diseases had medical bases, according to Dr. Cartwright, which could only be cured by enslavement, whipping, and paternalistic treatment. In Dr. Cartwright's report it can be seen that, once again, medical science had been used to justify coercive actions by the state. By dehumanizing the slave, enslavement could be justified.

Dr. Cartwright's report illustrates a principle that, while easier to identify historically, is readily practiced today. Mental health professionals assert their authority and invoke their specialized terminology as a form of propaganda to justify the coercive control of those in modern-day society who threaten the status quo (psychotics, sexual psychopaths, addicts, etc.). Of course, predictions about dangerousness are made throughout the criminal justice system on a daily basis, and several courtroom participants have a hand in making those predictions. When clinical predictions are made in capital trials, however, they are especially crucial because whether the defendant lives or dies hinges on them. Further, jurors are unlikely to question the conclusions of clinicians testifying in capital cases, as lay persons have a tendency to rely on and to follow the instructions of authority figures such as psychiatrists and judges (Milgram 1974; Garza 1996).

Psychiatrists have been relied on extensively in capital trials in Texas to make predictions about the future dangerousness of defendants. Prior to 1981, those predictions had usually been made on the basis of a short evaluation. However, since the U.S. Supreme Court required *Miranda* warnings (see *Miranda v. Arizona* 1966) be given prior to psychiatric examinations where the information was to be used in the penalty trial (*Estelle v. Smith* 1981), most psychiatric predictions of future dangerousness have been based on "hypotheticals." In a "hypothetical," a prosecutor simply summarizes the defendant's previous conduct before asking the doctor for a prediction about his or her future dangerousness. Although a variety of information can be used in making the dangerousness determination, such as a previous record of violence or any particularly heinous circumstance of the current offense, expert psychiatric opinion is used as a supplement, especially when other factors are absent, to show that the defendant is a future threat to society.

One particular psychiatrist, James Grigson, has earned a reputation as being a "hired gun" for the prosecution. Grigson has been dubbed "Dr. Death" because of the number of capital trials in which he has testified and the unequivocal nature of his testimony. The pattern of his testimony is similar from one trial to the next. After listening to a lengthy narrative about a hypothetical person (a.k.a. the defendant) given by the prosecutor, Dr. Grigson begins by classifying the defendant as a sociopath. He then discusses the characteristics of a sociopath: a highly skilled manipulator who, lacking a conscience, kills without remorse. The prosecutor then proceeds to ask what type of medical treatment is available. After indicating that there is no known cure for sociopathy, Grigson testifies with absolute certainty that the defendant will kill again. Consider the following typical exchanges:

Prosecutor: In your opinion will he kill again?

Grigson: Yes, he certainly will if there is any way at all he was given the opportunity to, he certainly will... Well, society can restrict him, confine him; yet even in areas of confinement, this behavior [killing people] will continue (*Boulware v. State* 1974:1991–1992).

Prosecutor: Can you tell us whether or not, in your opinion, having killed in the past, he is likely to kill in the future, given the opportunity?

Grigson: He absolutely will, regardless of whether he's inside an institutional-type setting or whether he is outside. No matter where he is, he will kill again.

Prosecutor: Are you telling me, then, that even if he were institutionalized, put in a penitentiary for a life sentence—would he still be a danger to guards, prisoners, and other people around him?

Grigson: Yes. He would be a danger in any type of setting, and especially to guards or to other inmates. No matter where he might be, he is a danger (*Rodriguez v. State* 1978:2136).

Prosecutor: Doctor, based upon that hypothetical, those facts that I explained to you, do you have an opinion within reasonable medical probability as to whether the defendant, Aaron Lee Fuller, will commit criminal acts of violence that will constitute a continuing threat to society?

Grigson: Yes sir, I most certainly do have an opinion with regard to that.

Prosecutor: What is your opinion, please, sir?

Grigson: That absolutely there is no question, no doubt whatsoever, that the individual you described, that has been involved in repeated escalating behavior of violence, will commit acts of violence in the future, and represents a very serious threat to any society which he finds himself in.

Prosecutor: Do you mean that he will be a threat in any society, even the prison society?

Grigson: Absolutely, yes sir. He will do the same thing that he will do outside (Rosenbaum 1990:166).

This testimony reveals very explicitly the goal of incapacitating offenders to keep society safe from their future acts of violence. Also, it is obvious that it is not enough just to lock them away with life sentences because they will still be dangerous to guards and other inmates. Much like Dr. Thomas Browne's "witch" and Dr. Cesare Lombroso's "born criminal," Dr. James Grigson's "sociopath" must be executed for the protection of all. By labeling defendants in these ways, they are dehumanized, allowing jurors to set them outside the boundaries of the human community. This makes it easier to decide that they are simply too evil and dangerous to be allowed to live. It also eases the consciences of jurors because they are doing the only thing that seems reasonable: incapacitating an "animal" who has no hope for rehabilitation and would kill again given any opportunity to do so.

Gone are the days when medical experts are asked to determine whether the accused are possessed by demons or their acts the result of witchcraft. No longer are the skulls of criminals measured to determine if they are candidates for capital punishment. However, in many instances, psychiatrists and other clinicians have entered into the modern-day witch hunt, a capital trial in which predictions are made regarding future dangerousness.

Discourse on Dangerousness: Overcoming Ambivalence

Despite the relative lack of merit of utilitarian arguments and the vast amount of empirical evidence showing the inability to accurately predict future dangerousness, the terminology of dangerousness continues to serve as a justification for the death penalty. Such discourse also alleviates reservations of jurors in their deliberations. After all, the idea of executing someone presents very intense moral difficulties for most Americans. Although general item public opinion polls show a high level of support for capital punishment, actual executions are still offensive to many people's sensibilities (see Spierenburg 1984).

In practice, only a small proportion of potential death penalty cases are brought before a death qualified jury, generally less than one quarter of the total pool of death-eligible homicides. Second, a large proportion of life sentences are returned by jurors during the punishment phase of capital trials; generally only about one half of the penalty trials in guided discretion states result in death sentences. Third, the level of legal protection provided in capital cases during trial and appeal is extensive and has resulted in an extremely complex legal process. Fourth, executions are carried out at a slow pace; inmates live on death row many years before being executed. Finally, most death row inmates are not executed, but instead are eventually returned to the general prison population or even released.

One reason for the public's apparent ambivalence about the death penalty can be isolated by examining the answers to more specific questions asked in public opinion polls and studies of capital jurors. Recent public opinion polls conducted by Bowers and colleagues (Bowers, Vandiver, and Dugan 1994) of the residents of several states have found that when respondents are given an option of life without parole (LWOP) as an alternative to the death penalty, only a minority still support capital punishment.

An ongoing nationwide study has found that among various issues discussed by jurors in the punishment phase of capital trials, the possibility of early release of offenders sentenced to LWOP has had the most pernicious influence on jury deliberations (Bowers and Steiner 1996). The researchers found that among jurors considering life in the early stages of deliberation but eventually returning a death sentence, the key to changing their minds nearly always was their mistaken belief that those sentenced to LWOP would be released early. Haney et al. (1994) found that the possibility of early release of those sentenced to LWOP played a role in the deliberations of 8 of the 10 juries studied in California. A study of Oregon jurors—a state which at that time only offered a life sentence with a 20 year mandatory minimum, but now offers LWOP—found that 23 of the 27 jurors interviewed felt that the possibility of parole was an important factor when considering the defendant's sentence

(Costanzo and Costanzo 1994). These studies reveal that members of the general public and those sitting on capital juries want to be protected, but that the ends of justice can be better served by an alternative to the death penalty.

Because the goal of incapacitation seems to be an overriding concern in the minds of capital jurors, any statutory language, jury instructions, or assertions made by counsel can be very influential on jurors' decisions to impose a death or life sentence. In all states, but especially those with explicit directions to consider the future conduct of the defendant, discourse on dangerousness serves to make the death sentence a more viable option for the jury. While jurors in other states use a balancing approach that focuses on the deservedness of the crime, jury deliberations in Texas and Oregon tend to focus almost entirely on the issue of future dangerousness. This focus nearly precludes discussions of potentially mitigating factors and the deservedness of the offense. A study comparing jury deliberations in California (which use a weighing model) to those made in Oregon (which relies on a special issues model) found that the deliberations in California tended to be much broader in scope and focused on the nature of the crime, whereas jurors in Oregon tended to be much more constricted in the range of information they considered (Haney et al. 1994:160). As Haney et al. (1994:160) state, "there was a marked tendency for Oregon jurors to focus all of their attention on a single question or issue (future dangerousness)."

In death-penalty systems that rely on predictions of future dangerousness, the process becomes more mechanical than moral; the jury simply answers the special issues to the best of its ability, from which the sentence naturally follows. The studies of jurors in Oregon (Haney, Sontag and Costanzo 1994; Costanzo and Costanzo 1994) found that jurors felt less responsibility for their sentencing decisions under the special issues framework. Paired with psychiatric testimony of the type discussed previously and a misguided concern over the protection of the community, answering a special issue on future dangerousness affirmatively almost totally alleviates the jurors of having to deal with the painful reality of sentencing someone to death. In their minds, jurors are often simply doing what the law requires them to do.

Dangerousness is an inherently uncertain phenomenon; yet, laws are written, juries instructed, and testimony provided treating dangerousness as an objective reality. The successful application of the label "dangerous" serves to set the defendant aside, just as do the labels "witch," "born criminal," "sexual offender," "drug addict," and "psychopath," negating the societal protections normally recognized. Thus labeled, the defendant is placed outside the boundaries of our protective community. The media presents hyped accounts of extremely bizarre serial killings, the perpetrators of which are painted as elusive, calculating, unremorseful monsters who will kill again given any opportunity to do so (Barak 1995). Fictional movies and true crime detective shows set the stage for a morality play between good and evil. Crimes of fiction become mixed with sensationalized accounts. Together these images constitute a false conception of reality with real consequences. While in reality capital defendants will be incarcerated for their entire life, or at least until they are aged, within a prison setting that is quite effective in minimizing their risk to other inmates and staff, defendants labeled "dangerous" in the courtroom are effectively placed within the realm of the distorted images of television hyperreality. Jurors caught up in a situation akin to a moral panic have little choice but to protect society by incapacitating these "dangerous sociopaths." Ambivalence is easily overcome, thus justifying the state's ultimate form of social control—the death penalty.

References

American Correctional Association (2002) "Survey Summary: Riots, Disturbances, Violence, Assaults, and Escapes." *Corrections Compendium* 27(5):6–19.

Baldus, D.C., G. Woodworth, and C. Pulaski (1990) *Equal Justice and the Death Penalty.* Boston: Northeastern University Press.

Barak, G. (1995) "Media, Crime, and Justice: A Case for Constitutive Criminology." Pp. 142–166 in J. Ferrell and C.R. Sanders (eds.), *Cultural Criminology.* Boston: Northeastern University Press.

Barefoot v. Estelle (1983) 463 U.S. 880.

Black, C.L. (1976) "Due Process for Death: Jurek v. Texas and Companion Cases." *Catholic University Law Review* 26:1–16.

Boulware v. State (1974) No. 52,139 (Tex. Crim. App.).

Bowers, W.J. and B.D. Steiner (1996) *The Pernicious Illusion of Early Release for First Degree Murderers not Sentenced to Death.* Paper Presented at the annual meeting of the American Society of Criminology, Chicago.

Bowers, W.J. and B.D. Steiner (1999) "Death by Default: An Empirical Demonstration of False and Forced Choices in Capital Sentencing." *Texas Law Review* 77:606–717.

Bowers, W.J., M. Vandiver, and P.H. Dugan (1994) "A New Look at Public Opinion on Capital Punishment: What Citizens and Legislators Prefer." *American Journal of Criminal Law* 22:77–150.

Brock, D.E., J. Sorensen, and J.W. Marquart (2000) "Tinkering with the Machinery of Death: An Analysis of the Impact of Legislative Reform on the Sentencing of Capital Murderers in Texas." *Journal of Criminal Justice* 28:343–349.

Brown v. Texas (1997) 522 U.S. 940.

Calderon v. Coleman (1999) 525 U.S. 141.

Costanzo, S. and M. Costanzo (1994) "Life or Death: An Analysis of Capital Jury Decision Making Under the Special Issues Sentencing Framework." *Law and Human Behavior* 18:151–170.

Cunningham, M.D. and T.J. Reidy (1999) "Don't Confuse Me with the Facts: Common Errors in Violence Risk Assessment at Capital Sentencing." *Criminal Justice and Behavior* 26:20–43.

Dugdale, R. (1877) *The Jukes: A Study in Crime, Pauperism, Disease, and Heredity.* New York: G.P. Putnam's Sons.

Estelle v. Smith (1981) 451 U.S. 454.

Federal Bureau of Investigation (2001) *Crime in the United States: Uniform Crime Reports.* Washington DC: U.S. Government Printing Office.

Furman v. Georgia (1972) 408 U.S. 238.

Garza, R. (1996) *The Lone Juror.* Unpubl. Man. San Antonio: St. Mary's School of Law.

Geis, G. and I. Bunn (1981) "Sir Thomas Browne and Witchcraft: A Cautionary Tale for Contemporary Law and Psychiatry." *International Journal of Law and Psychiatry* 4:1–11.

Goddard, H.H. (1912) *The Kallikak Family: A Study in the Heredity of Feeblemindedness.* New York: Macmillan.

Gould, S.J. (1981) *The Mismeasure of Man.* New York: W.W. Norton.

Gregg v. Georgia (1976) 428 U.S. 153.

Haney, C., L. Sontag, and S. Costanzo (1994) "Deciding to Take a Life: Capital Juries, Sentencing Instructions, and the Jurisprudence of Death." *Journal of Social Issues* 50(2):149–176.

Hooton, E. (1939) *The American Criminal.* Cambridge: Harvard University Press.

Jurek v. Texas (1976) 428 U.S. 262.

Marquart, J.W., S. Ekland-Olson, and J.R. Sorensen (1989) "Gazing into the Crystal Ball: Can Jurors Accurately Predict Dangerousness in Capital Cases?" *Law and Society Review* 23:449–468.

Marquart, J.W. and J.R. Sorensen (1989) "A National Study of the *Furman*-Commuted Inmates: Assessing the Threat to Society from Capital Offenders." *Loyola of Los Angeles Law Review* 23:5–28.

Milgram, S. (1974) *Obedience to Authority.* New York: Harper and Row.

Miranda v. Arizona (1966) 384 U.S. 436.

Monahan, J. (1981) *Predicting Violent Behavior: An Assessment of Clinical Techniques.* Beverly Hills: Sage.

Oregon Revised Statute (1988) Section 163.150.

Penry v. Lynaugh (1989) 492 U.S. 937.

Peterson, R. D. and W. C. Bailey (2003) "Is Capital Punishment an Effective Deterrent for Murder? An Examination of Social Science Research" (This volume.)

Petrunik, M. (1982) "The Politics of Dangerousness." *International Journal of Law and Psychiatry* 5:225–253.

Proffitt v. Florida (1976) 428 U.S. 242.

Radelet, M.L. and J.W. Marquart (1990) "Assessing Nondangerousness During Penalty Phases of Capital Trials." *Albany Law Review* 54:845–861.

Ramdass v. Angelone (2000) 530 U.S. 156.

Reidy, T.J., M.D. Cunningham, and J.R. Sorensen (2001) "From Death to life: Prison Behavior of Former Death Row Inmates in Indiana." *Criminal Justice and Behavior* 28:62–82.

Roberts v. Louisiana (1976) 428 U.S. 325.

Rodriguez v. State (1978) No. 62,274 (Tex. Crim. App.).

Rosenbaum, R. (May 1990) "Travels with Dr. Death." *Vanity Fair:*141–147, 161–174.

Senate Bill, Texas (1965) S.B. 145, 60th Leg., Reg. Sess., Chap. 659.

Senate Bill, Texas (1999) S.B. 39, 76th Leg., Reg. Sess.

Shafer v. South Carolina (2001) 532 U.S. 36.

Sicola, M.K. and R.R. Shreves (1988) "Jury Consideration of Mitigating Evidence: A Renewed Challenge to the Constitutionality of the Texas Death Penalty Statute." *American Journal of Criminal Law* 15:55–68.

Simmons v. South Carolina (1994) 512 U.S. 154.

Skipper v. South Carolina (1986) 476 U.S. 1.

Sorensen, J.R. and R.L. Pilgrim (2000) "An Actuarial Assessment of Violence Posed by Capital Murder Defendants." *Journal of Criminal Law and Criminology* 90:1251–1270.

Sorensen, J.R. and R.D. Wrinkle (1996) "No Hope For Parole: Disciplinary Infractions Among Death-Sentenced and Life-Without-Parole Inmates." *Criminal Justice & Behavior* 23:542–552.

Sorensen, J.R., R.D. Wrinkle, and A. Gutierrez (1998) "Patterns of Rule-Violating Behaviors and Adjustment to Incarceration among Murderers." *Prison Journal* 78:222–231.

Spierenburg, P. (1984) *The Spectacle of Suffering.* Cambridge: Cambridge University Press.

Steadman, H.J. (1983) "Predicting Dangerousness Among the Mentally Ill: Art, Magic, and Science." *International Journal of Law and Psychiatry* 6:381–390.

Szasz, T.S. (1972) "The Sane Slave: Social Control and Legal Psychiatry." *American Criminal Law Review* 10:337–356.

Texas Code of Criminal Procedure (1985) Article 37.071.

Texas Government Code (2002) Section 508.145(b).

Wolfson, W.P. (1982) "The Deterrent Effect of the Death Penalty Upon Prison Murder." Pp. 159–173 in H.A. Bedau (ed.), *The Death Penalty in America, 3rd. Ed.* New York: Oxford University Press.

Woodson v. North Carolina (1976) 428 U.S. 280.

Chapter 10

Executing Women, Juveniles, and the Mentally Retarded: Second Class Citizens in Capital Punishment

Victor L. Streib

Although we think of the United States as one of the few remaining death penalty countries, American murderers have a 99% chance of never being executed for their crimes. The screening begins early, with about 98% of those arrested for murder never getting sentenced to death by a trial court. Of those few who do get sentenced to death at the trial level, less than half are ever executed. This results in less than 1% of all murder arrestees actually being executed for their crimes.

Many factors and patterns have been studied and evaluated to determine how and why this capital punishment exclusion factor operates at such a remarkable level. The American experience reveals that prominent among the many excluded from capital punishment are women (almost always), juveniles (usually), and the mentally retarded (always). This chapter explores the similarities and differences between the express and implicit policies and social realities that produce these results. The overarching questions addressed include the following:

(1) While it may be appropriate to assume that juveniles are not fully responsible for their behavior, is such an assumption also appropriate for women?

(2) If we want to mainstream the mentally retarded in society as much as possible, should that include eligibility for the death penalty?

(3) Are the operative factors that limit executions of these three classes of offenders legally acceptable or are they unacceptable and discriminatory?

This chapter examines each category (women, juveniles, and mentally retarded) separately to highlight the basic issues involved in each category and the most apparent factors causing differential treatment of such persons. The last section of the chapter brings these three sets of basic issues and causative factors together to determine if they are the same or different, and why.

The primary focus of this chapter is the current American death penalty era. This era began when new death penalty statutes were passed following the Supreme Court's decision in *Furman v. Georgia* (1972) which in effect struck down all then-existing death penalty statutes. However, almost all traditional death penalty states passed new death penalty statutes within a very short time after *Furman*. Sentencing began under at least some of the new statutes in 1973 and continues through today. Although the constitutionality of these current era statutes was not recognized formally by the United States Supreme Court until *Gregg v. Georgia* (1976) and actual executions did not begin until 1977, the current era of death sentencing began in 1973.

Executing Female Offenders

In general, both the death sentencing rate and the death row population for female offenders remain very small in comparison to that for males. Actual execution of female offenders is quite rare, with only 566 documented instances beginning with the first in 1632. These 566 female executions constitute less than 3% of the total of about 20,000 confirmed executions in the United States since 1608 (Rivkind & Shatz 2001: 19). In fact, women are more likely to be dropped out of the system the further the capital punishment system progresses. They are arrested for about 10% of all murders but receive only 1% of all actual executions. In sum, women are unlikely to be arrested for murder, extremely unlikely to be sentenced to death, and almost never executed. While some legitimate explanations for this exist, an apparent sex bias is at least partly the cause of this discrepancy. (Streib 2002c).

Historical Background

During essentially the last century (January 1900 to October 2002), a total of 8,131 persons have been executed in the United States. However, only 49 (0.6%) of them have been females (Streib 2002a). Table 1 lists the ten women executed in the current death penalty era.

Perhaps the most remarkable aspect of these current-era executions is that they broke long-standing traditions of not executing female offenders. For example, North Carolina's execution of Velma Barfield in 1984 followed a forty-year lull in such executions, with the last execution of a woman in North Carolina occurring in 1944 (Bessie May Williams). Texas executed two women recently (1998 and 2000), but the previous execution of a woman in Texas was in 1863 (Chipita Rodriguez). Florida began executing women again in 1998, but the last woman executed in Florida was Celia Bryan (1848). Christina Riggs volunteered for execution in Arkansas in 2000, with the last execution of a woman in Arkansas being in 1868 (Mrs. Moses Dean). Finally, Oklahoma

Table 1
Executions of Female Offenders by State,
January 1, 1973, through October 9, 2002

Name	Date of Execution	Place of Execution	Race & Sex of Offender/Victim	Age at Crime	Age at Execution
Velma Barfield	11-02-1984	No. Carolina	WF / WM	52	58
Karla Faye Tucker	02-03-1998	Texas	WF / WF, WM	23	38
Judias Buenoano	03-30-1998	Florida	WF / 2WM	28	54
Betty Lou Beets	02-24-2000	Texas	WF / WM	46	62
Christina Marie Riggs	05-02-2000	Arkansas	WF / WF, WM	26	29
Wanda Jean Allen	01-11-2001	Oklahoma	BF / BF	29	41
Marilyn Kay Plantz	05-01-2001	Oklahoma	WF / WM	27	40
Lois Nadean Smith	12-04-2001	Oklahoma	WF / WF	41	61
Linda Lyon Block	05-10-2002	Alabama	WF / WM	45	54
Aileen Carol Wuornos	10-09-2002	Florida	WF / 6WM	33	46

feverishly executed women in 2001, with its last previous execution of a woman being in 1903 (Dora Wright).

Nine of these ten cases follow a very clear pattern: white women killing white victims. Following the patterns well-established by death penalty researchers, race bias in the death penalty system follows much more the race of victim than race of offender. Given that our legal system clearly values the lives of white victims over those of victims of color, it is not surprising to see that seventeen (94%) of the eighteen victims in these ten capital cases were white. By the way, the victims in eight of the ten cases were family members or friends of the offender. The Allen case in Oklahoma is odd in so many ways, in that this was a black woman who killed her black lesbian lover, an extremely unusual set of facts in women's executions. The Riggs case in Arkansas is also unusual, in that she was a mother who killed her young children. If Riggs had not volunteered for execution, it almost undoubtedly would not have happened, given that executions of mothers who kill their children have been extremely rare. The two women executed most recently (Linda Block and Aileen Wuornos) also volunteered for execution and refused to allow appellate challenges of their cases, making a total of three of the ten executions of women being of volunteers.

Unlike for the categories of the death penalty for juveniles and the mentally retarded, little or no primary sources of law even address the death penalty for women. Sex of offender is not mentioned in any death penalty statute, and no Supreme Court case has directly considered a challenge of sex bias in the death penalty system. Even though girls and women arrested for murder are screened out of the death penalty system even more completely than are juveniles and the mentally retarded, no express and above-board justification for this can be found in American law (Streib 2002c).

Women's Death Sentences in the Current Era

The annual rate of death sentences for female offenders nationally has remained around five or six (2% of the annual total) for many years but may be dropping slightly since 2000. (Streib 2002a). A total of 142 female death sentences have been imposed in the current era, about 2% of the estimated 7,325 death sentences for all offenders (U.S. Department of Justice 2001). Table 2 lists the sentences imposed each year according to the Bureau of Justice Statistics and my own research.

Despite some fluctuations particularly in the early years of this current era, the death sentencing rate for female offenders was typically about five per year beginning in the 1980s. In 1989 this annual death sentencing rate doubled for reasons unknown. In 1990 and 1991, the sentencing rate seemed to have returned to just above the pre-1989 levels. Then the rate surged to ten in 1992, portending an annual rate again nearly double that of the 1980s. However, four of those ten female death sentences in 1992 were imposed on the same person (Aileen Wuornos in Florida), leaving only six other female death sentences during 1992. Total female death sentences then returned to the normal level—about five to seven each year. However, this death sentencing rate for female offenders has fluctuated from one-a-year to ten-a-year during the past decade. In any event, the number of female offenders sentenced to prison death rows each year remains under 0.2% of the approximately 3,700 women sentenced to prison each year.

Of the 142 death sentences for female offenders, only fifty-one sentences remain currently in effect (Streib 2002a). Ten such sentences resulted in an execution (see Table 1) and another eighty-one death sentences were reversed or commuted to life imprisonment. Thus, for the total of ninety-one death sentences finally resolved (excluding the fifty-one still in effect and still being litigated), the reversal rate for women's death sentences in the current era is 89% (81/91).

These 142 death sentences for female offenders have been imposed in twenty-three individual states, comprising well over half of the death penalty jurisdictions during this time period. Table 3, taken from Streib (2002a), lists all death penalty jurisdictions which have imposed death sentences on female offenders since 1973. As Table 3 indicates, four states (North Carolina, Florida, California, and Texas) account for 42% of all such sentences. The first ten states have imposed three-quarters of female death sentences. These dominant sentencing states range from North Carolina to California and from Texas and Florida to Ohio (NAACP 2002).

As of October 2002, fifty-one female offenders remain on the death rows of seventeen states (Streib 2002a). The present ages of those fifty-one female

Table 2
Death Sentences Imposed upon Female Offenders,
January 1, 1973, through September 30, 2002

Year	Total Death Sentences	Female Death Sentences	Percentage of Total
1973	42	1	2.4%
1974	149	1	0.7%
1975	298	8	2.3%
1976	233	3	1.3%
1977	137	1	0.7%
1978	185	4	2.1%
1979	152	4	2.6%
1980	173	2	1.1%
1981	224	3	1.3%
1982	266	5	1.8%
1983	252	4	1.6%
1984	285	8	2.8%
1985	267	5	1.8%
1986	300	3	1.0%
1987	289	5	1.7%
1988	292	5	1.7%
1989	259	11	4.2%
1990	253	7	2.7%
1991	266	6	2.2%
1992	288	10	3.5%
1993	289	6	2.0%
1994	318	5	1.6%
1995	320	7	2.2%
1996	318	1	0.3%
1997	278	3	1.1%
1998	303	7	2.3%
1999	280	5	1.8%
2000	214	7	3.3%
2001	225*	2	0.9%
2002	170*	3	1.8%
Totals:	7,325*	142	1.9%

* Estimates as of September 30, 2002.

death row inmates range from twenty-three to seventy-three years old. They have been on death row from a few months to over twenty years.

Executing Juveniles

Juvenile offenders can and do commit terrible crimes despite their youthful age. In this context, a "juvenile" offender is one who commits a crime before his or her eighteenth birthday. A very small portion of such juvenile offenders

Table 3

State-by-State Breakdown of Death Sentences for
Females Offenders, January 1, 1973, through September 30, 2002

			Race of Offender	American		Total Female
Rank	Sentencing State	White	Black	Latin	Indian	Sentences
1	North Carolina	10	4	0	2	16
2	Florida	11	3	1	0	15
	California	7	3	5	0	15
4	Texas	10	4	0	0	14
5	Ohio	3	6	0	0	9
	Alabama	6	3	0	0	9
7	Illinois	1	4	2	0	7
	Mississippi	5	2	0	0	7
	Oklahoma	6	1	0	0	7
10	Georgia	5	1	0	0	6
	Pennsylvania	3	3	0	0	6
12	Missouri	4	0	1	0	5
13	Indiana	2	2	0	0	4
14	Kentucky	3	0	0	0	3
	Maryland	1	0	0	2	3
16	New Jersey	3	0	0	0	3
17	Arizona	2	0	0	0	2
	Arkansas	2	0	0	0	2
	Idaho	2	0	0	0	2
	Louisiana	1	1	0	0	2
	Nevada	1	1	0	0	2
	Tennessee	2	0	0	0	2
23	South Carolina	1	0	0	0	1
	Totals:	91	38	9	4	142

have been subjected to the death penalty since our earliest colonial days (Streib 1987). Recent years have seen considerable curtailing of this practice, but we still lead the world in executing juvenile offenders.

Historical Background

Actual execution of such condemned juveniles began in 1642 (Thomas Graunger, Plymouth Colony, Massachusetts) (Streib 1987:73). In the over three and one-half centuries since that time, at least 365 juvenile offenders have been executed for crimes (Streib 2002b). While these 365 executions of juveniles were imposed by thirty-eight states and the federal government, they constitute less than 2% of the total of about 20,000 confirmed American executions since 1608.

The sentencing to death of juvenile offenders has remained fairly consistent during the current era, but the actual execution of such offenders has been much more sporadic. For example, the early 1990s experienced an increase in executions of juvenile offenders. Then following a drought of almost five years, juvenile executions returned with vigor from 1998 to the present. The twenty-one juvenile offenders executed in the current era are listed in Table 4. They constitute only 2.6% of the total of 805 executions during this period (as of October 2002), an execution rate somewhat higher than had been experienced prior to 1973. Their periods on death row awaiting executions ranged from six years to over twenty years, resulting in ages at execution from twenty-three to thirty eight. Texas accounts for nearly two-thirds (13/21) of these current era executions, and nearly three-quarters of these executions have occurred in Texas and Virginia combined. No other state has had more than one execution of a juvenile offender in the current era.

All but one of these twenty-one juvenile offenders executed since 1973 were seventeen years old at the time of their crimes, with only Sean Sellers in Oklahoma being sixteen. The last fifteen-year-old offender executed was on December 29, 1954 (Abraham Beard, Florida), and the last fourteen-year-old offenders were executed on July 23, 1947 (James Lewis, Jr., and Charles Trudell, Mississippi) (Streib 1987). Offenders as young as ten to twelve at the times of their crimes have also been executed, but all before 1900. In the current era, the Supreme Court has ruled that offenders ages fifteen and younger can no longer be executed (*Thompson v. Oklahoma* 1988).

Returning to the twenty-one juvenile offenders executed since 1973, only 43% have been white offenders, while 56% of executed adult offenders were white. All (100%) executed juvenile offenders were male, while 99% of adult offenders were male. Race of victim is also very close between the two groups, with 80% being white in juvenile cases and 81% being white in adult cases. In the two juvenile execution cases with black victims, the victims also were both women, presumably resulting in the low value place on black victims by the death penalty system to be compensated for by the very high value placed on female victims. Executed juvenile offenders had 52% female victims, while executed adult offenders had 48% female victims (NAACP 2002).

Legal Context

The constitutionality of the death penalty for juveniles came to the attention of the Supreme Court only quite recently in the two and a quarter centuries of our country's existence. The very first time the issue emerged was in *Eddings v. Oklahoma* (1982). This was a case that was supposed to consider whether the death penalty for a sixteen-year-old offender violated the Eighth Amendment's prohibition of "cruel and unusual punishment," but in the end the Supreme Court never quite got to that ultimate issue. However, *Eddings* did establish that, at a minimum, "the chronological age of a minor is itself a relevant mitigating factor of great weight." That means that a sentencing judge and jury must

Table 4
Executions of Juvenile Offenders,
January 1, 1973, through September 30, 2002

Name	Date of Execution	Place of Execution	Race & Sex of Offender/Victim	Age at Crime	Age at Execution
Charles Rumbaugh	9-11-1985	Texas	WM / WM	17	28
J. Terry Roach	1-10-1986	So. Car.	WM / WM,WF	17	25
Jay Pinkerton	5-15-1986	Texas	WM / WF,WF	17	24
Dalton Prejean	5-18-1990	Louisiana	BM / WM	17	30
Johnny Garrett	2-11-1992	Texas	WM / WF	17	28
Curtis Harris	7-1-1993	Texas	BM / WM	17	31
Frederick Lashley	7-28-1993	Missouri	BM / BF	17	29
Ruben Cantu	8-24-1993	Texas	LM / LM	17	26
Chris Burger	12-7-1993	Georgia	WM / WM	17	33
Joseph John Cannon	4-22-1998	Texas	WM / WF	17	38
Robert A. Carter	5-18-1998	Texas	BM / LF	17	34
Dwight A. Wright	10-14-1998	Virginia	BM / BF	17	26
Sean R. Sellers	2-4-1999	Oklahoma	WM / WM,WM,WF	16	29
Christopher Thomas	1-10-2000	Virginia	WM / WF	17	26
Steve E. Roach	1-19-2000	Virginia	WM / WF	17	23
Glen C. McGinnis	1-25-2000	Texas	BM / WF	17	27
Gary L. Graham	6-22-2000	Texas	BM / WM	17	36
Gerald L. Mitchell	10-22-2001	Texas	BM / WM	17	33
Napoleon Beazley	5-28-2002	Texas	BM / WM	17	25
T.J. Jones	8-8-2002	Texas	BM / WM	17	25
Toronto Patterson	8-28-2002	Texas	BM / BF	17	24

consider the youthfulness of the offender in deciding whether to impose the death penalty, but the death penalty for juveniles is not absolutely prohibited.

Six years later in *Thompson v. Oklahoma* (1988), the Supreme Court held that executions of offenders under age sixteen at the time of their crimes are prohibited by the Eighth Amendment to the United States Constitution. Wayne Thompson was only age fifteen when he was involved in a capital murder. The combined effect of the four-Justice plurality opinion by Justice Stevens and the concurring opinion by Justice O'Connor in *Thompson* is to hold that no state without a minimum age in their death penalty statute can go below age sixteen without violating the Constitution, and in fact no state with a minimum age in its death penalty statute uses an age less than sixteen.

One year later, the Supreme Court decided *Stanford v. Kentucky* (1989), examining the combined cases of a sixteen-year-old offender (Heath Wilkins) and a seventeen-year-old offender (Kevin Stanford). *Stanford* left the minimum age at sixteen, declining to find a federal constitutional mandate placing that minimum age at seventeen or eighteen. Again it took the combined effect of a Justice Scalia's four-Justice plurality opinion and Justice O'Connor's concurring opinion to reach this holding. Highly sensitive to states' rights to determine their own death penalty policies and procedures, the Supreme Court in *Stanford* declined to find a national consensus establishing the minimum age at eighteen.

All three cases were decided by the narrowest of margins: *Eddings* was a five-four decision, *Thompson* was a four-one-three decision, and *Stanford* was a four-one-four decision. In fact, the Supreme Court has never in its entire history generated a five-justice majority on the constitutionality of the death penalty for juvenile offenders. Nonetheless, state courts have uniformly recognized and enforced these Supreme Court holdings without questioning their validity or staying power. The constitutionality of the death penalty for juvenile offenders appeared to be settled in the 1990s, at least so far as making youthfulness a mitigating factor of "great weight" and prohibiting executions for crimes committed below age sixteen. However, challenges to *Stanford* continue to be brought by sixteen-year-old and seventeen-year-old offenders, seeking to raise the minimum age to eighteen. The Supreme Court's decision in *Atkins v. Virginia* (2002) relied heavily on *Thompson* and *Stanford* by analogy in prohibiting the death penalty for the mentally retarded, so the juvenile death penalty issue will continue to be pushed before legislatures and courts. As of late 2002, three Supreme Court Justices have gone on record in *Patterson v. Texas* (2002) as wanting that Court to revisit the issue of the death penalty for juveniles.

Quite aside from the mandates of the Eighth Amendment to the United States Constitution, state constitutions are also a source of regulation for the juvenile death penalty. In *Brennan v. State* (1999), the Florida Supreme Court interpreted the Florida Constitution as barring the execution of Keith Brennan because he was only sixteen years old at the time of his crime. Noting they were not bound by the rulings of *Thompson* and *Stanford* in interpreting the requirements of the Florida Constitution, the Florida Court nonetheless did follow much of the same analytical approach. While the Florida Supreme Court paid due deference to the United States Supreme Court's interpretation of the United States Constitution, the ultimate interpreter of the Florida Constitution is, of course, the Florida Supreme Court. Similar state constitutional issues are being raised before other state supreme courts in additional juvenile death penalty cases.

Despite the significance of those federal and state cases, the minimum age for the death penalty today tends to be more a function of express statutory provision than of federal or state constitutional mandate. Thirty-eight state statutes and two federal statutes (civilian and military) provide for the death penalty for designated crimes. Among those forty death penalty statutes, both federal statutes and sixteen of the state statutes expressly provide for a minimum age of eighteen at the time of the crime. Age seventeen is specified by five other state statutes, and all other death penalty statutes have either an express minimum age of sixteen or that age implied by *Thompson*. However, state legislatures are showing a great amount of interest in this minimum age issue. Since *Stanford* was decided, Kansas (1994) and New York (1995) have reenacted the death penalty and have included a minimum age of eighteen. Montana (1999) and Indiana (2002) both amended their existing death penalty statutes to raise the minimum age to eighteen. As of 2002, about ten other state legislatures are considering similar amendments to their existing death penalty statutes. Specific jurisdictions and their present minimum ages are as follows:

Age Eighteen: California, Colorado, Connecticut, Illinois, Indiana, Kansas, Maryland, Montana, Nebraska, New Jersey, New Mexico, New York, Ohio, Oregon, Tennessee, Washington, and Federal (both civilian and military)

Age Seventeen: Florida, Georgia, New Hampshire, North Carolina, and Texas

Age Sixteen: Alabama, Arizona, Arkansas, Delaware, Idaho, Kentucky, Louisiana, Mississippi, Missouri, Nevada, Oklahoma, Pennsylvania, South Carolina, South Dakota, Utah, Virginia, and Wyoming

No Death Penalty: Alaska, District of Columbia, Hawaii, Iowa, Maine, Massachusetts, Michigan, Minnesota, North Dakota, Rhode Island, Vermont, West Virginia, and Wisconsin

Globally, the United States is the only country in the world which still permits the execution of offenders under age eighteen. Many treaties and international agreements prohibit this practice, to the point now that this prohibition has become *jus cogens* or international common law. Despite this international law and the considerable global pressure opposing the death penalty for sixteen year olds and seventeen year olds, the United States continues to permit this practice. However, actual execution of such juvenile offenders occurs essentially only in Texas and occasionally in one or two other states. To the degree that a jurisdiction is out of step with the rest of the world, it may be more correct to identify that rogue jurisdiction as Texas and not as the entire United States.

Juvenile Death Sentences Imposed in Current Era

Table 5 lists the sentences imposed each year on juveniles according to the Bureau of Justice Statistics (U.S. Department of Justice 2001) and my own research (Streib 2002b). A total of 221 death sentences have been imposed on juveniles between 1973 and late 2002, only 2.9% of the total of the about 7,325 death sentences imposed for offenders of all ages. Over two-thirds of those ju-

Table 5
Death Sentences Imposed for Crimes Committed As Juveniles, January 1, 1973, through September 30, 2002

| Year | Total Death Sentences[1] | Juvenile Death Sentences (Age at Crime) | | | Totals | Juvenile Sentences as a Percentage of Total Sentences |
		15	16	17		
1973	42	0	0	0	0	0.0%
1974	149	1	0	2	3	2.0%
1975	298	1	6	4	11	3.7%
1976	233	0	0	3	3	1.3%
1977	137	1	3	8	12	8.8%
1978	185	0	1	5	6	3.2%
1979	152	0	1	2	3	2.0%
1980	173	2	0	4	6	3.5%
1981	224	0	2	6	8	3.6%
1982	266	0	1	13	14	5.3%
1983	252	0	4	4	8	3.2%
1984	285	3	0	3	6	2.1%
1985	267	1	1	4	6	2.2%
1986	300	1	3	5	9	3.0%
1987	289	1	0	1	2	0.7%
1988	292	0	0	5	5	1.7%
1989	259	0	0	1	1	0.4%
1990	253	1	3	5	9	3.6%
1991	266	1	0	4	5	1.9%
1992	288	0	1	5	6	2.1%
1993	289	0	1	6	7	2.4%
1994	318	0	4	14	17	5.3%
1995	320	0	2	10	13	4.1%
1996	318	0	4	8	12	3.8%
1997	278	0	4	4	8	2.9%
1998	303	0	4	7	11	3.6%
1999	280	0	3	12	15	5.4%
2000	214	0	3	4	7	3.3%
2001	225*	0	0	6	6	2.7%
2002	170*	0	0	2	2	1.2%
Total:	7,325*	13	51	157	221	3.0%

1 The source of the data for total annual death sentences is the UNITED STATES DEPARTMENT OF JUSTICE, CAPITAL PUNISHMENT 2000 at 13, appendix table 1 (2001).
* Estimates as of September 30, 2002.

venile death sentences have been imposed on seventeen-year-old offenders, the other third on offenders ages sixteen and fifteen, and none on offenders age fourteen or younger at the time of their crimes.

The rate of juvenile death sentencing fluctuated considerably in the early years of this current era but then settled into a consistent annual rate of a little over 2% of total death sentences in the mid-1980s. A change occurred from 1987 to 1989 when the juvenile death sentencing rate dropped considerably, presumably deterred by the cases then pending before the United States Supreme Court. In the mid- to late-1990s, death sentencing of juvenile offenders stayed at a steady annual rate of about 3% to 5% of all death sentences. During the last few years, the juvenile death sentencing rate appears to have declined significantly. The six seven such sentences per year recently are only half of the typical rate in the preceding six years. Only two juvenile death sentences for 2002 have been verified anywhere in the United States as of October 2002.

These 221 juvenile death sentences have been imposed in twenty-two individual states, comprising well over half of the death penalty jurisdictions during this time period. Table 6 lists all death penalty jurisdictions which have imposed juvenile death sentences since 1973. Texas (57 sentences) is the clear leader in this practice, followed somewhat at a distance by Florida (31 sentences) and then Alabama (22 sentences). These three states together account for over half (110/221) of all juvenile death sentences, and only seven states have imposed ten or more juvenile death sentences in the current era.

Almost all (98%) juvenile offenders sentenced to death are males. The five cases involving female juveniles were either in the deep south (Mississippi, Alabama, and Georgia) or in Indiana. The thirteen youngest offenders (age fifteen at crime) were scattered across ten different states. Juvenile death sentences for black and white juvenile offenders appear to be spread around the sentencing jurisdictions fairly evenly, but all but one of the Latin offenders are in Texas, Arizona, Florida and Nevada.

Of these 221 juvenile death sentences imposed in the current era, only eighty-two (37%) remain currently in force. Only twenty-one (10%) have resulted in execution, and 118 have been reversed or commuted to life imprisonment. Therefore, for these 139 juvenile death sentences finally resolved either by reversal or execution, the reversal rate is 85% (118/139), excluding the eighty-two current death row inmates remaining under juvenile death sentences but still litigating them. Conversely, only 15% (21/139) of finally-resolved cases have resulted in actual execution.

Current Death Row Inmates under Death Sentences Imposed while They Were Juveniles

As of September 30, 2002, eighty-two persons were on death row under death sentences received for juvenile crimes (Streib 2002b). These eighty-two condemned juvenile offenders constituted 2% of the total death row population of 3,718 (NAACP 2002). Given an inherent under-reporting tendency, a few others of those 3,718 currently on death row actually may have been under age eighteen at the time of their crimes, but their ages are not yet verified for

Table 6
State-by-State Breakdown of Juvenile Death Sentences,
January 1, 1973, through September 30, 2002

Rank & State	Race of Offender				Sex of Offender		Age at Crime			Totals
	Asian	Black	Latin	White	Male	Female	15	16	17	
1: Texas	1	25	17	14	57	0	0	0	57	57
2: Florida	0	8	2	21	31	0	3	9	19	31
3: Alabama	0	11	0	11	20	2	1	9	12	22
4: Louisiana	0	16	0	1	17	0	2	7	8	17
5: Mississippi	0	7	0	6	12	1	0	5	8	13
6: Georgia	0	5	0	6	10	1	1	0	10	11
North Carolina	0	7	1	3	11	0	1	0	10	11
8: Oklahoma	0	0	0	7	7	0	1	3	3	7
Pennsylvania	0	6	0	1	7	0	1	2	4	7
South Carolina	0	3	0	4	7	0	0	3	4	7
11: Arizona	0	0	3	3	6	0	0	3	3	6
Ohio	0	5	0	1	6	0	0	1	5	6
13: Virginia	0	3	0	2	5	0	0	2	3	5
14: Missouri	0	2	0	2	4	0	0	2	2	4
15: Indiana	0	2	0	1	2	1	1	0	2	3
Kentucky	0	1	0	2	3	0	1	0	2	3
Maryland	0	2	0	1	3	0	0	0	3	3
Nevada	0	1	2	0	3	0	0	3	0	3
19: Arkansas	0	2	0	0	2	0	1	1	0	2
20: Nebraska	0	1	0	0	1	0	0	1	0	1
New Jersey	0	1	0	0	1	0	0	0	1	1
Washington	0	0	0	1	1	0	0	0	1	1
Totals:	1	108	25	87	216	5	13	51	157	221

purposes of this report. Although all were ages sixteen or seventeen at the time of their crimes, their current ages range from eighteen to forty-one. Race of offender for these juvenile cases differs from the adult offenders currently under sentences of death. Although 45% of the adult offenders are white, only 33% of the juvenile offenders are white. Another major difference is that only 9% of adults are Latin, while 16% of the juveniles are Latin. (NAACP 2002).

These eighty-two juvenile offenders currently are under death sentences in only fourteen of the twenty-three states which authorize the death penalty for juvenile offenders, and they have been on death row from one month to twenty-three years. Texas has by far the largest death row for juvenile offenders, holding twenty-eight (34%) of the national total of eighty-two juvenile offenders. All juvenile offenders currently under death sentences are male and have been convicted and sentenced to death for murder. Over three-quarters of these cases involve seventeen-year-old offenders, and two-thirds of them are offenders of color. In contrast, 80% of the victims are adults. Almost three-quarters of the victims are white, and just over half are females.

The total number of persons under death sentences has increased by 208% in the past fifteen years, reflecting an essentially steady rise from 1,209 (1983) to 3,718 (2002). In contrast, the number of juvenile offenders under death sentences has risen much more slowly. Only thirty-three juvenile offenders were under death sentences at the close of 1983, compared to eighty-two juvenile offenders as of September 30, 2002 (a 148% increase). Given the clear decrease in the annual death sentencing rate for juvenile offenders since 2000, presumably this number of juvenile offenders on death row will rise even more slowly than it has in past years.

Executing Mentally Retarded Offenders

A first cousin to the juvenile death penalty issue is the concern about the death penalty for mentally retarded offenders. One simplistic characterization of mental retardation is that it is comparable to having the mental age of a ten-year-old or a fourteen-year-old. If so, opponents argue, then mental age should determine death penalty eligibility, and mentally retarded offenders should be excluded just as juvenile offenders under the chronological age of sixteen are excluded. Apparently, mentally retarded persons comprise only about 1% to 3% of the general population but about 10% of death row inmates (*Atkins v. Virginia* 2002:2254, 2264). However, nothing like the detailed data we have for women and juvenile capital offenders exist for mentally retarded capital offenders. In any event, the following analysis assumes that a significant number of capital offenders are mentally retarded and that mental retardation of the offender is a factor in the death penalty process.

Characteristics of Mentally Retarded Defendants

In 1992, the American Association on Mental Retardation (AAMR) revised its definition of this disability to read as follows:

> *Mental retardation* refers to substantial limitations in present functioning. It is characterized by significantly subaverage intellectual functioning, existing concurrently with related limitations in two or more of the following applicable adaptive skill areas: communication, self-care, home living, social skills, community use, self-direction, health and safety, functional academics, leisure, and work. Mental retardation manifests before age eighteen (AAMR 1992).

The component parts of this widely accepted definition are terms of art. "Significantly subaverage intellectual functioning" can be measured through intelligence tests which render an intelligence quotient (IQ) score. To meet the AAMR definition of mental retardation, one must score below seventy on an intelligence test for which the mean score is one hundred. In statistical terms, this means that any individual who is mentally retarded is in the lowest 2.5% of the population in measured intelligence (AAMR 1992).

The AAMR definition also requires that an individual possess an actual disability in an "adaptive skill area" that affects everyday life (AAMR 1992). This component reflects an attempt to focus the attention of public policy makers on the specific areas of disability found within the mental retardation classification (AAMR 1992). Such a focus is helpful in recognizing the wide range of behaviors affected by the disability. This awareness is especially important when assessing the ability of a mentally retarded offender to be adequately defended in a capital crime case.

"Mental age" is an additional technique used to assess the severity of a person's mental retardation (Ellis and Luckasson 1985:434). It is an attempt to compare the intellectual functioning of the individual being tested with that of a mentally typical person. This is accomplished by identifying for each item on an IQ test the age level at which a typical person can successfully answer the question. For example, if a person with a chronological age of twenty receives a similar IQ score as a non-retarded child with a chronological age of eleven, the twenty-year-old is said to have a mental age of eleven. The death penalty arguments that flow from this mental age assessment of mentally retarded defendants are obvious. If an extremely mature murderer with the chronological age of fifteen or lower is not eligible for the death penalty under *Thompson*, then a mentally retarded murderer with the mental age of fifteen or lower is similarly ineligible for the death penalty.

The perceived inability of the mentally retarded to adequately negotiate the workings of the judicial system is often cited as a justification for their exclusion from the death penalty. Research on the moral development of the mentally retarded establishes that some mentally retarded individuals possess incomplete or immature concepts of blameworthiness and causation (Ellis and Luckasson 1985). As a result, a mentally retarded defendant may plead guilty to a crime he or she did not commit simply because he or she thinks that blame should be delegated to someone, and he or she is unable to master the idea of causation and his or her role in the incident. Similarly, a mentally retarded defendant may eagerly assume blame in an effort to please an accuser, which may result in an unfounded confession.

Further difficulties confront a mentally retarded defendant when he or she seeks to deny his or her disability or enhance his or her status in the courtroom. Such a defendant may boast of his or her strength or how he or she outsmarted the victim, when neither assertion is true. Few mentally retarded defendants acknowledge their disability when arrested or at any other time during their encounter with the criminal justice system. This halted moral development also is a factor in assessing culpability. Opponents of the death penalty for mentally retarded offenders argue that when a mentally retarded defendant's full moral reasoning ability is compromised, he or she cannot be held to have the level of culpability that would justify punishment by death (Ellis and Luckasson 1985).

Legal Context

The exemption of the mentally retarded from the death penalty apparently was firmly established in English and American common-law jurisprudence (Rumley 1993). Early definitions of "idiocy" focused on both intellectual impairment and its resulting impact on functional ability, making these definitions not dissimilar from today's AAMR definition. The basic point of disagreement has always been in the determination of what level of mental disability is sufficient for exemption from criminal responsibility. The sixteenth century "counting-twenty-pence" test defined an idiot as one who could not count to twenty, identify his parents, or cite his age (Ellis and Luckasson 1985). Early eighteenth century courts promulgated the "wild beast" test which exonerated from the death penalty those individuals whose awareness of their actions was no more than that of an infant, brute, or wild beast (Rumley 1993:1307).

Prior to 1986, apparently no death penalty statute had addressed mental retardation either as a mitigating circumstance or as a precluding factor. The Georgia legislature amended its death penalty statute in 1986 to preclude the death penalty for mentally retarded offenders, due in large part to extensive media coverage of Georgia's 1986 execution of Jerome Bowden who had an IQ of 65. The federal death penalty statute followed suit in 1988, and Maryland enacted a similar provision in 1989. However, all other death penalty jurisdictions in the United States at that time made no mention of mental retardation (*Atkins v. Virginia* 2002).

The Supreme Court first considered this issue in *Penry v. Lynaugh* (1989). Johnny Paul Penry was sentenced to death for rape and murder in Texas. Evidence that Penry was mentally retarded and brain damaged was presented, but he was found competent to stand trial. John Paul Penry had an IQ of fifty and the mental age of six, never having finished the first grade. In *Penry*, however, the Supreme Court found no constitutional bar to the death penalty for mentally retarded capital defendants, primarily because at that time (1989) only three death penalty jurisdictions expressly prohibited it. This did not constitute a national consensus opposing the death penalty for the mentally retarded under the Supreme Court's "evolving standards of decency" analysis.

However, the issue did not fade away after 1989. An intensive political action campaign kept the death penalty for the mentally retarded in the news media, and state legislatures in death penalty states were asked to address the issue. As a result, nearly half of the death penalty jurisdictions amended their death penalty statutes in the 1990s to exclude mentally retarded offenders, generally using an IQ cutoff of seventy, and this legislative movement continued to grow steadily in the early years of the twenty-first century. Mentally retarded defendants in death penalty cases continued to litigate this issue, and the Supreme Court entered this arena once again.

The Supreme Court's ruling in *Atkins v. Virginia* (2002) moved Eighth Amendment law on this issue. Daryl Atkins and an accomplice had committed a robbery-murder, but Atkins had an IQ of fifty-nine and the mental age of a nine- to twelve-year-old child. Concluding that the flurry of legislative activity, in conjunction with other indicators, establish a national consensus opposing the death penalty for the mentally retarded, the Supreme Court in *Atkins* held that this application of capital punishment is now cruel and unusual under the Eighth and Fourteenth Amendments. In addition to being rejected by a growing number of state legislatures, the actual imposition of death sentences and actual executions upon mentally retarded offenders is quite rare even in states which permit it, providing yet further indication of a national consensus against it. One lesser issue involved the opposition to this practice found in public polls, in the positions of leading organizations, and in comparative and international law. The majority in *Atkins* relied in small part on these findings, but the three dissenting Justices thought that a "national consensus" in constitutional law should not be built upon the whims of public opinion or upon the practices of other countries.

In establishing this national consensus under the evolving standards of decency, the Court in *Atkins* also measured it against the social purposes served by the death penalty: retribution and deterrence of capital crimes by prospective offenders. The Court held that mentally retarded offenders have less culpability for their crimes and therefore do not merit maximum retribution. The Court in *Atkins* also evaluated potential offenders' ability to deliberate and premeditate their murders, finding "that sort of calculus is at the opposite end of the spectrum from behavior of mentally retarded offenders." Given this basic truth, they were unlikely to be deterred from murderous conduct.

While *Atkins* held that the Eighth and Fourteenth Amendments prohibit execution of the mentally retarded, the Supreme Court left to the States the task of describing this category more precisely beyond the basic AAMR definition. This smacks of a macabre game of "you can't execute them but we won't tell you who they are," but it is the same approach used by the Court in regard to executing the insane. Following *Atkins*, we can expect a flurry of state legislative activity to amend death penalty statutes, both to prohibit the execution of the entire category of mentally retarded offenders and to define who is and is not in that category. The *Atkins* case appeared to endorse the common definition of mental retardation as having an IQ under seventy and having significant limitations in adaptive functioning in skill areas such as communication, self-care, home-living, and work, all of which manifested prior to age eighteen. The several hundred apparently mentally retarded inmates on death row at the time *Atkins* was decided also will have to litigate their cases individually to see if they fall within the protection of *Atkins*.

Comparing and Contrasting Issues and Factors

Many, perhaps most, of the reasons why women, juveniles, and the retarded are or are not screened out of the death penalty process are unknown to us. However, both the historical development of law and the general assumptions of American society provide standards by which we might measure these phenomena. The overriding question is whether the same or even similar death sentencing standards should apply alike to women, juveniles, and the mentally retarded.

Basic Culpability for Criminal Liability

The severity of criminal punishment under American criminal law is based not only on the amount of the harm inflicted but also on the maturity and clarity of the mental and emotional state of the offender at the time of the crime. This premise appears to be particularly significant for juvenile and mentally retarded offenders. Indeed, for individuals with ages less than sixteen or with IQs less than seventy combined with limited adaptive skills, the United States Constitution forbids capital punishment. Nothing so obvious and above board exists as to women offenders, but there is reason to believe that women offenders inadvertently benefit from the way the aggravating and mitigating factors are written in typical death penalty statutes (Streib 2002c).

The Supreme Court's Eighth Amendment opinions establish that imposition of the death penalty must be "directly related to the personal culpability of the criminal defendant" (*California v. Brown* 1987:544, O'Connor, J., concurring). Advocates for the mentally retarded assert that the effects of their disability in the areas of cognitive impairment, moral reasoning, control of impulses, and the ability to understand basic relationships between cause and effect make it impossible for them to possess that level of culpability essential in capital cases. Juveniles, particularly those of younger years, have very similar characteristics.

Another fundamental premise is that capital punishment is reserved for only the worst 1% of all murderers. The American death penalty system shunts aside the arguments either that *all* murderers should be executed or that *no* murderers should be executed. Essentially, the system must develop and utilize criteria that separate the top or "worst" 1% of all murderers from the bottom or "not-so-bad" 99% of all murderers. Do the immature mental and emotional characteristics of juveniles and the mentally retarded render them categorically incapable of being in that worst 1%? Even if this issue raises serious questions for those two categories, can we say that female offenders could never be in the worst 1%?

Evolving Standards of Decency

Although the Eighth Amendment prohibits cruel and unusual punishments, this concept is not fixed but is said to change over time, i.e., to be based on an "evolving standard of decency" (*Gregg v. Georgia* 1976). In deciding whether the death penalty for any of the three groups discussed in this chapter has become other than "decent" over the passage of time, courts tend to examine the current status of the statutory law, the frequency of imposition of the punishment by juries and trial courts, the positions of leading organizations knowledgeable about these issues, and the laws of other countries.

As has been discussed previously, most death penalty statutes have minimum ages with the most common minimum age being eighteen. As the offender's age goes down to seventeen and sixteen, more and more statutes forbid the death penalty for such offenders. Similarly, at the time *Atkins* was decided, about half of the death penalty statutes prohibited the death penalty for mentally retarded offenders. No American statutes forbid the death penalty for female offenders. Thus, if these official legislative actions are to serve as a guide, it would appear that executing juveniles (at least at some minimum age) and the mentally retarded fall below our standards of decency, but executing females is not an issue.

Reported previously are the frequencies of death penalties for women and for juvenile offenders. Essentially, women receive about 2% of the death sentences and 1% of the executions. Juveniles receive 3% of the death sentences and 2.4% of the executions. No such precise data exist for the mentally retarded, but the proportions probably are higher, perhaps around 10% for death sentences and for executions. These very small percentages can and are interpreted in several ways. One camp argues that these numbers reveal that juries generally are unwilling to sentence such offenders to death, with only a very few aberrant cases slipping by this barrier. The opposing camp argues that these numbers reveal that juries are laudably concerned and careful in such cases, but that juries are willing nonetheless to impose death sentences in such cases when they are warranted.

The death penalty for juveniles and the mentally retarded is opposed by many organizations and political action groups. No organizations specifically oppose the death penalty for female offenders unless they also oppose it for all offenders. While the viewpoints of these groups and their spokespersons tend to fill the media, should such political opinions be used to measure and determine the basic constitutional provisions of our criminal justice system?

Public opinion polls typically indicate that while about three-quarters of Americans support the idea of the death penalty in general, only about one-quarter support the death penalty for juveniles or for the mentally retarded. In the world community, the juvenile death penalty is almost nonexistent, causing America to be under attack as denying fundamental rights to children. A similar, although less developed world-wide viewpoint exists about the mentally retarded. No such identified viewpoint exists about female offenders, even though some other countries (such as Russia) expressly forbid the death penalty for women. The question remains whether the practices in other countries should be used to measure the evolving standards of decency in this country.

Incapacitation

The one sentencing goal that the death penalty fulfills perfectly is incapacitation. An executed offender is permanently incapacitated from committing any future crimes. This primary justification for the death penalty applies equally to all three categories of the capital offenders discussed in this chapter, as it does to all other categories of capital offenders. Therefore, although incapacitation is a key issue in the consideration of the death penalty, it would seem to provide no insights for consideration specific to the three categories considered in this chapter.

The incapacitation issue does affect these categories of offenders in different ways in one respect. Juvenile offenders can be argued to be at a stage of maturation and change, moving from a violent adolescent stage to a calmer adult stage. Therefore, at some point—perhaps in twenty or thirty years—they will no longer be a threat. This analysis pushes toward long-term incarceration as a satisfactory incapacitant. For the mentally retarded, the very nature of their retardation means that they are not maturing and changing mentally. They will have essentially the same mental level and abilities in twenty or thirty years as they do now. Simply incarcerating them "until they grow up," as we might do with juvenile murderers, would not be nearly as reasonable an alternative as it is for juveniles.

The need to incapacitate women who commit murder points also to long term incarceration in a women's prison. Most of the women on death row currently are there for killing their husbands or their children. They have no record and no tendencies toward killing strangers, including other prison inmates or guards. Being locked up in prison will almost completely prevent any opportunity to repeat their crimes.

Deterrence

The death penalty has always been and is likely always to be extremely rare, and thus its ineffectiveness as a deterrent stems in part from the knowledge that more than 99% of offenders who kill will never face execution. This is true for women, juveniles, and the mentally retarded as well. Therefore, any possible deterrent effect for these specific groups is greatly limited by this overall phenomenon.

Beyond that, there is reason to believe that juveniles and the mentally retarded do not react as a group to the general, rhetorical threat of severe consequences for their acts. The research commonly indicates that few murderers carefully plan and execute their homicides, but instead that most are impulsive and often emotion-driven. In such instances, the about-to-be-murderer does not engage in a careful cost/benefit analysis but instead just acts impulsively.

Where juveniles and the mentally retarded are involved, this impulsiveness and emotionalism is likely to be even more prevalent. For those few rational juvenile murderers who do calculate their crimes and thus might be deterred by any threatened punishment, long-term imprisonment may be a greater deterrent than is the death penalty. Juveniles hate to be grounded for Saturday night, let alone for a week or two. For a sixteen-year-old who loves life on the streets, grounding him or her for life by putting him or her in prison might be the ultimate punishment.

Women's homicides tend to be domestic and emotional, and less likely to be cold and calculating. The nature of such homicides means that any possible punishment simply is unlikely to be considered by them before they act.

Retribution

Everyone is sympathetic to the emotional outrage felt by the victim's family and community, but any choice of criminal sentence should be made in a logical, rational, cool-headed manner rather than by emotional outrage. The harm inflicted by female, juvenile, or mentally retarded murderers is enormous and gives rise to a strong desire for retribution and justice, yet life imprisonment for an offender should satisfy that need. When the offender is a juvenile—actually a child under law—the societally-acceptable demand for retribution is blunted, at least somewhat. When the offender is a mentally retarded adult, some might seek less retribution but others might not moderate their feelings.

When women are offenders, society may be less willing to wreak horrible punishments on them than upon males. When the ship is sinking, we put women in the lifeboats first. When women enter the armed forces, they are kept away from the firing line. Generally, it might be argued, we are uncomfortable with subjecting women to death or even danger (Streib 2002c).

Conclusions

It is true that women and juveniles are screened out of the death penalty system in about the same numbers, with death sentences or actual executions being quite rare for such individuals. It may be that mentally retarded offenders also are screened out to some degree, but the data regarding these offenders simply are not available to make this conclusion.

Still, it does appear that the reasons for screening out juveniles are much more justifiable than those for screening out women. A plausible argument can be made to treat mentally retarded offenders somewhat as we do juvenile offenders, but lumping together these two groups is inaccurate at best and fraught with difficulties. At the grossest levels, however, if a bright fifteen-year-old is ineligible for the death penalty because of his chronological youth, then a mentally retarded twenty-year-old with the mental age of ten or twelve also should be ineligible.

Making women ineligible for the death penalty, as Russia has done expressly and as the United States has done in practice, seems harder to defend. This practice, while explainable in some of its dimensions, seems at bottom to be unvarnished gender bias—a queasiness among criminal justice officials for putting a woman to death (Streib 2002c). One need not be a supporter of the death penalty to observe that if men are eligible for it, then women should be also. Otherwise, women are lumped in with juveniles and the mentally retarded as not fully responsible human beings.

References

American Association on Mental Retardation (1992) *Mental Retardation: Definition, Classification, and Systems of Supports.* (9th ed.) New York: American Association on Mental Retardation.

Atkins v. Virginia (2002) 122 S.Ct. 2242.

Bing, J.L. (1996) "Protecting the Mentally Retarded from Capital Punishment: State Efforts Since *Penry* and Recommendations for the Future." *New York University Review of Law and Social Change* 22:59–151.

Brennan v. State (1999) 754 So.2d 1 (Fla.).

California v. Brown (1987) 479 U.S. 538.

Eddings v. Oklahoma (1982) 455 U.S. 104.

Ellis, J.W. (1992) "Decisions By and For People With Mental Retardation: Balancing Considerations of Autonomy and Protection." *Villanova Law Review* 37:1779–1809.

Ellis, J.W. and R.A. Luckasson (1985) "Mentally Retarded Criminal Defendants." *George Washington Law Review* 53:414–493.

Furman v. Georgia (1972) 408 U.S. 238.

Gregg v. Georgia (1976) 428 U.S. 153.

Lockett v. Ohio (1978) 438 U.S. 586.

NAACP Legal Defense and Educational Fund, Inc. (2002) "Death Row, U.S.A." (Summer 2002). New York: NAACP Legal Defense and Educational Fund, Inc.

Patterson v. Texas (2002) 123 S.Ct. 24.

Penry v. Lynaugh (1989) 492 U.S. 302.

Rivkind, N. and S.F. Shatz (2001) *Cases and Materials on the Death Penalty.* St. Paul, MN: West Group.

Rumley, D.L. (1993) "A License to Kill: The Categorical Exemption of the Mentally Retarded from the Death Penalty." *St. Mary's Law Journal* 24:1299–1360.

Stanford v. Kentucky (1989) 492 U.S. 361.

Streib, V.L. (1987) *Death Penalty for Juveniles.* Bloomington, IN: Indiana University Press.

Streib, V.L. (1998) "Moratorium on the Death Penalty for Juveniles." *Law & Contemporary Problems* 61:55–87.

Streib, V.L (2002a) "Capital Punishment of Female Offenders: Present Female Death Row Inmates and Death Sentences and Executions of Female Offenders, January 1, 1973, to October 9, 2002" (October) (available at www.law.onu.edu/faculty/streib).

Streib, V.L. (2002b) "The Juvenile Death Penalty Today: Present Death Row Inmates Under Juvenile Death Sentences and Death Sentences and Executions for Juvenile Crimes, January 1, 1973, to September 30, 2002" (October) (available at www.law.onu.edu/faculty/streib).

Streib, V.L. (2002c) "Gendering the Death Penalty: Countering Sex Bias in a Masculine Sanctuary." *Ohio State Law Journal* 63:433–475.

Thompson v. Oklahoma (1988) 487 U.S. 815.

United States Department of Justice (2001) "Capital Punishment 2000." Washington, D.C.: United States Department of Justice.

Chapter 11

The Execution of the Innocent

Michael L. Radelet
Hugo Adam Bedau

Introduction

Elsewhere, we have published accounts of over four hundred cases where persons were wrongfully convicted in capital (or potentially capital) cases and we described several dozen of these cases in detail (Bedau and Radelet 1987; Radelet and Bedau, 1998, 2001; Radelet, Bedau, and Putnam 1992; Radelet, Lofquist, and Bedau 1997). In just the last few years, DNA technology has provided definitive proof of the innocence of over 100 prisoners (Scheck, Neufeld, and Dwyer 2000), and much has been learned about some of the major causes of these and other miscarriages of justice (Westervelt and Humphrey 2001). Our discussion in this Chapter falls into three parts. First, we explore the conceptualization of the term "innocence." Without precise conceptualization we have no suitable criterion for deciding who should and should not be considered innocent despite a criminal homicide conviction. Second, we review the kinds of evidence on which we have relied in previous research that led us to conclude that some defendants sentenced to death and executed were in fact innocent. Finally, we offer some observations on how government officials and the general public are currently reacting to the problem of executing the innocent and the relevance of this issue to contemporary death penalty debates.

Conceptualizing the Problem of Innocence

If we are to study how often innocent people are convicted of murder, sentenced to death, and executed, special care must be taken in conceptualizing "innocence" and in determining when this term ought to be applied to—or withheld from—a given convicted defendant. Previous work on this latter problem (e.g., Huff, Rattner, and Sagarin 1996; Radelet et al. 1992) touches only the tip of the iceberg. Undoubtedly, there are many more cases in which innocent persons have been convicted of homicide that have yet to be thoroughly documented and acknowledged by government officials, much less publicized in a way that will allow those who care to learn lessons from them.

In our initial research on this topic, we included in our inventory of exonerated defendants only those who were totally uninvolved in the capital offense of which they were convicted, or who were convicted of a capital crime that never occurred (e.g., consensual sexual relations tried in court as capital rape, or a criminal homicide in which the victim later turned up alive—which happened, most recently, to our knowledge, in 1974, see the case of Rivera and Walpole in Radelet et al. 1992:269–270). Such narrow inclusion criteria yield an extremely conservative set of cases. Almost any other plausible conceptualization of innocence yields a much larger set.

Of course, our conceptualization of innocence would be even more conservative if we included only cases where government officials admitted error. To be sure, in some 90 percent of the cases described in our previous publications there is some official acknowledgment by officials in one or another branch of government that the trial court's judgment of guilt was erroneous. But, as we believed when we began our work and confirmed by our investigations, never in the twentieth century has a government official in this country admitted that an execution carried out under his/her authority, or that of a predecessor, took the life of an innocent victim. That does not mean that innocent defendants have not been executed.

The conceptualization of innocence can be broadened from the conservative definition we have used in our research in several different ways. We have made no attempt to do so or to investigate and identify the new types of miscarriages that would result; the task is simply overwhelming. But we can cite examples of cases that illustrate each of these additional categories of innocent persons.

One way to broaden our definition would be to include all cases where indictment of the defendant was ultimately dismissed or where the defendant was found not guilty at retrial. A dismissal of charges after reversal of a defendant's conviction, or a verdict of acquittal at retrial, is evidence of innocence, but we do not regard it as conclusive evidence. Sometimes, a prosecutor fails to retry a defendant after a reversal not because of doubt about the accused's guilt ("beyond a reasonable doubt") or because of belief in the defendant's innocence, but for reasons wholly unrelated to guilt or innocence (e.g., the prosecution's sole witnesses have disappeared). We have not included such cases among our miscarriages. However, if conviction is to be treated as conclusive evidence of (legal) guilt, then by parity of reasoning *nolle prosequi* after a reversal could reasonably be treated as some evidence of (legal) innocence. We do not do this, but other reasonable observers have. Hence, the authors of a 1993 House Subcommittee Staff Report on innocence and the death penalty collapse the distinction between being acquitted of charges and being innocent, arguing that "[u]nder the law, there is no distinction between the definitely innocent and those found innocent [i.e., acquitted] after a trial but about whom there may remain a lingering doubt" (Subcommittee on Civil and Constitutional Rights 1993:13).

Other ways to expand the concept of innocence would permit us to include cases where homicides were indeed committed, but by accident, or in self-defense,[1] or by people who are certifiably mentally ill. We will also discuss cases in which defendants were probably guilty of second degree murder, but because of various blunders and shortcomings, were erroneously convicted of capital murder.

Accidental Killings

There are many cases in which a person, after being convicted of homicide and even sentenced to death, wins a retrial and is acquitted after persuading the jury that the homicide was accidental. Legally, the defendant is innocent of murder and always was, and it was a miscarriage of justice to have convicted him of criminal homicide in the first place.

An example is the Florida case of Clifford Hallman, sentenced to death for killing a waitress in a barroom brawl in Tampa in 1973. Hallman's death sentence was eventually commuted to life imprisonment after it was shown that with proper medical care, the victim would not have died (indeed, the victim's family successfully sued Tampa General Hospital for malpractice). Hallman unquestionably cut the victim during the brawl, but almost certainly did not intend for her to die. Despite being guilty only of accidental death, he remains imprisoned (Radelet and Zsembik 1993:309).

Homicides in Self-Defense

Depending on what theory of excuse and justification one accepts, homicide in self-defense is either excusable or justifiable; in either case, it is not criminal. Yet, persons have been sentenced to death for killing another in self-defense. In 1979 Patrick "Hooty" Croy was sentenced to death in California for killing a police officer, but at retrial in 1990 he was acquitted when he was able to show his jury that the killing had been done in self-defense (Radelet et al. 1997). In South Carolina in 1979, Michael Linder was sentenced to death for killing a highway patrol officer, but he was acquitted two years later at retrial when ballistics evidence supported Linder's self-defense claims (Radelet et al. 1997).

---

1. Our most recent work extends our prior parameters slightly by including three cases in which the defendant, initially sentenced to death, was later able to show that the homicide was committed in self-defense (Radelet et al. 1997).

Homicide by the Mentally Ill

In another class of cases, the defendant did kill another person but lacked the requisite *mens rea* to be held responsible for the crime. Nevertheless, the trial court convicted the defendant and sentenced him or her to death. Why? Because of attorney incompetence, or the absence or incompetence of expert psychiatric witnesses, or the jury's refusal to believe defense experts, or for other reasons. The result in any case is the same: Innocent defendants (that is, defendants not properly held responsible for their acts) are convicted and sometimes sentenced to death.

A classic example of this type of error involves Erwin Charles Simants, sentenced to death in 1976 for killing six members of a Nebraska family (Friendly 1976). At retrial in 1979, he was found not guilty by reason of insanity (Associated Press 1979). Not so lucky was Varnall Weeks. On May 13, 1995, readers of the *New York Times* awoke to read:

> Varnall Weeks, a convicted killer described by psychiatric experts as a paranoid schizophrenic who believed he would come back to life as a giant flying tortoise that would rule the world, was put to death this morning in Alabama's electric chair (Bragg 1995).

At trial, Mr. Weeks's inexperienced court-appointed attorney never raised the issue of the defendant's insanity. As the *Times* editorialized a few days before the execution, "If Alabama is allowed to take this sorry life, it will...expose just how barbaric and bloodthirsty this nation has become in its attempt to see justice done" (Shapiro 1995). No one knows how many mentally ill convicts on America's death rows do not deserve to be punished, but the number is unquestionably significant (Lewis *et al.* 1986; Miller and Radelet 1993).

These three categories of cases are familiar and have been discussed before by others, notably Charles Black, Jr. All illustrate what he rightly called the "caprice and mistake" in the criminal justice system where the death penalty is used (Black 1981). Three other less recognized categories of innocent defendants also deserve attention.

Non-Capital Murderers

David Baldus and his colleagues have estimated that "death-eligible" cases each year number at present around 2,000–5,000, or 10–25 percent of all murders and nonnegligent manslaughters in the nation (Baldus, Woodworth, and Pulsaki 1990:22). Death penalty abolitionists and retentionists alike agree that capital punishment is not supposed to apply to all murderers; it is to be applied only to the worst among the bad. Data on death sentencing practices in Florida suggest the number of death-eligible murderers may be even smaller; in any case, the system transforms only a few of the death-eligible defendants into death row prisoners. In Florida, for example, there are about a thousand homicides per year. Yet, despite the popularity of the death penalty, only about three dozen persons (3.6 percent) are actually convicted of first-degree murder and sentenced to death (Radelet and Pierce 1991:20). If we arrange the thousand murders per year on a scale from the most aggravated (perhaps a multiple rape-murder) to the least aggravated (perhaps a mercy killing), we can define "capital murder" (based on the verdicts and sentences of the trial courts themselves) as the crimes committed by the worst 3 or 4 percent.

However, some portion of the worst 3 percent are not sentenced to death, and some portion of the other 97 percent are. Ted Bundy, for example, was offered a plea bargain in both of his Florida murder trials (Mello 1990–91:900). Had he wished to do so, he could have escaped a death sentence. His case is not unique. Defendants accused of some of the worst murders often escape the death penalty through plea bargaining. Sometimes the prosecution has little choice: Either accept a plea bargain or risk not getting a conviction because of lack of convincing evidence. As the O.J. Simpson case showed, prosecutors may quickly decide not to seek the death penalty—even for those they believe are multiple murderers—when they learn the defendant is able to employ top-notch attorneys.

Other defendants, however, are not so lucky. If measured by statutory "aggravating" circumstances, their crimes (arguably) do not place them among the worst 3 percent, yet they end up on death row anyway. Many examples could be cited here, but space allows us to present only one: the case of Ernest Dobbert, who was executed in Florida on September 7, 1984. He had been convicted of killing his nine-year-old daughter. His Jacksonville jury, obviously troubled, recommended life imprisonment by a vote of 10–2. Florida's liberal death sentencing law allows the trial judge to reject the jury's recommendation, and so the judge sentenced Dobbert to death. The key witness at trial was Dobbert's 13-year-old son, who testified that he saw his father kick his daughter.[2] In a dissent from the Supreme Court's denial of certiorari written just hours before Dobbert's execution, Justice Thurgood Marshall argued that although there was no question that Dobbert abused his children, there was substantial doubt about whether he was guilty of premeditated murder: "That may well make Dobbert guilty of second-degree murder in Florida, but it cannot make him guilty of first-degree murder there. Nor can it subject him to the death penalty in that State" (*Dobbert v. Wainwright* 1984:1246). If Justice Marshall's assessment was correct, then Dobbert was not guilty of a capital offense, and—in this qualified sense—Florida executed an innocent man.

Although these defendants are unquestionably guilty of some form of criminal homicide, they are not guilty of capital murder. They do not belong among the death-eligible defendants. We rarely think about this category when

---

2. He later recanted and said his sister had actually died from choking on food.

discussing innocence and the death penalty, but it is relevant and extremely important. The problem has been with us for at least two centuries, ever since the invention of the distinction between first-degree (or capital) murder and second-degree (or non-capital) murder. Proper administration of the death penalty requires us to draw careful lines in several different dimensions simultaneously, but there is a substantial amount of evidence that shows we are doing a poor job distinguishing between those who do and those who do not deserve to be found guilty of capital murder and sentenced to death (Baldus et al. 1990; Bedau 1997; Bright 1994). This point is underscored by recent research that shows that two-thirds of the death sentences imposed in the U.S. from 1973 to 1995 were later overturned by appellate courts due to errors so severe that the conviction or the death sentence lacked reliability (Liebman, Fagan, West, and Lloyd 2000).

Some of those who are guilty of murder but factually innocent of capital murder end up on death row because of a politically ambitious prosecutor, a lazy or angry jury, an incompetent or over-worked defense counsel, or just bad luck (Bright 1992, 1994, 1995). Others are there not out of arbitrariness, but because of systematic bias and discrimination. In Florida (Radelet and Pierce 1991) and in several other states (Baldus et al. 1990; Gross and Mauro 1989; Pierce and Radelet 2002), taking into account all the relevant facts, those who kill whites are between three and four times more likely to end up on death row than are those who kill blacks. In short, race of victim is a strong predictor of which defendants end up on death row, and it explains why some who are innocent of capital murder are nonetheless sentenced to death.

Sentencing defendants to death who are innocent of capital murder—or innocent of any homicide—is especially risky in states where the trial judge has the authority to disregard the trial jury's advisory sentence recommendation, as the law allows in Alabama, Delaware, Florida, and Indiana. After interviewing 54 jurors from a dozen Florida capital juries, including those who judged Ernest Dobbert, Geimer and Amsterdam (1987–1988:28) concluded: "The existence of some degree of doubt about the guilt of the accused was the most often recurring explanatory factor in the life recommendation cases studied." Clearly, jurors may believe that certain defendants are "guilty beyond a reasonable doubt," but their lingering doubts about the defendant's guilt of a capital crime makes them reluctant to recommend the extreme penalty.

Innocent Victims in the Death Row Inmate's Family

No discussion of innocence and the death penalty can be complete without considering how the death penalty affects the inmate's family.

Governor Ronald Reagan) presided over the next to last *Furman*[3] execution in America (Seneker 1967), ordered the Justice Department prepare an immediate response (Bedau and Radelet 1988; Markman Cassell 1988). We evidently hit a sore spot in the administration's support the death penalty. Neither before nor since has the Attorney General's office an such an interest in academic research on the death penalty.[4] The government's response was not, as one might naively have hoped, to throw its resources behind a more comprehensive study of the problem. (We carried out our initial research over four years on a budget of $9,000.) It is anyone's guess what could have been discovered if the vast resources of the Justice Department had been available for a more comprehensive study of the problem. Instead the Attorney General's office designed its response solely to discredit our work and by implication to insulate the death penalty from the charge that even our society, with all the legal protections afforded the accused/convicted/sentenced capital defendant, there is still an undeniable risk of executing the innocent. As events would prove, the government's hostile reaction to our work was far different from that of other informed observers (see, e.g., Acker et al. 2001; Kaminer 1992; Marshall 1994).

The Justice Department's response focused on ten of the 23 cases where we declared our belief that the executed defendant was innocent. Our critics did little more than restate the case for the prosecution (as though we had denied or forgotten that these defendants had been found guilty "beyond a reasonable doubt"). Our judgment to the contrary was explained as the result of our careless methodology and excessive anti-death penalty zeal. In 1994, the conservative magazine, *National Review*, recycled the views of our critics (Markman 1994). At about the same time, however, Supreme Court Justice Harry Blackmun used our research to support (in part) his decision to abandon any further tinkering with "the machinery of death," as he called it, in the futile hope to make the administration of the death penalty in our society fair and efficient (*Callins v. Collins* 1994:1159). By 2000, one of the critics, Stephen Markman, had been appointed to the Michigan Supreme Court, and the other, Paul Cassell, to a seat on the U.S. District Court.

---

3. In the 1972 case of *Furman v. Georgia*, the Supreme Court invalidated all but a few death penalty statutes in the United States. Thereafter, states drew up new capital laws and procedures, making *Furman* the demarcation of the "modern" era of the death penalty in the United States.

4. A somewhat similar distortion of academic scholarship occurred in 1975, when Solicitor General Robert Bork submitted an amicus brief in *Fowler v. North Carolina* (1976). Bork asserted that all research purporting to show the death penalty had no deterrent effect was severely flawed, and that the recent research of Isaac Ehrlich, which found each execution deterred seven murders, provided "a reliable basis for judging whether the death penalty has a deterrent effect" (Baldus and Cole 1975:170). The inadequacies and inconclusiveness of Ehrlich's research has been extensively demonstrated; see, e.g., Bailey and Peterson 1997.

Consider moment why some Americans want the death pena
than life impment. They argue that the inmate does not suffer
punished on life imprisonment. What is it about the death pe
makes the in suffer more than if he had been sentenced inste:
imprisonmer many cases, the primary pain felt by men facing e:
seeing what t light and their anticipated execution does to the
life in prison niserable life; the inmate knows that even if he w
death row via mutation of the sentence, he would be resenter
without possit of parole and would die in prison. Given the
availability of I without-parole sentences, almost all prisoners gui
degree murder die in prison. Being executed would end the pair
onment sooner her than later.

But the paint by the inmate anticipating his own execution is
shadowed by th ain that innocent family members experience in
the death of the ved one. Their pain arises out of their helplessne:
directed at the m nd their experiences immediately prior to, durir
the execution it f (King and Norgard 1999; Radelet, Vandiver, :
1983). Families o death row inmates are often indigent and almost
erless in their abily to resist public and political outcries aimed at th
ated loved one. While the inmate's suffering is terminated at the inst
the family's goes on, from the moment they learn the death senter
carried out through the years of living with the memories and secor

Sentimental though this may seem to some, we make this poin
text of discussing executing the innocent for the following reasor
main justification for retaining the death penalty is retribution (E
Gross 1994; Gross 1998). Retribution gives us the simplest and m
gument for the death penalty: Execute the convicted killers becaus
it. But the death penalty inflicts its harm not with a laser but wi
injuring the guilty and the innocent alike. In ways very unlike pri:
the death penalty creates an ever-widening circle of victims. And i
caught in the circle as it widens do not deserve it. Obviously, fam
cide victims do not deserve their pain either, but the discussion at
penalty is foremost a discussion of what pain we should inflict in t
what pain has already been inflicted in the past (and is therefore i

Have Innocent Defendants
Really Been Executed?

In 1985, when we released the first draft of our research on ε
victions in capital cases (Margolick 1985), the reaction took
Then Attorney General Edwin Meese III, who in California in 1

Consider for a moment why some Americans want the death penalty rather than life imprisonment. They argue that the inmate does not suffer enough if punished only by life imprisonment. What is it about the death penalty that makes the inmate suffer more than if he had been sentenced instead to long imprisonment? In many cases, the primary pain felt by men facing execution is seeing what their plight and their anticipated execution does to their families. Life in prison is a miserable life; the inmate knows that even if he were to leave death row via commutation of the sentence, he would be resentenced to life without possibility of parole and would die in prison. Given the widespread availability of life-without-parole sentences, almost all prisoners guilty of first-degree murder will die in prison. Being executed would end the pain of imprisonment sooner rather than later.

But the pain felt by the inmate anticipating his own execution is often overshadowed by the pain that innocent family members experience in anticipating the death of their loved one. Their pain arises out of their helplessness, the scorn directed at them, and their experiences immediately prior to, during, and after the execution itself (King and Norgard 1999; Radelet, Vandiver, and Berardo 1983). Families of death row inmates are often indigent and almost always powerless in their ability to resist public and political outcries aimed at their incarcerated loved one. While the inmate's suffering is terminated at the instant of death, the family's goes on, from the moment they learn the death sentence has been carried out through the years of living with the memories and second-guesses.

Sentimental though this may seem to some, we make this point in the context of discussing executing the innocent for the following reason. Today, the main justification for retaining the death penalty is retribution (Ellsworth and Gross 1994; Gross 1998). Retribution gives us the simplest and most direct argument for the death penalty: Execute the convicted killers because they *deserve* it. But the death penalty inflicts its harm not with a laser but with a shotgun, injuring the guilty and the innocent alike. In ways very unlike prison sentences, the death penalty creates an ever-widening circle of victims. And many of those caught in the circle as it widens do not deserve it. Obviously, families of homicide victims do not deserve their pain either, but the discussion about the death penalty is foremost a discussion of what pain *we* should inflict in the future, not what pain has already been inflicted in the past (and is therefore unretractable).

Have Innocent Defendants Really Been Executed?

In 1985, when we released the first draft of our research on erroneous convictions in capital cases (Margolick 1985), the reaction took us by surprise. Then Attorney General Edwin Meese III, who in California in 1967 (with then

Governor Ronald Reagan) presided over the next to last pre-*Furman*[3] execution in America (Seneker 1967), ordered the Justice Department to prepare an immediate response (Bedau and Radelet 1988; Markman and Cassell 1988). We evidently hit a sore spot in the administration's support of the death penalty. Neither before nor since has the Attorney General's office taken such an interest in academic research on the death penalty.[4] The government's response was not, as one might naively have hoped, to throw its resources behind a more comprehensive study of the problem. (We carried out our initial research over four years on a budget of $9,000.) It is anyone's guess what could have been discovered if the vast resources of the Justice Department had been available for a more comprehensive study of the problem. Instead, the Attorney General's office designed its response solely to discredit our work and by implication to insulate the death penalty from the charge that even in our society, with all the legal protections afforded the accused/convicted/sentenced capital defendant, there is still an undeniable risk of executing the innocent. As events would prove, the government's hostile reaction to our work was far different from that of other informed observers (see, e.g., Acker *et al.* 2001; Kaminer 1992; Marshall 1994).

The Justice Department's response focused on ten of the 23 cases where we declared our belief that the executed defendant was innocent. Our critics did little more than restate the case for the prosecution (as though we had denied or forgotten that these defendants had been found guilty "beyond a reasonable doubt"). Our judgment to the contrary was explained as the result of our careless methodology and excessive anti-death penalty zeal. In 1994, the conservative magazine, *National Review*, recycled the views of our critics (Markman 1994). At about the same time, however, Supreme Court Justice Harry Blackmun used our research to support (in part) his decision to abandon any further tinkering with "the machinery of death," as he called it, in the futile hope to make the administration of the death penalty in our society fair and efficient (*Callins v. Collins* 1994:1159). By 2000, one of the critics, Stephen Markman, had been appointed to the Michigan Supreme Court, and the other, Paul Cassell, to a seat on the U.S. District Court.

---

3. In the 1972 case of *Furman v. Georgia*, the Supreme Court invalidated all but a few death penalty statutes in the United States. Thereafter, states drew up new capital laws and procedures, making *Furman* the demarcation of the "modern" era of the death penalty in the United States.

4. A somewhat similar distortion of academic scholarship occurred in 1975, when Solicitor General Robert Bork submitted an amicus brief in *Fowler v. North Carolina* (1976). Bork asserted that all research purporting to show the death penalty had no deterrent effect was severely flawed, and that the recent research of Isaac Ehrlich, which found each execution deterred seven murders, provided "a reliable basis for judging whether the death penalty has a deterrent effect" (Baldus and Cole 1975:170). The inadequacies and inconclusiveness of Ehrlich's research has been extensively demonstrated; see, e.g., Bailey and Peterson 1997.

We should mention in passing that apart from any substantial effect on the integrity and reliability of our research, the Justice Department's critique of that work has been very effective. The critique is frequently cited by those who support executions; they give no evidence of having read the critique, much less having read either our law review article or our book. Perhaps this is another example of the complacency that surrounds the public's attitude toward the death penalty and to issues of fact on which that attitude ought to depend.

Again and again, our critics point out that no capital jurisdiction in this country has ever admitted to executing an innocent person in this century—a point we were the first to make, thanks to our extensive research into the question.[5] Obviously, the government's failure or refusal to acknowledge that an innocent defendant has been executed is hardly evidence that none such have been executed.

Getting the state to concede that it has convicted (let alone executed) an innocent defendant is no easy matter. Once an innocent person is convicted, it is almost impossible to get that conviction reversed on grounds of the accused's innocence. And even if the prisoner does get released, usually the prosecutor or some other state official will continue to insist publicly that the prisoner really was guilty. The Jacobs-Tafero case powerfully and painfully illustrates this point.

In May 1990, Jesse Tafero was executed in Florida. His case gained notoriety because the electric chair malfunctioned and he burst into flames before he died. Two years later, Jesse's wife and co-defendant, Sonia Jacobs, who had been convicted and sentenced to death on exactly the same evidence that sent Tafero to his death, was released after a U.S. Circuit Court concluded that her conviction was based on prosecutorial suppression of exculpatory evidence and perjury by a prosecution witness (who was the real killer) (*Jacobs v. Singletary* 1992). Jacobs now lives in Ireland, and in early 1996 a television movie about her case was aired. But Tafero is dead. His is an extremely strong case of innocence. Had he been alive the evidence that led to Jacobs's release would have led to his release, too.

Did Jacobs's vindication and release cause any Florida official to apologize on behalf of the State, or even to express second thoughts about the execution? No. To be sure, a few newspaper articles pointed out the blunder (e.g., Barnett 1992), but no politician, prosecutor, judge, or ex-juror has so far made any public comment on Tafero's fate in light of Jacobs's vindication. Tafero's aged mother, living impoverished in Pennsylvania, does not have the resources to clear her son's name. His attorneys have long moved on to other cases.

So, given that we cannot point to admission of erroneous executions by government officials involved in the case, on what grounds can we confidently infer that innocent defendants have been executed? Apart from rare cases like

---

5. "[W]e have found no instance in which the government has officially acknowledged that an execution carried our under lawful authority was in error" (Bedau and Radelet 1987:25).

Tafero-Jacobs (where one codefendant is executed before the other codefendant is exonerated), there are at least three kinds of evidence that we believe ought to convince any reasonable person that innocent defendants are executed: Close Calls, Calculation of the Odds, and the Role of Lady Luck.

Close Calls

Between 1972 and the end of 1996, 68 death row inmates in the nation were released because of doubts about their guilt (Radelet et al. 1997). In early 2002, the number exceeded 100.[6] These releases do not prove that the system works, as some defenders of the death penalty would argue. If the system "worked," the defendants would be dead. In virtually all of these cases, the defendants were released only after an expensive and exhausting uphill struggle, and almost always fiercely resisted by the prosecution. Some of these prisoners, now free, came within a few days of being executed. Randall Adams, sentenced to death in Texas in 1977 and exonerated in 1989, came within one week of being executed (Radelet et al. 1992:67). Andrew Mitchell was sentenced to death in Texas in 1981, and once came to within five days of lethal injection before being vindicated in 1993 (Radelet et al. 1997). Two half-brothers in Florida, William Jent and Ernest Miller, came within 16 hours of execution before they were released from prison in 1988 (Radelet et al. 1992:318).

In mid-2003 there were some three thousand seven hundred prisoners on America's death rows. As things stand, it would be preposterous to believe that all the innocent defendants currently on death row have been identified and exonerated. If the history of the last twenty years is any guide to the future, an average of three death row inmates per year will continue to be vindicated and released. How many equally innocent death row inmates will be unsuccessful in obtaining relief is impossible to know, but the number most certainly is not zero.

Calculation of the Odds

Assume we execute two death row inmates, each of whom we believe is guilty "beyond a reasonable doubt" on the evidence. Let belief in guilt "beyond a reasonable doubt" mean that we are in effect 90 percent confident of the defendant's guilt, and that our belief in both these cases is correct. Nevertheless, we are not (and rarely could be) 100 percent certain, and so on these assumptions we are implicitly accepting a ten percent error rate even when we are 90 percent confident of guilt. But because the odds of error are multiplicative, the

---

6. Our list of innocent prisoners freed from death row is now updated and maintained by the Death Penalty Information Center; see <http://www.deathpenaltyinfo.org/innocencelist.html>

probability that *both* these defendants are guilty is not 90 percent (0.9), but only 0.81 percent (0.9 x 0.9). Thus, the probability that *all* 3,700 death row inmates today are guilty, even if we are 90 percent confident of guilt in each case, is minuscule.

To put this another way, if we executed 100 inmates and we were 95% confident of guilt in each case, we would be implicitly accepting a 5% error rate. We are willing to execute five innocent inmates out of the hundred (even though, of course, we would not know which five are innocent). If our perceptions on the odds of error are accurate reflections of the real occurrences of error, the number of innocent persons legally executed is quite high—and much higher than our research into identifiable cases suggests.

The Role of Lady Luck

In the heat of their attack on our claim that some two dozen of the several hundred cases we studied involve execution of the innocent, the Justice Department simply ignored the vast majority of cases where we claim an innocent person was convicted of a capital offense but was not executed (Markman and Cassell 1988). In effect they tacitly concede that our judgment is correct in 95 percent of all the cases and dead wrong in only 5 percent—as though only these 5 percent mattered. Markman and Cassell overlook scores of cases in which they do not—and could not—dispute our claim that an innocent person was convicted, and that the convict might have been executed except for extraordinary good fortune. Perhaps the defendant's release was owing to the timely discovery of a hitherto unknown eyewitness (e.g., the case of Jerry Banks in Radelet et al. 1992:171–188). But what if that witness had not stepped forward? Perhaps the true culprit confesses in time to save the innocent person (e.g., the case of James Foster in Radelet et al. 1992:23–39). But suppose he or she had kept silent about being involved? Perhaps a dedicated journalist takes up the cause and vindicates the convicted but innocent defendant (e.g., the case of Freddie Pitts and Wilbert Lee in Bedau and Radelet 1987:139–140). But what if there had been no journalist with an interest in the case? In 1993, Kirk Bloodsworth was freed from death row in Maryland when technology not widely available at the time of his trial (DNA) proved his innocence. Had this technology not been developed for another decade, had semen from the crime scene not have been preserved, and had the victim not been raped as well as murdered, Bloodsworth could easily have been executed. In one way or another, virtually every case in which death row inmates are able to prove their innocence is a story of exceptional luck.

Only when we realize how lucky the exonerated death row defendants have been do we realize how easy it is for fatal mistakes to go undetected. The more such cases are discovered the greater the likelihood that there are other cases so far undetected—and that some of them involve the execution of the innocent.

Given that boats filled with cocaine are regularly apprehended near our shores, it would be preposterous to argue that *all* boats carrying illegal drugs have been stopped.

Actual and Possible Remedies

The fact that innocent persons (in one or another sense of "innocence") are executed seems to have had (so far) little if any real impact on American opinion about the death penalty. Four deaf audiences can be identified: the appellate courts, clemency boards, legislatures, and the general public.

The Courts

The Supreme Court has in effect said that appellate courts need not listen to post-conviction evidence of a defendant's innocence, unless there are truly exceptional circumstances—as when the inmate has a videotape showing that he could not have been at the scene of the murder. A ruling of this very sort came in 1995 in the case of Lloyd Schlup, who, while incarcerated at the Missouri State Penitentiary, was accused of, and eventually sentenced to death for, the murder of a fellow inmate. Scheduled to be executed in 1993, he came to within nine hours of his death before Governor Mel Carnahan granted a stay and appointed a panel to reinvestigate the case. In addition to the videotape, Schlup had affidavits from twenty other prisoners and a former guard saying he was not the killer (Terry 1993). Schlup's demand for a full hearing on innocence prevailed in the Supreme Court by a narrow 5 to 4 vote (*Schlup v. Delo* 1995). The Court, continuing its strong effort to narrow access to review via federal habeas corpus by raising the threshold for relief, ruled that before an inmate could present evidence of his or her innocence in federal courts in search of a hearing to reopen the case it must be shown that "a constitutional violation has probably resulted in the conviction of one who is actually innocent" (at 867). By "probably" the Court meant "more likely than not" (at 867). Prior to this case, the defendant seeking habeas corpus relief in federal courts had to show by "clear and convincing evidence" that "no reasonable juror would have found him guilty except for a constitutional error at his trial" (*Sawyer v. Whitley* 1992:348) Although this was a victory for Schlup (a victory, thanks to Congress, that other inmates will not secure, as we will discuss below), it does demonstrate how reluctant the appellate courts are to hearing evidence of innocence. Had there been no videotapes, Schlup would be dead.

Clemency Officials

Government officials with the power to commute death sentences to terms of imprisonment generally have not been receptive to arguments of the condemned defendant's innocence. In the 20 year period, 1973–1992, there were only 29 death sentences that were commuted to prison terms by executive clemency (Radelet and Zsembik 1993). During the next decade, 19 more death sentences were commuted by executive powers.[7] Doubt about the defendant's guilt was a factor in 16 of those cases. Only one of those cases came from Texas or California—the two states with the largest death row populations. In Florida, the only other state with more than three hundred prisoners on death row, there has not been a commutation of a death sentence in twenty years. It is almost as if the defendant's possible innocence has become an argument *against* clemency: If he or she is innocent, let's carry out the execution right away lest the state officials who worked to get the conviction, sentence, and execution be embarrassed.

On the other hand, some governors in recent years have had the courage to step forward and commute numerous death sentences to terms of life imprisonment. In 1986, Governor Toney Anaya in New Mexico commuted the death sentences of all five men on death row in that state (Anaya, 1993), and in 1991 Governor Richard Celeste commuted eight death sentences in Ohio. More central to the issue of erroneous convictions, in February 2000, Republican Governor George H. Ryan of Illinois, faced with evidence that 13 death row inmates in that state turned out to be innocent, imposed an immediate moratorium on all executions. He then appointed a commission to study the causes of these errors and other aspects of the death penalty in Illinois. Among other problems, a study conducted for that commission discovered widespread race-of-victim and regional biases in Illinois death sentencing (Pierce and Radelet, 2002). In April 2002, the commission recommended 85 reforms in the way that capital cases are handled. In January 2003, Governor Ryan commuted the death sentences of all of the 167 death row inmates in Illinois to life imprisonment.

Legislatures

State legislators have not been persuaded to create tighter standards for death sentencing, much less to repeal the death penalty, out of worry about the innocent being executed. In 1994, Kansas re-enacted the death penalty; New York's legislature did so in 1995. In the latter case, extensive protections demanded by concerned legislators were built into the new death penalty law, with what effect remains to be seen. But New York's history of wrongful convictions in capital cases (Rosenbaum 1990–1991)—virtually placed in the

---

7. For an updated list of commutations, see <http://www.deathpenaltyinfo.org/clemency.html#list>

hands of every member of the state legislature prior to their vote—did not in the end persuade them against re-enacting the death penalty. There is little reason to believe that if Governor George Pataki (who was elected in part for his vigorous pro-death penalty stance) is confronted with a plea for clemency from a death row prisoner, he will follow the lead of such predecessors as Alfred E. Smith and Herbert H. Lehman. While Smith (1923–1928) and Lehman (1933–1942) served as governors, death sentences were routinely commuted every time one or more appellate court judge dissented from the ruling affirming the conviction (Abramowitz and Paget 1964:170).

In recent years Congress, like the courts, has made it easier to execute the innocent. In 1995, federal funding for attorneys for indigent death row inmates was severely cut, resulting in the closing of "Resource Centers" that provided legal services for condemned inmates in twenty states (Wiehl 1995). Congress has also restricted the ability of federal courts to hear claims of innocence. Several new barriers to obtaining habeas corpus relief are contained in the Anti-Terrorism and Death Penalty Act of 1996. For example, the Act includes a provision that requires "clear and convincing" evidence of innocence rather than simply evidence of "probable" innocence (Coyle 1996; Tabak 1996a, 1996b). This nullifies the broader standard articulated by the Supreme Court in the Schlup case discussed previously. After this legislation, even with his videotapes, Schlup would be dead.

But there is some hope. By mid-2002, fully half of the House of Representatives and twenty-five members of the Senate were co-sponsoring the "Innocence Protection Act." Among other things, this legislation would guarantee access by convicted defendants to biological crime-scene material which, through DNA analysis, might be used to prove their innocence (Leahy 2001; Yackle 2001).

General Public

Public support for the death penalty in the United States has dropped in the past few years. In 1994, Gallup polls found that approximately 80 percent of Americans supported the death penalty. This support fell to 72 percent in 2002. More importantly, the 2002 poll showed that only 52 percent of Americans support the death penalty given the alternative of "life without parole" sentences, which are available in virtually all death penalty jurisdictions.

One reason for the drop in death penalty support, particularly given the alternative of life sentences, is concern over the fairness of the death penalty. In the 2002 poll, 40 percent of the respondents expressed a belief that the death penalty was applied unfairly. Indeed, a 2000 poll by the Peter Hart research firm found that 64 percent of Americans favor a moratorium on executions until questions of its fairness can be resolved. The poll showed 89 percent supported increased access to DNA evidence in capital cases. A poll taken in 2000 by NBC News/Wall Street Journal found that 80 percent of all Americans believed that innocent prisoners had been executed in the previous five years.

In the end, arguing that the death penalty should be abolished because it will occasionally take the lives of innocent defendants may not be the most effective kind of argument to make, just as it is wrong to argue against torture on the ground that some false confessions will result. Opposing the death penalty for the innocent does not make one a death penalty abolitionist; the true test is whether one opposes it for the guilty. The importance of the innocence argument is that it undermines the justification of capital punishment on the grounds of retributive justice.

As things stand now, we have little or no knowledge about the effect on the public's support for the death penalty of information about wrongful convictions of innocent capital defendants. Here as elsewhere, the "Marshall Hypothesis" (suggesting that the public is ignorant of the basic facts about the death penalty, and claiming that an informed public tends to oppose the death penalty) remains untested in recent years (but see Bohm, Clark, and Aveni 1991; Sarat and Vidmar 1976). In the fifteen years since our research was first published, we have some vivid anecdotal evidence from various conversations and courtroom testimony showing that those who learn about wrongful convictions find themselves rethinking their support for the death penalty (Radelet 1987). More systematic research confirms that knowledge about miscarriages of justice leads to reduced support for the death penalty (Clarke, Lambert, and Whitt 2000/01). However, more research is still needed before we can definitively gauge the effect of such knowledge on the general public.

It appears that for the foreseeable future, most Americans will either ignore the risks of executing the innocent or will accept its inevitability. Consider, for example, a recent letter to the *Houston Post* by Rex L. Carter (1994). In November 1994, we wrote to the paper, pointing out the inevitability of executing the innocent and mentioned the case of Gary Graham. Graham had admitted to a string of armed robberies but denied he was guilty of the murder that sent him to Texas's death row. Indeed, much of the evidence of his guilt of that crime was suspect (Blaustein 1993). Here is Mr. Carter's response:

> As a defender of the death penalty, I have no problem in admitting "innocent people can be executed" and couldn't care less what happens to Gary Graham. He should have been executed for what he confessed to.
>
> There is a war going on in our own country—against crime and thugs like Graham. It is sad that innocent people get killed in war, but that is the way it is. Ask any wartime veteran.
>
> Try 'em, give 'em 90 days for appeal and then hang 'em slowly at noon on the courthouse lawn. Just maybe killers-to-be will get the message, just as Japan did when we dropped the A-bomb.

Mr. Carter's logic could use some polish, but we have no doubt that he articulates the way many citizens and politicians feel. Despite the doubts about Gary Graham's guilt, he was executed on June 22, 2000.

Dale Volker, the state senator from New York whose ten year quest to reinstate the death penalty in the Empire State finally succeeded in 1995, had this to say about executing the innocent: "I would never think it's impossible. You would hope that it would never happen, but the mere fact that you might fail does not argue that you shouldn't do it" (Verhovek 1995). This reminds us of the movie "Dr. Strangelove," when the Chairman of the Joint Chiefs of Staff (played by George C. Scott) tells the President (played by Peter Sellers) that a 40 megaton nuclear bomb is about to be dropped on a target in Russia:

> The President: General Turgidson, when you instituted the human reliability tests you assured me there was no possibility of such a thing ever occurring.
>
> General Turgidson: Well, ahh, I don't think it's quite fair to condemn the whole program because of a single slip-up.

Consider the comments of Paul D. Kamenar, executive director of the conservative Washington Legal Foundation, who early in 1995 was quoted in the *New York Times*, saying: "I would gladly give them a couple of questionable cases that they are harping about in return for their agreeing to recognize that in the vast majority of cases, there is no question of the guilt of those being executed" (Verhovek 1995). This is an interesting trade, as few would deny that most of those on death row are guilty. Would most retentionists agree that the vast majority of murderers on death row are *not* genocidal maniacs, psychopathic serial or multiple murderers, recidivist killers and so do not belong there? We doubt it.

Finally, consider the comments of Florida State University criminologist Larry Wollan. Although a supporter of the death penalty, Wollan realizes that the risk of executing the innocent is undeniable, and he phrases the argument in a responsible way: "Innocent people have been executed," he concedes. "The value of the death penalty is its rightness vis-a-vis the wrongness of the crime, and that is so valuable that the possibility of the conviction of the innocent, though rare, has to be accepted" (Verhovek 1995). Elsewhere, Ernest van den Haag makes the same point when he says that our documentation of 23 erroneous executions this century "does not tell us anything unexpected" (van den Haag 1990:512), and this liability does not outweigh the deterrent and moral benefits of the death penalty. Because, in our judgment, those benefits of the death penalty are entirely illusory—we gain nothing in public safety or moral rectitude by the practice of the death penalty—the constant and unavoidable risk of executing the innocent cannot be so complacently tolerated.

We close on an ironic note. One of the amazing things that has happened in the fifteen years since our research was first released to the public is that those who defend the death penalty now concede the inevitability of executing the innocent—even if they challenge individual cases that we and others have identified as probably involving the execution of an innocent person. In large part this change has resulted from incontrovertible evidence provided by DNA testing (Scheck et al. 2000). It is a *major* concession. We know of no defender of the death penalty who, prior to 1987, was willing to make such a concession in public. This issue has the effect of forcing responsible defenders of capital punishment to rethink their retributive argument (surely, they must agree that on their assumptions executing the innocent—those who do *not* deserve to die—is a terrible wrong) as well as their cost/benefit argument (exactly what are the benefits from the death penalty that outweigh the admitted cost of executing the innocent?). Elsewhere, we have shown why we believe these arguments must fail (Radelet et al. 1992:271–281). Meanwhile, how will future generations of historians look back and evaluate America's current love for the executioner?

References

Abramowitz, E., and D. Paget (1964) "Executive Clemency in Capital Cases." *New York University Law Review* 39:131–192.

Acker, J.R., T. Brewer, E. Cunningham, A. Fitzgerald, J. Flexon, J. Lombard, B. Ryn, and B. Stodghill (2001) "No Appeal from the Grave: Innocence, Capital Punishment, and the Lessons of History." Pp. 154–173 in S.D. Westervelt and J.A. Humphrey (eds.), *Wrongly Convicted: Perspectives on Failed Justice.* New Brunswick, N.J.: Rutgers University Press.

American Bar Association (1997) "A Report from the IR&R Death Penalty Committee." *Human Rights* (Winter):22–25.

Anaya, T. (1993) "Statement by Toney Anaya on Capital Punishment." *University of Richmond Law Review* 27:177–183.

Associated Press (1979) "Man Guilty of Oklahoma Murders; Defendant in Nebraska Acquitted." *New York Times,* Oct. 18, p. 16.

Bailey, W.C., and R.D. Peterson (1997) "Murder, Capital Punishment, and Deterrence: A Review of the Literature." Pp. 135–161 in H.A. Bedau (ed.), *The Death Penalty in America: Current Controversies.* New York: Oxford University Press.

Baldus, D.C., and J.W.C. Cole (1975) "A Comparison of the Work of Thorsten Sellin and Isaac Ehrlich on the Deterrent Effect of Capital Punishment." *Yale Law Journal* 85:170–186.

Baldus, D.C., G.G. Woodworth, and C.A. Pulaski, Jr. (1990) *Equal Justice and the Death Penalty: A Legal and Empirical Analysis.* Boston: Northeastern University Press.

Barnett, C. (1992) "New Evidence Might Have Spared Killer." *Gainesville Sun,* Nov. 21, p. 1.

Bedau, H.A. (1997) *The Death Penalty in America: Current Controversies.* New York: Oxford University Press.

Bedau, H.A. and M.L. Radelet (1987) "Miscarriages of Justice in Potentially Capital Cases." *Stanford Law Review* 40:21–179.

Bedau, H.A. and M.L. Radelet (1988) "The Myth of Infallibility: A Reply to Markman and Cassell." *Stanford Law Review* 41:161–170.

Black, C.L., Jr. (1981) *Capital Punishment: The Inevitability of Caprice and Mistake, Second Edition.* New York: W.W. Norton & Co.

Blaustein, S. (1993) "The Executioner's Wrong: Texas Will Execute Gary Graham for a Murder He Almost Certainly Didn't Commit." *The Washington Post*, Aug. 1, p. C1.

Bohm, R.M., L.J. Clark, and A.F. Aveni (1991) "Knowledge and Death Penalty Opinion: A Test of the Marshall Hypothesis." *Journal of Research in Crime and Delinquency* 28:360–387.

Bragg, R. (1995) "A Killer Racked by Delusions Dies in Alabama's Electric Chair." *New York Times*, May 13, p. 7.

Bright, S.B. (1992) "In Defense of Life: Enforcing the Bill of Rights on Behalf of Poor, Minority and Disadvantaged Persons Facing the Death Penalty." *Missouri Law Review* 57:849–870.

Bright, S.B. (1994) "Counsel for the Poor: The Death Sentence Not for the Worst Crime but for the Worst Lawyer." *Yale Law Journal* 103:1835–1883.

Bright, S.B. (1995) "The Politics of Crime and the Death Penalty: Not 'Soft on Crime,' But Hard on the Bill of Rights." *Saint Louis University Law Journal* 39:479–503.

Callins v. Collins (1994) 510 U.S. 1141.

Carter, R.L. (1994) "Letter to the Editor." *Houston Post*, Nov. 13.

Clarke, A.W., E. Lambert, and L.A. Whitt (2000/01) "Executing the Innocent: The Next Step in the Marshall Hypothesis." *New York University Review of Law and Social Change* 26:309–344.

Coyle, M. (1996) "Law: Innocent Dead Men Walking?" *National Law Journal*, May 20, p. 1.

Dobbert v. Wainwright (1984) 468 U.S. 1231.

Ellsworth, P.C., and S.R. Gross (1994) "Hardening of the Attitudes: Americans' Views on the Death Penalty." *Journal of Social Issues* 50 (Summer):19–52.

Fowler v. North Carolina (1976) 428 U.S. 904.

Friendly, F.W. (1976) "A Crime and Its Aftershock." *New York Times Magazine*, March 21, 11–18, 85–95.

Furman v. Georgia (1972) 408 U.S. 238.

Gallup, A., and F. Newport (1991) "Death Penalty Support Remains Strong." *The Gallup Poll Monthly* 309 (June):40–45.

Geimer, W.S., and J. Amsterdam (1987–1988) "Why Jurors Vote Life or Death: Operative Factors in Ten Florida Death Penalty Cases." *American Journal of Criminal Law* 15:1–54.

Gross, S.R. (1998) "Update: American Public Opinion on the Death Penalty—It's Getting Personal." *Cornell Law Review* 83:1448–1475.

Gross, S.R., and R. Mauro (1989) *Death & Discrimination: Racial Disparities in Capital Sentencing.* Boston: Northeastern University Press.

Huff, C.R., A. Rattner, and E. Sagarin (1996) *Convicted But Innocent: Wrongful Conviction and Public Policy.* Thousand Oaks, CA: Sage Publications.

Jacobs v. Singletary (1992) 952 F.2d 1282 (11th Cir.).

Kaminer, W. (1992) "The Wrong Men," *The Atlantic* 147 (Dec.):147–149.

King, R., and K. Norgard (1999) "What About Our Families? Using the Impact on Death Row Defendants' Family Members as a Mitigating Factor in Death Penalty Sentencing Hearings." *Florida State University Law Review* 26:1119–1175.

Leahy, Senator P. (2001) "The Innocence Protection Act of 2001." *Hofstra Law Review* 29:1113–1154.

Lewis, D.O., J.H. Pincus, M. Feldman, L. Jackson, and B. Bard (1986) "Psychiatric, Neurological, and Psychoeducational Characteristics of 15 Death Row Inmates in the United States." *American Journal of Psychiatry* 143:838–845.

Liebman, J., J. Fagan, V. West, and J. Lloyd (2000) "Capital Attrition: Error Rates in Capital Cases, 1973–1995." *Texas Law Review* 78:1839–1865.

Margolick, D. (1985) "25 Wrongfully Executed in U.S., Study Finds." *New York Times*, Nov. 14, p. 13.

Markman, S.J., and P.G. Cassell (1988) "Protecting the Innocent: A Response to the Bedau-Radelet Study." *Stanford Law Review* 41:121–160.

Markman, S.J. (1994) "Innocents on Death Row?" *National Review*, Sept. 12, 72–77, 92.

Marshall, L.C. (1994) "Book Review." *Journal of Criminal Law and Criminology* 85:261–280.

Mello, M. (1990–91) "On Metaphors, Mirrors, and Murders: Theodore Bundy and the Rule of Law." *New York University Review of Law and Social Change* 18:887–938.

Miller, K.S., and M.L. Radelet (1993) *Executing the Mentally Ill.* Newbury Park, CA: Sage.

Pierce, G.L., and M.L. Radelet (2002). "Race, Region, and Death Sentencing in Illinois, 1988–1997." *Oregon Law Review* 81:39–96.

Radelet, M.L. (1987) "Sociologists as Expert Witnesses in Capital Cases: A Case Study." Pp. 119–134 in P.R. Anderson and L.T. Winfree, Jr., (eds.) *Expert Witnesses: Criminologists in the Courtroom.* Albany: State University of New York Press.

Radelet, M.L., and H.A. Bedau (1998) "The Execution of the Innocent." *Law and Contemporary Problems* 61:105–124.

Radelet, M.L., and H.A. Bedau (2001) "Erroneous Convictions and the Death Penalty." Pp. 269–280 in S.D. Westervelt and J.A. Humphrey (eds.), *Wrongly Convicted: Perspectives on Failed Justice.* New Brunswick, N.J.: Rutgers University Press.

Radelet, M.L., H.A. Bedau, and C.E. Putnam (1992) *In Spite of Innocence.* Boston: Northeastern University Press.

Radelet, M.L., W.S. Lofquist, and H.A. Bedau (1997) "Prisoners Released from Death Rows Since 1970 Because of Doubts About Their Guilt." *Thomas M. Cooley Law Review* 13:907–966.

Radelet, M.L., and G.L. Pierce (1991) "Choosing Those Who Will Die: Race and the Death Penalty in Florida." *Florida Law Review* 43:1–34.

Radelet, M.L., M. Vandiver, and F. Berardo (1983) "Families, Prisons, and Men with Death Sentences: The Human Impact of Structured Uncertainty." *Journal of Family Issues* 4:593–612.

Radelet, M.L., and B.A. Zsembik (1993) "Executive Clemency in Post-*Furman* Capital Cases." *University of Richmond Law Review* 27:289–314.

Rosenbaum, M.I. (1990–1991) "Inevitable Error: Wrongful New York State Homicide Convictions, 1965–1988." *New York University Review of Law & Social Change* 18:807–830.

Sarat, A., and N. Vidmar (1976) "Public Opinion, the Death Penalty, and the Eighth Amendment: Testing the Marshall Hypothesis." *Wisconsin Law Review* 1976:171–206.

Sawyer v. Whitley (1992) 505 U.S. 333.

Scheck, B., P. Neufeld, and J. Dwyer (2000) *Actual Innocence.* New York: Doubleday.

Schlup v. Delo (1995) 513 U.S. 298.

Seneker, C.J. (1967) "Governor Reagan and Executive Clemency." *California Law Review* 55:412–418.

Shapiro, A.L. (1995) "An Insane Execution." *New York Times*, May 11, p. 29.

Subcommittee on Civil and Constitutional Rights, Committee on the Judiciary (1993) *Innocence and the Death Penalty: Assessing the Danger of Mistaken Executions.* Staff Report, 103 Cong., 1st Sess. (Oct. 21).

Tabak, R.J. (1996a) "Panel Discussion: Is There Any Habeas Left in This Corpus?" *Loyola University—Chicago Law Review* 27:523–614.

Tabak, R.J. (1996b) "Habeas Corpus as a Crucial Protector of Constitutional Rights: A Tribute Which May Also Be a Eulogy." *Seton Hall Law Review* 26:1477–1492.

Terry, D. (1993) "Despite New Evidence, A Prisoner Faces Death." *New York Times*, Nov. 15, p. A8.

van den Haag, E. (1990) "Why Capital Punishment?" *Albany Law Review* 54:501–514.

Verhovek, S.H. (1995) "When Justice Shows Its Darker Side." *New York Times*, Jan. 8, p. 6E.

Westervelt, S.D. and J.A. Humphrey (2001) *Wrongly Convicted: Perspectives on Failed Justice.* New Brunswick, N.J.: Rutgers University Press.

Wiehl, L. (1995) "A Program for Death-Row Appeals is Facing Elimination." *New York Times*, Aug. 11, p. B16.

Yackle, L. (2001) "Congressional Power to Require DNA Testing." *Hofstra Law Review* 29:1173–1209.

Part IV

The Administration of the Death Penalty

Chapter 12

Closing the Circle:
The Illusion of Lawyers
for People Litigating for Their
Lives at the *Fin de Siècle*

Michael Mello
Paul J. Perkins

Representing Death Row:
The Real Capital Punishment

> My seven years studying the death penalty taught me, however,
> that the guts of our American death penalty are not to be found in
> prison. Death row—with its prisoners and wardens and pastors—
> is a dull, slow hell of waiting and despair. The real death penalty
> enterprise is a bustling, frantic mill of investigation, litigation, brief
> drafting, strategy, oral and written argument, a Rube Goldberg
> contraption kept clanking perpetually by the fuel of caffeinated
> lawyers and their cousins, the poll-driven politicians. It is a mad-
> house (Von Drehle 1997:iii).

This chapter will attempt to summarize the seven-decades-long story of the
right to and availability of effective, court-appointed counsel in death penalty
cases. This narrative is a more-or-less linear history of the provision of legal aid
at state capital trials and after trial, in post-conviction *habeas corpus* proceedings.

We make a distinction between trial and *habeas corpus* because that distinction is of constitutional magnitude; according to a strong majority of the
United States Supreme Court, the Sixth Amendment guarantees a right to
counsel at felony trials (capital and noncapital), and due process requires that
indigents be appointed counsel on the first automatic appeal—but not beyond, and not in *habeas corpus* proceedings. We limit our inquiry to cases tried
in state court because the overwhelming majority of death row inmates in

347

America today were convicted and condemned to die at state trials rather than federal trials.

Our narrative of the history of the right to counsel in capital cases is inseparable from the somewhat parallel judicial development of *habeas corpus* as a procedural vehicle through which state prisoners may raise in federal court, and litigate in state court, legal errors of constitutional magnitude—including violation of the Sixth Amendment right to counsel. *Habeas* is the remedial vehicle for violations of the right to counsel at trial. It is also inseparable from the history of the litigation campaign to use the courts to outlaw or limit capital punishment in America.

The Right to Court-Appointed Counsel at Trial and in *Habeas,* and the Availability of *Habeas*: of Ratchets and Accordions

What can I unbury?...
I have erected
A barrier, that my soul might be protected
Against the invading ghosts of what I saw
In years when Murder wore the mask of Law
(Sassoon, *Songbook on the War* 1926:147).

The developmental trajectories of the right to court-appointed counsel and the availability of *habeas* have differed in one important respect. The right to court-appointed counsel, once recognized to apply to a class of cases, has never been retracted; the history of the right to court-appointed counsel has been one of expansion only, from *Scottsboro* in 1932 until today. By contrast, the ready availability of *habeas* has expanded (in the 1960s and early '70s) and then contracted (mid-1970s to present). If the right to counsel has been a ratchet, then access to *habeas* has been an accordion.

As of mid-century, the right to court-appointed counsel and availability of *habeas* evolved more or less in tandem. Both were equally unavailable.

The Right to Counsel at Trial:
The Road from Scottsboro to Gideon

Scottsboro's just a little
place:
No shame is writ across
its face—
It's court, too weak to

stand against a mob,
It's people's heart, too small
to hold a sob.

(Hughes, *The Town of Scottsboro* 1932:168).

It was not until the *Scottsboro* case in 1932 that the Supreme Court recognized a constitutional right to court-appointed counsel in capital trials in state court. This state of affairs possessed the virtue of consistency: Since, pre-*Scottsboro* there was no right to court-appointed counsel, there was no need for a procedural mechanism, like *habeas*, to enforce that nonexistent right to counsel. No right, so no remedy.

When the court decided *Scottsboro*, it looked to the history of the right to counsel and court-appointed counsel from the English common law to 1932 (*Powell v. Alabama* 1932:60). In 1836, England granted felony defendants the right to counsel in all matters (*Powell* 1932:60). Before that, however, England granted the right only to those accused of misdemeanors. This anomaly was defended by Lord Coke in writings prescient of the *Scottsboro* judge's rationalization used to deny the nine young men a lawyer—that in felonies, the court itself was counsel for the defendant (*Powell* 1932:61). While the English rule was still in practice, most colonies in America recognized the defendant's right to counsel in all criminal matters (*Powell* 1932:60–61). And even those that did not expressly recognize the right in their charters or constitutions, or both, either implicitly recognized the right as consistent with the English Declaration of Rights or expressly recognized it by statute (*Powell* 1932:61–65). Yet in the colonies, except New Jersey and Connecticut, the right to counsel meant only that criminal defendants had the right to hire or retain lawyers (Note 1989:1604). When the First Congress convened, James Madison proposed that one amendment that should be added to the Constitution was the guarantee that "in all criminal prosecutions, the accused shall enjoy the right to...have the assistance of counsel for his defense" (Note 1989:1604). Yet, there was little debate about this proposed amendment in the House and in the Senate (Bahl 1991:423, 454), which raises the inference that the right to counsel expressed in the Sixth Amendment grants the very same right to hire or to retain an attorney in criminal prosecutions that was recognized by the majority of colonies in their own charters and constitutions (Bahl 1991:455). Thus, when the Bill of Rights was ratified, United States citizens who could not retain or hire a lawyer had no real right to counsel unless they lived in New Jersey or Connecticut where counsel was granted even to those who could not afford it (Bahl 1991:455).

The United States Supreme Court did not limit the actions of the States in criminal procedural matters for the next 80 years after the Constitution was ratified (Bahl 1991:425). Even after the Fourteenth Amendment was added to the Constitution in 1868, the Court showed in a number of decisions that it would not intervene in state criminal procedure matters for the next sixty years.

One such decision seemed to prevent the Court ever from reasoning that the Sixth Amendment's guarantee of the right to counsel applied to the states. In *Hurtado v. California* (1884), the Court held that the right to indictment before a grand jury, although expressly contained in the Fifth Amendment, did not apply to the states. The Court reasoned that although the Fifth and Fourteenth Amendments contain a due process clause, only the Fifth Amendment expressly grants the right to indictment before a grand jury; therefore, since due process itself does not require the grand jury procedure, the Fourteenth Amendment could not be read to require that states recognize the right of their citizens to receive a grand jury indictment (*Hurtado v. California* 1884:534–535).

Such reasoning clearly would prove an obstacle to the argument that indigent criminal defendants had a cognizable right under state and federal law to the assistance of counsel: The Fourteenth Amendment only provided for due process; hence, the argument would go, since due process itself does not require that counsel be provided to criminal defendants, and since the Fourteenth Amendment contains no express provision for the right to counsel, defendants indicted under color of State law would not even merit the right to hire or retain counsel, let alone have it provided for them.

Then came *Scottsboro* (*Powell v. Alabama* 1932:45; Lewis 1964:104–110; Carter 1969; Goodman 1994). Nine young black men (Charlie Weems, Ozie Powell, Clarence Norris, Olen Montgomery, Willie Roberson, Haywood Patterson, Andy and Roy Wright, and Eugene Williams, ages 13 to 21), were arrested on March 3, 1931, for allegedly raping two white women (Ruby Bates and Victoria Price). Accuseds and accusers had all been riding the rails.

Professor Francis Allen describes the case as starting in a freight train "slowly moving across the countryside of northern Alabama." It was

> ...a time of economic distress and social unrest. As if in response to some common impulse, thousands of young people—no one knows how many—left their homes and communities to drift across the land by train and on foot, presumably in search of work, but, in reality, often without any defined or definable objective. In a gondola car of the train rode two groups of youths, one composed of Negroes, the other whites. Among the latter were two white girls. What occurred has ever since been the subject of sharp controversy. It is at least established that a dispute broke out between the Negroes and the whites. There was a fight and all but one of the white boys were thrown off the slow-moving train. Word was sent ahead, and when the freight train approached the village of Scottsboro, the Negroes were met by the sheriff and a

pose. The charge was rape of the white girls. Fearing the violence
of the community, the sheriff moved the defendants to the neighboring town of Gadsden. The militia was called to Scottsboro to
maintain order. A few days later the defendants were tried in three
separate proceedings. Each of the three trials was completed in the
space of a single day. All the defendants were convicted of rape,
and the juries imposed the sentence of death on each (Allen
1958:191).

The Scottsboro defendants appealed to the United States Supreme Court,
arguing that they had received ineffective assistance of counsel. They were put
on trial only six days after their indictment. And for all practical purposes they
had no lawyer during their capital trial. The Alabama trial judge had "appointed all members of the bar" for purposes of arraigning the defendants,
and he expected them to represent the Scottsboro Boys—as they were
called—at the trial if no one else turned up to represent the accused. What
this meant, of course, was that no lawyer had responsibility for the defense.

The United States Supreme Court opinion voiding the convictions and sentences and ordering a retrial was written by Justice George Sutherland, one of
the "Four Horsemen" on the Court who were anathema to President Roo-
sevelt's New Deal. For the Court he explained why the right to counsel was a
fundamental constitutional element of "due process of law":

> The right to be heard would be, in many cases, of little avail if it did
> not comprehend the right to be heard by counsel. Even the intelli-
> gent and educated layman has small and sometimes no skill in the
> science of law. If charged with crime, he is incapable, generally, of
> determining for himself whether the indictment is good or bad. He
> is unfamiliar with the rules of evidence. Left without the aid of
> counsel he may be put on trial without a proper charge, and con-
> victed upon incompetent evidence, or evidence irrelevant to the
> issue or otherwise inadmissible. He lacks both the skill and knowl-
> edge adequately to prepare his defense, even though he have a per-
> fect one. He requires the guiding hand of counsel at every step in the
> proceedings against him. Without it, though he be not guilty, he
> faces the danger of conviction because he does not know how to es-
> tablish his innocence. If that be true of men of intelligence, how
> much more true is it of the ignorant and illiterate, or those of feeble
> intellect (*Powell v. Alabama* 1932:68–69).

The 1932 *Scottsboro* decision did not require court-appointed counsel in *all*
felony trials in state court. *Scottsboro* was a capital case, and although a fair
reading of the Court's opinion limited it to trials where death was a possible
punishment, it wasn't clear that *Scottsboro* required counsel in all *capital* cases.

The Court expressly limited its holding to cases involving capital defendants who could not afford to retain counsel and who could not be expected to carry out their own defenses:

> All that is necessary now to decide, as we do decide, is that in a capital case, where the defendant is unable to employ counsel, and is incapable adequately of making his own defense because of ignorance, feeble-mindedness, illiteracy, or the like, it is the duty of the court, whether requested or not, to assign counsel for him... (*Powell v. Alabama* 1932:71).

The uniquely hideous facts of the *Scottsboro* trial had clearly made an impression upon Justice Sutherland: the farcical appointment of "all members of the bar" as counsel, the fact that the trials "immediately proceeded. The defendants [were] young, ignorant, illiterate, surrounded by hostile sentiment, haled back and forth under guard of soldiers, charged with an atrocious crime regarded with especial horror in the community where they were to be tried," and were thus put in jail (*Powell v. Alabama* 1932:57–58). Take away any one or more of these special conditions, and it became unclear whether the Supreme Court would still have regarded counsel as "fundamental" to "due process of law."

With the question of whether a right to court-appointed counsel existed in all felony trials left open since *Scottsboro,* in 1942, in *Betts v. Brady,* the Supreme Court resolved this issue in the negative. Smith Betts, a farm hand in rural Carroll County, Maryland, was charged with robbery, a non-capital offense (*Betts v. Brady* 1942:456). Because he lacked the funds to hire a defense lawyer, Betts asked the court to appoint one. The Maryland trial judge refused, explaining to Mr. Betts that in Carroll County attorneys were appointed only in capital cases—rape and murder. At Betts' trial, the main dispute involved eyewitness identifications. Mr. Betts did the best he could acting as his own lawyer, but the judge who presided at the trial (there was no jury) disbelieved Betts, found him guilty, and sentenced him to eight years in prison (at 457).

The Supreme Court decided in Smith Betts' case that there was no generalized right to counsel in noncapital trials. But, if "special circumstances" were present in the case, then there *was* a right to counsel. Circumstances deemed "special" by the Court included "the age and education of the defendant, the conduct of the court or prosecuting officials, and the complicated nature of the offense charged, and the possible defenses thereto" (Lewis 1964:113). And, of course, the "gravity of the crime" (at 113).

These elements seemed to have been lifted, somewhat, from the facts of *Scottsboro*: the ages of the defendants there ranged from 13 to 21; the court's behavior seemed an aberration—appointing all members of the bar to represent the defendants (*Powell v. Alabama* 1932:49); although the charges and defenses thereto did not seem complicated, the gravity of the crime, rape, was substantial, for at that time it was a capital offense (at 50). Yet the Court in *Scottsboro* had been explicit about the limit of its holding—only to capital defendants who could not provide for their own defenses. The Court did not delineate the elements of the circumstances in its holding sufficiently to make the *Betts* decision a natural extension thereof. Nor could it, for the *Powell* Court was explicit that the crime had to be a capital offense to apply its holding (at 71).

Betts threw the continued validity of *Scottsboro* into doubt, by raising the question: If a capital case did not present "special circumstances," then did the *Scottsboro* decision apply (requiring court-appointed counsel) or would *Betts* apply (not requiring counsel, because no "special circumstances" present, even though it's a capital case)? In other words, did *Scottsboro* establish a per se rule of right to counsel in capital trials where the defendants could not provide for their own defenses? Or was the *Scottsboro* rule limited to cases with facts as howlingly unfair as *Scottsboro*? Did the *Betts* "special circumstances" requirement apply equally across the board, to capital and noncapital cases alike?

In the years following *Betts*, the Court, in case after case, always found that capital trials did present "special circumstances." As a practical matter, the fact that the trial was *capital* represented a *per se* "special circumstance" requiring the appointment of counsel. In 1945 two capital cases reached the Supreme Court raising "special circumstances" issues, and in both cases the Court, 7–2, held such circumstances to be present (*Williams v. Kaiser* 1945; *Tomkins v. Missouri* 1945). In 1961 the justices made clear that they were drawing a line between capital and non-capital cases: "When one pleads to a capital charge without benefit of counsel, we do not stop to determine whether prejudice resulted" (*Hamilton v. Alabama* 1961:55). The *Scottsboro* decision lived.

The bright-line distinction between capital and non-capital cases, however, was artificial. In case after "special circumstances" case, the justices struggled to fashion a coherent definition of "special circumstances." This effort was not a happy one, as Justice Hugo Black, who dissented in *Betts*, seldom lost an opportunity to remind his brethren. By the early 1960s the justices' frustration with *Betts'* "special circumstances" rule had increased to the point where overruling *Betts* became a distinct possibility. All the Court needed was the right case to use as a vehicle to reconsider *Betts*.

Enter Clarence Earl Gideon, a small time Florida criminal who had been convicted of breaking into and robbing the coin machine in a Pensacola pool hall. At his felony trial, Gideon had asked for a lawyer. The trial judge refused, because Gideon's was not a capital case. The Florida Supreme Court affirmed.

At this point Clarence Gideon's case becomes the stuff of legends, best told by Anthony Lewis' book *Gideon's Trumpet* (1964). Gideon wrote and filed, in the U.S. Supreme Court, a petition asking the justices to throw out his felony conviction because he had been denied the right to counsel at trial. Gideon was wrong, of course; under *Betts* he *wasn't* entitled to counsel unless he could show "special circumstances." He probably couldn't. Gideon wasn't retarded or illiterate, and, in fact, he didn't do so bad as his own lawyer at trial, especially since the presiding judge did the best he could to help Gideon make his case of innocence. But the very apparent *absence* of special circumstances made Gideon's case a good vehicle with which the justices could revisit the *Betts* rule itself. Here was a case lacking in special circumstances: If *Betts* remains the law, then Gideon loses; for Gideon to win, *Betts* must be overruled.

The Court invited Abe Fortas, of the D.C. superfirm Arnold, Fortas and Porter, to serve as Gideon's lawyer. The justices told Fortas to address the question whether *Betts v. Brady* should be overruled. It was an invitation to Fortas (and his partner Abe Krash and his summer associate John Hart Ely) to take part in constitutional history.

In autumn 1962, Fortas' hand was strengthened significantly by the publication of a definitive article written by law professor Yale Kamisar and published in the *Chicago Law Review*. The article would appear too late to use in Fortas' brief, but Kamisar, knowing about the Gideon case, telephoned Krash in September and offered to send him a copy of the manuscript. The offer was gladly accepted (Lewis 1964:132).

Kamisar's article filled an important empirical hole in Gideon's argument: What would be the practical, real world consequences of overruling *Betts*? Rhetoric about "constitutional revolutions" notwithstanding, the U.S. Supreme Court has never been packed with revolutionaries. Only a few years earlier, in *Brown v. Board of Education* (1954), the Court had sparked a social upheaval still very visible in 1962, when the Court granted review in Gideon's case. The justices might well have felt squeamish about doing it again.

Kamisar's article demonstrated that the consequences of overruling *Betts* would not be momentous. Kamisar showed that 37 states already formally provided court-appointed counsel as a matter of right in all felony cases. Of the remaining 13 that didn't, in eight states a rule of court-appointed counsel existed *de facto*, notwithstanding the absence of statute or court rule. That left only five states that would have been affected by overruling *Betts*.

In its landmark ruling in *Gideon v. Wainwright* (1963), the Supreme Court scrapped *Betts* altogether, including the capital/noncapital distinction that had proved so vexing. Justice Hugo Black, the *Betts* dissenter, wrote the Court's opinion in *Gideon*, deciding that Clarence Earl Gideon did indeed have a Sixth Amendment right to court-appointed counsel in his noncapital trial for breaking into and robbing the coin machine in a Pensacola pool hall. Henceforth, all felony prosecutions in state court required the appointment of counsel. Clarence Gideon's case did not affect the *Scottsboro* rule that counsel must *always* be appointed in capital trials; Gideon's case simply extended *Scottsboro's per se* rule to include noncapital felony trials.

The right to counsel recognized in the *Scottsboro* case was not the only federal constitutional right the Supreme Court extended to include in state criminal trials as well as federal. *Scottsboro* was emblematic of what some have termed the Court's "revolution" in constitutional criminal procedure—the application of the procedural rights enumerated in the Constitution to state criminal trials. Meanwhile, as the range of available constitutional criminal procedure rights expanded, so did the availability of *habeas* to provide a federal judicial forum for vindication of those rights. According to a treatise on *habeas* corpus (Liebman and Hertz 1994:§ 2.4d), the Court's decision in *Brown v. Allen* (1953) reaffirmed the cognizability in *habeas* of all federal constitutional claims presented by state prisoners, including, of course, the constitutional right to court-appointed counsel in capital cases recognized in *Scottsboro*. As the Court recognized new rights, *habeas* kept pace and remained as a mechanism to vindicate those rights in federal court.

No Constitutional Right to Counsel
in Capital *Habeas*

> There were two...things I was always thinking about: the dawn and my appeal (Camus 1989:111).

Many scholarly treatments of *habeas corpus* in the twentieth century begin with the infamous Leo Frank case. Leo Frank, a New York Jew, had gone to Georgia to manage a pencil factory, and had been indicted for the rape and murder of a 14-year-old child. The brutal nature of the killing—along with his religion and northern origin—aroused violent local prejudices (*Frank v. Mangum* 1915). Justice Oliver Wendell Holmes described the atmosphere of terror and violence that permeated the courtroom and jury deliberations:

> The trial began on July 28, 1913, at Atlanta, and was carried on in a court packed with spectators and surrounded by a crowd outside, all strongly hostile to [Frank]. On Saturday, August 23, this hostility was sufficient to lead the judge to confer in the presence of the jury with the Chief of Police in Atlanta and the Colonel of the Fifth Georgia Regiment stationed in that city, both of whom were known to the jury.
>
> On the same day, the evidence seemingly having been closed, the public press, apprehending danger, united in a request to the Court that the proceedings should not continue on that evening. Thereupon the Court adjourned until Monday morning.
>
> On that morning when the Solicitor General entered the court he was greeted with applause, stamping of feet and clapping of hands, and the judge before beginning his charge had a private conversation with [Frank's] counsel in which he expressed the opinion that there would be "probable danger of violence" if there should be an acquittal or disagreement [i.e., a hung jury], and that

it would be safer for not only [Frank] but his counsel to be absent from Court when the verdict was brought in.

At the judge's request they agreed that [Frank] and they should be absent, and they kept their word. When the verdict was rendered, and before more than one of the jurymen had been polled there was such a roar of applause that the polling could not go on till order was restored. The noise outside was such that it was difficult for the judge to hear the answers of the jurors although he was only ten feet from them (*Frank v. Magnum* 1915:345–346).

The jury convicted Leo Frank, of course, and the trial judge sentenced him to death. When the Georgia Supreme Court affirmed, Frank filed a petition for writ of *habeas corpus* in federal court. Ultimately, a majority of the United States Supreme Court refused to second-guess the Georgia state courts.

Holmes dissented. Holmes' dissenting opinion was blunt: "Mob law does not become due process of law by securing the assent of a terrorized jury. We are not speaking of mere disorder, or mere irregularities in procedure, but of a case where the processes of justice are actually subverted.... Any judge who has sat with juries [as Holmes had] knows that in spite of forms they are extremely likely to be impregnated by the environing atmosphere" (*Frank v. Magnum* 1915:347). Leo Frank almost certainly was innocent of the rape and killing for which he was convicted and, in the end, lynched (Rawls 1982:A12).

In 1923, however, in another case involving capital juries intimidated by the threat of mob violence, the Court reviewed the convictions of five African-Americans. African-Americans had been systematically excluded from both grand and petit jury panels. The trial, which had lasted about 45 minutes, was a mask for lynch law, with all major players swept along by an "irresistible wave of public passion" (*Moore v. Dempsey* 1923:90; Cortner 1988). Justice Holmes, writing for the Court, observed, "No juryman could have voted for an acquittal and continued to live in [the county]" (*Moore v. Dempsey* 1923:89). The Court decided that federal relief was available:

[I]f the case is that the whole proceeding is a mask—that counsel, jury, and judge were swept to the fatal end by an irresistible wave of public passion, and that the state courts failed to correct the wrong—neither perfection in the machinery for correction nor the possibility that the trial court and counsel saw no other way of avoiding an immediate outbreak of the mob can prevent this court from securing to the [defendants] their constitutional rights (at 91).

The year *Gideon v. Wainwright* was decided (1963), also marked the high-water mark of the Warren Court's expansion of *habeas* (*Fay v. Noia* 1963). But in 1966 Congress stepped in and scaled back the availability of *habeas* to state prisoners. It limited the discretion of federal judges to entertain *habeas* peti-tions "only on the ground that [the petitioner] is in custody in violation of the Constitution or laws or treaties of the United States" (28 U.S.C. § 2254). Con-gress also created a presumption that any issue of fact determined by a state court after a hearing on the merits is correct, and required the petitioner to es-tablish by convincing evidence that the state court's ruling was erroneous. The post-Warren Court contracted the scope of habeas further, as did Congress in the 1990s (Liebman and Hertz 1994:§ 2.4d).

The right to counsel in capital *habeas* has yet to be recognized by the Supreme Court, but as a practical matter it has existed since the early 1960s, when the NAACP Legal Defense and Educational Fund, Incorporated (LDF), guided by Anthony Amsterdam and his colleagues, decided to challenge every death sentence in every capital case (Wolfe 1973; Meltsner 1973). This decision led directly to the decade-long moratorium on executions between 1967 and 1977. And although the moratorium ended in 1977, with Gary Gilmore's exe-cution by a Utah firing squad, the reality of counsel in *habeas* did not: Since 1967 no death row prisoner who has wanted a *habeas* lawyer to fight his execu-tion has not had one.

In the years following *Gideon* in 1963, the Court made it increasingly clear that there was no constitutional right to counsel in *habeas* proceedings, capital as well as noncapital. But by 1963 a whole new set of forces were about to enter the picture: the first sustained and national effort to challenge, in federal court, the constitutionality of capital punishment itself.

Looking back on it now, from the vantage point of 1997 — with more than 3,000 people on death row in 38 states — it's important to keep in mind that by any measure, LDF's use of the federal courts and the Constitution to shut down capital punishment as a legal system was a breathtaking success. Be-tween 1967 and 1977, LDF and its allies secured and held a moratorium on executions in America while the Supreme Court sorted through and resolved LDF's challenge to the legality of the death penalty.

Perhaps LDF's most important ally in Florida was a brilliant, courageous, eccentric — in the best John Stuart Mill-ian sense of the word — Miami attor-ney named Tobias Simon. In states other than Florida and California, courts and politicians seemed willing to hold off executions until the Supreme Court had a chance to consider and decide LDF's constitutional challenges to capital punishment as a legal system. But not in Florida and California, the two states with by far the largest death row populations at the time (50 in Florida and 70 in California). Florida and California had elected new "law and order" gover-nors in 1965, and both Florida Governor Claude Kirk and California Governor Ronald Reagan had made campaign promises to enforce the death penalty.

Until 1967, LDF had persuaded its affiliated attorneys to represent individ-ual death row prisoners in individual cases only and to raise LDF's constitu-tional claims in individual case by individual case. That approach could only work if every condemned prisoner had a lawyer to raise LDF's constitutional issues in the proper court at the proper time and in the procedurally proper way, and, in most cases in most states, they did.

But not in Florida—the state that had only four years previously, in 1963, given the world *Gideon v. Wainwright*. As depicted in Michael Meltsner's indispensable 1973 book, *Cruel and Unusual*, Toby Simon and his associate, Alfred Feinberg, had realized by 1967 that:

> ...the most pressing concern was the death-row inmates who were not represented by lawyers. Angered by Kirk's posturing, they feared that he would execute one of the many men on death row who had no lawyer, no concerned friends, and no pending lawsuit. There were men on the row who risked execution simply because they did not know how to file a suit to block it. The lawyers' anxiety grew after state officials refused to divulge the name and status of every death-row inmate.
>
> If there was anything unconstitutional in the state's administration of the death penalty, Simon and Feinberg reasoned, all Florida death penalties suffered from identical defects of unconstitutional procedure. On this premise, Simon decided that death-row inmates represented a class of persons whose constitutional objections to death case procedures and execution itself could be joined and resolved in one proceeding. Why not present a petition for a writ of *habeas corpus* to a federal judge in the name of the men Simon represented personally, and ask that it be treated as though it had been filed on behalf of all death-row prisoners? If such a suit was proper, the courts would have to postpone all executions until they finally decided whether the legal rights of the inmates had been infringed (Meltsner 1973:129).

"Simon's Frolic," Meltsner and LDF called the class action idea. Meltsner describes what happened next:

> Four months later [Federal District Judge] McRae concluded that a full factual inquiry was necessary before he could decide whether or not to entertain the class suit. The use of a class action, he agreed, depended on whether or not death-row inmates had effective access to the courts. Were they without lawyers? Were they poor, ignorant, or illiterate, and thereby unable to protect themselves by retaining an attorney or filing their own *habeas corpus* petition in court? If the answer to these questions was yes, a class suit might be the only way they could assert their legal claims.
>
> In order to find out the answers, McRae accepted an ACLU-LDF offer to interview each consenting death-row inmate and to

report back to the court. Amsterdam prepared a questionnaire, Simon scheduled the interviews, and they both put together a task force of ACLU volunteers, LDF cooperating lawyers, and law students who went to Raiford to inquire into the background, employment, education, prior criminal record, financial status, and legal representation of each inmate who agreed to talk to them.

When the job was done, Simon had a profile of forty of the fifty-two men on death row to present to Judge McRae. Of these, thirty-four inmates had already lost their appeals to the Florida Supreme Court and were subject to electrocution at Governor Kirk's whim unless new legal proceedings were brought on their behalf. As Simon had feared, half of these thirty-four had no lawyers or means to hire them; all but six of the other half were represented by the small group of ACLU-LDF lawyers. Fourteen of the men were unskilled laborers; seven were farm laborers; thirty-seven of the forty were entirely destitute; and the remaining three reported having less than a hundred dollars.

At the time of the interviews, death-row inmates were given the Beta test, a nonverbal IQ test commonly used to test prisoners, in order to measure their likely understanding of legal proceedings. If sufficient numbers were of subnormal intelligence, it would be strong evidence that they could not have taken even the initial steps necessary to bring their cases to court and that therefore a class action was necessary to protect their interests. Here again, Simon's position was vindicated. The mean IQ for the group of forty men was 88.35 (80 to 89 is considered "low average"), and the mean number of years of school attendance was 8.62. Further, when the inmates were divided into three groups, those with non-ACLU-LDF counsel had had the highest IQ—almost normal; those without counsel had lower IQ's—distinctly subnormal; and those with ACLU-LDF counsel had the lowest IQ's of all. The lawyers later argued that the results demonstrated that helpless men were without help—though the private joke was that any death-row inmate with any brains was too smart to want ACLU-LDF counsel.

The results of the interviews and tests were forwarded to Judge McRae and a court hearing scheduled. Amsterdam flew to Jacksonville to tell McRae why the facts adduced required treatment of death-row inmates as a class. He told the Judge that the unrepresented, ignorant, and indigent men of Raiford's death row must be heard in one case for want of the ability to institute and maintain individual legal proceedings designed to secure their rights. The punch line of his plea was: "They will be heard together or they will be electrocuted individually. There is no third possibility." One simply could expect no other result, Amsterdam insisted, given their level of intelligence, their poverty, and the fact that their communication with the outside world was totally dependent on the will of their keepers.

Months later McRae decided that the class action was proper. He continued the prohibition on execution and told the lawyers that he would consider their arguments about Florida capital punishment laws (Meltsner 1973:132–133).

In 1972, in the *Furman* decision, LDF persuaded the Court to strike down every capital statute and every extant death sentence in the United States— clearing more than 600 people from death row. In 1976, the Supreme Court upheld the abstract constitutionality of certain types of retooled capital statutes. Between 1976 and 1983, the Court took LDF's contention that "death is different" seriously, and struck down various aspects of the refitted death penalty statutes; only a handful of executions occurred between 1976 and 1983. However, between 1983 and today, the Supreme Court seems to have more or less given up on its project of requiring that states' capital punishment systems produce fair, consistent and reliable sentences of death as a punishment (Steiker and Steiker 2003). Yet, even in this age of "deregulated death," the justices take capital cases far more seriously than the Court ever did prior to 1963; this, in the end, may be the LDF's most enduring achievement in its three-decades-plus effort to use the courts to bring capital punishment within the rule of law.

In 1977 Gary Gilmore became the first execution since 1967. In 1979 John Spenkellink became the first non-consensual execution since 1967. Spenkellink was executed in Florida. Over the next few years, a handful of people were executed in Florida, Texas, Virginia and Louisiana. By the late 1980s, and continuing into the 1990s and through today, executions became more and more frequent.

Note that the fundamental systemic changes wrought by *Furman* were *procedural* in nature. *Furman* had invalidated the existing capital punishment systems because those systems were defective procedurally. The post-*Furman* statutes upheld in 1976 set out a complex array of new procedures for deciding who dies. Before *Furman*, capital trials were fairly straightforward: one trial, one verdict, one appeal, not a lot of procedural requirements. After *Furman*, capital trials would become vastly more complicated procedurally: bifurcated trials, listed aggravating and mitigating circumstances, proportionality review, more careful automatic appeals, and the like (Acker and Lanier 2003). At every stage—from pre-trial, through trial, automatic appeal, post-conviction, *habeas*, and executive clemency, the rules had suddenly become far more complicated.

The procedural sea-change brought about by *Furman* greatly increased the importance of defense lawyers at trial and beyond. Only a skilled, experienced, and sufficiently resourced defense lawyer could be expected to figure out and then to navigate her client through the new procedural maze of capital punishment as a legal system—a maze with no map and a labyrinth with no Ariadne. Trial lawyers had to figure it out as they went along; *no one* had any real experience working under the new procedural requirements. Indeed, few lawyers had much meaningful experience with the old, obsolete statutes invalidated in *Furman*. An entire generation of lawyers, those who came of age during the 1967–77 moratorium, had no experience with capital punishment at all.

The capital trials during the early years of the post-*Furman* era reflected this understandable lawyerly inexperience and justifiable confusion over how the new procedures would work. The transcripts in many of these early cases are almost painful to read. For instance, bifurcated trials required defense attorneys prior to trial to emphasize the penalty stage as much as the guilt phase, something many trial lawyers found extremely counterintuitive. In trial after trial, capital defense lawyers took their clients into the punishment phase with very little mitigating evidence to present, because the lawyers didn't investigate mitigating circumstances, because they never expected to lose at the guilt phase and ever *get* to the penalty phase.

Given the procedural confusion that reigned at many capital trials, the availability of *habeas* as a safety valve to fix the mistakes of the lawyers at trial became critically important. As of 1983, federal courts in *habeas* were invalidating 60 percent of state death sentences due to trial errors of constitutional magnitude. In the few years following Gary Gilmore's execution in 1977, capital *habeas* cases were able to attract the best such lawyers in the nation. As described in David von Drehle's magnificent 1995 book, *Among the Lowest of the Dead*, John Spenkellink (executed in Florida in 1979) was represented by Anthony Amsterdam, David Kendall, Millard Farmer and LDF. No Fortune-500 company ever received better legal aid than did John Spenkellink.

Soon, however, the cases piled up. Spenkellink's 1979 execution meant that more executions would follow, and they did.

At the same time, the U.S. Supreme Court began sharply constricting death row's access to the *habeas corpus* federal courts, and, beginning in 1984, telling the states that death cases need receive no more effective representation at trial than non-death cases: So long as the court-appointed trial lawyer can fog up a mirror, the Sixth Amendment right to counsel is satisfied. And states need not provide any lawyer at all in capital *habeas* cases. Thus, at trial you only get a lousy lawyer. And that lousy lawyer's mistakes won't be fixed in *habeas*, because you don't have a right to any lawyer at all and, even if you had a *habeas* lawyer, she probably wouldn't succeed in winning you a new trial, because the scope of *habeas* review has become so constricted.

One might conclude that the story of legal aid for death row was over by 1967. Either *de jure* (at trial) or *de facto* (in *habeas*), capital defendants at trial and capital prisoners in *habeas* got lawyers if they wanted them. On paper, that appeared to be the case.

The reality on the ground was far different, however. The reality was that the "right" to counsel at trial was a paper right only, because of the abysmal *quality* of the legal aid to which one was entitled. *Gideon's* promise of effective assistance of counsel at trial turned out to have been a false one.

The Right to Some Kind of Lawyer

Real evil
at its worst does not declare
itself.
It cowers like the smallest
of the smallest cancers on a slide,
happy if it's never seen
or else mistakenly identified.
Basic humanity and the inability
to live with guilt prevent
the basest criminals from saying
what they are
              (Hazo 1997:*The Face of Evil in Our Time* (March 4 Draft)).

The scholarly literature (Liebman and Hertz 1994), organizations such as the ABA, and the witness of countless participants in capital punishment as a legal system have demonstrated again and again that people on trial for their lives very often receive lawyers so grotesquely inept, inexperienced and incompetent as to be laughable were it to occur in any other context than a life-or-death trial. We are not here talking about trial lawyers who aren't F. Lee Bailey. We are talking about lawyers who are "trying their first cases or with little or no experience in trying serious cases, lawyers who were senile or intoxicated or under the influence of drugs while trying the cases, lawyers who were completely ignorant of the law and procedures governing a capital trial, lawyers who used racial slurs to refer to their clients, lawyers who handled cases without any investigative or expert assistance, lawyers who slept or were absent during crucial parts of the trial..." (Bright and Keenan 1996:800–801; Bright 1994:1835).

As Ira Robbins and the ABA (Robbins 1990:1; *McFarland v. Scott* 1994a (Blackmun, J., dissenting from denial of cert.); Bright 1994; Berger 1990–91; Geimer 1994) and others have shown, part of the problem here is resources— the legal system in capital trials gets what it pays for. And what it pays is often the equivalent of sub-minimum wage. You could make more money flipping burgers at McDonald's than you'd make trying capital cases in many southern States enthusiastic about enforcing capital punishment.

But wait. Even if the lawyer at trial were an incompetent hack, won't the *habeas* courts identify the problem and fix it by ordering a new trial at which the defendant would be represented by a lawyer able at least to fog up a mirror? The answer is no. This is so for two reasons. First, the Supreme Court has made it extremely difficult to prove that a capital trial lawyer failed to render "effective" assistance of counsel. Second, to meaningfully challenge the quality of your trial lawyer, you must have a lawyer at the *habeas* level. That *habeas* lawyer must herself possess sufficient skill, experience and resources to allow her to prove how lousy your trial attorney performed.

In other words, for a condemned person to prove his trial lawyer was constitutionally lousy, that person must have a good lawyer at the *habeas* stage. But there is no constitutional "right" to counsel in *habeas* at all: Death row prisoners' access to legal aid depended entirely on the ability of the LDF and other organizations (such as Team Defense in Atlanta) to find attorneys willing and able to take on these cases. Since the early 1980s, when the LDF took itself out of death work in a big way, the pool of lawyers willing to represent capital prisoners *pro bono* has run dry.

Once again, it is useful to distinguish between the right to counsel at trial and the "right" to, or availability of, counsel in *habeas* corpus proceedings.

The Right to a Real Attorney at Trial: *Gideon* Betrayed

> We lay in wet snow. I kept alive on brandy, the fear of death, and the glorious fact of the cathedral town just below us, Glittering with the morning.
>
> Letter by Wilfred Owen to his mother, March 23, 1917, from the Western front

In 1963 *Gideon* guaranteed the right to counsel at trial. Twenty-one years later, in David Leroy Washington's case, the Supreme Court would decide what quality of lawyering was required by *Gideon*. Like Clarence Earl Gideon's case, David Washington's reached the United States Supreme Court by way of a Florida trial and a Florida Supreme Court appeal.

The David Leroy Washington case was an unfortunate vehicle by which to resolve the issue of what standards should govern claims of ineffective assistance of trial counsel in criminal prosecutions. Many of the systemic problems described above were not present in Washington's trial. Yet, the doctrinal standards articulated by the Supreme Court in his case now control claims of ineffective assistance in all cases, capital and noncapital alike.

During a ten-day crime spree, Washington planned and committed three groups of crimes, which included three stabbing murders, torture, kidnaping, assaults, attempted murder, attempted extortion, and theft. Washington surrendered to police after his two accomplices were arrested for one of the murders. He gave the police a lengthy confession to one of the murders, and an experienced Miami criminal defense lawyer was subsequently appointed to be his attorney.

Acting against his lawyer's advice, Washington confessed to the other two murders. Following his indictment for all three homicides, Washington waived his right to a jury trial and, again contrary to the advice of his attorney, pleaded guilty to the three killings and accepted responsibility for his crimes. Counsel advised Washington to invoke his right under Florida law to an advisory jury at his capital sentencing hearing. Washington rejected the advice. He chose instead to be sentenced by the trial judge without a jury recommendation. The judge sentenced Washington to death on each of the three counts of first-degree murder.

The Supreme Court later found that Washington's trial attorney conducted only minimal investigation into the existence of possible mitigating evidence. Although "counsel spoke with [Washington] about his background," and had telephone conversations with Washington's wife and mother, "[h]e did not follow up on the one unsuccessful effort to meet with them. He did not otherwise seek out character witnesses.... Nor did he request a psychiatric examination" (*Strickland v. Washington* 1984:672–673). At the sentencing hearing, "[c]ounsel decided not to present and hence not to look further for evidence concerning [Washington's] character and emotional state" (at 672–673). As the Court noted, "[t]hat decision reflected trial counsel's sense of hopelessness about overcoming the evidentiary effect of [Washington's] confessions to the gruesome crimes. It also reflected the judgment that it was advisable to rely on the plea colloquy for evidence about [Washington's] background and about his claim of emotional stress..." (at 668, 672–673). Counsel's dependence on the plea colloquy was due at least in part to a statement made by the trial judge that he had "a great deal of respect for people who are willing to step forward and admit their responsibility" (at 672).

Washington claimed in collateral proceedings that his lawyer rendered ineffective assistance because the attorney failed to conduct a meaningful investigation into his background and character. The state courts and federal district court rejected Washington's claims (*Washington v. Strickland* 1982:1247–1249). A panel of the former Fifth Circuit ordered the case remanded for an evidentiary hearing. The en banc court decided that the case was worthy of review.

In its opinion, the en banc Fifth Circuit attempted to elucidate the proper standards for evaluating claims of ineffective assistance of counsel based upon allegations of inadequate trial preparation. In addressing Washington's principal contention, that his trial attorney's assistance was not reasonably effective because counsel breached his duty to investigate mitigating circumstances, the lower court agreed with Washington that the Sixth Amendment imposes on counsel a duty to investigate. Reasonably effective assistance must be based on informed professional deliberation, and informed legal choices can be made only after investigating the options. Recognizing that "[t]he amount of pretrial investigation that is reasonable defies precise measurement" (at 1251), the heart of the Fifth Circuit's opinion was a typology that classified cases presenting issues concerning the scope of the duty to investigate before proceeding to trial.

The Fifth Circuit reasoned that if there is only one plausible line of defense, trial counsel must conduct a "reasonably substantial investigation" (at 1252) into that line of defense, since there can be no strategic choice that renders such an investigation unnecessary. The same duty exists if counsel relies at trial on only one line of defense, although others were available. In either case, the investigation need not be exhaustive. Although the scope of counsel's duty depends on such facts as the strength of the government's case and the likelihood that pursuing certain leads may prove more harmful than helpful, it must at a minimum include "an independent examination of the facts, circumstances, pleadings and laws involved" (at 1253).

In cases where more than one possible line of defense exists, counsel ideally should investigate each one substantially before making a strategic decision about which defenses to raise at trial. If the attorney conducts such an investigation, the strategic choice made as a result would "seldom if ever" (at 1254) be found to be the result of ineffective assistance of counsel. Given that legal advocacy is more art than science, and that the adversarial system requires deference to counsel's informed tactical decisions, strategic choices must be respected in these circumstances if they are based on reasonable professional judgment. If counsel does not conduct a substantial investigation into each of several plausible lines of defense, however, assistance may nonetheless be effective if the lawyer excludes certain lines of defense only for strategic reasons. Financial and caseload limitations may force attorneys to make early strategic choices, often based solely on conversations with the client and review of the prosecutor's evidence.

These strategic choices about which lines of defense to pursue would receive deference only to the extent to which they were reasonable. Thus, "when counsel's assumptions are reasonable given the totality of the circumstances and when counsel's strategy represents a reasonable choice based upon those assumptions, counsel need not investigate lines of defense that he has chosen not to employ at trial" (at 1255). Factors relevant to deciding whether particular strategic choices are reasonable would include the experience of the attorney, the inconsistency of unpursued and pursued lines of defense, and the potential for prejudice from taking an unpursued line of defense.

The Fifth Circuit's opinion then addressed the prejudice to the defense that must be shown before counsel's errors would be held to justify invalidation of the conviction or sentence. A special showing of prejudice would be required except in cases of outright denial of counsel, of affirmative government interference in the representation process, or of inherently prejudicial conflicts of interest. For cases of deficient performance by counsel when the government is not directly responsible for the deficiencies and when evidence of deficiency may be more accessible to the defense than to the prosecution, a prisoner must show that counsel's errors "resulted in actual and substantial disadvantage to the course of his defense" (at 1262). The requisite showing of prejudice would result in reversal of the judgment unless the prosecution could show that the constitutionally deficient performance, in light of all of the evidence, was harmless beyond a reasonable doubt. A majority of the Fifth Circuit judges sitting en banc agreed that David Washington's case should be remanded to the district court for application of the newly announced standards governing ineffective assistance of counsel.

The Supreme Court reversed. (Several states joined Florida in its petition for plenary review of *Washington v. Strickland.*) Writing for seven members of the Court, Justice O'Connor noted at the outset that no special standards apply in determining ineffective assistance of counsel claims in capital cases such as the one before it. As Judge Vance had done in his opinion for the Fifth Circuit, the Supreme Court treated the punishment that the defendant faces as merely one factor in the totality of circumstances to be considered in determining whether counsel was reasonably effective (*Strickland v. Washington* 1984:680). The lawyer in a capital sentencing proceeding occupies a place "comparable" to that at trial (at 687). "The benchmark for judging any claim of ineffectiveness must be whether counsel's conduct so undermined the proper functioning of the adversarial process that the [proceeding] cannot be relied on as having produced a just result" (at 686).

The Supreme Court held that to prevail on a claim of constitutionally ineffective assistance of counsel, a prisoner must make a two-pronged showing (*Strickland v. Washington* 1984:687). First, she must establish that counsel's performance was deficient. To do this, a claimant must prove that the lawyer's representation fell below an objective standard of reasonableness, measured by "prevailing professional norms" (at 688). Critically, Justice O'Connor exhorted reviewing courts to adhere to a standard "that counsel is strongly presumed to have rendered" constitutionally adequate assistance (at 690).

In addition to showing substandard performance, a claimant must show that counsel's deficient performance caused her prejudice (*Strickland v. Washington* 1984:687). Prejudice for O'Connor requires a demonstration that the attorney's errors were "so serious as to deprive the defendant of a fair trial, a trial whose result is reliable"(at 687). It is not enough to show that counsel's defective performance "had some conceivable effect on the outcome of the proceeding" (at 693). Conversely, a petitioner need not demonstrate that counsel's substandard performance "more likely than not altered the outcome in the case" (at 693.). Rather, the Court articulated what it viewed as an intermediate standard. "The defendant must show that there is a reasonable probability that, but for counsel's unprofessional errors, the result of the proceeding would have been different. A reasonable probability is a probability sufficient to undermine confidence in the outcome" (*Strickland v. Washington* 1984:694).

Applying this two-pronged standard to the facts of David Washington's case, the Court concluded that Washington's trial lawyer passed muster under both criteria at the sentencing hearing. According to the Court, counsel's "tactical" choices fell within the range of reasonableness, and the omitted mitigating evidence could not by any reasonable probability have changed the sentence due to the aggravating factors in the case (*Strickland v. Washington* 1984:699). David Leroy Washington was executed several months after the Court issued its opinion in his case.

Perhaps the most pernicious aspect of the constitutional standard adopted by Justice O'Connor in *Washington* was her strong presumption in favor of attorney competence. Her opinion established the standard of "reasonably effective assistance" (*Strickland v. Washington* 1984: 687–691), assumed reasonable performance by the defense attorney (at 689–691), and required a showing of clear prejudice to the defendant (at 691–696). At the same time Justice O'Connor gave virtually no guidelines, beyond the opaque requirement of "reasonableness," for determining what an attorney must do to be considered effective (at 688–89). Further, Justice O'Connor's prejudice standard requires too much: "This is 'far less a standard for effective assistance of counsel than a standard for disposing of effective assistance of counsel claims'" (Kamisar 1990:368). Applying Justice O'Connor's prejudice test to capital sentencing proceedings, when juries are called upon to make the highly subjective determination of whether a fellow human being has lost her moral entitlement to live, struck Professor Kamisar as "particularly anomalous—almost bizarre" (at 370).

As a result, claims of ineffective assistance can be brushed away by the federal courts. In fact, they have been. This would be less troubling if the quality of legal aid were high. It is not.

The right to effective assistance of counsel is no technicality. It has been called the "most pervasive right" because it defines one's ability to assert any other rights (Bazelon 1973:5). "Counsel serves to insure the operation of procedural and constitutional protections guaranteed to a criminal defendant" (Klein 1986:625–626). The Supreme Court in *Powell v. Alabama* (1932) recognized over half a century ago that without counsel capital defendants face conviction and condemnation not because they may be guilty but because they lacks the tools to prove their innocence. This is especially so when they are ignorant, illiterate, of feeble intellect, or on trial for their life (*Powell v. Alabama* 1932:57–59). The right to counsel is not simply a supplemental right. Because this right cuts to the heart of our judicial system, the right to counsel deserves protection proportional to its stature.

That is the myth. The reality is very different. Notwithstanding the ringing aspirational rhetoric of *Powell* and its progeny such as *Gideon v. Wainwright* (1963), and notwithstanding the functional importance of the right to counsel, violations of the right are routine, if not assumed (albeit not admitted) as a matter of course. In the years limning the *Washington* decisions, there was a clear recognition that a problem existed.

Former Chief Justice Warren Burger publicized the counsel predicament. He wrote in 1980 that "a broad consensus has now emerged that a significant problem concerning the quality of a substantial number of lawyers' performances in the trial courts does indeed exist" (Burger 1980:1). Between one-third and one-half of courtroom attorneys are "not really qualified" to represent their clients adequately (Burger 1977:170). So who is this professional entrusted with the responsibility for protecting the rights and establishing the innocence of the indigent client? Professor Vivian Berger answered in 1986: "Apparently, a presumptive incompetent, an agent all too frequently unfit to discharge her high obligations to her principal" (Berger 1986:11).

Former D.C. Circuit Chief Judge David Bazelon agreed. Bazelon wrote in 1973 that "no one could seriously dispute that ineffective assistance is a common phenomenon" (Bazelon 1973:2). He crystallized the gap between lofty doctrinal theory and grimy everyday reality in a frequently quoted passage: "[A]lthough we generals of the judiciary have designed inspiring insignia for the standard, the battle for equal justice is being lost in the trenches of the criminal courts where the promise of *Gideon* and *Argersinger* goes unfulfilled" (Bazelon 1976:811). The military imagery is problematic but the point powerfully made.

After twenty-three years on the bench Judge Bazelon believed that "a great many—if not most—indigent defendants do not receive the effective assistance of counsel guaranteed them by the 6th Amendment" (Bazelon 1973:2). The right to effective assistance of counsel too often translates into "little more than pro forma representation" (at 2).

Empirical data tend to support Justice Burger's and Judge Bazelon's experiential conclusions. Collectively these statistical studies "provide positive documentation for the position that a serious problem indeed exists and demands a remedy" (Burger 1980:9).

The first relevant poll was conducted of federal judges in 1978 by the Committee on Qualifications to Practice Before the United States Courts in the Second Circuit. The Second Circuit judges responded that more than 7.1 percent of the attorneys appearing before them were incompetent, and that a larger number were leaning toward inadequacy (ABA 1977:1525).

In that same year the Federal Judicial Center released the results of its own survey of nearly 400 federal district judges. The results were depressing. "Of those responding, 41.3 percent believed that the quality of advocacy in their courts was a 'serious problem'" (Burger 1980:9).

The American Bar Foundation followed these studies with one of its own. The foundation sent questionnaires to 5,515 state and federal trial judges (Maddi 1978:109–110). Of the 1,442 responding, 87 percent rated at least 50 percent of attorneys fully competent (at 110). However, only 4 percent said they could be confident that all of the attorneys in their courtrooms were competent (at 116). The author concluded from this study that a typical response was that slightly below 80 percent of the attorneys were competent (at 116). The flip side was that at least 20 percent were not.

In 1978, Anthony Partridge and Gordon Bermant conducted, for the Federal Judicial Center, one of the most sophisticated studies yet completed on attorney performance (Partridge and Bermant 1978). Questionnaires were sent to all federal district and circuit judges, along with a request for case reports evaluating the performance of lawyers appearing in their courtrooms during a specified time period. The district judges rated 8.6 percent of all trial lawyer performances they saw to be less than adequate (at 13). More importantly, 41.3 percent responded affirmatively when asked if they believed that a serious problem of inadequate representation existed in their courts (at 16).

More recently, studies have shown that in the nine southern states that constitute the "death belt," more than 10 percent of the attorneys who have represented indigent capital defendants have subsequently been "disbarred, suspended, or otherwise disciplined at a rate three to forty-six times the average for those states" (Note 1994:1925). Certainly, lack of training is at least partly to blame for these sad statistics. In the death belt, one-third of the attorneys whose clients received death sentences practiced civil, not criminal law; indeed, most had never handled a capital case before (at 1928). These states have no training programs for capital defenders and they do not screen appointed defense attorneys for incompetency (at 1928).

These studies provide disturbing quantification for Justice Burger's and Judge Bazelon's anecdotal reports of the general defectiveness of counsel. "A realistic, rough estimate of the amount of poor trial lawyer performance ranges anywhere from 9% to 22%, depending on the norms of the rater" (Levine 1984:1299). The studies suggest that "it is clearly plausible to hypothesize that as many as one in seven criminal defendants receive less than adequate representation" (at 1299). The "prime casualties" of this problem are the "poor, uneducated and unemployed" (Bazelon 1976:812). It is the indigent defendant who is represented all too often by "walking violations of the Sixth Amendment" (at 812).

Why are things so bad? Any fair answer must focus upon the system of delivery of legal services to indigents, rather than upon the poor performance of individual defense lawyers. The systemic problems include inadequate compensation and underfunding, pressures of crushingly oppressive caseloads, and lack of motivation supplemented by plea-hungry judges (Robbins 1990:1).

Too many members of the criminal defense bar are inexperienced lawyers who learn by trial and error with real cases and real lives (Berger 1986:61–62). On the other side, those who do become "pros" and who are able and dedicated champions often face high burnout rates and become cynical and/or contemptuous of their clients (at 62). This creates a rapid turnover and opens the door to an increasing number of neophytes into the defense of the indigent. Criminal representation is complex and difficult even for the experienced and well outfitted lawyer. It is nearly impossible for the lawyer just out of law school, with little or no experience, to be an effective defense lawyer (Bazelon 1973:13).

The neophyte, although generally dedicated and increasingly well trained in law school, simply lacks both familiarity with the system and experience in trial advocacy (Bazelon 1976:812). Yet, due to the inability of many public defender offices to provide apprenticeships or training periods similar to those provided by private law firms (Burger 1980:7), the criminal defense lawyer may have her first solo case within a few short weeks of passing the bar (Bazelon 1973:14). This bad start more often than not does not lead to acquired skills but rather to repeated and unguided poor performance (Levine 1984:1381). The process operates at the expense of the hapless client who is left with no redress and who began with no choice of counsel in the first place.

Beyond the lack of sound training programs, poor people's lawyers may face crushing caseloads and cut-rate fees which promote lackluster performance and discourage careful investigation (Berger 1986:61). Lack of financial resources can cripple an indigent defense office (Klein 1986:658). In some major American cities, public defenders carry annual caseloads of over 500 cases per attorney (Bazelon 1973:6). Some offices have inadequate investigators, social workers, and support staff (Bazelon 1976:815). Lawyers in such offices have little chance to prepare and investigate their cases. They spend most of their time in court. "[W]itnesses are interviewed only in the corridors of courthouses; legal research is done by flipping through the penal code during recesses; time for reading, consulting, investigating, or making discovery and other motions is scarce; and there is not even adequate opportunity to consult fully with clients" (at 815). The result is that the defendant is likely to be ineffectively represented. The attorney, through no real fault of her own, is unprepared, uninformed, or otherwise ill equipped to establish innocence or even to plea bargain effectively for the client's best interest. "Despite the Criminal Justice Standards and court pronouncements, caseload pressures and insufficient funding have led to widespread failings by defenders of their duty to investigate" (Klein 1986:666).

Judges can be part of the problem faced by the public defender or court-appointed attorney. Consciously or not, judges may look for the "sweetheart" lawyer who will not rock the boat. Judges worried about crowded dockets may not want to see lawyers who make numerous motions or who demand lengthy trials. Judges have the power of appointing counsel, and they can fall into the habit of rewarding quick plea bargained cases. Judges may paper over inadequacy or focus only on the defendant's guilt and not on the attorney's inadequacy (Bazelon 1973:15–16). Thus, new attorneys may be given wrong cues and be encouraged to develop bad habits based on speed instead of effectiveness: Newcomers often learn too quickly how to play the game that will turn over the most cases, thus bringing in the most cash. These new attorneys thus become part of "the 'cop-out-bar' by either the economic necessity of inadequate fee structures or the need to curry favor with plea-hungry judges who have the professional life-and-death power to appoint counsel and fix their compensation" (Bazelon 1976:813).

Defense attorneys resist these problems in a number of ways. Two popular responses are the zone defense and the contract system. Under the zone defense, the attorney is assigned to courtrooms rather than to clients (Klein 1986:676). The client therefore faces a different defense lawyer at each stage of the process. This may be economical for the law office, since it reduces the time an attorney spends shuffling around town, but it is detrimental to the client. No lawyer ever takes full responsibility for her client; therefore, trust in the attorney is diminished and communication with clients greatly impeded (at 677). No meaningful attorney/client relationship is created.

The contract system is equally unsatisfying. Under this approach the county contracts out large numbers of indigent cases, on a flat sum compensation scheme, to the lowest bidder (Klein 1986:679). The attorneys winning the bid must then squeeze the cost of representing those clients into a budget that falls below their bid in order to make a profit. This breeds environments in which cases are dealt with in terms of overhead instead of preparation needed. Lawyers are pressured to dispose of each case as quickly as possible, irrespective of the consequences to the client. Professor Vivian Berger, whose words bear repeating, described it well: "[J]ust who is this professional to whom, because of her vaunted expertise, the system entrusts such responsibility for protecting the ignorant and vulnerable client? Apparently, a presumptive incompetent, an agent all too frequently unfit to discharge her high obligations to her principal" (Berger 1986:11).

One might think that these problems are less prevalent when defendants are on trial for their lives. One would be wrong. Bruce Shapiro calls it the "sleeping lawyer syndrome," and his metaphor is apt. Describing the 1992 Texas capital trial of George McFarland, Shapiro (quoting the *Houston Chronicle*) writes:

> Seated beside his client...defense attorney John Benn spent much of Thursday afternoon's trial in apparent deep sleep.
>
> His mouth kept falling open and his head lolled back on his shoulders, and then he awakened just long enough to catch himself and sit upright. Then it happened again. And again. And again.
>
> Every time he opened his eyes, a different prosecution witness was on the stand describing another aspect of the...arrest of George McFarland in the robbery-killing of grocer Kenneth Kwan.
>
> When state District Judge Doug Shaver finally called a recess, Benn was asked if he truly had fallen asleep during a capital murder trial.

It's boring," the 72–year-old longtime Houston lawyer explained....

Court observers said Been seems to have slept his way through
virtually the entire trial (Shapiro 1997:27–28).

The point isn't that most capital defense lawyers sleep through their clients'
trials. Most don't. The point is that not even a problem as objectively and iden-
tifiably obvious as a sleeping lawyer isn't necessarily enough to invalidate a
death sentence. At least not in Texas. Between April 1996 and April 1997, the
Texas Court of Criminal Appeals has turned down three petitions from condemned inmates whose lawyers "slept through significant portions of their trials" (Shapiro 1997:28). Shapiro quotes Texas District Judge Doug Shaver: "The
Constitution says that everyone's entitled to an attorney of their choice. But
the Constitution does not say that the lawyer has to be awake" (at 27).

Indeed. Even in capital prosecutions many states expect defense lawyers essentially to donate their time (Kamisar 1990:365). Professor Kamisar quotes
Stephen Bright, director of the organization formerly known as the Southern
Prisoner's Defense Committee, as saying: "I know a Mississippi lawyer who has
spent 400 hours working on [a capital trial] and can only get $1,000. I can
make more money pumping gas than working a capital case" (Kamisar
1990:366). This dismal conclusion echoes the findings of other students of the
issue (Robbins 1990). It also reinforces the senior author's own experience as a
capital post-conviction litigator.

No Right to Counsel in *Habeas Corpus* Proceedings, Except When Congress Says There Is

> Yet those who cling to life with stubborn hands,
> Can grin through storms of death and find a gap
> In the clawed, cruel tangles of his defense
>> (Siegfried Sassoon 1917: *Prelude and the Troops*
>> (Craig Lockhart)).

The Landscape Pre-1996 Antiterrorism and Effective Death Penalty Act

What we have today, and will have for the foreseeable future, is the illusion
of counsel at trial and in *habeas*. To see how this came to be so, we will summarize the history of the campaign to use the courts to abolish or limit capital
punishment as a legal system beginning in the early 1960s, when Anthony Amsterdam and LDF were first firing up their campaign to outlaw capital punishment by use of the federal courts.

As capital punishment emerged once again as a reality in America, so did the counsel crisis. For much of the 1980s the situation on the ground was strikingly similar to the world at the time around *Gideon v. Wainwright*. And, as *Gideon* reached the United States Supreme Court from Florida, the modern crisis in counsel also played itself out in the sunshine state.

Think of it as "Simon's Frolic II." As discussed above, the 10-year moratorium on executions in America came about in Florida because maverick ACLU attorney Tobias Simon disregarded LDF's advice and filed a 1967 class action on behalf of all Florida death row inmates, many of whom were illiterate and without counsel. When the national moratorium ended with Gilmore's 1977 execution in Utah and John Spenkellink's 1979 execution in Florida, Simon and his Florida colleagues filed a new class action lawsuit, again against the advice of LDF. Simon filed his class action lawsuit in 1979, at the beginning of the crisis, when only three Florida death warrants had been signed in the post-*Furman* era: two against John Spenkellink and one against Willie Jasper Darden (Mello 1997). The lawsuit, styled *Graham v. State*, was brought as an original proceeding in the Florida Supreme Court on behalf of nine condemned inmates with volunteer or public defender lawyers. The suit sought appointment of counsel for state post-conviction and federal *habeas* corpus proceedings. The actual petitioners were volunteer attorneys who either represented one of the nine condemned men or who had represented John Spenkellink. Five of the nine condemned inmates had previously filed state post-conviction motions, and one had filed a federal *habeas* petition. The petitioners/attorneys had examined the records of the nine condemned men and argued to the court that each record contained issues that had sufficient merit to warrant collateral reviews.

Toby Simon's petition catalogued the legal steps taken by LDF and other volunteers to attempt to prevent the execution of John Spenkellink. The petition specified that LDF was unable to continue the support it had provided during the Spenkellink litigation and discussed other possible sources of lawyers. As to volunteer counsel, the petition said:

> The petitioners herein represent the bulk of Florida attorneys willing to volunteer time and expertise to secure collateral review in death cases. The volunteer attorneys have learned, as a result of the Spenkellink/Darden experience, that a single lawyer is wholly insufficient in a death case. Additionally, because of Spenkellink and Darden, the volunteers are exhausted and their funds depleted. In short, volunteers are incapable of seeking the collateral review required to be sought on behalf of the condemned. It is unfair and unreliable that condemned persons must rely upon representation by unpaid volunteer attorneys (Mello 1997:183).

The petition gave two reasons why public defenders could not assume responsibility for such representation. First, the public defenders' authority to represent inmates in federal courts was questionable. Second, "the public defenders are simply not equipped to expend the effort and resources that the Spenkellink execution proved mandatory. Neither the budget nor the staff of the public defenders' offices are adequate to handle such cases" (Mello 1997:183).

The petition was based solely upon the due process clause of the Fourteenth Amendment. No claim based on the Eighth Amendment or on the state constitution was advanced. The Florida Supreme Court denied the petition, holding that "no court has determined that there is a constitutional right to the assistance of counsel to aid in the preparation of a petition for post-conviction relief" (*Graham v. State* 1979:1364). The court appeared to deny the existence of a counsel problem in Florida, noting that the petitioners in *Graham* were all persons who, in the court's view, had had considerable judicial attention given to their cases.

The court did seem to recognize that counsel ought to be appointed generously: "The adversary nature of the proceeding, its complexity, the need for an evidentiary hearing, or the need for substantial legal research are all important elements which may require the appointment of counsel" (at 1366). Nevertheless, the court reiterated that the State of Florida has no obligation to provide counsel or pay the costs of federal proceedings.

The court analyzed in more detail the need to provide counsel for state post-conviction proceedings. The court explained that Florida had been progressive on the right to counsel issue ever since *Gideon v. Wainwright*, noting that the state had established a public defender system within weeks of that decision, as well as comprehensive post-conviction relief procedures. Given that the state also supplied counsel in post-conviction proceedings once a defendant was able to make a prima facie case for relief, the court concluded that "there is no constitutional requirement for the appointment of individual counsel for an application for post-conviction relief until a colorable or justiciable issue or meritorious grievance…appears in the appellant's petition" (at 1366).

The second attempt to secure a system wide solution to the then-growing counsel crisis in Florida occurred in 1982. Timothy Palmes, a condemned inmate facing impending execution, sought a stay of execution and appointment of counsel based on the decision in *Hooks v. Wainwright* (1982a). The federal district court in *Hooks* had entered an order finding that the Florida Department of Corrections was denying inmates the constitutionally guaranteed right of meaningful access to the courts. The court found that to satisfy the inmates' right to access, Florida must provide a plan that would give indigent inmates access to attorneys for the purpose of representing and advising them in state and federal judicial proceedings attacking their convictions and sentences. At the time Palmes filed his action, all proceedings in *Hooks* had been stayed pending appeal. Palmes was a member of the *Hooks* class, and his motions for stay of execution and appointment of counsel were brought as part of the *Hooks* litigation.

Palmes' case was an appropriate vehicle to raise the constitutional implications of Florida's counsel crisis: He was facing an imminent execution date and he had no lawyer (Mello 1997:184). On May 18, 1982, the clemency attorneys representing Palmes and Ronald Straight, Palmes' co-defendant, telephoned the Florida Clearinghouse on Criminal Justice and left messages for Scharlette Holdman, the clearinghouse's director. Before Holdman could return their phone calls, Mrs. Anna Palmes, Timothy Palmes' mother, telephoned the Clearinghouse to tell Holdman that she had learned that the governor had signed death warrants against her son, Timothy, and Ronald Straight, and that they were to be executed on June 15. Holdman told her not to worry, because Palmes' clemency attorney had assured Holdman that he would represent Palmes in post-conviction proceedings and in obtaining a stay of execution so that those proceedings could go forward.

By the next day, Holdman had talked with the clemency attorneys. Both told her that they would not represent Palmes or Straight, and that Holdman should try to find other volunteer counsel. She asked both attorneys to help find counsel for these men.

Holdman immediately began telephoning members of the private bar, asking them to consider representing either Palmes or Straight, and asking for names of other attorneys whom she might contact to ask for assistance. During the next week, she spoke with 40 attorneys and explained the dire need for *pro bono* help for these two men who faced imminent execution with no counsel. She explained that neither prisoner had been represented in any state post-conviction or federal collateral proceeding and that, given their own educational backgrounds and abilities and the conditions of confinement at Florida State Prison, it was virtually impossible for them to represent themselves. She also explained that no state-funded agency provided counsel to death-sentenced prisoners after the Florida Supreme Court affirmed their convictions and sentences on direct appeal. She explained that these two prisoners, like others on death row, were entirely dependent on the private bar to provide representation as part of their *pro bono* obligation, and that there were no guaranteed financial resources, either state or private, to offset the substantial out-of-pocket expenses related to the cases.

Several of the attorneys agreed to consider representing one of the two prisoners if their law firms agreed. Only one attorney, Raymond Makowski, agreed to represent either prisoner. Makowski agreed to represent Ronald Straight.

Attorneys frequently gave Holdman the same reasons for not representing either Palmes or Straight:

1. Inexperience with the prevailing law. Some criminal defense attorneys felt they did not have sufficient experience in capital law and habeas litigation to allow them to research and review relevant state and federal law; review the transcripts; interview the client, his prior counsel, co-defendants, and other relevant people; and investigate and prepare the

pleadings necessary to obtain the stay of execution in the time available before the execution.

2. Financial costs. Some attorneys did not have the financial resources to cover out-of-pocket expenses such as printing, travel, telephone, and express mail, all necessary for investigation and consultation with the inmate, his prior counsel, potential witnesses, and potential experts.

3. Scheduling. Several attorneys expressed deep concern and said they wished they could offer their services. But their immediate calendar and commitments to fee-paying clients precluded their representing these two men on such short notice when it was apparent that a tremendous amount of time would have to be spent reviewing the record, interviewing the client, researching the law, investigating the merits of possible claims, and preparing the multiple pleadings that would have to be filed in several courts.

4. Conflicts. Some attorneys had been employed by the state prosecutor's office at the time the cases were prosecuted and thus had a conflict of interest. Others had represented one of the co-defendants who received immunity in exchange for testifying for the state. Others had personal relationships with the victim's family (Mello 1997:185).

Two lawyers eventually agreed to represent Palmes in his efforts to secure counsel. These lawyers refused, however, to represent Palmes in his underlying challenges to his conviction and sentence. The lawsuit seeking counsel (and stay of Palmes' execution) was brought as part of the ongoing *Hooks* litigation.

The district court eventually granted a stay but denied Palmes' claim under *Hooks*. The court treated Palmes as moving through his attorneys and noted that "it was certainly somewhat incongruous that a person claiming he is unable to obtain the assistance of counsel is currently represented by at least two able attorneys" (*Hooks v. Wainwright* 1982b:654, n.1). This view clearly influenced the court's reasoning in rejecting Palmes' claims:

> Accompanying his motion is a well-orchestrated array of affidavits intended to show that all efforts to secure counsel to represent him have been unsuccessful. The affidavits include veiled pleas for judicial assistance on behalf of various organizations devoted to representing defendants convicted of capital crimes. The content of these affidavits reflects a broader purpose than merely securing the assistance of counsel for Timothy Palmes. They are replete with general information as to the burgeoning number of capital cases and the inability of the organizations to obtain adequate funds to cover even the expenses of volunteer attorneys (at 654).

The motion and attached affidavits are "well-intentioned but, unfortunately, misdirected" (at 654). The court held that it lacked jurisdiction to issue a stay of execution absent a pending *habeas* petition. It reasoned that particularly during "these times of growing friction and disagreement concerning the proper working relationship between the state and federal courts," federal courts ought to operate only through "prescribed mechanisms," such as *habeas* corpus proceedings (at 655).

The court was careful to stress that it was in no way adjudicating the merits of Palmes' claim that he was entitled to counsel. The court recognized that its opinion in *Hooks* was "certainly relevant" to Palmes' claim and found the idea that a person might be executed without the benefit of some form of attorney-assistance to aid him in pursuing remedies prescribed by law "repugnant to the spirit, if not the letter, of the federal Constitution" (at 656). In addition, the court found it difficult to discern how a person confined to death row could be afforded meaningful access to the courts without the benefit of some professional legal assistance.

The court put the burden right back where it always had been: on the backs of the volunteer lawyers. "Fortunately," the court wrote with a wink to reality, "at least in the past, there have been adequate numbers of qualified volunteer attorneys to represent capital defendants in post-conviction proceedings" (at 656). The court "trusted" that Palmes' present counsel would continue to represent him until a *habeas* petition had been filed, which most likely also meant until exhaustion could be completed, at which time a determination of appointment of counsel would be appropriate.

Eventually, Thomas McCoun, who had represented Anthony Antone, volunteered to represent Palmes. He did so throughout two rounds of state and federal post-conviction proceedings. Palmes was executed in 1984, two years before his co-defendant, Ronald Straight.

Despite the outcome of the *Palmes/Hooks* litigation, change was in the air. In 1982, the ABA approved a resolution calling for the appointment of counsel for capital post-conviction litigation in state and federal court. In January 1984, the Florida State-Federal Judicial Council, led by Eleventh Circuit Chief Judge John Godbold, squarely addressed the counsel problem. Concluding that the basic problem with the capital post-conviction process was the inadequate number of volunteer lawyers, the Council passed a unanimous resolution to ask the Florida bar to create a mechanism within the bar to recruit private counsel in this area. In May 1984, in response to this request, the Florida bar appointed a Special Committee on Representation of Death Sentenced Inmates in Collateral Proceedings. The Committee consisted of 15 lawyers representing 15 of the largest civil law firms in the state.

The Committee first met in June 1984, and developed a plan of action centering on the recruitment of volunteer attorneys, particularly from large civil law firms in Florida. The idea behind tapping the resources of civil law firms was twofold. First, the small pool of criminal defense attorneys able and willing to handle collateral proceedings in capital cases had been exhausted. Second, large civil law firms were in a better position, relative to small firms or sole practitioners, to absorb the huge expenditures of time and money required by such litigation. To provide advice and guidance, Florida would create a volunteer lawyers resource center located at Florida State University Law School.

But it was too little too late. The center and it's brilliant director, Mark Olive, were soon swamped with cases. In spring 1985, the Florida legislature created a statewide public defender office, the Office of the Capital Collateral Representative ("CCR") to provide post-conviction legal aid for Florida's death row. With Olive as litigation director and Holdman as chief investigator, CCR was the best office of its kind in the nation. But when CCR's director, Larry Spalding, fired Holdman, knowing Olive would be compelled to resign in protest, the quality of CCR's representation began a slow decline until, by 1995, the agency was but a shadow of the original office. CCR complained it was overloaded with cases; at least one observer concluded that CCR's "overload" claims could not be substantiated (Mello 1997).

By February 1997, most observers had concluded that the CCR experiment had been a failure. On February 13, 1997, a commission created to study CCR concluded that the agency should be abolished and replaced with a model that works. A prime impetus for the commission's formation was a class action civil rights lawsuit—"Simon's Frolic III," if you will—challenging the applicability of the opt-in provisions of the 1996 Antiterrorism and Effective Death Penalty Act. CCR argued that the agency could not provide the quality of state post-conviction counsel required by the 1996 Act (discussed below). The federal district court agreed (*Hill v. Butterworth* 1996; *Florida Flunks Death Counsel Test* 1996), and on January 16, 1997, certified the class. Three weeks after the district court's decision giving class-wide treatment pursuant to CCR's claim that the agency itself was indeed incompetent, the special commission released its report recommending that CCR be abolished (Poynter 1995; Judd, Jan. 1, 1997; Poynter 1997; Letter 1997; Judd, March 1, 1997).

And Florida isn't the only capital punishment state with a counsel crisis. The ABA's 1997 resolution calling for a national moratorium on executions was based on the lack of adequate legal aid in capital trials and beyond (Resolution 1997; Podgers 1997:26). States with the death penalty must decide whether condemned inmates wishing to pursue post-conviction remedies should be provided lawyers at the states' expense. This aspect of capital punishment was masked during the de facto moratorium on executions between 1967 and 1977, and by the slow resumption of executions in the late 1970s and 1980s. But as capital punishment becomes a genuinely national phenomenological reality, and as executions resume in earnest, the counsel question takes on increasing urgency. It is an urgency with two quite different aspects. The state must decide whether to give condemned people lawyers. And lawyers must decide whether they can, and should, do this work.

Texas is experiencing a post-conviction counsel crisis of escalating magnitude caused by the shrinking pool of volunteer lawyers and the accelerated scheduling of execution dates for unrepresented death row inmates. Roughly 125 of Texas's death row prisoners remained lawyerless as of May 1996. In a situation eerily reminiscent of Florida in the mid-1980s, almost all the lawyers in Texas capital post-conviction proceedings are volunteers. In Texas, the extraordinary numbers of post-appeal execution orders, accelerated post-conviction litigation schedules, and decreasing numbers of volunteer attorneys effectively nullify the state post-conviction process for many death-sentenced prisoners. These problems are magnified when execution dates have been set. To stay the execution, counsel must master a substantial record and a complex area of law, while simultaneously litigating both the merits and the stay request in federal and state forums, often before more than one court in each. This sometimes involves a literal race from court to court to meet deadlines (Mello 1997:133 (collecting sources)).

As of January 1996, Pennsylvania had 187 inmates on its death row, of whom 100 to 125 have no post-conviction lawyers. Nine months earlier, a state supreme court justice, speaking before the Philadelphia Bar Association Criminal Justice Section, estimated that 57 of the 187 are "probably" underrepresented, and 130 of them may or may not have completed their full appeals. A Pittsburgh School of Law professor said, "There are about 190 people on death row right now, and almost none are represented after the direct appeal stage" (Mello 1997:134–135). Of the 401 inmates on California's death row as of May 1995, 108 (27 percent) were without counsel (Mello 1997:135).

Nationally, hundreds more are already in the post-conviction process, and many more will be there soon. Virtually all of these inmates are indigent and cannot afford to hire lawyers. The ABA has estimated that 99 percent of death row prisoners are poor; because many of them can neither read nor write, it is virtually impossible for them effectively to investigate and to file meaningful petitions and otherwise pursue remedies in the post-conviction process. As Steve Bright testified before Amnesty International's Commission of Inquiry into the Death Penalty, poverty is a

> ... crucial factor that determines who receives the death penalty. The major consequence of poverty for those facing the death penalty is having a court-appointed lawyer. Just having a judge who may have made his way from district attorney to judge by discriminating, by seeking and using the death penalty as a political tool, and who is now the person who appoints the lawyer for the poor person accused of a death-eligible crime. Poor people accused of crimes do not pick their lawyers. They are stuck with their lawyers. But any mistake the lawyer makes is held against the person accused, not against the lawyer (Bright 1995:124–125).

The World According to Congress:
The 1996 Antiterrorism and Effective Death Penalty Act

Into the capital *habeas* counsel crisis described above rode Congress and President Bill Clinton. The result of their intervention was the 1996 Antiterrorism and Effective Death Penalty Act (AEDPA).

The direct, linear history of the counsel dimensions of the 1996 AEDPA actually begins in 1988. Congress enacted and President Bush signed a bill authorizing capital punishment for drug "kingpins" (Liebman and Hertz 1994). A little-noticed provision of the 1988 Act authorized the federal courts to appoint counsel for death row prisoners in *habeas* corpus proceedings and in advance of the actual filing of a *habeas* petition. The Supreme Court held that the 1988 Act meant exactly that. When the Texas counsel crisis reached the Court in *McFarland v. Scott* (1994), the Court upheld the counsel provisions of the 1988 Act.

The 1988 Act only solved one part of the counsel conundrum, however: It provided lawyers for capital prisoners in federal *habeas* court. It didn't provide counsel for state *habeas*. Completion of state *habeas* was a necessary precondition to seeking federal *habeas*. Congress addressed the question of state post-conviction counsel in the 1996 AEDP Act.

The AEDPA's intent was to "streamline" capital *habeas*, to "curb the abuse of the statutory writ of *habeas corpus*" by lawyers for death row prisoners and to "address the 'acute problems of unnecessary delay and abuse in capital cases' by death row and its lawyers" (Liebman and Hertz 1996 Supp.:§ 2.7a, p. 10). Among other reforms, the Act sets a one-year limitation period on application for the *habeas* writ, time limits within which the federal district court must act on *habeas* petitions, limits the issues properly brought in a *habeas* petition, and sharply limits prisoners' ability to receive meaningful federal judicial review of successive *habeas* petitions.

However, there is a catch, and the catch concerns counsel. For states to receive the benefits of these restrictions on the availability of *habeas*, those states must first "opt in" to the new *habeas* regime by

> ...establishing, in a statutorily specified way, "a mechanism for the appointment and compensation and reimbursement of [state post-conviction] counsel" that satisfies certain statutory standards. In essence, that is, states that "opt in" receive certain advantages in the way of restricted federal *habeas* corpus review of their capital prisoners as a *quid pro quo* for their having provided the affected capital prisoners with certain procedural advantages during state post-conviction [sic] proceedings" (Liebman and Hertz 1996 Supp.: § 2.7a, p. 15).

Thus, for example, for Texas to obtain the procedural goodies of restricted *habeas* review for its death row prisoners, Texas must "opt in" by providing those prisoners with counsel in the state post-conviction process. Texas gets to kill them faster, but only by giving them lawyers first.

To qualify for the opt-in provisions, a state must establish a system to provide post-conviction counsel for death row prisoners. The state must "create a mechanism for the appointment, compensation, and payment of reasonable litigation expenses of competent counsel in state post-conviction proceedings brought by indigent prisoners whose capital convictions and sentences have been upheld on direct appeal" (Liebman and Hertz 1996 Supp.:§2.7c, p. 31, quoting Act) by the state's highest court. In addition, the state must "provide standards of competency for the appointment of such counsel"(at §2.7c, p. 31). As of this writing, no state had been held to qualify for opt-in status.

The 1996 Act creates the possibility that competent and reasonably well-funded post-conviction legal aid will be provided to capital prisoners. However, it is difficult to be optimistic. Ultimately, the same U.S. Supreme Court that decided and enforces *Strickland v. Washington* will do to the 1996 Act what it did to *Gideon v. Wainwright*: recognize a formalistic "right to counsel," but allow the states to administer that "right" however they like, with virtually no federal judicial oversight of how meaningful the "right" is in the real world, day-to-day reality of capital post-conviction litigation. The Rehnquist Court will gut the 1996 Act's counsel requirements as it gutted *Gideon* in *Strickland v. Washington*.

After all, as the Rehnquist Court has put it, the trial is the "main event." All the "counsel" to which one is entitled at that main event is set out in *Strickland v. Washington*. It's hard to imagine that a court that gives so little to capital defendants at the main event would give them anything *more* than that in the sideshow of post-conviction review. Thus, when you're on trial for your life, *Strickland v. Washington* is all you get at trial and, at the most, all you get in capital post-conviction as well. In either arena, it's not much.

Conclusion: Fighting for the Light

> Do not go gentle into that good night;
> Old age should burn and rage at close of day;
> Rage, rage against the dying of the light
>
> Dylan Thomas (1951)

Before *Gideon* in 1963, there was no constitutional right to court-appointed counsel in non-capital felony trials except when due process required in cases presenting "special circumstances." After *Gideon* there was a right to counsel in capital and non-capital felony trials, but the cases following *Gideon* have made increasingly clear that the "right to counsel" doesn't mean the right to an attorney who is any good. In the early 1960s, death row prisoners had no right to counsel in *habeas*, but, as a practical matter, LDF and other groups usually managed to find the necessary lawyers. Today, as in Florida in 1966 and 1967, large numbers of condemned inmates have no lawyers.

There is one difference between then and now. In the 1960s, a death row prisoner with a *habeas* lawyer meant he likely wouldn't be executed. Today, even having a good *habeas* lawyer won't likely save him. But that is for another book.

Sources

Several landmark court cases discussed in this chapter have been the subject of some of the best books ever written on the anatomy of judicial decision-making. On *Gideon v. Wainwright* and *Betts v. Brady*, there is Anthony Lewis' *Gideon's Trumpet*. On *Furman v. Georgia* and the campaign by Anthony Amsterdam and the NAACP Legal Defense and Educational Fund, Inc., to outlaw capital punishment there are Burton Wolfe's *Pileup on Death Row* (1973), Michael Meltsner's *Cruel and Unusual* (1973), and Herbert Haines' *Against Capital Punishment* (1996). On the infamous Scottsboro case, there is an extensive and excellent literature, including James Goodman's *Stories of Scottsboro* (1994) and Dan Carter's *Scottsboro* (1969). And on the Arkansas riot case there is Richard Cortner's *A Mob Intent on Death* (1988).

References

ABA (1977) "Just How Good (or Bad) are Federal Trial Lawyers?" *ABA Journal* 63:1525, 1540–1543.

Acker, J.R. and C.S. Lanier (2003) "Beyond Human Ability?" The Rise and Fall of Death Penalty Legislation." (This volume).

Allen, F. (1958) "The Supreme Court and State Criminal Justice." *Wayne Law Review* 4:191–204.

Antiterrorism and Effective Death Penalty Act (1996) Pub.L.104-138, 110 Stat. 1214.

Bahl, M. (1991) "The Sixth Amendment Right to Counsel Under the Massiah Line of Cases." *Journal of Criminal Law and Criminology* 82:423–463.

Bazelon, D. (1976) "The Realities of Gideon and Argersinger." *Georgia Law Journal* 64:811–838.

Bazelon, D. (1973) "The Defective Assistance of Counsel." *University of Cincinnati Law Review* 64:1–46.

Berger, V. (1990–1991) "The Chiropractor as Brain Surgeon." *New York University Review of Law and Social Change* 18:245–254.

Berger, V. (1986) "The Supreme Court and Defense Counsel." *Columbia Law Review* 86:9–116.

Betts v. Brady (1942) 316 U.S. 455.

Bright, S.B. and P.J. Keenan (1996) "Judges and the Politics of Death." *Boston University Law Review* 75:759–835.

Bright, S.B. (1995) "Race, Poverty and Disadvantage in the Infliction of the Death Penalty in the Death Belt." In Amnesty International (ed.), *The Machinery of Death*. New York: Amnesty International.

Bright, S.B. (1994) "Counsel for the Poor." *Yale Law Journal* 103:1831–1883.

Brown v. Allen (1953) 344 U.S. 443.

Brown v. Board of Education (1954) 347 U.S. 483.

Burger, W.E. (1980) "Some Further Reflections on the Problem of Adequacy of Trial Counsel." *Fordham Law Review* 49:1–25.

Burger, W.E. (1977) "The Special Skills of Advocacy." *Journal of Contemporary Law* 3:163–176.

Camus, A. (1946) *L'Etranger* in M. Ward (Trans.) (1989) *The Stranger*. New York: Knopf.

Carter, D.T. (1969) *Scottsboro: Tragedy of the American South*. Baton Rouge: Louisiana State University Press.

Cortner, R.C. (1988) *A Mob Intent on Death: The NAACP and the Arkansas Riot Cases*. Middletown, CT: Wesleyan University Press.

Fay v. Noia (1963) 372 U.S. 391.

"Florida Flunks Death Counsel Test." (September 30, 1996) *National Law Journal*:A16.

Frank v. Mangum (1915) 237 U.S. 309.

Geimer, W. (1995) "A Decade of Strickland's Tin Horn." *William and Mary Bill of Rights Journal* 4:91–178.

Gideon v. Wainwright (1963) 372 U.S. 335.

Goodman, J. (1994) *Stories of Scottsboro*. New York: Pantheon Books.

Graham v. State (1979) 372 So.2d 1363 (Fla.).

Haines, H.H. (1996) *Against Capital Punishment: The Anti-Death Penalty Movement in America, 1972–1994*. New York: Oxford University Press.

Hamilton v. Alabama (1961) 368 U.S. 52.

Hazo, S. (1997) *The Face of Evil in Our Time*. (Unpublished manuscript).

Hill v. Butterworth (1996) 941 F.Supp. 1129 (N.D. Fla.).

Hooks v. Wainwright (1982a) 536 F.Supp. 1330 (M.D. Fla.).

Hooks v. Wainwright (1982b) 540 F.Supp. 652 (M.D. Fla.).

Hughes, L. (1932) *The Town of Scottsboro*, reprinted in A. Rampersad and D. Roessel (eds.) (1994) *The Collected Poems of Langston Hughes*. New York: Knopf.

Hurtado v. California (1884) 110 U.S. 516.

Judd, (March 1, 1997) "Proposals Would Replace CCR With Regional Office." *Florida Bar News*:10.

Judd, (January 1, 1997) "CCR Faces Legislative Battle." *Florida Bar News*:1.

Kamisar, Y. (1990) "Gideon v. Wainwright: A Quarter-Century Later." *Pace Law Review* 10:343–378.

Klein, R. (1986) "The Emperor Gideon Has No Clothes." *Hastings Constitutional Law Quarterly* 13:625–694.

Letter from McDonald Commission for the Review of Post-conviction Representation to Gov. Lawton Chiles, Sen. Pres. Toni Jennings and Speaker of the House Daniel Webster, Feb. 13, 1997.

Levine, B. (1984) "Preventing Defense Counsel Error." *University of Toledo Law Review* 15:1275–1455.

Lewis, A. (1964) *Gideon's Trumpet*. New York: Random House.

Liebman, J., and R. Hertz (1994) *Federal Habeas Corpus Practice and Procedure.* Charlottesville: Michie Co.

Maddi, D.L. (1978) "Trial Advocacy Competence: The Judicial Perspective." *American Bar Foundation Research Journal.* 1978:105–151.

McFarland v. Scott (1994) 512 U.S. 849.

Mello, M. (1997) *Dead Wrong.* Madison: Wisconsin University Press.

Meltsner, M. (1973) *Cruel and Unusual Punishment.* New York: Random House.

Moore v. Dempsey (1923) 261 U.S. 86.

Note (1989) "The Right to Counsel Clause As Constitutional Theory." *American Criminal Law Review* 26:1599–1616.

Note (1994) "Ineffective Assistance of Counsel." *Harvard Law Review* 107:1923–1940.

Owen, W. (1917) Letter to Mrs. Owen March 23, 1917, reprinted in D. Day Lewis (ed.) *The Collected Poems of Wilfred Owen.* New York: New Directions (1983).

Partridge, A. and G. Bermant (1978) *The Quality of Advocacy in the Federal Courts.* Washington: Federal Judicial Center.

Podgers, J. (April, 1997) "Time Out for Executions." *ABA Journal.* 83:26.

Powell v. Alabama (1932) 287 U.S. 45 (1932).

Poynter (January 5, 1997) "Legislature Set to Judge Death Row Appeals Unit." *Tallahassee Democrat:*1A.

Poynter (December 15, 1995) "Justice Delayed?" *Tallahassee Democrat:*1A.

Rawls (March 8, 1982) "After 69 Years, Lynching Victim is Cleared." *New York Times.*

Resolution and Reports, ABA House of Delegates (San Antonio, Texas Feb. 3, 1997).

Robbins, I. (1990) "Toward a More Just and Effective System of Review in State Death Penalty Cases." *American University Law Review* 40:1–296.

Sassoon, S. (1926) *A Footnote on the War,* reprinted in R. Hart-Davis (ed.) (1983) *Siegfried Sassoon: The War Poems.* London: Faber and Faber.

Shapiro, B. (April 7, 1997) "The Sleeping Lawyer Syndrome." *The Nation:*27.

Steiker, C.S. and J.M. Steiker (2003) "Judicial Developments in Capital Punishment Law." (This volume.)

Strickland v. Washington (1984) 466 U.S. 668.

Tomkins v. Missouri (1945) 323 U.S. 485.

Von Drehle, D. (1997) Foreword in M. Mello, *Dead Wrong.* Madison: University of Wisconsin Press.

Von Drehle, D. (1995) *Among the Lowest of the Dead.* New York: Random House.

Washington v. Strickland (1982) 593 F.2d 1243 (5th Cir.).

Williams v. Kaiser (1945) 323 U.S. 471.

Wolfe, B.M. (1973) *Pileup on Death Row.* Garden City, NY: Doubleday.

Chapter 13

Stacking the Deck for Guilt and Death: The Failure of Death Qualification to Ensure Impartiality

Marla Sandys
Scott McClelland

Jurors are faced with the enormous responsibility of deciding whether a defendant deserves to live or die. Who are these people selected to make this life or death decision? How are they selected? Is the process fair? Are their decisions rendered in accordance with the law? These are the questions that guide this chapter; the answers help to evaluate the success or failure of this country's 30-year experiment with capital punishment.

The Uniqueness of Capital Juries

The modern era of capital punishment is replete with U.S. Supreme Court cases pointing to the jury as both the problem and the solution to alleged arbitrariness in capital sentencing. Capital juries have been the focus of so much attention (in the law) because they are charged with deciding not only whether the defendant is guilty, as is the norm in non-capital cases, but also the sentence to be imposed on defendants they find guilty of a capital offense. Until recently, judges either acting alone (in five states—Arizona, Colorado, Idaho, Montana, and Nebraska) or based on the recommendation from a jury (in four states—Alabama, Delaware, Florida, and Indiana) also were responsible for making sentencing decisions in capital cases; *Ring v. Arizona* (2002) changed that. Although it is too early to know all of the implications of the Court's decision, *Ring* makes it clear that jurors, not judges, must decide the essential facts that determine whether a person convicted of a capital crime will live or die.

The role that capital juries play in sentencing decisions is importantly shaped by an additional distinctive characteristic: jurors must be death-qualified[1] prior to being found suitable to serve on a capital case. In its most generic form, being death-qualified means that a person must be able to abide by the rules that govern jurors in capital cases. In reality, however, the only rules that are unique to capital jurors concern the decision of whether to sentence a defendant to death or a lesser punishment. Consequently, the procedures employed to determine death-qualification status are targeted to a prospective juror's ability to vote for a sentence of death.

The U.S. Supreme Court's Battle with Death-Qualification

In all jury trials, prospective jurors are questioned, through the process known as voir dire, to ascertain whether they will be impartial triers of fact. Those prospective jurors whose responses intimate that they could not be impartial are/should be challenged for cause: one of the attorneys asks the judge to excuse the prospective juror because of his or her inability to be impartial. The judge, at his or her discretion, decides whether to grant the challenge and thus excuse the prospective juror, or to deny the challenge and let the person remain in the pool of eligible jurors. For instance, if a prospective juror knows the victim, the defense attorney is likely to challenge that person for cause, alleging that the prospective juror's ability to evaluate the evidence objectively would be compromised. In capital cases, prospective jurors' death-qualification status also serves as the basis for a challenge for cause: an attorney will challenge for cause any prospective juror he or she believes would not follow the law in determining the appropriate sentence. The decision as to whether a juror is death-qualified or successfully challenged for cause resides with the trial judge. Challenges for cause are unlimited in number because the Sixth Amendment requires that defendants be tried by an impartial jury. Prospective jurors who survive this stage of voir dire, who are not successfully challenged for cause, are considered impartial and thus qualified jurors. From this group, attorneys have the opportunity to winnow out those potential jurors who, although considered impartial by the judge, the attorneys feel may be biased against them. These exclusions are accomplished through peremptory challenges, which are limited in number and do not require the approval of a

---

1. The term death-qualification initially referred to the general requirements determining whether jurors were qualified to serve on a death penalty case. The term also came to encompass the fact that prospective capital jurors used to be asked about only their views on the death penalty, not the alternative punishments. Life-qualification, in contrast, is a newer concept, one designed specifically to address prospective jurors' ability to vote for a life sentence, or any sentence less than death.

judge: the only recognized exceptions to attorneys' freedom to use a peremptory challenge to remove a juror are that the strike of the juror cannot be based on race (*Batson v. Kentucky* 1986; *Georgia v. McCollum* 1992) or gender (*J.E.B. v. Alabama* 1994).

Consistent with its determination that " 'the penalty of death is qualitatively different' from any other sentence" (*Lockett v. Ohio* 1978:604, quoting *Woodson v. North Carolina* 1976), the U.S. Supreme Court has set the minimum standards that capital jurors mut satisfy. In recent years, there have been three such standards—pre*Witherspoon*, *Witherspoon*, and *Witt*. The importance of these standards cannot be overstated because they determine who is eligible to serve as a capital juror.

The first standard, pre*Witherspoon*, asked prospective jurors whether they had any "conscientious scruples against the death penalty." Any person who answered in the affirmative was excused from serving in a capital case. The result, of course, was that opponents of capital punishment were precluded from serving as jurors in cases where the death penalty was an option. Prospective jurors found death-qualified under the pre*Witherspoon* test might be expected overwhelmingly to be proponents of capital punishment and thus differ in significant ways from those excluded from service due to their opposition to capital punishment. This was the exact issue the U.S. Supreme Court confronted in *Witherspoon v. Illinois* (1968).

Witherspoon v. Illinois

The Illinois statute in existence at the time of Witherspoon's trial recognized "a cause for challenge of any juror who shall, on being examined, state that he has conscientious scruples against capital punishment, or that he is opposed to the same" (*Witherspoon v. Illinois* 1968:512). Hence, Witherspoon was tried, convicted, and sentenced to death by a jury comprised solely of proponents of capital punishment. When his case was reviewed by the U.S. Supreme Court, Witherspoon argued that:

> ...such a jury...must necessarily be biased in favor of conviction, for the kind of juror who would be unperturbed by the prospect of sending a man to his death...is the kind of juror who would too readily ignore the presumption of the defendant's innocence, accept the prosecution's version of the facts and return a verdict of guilt (at 516).

Witherspoon presented the Court with three unpublished studies that supported his contention of conviction-proneness among death-qualified jurors. The Court was not persuaded, referring to the studies as "too tentative and fragmentary to establish that jurors not opposed to the death penalty tend to favor the prosecution in the determination of guilt" (*Witherspoon v. Illinois* 1968:517). However, the Court did decide, without benefit of any empirical evidence, that a jury so selected resulted in "a tribunal organized to return a verdict of death" (at 521) and declared this consequence of the Illinois statute to be unconstitutional. The Court did not find that any of the individual jurors who decided Witherspoon's case were partial, or improperly seated on the jury. Rather, the resultant *jury* violated the Sixth and Fourteenth Amendments because its members were not drawn from the entire spectrum of viewpoints that existed in the community: opponents of capital punishment who could nonetheless obey the law were systematically excluded from serving on the case. Consequently, the Court established a new death-qualification standard, finding it constitutional for:

> ...the State to execute a defendant sentenced to death by a jury from which the only veniremen excluded for cause were those who made unmistakably clear (1) that they would *automatically* vote against the imposition of capital punishment without regard to any evidence that might be developed at the trial before them, or (2) that their attitude toward the death penalty would prevent them from making an impartial decision as to the defendant's guilt (at 522, n. 21, emphasis in original).

Hence, a prospective juror's mere opposition to, or conscientious scruples against the death penalty no longer would support a successful challenge for cause. Prospective jurors would now have to make it "unmistakably clear" that they would "automatically vote against" the death penalty before they could be excluded for cause. Thus, a much smaller group of individuals with reservations against capital punishment would be excluded under this test than under the pre*Witherspoon* standard.

The *Witherspoon* opinion was important in another respect, in addition to changing the death-qualification standard. Although the Justices rejected Witherspoon's contention of conviction-proneness, they did so "[i]n light of the presently available information" (*Witherspoon v. Illinois* 1968:518). The majority opinion, in effect, invited further investigation into the relationship between death qualification and conviction-proneness when it stated that another capital defendant "might still attempt to establish that the jury was less than neutral with respect to guilt" (at 520, n.18). Social scientists obliged the Court with increasingly rigorous studies, the results of which are discussed below.

Wainwright v. Witt (1985)

The U.S. Supreme Court next addressed the appropriate standard for excluding prospective jurors from serving on capital cases in *Wainwright v. Witt* (1985). In a curious fashion, the majority opinion in *Witt* articulated a new standard for death-qualification that it claimed did not alter the current law (see Thompson 1989):

the proper standard for determining when a prospective juror may be excluded for cause because of his views on capital punishment is whether the juror's view would "prevent or substantially impair the performance of his duties as a juror in accordance with his instructions and his oath" (at 582, quoting *Adams v. Texas* 1980).

Hence, the Court claimed that *Adams*, not *Witherspoon*, had been the operative standard for the previous five years. Thompson (1989) argues persuasively that the Court took this position, at least in part, to avoid having to justify its invalidation of *Witherspoon*. More importantly, however, the *Witt* opinion signified the Court's reluctance to continue evaluating impartiality in terms of the resultant jury rather than the individual jurors selected to serve on the case:

> Here, as elsewhere, the quest is for *jurors* who will conscientiously apply the law and find the facts. That is what an "impartial" *jury* consists of... (*Wainwright v. Witt* 1985:423, emphasis added).

Regardless of the Court's reluctance to acknowledge the change in death-qualification standards, there is no denying that *Witt* differs substantially from *Witherspoon*. In particular, prospective jurors no longer have to make it "unmistakably clear" that they would "automatically" vote against the death penalty before they can be successfully challenged for cause. *Witt* relaxes the standard, thereby increasing the range of prospective jurors who may be dismissed from serving on a capital case. In addition, McNally (1985) argued that *Witt* empowered the defense to challenge for cause extreme proponents of capital punishment whose views would prevent them from performing the duties of a juror. These jurors are known as Automatic Death Penalty (ADPs) voters, or California-excludable jurors (*Hovey v. Superior Court* 1980), because they indicate that they would vote for a sentence of death in every case in which they found the defendant guilty of a capital offense.

Witt also accords judges wide latitude in evaluating challenges for cause. Unlike *Witherspoon*, which required prospective jurors to state explicitly that they would "automatically" vote against the death penalty, *Witt*'s standard is substantially more amorphous (Dillehay and Sandys 1996; Haney, Hurtado, and Vega 1994; Thompson 1989). How impaired does a person's ability to perform the duties of a juror have to be before being ineligible to serve on the case? What constitutes being impaired? The Justices acknowledged the futility of appellate courts attempting to answer these questions, instead preferring to rely on trial court judges' decisions:

> ...many veniremen simply cannot be asked enough questions to reach the point where their bias has been made "unmistakably clear".... Despite this lack of clarity in the printed record, however, there will be situations where the trial judge is left with the definite *impression* that a prospective juror would be unable to

faithfully and impartially apply the law (*Wainwright v. Witt* 1985:424–425, emphasis added).

An obvious effect of this deference to trial judges' impressions is that it becomes increasingly difficult to obtain relief at the appellate level on juror qualification issues. How is it possible to recreate the situation that led to the judge's impression if the "printed record" may be devoid of "clarity"? An additional effect, perhaps desired by the Court, was first predicted by Thompson (1989): *Witt*'s lack of precision would be accompanied by a decline in social science research on the issue. As Dillehay and Sandys (1996) note, this is a reasonable response if the purpose of the research is "to predict the rate of dismissals for cause made by judges" (at 164). However, it is still possible to conduct research, based on *Witt*, that "identifies the prevalence and strength of assessed dispositions as baseline information about juror-eligible citizens" (at 164), which is what they did.

Dillehay and Sandys (1996) interviewed 148 previous jurors who had served on felony cases in Kentucky, which is one of the handful of states in which jurors in non-capital cases render sentencing decisions. The jurors' ADP status was assessed, they were classified as either includable or excludable under *Witt*, and they answered the Capital Juror Role Performance scale to assess their ability to perform the duties of a capital juror. The overall conclusion, based on a variety of comparisons of the general *Witt* question with the more specific task-oriented items, revealed that 36 percent of the respondents would be "misidentified using the *Witt* criterion" (at 159). Clearly, as a general standard, *Witt* fails woefully to determine who could and who could not perform the duties of a juror. Moreover, this finding is based on the jurors' own predictions of their behavior in unknown circumstances, which is a questionable task to begin with. It only stands to reason that judges, who lack the self-knowledge the jurors possess, would be even more ineffectual at predicting who would be substantially impaired by their views about capital punishment.

Additional survey research reveals that the *Witt* standard has not eliminated the previously documented differences between includable and excludable juror-eligible citizens (Gershowitz 1999; Haney, Hurtado, and Vega 1994; Neises and Dillehay 1987). For instance, Haney, Hurtado, and Vega (1994) found significant differences between includables and excludables, whether they were classified by *Witherspoon* or *Witt*, on the 26 issues examined. As expected, excludables (both *Witherspoon* and *Witt*) were less punitive, more concerned with due process, more receptive to mitigation, and less receptive to aggravation than were the includable respondents. This same pattern of findings emerged in a recent study of 450 persons called for jury duty in Miami, Florida. Butler and Moran (2002) assessed *Witt* death-qualification status by asking participants "if they felt so strongly about the death penalty (either for or against it) that their views would prevent or substantially impair the performance of their duties as a juror in a capital case. Participants who answered 'No' to the aforementioned question were classified as death-qualified according to *Witt*; those who answered 'Yes' were classified as excludable" (p. 179). Participants then read a case scenario that spoke to both guilt and penalty issues. In particular, the participants read about aggravating and mitigating circumstances that the state and the defense argued, respectively. The respondents were then asked to indicate their penalty preference and to provide their degree of agreement with the alleged aggravators, statutory mitigators and the non-statutory mitigators.[2] The *Witt* excludables were significantly less likely than the *Witt* death-qualified respondents to endorse a sentence of death. Moreover, the death-qualified respondents were significantly more likely to agree with each of the aggravators while the excludables were significantly more likely to endorse each of the nonstatutory mitigators. Interestingly, there was only one significant difference between death-qualified and excludable respondents in regard to the statutory mitigators: excludable participants were more likely to see the "person suffering from mental/emotional disturbance" as a mitigator.

In short, jurors who decide the guilt/innocence of capital defendants and hence whether these persons will be eligible for the death penalty remain decidedly different from jurors who are allowed to serve on any other kind of case.[3] Moreover, the current death-qualification standard, *Witt*, is so ambiguous that it does little to ensure that capital defendants will be tried by jurors who could in fact perform the duties required of them

Conviction-Proneness Revisited

Hovey v. Superior Court of Alameda County (1980)

In the years following *Witherspoon*, defendants continued to present state and lower federal courts with social science evidence that supported the relationship between being death qualified and conviction-proneness. The courts,

---

2. Statutory mitigators are those factors that are stated explicitly in the law. For example, in Indiana jurors are told that if the defendant has no significant history of prior criminal conduct, the law considers that to be a mitigator. In contrast, a non-statutory mitigator is anything that the juror him or herself considers in support of a sentence of less than death, as is required by *Lockett v. Ohio* (1978). In Indiana, this is accomplished by informing jurors that they can consider any other circumstance, beyond those explicitly presented in the statute, that supports a sentence of less than death.

3. The resultant non-representativeness of this procedure calls into question the reliability of the Supreme Court's reliance on capital jury outcomes as indicative of community standards or popular opinion when evaluating Eighth Amendment claims (*Gregg v. Georgia* 1976).

however, were not receptive, interpreting *Witherspoon*'s evaluation of the then-available evidence—as "too tentative and fragmentary"—as "a judgment on any data that might be presented" (Gross 1984:12). That changed in 1980, in *Hovey v. Superior Court*, wherein the petitioner claimed that:

> prospective jurors, who would automatically vote against death at the *penalty* phase, cannot constitutionally be excused from sitting at the *guilt* phase if they can be fair and impartial *at that phase* (*Hovey* 1980:1308, emphasis in original).

In deciding this issue, the *Hovey* court conducted a thorough, thoughtful analysis of the extant research. Its analysis distinguished between those studies directly related to conviction-proneness (*e.g.*, studies that included some measure of how the participants voted) and general surveys that addressed the constellation of attitudes associated with those specific attitudes toward capital punishment. The *Hovey* court viewed the attitude studies as relevant to the issue of conviction-proneness "since it would reasonably be anticipated that persons who differ on both capital punishment attitudes and voting behavior would also differ with respect to a number of other, related attitudes" (at 1326–1327). The attitude surveys also were viewed as critical to an evaluation of whether exclusion by death qualification "tends to reduce 'the presence of minority viewpoints' on the jury" (*Hovey*:1327, quoting *Ballew v. Georgia* (1980), citations omitted).

The most sophisticated studies presented to the court, not surprisingly, received the most praise in the *Hovey* opinion. For instance, the court devoted considerable attention to the procedures and materials used by Cowan, Thompson, and Ellsworth (1984) to assess conviction-proneness, noting that Professor Hans Zeisel testified during the evidentiary hearing that "[t]here's no way of doing it better" (*Hovey* 1980:1325). Cowan *et al.* presented eligible jurors, who had been previously classified as either death qualified or *Witherspoon* excludables, with a two and one-half hour long videotaped reenactment of a homicide trial. The subjects completed an initial verdict questionnaire, after which they were placed in groups of 12 to deliberate about the case for one hour. They then completed an extensive post-deliberation questionnaire. Consistent with *Hovey*'s claim, Cowan *et al.* found the *Witherspoon* excludables significantly less conviction-prone, on both the pre- and post-deliberation measures, than the death-qualified subjects. For instance, 34.5 percent of the excludable subjects, compared with 13.7 percent of the death-qualified subjects, voted not guilty following deliberation (chi-square (1) = 7.79, $p<.01$). Similarly, the excludable subjects evaluated the prosecution witnesses as both less credible and less helpful, and they saw the prosecutor as less believable than did the death-qualified subjects. Finally, Cowan *et al.* (1984) found that the groups comprised of both excludables and death-qualified subjects were "more critical in their evaluations of the witnesses" (at 75) than were the death-qualified only groups.

The attitude surveys were similarly praised by the *Hovey* court, especially the one conducted by Fitzgerald and Ellsworth (1984). In this study, the subjects' death-qualification status, under both prongs of *Witherspoon*, was assessed, as was their endorsement of a due process or crime control orientation. The interview also included items to assess "respondents' punitiveness, willingness to consider the insanity defense, and feelings about the opposing counsel" (at 41), in addition to information about the demographic characteristics of the respondents. The results consistently point to the detrimental effects of death qualification: 17.2 percent of the 717 fair and impartial jurors were found excludable under *Witherspoon*. Excludables were more likely "to agree that it is better for society to let some guilty defendants go free than to risk convicting an innocent person" (at 42), which reflects a basic premise of our criminal justice system. In addition, death-qualified subjects were more inclined to believe that failure to testify on one's own behalf implies guilt; they were both more trusting of the prosecutor and less trusting of the defense attorney than the excludables; and they were significantly less receptive to evidence in support of an insanity defense. Likewise, the *Witherspoon* death qualified subjects were more inclined than the excludables to see harsh punishment as the answer to crime. In addition, Fitzgerald and Ellsworth (1984) found that death qualification "threatens the representativeness of the jury by disproportionately eliminating certain demographic categories of people" (at 46), including women, African Americans, Democrats, those who are self-employed, Jews, atheists, agnostics, and those with lower family incomes. As these authors conclude: "death qualification systematically distorts the attitudes of the jury in a direction that discriminates against the defendant and undermines the protections of due process" (at 48).

The *Hovey* court was presented with several other studies (*e.g.,* Bronson 1970; Goldberg 1970; Jurow 1971; Zeisel 1968), all except one of which (Osser and Bernstein 1968) supported the petitioner's claim. The court, with commendable sophistication, evaluated the strengths and weaknesses of each of the studies and concluded that most of the Attorney General's "major methodological arguments to attack the conclusions which petitioner would draw from these studies...do not have merit" (*Hovey* 1980:1341). For instance, the Court referred to the State's claim that the studies should be dismissed "because the subjects involved were not representative of the general population" (at 1342), as reflecting "a fundamental misunderstanding of the conclusions sought to be drawn from these studies..." (at 1342). Ultimately, the Court accepted the research findings, noting that "[t]he prosecution has not sought...to adduce evidence that there is no correlation between conviction proneness and attitudes toward capital punishment" (at 1325).

It might be assumed that, at least in California, *Hovey* resulted in a fundamental change in death-qualification practices; one that required distinct qualifications of the jurors for the guilt and sentencing stages of the trial. That would be wrong. Although the Court accepted the conclusion of conviction-proneness among *Witherspoon* death-qualified jurors, none of the studies assessed conviction-proneness among California death-qualified jurors. California, of course, followed the language of *Witherspoon*, but its statute also mandated the exclusion for cause of ADPs, those who would automatically vote *for* the death penalty, without regard for the evidence, upon convicting the defendant of a capital offense. Hovey attempted to persuade the Court that the number of ADP jurors was so small that their exclusion would not significantly affect the established pattern of conviction-proneness. The Court was not moved. It concluded that:

> [t]he lack of reliable evidence on the effect of California's exclusion of "automatic death penalty" jurors from capital cases means petitioner has not made any reliable showing that a pool of "California death-qualified" jurors differs from the pool of jurors who are eligible to serve at noncapital trials (*Hovey* 1980:1344, footnotes omitted).

Results of subsequent attempts to determine the percentage of ADPs in the population have varied greatly. For instance, Kadane (1984) reports the results of a national Harris Poll that found only one percent of the population to be ADPs. Kadane's re-analysis of Cowan *et al.* (1984) and Fitzgerald and Ellsworth's (1984) data, in light of the Harris Poll, found that the exclusion of ADPs would not alter the finding of conviction-proneness. Likewise, Seltzer, Lopes, Dayan, and Canan (1986) report that "only one respondent (of the 496 respondents who said he/she could be fair and impartial during the guilt-innocence stage) said s/he would automatically vote for the death penalty in all cases" (at 604). Although they did not include an assessment of conviction-proneness in their study, Dillehay and Sandys (1996), in contrast, found that almost 30 percent of the previous felony jurors in their sample were classified as ADPs. They also established that ADPs are likely missed by the traditional questions used to determine death-qualification status: ADPs often are erroneously found to be death-qualified, which in turn would exaggerate the finding of conviction-proneness.

The court in *Hovey* was presented with evidence on one other issue upon which it granted the petitioner relief: the process effect of death-qualification. Briefly stated, Haney (1984) conducted a creative study to demonstrate that mere exposure to death-qualification voir dire engenders bias against the defendant. Eligible capital jurors from California were randomly assigned to view one of two videotapes of a simulated voir dire. The videotape viewed by subjects in the experimental group differed from the control group's only in that it included a 30 minute segment on death qualification. Results revealed that subjects in the experimental group were significantly more likely than those in the control group to believe that the defendant was guilty, that he would be convicted of first-degree murder, and that he would receive a sentence of death. The court, persuaded by the negative effects of exposure to death qualification, ordered that

> [i]n order to minimize the potentially prejudicial effects identified by the Haney study, this court declares...that in future capital cases that portion of the voir dire of each prospective juror which deals with issues which involve death-qualifying the jury should be done individually and in sequestration (*Hovey* 1980:1354, footnotes omitted).

The wisdom of this aspect of the *Hovey* opinion has been substantiated by Allen *et al.'s* (1998) meta-analysis of 14 studies that examine the relationship between potential jurors' attitudes toward capital punishment and "some means of evaluating how likely the persons were to convict or evaluate a criminal legal proceeding" (at 721). In addition, these authors coded each study for the presence of voir dire: five of the studies did and nine of the studies did not include some means of determining whether participants would be eligible to serve as a capital juror. The general finding of the meta-analysis is that the more a person favors the death penalty, the more likely he or she is to favor conviction. This finding, however, is even more pronounced in those studies that included a voir dire component. Thus, when attitude toward capital punishment was operationalized as the outcome of death qualification, there was an even stronger relationship between attitudes (excludable or not) and preferences for conviction: "The results indicate that the use of a voir dire process increases the impact of attitudes toward the death penalty on attitudes toward guilt and punishment of the defendant" (p. 724). Moreover, research also finds that defense attorneys are more likely to initiate, and judges are more likely to grant defense-inspired challenges for cause when jurors are questioned individually during voir dire (Nietzel and Dillehay 1982; Nietzel, Dillehay, and Himelein 1987).

Lockhart v. McCree (1986)

The *Hovey* opinion was an encouraging sign that the courts might be receptive to the evidence of conviction-proneness. The issue, and all the evidence, finally were presented to the U.S. Supreme Court in *Lockhart v. McCree* (1986):

> In this case we address the question left open by our decision nearly 18 years ago in *Witherspoon v. Illinois* (citations omitted): Does the Constitution prohibit the removal for cause, prior to the guilt phase of a bifurcated capital trial, of prospective jurors whose opposition to the death penalty is so strong that it would prevent or substantially impair the performance of their duties as jurors at the sentencing phase of the trial? (at 165)

Justice Rehnquist, writing for the majority, concluded that the Constitution did not prohibit the practice.

The legacy of *McCree* is twofold: it is both the perpetuation of conviction-proneness and its slap in the face to social science research. As Acker (1993) concluded, in referring to *McCree*: "A more complete repudiation of social science research could hardly have been accomplished" (at 76, n. 9). There have been several excellent criticisms of the *McCree* opinion, the gist of which will be summarized below (see Acker 1993; Ellsworth 1988, 1991; Haney and Logan 1994; Seltzer *et al.* 1986; Thompson 1989).

In *McCree*, the Court was presented with 15 published studies that all found death-qualified jurors to be more conviction-prone than excludable jurors. The Court also was presented with the complete records of *Hovey* and *Grigsby v. Mabry* (1983), in which the U.S. District Court for the Eastern District of Arkansas held that death qualification violated the Sixth and Fourteenth Amendments because of the evidence of conviction-proneness. This finding was upheld by the Eighth Circuit (*Grigsby v. Mabry* 1985). As Haney and Logan (1994) note, the research "was perhaps the most elaborate and carefully assembled psychological record brought before the Court to date" (at 91). That did not matter to the Court. In stark contrast to the courts in *Hovey* and *Grigsby*, the majority opinion in *McCree* suggests the justices "had either not understood [the research] or had not read [the research], or that they just didn't care" (Ellsworth 1988:193).

Prior to addressing the legal issues in *McCree*, the opinion discussed "several serious flaws in the evidence upon which the courts below reached the conclusion that 'death qualification' produces 'conviction-prone' juries" (at 168). In the space of five brief paragraphs, the Court dismissed all but one of the studies as being inadequate to address the issue and then concluded, "[s]urely a '*per se* constitutional rule' as far reaching as the one McCree proposes should not be based on the results of the lone study that avoids this fundamental flaw" (at 172–173). What exactly were the "serious flaws" that rendered the research irrelevant? First, the Court summarily excluded from consideration all the surveys ($n = 8$) that did not require respondents to render a verdict on guilt: "Eight [studies]…dealt solely with generalized attitudes and beliefs about the death penalty and other aspects of the criminal justice system, and were thus, at best, only marginally relevant to the constitutionality of McCree's conviction" (at 169). In contrast, the *Hovey* court expressly acknowledged the importance of these studies to an accurate evaluation of the fair cross-section requirement of the Sixth Amendment. Moreover, all of the surveys show a general pro-prosecution bias, which obviously correlates with a pro-conviction bias (Ellsworth 1988; *Hovey* 1980).

The Court then dismissed Haney's (1984) study on the process effect of death qualification, noting "McCree raised [this issue] in his brief to this Court but that counsel for McCree admitted at oral argument [this claim] would not, *standing alone*, give rise to a constitutional violation" (at 170, emphasis added). The Court had considered three of the remaining six studies in *Witherspoon*. These also were deemed irrelevant because "if these studies were 'too tentative and fragmentary' to make out a claim of constitutional error in 1968, the same studies, unchanged but for having aged some 18 years, are still insufficient to make out such a claim in this case" (at 171). The Court neglected to acknowledge that two of the three studies had changed; they had survived the rigors of peer review and had been published. Moreover, the results of the studies had since been replicated by several other researchers.

Two of the final three studies were then criticized for not including a deliberation component, and all of them were criticized for not being able to state explicitly how the "presence of one or more '*Witherspoon*-excludables' on a guilt-phase jury would have altered the outcome of the guilt determination" (at 171–172). The "fatal flaw" that applied to all but one of the six conviction-proneness studies (Cowan *et al.* 1984) was that they did not account for jurors who, because of their opposition to capital punishment, could not be fair and impartial in the determination of guilt. However, several of the studies that had already been dismissed, the attitude surveys, *did* take such prospective jurors into account and the results were the same. Finally, in perhaps its most disingenuous criticism, *all* of the studies were criticized for using randomly selected juror-eligible citizens rather than actual jurors. Aside from the fact that one of the studies presented to the Court was based on actual jurors (non-capital, of course), all jurors on capital cases should have been death-qualified and thus there is no means for comparing their verdict to those reached by excludable jurors on the same case.

As Ellsworth (1988, 1991) and others (Haney and Logan 1994; Thompson 1989) have noted, the *McCree* opinion reflects a fundamental misunderstanding of one of the basic concepts taught in every introductory research methods class: convergent validity. There is no such thing as a perfect study. Rather, knowledge is accumulated, and confidence in a finding established, when numerous different researchers, employing different methods and materials, produce a similar pattern of findings. That clearly was the case with the research presented to the Court in *McCree*. However, the Court took the easy way out, avoiding the possibility of having to reverse convictions returned by death-qualified juries, and ignored the evidence. As Ellsworth (1988) has noted, "the Court's opinions are a product of the Justices' attitudes toward capital punishment" (at 207) and "the outcome of these cases is frequently a foregone conclusion" (at 207). Justice Marshall's dissent in *McCree* reflects a similar sentiment:

> I cannot help thinking that respondent here would have stood a far better chance of prevailing on his constitutional claims had he not been challenging a procedure peculiar to the administration of the death penalty. For in no other context would a majority of

this Court refuse to find any constitutional violation in a state practice that systematically operates to render juries more likely to convict, and to convict on the more serious charges. I dissent (at 206).

Ultimately, the issue of conviction-proneness was irrelevant to the *McCree* opinion:

> ...we will assume for purposes of this opinion that the studies are both methodologically valid and adequate to establish that 'death qualification' in fact produces juries somewhat more 'conviction-prone' than 'non-death-qualified' juries. We hold, nonetheless, that the Constitution does not prohibit the States from 'death qualifying' juries in capital cases (at 173).

The Court based its decision on a different interpretation of impartiality. It concluded "that an impartial *jury* consists of nothing more than '*jurors* who will conscientiously apply the law and find the facts'" (at 178, emphasis in original, quoting *Witt*). This reasoning, or lack thereof, negates the larger issue of the pool from which these so-called impartial jurors are selected to serve on the case. As Justice Marshall observed in dissent:

> ...I am puzzled by the difficulty that the majority has in understanding the "logic of the argument...." Here, respondent adopts the approach of the *Witherspoon* Court and argues simply that the State entrusted the determination of his guilt and the level of his culpability to a tribunal organized to convict (at 194).

It is clear that the *McCree* majority's opinion was rendered to lock the door that *Witherspoon* had opened years before. Its reliance on the individual-level requirement of impartiality all but eliminated possible future contributions by social scientists to this area of inquiry (Thompson 1989). And, in fact, the Court has not decided another case on conviction-proneness since *McCree*.

Automatic Death Penalty Voters Revisited

What does it mean to be an automatic death penalty voter? How does the law differentiate between those who are generally in favor of capital punishment and those who are not willing to consider any option other than death? In other words, what does the law require of a potential capital juror in order to become "qualified" to serve? Doubtless, most people do not believe that they would always vote for the death penalty in a murder case. As Seltzer *et al.* (1986) noted, only one of 496 of their respondents claimed that s/he would automatically vote for the death penalty. And yet, actual capital jurors appear uncommonly willing to see death as the only acceptable penalty for various types of murders (Bowers, Sandys, and Steiner 1998; Bowers, Fleury-Steiner, and Antonio 2003).[4]

For the past 17 years, *Witt* has remained the general standard for death qualification. The virtual dearth of empirical assessments of *Witt*'s effects suggests that the situation is unlikely to change. However, there have been cases that help to clarify the applicability of the *Witt* standard.

Prior to *Witt*, death qualification was applied only to opponents of capital punishment. It was not until *Hovey* (1980) that the prospect of excluding extreme proponents of capital punishment even became an issue.[5] Haney, Hurtado, and Vega (1994:621), however, claim that ADPs rarely were excluded in practice, even in California where it was the law.

Not until 1988, in *Ross v. Oklahoma*, did the U.S. Supreme Court address the constitutionality of empanelling ADP voters on capital juries. The trial judge in *Ross* had refused to grant the defendant's challenge for cause of a prospective juror who indicated that he would automatically vote for death if the defendant were convicted of a capital offense. The Supreme Court did not grant the petitioner relief in *Ross* because his attorney had used a peremptory challenge to remove the ADP prospective juror. The *Ross* opinion, however, stated that "[h]ad [this juror] sat on the jury that ultimately sentenced petitioner to death, and had petitioner properly preserved his right to challenge the trial court's failure to remove [the juror] for cause, the sentence would have to be overturned" (at 85).

True to its word, in *Morgan v. Illinois* (1992), the Supreme Court vacated the sentence of a condemned offender because the trial court (which, by law, conducts the voir dire in Illinois) granted the State's request to ask prospective jurors whether they would never vote to impose the death penalty (*Witherspoon*), yet refused the defense's request to determine whether any of the prospective jurors would always vote for the death penalty. The Illinois Supreme Court affirmed the sentence, concluding that (1) all the jurors who served on the case

---

4. Bowers *et al.* (1998), as part of the Capital Jury Project, asked close to 900 former capital jurors to indicate whether they thought death was the "only acceptable," "sometimes acceptable," or "unacceptable" sentence for a variety of different types of murder: "Astonishingly, more than half of the jurors said that they believed that death was the only acceptable punishment for three of the seven kinds of murder: repeat murder, premeditated murder, and multiple murder" (at 1504).

5. See *Grigsby v. Mabry* (1983) for the earliest discussion of this issue in the federal courts.

stated that they could be fair and impartial, and (2) the trial court is not required to life-qualify, or reverse-*Witherspoon* prospective jurors. The U.S. Supreme Court disagreed, announcing that "based on [the requirement of] impartiality...a capital defendant may challenge for cause any prospective juror" who will automatically vote for the death penalty (at 729). Such a juror "will fail in good faith to consider the evidence of aggravating and mitigating circumstances as the instructions require" (at 729, citing *Witt*). The *Morgan* Court, again citing *Witt*, also declared that only *"through questioning"* (at 733, emphasis in original) can partiality be determined. Hence, *Witt* does preclude ADPs from serving on capital cases, and the defense has the right to life qualify (or reverse-*Witherspoon*) prospective jurors.[6] To the extent that ADPs can be accurately detected, this marks an important step toward balancing capital defendants' rights with those of the State (*cf.*, Dillehay and Sandys 1996).

But to what extent are ADPs accurately detected? Experienced capital litigators recognize that what people offer as the conditions under which they would and would not vote for death are inconsistent with the legal requirements. For instance, prospective capital jurors who have survived questioning by the judge and the prosecutor have offered the defense the following conditions under which they would not vote for the death penalty:

> war time
> children playing with a gun
> hunting accident
> If the guy was not guilty[7]

Clearly, these examples would never be charged as capital offenses; these are examples from jurors who do not understand that the only time that they would be asked to consider voting for a sentence of death is if they were convinced that the person was guilty of the murder plus the aggravating circumstances. Can we be confident that these jurors are not automatic death penalty voters? No. Is it cause for concern that such jurors slipped by the judge and the prosecutor? Yes. It is perhaps due to this obvious difficulty in discerning automatic death penalty voters that the majority opinion in *Morgan* noted that "[i]t may be that a juror could, in good conscience, swear to uphold the law and yet be unaware that maintaining such dogmatic beliefs about the death penalty would prevent him or her from doing so" (at 735). Hence, a person who fits

---

6. The trend in lower courts, however, is to treat the inquiries differently. Many courts have interpreted *Morgan* much more narrowly, as requiring only the exclusion of prospective jurors who will automatically vote for the death penalty, and not those whose ability to consider a life sentence is substantially impaired (Holdridge 1999:290–291).

7. These examples were compiled by the first author from conversations with attorneys.

the legal definition of an automatic death penalty voter may be unaware of his or her biases:

> But such jurors—whether they be unalterably in favor of, or opposed to, the death penalty in every case—by definition are ones who cannot perform their duties in accordance with law, their protestations to the contrary notwithstanding (*Morgan v. Illinois* 1992:735).

Morgan thus recognizes that a verbal statement on the part of a prospective juror, that s/he could be fair, is no guarantee that such an individual should be qualified to serve on a capital case. The Court articulated the true characteristics of an automatic death penalty voter:

> A juror who will automatically vote for the death penalty in every case will fail in good faith to consider the evidence of aggravating and mitigating circumstances as the instructions require him to do. Indeed, because such a juror has already formed an opinion on the merits, the presence or absence of either aggravating or mitigating circumstances is entirely irrelevant to such a juror.... [A] capital defendant may challenge for cause any prospective juror who maintains such views (at 729).

Thus, an automatic death penalty voter is someone for whom mitigating circumstances are "entirely irrelevant."[8] We can therefore think of such jurors as being "mitigation impaired" because they will not consider mitigating circumstances in support of a sentence less than death, as the law requires (Garvey 1998; Blume *et al.* 2001:1228).[9]

---

8. ADPs, however, are not the only prospective jurors that are cause for concern. "Burden-shifting" jurors may create an even more nuanced problem in that while they will not say that mitigating circumstances are completely irrelevant to their decision-making process, they will nonetheless enter the sentencing phase, "possessed of the presumption that the conviction for murder means they should impose the death penalty, and (at best) that the defendant had better wise up with some *really good* reason for them to conclude otherwise" (Blume, *et al.* 2001).

9. Holdridge (1999:302–303) makes an argument that many lower courts are conflating the question of whether prospective jurors *can* consider aggravating and mitigating circumstances (are they mitigation-impaired?) with the question of what weight prospective jurors will assign aggravating and mitigating circumstances. According to Holdridge, "under modern Eighth Amendment jurisprudence, capital jurors are free to make an individual assessment of the appropriate penalty and to assign *whatever weight they deem appropriate to aggravating and mitigating circumstances*" (emphasis added) (1999:300). According to his argument, prospective jurors who state during voir dire that specific aggravating (*e.g.*, rape) or mitigating (*e.g.*, under influence of alcohol) circumstances will prevent them from imposing particular penalties are capable jurors, and indeed are following the law. So, for example, if a juror wants to automatically vote for death upon proof of a specific aggravator, Holdridge argues that is constitutionally

Capital Jurors and Mitigation Impairment

The work of the Capital Jury Project (CJP) sheds light on the extent to which capital jurors are mitigation impaired. As described in the following chapter by Bowers, Fleury-Steiner and Antonio (2003), the CJP is a national study involving some 1200 capital jurors. One component of the interview with these jurors focuses on the role of aggravating and mitigating circumstances in their sentencing decisions. Specifically, the jurors were presented with 39 circumstances that might have been present in the case on which they served. For each circumstance, the juror was asked whether it was a factor in the case. For those jurors who indicated that any of the circumstances were *not* a factor in their case, the interviewer was instructed to ask the juror to surmise how the circumstance would have influenced his or her penalty decision in another case. Specifically, the juror was asked: "In another case, if this had been a factor, *would it have made you* much more likely to vote for death, slightly more likely to vote for death, no more or no less likely to vote for death, slightly less likely to vote for death or much less likely to vote for death?"[10] Thus, we have the jurors' own best estimates of the influence these circumstances would have on their voting preferences. This situation is akin to that of voir dire, except in one respect: the jurors interviewed as part of the CJP had actually served on a capital case and therefore might be expected to give a more reliable judgment of whether and to what extent such circumstances would influence their sentencing decisions. In the language of the CJP interview, mitigators are those circumstances that jurors said would make them less likely to vote for death.

Table 1 shows the percent who said the circumstance would make them less likely to vote for death, more likely to vote for death, or not affect their punishment decision for the 15 of the 39 circumstances that are interpreted, on balance, as mitigators. The percentages in Table 1 are based only on those jurors who were not presented with evidence or argument in support of the circumstance in their case.

---

permissible, providing that the juror has not been precluded from considering any factor in mitigation. Clearly, this view is consistent with Justice Scalia's dissent in *Morgan v. Illinois*, but not the majority opinion, which is more in line with Blume *et al.'s* (2001) conception of mitigation-impaired jurors as yet another variation of an ADP.

10. Jurors who indicated that the circumstance was a factor in their case were then asked whether the factor made them much more likely to vote for death, slightly more likely to vote for death, no more or no less likely to vote for death, slightly less likely to vote for death, or much less likely to vote for death.

Table 1
Jurors' Anticipated Effect of Circumstances
on Penalty Voting Preferences

Circumstance	% less likely to vote for death	% no more or no less likely to vote for death	% more likely to vote for death	Not a factor (N)
Lingering doubt	81.3	16.1	2.7	902
DEF mentally retarded	80.6	17.1	2.2	980
DEF mentally ill	67.7	29.6	2.6	894
DEF under extreme emotional disturbance	63.3	29.6	7.1	771
DEF placed in institutions in past, no help	50.9	46.8	2.3	725
DEF under 18 at time of crime	46.3	51.3	2.5	975
DEF seriously abused as child	43.9	55.1	1.0	675
DEF no previous criminal record	35.3	55.7	9.0	654
Crime not premeditated, committed during other crime	34.7	38.3	27.0	614
DEF hardworking, well behaved inmate	27.8	70.5	1.7	723
DEF under influence of alcohol	27.2	57.5	15.3	738
DEF—under influence of drugs	25.8	57.0	17.2	756
VIC known troublemaker	24.1	68.0	7.9	959
Accomplice testified for deal	21.9	70.3	7.8	799
VIC had a criminal record	20.9	70.8	8.3	927

While lingering doubt[11] and the defendant being mentally retarded[12] are the strongest anticipated mitigators[13], even here one in five jurors (18.8% and 19.3%, respectively) said that these factors would have either no effect on their sentencing vote preference or that they would actually make them more likely to vote for death. These findings are especially poignant give the Court's recent determination in *Atkins* (2002), that persons who are mentally retarded are ineligible for the death penalty: almost one in five of these actual capital jurors appears unmoved by a fact that now renders a person ineligible for a sentence of death.

---

11. The actual wording of the item was as follows: "Although the evidence was sufficient for a capital murder conviction, you had some lingering doubt that the defendant was the actual killer."

12. In 2002, the U.S. Supreme Court ruled that mentally retarded offenders are ineligible for capital punishment (*Atkins v. Virginia*).

13. It is important to note that lingering doubt may refer to the degree of culpability and not innocence per se (Bowers *et al.* 1998; Sundby 1998).

For only three additional items did more than half of these jurors believe the circumstance would make them less likely to vote for death: (1) the defendant had a history of mental illness; (2) the killing was committed while the defendant was under the influence of an extreme mental or emotional disturbance; and (3) the defendant had been placed in institutions in the past but never given any real help or treatment for his problems. In contrast, most jurors said that each of the remaining ten circumstances questioned would not make them less likely to vote for death. Four of these 10 circumstances were rejected as mitigators by 50% to 65% of the jurors:

1. The defendant was under 18 when the crime occurred.
2. The defendant had been seriously abused as a child.
3. The defendant had no previous criminal record.
4. The killing was not premeditated but was committed during another crime, such as a robbery, when the victim tried to resist.

And the remaining six circumstances were seen as mitigating by an even smaller minority—fewer than one in three of the jurors:

1. The defendant would be a hardworking well behaved inmate and would make positive contributions in prison.
2. The killing was committed while the defendant was under the influence of alcohol.
3. The killing was committed while the defendant was under the influence of drugs.
4. The victim was a known troublemaker.
5. The defendant was convicted with evidence from an accomplice who testified against him/her in return for a reduced charge or sentence.
6. The victim had a criminal record.

The most common reaction of jurors to these circumstances is no reaction at all. For 10 of these 15 circumstances, over half of these former capital jurors say that had the circumstance been present in their case it would have made them no more or no less likely to vote for death. And while the percentages are relatively small—unless of course one of these jurors is serving on your case— at least one percent of jurors viewed each of these 15 potential mitigating circumstances as an aggravator.

The pattern reflected in Table 1 suggests that some jurors believe that it is inappropriate to consider all but a few of these circumstances as mitigating in their sentencing decisions. To determine whether the apparent reluctance to consider these factors in mitigation is a function of the particular circumstance in question or the jurors themselves, we now ask a slightly different question: what percentage of these actual capital jurors would meet the criterion of *Morgan* by indicating that they would consider all of these circumstances mitigating? Given our focus, the selection of capital jurors, we elected to look only at the subsample of jurors who indicated that none of the mitigators in question were factors in their case. In this way, we are not confounding evidence presented in a particular case with general assessments of influence of the circumstance. Moreover, by excluding jurors who were presented with evidence of these factors our sample comes closer to resembling an actual venire that has not been presented with or used these circumstances in reaching a capital sentencing decision.

For the purpose of this analysis, we distinguish between "strong" and "weak" mitigators. Strong mitigators are the five circumstances, listed in Table 1, that over 50% of the jurors reported would make them less likely to vote for death. The remaining 10 circumstances presented in Table 1 are the weak mitigators in this analysis.

In the case of the strong mitigators, 436 jurors reported that none of these five circumstances were factors in their cases.[14] We then determined how many of these jurors anticipated that each of these five circumstances would make them less likely to vote for death. Almost one in three (129, or 29.6%) of the 436 jurors predicted that they would be less likely to vote for death if any one of these five strong mitigators had been proffered in their case. Stated differently, less than one in three of these jurors meets the requirement of *Morgan* by indicating that they would interpret all of these circumstances as mitigating. While the majority of the jurors expect that at least some of these strong mitigators would in fact make them less likely to vote for death[15], 4.6% (20) of these jurors said that none of the five strong mitigators would make them less likely to vote for death. These jurors' absolute repudiation of the strong mitigators suggests that they fall beyond being mitigation impaired. They could more accurately be described as mitigation deniers.

Only 84 jurors were exposed to none of the ten circumstances considered to be weak mitigators. None of these 84 jurors said that they would be less likely to vote for death in response to all ten of these circumstances. At the other extreme, 16.7% (14) of these jurors said that none of these weak mitigators would make them less likely to vote for death. All told, only 34.5% (29) of these 84 jurors predicted that they would be less likely to vote for death in re-

---

14. This does not mean that the rest of the jurors all evaluated as least some of these circumstances as mitigation; all we know at this time is that the remaining jurors acknowledged that one or more of these circumstances were present in their case.

15. The actual breakdown is as follows:
Number of Strong Mitigators

	0	1	2	3	4	5	Total
%	4.6	9.6	11.7	17.4	27.1	29.6	100
(#)	(20)	(42)	(51)	(76)	(118)	(129)	(436)

sponse to four or more of these 10 weak mitigators. Thus, even among former capital jurors, those who should understand how to interpret mitigation, very few appear ready to be moved by the very circumstances that commonly comprise defense stories of mitigation.

Implications

A range of proposals could be implemented to bring current practices in line with the underlying spirit of the law. At one extreme, one could endorse Justice Scalia's notion, expressed in dissent in *Morgan*, that the law merely requires that capital jurors not be precluded from considering mitigation evidence, not that they be required to give factors proffered by the defense mitigating effect. In short, this proposal means that we do nothing and that we endorse practices that allow jurors who cannot consider circumstances to be mitigating to decide whether the appropriate sentence in a given case is life or death.

On the other end of the spectrum, one might endorse a scheme where a capital jury would not be "death qualified" until the guilt phase of a trial is complete and an aggravating circumstance has been unanimously agreed upon. Capital cases must be tried as bifurcated proceedings and sentencing decisions are expected to be guided by considerations of aggravating and mitigating circumstances (*Gregg v. Georgia* 1976). We also know that the jury must agree unanimously on at least one aggravator charged by the state before the defendant becomes eligible for the death penalty (*Ring v. Arizona* 2002). Thus, it is only after the jury finds unanimously, beyond a reasonable doubt, guilt of capital murder plus an aggravator that a person becomes eligible for a sentence of death. In short, the jury must first determine guilt and eligibility before selection of the penalty becomes an issue (*Tuilaepa v. California* 1994). Hence, it stands to reason that jurors' views of the death penalty are likewise irrelevant unless and until the jury reaches the penalty-selection phase of the trial.

The current structure to death qualification focuses jurors' attention unnecessarily on the penalty from the outset of the trial, rendering penalty considerations the lens through which jurors view the evidence of guilt (Haney 1984). The only way to eliminate penalty considerations from framing interpretations of evidence of guilt is to postpone the death- and life-qualification of the jurors, to wait until the court knows for certain that a sentence of death is a legitimate possible outcome. In short, the qualification would occur if and when the case reaches the penalty-selection phase. Jurors could be selected with the same care and concern for impartiality as they are now for murder cases where death is not a possibility. As such, prospective jurors would be questioned about their familiarity with the case, their knowledge of any of the witnesses or other actors involved in the case, and so on, without being questioned about their views on the death penalty or any other penalty. The jury would then proceed to determine whether the defendant was guilty of the murder and the aggravating factor. If the jury did not agree unanimously about both such issues, death would not be a possible sentence and the jury's duty would be fulfilled. If, on the other hand, the jury did agree unanimously on the murder charge and the aggravator, the jurors would then go through the process of death- and life-qualification. It is only then, after hearing the evidence in support of guilt and the aggravator(s), that a juror would know and the court could determine accurately whether the juror stands willing to consider evidence in support of all possible sentences as *Morgan* requires.

There is at least one obvious obstacle to implementing this proposal: it is unlikely that all jurors who serve on the guilt/eligibility phases would remain qualified to serve at the selection phase of the trial.[16] What this means, of course, is that additional court time and money will be required to empanel a jury for the selection phase. There are at least three possible solutions to this challenge. First, the court could qualify substantially more jurors for the guilt/eligibility phases and thereby conduct the death- and life-qualification on this larger pool of jurors who have thus heard all phases of the trial (though most of the jurors would have served as alternates during the previous stages of the trial). Alternatively, the court could treat the selection phase as a resentencing hearing, thereby empanelling a new jury, one that has been death qualified, to decide on the sentence. While this option requires additional work on the part of court actors, resentencing hearings are routine in cases where the sentence but not the conviction has been reversed on appeal.[17] One final option would be a hybrid of the two previous proposals: Rather than having numerous alternates sit through the initial phases of the trial, the court could conduct the death- and life-qualification of the original jurors and then supplement the jury with whatever number of new jurors is needed. In this scheme, the jury that decides on the appropriate penalty would be comprised both of jurors who had served on the guilt/eligibility phases and additional jurors who were brought in as though being called for a standard resentencing trial.

A compromise between the two proposals noted above is suggested by New York law, under which jurors who are death qualified prior to trial are subject to a second round of voir dire questioning after the guilt determination to test

---

16. If this is in fact the case, as we suspect it is, it begs the question of the fairness of current practice. If there are no concerns about the fairness of the current practice, there should likewise be no opposition to implementing this new proposal.

17. It is conceivable that there would be fewer such reversals on appeal if there were more fairness at the guilt and eligibility phases of the trial.

their impartiality about making the punishment decision. The purpose is to prevent those jurors who have picked up any biases as a result of the guilt-phase trial from participating in the sentencing decision.[18] "Thoroughgoing and sensitive questioning might detect the often unspoken influences of the guilt trial experience, including even pro-death biasing effects of exposure to the first round of jury selection" (Bowers *et al.* 1998:1542). Alternatively, emphasis could be placed on discerning what is required of jurors in order for them to remain eligible for service. Instead of attempting to reject jurors, an effort could be made to educate the jurors about their sentencing obligations, to acknowledge that the guilt phase may have been an ordeal, and to stress that their focus must now change and that they must remain open to all possible sentencing options. This re-education effort should be agreed upon by both the prosecution and the defense, and delivered in the form of an instruction by the judge at the outset of the selection phase, as a means of reframing the jurors' orientation to the evidence presented during the penalty-selection phase of the trial.

Conclusion

Death-qualification standards theoretically exist to ensure that capital defendants will be tried by impartial jurors who will follow the law. The research, however, demonstrates that there is a deep chasm between the law's intentions and the result of death qualification in practice. Rather than ensuring impartiality, the result can more accurately be described as a stacked deck against the defendant: death-qualified jurors, regardless of the standard, are more conviction-prone, less concerned with due process, and they are more inclined to believe the prosecution than are excludable jurors. Moreover, evidence suggests that actual capital jurors, who have survived death qualification, often are unwilling or unable to consider mitigation evidence. In addition, we have evidence that the bifurcated proceedings endorsed by the *Gregg* Court have failed to curtail the influence of penalty considerations from contaminating guilt/eligibility decisions (Bowers *et al.* 1998). Bifurcation does little to reduce arbitrariness in capital sentencing if the current practice simply physically separates, but does not keep psychologically separate, these difficult and distinct decisions to be made by the jury. True bifurcation of proceedings requires that

---

18. N.Y.Crim.Proc. Law, sec. 400.27(2): "Before proceeding with the jury that found the defendant guilty, the court shall determine whether any juror has a state of mind that is likely to preclude the juror form rendering an impartial decision based upon the evidence adduced during the proceeding."

considerations of penalty do not contaminate decisions of guilt. Until the spirit of *Gregg* and *Morgan* is fully realized, the use of capital punishment will be plagued by concerns about biased and partial jurors

References

Abramson, J. (1994) *We, the Jury: The Jury System and the Ideal of Democracy.* New York: Basic Books.

Acker, J.R. (1993) "A Different Agenda: The Supreme Court, Empirical Research Evidence, and Capital Punishment Decisions 1986–1989." *Law & Society Review* 27:65–88.

Adams v. Texas (1980) 448 U.S. 38.

Allen, M., E. Mabry, and D. McKelton (1998) "Impact of Juror Attitudes about the Death Penalty on Juror Evaluations of Guilt and Punishment: A Meta-Analysis." *Law and Human Behavior* 22:715–731.

Atkins v. Virginia (2002) 122 S.Ct. 2242.

Ballew v. Georgia (1978) 436 U.S. 962.

Batson v. Kentucky (1986) 476 U.S. 79.

Blume, J.H., S.L. Johnson, and A.B. Threlkheld (2001) "Probing 'Life Qualification' Through Expanded Voir Dire." *Hofstra Law Review* 29:1209–1264.

Bowers, W.J., B. Fleury-Steiner, and M.E. Antonio (2003). "The Capital Sentencing Decision: Guided Discretion, Reasoned Moral Judgment, or Legal Fiction?" (This volume.)

Bowers, W.J., M. Sandys, and B. Steiner (1998) "Foreclosed Impartiality in Capital Sentencing: Jurors' Predispositions, Guilt-Trial Experience, and Premature Decision Making." *Cornell Law Review* 83:1476–1556.

Bronson, E.G. (1970) "On the Conviction Proneness and Representativeness of the Death Qualified Jury: An Empirical Study of Colorado Veniremen." *University of Colorado Law Review* 42:1–32.

Butler, B.M. and G. Moran (2002) "The Role of Death Qualification in Venirepersons' Evaluations of Aggravating and Mitigating Circumstances in Capital Trials." *Law and Human Behavior* 26: 175–184.

Cowan, C.L., W.C. Thompson, and P.C. Ellsworth (1984) "The Effects of Death Qualification on Jurors' Predisposition to Convict and on the Quality of Deliberation." *Law and Human Behavior* 8:53–79.

Dillehay, R.C. and M.R. Sandys (1996) "Life Under *Wainwright v. Witt*: Juror Dispositions and Death Qualification." *Law and Human Behavior* 20:147–165.

Ellsworth, P.C. (1991) "To Tell What We Know or Wait for Godot?" *Law and Human Behavior* 15:77–90.

Ellsworth, P.C. (1988) "Unpleasant Facts: The Supreme Court's Response to Empirical Research on Capital Punishment." Pp. 177–211 in K.C. Haas and J.A. Inciardi (eds.), *Challenging Capital Punishment: Legal and Social Science Approaches.* Newbury Park, CA: Sage.

Fitzgerald, R. and P.C. Ellsworth (1984) "Due Process vs. Crime Control: Death Qualification and Jury Attitudes." *Law and Human Behavior* 8:31–51.

Garvey, S.P. (1998) "Aggravation and Mitigation in Capital Cases: What do Jurors Think?" *Columbia Law Review* 98: 1538–1576.

Georgia v. McCollum (1992) 505 U.S. 42.

Gershowitz, A.M. (1999) "Delaware's Capital Jury Selection: Inadequate Voir Dire and the Problem of Automatic Death Penalty Jurors." *Delaware Law Review* 2:235–269.

Goldberg, F. (1970) "Toward Expansion of *Witherspoon*: Capital Scruples, Jury Bias, and the Use of Psychological Data to Raise Presumptions in the Law." *Harvard Civil Rights-Civil Liberties Review* 5:53–69.

Grigsby v. Mabry (1985) 758 F.2d 226 (8th Cir.).

Grigsby v. Mabry (1983) 569 F.Supp. 1273 (E.D. Ark.).

Gross, S.R. (1984) "Determining the Neutrality of Death-Qualified Juries: Judicial Appraisal of Empirical Data." *Law and Human Behavior* 8:7–30.

Haney, C. (1984) "On the Selection of Capital Juries: The Biasing Effects of the Death-Qualification Process." *Law and Human Behavior* 8:121–132.

Haney, C. and D.D. Logan (1994). "Broken Promise: The Supreme Court's Response to Social Science Research on Capital Punishment." *Journal of Social Issues* 50:75–101.

Haney, C., A. Hurtado, and L. Vega (1994) "'Modern' Death Qualification: New Data on its Biasing Effects." *Law and Human Behavior* 18:619–633.

Holdridge, J. (1999) "Selecting Capital Jurors Uncommonly Willing to Condemn a Man to Die: Lower Courts' Contradictory Readings of *Wainwright v. Witt* and *Morgan v. Illinois*." *Mississippi College Law Review* 19:283–303.

Hovey v. Superior Court (1980) 616 P.2d 1301 (Cal.).

J.E.B. v. Alabama (1994) 511 U.S. 127.

Jurow, G.L. (1971) "New Data on the Effect of a Death Qualified Jury on the Guilt Determination Process." *Harvard Law Review* 84:567–611.

Kadane, J.B. (1984) "After *Hovey*: A Note on Taking Account of the Automatic Death Penalty Jurors." *Law and Human Behavior* 8:115–120.

Levine, J.P. (1992) *Juries and Politics*. Pacific Grove, CA: Brooks/Cole.

Lockett v. Ohio (1978) 438 U.S. 586.

Lockhart v. McCree (1986) 476 U.S. 162.

McNally, K. (1985) "Rehnquist's Revenge." *The Advocate* 7 (April):14–18.

Morgan v. Illinois (1992) 504 U.S. 719.

Neises, M.L. and R.C. Dillehay (1987) "Death Qualification and Conviction Proneness: *Witt* and *Witherspoon* Compared." *Behavioral Sciences and the Law* 5:479–494.

Nietzel, M.T. and R.C. Dillehay (1982) "The Effects of Variations in Voir Dire Procedures in Capital Murder Trials." *Law and Human Behavior* 6:1–13.

Nietzel, M.T., R.C. Dillehay, and M.J. Himelein (1987) "Effects of Voir Dire Variations in Capital Trials: A Replication and Extension." *Behavioral Sciences & the Law* 5:467–477.

Osser, A.I. and B. Bernstein (1968) "The Death-Oriented Jury Shall Live." *San Fernando Valley Law Review* 1:253–258.

Radelet, M.L. and M. Mello (1992) "Death-to-Life Overrides: Saving the Resources of the Florida Supreme Court." *Florida State University Law Review* 20:196–228.

Ring v. Arizona (2002) 122 S.Ct. 2248.

Ross v. Oklahoma (1988) 487 U.S. 81.

Seltzer, R., G.M. Lopes, M. Dayan, and R.F. Canan (1986) "The Effect of Death Qualification on the Propensity of Jurors to Convict: The Maryland Example." *Howard Law Journal* 29:571–607.

Sundby, S.E. (1998) "The Capital Jury and Absolution: The Intersection of Trial Strategy, Remorse, and the Death Penalty." *Cornell Law Review* 83:1557–1598.

Thompson, W.C. (1989) "Death Qualification after *Wainwright v. Witt* and *Lockhart v. McCree*." *Law and Human Behavior* 13:185–215.

Tuilaepa v. California (1994) 512 U.S. 967.

Wainwright v. Witt (1985) 469 U.S. 412.

Witherspoon v. Illinois (1968) 391 U.S. 510.

Woodson v. North Carolina (1976) 428 U.S. 280.

Zeisel, H. (1968) *Some Data on Juror Attitudes Toward Capital Punishment.* Monograph. Center for Studies in Criminal Justice, University of Chicago Law School.

Chapter 14

The Capital Sentencing Decision: Guided Discretion, Reasoned Moral Judgment, or Legal Fiction

William J. Bowers
Benjamin D. Fleury-Steiner
Michael E. Antonio

Legal Context

The capital jury is unique. It makes the fundamentally moral decision of whether a convicted defendant should live or die.[1] Yet, it is not free to make this decision however it pleases. Indeed, it was the "arbitrary" and "capricious" way juries were making such decisions that brought capital punishment to a halt in 1972 when the U.S. Supreme Court held, in *Furman* v. *Georgia* (1972), that the death penalty, as applied, was unconstitutional. Seeking to remedy such arbitrariness and capriciousness, most state legislatures enacted new capital statutes that separated the trial into guilt and sentencing phases and provided standards or directions to guide jurors' exercise of discretion at the sentencing stage of the trial. Four years after *Furman*, the Supreme Court endorsed these "guided dis-

---

1. In death penalty states, the capital sentencing decision is typically made by the same jury that convicted the defendant of capital murder. Two states (Alabama and Florida) permit the trial judge to override a jury death or life verdict; two others (Delaware and Indiana) did so until 2002. Five states (California, South Carolina, Virginia, Ohio, and Kansas) permit the judge to override a jury's sentence of death but not of life. Five states (Arizona, Colorado, Idaho, Montana, and Nevada) gave sole sentencing responsibility to the trial judge (with no jury participation) until the Supreme Court ruled in *Ring* v. *Arizona* (2002) that the capital sentencing decision must not be made without jury participation. Few states give juries sentencing responsibility in non-capital cases (e.g., Kentucky and Texas).

cretion" capital statutes[2] in *Gregg* v. *Georgia* (1976) and companion cases[3]—saying such a bifurcated system "is more likely to ensure elimination of the constitutional deficiencies identified in *Furman*" (at 192).

Writing for the Court in *Gregg*, Justice Stewart explained how these statutory guidelines are presumed to remedy the *Furman* ills:

> Left unguided, juries imposed the death sentence in a way that could only be called freakish. The new Georgia sentencing procedures, by contrast, focus the jury's attention on the particularized nature of the crime and the particularized characteristics of the individual defendant.... In this way the jury's discretion is channeled. No longer can a jury wantonly and freakishly impose the death sentence; it is always circumscribed by the legislative guidelines (Id. at 206–207, plurality opinion).

At the same time that the Supreme Court endorsed "guided discretion" capital statutes it rejected statutes that made the death penalty mandatory upon conviction for capital murder in *Woodson* v. *North Carolina* (1976) and *Roberts* v. *Louisiana* (1976) on the ground that "individualized treatment" in capital sentencing was constitutionally indispensable. This requirement of individualized treatment became an essential ingredient in later rulings that relaxed the force of statutory guidelines,[4] and in the Court's emergent conception of the capital sentencing decision.

---

2. This represented a turnaround in the Court's thinking about sentencing guidelines. Only five years earlier in *McGautha v. California* (1971) it had concluded that the task of devising such guidelines was "beyond present human ability" (at 204).

3. The Supreme Court approved three forms of guided discretion—threshold, weighing, and directed statutes—in *Gregg* v. *Georgia* (1976), *Proffitt* v. *Florida* (1976), and *Jurek* v. *Texas* (1976), respectively. Most states adopted "weighing statutes," like Florida's, which list aggravating and mitigating considerations and require jurors (in different ways) to weigh the aggravating against the mitigating factors in making their punishment decision. Some states followed Georgia's "threshold statute" in which only aggravating considerations are listed and jurors may impose death if they find at least one such aggravator and have considered the evidence in mitigation. A few states have "directed statutes" like Texas', which single out specific aggravating factors, such as the defendant's future dangerousness or the heinousness of the crime, that jurors must consider, together with mitigation, in making their penalty decision. The terms "weighing," "threshold," and "directed" were first assigned to these kinds of statutes in a 1974 article (Note at 1699–1712). See also Gillers (1980) and Acker and Lanier (1995:33–52) for detailed discussions of these statutory distinctions.

4. The Court eased the role of statutory guidelines by allowing the consideration of any mitigating factors, not just those enumerated in the statutes (*Lockett* v. *Ohio* 1978); by permitting the sentencing decision to be unguided once the jury finds a single statutory aggravating factor and considers mitigation (*Zant* v. *Stephens* 1983); and by not requiring states to monitor the proportionality or evenhandedness of capital sentencing under their statutes (*Pulley* v. *Harris*

Beyond sentencing guidelines, individualized treatment, and a separate penalty stage of the trial, the Supreme Court has articulated a conception of the capital sentencing decision as a "reasoned moral choice" in *Penry* v. *Lynaugh* (1989).[5] Accordingly, the decision must be an "individualized assessment" of the character and record of the particular offender and the circumstances of the particular offense, unencumbered by ignorance or emotion, and supported with information sufficient and relevant for reliable rational decision-making. At sentencing:

> [f]ull consideration of evidence that mitigates against the death penalty is essential if the jury is to give a " 'reasoned moral response to the defendant's background, character, and crime.' " In order to ensure "reliability in the determination that death is the appropriate punishment in a specific case," the jury must be able to consider and give effect to any mitigating evidence relevant to a defendant's background and character or the circumstances of the crime (at 328, citations and internal quotation marks omitted).

The conception of the capital sentencing decision as a reasoned moral response is reflected in Court decisions about who is qualified to serve as a capital juror, how they must approach the sentencing task, what legal rules govern

---

1984). These and related decisions that had the effect of circumscribing the role of such guidelines, have been described by Weisberg (1984) as "deregulating death" to the point, he contends, where capital juries function much as they did before *Furman* ruled standardless decision-making unconstitutional (See, Weisberg 1984; also Gey 1992).

5. In *Penry* (1989:319) the Court described how a reasoned moral response embodies individualized treatment, sentencing reliability, and the retributive element of personal culpability:

> Underlying Lockett and Eddings is the principle that punishment should be directly related to the personal culpability of the criminal defendant. If the sentencer is to make an individualized assessment of the appropriateness of the death penalty, "evidence about the defendant's background and character is relevant…" [*quoting California v. Brown* 1987:545, O'Connor, J., concurring]. Moreover, Eddings makes clear that it is not enough simply to allow the defendant to present mitigating evidence to the sentencer. The sentencer must also be able to consider and give effect to that evidence in imposing sentence [*Hitchcock v. Dugger* 1987]. Only then can we be sure that the sentencer has treated the defendant as a "uniquely individual human bein[g]" and has made a reliable determination that death is the appropriate sentence [*quoting Woodson v. North Carolina* 1976:304–305]. "Thus, the sentence imposed at the penalty stage should reflect a reasoned *moral* response to the defendant's background, character, and crime" [*quoting California v. Brown* 1987:545, O'Connor, J., concurring, emphasis in original].

For further discussions and analyses of the Court's evolving conception of a "reasoned moral" decision, see, e.g., Bilionis (1991); Steiker and Steiker (1992); Sundby (1991).

their decision making, what kinds of information they need for a reliable decision, the need for them to accept responsibility for the defendant's punishment, and the need for their decision-making to be race neutral. Since it is essential to the task of deciding punishment and since it contrasts with the essence of deciding guilt, we review in more detail what the Court has in mind as a reasoned moral choice.

The Sentencing Decision As a Reasoned Moral Choice

Unlike the guilt decision, which entails assessing whether the facts that establish every legal element of the crime charged have been proven beyond a reasonable doubt to all twelve jurors, the punishment decision is directed and constrained by a very different set of considerations and procedures, appropriate for a fundamentally moral judgment. Generally, the jury must unanimously find an aggravating factor beyond a reasonable doubt for the defendant to be death-eligible.[6] But, the fact that the defendant is guilty of capital murder must not, in and of itself, be a reason that he or she should be sentenced to death (*Sumner* v. *Shuman* 1987; *Woodson* 1976). Nor may the presence or strength of aggravating factors alone mandate the death penalty.[7] Hence, jurors must be open to imposing a life sentence despite the presence and strength of aggravating circumstances. Capital jurors must, therefore, approach the sentencing task with a different frame of mind from the one they employed in reaching the guilty verdict.

An individualized assessment of personal culpability based on the defendant's background and character is constitutionally required in capital sentenc-

---

6. Most (but not all) state capital statutes explicitly require that aggravators be proven beyond a reasonable doubt to all jurors (Acker and Lanier 1993:309–310; Acker and Lanier 1995:34–35). While the Supreme Court has not ruled on whether aggravating circumstances must be proven beyond a reasonable doubt, or whether a jury's finding of aggravation must be unanimous, the rationale for requiring proof beyond a reasonable doubt in criminal trials articulated in *In re Winship* 397 U.S. 358 (1970) arguably would require that this high standard be met for establishing aggravating circumstances in capital sentencing. Moreover, the Court's ruling in *Ring* v. *Arizona* (2002) holds that statutory aggravating factors in capital sentencing are properly understood as factual elements of the crime that must be determined by jury rather than judge in accord with the Sixth Amendment. As such, they are presumably subject to the requirement that they be found beyond a reasonable doubt in capital cases.

7. The Supreme Court has approved capital statutes that require the jury to impose a death sentence if it finds that aggravating circumstances outweigh mitigating circumstances (*Boyde v. California* 1990:374, 386) or when it finds aggravation but no mitigation (*Blystone v. Pennsylvania* 1990:305) but the assessment of mitigation—whether it is present and what weight it should be given—is up to each individual juror. Hence these statutes require a death sentence only if no jurors find mitigation or none find that mitigation is not outweighed by aggravation.

ing because "defendants who commit criminal acts that are attributable to a disadvantaged background, or to emotional and mental problems, may be less culpable than defendants who have no such excuse" (*Penry* 1989:319, quoting *California v. Brown* 1987:545). Accordingly, jurors are required to consider mitigating evidence even if it does not "relate specifically to the [defendant's] culpability for the crime he committed" (*Skipper v. South Carolina*, 1986:4). They may not dismiss mitigating factors on the basis that they do not "excuse" the crime (*Eddings v. Oklahoma* 1982:113). The concept of mitigation in capital sentencing is thus far broader than the notion of reduced responsibility in the criminal law, generally.[8] Capital jurors are free to assess the appropriate weight to be given to particular evidence offered in mitigation, but under the Eighth Amendment "they may not give it no weight by excluding such evidence from their consideration" (*Eddings* 1982:115). In other words, to comply with the Constitution, jurors must at least consider any evidence in mitigation that might call for a sentence less than death (*Lockett* 1978). While the weight to be given to any mitigating factor is up to the sentencer, it is not permissible to give mitigating evidence no weight (*Eddings* 1982:114–115; *Morgan v. Illinois* 1992:738).

Moreover, capital jurisprudence has cast the capital sentencing decision as fundamentally an individual moral judgment. Each juror is responsible for making the punishment decision on the strength of his own personal satisfaction with the evidence of mitigation and his own moral consciousness about the appropriateness of the punishment. Thus, in selecting the punishment, a juror is not required to agree with others on the presence or weight he or she assigns to various aspects of mitigation. Nor must he or she observe the standard of reasonable doubt in assessing the evidence of mitigation.[9] The standards of proof beyond a reasonable doubt and of unanimous jury findings of fact generally required for the determination of guilt and of aggravation simply do not apply to the consideration of mitigation (*McKoy v. North Carolina* 1990; *Mills v. Maryland* 1988).

Defining the punishment decision as a reasoned moral choice also implies that jurors must understand the alternative punishments from which they choose, that they must accept responsibility for the choice they make, and that the choice they make must not be biased by improper considerations such as

---

8. See, e.g., Fletcher (1996) observing that lack of full responsibility and excuse may diminish punishment, without any reference to mitigation.

9. Indeed, most capital jurisdictions leave the level of proof for evidence of mitigation wholly unspecified. The exceptions are Maryland, New Hampshire, Pennsylvania, Wyoming, and federal law for drug related killings; they specify that jurors must find mitigating circumstances by a "preponderance of the evidence," but it is not clear that this is a distinction of any consequence (Acker and Lanier 1994:342, n. 225).

race. Understanding the alternatives means that jurors should not have misleading impressions about the available punishment options. They should have information about the alternatives that will prevent them from making a "false choice" (*Simmons* v. *South Carolina* 1994).[10] Accepting responsibility means that jurors must assume personal responsibility for the punishment they impose. They should not see the law as the responsible agent, or believe that others who may review their verdict thereby relieve them of responsibility for the punishment (*Caldwell* v. *Mississippi* 1985). And in choosing between life or death, jurors must not be influenced, consciously or unconsciously, by the race of the defendant, by the race of the victim, or by their own race (*Turner* v. *Murray* 1986).

We now turn to what is known about how capital jurors make their sentencing decisions, and to whether or how well they abide by the standards for a reasoned moral choice. We begin with the development of this research and review the findings of early investigations, especially their efforts to learn about the role of statutory sentencing guidelines. We then review the results of a national program of research on the decision-making of capital jurors known as the Capital Jury Project (CJP) for an account of how well juries in the post-*Furman* era comport with constitutionally grounded sentencing requirements.

Research Background

The first systematic look at the capital jury came through the eyes of trial judges. Kalven and Zeisel (1966), in their pioneering study of the American jury, devoted a chapter to juries in capital cases. They compared the sentencing decisions of capital juries, as reported by the presiding trial judges, with the sentences those judges said they would have imposed in 111 pre-*Furman* capital cases. They found, as the *Furman* Court did six years later, that the sentencing decisions of these juries were arbitrary. Judges and juries disagreed about whether death should be the punishment more often than they agreed on the death penalty. Beyond this, Kalven and Zeisel observed, "many of the murder cases in which the judge and jury disagree on the death penalty appear no less heinous than those in which they agree" (at 439). Their research also documented that race of victim was a source of disparity in sentencing; a judge who disagreed with the jury's life vote in a black on black murder case said, "A

---

10. The Court has so far made this a constitutional requirement only when the prosecution has alleged the future dangerousness of the defendant and the death penalty alternative is a sentence of life without the possibility of parole. For evidence that knowledge of the death penalty alternative influences jurors' decision-making in cases not limited to these conditions, see, Bowers and Steiner (1999:Table 6).

Negro killing a Negro, that is, the jury did not attach enough importance to the value of human life due to race" (at 442).

After this glimpse at the capital jury through the eyes of trial judges, it escaped empirical scrutiny until the late 1980s.[11] Ironically, the work of Kalvin and Zeisel may have been partly responsible for this hiatus. Their research prompted lawmakers to block the direct observation of real juries for research purposes.[12] Studies of sentencing outcome in capital cases (reviewed in Baldus and Woodworth 2003) may also have diverted research attention from the decision-making process. This line of research on sentencing outcomes which culminated in the Baldus, Woodworth, and Palaski (1990) study presented to the Supreme Court in *McCleskey* v. *Kemp* (1987), demonstrated, many thought, that Georgia's guided discretion capital statute—the model the Supreme Court upheld in *Gregg* as a remedy for the *Furman* ills—failed the test of purging racial bias from the capital sentencing process, and would thus end America's post-*Furman* experiment with capital punishment.

At the time there was little interest in the arduous task of studying the sentencing process—how jurors reached their sentencing decision, whether they followed statutory guidelines, whether they understood sentencing instructions, and just how race or other prohibited considerations might have crept into their decision-making. All this changed, however, in 1987 when the Supreme Court, by a single vote in *McCleskey*, acknowledged the evidence of system-wide racial disparities in sentencing outcomes but denied that such patterns were sufficient to impeach the decision-making of capital jurors. The Court reaffirmed its faith in the capital jury, saying:

> The capital sentencing decision requires the individual jurors
> to focus their collective judgment on the unique characteristics of

---

11. Mock jury studies of the capital sentencing decision were, of course, an option, but one with the serious drawback of having to simulate the reality of making the life or death decision. Some researchers did devote attention during this period to the more limited but more manageable task of studying whether jury selection procedures in capital cases, particularly the "death qualification" requirement, actually yield an unbiased jury for making the guilt decision (e.g., Fitzgerald and Ellsworth 1984; Haney 1984). Despite the merits of this research (Ellsworth 1988) the Supreme Court in *Lockhart* v. *McCree* (1986) rejected the evidence that jury selection procedures in capital cases produced guilt prone juries. See, Sandys and McClelland (2003) for a discussion of "death qualification" and a review of the related research.

12. Following the disclosure in 1955 of the audio taping of jury deliberations in connection with Kalven's and Zeisel's research, the U.S. Attorney General publicly censured "eavesdropping" on jury deliberations. Congress and more than 30 states responded by enacting statutes prohibiting jury taping (Kalven and Zeisel 1966:xv). Such barriers have occasionally been relaxed for media interests (e.g., the airing of video taped deliberations of a Wisconsin criminal jury on the PBS "Frontline" program, April 11, 1986; and of four Arizona juries on a two hour NBC Special, April 16, 1997).

a particular criminal defendant. It is not surprising that such collective judgments often are difficult to explain. But the inherent lack of predictability of jury decisions does not justify their condemnation. On the contrary, it is the jury's function to make the difficult and uniquely human judgments that defy codification and that "buil[d] discretion, equity, and flexibility into a legal system"[13] (at 311).

This made it clear that, in the Court's mind, the analysis of sentencing outcomes would not suffice. To demonstrate unconstitutional arbitrariness or discrimination in capital sentencing, researchers would need to learn how capital jurors actually made their sentencing decisions. Given the legal taboo on observing jurors in the process of making decisions, even by means of unobtrusive or concealed filming or listening devices, and given the Court's premium on the experience of actual jurors in actual cases, this would mean interviewing former jurors about their decision-making. Thus, it was the *McCleskey* Court's affirmation of its faith in the capital jury, despite the demonstrated racial disparities in sentencing outcomes, that drew research attention to persons who had served as capital jurors.

Soundings in Florida, California, and Oregon

Shortly after the *McCleskey* decision, researchers undertook studies based on in-depth interviews with persons who had served on capital juries in Florida, California, and Oregon. These interviews focused on how jurors actually made their decisions and whether, or to what extent, they were guided by the capital statutes in their respective states. The questioning was largely an open ended inquiry into what factors influenced the sentencing decision, and whether jurors' decision-making was being guided by statutory provisions and the Court's conception of the sentencing decision as a reasoned moral choice.

In Florida, Geimer and Amsterdam (1987–88) interviewed some 54 jurors from 10 trials, five in which the jurors voted for death, and five in which they voted for life. They asked jurors to explain the reasons for their life or death sentencing decisions and to evaluate the role or influence of Florida's statutory aggravating and mitigating considerations on their decisions. Two out of three jurors (65%) indicated that Florida's statutory aggravating and mitigating guidelines had "little or no influence" on their sentencing decisions.

From jurors' explanations of how they did make their decisions, Geimer and Amsterdam identified what they called the "operative factors" that actually

---

13. Quoting Kalven and Zeisel (1966:498) concerning guilt, not sentencing, decisions.

shaped jurors' sentencing decisions. While most of the jurors who voted for death (64%) cited the "manner of the killing" as an operative factor, more than half (54%) gave the impermissible "presumption of death" as a factor, the constitutionally forbidden belief that the death penalty was the correct or appropriate punishment, unless they could be persuaded otherwise (at 41). As one juror bluntly put it, "[o]f course he got death. That's what we were there for" (at 45–46). Next in line as influential operative factors in the death decision were "defendant's demeanor" and "defense attorney performance" (32% and 21% of the jurors in death cases, respectively). The former was illustrated by a juror's comment that the "[defendant] seemed callous, indifferent. Nobody saw a heartbeat of regret. He didn't move a muscle except for crossing his legs. By the time of the penalty phase, the jury was not inclined to feel sorry for him. Minds were already colored" (at 52).

Likewise, Geimer and Amsterdam identified operative factors among the jurors who voted for life. Most common (65%) was "lingering doubt" about the capital murder verdict. An example of this explanation was "we found him guilty, there wasn't anybody else to put it on.... But we didn't want to execute him because some evidence might come out in the future about the other guy" (at 29). Concerning the defense attorney's performance, a juror said, "I shouldn't say it, but I feel it in my heart and always have, his lawyer left a lot to be desired. I realize he was hired by the state to do a job and probably not paid much.... I didn't mention it at the jury room but I think he was not determined enough. He didn't try enough and that affected the jury" (at 53).

In California, Sontag (1990) interviewed 30 jurors drawn from one death and one life case in each of five counties throughout the state. In Oregon, Costanzo (1990) interviewed 27 jurors from five death and four life cases from a single urban county responsible for the majority of Oregon's capital trials. The findings of these two studies are reviewed and contrasted in Haney, Sontag, and Costanzo (1994).

Under California's statute, which lists "special circumstances" without specifying whether those factors are to be considered as aggravating or mitigating, and without indicating how the factors are to be weighed in deciding on the defendant's punishment, juries seemed quite confused about how to make the sentencing decision. Sontag found that California juries deliberated with much broader and less coherent agendas, and took approximately three times longer to reach a sentencing verdict than did the Oregon juries studied by Costanzo. Many California jurors tended to search for a key factor that would make the decision clear-cut. They typically narrowed the decision by focusing almost exclusively on the crime and on issues which had already come up in the guilt phase of the trial. Haney et al. (1994) reported that "fully one-third of our sample refocused the penalty phase inquiry entirely on the nature of the crime itself, and did so in a way that amounted to a presumption in favor of death" (at 162)—quite comparable to what Geimer and Amsterdam identified as the most common operative factor among Florida jurors who voted for death.

This tendency to reduce the complex question of life or death to one decisive point among California jurors is illustrated in the comments of a few jurors. For example, one death-jury member recalled the nature of the penalty decision as a matter of determining premeditation: "[A]ccording to the instructions, the main thing was, was it premeditated? Did he deliberately, did he intend to kill these people? If so, then we should give him the death penalty. If not, then we should give life without the possibility of parole" (at 162). Another juror confused the penalty decision with the legal standard of insanity: "I think the bottom line was, at the time he was committing [the crimes], did he know what he was doing? Did he know right from wrong? That's the whole thing" (at 162).

Oregon's directed statute, modeled on that of Texas, made the life or death sentence rest heavily upon jurors' answers to a single question: "whether there is a probability that the defendant would commit criminal acts of violence that would constitute a continuing threat to society." Oregon juries, compared to those in California, appeared more coherent in their decision-making but were much more constricted in the range of information they considered. The directed statutes used in Oregon and Texas have been challenged for discouraging the consideration of mitigating evidence. In this connection, Costanzo reported that many of the jurors' comments underscored the narrowing effect of the directed statute on the range of issues they considered: "We just had to stick to those four [sic] basic criteria. We couldn't deviate with this mitigating circumstance, or testimony of people that had spoken on his behalf or against him. We just had to go by those guidelines that they give you when you make that decision" (at 165–166).

Oregon jurors relied upon the sentencing instructions not only to narrow the scope of the evidence they considered but also to minimize their responsibility for the outcome of their deliberations: "We are not sentencing him to death—we are just answering these questions. We talked about it. We are just answering these questions—to get a clear mind so as not to feel guilty that I sentenced him to die. That's how the law has it—just answer these questions" (at 161–167). Oregon jurors also generally underestimated how long convicted defendants who were not given the death penalty would spend in prison before returning to society, and fully one-half of the Oregon jurors did not believe that the death penalty would actually be carried out.

Concerning both the California and Oregon studies, the investigators observed that "there was a tendency among jurors from both samples to shift or abdicate responsibility for the ultimate decision—to the law, to the judge, or to the legal instructions—rather than to grapple personally with the life and death consequences of the verdicts they were called upon to render" (Haney et al. 1994:160). In addition, the researchers concluded:

Capital penalty instructions fail to acknowledge (let alone clearly frame or carefully guide) the inherently moral nature of the task that they direct jurors to undertake. They seem to imply that death sentencing involves nothing more than simple accounting, an adding up of the pluses and minuses on the balance sheet of someone's life (at 172).

These studies raised serious questions about the operation of post-*Furman* capital statutes. Jurors appear to understand sentencing instructions poorly, especially their obligation to give effect to mitigation. Many appear to presume that death is the appropriate punishment for capital offenses without regard for mitigation. They seem to focus narrowly on a single issue to simplify decision-making and to reach consensus on punishment. In explaining the decision to impose the death penalty, they invoke guilt related considerations as if the sentencing process was merely a replay of the guilt decision. These soundings were sufficiently ominous to justify a more extensive investigation of the capital sentencing process, one that would take a more systematic look into the black box of jury decision-making.

The Capital Jury Project (CJP)

The Capital Jury project is a national program of research on the decision-making of capital jurors conducted by a consortium of university based researchers with the support of the National Science Foundation.[14] The findings of the CJP are based on in-depth interviews with persons who have actually served as jurors in capital trials. The interviews chronicle the jurors' experiences and decision-making over the course of the trial, identify points at which various influences come into play, and reveal the ways in which jurors reach their final sentencing decisions.[15]

---

14. The CJP was undertaken by university-based investigators specializing in the analysis of data collected in their respective states and collaborating to address the following objectives of the Project: (1) to examine and systematically describe jurors' exercise of capital sentencing discretion; (2) to identify the sources and assess the extent of arbitrariness in jurors' exercise of capital discretion; and (3) to assess the efficacy of the principal forms of capital statutes in controlling arbitrariness in capital sentencing. This project was supported by the Law and Social Sciences Program of the National Science Foundation, grant NSF SES-9013252.

15. The research is based on a common core of data collected in the participating states. The investigators cooperatively developed a core juror interview instrument and enhanced the usefulness of this instrument in their respective states by adding to the information gathered in the core interviews, conducting additional interviews in selected cases of special interest, and incorporating additional case-specific data from other sources. The juror inter-

The CJP began in eight states and has since grown to include six more, for a total of fourteen states in which interviews have been conducted. States were chosen for this research to reflect the principal variations in guided discretion capital statutes.[16] Within each state, 20 to 30 capital trials were picked to represent both life and death sentencing outcomes.[17] From each trial, a target sample of four jurors was systematically selected for in-depth three-to-four-hour personal interviews.[18] Interviewing began in the summer of 1991. The present CJP working sample includes 1,201 jurors from 354 capital trials in 14 states.[19] These 14 states are responsible for 76.1% of the 3,718 persons on

---

views obtained data on some 700 variables through structured questions used in all states, and also included open-ended questions that called for detailed narrative accounts of the respondents' experiences as capital jurors. Advanced law and social science students working under the supervision of the various faculty investigators carried out much of the interviewing and other data collection in the respective states. All jurors selected for interviews were guaranteed confidentiality. The preparation of the interview data for state-level and project-wide statistical analyses was carried out at the College of Criminal Justice, Northeastern University under the direction of William J. Bowers, Principal Investigator of the CJP (See Bowers 1995:1082, n. 206 for further information on the interview questions and methods used).

16. The sample was designed to include (1) states with "threshold," "balancing," and "directed" statutory guidelines for the exercise of sentencing discretion; (2) states with "traditional" and "narrowing" statutory definitions of capital murder; and (3) states that make the jury sentencing decision binding and those that permit the judge to override the jury's decision. For further details about sampling states, see Bowers (1995:1077–1079).

17. The sample of trials was restricted to those in which the defendant was charged with a murder punishable by death, convicted of that murder in the guilt phase of the trial, and sentenced to life or death by a jury in the sentencing phase of the trial. The sampling plan for each state called for an equal representation of trials that ended in life and death sentencing decisions to maximize the potential for comparing and contrasting jurors in "life" and "death" cases within each state. Hence, trials were not sampled to be strictly representative within states or within the nation as a whole, but to facilitate analytic comparisons (See, Bowers 1995:1079, 1080 nn. 200–203 for further details about sampling trials within states).

18. Investigators had discretion to conduct additional interviews in cases where the initial interviews raised questions that further interviews might help to resolve. In two states (Kentucky and Virginia), samples of more than four jurors were drawn from cases where the minimum sample of trials with life or death outcomes could not be met within the initial time frame for data collection. The target sample of four jurors per case was not always met due to difficulties in applying the sampling and replacement protocol, locating jurors whose addresses and phone numbers had changed or were not initially correct or sufficiently detailed, and unwillingness of some jurors to be interviewed, despite a $20 incentive payment. Of the 354 trials in the sample, 39 trials are represented by a single juror, 45 by two, 72 by three, 152 by four, 31 by five, 13 by six, and 1 each by seven and eight jurors.

19. The number of jurors interviewed and the number of trials from which they were drawn in each state are shown below:

death row as of June 1, 2002, and for 79.0% of the 795 persons who were executed between 1977 and September 1, 2002.[20]

Since 1993, some 30 articles presenting and discussing the findings of the CJP have been published in scholarly journals.[21] In the pages that follow we review the principal findings of this research on jurors' comportment with constitutional standards. The finding are presented under three major headings: "premature," "misguided," and "race-linked" punishment decision-making. The findings, statistical tabulations, and excerpts from jurors' interviews we present below come principally from four of these publications (Bowers 1995; Bowers, Sandys, and Steiner 1998; Bowers and Steiner 1999; Bowers, Steiner, and Sandys 2001; they are accessible on www.cjp.neu.edu). The statistics from the first three of these sources have been updated in the text and tables below with the data now available.[22]

Premature Punishment Decision-Making: Deciding on punishment at the guilt trial

Every jurisdiction that authorizes capital punishment requires the sentence to be determined at a separate penalty phase of the trial according to sentencing guidelines set forth in its capital statute. This bifurcated procedure assumes that jurors can and do make independent decisions, first, about guilt, and then

	Number of jurors	Number of trials
Alabama	59	20
California	152	36
Florida	117	30
Georgia	77	25
Indiana	101	32
Kentucky	113	31
Louisiana	30	10
Missouri	61	19
North Carolina	83	26
Pennsylvania	78	29
South Carolina	114	31
Tennessee	49	15
Texas	120	38
Virginia	47	12

20. See, NAACP Legal Defense and Educational Fund, Inc., "Death Row, U.S.A." at http://www.deathpenaltyinfo.org/DEATHROWUSArecent.pdf (last visited September 4, 2002).

21. See the Capital Jury Project Website at http://www.cjp.neu.edu for an updated listing of CJP related articles, commentaries, and doctoral dissertations.

22. Statistical analyses were based on interviews with 684 jurors from seven states in Bowers (1995), and on 916 jurors from 11 states in Bowers et al. (1998) and Bowers and Steiner (1999).

Table 1*
Capital Jurors' Stands on Punishment at the Guilt Stage
of the Trial in 13 States and the Full Sample

State	Death %	Life %	Undecided %	No. of Jurors (N)
Alabama	21.2	32.7	46.2	(52)
California	26.1	16.2	57.7	(142)
Florida	24.8	23.1	52.1	(117)
Georgia	31.8	28.8	39.4	(66)
Indiana	31.3	17.7	51.0	(96)
Kentucky	34.3	23.1	42.6	(108)
Missouri	28.8	16.9	54.2	(59)
North Carolina	29.2	13.9	56.9	(72)
Pennsylvania	33.8	18.9	47.3	(74)
South Carolina	33.3	14.4	52.3	(111)
Tennessee	34.8	13.0	52.2	(46)
Texas	37.5	10.8	51.7	(120)
Virginia	17.8	31.1	51.1	(45)
All states	30.3	18.9	50.8	(1,135)

* Source: Bowers et al. (1998:Table 1), updated.

about punishment. If jurors are to be guided in their exercise of capital sentencing discretion by statutory provisions, as constitutionally required, it goes without saying that they must wait until the penalty stage of the trial to decide what the punishment should be. A juror should reach a decision concerning punishment only after hearing and giving effect to the evidence, the arguments, and the instructions for making that decision.

To learn when jurors reached their decisions about the defendant's punishment, we asked them what, at various stages of the trial, they thought the defendant's punishment should be. The first of these questions came in the section of the interview that dealt with the guilt trial. It read, "After the jury found [defendant's name] guilty of capital murder but before you heard any evidence or testimony about what the punishment should be, did you then think [defendant's name] should be given: a death sentence, a life sentence, [or were you] undecided?" Table 1 displays the jurors' responses to this question for 13 participating states[23] and for the total sample.

Remarkably, half of the capital jurors (49.2%) thought they knew what the punishment should be at the guilt stage of the trial. Three of ten (30.3%) said

23. We omit the data from Louisiana in breakdowns by state (Table 1, 3, and 4) because there are too few interviews with Louisiana jurors (N=29) for reliable percentages. In all other participating states, interviews were completed with a sample of at least 40 jurors from a minimum of 10 capital trials.

it should be death, two of ten (18.9%) said it should be life, only five out of ten jurors (50.8%) remained undecided. Moreover, this premature decision-making is pervasive; no CJP state is spared. In fact, nine of the thirteen states are within five points of the sample wide percent saying undecided; only Georgia departs by as much as ten percentage points from the level for all states. Nor is there much variation in taking an early pro-death stand. Again, nine states are within five points of the sample wide percent saying the punishment should be death; only Virginia is more than ten points from the percentage for all states, and with the smallest sample of jurors (N=45) its percentages are least reliable. Evidently, no state effectively curbs premature punishment decision-making.

According to the data in Table 1, post-*Furman* capital statutes are not operating as the constitution requires. Many jurors appear not to wait for the penalty stage evidence and arguments regarding the appropriate punishment or for the guidance of sentencing instructions before making their punishment decisions. Could it be, however, that jurors who said they took a stand on punishment at guilt were actually doubtful or tentative about the punishment they chose at this early point in the trial?

To assay this possibility, we asked jurors who said they thought at the guilt stage of the trial that the punishment should be death or life, "How strongly did you think so?" They could answer that they were "absolutely convinced," "pretty sure," or "not too sure." Seven out of ten jurors who took a pro-death stand (70.4%) and six of ten who said the punishment should be life (57.7%) characterized themselves as "absolutely convinced." Furthermore, nearly all of the remaining jurors who took an early punishment stand were "pretty sure." Only a meager 2.6% and 4.8% of the early pro-death and early pro life jurors characterized themselves as "not too sure" (Bowers et al. 1998:Table 2, updated). Hence, these early stands on punishment were not tentative or doubtful. To the contrary, most jurors who held them boldly affirmed without reservations that they were convinced of what the punishment should be before hearing the evidence and arguments at the sentencing stage of the trial, before hearing the judge's sentencing instructions, and before hearing the opinions and arguments of their fellow jurors.

A further test of the firmness of these early stands on punishment is the degree to which they dominate jurors' subsequent thinking about the punishment. Do jurors hold tenaciously to their early punishment stands for the rest of the trial? We asked jurors about their stands on punishment at three later points in the trial: during the penalty stage but before punishment deliberations, and at the first and the final jury votes on punishment. Their responses reveal that most jurors who thought that either death or life was the right punishment at the guilt stage of the trial held steadfastly to that conviction for the rest of the proceedings (Bowers et al. 1998:Table 3, updated). In particular, four of five early pro-death jurors (79.6%) followed an unbroken pro-death pathway until the jury's final vote on punishment. And, the eleventh-hour conversion to life of one in five such jurors (20.1%) was typically a step they took reluctantly to avoid being a hung jury on punishment rather than a genuine conversion to the belief that the defendant deserved a life sentence (e.g., Sandys 1995:1196).

The tendency of most jurors who take an early stand on punishment to be absolutely convinced of it and to stick with it thereafter strongly suggests that their minds were closed to evidence and arguments presented later in the trial. In this connection, we posed the following question: "Some jurors feel that the decisions about guilt and punishment go together once they understand what happened and why; other jurors feel these are separate decisions based on different considerations. Which comes closest to the approach you took?" The jurors who took an early pro-death and early pro life stand on punishment were roughly twice as likely as undecided jurors (40.9% and 34.0% vs. 19.1%) to concede that they made the guilt and punishment decisions at the same time on the same grounds (Bowers et al. 1998:Table 4, updated). Thus, jurors' own perceptions of how they made their punishment decisions confirm the distinctive failure of many premature punishment decision makers to give effect to different considerations in sentencing than in guilt—thus rendering the penalty phase evidence, arguments, and instructions irrelevant.

These early pro-death stands clearly violate the Court's rulings in *Lockett* (1978), *Eddings* (1982), *Skipper* (1986), and *Morgan* (1992) that the sentencer be presented with, and give effect to, all relevant evidence of mitigation in making the sentencing decision. Because the defendant may not present such evidence until the later sentencing stage of a capital trial, deciding that death is the appropriate punishment at guilt, without even being exposed, much less giving effect, to mitigation, obviously violates this requirement.

The contours of early pro-death decision-making

The prevalence of premature pro-death decision-making, its substantial presence in all CJP states, the certainty that jurors feel about their early pro-death stands, the consistency with which they stick to their initial stands thereafter, and their acknowledgment that they made their guilt and punishment decisions on the same grounds, suggest that many jurors found something during the guilt trial decisive and compelling, something that removed all doubt about what the punishment should be. Are there features of the evidence or arguments at the guilt stage of the trial that convince jurors of what the punishment should be? Are early pro-death jurors exposed to especially egregious crimes or captivating evidence? Or, is there something in the personal predispositions jurors bring with them to the trial that disposes them to premature decision-making? In this section, we examine jurors accounts of what at the guilt trial persuaded them that death was the right punishment, and consider the possibility that selective exposure to certain kinds of crimes or evidence might account for such early decision-making. In the next section, we examine whether some jurors come to the trial predisposed to make a hasty punishment decision.

After jurors who took a life or death stand on punishment at the guilt stage of the trial had indicated how convinced they were of their stands, the interviewer was instructed to ask them at what point during the guilt phase of the trial they reached their punishment decision. During "the presentation of evidence" was the most common response, more so among early pro-death (54.6%) than early pro life (39.0%) jurors (Bowers et al. 1998:Table 5). Beyond convincing jurors of the defendant's guilt, then, the presentation of guilt evidence appears to have the substantial additional effect of persuading them of what the punishment should be, more often that it should be a death than a life sentence.

Of the jurors who indicated when during the guilt trial they took a stand on punishment, three out of ten went on to volunteer the reason or an explanation for their decision. Many of the early pro-death jurors cited convincing proof of guilt as the reason for their early pro-death stands:

FL: When I was convinced he was guilty—when we were going through the hard evidence.

NC: After the pathologist report, after I was convinced he was the one who did it.

FL: When I knew in my heart that he was guilty.... This was after hearing the forensic evidence from prosecution.

KY: I again believed in the death sentence, believe in it, so in my mind I knew what my vote would be. When he was found guilty. When everybody agreed on guilt.

TX: Uh, before we actually voted, before we went in there. I was pretty sure, I mean, I was absolutely sure, because I truly believe in what the Bible says and I think I told them this when they chose me.

For some jurors, it was the grotesque or gruesome nature of the crime that convinced them that death should be the punishment:

KY: Once guilt was established that [defendant] had committed this gruesome crime. I had no problem at all determining what punishment was applicable.

MO: Um, I'd say probably right when the prosecutor made the statement. She was stabbed twenty-two times.

SC: When they started to talk about the brutality of the crime.

Many jurors' stressed the role of physical evidence, especially photographs or video tapes as critical in their punishment decisions:

AL: When the D.A. handed us the pictures.

CA: Video tape portion of the trial. [When the jury viewed a video tape of the killing that a store monitoring system had recorded.]

KY: After I saw pictures and hair and semen analysis.

MO: [After] looking at the pictures and seeing you know, the crime, the autopsy photos.

FL: During the evidence—when [I] saw the pictures of the victim.

MO: After I knew, when they showed us the photographs of [the victim] and how he had been murdered. I knew [the defendant] had done it by the video tape but I didn't know how severe and how gruesome it was.

In a few instances they gave vivid accounts of how photo or video evidence had affected them:

NC: During the trial. I can tell you...when we saw pictures of this woman's body, burned.... Where her feet were burned off.... Horrible, horrible pictures of this. That convinced me.

CA: Just sitting there watching [a video tape of the killing from a store monitoring system]. I've seen a lot [of] stuff, but I never.... Even Arnold Schwarzenegger movies didn't affect me like that, you know? This wasn't make-believe, watching that video tape. The video tape was very powerful.

Thus, many jurors attribute their early stands for death to unquestionable proof of guilt, heinous aspects of the crime, and physical evidence, especially in photographs and on audio or video tape.

In addition to the nature of the crime and the evidence of guilt, some early pro-death jurors focused on the defendant to explain what caused them to take a stand for death during the guilt stage of the trial. These accounts typically concerned the demeanor of the defendant and the juror's perception of his future dangerousness if not sentenced to death:

CA: Once I was convinced that he did it, I was convinced that he was kind of cold-blooded and didn't have any feelings, basically.

KY: I can't explain to you how he looked but I guess that's when I knew...the way he sat there.

TX: I think this feeling came about over days of watching him and knowing he could do something like that again.

The defendant's likely future dangerousness is an especially prominent theme—the likelihood that "he could do something like that again," in the words of the juror just quoted:

SC: When we heard all of the evidence I thought he would be dangerous if he got out and in thirty years he might still be dangerous.

CA: I feel he's like a dangerous snake. I feel that he might be a threat.

TX: Well while he was in jail waiting to go to trial for this he got in a fight. And I could see that to me, or it looked like somebody, he wasn't going to change. And if he was let back into society he would continue with his path of crimes.

CA: ...we didn't want him to get back out on the street again.

Early pro-death jurors found the fact of guilt and the nature of the crime compelling. They believe the death penalty is called for when the crime is egregious, the evidence is explicit, the defendant appears unrepentant, or seems apt to repeat his crime. To be sure, the heinousness of the crime and the dangerousness of the defendant may be relevant to the punishment decision, but they must not be the basis of such a decision prior to hearing evidence of mitigation at the punishment stage of the trial (see Bentele and Bowers (2001) for an examination of the decision-making of jurors whose final votes were for death).

Of course, it is possible that early pro-death or pro-life jurors were exposed to different kinds of crimes or evidence than the jurors who remained undecided. Could it be, for example, that early pro-death jurors were more commonly confronted with egregious crimes, graphic crime scene photographs, or indications of guilt backed up by forensic analysis, fingerprint samples, eyewitness identification, etc. To test this possibility, we examined a wide range of questions the interview asked about the nature of the crime, the number involved as victims and perpetrators, the relationship between offender and victim, and the kinds of evidence presented at the trial. Yet, the extensive data jurors provided on the characteristics of the crime and on the evidence of guilt reveal no sizable or consistent differences between early death or early life decision-makers and those who, in accord with the law, waited until the sentencing stage of the trial to make their punishment decisions (Bowers et al. 1998:Appendix B). Hence, the evidence indicates that early pro-death decision-making did not occur because jurors served on cases with more aggravated kinds of killings, more convincing evidence of guilt, or more dangerous defendants than did those who remained undecided or took a pro-life stand at guilt.

Since early pro-death jurors were not exposed to stronger evidence, more vivid or graphic depictions of the crimes, or more aggravated kinds of crimes at the guilt trial, something else must be at work. It might be that jurors who take an early stand on punishment do so because they come to the trial with a predisposition to see death as the only acceptable punishment for capital murder—a predisposition that is activated by gruesome details of the crime, details made especially vivid in physical evidence, pictures, video tapes and the like, a predisposition that overrides the requirement to wait for the sentencing stage of the trial before taking a stand on punishment.

Table 2*

Capital Jurors' Feelings That the Death Penalty Is the Only
Acceptable Punishment, Sometimes Acceptable As Punishment,
or an Unacceptable Punishment for Various Crimes**

	Only acceptable %	Sometimes acceptable %	Un-acceptable %
Murder by someone previously convicted of murder	71.6	26.1	2.3
A planned, premeditated murder	57.1	40.3	2.6
Murders in which more than one victim is killed	53.7	43.7	2.6
Killing of a police officer or prison guard	48.9	47.8	3.3
Murder by a drug dealer	46.2	50.4	3.4
A killing that occurs during another crime	24.2	68.9	6.9
When an outsider to the community kills an admired and respected member of the community	22.3	72.6	5.1

* Source: Bowers et al. (1998:1505, Table 6), updated.
** Row Percentages are based on 1,159 to 1,171 jurors.

The predisposition toward death as punishment

Do jurors come to the capital trial with an open mind about punishment? If they are to give effect to aggravating considerations in their decision-making, they cannot regard the death penalty as an unacceptable option (*Witherspoon v. Illinois* 1968:519–520). Likewise, if they are to give effect to mitigating considerations, they must not regard the death penalty as the only acceptable punishment (*Woodson* 1976:305). Instead, they must regard the death penalty as sometimes acceptable for such an offense and give effect to both aggravating and mitigating considerations in deciding whether it is the appropriate punishment in the case at hand (*Morgan* 1992).

To detect jurors' personal feelings or predispositions that might impair their proper functioning as members of a capital jury, we asked them about the acceptability of the death penalty to them for seven specific kinds of murder. The question read, "Do you feel that the death penalty is the only acceptable punishment, an unacceptable punishment, or sometimes acceptable as punishment for the following specific kinds of murder..." Table 2 shows jurors' responses for each of these crimes.

These data make it clear that many persons chosen to serve as capital jurors fail to appreciate or to personally accept the principle, established in *Woodson* (1976), that the death penalty is never the "only acceptable" punishment for a capital offense. More than half of the jurors believed that death was the only acceptable punishment for repeat murder, premeditated murder, and multiple murder. Nearly half identified death as the only acceptable punishment for the killing of a police officer or prison guard, or for a murder by a drug dealer. A quarter of the jurors said that death was the only acceptable punishment for felony related killing and the killing of a respected citizen by a stranger to the community. By contrast, very few jurors (between 2.3% and 6.9%) believed that death was unacceptable as punishment for any of the seven kinds of murder in Table 2.

Contrary to *Morgan's* requirement that jurors give effect to both aggravation and mitigation in sentencing, this predisposition of many jurors to see death as the "only acceptable" punishment leaves no room for mitigation.[24] Indeed, once jurors with such a predisposition are convinced of guilt and prompted by physical evidence that lends credence to the egregious or heinous character of the crime, they might be expected to decide that death is the "right" punishment without waiting for further evidence or arguments. And, the more crimes for which they see death as the only acceptable punishment, the stronger such a predisposition is apt to be—a predisposition that might be expected to foster a precipitous pro-death punishment decision.

The CJP research confirms that there is a strong association between feeling that death is the only acceptable punishment for these kinds of crime and taking a pro-death stand at the guilt stage of the trial (Bowers et al. 1998:Table 7, updated). The more of these offenses for which a juror believed death is the only acceptable punishment, the more likely he or she was to take an early pro-death stand. In fact, early pro-death stands are five times as common (52.2% vs. 10.0%) among those who believe death is the only acceptable punishment for all seven of these kinds of killings as compared to those who said it was the only acceptable punishment for none of these offenses.[25]

---

24. See Sandys and McClelland (2003) for evidence that many jurors are "mitigation impaired," and see Bentele and Bowers (2001:1041–1053, Part 3C) for evidence that many jurors who impose the death penalty disregard or disparage mitigation.

25. Since we asked jurors about the acceptability of the death penalty not before but after they had served on a capital case, it might be that their responses are the product of having served rather than an indication of their feelings or predispositions prior to this service (i.e., that they mistakenly recall their initial stands to be consistent with their final votes on punishment), a tendency known as "hind sight bias" (Nisbet and Wilson 1977). As noted earlier, we asked jurors about their stands on punishment at four points during the trial. If the association between the feeling that death is the only acceptable punishment and taking an early pro-death stand on punishment is the product of jury service, we would expect to see that this association increases over the course of the trial. The contrary is true, however. The association between believing that the death penalty was the only acceptable punishment and the stand jurors took at various points during the trial is strongest at the initial guilt stage of the trial and diminishes at successive points thereafter (Bowers et al. 1998:Appendix A). The pattern of associations thus supports the inference that the hasty pro-death stand taken by roughly a third of the capital jurors at the guilt stage of the trial is the result of a predisposition jurors bring with them to the trial, a predisposition that encourages an early pro-death stand on the defendant's punishment,

The obvious implication is that voir dire questioning has failed to detect many jurors who, because of their pro-death predispositions, should fail the "life qualification" test for capital jury service. They may say under oath that they can disregard their personal feelings and beliefs, but the evidence shows that in practice they do not. Perhaps this is because abstract questions are an unrealistic test of the realities of jury service. Clearly, the range or kinds of questions now employed or even permitted, the discretion judges exercise in culling out biased jurors, and attorneys' skills in conducting voir dire questioning are not sufficient to purge prospective jurors who will not abide by sentencing standards.[26] The reality is that pre-existing feelings that death is the only acceptable punishment for many kinds of aggravated murder substantially contribute to taking a firm pro-death stand at the guilt stage of the trial, and this reality is manifestly contrary to the principles of capital sentencing in *Lockett* (1978), and to the qualifications for capital jury service in *Morgan* (1992).

The contamination of guilt with punishment considerations

The fact that many jurors had decided on punishment during the guilt trial means that they might possibly have voiced their views about the defendant's punishment during guilt deliberations, with adverse implications for the guilt verdict. The very danger that the guilt decision might be contaminated by pun-

---

and not the result of hind sight bias, or, a tendency for jurors' responses to be a reflection of their final votes (rather than their initial stands) on punishment.

26. In many cases it simply may not be possible at jury selection to determine whether a prospective capital juror will consider aggravating and mitigating factors or otherwise follow sentencing guidelines in good faith when making the life or death punishment decision. During jury selection, judges and attorneys necessarily rely upon a limited range of questions for this purpose. These questions typically ask whether jurors can follow the judge's instructions, and of course, the socially desirable answer jurors are naturally motivated to give is that they can—especially since they usually have had no experience of trying and failing to do so. In *Witt* (1985), the Court itself acknowledged this point:

> Determinations of juror bias cannot be reduced to question-and-answer sessions which obtain results in the manner of a catechism. What common sense should have realized experience has proved: many veniremen simply cannot be asked enough questions to reach the point where their bias has been made "unmistakably clear"; these veniremen may not know how they will react when faced with imposing the death sentence, or may be unable to articulate, or may wish to hide their true feelings (*Wainwright v. Witt* 1985:424–425).

For evidence that a single question or a narrow line of questioning may be a poor means of determining how prospective jurors think in ways that may impede their compliance with the constitutionally imposed standard, see, Dillehay and Sandys (1996:148–152).

ishment considerations is what prompted the Supreme Court to require in *Witherspoon* (1968) that prospective jurors be able to make the guilt decision apart from their attitudes or beliefs about the death penalty.

Despite this insistence that guilt and punishment considerations be kept apart, most jurors reported that during guilt deliberations they did discuss the legally irrelevant and likely confounding matter of the defendant's punishment (Bowers et al. 1998:Table 11, updated). One-half (49.0%) said "jurors' feelings about the right punishment" were discussed "a great deal" during guilt deliberations. Beyond expressions of feelings, four of ten jurors (38.7%) indicated an element of advocacy in these discussions, answering "yes" to the question, "In deciding guilt, did jurors talk about whether or not the defendant would, or should, get the death penalty?"

The jurors who made premature punishment decisions were the ones more apt to say that the defendant's punishment came up during guilt deliberations. They also reported that the discussion during guilt deliberations focused a great deal on elements of aggravation, typically of relevance to the determination of punishment, such as the cruel brutal nature of the crime, the pain and suffering of the victim, and the future dangerousness of the defendant (Bowers et al. 1998:1521, n. 87). Because they were more likely than others to see the death penalty as the only acceptable punishment, and because they were more likely than others to have decided what the punishment should be during the guilt trial, their pro-death advocacy may, in many cases, have dominated guilt deliberations.

Does jurors' punishment advocacy actually influence the jury's verdict on guilt? The jurors themselves provide answers. After the question, "In deciding guilt, did jurors talk about whether or not [the defendant] would, or should, get the death penalty," interviewers were instructed to ask the jurors who answered "yes" the further question: "What did they say?" Sometimes quite explicitly, their responses indicated a contamination of the guilt decision with punishment considerations, as illustrated in the following accounts (Bowers et al. 1998:1522):

SC: It was almost a—this may sound petty—but it was almost a trade off, with the juror, with the other jury members. We'll go along with the [capital] guilty [verdict] but there won't be a death [sentence]. I mean it was like four days deliberation on guilt and two hours on sentencing.

AL: Uh, it was probably contrary to the rules and it was certainly contrary to the judge's instructions. But the discussion came up when we were trying to determine guilt or innocence of a capital crime. At that stage, we discussed the possible penalties and [a] very unusual situation arose in the jury room.... A couple of the jurors,...one in particular...were disposed not to find him guilty of a capital crime.... So in order to get a verdict, we had to discuss the penalty prematurely.... Um everybody was finally convinced that he shot the victim intentionally, and that it was not accidental. But even acknowledging that, we still had two people who in the face of that evidence, and after themselves acknowledging it, were still not inclined to find him guilty of a capital crime unless the other jurors agreed not to recommend the death penalty. . . .

In these cases, jurors with doubts, about a capital murder verdict agreed to vote guilty of capital murder in exchange for an agreement with early pro-death jurors to abandon their pursuit of the death penalty. Such a guilt for punishment trade-off not only forfeits the punishment decision to guilt considerations, but also confounds the guilt decision with punishment concerns, thus nullifying a guilty verdict for a lesser crime.

Jurors experience a strong temptation, if not pressures, to talk about punishment at guilt, even when they know it is inappropriate. In some instances they manage to overcome the temptation; in others, the temptation prevails. When punishment is part of the discussion, pro-death jurors often declare—sometimes in forceful, impassioned words—that the law requires death or that the character of the crime or of the defendant demands it. They emphasize the cruelty or the premeditation of the offender and the aggravated character of the crime; they stress the need for incapacitation as well as retribution (Sarat 1995). They argue that the jury was selected for its ability to impose death, and they allay others' reluctance to impose death by saying that jurors must not feel personally responsible for the defendant's punishment, that judges are the ones who actually impose the sentence, and that the death penalty is seldom carried out (Hoffmann 1995).

The evidence here from the experience of real jurors in real cases reveals not only the failure to achieve impartiality in sentencing, but also the failure to protect the guilt decision from the confounding effect of premature stands on punishment voiced in guilt deliberations. The presumed insulation of guilt and punishment decisions by means of a bifurcated capital trial is in many cases a legal fiction—leaving jurors to make the guilt and sentencing decisions with the same arbitrariness and caprice condemned by *Furman* (1972).

Misguided Punishment Decision-Making

Misunderstanding the standards for considering mitigation

When a capital trial moves from the guilt to the punishment stage, the decision rules change. Unlike the guilt decision, the punishment decision is to be a reasoned moral choice on the part of each individual juror. While the standard of proof beyond a reasonable doubt and the agreement of all 12 jurors are generally necessary for a guilt verdict and for findings of aggravation, not so for mitigation. The Supreme Court's rulings in *McKoy* (1990) and *Mills* (1988) hold that the individual juror may judge that mitigation is sufficient to block a death sentence without the concurrence of other jurors if he finds that it is proven to his own personal satisfaction.[27] This difference respects the critical role of mitigation as the essence of the punishment decision, once findings of aggravation have narrowed the class of death eligible offenders (*Zant* 1983:878).[28] The sentencing decision is thus an individual moral judgment; each juror's stand on the defendant's punishment should be a "reasoned moral response," apart from the judgments of other jurors (*Penry* 1989:319).[29]

Once jurors have heard the evidence and arguments presented at the sentencing stage of the trial, they are instructed by the judge on how to make their sentencing decision. Experimental studies of prospective jurors raise serious questions about the comprehensibility of such instructions, and point in particular to an apparent pro-death bias in sentencing decisions owing to jurors' misunderstandings concerning mitigation (Diamond and Levi 1996; Luginbuhl 1992; Wiener et al. 1998; Zeisel 1990). The possibility that capital jurors make their sentencing decisions with distorted or biased understandings of the guidelines they are to follow is an unsettling proposition that the CJP is well suited to test with persons who have actually served as capital jurors.

The CJP investigators for North Carolina (Luginbuhl and Howe 1995) and for South Carolina (Eisenberg and Wells 1993) have examined jurors' understanding of sentencing instructions in those states and found that many jurors are wrong about which factors can and cannot be considered, what level of proof is needed, and what degree of concurrence is required for findings of aggravation and mitigation. Critically, both studies found that the nature of those misunderstandings would lead jurors to improperly accept aggravating and improperly reject mitigating considerations.

This pro-death bias is most conspicuously the product of jurors' mistaken views about mitigation and it is not limited to these two states where it was first confirmed. Two questions in the CJP interviews dealt specifically with rules governing the consideration of mitigation. One asked, "For a factor in favor of a life or lesser sentence to be considered, did it have to be proved 'beyond a reasonable doubt,' by 'a preponderance of the evidence,' or only to 'a juror's personal satisfaction.'" Proof beyond a reasonable doubt is clearly mis-

---

27. Or by a preponderance of the evidence in Pennsylvania (*supra* note 9).

28. *Zant* (1983) recast the sentencing process as one of narrowing the class of death-eligible defendants by requiring a finding of at least one statutory aggravating factor and then permitting the unguided exercise of discretion in selecting the punishment, except insofar as *Lockett* mandates the consideration of mitigation.

29. Quoting *California* v. *Brown*, 479 U.S. 538, 545 (1987) (O'Connor, J., concurring). This decision is in accord with the view in *Lockett* that "the risk that the death penalty will be imposed in spite of factors which may call for a less severe penalty…is unacceptable and incompatible with the commands of the Eighth and Fourteenth Amendments" 438 U.S. at 605 (opinion of Burger, C.J.).

Table 3*
Capital Jurors' Misunderstanding of Rules for
the Consideration of Mitigating Evidence

State	Mitigating factors must be proved beyond a reasonable doubt		All jurors must agree on mitigating factors	
	%	(N)	%	(N)
Alabama	53.8	(52)	32.7	(52)
California	37.6	(149)	49.7	(149)
Florida	48.7	(117)	23.1	(117)
Georgia	62.2	(74)	74.0	(73)
Indiana	58.2	(98)	57.1	(98)
Kentucky	61.8	(110)	69.7	(109)
Missouri	34.5	(58)	51.7	(58)
North Carolina	43.0	(79)	43.8	(80)
Pennsylvania	32.0	(75)	58.7	(75)
South Carolina	48.7	(113)	66.7	(114)
Tennessee	46.7	(45)	67.4	(46)
Texas**	66.0	(47)	56.3	(48)
Virginia	51.2	(43)	72.7	(44)
All states	49.2	(1,085)	54.7	(1,089)

* Source: Luginbuhl and Howe (1975:Table 1), updated with breakdown by state added.
** The number of Texas jurors is reduced in this table because these two questions were replaced with others while the interviewing in Texas was underway.

taken. The other question asked, "For a factor in favor of a life or lesser sentence to be considered, did all jurors have to agree on that factor, or did jurors not have to agree unanimously on that factor?" For the CJP states and the sample as a whole, Table 3 shows the extent to which jurors are mistaken about the level of proof and level of agreement for considering mitigation.

Most jurors in the full sample are either wrong or ignorant about each of these rules for the consideration of mitigating evidence, and the mistaken ones assume rules that tend to block findings of mitigation. Half of the jurors (49.2%) wrongly believed that a mitigating factor had to be proved beyond a reasonable doubt, and even more (54.7%) mistakenly believed that jurors had to agree unanimously on a mitigating factor for it to be considered in mitigation. Although not shown in Table 3, another 15.4% and 11.8% indicated that they did not know the required level of proof or degree of agreement, respectively. Thus, only about a third of the jurors were correct about either of these standards; 35.4% about the level of proof (including either "personal satisfaction" or "preponderance of the evidence" as acceptable responses) and 33.5% about the degree of agreement for a finding of mitigation.

As with premature punishment decision-making, the breach is pervasive; no state is spared. Here, there is more variation from state to state in the percent mistaken about level of proof and level of agreement concerning mitigation, yet the differences do not identify the jurors of any states as substantially and consistently better informed in both respects. North Carolina is the only state that is more than five points below the mistaken responses in the sample as a whole on both mitigation rules; California is more than five points below on one and at five points below on the other.

By contrast, two states do consistently worse than the rest. Georgia and Kentucky are more than ten points above the sample wide figures on both rules, suggesting that the absence of enumerated mitigating factors in these threshold statutes may foster such mistaken impressions. South Carolina, the other threshold state, is ten points above the rest on one but not on both of these rules. The greatest departures from the sample wide statistics come with Alabama and Florida on the unanimity requirement. To be sure, only in these two states may juries recommend a death sentence, without being unanimous, but this has nothing to do with the level of agreement required for considering mitigation. Some Alabama and Florida jurors may simply have generalized the application of the nonunanimous standard from the penalty verdict to findings of mitigation. No states are giving their jurors substantially and consistently better, not to say correct, understandings of the distinctive rules supposed to govern the consideration of mitigation.

Clearly, a great many jurors wrongly believe that the fact finding rules for decision-making about guilt and aggravation apply as well to mitigation. No doubt, some of this "tilt toward death" in jurors' understanding of sentencing instructions is due to a "carry-over" of the guilt decision rules to the sentencing phase of the trial in the minds of jurors. It is a matter of folk knowledge that jurors in a criminal trial must unanimously agree that specifically enumerated factors are proved beyond a reasonable doubt for the jury to hand down a guilty verdict. Obviously, many jurors wrongly assume that the same require-ments of unanimity and reasonable doubt also apply to the consideration of mitigation in sentencing. They fail to appreciate that the decision rules are dif-ferent for evidence of mitigation, probably because they do not realize that they are being called upon not for a finding of facts but for a reasoned moral judgment. They do not understand that for such a reasoned moral choice the Constitution requires that each capital juror independently decide whether mitigation is sufficient to reject a death sentence, whatever the aggravation, and whatever the punishment decisions of other jurors. When a juror becomes convinced that the death penalty is not appropriate in light of mitigating con-siderations, that juror is morally obligated to vote for a life sentence.

Mistakenly believing a death sentence is required

As fundamental to capital sentencing as which factors can be considered, what level of proof is needed, whether unanimity is required, or how the weighing of factors must be conducted and interpreted, is the prohibition against having the death sentence be, or be seen by jurors as, "mandatory." In *Woodson* (1976) the Supreme Court established that no state can require the death penalty simply or solely upon the finding of a particular aggravating factor or given level of aggravation. The punishment decision must always entail the consideration of mitigation.

To test jurors' understanding of this basic principle, CJP investigators asked jurors about two relatively common aggravating factors. The question asked whether they believed, after hearing the judge's sentencing instructions, that the death penalty was required (a) "if the evidence proved that the defendant's conduct was heinous, vile or depraved," or (b) "if the evidence proved that the defendant would be dangerous in the future." Jurors' responses reveal that many capital jurors mistakenly believed that the death penalty was "required" when these aggravating circumstances were present (Bowers 1995:Table 7, updated). Four out of ten jurors (43.9%) wrongly believed that they were required to impose the death penalty if the evidence proved that the crime was heinous, vile, or depraved, and only somewhat fewer (37.0%) mistakenly thought the death penalty was required if the evidence proved the defendant would be dangerous in the future. Half of the jurors (50.3%) believed that the death penalty was required under one or the other of these two aggravating conditions. This misunderstanding of statutory standards obviously biases the sentencing decision in favor of the death penalty to the extent that jurors do, in fact, find that the evidence proves these allegations.

Jurors' answers to a further question are relevant here. Concerning the particular case on which the jurors sat, the interview asked whether the evidence proved that the crime was heinous, vile, or depraved, and whether it proved that the defendant would be dangerous in the future. The overwhelming majority of jurors believed that the evidence did, in fact, prove these factors (Bowers 1995:Table 8, updated). Some 81.5% said the evidence proved that the defendant's crime was "heinous, vile, or depraved," and 78.2% said it proved that the defendant would be "dangerous in the future." Some 84.7% of the jurors believed that the evidence in their case proved at least one of these two aggravating circumstances. As a consequence, 44.6% of the capital jurors entered sentencing deliberations with the misimpression that the death penalty was required by law in the case before them (This represents the percent of jurors who believed that the death penalty was required for one or the other of these two factors, a factor which they also believed was proved by the evidence).

Hence, the presence of an aggravating factor, which should merely make a defendant eligible for a death sentence, operates as a mandate for the death penalty in the minds of many jurors. This is illustrated in their responses to questions about how the jury arrived at its decision to sentence the defendant to death (Bentele and Bowers 2001):

NC: if you answer two questions "yes" you have to give the death penalty. That would automatically require the death penalty.

TX: I don't remember the specifics, but he made it very clear to us what the law prescribed. It was like; "If…, then…."

SC: What would the defendant do if set free? Would [the defendant] kill again? The law said the defendant must get death…[the] solicitor explained that this was required by law.

CA: I think she [an almost holdout juror] finally had to admit that he would easily hurt someone else and that our instructions said in that case we were required to give death.

Believing that death is required by law when certain commonly found aggravating factors are present in a case goes hand in hand with being predisposed to vote for death, with making the punishment decision prematurely, and with failing to understand the standards for considering mitigation. Indeed, these faults are self reinforcing. The belief that the death penalty is required by law when aggravation is proven obviates the need to understand the rules for considering mitigation, and insulates an early pro-death stand on punishment from later evidence and arguments for a life sentence. Surely, the predisposition of many jurors to see death as the "only acceptable punishment" for various kinds of aggravated murder nourishes the belief that the law requires death when these relatively common aggravators are present.

This constellation of faults—pro-death predispositions, premature punishment decision-making, mistakenly believing a death sentence is required, and misunderstanding mitigation rules—suggests that the statutory guidelines as conveyed in the judge's sentencing instructions may serve more as a foil than a guide for the punishment decisions of most jurors. One question asked by the CJP investigators bears on this point. It asked, "Would you say the judge's sentencing instructions to the jury…simply provided a framework for the decision most jurors had already made?"

Virtually three out of four jurors (74.2%) acknowledged that sentencing instructions did not guide the jury's decision-making on punishment but served instead as a rationale for a decision most jurors made without regard for the instructions (Bowers 1995:Table 9, updated). For many jurors the judge's sentencing instructions obviously serve to rationalize in legalistic terms a decision arrived at contrary to what constitutional law requires.

Underestimating the death penalty alternative

If jurors are to make a reasoned, responsible sentencing decision, should they not be fully and accurately informed of the punishment options from which they must choose? The Court in *Gregg* (1976:190) asserted that "accurate sentencing information is an indispensable prerequisite to a reasoned de-

Table 4*
Capital Jurors' Estimates and Mandatory Minimums of
Time Served before Release from Prison for Capital Murderers
Not Sentenced to Death in 13 States and the Full Sample

State	Median estimate**	(N)	Mandatory minimum***
	Years in prison if not given death		
Alabama	15.0	(35)	LWOP
California	17.0	(98)	LWOP
Florida	20.0	(104)	25
Georgia	7.0	(67)	15
Indiana	20.0	(75)	30
Kentucky	10.0	(74)	12, 25****
Missouri	20.0	(47)	LWOP
North Carolina	17.0	(77)	20
Pennsylvania	15.0	(63)	LWOP
South Carolina	17.0	(99)	30
Tennessee	22.0	(42)	25
Texas	15.0	(106)	20
Virginia	15.0	(36)	21.75
All states	15.0	(943)	—

* Source: Bowers and Steiner (1999:Table 1), updated.
** Median estimates exclude "no answers" and unqualified "life" responses but include responses indicating "life without parole" or "rest of life in prison."
*** These are the minimum periods of imprisonment before parole eligibility for capital murderers not given the death penalty at the time of the sampled trials in each state.
**** Kentucky gives capital jurors different sentencing options with 12 years and 25 years before parole eligibility as the principal alternatives (See Bowers and Steiner 1999:646, n. 198).

termination of whether a defendant shall live or die by a jury of people who may never before have made a sentencing decision." Georgia capital trial transcripts reveal that the most common question jurors ask judges during sentencing deliberations is how long would the defendant actually spend in prison if not given the death penalty (Lane 1993). The jurors typically return a death sentence soon after being denied an answer (at 336). Could it be that Georgia jurors often vote for death in such cases because they mistakenly underestimate what the alternative punishment would be?

The CJP investigators asked jurors "How long did you think someone not given the death penalty for a capital murder in this state usually spends in prison?" In Table 4 we show jurors' median estimates in response to this question, and the legally established mandatory minimums before parole consideration for persons convicted of capital murder but not sentenced to death by state and for the full sample.

The CJP interviews reveal that capital jurors consistently and substantially underestimate the death penalty alternative. In every state, the median estimate was well below the mandatory minimum for parole eligibility. That is to say, most jurors believe that capital murderers not given the death penalty will usually be back on the streets even before completing the legally mandated minimum sentence for parole consideration in their state.

Do these usually mistaken impressions about the alternative punishment influence jurors' sentencing decisions? The CJP data show that the shorter jurors think prison confinement would be, if they did not impose the death penalty, the more likely they are to vote for death (Bowers and Steiner 1999:Table 3). Between jurors who say the alternative is less than 10 years and those who say 20 or more years, the difference in pefcent voting for death is 16 points (66.7% vs.50.3%) at the first ballot on punishment, and 25 points (71.5% vs. 46.4%) at the final sentencing decision. Before the sentencing stage of the trial and before sentencing deliberations, the corresponding differences in pro-death stands are 11 and 9 percentage points.[30] The data thus show that the more jurors underestimate the death penalty alternative the more likely they are to vote for death, and this pro-death leaning becomes more pronounced later in the trial. In particular, misimpressions about the alternative to the death penalty appear to become critical in the final give and take of punishment deliberations.

Jurors' narrative responses reveal the sources of their estimates of the death penalty alternative:

SC: We were discussing our prisons are so overcrowded now it's already a fact that there are people being released that would'a been there a lot longer had we not had an overcrowding situation...[I know this because] my boyfriend's mother works at the South Carolina department of corrections. And I mean [I] know that you hear, just you know, street talk. You know, anybody knows that you can commit a murder these days and be [out] in no time.

AL: I read the papers everyday, just about it, and I'd say 60% to 70% of the crime committed in Birmingham, this area here, is committed by people who've been in prison, get out several different times. We've had quite a few murders, now that's the cause of it.

Fear of the defendant's recidivism led jurors to impose a death sentence even when they believed a life sentence was deserved:

GA: Unanimous[ly], we'd have voted for life without parole but that wasn't an option, and we felt sure that if he was given life, he'd be given parole....

---

30. Owing to the exceptionally low release estimates of Georgia jurors, they were excluded from this tabulations in order to obtain representative statistical comparisons for the remaining twelve states. See Steiner, Bowers, and Sarat (1999:Table 4, Part B) for the association between release estimates and jurors' stands on punishment in Georgia.

We all felt like that he did not deserve...[that] there wasn't enough evidence to feel like he deserved...I mean death.

NC: We all had decided if we were absolutely sure that he would never have gotten out of prison we wouldn't have given him the death penalty. But we were not sure of that. That's why we imposed the death penalty.

VA: We all knew that he's (sic) probably be in prison for a considerable amount of time but the other thing we looked at is that because he was very quiet, because he appeared, apparently could contain himself very well, especially in an environment where he was restricted. That he would end up being a model prisoner and be out in 15 to 20 years....

Claims of early release may be the trump card for convincing life holdouts to vote for death:

KY: It was two guys. I just think they felt really bad about putting another person to death, but then they realized. Well, another factor was, we also told them that if he was to be put to death, he would probably never be put to death. He was going to be on death row probably till he dies. But that was the only way to keep him in prison.

TX: One of the jurors held out.... Very intelligent man. But I don't think he appreciated a lot of the unsaid things about the American justice system (laughs). Such as life does not mean life. And frankly, if there had been a complaint, at that time. There probably would have been a mistrial.... Seriously, because I kind of felt kind of like the jury badgered him to the point to where he changed his vote.... There was a lot of hostility. A lot of frustration and a lot of hostility towards this person.... I wouldn't say there was anything physical about it.... Well I think there was a basic frustration on the part of the jurors that this guy.... We were like..."What the hell are you even doing here?"

In *Simmons v. South Carolina* (1994), the Supreme Court ruled that a capital defendant was protected from having his jury make a "false choice," that is, making a choice between the death penalty and a false or incorrect understanding of the alternative. It limited the application of this principle, however, to situations, such as Simmons', in which the death penalty alternative was a life sentence without parole and the prosecution argued the defendant's future dangerousness. While the CJP data do indeed show that jurors are more apt to vote for death if they underestimate the alternative under this circumstance, the data show as well that underestimating the alternative also leads to a vote for death when the alternative is not life without parole and the defendant is not alleged to be dangerous (Bowers and Steiner 1999:Table 6). Hence, to inform jurors as provided by *Simmons* is, at best, a partial corrective to a widespread tilt toward death in capital sentencing.

Since the CJP interviews were conducted, additional states have adopted life without parole (LWOP) as the death penalty alternative.[31] To the extent that jurors are aware of such changes and believe that the new legislation means what it says the pro-death bias of underestimating the death penalty alternative may recede. Yet, jurors in three of the four CJP states with LWOP were virtually unaware of this fact; in Alabama, Missouri, and Pennsylvania a total of only three jurors said the alternative was life without parole, or explicitly indicated that the defendant would spend the rest of his life in prison. In California, only one in five jurors correctly identified LWOP as the alternative, and many were still not confident that the law meant what it said.[32] The median release estimate was 17 years. Jurors bring their own ideas about criminal sentences, parole, and the death penalty alternative to jury deliberations, ideas which appear to be firmly imbedded in "folk knowledge" and reinforced by selective media coverage of crime and punishment (Steiner et al. 1999). When they read or hear about released murderers killing again, they may not consider whether the offender was imprisoned for capital murder. And when judges tell them what the alternative is they may have doubts if what they hear does not conform to their own beliefs about how the law actually works. The substantial and widespread underestimates of the death penalty alternative documented in Table 4, place the burden of proof on those who claim that capital jurors are not making false choices but reasoned moral judgments. They cannot, as before, simply adopt the legal fiction that jurors correctly understand the death penalty alternative.

Denying responsibility for the punishment

The U.S. Supreme Court in *Caldwell* v. *Mississippi* (1985) said it is an "intolerable danger" for jurors to believe that "the responsibility for any ultimate determination of death will rest with others." The Court reasoned, "A capital sentencing jury is made up of individuals placed in a very unfamiliar situation and called on to make a very difficult and uncomfortable choice.... Given such a situation, the uncorrected suggestion that the responsibility for any ultimate determination of death will rest with others presents an intolerable danger that the jury will in fact choose to minimize the importance of its role" (at 333).

The mistaken beliefs of many jurors that the law requires the death penalty if the evidence proves the crime is heinous or the defendant is dangerous is

---

31. All but three of the 38 death penalty states (Kansas, New Mexico, and Texas) are reported to have LWOP as a death penalty alternative under at least some circumstances. See, http://www.deathpenaltyinfo.org/lwop.html (last visited September 4, 2002).

32. See Bowers and Steiner (1999:666–671) for excerpts from juror interviews in six California cases that underscore their mistrust of claims that defendant's not sentenced to death will spend the rest of their lives in prison.

Table 5*
Percent Ranking Five Sources or Agents of Responsibility for the Defendant's Punishment from Most "1" to Least "5" Responsible.

	Most >				< Least
	1	2	3	4	5
The defendant because his/her conduct is what actually determined the punishment	49.3	10.7	6.0	7.8	26.3
The law that states what punishment applies	32.8	40.0	8.6	12.4	6.2
The jury that votes for the sentence	8.9	23.6	38.2	25.4	3.8
The individual juror since the jury's decision depends on the vote of each juror	5.5	14.2	27.1	28.4	24.8
The judge who imposes the sentence	3.6	11.2	20.5	25.8	39.0

* Source: Bowers (1995:Table 10), updated. Percentages are based on the 1,095 jurors who ranked all five options (i.e., ranks sum to 15).

consistent with the notion that many jurors see the law, rather than themselves, as responsible for the defendant's punishment. Indeed, Weisberg (1984:383) has argued that the very sentencing guidelines jurors are instructed to follow, by appearing to provide an authoritative formula for the "correct" or "required" punishment, may actually diminish jurors' sense of responsibility for the punishment they impose.[33]

To see where capital jurors place responsibility for the defendant's punishment, CJP investigators asked jurors about five sources or agents of responsibility. Jurors were asked to rank these five options from most to least responsible for the defendant's punishment. The percent giving ranks 1–5 (for "most" to "least" responsible) are shown for each of the five options in Table 5.

Overwhelmingly, jurors deny that they are primarily responsible for the defendant's punishment. As the *Caldwell* Court feared, they place responsibility for the defendant's punishment elsewhere. Four of five jurors assigned foremost

---

33. Weisberg argues that the penalty phase juror, deciding whether to sentence the defendant to death, is in a position similar to that of the subjects in Stanley Milgram's (1974) classic program of research on obedience to authority in which subjects were instructed by an authority figure to inflict what they were told was "painful" punishment on a "learner" in an adjacent room (at 305). Milgram found that his subjects were willing to increase the pain-inducing electric shocks despite the ersatz sounds of their victims suffering.... Milgram's interpretation of his findings was that, in response to instructions from an authority figure, a moral state is induced which he called an "agentic shift," a state of mind in which a man feels responsible to the authority directing him but feels no responsibility for the content of the actions that the authority prescribes (at 132–134). Weisberg postulates that the instructions given the capital sentencing jury, which have the appearance of legal rules, dilute the jury's sense of responsibility, rather than guiding discretion.

responsibility to the defendant (49.3%) or to the law (32.8%). The idea that the defendant's punishment is his own responsibility has the attraction that it blames the culprit for what the jury must do. Note, however, that a quarter of the jurors (26.3%) see him as the least responsible. They appear to distinguish between blaming the defendant for his crime and for his punishment.

By contrast, only a tiny minority (5.5%) believed that the individual juror was most responsible for the defendant's punishment. Only a few more (8.9%) believed that the jury as a body was most responsible. Altogether, only three out of twenty jurors (14.4%) believed that either the jurors, as a group or individually, were the agents most responsible for the defendant's punishment. In responsibility for the punishment, the jury ranked third, the individual juror fourth, and the judge fifth (as indicated by the percent assigning rank "1," and by the modal ranks of the five options).

Consistent with Weisberg's (1984) argument that statutory guidelines serve to replace jurors' sense of responsibility with the authority of law, the law even more consistently than the defendant outranks the jury or the individual juror in responsibility for the defendant's punishment. Indeed, the law was the most responsible agent in the minds of jurors if both first and second ranks are considered. Specifically, three of four jurors (72.8%) rank the law as either first or second in responsibility, as compared to one in three for the jury (32.5%) and one in five for the individual juror (19.7%). This preeminence of the law, over the juror or the jury, is an apparent testimony to the desire of jurors to defer to the law or to see themselves as simply "following the law," whether they understand its requirements or directives. Though jurors may misunderstand statutory guidelines, they still seek the cover of law for the awesome responsibility of their life or death decision.

The *Caldwell* Court worried particularly about one way that jurors might minimize the importance of their role: "[O]ne can easily imagine that in a case in which the jury is divided on the proper sentence, the presence of appellate review could effectively be used as an argument for why those jurors who are reluctant to invoke the death sentence should nevertheless give in" (at 333). Concerning this issue, the CJP asked jurors whether during their sentencing deliberations they thought responsibility for deciding what the defendant's punishment should be belonged strictly to the jury or was shared with trial or appellate judges; the defendant and the law were excluded from consideration. Only one in four jurors (27.2%) believed that "strictly the jury and no one else" was responsible for the punishment. Among the remaining jurors, 31.0% believed jurors were mostly responsible, 22.9% said jurors and judges were each partly responsible, and 19.0% said the responsibility was mostly in the hands of judges (Bowers 1995, updated; cf. Eisenberg, Garvey, and Wells 1996). Thus, when jurors are asked specifically about the allocation of responsibility between themselves and judicial authorities, the great majority of jurors see responsibility as shared with trial and appellate judges.

Jurors' commentaries on reaching their final sentencing decisions (from Sandys 1995:1217 and Sarat 1995:1133) aptly illustrate the *Caldwell* Court's concern:

Ky: It was an awareness that it would be, it was an awareness that it would be appealed, appeals mandated by law. If it had not been appealed, if I had not been aware that there would be a necessary appeal, I might not have changed my mind.

Ga: But there were still a couple who didn't want [the defendant] to die.... That meant that we had to talk about the fact that this, just for the reason that we voted for death, did not necessarily mean that [he] would die at the hands of the state. And I think we talked a good bit about the fact that this would go to the Georgia Supreme Court and it would be reviewed and that if anything was out of the ordinary then it would be thrown out, and that even after then the man would have many opportunities to appeal. And I think that probably that discussion helped more than anything to persuade the two that was reluctant.

At the time of the interviews, three of the CJP states—Alabama, Florida, and Indiana[34]—had capital statutes that permitted the trial judge to "override" the jury's sentencing decision; the judge could impose either a death or a life sentence, contrary to the jury's recommendation. In these three judge override states, as compared to the ten "jury binding" states, one might expect even fewer jurors to see themselves as responsible for the defendant's punishment. In fact, only a fourth as many jurors said the jury alone is responsible in the judge override as compared to the jury binding states (7.7% vs. 29.8%); twice as many said responsibility was mostly in the judge's hands (32.9% vs. 17.0%).[35] Allowing the trial judge to override the jury's sentencing decision unmistakably diminishes jurors' sense of responsibility for the defendant's punishment.

Clearly, most capital jurors are uneasy about responsibility for the awesome life or death decision they must make. Many see the defendant as responsible for his own punishment but even more see the law first or second in responsi-

---

34. Indiana abandoned its judge override provision in 2002 as indicated in note 1.

35. The tendency of jurors in override states to transfer responsibility from themselves to judges is further evident in the ranks they designate for the five agents of responsibility in Table 5. They assign much greater responsibility to the trial judge and considerably less to the individual juror than do jurors in other states. In these three states, the percent ranking the trial judge 1–3 is higher by 29.8 points (58.4% vs. 28.6%) and the percent ranking the individual juror 1–3 is lower by 20.8 points (30.7% vs. 51.5%) than in the other states. Furthermore, the impact of override is virtually confined to these two agents of responsibility. The distributions of jurors' responsibility ranks for the defendant, the law, and the jury as a group are essentially the same in the judge override and jury binding states (none of the differences between the corresponding 15 percentages exceed 5 points).

bility. They want to believe that the law is responsible and that they are simply its agents. They want the cover of law for their decision, although they often make their decision before learning what the law says they should consider, or without correctly understanding what the law requires of them. Significantly, this tendency to deny responsibility for the defendant's punishment appears to make it easier for jurors to vote for death. Hoffmann's (1995) examination of Indiana jurors' narrative accounts of their sentencing decisions documents the importance to jurors of "higher authority" for guidance in the momentous life or death decision. Not infrequently, they seek "divine guidance"—hardly, we think, what the Supreme Court had in mind as "guided discretion."

Race Linked Punishment Decision-Making

Racial bias: Statistical evidence

Shortly after the Supreme Court endorsed the guided discretion capital statutes in *Gregg* and companion cases, studies of the application of these rewritten statutes showed disparities in the use of the death penalty by race of defendant, and especially by race of victim (See Baldus and Woodworth 2003). Consistent with this evidence, the Supreme Court in *Turner* (1986) explicitly acknowledged the danger that both conscious and unconscious racial sentiments are apt to influence jurors' sentencing decisions in capital cases, and it singled out black defendant/white victim (B/W) cases as the ones in which jurors' racial attitudes are especially apt to confound the sentencing decision. It ruled that "a capital defendant accused of an interracial crime is entitled to have prospective jurors informed of the race of the victim and questioned on the issue of racial bias" (at 37). The Court declared that this judgment was "based on a conjunction of three factors: the fact that the crime charged involved interracial violence, the broad discretion given the jury at the death-penalty hearing, and the special seriousness of the risk of improper sentencing in a capital case" (at 37).

The CJP has made it possible to examine the role of jurors' race, both the racial composition of the jury[36] and the race of the individual juror[37] in capital sentencing. In the critical black defendant/white victim cases where *Turner*

---

36. The sample of trials from which jurors have been interviewed is large enough to permit extensive statistical analyses. After dropping cases with exclusively hispanic or asian defendants or victims, we have 165 W/W cases, 74 B/W cases, and 60 B/B cases.

37. With a target sample of four jurors per case, we have interviews with both black and white jurors in 33 W/W cases, 25 B/W cases, and 13 B/B cases, large enough samples to permit reliable comparisons of black and white jurors who served on the same cases. Restricting the analysis to W/W, B/W, and B/B cases from which both black and white jurors were interviewed avoids the mistake of attributing observed differences between black and white jurors to race

Table 6*
Percent of Black Defendant White Victim Capital Trials in which
Death Sentences were Imposed by Number of White Male,
White Female, Black Male, and Black Female Jurors

Number of Jurors who were:	White Males % N	White Females % N
0–3	35.3 (17)	54.2 (24)
4	23.1 (13)	50.0 (10)
5	63.2 (19)	61.5 (13)
6+	78.3 (23)	52.0 (25)
Number of Jurors who were:	Black Males % N	Black Females % N
0	71.9 (32)	55.5 (27)
1	42.9 (21)	61.9 (21)
2	36.4 (11)	60.0 (10)
3+	—— (3/8)	35.7 (14)

* Source: Bowers et al. (2001:Table 1).

warned of the dangers of both conscious and unconscious racism in jurors' decision-making, the CJP finds, indeed, that the likelihood of a death sentence is
strongly linked to the racial composition of the jury. The data reveal a pronounced pro-death "white male dominance" effect, and an almost equally pronounced pro-life "black male presence" effect, as shown in Table 6.

Observe first, that the number of white males on the jury was strongly associated with the imposition of a death sentence. Deaths sentences were imposed
in more than twice as many of the cases with five or more white males (70.7%)
than in those with four or fewer white males (30.0%). Note as well that the
presence of a black male juror was strongly associated with the imposition of a
life sentence. In the absence of black male jurors, a death sentence was almost
twice as likely (71.9%) than in the presence of at least one black male (37.5%).[38]

Furthermore, when we examined black and white jurors who served on the
same B/W cases,[39] it was evident that the black and white jurors became polarized on punishment—whites for death and blacks for life—over the course of

when they might actually reflect differences in the kinds of cases from which the full complements of black and white jurors were drawn.

38. In intra-racial W/W and B/B cases, jury composition had comparatively little influence
on sentencing outcomes (Bowers et al. 2001:Table 1).

39. To minimize the possibility that observed differences in the responses of black and white
jurors were due to differences in the cases on which they served, the analysis of individual jurors'
responses was confined to the 24 B/W cases from which both black and white jurors were interviewed.

the trial. At the guilt phase, whites were three times more likely than blacks to take a pro-death stand on punishment (42.3% vs. 14.7%). After sentencing instructions they were four times more likely to do so (58.5% vs. 15.2%). By the first vote on punishment, the differential between white and black jurors reached more than seven to one (67.3% vs. 9.1%)(Bowers et al. 2001:Table 2).

This progressive divergence of black and white jurors' punishment stands in the same B/W cases raises the question of what they may have seen differently in these cases, and how such differences may have become exacerbated over the course of the trial. The CJP data reveal differences of perspective between black and white jurors in three kinds of punishment related considerations: lingering doubt about the defendant's guilt, impressions of the defendant's remorsefulness, and perceptions of the defendant's future dangerousness.

First, black jurors were far more likely than their white counterparts to have lingering doubts about the defendant's guilt when making their punishment decisions (Bowers et al. 2001:Table 3). These doubts, generated during the guilt stage of the trial, were manifest in jurors' thinking about whether the defendant was actually guilty of capital murder and whether he was even involved in the crime (i.e., the possibility of mistaken identity). In fact, more than half of black jurors (52.9%) as compared to less than one in five white jurors (17.0%) acknowledged at least some doubts about the capital murder verdict, and there was a comparable black-white difference (45.5% vs. 5.9%) in having some doubt that the defendant was the actual killer. Given the sordid history of all-white juries, sheriff's posses, and lynchings associated with black-on-white killings, this concentration of mistrust among black jurors in these B/W cases might be anticipated.

Second, black jurors were much more likely than their white counterparts in B/W cases to see the defendant as remorseful (Bowers et al. 2001:Table 4, Panel A). More than three of five blacks (64.7%) and fewer than one of five whites (17.3%) said that "sorry" characterized the defendant "very" or "fairly" well; there was a corresponding black-white difference (52.9% vs. 14.8%) in "yes" responses to a question about whether the defendant "appeared sorry during the trial." Personal identification with the defendant, and feelings that the defendant deserved mercy also divided black and white jurors in these cases (Bowers et al. 2001:Table 4, Panels B and C). The greater identification with the defendant and with his situation among black jurors in these cases may make them more sensitive to subtle indications of his sorrow or remorse, and believing that the defendant is sorry may, in turn, encourage black jurors to feel that the defendant deserves mercy. By contrast, the tendency of white jurors not to be reminded of someone by a black defendant and not to imagine themselves in the situation of a black defendant's family may make them less sensitive to such indications, and hence less willing to grant mercy to a black defendant on grounds of remorse.

Third, white jurors were more likely than their black counterparts to see the defendant in B/W cases as dangerous and to regard his dangerousness as a reason for the death penalty (Bowers et al. 2001:Table 5). Both black and white jurors in these cases reported that a great deal of discussion during punishment deliberations focused on the defendant's likely dangerousness. But white jurors believe that in the absence of a death sentence, such defendants will usually be back on the streets far sooner than do black jurors. This may, in part, explain why they were especially likely to stress the defendant's dangerousness as a reason for the death penalty. Six of ten white jurors (57.2%) said that the defendant's dangerousness made them more likely to vote for death; four of ten (42.9%) said it made them "much more likely" to do so. For their part, black jurors were less willing to concede that the defendant was dangerous or to believe that such offenders soon return to society if not given the death penalty. They were conspicuous in rejecting the consideration of the defendant's dangerousness in deciding to vote for life or death. Only one in five (20.0%) of the black jurors said that the defendant's dangerousness made them more likely to vote for death, less than one in ten (8.0%) said "much more likely" to do so. Perhaps their reticence was a reaction to pressure they felt from white jurors to make dangerousness the rationale for a final death verdict.

The magnitude of these differences between black and white jurors are even more astonishing when we compare the males of each group. That is, the black-white differences in B/W cases (shown in Bowers et al. 2001:Tables 3–5) were even more pronounced when the comparisons were between males of the respective races, as shown in Table 7.[40]

Black males were the most likely and white males were the least likely to have lingering doubt about the defendant's guilt, chiefly about the extent of the defendant's involvement or responsibility for the crime. Again, black males were the most likely, and white males the least likely, to see the defendant as remorseful, and to identify with the defendant's or his family's situation. And on the flip side, white males were the most likely, and black males the least likely, to see the defendant as dangerous and to believe that he would be released from prison soon if not given the death penalty. Finding the males of each race at such extremes in these punishment-related considerations helps to account for the revelation in Table 6 that the effect of jury composition on sentencing outcomes is due above all to the number of males of each race on the jury.

The contrasting perceptions of the defendant's dangerousness and remorsefulness and of lingering doubts about his guilt between black and white jurors in the same B/W cases are surely grounded in their "folk knowledge" of the causes of crime and of the trustworthiness of the criminal justice process

---

40. When the data are broken down by jurors' race and gender, the number of jurors is reduced so that only the most sizeable and consistent percentage differences are statistically reliable. Therefore, we present only those data that show sizeable and consistent differences by jurors' race and gender in Table 7.

Table 7*
Elements of (a) Lingering Doubts (b) the Defendant's Remorse and Identification, and (c) Dangerousness and Release Estimates by Jurors' Race and Gender in Black Defendant-White Victim Cases (Percent by Column)

	White Males	White Females	Black Males	Black Females
A. Lingering doubts				
1. Importance of lingering doubts about the defendant's guilt for you in deciding on punishment				
Very	—	12.5	26.7	21.1
Fairly	6.9	—	26.7	15.8
Not Very	6.9	8.3	—	15.8
Not At All	86.2	79.2	46.7	47.4
(No. of jurors)	(29)	(24)	(15)	(19)
2. When considering punishment, did you think the defendant might not be the one most responsible for the killing?				
Yes	10.3	4.0	60.0	36.8
No	86.2	96.0	40.0	52.6
Not Sure	3.4	—	—	10.5
(No. of jurors)	(29)	(25)	(15)	(19)
B. Remorse and identification				
1. How well does "Sorry for what s/he did" describe the defendant?				
Very Well	7.4	20.0	46.7	31.6
Fairly Well	7.4	—	33.3	21.1
Not So Well	33.3	40.0	6.7	15.8
Not At All	51.9	40.0	13.3	31.6
(No. of jurors)	(27)	(25)	(15)	(19)
2. Did you imagine yourself in the defendant's situation?				
Yes	26.7	28.0	53.3	31.6
No	73.3	72.0	46.7	68.4
(No. of jurors)	(30)	(25)	(15)	(19)
3. Did you imagine yourself in the defendant's family's situation?				
Yes	30.0	48.0	80.0	47.4
No	60.0	48.0	13.3	47.4
Not Sure	10.0	4.0	6.7	5.3
(No. of jurors)	(30)	(25)	(15)	(19)
C. Dangerousness and early release				
1. "Dangerous to Other People" describes the defendant…				
Very Well	63.3	52.0	26.7	42.1
Fairly Well	30.0	32.0	53.3	36.8
Not So Well	3.3	8.0	—	10.5
Not At All	3.3	8.0	20.0	10.5
(No. of jurors)	(30)	(25)	(15)	(19)
2. How long did you think someone not given the death penalty for a capital murder in this state usually spends in prison?				
0–9 years	30.0	17.6	7.7	7.1
10–19 years	30.0	52.9	30.8	57.1
20 or more years	40.0	29.4	61.5	35.7
(No. of jurors)	(20)	(17)	(13)	(14)

* Source: Bowers et al. (2001), Table 7.

(Steiner et al. 1999), and in what the *Turner* Court identified as both conscious and "less consciously held" racial attitudes (at 42). These race linked differences of experience, perspective, and attitude may undercut the compatibility of blacks and whites as jury members and contaminate the deliberative process with mistrust, hostility, and invective. Far from a reasoned moral choice, jury deliberations on punishment may take on the character of a pernicious struggle to subdue opposition. Jurors' narrative accounts of the decision making process provide a window on such sentencing dynamics (Fluery-Steiner, 2002).

Racial bias: Narrative evidence

In addition to the many structured questions that provide extensive statistical data, the CJP interviews also included open ended questions about jurors' thinking and experience in their role as capital jurors. The CJP interviewers were instructed to probe for details and explanations that would refine and elaborate jurors' initial responses to these open ended questions. We have selected excerpts from interviews with both white and black jurors in two black defendant/white victim cases[41] that show how black and white jurors in the same cases viewed the evidence, the defendant, and one another, and how these views influenced the decision-making process.

CASE A: A Florida jury with one black and six white males recommended the death penalty for a black man who, with one black and one white co-perpetrator, killed a police officer.

The only black male juror on a Florida jury that included six white male jurors saw the white jurors as bent on the death penalty from the very beginning of the trial. He saw them as impatient to get home, unwilling to deliberate seriously. He felt that the white-male-dominated jury wanted the death penalty because the defendant was a black man and the victim was white:

Q: In deciding guilt, did jurors think about whether or not the defendant would or should get the death penalty? If yes, what did they say?

J: They wanted to burn both of them black boys. I'm serious, that's the impression I got. I felt like, I was the only black male on the jury.... I felt like they didn't give a shit one way or the other. They wanted to go to the football game and they wanted to go home to their husbands and all this type of stuff, and not worry about whether these people were gonna die or not. They felt like hell, these two black boys took a white man's life: "We're going to burn them." That's the impression I got from a lot of the jurors.... I really felt like they wanted to burn both those guys because

---

41. The excerpts for Cases A and B below were drawn from more extensive accounts in Bowers et al. (2001:244–246) and Bowers et al. (2001:248–250), respectively.

they were black, well because the white guy in the case [had a plea bargain], and we didn't even hear his testimony. He was there just as much as the other black guy was.

Q: Can you think of anything more about the jury that helps to explain how or why it reached its decision?

J: ... What I'm saying is that they had no respect for a black male and they didn't know how to really judge him. They wanted the death penalty, give him the death penalty 'cause he killed a white man. Boom, that was it.

This black juror had lingering doubt that the defendant on trial was the one most responsible for the killing:

Q: Can you think of anything more we haven't talked about yet that was important in understanding the jury's guilt decision?

J: I felt that two people did not pull the trigger, only one did. I think it's wrong to try somebody for something somebody else done. I think it was unjust that he was charged with a capital crime for this.... He tried to keep this other guy from killing, but he was too late; the other guy had already shot before he could say anything.... Every man should pay his own [dues]—'cause [the defendant] was not holding that guy by the hand saying you pull [the] trigger or you don't pull [the] trigger.

The words of a white female juror tend to confirm the black juror's belief that at least some white jurors made the punishment decision before the sentencing stage of the trial, that they ignored, discounted, or trivialized sentencing evidence and arguments, and that they were in a hurry to be done with the sentencing decision:

I: When did you first think [the defendant] should be given the death penalty?

J: I think when we went in for [guilt] deliberations and we got the instructions.

I: So before guilt deliberations, but after you got the judge's instructions.

J: Agreed.

Q: What prosecution evidence or witness at the punishment stage of the trial was most important or influential, in your mind, and why?

J: Can't remember.

Q: What defense evidence or witness at the punishment stage of the trial was most important or influential, in your mind, and why?

J: [The] defendant had received a certificate from the PTL [Praise The Lord] Club. We all thought that was hysterical. It was very difficult not to laugh.

Q: In your own words, can you tell me what the jury did to reach its decision about defendant's punishment? How did the jury get started; what topics did it discuss, in what order; what were the major disagreements and how were they resolved?

J: [We] did not spend a lot of time on it because we were told it was only a recommendation. [We] wanted to go home. That was the feeling of most jurors.

In Florida, the jury may recommend the death penalty by a majority vote. It did so in this case, despite the black male juror's vote for a life sentence.

CASE B: A South Carolina jury with one black and five white males sentenced a black man to death for the robbery related murder of a white woman.

White and black jurors made diametrically opposed interpretations of the defendant's human qualities and remorsefulness. A white male juror perceived the defendant as emotionless, afraid that he would be dangerous in the future, and worried about what the neighbors would expect them to do. A white female juror saw the defendant's statement of remorse as pretense and felt the "boy's" execution might actually be good for his mother. The black juror was mistakenly convinced that the death penalty was required, though he wished he had voted for life. The white male juror was asked:

Q: What defense evidence or witness at the punishment stage of the trial was most important or influential, in your mind, and why?

J: His mother, really his reaction to his mother's testimony, he was very unemotional through the whole trial and when his mother got on the stand and pleaded for his life he didn't bat an eye, not a tear, no emotion at all, that pretty much put him in the electric chair.... The point was brought up that our friends and neighbors were expecting us to do the right thing and if this guy were to ever get out, he was so violent, his episodes of violence, we were really afraid of what might happen if he is ever allowed out into society again.

A white female juror echoed and elaborated upon the "coldness of the man," despite his responsiveness to his girlfriend, and upon his pretense of being sorry:

Q: Did any of the testimony by defense witnesses at the punishment stage of the trial "backfire," or actually hurt their case?

J: Well, I would have to say the one was putting the girlfriend on the stand, because she followed the mother.... The girlfriend told about how good he was with her two children although they were not his children, and how, what a good person he was. It was all well and good to hear that, but he perked up when the girlfriend got off the stand, and even when she walked off the stand he looked at her and gave her this grin and winked at her, and I mean he had no response for his mother who was up there shedding all these tears for him and yet had this response for his girlfriend, to me it really showed the coldness of the man.

Q: Did defendant testify or make a closing statement at the punishment stage of the trial?

J: It was poor.... One reason was because he came up to this podium that they had set up in front of us, very nicely dressed with a legal, long, legal pad and a Bible in his hand, and he stood up there, and he read a statement that was obviously prepared by his lawyer where he said how sorry he was for this family and the other people that had survived, the trauma that they had to go through, the families of the victim herself, and he expressed appreciation for his family members and friends and all that had come out and supported him, but they were not his words. I mean it was so obvious that they were not his words.

This juror took the paternalistic view that the death penalty might actually be a good thing for the defendant's mother:

Q: What were the strongest factors for and against a life [or death] sentence?
J: His manner in the courtroom, and I think the fact that I really believe the justice system does not have a very good rehabilitation record.... I tell you I also think...about this boy's mother at that time, to watch her son behind bars for 30 years, I don't know whether that would have been any less merciful or any more merciful I should say for her than to have the boy executed and then his life is over with. Time does a healing for people and their grief, not that she wouldn't have more grief at the time [of his execution, but it would not] burden her with this boy being behind prison [bars] and what he would go through.

Note that this juror began referring to the defendant as "boy" in her patronizing explanation of why his execution would probably be good for his mother. She later interrupted the flow of the interview to say that she was insulted at being asked whether she could be racially unbiased as a juror:

J: I want to tell you in the sentencing, excuse me, in the choosing of the jury, they, his lawyer asked me if it mattered to me that the defendant sitting here was a black man and the victim was a white woman, would that make a difference to me that was the facts in the case. And I thought that was an insulting question for that man to ask. Apparently he asked that of everybody, but I just, a life is a life, and if the man committed a crime I don't think that those things ought to weigh into it. And I told him so, I said, I mean, the person that died, whether the person was white or black or male or female just should not bear into this. And I don't think it would in my case, and I was insulted.

The black male juror saw the defendant in a very different light than did the white jurors. He was opposed to the death penalty until the final jury vote, when he seems to have become convinced that the law required a death sentence:

I: In your mind, how [would you] describe the killing?

J: Accidental.

I: How did [the defendant] appear to you during the trial?

J: Psychotic, dual personality…and a drug addict.

Q: In deciding guilt, did jurors talk about whether or not [the defendant] would, or should, get the death penalty?

J: One person [apparently referring to himself] didn't think he should get it.

Q: Was there any discussion among the jurors about the meaning of proof beyond a reasonable doubt?

J: Defendant would get the death penalty if this was found.

When the questioning turned to the punishment stage of the trial, he was asked:

Q: Did [the defendant's] mood or attitude change after the guilty verdict was handed down and the focus of the trial shifted to what the punishment should be?

J: [He] seemed sorry and pled for [his] life.

I: Did [the defendant] testify or make a closing statement at the punishment stage of the trial?

J: [He] told the jury that he had good qualities and could change.

Q: What did the defense attorney stress most as the reason why [the defendant] should not get the death penalty?

J: Because he was human, not an animal.

According to this lone black juror, the defendant's dangerousness and the impression that the death penalty was required by law influenced the jury's death penalty recommendation. In retrospect he wished that he had not been "so vicious" and gone along with the death penalty:

Q: In your own words, can you tell me what the jury did to reach its decision about [the defendant's] punishment?

J: What would defendant do if set free? Would [the defendant] kill again? The law said the defendant must get death…. The prosecutor explained that this was required by law.

Q: When you think back about serving as a juror on [this] case, is there anything you wish you had said or done differently?

J: Yes.

I: What was it?

J: [I] wouldn't have been so vicious, [I] may not have given death.

Racial bias: Implications

The CJP data from capital jurors, themselves, unmistakably exposes the influence of race in capital sentencing. This influence is felt foremost in the B/W cases, where the death penalty has long served to reinforce the color line. Historical analysis suggests that these are the kinds of crimes that have been lightning rods for the expression of white rage over the crossing of racial boundaries. The death penalty in these cases has been the vehicle for demonstrating white racial dominance. These cases most poignantly represent what Gunnar Myrdal (1962), in his epochal examination of America's race problem, identified as the "American Dilemma."

The make-up of the jury, we now see, is integral to this racial influence. When juries were all-white and all-male, as they were for most of our nation's history, it was impossible to see this bias through the lens of jury racial composition. Now that the racial and gender composition of juries varies, we can see what difference it makes to have (and not to have) blacks or women on a capital jury. In fact, we have seen that the chances of a death sentence for a black defendant whose victim is white are dramatically affected by the race and gender of his jurors. The death penalty is more than twice as likely for the defendant in a B/W case who draws five or more white male jurors as for the one who draws fewer. A life sentence is almost twice as likely for the defendant who draws a black male juror than for the one who fails to do so. These are far from trivial odds in this sizeable sample of seventy-four B/W cases from fourteen different states. Indeed, the role that a juror's race plays in this sample of cases is significant well beyond a chance occurrence in a sample of this size.

Jurors' narrative accounts yield further insights into their decision-making. They reveal a lack of receptivity to mitigating evidence among white jurors when the defendant is black. White jurors often appear unable or unwilling to consider the defendant's background and upbringing in context. As one minority juror put it: "they [the white jurors] were not considering what background this kid [the defendant] came out of. They were looking at it from a white middle-class point of view.... We had to look at it like the lifestyle he came out of, the background he came out of. But nobody wanted to listen" (Bowers et al. 2001: 251). Another black juror said, "they [the white jurors] had no respect for a black male, and they didn't know how to judge him. They wanted the death penalty, give him the death penalty, because he killed a white man. That was it" (Bowers et al. 2001:245). Indeed, what black jurors see as mitigating circumstances, white jurors often see in a contrary light. Where a black juror said the defendant "seemed sorry and pled for his life," a white juror saw "the coldness of the man." Evidently, a predilection of whites to see black defendants as arrogant, frightening, or dangerous, blunts or blocks their receptivity to mitigating evidence and arguments, especially their willingness to see the defendant as remorseful. The failure of jurors to give effect to mitigating evidence in their decision-making on punishment runs contrary to the Supreme Court's conception in *Lockett* of the role of mitigating circumstances in the sentencing decision, and to its ruling in *Morgan* concerning qualifications for capital jury service.

What is more, these data paint a picture at odds with the notion of a "deliberative jury" (Abramson 1994) that scrupulously weighs aggravating and mitigating considerations to arrive at what the Supreme Court has extolled as "a reasoned moral response." In their narrative accounts, black jurors report that their white fellow jurors came to the trial with their minds made up about punishment and that they treated evidence of mitigation as trivial or ignored it. According to the statistical data, black jurors feel that the jury was in a rush to reach a verdict and intolerant of disagreement (Bowers et al. 2001:Table 6); and they feel more emphatically so in cases with five or more white male jurors (Bowers et al. 2001:Table 8). Further, these white-male-dominated juries appear to exacerbate the fissures between black and white jurors in lingering doubt, remorse, and dangerousness. Uniquely, jurors' narrative accounts reveal tactics of ostracism, deception, and intimidation in the B/W cases. These decision-making dynamics appear to be driven by a determination to impose a particular verdict, not by a commitment to reach consensus by reviewing and deliberating about the evidence—"verdict driven" rather than "evidence driven" deliberations (Hastie, Penrod, and Pennington 1983). Jurors' accounts reflect tension, hostility, mistrust, and misunderstanding between black and white jurors—far from the ingredients for the "reasoned moral response" called for by the U.S. Supreme Court.

The Supreme Court acknowledged in *Turner* that jurors' racial sentiments are apt to confound the capital sentencing decision in B/W cases. Indeed, the Court's thinking in *Turner* about how racial sentiments might come to bear foreshadows the CJP findings:

> Because of the range of discretion entrusted to a jury in a capital sentencing hearing, there is a unique opportunity for racial prejudice to operate but remain undetected.... [A] juror who believes that blacks are violence prone or morally inferior might well be influenced by that belief in deciding whether petitioner's crime involved [such] aggravating factors.... Such a juror might also be less favorably inclined toward [a] petitioner's evidence of mental disturbance as a mitigating circumstance. More subtle, less consciously held racial attitudes could also influence a juror's decision.... Fear of blacks, which could easily be stirred up by the violent facts of petitioner's crime, might incline a juror to favor the death penalty (at 35).

The Court emphasized that the sentencing determination is especially vulnerable to the influence of racial attitudes and prejudices because "in a capital sentencing proceeding before a jury, the jury is called upon to make a highly subjective, unique, individualized judgment regarding the punishment that a particular person deserves" (at 33–34). The Court explained, "we are convinced that such discretion gives greater opportunity for racial prejudice to operate than is present when the jury is restricted to fact-finding" (at 36, n. 8). It continued, "as we see it, the risk of racial bias at sentencing hearings is of an entirely different order, because the decisions that sentencing jurors must make involve far more subjective judgments than when they are deciding guilt or innocence" (at 38, n. 12).

Yet, the remedy was insufficient—reliance on voir dire questioning to detect such deeply ingrained and often unconscious racial attitudes was wishful thinking. The failure of *Turner* to purge sentencing decisions of race-linked attitudes is manifest in this research by the fact that virtually all of the cases examined in the statistical and qualitative analyses of the CJP data were tried after *Turner* (1986) became effective.

The CJP evidence of racial influence goes a critical step beyond what Baldus and his colleagues were able to show in *McCleskey*. Baldus et al. (1990) demonstrated that the likelihood of juries imposing the death penalty differed depending upon the race of defendant and victim; in particular, they showed that jurors were most likely to impose death sentences when the defendant was black and the victim was white, as in the *McCleskey* (1987) case. Further, Baldus showed that the greater use of the death penalty in such cases could not be accounted for by any one or all of a vast and comprehensive set of legally relevant considerations. He thus established that the race of defendant and victim were implicated in the sentencing decisions of jurors. He did this, however, without being able to show how jurors' race or race-linked attitudes figured into the decision-making process.[42] The majority in *McCleskey* averred that the Baldus data linking defendant and victim race to sentencing outcome did not impeach the exercise of sentencing discretion by capital jurors, and that statistical patterns of sentencing outcomes were no substitute for knowing how individual jurors focus their collective judgment.

That is precisely what we have here—data not merely on the race of the defendants and their victims, but on real black and white jurors in actual cases who have told us how they made the life or death sentencing decision. These data flesh out the ways in which the race of individual jurors and the racial composition of the jury, in connection with the race of defendant and victim, figure into the capital sentencing decision. And, these are differences of the kind that the Court in *Turner* said would constitute an unacceptable risk of race-linked arbitrariness in the sentencing decisions of capital jurors. In particular, the evidence here shows that gross race-linked differences in the critical sentencing considerations of lingering doubt, remorse, and dangerousness are most manifest and egregious precisely in the black defendant/white victim cases where the Court in *Turner* was afraid that they might occur. The conse-

---

42. In their subsequent research on capital sentencing in Philadelphia, Baldus, Woodworth, Zuckerman, Werner, and Broffitt (2001) have demonstrated a link between jury racial composition and the sentencing decision of these juries, including the extent to which age and gender of minority jurors influences the sentences imposed (see Figure 10).

quence is that the decision-making process is a glaring departure from the Court's repeated admonition that the "qualitative difference between death and other penalties calls for a greater degree of reliability when the death sentence is imposed" (at 35).

Conclusion

Fundamental to America's post-*Furman* experiment with capital punishment is the premise that the punishment decision be made at a separate sentencing stage of the trial held after a capital murder verdict where jurors approach that decision with an open mind so they can give effect to both aggravating and mitigating evidence and argument. The CJP finds, to the contrary, that before the sentencing stage of the trial, many jurors think they know what the defendant's punishment should be, that most who take such an early stand on punishment are "absolutely convinced" of that stand, that these premature stands on punishment remain relatively unaltered thereafter, that early pro-death stands are prompted by graphic crime evidence presented at the guilt stage of the trial, that such stands have roots in a predisposition to see death as the "only acceptable punishment" for aggravated murder that many jurors bring to the trial, and that jurors' premature stands on punishment contaminate the guilt decision process. All this runs contrary to the purpose of the bifurcated trial in which the fact finding guilt decision is separated from the reasoned moral choice of punishment decisions so that each can be made in its own time according to its distinctive rules and procedures without the confounding influence of the other.

Equally fundamental to the post-*Furman* experiment is the premise that jurors sentencing decisions be guided by understandings and procedures that will make the punishment a reasoned moral choice. The CJP interviews reveal that many jurors misunderstand sentencing guidelines, that they wrongly apply the fact finding decision rules for guilt to the punishment decision, and consequently approach the punishment decision with a "tilt" toward death. In particular, jurors do not understand that they are being called upon individually to make a reasoned moral choice and that this choice is governed by distinct standards for considering mitigation. They fail to understand that a mitigating factor need not be proved beyond a reasonable doubt, and that all jurors need not agree upon a mitigating factor for a juror to consider it in his or her sentencing decision. Additionally, many jurors believe the law requires a death sentence when it does not. They fail to understand that the punishment decision is never dictated by the presence of a particular aggravating factor such as the heinousness of the crime or the dangerousness of the defendant, and that a death sentence is never required by law. In reality, the chief function of sentencing guidelines may be to rationalize decisions made in other ways, as suggested by the agreement of three out of four jurors that the judge's sentencing instructions, "simply provided a framework for a decision most jurors had already made."

Further, a reasoned moral judgment in capital sentencing implies that jurors correctly understand the options from which they must choose and that they take responsibility for the choice they make. Yet, CJP investigators found that most jurors underestimated the death penalty alternative, and that such misperceptions made them more likely to vote for death. A number of jurors said they voted for death not because they thought it was the right punishment, but because they found it more appropriate than what they misunderstood the alternative to be. And, despite having deliberated and decided on the defendant's punishment, fewer than one in five capital jurors saw themselves as primarily responsible, individually or as a group, for the defendant's punishment. Twice as many said the law and three times as many said the defendant was primarily responsible. Jurors who made the life or death decision were obviously uncomfortable with the idea that they are responsible for whether the defendant will live or die.

Beyond this, the decision-making of capital jurors must also be free of racial bias. Accusations and evidence of racism have stalked capital punishment in America since colonial times. The use of the death penalty since *Furman* has been racked with disparities by race of defendant and victim, disparities in sentencing outcomes which the Court has acknowledged but refused to accept as dispositive evidence of a constitutional fault. Still, the Court has explicitly recognized that jurors' conscious and unconscious racial attitudes could pose an unconstitutional risk of failing to deliver evenhanded capital sentencing. The CJP has now demonstrated that jurors' race, in conjunction with race of defendant and victim, plays a substantial role in sentencing decisions. Specifically, it has shown systematic differences in the way black and white jurors in the same cases see critical aggravating and mitigating circumstances particularly the defendant's dangerousness and remorsefulness, differences that contribute to known racial disparities in sentencing outcomes. By showing that the likelihood of a death sentence for a black defendant whose victim was white is significantly affected by the racial composition of his jury, and by linking these differences in the likelihood of a death sentence to stark differences in how black and white jurors in these cases think about aggravation and mitigation, the CJP findings obviate the challenge of constitutional insufficiency leveled at evidence of disparities in sentencing outcomes alone.

The capital jury is the focal point of the post-*Furman* experiment with capital punishment. New statutes supposed to guide jurors' exercise of sentencing discretion were the remedy to the ills of arbitrariness and caprice under pre-*Furman* statutes. The Supreme Court has so far rebuffed evidence that jurors are not now performing as the Constitution requires. In *Lockhart* (1986) it rejected evidence that jury selection procedures in capital cases yield death-prone juries, and in *McCleskey* (1987) it was unmoved by evidence that sentencing outcomes were influenced by race of defendant and victim. The Court was unwilling to accept inferences about the decision-making of real jurors on the basis of experiments with mock jurors in *Lockhart* and on the basis of statistics about sentencing outcomes in *McCleskey*. It complained in *Lockhart* that the evidence was flawed because it was not about real jurors in real cases. The CJP evidence is about real jurors in real cases, and it bears directly upon the exercise of discretion in capital sentencing—the issue at the heart of the post-*Furman* experiment with capital punishment.

References

Abramson, J. (1994) *We, the Jury: The Jury System and the Ideal of Democracy*. New York: Basic Books.

Acker, J. R. and C. S. Lanier (1993) "Capital Murder From Benefit of Clergy to Bifurcated Trial: Narrowing the Class of Offenses Punishable by Death." 29 *Criminal Law Bulletin* 291–316.

Acker, J. R. and C. S. Lanier (1994) "In Fairness and Mercy: Statutory Mitigating Factors in Capital Punishment Law." 30 *Criminal Law Bulletin* 299–345.

Acker, J. R. and C. S. Lanier (1995) "Matters of Life or Death: The Sentencing Provisions in Capital Punishment Statutes." 31 *Criminal Law Bulletin* 19–60.

Baldus, D.C. and G. Woodworth (2003) "Race Discrimination and the Death Penalty: An Empirical and Legal Overview." (This volume.)

Baldus, D.C., G. Woodworth, D. Zuckerman, N. A. Weiner, and B. Broffitt (2001) "The Use of Peremptory Challenges in Capital Murder Trials: A Legal and Empirical Analysis." 3 *U. Pa. J. Const. L.* 3–170.

Baldus, D.C., G. Woodworth, and C.A. Pulaski, Jr. (1990) *Equal Justice and the Death Penalty: A Legal and Empirical Analysis*. Boston: Northeastern University Press.

Bentele, U. and W.J. Bowers (2001) "How Jurors Decide on Death: Guilt is Overwhelming; Aggravation Requires Death; and Mitigation is No Excuse." 66 *Brooklyn Law Review* 1013–1080.

Bilionis, L.D. (1991) "Moral Appropriateness, Capital Punishment, and the Lockett Doctrine." 82 *J. Crim. L. & Criminology* 283–333.

Blystone v. *Pennsylvania* (1990) 494 U.S. 299.

Bowers, W.J. (1995) "The Capital Jury Project: Rationale, Design, and Preview of Early Findings." 70 *Indiana Law Journal* 1043–1102.

Bowers, W.J., M. Sandys, and B.D. Steiner (1998) "Foreclosed Impartiality in Capital Sentencing: Jurors' Predispositions, Guilt-Trial Experience, and Premature Decision Making." 83 *Cornell Law Review* 1474–1556.

Bowers, W.J. and B.D. Steiner (1999) "Death by Default: An Empirical Demonstration of False and Forced Choices in Capital Sentencing." 77 *Texas L. Rev.* 605–645.

Bowers, W.J., B.D. Steiner, and M. Sandys (2001) "Death Sentencing in Black and White: An Empirical Analysis of the Role of Jurors' Race and Jury Racial Composition." 3 *U. Pa J. Const. L.* 171–274.

Boyde v. *California* (1990) 494 U.S. 370.

Caldwell v. *Mississippi* (1985) 472 U.S. 320.

California v. *Brown* (1987) 479 U.S. 538.

Costanzo, S. (1990) *Penalty Decision Making Under the Special Issues Framework: A Social Psychological Analysis.* (Unpublished Ph.D. dissertation, University of California (Santa Cruz), reprinted by UMI Dissertation Services).

Diamond, S.S. and J.N. Levi (1996) "Improving Decisions on Death by Revising and Testing Jury Instructions." 79 *Judicature* 224–232.

Dillehay, R. C. and M. R. Sandys (1996) "Life Under *Wainwright v. Witt*: Juror Dispositions and Death Qualification." 20 *Law and Human Behavior* 147–165.

Eddings v. Oklahoma (1982) 455 U.S. 104.

Eisenberg, T., S.P. Garvey, and M.T. Wells (1996) "Jury Responsibility in Capital Sentencing: An Empirical Study." 44 *Buffalo Law Review* 339–380.

Eisenberg, T. and M.T. Wells (1993) "Deadly Confusion: Juror Instructions in Capital Cases." 79 *Cornell Law Review* 1–17.

Ellsworth, P.C. (1988) "Unpleasant Facts: The Supreme Court's Response to Empirical Research on Capital Punishment." Pp. 177–212 in K.C. Haas and J.A. Inciardi (eds.), *Challenging Capital Punishment: Legal and Social Science Approaches.* Newbury Park: Sage Publication.

Fitzgerald, R. and P.C. Ellsworth, (1984) "Due Process vs. Crime Control." 8 *Law and Human Behavior* 31–51.

Fletcher, G. (1996) *Basic Concepts of Legal Thought.* New York: Oxford University Press.

Furman v. Georgia (1972) 408 U.S. 238.

Gey, S.G. (1992) "Justice Scalia's Death Penalty." 20 *Florida State University Law Review* 67–132.

Geimer, W.S. and J. Amsterdam (1987–88) "Why Jurors Vote Life or Death: Operative Factors in Ten Florida Death Penalty Cases." 15 *American Journal of Criminal Law* 1–54.

Gillers, S. (1980) "Deciding Who Dies." 129 *U. P. L. Rev.* 1–124.

Gregg v. Georgia (1976) 428 U.S. 153.

Haney, C.(1984) "On the Selection of Capital Juries: The Biasing Effects of the Death-Qualification Process." 8 *Law and Human Behavior* 121–132.

Haney, C., L. Sontag, and S. Costanzo (1994) "Deciding to Take a Life: Capital Juries, Sentencing Instructions, and the Jurisprudence of Death." 50 *Journal of Social Issues* (2):149–176.

Hastie, R., S. Penrod, and N. Pennington (1983) *Inside the Jury.* Cambridge, MA: Harvard University Press.

Hitchcock v. Dugger (1987) 481 U.S. 393.

Hoffmann, J.L. (1995) "Where's the Buck?—Juror Misperception of Sentencing Responsibility in Death Penalty Cases." 70 *Indiana Law Journal* 1137–1160.

In re *Winship* (1970) 397 U.S. 358.

Jurek v. Texas (1976) 428 U.S. 262.

Kalven, H. and H. Zeisel (1966) *The American Jury.* Chicago: University of Chicago Press.

Lane, J.M. (1993) "'Is There Life without Parole?': A Capital Defendant's Right to a Meaningful Alternative Sentence." 26 *Loyola of Los Angeles Law Review* 327–393.

Lockett v. Ohio (1978) 438 U.S. 586

Lockhart v. McCree (1986) 476 U.S. 162.

Luginbuhl, J. (1992) "Comprehension of Judges' Instructions in the Penalty Phase of a Capital Trial: Focus on Mitigating Circumstances." 16 *Law and Human Behavior* 203–218.

Luginbuhl, J. and J. Howe (1995) "Discretion in Capital Sentencing Instructions: Guided or Misguided?" 70 *Indiana Law Journal* 1161–1181.

Lynch, M. and C. Haney (2000) "Discrimination and Instructional Comprehension: Guided Discretion, Racial Bias, and the Death Penalty." 24 *Law and Human Behavior* 337–358.

McCleskey v. *Kemp* (1987) 481 U.S. 279.

McGautha v. *California* (1971) 402 U.S. 183.

McKoy v. *North Carolina* (1990) 494 U.S. 433.

Mills v. *Maryland* (1988) 486 U.S. 367.

Milgram, S. (1974) *Obedience to Authority: An Experimental View.* New York: Harper & Row.

Morgan v. *Illinois* (1992) 504 U.S. 719.

Myrdal, G. (1962) *An American Dilemma: The Negro Problem and Modern Democracy.* New York: Harper-Collins Publishers.

NAACP (2002) Legal Defense and Educational Fund, Inc., "Death Row, U.S.A." at http://www.deathpenaltyinfo.org/DEATHROWUSArecent.pdf.

Nisbet, R.E. and T.D. Wilson (1977) "The Halo Effect: Evidence for Unconscious Alteration of Judgments." 35 *Journal of Personality and Social Psychology* 250–256.

Note (1974) "Discretion and the Constitutionality of the New Death Penalty Statutes." 87 *Harvard Law Review* 1690–1719.

Penry v. *Lynaugh* (1989) 492 U.S. 302.

Proffitt v. *Florida* (1976) 428 U.S. 242.

Pulley v. *Harris* (1984) 465 U.S. 37.

Ring v. *Arizona* (2002) 122 S.Ct. 2428.

Roberts v. *Louisiana* (1976) 428 U.S. 325.

Sandys, M. and S. McClelland (2003) "Stacking the Deck for Guilt and Death: The Failure of Death Qualification to Ensure Impartiality." (This volume.)

Sandys, M. (1995) "Cross-Overs—Capital Jurors Who Change Their Minds About the Punishment: A Litmus Test For Sentencing Guidelines." 70 *Indiana Law Journal* 1183–1221.

Sarat, A. (1995) "Violence, Representation, and Responsibility in Capital Trials: The View From the Jury." 70 *Indiana Law Journal* 1103–1135.

Simmons v. *South Carolina* (1994) 512 U.S. 154.

Skipper v. *South Carolina* (1986) 476 U.S. 1.

Sontag, L. (1990) *Deciding Death: A Legal and Empirical Analysis of Penalty Phase Jury Instructions and Capital Decision-Making.* (Unpublished Ph.D. dissertation, University of California (Santa Cruz), reprinted by UMI Dissertation Services).

Steiker C.S. and J.M. Steiker (1992) "Let God Sort Them Out: Refining the Individualization Requirement in Capital Sentencing." 102 *Yale L.J.* 835–870.

Fluery-Steiner, B.D. (2002) "Narratives of the Death Sentence: Toward a Theory of Legal Narrativity." 36 *Law and Society Review* 549–576.

Steiner, B.D., W.J. Bowers, and A. Sarat (1999). "Folk Knowledge as Legal Action: Death Penalty Judgments and the Tenet of Early Release in a Culture of Mistrust and Punitiveness." 33 *Law and Society Review* 461–505.

Sumner v. *Shuman* (1987) 483 U.S. 66.

Sundby, S.E. (1991) "The Lockett Paradox: Reconciling Guided Discretion and Unguided Mitigation in Capital Sentencing." 38 *UCLA L. Rev.* 1147–1208.

Turner v. *Murray* (1986) 476 U.S. 28.

Wainwright v. *Witt* (1985) 469 U.S. 412.

Weiner R.L., L.E. Hurt, S.L. Thomas, M.S. Sadler, C.A. Bauer, and T.M. Sargent (1998) "The Role of Declarative and Procedural Knowledge in Capital Murder Sentencing." 28 *Journal of Applied Social Psychology* 124–144.

Weisberg, R. (1984) "Deregulating Death." Pp. 305–395 in P.B. Kurland, G. Casper, and D.J. Hutchinson (eds.),*The Supreme Court Review 1983*. Chicago: University of Chicago Press.

Witherspoon v. *Illinois* (1968) 391 U.S. 510.

Woodson v. *North Carolina* (1976) 428 U.S. 280.

Zant v. *Stephens* (1983) 462 U.S. 862.

Zeisel, H. (1990) Affidavit (21 August, 1990). United States District Court, Northern District of Illinois, Eastern Division. Case No. 89C3765.

Chapter 15

Mitigation and the Study of Lives: On the Roots of Violent Criminality and the Nature of Capital Justice

Craig Haney

Introduction

In this chapter I address the elusive concept of "mitigation" and the way in which attempts to assemble and present mitigating evidence to capital juries that might engender compassion and lead to merciful decisions has involved experts, attorneys, and investigators in the study of lives—the lives of capital defendants. Among social scientists, at least, the criminal law is notorious for its extremely narrow focus on decontextualized criminal acts and what seem to be arbitrarily defined states of mind. Much that a social scientist would want to know about the historical, social contextual, and even immediate situational influences on criminal behavior—knowledge that otherwise would be crucial to meaningfully analyze and truly understand the actions of a criminal offender—is deemed irrelevant by the criminal law. This narrowness has been the source of great frustration among social scientists, most of whose work has been systematically excluded from individual trials, appellate opinions, and the drafting of criminal statutes and codes. Because it has led legal decision-makers to ignore most of the racial, socioeconomic, and social psychological differentials that play such a crucial role in the etiology of crime in our society, this myopic focus probably also has been at the root of much injustice in the criminal system (e.g., Haney 1983).

There is one exception to this general rule—a capital penalty trial. A line of United States Supreme Court cases beginning some 20 years ago established the right of capital defendants to present a broad range of potentially mitigating evidence—evidence intended to produce life rather than death verdicts—

in the final stage of a capital sentencing proceeding.[1] Although chronically scarce resources and, in some jurisdictions, widespread attorney incompetency mean that this rule often is honored only in the breach, the range of potentially relevant evidence has been greatly expanded to include what amounts to, in essence, a psychobiographical account of the defendant's life. As one legal commentator summarized it: "At the penalty phase of a capital trial, the central issue is no longer a factual inquiry into whether the defendant committed any crimes; it is the highly-charged moral and emotional issue of whether the defendant, notwithstanding his crime, is a person who should continue to live (Goodpaster 1983:334–335). To address this issue, the capital jury must be informed about who the defendant is and, to the extent that it is possible to know, how he got to be that way. Psychologically informed social histories are invaluable to this process.

Of course, these psychobiographical stories are not told to jurors who approach the topic of violent criminality as blank slates. In fact, most jurors enter the courtroom already holding a conventional view of crime and criminals that they have gleaned from the media and, to a certain extent, from the law itself. Armed with this conventional and pre-existing narrative about why people do bad things, jurors are predisposed to posit violent acts as the product of an odd combination of equally free and unencumbered evil choices, on the one hand, and monstrously deranged, defective traits, on the other. Indeed, in most of the "crime stories" that form the basis of jurors' "common knowledge" about these issues, they are taught that extreme violence of the sort that they confront and attempt to comprehend in capital cases is carried out by de-

---

1. Indeed, much of what I will present in this chapter about "modern" penalty phase practice and its reliance upon social histories predates even this line of capital cases. More than 30 years ago the California Supreme Court described the nature and function of a capital penalty trial this way:

> The emphasis must be upon the individual rather than the offense; such insistence upon the importance of the individual symbolizes a basic value of our society that contrasts with a totalitarian denigration of the individual as an appendage of the state. Our insistence upon the dignity and worth of the individual must surely be strictly and steadfastly applied in the crucial context of the individual's life or death. The jury decides whether the individual should be permitted to live upon the basis of a complete and careful analysis of that person as a human composite of emotional, psychological and genetic factors. The jury looks at the individual as a whole being and determines if he is fit to live. The jury is entitled to weigh psychiatric and other testimony as to his susceptibility to rehabilitation and reformation (*People v. Morse* 1964: 647).

Thus, although much of the research that I will cite on social historical factors is of relatively recent origin, recognition of the importance of taking a comprehensive approach to capital penalty trials and the basic respect for persons that it embodies are not.

humanized, anonymous figures or monsters rather than real people. If the victim of violent crime is depicted as "everyman," then the perpetrator is "other" personified. Elsewhere I have termed this the "myth of demonic agency" (Haney 1995), because it serves to deny the humanity of the persons who commit capital murder by substituting the heinousness of their crimes for the reality of their personhood. This myth is essential to maintaining the system of death sentencing in the United States, and its dehumanizing effects are amplified by procedures and practices that occur within the trial itself.[2] "Mechanisms of moral disengagement" further distance jurors from the personhood of the capital defendant and disengage them from the moral complexities of the actions they are being asked by the state to authorize (Haney 1997c).

A capital penalty trial provides a rare opportunity to confront this mythology directly and to counter the partial and misleading stereotypes that plague the public's view of criminality. Properly conducted penalty phases present capital jurors with a fuller and more accurate view of the causes of violence and enrich their understanding of the person whose life they must judge. The presentation of mitigation requires the construction of an empathetic narrative, one that may include the broad sociological forces that constitute the larger context of the crime, the background and developmental history of the defendant and, in some cases, the deeper psychological issues that help to account for why a particular crime was committed by a specific defendant. As I will suggest in this chapter, the pre-existing biases with which they approach the penalty trial and the virtually incomprehensible sentencing instructions they are given at its conclusion mean that most jurors will need extensive education about how and why these things are relevant. Also, because they have few if any alternative sources of information about such issues, the patient, coherent, elaborate presentation of social history evidence in the penalty trial is absolutely indispensable to any claim that might be made about fair, reliable, and morally defensible capital verdicts.

Crime Stereotypes and Social Histories

The task of presenting a humanizing, empathetic narrative that will enable jurors to understand not only the harm that a capital defendant has inflicted, but also the circumstances from which he has come and the social history that has helped to produce his actions, is rendered more difficult by the elusiveness

---

2. A framework of what can be termed "structural aggravation" is built into death penalty trials as a whole. Structural aggravation stems from the ways in which capital trial practice, procedures, and instructions combine to differentially highlight and underscore those things that would push capital juries in the direction of death verdicts and neutralize or de-emphasize those things that favor life.

of the concept of capital "mitigation." Mitigation is the legal category into which penalty phase evidence must be placed before it can be used by jurors in reaching merciful and compassionate decisions that can spare capital defendants' lives. Its elusiveness derives from two basic sources: the miseducation of the American juror and the inadequacies of the capital trial process.

As I already have suggested, many jurors come to the courthouse with firmly entrenched, preconceived ideas about the roots of violent criminality. As one commentator has argued, these familiar mental constructs not only "help shape the outcome of criminal cases and predispose us to play out certain scripts, schemata, and stereotypes," but they also "demand those narrative genres that best reflect a preferred sense of truth and justice" (Sherwin 1994:54). Most of the information from which such mental constructs and narrative genres are built derives from media accounts of crime and punishment that are terribly incomplete when they are not simply wrong. Like most citizens, then, capital jurors are not used to thinking about crime in terms of the social and developmental factors that may have contributed to it. For many, a capital penalty trial will be their first encounter with the tragic life history of someone who has committed a violent crime. It will also be their first opportunity to consider the ways in which these powerful social historical forces and influences—sometimes so extreme and traumatic that it will be difficult for jurors to fully appreciate or comprehend them—should be taken into account as "mitigation" in deciding whether the defendant should live or die.

This is in part because of the narrow and misleading information they have been provided as citizens about the nature of crime and criminals. Social and economic context is typically ignored by the news media in crime reporting (e.g., Barlow, Barlow, and Chiricos 1995; Humphries 1981) as well as television crime drama (e.g., Haney and Manzolati 1980). By the time information about the background and social history of the defendant has been gathered and becomes publicly accessible in a criminal trial—in those comparatively few cases in which it ever does—most cases are no longer "news" and—again, except for the most highly publicized cases—are no longer of interest to the press. For example, one study analyzed the content of newspaper crime reporting in a major city during a one year period and found that over two-thirds of the articles related to only the beginning stages of criminal justice system processing (e.g., crime incidents, arrests, charges being lodged against suspects). In addition, the study found that the commission of the crime itself accounted for the major details contained in the articles, and that post-arrest stages of criminal justice processing were seldom mentioned. It also found that "[s]urprisingly, suspects were seldom described in detail. The typical information given about them was their name, age, and address" (Sherizen 1978:218). Meaningful social and developmental history, context, and explanation are simply lacking in these accounts.

Prospective jurors are unlikely to find contextualized explanations of crime anywhere else in public discourse about the topic. Fictionalized portrayals and popularized scholarship on the question of violent crime are of little help in educating the public about how criminogenic background and history can explain individual-level violence. Instead, citizens are treated to widespread media mystifications about "natural born killers" that even seep into contemporary academic commentary on the issue (cf. Harris 1988; McNulty 1995; Tarantino 1995). Serious-looking but oversimplified treatments of the topic have instructed members of the public that much crime reduces to the problem of "evil people" (Wilson 1975), is caused in part by the defective biology of its perpetrators (Wilson and Herrnstein 1985), and warn that our society is at risk of being overwhelmed by an epidemic of the "disease" of murder (Norris 1988). Thus, notwithstanding the extensive literature to which I will refer later in this chapter, the message that truly meaningful explanations for capital violence are rooted in the structure of the lives of those who commit it can rarely be found in the news media, dramatic renderings of crime and punishment, or popularized academic analyses of the topic.

For these reasons, teaching jurors to look carefully at the social histories of capital defendants to reach mitigating conclusions about the causes of crime and the culpability of capital offenders requires a special effort on the part of attorneys. Jurors must learn and then apply psychologically valid lessons that are nonetheless very much at odds with the stereotypes created by the media and nourished by the system of capital punishment that prevails in our society. Compared to the lifetime of learning that must be overcome, jurors must integrate these lessons within a relatively short period of time. And they must do so without much direct help from the legal system that has brought them to the capital jury box and structured a life and death decision for them to make.

Presenting the social history of the defendant—through lay and expert testimony—has become the primary vehicle by which capital defense attorneys attempt to correct the misinformed and badly skewed views of violent crime and violent criminals that many jurors hold (e.g., Haney 1995; 1997a; White 1987). But, despite the constitutional mandate that capital defendants must be permitted to present a broad range of potentially mitigating testimony—virtually anything that speaks to the background and character of the defendant—standard death penalty practices and procedures in many ways hinder the meaningful use to which this information is put. This occurs for several reasons, including the failure of the courts to *require* (rather than simply permit) that a detailed, in-depth, and psychologically-informed social history be compiled in every case; an apparent judicial inability or unwillingness to effectively *define* the concept of mitigation for jurors; and the failure of judges to further assist jurors in identifying specific and meaningful examples of the kinds of testimony that can and should legitimately be considered mitigating *in the case at hand* by providing tailored or "pinpoint" instructions rather than the abstract, generic, "boilerplate" versions presently in use. Instead, confusing and often incomprehensible capital sentencing instructions too frequently hinder the jury's understanding of whether and how it is supposed to use social history testimony to understand the lives and contextualize the criminal behavior of those still too-few capital defendants who are fortunate enough to have it presented in their penalty trials.

Instructional Incomprehension and Capital Mitigation

It is now widely understood that *Furman v. Georgia* (1972) effected radical changes in the administration of the death penalty in the United States. To supposedly remedy the problems of arbitrariness and discrimination in the system of capital punishment that were identified in *Furman*, death-sentencing states devised new laws ostensibly designed to guide the discretion of the jury and regularize its decision-making. Although the "modern" death penalty differs from its pre-*Furman* predecessor in several ways, perhaps the most psychologically interesting and important is the role played by capital instructions in the attempt to structure and channel the capital jury's collective thought process. By Supreme Court mandate the "unbridled" discretion that previously characterized capital jury decision-making was to be eliminated by telling jurors what to think about, consider, and be guided by (and, by implication, what to ignore) in deciding between life and death. In many ways, these sentencing instructions became the key legal device by which the death penalty was to be made fair. For example, in *Pulley v. Harris* (1984), the Court seemed so certain that a sentencing template of factors for capital jurors to consider would "provide jury guidance and lessen the chance of arbitrary application of the death penalty... [and thereby] guarantee that the jury's discretion will be guided and its consideration deliberate" (at 51) that it concluded a proportionality review (comparing each case in which a death sentences was rendered to similar others) was not necessary.

Because of the emphasis placed on sentencing instructions to guide the discretion of the capital jury under the *Furman*-inspired reforms, these instructions have been the focus of intense legal scrutiny and scholarly attention (e.g., Diamond 1993; Haney and Lynch 1994; 1997b; Weisberg 1984; Wiener, Pritchard, and Weston 1995). Empirical studies of the capital sentencing process now indicate that these instructions do not accomplish in fact what they were designed to achieve in principle. The most significant problems stem from the general incomprehensibility of the instructions and, more pointedly in the present context, their failure to clarify the meaning of mitigation and provide jurors with guidance about how to find and use it in any of the evidence that typically is presented in a capital penalty trial.

Let me be more specific. Out of the frank recognition that "death is different," the Court has required states to specify those things that jurors may consider as reasons for taking a defendant's life. Further, to prevent a range of idiosyncratic and impermissible factors from playing an explicit part in the process, aggravating circumstances must be specified by statute. But the court has given defendants wide latitude in presenting a vast array of potentially mitigating factors.[3] As Justice O'Connor once noted: "The heart of the retributive rationale is that a criminal sentence must be directly related to the personal culpability of the criminal offender" (*Tison v. Arizona* 1987:148). In slightly different but related terms, the Court has stated that the capital jury's decision about whether or not a defendant should receive a death sentence must turn in part on an "individualized determination on the basis of the character of the individual [defendant]...." (*Zant v. Stephens* 1983:879). That determination is conceptualized very broadly: individualized capital sentencing "is satisfied by allowing the jury to consider *all relevant mitigating evidence*" (*Blystone v. Pennsylvania* 1990:299; emphasis added) in a process that is "expansive enough... to assure an assessment of the defendant's culpability" (*Tuilaepa v. California* 1994:973).

The good news is that this individualization requirement has placed the background and life circumstances of the defendant center stage in a capital penalty trial in a way that is replicated nowhere else in the criminal law. The

---

3. As I have mentioned, the line of United States Supreme Court cases establishing this right began more than two decades ago. In *Woodson v. North Carolina* (1976) the Court wrote that: "[I]n capital cases the fundamental respect for humanity underlying the Eighth Amendment... requires consideration of the character and record of the individual offender and the circumstances of the particular offense as a constitutionally indispensable part of the process of inflicting the penalty of death" (at 304). Over the next 20 plus years a series of cases has consistently reaffirmed that principle. Thus, the Court ruled in *Lockett v. Ohio* (1978) that the capital sentencing authority must "not be precluded from considering, as a mitigating factor, any aspect of a defendant's character or record... that the defendant proffers as a basis for a sentence less than death" (at 604); and in *Eddings v. Oklahoma* (1982) that the sentencer may not be precluded from considering and may not "refuse to consider, as a matter of law, any relevant mitigating evidence... [including] evidence of a turbulent family history, of beatings by a harsh father, and of severe emotional disturbance" (at 877). It found in *Skipper v. South Carolina* (1986) that even evidence of positive post-offense prison or jail adjustment could not be excluded from the penalty trial if the defendant elected to present such testimony because a jury might interpret it to mean that defendant "would pose no undue danger to his jailers or fellow prisoners and could lead a useful life behind bars if sentenced to life imprisonment" (at 7). The Court noted in *California v. Brown* (1987) that "evidence about the defendant's background and character is relevant because of the belief, long held by this society, that defendants who commit criminal acts that are attributable to a disadvantaged background, or to emotional and mental problems, may be less culpable than defendants who have no such excuse" (at 545); and concluded in *Penry v. Lynaugh* (1989) that because "mitigating evidence of mental retardation and childhood abuse has relevance to [the defendant's] moral culpability" (at 322), the capital jury must at least be able to consider and, if it so chooses, give it mitigating effect.

bad news is that the capital instructions that are intended to structure the jury's penalty decision-making—supposedly providing them with much needed guidance about what to make of social history and other background testimony in the penalty trial—border on incomprehensible in most respects. For example, my colleagues and I have conducted research indicating that California's entire penalty instruction is very poorly understood by upper-level college students (Haney and Lynch 1994), that these problems are not clarified in actual cases through attorney arguments (Haney and Lynch 1997b), and that jurors who had served in actual capital cases were plagued by fundamental misconceptions about what the instructions meant (Haney, Sontag, and Costanzo 1994). However, we also found that, in addition to the *overall* lack of clarity and difficulty in comprehension, these instructions were especially vague, unhelpful, and confusing with respect to the crucial concept of mitigation. Indeed, mitigation stood out as the least well understood and most difficult of the specific factors to correctly identify. Thus, the typical capital juror is given virtually no clear instruction on what mitigation is, little or no help on how to find it amidst the evidence that is presented in the typical penalty trial, and no real guidance on how to use it in reaching a merciful and just sentencing verdict.

Moreover, specific statutory mitigating factors are defined in most states in such a way as to be rarely if ever applicable. Factors like the possibility that the victim was an accomplice in his or her own demise really never come into play in any capital case. Rather, most defense attorneys must depend upon an expansive, catchall or "anything else the defendant offers as a reason for a sentence less than death" factor as the vehicle by which meaningful mitigating testimony can be introduced. This factor has the advantage of giving counsel the widest possible evidentiary swath with which to approach the question of mitigation, but the disadvantage of giving jurors no clue about whether and which parts of such testimony *are* mitigating, how much weight (if any) to give them (individually or overall), and how to combine the evidence introduced under this "catchall" rubric with other statutorily enumerated factors to produce a final sentencing verdict. Geimer (1990–91) has noted that "[t]he law would seem a likely source from which to derive elements of an entitlement to life. However, death penalty statutes are barren of helpful guidelines" (at 284). Unlike aggravation—which is both a more commonly understood general concept and represented in specifically enumerated factors that are far more likely to apply in the typical case—mitigation is left largely to the various and sundry subjective interpretations that jurors bring with them or can be persuaded by attorneys to apply.

Yet, despite the systematic miseducation they have received at the hands of the media and the lack of instruction and clarification they will receive from the courts, capital jurors and other citizens are *not* impenetrably insensitive or unsympathetic to properly presented mitigating testimony. Indeed, although attitude surveys conducted throughout the United States document overwhelming support for the death penalty, careful examination of these data suggest that support is largely symbolic and generic. Americans support the *idea* of the death penalty, and hold the general belief that it should be implemented, but they differ widely in their views about when and how it should be used and the kind of defendant on whom it should be imposed (e.g., Haney, Hurtado, and Vega 1994). Moreover, in response to a variety of specific factors that are present in the social histories of many capital defendants, but absent any education about why or how these things should be taken into account and without any contextualizing framework to demonstrate the ways in which they fit together in a social history, many persons reported that they would be influenced toward life verdicts by factors like the defendant's history of child abuse, the fact that he had never received treatment for his problems, and evidence that he would adjust well in prison.

Thus, media mystifications and political distortions about the nature of violent criminality ensure that most jurors will have no real theory of mitigation themselves, and our current capital jurisprudence ensures that they will not be given one via judicial sentencing instructions. Both facts place a special burden on attorneys to assemble, present, and explain the defendant's social history and its mitigating significance. Since mitigation is very difficult for most jurors to define accurately, many people who do not comprehend the concept at all may well ignore it in their penalty calculations. Others who have idiosyncratic and incorrect definitions may employ the concept in a way that narrows the focus of penalty deliberations or introduces a randomness or arbitrary quality to the outcome of the cases. Rather than a life-giving effect, mitigation therefore may function as a kind of error term in the death penalty equation. The coherent presentation of a capital defendant's social history, along with a clear explanation about its meaning and significance to the task at hand, can help to reduce the size of that error term. The effort adds fairness and predictability to capital sentencing.

The Normative Structure of the Lives of Capital Defendants[4]

It is important to acknowledge that mitigating evidence—here the psychobiographical summary of a capital defendant's life and the account of his social history that is presented at the penalty trial—is *not* intended to excuse,

---

4. A more detailed discussion of this issue can be found in Haney (1995).

justify, or diminish the significance of the crimes that he has committed. Instead, it is used as an indispensable aid in understanding the defendant's "background and character" in a way that hopefully will illuminate critical issues in the decision capital jurors must make about sentencing. Mitigating social histories are not intended to in any way diminish the significance of the defendant's actions, his responsibility for the harm that he has perpetrated, or the human tragedy that capital violence represents for victims and their families. Quite the contrary, I do not believe that we can begin to acknowledge and pay fitting tribute to the victims of these crimes without honestly and comprehensively addressing their causes. As Robin West (1990) has argued, we must learn about the life circumstances of capital defendants, as well as the social realities that created those circumstances, "because the victims of crime deserve it, the communities that fear crime need it, and the intractable problem of violent crime demands it" (at 176).[5] Looking carefully and deeply at the lives of those who commit capital crimes allows us to overcome the fictionalized, demonized caricatures the media has concocted for us—including those of us who will sit on capital juries. This is an important step in learning the necessary lessons by which future victims can be spared.

Social histories, then, are not excuses but explanations. An explanation does not necessarily dictate a judgment. In this context, as attorneys who have employed them can attest, some explanations lead to life verdicts and some do not. However, social history testimony is offered out of the belief that no jury can render justice in the absence of an explanation of the life of the person whose fate is being decided. In each such case, the goal of a mitigating social history is to place the defendant's life in a larger social context and, in the final

---

5. In an otherwise especially insightful discussion of these issues, Professor West seemed to suggest that the "defense narrative" in a capital penalty trial was one that categorically excluded individual responsibility. It does (or, at least, should) not. Because the model of individual responsibility that dominates our criminal law is so pervasive and omnipresent, many capital defense attorneys may simply assume that jurors will employ it without any special prompting from them. That does not mean that these attorneys categorically reject their client's legal responsibility for his actions nor that, in asking the jury to spare his life, they are inviting jurors to ignore his blameworthiness or shift all of the responsibility to his family or society at large. A social historical approach to these issues serves instead to balance a prosecutorial narrative that typically acknowledges *only* personal ill-will and evil (Cf. Lynch and Haney 1997). The same kind of incorrect caricature of the social historical approach was reflected in Alfieri's (1996) discussion of these issues. An honest and meaningful social history—the only kind that discharges an attorney's duties to both the client and the jury—is precisely one that emphasizes "throughout the capital proceedings the defendant's human vulnerability to both good and bad motive and the possibility of redemption" (Alfieri 1996:348). Yet, even a narrative that emphasized societal deprivation—so long as it was accurate and true—would enrich rather than impoverish a model of moral blameworthiness.

analysis, to reach conclusions about how someone who has had certain life experiences, been treated in particular ways, and experienced certain kinds of psychologically-important events has been shaped and influenced by them. It reflects a turning away from a century-old bias that located the causes of violent criminality exclusively inside the individuals who engaged in it (Haney 1982). It urges the application of a more contemporary theoretical and empirically well-documented framework in its place.

This new framework conceptualizes the roots of violent behavior as extending beyond the personality or character structure of those people who perform it, and connecting historically to the brutalizing experiences they have commonly shared as well as the immediately precipitating situations in which their violence transpires. The study of the lives of capital defendants yields important truths about the social and developmental roots of extreme violence in our society. Ironically, capital penalty trials have become unique legal forums in which these truths can be told. This approach can assist in understanding the causes of capital murder as well as providing a psychological framework for comprehending a single, violent social history. Moreover, the lessons contained in these psychobiographies can serve as the basis for a responsible social policy of violence prevention in lieu of the categorically punitive approach with which our society recently has become so enamored.

This way of understanding capital defendants also connects directly with a renewed emphasis in the discipline of psychology on the use of social historical techniques (e.g., Elder 1981; Gubrium and Holstein 1995), or what is sometimes called "the study of lives" (cf. Polkinghorne 1996; Runyan 1983; White 1992). It is based in part on the vast and growing literature on the importance of past and present social context in understanding human behavior (e.g., Mischel 1968; Moen, Elder, and Luscher 1995; Ross and Nisbett 1991), as well as on studies of the ways in which certain kinds of past experiences can shape and influence human development over the life course (e.g., Caspi, Bem, and Elder 1989; Sroufe, Egeland, and Kreutzer 1990). As one researcher has noted, the social or life history approach "implies a holistic stance to social reality" and is the "method of choice when complex human events are at stake, when inquiries into the subjective realm of human beliefs, motives and actions in complex social matrices are involved" (Ortiz 1985:100). This method is in many ways uniquely suited to the task of providing capital jurors with insights into how the background of the defendant has helped to shape his character, influenced the course of his development, and affected his actions as an adult—and to do so in ways that speak directly to the critical issue of individualized culpability.

The compilation of a detailed and in-depth social history is also a labor intensive, time consuming, emotionally draining, and psychologically complex undertaking. It cannot be done quickly and it cannot be done effectively by someone who lacks training or experience in relevant aspects of developmental, social, or clinical psychology. One commentator has summarized the complexity of the "complete background investigation" of the capital defendant's life that must be performed by investigators and experts in the construction of a social history:

> This typically requires counseling with members of the [defendant's] family, loved ones, and friends in order to uncover intimate information which could be critical to the litigation. The investigation must cover the inmate's childhood, family life, education, relationships, important experiences, and overall psychological make-up. Crucial witnesses such as childhood friends, teachers, employers, religious advisors, and neighbors may be 'scattered like a diaspora of leaves along the tracks of the defendant's travels'; nevertheless, they must be located and interviewed in order to determine whether they can provide favorable...evidence (Mello 1990–91:895, footnotes omitted).

When done properly, this background and social history investigation and analysis provides the experts who conduct it and the jurors to whom it is presented an extraordinary amount of in-depth information with which to understand a capital defendant's life course. Indeed, it represents an investigatory and analytical effort that is rarely matched in any other setting, including academic research or clinical practice.

The Risk Factors Model in Social History Evaluation

It is often helpful to frame the social history of a capital defendant with a "risk factors" model of the sort that is employed in developmental and social psychology as well as by epidemiologists and medical researchers. Here, "risk factors" can be defined as those events whose presence in one's background indicates "a higher probability for the development of a disorder; as such, these factors are statistically associated with higher incidence rates" (Masten and Garmezy 1985:3). Under this rubric, "stressors" refer to "any change in the environment which typically—i.e., in the average person—induces a high degree of continual tension and interferes with normal patterns of response" (at 6). Because it allows for the analysis of many of the background experiences that are so commonplace in the lives of capital defendants—recognized as "risk factors"—along with the immediate situational pressures under which they act—here conceptualized as "stressors"—this model often provides an especially valid and meaningful way of establishing and illuminating the complex interplay of a defendant's social history and adult behavior. Indeed, Masten and Garmezy have summarized a portion of the developmental literature on risk factors in terms that regularly apply to capital defendants: "Children who pursue delinquent careers may have been exposed to very severe stresses and harmful life events, genetic disadvantage, inappropriate parental models, selective reinforcement by parents of the child's maladaptive behavior, and chronic low self-esteem" (at 25).

Moreover, when added up over the course of a life, the risk factors that can be identified in a capital defendant's social history form a whole that is greater than its individual parts. This way of conceptualizing social histories allows juries to understand and appreciate the role that one or (typically) many of these risk factors that distinguish a capital defendant's life history from others play in accounting for his presence in the courtroom. Along with the numerous stressors that typically are present as precipitating factors, these forces constitute the psychological context of capital crime. The model also helps to account for individual variations in responding to the same or similar risk factors and stressors by acknowledging, on the one hand, different "vulnerabilities" to certain kinds of problems for certain children and, on the other hand, the role of so-called "protective factors" (like warm and supportive family milieus, or the presence of an extended support system) that can buffer children from otherwise damaging elements in their environment.

The Longterm Effects of Childhood Trauma

The lives of many capital defendants are bereft of the things we now know are essential to normal psychological development—"dependable attachment, protection, guidance, stimulation, nurturance, and ways of coping with adversity" (Hamburg 1993:60). Instead, they often confront the multiple risk factors of poverty, chronic neglect, emotional and physical abuse, and extreme familial instability with little to buffer them from the predictable harm.

The Effects of Poverty on the Lives of Capital Defendants

Some capital defendants are the children of profound poverty and deprivation. They are the legacy of a society that has, over the last 20 years, systematically turned its back on its poor and on their children. Indeed, the widespread poverty of capital defendants is so generally accepted that it has escaped much academic commentary (e.g., Egelko 1994), except as it affects the quality of their legal representation (Bright 1992). But poverty also affects their quality of life, and plays an important role in the social histories that surround the crimes for which they may be put to death. Although we are just beginning to assess the long-term consequences of childhood poverty, researchers have documented the persistent despair that profound economic deprivation can inflict. Not surprisingly, children who grow up in economically deprived households are less likely to be hopeful, self-directed, and confident about their future than those who grow up under better economic conditions (e.g., Duncan, Brooks-Gunn, and Klebanov 1994; Elder 1979). One national survey found that welfare status or perceived financial stress was significantly related to children's emotional and behavioral problems—specifically, to higher levels of depression, antisocial behavior, and impulsivity (Takeuchi, Williams, and Adair 1991).

Consistent with these and other findings, unemployment and employment in poor quality jobs are systematically related to the arrest rates among juveniles and young adults (Allen and Steffensmeier 1989). In the United States, of course, poverty and unemployment are inextricably interrelated with race. Thus, one study found that although single year poverty rose about the same amount among both Black and White children between 1970 and the mid-1980s, the differences between them remained quite large. That is, the average percentage of those considered poor rose from 10.5 percent to 12.9 percent during this period among White children, and a staggering 42.5 percent to 45.1 percent among Black children (Duncan and Rodgers 1991). Moreover, African American children are more likely to live under conditions of *chronic* poverty (e.g., Bane and Ellwood 1986).

Over the last several decades, researchers have given increased attention to the mechanisms by which the structural variable of poverty translates into significant psychological consequences for children who experience it. We have learned that poverty forces family members to adapt to scarcity in ways that influence interpersonal relationships and, in turn, adversely affects child development. One ethnographer studying children growing up in a poor urban neighborhood concluded that despite their resourcefulness, children are "no match for the physical toll of poverty and its constant frustrations and humiliations." Specifically:

> A number of the children I know came into the world already victimized by prenatal undernourishment and, as a result, by premature birth or a low birth weight. Since then, inconsistent mealtimes, punctuated by feasts on hunger-numbing junk food bought with proceeds from odd jobs or the leftovers from welfare checks, have left many kids alternately drained, hyperactive, and irritable. Frustration at their parents inability to provide and memories of those adults' defensive responses to requests for food and clothes inevitably help engender...mistrust and manipulative behavior.... Poverty also often engenders a deep sense of personal failure and humiliation (Nightingale 1994:55).

We also have learned that poverty pushes children too rapidly toward adult status and roles. Because interpersonal resources within the family must be devoted more to survival than to child rearing, younger children tend to grow up "undersocialized" (e.g., Elder and Caspi 1988). Other researchers have documented an absolutely critical issue—the ways in which economic hardship produces psychological distress for both parents and children. It is this distress — more than the direct effect of poverty — that undermines parents' ability to provide nurturant care and increases tendencies toward inconsistent discipline. These problematic parenting styles are, correspondingly, associated with increased depression, drug use, and delinquency among adolescent children (e.g., Lempers, Clark-Lempers, and Webb 1989).

In any individual social history, the linkages from childhood poverty to adult violence may be complex but they are rarely difficult to comprehend. There are indirect routes by which poverty can have long-term effects on adult criminal behavior. Thus, persistent poverty is predictive of severe and recurrent child abuse — family "[v]iolence does occur at all income levels but it is more often repeated among the persistently poor" (Kruttschnitt, McLeod, and Dornfeld 1994:310) — which in turn predicts higher levels of delinquency and adult criminality, including violence. In addition to the role that poverty plays in increasing despair and undermining self-esteem, in forcing the undersocialization of children, and in interfering with consistent and nurturant parenting — all of which put children at greater risk of delinquent behavior — poverty can result in increased levels of frustration. Of course, chronic poverty can result in chronic frustration. Research reveals that, depending on the circumstances — particularly, the *reasons* a person perceives his or her desired goals are blocked — such frustration can produce greater levels of "angry aggression" (Berkowitz 1989). Not surprisingly, then, we know that economic inequality is statistically associated with violence, and that severe poverty is associated with high rates of lethal aggression (e.g., Huff-Corzine, Corzine, and Moore 1991; Williams 1984).

In this context, race-based poverty forces minority group members to confront higher levels of frustration as well as exposing them to a higher number of other risk factors that are associated with poverty. For example, higher rates of poverty create greater levels of psychological distress for parents and children alike, which can adversely affect the quality of parenting and the development of the child (e.g., McLoyd 1990). We already know that, as one researcher put it: "Black children suffer disproportionately from virtually every form of stress affecting full and healthy development..." (Lassiter 1987:39). Yet, as this same researcher concluded, "none of these stressors is more threatening to the healthy development of black children and to the stability of their families than intrafamilial child abuse" (at 39).

Two interrelated and very significant risk factors in the lives of many capital defendants — familial instability and lack of predictable structure — often are related to poverty, but also can occur for a variety of other reasons. Indeed, the structure of the lives of capital defendants is often pervaded by personal and social chaos and instability. Their family structure is erratic, fluid, and unpredictable; their parents separate and divorce often, and there are numerous new adults who come in and out of their lives. As children, they move because of poverty, they move because of their parents' chronic instability and interpersonal conflicts, they move because of the restlessness and whimsy of those adults who are in charge of them, and they move because their families have such a tenuous grasp on harsh labor markets that they are buffeted around from job to job at the slightest economic shift. All of this external chaos and instability makes the critical developmental tasks of creating internal anchors or controls and a stable sense of self more difficult to accomplish. Moreover, it creates an internal environment in which other forms of maltreatment are more likely. Thus, one study of abused children reported that: "[T]he homes of many of these children are characterized by chaos, disruption, and disorganization" (Egeland and Erickson 1987:115).

Childhood Abandonment and Neglect

In addition to the abject poverty, economic and emotional deprivation and instability that they often confront, there are other risk factors that routinely appear in the social histories of capital defendants. Many have experienced abandonment and chronic neglect. Abandonment may occur because of divorce, parental incarceration, or the overwhelmingness of parenting and other responsibilities. Whatever its causes, it can have profound effects on a child's life course (e.g., Mishne 1992; Wolfenstein 1976). Indeed, studies of its psychological sequelae indicate that abandoned children are at high risk for mood disorders such as depression (e.g., Schonfeld 1995) and related problems (e.g., Crouch and Milner 1993; Freudenberger and Gallagher 1995), and that they also are more likely to manifest a specific set of behaviors that are can be related to subsequent criminality—aggressiveness, rebelliousness, and disobedience (e.g., Burnstein 1981).

Emotional abandonment—in the form of parental withdrawal and chronic neglect—is another risk factor that frequently pervades the lives of capital defendants. Because it often results from the fact that parents are themselves grappling with overwhelming economic circumstances, interpersonal problems, alcohol and drug addictions and the like, neglect is often not the product of any conscious or intentional desire to do harm. Its consequences are nonetheless profound. Indeed, one study acknowledged that neglectful parenting was "often the result of chronic stress, situations arising from frequent or prolonged spells of unemployment, physical or mental disabilities among members of the family, and an often permanent condition of poverty..." (Wilson 1980:232). This study also concluded that neglectful parenting was "highly likely" to contribute to patterns of delinquency and should, therefore, be regarded as creating "severe social handicap" in children exposed to it (at 233). Another study found that "psychologically unavailable caregiving" in which parents passively rejected children, were detached and uninvolved with them except when absolutely necessary, had dramatic consequences. At two years these children were "angry, extremely frustrated, noncompliant and displayed a great deal of negative affect." As they got older they "were less persistent and enthusiastic" than other children and also "expressing a great deal of negative emotion, lacking impulse control, and [were] highly dependent" (Egeland and Erickson 1987:115). Similarly, Gerald Patterson and his colleagues have identified a causal connection between poor parenting (e.g., harsh, inconsistent discipline, little positive involvement, and inadequate monitoring and supervision) and coercive, socially unskilled behavior on the part of children that often leads, through a series of intervening steps, to delinquency and substance abuse problems (e.g., Patterson, DeBaryshe, and Ramsey 1989).

Physical Abuse and Maltreatment in the Lives of Capital Defendants

Child neglect occurs in conjunction with physical abuse in a high percentage of cases and, unfortunately, both co-occur with unusual frequency in the lives of capital defendants. We now know that: "Inappropriate parental behavior may produce physical, emotional, or sexual damage. Although we cannot always accurately predict what effects maltreatment will produce, victims most often suffer multiple damage, and individual susceptibilities to harm differ" (Garbarino 1989:221; see also, Wolfe 1987). Although it is difficult to predict precisely which of the harmful effects of maltreatment any particular child will manifest, studies show that juveniles who have become involved in delinquency "have endured child abuse and neglect at far greater rates than estimates for the population as a whole and for the low-income groups in particular" (Garbarino 1989:251). We certainly know that abused children are much more likely to engage in violence as adults, giving rise to what is now routinely referred to as a "cycle of violence" (Dodge, Bates, and Petit 1990; Widom 1989a; 1989b). As one early study concluded: "Violence does appear to breed violence.... The child who experiences violence... has the potential of becoming a violent member of society in the future" (Silver, Dublin, and Lourie 1969:407).

Some research has suggested that aggressive fathers may create a social environment that is conducive to aggressive behavior (McCord 1991; 1994a). Similarly, one study that documented the neurological, cognitive, socioemotional consequences of physical abuse focused on the "interpersonal" nature of the transgression and the way in which it adversely affected children's social behavior and their understanding of social relationships. Specifically, "[g]iven the child's exposure to parental violence as a legitimate means of interacting with other people," these researchers were not surprised to find that "abused children are more aggressive, showing more hostile, externalizing and negative social behavior with other people than nonabused children" (Salzinger, Feldman, Hammer, and Rosario 1991:74). Other studies suggest that these violent patterns may be psychologically encoded through "identification with the aggressor," wherein abused children learn to model the behavior of the powerful parent figures who mistreat them. Other researchers have focused more specifically on the developmental role of aggression in protecting the more fragile self against a hostile, seemingly psychologically life-threatening environment of the sort that is created by an abusive parent. That is: "Faced with profoundly insensitive or cruel parenting, the young child's representation of all mental life will be fragile. Ordinary frustration of aims will signal potential destruction of the reflective self, accompanied by intolerable anxiety" (Fonagy, Moran, and Target 1993:475). Others have interpreted the cycle of violence as "reenactment behavior" that is "an attempt to manage the confusion and stress" that are generated by the abuse (McCormack, Rokous, Hazelwood, and Burgess 1992:226).

However, despite these different perspectives about exactly how and why aggression appears to recur in subsequent generations, there is little doubt "that violence is transmitted intergenerationally from parents to their adolescent offspring and that psychological mechanisms are, at least in part, a feature of this transmission" (Truscott 1992:332; see also, Rutter, Quinton, and Liddle 1983; Tolman and Bennett 1990). These mechanisms are useful in understanding the intergenerational transmission of violence and abuse that characterizes the lives of so many capital defendants. It is a destructive legacy that continues to plague its victims through adolescence and into adulthood. Thus, as one study concluded: "[e]ven among a relatively homogeneous group of youthful offenders, the majority of whom had substantial criminal records, evidence of family violence, parental criminality, and parental neglect or poor supervision significantly increased parolees' risk of rearrest for violent crimes" (Lattimore, Visher, and Linster 1995:76; see also, Lake 1995). Similarly, Rivera and Widom (1992) found that neglected and abused African American male children have a higher likelihood of arrests for delinquency, adult criminality, and violent criminal behavior.

In addition to the harmful effects of direct physical abuse, we also know that *witnessing* the abuse of others can be an extremely damaging psychological risk factor (e.g., Rosenberg 1987; Rosenberg and Giberson 1991). Thus, one study found that boys appeared to be more vulnerable to the effects of marital discord and, although they could make no simple causal connections between witnessing abuse and subsequent adjustment problems, the researchers concluded that "[b]esides inappropriate modeling of conflict resolution, these children are affected by their mothers' diminished effectiveness as a parent, negative changes in family status, and related factors that result from family violence" (Wolfe, Jaffe, and Wilson 1988:239). Other researchers have found that exposure to parental conflict and aggression was one of the "instigating conditions" to adult criminality (e.g., McCord 1994a; 1994b). This risk factor is common in the lives of many capital defendants. Indeed, many capital defendants come from chronically abusive homes in which their mothers and other siblings have been physically attacked in their presence, sometimes despite their noble but typically ineffective attempts to intervene.

Institutional Failure and Capital Mitigation

This pattern of childhood poverty, familial instability, and parental neglect and abuse predictably results in higher rates of juvenile institutionalization among capital defendants. Indeed, for many of them, as they approach their teenage years, their social history merges into an institutional history. Although intended as agencies of resocialization and enhanced social control, supposedly designed to produce conforming behavior and to decrease unlawful activity, juvenile and adult penal institutions often constitute their own kind of risk factor, independently increasing rather than decreasing the likelihood of subsequent reoffending. The literature on the failure of our adult prison system is clear, although the impact of this failure on the problem of worsening violence in our society has yet to be adequately told (e.g., Christie 1993; Haney 1997b). Indeed, *institutional failure* is another theme that is prominent in the lives of many capital defendants — ranging from the lack of desperately needed intervention, to intervention that is ill-conceived, poorly and inadequately funded and staffed, and intervention that is terribly destructive of the human psyche and spirit.

Nowhere is the price of institutional failure clearer and more painful to contemplate than in the case of children who are confined by agencies of social control, only to have that experience worsen, sometimes irreparably, the very problems their incarceration was designed to remedy. However inadequate the dominant "free choice" rhetoric has proven for understanding adult criminality, it does not even begin to explain most juvenile crime. Yet, far too often in the lives of capital defendants, juvenile institutionalization represents a kind of "turning point," an experience that helps them resolve the internal struggle over who to be — indeed, over who they can be — in a profoundly negative way. Destructive juvenile incarceration forces children to commit to a value system and a way of being that is angry and rejecting, and which places individualistic survival above all else.

The potentially destructive effects of normatively ineffective, stigmatizing juvenile justice system processing has been recognized for some time (e.g., Forer 1970; Schur 1973). For example, a study of California's vast "youth authority" began with the observations: "The institutional environment at California Youth Authority training schools is in many ways detrimental to the health and behavior of the 5,700 young men and women who are detained in these facilities.... It is the thesis of this report that not enough attention has been paid to the negative impact which remarkably stressful living conditions at the Youth Authority have on its institutionalized population" (Lerner 1982:8). Similarly, a nationwide examination of juvenile justice facilities concluded with a series of scathing observations, including the fact that "[y]oungsters sent to juvenile de-

tention centers and training schools are likely to be brutalized rather than rehabilitated" (Silberman 1978:312) and that the "overwhelming majority of detained juveniles receive no help worthy of the name" (at 330). Studies continue
to document the absence of adequate and appropriate services for children who
suffer from serious emotional problems (e.g., Cohen, Preiser, Gottlieb, Harris,
Baker, and Sonenklar 1993). Many such children are inadequately or badly
treated by juvenile justice institutions that have too little in the way of resources,
time, and expertise with which to reverse years of pre-existing trauma and address the consequences of exposure to substantial numbers of risk factors (e.g.,
Greene 1993; Zigler, Taussig, and Black 1992).

There is a second form of institutional failure that extends beyond the lack of
treatment for pre-existing problems—the proactive harm that may be inflicted
on young people by harsh and degrading conditions of confinement. The early
sociological literature on juvenile justice institutions underscored their destructive potential (e.g., Zald 1960), including their tendency to undermine self-esteem (Fetrow and Fetrow 1974) and subject young offenders to brutalizing experiences from which they may never recover (Bartollas, Miller, and Dinitz 1976).
In many of the facilities in which adult capital clients were confined as juveniles,
this conclusion—reached more than 20 years ago—has remained accurate:

> [T]he bare fact remains that some of the [living units] are worse
> than the streets; that some of the strong in the streets become the
> meek in the institution; that the juvenile correctional institution is
> a misnomer, as is the industrial school, the training school, the ad-
> justment center. All are euphemisms. No matter how pleasant the
> place may seem, very little correction, training, or adjustment oc-
> curs—or can, in fact, occur under present circumstances and so-
> cial policies (Bartollas, Miller, and Dinitz 1976:271).

Other researchers have reached similar conclusions about other juvenile facilities. Moreover, Nightingale (1994) has written about the way in which institutions of social control now have begun to play increasingly larger roles in the
lives of inner-city children, their harshness reinforcing the lessons of what he
euphemistically refers to as the "forceful parenting" many have already received at home. Further: "[B]y equating child punishment with jails and being
prepared to employ the police, parents demonstrated just how closely their
philosophies resonated with those of mainstream institutions of law and
order" (at 95). Not surprisingly, institutional placement appears to adversely
affect subsequent parole adjustment, especially among youthful offenders
whose family life is problematic (Fendrich 1991). Indeed, one study of California juvenile institutions reached the "specific and urgent" recommendation
that "our present system for dealing with youthful offenders needs drastic
overhauling," in large part because of the extent to which it "returns[s] to freedom young men and women who have been brutalized by their institutional

experience" (Lerner 1986:46). This fact led to the conclusion that such institutions actually "promote crime rather than deter it, and increase the criminal population at great expense to the rest of us" (at 47).

Institutional failure extends with a vengeance to adult correctional institutions. Some commentators have speculated that, over the long run, increasingly high levels of imprisonment will worsen rather than reduce the problem of violent crime (Haney 1997b). In addition to the direct effects of institutionalization on persons who will subsequently be released (e.g., Goodstein 1980; Orsagh and Chen 1988), especially high levels of incarceration in some communities will have disastrous effects on family formation, maintenance, and survival. Incarceration intensifies many of the problems of poverty and instability described earlier, indirectly contributes to increases in criminality, and amplifies the structural linkages between unemployment, economic deprivation, family disruption and criminal behavior (e.g., Sampson 1987). Indeed, one commentator has warned that "imprisonment will become the most significant factor contributing to the dissolution and breakdown of African American families during the decade of the 1990s" (King 1993:145).

Moreover, the causes of escalating violence following incarceration are all the more apparent for those defendants whose prison sentences were accompanied by pre-existing psychiatric disorders and substance abuse problems that either went unrecognized, or whose recommendations for treatment simply went unheeded. The lack of mental health services for prisoners continues to plague our nation's prison system. A recent federal case provided a description of the shocking inadequacies in mental health services available to psychologically troubled and psychiatrically disturbed California prisoners (see *Coleman v. Wilson* 1994 and the related discussion in Specter 1994). Unfortunately, the California system is not alone in failing to provide the resources with which to treat its mentally-ill prisoners, or in employing the practice of putting emotionally disturbed prisoners in punitive isolation rather than treatment facilities (Haney and Lynch 1997a; Toch 1982; *Madrid v. Gomez* 1994).

Nor is it alone in exposing citizens to the increased risk of capital violence committed by persons inadequately treated, psychologically harmed, or otherwise brutalized by criminal justice institutions that achieve the opposite of their intended effect. Prisons often fail by not providing meaningful vocational or educational training, so that the scars of poverty cannot be overcome. They can fail because they create destructive and hostile environments where the damage of earlier mistreatment worsens. They can produce criminalizing habits of mind and behavior that, along with the persistent stigma of past incarceration, may disable prisoners once they are released (see Haney 1997b, for a more detailed discussion). And they can neglect to provide badly needed psychological counseling and, especially, treatment for the drug and alcohol problems that are so clearly implicated in much violent crime. The lives of capital defendants too often bear the marks of all these institutional failures.

Criminogenic Adaptations to Childhood Trauma: Alcohol, Drugs, and Gangs

The residue of early developmental history interacts with current circumstances to shape behavioral patterns over a life course. The legacy of a child's prior treatment persists, such that "children with early internal models of available care and self-worth are more responsive to positive features of the environment and more resilient to stress" (Sroufe, Egeland, and Kreutzer 1990:1371). Not only does past experience influence present decision-making, but it can lead in some cases to the development of self-fulfilling interactional patterns and styles. Thus, some adolescents react to the memory of past mistreatment and rejection by becoming aggressive or emotionally distant which, in turn, leads to further mistreatment and rejection and the possibility of ever-escalating misbehavior and disconnection from others (e.g., Patterson, DeBaryshe, and Ramsey 1989).

Other adaptations provide short term relief from the pain of one's past or the press of intolerable present circumstances, but lead to long-term destructive consequences later in life. Thus, many victims of early abuse and neglect turn to drugs and alcohol as a form of "self-medication" that promises to reduce their emotional pain. Indeed, often their own parents' drug and alcohol abuse provides them with their most available and salient model for reducing intolerable stress, relieving depression, and resolving interpersonal conflict. Yet, we know that alcohol and drug use represent major risk factors for subsequent criminality, including violence (Langevin, Paitich, Orchard, Handy, and Russon 1982; Langevin, Ben-Aron, Wortzman, Dickey, and Handy 1987; Parker 1995). For example: "Although drug use does not appear to initiate a criminal career, a large volume of research clearly indicates that frequency of drug use has a strong impact on the extent, direction, and duration of that (criminal) career" (McBride and McCoy 1994:268). Indeed, "[i]t is generally acknowledged that drug use is an important factor in crimes of violence, including homicide" (Spunt, Brownstein, Goldstein, Fendrich, and Liberty 1995:125). Drug abuse may have direct effects on behavior that may further marginalize users, undermine school or job performance and, depending upon the particular drug, increase aggressive reactivity (e.g., Miller and Potter-Efron 1989). It also places users in direct contact with a subculture in which both criminal and violent behavior are more normative (e.g., McCarthy and Hagan 1995). Particularly in cases of addiction, high levels of drug use may create an economic strain for addicts that can only be met through illicit activity (see generally, Goldstein 1989; Stephens 1991).

Gang membership represents another short term adaptation taken in adolescence and young adulthood by some capital defendants to overcome the legacy of their early developmental problems and the pressures of the communities in which they live. It often exacts a significantly negative, life-altering long-term price. Early studies of urban Latino gangs noted that membership could be explained in part by the "absence of a secure cultural (and personal) identity" brought about by the marginality of the groups from which their members originated (Vigil 1983:47). Researchers talked about turning to gangs as a way of coping with the "multiple marginality" of the rest of their existence. Indeed, the multiple marginality that Vigil (1983) described applies to many capital defendants who must cope with the effects of "low socioeconomic status, culture conflict, and impaired development of self-esteem which arise in a complex of ecological, socioeconomic, cultural, and psychological factors" (at 46). Luis Rodriguez (1994), who has written eloquently about the pull of gang life, has noted that for many young people "a gang embraces who they are, gives them the initiatory community they seek and the incipient authority they need to eventually control their lives" (at 605). Indeed, they turn to gangs in large part because "[t]hese are things other institutions, including schools and families, often fail to provide" (at 605; see also, Hagedorn 1988; Sanchez-Jankowski 1991; Smith and Tarallo 1995; Vigil 1988).

This reliance by young people upon gangs to fulfill needs and provide opportunities that are otherwise denied them sometimes occurs in conjunction with, and serves to facilitate, alcohol and drug use (e.g., Fagan 1989; Sullivan 1989; Williams 1989), so that the negative consequences of both adaptations are compounded. This interaction also increases the likelihood that juvenile and adult institutionalization will follow. A kind of social historical cycle begins to develop in which risk factors amplify each other's effects. Attempts to overcome the legacy of one risk factor sometimes leads to a new and more powerful criminogenic influence as lives begin to spin dangerously out of control.

Indeed, the nexus between poverty, childhood abuse and neglect, social and emotional dysfunction, alcohol and drug abuse, and crime is so tight in the lives of many capital defendants as to form a kind of social historical "profile." The social ecology of crime is shaped by the neighborhoods in which its perpetrators are raised. The demographic mix of these communities determines the nature of the class and race conflict to which participants become accustomed. Criminal opportunities and social and economic pressures to succumb vary by neighborhood and family. In fact, recently published autobiographical and ethnographic accounts of the structural disadvantages of race and class underscore many of the cumulative difficulties that capital defendants have confronted (e.g., Canada 1995; Coyle 1993; Kotlowitz 1991; Frey 1994; Ladd 1994; McCall 1994; Rodriguez 1993; Staples 1994; Sullivan 1989).[6] These new urban ethnographies depict the influence of sociopolitical and economic

---

6. For a lengthy response to the claim that the role of social historical disadvantage in mitigating capital crime is minimized or eliminated by virtue of the fact that "not everybody" who endures them also succumbs to criminal violence, see Haney (1995:589–608).

forces as they shape the choices of individual actors; choices that are often less a product of rational or conscious decision-making processes than attempts to struggle with "[f]eelings of sheer humiliation and embarrassment, disappointment and frustration, grief and loneliness, and fear and anxiety (especially concerning suspicion, rejection, and abandonment)" (Nightingale 1994:40). The consequences of such a combination of early, often prolonged abuse and neglect, continued economic and social marginalization, and juvenile and adult institutionalization in the lives of many capital defendants may even amount to what has been called "complex PTSD" [post traumatic stress disorder], reflecting chronic and repeated exposure to trauma that inflicts a deeper and broader pattern of psychic harm (e.g., Herman 1992a; 1992b).

Conclusion

Cornel West has written eloquently about the interrelationship between the structural and individual determinants of social behavior. He urged social scientists and policy makers to:

> [a]cknowledge that structures and behavior are inseparable, that institutions and values go hand in hand. How people act and live are shaped—though in no way dictated or determined—by the larger circumstances in which they find themselves. These circumstances can be changed, their limits attenuated, by positive actions to elevate living conditions (West 1993:12).

This observation counsels not only in favor of social and political action to elevate the depressed circumstances in which many people are forced to live and to improve the structures and the values that shape and delimit their life chances, but also to acknowledge the importance of these social historical factors in legal decision-making about moral culpability and personal blameworthiness. Capital penalty trials provide an important and, in many ways, unique forum in which these issues can and should be addressed.

The social historical patterns I have discussed that emerge from the lives of capital defendants—and the trauma and the risk factors that accumulate within them—reflect the deep roots of violence in our society. The sins of the parents and the larger society in which these children are raised are visited not only on the children themselves but, with uncanny regularity, on the future victims of those children grown up. When many of us began examining the lives of capital defendants, now 20 or more years ago, we were struck by the frequency with which these men were brutalized and neglected as children, pushed to the social and economic margins of our society, and often mistreated by the very institutions we had entrusted with the task of helping them. The patterns were striking in the lives of these defendants and many others and, after years of carefully documenting these effects, there is now little question about the causal connections. Study after study has confirmed the cycles of desperation, hopelessness, and violence; cycles in which many capital defendants have become enmeshed.

It is difficult to imagine how any jury could begin to meaningfully analyze and fairly assess a capital defendant's moral culpability and blameworthiness absent a painstakingly researched, thoughtfully assembled, and carefully and comprehensively presented chronicle of his life. In this regard, capital penalty instructions also must be revised and reframed in such a way as to legitimate such explanations and acknowledge their mitigating force. A social history—the in-depth and psychologically-informed study of a capital defendant's life—and judicial instructions that specifically underscore its importance add minimal fairness and a quantum of essential predictability to capital sentencing that are said by death penalty supporters to be its constitutional hallmarks. Absent either one, not even the pretense of having done justice can be claimed.

References

Alfieri, A. (1996) "Mitigation, Mercy, and Delay: The Moral Politics of Death Penalty Abolitionists." *Harvard Civil Rights-Civil Liberties Law Review* 31:325–352.

Allen, E. and D. Steffensmeier (1989) "Youth, Underemployment, and Property Crime: Differential Effects of Job Availability and Job Quality on Juvenile and Young Adult Arrest Rates." American Sociological Review 54:107–123.

Balkwell, J. (1990) "Ethnic Inequality and the Rate of Homicide." *Social Forces* 69:53–70.

Bane, M. and D. Ellwood (1986) "Slipping In and Out of Poverty: The Dynamics of Spells." *Journal of Human Resources* 21:1–23.

Barlow, M., D. Barlow, and T. Chiricos (1995) "Mobilizing Support for Social Control in a Declining Economy: Exploring Ideologies of Crime Within Crime News." *Crime and Delinquency* 41:191–204.

Bartollas, C., S. Miller, and S. Dinitz (1976) *Juvenile Victimization: The Institutional Paradox*. New York: Halsted.

Berkowitz, L. (1989) "Frustration-Aggression Hypothesis: Examination and Reinterpretation." *Psychological Bulletin* 106:59–73.

Blau, J. and P. Blau (1982) "The Cost of Inequality: Metropolitan Structure and Violent Crime. *American Sociological Review* 47:114–129.

Blystone v. Pennsylvania (1990) 494 U.S. 299.

Bright, S. (1992) "In Defense of Life: Enforcing the Bill of Rights on Behalf of Poor, Minority and Disadvantaged Persons Facing the Death Penalty." *Missouri Law Review* 57:849–861.

Burnstein, M. (1981) "Child Abandonment: Historical, Sociological and Psychological Perspectives." *Child Psychiatry and Human Development* 11:213–221.

California v. Brown (1987) 479 U.S. 538.

Canada, G. (1995) *Fist Stick Knife Gun: A Personal History of Violence in America*. Boston: Beacon Press.

Caspi, A., D. Bem, and G. Elder (1989) "Continuities and Consequences of Interactional Styles Across the Life Course." *Journal of Personality* 57:375–406.

Christie, N. (1993) *Crime Control as Industry: Towards Gulags, Western Style?* London: Routledge.

Cohen, R., L. Preiser, S. Gottlieb, R. Harris, J. Baker, and N. Sonenklar (1993) "Relinquishing Custody as a Requisite for Receiving Services for Children with Serious Emotional Disorders: A Review." *Law and Human Behavior* 17:121–134.

Coleman v. Wilson (1994) CIV S-90-0520 (E.D. Cal.).

Coyle, D. (1993) *Hardball: A Season in the Projects.* New York: G.P. Putnam.

Crouch, J. and J. Milner (1993) "Effects of Child Neglect on Children." *Criminal Justice and Behavior* 20:49–65.

Diamond, S. (1993) "Instructing on Death: Psychologists, Judges, and Juries." *American Psychologist* 48:423–434.

Dodge, K., J. Bates, and G. Petit (1990) "Mechanisms in the Cycle of Violence." *Science* 250:1678–1683.

Dubrow, N. and J. Garbarino (1989) "Living in the War Zone: Mothers and Young Children in a Public Housing Development." *Child Welfare* 68:3–20.

Duncan, G., J. Brooks-Gunn, and P. Klebanov (1994) "Economic Deprivation and Early Childhood Development." *Child Development* 65:291–316.

Duncan, G. and W. Rodgers (1991) "Has Children's Poverty Become More Persistent?" *American Sociological Review* 56:538–550.

Dutton, D. and S. Hart (1992) "Evidence for Long-term, Specific Effects of Childhood Abuse and Neglect on Criminal Behavior in Men." *International Journal of Offender Therapy and Comparative Criminology* 36:129–137.

Eddings v. Oklahoma (1982) 455 U.S. 104.

Egeland, B. and M. Erickson (1987) "Psychologically Unavailable Caregiving." Pp. 110–120, in M.R. Brassard, R. Germain, and S. Hart (eds.), *Psychological Maltreatment of Children and Youth.* New York: Pergamon.

Egelko, B. (August 14, 1994) "One Thing Constant on Death Row: Inmates Are Poor." *San Jose Mercury News*:3B.

Elder, G. (1981) "Social History and Life Experience." Pp. 3–31, in D. Eichorn, J. Clausen, N. Haan, M. Honzik, and P. Mussen (eds.), *Present and Past in Middle Life.* New York: Academic Press.

Elder, G. (1979) "Historical Change in Life Patterns and Personality." Pp. 117–159, in P. Baltes and O. Brim (eds.), *Life-Span Development and Behavior* (Vol. 2). New York: Academic Press.

Elder, G. and A. Caspi (1988) "Economic Stress in Lives: Developmental Perspectives." *Journal of Social Issues* 44:25–45.

Fagan, J. (1989) "The Social Organization of Drug Use and Drug Dealing Among Urban Gangs." *Criminology* 27:633–669.

Feldman, M., K. Mallouh, and D. Lewis (1986) "Filicidal Abuse in the Histories of 15 Condemned Murderers." *Bulletin of the American Academy of Psychiatry and Law* 14:345–352.

Fendrich, M. (1991) "Institutionalization and Parole Behavior: Assessing the Influence of Individual and Family Characteristics." *Journal of Community Psychology* 19:109–122.

Fetrow, R. and A. Fetrow (1974) "How a Pre-trial Facility can Destroy the Self-esteem of the Juvenile." *International Journal of Offender Therapy and Comparative Criminology* 18:227–232.

Fonagy, P., G. Moran, and M. Target (1993) "Aggression and the Psychological Self." *International Journal of Psycho-Analysis* 74:471–485.

Forer, L. (1970) *No One Will Listen: How Our Legal System Brutalizes the Youthful Poor.* New York: John Day.

Freudenberger, H. and K. Gallagher (1995) "Emotional Consequences of Loss for Our Adolescents. Special Issue: Adolescent Treatment: New Frontiers and New Dimensions." *Psychotherapy* 32:150–153.

Frey, D. (1994) *The Last Shot: City Streets, Basketball Dreams.* Boston: Houghton Mifflin.

Furman v. Georgia (1972) 408 U.S. 238.

Garbarino, J. (1989) "The Incidence of and Prevalence of Child Maltreatment." Pp. 219–261, in L. Ohlin and M. Tonry (eds.), *Family Violence.* Chicago: University of Chicago.

Geimer, W. (1990–91) "Law and Reality in the Capital Penalty Trial." *New York University Review of Law and Social Change* 28:273–295.

Goldstein, P. (1989) "Drugs and Violent Crime." Pp. 11–48, in N. Wiener and M. Wolfgang (eds.), *Pathways to Criminal Violence.* Newbury Park, CA: Sage.

Goodpaster, G. (1983) "The Trial for Life: Effective Assistance of Counsel in Death Penalty Cases." *New York University Law Review* 58:299–362.

Goodstein, L. (1980) "Inmate Adjustment to Prison and the Transition to Community Life." *Journal of Research on Crime and Delinquency* 10:241– 265.

Greene, M. (1993) "Chronic Exposure to Violence and Poverty: Interventions That Work for Youth." *Crime and Delinquency* 39:101–124.

Gregg v. Georgia (1976) 428 U.S. 153.

Gubrium, J. and J. Holstein (1995) "Biographical Work and New Ethnography." Pp. 45–58, in R. Josselson and A. Lieblich (eds.), *Interpreting Experience: The Narrative Study of Lives.* Thousand Oaks, CA: Sage.

Hagedorn, J. (1988) *People and Folks: Gangs, Crime and the Underclass in Rust Belt City.* Chicago: Lakeview.

Hamburg, D. (1993) "The American Family Transformed." *Society* 30 (January–February):60–69.

Haney, C. (1982) "Psychological Theory and Criminal Justice Policy: Law and Psychology in the 'Formative Era.'" *Law and Human Behavior* 6:191–235.

Haney, C. (1983) "The Good, the Bad, and the Lawful: An Essay on Psychological Injustice." Pp. 107–117, in W. Laufer and J. Day (eds.), *Personality Theory, Moral Development, and Criminal Behavior.* Lexington, MA: Lexington Books.

Haney C. (1995) "The Social Context of Capital Murder: Social Histories and the Logic of Mitigation." *Santa Clara Law Review* 35:547–609.

Haney, C. (1997a) "Psychological Secrecy and the Death Penalty: Observations on 'the Mere Extinguishment of Life.'" *Studies in Law, Politics, and Society* 16:3–69.

Haney, C. (1997b) "Psychology and the Limits to Prison Pain: Confronting the Coming Crisis in Eighth Amendment Law." *Psychology, Law, and Public Policy* 3:499–588.

Haney, C. (1997c) "Violence and the Capital Jury: Mechanisms of Moral Disengagement and the Impulse to Condemn to Death." *Stanford Law Review* 49:801–840.

Haney, C., A. Hurtado, and L. Vega (1994) "'Modern' Death Qualification: New Data on its Biasing Effects." *Law and Human Behavior* 18:619–634.

Haney, C. and M. Lynch (1994) "Comprehending Life and Death Matters: A Preliminary Study of California's Capital Penalty Instructions." *Law and Human Behavior* 18:411–434.

Haney, C. and M. Lynch (1997a) "'Regulating Prisons of the Future: A Psychological Analysis of Supermax and Solitary Confinement." 23 *New York University Review of Law and Social Change* 477–570.

Haney, C. and Lynch, M. (1997b) "Clarifying Life and Death Matters: An Analysis of Instructional Comprehension and Penalty Phase Arguments." *Law and Human Behavior* 21:575–595.

Haney, C. and J. Manzolati (1980) "Television Criminology: Network Illusions of Criminal Justice Realities." Pp. 125–136, in E. Aronson (ed.), *Readings on the Social Animal.* San Francisco, CA: W.H. Freeman.

Haney, C., L. Sontag, and S. Costanzo (1994) "Deciding to Take a Life: Capital Juries, Sentencing Instructions, and the Jurisprudence of Death." *Journal of Social Issues* 50:149–176.

Harris, T. (1988) *The Silence of the Lambs.* New York: St. Martin's Press.

Harvey, W. (1986) "Homicide among Black Adults: Life in the Subculture of Exasperation." Pp. 153–171, in D. Hawkins (ed.), *Homicide Among Black Americans.* Lanham, MD: University Press of America.

Herman, J. (1992a) "A New Diagnosis." Pp. 115–129, in J. Herman (ed.), *Trauma and Recovery.* New York: Basic Books.

Herman, J. (1992b) "Complex PTSD: A Syndrome in Survivors of Prolonged and Repeated Trauma." *Journal of Traumatic Stress* 5:377–391.

Huff-Corzine, L., J. Corzine, and D. Moore (1991) "Deadly Connections: Culture, Poverty, and the Direction of Lethal Violence." *Social Forces* 69:715–732.

Humphries, D. (1981) "Serious Crime, News Coverage, and Ideology: A Content Analysis of Crime Coverage in a Metropolitan Paper." *Crime and Delinquency* 27:191–205.

King, A. (1993) "The Impact of Incarceration on African American Families: Implications for Practice." *Families in Society: The Journal of Contemporary Human Services* 74:145–153.

Kotlowitz, A. (1991) *There Are No Children Here.* New York: Doubleday.

Kruttschnitt, C., J. McLeod, and M. Dornfeld (1994) "The Economic Environment of Child Abuse." *Social Problems* 41:299–315.

Ladd, J. (1994) *Out of the Madness: From the Projects to a Life of Hope.* New York: Warner.

Lake, E. (1995) "Offenders' Experiences of Violence: A Comparison of Male and Female Inmates as Victims." *Deviant Behavior* 16:269–290.

Langevin, R., D. Paitich, B. Orchard, L. Handy, and A. Russon (1982) "The Role of Alcohol, Drugs, Suicide Attempts and Situational Strains in Homicide Committed by Offenders Seen for Psychiatric Assessment." *Acta Psychiatrica Scandinavica* 66:211–228.

Langevin, R., M. Ben-Aron, G. Wortzman, R. Dickey, and L. Handy (1987) "Brain Damage, Diagnosis, and Substance Abuse among Violent Offenders." *Behavioral Sciences and the Law* 5:77–94.

Lassiter, R. (1987) "Child Rearing in Black Families: Child-Abusing Discipline?" Pp. 39–54, in R. Hampton (ed.), *Violence in Black Families.* Lexington, MA: Lexington Books.

Lattimore, P., C. Visher, and R. Linster (1995) "Predicting Rearrest for Violence among Serious Youthful Offenders." *Journal of Research on Crime and Delinquency* 32:54–83.

Lempers, J., D. Clark-Lempers, and V. Webb (1989) "Economic Hardship, Parenting, and Distress in Adolescence." *Child Development* 60:25–39.

Lerner, S. (1986) *Bodily Harm: The Pattern of Fear and Violence at the California Youth Authority.* Bolinas, CA: Commonweal Research Institute.

Lerner, S. (1982) *The CYA Report: Conditions of Life at the California Youth Authority.* Bolinas, CA: Common Knowledge Press.

Lewis, D., R. Lovely, C. Yeager, G. Ferguson, W. Friedman, G. Sloane, H. Friedman, and J. Pincus (1988) "Intrinsic and Environmental Characteristics of Juvenile Murderers." *Journal of the American Academy of Child and Adolescent Psychiatry* 27:582–587.

Lockett v. Ohio (1978) 438 U.S. 586.

Lynch, M. and C. Haney (1997) "Arguing Life and Death: The Narrative Structure of the Debate over Whether a Defendant Lives or Dies." Unpublished manuscript, University of California, Santa Cruz.

Madrid v. Gomez (1995) 889 F.Supp. 1146 (N.D. Cal.).

Masten, A. and N. Garmezy (1985) "Risk, Vulnerability and Protective Factors in Developmental Psychopathology." Pp. 1–52, in F. Lahey and A. Kazdin (eds.), *Advances in Clinical Child Psychology.* New York: Plenum.

McBride, D. and C. McCoy (1994) "The Drugs-Crime Relationship: An Analytical Framework." *Prison Journal* 73:357–278.

McCall, N. (1994) *Makes Me Wanna Holler: A Young Black Man in America.* New York: Random House.

McCarthy, B. and J. Hagan (1995) "Getting into Street Crime: The Structure and Process of Criminal Embeddedness." *Social Science Research* 24:63–95.

McCord, J. (1994a) "Aggression in Two Generations." Pp. 241–251, in L. Huesmann (ed.), *Aggressive Behavior: Current Perspectives.* New York: Plenum.

McCord, J. (1994b) "Inner City Life: Contributions to Violence." Pp. 100–104, in National Research Council (eds.), *Violence in Urban America: Mobilizing a Response.* Washington, D.C.: National Academy Press.

McCord, J. (1991) "The Cycle of Crime and Socialization Practices." *Journal of Criminal Law and Criminology* 82:211–228.

McCormack, A., F. Rokous, R. Hazelwood, and A. Burgess (1992) "An Exploration of Incest in the Childhood Development of Serial Rapists." *Journal of Family Violence* 7:219–228.

McLoyd, V. (1990) "The Impact of Economic Hardship on Black Families and Children: Psychological Distress, Parenting, and Socioemotional Development." *Child Development* 61:311–346.

McNulty, P. (1995) "Natural Born Killers: Preventing the Coming Explosion of Teenage Crime." *Policy Review* 71:84–87.

Mello, M. (1990–91) "On Metaphors, Mirrors, and Murders: Theodore Bundy and the Rule of Law." *New York University Review of Law and Social Change* 18:887–938.

Miller, M. and R. Potter-Efron (1989) "Aggression and Violence Associated with Substance Abuse." *Journal of Chemical Dependency Treatment* 3:1–36.

Mischel, W. (1968) *Personality and Assessment.* New York: Wiley.

Mishne, J. (1992) "The Grieving Child: Manifest and Hidden Losses in Childhood and Adolescence." *Child and Adolescent Social Work Journal* 94:471–490.

Moen, P., G. Elder, and K. Luscher (eds.) (1995) *Examining Lives in Context: Perspectives on the Ecology of Human Development*. Washington, DC: American Psychological Association.

Nightingale, C. (1994) *On the Edge: A History of Poor Black Children and Their American Dreams*. New York: Basic Books.

Norris, J. (1988) *Serial Killers: The Growing Menace*. New York: Doubleday.

Orsagh, T. and J. Chen (1988) "The Effect of Time Served on Recidivism: An Interdisciplinary Theory." *Journal of Quantitative Criminology* 4:155–171.

Ortiz, K. (1985) "Mental Health Consequences of Life History Method: Implications from a Refugee Camp." *Ethos* 13:99–120.

Parker, R. (1995) "Bringing 'Booze' Back In: The Relationship Between Alcohol and Homicide." *Journal of Research in Crime and Delinquency* 32:3–38.

Patterson, G., B. DeBaryshe, and E. Ramsey (1989) "A Developmental Perspective on Antisocial Behavior." *American Psychologist* 44:329–335.

Penry v. Lynaugh (1989) 492 U.S. 302.

People v. Morse (1964) 338 P.2d 33 (Cal.).

Polkinghorne, D. (1996) "Narrative Knowing and the Study of Lives." Pp. 77–99, in J. Birren, G. Kenyon, J. Ruth, J. Schroots, and T. Svensson (eds.), *Aging and Biography: Explorations in Adult Development*. New York: Springer.

Pulley v. Harris (1984) 465 U.S. 37.

Rivera, B. and C. Widom (1992) "Childhood Victimization and Violent Offending." *Violence and Victims* 5:19–35.

Rodriguez, L. (November 21, 1994) "Throwaway Kids: Turning Youth Gangs Around." *The Nation* 259:605–609.

Rodriguez, L. (1993) *Always Running, La Vida Loca: Gang Days in L.A.* Los Angeles: Curbstone.

Rosenberg, M. (1987) "Children of Battered Women: The Effects of Witnessing Violence on Their Social Problem-Solving Abilities." *Behavior Therapist* 10:85–89.

Rosenberg, M. and R. Giberson (1991) "The Child Witness of Family Violence." Pp. 231–253, in R. Ammerman and M. Hersen (eds.), *Case Studies in Family Violence*. New York: Plenum Press.

Ross, L. and R. Nisbett (1991) *The Person and the Situation: Perspectives of Social Psychology*. New York: McGraw-Hill.

Runyan, M. (1983) "Idiographic Goals and Methods in the Study of Lives." *Journal of Personality* 51:413–437.

Rutter, M., D. Quinton, and C. Liddle (1983) "Parenting in Two Generations: Looking Backwards and Looking Forwards." Pp. 60–98, in N. Madge (ed.), *Families at Risk*. London: Heinemann.

Salzinger, S., R. Feldman, M. Hammer, and M. Rosario (1991) "Risk for Physical Child Abuse and the Personal Consequences for its Victims." *Criminal Justice and Behavior* 18:64–81.

Sampson, R. (1987) "Urban Black Violence: The Effect of Male Joblessness and Family Disruption." *American Journal of Sociology* 93:348–382.

Sanchez-Jankowski, M. (1991) *Islands in the Street: Gangs and American Urban Society*. Berkeley: University of California Press.

Schonfeld, W. (1995) "Depression in Adolescence." Pp. 31–38, in R. Marohn, and S. Feinstein (eds.), *Adolescent Psychiatry: Developmental and Clinical Studies* (Vol. 20). Annals of the American Society for Adolescent Psychiatry. Hillsdale, NJ: Analytic Press.

Schur, E. (1973) *Radical Nonintervention: Rethinking the Delinquency Problem.* Englewood Cliffs, NJ: Prentice-Hall.

Shengold, L. (1989) *Soul Murder: The Effects of Childhood Abuse and Deprivation.* New Haven, CT: Yale University Press.

Sherizen, S. (1978) "Social Creation of Crime News: All the News Fitted to Print." Pp. 203–224, in C. Winick (ed.), *Deviance and Mass Media.* Beverly Hills, CA: Sage.

Sherwin, R. (1994) "Law Frames: Historical Truth and Narrative Necessity in a Criminal Case." *Stanford Law Review* 47:39–83.

Silberman, C. (1978) *Criminal Violence, Criminal Justice.* New York: Random House.

Silver, L., C. Dublin, and R. Lourie (1969) "Does Violence Breed Violence? Contributions from a Study of the Child Abuse Syndrome." *American Journal of Psychiatry* 126:404–407.

Skipper v. South Carolina (1986) 476 U.S. 1.

Smith, M. and B. Tarallo (1995) "Who Are the 'Good Guys'? The Social Construction of the Vietnamese 'Other.'" Pp. 50–76, in M. Smith and J. Feagin (eds.), *The Bubbling Cauldron: Race, Ethnicity, and the Urban Crisis.* Minneapolis, MN: University of Minnesota Press.

Specter, D. (1994) "Cruel and Unusual Punishment of the Mentally Ill in California's Prisons: A Case Study of a Class Action Suit." *Social Justice* 21:109–116.

Spunt, B., H. Brownstein, P. Goldstein, M. Fendrich, and H. Liberty (1995) "Drug Use by Homicide Offenders." *Journal of Psychoactive Drugs* 27:125–134.

Sroufe, L., B. Egeland, and T. Kreutzer (1990) "The Fate of Early Experience Following Developmental Change: Longitudinal Approaches to Individual Adaptation in Childhood." *Child Development* 61:1363–1373.

Staples, B. (1994) *Parallel Time: Growing Up in Black and White.* New York: Pantheon.

Steiker, C. and J. Steiker (1995) "Sober Second Thoughts: Reflections on Two Decades of Constitutional Regulation of Capital Punishment." *Harvard Law Review* 109:355–438.

Stephens, R. (1991) *The Street Addict Role.* New York: State University of New York Press.

Sullivan, M. (1989) *"Getting Paid": Youth Crime and Work in the Inner City.* Ithaca, NY: Cornell University Press.

Takeuchi, D., D. Williams, and R. Adair (1991) "Economic Distress in the Family and Children's Emotional and Behavioral Problems." *Journal of Marriage and the Family* 53:1031–1041.

Tarantino, Q. (1995) *Natural Born Killers.* London: Faber and Faber.

Tison v. Arizona (1987) 481 U.S. 137.

Toch, H. (1982) "The Disturbed Disruptive Inmate: Where Does the Bus Stop?" *Journal of Psychiatry and Law* 10:327–349.

Tolman, R. and L. Bennett (1990) "A Review of Quantitative Research on Men Who Batter." *Journal of Interpersonal Violence* 5:87–118.

Truscott, D. (1992) "Intergenerational Transmission of Violent Behavior in Adolescent Males." *Aggressive Behavior* 18:327–335.

Tuilaepa v. California (1994) 512 U.S. 967.

Vigil, J. (1988) *Barrio Gangs: Street Life and Identity in Southern California.* Austin, TX: University of Texas Press.

Vigil, J. (1983) "Chicano Gangs: One Response to Mexican Urban Adaptation in the Los Angeles Area." *Urban Anthropology* 12:45–75.

Weisberg, R. (1984) "Deregulating Death." Pp. 305–395, in P.B. Kurland, G. Casper, and J. Hutchinson (eds.), *The Supreme Court Review 1983.* Chicago: University of Chicago Press.

West, C. (1993) *Race Matters.* Boston, MA: Beacon.

West, R. (1990) "Narrative, Responsibility and Death: A Comment on the Death Penalty." *Maryland Journal of Contemporary Legal Issues* 1:161–177.

White, R. (1992) "Exploring Personality the Long Way: The Study of Lives." Pp. 3–21, in R. Zucker, A. Rabin, J. Aronoff, and S. Frank (eds.), *Personality Structure in the Life Course: Essays on Personology in the Murray Tradition.* New York: Springer.

White, W. (1987) *The Death Penalty in the Eighties: An Examination of the Modern System of Capital Punishment.* Ann Arbor, MI: University of Michigan Press.

Widom, C. (1989a) "Child Abuse, Neglect, and Adult Behavior: Research Design and Findings on Criminality, Violence, and Child Abuse." *American Journal of Orthopsychiatry* 59:355–367.

Widom, C. (1989b) "The Cycle of Violence." *Science* 244:160–166.

Wiener, R., C. Pritchard, and M. Weston (1995) "Comprehensibility of Approved Jury Instructions in Capital Murder Cases." *Journal of Applied Psychology* 80:455–467.

Williams, K. (1984) "Economic Sources of Homicide: Reestimating the Effects of Poverty and Inequality." *American Sociological Review* 49:283–289.

Williams, T. (1989) *The Cocaine Kids: The Inside Story of a Teenage Drug Ring.* Reading, MA: Addison-Wesley.

Williams, T. and W. Kornblum (1994) *The Uptown Kids: Struggle and Hope in the Projects.* New York: Grosset/Putnam.

Wilson, H. (1980) "Parental Supervision: A Neglected Aspect of Delinquency." *British Journal of Criminology* 20:203–234.

Wilson, J. (1975) *Thinking About Crime.* New York: Basic Books.

Wilson, J. and R. Herrnstein (1985) *Crime and Human Nature.* New York: Simon and Schuster.

Wolfe, D. (1987) *Child Abuse: Implications for Child Development and Psychopathology.* Newbury Park, CA: Sage.

Wolfe, D., P. Jaffe, and S. Wilson (1988) "A Multivariate Investigation of Children's Adjustment to Family Violence." Pp. 228–239, in G. Hotaling and D. Sugarman (eds.), *Family Abuses and Its Consequences.* Newbury Park, CA: Sage.

Wolfenstein, M. (1976) "Effects of Adults on Object Loss in the First Five Years." *Journal of the American Psychoanalytic Association* 24:659–668.

Woodson v. North Carolina (1976) 428 U.S. 280.

Zald, M. (1960) "The Correctional Institution for Juvenile Offenders: An Analysis of Organizational 'Character.'" *Social Problems* 8:57–67.

Zant v. Stephens (1983) 462 U.S. 862.

Zigler, E., C. Taussig, and K. Black (1992) "Early Childhood Intervention: A Promising Preventative for Juvenile Delinquency." *American Psychologist* 47:997–1006.

Chapter 16

Race Discrimination and the Death Penalty: An Empirical and Legal Overview

David C. Baldus
George Woodworth

Introduction

The issue of race discrimination and the death penalty has been a matter of scholarly and legal interest since the 1930s. Indeed, every court that has addressed the issue has condemned the idea of race discrimination in the administration of the death penalty as having no place in a society dedicated to the rule of law. Nevertheless, in this century, no American court has upheld a legal claim alleging race discrimination in the use of the death penalty (as contrasted with claims of discrimination in the selection of capital juries, which have been sustained). Moreover, only one American legislative body has adopted legislation that would give a capital defendant the right to advance a claim of racial discrimination in the manner that racial minorities and women are empowered to present legal claims of race discrimination in employment, housing, and public accommodations.

This article focuses on four issues related to race discrimination in the administration of the death penalty in America: (1) the link between discretion and discrimination in the post-*Furman* v. *Georgia* (1972) era, (2) the ethical, moral, and legal concerns associated with race discrimination in the administration of the death penalty, (3) the evidence of discrimination, past and present, and (4) judicial and legislative responses to claims of discrimination in the post-*Furman* period.

Discretion and Discrimination

The issue of race and the death penalty has its roots in the broad exercise of discretion that state laws grant prosecutors and the sentencing authority, typically a jury, in their administration of the death penalty: specifically, the power to treat similarly situated "death-eligible" defendants differently because of the race of the defendant or the race of the victim in the case.[1] (A death-eligible case refers to one in which the facts are sufficient under state law to sustain a capital murder conviction and death sentence, whether or not the state actually seeks a death sentence or the jury actually imposes a death sentence in the case.)

Three actors in the typical state charging and sentencing system exercise broad discretion. First is the prosecutor, whom the law gives complete discretion either to seek a death sentence in death-eligible cases or to waive the death penalty, unilaterally or by way of a negotiated plea bargain. For cases that advance to a penalty trial, the sentencing authority, typically a jury, exercises

---

1. During slavery, state criminal codes explicitly authorized stronger punishments for slaves and emancipated blacks than for whites. In addition, state laws permitted stronger punishments for crimes committed against whites than for crimes against blacks (Radelet and Vandiver 1986:97). (In legal parlance, we refer to discrimination that is expressly authorized by state law as "facial" discrimination.) Facially discriminatory laws continued after the Civil War, until the adoption of the Fourteenth Amendment in 1868. Moreover, in the enforcement of the laws enacted after the war, crimes committed against black victims continued to be treated more leniently or not prosecuted at all, especially if the defendant were white. Crimes by black defendants on the other hand, were punished more harshly, especially if the victim were white. A scholar of the reconstruction period, Professor Leon Litwack notes:

> The double standard of white justice was nowhere clearer, in fact, than in the disparate punishments meted out to whites and blacks convicted of similar crimes.... [A] Freedmen's Bureau officer in Georgia despaired of any early or mass conversion to [the]...principle...that killing a black person amounted to murder.... The best men in the State admit that no jury would convict a white man for killing a freedman, or fail to hang a Negro who had killed a white man in self defense (Litwack 1979:285–86).

Although the Fourteenth Amendment put an end to facial discrimination, it did not sever completely the link between the death penalty and race, even at the legislative level. Indeed, the potential of the death penalty as a means of intimidating and subordinating the black community was clearly perceived and contributed to the strong community support for the use of the death penalty that continues to this day in the deep South. In addition, the availability of a highly discretionary death penalty was useful in combating lynching, a practice that tarnished the image of many states, both North and South, well into this century. Thus, a "lawful" conviction and sentencing (by an all white jury), followed by a swift execution, was substituted for the more unseemly lynching, with the same practical effect (Cook and Kende 1996:821). Lawful executions also reduced Congressional pressure for the enactment of federal anti-lynching legislation in the 1920s (Colbert 1990:80).

With the decline of such blatant racism in the 20th century, the link between race and the death penalty has become much more subtle. Nevertheless, the broad powers of discretion in the late 19th century systems of justice, both North and South, continue to this day with only slight modification. Therein lies the continuing risk of race discrimination in contemporary death sentencing systems.

complete discretion on the life or death decision once it finds that a statutory aggravating circumstance is present in the case. The third actor is the governor or board of pardons and paroles who generally have complete discretion to commute a death sentence to life without possibility of parole or a term of years.

The scope of prosecutorial and jury discretion in current systems is illustrated in Figure 1, which presents a flow chart of the capital charging and sentencing system in Philadelphia, Pennsylvania during the period 1983–93 (Baldus et al. 1998:1645). The Pennsylvania death-sentencing statute is typical in many ways of statutes found in "weighing" death penalty jurisdictions, in which the sentencing authority weighs aggravating and mitigating circumstances as a predicate for its sentencing decision. Aggravating circumstances refer to the particularly serious features of a case, for example, evidence of extensive premeditation and planning by the defendant, or torture of the victim by the defendant. Mitigating circumstances in contrast, refer to features of a case that explain or particularly justify the defendant's behavior, even though they do not provide a defense to the crime of murder. Mitigating circumstances include such things as the youth or immaturity of the defendant.

As is typical in all states, the breadth of prosecutorial and jury discretion under Pennsylvania law is limited at the outset by the legislature's definition of the offense of capital murder and its specification of a discrete list of statutory aggravating circumstances, one of which must be found by the sentencing authority as a basis for the imposition of a death sentence. Another requirement of each state's death penalty law is that the defendant's conduct and mental state also must satisfy the requirements of state law for capital murder. In Pennsylvania, this means that, in addition to the presence of a statutory aggravating circumstance, a case is "death eligible" only if the facts of the case are also sufficient to support a finding of liability for first degree-murder.

Pennsylvania law prescribes 18 such aggravating circumstances. They include such factors as multiple victims, murder for hire, and a prior murder conviction. The limitation on discretion imposed by these aggravating circumstances satisfies the requirement of *Furman v. Georgia* that death-sentencing systems must provide standards to guide the exercise of discretion if they are to satisfy the requirements of the Eighth Amendment.

Pennsylvania law also specifies eight statutory mitigating circumstances that may be considered by the sentencing authority if it finds a statutory aggravating circumstance present in the case.

Figure 1 presents a flow chart of the death-eligible cases processed in Philadelphia during the period 1983–93. Decision Points 1–2 indicate two points at which a defendant can avoid altogether the risk of receiving a death sentence. At decision point 1, the prosecutor may consent to a guilty plea and waive the death penalty (Box 1B) or advance the case to a guilt trial. At deci-

Figure 1
Decision Points in Philadelphia Capital Charging and Sentencing System
(Philadelphia: 1983–93) (N = 707)

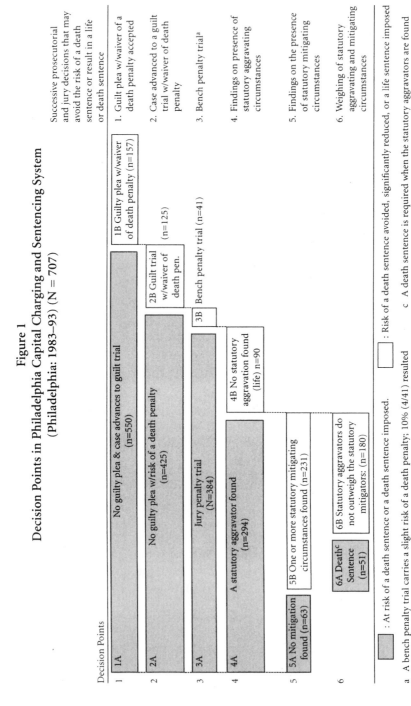

Successive prosecutorial and jury decisions that may avoid the risk of a death sentence or result in a life or death sentence

1. Guilt plea w/waiver of a death penalty accepted

2. Case advanced to a guilt trial w/waiver of death penalty

3. Bench penalty trial[a]

4. Findings on presence of statutory aggravating circumstances

5. Findings on the presence of statutory mitigating circumstances

6. Weighing of statutory aggravating and mitigating circumstances

Decision Points

1   No guilty plea & case advances to guilt trial (n=550) | 1B Guilty plea w/waiver of death penalty (n=157)

2   2A No guilty plea w/risk of a death penalty (n=425) | 2B Guilt trial w/waiver of death pen. (n=125)

3   3A Jury penalty trial (N=384) | 3B Bench penalty trial (n=41)

4   4A A statutory aggravator found (n=294) | 4B No statutory aggravation found (life) n=90

5   5A No mitigation found (n=63) | 5B One or more statutory mitigating circumstances found (n=231)

6   6A Death[c] Sentence (n=51) | 6B Statutory aggravators do not outweigh the statutory mitigators: (n=180)

▨ : At risk of a death sentence or a death sentence imposed.

☐ : Risk of a death sentence avoided, significantly reduced, or a life sentence imposed

▨ : A bench penalty trial carries a slight risk of a death penalty; 10% (4/41) resulted in a death sentence.

☐ : A death sentence is required when the statutory aggravators are found to outweigh the statutory mitigators.

a   A bench penalty trial carries a slight risk of a death penalty; 10% (4/41) resulted in a death sentence.

b   When no mitigation is found a death sentence is required by law.

c   A death sentence is required when the statutory aggravators are found to outweigh the statutory mitigators.

sion point 2, the prosecutor may unilaterally waive the death penalty pre-trial, in which event the case advances to trial as a non-capital case (Box 2B).

The remaining cases, which constitute 60% (425/707) of all of the death-eligible cases, advanced to trial with the Commonwealth seeking a death sentence. In these cases, the defendant, at decision point 3, has the option of waiving a jury guilt and penalty trial (Box 3B). Only a small fraction of defendants take this option, but for those who do, the risk of a death sentence is sharply reduced if they are convicted of first-degree murder. Specifically, the risk of a death sentence in a penalty trial before a judge is .10 (4/41) in contrast to .30 (114/384) before a jury. However, most defendants opt for a jury trial in the hope that, before a jury, they will be acquitted or convicted of an offense less serious than murder 1 or 2, both of which carry a mandatory life-without-parole sentence.

For the jury cases that result in a murder 1 conviction, decision points 4–6 reflect the jury's penalty-trial decisions. They focus on three specific issues. The first, at decision point 4, is whether the case includes one or more aggravating circumstances. If the jury finds none present, which occurred 23% (90/384) of the time (Box 4B), the defendant is sentenced to life without possibility of parole.

For the cases in which one or more aggravating circumstances is found, the jury is further instructed to determine whether a statutory mitigating circumstance is also present in the case. If this question is answered in the affirmative (which requires the affirmative vote of only a single juror), the jurors move on to the final weighing decision (Box 5B). In spite of this low threshold for advancing the case to the final stage of decision, Philadelphia juries failed to find any mitigation present 21% (63/294) of the time. It is at this point that the law of Pennsylvania differs from the law of most other weighing jurisdictions. The difference is that if the jury fails to find mitigation at this stage in the proceedings, it is instructed that it *must* return a death sentence, whether or not it considers a death sentence appropriate or just. Thus each finding of no mitigation present at decision point 5 resulted in the mandatory imposition of a death sentence (Box 5A). The importance of this decision point is reflected in the fact that 55% (63/114) of the Philadelphia jury death sentences were imposed on this basis.

For the cases in which mitigation is found at level 5, the jury at level 6 weighs the aggravating and mitigating factors and is instructed to return a verdict of death if it finds that the aggravating circumstances outweigh the mitigating circumstances. In 22% (51/231) of the weighing cases, the jury returned a death verdict (Box 6A).[2]

---

2. When the focus is on the total death-sentencing rate among all of the penalty trials indicated in Box 3A, the death sentencing rate is .30 (114/384). Among all of the death-eligible cases in Row 1, the rate is .16 (114/707).

Most striking about the exercise of prosecutorial and jury discretion in contemporary death-sentencing systems process is that their decisions to seek and impose death sentences are essentially unreviewable with respect to the issue of discrimination. In the absence of an admission by the prosecutor or individual jurors that race was a factor in their decisions, (which is virtually unheard of) discriminatory behavior by either of these actors is essentially outside the scope of appellate review in the numerous appeals that generally follow the imposition of a death sentence.

As noted above, the third possible actor on the life/death issue is the governor or another statewide body, such as a board of pardons and paroles, who exercises complete discretionary power to commute death sentences to life in prison or a term of years. (This discretion is also beyond any sort of meaningful review by appellate courts.) In the not-so-recent past (pre-1970), governors in death-sentencing states routinely commuted to life imprisonment or a term of years up to one third of the death sentences that they reviewed. Today, however, commutations of death sentences by governors and review boards rarely occur unless they are mandated by a judicial decision.

Early Questions About and Challenges to the Scope of Discretion in Death Cases

In the 1960s, concerns about the link between broad discretion in the administration of the death penalty and the risk of arbitrariness, especially racial discrimination, prompted proposals to limit the discretion of sentencing juries. For example, the American Law Institute (ALI), a distinguished group of lawyers, judges, and academics, proposed in the Model Penal Code (a recommendation to state legislatures) that the death penalty be limited to narrow, statutorily defined categories of cases. The ALI also proposed that juries be empowered to impose death sentences only after they made "factual" findings about the presence of (a) statutory "aggravating circumstances," such as the presence of an armed robbery or rape, and (b) statutory "mitigating circumstances," such as the defendant's youth or the absence of a prior criminal record, and (c) found "that there were no mitigating circumstances sufficiently substantial to call for leniency."

In spite of these recommendations, the United States Supreme Court rejected the argument that those procedures were required by the United States Constitution (*McGautha v. California* 1971). Nevertheless, in the following year, *Furman v. Georgia* (1972) invalidated the death-sentencing systems of every American jurisdiction on the grounds that the "untrammeled" discretion that the systems delegated to sentencing juries, combined with what appeared to be an arbitrary pattern of death-sentencing decisions that they produced, was unacceptable under the "cruel and unusual punishments" provision of the Eighth Amendment of the Constitution.

Although *Furman* was perceived by some as the end of the death penalty in America, the decision had the opposite effect and galvanized state legislative support for the death penalty. Within two years of the decision, more than 30 states had amended their statutes in an effort to address the concerns expressed in *Furman*. Shortly thereafter, the Supreme Court approved amendments in the states that either adopted weighing procedures modeled after the earlier recommendation of the American Law Institute, or required the jury to find at least one statutorily-defined aggravating circumstance as a predicate to the imposition of a death sentence.[3] The upshot of those procedures was that the jury's discretion was limited to a narrower group of murder cases than it could consider before *Furman* and the jury was required to consider any mitigating circumstances that the defendant presented. Beyond those changes, however, the jury's discretion on the question of whether the defendant should live or die was unlimited and essentially unreviewable by appellate courts.

The issue of prosecutorial discretion was not explicitly considered in *Furman*, but it was, four years later, in *Gregg v. Georgia* (1976). The Court ruled there that the imposition of limitations on the exercise of prosecutorial discretion, beyond the statutory classifications that defined the classes of cases in which the death sentence could be imposed was not required because it would require fundamental changes in the American criminal justice system that were neither contemplated nor required by the Constitution.

Thus, by the end of 1976, the Supreme Court had approved a series of state death penalty statutes on the ground that their newly enacted procedural standards appeared capable of minimizing to constitutionally acceptable levels the risk of arbitrariness and discrimination in the administration of the death penalty. In none of those cases, however, did the Court consider any empirical evidence about how the systems actually operated. A significant issue at the

---

3. The "weighing" death sentencing model was approved by the United States Supreme Court in *Proffitt v. Florida* (1976). Although the weighing statutes are the most common procedure in America, another fairly common approach is to require the finding of at least one statutory aggravating circumstance and then give the sentencing authority complete discretion in terms of what factors it considers and how it considers them in the sentencing decision. Georgia is a good example of this system which was approved by the Supreme Court in *Gregg v. Georgia* (1976). Another important alternative is the Texas system which narrowly defines capital murder and upon a capital murder conviction, presents a narrow list of statutory aggravating circumstances, the most important of which is "whether there is a probability that the defendant would commit criminal acts of violence that would constitute a continuing threat to society." This system was approved in *Jurek v. Texas* (1976). The only alternative approach that has been disapproved by the Supreme Court is a mandatory death sentence upon a jury's finding a defendant guilty of first-degree murder. *Woodson v. North Carolina* (1976).

end of the 1970s, therefore, was whether the post-*Furman* reforms had altered the levels of discrimination that many suspected existed pre-*Furman* and whether the new systems were constitutionally acceptable on this issue.

Ethical, Moral, and Legal Concerns Implicated by Race Discrimination in the Administration of the Death Penalty

Ethical and Moral Concerns

The "issue" of race discrimination in the administration of the death penalty does not primarily relate to the conviction of factually innocent defendants because of their race. To be sure, there is evidence that many of the miscarriages of justice that occurred both before and after *Furman* were racially motivated. For example, in a famous recent case, Walter McMillian, an African American, was framed and sentenced to death in Alabama for the murder of a white woman by false testimony generated by law enforcement officials. It is clear that both McMillian's race, his history of dating a white woman, and the race of his alleged victim made him an easier target (Radelet et al. 1996:949–950). Nevertheless, the best research on miscarriages of justice in the post-*Furman* period suggests that white and black defendants, who are factually innocent of any crime, are equally at risk of being falsely convicted and sentenced to death (at 917).

In contrast to the miscarriage of justice issue, the principal concern about race discrimination in the administration of the death penalty relates to the differential treatment of similarly situated defendants who are in fact guilty of capital murder. The core ethical concern is fairness—treating like cases alike, especially when the consequences of the decision are so severe. There is a strong consensus that governments, in particular, have a profound duty to treat all of their citizens with equal care and concern, without regard to factors in their cases that have no bearing on the defendant's criminal culpability (Dworkin 1977). Given the legacy of slavery and race discrimination in our history, this concern has special force with respect to discrimination based on the race of the defendant, a factor over which he or she has no control (Nathanson 1985). However, when a defendant's allegation of discrimination is based on the race of the victim, the moral appeal of the claim may be weakened with a reminder that the defendant, not society, selected the victim.

Concerns about race discrimination also resonate at the group level. Such a concern underlies the claim of an "adverse disparate impact" which arises when non-discriminatory practices, most commonly those of prosecutors, adversely affect minority defendants or defendants in white-victim cases. In the death penalty context, there is both statistical and anecdotal evidence in several states that prosecutorial policies are more punitive in counties with above average proportions of minority defendants and above average proportions of white victims, even though the evidence suggests that within these communities death-eligible offenders are treated evenhandedly with respect to the race of the defendant and victim. This means that while there may be no purposeful discrimination against minority defendants or defendants whose victims are white, statewide, defendants in those cases are at greater risk of advancing to a penalty trial because of the place of their prosecution.

At a broader level, claims of race-of-victim discrimination (which exist, for example, when white-victim cases are treated more punitively than black-victim cases) raise an ethical concern that the state's failure to allocate resources equally in the prosecution of both black- and white-victim cases denies the black community equitable access to any possible benefits the death penalty may provide (Carter 1988; Kennedy 1988). Also, even if it were clear that black and non-black defendants were treated fairly and consistently in America's death-sentencing system, there are also concerns about the substantial overrepresentation of blacks on death row in America (12 percent of the nation's civilian population versus 40 percent of the death row population). Many citizens consider it insensitive and unseemly, if not immoral, for a country with our historical record on slavery and race discrimination, to persist in using a punishment that is administered and controlled almost exclusively by whites and serves no demonstrated penological function, but has a profound adverse impact, physically, psychologically, and symbolically on its black citizens.

For many others, however, ethical concerns about race discrimination relate strictly to the extent to which equally culpable defendants are treated differently because of the race of the defendant or victim. Moreover, for some people within this group, the level of ethical and moral concern depends on the extent to which the cause of the differential treatment is the product of conscious racial animus, the influence of stereotypical or non-conscious perceptions of comparative dangerousness of black and non-black defendants, or the influence of community perceptions of the heinousness of crimes that happen to be correlated with the racial aspects of the cases.

Proponents of the death penalty offer several counter ethical arguments. The principal one is that concerns about the equal treatment of similarly situated defendants is trumped by society's interest in retribution, justice, and concern for the victims of crime and their families (McAdams 1998:168; van den Haag 1985). It is further argued that the fact of racial discrimination in no way diminishes either the culpability of the defendants who are sentenced to death for racial reasons or society's justification for executing them.

Two other counter arguments proceed from quite different premises. The first asserts that concerns about race discrimination are misplaced because there is no convincing evidence that race is an influence in the system. The second argument is that race discrimination is inevitable and endemic in all of our social institutions (the death penalty being no exception), and there is nothing that the law can do about it short of abolishing the death penalty, a move that, in their view, cannot be morally justified on this ground (Baldus et al. 1994). Adherents to this second position believe that the costs of eliminating the death penalty clearly outweigh any harms caused by race discrimination. This belief no doubt explains why most citizens who support the death penalty in opinion polls maintain that support even if they believe the system is racially discriminatory.

Legal Concerns

At a strictly doctrinal level, the law is less conflicted than is ethical and moral opinion on the question. First, the United States Supreme Court has repeatedly stated that the Fourteenth Amendment of the Constitution forbids "purposeful" or "disparate treatment" discrimination by all public officials, which definitely includes prosecutorial and jury decisions to seek and impose death sentences (*Washington v. Davis* 1976). This position rests on the proposition that the Fourteenth Amendment prohibits consideration of race as a basis for official decisions, unless the consideration can be justified by a compelling state interest, which could never be established in the capital charging and sentencing context.

The Court has explicitly ruled that the prohibition against purposeful/disparate treatment discrimination applies to differential treatment based on the race of the defendant and the victim (*McCleskey v. Kemp* 1987). Thus, even though a defendant claiming race-of-victim discrimination may not be able to show a nexus between *his* race and an adverse decision in his case, he may raise the issue because he is entitled to decisions in his case that are free of the influence of any person's race, including that of his victim.

A legal consensus also exists that decisions to seek or impose the death penalty that are consciously motivated by racial animus constitute "purposeful" discrimination under the Fourteenth Amendment. Consensus breaks down, however, over whether decisions that treat black defendants more punitively than similarly situated non-black defendants constitute "purposeful" discrimination under the Amendment, when those decisions are driven by stereotypical ideas about black defendants and white victims (Lee and Bhagwat 1998). A similar issue arises when the decisions of prosecutors or sentencing authorities represent a response to a community's demand for a more punitive response in cases involving, for example, black defendants and white victims.

It is also clear that purposeful race discrimination constitutes a violation of the "cruel and unusual punishments" provision of the Eighth Amendment (*McCleskey v. Kemp* 1987). Indeed, the Supreme Court has stated that even a demonstrated "risk" that racial considerations may have influenced a death sentencing decision is a sufficient basis for granting judicial relief. The theory underlying this rule is that a decision either to seek or impose a death sentence, which is at substantial risk of being influenced by the race of the defendant or victim, is arbitrary within the meaning of the Eighth Amendment, because it is not based on the criminal culpability of the defendant, the only constitutionally permissible basis for a sentence of death.

We mentioned above a legal theory known as an adverse disparate impact, which is implicated when the application of evenhanded practices, such as prosecutorial charging policies, produce a statewide adverse impact on minority defendants or defendants in white victim cases. Existing anti-discrimination employment law recognizes such claims, but it does not bar a facially neutral standard that produces an adverse disparate impact, such as height and weight requirements for fire-fighting positions, if the standard can be justified in terms of "business necessity." Under the existing constitutional doctrine that regulates the administration of the death penalty, there is no basis for the judicial application of a disparate impact theory that is analogous to the disparate impact theory applied in employment law. However, when the evidence indicates that an adverse disparate impact is produced by the evenhanded administration of the law, it is certainly appropriate for the legislature to address the issue with standards designed to bring geographic uniformity to the administration of the law. Indeed, in the eyes of some legislatures geographic uniformity in the administration of the death penalty is an important interest independently of whether geographic disparities also produce an adverse impact on minority defendants or defendants in white victim cases.

Evidence of Race Discrimination

Pre- and Post-*Furman* Issues and Interpretations

When considering the issue of purposeful/disparate treatment discrimination, a useful threshold distinction is drawn between a claim of "systemic" or "pattern and practice" racial discrimination and a claim of disparate treatment discrimination in individual cases.[4] The principal focus of this chapter is on systemic disparate treatment discrimination.

---

4. A claim of disparate treatment discrimination in an individual case alleges that the race of the defendant or the race of the victim was a "factor," a "substantial factor," or a "but for factor" in the claimant's case (Baldus et al. 1994:389). Proof of discrimination in an individual case may be based on "direct," smoking gun evidence, for example, an admission or racial slur by a prosecutor or juror. Proof of such discrimination may also be based on a combination of quantitative and qualitative evidence. In the context of capital charging and sentencing, such a claim has never been successful. Nor has a claim of systemic discrimination ever been successful.

A claim of systemic discrimination alleges, that the impact of race is a pattern and practice in a substantial proportion of prosecutorial decisions to seek and/or jury decisions to impose the death sentence. Proof of systemic racial discrimination is normally established with statistical evidence demonstrating, for example, that, on average, black defendants or defendants with white victims are treated more punitively than similarly situated white defendants and defendants with black victims, as the case may be. The claim does not allege that *all* black defendants or all defendants whose victims are white are treated more punitively. Proof of a pattern and practice of discrimination is circumstantial and its inferential power depends on (a) the magnitude of the disparities in the treatment of the different, racially defined groups of cases, and (b) the plausibility that the differences in treatment along racial lines are not the product of either chance or different case characteristics within the two racial groups that could reasonably explain the disparities on legitimate grounds (Baldus and Cole 1980; Paetzold and Willborn 1994; Spriggs 1994).

Employment discrimination cases involving claims of systemic discrimination provide a model of proof that is directly applicable to the death-sentencing context. (As we point out below, however, courts have not applied this model in capital cases.) Proof of disparate treatment discrimination in employment cases typically commences with a statistical demonstration of systemic discrimination among a large group of cases that includes the individual plaintiffs who are claiming discrimination in their particular cases. Compelling evidence of a pattern and practice of discrimination supports an inference of purposeful discrimination in the case of each minority or woman who was adversely affected by a decision of the defendant, usually in hiring or promotion. At this point, Title VII, a federal law which prohibits race and gender discrimination in employment places on the defendant-employer the burden of establishing that race or gender was not a factor in the case of each adversely affected minority or woman. This final inquiry, therefore, focuses on the legitimate facts of the individual cases that are offered to rebut the inference of discrimination and considers whether these facts appear plausible as an explanation for the adverse decision in the plaintiff's case. For example, if a rejected minority group member had very weak qualifications for the job, the "rival" non-discriminatory hypothesis would likely appear quite plausible and relief would likely be denied. But if the minority group member had qualifications that exceeded those of most of the whites hired, the rival non-discriminatory hypothesis would appear implausible and relief would likely be forthcoming (Baldus et al. 1994; Blume et al. 1998:1798–1807; Graines and Wyatt 2000).

When one considers claims of systemic purposeful discrimination in the application of the death penalty, it is useful to distinguish between evidence of "unadjusted" racial disparities and "adjusted" disparities. Unadjusted disparities are estimated without regard to the influence that legitimate case characteristics, such as the presence of aggravating circumstances that affect the perceived "criminal culpability" (*State v. Papasavvas* 2002) and "blameworthiness" of the defendants in the analysis, may have in the cases. A 10-percentage-point difference (.25–.15) in death-sentence rates in white versus non-white victim cases is an example of an unadjusted disparity. The disparity is unadjusted because it does not take into account the possibility that the white-victim and black-victim cases may have quite different levels of criminal culpability, which in fact explain the differences in the death sentencing rates for the two groups of cases. In contrast, adjusted disparities are estimated after controlling for the presence of aggravating and mitigating factors that clearly influence prosecutorial and jury perceptions of defendant criminal culpability and blameworthiness. Adjusted disparities avoid the risk that the influence of race and defendant culpability will be confounded and lead to faulty inferences about the impact of race on decision-making.

There are several methods for calculating adjusted race disparities. The most commonly used is a regression coefficient for the race of the defendant or victim, computed in a logistic multiple regression analysis, which estimates the extent to which, on average, a defendant's odds of being charged capitally or sentenced to death are enhanced by virtue of the race of the victim or defendant in the cases, after controlling for other legitimate case characteristics. For example, in a large study from Georgia, the results of a logistic regression analysis indicated that after controlling for 39 legitimate case characteristics, on average, defendants with white victims faced odds of receiving a death sentence that were 4.3 times higher than the odds faced by defendants whose victims were black.

There are also alternative ways of computing adjusted disparities, such as direct and indirect standardization procedures, which are easier to interpret because they do not rely on or require an understanding of multiple regression analyses. (Baldus et al. 2001:162–66). The results of these procedures might indicate, for example, that after adjustment for all statutory aggravating and mitigating circumstances in the cases, the adjusted death-sentencing rate was .26 for the white victim cases and .13 for the black victim cases, a 13-percentage-point difference (.26–.13), and a 2 to 1 (.26/.13) ratio of death-sentencing rates, or a 2.35 to 1 (.26/.74 ÷ .13/.87) odds ratio.

The failure of a statistical analysis to adjust estimated race disparities by taking into account the distribution of aggravating and mitigating factors in the case introduces the risk of an erroneous inference about the influence of race in the system. The risk of such an error is illustrated in a well known study of sex discrimination in the graduate programs of a leading university (Bickel et al. 1977). A large, unadjusted statistical "disparity" indicated that female applicants were admitted to graduate school (the "outcome" or "dependent" variable) at a much lower rate than male applicants, thereby suggesting the possibility of sex discrimination. However, on closer examination it became apparent that the great bulk of women applied to departments with very low admission rates (e.g., English and history), while most of the men applied to departments with very high admission rates (e.g., science and engineering). Thus, the "independent" variable—department of application—was strongly correlated with *both* the sex of the applicants and the probability of admission. The failure to "control" for department of application fatally undercut the validity of the unadjusted disparity as a basis for inferring the presence of systemic gender discrimination in graduate school admission rates. Moreover, when the researchers did control for the department of application, the evidence showed that, on average, women were more likely to be admitted to graduate school than were the men. The moral of the story is that a failure to control for a legitimate case characteristic introduces a risk of error in the analyses, if and only if, the omitted variable has two properties: (1) it is correlated with the decision-making outcome of interest, and (2) it is also correlated with the claimant's membership in a protected class, such as racial minorities or women. Both of those conditions were met in the graduate school example because the department of application variable was correlated with both the probability of admission *and* the gender of the applicants.

It is for this reason that gross racial disparities in death-sentence rates that fail to control for factors that may legitimately influence death-sentencing decisions, especially when they are based on the entire nation, are highly suspect as a basis for inferring race discrimination in the treatment of similarly situated defendants. For example, evidence that blacks constitute 12 percent of the national population, but 40 percent of the nationwide death row population, is sometimes offered as evidence of systemic race-of-defendant discrimination. This unadjusted disparity is highly misleading because it fails to control for the disproportionately high proportion of blacks (about 50 percent) among citizens arrested for homicide nationally (U.S. Department of Justice, Federal Bureau of Investigation 2000:234). As a result, the comparison fails to control for the differential rates at which black and non-black citizens are likely to have committed death-eligible homicides.

Apologists for the current system make a similarly misleading argument when, on the basis of evidence that blacks constitute about 50 percent of homicide arrestees but only 40 percent of the death row population, they assert that white defendants are discriminated against nationally. The flaw in the argument is its failure to compare the treatment of similarly situated black and non-black defendants in death-eligible cases (in most death-sentencing states only about 10 to 15 percent of defendants arrested for homicide have committed death-eligible crimes). Moreover, the argument fails to account for the effects of race-of-victim discrimination, which by lowering the death-sentencing rate in black-victim cases, has the additional effect of reducing the overall rate of death-sentencing for black defendants, who are responsible for the vast majority of black-victim murders. Only by comparing the differential treatment of black and non-black offenders whose victims are non-black can one validly test for race-of-defendant discrimination in the system. (The number of white versus black death-eligible homicides is generally too small to permit a similar comparison of black versus black and white versus black homicides.)

Thus, unadjusted disparities are only suggestive. Also, experience indicates that when the disparities in death-sentencing rates are adjusted for legitimate case characteristics, the unadjusted disparities often, but not always, decline. The most reliable evidence of discrimination, therefore, consists of racial disparities that are adjusted to reflect the different levels of culpability of the cases in the different racial groups. But here one must beware of the "average overall culpability" fallacy, which can be illustrated with two examples. In the first analysis, there is evidence that the death-sentencing rate is higher for black than it is for white defendants. The defense to a claim of discrimination points to evidence that overall, the black-defendant cases are more aggravated than the white-defendant cases, which allegedly explains the unadjusted racial disparity in death sentencing rates. In the second case, there is evidence that the death-sentencing rate is greater in the white victim than it is in black-victim cases. The defense offered here is evidence that, on average, the white-victim cases are more aggravated than the black-victim cases, which allegedly explains the unadjusted race-of-victim disparity.

Both of these arguments are flawed because there is no necessary correlation between the average culpability level for the different racial groups of cases and the extent to which similarly situated defendants in the different racial groups are treated similarly or differently. For example, the *average* culpability level of black- and white-victim cases tells us nothing about the extent to which subgroups of black- and white-victim cases with, for example, average or above average levels of culpability, are treated the same or differently in the system. Nor does evidence that black-defendant cases are on average more aggravated than white-defendant cases tell us anything about the extent to which subgroups of black and white defendants with, for example, high or low levels of culpability, are treated the same or differently.

In Baldus, Woodworth, and Pulaski (1990), for example, evidence from Georgia clearly shows that white-victim cases were, on average, more aggravated than the black-victim cases. Nevertheless, when similarly culpable cases were compared, the white-victim cases were at greater risk of receiving a death sentence than black-victim cases with similar levels of culpability; indeed the strongest race-of-victim effects were observed among the cases with average levels of defendant culpability.

Good practice suggests, therefore, that the greatest weight be placed on the results of controlled studies that estimate racial disparities among cases with similar levels of criminal culpability. A problem with this practice, however, is that well-controlled studies are expensive and time consuming to execute, and as a result, relatively few have been conducted. It is necessary, therefore, in speculating about the American system as a whole, to consider all of the available evidence, which, in addition to the results of the controlled studies, includes unadjusted disparities and anecdotal testimony provided by the principal participants in the process—defense lawyers, prosecutors, and judges. The sparseness of the available data encourages skepticism about sweeping claims concerning the level of race discrimination in jurisdictions where systematic studies have not been conducted.

Pre-*Furman* Data

Detailed pre-*Furman* data are limited. However, a study of Southern capital rape trials in the 1950s and early 1960s showed strong race-of-defendant and race-of-victim effects. Specifically, black defendants with white victims were at much greater risk of receiving a death sentence than any other racial category of cases (Wolfgang and Riedel 1973, 1975). Those results were consistent with unadjusted data from 1930–1970 indicating that 89 percent of the 455 defendants executed for rape nationwide, largely in the South, were black, a statistic that came as no surprise, given the historical preoccupation in the South with the rape of white women by black men (Williamson 1984:116, 183–84).

The unadjusted data for murder pre-*Furman*, indicate that 49 percent of the 3,334 defendants executed for murder during this same period were black. Indeed, data collected by Watt Espy indicates that from the 1910s to the 1950s, from 60 percent to 70 percent of the people executed for murder in the South were black (Bohm 1991:73–74; Schneider and Smykla 1991:12). Also, a well-controlled study of Georgia just prior to *Furman* revealed strong race-of-defendant and race-of-victim effects among defendants convicted of murder (Baldus et al. 1990: 248–53). However, a detailed study of pre-*Furman* California penalty trials in murder cases showed no race effects whatever during the 1960s (Special Issue 1969).

Post-*Furman* Data

Available post-*Furman* data suggest improvement in the South. In contrast to the nearly 70 percent representation rate of blacks executed pre-*Furman*, the post-*Furman* data from the South reveal the proportion of blacks, both on death row and among those actually executed, is at the national average of about 40 percent. Although the data in this pre- versus post-*Furman* comparison are not well-controlled, it is unlikely that differences of this magnitude would appear unless something is going on beyond chance (the proportion of blacks in the South has not declined sufficiently in the post-*Furman* period to explain this difference; nor have the comparative homicide rates in the black and white communities changed significantly). Also, a controlled pre- and post-*Furman* (the 1970s) study showed a marked decline in the evidence of race-of-defendant discrimination, although the race-of-victim effects were the same in both periods (Baldus et al. 1990:150).

The post-*Furman* data fall into two periods—before and after 1990, the year that the United States General Accounting Office (GAO) published a synthesis and analysis of empirical studies conduct in the early post-*Furman* years (U.S. General Accounting Office 1990). The GAO's 1990 report, compiled at the request of the United States Senate, presents a systematic review of the empirical studies conducted by a variety of investigators in the 1970s and early 1980s. The GAO initially considered conducting one or more empirical studies itself, but finally opted for "an evaluative synthesis," which consisted of a review and critique of the existing research.[5] In its review, the report sought to assess the extent to which the existing literature supported (a) claims of "race-of-defendant" discrimination, for example, black defendants are treated more punitively than similarly situated non-black defendants, and (b) claims of "race-of-victim" discrimination, for example, defendants whose victims are white are treated more punitively than similarly situated defendants whose victims are black. On the issue of race-of-victim discrimination, the agency reported that:

> In 82% of the studies, race-of-victim was found to influence the likelihood of being charged with capital murder or receiving a death sentence, i.e., those who murdered whites were found to be more likely to be sentenced to death than those who murdered blacks. This finding was remarkably consistent across data sets, states, data collection methods, and analytic techniques. The finding held for high, medium, and low quality studies.
>
> The race-of-victim influence was found at all stages of the criminal justice system process, although there were variations among studies as to whether there was a race-of-victim influence at specific stages. The evidence for the race-of-victim influence was stronger for the earlier stages of the judicial process (e.g., prosecutorial decision to charge defendants with a capital offense, decision to proceed to trial rather than plea bargain) than in later stages. This was because the earlier stages were comprised of larger sam-

---

5. Arkin 1980; Baldus et al. 1986; Baldus et al. 1990; Barnett 1985; Berk and Lowery 1985; Bienen et al. 1988; Bowers 1983; Bowers and Pierce 1980; Ekland-Olson 1988; Foley 1987; Foley and Powell 1982; Gross and Mauro 1989; Keil and Vito 1989; Klein et al. 1987; Klemm 1986; Lewis et al. 1979; Murphy 1984; Nakell and Hardy 1987; Paternoster and Kazyaka 1988; Radelet 1981; Radelet and Pierce 1985; Reidel 1976; Smith 1987; Zeisel 1981. The pre-*Furman* studies and post-*Furman* studies published before 1990 are summarized in Baldus et al. 1990:248–266.

ples allowing for more rigorous analyses.[6] However, decisions made at every stage of the process necessarily affect an individual's likelihood of being sentenced to death (U.S. General Accounting Office 1990:5–6).

The largest of the studies reviewed by the GAO focused on 2,400 cases processed in the Georgia charging and sentencing system in the period 1973–80 (Baldus et al. 1990). These results, which were the basis of the petitioner's claim of racial discrimination in *McCleskey v. Kemp*, indicated that after controlling for the presence or absence of hundreds of variables for legitimate case characteristics, such as the level of violence and the defendant's prior record, defendants whose victims were white faced, on average, odds of receiving a death sentence that were 4.3 times higher than similarly situated defendants whose victims were black.

On the issue of race-of-defendant discrimination, the GAO study concluded:

> The evidence for the influence of the race-of-defendant on death penalty outcomes was equivocal. Although more than half of the studies found that race-of-defendant influenced the likelihood of being charged with a capital crime or receiving the death penalty, the relationship between race-of-defendant and outcome varied across studies. For example, sometimes the race-of-defendant interacted with other factors. In one study, researchers found that in rural areas black defendants were more likely to receive death sentences, and in urban areas white defendants were more likely to receive death sentences. In a few studies, analyses revealed that the black defendant/white victim combination was the most likely to receive the death penalty. However, the extent to which the finding was influenced by race-of-victim rather than race-of-defendant was unclear (U.S. General Accounting Office 1990: 4).

We have identified 18 empirical studies of death penalty systems published or reported since the GAO report. The methodology and results of these studies are summarized in Appendix A of this Chapter. The results range from simple tabulations demonstrating unadjusted racial disparities to well controlled multivariate analyses (see also Baldus et al. 1998:1660-1662, 1742–1745 for a state-by state tabulation of all the relevant post-*Furman* studies prior to 1998). The post-1990 results are consistent with those summarized in the GAO report, i.e., two document no race effects at all—Baldus et al. 2002 (Nebraska) and Baime 2001 (New Jersey); three report both race-of-defendant and race-

---

6. This is one possible explanation but it is also possible and plausible that discrimination is greater in prosecutorial decisions because they are less constrained and less visible than jury penalty trial decisions.

of-victim effects—Baldus et al. 1998 (Philadelphia, PA); U.S. Department of Justice 2000 (federal death penalty), and *State v. Cobb* 1995 (Connecticut); two report disparities in black defendant/white victim cases—Keil and Vito 1995 (Kentucky) and Paternoster and Brame 2003 (Maryland); and twelve report race-of-victim effects but no race-of-defendant effects—Bortner and Hall 2002 (Arizona); Klein and Rolph 1991 (California); Radelet and Pierce 1991 (Florida); Pierce and Radelet 2002 (Illinois); Ziemba-Davis and Myers 2002 (Indiana); Baldus and Woodworth 2001 (Maryland); Paternoster and Brame 2003 (Maryland); Lenza, Keys, and Guess 2003 (Missouri); Unah and Boger 2001 (North Carolina); McCord 2002 (South Carolina); Brock et al. 2000 (Texas); and Joint Legislative Audit and Review Commission 2002 (Virginia).

Geographic Scope of the Post-*Furman* Race Disparities

Our review of the studies before and after the GAO report reveals that relevant data are not available on charging and sentencing practices for all death-sentencing states. Nevertheless, for 77% (30/39) of the nation's 39 death-sentencing jurisdictions (including the federal government) in which a death sentence has been imposed (no sentences have been imposed in New Hampshire), we were able to locate some relevant data for at least one period of time since 1973. In 83% (25/30) of the jurisdictions with relevant data, there is some evidence of race-of-victim disparities (adversely affecting defendants whose victims are white), and in 33% (10/30) of these jurisdictions, there is some evidence of race-of-defendant disparities (adversely affecting black defendants).

As the GAO survey points out, there are considerable differences in the extent to which empirical studies of race discrimination control for legitimate case characteristics, such as the level of violence in the case and the defendant's prior criminal record. Because the cost and complexity of conducting reasonably well-controlled empirical studies is substantial, such studies have been conducted in only eleven jurisdictions (CA, CO, GA, KY, MD, MS, NE, NJ, NC, Philadelphia, PA, and SC). (We define a "reasonably well-controlled" study as one having statistical controls for 10 or more legitimate non-racial case characteristics.). However, the results from less well-controlled studies are also relevant and instructive. Not uncommonly, their results are consistent with the results of a well-controlled study conducted in the same jurisdiction.

In assessing the most plausible inferences that the post-*Furman* research can support, most significant in our judgment is the overall pattern across so many jurisdictions and the implausibility of non-racial factors as a causal explanation, especially with respect to race-of-victim discrimination. In this regard, it is useful to consider the opinion of John C. McAdams, a methodologically sophisticated supporter of capital punishment who has evaluated this literature through a skeptical and critical lens. In his words: "There is a general and quite robust bias against [using the death penalty in cases with] black victims, and there is no general bias against black defendants... [although] there might be bias [against black defendants] in some places, under some circumstances."[7] We believe this is a fair assessment of the literature.

The Variety, Magnitude, and Practical Consequences of Post-*Furman* Race Disparities

The evidence suggests quite different levels of race effects *within* individual states. For example, both anecdotal evidence and a few studies indicate that in some states, death-eligible cases are settled by center-city prosecutors for sentences less than death under circumstances in which suburban prosecutors commonly insist upon a capital trial and often secure a death sentence. Because center-city cases are more likely to involve black victims and suburban cases are more likely to involve white victims, the overall effect statewide may be a race-of-victim disparity in the rates that the state seeks a death sentence, i.e., a higher penalty trial rate in white-victim cases than in black-victim cases.

What is unclear in these situations, and calls for further analysis within the separate communities involved, is whether within each community, the white-victim cases are treated more punitively than the black-victim cases. If this were the case in either or both communities, the evidence would support a finding of disparate treatment, i.e., the statewide race-of-victim disparity reflects differential treatment of white- and black-victim cases within one or more communities. However, if the evidence documents evenhanded treatment within the different localities, the data would only support an inference of statewide disparate impact. The studies summarized in Appendix A from Maryland, Nebraska, and Virginia are instructive on this issue.

There are also differences in the magnitude of race effects at different decision-making levels in the various state systems, that is, there may exist differential race effects in prosecutorial decisions to seek death, jury decisions to impose death, and the overall combined effects of these two stages of decision. Sometimes race effects at the prosecutorial and jury points of decision cancel one another out, while in other situations, the race effects are in the same di-

---

7. McAdams 1998:166 & n. 53. The author, a political scientist, favors capital punishment in America today because "[b]etween an inequitable death penalty and no death penalty, I would prefer an inequitable death penalty...." He justifies this position with his belief in the deterrent effect of the death penalty, the majority support for the death penalty in both the black and white communities, and his belief that with an abolition of capital punishment "we would have a ratcheting down of punishment, with the inequities remaining" (at 168).

rection and produce an enhanced overall race disparity that reflects the impact of both those decision points.

There is also persuasive evidence that the magnitude of race disparities sometimes correlates with the culpability or aggravation level of the cases. A well-controlled study of Georgia's system, demonstrated that the race-of-victim effects were very low in the most aggravated cases in which almost all jurors would be persuaded by the facts of the case that a death sentence was appropriate (Baldus et al. 1990:152–54, 321). However, in the less aggravated "mid-range" cases, in which the "correct" sentence was less clear, and the room for the exercise of discretion was much broader, the race effects were much stronger (Spohn and Cederblom: 1991).

The Impact of Race Disparities on Capital Charging and Sentencing Outcomes

Two distinct but related measures focus on the extent to which the race of the defendant and the victim appear to enhance the likelihood that defendants will be sentenced to death. The first approach focuses on the impact that defendant or victim race appears to have on the *odds* that the average individual black defendant will be sentenced to death, i.e., the odds of a death sentence for black defendants or defendants with white victims are compared to the odds faced by similarly situated non-black defendants and defendants with black or minority victims.[8] For example, the data before the Supreme Court in *McCleskey* indicated that the odds of receiving a death sentence, after controlling for key aggravating and mitigating circumstances, were on average enhanced by a factor of 4.3 if the victim in the case were white. The other controlled studies that document significant race effects suggest similar levels of "practical" impact on the sentencing outcomes—on the order of 3 to 10 times.

A related measure estimates the impact of race on the *probability* that defendants, with a typical level of culpability, will be treated differently because of the race of the defendant or victim. This impact may be usefully expressed as the arithmetic difference in adjusted death-sentencing rates between similarly situated defendants. For example, a recent Nebraska study, documents a 19-percentage-point (.51–.32) disparity in the adjusted rates that white and minority defendants terminate death-eligible cases in a negotiated plea agreement. In other words, this measure indicates that, on average, white defendants have a probability of negotiating a favorable plea agreement, which will avoid the risk of a death sentence, that is 19 percentage points higher than similarly situated minority defendants (Baldus et al. 2002: Fig. 8 n. 1).

---

8. The relationship between "odds" and "probabilities" is as follows: Odds = Probability/(1 - Probability), while Probability = Odds/(1 + Odds).

Another highly relevant measure, the ratio of adjusted death-sentencing rates, expresses the *relative* risk that various subgroups of similarly situated defendants face of gaining favorable or unfavorable decisions in their cases. For example, in the Nebraska plea bargaining example noted above, the ratio of the adjusted death-sentencing rates for the white and minority defendants is 1.6 (.51/.32).[9] This ratio indicates that, on average, white defendants are 1.6 times more likely than similarly situated minority defendants to negotiate a plea agreement with a waiver of the death penalty.

Measures of the Practical Importance of Race in Charging and Sentencing Decision-Making

One measure of the practical importance of race in the system is the relative disparity, i.e., the extent to which the magnitude of the adjusted race disparity *exceeds* the average overall charging or death-sentencing rate, as the case may be, for all cases. This measure expresses the adjusted difference between the death sentencing rates for the two groups as a percentage of the overall rate. For example, in a state with an overall average death-sentencing rate of 24%, an adjusted race-of-victim disparity of 7 percentage points indicates that the death sentencing rate in the white victim cases exceeds the overall death-sentencing rate by 29% (7/24).

A related measure expresses the degree to which the level of adverse treatment of the disadvantaged group exceeds the treatment of the more favored group. For example, in a recent Philadelphia study, at one stage in the penalty trial decision-making process, the death sentencing rate was 22% for the black victim cases and 31% for the white victim cases, a nine-percentage point difference. Accordingly, the death-sentencing rate for the white victim cases in this example exceeds the rate for similarly situated defendants in black victim cases by 41% (9/22) (Baldus et al. 1998:1727).

An excess death-sentencing analysis may also focus on the extent to which the *number* of death sentences juries actually imposed on black defendants or in white-victim cases exceeds what one would expect to see in an evenhanded system. Recent research in Philadelphia used this approach to estimate that the number of death sentences juries imposed against black defendants in jury

---

9. A drawback of this measure is its sensitivity to the magnitude of the overall death-sentencing rate (for the two groups of defendants). For example, a 5-percentage point disparity, when the overall death-sentencing rate is low, may produce a quite different ratio estimate than when the overall rate is high, e.g., rates of .10 and .05 will produce a ratio of 2.0 (10/5), while rates of .55 and .50 will produce a ratio of 1.1 (55/50), even though the deprivation in the average *probability* of being sentenced to death for the members of the disadvantaged group is identical in both situations.

weighing decisions was 63% in excess of the number one would expect to see in an evenhanded system; in this analysis, the measure of what one would expect to see in an evenhanded system was the death sentencing rate in the non-black defendant cases. In an alternative analysis, the measure of what one would expect to see in an evenhanded system was the average death-sentencing rate for all defendants; with this assumption, the results indicated that the number of death sentences imposed against black defendants was 13% in excess of what one would expect to see in an evenhanded system (Baldus et al. 1998:1728).[10]

Another basis for estimating the practical impact of race in a system is a comparison of (a) the magnitude of the coefficients estimated in a logistic regression analysis for the race variables with (b) the magnitude of the coefficients estimated for other legitimate case characteristics. These comparisons enable one to compare the average overall impact of the race of the victim or defendant on charging and sentencing outcomes with the impact of important aggravating circumstances, such as multiple victims. For example, in such an analysis of death-sentencing decisions among all death-eligible cases in Philadelphia, that included all of the statutory aggravating and mitigating circumstances, the odds multiplier associated with a defendant's being black, 3.1, was larger than the odds multipliers estimated for the following three statutory aggravating circumstances: ransom or hostage victim, contemporaneous felony in the case, and the defendant knowingly created a grave risk of death to another (Baldus et al. 1998:1760–61).

---

10. The substantial drop in the number of excess death sentences when the measure for an evenhanded system is the average death sentencing rate for all cases is explained by the fact that 90% of the defendants whose cases advanced to the weighing stage of the penalty trial were black.

Although we have presented a bewildering array of ways of quantifying discrimination, they are all ways of expressing the relationship between the same two numbers: the (adjusted) death sentencing rates among two classes of defendants. The measures fall into two broad categories: absolute and relative. For example, suppose the adjusted death sentencing rates are 22% (.22) for black victim cases, 31% (.31) for white victim cases and 24% (.24) for all cases. The *absolute difference* is 9 percentage points (31–22); the *relative risk* is the ratio of the rates: 1.41 (31/22); the *increased risk*, 41% (100 x 9/22), is the difference expressed as a percent of the rate in the favored group; and the *relative increase*, 38% or 100 x 9/24, is the increase expressed as a percent of the overall rate. The latter two measures predict the percent reduction in white victim death sentences or all death sentences, respectively, that would occur in an even-handed system which sentenced white victim cases to death at the same rate as comparable black victim cases.

The *odds ratio*, 1.59 (31/69 ÷ 22/78), is another relative measure closely related to the relative risk. Odds ratios are favored by statisticians and epidemiologists for technical reasons (unlike relative risks they can be computed in case-control studies and can be adjusted more easily for larger numbers of confounding variables). Odds ratios are numerically comparable to but somewhat larger than relative risks; here for example the odds ratio is 1.59 and the relative risk is 1.41.

In the mid-range of cases in terms of defendant culpability, the racial disparities are often in the 15- to 30-percentage-point range, which represents about 30 to 40% of the average rate for all cases in this category. For example, if the average death-sentencing rate in the mid-range of cases were 50%, a 20-percentage point disparity in this range of cases would represent 40% (20/50) of the mid-range average.

Beneficiaries and Explanations

As noted above, the overall pattern in the post-*Furman* period, especially as it relates to race-of-victim discrimination, supports an inference that there exists in a number of jurisdictions a significant risk that race, particularly the race of the victims, is influencing decisions. These data suggest that the observed death sentencing results would likely be quite different if all decisions were taken in an evenhanded manner with respect to race.

Some observers have noted that the principal beneficiaries of race-of-victim discrimination are black defendants. The reason is that the vast majority of death-eligible cases involving black victims also involve black defendants. Thus, if black victim cases are on average treated less punitively than white victim cases, fewer black defendants will be sentenced to death than would be the case in an evenhanded system that sentenced all cases at the white victim rate. However, if an evenhanded system sentenced all cases at the *black victim* rate, there would be no increase in the number of black defendants sentenced to death and a decline in the number of non-black defendants sentenced to death. Nevertheless, it is clear that if an evenhanded policy were applied to the black and white victim cases (at the current rate for either black or white victim cases), the *proportion* of black defendants on death row would increase.

In jurisdictions that currently treat black defendants more punitively than similarly situated non-black defendants, an evenhanded system would reduce the absolute number of black defendants sentenced to death. Moreover, an evenhanded system that applied the current death sentencing rate, for either black or non-black defendants, would reduce the proportion of black defendants on death row.

Why might this be the case? Like many important issues, this question cannot be answered solely through statistical analyses. Nevertheless, there is a considerable body of psychological, sociological, and political science literature (Gross and Mauro 1989:109–17), the reported experience of legal practitioners (Bright 1995; Stevenson and Friedman 1994), newspaper reports (Henderson and Taylor 1985), and common experience that suggests the following explanation.

The results observed pre-*Furman*, particularly in the South, were likely in significant part the product of overt racial animus—hostility toward black defendants—especially if the victim were white, and the belief that black victims were worth less than white victims. During the post-*Furman* period, the level of overt racial animus appears to have declined throughout the nation. As a result, the mechanisms producing the current race effects appear to be more complex and less conscious than in the pre-*Furman* period (Johnson 1988; Lawrence 1987).

The most important determinant of race disparities in charging and sentencing outcomes appears to be community outrage and public pressure to avenge highly visible murders as perceived by prosecutors, judges, and juries. High visibility is often correlated with the defendant/victim racial composition of the cases; white victim cases, especially if they are interracial cases, continue to attract the most media coverage. This attention in turn influences the allocation of prosecutorial resources to those cases, especially if reelection or a run for higher political office is on the horizon. Also, when the victim is white, some prosecutors are more solicitous of a request by the victim's family that death be sought. In addition, when the families of black victims are consulted, they are generally less likely to seek a death sentence.

In some communities, it is still generally accepted that black-on-black homicides do not warrant the resources required for capital trials, and that plea-bargains with relatively light sentences are appropriate. Such perceptions may, in many black-victim cases, result in perfunctory investigations by law enforcement officials, which in turn may lead some prosecutors to believe that the prospects of obtaining a death sentence are too low to justify the cost. In addition, some prosecutors may believe that the low level of cooperation expected from the black community in the investigation of black-on-black homicides may significantly reduce the chance of obtaining a capital murder conviction at trial, thereby encouraging acceptance of a plea to a lesser offense. Furthermore, the perception in the black community that defendants in black-on-black cases are likely to receive light sentences, and be back on the streets in a relatively short period of time, may inhibit witnesses from coming forward with incriminating evidence against capital defendants in such cases.

In many places prosecutors, judges, and penalty trial jurors are predominantly white even though the defendants whose cases they hear are not. White jurors are less likely to sympathize with black defendants and identify with black victims (Rand 2000). Convincing evidence also exists that many participants in the system, both black and non-black, consider young black males more deserving of severe punishment because they are viewed as violence prone, morally inferior, and a threat to the community (Steffensmeier 1998). The danger for black defendants in the system is particularly acute when the attorneys who represent them entertain racial stereotypes and assumptions that diminish the quality and vigor of their representation.

The risk of both race-of-defendant and race-of-victim discrimination is also enhanced when the jury selection process results in the serious underrepresentation of blacks on criminal trial juries (Kennedy 1997: Ch. 6). This has multiple causes. First, blacks are underrepresented on the voter and automobile registration lists from which most jury venires are drawn. Second, low income citizens are less likely to appear for jury service and more likely to be excused for hardship. Most important, however, is the wide-ranging discretion of prosecutors to strike prospective black jurors through the exercise of "peremptory" challenges. The result is that many black defendants are sentenced by jury panels with no or only a few black jurors. This problem is particularly acute when the attorneys assigned to represent indigent defendants are inexperienced or indifferent, with the result that prosecutorial efforts to strike minority group members from the jury may not be effectively challenged (Baldus et al. 2001b; Bowers et al. 2001; Stevenson and Friedman 1994).

Finally, the risk of race discrimination may be exacerbated by explicit prosecutorial references to the race of the defendant or the victim (e.g., "the victim before her death was sexually assaulted by a person of another race"), as well as racial slurs and other appeals to racial prejudice, such as the use of animal metaphors in describing the defendant (e.g., "the defendant is no more than a wild beast") to the jury. Slurs of this type have come from prosecutors, judges, and defense counsel.

Judicial, Legislative, and Gubernatorial Responses to Claims of Racial Discrimination

The United States Supreme Court

The Supreme Court did not directly address a constitutional claim that the death penalty is administered in a racially discriminatory pattern until *McCleskey v. Kemp* (1987). The justices, however, have been aware of the issue for decades. In fact, many of the procedural protections that the Court has established in criminal cases since the 1930s were announced in capital cases involving African-American defendants from the South (Klarman 2000). Moreover, although the Court was aware of empirical studies suggesting racially discriminatory patterns, especially in southern states, it has demonstrated a persistent reluctance to confront the race question directly. In a number of capital cases between 1962 and 1986, the Court either declined requests to hear issues of racial discrimination by denying certiorari or resolved the case on other grounds.

A noteworthy example of the Court's diffidence on this issue is *Maxwell v. Bishop* (1970). Maxwell, a black male, received a death sentence from an Arkansas jury for the nonfatal rape of a white woman. The case received particular attention because Maxwell's attorneys supported their claim with statistical evidence that Maxwell's death sentence was part of a racially discriminatory pattern. Most telling were results from an Arkansas study showing that, between 1945 and 1965, the probability that a black male convicted of raping a white woman would receive the death sentence in Arkansas was about 50 percent, while the death-sentencing rate for cases involving a conviction for intraracial rape was only 14 percent. Maxwell's experts further established that this disparity could not be explained by nonracial factors, such as the level of violence involved or the defendant's prior criminal record. Despite this evidence, the Court of Appeals for the Eighth Circuit ruled that Maxwell's statistics were insufficient to invalidate his death sentence on equal protection grounds. The Supreme Court agreed to review, and ultimately vacated, the Eighth Circuit's decision on another constitutional ground, but the Court pointedly declined to review Maxwell's statistically based, Equal Protection claim.[11]

Two years after it decided *Maxwell*, the Supreme Court again confronted claims of racial discrimination in *Furman v. Georgia* (1972). The Court's brief per curiam opinion did not directly address the claims of racial discrimination asserted by Furman and a companion case petitioner, both of whom were African-American. However, three concurring justices and one dissenting justice expressed in separate opinions their concerns that the jury sentencing practices under scrutiny created a dangerous opportunity for racial discrimination. Justice Thurgood Marshall's concurring opinion gave the question the greatest attention. He recited in detail the national statistics previously presented showing a disproportional overrepresentation of blacks among the people executed in America from 1930 through 1970. Evidence on the issue from well-controlled studies unfortunately was simply unavailable.

As noted previously, the decade following *Gregg v. Georgia* (1976) saw the publication of a number of empirical studies, primarily in southern jurisdictions that were designed to test the discrimination hypothesis in murder cases. One of the largest of those studies was commissioned by the NAACP Legal Defense Fund (LDF) in the early 1980s. This study, conducted by David Baldus, George Woodworth, and Charles Pulaski, Jr., analyzed the relationship between sentencing outcomes and racial characteristics in 2,484 homicide cases charged and sentenced in Georgia from 1973 to 1979. The following unadjusted tabulation, from what the courts have described as "the Baldus study," indicates how death-sentencing outcomes correlated with the defendant/victim racial combination among all cases in the study:

Black Defendant/White Victim:	21 percent	(50/233)
White Defendant/White Victim:	8 percent	(58/748)
Black Defendant/Black Victim:	1 percent	(18/1,443)
White Defendant/Black Victim:	3 percent	(2/60)

---

11. These same data were brought to the Court's attention in *Coker v. Georgia* (1977), which challenged the penalty for the crime of rape. The Court barred the use of capital punishment for rape on Eighth Amendment "excessiveness" grounds, and it pointedly made no reference to the racial issue presented by the case.

Those data suggest strong race-of-victim discrimination as well as more punitive treatment of black offenders in white-victim cases. The data were further subjected to extensive multivariate statistical analysis designed to estimate racial disparities after adjustment for a large variety of legitimate case characteristics, such as the number of victims, contemporaneous offenses such as rape or robbery, and the defendant's prior record. The results of the statewide logistic regression analysis indicate that among death-eligible cases, the average defendant's odds of receiving a death sentence were 4.3 times higher if the victim in the case were white. The study also showed (a) that the race-of-victim disparities were largest in the "mid-range" cases, which gave prosecutors and sentencing juries the largest degree of discretion, and (b) that the observed race-of-victim disparities in death sentencing were primarily the product of prosecutorial rather than jury decision-making.

After adjustment for 39 legitimate variables in the core regression analysis the results provided no evidence of systematic, statewide discrimination against black defendants. To be sure, in rural areas, blacks were at greater risk of a capital prosecution and death sentence than similarly situated whites. But in urban areas, the opposite was the case and the two effects canceled each other out statewide.

LDF's Georgia study provided the basis for *McCleskey v. Kemp* (1987), a federal habeas corpus proceeding commenced in 1982 with the intention of reversing Warren McCleskey's death sentence. McCleskey was a black male whom a jury had sentenced to death for killing a white police officer in Atlanta. In the case, LDF attorneys alleged that the Georgia study of death sentencing demonstrated a pattern of purposeful and intentional discrimination, and that McCleskey's sentence consequently violated the Equal Protection Clause of the Fourteenth Amendment. McCleskey's lawyers also claimed that the Georgia study demonstrated a sufficient showing of arbitrariness and caprice in Georgia's administration of its capital statute to violate the cruel and unusual punishment prohibition of the Eighth Amendment, as interpreted by *Furman*.

The Supreme Court rejected both of those constitutional claims by a vote of 5 to 4. The majority opinion, written by Justice Lewis Powell, declared that, because the Baldus study did not establish "with exceptionally clear proof... that the decision makers in McCleskey's case acted with discriminatory purpose," no Equal Protection violation had been established (*McCleskey v. Kemp* 1987:297). Of particular importance was the Court's unwillingness to apply the methods for proving discrimination, both systematically and in McCleskey's case, that are commonly used in jury discrimination and employment discrimination cases.[12] One surprising effect of *McCleskey*, therefore, is

---

12. The dissenting opinions of Justices Blackmun and Stevens are of particular interest because they perceived the remedy for the discrimination in *McCleskey* to be a limitation of the

that equal protection claims of purposeful race discrimination in death sentence cases are now subjected to a far heavier burden of proof than is applied to evaluate claims in ordinary jury and employment discrimination cases and claims of discrimination by white voters challenging racially motivated legislative redistricting (Cook and Kende 1996; Leipold 1998; Selmi 1997).

In response to McCleskey's Eighth Amendment arbitrariness claim, Justice Powell's opinion accepted the validity of his data but rejected McCleskey's claim that his sentence was excessive because racial considerations may influence capital sentencing decisions in Georgia, on the ground that the statistical evidence he offered failed to establish "a constitutionally significant risk" that racial factors had, indeed, infected Georgia's death-sentencing process (*McCleskey v. Kemp* 1987:313). There is some intimation in the Court's opinion that statistical evidence might possibly support an Eighth Amendment claim of excessiveness, but only if the proven disparities were much more severe than those documented by McCleskey. There is also a suggestion in the opinion that since statistics, "at most may show only a likelihood that a particular factor entered into *some* decisions" (emphasis added), statistical proof can never provide a sufficient base for inferring a constitutional risk of excessiveness in an individual case. The opinion further suggests that when "constitutional [procedural] guarantees are met" empirical evidence is irrelevant to a claim of excessiveness under the Eighth Amendment. This point is underscored by the Court's failure to specify in any way why McCleskey's proof was not constitutionally "significant" (*McCleskey v. Kemp* 1987:308, 313).

Justice Powell's opinion is couched largely in terms of McCleskey's failure of proof. But he also addressed and alluded to several concerns that do not fit within any recognizable legal categories, but appear to have been important to the decision. One factor working against McCleskey's equal protection argument may have been that the principle of racial equality underlying the Equal Protection Clause of the 14th Amendment was not as heavily implicated in his case as it is in a more typical civil rights case. As a convicted murderer, McCleskey did not enjoy same status of an "oppressed minority" as would a blameless claimant seeking equal access to housing, employment, or schools. In addition, McCleskey's claim primarily pointed not to discrimination on the basis of his race (over which he had no control) but rather to discrimination on the basis of the victim's race. As noted earlier, it was McCleskey who "chose" his victim, a fact that weakened the moral appeal of his claim.

At one level, it may come as a surprise to see the Court reject a claim of arbitrariness in the face of the strong empirical evidence presented by McCleskey. On several earlier occasions, it has invalidated a death sentence on the ground

---

Georgia death-sentencing system to the most aggravated cases in which no race effects were apparent.

that the record indicated an unacceptable "risk" of arbitrariness in the case, when in fact, unlike in *McCleskey*, there was little to support such an inference beyond the justices' hunches and intuition. This preference for hunches and intuition may very well reflect an insecurity about the justices' own abilities to assess properly statistical evidence of the type presented in *McCleskey*. The Court may fear that if it bases its findings on empirical data, subsequent analyses could demonstrate that it incorrectly interpreted the empirical data on which its findings were based. One can understand why judges, relatively untrained in statistics and confronted with conflicting opinions about the validity of the data, might have greater confidence in their intuitively derived conclusions than in the pronouncements of statisticians.

It is likely that even more important than those considerations was a concern that a finding of unconstitutional discrimination in McCleskey's case would have had a significant disruptive effect on the criminal justice systems of Georgia and other states. Justice Powell's opinion alludes to this possibility by his suggestion that a finding in favor of McCleskey could throw "into serious question the principles that underlie our entire criminal justice system." Such a ruling, he explained, could validate, under the Eighth Amendment, not only claims of racial discrimination, but also claims of discrimination based on sex, or on such allegedly arbitrary factors as the "defendant's facial characteristics, or the physical attractiveness of the defendant or the victim, that some statistical study indicates may be influential in jury decision-making" (*McCleskey v. Kemp* 1987:317–18; Dorin 1994).

Even more important in the Court's thinking may have been a concern that recognition of a racial claim in a death case by the high court would discredit the death penalty and enhance public perceptions that the Court was responsible for the "failure" of the death penalty in the post-*Furman* period. This concern was underscored by a memo written by Justice Scalia while *McCleskey* was pending in the Court. Addressing the entire Court, he stated his belief that racial discrimination in the administration of the death penalty is "real, acknowledged in the decisions of this court, and ineradicable" (Baldus et al. 1994:371). From this perspective, any effort by the Court to cure the effects of discrimination could obviously have significant potential repercussions for the future of the death penalty in America.

If the purpose of *McCleskey* was to provide closure, it certainly was successful in the federal courts. The decision has eliminated the federal courts as a forum for the consideration of statistically based claims of racial discrimination in capital sentencing. *McCleskey* has also been used to reject such claims in state courts (Blume et al. 1998:1780–98).

Another effect of *McCleskey* has been to stimulate an alternative focus in academic research on the death penalty. In addition to statistical evidence, several important projects now also focus on extended interviews with jurors who have participated in the life-and-death decision making of penalty trials. The early results indicate that this research will shed substantial light on the extent to which jurors understand both the facts and law that underlie their decisions and follow the instructions given them by the court (Symposium 1995; Bowers 1995)

McCleskey has drawn considerable criticism (Bassett 2002:1; Amsterdam 1988). Numerous commentators have expressed serious concern with the Court's placement of an implicit imprimatur on racial discrimination in such an important area of the criminal law. Particularly offensive to African-Americans is the perception, based upon *McCleskey*, that the Constitution authorizes prosecutors and jurors to provide minority communities with less protection than it provides white communities (Kennedy 1988). In spite of these criticisms, however, *McCleskey* remains the law.

The reluctance of the Supreme Court to consider claims of racial discrimination in the administration of the death penalty has also been evident in two federal cases, one capital (*United States v. Bass* 2002) and one non-capital (*United States v. Armstrong* 1996), in which a defendant alleged before trial that the prosecutors in his case had selected him for federal prosecution (in the non-capital case), and for capital prosecution (in the death penalty case) because he was African-American. In each case, the defendant sought discovery of the prosecution's files to document that race-of-defendant disparities existed in prosecutorial charging decisions among comparable cases. In each case the Court held that discovery would be permitted only if the defendant could establish independently of the information he sought through the discovery disparate treatment in the exercise of prosecutorial discrimination among similarly situated cases. These rulings reflect judicial deference to the executive branch and great hesitancy to examine prosecutorial charging decisions, a policy that also exists in state criminal courts.

Congressional Reform Efforts

Although *McCleskey* has closed down federal court discussion of race in capital cases, it did not block further consideration of the issue by Congress. Indeed, Justice Powell's opinion for the Court in *McCleskey* suggested that claims of discrimination might best be presented for corrective action to legislatures.

In *McCleskey's* wake, congressional concerns first stimulated a formal assessment of the scope of the problem in American capital charging and sentencing systems. This produced the GAO report mentioned previously, which clearly suggested that there is a problem, especially with respect to race-of-victim discrimination. Continuing congressional concerns led to a series of efforts to bypass *McCleskey* by relying on the legislative power granted Congress under the Enabling Clause of the Fourteenth Amendment (Baldus et al. 1994). The two resulting proposals were known as the Racial Justice Act and the Fairness in Death Sentencing Act. Neither specifically addressed the situation in Georgia or in any other state. Nor did they specifically seek to impose on the states structural remedies of the type suggested by Justices Blackmun and Stevens in *McCleskey* that would limit the exercise of prosecutorial and jury discretion to the most highly aggravated cases in which no race effect was apparent. Instead, the measures were designed to give offenders condemned to death the same right to challenge their individual death sentences as racially motivated as is currently enjoyed by individuals claiming discrimination under federal employment and housing laws.

Under the two proposals, a black defendant, or a defendant whose victim was white, could establish a prima facie case by showing a racially discriminatory pattern of death sentencing, presumably after adjustment for the leading aggravating circumstances. The State could rebut this showing by demonstrating by a preponderance of the evidence that identifiable and pertinent nonracial factors persuasively explain the observable racial disparities comprising the pattern. Absent such a rebuttal by the State, defendants would be entitled to relief from their death sentences if their cases fell within a category of cases in which a racial disparity existed to their disadvantage.

The second proposal, the Fairness in Death Sentencing Act, was adopted by the U.S. House of Representatives in 1990 and, with only slight modification, in 1994, but in each instance, it was rejected by the Senate in a House-Senate Conference Committee (Baldus et al. 1994:404). On both occasions, the measure attracted strong opposition from state attorneys general and prosecutors in death penalty states who argued, on the one hand, that race discrimination did not exist and therefore the act was unnecessary, and on the other hand, that the provision would necessarily result in either the use of quotas or the de facto abolition of capital punishment in America (Lungren and Krotoski 1995; Edwards and Conyers 1995; Rothman and Powers 1994). The latter argument was premised on claims that race discrimination in the use of the death penalty was inevitable and impossible to prevent, detect, or remedy; thus, the choice between quotas and abolition. Although we consider those arguments spurious red herrings, they had considerable force with legislators who feared that a vote in support of the Act might be characterized at home as an action that could lessen the viability of the death penalty in their states.[13]

State Court Claims

Although state supreme courts are not bound by *McCleskey* and are free to entertain claims of racial discrimination under their state constitutions, the idea is distinctly unappealing to nearly all such courts (Blume et al.

---

13. Racial Justice Act provisions have also been presented without success in the Kentucky and Maryland legislatures.

1998:1780–98). The reasons are quite clear. Most important is the power of the death penalty as a symbol in contemporary American life, especially in the South (Baldus 1996).

Indeed, many judges are even reluctant to vacate death sentences for legal error when the Constitution clearly calls for such action. The unpleasant fate of elected judges who have been perceived by the public to be resistant or unsympathetic to the death penalty are widely known in the profession (Bright and Keenan 1995). The idea of upsetting even a single death penalty on racial grounds, particularly in the South, would carry unacceptable personal risks for most judges (Hall 1992).

It is no surprise, therefore, that the two state supreme courts (Connecticut and New Jersey) that have thus far expressed a possible interest in the issue are found in northeastern jurisdictions with strong traditions of concern about racial discrimination. Moreover, the members of the only state supreme court to have actually adjudicated a race claim (New Jersey) enjoy the protection of tenure until retirement at age 70. In the first New Jersey case, *State v. Marshall* (1992), the court rejected the *McCleskey* approach and ruled that under the equal protection clause of the New Jersey constitution claims of race-of-victim and race-of-defendant discrimination are cognizable. It also recognized the standing of a white defendant to present a "structural challenge to the constitutional fairness" of New Jersey's death sentencing system as that system is actually applied by the state's prosecutors and juries. In what the New jersey court now refers to as "systemic proportionality review," the issue is whether the race of the victim or the race of the defendant "played a significant part in capital-sentencing decisions" in New Jersey. The focus in the *Marshall* case was on the constitutional legitimacy of the system as a whole, rather than on the risk that race might have adversely influenced the decision of the prosecutor or jury in an individual case.

The *Marshall* opinion is less developed regarding potential remedies because the New Jersey court did not find evidence of unconstitutional discrimination. The court did state that, if it found such discrimination to exist, it would "seek corrective measures" whose impact the court could observe through its system of judicial oversight. The most likely possibilities would be a limitation on the class of death eligible cases or the promulgation of more objective and detailed standards to guide the exercise of prosecutorial discretion. The court further stated that if the corrective measures failed to correct the discrimination, it "could not...tolerate" such a system and would presumably declare it unconstitutional. However, in spite of the New Jersey court's willingness to consider race claims, it has rejected, as not yet proven, all of the claims it has thus far heard.[14] Moreover, in *State v. Loftin II (1999)*, the Court adopted a requirement that to obtain relief on a racial theory, the defendant must "re-

14. The Supreme Court of Minnesota, an abolitionist state, has also rejected *McCleskey*, in the context of non-capital sentencing (*State v. Russell* 1991), as did a three-person minority of

lentlessly document the risk of racial disparity in the imposition of the death penalty," a standard that represents a more onerous burden of proof than was suggested in *Marshall* (Proportionality Review Project II 2000; Folster 1999:516–17; Sawyer 1997:716–20).

State Legislative and Gubernatorial Action

Two state legislatures have responded to concerns about the risk of race discrimination in the administration of the death penalty. In 1995, New York reinstated the death penalty and in the process adopted a proportionality review provision that requires the Court of Appeals to determine, when requested to do so by the defendant, whether the "sentence of death is excessive or disproportionate to the penalty imposed in similar case by virtue of the race of the defendant or a victim of the crime" for which the defendant was convicted (Crim. Proc. Law Sec. 470.30 3. (b)). This statute authorized the Court of Appeals to engage in the same kind of systemic analysis of race effects in the system that is currently conducted by the New Jersey Supreme Court described above. In anticipation of such reviews, the New York court has created a data collection system for all cases charged with first-degree murder. However, to date the New York court has had no occasion to conduct such a review.

In the mid-1990s, the Kentucky legislature, acting out of concerns about the risk of racial discrimination in the administration of the state's death penalty commissioned an empirical study of its death penalty system, which documented a pattern and practice of disparate charging and sentencing practices in cases with black defendants and white victims.[15] In response to the evidence produced in the Kentucky study, the Kentucky legislature in 1998 adopted a variant of the Racial Justice Act that had been considered earlier by Congress. The Kentucky measure authorizes a pre-trial claim that "race was the basis of the decision to seek a death sentence" in a capital defendant's case. However, in contrast to the proposed federal law, the Kentucky measure does not appear to permit a challenge to discrimination at the sentencing stage of the proceedings.[16]

Over the past decade the movement to declare statewide moratoria on executions and study the administration of the death penalty has gained support in principal part because of concerns about miscarriages of justice but also because of concerns about arbitrariness and discrimination in the administration of the death penalty (Kirchmeier 2002). In 1999, the Nebraska legislature

---

the seven-member Florida Supreme Court in 1992 (*Foster v. State* 1992). The Connecticut court agreed in principle to hear a race claim in 1995 (*State v. Cobb* 1995), but has not yet done so.

15. During 1999 the Maryland legislature failed to approve comparable measures for the study of its system (House Bill 538 1999).

16. Ky. Rev. Stat. Ann. Sec. 532.300 (Banks-Baldwin 1998) ("Prohibition Against Death Sentence Being Sought Or Given On The Basis Of Race; Procedures For Dealing With Claims").

adopted a moratorium on executions in large part because of concerns about the risk of racial and geographic disparities in the system. However, the Governor vetoed this measure and there were insufficient votes to override the veto. In. its place, the legislature appropriated funds for an empirical study of the system. (Baldus et al. 2002).

The well-publicized moratorium on executions ordered in 2000 by Illinois Governor George H. Ryan was motivated principally by his concern about the large number of Illinois death row prisoners who had been exonerated as factually innocent. The commission he created to study the Illinois system focused primarily on this issue, but in addition it commissioned a study of the impact of race in the Illinois system. The resulting study documented significant race-of-victim and geographic disparities (Pierce and Radelet 2002). In January 2003, Governor Ryan pardoned or commuted to life imprisonment the death sentences of everyone on Illinois's death row. His speech justifying this action referred to the evidence of race and geographic disparities in Illinois, but his principal motivation appears clearly to have been a concern about fundamental miscarriages of justice associated with the execution of factually innocent people.

In May 2002, Maryland Governor Parris N. Glendening ordered a moratorium on executions pending completion of an empirical study of the administration of the Maryland death penalty, which his office had commissioned the previous year, and its consideration by the Legislature. In so doing he stated his belief that miscarriages of justice did not appear to be a significant problem in Maryland, even though at least one factually innocent person had been released from Maryland's death row since 1973. What concerned him was the risk of race discrimination and. geographic disparities, which were to be the principal focus of the study he had commissioned. The study, which was released in January 2003, revealed no race-of-defendant effects but documented significant statewide white-victim and black-defendant/white-victim disparities in death-sentencing rates among all death-eligible cases, which reflect disparate treatment in prosecutorial charging practices (Paternoster and Brame 2003: tbls. 12E, 12F, and 13F). The data also revealed significant geographic disparities in charging practices that produce significant geographic disparities in death sentencing outcomes among all death eligible cases. The significance of these findings is under consideration by the both the legislature and the newly elected Governor, Robert L. Ehrlich. As of February 2003, executions had not been resumed in Maryland, but Governor Ehrlich had stated that he would rescind the moratorium imposed by his predecessor and no action on the issue had been taken by the legislature.

Conclusion

The history of race discrimination and the death penalty in the past century has been largely a tale of denial and avoidance by state and federal courts, Congress, and state legislatures. As a result, the civil rights movement, which has hardly touched the American criminal justice system in general, has almost completely by-passed the core discretionary decisions of the American capital sentencing system. Given the importance of the death penalty as a symbol in American life and the perceived political risk to public officials who appear unsympathetic to the use of the death penalty, this record comes as no great surprise. Nevertheless, for a nation with a historical commitment to equal justice under the law, the story is a disappointment. This concern is highlighted by the record of the last twenty-five years, which indicates that the problems of discrimination in the use of the death penalty are as susceptible to identification, adjudication, and correction as are the practices of discrimination in other areas of American life that the civil rights movement has already addressed.

Appendix A

Summaries of Empirical Studies of Death Sentencing Systems
Published/Reported since 1990

1. Arizona—Bortner and Hall (2002). This is a report prepared by Arizona State University's Center for Urban Inquiry, College of Public Programs for the Arizona Attorney General's 30-member Arizona Capital Case Commission. The database includes 971 cases indicted for first-degree murder statewide between 1995 and 1999; 143 of these cases advanced to a penalty trial with exclusively judge sentencing and 31 resulted in a death sentence (at v). The report presents two tables with statewide race data. The race of the defendant is known in 98% of the cases and race of defendant *and* the race of the victim are known in 68% of the cases (at 16–17, 34, Exhibits 15 & 34). The only control for the death-eligibility of defendants is whether the case was death noticed. Nor are there controls for the comparative criminal culpability of the defendants who were death noticed. The report presents no substantive analysis of the racial data. In our analysis of these data, we focus on the race disparities (and their level of statistical significance) in the rates that death-noticed cases advance to a penalty trial and result in a judicially imposed death sentence. White/Anglo defendants were much more likely than "defendants-of-color" (Hispanic, African American, Native American and Asian) to advance to a penalty trial and receive a death sentence. For example, the death-sentencing rate among all death-noticed cases was .10 (20/201) for white defendants v. .06 (11/175) for defendants-of-color ($p = .20$) (at 34). This is explained by the substantially more punitive treatment of white-victim cases in the system and the fact that 81% (71/88) of the white-victim cases that advanced to a penalty trial had a white defendant. Among the death-noticed cases there is an unadjusted 9-percentage point white-victim disparity (.54–.45) ($p = .11$) in the rates that cases advanced to a capital trial. For the cases that advanced to a penalty trial there is a 20-percentage point unadjusted white-victim disparity (.34–.14) ($p = .03$) in judicial death-sentencing rates. Among all of the death-noticed cases, there is an 11-point white-victim disparity (.15–.04) ($p = .002$) in death-sentencing rates.

This means that death-noticed white-victim cases are 3.75 times (15/4) more likely than victim-of-color cases to result in a death sentence (at 16–17, Exhibit 15). Because the study cannot identify death-eligible cases that were not death-noticed, the white-victim disparity in death sentencing rates among all death eligible cases is probably much larger than the disparity estimated among the death-noticed cases. It would be useful, therefore, for the commission to sponsor an additional phase of this research that estimates race effects after adjustment for offender criminal culpability.

2. California—Klein and Rolph (1991). An analysis of 496 California jury penalty trials conducted between 1977 and 1983 in which juries returned death verdicts in 29% of the cases. The unadjusted data show no race-of-defendant effects but reveal a 9-percentage point (.32–.23) race-of-victim disparity, significant at the .024 level (at 38, tbl. 1). In a multivariate Classification and Regressions Trees ("CART") analysis, which controls for 15 cases characteristics, the inclusion of a variable for the race-of-victim increased the number of correctly predicted sentencing outcomes by 1% (at 43–44, tbl.4). Because the study is limited to penalty trials, the authors make clear that their findings cannot be generalized to prosecutorial decision making (at 34, 44). For a critique of the CART methodology used in this study, see Baldus et al. 1998: 1665–66 n. 80.

3. Connecticut—*State v. Cobb* (1995). Unadjusted data for the period 1973–94 presented to the court in the appeal of a capital murder conviction document a guilt-trial capital-murder conviction rate of .62 (13/21) in black-defendant cases and .33 (14/45) in non-black-defendant cases. The data also indicate that while 40% of murder victims were black, black victims constituted 14% of the victims in the cases that resulted in a capital murder conviction, 5.5% of the victims in the cases that advanced to a penalty trial, and none of the victims in the cases that resulted in a death sentence (at 964 nn. 7–8).

4. Florida—Radelet and Pierce (1991). An analysis of 10,142 homicides committed between 1976 and 1987, 415 of which resulted in a death sentence (at 18). The unadjusted results document that 5.9% of those who killed whites and 1% of those who killed blacks were sentenced to death (at 21) despite the absence of any greater probability that the white-victim cases involved additional felony circumstances. Among the homicides with a contemporaneous felony, 16.2% of those who killed whites and 3.3% of those who killed blacks were sentenced to death (at 23). The authors also tested whether the race-of-victim effects could be explained by the defendant-victim relationship, the number of victims, the victim's sex, the type of weapon, or the location of the crime. Individually none of these variables could explain away the race effects. When the authors assessed the same variables collectively using a logistic regression analysis, they found that, on average, the odds of receiving a death sentence in the white-victim cases were 3.42 times higher than they were in the black-victim cases (at 28).

5. Illinois—Pierce and Radelet (2002). An analysis of 4,182 Illinois first-degree murder convictions between 1988 and 1997 in which 76 death sentences were imposed producing an overall death sentencing rate of 1.6% (67/4182) (at 60). The study examined the combined impact of capital charging and sentencing decisions and documented a statistically significant unadjusted 2.6-percentage point race-of-victim effect (a 3.8% rate for white-victim cases v. 1.2% rate for black- and Hispanic-victim cases combined (at 93, tbl. 27). A multivariate logistic regression analysis tested the impact of 28 other variables including the number, age, and race of victims, the presence of a variety of contemporaneous crimes, the defendant's prior record, and the race and sex of the defendant (at 95, tbl. 31a). The results revealed statistically significant race-of-victim and geographic disparities. Specifically, after adjustment for all of the legitimate and illegitimate factors in the analysis, the documented odds of receiving a death sentence were 60% lower if the victim was black ($p = .009$) and 84% lower if the crime occurred in Chicago compared to a rural county ($p.= .0001$) (at 65, tbl. 31a). Although an unadjusted analysis reports black defendants were at a *lower* risk of receiving a death sentence than white defendants, in the logistic regression analysis, noted above, that controls for the race of the victim, on average, the odds of receiving a death sentence were 1.2 time *higher* in black-defendant cases, but this disparity is not statistically significant ($p = .58$).

6. Indiana—Ziemba-Davis and Myers (2002). An analysis of a sample of 224 murder convictions drawn from a universe of 975 defendants convicted of murder from 5/1/93 to 8/10/01. The death-sentencing rate in the sample was .04 (10/224), while among the universe of all murder cases it was .09 (86/975) (at pp. A–B, D, n. 7). The study does not indicate the number of death-eligible defendants among those in the sample who received either sentences of life without parole (26%) or a determinate term of years (70%). Nor does the study include any measures of the comparative culpability of the offenders in the sample.

Among the sample cases, the death-sentencing rate was .07 (9/125) for white defendants and .01 (1/99) for minority defendants ($p = .02$) (at pp. E–F, tbls. 2 & graph A). The death-sentencing rate was .06 (9/143) for the white-victim cases v. .01 (1/77) for the minority-victim cases ($p = .09$) (at p. H, tbl. 3).

The authors state their intention to conduct multivariate analyses in the future that will control for "the offender's culpability and the aggravating and mitigating circumstances that characterize" the crimes in their database. Nevertheless, they state that while sentencing outcomes may "appear to be less severe for Non-White offenders than for White offenders, this observation may have more to do with the victim's race than the offender's race [for]...when the victim is Non-White, Non-White offenders appear to be sentenced less severely than White offenders" (at pp. J–K, referring to both capital and non-capital sentencing). The authors also report the findings of a logistic regression analysis of prosecutorial charging decisions in Marion County, Indiana, between 1979 and 1989. Although the authors do not state the extent to which the Marion County study controlled for offender culpability, they report its finding that "the odds of the death penalty being charged was 3.7 times higher in cases involving White victims than in cases involving Black victims" (at p. B, n.3).

7. Kentucky—Keil and Vito (1995). An analysis of 577 death-eligible cases prosecuted during the period 1976–91. The core analyses were logistic regressions that controlled for six legitimate case characteristics related to the defendant and the circumstances of the crime. The analysis of prosecutorial decisions to seek a death sentence reported an odds multiplier of 1.26 when the case involved a black defendant and white victim ($p = .05$). The overall analysis, which reflects the combined effect of both prosecutorial decisions to seek and jury decisions to impose a death sentence, reported an odds multiplier of 1.41 for the black-defendant/white-victim cases significant at the .05 level.

8. **Maryland** (two studies)—a. Baldus and Woodworth (2001a). An analysis of 346 Maryland death-eligible cases that were "death noticed" by virtue of the state's service of a notice of its intention to seek a death sentence between 1978 and 1999. The study does not include an unknown number of death-eligible cases that were not death noticed. The unadjusted race-of-victim disparity in death-sentencing rates among these cases was a significant 12-percentage points (.29 for white-victim cases v. .17 for the black-victim cases) (at fig. 1A). The disparity estimated after adjustment for the number of statutory aggravating circumstances charged in the state's notice of intent to seek death was a significant 11 points (at fig. 3). The rates at which the death-noticed cases advanced to a penalty trial were .64 for the white-victim cases v. .35 for the black-victim cases, a significant 29-point disparity, which declined to a significant 27-point disparity after adjustment for the number of aggravating circumstances charged in the cases (at fig. 6). Because this research only controls for the number of statutory aggravators in the cases, a question remains whether the race-of-victim effects it documented will persist when stronger controls for defendant culpability and geography are introduced. On the latter point, nine of the thirteen offenders on death row were sentenced to death in a suburb of the City of Baltimore known as Baltimore County. In Baltimore County capital charging and death sentencing rates are substantially higher than they are in Baltimore city, which accounts for only one person on death row. Nine of the thirteen offenders on death row are black.

b. Paternoster and Brame (2003). An analysis of 1,311 death-eligible murder cases that were identified in a case-by-case screen of the facts of approximately 6,000 homicides committed between July 1, 1978 and December 31, 1999. The state filed a notice of its intention to seek a death sentence in 27% (353/1311) of the death-eligible cases and 51% (180/353) of the "noticed" cases advanced to a penalty trial. The sentencing authority imposed a death sentence in 42% (76/180) of the penalty trial cases, which produced a death sentencing rate of 6% (76/1311) among all death-eligible cases (at tbl. 1 & fig. 1).

The report documents large and significant unadjusted geographic disparities in prosecutorial charging decisions, with the death-notice rates ranging from 66% in Baltimore County to 5% in Baltimore City (at tbl. 8). However, the penalty trial death-sentencing rates are basically the same in these two jurisdictions, i.e., 46% in Baltimore County and 50% in Baltimore City, which means that among all death-eligible cases, the death-sentencing rate in Baltimore County is 22-percentage points higher (23% v. 1%) than it is in Baltimore City.

The report presents unadjusted race-of-defendant and race-of-victim disparities as well as adjusted race effects estimated in logistic multiple-regression analyses. The unadjusted analyses reveal no significant race-of-defendant disparities adverse to black defendants (at tbl. 1). The race-of-victim analyses document large and significant unadjusted white-victim disparities in charging decisions and in the death-sentencing rate among all death-eligible cases (at tbl. 2). For example, the race-of-victim disparity in the death-notice rates is 24-percentage points (43% for the white-victim cases v. 19% for the minority-victim cases) and the disparity in death-sentencing rates among all death-eligible cases is 9 points (11.6% v. 2.3%). Also, there is a 7-percentage point disparity in the penalty trial death-sentencing rates (44% for white-victim cases v. 37 for minority-victim cases), but it is not significant (id.). Finally, the black-defendant/white-victim unadjusted disparities are significant only in the state's charging decisions and in the death-sentencing outcomes among all death-eligible cases (at tbl. 3C). For example, there is a 20-percentage point disparity in the state's death-notice decisions—45% for black-defendant/white-victim cases v. 25% for all other cases—and a 10 point disparity in death-sentencing rates among all death-eligible cases—14 % for black defendant v. 4% for all other cases. In the penalty trial sentencing decisions, there is a non-significant 12-point disparity (49% for the black defendant/white victim case v. 37% for all other cases (at tbl. 3C).

The multivariate analyses applied logistic regression to the key decision points. In addition to the variables for race and geography, the models included variables screened from a file of 123 variables for statutory and non-statutory aggravating and mitigating circumstances and the strength of the evidence in the cases. Variables from this file were included in a given analysis if they showed a significant ($p < .05$) relationship with either a race or county of prosecution variable (at p.20). The multivariate models revealed no significant race-of-defendant disparities, which is consistent with the unadjusted results (at tbls. 11A–11F). (The penalty trial sentencing decisions reveal an adjusted 6-percentage point disparity, 44% for black v. 38% for non-black defendants, but it is not significant (at tbl. 11F)).

The more important issue is whether the unadjusted race-of-victim effects noted above would persist after controlling for offender culpability, the strength of the evidence, and the county of prosecution. The county of prosecution is particularly important because Baltimore County, which has the state's most punitive charging practices, also has the highest proportion of white-victim cases (79%) (at tbl. 18). Therefore, one might reasonably expect to see the statewide race-of-victim disparity diminish when controls are introduced for the county of prosecution. However, this did not occur and the results of the multivariate analyses were substantially consistent with the results of the unadjusted race-of-victim analyses. Specifically, the race-of-victim disparity remained significant in the state's notice decisions and in its decisions to advance cases to a guilt trial seeking a death sentence (at tbls. 12A &12B). The adjusted race-of-victim disparity in the penalty trial sentencing decisions was only 5 percentage points (43% v. 38%) and not significant (at tbl. 12G). In the analysis of death sentences imposed among all death-eligible cases, the principal analysis documented a 3.4 white-victim odds multiplier, significant at the .05 level, while an alternative analysis employing a stepwise regression model estimated a 2.1 odds multiplier, significant at the .07 level (at tbls. 12E &12F and p. 33). (In both of these analyses, the death-sentencing rate among all death-eligible cases is significantly higher in Baltimore County and significantly lower in Baltimore City.) What the report does not address is the extent to which separate analyses within these jurisdictions and other counties of the state would reveal significant race-of-victim effects in charging and sentencing outcomes within the individual jurisdictions.

Finally, in the multivariate analyses of black defendant/white victim effects, the disparities are significant only in the prosecutorial charging decisions (at tbls 13A &13B) and in the imposition of death sentences among all death-eligible cases (at tbl. 13F).

9. Missouri—Lenza, Keys, and Guess (2003). An analysis of 574 homicides that "were selected for prosecution as capital murder offenses" from a population of 9,857 homicides committed in the state between 1978 and 1996 in which 152 death sentences were imposed. 51% (281/551) of the capital prosecutions advanced to a guilt trial with the state seeking a death sentence and 54% (152/281) of the penalty trial cases resulted in a death sentence. The death-sentencing rate among the capitally charged cases was .26 (152/574) and among all homicides, it was .02 (152/9857) (at 3–4).

The source of data was reports of the trial court judges, which included information on the race of the defendant and victim, and control variables for the defendant's age, the sex of the defendant and victim, the weapon used, whether the defendant and victim were strangers, whether the defendant was represented by a public defender or a private attorney, and whether the defendant had a felony criminal record (at 4–5, 7). Due to its data sources, the study could not identify the entire universe of death-eligible offenses. However, among all homicides (which embraces many cases that are not death-eligible), black defendants were capitally charged 4% of the time compared to 9% of the time for the white defendants; white-victim cases were capitally charged 10% of the time, while the rate in the black-victim cases was 3%; in the black-defendant/white-victim cases, the rate was 15% and in black-defendant/black-victim homicides, the rate was 3% (at 6).

The study applies multivariate logistic regression analysis to (a) the prosecutorial decisions to advance capitally charged cases to a guilt trial and (b) the penalty-trial sentencing decision. The models included (a) variables for three defendant/victim racial combinations (B/B, B/W, and W/B), with the W/W combination serving as the reference category, and (b) variables for the eight control factors.

In the analysis of the prosecutorial decisions, compared to the W/W cases, the B/B cases were 60% less likely ($p = .00001$) than the W/W cases to advance to a guilt trial; the B/W and W/B cases were more likely to advance than the W/W cases, but the differences were not significant (at tbls. 1 & 2). In the penalty trial analysis, the B/B and B/W cases were less likely than the W/W cases to receive a death sentence and the W/B cases were slightly more likely, but none of the disparities was statistically significant (at tbls. 3 & 4).

10. Nebraska—Baldus et al. (2002). An analysis of 185 prosecutions in death-eligible cases from 1973 to 1999 in which 89 cases advanced to a penalty trial and 29 resulted in a judicially imposed death sentence. The overall death-sentencing rate among all death-eligible cases was .16 (29/185) and the penalty-trial death-sentencing rate was .33 (29/89). The study documented no race-of-victim or race-of-defendant effects in the rates that death sentences were imposed in the penalty trials or among all death-eligible cases. The only race effect in the system was in the rate that death-eligible cases advanced to penalty trial, i.e., .58 in minority defendant cases v. .44 in white defendant cases ($p = .10$) (at fig. 8). However, with the introduction of controls for the place of prosecution, i.e., in a major urban county (Douglas, Sarpy, Lancaster) or in a county of greater Nebraska, the race-of-defendant effect disappeared. There are two reasons for this effect. The first is that the penalty-trial rates in the major urban counties, which include Omaha and Lincoln, are much higher, .58, than they are in greater Nebraska, .28. The second explanation is that 90% of the minority death-eligible defendants are prosecuted in the major urban counties. When the authors examined separately the treatment of minority and white defendants within these two

areas the data revealed no race-of-victim effects in the rates that cases advanced to penalty trial. The only other significant unexplained disparity documented in the study concerns the socioeconomic status of the victim. Among all death-eligible cases, after adjustment for the defendant's criminal culpability, defendants in high socioeconomic status victim cases were more than five times as likely to receive a death sentence as those in low socioeconomic status victim cases, i.e., .28 v. .05 (at fig. 24).

11. New Jersey—Baime (2001) and Weisburd and Naus (2001). The principal report was prepared by Judge David S. Baime, the New Jersey Supreme Court's Special Master for Proportionality Review. It consists of an analysis of 445 death-eligible cases prosecuted since the establishment of New Jersey's death sentencing system in 1983, which resulted in 146 penalty trials and 46 death sentences imposed. This represents a penalty trial death-sentencing rate of 32% and a death-sentencing rate of 10% among all death-eligible cases. In both unadjusted and adjusted logistic regression analyses, the data show no race-of-defendant or race-of-victim effects in the penalty-trial death-sentencing rates or in the death-sentencing rates among all death-eligible cases (Baime at 33–43). The only significant race disparity in the system is the differential rate that cases advance to penalty trial in black and white-victim cases, i.e, .45 (86/190) for white-victim cases v. .22 (38/172) for the black victim cases (at 53).

This disparity remains after adjustment for defendant culpability, but it is sharply reduced with the introduction of a control for the place of prosecution, i.e., in a major urban county (Camden, Essex, and Union) or in a county of greater New Jersey. The explanation for the decline has two parts. The first is that the penalty-trial rate is two times higher in greater New Jersey (.42) than it is in the major urban counties (.21). The second part of the explanation is that 62% of the victims in greater New Jersey are white while only 20% of the victims are white in the major urban counties (Baime at 53). In statewide multivariate analyses of the rates that cases advanced to penalty trial, controlling for offender culpability *and* the county of prosecution, the magnitude and significance of the statewide white-victim disparities depends on the model specification. When the models included variables for both white-victim and Hispanic-victim cases, with the black-victim cases as the reference population, the white-victim odds multipliers are in the 1.6–1.8 range, but they are not significant beyond the .10 level (Weisburg and Naus at tbls. 26.1, 26.1.1, 26.2, 26.2.1). However, when Hispanic-victim cases, which constitute 12% (44/379) of the universe of cases are deleted and the comparison is strictly between the treatment of the white- and black-victim cases, the odds multipliers for the white-victim effects are in the 2.0–2.2 range, with levels of significance ranging from .05 to .07 (*Id.* at tbls. 27.1.1, 27.2, 27.2.1).

In addition to the statewide analysis, Judge Baime estimated race-of-victim disparities within individual counties and groups of counties. A county-by-county analysis of unadjusted penalty-trial rates indicates that in two of the three major urban counties, the unadjusted rate is *higher* in the black-victim cases. However, in the twelve counties of greater New Jersey with both black- and white-victim death-eligible cases, in nine counties the penalty-trial rate is higher in the white-victim cases (based on small samples). In two counties it is the same, and in one county it is lower in the white-victim cases (Baime at 56–57). The report concludes that these unadjusted race-of-victim disparities, based on small samples, are explained by "variables other than race, such as the killing of a police officer, other homicides, etc.," which "are not evenly distributed among the races of the defendants and/or the victims" (at 59).

12. North Carolina—Unah and Boger (2001). An analysis of a universe of 3,592 first and second degree murder convictions between 1993 and 1997 based on a stratified sample of 502 cases obtained from a random sample of 26 of the state's 44 judicial districts (which includes 57 of the state's 100 counties) (at 18–19, 23). The death-sentencing rate among all cases was .03 and among all death-eligible cases, the rate was .06. The unadjusted rate for the death-eligible white-victim cases was .08 v. .05 for the non-white-victim cases ($p = .01$). The unadjusted rates for the white and non-white offenders were .06 and .07 respectively (at 24, tbl. 2). In a logistic regression analysis of the death-eligible cases, which controlled for ten statutory aggravating and seven mitigating circumstances plus fifteen additional legitimate defendant and offense characteristics, the odds multiplier for the white-victim variable was 3.5, significant at the .05 level, while the odds multiplier for the non-white defendant variable was 2.0 but not significant (at 27, tbl. 4). The data indicate that these race effects are attributable to both prosecutorial charging and jury sentencing decisions, although the stronger effect appears to come from the prosecutorial decisions (at 29–33, tbls. 5–7).

13. Philadelphia, Pennsylvania—Baldus et al. (1998). This analysis of 707 prosecutions in Philadelphia death-eligible cases between 1983 and 1993 is based on a stratified sample of 672 cases. Of the 707 prosecutions, 384 advanced to a jury penalty trial in which 114 death sentences were imposed resulting in a penalty trial death-sentencing rate of .30 (114/384) and a jury death-sentencing rate among all death-eligible cases of .16 (114/707). Death sentences are mandatory when the jury finds statutory aggravation in a case but fails to find statutory mitigation present (63 death sentences were imposed at this stage). When both aggravation and mitigation are found, death sentences can be imposed in the weighing stage of the penalty trial (51 death sentences were imposed at this stage) (at 1645). In a logistic regression analysis, the results document race-of-victim effects in jury decisions to impose a death sentence for failure to find mitigation in the case (the odds multiplier when the victim is non-black is 3.9 but it is significant only when the hung cases are included in the analysis) (at 1685–870). In the jury weighing decisions, there is a significant and substantial black-defendant effect (at 1688–89). There is also a black-defendant effect among all jury-sentencing decisions and in the death sentences imposed among all death-eligible cases (at 1758–61).

14. South Carolina—McCord (2002). An analysis of the eleven most highly aggravated (four or more "depravity points") 1998 homicides on which the author was able to obtain data from public records and/or newspaper reports. (There were a total of 305 South Carolina homicides in 1998.) The eleven cases in the sample, which involved 20 defendants and 19 victims, accounted for the three death sentences imposed for murders committed in 1998 (at 294–96). Two of the death sentences (66.6%) were imposed against white defendants who constitute 45% (9/20) of the offenders. 39% (7/18) of the victims were white, but all of the death sentences were imposed in white-victim cases. While acknowledging the small samples involved, the author states that his results provide no evidence of race-of-defendant discrimination. As for race-of-victim discrimination, he concludes that while "[m]ore particular facts may justify the differential treatments" the results are "quite consistent with other studies that have concluded that there are significant race-of-victim effects in death sentencing (at 296–97).

15. Texas—Brock et al. (2000). An analysis of 28,286 individuals, 17 years of age or older, arrested for intentional homicide in Texas during the period 1980–96, which includes the 583 death sentences imposed during the same period (at 63). The measure of offender culpability and deathworthiness is a five-level scale based on a count of four case characteristics: contemporaneous felony committed by a stranger, weapon used was other than a gun, multiple victims, and a helpless victim on the basis of the age and sex of the victim (at 66–67). The measure of the degree to which prosecutors seek and juries impose death sentences in relevant subgroups of cases is the ratio of the proportion of death-sentences imposed to the proportion of arrestees among each subgroup of cases. For example, the ratio of death sentences to homicide arrests is 13.2 (7.9%/.6%) in the most aggravated cases and .03 (.7% / 28%) in the least aggravated cases (at tbl. 3). The unadjusted estimates show death penalty/arrest ratios of 1.4 for white defendants, 1.01 for black defendants, and .60 for Hispanic defendants. These results reflect, in part, the 2.04 death penalty/arrest ratio for the white-victim cases compared to ratios of .44 and .50 for the black- and Hispanic-victim cases. When account is taken of the defendant/victim racial combination, the cases most at risk of a death sentence are the black/white cases (a 4.31 ratio) and the cases least at risk are the white/black cases (a .13 ratio). When the authors adjust for the culpability levels of the cases, the white-victim effect persists but the effects are strongly associated with culpability level, i.e., a 2.42 ratio for the least culpable cases, a 1.73 ratio for the mid-range cases and a 1.43 ratio for the most aggravated cases (at 69, tbl. 6).

16. Virginia—Joint Legislative Audit and Review Commission (2001). An analysis of a sub-sample of 160 cases drawn from a larger stratified sample of 215 death-eligible cases prosecuted between 1995 and 1999. The larger sample was stratified to obtain a representative sample of major urban, suburban, and rural counties (at 19–23). Among the larger sample of 215 death-eligible cases, the state sought a death penalty 30% of the time, 21% of the cases advanced to a penalty trial, and 11% resulted in a death sentence (at 51, tbl. 17). Because of the small number of death sentences imposed, the analysis focuses on the prosecutorial decision to seek a death sentence in cases in which one or both of the statute's aggravating circumstances (vileness or future dangerousness) was present, in addition to liability for capital murder (at 40–41). The unadjusted results suggest no race-of-defendant effects but a race-of-victim effect, i.e., 70% white victims in cases with a death sentence sought v. 45% white victims in the cases with a death sentence not sought (at 37). The core of the analysis is a logistic regression model that includes, in addition to the race of the defendant and the race and gender of the victim, the following case characteristics: rape involved; DNA implicated the defendant; an eyewitness implicated the defendant; whether or not the victim was: of good character, related to or an intimate of the defendant, a drug acquaintance of the defendant, or a stranger; and whether the crime occurred in a major urban county, a suburban county, or a rural county (at 42, tbl. 7). In the logistic regression model, only two of these variables showed a statistically significant relationship to the decision to seek a death sentence, i.e., the victim and defendant were related/intimate and the crime occurred in a medium density county

(i.e., a suburb). Although the coefficient for the white-victim variable was not significant, it was the most aggravating case characteristic in the model, with an odds multiplier of 3.2. The lack of significance of the white-victim variable may be explained by a strong association between the suburban and white-victim variables and the unfortunate inclusion in the model of variables for black-defendant/white-victim cases, and white-victim cases, which substantially overlap.

17. **Federal Death Penalty**—DOJ (2000). A report of charging and sentencing decisions in the federal system since 1988. The principal focus of the report is on federal death-eligible crimes and capital prosecutions. For the 1995–2000 period, the report covers 682 death-eligible cases prosecuted from 1995 to 2000 that were charged with a capital offense; 25% were approved for capital prosecution by the Attorney General and 20 defendants were sentenced to death. Although the report is primarily descriptive, the data lend themselves to a reanalysis, which we conducted with a focus on race-of-victim and race-of-defendant effects. The unadjusted data reveal race-of-victim effects in the rates that U.S. Attorneys (USA) request authorization to seek a death sentence—.37 in white-victim cases v. .21 in minority-victim cases, a 16-percentage-point disparity, significant at the .01 level. Because there is a strong tradition at "main justice" in Washington of approving the recommendations of U.S. attorneys, 88% of their requests were ratified by the Attorney General. As a consequence, the race-of-victim effects in the USA requests were de facto ratified by the Attorney General, even though the participants in the main justice review process are unaware of the race of the defendants and victims in the cases they review. The DOJ report also documents unadjusted race-of-defendant effects in the rates that cases in which a capital prosecution has been authorized by the Attorney General subsequently obtain a death penalty waiver by the USA before trial (at tbls. 2A and 2B). This occurred in 50% of the white-defendant cases and 30% of the black-defendant cases ($p = .03$).

DOJ (2001) is an expanded analysis of the DOJ 2000 report, which embraces additional 231 death-eligible cases that were not included in the earlier report. The report focuses on differences in capital charging practices in different USA offices that may have been influenced by the racial characteristics of the cases. On the basis of a largely non-quantitative analysis, the report concludes that "the racial and ethnic proportions found in the general pool of potential federal cases, and differences among the racial and ethnic proportions in different districts, results from non-invidious causes" (at 12).

References

Amsterdam, A. (1988) "Race and the Death Penalty." *Criminal Justice Ethics* 7:2, 84–86.

Arkin, S. (1980) "Discrimination and Arbitrariness in Capital Punishment: An Analysis of Post-*Furman* Murder Cases in Dade County, Florida, 1973–1976." *Stanford Law Review* 33:75–101.

Baime, D. (2001) *Report to the New Jersey Supreme Court Systemic Proportionality Review Project*. Trenton, N.J.: New Jersey Supreme Court.

Baldus, D. (1996) "When Symbols Clash: Reflections on the Future of the Comparative Proportionality Review of Death Sentences." *Seton Hall Law Review* 26:1582–1606.

Baldus, D. and J. Cole (1980) *Statistical Proof of Discrimination*. Colorado Springs: Shepard's McGraw-Hill.

Baldus, D., C. Pulaski, Jr., and G. Woodworth (1986) "Arbitrariness and Discrimination in the Administration of the Death Penalty: A Challenge to State Supreme Courts." *Stetson Law Review* 15:133–261.

Baldus, D. and G. Woodworth (2001). *Race-of-Victim and Race-of-Defendant Disparities in the Administration of Maryland's Capital Charging and Sentencing System (1978–1999): Preliminary Findings* (unpublished manuscript on file with the authors).

Baldus, D., G. Woodworth, C. Grosso, and A. Christ (2002) "Arbitrariness and Discrimination in the Administration of the Death Penalty: A Legal and Empirical Analysis of the Nebraska Experience (1973–1999)." *Nebraska Law Review* 81:486–756.

Baldus, D., G. Woodworth, and C. Pulaski, Jr. (1994) "Reflections on the 'Inevitability' of Racial Discrimination in Capital Sentencing and the 'Impossibility' of Its Prevention, Detection and Correction." *Washington & Lee Law Review* 51:359–430.

Baldus, D., G. Woodworth, and C. Pulaski, Jr. (1990) *Equal Justice and the Death Penalty*. Boston: Northeastern University Press.

Baldus, D., G. Woodworth, D. Zuckerman, N. Weiner, and B. Broffitt (2001) "The Use of Peremptory Challenges in Capital Murder Trials: A Legal and Empirical Analysis." *U. of Pennsylvania Journal of Constitutional Law.* 3:1–169.

Baldus, D., G. Woodworth, D. Zuckerman, N. Weiner, and B. Broffitt (1998) "Racial Discrimination And The Death Penalty In The Post-*Furman* Era: An Empirical And Legal Overview, With Recent Finding From Philadelphia." *Cornell Law Review* 83:1683–1770.

Barnett, A. (1985) "Some Distribution Patterns for the Georgia Death Sentence." *University of California, Davis Law Review* 18:1327–1374.

Bassett, T. (2002) "Risking Cruelty: McCleskey v. Kemp, Retributivism, and Ungrounded Moral Judgment." *Syracuse Law Review* 52:1–49.

Berk, R. and J. Lowery (June 1985) "Factors Affecting Death Penalty Decisions in Mississippi." (Unpublished manuscript summarized in Baldus et al.1990: 258–69.)

Bickel, P., E. Hammel, and W. O'Connell (1977) "Sex Bias in Graduate Admission: Data from Berkeley." Pp. 113–130, in W. B. Fairley and F. Mosteller (eds.), *Statistics and Public Policy.* Reading, MA: Addison-Wesley.

Bienen, L., N. Weiner, D. Denno, P. Allison, and D. Mills (1988) "The Reimposition of Capital Punishment in New Jersey: The Role of Prosecutorial Discretion." *Rutgers Law Review* 41:327–372.

Blume, John H., Sherri Johnson, and Theodore Eisenberg (1998) "Post-*McCleskey* Racial Claims in Capital Cases." *Cornell Law Review* 83:1771–1810.

Bohm, R. M. (1991) "Race and the Death Penalty in the United States." Pp. 71–85, in M. Lynch and E. Patterson (eds.), *Race and Criminal Justice.* New York: Harrow and Heston.

Bortner, P., A. Hall (2002) *Arizona First-degree Murder Cases Summary of 1995–1999 Indictments: Data Set II Research Report to Arizona Capital Case Commission.* Phoenix AZ: Arizona Capital Case Commission.

8

Bowers, W. (1995) "The Capital Jury Project: Rationale, Design and a Preview of Early Findings." *Indiana Law Journal* 70:1043–1102.

Bowers, W. (1983) "The Pervasiveness of Arbitrariness and Discrimination Under Post-Furman Capital Statutes." *Journal of Criminal Law and Criminology* 74:3:1067–1100.

Bowers, W. and G. Pierce (1980) "Arbitrariness and Discrimination under Post-Furman Capital Statutes." *Crime and Delinquency* 26:563–635.

Bowers, W. B., Steiner, and M. Sandys (2001) "Death Sentencing in Black and White: An Empirical analysis of the Role of Jurors' Race and Jury Racial Composition." *U. of Pennsylvania Journal of Constitutional Law* 3:171–274.

Bright, S. (2001) "Will the Death Penalty Remain Alive in the Twenty-First Century?: International Discrimination, Arbitrariness, and the Risk of Executing the Innocent." *Wisconsin Law Review* 2001:1–27.

Bright, S. (1995) "Discrimination, Death and Denial: The Tolerance of Racial Discrimination in Infliction of the Death Penalty." *Santa Clara Law Review* 35:433–483.

Bright, D. and P. Keenan (1995) "Judges and the Politics of Death: Deciding Between the Bill of Rights and the Next Election in Capital Cases." *Boston University Law Review* 75:759–835.

Brock, D., N. Cohen, and J. Sorensen (2000) "Arbitrariness in the Imposition of Death Sentences in Texas: An Analysis of Four Counties by Offense Seriousness, Race of Victim, and Race of Offender" *American Journal of Criminal Law* 28: 43–71

Carter, S. (1998) "When Victims Happen to be Black." *Yale Law Journal* 97:420–447.

Coker v. Georgia (1977) 433 U.S. 584.

Colbert, D. (1990) "Challenging the Challenge: Thirteenth Amendment as a Prohibition Against the Racial Use of Peremptory Challenges." *Cornell Law Review* 76:1–128.

Cook, J. and M. Kende (1996) "Color-blindness in the Rehnquist Court: Comparing the Court's Treatment of Discrimination Claims by a Black Death Row Inmate and White Voting Rights Plaintiffs." *Thomas Cooley Law Review* 13:815–852.

Dorin, D. (1994) "Far Right of the Mainstream: Racism, Rights, and Remedies from the Perspective of Justice Antonin Scalia's McCleskey Memorandum." *Mercer Law Review* 45:1035–1088.

Dunlop, R. (1995–96) "Is Justice Color-Blind?" *The [Louisville] Courier Journal* (Dec. 31–Jan. 2).

Dworkin, R. (1977) *Taking Rights Seriously.* Cambridge: Harvard University Press.

Edwards, D. and J. Conyers Jr. (1995) "The Racial Justice Act—A Simple Matter of Justice." *Dayton Law Review* 20: 699–713.

Ekland-Olson, S. (1988) "Structured Discretion, Racial Bias and the Death Penalty: The First Decade After Furman in Texas." *Social Science Quarterly* 69:853–873.

Foley, L. (1987) "Florida After the Furman Decision: The Effect of Extra Legal Factors in the Processing of Capital Offense Cases." *Behavioral Sciences and the Law* 5:457–465.

Foley, Linda and Richard Powell (1982) "The Discretion of Prosecutors, Judges, and Juries in Capital Cases." *Criminal Justice Review* 7:2:16–22.

Foster v. State (1992) 614 So.2d 455 (Fla.).

Folster, K. (1999) "The New Jersey Supreme Court in the 1990's: Independence is Only Skin Deep. *Albany Law Review* 62:1501–1545.

Furman v. Georgia (1972) 408 U.S. 238.

Gise, R. (1999) "Note: Rethinking McCleskey v. Kemp: How U.S. Ratification of the International Convention on the Elimination of All Forms of Racial Discrimination Provides a Remedy for Claims of Racial Disparity in Death Penalty Cases" *Fordham International Law Review* 22:2270–2323.

Graines, S. and J. Wyatt (2000) "The Rehnquist Court, Legal Process Theory, and McCleskey v. Kemp." *American Journal of Criminal Law* 28:1–41.

Gregg v. Georgia (1976) 428 U.S. 153.

Gross, S. and R. Mauro (1989) *Death & Discrimination: Racial Disparities in Capital Sentencing*. Boston: Northeastern University Press.

Hall, M.B. (1992) "Electoral Politics and Strategic Voting in State Supreme Courts." *The Journal of Politics* 54:427–446.

Henderson and Taylor (1985) "Racist Justice: Discrimination Even in Death." Dallas *Times Herald* (November 17).

House Bill 538 (1999) (Study of the Administration of the Death Penalty: MD)

Johnson, S (1988). "Unconscious Racism and the Criminal Law." *Cornell Law Review* 73:1016–1037.

Joint Legislative Audit and Review Commission of the Virginia General Assembly (2002, January) *Review of Virginia's System of Capital Punishment*. Available at http://jlarc.state.va.us/reports/rpt274.pdf.

Jurek v. Texas (1976) 428 U.S. 262.

Keil, T.J. and G. Vito (1995) "Race and the Death Penalty in Kentucky Murder Trials: 1971–91." *The Advocate* 17:5–15.

Keil, T.J. and G. Vito (1989) "Race, Homicide, Severity, and Application of the Death Penalty: A Consideration of the Barnett Scale." *Criminology* 27:3:511–525.

Kennedy, R. (1997) *Race, Crime, and the Law*. New York: Pantheon Books.

Kennedy, R. (1988) "McCleskey v. Kemp: Race, Capital Punishment and the Supreme Court." *Harvard Law Review* 101:1388–1443.

Kirchmeier, J. "Another Place Beyond Here: The Death Penalty Moratorium Movement in the United States." *University of Colorado Law School* 76:1–116.

Klarman, M. (2000) "The Racial Origins of Modern Criminal Procedure." *Michigan Law Review* 99:48–97.

Klein, S., A. Abrahamse, and J. Rolph (1987) "Racial Equity in Prosecutor Requests for the Death Penalty." (Unpublished manuscript, The Rand Corporation.)

Klein, S. and J. Rolph (1991) "Relationship of Offender and Victim Race to Death Penalty Sentences in California" *Jurimetrics* 32:33–48.

Klemm, M. (1986) "The Determinants of Capital Sentencing in Louisiana, 1975–1984." Dissertation, University of New Orleans.

Lawrence, C. (1987) "The Id, the Ego, and Equal Protection: Reckoning With Unconscious Racism." *Stanford Law Review* 39:317–388.

Lee, E. and A. Bhagwat (1998). "The McCleskey Puzzle: Remedying Prosecutorial Discrimination Against Black Victims in Capital Sentencing." *Supreme Court Review* 1998:145–192.

Leipold, A. (1998) "Objective Tests and Subjective Bias: Some Problems of Discriminatory Intent in the Criminal Law." *Chicago Kent Law Review* 73:533–558.

Lenza, M., D. Keys, and T. Guess (2003) "The Prevailing Injustices in the Application of the Death Penalty in Missouri (1978–1996)." Available at http://www.umsl.edu/division/ artscience/forlanglit/mbp/Lenzal.html.

Lewis, P., H. Mannle, and H. Vetter (1979) "A Post-Furman Profile of Florida's Condemned—A Question of Discrimination in Terms of Race of the Victim and a Comment on Spenkelink v. Wainwright." *Stetson Law Review* 9:1–45.

Litwack, L.F. (1979) *Been in the Storm So Long: The Aftermath of Slavery*. New York: Random House.

Lungren, D. and M. Krotoski (1994) "The Racial Justice Act of 1994—Undermining Enforcement of the Death Penalty Without Promoting Racial Justice. *Dayton Law Review* 20:655–97.

Maxwell v. Bishop (1970) 398 U.S. 262.

McAdams, J. (1998) "Racial Disparity and the Death Penalty." *Law and Contemporary Problems* 61:152–70 (Autumn).

McCleskey v. Kemp (1987) 481 U.S. 279.

McCord, D. (2002) "A Year in the Life of Death: Murders and Capital Sentences in South Carolina." South Carolina Law Review 53: 250–359.

McGautha v. California (1971) 402 U.S. 183.

Murphy, E. (1984) "The Application of the Death Penalty in Cook County." *Illinois Bar Journal* 93:90–95.

Nakell, B. and K. Hardy (1987) *The Arbitrariness of the Death Penalty*. Philadelphia: Temple University Press.

Nathanson, S. (1985) "Does It Matter It the Death Penalty is Arbitrarily Administered?" *Philosophy and Public Affairs* 14:149–164.

Paetzold, R. and S. Willborn (1994) *The Statistics of Discrimination*. Colorado Springs: Shepard's/McGraw-Hill.

Paternoster, R. and R. Brame (2003) "An Empirical Analysis of Maryland's Death Sentencing System With Respect To The Influence Of Race And Legal Jurisdiction." Available at www.urhome.umd.edu/newsdesk/.

Paternoster, R. and A.M. Kazyaka (1988) "The Administration of the Death Penalty in South Carolina: Experiences Over the First Few Years." *South Carolina Law Review* 39:245–414.

Patterson, C. M. (1995) "Race and the Death Penalty: The Tension Between Individualized Justice and Racially Neutral Standards." *Texas Wesleyan Law Review* 2:45–95.

Pierce, G. and M. Radelet (2002). *Race, Region, and Death-Sentencing in Illinois, 1988–1997* 81 Or. L. Rev. 39.

Proffitt v. Florida (1976) 428 U.S. 242.

Proportionality Review Project (2000) 757 A.2d 168 (N.J.).

Radelet, M., W. Lofquist, and H. Bedau (1996) "Prisoners Released From Death Rows Since 1970 Because of Doubts About Their Guilt." *Thomas M. Cooley Law Review* 13:907–966.

Radelet, M. and G. Pierce (1991) "Choosing Those Who Will Die: Race and the Death Penalty in Florida." *Florida Law Review* 43:1–34.

Radelet, M. and G. Pierce (1985) "Race and Prosecutorial Discretion in Homicide Cases." *Law and Society Review* 19:587–621.

Radelet, M. and M. Vandiver (1986) "Race and Capital Punishment: An Overview of the Issues." *Crime & Social Justice* 25:94–113.

Radelet, M. (1981) "Racial Characteristics and the Imposition of the Death Penalty." *American Sociological Review* 46:918–927.

Rand, J. (2000). "The Demeanor Gap: Race, Lie Detection, and the Jury." *Connecticut Law Review* 33:1–76.

Rafferty, R. (1995) "Note: In the Shadow of McCleskey v. Kemp: The Discriminatory Impact of the Death Sentencing Process." *New England Journal of Criminal and Civil Confinement* 21:271–312.

Reidel, M. (1976) "Discrimination in the Imposition of the Death Penalty: A Comparison of the Characteristics of Offenders Sentenced Pre-Furman and Post-Furman." *Temple Law Quarterly* 49:261–287.

Rohrlich and Tulsky (1996) "Not All L.A. Murder Cases Are Equal." *L.A. Times* (Dec. 5).

Rothman, S. and S. Powers (1994) "Execution by Quota?" The Public Interest 116 (Summer 1994):3–17.

Sawyer, R. (1997) "Comment: The Last Line of Defense: A Comparative Analysis of United States Supreme Court and New Jersey Supreme Court Approaches to Racial Bias in the Imposition of the Death Penalty." *Seton Hall Constitutional Law Journal* 7:663–721.

Schneider, V. and J. Smykla (1991) "A Summary Analysis of Execution in the United States, 1608–1987: The Espy File." Pp. 1–15, in R.M. Bohm (ed.), *The Death Penalty in America: Current Research.* Cincinnati, OH: Anderson.

Selmi, M. (1997) "Proving Intentional Discrimination: The Reality of the Supreme Court." *Georgetown Law Journal* 86:279–350.

Smith, D. (1987) "Patterns of Discrimination in Assessments of the Death Penalty: The Case of Louisiana." *Journal of Criminal Justice* 15:279–286.

Special Issue (1969) "A Study of the California Penalty Trial in First-Degree-Murder Cases." *Stanford Law Review* 21:1297–1497.

Spohn, C. and J. Cederblom (1991) "Race and Disparities in Sentencing: A Test of the Liberation Hypothesis." *Justice Quarterly* 8:305–327.

Spriggs, K. (1994) *Representing Plaintiffs in Title VII Actions.* New York: Wiley.

State v. Cobb (1995) 663 A.2d 948 (Conn.).

State v. Loftin II (1999) 724 A.2d 129 (N.J.)

State v. Marshall (1992) 613 A.2d 1059 (N.J.).

State v. Papasavvas (2002) 790 A.2d 798 (N.J.).

State v. Russell (1991) 477 N.W.2d 886 (Minn.).

Steffensmeier, Darrell (1998) "The Interaction of Race, Gender, and Age in Criminal Sentencing: The Punishment Cost of Being Young, Black, and Male." *Criminology:* 36:763–797.

Stevenson, B. and R. Friedman (1994) "Deliberate Indifference: Judicial Tolerance of Race Bias in Criminal Justice." *Washington & Lee Law Review* 51:509–527.

Symposium (1995) *Indiana Law Journal* 70, 4 (Fall).

Unah, I. and J. C. Boger (2001). *Race and the Death Penalty in North Carolina— An Empirical Analysis: 1993–1997 available at* http://www.unc.edu/~jcboger/NCDeathPenalty Report2001.pdf.

U.S. Department of Justice (2000). *Survey of the Federal Death Penalty System (1988–2000)*. Washington, D.C. :Department of Justice.

U.S. Department of Justice (2001). *Survey of the Federal Death Penalty System: Supplementary Data, Analysis and Revised Protocols for Capital Case Review*. Washington, D.C.: Department of Justice.

U.S. Department of Justice, Federal Bureau of Investigation (2000) *Crime in the United States, 2001*. Washington, D.C.: U.S. Government Printing Office.

U. S. General Accounting Office (1990) *Death Penalty Sentencing: Resource Indicates Pattern of Racial Disparities*. Washington, D.C.: U.S. General Accounting Office.

van den Haag, E. (1985) "Refuting Reiman and Nathanson." *Philosophy & Public Affairs* 14:165–176.

Weisburd, D and J. Naus, (2001) *Report to Special Master Baime: Re Systemic Proportionality Review*.

Washington v. Davis (1976) 426 U.S. 229.

Wiley, M. (1995) "McCleskey v. Kemp: Race-Conscious Decision Making in Reforming Capital Sentencing." *Howard Scroll Social Justice Review* 3:81–106.

Williamson, J. (1984) *The Crucible of Race*. New York: Oxford University Press.

Wolfgang, M. and M. Reidel (1975) "Rape, Race, and the Death Penalty in Georgia." *American Journal of Orthopsychiatry* 45:658–688.

Wolfgang, M. and M. Reidel (1973) "Race, Judicial Discretion, and the Death Penalty." *Annals of the American Academy of Political and Social Science* 407:119–133.

Woodson v. North Carolina (1976) 428 U.S. 280.

Zeisel, H. (1981) "Race Bias in the Administration of the Death Penalty: The Florida Experience." *Harvard Law Review* 95:451–468.

Ziemba-Davis, M. and B. Myers, Indiana Criminal Justice Institute (January 10, 2002). *The Application of Indiana's Capital Sentencing Law: A Report to Governor Frank O'Bannon and the Indiana General Assembly* (January 10, 2002) (on file with the Indiana Criminal Justice Institute, Indianapolis, Indiana). Available at www.in.gov/cji/home.html.

Chapter 17

Federal Habeas Corpus in Capital Cases

Eric M. Freedman

Introduction:
Federalism and Injustice

In legal terms, habeas corpus is simply the name for the procedure by which a court inquires into the legality of a citizen's detention. But habeas corpus is rarely discussed in merely legal terms. The name carries a special resonance in Anglo-American legal and political history: habeas corpus is celebrated as the Great Writ of liberty.

The reason is straightforward. The availability of habeas corpus means that if an individual is found to have been restrained unlawfully, the court can release him or her—thus enforcing the rule of law and frustrating governmental oppression. Attempts to extend the range and efficacy of the writ have thus been inseparably connected for centuries with attempts to secure justice for those who at any particular moment find themselves execrated by the dominant forces in society.

The present discussion concerns the situations that arise when a state prisoner files a petition in federal court challenging his or her criminal conviction. Such a petition calls upon the federal court to decide, in the words of the federal habeas corpus statute, whether the prisoner is being held "in custody in violation of the Constitution or laws or treaties of the United States" (28 U.S.C. §2254(a)).

Thus, federal habeas corpus is inseparably connected to the idea of federalism—sometimes in our history rightly understood as a device for insuring liberty by dispersing power, and sometimes misunderstood as an excuse for inaction in the face of injustice. For the effect of the existence of federal habeas corpus is that even though the Supremacy Clause of the Constitution (U.S. Const., Art. VI) already requires state courts to insure that state criminal defendants receive every protection afforded by the Constitution, treaties, or federal law, those defendants are also entitled to insist that a federal court review the state court proceedings in order to insure that the conviction and sentence are lawful.

Figure 1
Typical State and Federal Trial and Post-Conviction Procedure

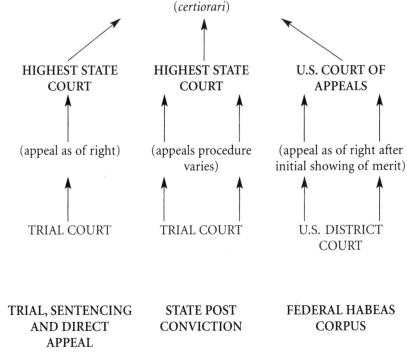

UNITED STATES SUPREME COURT

(*certiorari*)

| HIGHEST STATE COURT | HIGHEST STATE COURT | U.S. COURT OF APPEALS |

(appeal as of right) | (appeals procedure varies) | (appeal as of right after initial showing of merit)

TRIAL COURT | TRIAL COURT | U.S. DISTRICT COURT

| TRIAL, SENTENCING AND DIRECT APPEAL | STATE POST CONVICTION | FEDERAL HABEAS CORPUS |

(Association of the Bar 1996:199)

Stated slightly more completely, as shown in Figure 1, a state criminal defendant has the right after conviction in a state trial court to pursue a direct appeal to one or more state appellate courts (typically in capital cases directly to the state's supreme court), and then to seek discretionary review in the United States Supreme Court by a procedure known as *certiorari*. Thereafter, most states provide for some form of state post-conviction review. Where such procedures exist, defendants must utilize them before seeking the federal habeas corpus remedy.

Federal Habeas Corpus and the American Past Origins

However illogical such a dual system may appear in the abstract, it makes perfectly good sense when viewed in the context of American history, American government, and American reality—especially with respect to the death penalty.

The founders of this country were quite familiar with the tyrannical potential of the criminal law (Hamilton 1788b). As I have elaborated in greater detail elsewhere (Freedman 1996), one important manifestation of their concern is the Suspension Clause of the Constitution (U.S. Const., Art. I, Sec. 9, cl. 2): "The Privilege of the Writ of Habeas Corpus shall not be suspended, unless when in Cases of Rebellion or Invasion the public Safety may require it."

The issue was brought to the floor of the Philadelphia Convention by Charles Pinckney of South Carolina. As James Madison's notes of August 28, 1787 record (Farrand 1966:438):

> Mr. Pinkney, urging the propriety of securing the benefits of the Habeas corpus in the most ample manner, moved 'that it should not be suspended but on the most urgent occasions, & then only for a limited time not exceeding twelve months'.
>
> Mr. Rutlidge was for declaring the Habeas Corpus inviolable— He did not conceive that a suspension could ever be necessary at the same time through all the States—
>
> Mr. Govr Morris moved that 'The privilege of the writ of Habeas Corpus shall not be suspended, unless where in cases of Rebellion or invasion the public safety may require it'.
>
> Mr. Wilson doubted whether in any case a suspension could be necessary, as the discretion now exists with Judges, in most important cases to keep in Gaol or admit to Bail.
>
> The first part of Mr. Govr. Morris's motion, to the word 'unless' was agreed to nem: con:—on the remaining part; N.H. ay. Mass ay. Ct. ay. Pa. ay. Del. ay. Md. ay. Va. ay. N.C. no. S.C. no. Geo. no. [Ayes—7; noes—3.]

Luther Martin of Maryland has left us further details of the debate on this last motion (in which he sided with the minority)(Martin 1788:434):

> As the State governments have a power of suspending the habeas corpus act [in cases of rebellion or invasion], it was said there could be no good reason for giving such a power to the general government, since whenever the *State* which is invaded or in which an insurrection takes place, finds its safety requires it, *it* will make use of that power—*And* it was urged, that if we gave this power to the general government, it would be an engine of oppression in its hands, since whenever a State should oppose its views, however arbitrary and unconstitutional, and refuse submission to them, the general government may declare it to be *an act of rebellion*, and suspending the habeas corpus act, may *seize* upon the persons of

those *advocates of freedom*, who have had *virtue* and *resolution* enough to excite the opposition, and may *imprison* them during its pleasure in the *remotest* part of the union, so that a citizen of Georgia might be *bastiled* in the furthest part of New-Hampshire-or a citizen of New-Hampshire in the furthest extreme to the south, cut off from their family, their friends, and their every connection-These considerations induced me, Sir, to give my negative also to this clause.

When the debate moved to the state ratification processes, the same set of concerns emerged. There was universal agreement that, because human nature was inherently power-seeking, any grant of authority to government office-holders must be scrutinized with extreme care since they would inevitably attempt to abuse their positions. Opponents of the Suspension Clause, who pointed out that—despite its negative phraseology—it was in fact a grant of power to the federal government, denounced it as dangerous. As the French chargé d'affaires wrote home in summarizing this view: "The Congress will suspend the writ of *habeas corpus* in case of rebellion; but if this rebellion was only a resistance to usurpation, who will be the Judge? the usurper" (Otto 1787:424).

The Federalists' response was that they shared the views of their opponents—which were fully implemented by the Constitutional text. Thus, in a speech to the Maryland legislature reporting on his doings as a Convention delegate (and responding to the views of Luther Martin), James McHenry said: "Public safety may require a suspension of the Ha: Corpus in cases of necessity: when those cases do not exist, the virtuous Citizen will ever be protected in his opposition to power, 'till corruption shall have obliterated any sense of Honor & Virtue from a Brave and free People" (McHenry 1787:283).

As subsequent developments show, it seems fairly clear that the Federalists won this debate. In ratifying the proposed Constitution, a number of states passed sets of amendments that they wished to see incorporated; James Madison collated these, and those that had achieved a reasonable degree of consensus among the states eventually became the Bill of Rights. There were explicit safeguards for numerous rights—from freedom of press and religion, to protections for the civil jury trial and a ban on cruel and unusual punishments—that the Anti-federalists had warned would be in jeopardy under the Constitution as originally proposed, and the entire project thus represented a repudiation of the Federalist position that those and other rights had already been sufficiently safeguarded. But there was not a word about the right to habeas corpus, reflecting the fact that (with one minor exception) the states had not proposed any further protection for that right.

A fair conclusion is that the ratification debates had convinced all parties that the Clause as proposed would meet the aims they agreed that they shared:

to protect the liberties of those who might fall afoul of the organs of power. It follows from this premise that, were they present among us today, the debaters would reject modern formulations that see the federal writ of habeas corpus for state prisoners as an assault on state sovereignty.

Plainly, the Federalists were not worried about preserving state sovereignty—neither in the sense of the dignity of the states as against the federal government, nor in the sense of preserving the rights of state-wide majorities to act as they pleased toward their own citizens. With regard to the first, it was the over-abundance of reserved power in the states that led to the need to write the Constitution in the first place. With regard to the second, it is clear that checking the excesses of local majorities (like Rhode Island's) that might act oppressively towards local minorities (like creditors) was a major Federalist goal.

As for the Anti-federalists, their contributions to the debate over the Clause clearly show that they, unlike some modern Supreme Court Justices, were not worried about whether the states would sufficiently retain their sovereign rights to imprison or execute people, but were, rather, worried about whether the states would retain their sovereign rights to release them. In particular, they were concerned that federal power might be exerted so as to keep unpopular prisoners—rightly or wrongly branded by the authorities as criminals—from vindicating their rights to freedom. From the Anti-federalist point of view, a power in the general government to release state prisoners, as opposed to a power in the general government to forestall their release, would be an example of federalism as a preserver of liberty—an instance of the virtue of a federal, as opposed to a national, government.

Furthermore, Federalists and Anti-federalists shared an appreciation of the fact that, to the extent that the Constitution had, through such devices as life tenure and guaranteed salaries, improved on the English model in safeguarding the independence of the judicial branch from overt political pressures (Hamilton 1788a), habeas corpus proceedings could be expected to inquire impartially into executive and legislative actions.

As famously expressed by James Madison in No. 51 of The Federalist (Madison 1788:323), "In the compound republic of America, the power surrendered by the people is first divided between two distinct governments, and then the portion allocated to each subdivided among distinct and separate departments. Hence a double security arises to the rights of the people. The different governments will control each other, at the same time that each will be controlled by itself."

The Civil War and Its Aftermath

Of course, in practice, as many of the founders had foreseen, "the rights of the people" came under unremitting stress from the philosophical and political challenges generated by the peculiar institution of slavery:

During the period that slavery existed in a colony or state, African-Americans were usually judged and summarily punished in special courts by all-white judges or juries for alleged crimes committed against whites. Violent acts by whites against blacks were rarely defined as criminal and then only as property crimes committed against the slave's white owner. Not only did the legal structure of slavery fail to protect blacks against the violent acts of whites, but it denied African-Americans the right to seek legal redress, or to testify as a witness against whites (Colbert 1990:13).

The 13th, 14th, and 15th Amendments, passed in the aftermath of the Civil War, were designed to end this two-tier system within the states. But the framers of those Amendments had little faith in the willingness of the state courts to discharge the responsibility of guaranteeing the rights of equal protection and due process of law to all citizens. It was in this context that Congress passed the federal habeas corpus act of 1867 (Amsterdam 1965), whose basic structure survives to this day. In the face of "the state courts' expected systematic resistance," the "Congress sought to assure prisoners of one full opportunity to enforce their newly given national rights in a national court" (Liebman and Hertz 1994a:43).

The Supreme Court's initial response was to recognize that the 1867 act was written "in language as broad as could well be employed," and to implement fully "the purpose of Congress to invest the courts of the Union...with power upon writ of habeas corpus to restore to liberty any person...who is held in custody, by whatever authority, in violation of the Constitution or any law or treaty of the United States" (Ex parte Royall 1886:247–248; Liebman and Hertz 1994a:44–46).

But as Congress retreated from Reconstruction, so did the Court diminish in its enthusiasm for the enforcement of federal constitutional rights against state authorities. Mirroring its performance across the range of issues presented by the Civil War Amendments, the Court, ruling in a series of technically complex cases whose true underpinnings remain obscure, increasingly began to announce rules of its own devising whose effect was to limit the access of state prisoners to federal habeas corpus (Liebman and Hertz 1994a:47–52).

In terms of outcome, if not of doctrine, the nadir was reached in 1915 in *Frank v. Magnum*. In a famous case that drew intense national attention at the time and has been the subject of extensive historical writing (e.g., Dinnerstein 1991), Leo Frank was convicted in Georgia under circumstances of extreme anti-Semitic hostility of a murder that it is now universally agreed he did not commit. The Supreme Court, however, refused to re-examine on habeas corpus the determination of the Georgia Supreme Court that the trial jury had not been swayed by the threat of mob violence should it fail to convict.

Thus, as far as the Supreme Court was concerned, Georgia was free to execute the death sentence it had pronounced on Frank. In fact, the Governor, convinced of his innocence, commuted the sentence to life imprisonment. But a vigilante committee composed of leading citizens of Georgia—including a minister, two former supreme court justices and an ex-sheriff—broke into the prison, kidnapped Frank and lynched him to much local jubilation. Although the identities of the members of the committee were well-known, "the coroner's jury investigating the murder of Leo Frank concluded that it was unable to identify any of the perpetrators. This was typical of lynching in the South during that era. The only difference is that this victim was not black" (Dershowitz 1991).

Plainly, the situation was unconscionable. And in 1923, in *Moore v. Dempsey*, the Supreme Court granted habeas corpus relief in virtually identical circumstances. The black petitioners there alleged that they had been meeting to discuss their grievances against local white landowners when they were attacked by a white mob, leading to several days of rioting that resulted in the deaths of over 200 black men, women, and children, and five white men. Moore and a number of other blacks were arrested for murdering one of the whites.

As the Court summarized their account: "Shortly after the arrest of the petitioners a mob marched to the jail for the purpose of lynching them but were prevented by...the promise of...leading officials that if the mob would refrain,...they would execute those found guilty in the form of law" (*Moore v. Dempsey* 1923:88–89). The officials then "made good their promise by calling colored witnesses and having them whipped and tortured until they would say what was wanted" (p. 89).

Within a few days:

> [T]he petitioners were brought into Court, informed that a certain lawyer was appointed their counsel and were placed on trial before a white jury—blacks being systematically excluded from both grand and petit juries. The Court and neighborhood were thronged with an adverse crowd that threatened the most dangerous consequences to anyone interfering with the desired result. The counsel did not venture to demand delay or a change of venue, to challenge a juryman or to ask for separate trials. He had had no preliminary consultation with the accused, called no witnesses for the defense although they could have been produced, and did not put the defendants on the stand. The trial lasted about three-quarters of an hour and in less than five minutes the jury brought in a verdict of guilty of murder in the first degree.... [T]here never was a chance for the petitioners to be acquitted; no juryman could have voted for an acquittal and continued to live in Phillips County and

if any prisoner by any chance had been acquitted by a jury he could not have escaped the mob (*Moore v. Dempsey* 1923:89–90).

Having been sentenced to death and denied relief by the Arkansas courts, the defendants presented a habeas corpus petition to the federal district court—which dismissed it summarily. Undeterred by the dissent's charge that it was abandoning the rule of deference to state court processes that it had erected in *Frank*, the Supreme Court reversed, holding that the federal courts had the duty of inquiring into allegations of basic constitutional violations in state court criminal proceedings. Not surprisingly, in the wake of this ruling the prosecution soon ran out of steam, and all the defendants were released within two years (Cortner 1988).

The Present

The Special Problems of Capital Cases

Moore's re-articulation of first principles was soundly based, and of special importance to capital cases. As other chapters in this volume show in detail, the factors that led to repeated unjust death sentences in the era of *Moore* and the Scottsboro Boys (*Powell v. Alabama* 1932) remain powerful today. The current operation of our criminal justice system is still such that—in defiance of every dictate of fundamental fairness—capital defendants systematically receive less due process than others. Their cases are more likely than those of defendants not facing execution to have been infected by distortions arising from racism, the incompetence of defense counsel, their own mental limitations, public passion, political pressures, or jury prejudice or confusion (Baldus and Woodworth 2003; Bowers, Fleury-Steiner and Antonio 2003; Bright 2003; Mello and Perkins 2003; Sandys and McClelland 2003).

Of course, the result is a dangerous increase in the risk that the system will make a fatal error (Freedman 1990–91; Gross 1996; Radelet and Bedau 2003). And whatever may be the benefits of bringing criminal proceedings to closure promptly, there is, in the words of Justice Harlan's 1971 separate opinion in *Mackey v. United States*: "little societal interest in permitting the criminal justice process to rest at a point where it ought properly never to repose" (1971:693).

For these reasons, the "policies favoring a meaningful federal habeas corpus remedy for state prisoners apply with particular force in capital cases" (Liebman and Hertz 1994a:88). As the Association of the Bar of the City of New York documented in a major study, time and time again only federal habeas corpus stands between death row inmates and grievous injustice. Consider some examples drawn from judicial opinions published just since 1980 (Association of the Bar 1996:177–181):

- A mentally deficient man gave the police two vastly different statements during 42 hours of uncounselled questioning. The latter of the two confessions used words beyond the defendant's capability and, unlike the first confession, distinctly recited facts which qualified defendant for the death penalty.
- The grand jury that indicted the defendant was selected in a process that systematically excluded African-Americans.
- The prosecution knowingly presented misleading evidence by using an expert witness to testify at the defendant's trial that he must have been the sole triggerman, when that same expert had previously testified at the co-defendant's trial that the co-defendant must have been the sole triggerman.
- The prosecution withheld its most crucial witness' prior statement, which corroborated evidence favorable to the defendant and would have been material in challenging the witness' trial testimony; after the federal court ordered a retrial, the charges were dropped and the defendant released.
- The prosecutor (i) deliberately withheld the fact that his chief witness had received a deal for his trial testimony, and then (ii) misled the jury by stating in his closing argument that the absence of such a deal favorably reflected upon the veracity of the witness.
- The defendant was insane at the time of the trial and thus was not competent to assist his attorney. After the federal court ordered a retrial and the defendant was restored to sanity, he was acquitted.
- The district attorney devised a secret scheme by which he got the jury commissioners to under-represent African-Americans and women.
- Massive pretrial publicity in a small town compromised nearly all jurors, many of whom had attended the victims' funeral.
- The local sheriff handpicked the jury in a case involving the murder of a police officer.
- The judge's charge to the jury unconstitutionally placed on the defendant the burden of proof on a key element of the alleged crime.
- The prosecutor based his argument in favor of a death sentence on prior felony convictions that he knew did not exist, even though defense counsel agreed that they did.
- The defendant was sentenced to death by a jury that had been unconstitutionally instructed that it could not consider his brain damage, his full cooperation with the police, or his favorable prospect for rehabilitation as mitigating factors.
- The prosecutor inaccurately told the jury that a verdict of death would not be final because the appellate courts would correct any mistakes it made.
- The defendant's attorney failed to inform the jury that convicted and sentenced the defendant to death that the State's only witness—the ad-

mitted killer, who testified in return for a lesser sentence—did not link the defendant to the murder in his detailed confession to police.

- Defense counsel filed no pretrial motions, did not try to locate any defense witnesses, did not interview the defendant's family or the State's witnesses, did not visit the crime scene, failed to use possibly exculpatory evidence available from the State's scientific tests, and failed to seek a new trial after evidence emerged that the victims were alive after the last time that the defendant could have been in contact with them.

- Neither defense lawyer conducted any investigation seeking evidence that might persuade the jury not to impose the death sentence, because "[e]ach lawyer…believed…the other was responsible for preparing the penalty phase."

- Defense counsel did not investigate or otherwise prepare for the capital sentencing hearing because he was confident that he could negotiate a sentence other than death.

- Defense counsel failed to bring to the jury's attention evidence relating to the defendant's mental retardation, the fact that his I.Q. was below 41, that he was only 17 years old at the time of the crime, and was not proven to have had any intent or played any role in the homicide.

- The prosecution withheld information that three individuals, known to be associates in criminal activity, had previously been identified as being at the scene of the crime; that one of the individuals identified had confessed committing the crime to his cellmate; that the same individual was positively identified as having forged endorsements on the money orders taken during commission of the crime; and that the same individual had committed manslaughter by using a weapon of similar caliber to the one used in commission of the crime.

As improbable as it may seem at first, these examples (and numerous similar ones to be found in the Bar Association's report) are typical—not aberrational. The most reliable published data show that, notwithstanding the strong political, institutional and legal pressures on the federal courts to leave state death cases undisturbed, those courts felt compelled to grant habeas corpus relief (i.e., to overturn either the conviction or the death sentence) in 21 percent of the capital cases they reviewed between 1973 and 1995 (Liebman et al. 2000) (emphasizing the importance of vigorous review at the state level as well, the reversal rate there is 47 percent—for an overall reversal rate of 68 percent). These figures are astoundingly high. By the most generous estimates, the rate in non-capital cases does not exceed 7 percent, and, if the appropriate statistical methodology is applied, the actual number may be less than 1 percent.

In short, the systemic problems with the administration of capital punishment in this country that are canvassed elsewhere in this volume are real. And federal habeas corpus proceedings have for a good part of this century served to reveal those problems and, to some extent, to ameliorate them.

The Legal System Refuses to Confront Injustice

A real attack on the multiple sources of injustice in death penalty proceedings would require much in the way of resources and political will. Even then, it might not succeed. It is certainly more than possible that Justice Blackmun was right in his conclusion in *Callins v. Collins* that "the death penalty cannot be administered in accord with our Constitution" (1994:1157).

Moreover, any serious exploration of that issue would raise the uncomfortable prospect of discovering that the problems endemic to capital cases are widespread in non-capital ones as well. Thus, for example, in rejecting an impeccably-documented attack on the racial disparities in Georgia's death penalty system, Justice Powell wrote in the 1987 case of *McCleskey v. Kemp* (1987:315–316): "McCleskey's claim, taken to its logical conclusion, throws into serious question the principles that underlie our entire criminal justice system.... [I]f we accepted McCleskey's claim that racial bias has impermissibly tainted the capital sentencing decision, we could soon be faced with similar claims as to other types of penalty."

Under the pressure of those considerations, both the courts and Congress over the past twenty years or so have shown a consistent inclination to shoot the messenger: to respond to the injustices revealed in capital habeas proceedings by devising mechanisms to restrict such proceedings, rather than ones to remedy the injustices.

For an example, one need look no further than the saga of Warren McCleskey himself, which may someday come to symbolize criminal justice in the Rehnquist era. McCleskey had participated in an armed robbery in which a policeman was killed. Although he maintained that he was not the triggerman, the evidence against him at trial included a purported jailhouse confession to one Offie Evans, an inmate housed near him, in which McCleskey was said to have admitted shooting the officer.

In his original habeas corpus petition in the Georgia courts, McCleskey asserted that Evans had been deliberately sent into his cell by the government to elicit a confession. If this in fact occurred, it indisputably violated McCleskey's Sixth Amendment right to counsel. But the state denied the allegation. The prosecuting attorney stated at a deposition that he was unaware of any prior arrangement with Evans, and a set of documents represented as containing the complete prosecutor's file contained no supporting evidence. Counsel, who had tried but failed to gain any further substantiation, thereupon omitted the claim from the federal habeas corpus petition he filed following denial of relief by the state courts.

That federal proceeding was the one that reached the Court in 1987, and resulted in the 5–4 decision written by Justice Powell that rejected the claim that the statistical evidence of overwhelming racial disparities in the administration of Georgia's capital punishment system was an Equal Protection violation (*McCleskey v. Kemp*).

Following the decision, McCleskey again sought habeas corpus relief on his claim concerning Evans—this time armed with a 21-page report from Evans to the government on his conversations with McCleskey, a document that had not been included when the prosecution turned over to the defense what purported to be the government's "complete" file. McCleskey had obtained the document from the Atlanta police in the weeks following the Court's decision only as a result of a new interpretation of the Georgia Open Records Act by the Georgia Supreme Court.

After conducting an evidentiary hearing, including the testimony of a jailer whose identity was discovered through the document, the District Court granted habeas relief, concluding that the failure to present the claim earlier was justifiable, and that, since Evans had indeed been deliberately planted by the government, McCleskey was entitled to prevail on the merits.

Without reaching the merits, the Eleventh Circuit reversed, holding that the petition should have been dismissed as an "abuse of the writ." McCleskey again sought Supreme Court review.

As of that moment, the law concerning procedural missteps by counsel during habeas corpus proceedings was divided into three categories:

1. *Procedural Default.* These cases occurred when a prisoner had failed to properly present a claim to a state court that he or she later sought to assert on federal habeas corpus, and the state court had applied its own procedural rules to deny review of the merits. As a matter of comity, the Supreme Court had held (*Wainwright v. Sykes* 1977) that federal courts would not review such claims either, unless the petitioner surmounted the difficult hurdle of showing both "cause" for the default—i.e., "some objective factor external to the defense [that] impeded counsel's effort to comply with the State's procedural rule" (*Murray v. Carrier* 1986:488)—and "prejudice" arising from it.

Since McCleskey had properly presented his claim to the Georgia courts, which had rejected it on the merits, the category seemingly had no application to his case.

2. *Abuse of the Writ.* Where a second federal petition presented a claim that had not been made previously, controlling authority required an inquiry into whether there had been subjective bad faith on the part of the petitioner, that is, whether he or she had deliberately withheld the newly asserted ground in an effort to multiply bites at the habeas corpus apple (*Sanders v. U.S.* 1963; *Fay v. Noia* 1963). As noted, the District Court in McCleskey's case had held that there was no deliberate withholding, and the case proceeded to the Supreme Court to review the contrary ruling of the Eleventh Circuit.

3. *Ends of Justice*. In cases where a claim had previously been presented and adjudicated on federal habeas corpus, existing doctrine required an inquiry into whether the "ends of justice" would be served by allowing its re-litigation. This cloudy term had not been clarified by the Supreme Court in recent years, and apparently had nothing to do with McCleskey's case, inasmuch as his Sixth Amendment claim had not been presented in his first federal petition.

In deciding McCleskey's second appeal in 1991 (*McCleskey v. Zant* 1991), the Court, without the benefit of argument from the parties, simply obliterated these distinctions (Freedman 1991). Henceforth, it announced in a 6–3 decision by Justice Kennedy, the standard to be applied in all three situations would be that least favorable to petitioners, namely the "cause and prejudice" standard of the procedural default cases.

"Cause and prejudice" is a standard that falls particularly harshly on death penalty defendants. Only rarely would they have difficulty in demonstrating "prejudice," but they virtually never get that far. Attorney ineffectiveness pervades capital cases to the point of undermining the fairness of the entire system of death penalty adjudication (Association of the Bar 1996:183–87; Mello and Perkins 2003). However, the courts do not tackle the problem "realistically and pragmatically"; rather, they view claims that defense lawyers were incompetent at trial and on direct appeal through the distorting lens of "the strong presumptions of attorney effectiveness mandated by *Strickland v. Washington*" (1984) (Association of the Bar 1989). Moreover, they do not recognize ineffectiveness claims arising from later stages of the proceedings at all.

Thus, deficient attorney performance almost never qualifies as "cause," meaning that, as a practical matter, the courts almost never find "cause" for any procedural error they discern in a capital case. And, without "cause," the court does not consider "prejudice"—much less the underlying merits of the petitioner's claim of constitutional error.

That is precisely what happened in McCleskey's case. Notwithstanding the State's deceptive response to his discovery requests, and a lawyer's obligation to assert only those claims for which a reasonable basis exists, the majority wrote that McCleskey's attorney was at fault for not continuing to assert his claims about Offie Evans. That, however, did not make the lawyer's performance defective under *Strickland*, because the failure took place during post-conviction proceedings, where there is no right to effective counsel.

Thus, McCleskey had failed to show "cause"; his petition had been properly dismissed; and he should be executed (as indeed he was) regardless of whether the government had in fact acted unconstitutionally. "Finality," the Court said, "has special importance in the context of a federal attack on a state conviction," because "the power of a State to pass laws means little if the State cannot enforce them" (*McCleskey v. Zant* 1991:491).

This reification of the "State" as an entity with rights independent of We the People who created it has been pervasive in the recent habeas corpus jurisprudence of the Supreme Court (and, indeed, in its constitutional jurisprudence generally), with most unfortunate results—not just for individuals like Mc-Cleskey, but for our system of justice as a whole.

The 1989 decision in *Teague v. Lane* (1989), which has been unanimously condemned by practitioners, judges, and scholars alike as "arbitrary and perverse" (Association of the Bar 1989: 852; Liebman and Hertz 1994b: 715–805), epitomizes the problem. The workings of *Teague* may be illuminated by the following hypothetical (drawn from, but not identical to, a famous real case). A defendant named Miranda is arrested and confesses to a crime of which he is subsequently convicted. He claims, though, that the use of the confession at his trial violated the Fifth and Sixth Amendments, because the police never warned him that it could be used against him nor that he had the right to consult with counsel before talking with the police. This claim, being unsupported by any decisional law, is rejected by every court to consider it on direct appeal, on state post-conviction review, and in federal habeas corpus—until ultimately being accepted by the Supreme Court on consideration of Miranda's federal habeas corpus petition.

Under traditional concepts of the judicial role, *viz.* that the Court is indeed describing what the Fifth and Sixth Amendments mean (and, implicitly, always have meant), the effect of this ruling should be that every criminal defendant in the country who did not get the required warnings is entitled (unless the error was harmless due to overwhelming other evidence) to have his or her conviction overturned as unconstitutional—through direct appeal if the case is still at that stage, state post-conviction proceedings if available, or a federal habeas corpus petition. Knowledge of this systemwide effect was, until the middle of this century, thought to be a salutary restraint on judicial inclinations to read new individual rights into the Constitution. While perhaps leading to fewer pro-defendant rulings, the rule of full retroactivity meant that every defendant who had been the victim of the same governmental conduct would get relief.

But, under the impact of a number of mid-century opinions by Justice Harlan, who complained that a rule of full retroactivity imposed large costs on states that had in good faith complied with prior law, the Supreme Court began in a series of decisions to adopt a multi-factor test. This test considered such matters as the importance of the new rule and the degree to which the states could have anticipated it. The Court would then determine (usually in a case subsequent to the one announcing the rule itself) whether the rule would apply retroactively to people whose convictions had become final in state court before the Court's decision.

In *Teague*, the Court decided that this provided insufficient protection to the states. Henceforth, it announced, all federal courts adjudicating habeas corpus petitions were (unless one of two narrow exceptions applied) disabled from announcing any "new" rules of constitutional law, thus giving the states virtually perfect protection from the imposition of any retroactive obligations. Moreover, this would be a threshold issue in each case; a federal court must first decide whether a ruling in petitioner's favor would require it to declare a "new" rule, and, if so, stop at that point (without ruling on the merits of the petitioner's contention).

Of course, this formulation made central the issue of what constituted a "new" rule, and the Court proved entirely unable to provide a consistent answer to that question, either in *Teague* itself or subsequently. Sometimes it would hold that a rule was new only if it constituted a clear break with the past—acknowledging that an important element of retroactivity doctrine is giving the states an incentive to err in favor of, rather than against, recognizing nascent constitutional rights. At other times, in contrast, it would hold that a rule was new unless directly dictated by precedent.

More broadly, the result of *Teague's* limitation on federal habeas corpus was that "new" rules of constitutional law, however defined, could only be created on direct appeal. Because (as a glance back at Figure 1 will show) the Supreme Court is the only federal court that hears direct appeals of state criminal cases (which it does a mere handful of times a year), the effect of *Teague* was to eliminate the lower federal courts from the development of new rules of constitutional law in the criminal context. This deprives not only prisoners, but the country and the Supreme Court itself, of the benefit of those courts' insights.

Moreover, *Teague* gave litigants, especially capital litigants, every incentive to delay. Once a defendant's case had progressed to the federal system, he or she could no longer benefit from any favorable changes in the law. So "a prisoner who has somehow managed to keep his or her case tied up in the state courts will benefit from favorable changes in the law, while his or her more diligent co-defendant, convicted on the same day of the same crime, will not" (Association of the Bar 1989:852).

Despite these criticisms and many more, the Court—determined to protect the states against the costs of complying with rules of constitutional law that the Court itself is willing to adopt—has so far been unwilling to re-evaluate *Teague*.

Nor are *McCleskey* and *Teague* atypical. Time and time again over the last two decades, the rationale for the creation of a legalistic maze of restrictions on the availability of the habeas corpus remedy has been federalism, but the statement of this rationale has not been accompanied by an explanation of how it justifies the results reached in the case at hand.

Another stark example of this problem came a few months after *McCleskey* in *Coleman v. Thompson* (1991). There, the Court ruled that a capital prisoner whose lawyer had filed his state habeas corpus appeals papers three days late had thereby forfeited federal habeas corpus review. This decision was premised on the explicit view that the outcome represented the appropriate "allocation of costs" between the interests of the State avoiding a federal review of its conviction that might lead to an expensive retrial and those of the prisoner in not being executed pursuant to a possibly unconstitutional judgment. In a dictum that will live in infamy, the Court began its opinion, "This is a case about federalism" (p. 726).

To reach such results in the name of federalism is untenable, both intellectually and practically. Intellectually, as already discussed (and as well elaborated by Justice Blackmun in his dissent in *Coleman*), the view of federalism that animated the framers supports careful federal review of state court criminal convictions, not deference to the sovereign rights of states to deprive citizens of Constitutionally protected liberty.

Practically, the problem is that an unrealistic reliance on the quality of justice in state judicial systems will inevitably (as in the Leo Frank case) lead to outrageous outcomes. These in turn are not only morally indefensible, but invariably will produce a backlash whose certain result will be legislative or judicial action to insure more extensive habeas corpus review (as in *Moore v. Dempsey*), and whose possible result may be to undermine public support for the death penalty itself.

Yet, apparently operating on the premise that a wrong not heard is one that does not exist, the Congress in 1995 cut off funding for the post-conviction defender organizations that had provided counsel to the death row inmates in many of the cases described above (Association of the Bar 1996:188–191, 200–205).

AEDPA

Against this background, there was considerable concern when Congress went to work on the habeas corpus reform statute that eventually became the Antiterrorism and Effective Death Penalty Act of 1996 (AEDPA) (Pub. L. 104–132; Yackle 1996:383–384). And, indeed, some of the early proposals could only be described as radical. For instance, Senator Kyl offered a provision that was designed to eliminate habeas corpus review of state convictions outright. But although Senator Lott praised this idea, on the grounds that it would solve the "problems of delay and abuse by eliminating these habeas corpus reviews of state judgments," the Senate defeated the amendment by a vote of 61 to 38 (Yackle 1996:398–401).

Instead, Congress ultimately enacted a relatively modest set of reforms. Amid a welter of technical changes (Liebman and Hertz 1996: 12–14), the legislation sought to speed up habeas proceedings in two basic ways: directly, by setting time limits on various procedural steps, and indirectly, by providing that the federal courts should not grant the writ unless the state proceedings "resulted in a decision that was contrary to, or involved an unreasonable application of, clearly established federal law as determined by the Supreme Court of the United States" (28 U.S.C. §2254(d)).

Thus, Congress heeded some of the important lessons that history teaches about the critical role of federal habeas corpus in assuring adherence to the rule of law. It chose to accomplish its purpose of speeding up habeas litigation by rewriting the procedural rules while making no fundamental alteration in the existing role of the federal courts in inquiring into state capital convictions.

As President Clinton said in signing the legislation, it was designed "to stream-line Federal appeals for convicted criminals sentenced to the death penalty," while preserving "independent review of Federal legal claims and the bedrock constitutional principle of an independent judiciary" (Liebman and Hertz 1996:346).

As to the Supreme Court, its developing jurisprudence under the statute has sent a clear message: the Court had shaped the field to its liking prior to 1996 and—regardless of what Congress may or may not have desired—it is unwilling to read AEDPA as imposing any significant additional limitations. Hence, it has consistently rejected restrictive readings proposed by the government (Freedman 2001:177 n.8).

The Future: Achieving Justice within a Federal System

Still, if the law has not become significantly worse for capital prisoners seeking to vindicate claims of constitutional right, it has certainly not become better. And, in the wake of September 11, both Court and Congress may be buffeted in the future, as they have been in the past, by calls for the repression of particularly dangerous-seeming groups (Freedman 2002). Moreover, law aside, the constricted ability of death row inmates to have a meaningful day in court resulting from the paucity of available competent counsel remains a public scandal (Mello and Perkins 2003).

Nonetheless, particularly in light of the growing public concern over the possibility of executing the innocent (Radelet and Bedau 2003) and the resulting renewed appreciation for a judicial process that looks "through the form and into the very heart and substance of the matter" (*Frank v. Magnum* 1915: 332), there are sound reasons to believe that the country is beginning to learn the clear precept for the future that emerges from the past and present of the federal writ of habeas corpus in capital cases: defending injustice on the basis of federalism disserves both federalism and justice.

References

Amsterdam, A.G. (1965) "Criminal Prosecutions Affecting Federally Guaranteed Civil Rights: Federal Removal and Habeas Corpus Jurisdiction to Abort State Court Trial." *University of Pennsylvania Law Review* 113:793–912.

Association of the Bar of the City of New York (1989) "Legislative Modification of Habeas Corpus in Capital Cases." *Record of the Association of the Bar of the City of New York* 44:848–864.

Association of the Bar of the City of New York (1996) "The Crisis in Capital Representation." *Record of the Association of the Bar of the City of New York* 51:169–206.

Baldus, D.C. and G. Woodworth (2003) "Race Discrimination and the Death Penalty: An Empirical and Legal Overview." (This volume.)

Bowers, W.J., B.D. Fleury-Steiner and M.E. Antonio (2003) "The Capital Sentencing Decision: Guided Discretion, Reasoned Moral Judgment, or Legal Fiction?" (This volume.)

Bright, S.B. (2003) "The Politics of Capital Punishment: The Sacrifice of Fairness for Executions." (This volume.)

Callins v. Collins (1994) 510 U.S. 1141.

Colbert, D.L. (1990) "Challenging the Challenge: The Thirteenth Amendment as a Prohibition Against the Racial Use of Peremptory Challenges." *Cornell Law Review* 76:1–128.

Coleman v. Thompson (1991) 501 U.S. 722.

Cortner, R.C. (1988) *A Mob Intent on Death*. Middletown: Wesleyan University Press.

Dershowitz, A.M. (1991) "Introduction." In *The Leo Frank Case*. Birmingham: Notable Trials Library.

Dinnerstein, L. (1991) *The Leo Frank Case*. Birmingham: Notable Trials Library.

Ex parte Royall (1886) 117 U.S. 241.

Farrand, M. (1966) *The Records of the Federal Convention of 1787*. Vol. 2. Revised edition. New Haven: Yale University Press.

Fay v. Noia (1963) 372 U.S. 391.

Frank v. Magnum (1915) 237 U.S. 309.

Freedman, E.M. (1990–91) "Innocence, Federalism, and the Capital Jury: Two Legislative Proposals for Evaluating Post-Trial Evidence of Innocence in Death Penalty Cases." *New York University Review of Law and Social Change* 18:315–324.

Freedman, E.M. (1991) "Habeas Cases Rewrote the Doctrine." *The National Law Journal*: Aug. 19.

Freedman, E.M. (1996) "The Suspension Clause in the Ratification Debates." *Buffalo Law Review* 44:451–468.

Freedman, E.M. (2001) *Habeas Corpus: Rethinking the Great Writ of Liberty*. New York: New York University Press.

Freedman, E.M. (2002) "The Bush Military Tribunals: Where Have We Been? Where Are We Going?," *Criminal Justice*: Summer.

Gross, S.R. (1996) "The Risks of Death: Why Erroneous Convictions are Common in Capital Cases." *Buffalo Law Review* 44:469–500.

Hamilton, A. (1788a) "The Federalist, No. 78." Pp. 564–572, in C. Rossiter (ed.), *The Federalist Papers*. New York: Mentor Publishing.

Hamilton, A. (1788b) "The Federalist, No. 84." Pp. 510–520, in C. Rossiter (ed.), *The Federalist Papers*. New York: Mentor Publishing.

Liebman, J.S. et al. (2000), *A Broken System: Error Rates in Capital Cases*. New York: Columbia University.

Liebman, J.S. and R. Hertz (1994a) *Federal Habeas Corpus Practice and Procedure*. Vol. 1. Second edition. Charlottesville: The Michie Company.

Liebman, J.S. and R. Hertz (1994b) *Federal Habeas Corpus Practice and Procedure*. Vol. 2. Second edition. Charlottesville: The Michie Company.

Liebman, J.S. and R. Hertz (1996) *Federal Habeas Corpus Practice and Procedure*. Cumulative Supplement. Charlottesville: The Michie Company.

Mackey v. United States (1971) 401 U.S. 667.

Madison, J. (1788) "The Federalist, No. 51." Pp. 320–325, in C. Rossiter (ed.), *The Federalist Papers*. New York: Mentor Publishing.

Martin, L. (1788) "The Genuine Information Delivered to the Legislature of the State of Maryland Relative to the Proceedings of the General Convention Lately Held at Philadelphia, VIII." Pp. 433–437, in J.P. Kaminski and G.J. Saldino (eds.), *Documentary History of the Ratification of the Constitution*. Vol. 15. Madison: Historical Society of Wisconsin.

McCleskey v. Kemp (1987) 481 U.S. 279.

McCleskey v. Zant (1991) 499 U.S. 467.

McHenry, J. (1787) "Speech to the Maryland House of Delegates." Pp. 279–284, in J.P. Kaminski and G.J. Saldino (eds.), *Documentary History of the Ratification of the Constitution*. Vol. 14. Madison: Historical Society of Wisconsin.

Mello, M. and P. Perkins (2003) "Closing the Circle: The Illusion of Lawyers for People Litigating for Their Lives at the *Fin de Siècle*." (This volume.)

Moore v. Dempsey (1923) 261 U.S. 86.

Murray v. Carrier (1986) 477 U.S. 478.

Otto, L.G. (1787) "Letter to Comte de Montmorin." Pp. 422–525, in J.P. Kaminski and G.J. Saldino (eds.), *Documentary History of the Ratification of the Constitution*. Vol. 13. Madison: Historical Society of Wisconsin.

Powell v. Alabama (1932) 287 U.S. 45.

Public Law 104-132 (1996) Amending 28 U.S.C. §§2244, 2253, 2254, 2255, and adding 28 U.S.C. §§2261–2266 (eff. April 24).

Radelet, M.L. and H.A. Bedau (2003) "The Execution of the Innocent." (This volume.)

Sanders v. United States (1963) 373 U.S. 1.

Sandys, M. and S. McClelland (2003) "Stacking the Deck for Guilt and Death: The Failure of Death Qualification to Ensure Impartiality." (This volume.)

Strickland v. Washington (1984) 466 U.S. 668.

Teague v. Lane (1989) 489 U.S. 288.

United States Code (1994) tit. 28 §2254(a).

United States Code (1994) tit. 28 §2254(d).

Wainwright v. Sykes (1977) 433 U.S. 72.

Yackle, L.W. (1996) "A Primer on the New Habeas Corpus Statute." *Buffalo Law Review* 44:381–449.

Chapter 18

The Economic Costs of Capital Punishment: Past, Present, and Future

*Robert M. Bohm**

Many Americans have an opinion about the death penalty despite knowing little about the way the punishment is administered. What little they think they know, moreover, often is wrong (see Bohm 2003). One of the most common myths about capital punishment is that it is cheaper than alternative punishments such as life imprisonment without opportunity for parole (LWOP). For example, Political Science Professor John Culver claims that "the execution of an individual in his or her 30s is less expensive than maintaining that person in prison for 30 or more years until a natural death occurs" (1985:574). In a recent Gallup poll, 20 percent of supporters of capital punishment selected "save[d] taxpayers money/[c]ost associated with prison" as a reason for their support. It was the second most frequently selected reason behind retribution at 48 percent (Jones 2001).

The principal purpose of this chapter is to compare the economic costs of capital punishment with the economic costs of alternative punishments, especially LWOP (which is presumed to be the next most expensive punishment). Implicit in the analysis are comparisons of three types: (1) capital punishment vs. an alternative punishment applied after a successful plea bargain, (2) capital punishment vs. an alternative punishment imposed after a trial only, and (3) capital punishment vs. an alternative punishment imposed after a trial and post-conviction review. Assuming the same alternative punishment, the comparisons are listed in descending order from largest to smallest cost differential. The first comparison reveals the largest cost differential because the costs of the alternative punishment do not include trial or post-conviction review expenses, all of which are invariably incurred in capital cases (unless post-conviction proceedings are waived). Also briefly discussed in the chapter are past practices and their costs (which may help explain why some people believe in the myth), financial and other ramifications of recent efforts to streamline the process, the costs of mistakes, "start-

* Thanks to my co-editors for their many helpful suggestions.

up" costs for jurisdictions contemplating reinstatement of the death penalty, and some of the consequences if capital punishment were to be replaced with LWOP in the future.

The Past: Business as Usual

Prior to the *Furman v. Georgia* decision in 1972, the costs of capital punishment were not an issue. The death penalty was not an expensive punishment relative to LWOP because capital cases were disposed of quickly, no extraordinary procedures were followed, reversals were relatively rare, and the costs associated with executions alone were minimal. Regarding the relatively quick disposal of capital cases, in 1934, for example, Doc Williams was executed in Florida 33 days following his apprehension and only 45 days after the crime was committed (McGovern 1982:10). Data from 1956–1960 show that the average time between death sentence and execution was 14.4 months (Peterson and Bailey 2003); however, by yearend 2000, the average had risen to 137 months (Snell 2001:12, Table 12). A primary reason for the 851 percent increase in time between conviction and execution in capital cases is the "super due process" (Radin 1980) now required by the Supreme Court's "death is different" doctrine. "Super due process" refers to the unique procedural safeguards afforded people charged with capital crimes.[1] Those safeguards apply primarily to the trial and post-conviction stages of the process.

---

1. The general elements of "super due process" are: (1) bifurcated trials, with separate guilt and penalty phases; (2) "guided discretion" statutes; (3) finding at least one of the aggravating circumstances listed in a death penalty statute before the crime is death-eligible; (4) allowing the presentation of relevant mitigating evidence during the penalty phase of bifurcated trials; (5) automatic appellate review; and (6) proportionality review. Although the Supreme Court considers all of the safeguards desirable, it does not require them all. Also, as will be discussed in greater detail in a later section of this chapter, the Supreme Court in recent years has attempted to speed up the process by altering some of the "super due process" protections.

The primary justification for "super due process" is the "death is different" doctrine advocated by Supreme Court Justice William Brennan and first articulated in *Furman v. Georgia* (1972; also see Bedau 1987). In *Furman*, Justice Brennan observed that death is "an unusually severe punishment, unusual in its pain, in its finality, and in its enormity" (at 287). Later, in *Gardner v. Florida* (1977), the Court elaborated:

> [F]ive Members of the Court have now expressly recognized that death is a different kind of punishment from any other which may be imposed in this country. From the point of view of the defendant, it is different both in its severity and its finality. From the point of view of society, the action of the sovereign in taking the life of one of its citizens also differs dramatically from any other legitimate state action. It is of vital importance to the defendant and

The Present: Death Is Different and Super Due Process

Although it may be relatively inexpensive to put people to death, it is quite costly to put them to death legally in the United States under post-*Furman* statutes. As noted above, the Supreme Court requires that defendants charged with capital crimes be provided with "super due process," and "super due process" is expensive. According to the available evidence, the average cost per execution in the United States (that is, the entire process) ranges from about $2.5 million to $5 million (in 2000 dollars). (Also see Cook and Slawson 1993; Garey 1985; Hoppe 1992; Liebman, Fagan, and West 2000, n. 74; New York State Defenders Association 1982; Spangenberg and Walsh 1989).[2] In extraordinary cases the cost can be much more. For example, the state of Florida reportedly spent $10 million to execute serial murderer Ted Bundy in 1989 (Muwakkil 1989:6). It is estimated that the federal government spent more than $100 million to execute mass murderer Timothy McVeigh in 2001 (Michel and Herbeck 2001).

If the average annual cost of imprisonment in the United States is about $20,000 per inmate (see Bohm and Haley 2002:362),[3] and an inmate sentenced to LWOP lives 50 years,[4] then the cost of that LWOP sentence is roughly $1 million (assuming the LWOP sentence was the result of a successful plea bargain), making capital punishment, on average, approximately two and one-

---

to the community that any decision to impose the death sentence be, and appear to be, based on reason rather than caprice or emotion (at 357).
Also see *Woodson v. North Carolina* (1976) and *Gregg v. Georgia* (1976).

2. Between 1995, the year New York reinstated the death penalty, and 1999, New York spent an estimated $68 million on 37 death penalty cases. More than half of those cases resulted in plea deals and life sentences. Eight cases are still pending. Of the nine trials completed, five ended with death sentences and four with life without parole. By the time the first death row inmate is executed, the costs to New York of the five cases could reach $238 million. See "Death Penalty Expenses Adding Up" (1999).

3. The annual cost of confining an inmate on death row generally is somewhat greater than the annual cost of housing an LWOP inmate among the general population of a maximum security prison (see Brooks and Erickson 1996:883). Also, the $20,000 average annual cost of imprisonment does not include additional expenses that may be incurred because of the medical problems of elderly inmates. The amount of such costs is unknown. However, any added medical costs should be offset somewhat by the reduced security level needed for elderly inmates.

4. Because of the conditions of prison life, such as violence, HIV and other diseases, poor diets, and poor health conditions, it has been estimated that an inmate sentenced to LWOP will live an average of 31 years in prison (Brooks and Erickson 1996:883). At yearend 2000, the median age of a death row inmate at time of arrest was 27 (the median age of death row inmates was 38) (Snell 2001:9, Table 8).

half to five times more expensive than LWOP (imposed as a result of plea bargaining). Of course, if the LWOP sentence were imposed after a trial (and included other post-conviction proceedings), then the difference would be much smaller. Nevertheless, the costs of a death sentence will probably always be more expensive than the costs of an LWOP sentence because "super due process" is only required in capital cases (Paternoster 1991:279; also see *Harmelin v. Michigan* 1991). In North Carolina, for example, the cost differential between a capital case culminating in an execution and a noncapital case resulting in a 20-year sentence was estimated to be between $163,000 and more than $216,000 (Cook and Slawson 1993:97–98).

Why is "super due process" so expensive? That question is answered below. However, it must be emphasized that many of the costs reported below are estimates, that there can be great variation in the costs of specific services among different jurisdictions, that cost estimates are not available for every part of the process, and that not every cost or part of the process occurs in every case. Moreover, some costs can be duplicated when retrials or resentencings follow the vacation of a conviction or capital sentence on appeal or during the post-conviction review process. It should also be remembered that whenever a capital trial does not result in a death sentence and execution, the added costs associated with the death penalty process have been incurred without any "return" on the state's investment of resources.

The following analysis is divided into five general stages of the capital punishment process: (1) pretrial, (2) trial, (3) posttrial, (4) imprisonment, and (5) execution.

The Pretrial Stage

The costs of capital punishment begin to mount soon after a potentially capital crime (in most cases, an "aggravated" murder) has been reported to the police. The investigation of potentially capital crimes tends to be more rigorous than the investigation of other felonies. When the crime may be a capital offense, forensic experts tend to examine the crime scene more carefully. This greater attention to detail and the extra time it requires results in an added but unknown cost (New York State Defenders Association 1982; Spangenberg and Walsh 1989).

Investigation of the case frequently continues through trial and can last several years (Garey 1985:1252; Spangenberg and Walsh 1989:49). The investigation of potentially capital crimes has been estimated to take three to five times longer than for other felonies, primarily because the prosecution as well as the defense must prepare for both stages of the bifurcated trial—the guilt and penalty phases (Brooks and Erickson 1996:893; Garey 1985:1252; Spangenberg and Walsh 1989:49). Because defense counsel can present any relevant mitigating evidence during the penalty phase of a capital trial (see *Lockett v. Ohio*

1978), a thorough investigation of possible mitigators is time-consuming and expensive. In North Carolina, investigators working for the state were paid $22.16 per hour in 1991–92 (Cook and Slawson 1993:44, Table 5.3). Experienced private investigators, who frequently are hired by the defense, are paid between $75 and $200 an hour (Spangenberg and Walsh 1989:49).

Once a suspect has been identified and an arrest is made, a bond hearing is held. The costs of those processes probably do not differ greatly for potentially capital crimes and other serious felonies, but estimates of those costs have not been reported. However, if bond is denied and the suspect is incarcerated, which is nearly always more likely with potentially capital crimes, then additional costs will be incurred as a result of the tighter security that will be provided through the entire process (Brooks and Erickson 1996:901; Spangenberg and Walsh 1989:48). There are no estimates for those extra security costs.

If the prosecutor believes that there is evidence to convict the suspect of the crime, and the crime is an "aggravated" murder (or other capital offense), then the prosecutor will seek an indictment for capital murder in jurisdictions that employ grand juries.[5] In those jurisdictions that do not use grand juries, formal charges are filed through an information. The costs of each capital indictment are believed to be "enormous" (though no dollar figure has been cited) because each indictment must be prepared even though only about 20 percent of them will reach trial (Spangenberg and Walsh 1989:49).

The most expensive part of the pretrial process frequently involves the motions filed in death penalty cases. Defense counsel has both a professional and an ethical obligation to represent his or her client's interests by filing nonfrivolous motions which, at a minimum, create and preserve the defendant's record for appeal (Garey 1985:1251, n. 134). Extensive amounts of time can be devoted to researching and writing pretrial motions. The prosecution must respond to the motions as well as prepare and file its own. In North Carolina, at least 34 different motions have been made in recent capital litigation, plus an additional 11 different motions made during the penalty phase of the trial (Cook and Slawson 1993:28–29, n. 47). Those motions are in addition to the more standard ones that are frequently filed by both sides in other felony cases (Cook and Slawson 1993:30, n. 47). Typical motions filed in capital cases involve voir dire, jury composition, death qualification process challenges, change of venue, and challenges to the death penalty's constitutionality in general and to the state's death penalty statute in particular (Garey 1985:1249–1250; Cook and Slawson 1993:28–29, n. 47). It is estimated that two to six times more motions are filed in death penalty cases than in other felony cases (Garey 1985:1248; Spangenberg and Walsh 1989:50). Between five

5. Grand juries are involved in felony prosecutions in about half the states and in the federal system (Bohm and Haley 2002:287).

and seven motions are typically filed in noncapital cases in New York (New York State Defenders Association 1982:12). In a single North Carolina capital case in 1991, the cost of pretrial motions was $115,247 (Cook and Slawson 1993:81, Table 7.6).

A big part of the expense of motions is the costs of experts who are paid for both their research/consulting and testimony at trial. Experts are employed by both the defense and the prosecution. Among the experts used in capital cases are: (1) psychiatrists, who are paid about $100–$150 an hour or $500–$1,000 a day (Garey 1985:1253; Spangenberg and Walsh 1989:50); (2) medical examiners, who are paid about $700–$1,000 a day (Garey 1985:1253; Spangenberg and Walsh 1989:50); (3) polygraph experts, who are paid about $200–$300 a day for courtroom testimony and about $150–$250 per examination (Garey 1985:1253; Spangenberg and Walsh 1989:50); (4) experts on eyewitness identification, who are paid about $100 an hour or about $500 a day for courtroom testimony (Garey 1985:1253; Spangenberg and Walsh 1989:50); and (5) forensic scientists, juristic psychologists, and criminologists, who (in 1996) were paid a maximum of about $130 an hour in Florida (Orange County) unless special circumstances existed (author's own experience). Altogether, defense expert witnesses alone can easily cost more than $40,000 in capital cases (Brooks and Erickson 1996:895).

The Trial Stage

Most criminal cases—approximately 90 percent of them—never reach trial, but instead are resolved through plea bargaining. Capital cases are an exception; they are rarely plea bargained.[6] Because "death is different," death penalty cases go to trial ten times more often than do other felony cases (Garey 1985:1247, n. 114; Spangenberg and Walsh 1989:50).

As noted in other chapters of this book, the most striking difference between a capital trial and trials for other serious felonies is that capital trials are bifurcated or divided into two separate stages: a guilt phase and a penalty phase. In bifurcated trials, all of the expenses of the guilt phase can possibly be

---

6. In some cases, the threat of the death penalty may encourage guilty pleas; thus, providing substantial cost savings in comparison to capital cases that go to trial. However, the death penalty is not often used in that way (Brooks and Erickson 1996:890–891). In some jurisdictions district attorneys are prohibited by statute to plea bargain in first degree murder cases (Cook and Slawson 1993:2). If capital punishment were replaced with LWOP, on the other hand, it is unlikely that defendants would plead guilty to LWOP (what would they have to lose if they went to trial?). Consequently, in jurisdictions that provide for both capital punishment and LWOP sentences, the availability of capital punishment, as at least a threat, may sometimes reduce costs.

duplicated in the penalty phase (Brooks and Erickson 1996:897; Spangenberg and Walsh 1989:52). An average capital trial in California in 1983 was about 3.5 times or 30 days longer than an average noncapital murder trial, which required approximately 12 days (Garey 1985:1258 and 1258, n. 175). The average death penalty trial in Texas in 1992 lasted 14 weeks and cost $265,640 (Hoppe 1992). (Specific trial expenses, when available, are identified below.) The average death penalty trial in North Carolina in 1991–92 cost $84,099 and lasted 14.6 days (Cook and Slawson 1993:59 and 61, Tables 6.2 and 6.3). In North Carolina, the cost of death penalty trials ranged from a low of $24,777 to a high of $179,736 (Cook and Slawson 1993:59, Table 6.2). By contrast, the average noncapital murder trial in North Carolina cost $16,697 and lasted 3.8 days (Cook and Slawson 1993:59 and 61, Tables 6.2 and 6.3). The cost of noncapital murder trials in North Carolina ranged from a low of $7,766 to a high of $30,952 (Cook and Slawson 1993:59, Table 6.2).

In North Carolina, the guilt phase of the bifurcated capital trial was considerably more expensive than the penalty phase. The costs of only the guilt phase ranged from $9,802 to $137,500; the average guilt phase cost $52,290 and lasted 10.6 days (Cook and Slawson 1993:59 and 61, Tables 6.2 and 6.3). The guilt phase, in other words, accounted for about 62 percent of the costs and 73 percent of the time spent on the entire trial. The cost of a capital trial's guilt phase in North Carolina may be atypical, however. Paternoster (1991:198) claims that the penalty phase, and not the guilt phase, is "the single greatest cost inflator of a capital trial" (also see Garey 1985:1259). He explains that in most capital trials the prosecutor's overwhelming evidence makes the defendant's guilt obvious, so there is little to contest. Consequently, defense counsel focuses on saving his or her client's life in the penalty phase of the trial. To aid the effort, as noted previously, counsel is allowed to present mitigating evidence on his or her client's behalf, which requires a considerable, but unknown amount of time.

Among the specific costs of the guilt phase of a capital trial are voir dire, attorney hours, expert testimony, witnesses, and court costs. Most of those expenses involve payments for time expended on the case. Many prosecutors and defense attorneys believe that jury selection is the key element in a capital case. As an Erie County, New York district attorney observed, "All you have to do is find one person that doesn't want to go for the death penalty, and you've defeated it" (see "Death Penalty Expenses Adding Up" 1999). It is estimated that voir dire during the selection of the jury takes approximately five times longer in capital cases than in other felony cases (Garey 1985:1257; Spangenberg and Walsh 1989:52) and may increase the cost of the capital trial by nearly $90,000 (in 1985) (Garey 1985:1257). Jury selection in capital cases typically takes six weeks to complete (Brooks and Erickson 1996:896, n. 134). In two recent capital cases in New York, jury selection took ten weeks in the first case and seven weeks in the second case ("Death Penalty Expenses Adding Up" 1999). The average cost of empaneling a jury in capital cases in Texas in 1992 was $17,220 (Hoppe 1992). A survey of 20 California capital murder trials conducted in the early 1980s found that jury selection was the most expensive part of a capital trial (Kaplan 1983:571).

A major reason voir dire in capital cases is so costly is that many death penalty jurisdictions require that jurors not only be questioned individually, but that they also remain sequestered until the full jury is selected or they are dismissed (Garey 1985:1255; Spangenberg and Walsh 1989:51). Many jurisdictions allow defendants to waive this requirement. Although data on the frequency of such waivers are not available, they are probably not requested very often. Among other reasons why voir dire in capital cases takes longer and is more expensive are: (1) the increased number of peremptory challenges allowed in capital cases (Garey 1985:1256; Spangenberg and Walsh 1989:52), (2) the increased number of jurors who are likely to be dismissed for cause (Garey 1985:1256), (3) the increased number of jurors who try to disqualify themselves (Garey 1985:1257, n. 173), and (4) in some jurisdictions, the need to select jurors for both the guilt and penalty phase of the trial (Brooks and Erickson 1996:897; Garey 1985:1257, n. 173; Spangenberg and Walsh 1989:52).

Many states require that capital defendants have two attorneys; no state requires two attorneys in noncapital cases (Cook and Slawson 1993:15; Spangenberg and Walsh 1989:54). Attorneys can spend from nearly 300 to 1,000 hours on capital cases (Spangenberg and Walsh 1989:53). In North Carolina in 1991–92, for example, defense attorneys and prosecutors spent an average of 613 and 282 hours, respectively, on capital cases (Cook and Slawson 1993:61, Table 6.3). By contrast, they spent an average of 150 and 61 hours, respectively, on noncapital cases (Cook and Slawson 1993:61, Table 6.3).

Public defenders in North Carolina were paid an average of $68.31 an hour; assistant public defenders received an average of $48.34 an hour (Cook and Slawson 1993:44, Table 5.3). District Attorneys, on the other hand, were paid an average of $83.10 an hour; assistant district attorneys received an average of $55.63 an hour (Cook and Slawson 1993:44, Table 5.3). Based on those hourly rates, the average cost of a public defender in North Carolina capital cases in 1991–92 was about $42,000 per case; the average cost of an assistant district attorney (assuming most capital cases are handled by ADAs) was about $16,000 per case (it would be about $23,000 if handled by a DA).[7]

---

7. Although the hourly costs of district attorneys, public defenders, judges and others are usually "fixed" (because they receive salaries), and would be the same whether the case was capital or noncapital, the costs of those participants in the process are provided for two reasons. First is to allow the reader to gauge the costs of a capital case (or any case) that goes to trial (and is further reviewed) in comparison to the costs of a capital case that is plea bargained to LWOP. Second is to help in the estimation of some of the "hidden costs" of capital punishment. When district attorneys spend much of their time trying capital cases, when court time is consumed with

The cost of defense counsel through sentencing in Maryland in 1982 was estimated to range from $50,000 to $75,000 per capital case (Garey 1985:1258). In 1993, the Connecticut Public Defender's Office spent $138 to defend an average noncapital case (this included plea bargains) and approximately $200,000 to defend each death penalty case (Brooks and Erickson 1996:892). Private defense fees in a recent California capital trial involving three defendants cost the state $1.1 million (Brooks and Erickson 1996:894). Florida increased its fees for appointed defense attorneys in capital cases in January 1998. The hourly rate for the lead attorney was raised from $50 to $120, while assisting attorneys may receive as much as $100 an hour (Clary 2001). From 1995 through 1999, the New York Capital Defender's Office spent more than $34 million on 37 defendants charged with capital crimes. The costs included the Defender Office's annual budget and money paid to court-appointed defense attorneys, defense investigators, and defense experts. For fiscal year 1999, $14.75 million was allocated for capital defense costs. In two recent capital cases in New York, defense expenditures were nearly $600,000 and $900,000, respectively. The district attorneys in those cases spent nearly $800,000 and $750,000, respectively ("Death Penalty Expenses Adding Up" 1999). The federal government spent $13.8 million in public funds to hire private attorneys and cover other costs to defend Timothy McVeigh ("McVeigh Defense: $13.8 Million" 2001).

The hourly or daily rates of expert witnesses for in-court testimony were described previously and are not repeated here.

A larger number of witnesses usually are called in capital trials. Those witnesses must be interviewed, their testimony must be prepared, and they must be deposed by the other side. All of this requires considerable attorney time. Total costs for two defense attorneys, three prosecutors, investigators, and expert witnesses in capital cases in Texas in 1992 averaged $150,452 ($112,400 for the two defense attorneys, investigators, and expert witnesses, and $38,052 for the three prosecutors) (Hoppe 1992).

Court costs are estimated to be 3.5 times greater in capital cases than they are in other felony cases (Garey 1985:1258; Spangenberg and Walsh 1989:53). In North Carolina in 1991–92, for example, superior court judges were paid an average of $631 a day; court reporters were paid an average of $191 a day; deputy court clerks were paid an average of $146 a day; and bailiffs were paid an average of $125 a day (Cook and Slawson 1993:46, Table 5.4). Two bailiffs were generally assigned to each capital trial (Cook and Slawson 1993:45). In Texas in 1992, the average cost per judge in a capital case was $23,968 (Hoppe

---

lengthy death trials, and when appellate courts spend so much of their time reviewing death penalty appeals, other, noncapital cases are affected. For example, other serious cases receive less attention than they would otherwise, or cases that ordinarily would be tried are plea bargained, simply because there is not enough time to do otherwise.

1992). Additionally, courtroom space in North Carolina was estimated to cost $174 a day (Cook and Slawson 1993:46). In sum, the total per day cost of a capital trial in a North Carolina Superior Court in 1991–92 was estimated to be $1,416 (Cook and Slawson 1993:46); the cost of a capital trial per day in California in 1983 was approximately $2,186, not including extra security or transcript costs (Garey 1985:1255). In 1999, a criminal court case in New York City cost about $3,800 per day. At that rate, court costs in two death penalty cases in Queens totaled approximately $725,000. In Suffolk County, where the daily rate was $3,556, the court costs in one capital case were almost $650,000 ("Death Penalty Expenses Adding Up" 1999).[8]

As mentioned above, all of the expenses of the guilt phase could be duplicated in the penalty phase. At a minimum, the penalty phase will require additional expenditures for attorney time, expert testimony, witnesses, and court costs (Spangenberg and Walsh 1989:52). In some jurisdictions separate juries are sometimes required for the penalty phase of a capital trial, in which case the costs of voir dire also could be duplicated.

Capital trials can force local governments to make difficult choices. For example, a recent study in Illinois found that capital trials could increase county spending by as much as 1.8 percent per trial. Such trials are often financed through increased property taxes or funds taken from police and highway appropriations (cited in Governor's Commission on Capital Punishment 2002:199). A *Wall Street Journal* article reported that the Texas county where the three men convicted of the 1998 murder of James Byrd were tried was forced to raise property taxes 6.7 percent for two years to cover trial costs (cited in Governor's Commission on Capital Punishment 2002:199). In some death-eligible cases, prosecutors forego capital trials altogether rather than incur the expense.

The Posttrial Stage

The posttrial stage generally is the most expensive part of the entire process (Paternoster 1991:212). Automatic appeal of conviction and/or death sentence to the state supreme court is required in nearly all jurisdictions with capital punishment statutes (Spangenberg and Walsh 1989:52).[9] If the appellant wins,

---

8. See note 7 above.

9. At yearend 2000, the Federal Government was the only exception. In South Carolina, the defendant, if deemed competent, may waive right of sentence review. Idaho, Indiana, Kentucky, Oklahoma, and Tennessee only require review of the sentence. Review of conviction in Idaho has to be filed through appeal or forfeited. Review of conviction can be waived in Indiana and Kentucky. An appeal of trial court error may be waived in Virginia but not a review of sentence for arbitrariness and proportionality. The right to waive an automatic review has not been

the costs of the original trial, or at least part of those costs, could be replicated at the retrial or resentencing (Brooks and Erickson 1996:897–898; Spangenberg and Walsh 1989:53).

It is estimated that a typical capital appeal requires from 500 to 2,000 hours of attorney time, not including travel, photocopying, and other obligations. (Garey 1985:1263; Paternoster 1991:205; Spangenberg and Walsh 1989:52–53). In North Carolina in 1991–92, appellate defenders received an average of $61.89 an hour; assistant appellate defenders were paid an average of $43.80 an hour (Cook and Slawson 1993:48, Table 5.6). Appointed appellate defense attorneys in California received an average of $60 per hour in 1985 (Garey 1985:1263). North Carolina Supreme Court justices were paid an average of $96.92 an hour, while their law clerks received an average of $28.02 an hour (Cook and Slawson 1993:47, Table 5.5). The average cost of a North Carolina Supreme Court justice for a capital appeal was estimated to be $1,887; the average cost of a court clerk was $2,083 (Cook and Slawson 1993:79, Table 7.5). The average cost of the North Carolina Attorney General for a capital appeal was estimated to be $5,261 (Cook and Slawson 1993:79, Table 7.5).[10]

Although the Supreme Court does not require it (see *Pulley v. Harris* 1984), some states also provide proportionality review. Proportionality review is a process whereby state appellate courts compare the sentence in the case before it with sentences imposed in similar cases in the state (see, for example, Paternoster 1991:81–82). Its purpose is to identify disparities in sentencing. To perform proportionality review, data must be gathered and analyzed and a report must be written. The costs of proportionality review have not been estimated.

Besides the automatic appellate review, capital defendants may contest their conviction and/or sentence through both state and federal post-conviction proceedings. Including the automatic appeal, there are at least nine or ten possible levels of review following the guilt and penalty phase of a capital trial (Freedman 2003; Garey 1985:1263).[11] In Texas in 1992, the average cost of the state post-conviction process for capital cases was $94,240 (Hoppe 1992). The biggest expense was for attorney time. Although the U.S. Constitution does not require the appointment of attorneys for indigent capital defendants beyond the automatic appeal, that is, for state post-conviction collateral review (see *Murray v. Giarratano* 1989), many jurisdictions provide them anyway (Spangenberg and Walsh 1989:54). It has been estimated that attorneys spend

---

addressed in Mississippi. Neither statute nor case law precludes a waiver of appeal in Wyoming (Snell 2001:3).

10. See note 7 above.

11. See Figure 1 in Freedman (2003) for an illustration of the typical state and federal trial and post-conviction procedure.

an average of 700 to 1,000 hours on state post-conviction proceedings in capital cases (Spangenberg and Walsh 1989:55 for both state and federal post-conviction proceedings). A 1986 American Bar Association survey, for example, found that lawyers spent an average of 963 hours on state post-conviction appeals (Paternoster 1991:205). According to Hoppe (1992), specific cost averages in Texas were as follows: (1) defense costs = $15,000; (2) prosecution costs = $29,000; (3) cost of reproducing the trial record[12] = $20,000; and (4) court of criminal appeals (three-day estimate) = $30,240.

The cost of state post-conviction proceedings in two North Carolina cases was considerably higher—$293,393 and $216,387 per case (Cook and Slawson 1993:81–82, Tables 7.6 and 7.7)—although that may be due to the inclusion of stages, such as clemency/commutation proceedings, not included in the Texas costs. Specific costs in the more expensive North Carolina case included the following (years in which expenses were incurred are in parentheses): (1) state motion for appropriate relief = $29,957 (1985–87); (2) petition for certiorari to North Carolina Supreme Court = $6,188 (1987–88); (3) state motion hearing = $2,057 (1988); (4) motion for stay of execution in North Carolina Supreme Court = $833 (1989); (5) motions in North Carolina Supreme Court = $3,642 (1990); (6) motions in North Carolina Superior Court = $115,247 (1991); and (7) clemency/commutation proceedings = $84,888 (1991–92) (Cook and Slawson 1993:81, Table 7.6).

Federal post-conviction proceedings for Texas capital appellants averaged six years and cost about $1.7 million per appellant (Hoppe 1992). Unlike the situation for state post-conviction proceedings, the federal government requires legal representation for capital defendants pursuing federal habeas corpus appeals (21 U.S.C. §848 (q)(4), 1994; also see Howard 1996). The federal courts have/had three options in meeting this statutory requirement (see Howard 1996:903). First, they may appoint attorneys from the private bar. Those attorneys submit vouchers for payment to the Administrative Office of the United States Courts which allocates funds according to provisions in the Criminal Justice Act (18 U.S.C.§3006A, 1994). Although the Act does not prescribe any limitation on the amount that can be paid for services, in *In re Berger* (1991), the Court limited appointed counsel representing capital defendants before the Supreme Court to $5,000 in fees. A second option is to appoint attorneys employed by federal public defender organizations which are funded through grants made available by the Judicial Conference of the United States (18 U.S.C. §3006A(g)(2)(A), 1994; 28 U.S.C. §605, 1994). A problem

---

12. In 1981, it was estimated that the typical trial record in a capital case in California was 4,000 pages or more, while the opening brief averaged about 200 pages (Garey 1985:1263, n. 217). The cost for preparing 24 copies of the 22,000-page transcript of a 1999 capital trial in New York was $44,478.28 ("Death Penalty Expenses Adding Up" 1999).

with these first two options is that neither one guarantees the appointment of attorneys with expertise in capital jurisprudence (Howard 1996:903).

The third and best option (for capital defendants) is/was the appointment of attorneys employed by Post-Conviction Defender Organizations (PCDOs), which were originally called Death Penalty Resource Centers. Those agencies were created by Congress in 1988 and dealt only with capital cases and related post-conviction issues. They employed full-time, salaried attorneys, investigators, and support staff and operated in 20 of the 38 death penalty states (Howard 1996:904). The Judicial Conference funded PCDOs through grants that are contingent upon the receipt of state funding for any state court work PCDOs did. In fiscal year 1994, the 20 PCDOs received nearly $20 million for their work on capital cases (Howard 1996:904).

Because of the success of PCDO attorneys in getting convictions and death sentences overturned, the agencies have come under fire from death penalty proponents. It appears, moreover, that critics of the PCDOs have won the day. On January 6, 1996, President Clinton signed into law HR-1358 (Pub. L. No. 104–91, 110 Stat. 7). The law provided a budget of approximately $262 million for the Federal Judiciary's Defender Services but stipulated that none of the money was to be spent on PCDOs after April 1, 1996—to allow for an orderly end to the program (Howard 1996:914). After the 1996 fiscal year ended on September 30, no further federal funding of the PCDOs was to be provided (Howard 1996:914).

With the demise of PCDOs, the federal courts will be left with only the first two options of providing attorneys for capital defendants pursuing federal habeas corpus relief. The debate in Congress suggested that the abolition of PCDOs would save the government about $20 million annually (Howard 1996:915). However, Richard Arnold, Chief Judge of the U.S. Court of Appeals for the Eighth Circuit disagrees. He predicts "that elimination of the PCDOs will significantly increase delays in handling an ever-increasing death penalty caseload by creating an insufficient pool of qualified and experienced attorneys to handle the petitions" (Howard 1996:915). He estimates that "the cost of representing death row inmates would rise from the current expenditure of $21.2 million to 'between $37 million and $51.1 million' with the elimination of the PCDOs" (Howard 1996:915).

In any event, it has been estimated that attorneys in capital cases spend an average of 700 to more than 1,000 hours on federal post-conviction proceedings (Spangenberg and Walsh 1989:55 for both state and federal post-conviction proceedings). The 1986 American Bar Association survey, for example, found that lawyers spent an average of 1,037 hours on federal post-conviction litigation (Paternoster 1991:205). In Texas, defense attorneys received an average of $92,300 for their federal post-conviction work in capital cases, while it cost the Texas Attorney General's office an average of $19,600 per capital case challenged on federal habeas corpus (Hoppe 1992). The remainder of the estimated $1.7 million per federal post-conviction capital case went for court costs and outlays (Hoppe 1992).

Cost estimates by Cook and Slawson (1993:81, Table 7.6) of federal post-conviction proceedings for North Carolina capital prisoners included the following (years on which estimates are based are in parentheses): (1) certiorari petition to the U.S. Supreme Court = $7,885 (1984); motion for stay of execution in the federal district court = $757 (1989); (3) federal district court habeas proceedings = $17,383 (1989–90); and (4) federal appellate proceedings = $24,556 (1990–92).

Imprisonment

Under current practices, convicted capital offenders serve a long prison term on death row (now averaging more than 10 years) in addition to being sentenced to death.[13] Put somewhat differently, because of "super due process" protections, capital offenders typically serve more than 20 percent of what otherwise might be a "50 year" LWOP sentence before they are executed.

Due to added security precautions, including single cell confinement, it almost certainly is more expensive to house inmates on death row than to confine them with the general population in a maximum security prison (see Spangenberg and Walsh 1989:56). The available evidence, however, suggests that the difference in the annual costs of confinement is not great—approximately $1,000–$2,000 per inmate (see Brooks and Erickson 1996:883).[14] An additional and unique cost of confinement for death row inmates involves the death watch—the period just before the execution (see Gillespie 2003:45–50; Johnson 1990:Chap. 6). The extra costs of the death watch have not been estimated.

Executions

Executions, themselves, are relatively inexpensive. Regardless of the method employed, it is relatively cheap to put people to death. For example, the electricity needed for an electrocution is estimated to cost about 31 cents; the sodium cyanide pellets used in executions by lethal gas cost about $250; and the chemicals needed for a lethal injection cost anywhere from $71.50 to

---

13. Some death row inmates have served more than twenty years awaiting execution. For a description of the "living hell" that death row inmates experience, see Johnson (1990, 1989) and Gillespie (2003).

14. In 1999, the annual cost of incarcerating an inmate on death row in New York State was $44,000 ("Death Penalty Expenses Adding Up" 1999).

$600 or $700 (Denno 1994:655). The costs of the bullets and rope used in shooting and hanging executions have not been reported but must be minimal. The costs of the execution apparatuses also vary considerably and are not very expensive when averaged over a large number of executions. For example, the cost of an electrocution system is about $35,000; the cost of a gallows is about $85,000; the cost of a gas chamber is about $200,000; and the cost of a lethal injection system is around $30,000 (Denno 1994:655).[15] The aforementioned costs do not include payments to the "execution technicians," which may range from $150 to $500 per execution (Denno 1994:655, n. 705).

One last cost of capital punishment involves disposal of the body—a potential cost for any inmate who dies in prison. If the family of the executed offender does not make final arrangements, burial or cremation is left to the state. This final cost has not been estimated, but it is unlikely to be very expensive.[16]

The Future: Streamlining the Appellate and Post-Conviction Process, the Costs of Mistakes, "Start-Up" Costs, and the LWOP Alternative

Streamlining the Appellate and Post-Conviction Process

Proponents of capital punishment argue that the costs of the penalty could be reduced significantly if the appellate and post-conviction process were streamlined. They contend that most of the legal challenges filed by death row inmates or their attorneys are without merit—that they are nothing more than desperate attempts to keep the inmate alive. It is true that, until recently, it was possible for death row inmates to employ the dual system of collateral review numerous times, but it is no longer the case. Beginning in the 1980s, the Supreme Court began placing restrictions on the federal review process in state capital cases (see, for example, *Barefoot v. Estelle* 1983; *Clemons v. Mississippi* 1990; *Saffle v. Parks* 1990).

---

15. Denno (1994:655) notes that before 1990 states were increasingly buying "execution trailers" costing $100,000. The trailers included "a lethal-injection machine, a steel holding cell for the prisoner, and additional areas for witnesses, the chaplain, prison employees, and medical personnel."

16. This chapter's author called a local funeral home in Orlando, Florida, to get estimates. He was told that the least expensive cremation would cost about $1,400, while the least expensive burial would cost about $5,000.

In addition, the passage of the Antiterrorism and Effective Death Penalty Act of 1996 (AEDPA) and similar measures by state legislatures has made access to both the federal and state courts during the post-conviction process more difficult. The AEDPA, for example, requires that second or subsequent habeas petitions be dismissed when the claim had already been made in a previous petition. It also requires that claims involving alleged denials of rights that were not recognized before the offender's state appeals be dismissed, unless the Supreme Court announces a new rule of constitutional law and makes it retroactive to cases on collateral review. Under the Act, the only other way the federal courts will hear a claim not considered by the state courts is when the claim is based on new evidence not previously available. Even then, the new evidence must be of sufficient weight, by a clear and convincing standard of proof, to convince a judge that the capital defendant was not guilty of the crime or crimes for which he or she was convicted.

The Act also made the federal appellate courts "gatekeepers" for second or subsequent habeas corpus petitions. Thus, to file a second or subsequent claim under the new law, a capital defendant must first file a motion in the appropriate appellate court announcing his or her intention. The motion must then be heard by a panel of three judges within thirty days. The judges must decide whether the petitioner has a legitimate claim under the new Act. If the claim is denied, the new law prohibits any review of the panel's decision, either by a rehearing or writ of certiorari to the Supreme Court. So far, the Supreme Court has upheld the constitutionality of the new law (see *Felker v. Turpin* 1996).[17]

The evidence, moreover, shows that many of the habeas corpus petitions filed by death row inmates or their attorneys have merit. At least 32 percent and as many as 68 percent of all convictions or sentences in death penalty cases from 1973 through 2000 have been overturned on appeal.[18] These reversals have resulted from fundamental constitutional errors such as coerced confessions; ineffective assistance of counsel; denial of the right of an impartial jury; prosecutors withholding exculpatory evidence, suborning perjury, and use of tainted evidence; and unconstitutional jury instructions (Liebman et al. 2000; Paternoster 1991:208–209; Scheck, Neufeld, and Dwyer 2001). The percentage of death penalty cases overturned by the appellate courts since the reestablishment of capital punishment has far exceeded the percentage of appellate rever-

---

17. Although the recent restrictions on federal habeas corpus in capital cases may reduce costs at the federal level, they may not reduce costs overall. Costs likely will be shifted to the states and counties where post-conviction motions in state courts will be litigated more extensively (Brooks and Erickson 1996:900 and 902).

18. Approximately 7,000 death sentences were imposed in the United States from 1973 through 2000 (see Snell 2001:15, Appendix table 3 for the lower figure, and Liebman et al. 2000, for the higher figure).

sals of all other noncapital felony cases—in most states, this probably does not exceed one percent (White 1987:10).

In sum, despite a very elaborate process that includes "guided discretion" statutes and bifurcated trials, a large number of convictions and/or sentences in death penalty cases are reversed on appeal or during post-conviction review—a reversal rate many times higher than in noncapital cases. The errors that are discovered, moreover, are not insignificant "legal technicalities," but are the result of violations of fundamental constitutional protections. Under such circumstances, a likely result of restricting the access of death row inmates to judicial review of their cases is miscarriages of justice. In other words, without the ability to challenge arrests, charges, indictments, convictions, sentences, and pending executions in the courts, there likely will be an increase in the number of innocent people, or people not legally eligible for execution, involved in the capital punishment process. The subject of miscarriages of justice in capital cases is examined in detail by Radelet and Bedau (2003).

The Costs of Mistakes

Mistakes made in capital cases can add another monetary cost to the process. For example, Freddie Lee Pitts and Wilbert Lee were pardoned in Florida in 1975 after spending 12 years apiece on death row for a murder that somebody else committed (Amsterdam 1982:349). In 1997, after years of failed efforts, Pitts and Lee received a few hundred thousand dollars each as compensation from the state for its mistakes. Bobby Joe Leaster, received a check from Massachusetts for $75,000 in 1992. The money was the first installment of the $1 million annuity the state will pay him for wrongly imprisoning him for 15 years for a murder he did not commit (*The Charlotte Observer* November 13, 1992). Leaster was released from prison in 1986 after prosecutors declined to pursue a retrial. Because of the state's fiscal problems, it took several attempts before Massachusett's legislators approved the indemnification measure. The Ford Heights Four won a $36 million settlement from the Illinois county that wrongfully convicted them. They had spent 18 years in prison before DNA tests exonerated them in 1996 (Cohen 1999).

Sixteen states and the federal government have statutory provisions for indemnifying the wrongly convicted (in capital and non-capital cases). Most of those states are far from generous. For example, in California maximum compensation is $10,000 regardless of the length of prison sentence served. In other words, if a California death row inmate were exonerated after serving 20 years, which some death row inmates have served, then he would be compensated at a rate of $500 per year served. The federal government limits compensation to a maximum of $5,000 regardless of the amount of time served. Attorney expenses for preparing the necessary legal documents can take a third of the money. Getting the money from the state, even after it has been awarded, seldom is easy (Scheck et al. 2001:297–298). Nevertheless, mistakes made in capital cases can prove costly to the jurisdictions that make them.

"Start-Up" Costs

Another cost of capital punishment is the substantial "start-up" expense incurred when a jurisdiction decides to reinstate the death penalty. Those expenses are of three types: (1) building and facility costs, (2) judicial and attorney training costs, and (3) equipment costs (see Brooks and Erickson 1996). Because the costs of execution equipment were described previously, only the first two types of "start-up" costs are examined here.

Building and facility costs vary greatly, but jurisdictions can expect to spend hundreds of thousands and, in some cases, millions of dollars to construct death rows and execution chambers. For example, in 1993, the Wisconsin Department of Corrections estimated that "a new twelve-unit death row, including a lethal injection death chamber" would cost $1.4 million to construct (Brooks and Erickson 1996:886). Additionally, an estimated $144,600 would have to be spent on one-time start-up overhead costs, and about $500,000 annually for security personnel (Brooks and Erickson 1996:886).

When New York reinstated the death penalty in 1995, the legislature appropriated a little more than one million dollars for "start-up" costs: $389,000 for a twelve-cell death row, $190,000 to convert an old correctional hospital into a three-cell death row for women, and $475,000 for a death chamber, injection room, and three holding cells (Brooks and Erickson 1996:886, n. 62). By contrast, Florida spent $9.5 million in 1992 to build a new 331-unit death row (Brooks and Erickson 1996:886). In 1996, the federal government spent half a million dollars to build a lethal injection chamber at the new federal death row in Terre Haute, Indiana (Brooks and Erickson 1996:886–887).

Because "death is different," special training is needed for judges and attorneys involved in death penalty cases. A few jurisdictions require such training. When the New York legislature reinstated capital punishment in 1995, it appropriated about $3.5 million for a new agency responsible for training capital defense attorneys; another approximately $2 million was earmarked for the training of capital prosecutors (Brooks and Erickson 1996:887). In the second year after the Kansas legislature reinstated the death penalty in 1994, it budgeted $1.4 million for a death penalty defense agency (Brooks and Erickson 1996:892). In 1995, the Wisconsin legislature contemplated the reenactment of capital punishment. It considered spending $60,000–$70,000 to bring in national experts for a one-time seminar to train 50–100 lawyers (Brooks and Erickson 1996:887). It also estimated that attorney and judicial training costs for the first two years after reenactment would be about $400,000 and then $200,000 annually, thereafter (Brooks and Erickson 1996:887). In short, attorney and judicial training in capital jurisprudence involves both substantial "start-up" costs and ongoing expenses to keep both lawyers and judges abreast of changes in capital punishment law.

The LWOP Alternative

Currently, 35 of 38 death penalty states plus the federal government and the U.S. military also have LWOP. The only death penalty states without it are Kansas, New Mexico, and Texas (Death Penalty Information Center 2002).[19] As of the mid-1990s, LWOP was the only alternative to capital punishment in 16 death penalty jurisdictions in the United States; in 12 jurisdictions, the alternative to capital punishment was either LWOP or a lesser punishment, usually life imprisonment with parole eligibility (Acker and Lanier 1995:55). For a variety of reasons, it is less costly to sentence capital offenders to LWOP than it is to sentence them to death—in some cases, as much as two and one-half to five times less costly on average (see the preceding discussion).

The greatest savings of LWOP sentences are achieved when they are imposed following a guilty plea (but see note 6 above). In such cases, the bifurcated trial, the automatic appeal, and post-conviction processes are eliminated. As described previously, the costs of those stages in capital cases are substantial because "death is different" and "super due process" must be provided to capital defendants.

Even if LWOP sentences were imposed after trial (and post-conviction review), they would still be cheaper than capital punishment because the Supreme Court has ruled that LWOP sentences do not require the "super due process" procedures necessary when the penalty is death (*Harmelin v. Michigan* 1991; Paternoster, 1991:279). Thus, the replacement of death sentences with sentences to LWOP would reduce financial expenditures considerably.

Critics fear that such a strategy would have the undesirable effect of exacerbating the current prison overcrowding crisis. However, this has not been a problem for states with LWOP statutes. For example, less than 2 percent of Alabama and Kentucky prison inmates are serving LWOP sentences (Paternoster, 1991:280). Although that percentage would likely increase if all death sentences were replaced with LWOP, the increase would be small. If their sentences were changed to LWOP, the 200 to 300 offenders sentenced to death each year, together with the approximately 3,700 current death row inmates, would hardly be noticed among the more than one million inmates now confined in American prisons (but see note 3 above regarding the added costs of elderly inmates).

---

19. In addition, 11 of 12 states without the death penalty plus the District of Columbia have LWOP. Alaska is the only state without the death penalty not to have LWOP (Death Penalty Information Center 2002).

Another concern with replacing capital punishment with LWOP is the continuing threat capital offenders might pose in prison, or if they were released through error or oversight. Although such a concern is important in the death penalty debate, it does not directly bear upon the financial costs of the penalty and, thus, is not discussed here.[20]

In sum, death sentences could be replaced with LWOP at considerable cost savings to the taxpayer, with negligible impact on the current prison overcrowding crisis. LWOP sentences would also allow for the correction of miscarriages of justice when they were discovered and would eliminate any brutalizing effect of capital punishment[21]. North Carolina recently passed legislation that allows prosecutors to offer capital defendants the chance to plead guilty and accept an LWOP sentence (The Death Penalty Information Center 2002). Prosecutors previously did not have that option. The legislation likely will save the state millions of dollars by eliminating the costs of a capital trial and appellate and post-conviction review. Whether such a strategy is desirable for other reasons is another matter.

Conclusion

The evidence clearly shows that capital punishment systems in the United States are always more expensive than punishment systems without capital punishment because "super due process" is required in the former but not in the latter. As discussed in other chapters of this book, there are a variety of reasons given for supporting or opposing capital punishment. If the ultimate penal sanction is supported because of the belief that it is cheaper than noncapital punishments, this chapter establishes why such a belief is mistaken. Thus, a fair question in the capital punishment debate is whether the death penalty is worth the extra cost.

References

Acker, J. R. and C. S. Lanier (1995) "Matters of Life or Death: The Sentencing Provisions in Capital Punishment Statutes." *Criminal Law Bulletin* 31:19–60.

---

20. A recent study found that capital murderers sentenced to LWOP were no greater threat to other prisoners or correctional staff than death-sentenced inmates or other murderers sentenced to terms of imprisonment (Sorensen and Wrinkle 1996).

21. The brutalizing or counterdeterrent effect refers to the process by which the death penalty causes or provokes murders rather than deterring them (see Bowers 1988:57–61; 1984:273–274; Sellin 1959:65–69).

Amsterdam, A. G. (1982) "Capital Punishment." Pp. 346–358 in H. A. Bedau (ed.) *The Death Penalty in America*, Third Ed. New York: Oxford University Press.

Barefoot v. Estelle (1983) 463 U.S. 880.

Bedau, H. A. (1987) *Death is Different: Studies in the Morality, Law, and Politics of Capital Punishment.* Boston: Northeastern University Press.

Bohm, R. M. (2003) "American Death Penalty Opinion: Past, Present, and Future." (This volume).

Bohm, R. M. and K. N. Haley (2002) *Introduction to Criminal Justice*, 3rd Ed. Woodland Hills, CA: Glencoe/McGraw-Hill.

Bowers, W. J. (1988) "The Effect of Executions is Brutalization, Not Deterrence." Pp. 49–89 in K. C. Haas and J. A. Inciardi (eds.) *Challenging Capital Punishment: Legal and Social Science Approaches.* Newbury Park, CA: Sage.

Bowers, W. J. with G. L. Pierce and J. F. McDevitt (1984) *Legal Homicide: Death as Punishment in America, 1864–1982.* Boston: Northeastern University Press.

Brooks, J. and J. H. Erickson (1996) "The Dire Wolf Collects His Due While the Boys Sit by the Fire: Why Michigan Cannot Afford to Buy into the Death Penalty." *Thomas M. Cooley Law Review* 13:877–905.

Clary, S. (2001) "Killer's Defense Cost Will Set Record." *The Orlando Sentinel* (December 1), p. C1.

Clemons v. Mississippi (1990) 494 U.S. 738.

Cohen, S. (1999) "Mistakes Refocus Death-Penalty Debate." *The Orlando Sentinel* (August 15), p. A-4.

Cook, P. J. and D. B. Slawson with L. A. Gries (1993) *The Costs of Processing Murder Cases in North Carolina.* Raleigh, NC: North Carolina Administrative Office of the Courts.

Culver, J. H. (1985) "The States and Capital Punishment: Executions from 1977–1984." *Justice Quarterly* 2:567–578.

"Death Penalty Expenses Adding Up" (1999) *New York Daily News* (October 20) at www.th-record.com/1999/10/20/executio.htm.

Death Penalty Information Center (2002) www.deathpenaltyinfo.org/lwop.html.

Denno, D. W. (1994) "Is Electrocution an Unconstitutional Method of Execution? The Engineering of Death over the Century." *William and Mary Law Review* 35:551–692.

Felker v. Turpin (1996) 116 S.Ct. 2333.

Freedman, E. M. (2003) "Federal Habeas Corpus in Capital Cases." (This volume).

Furman v. Georgia (1972) 408 U.S. 238.

Gardner v. Florida (1977) 430 U.S. 349.

Garey, M. (1985) "The Cost of Taking a Life: Dollars and Sense of the Death Penalty." *University of California Davis Law Review* 18:1221–1273.

Gillespie, L. K. (2003) *Inside the Death Chamber: Exploring Executions.* Boston: Allyn and Bacon.

Governor's Commission on Capital Punishment (2002) State of Illinois. www.idoc.state.il.us/ccp/ccp/reports/commission_reports.html.

Gregg v. Georgia (1976) 428 U.S. 153.

Harmelin v. Michigan (1991) 501 U.S. 957.

Hoppe, C. (1992) "Life in Jail, or Death? Life Term is Cheaper." *The Charlotte [North Carolina] Observer* (March 22), p. 12A.

Howard, Jr., R. C. (1996) "The Defunding of the Post Conviction Defense Organizations as a Denial of the Right to Counsel." *West Virginia Law Review* 98:863–921.

In re Berger (1991) 498 U.S. 233.

Johnson, R. (1990) *Death Work: A Study of the Modern Execution Process.* Pacific Grove, CA: Brooks/Cole.

Johnson, R. (1989) *Condemned to Die: Life Under Sentence of Death.* Prospect Heights, IL: Waveland.

Jones, J. M. (2001) "Two-Thirds of Americans Support the Death Penalty." The Gallup Organization. www.gallup.com/poll/releases/pr010302.asp

Kaplan, J. (1983) "The Problem of Capital Punishment." *University of Illinois Law Review* 3:555–577.

Liebman, J. S., J. Fagan, and V. West (2000) "A Broken System: Error Rates in Capital Cases, 1973–1995." The Justice Project, www.justice.policy.net/jpreport.html

Lockett v. Ohio (1978) 438 U.S. 586.

McGovern, J. R. (1982) *Anatomy of a Lynching: The Killing of Claude Neal.* Baton Rouge: Louisiana State University Press.

"McVeigh Defense: $13.8 Million." (2001). *The Orlando Sentinel* (June 30), p. A17.

Michel, L. and D. Herbeck (2001) *American Terrorist: Timothy McVeigh & the Oklahoma City Bombing.* New York: Regan Books.

Murray v. Giarratano (1989) 492 U.S. 1.

Muwakkil, S. (1989) "The Death Penalty and the Illusion of Justice." *In These Times*, Vol. 13, No. 26 (May 24–June 6):6.

New York State Defenders Association (1982) *Capital Losses: The Price of the Death Penalty for New York State.* Albany, NY: New York State Defenders Association, Inc.

Paternoster, R. (1991) *Capital Punishment in America.* New York: Lexington.

Peterson, R. D. and W. C. Bailey (2003) "Is Capital Punishment an Effective Deterrent for Murder? An Examination of Social Science Research." (This volume).

Pulley v. Harris (1984) 465 U.S. 37.

Radin, M. J. (1980) "Cruel Punishment and Respect for Persons: Super Due Process for Death." *Southern California Law Review* 53:1143–1185.

Saffle v. Parks (1990) 494 U.S. 484.

Scheck, B., P. Neufeld, and J. Dwyer (2001) *Actual Innocence: When Justice Goes Wrong and How to Make It Right.* New York: Penguin Putnam.

Sellin, T. (1959) *The Death Penalty.* Philadelphia: The American Law Institute.

Snell, T. L. (2001) "Capital Punishment 2000." Bureau of Justice Statistics Bulletin (December). Washington, D.C.: U.S. Department of Justice.

Sorensen, J. and R. D. Wrinkle (1996) "No Hope for Parole: Disciplinary Infractions Among Death-Sentenced and Life-Without-Parole Inmates." *Criminal Justice and Behavior* 23:542–552.

Spangenberg, R. L. and E. R. Walsh (1989) "Capital Punishment or Life Imprisonment? Some Cost Considerations." *Loyola of Los Angeles Law Review* 23:45–58.

White, W. S. (1987) *The Death Penalty in the Eighties: An Examination of the Modern System of Capital Punishment.* Ann Arbor: University of Michigan Press.

Woodson v. North Carolina (1976) 428 U.S. 280.

Part V

Terminal Stages of the Penalty of Death

Chapter 19

"Above All, Do No Harm": The Role of Health and Mental Health Professionals in the Capital Punishment Process

Charles Patrick Ewing

By training, tradition and, in some cases, oath, health care providers (including mental health professionals) assume an ethical duty to enhance and maintain life whenever possible. For example, for centuries physicians have sworn to use their skills to help the sick and "above all, to do no harm" (Hippocrates c. 460–400 B.C.). Though not bound by the Hippocratic Oath, virtually all other health care and mental health care professionals have assumed a similar duty (Ewing 1987).

Until recently, there was little if any question that this duty existed or that it transcended virtually all competing social and legal concerns. Faced with the choice between terminating life and prolonging it, health care professionals routinely chose the latter course of action.

In recent times, the ethical duty to enhance and maintain life whenever possible has been strained by social and legal demands for the use of health care skills to terminate life. Physicians now routinely perform abortions, and at least some health care professionals actively (and in some cases publicly) engage in the practice of euthanasia. Though increasingly common, these activities remain controversial and continue to be the subject of lively ethical debate.

A third—and much less commonly considered—arena in which health care skills are currently being used to assist in the termination of life is capital punishment. This chapter examines the clash between professional ethics and the law when health care professionals actively participate in the death penalty process. Specifically, this chapter explores the ethics of health care professionals' involvement in state efforts to (1) secure a sentence of death; (2) assess and, where necessary, restore a death row inmate's competency to be executed; and (3) carry out a legally authorized execution.

Health Care Professionals and Capital Sentencing

Most of the expressed ethical concern about health care professionals participating in the death penalty process stems from their controversial involvement in the actual execution process. Much less attention has been paid to ethical issues which arise when health care professionals lend their expertise to the state earlier in the capital punishment process. Though the efforts of health care professionals at these earlier stages are less direct, they may be even more significant.

Current death penalty law in every American jurisdiction with such laws virtually guarantees that at least some health care professionals will be involved in the process by which the legal system decides whether to impose a sentence of death. For example, to be tried for capital murder, defendants must be competent to stand trial (i.e., capable of understanding the charges against them and assisting in their own defense). To convict a defendant of a capital crime, the trier of fact often must consider and reject one or more psychiatric defenses such as insanity or extreme emotional disturbance. Before sentencing a convicted capital defendant to death, the sentencing jury must weigh all mitigating evidence, including evidence regarding the defendant's psychological development and mental condition at the time of the offense. Generally, the jury may give such evidence whatever weight it deems appropriate, but a defendant found to be mentally retarded may not be sentenced to death. Finally, in some jurisdictions, the trier of fact must also weigh—and make a finding with regard to—specific aggravating evidence such as the convicted defendant's future dangerousness.

In each of these aspects of the capital sentencing process, health care professionals (usually psychologists and/or psychiatrists but sometimes other physicians as well) are called upon to evaluate the capital defendant and to present evidence which may help determine whether the defendant is sentenced to die.

Assessing Competency to Stand Trial

"Few principles are as firmly embedded in Anglo-American criminal jurisprudence as the doctrine that an 'incompetent' defendant may not be put to trial" (Perlin 1994:504). In *Dusky v. United States* (1960:402), the U.S. Supreme Court held that to be tried, a criminal defendant must have "sufficient present ability to consult with his lawyer with a reasonable degree of rational understanding" and a "rational as well as factual understanding of the proceedings against him."

Subsequently, in *Pate v. Robinson*(1966:385), the Court held that the due process clause requires a trial court to order an inquiry any time there is "bona fide doubt" as to a defendant's competency to stand trial. Finally, in *Drope v. Missouri* (1975:180) the Court ruled that there are "no fixed or immutable signs that invariably indicate the need for further inquiry to determine fitness to proceed...." To the contrary, "evidence of a defendant's irrational behavior, his demeanor at trial, and any prior medical opinion on competence to stand trial are all relevant in determining whether further inquiry is required" (p. 180).

As a practical matter, courts have almost universally read those cases along with relevant state laws to require that when there is doubt as to a defendant's fitness to proceed, that defendant is to be examined by one or more mental health professionals, who will report the results of the examination(s) to the court. In response, mental health professionals have developed numerous models and instruments specifically designed to assess competence to stand trial (see, e.g., Grisso 1988).

Although competency to stand trial is always an issue, and one that may be raised at any point in the proceedings by either side or *sua sponte* by the court, in the vast majority of criminal cases competency is never raised, much less formally evaluated. In the capital punishment context, however, competency to stand trial is frequently raised as a concern, and many if not most capital defendants are assessed for competency to stand trial.

In some of these cases, consideration of the competency issue reflects defense counsel's genuine concerns about issues of mental illness or mental retardation. In others, however, defense counsel's request for a competency evaluation may simply be *pro forma*, i.e., part of the standard procedure for insuring fairness and effective assistance of counsel in a capital case. On the other hand, a request for a competency evaluation may stem from judicial concern about the nature of the crime and possible punishment, or from the prosecution's desire to use the competency examination as a means of discovery.

Whatever its basis in fact, the competency examination will almost invariably be conducted by a licensed psychologist or psychiatrist. While the opinion of the mental health professional will not necessarily be dispositive, such opinions are generally given great weight and may, as a practical matter, be the deciding factor. Thus, for example, when a psychologist or psychiatrist examines a capital defendant and pronounces that defendant fit to proceed to trial, it might be argued that such professional has become an active participant in the capital punishment process.

The mental health expert who pronounces a capital defendant not competent to stand trial is also an active participant in the process, but his or her professional judgment will decrease rather than increase the likelihood that the defendant will ultimately be sentenced to die. Of course, the objective mental health professional has no way of knowing what opinion he or she will render prior to conducting the evaluation. Hence, whatever opinion the evaluator ultimately renders, he or she is an active participant in the capital punishment process.

Does the mental health professional's role in evaluating the trial competency of a capital defendant raise significant ethical issues? That depends upon two related issues: (1) how one views the significance of the competency evaluation in the overall capital punishment process and (2) how the data gathered in the competency evaluation is used by the courts and others.

At the extreme, it might be argued that the participation of mental health professionals "in any aspect of a capital case...is ethically objectionable" (Bonnie 1990:75). That argument, however, generally fails for a number of reasons, at least when applied to the issue of competence to stand trial.

To begin with, while an incompetent defendant may not be tried and thus cannot be sentenced to die, the input of the examining mental health professional(s) on this issue not only fails to be legally dispositive but its relationship to the ultimate decision in the case (life vs. death) is rather attenuated. The examining professional does contribute to the process, broadly conceived, but that contribution is usually extremely limited. Unless used for other purposes (as discussed below), at most the professional competency examination will lead to a legal conclusion that the defendant is fit to proceed to trial—a conclusion that may well be warranted by other evidence as well. Prior to being executed, the defendant will still have to be tried, convicted, sentenced to die, and exhaust all available levels of appellate review.

But beyond those issues, acceptance of this extreme ethical argument would, by logical extension, bar mental health professionals from any participation in the competency to stand trial decision-making process, indeed perhaps from any participation whatsoever in the process of criminal adjudication. As Bonnie (1990:76) observed:

> It is sometimes argued that the principle of nonmalfeasance, the duty to avoid harm, is fundamentally contradicted by any professional interaction with a client that might elicit information or opinion that could be used to support a death sentence. However, this same premise could be deployed against professional participation in any criminal case, when information elicited during the evaluation (and opinion based upon this information) could be used to support a criminal conviction and imprisonment.... It would seem difficult to sustain the argument, as a matter of principle, that forensic testimony that might lead to execution offends the tenet of nonmalfeasance even though the presentation of testimony that might lead to profoundly debilitating imprisonment does not.

Bonnie's argument is sensible, especially when applied to a legal issue that is not only fundamental to all criminal cases but virtually requires the expertise of mental health professionals. To put it more simply: in most cases, whatever the possible punishment, mental health expertise is essential to the proper adjudication of competency to stand trial.

Bonnie's argument, however, seems less forceful where information gathered by the competency examiner is later used for purposes other than determining whether the defendant is competent to stand trial. For example, at one time, it was fairly routine practice in Texas to have capital defendants examined for competency by a psychiatrist who would then appear at their sentencing hearings and pronounce them dangerous, thereby providing support for a statutory aggravating circumstance required to sentence a convicted capital defendant to death—i.e., the "probability that the defendant would commit criminal acts of violence that would constitute a continuing threat to society" (Ewing 1983).

That specific practice was effectively curbed by a U.S. Supreme Court ruling in *Estelle v. Smith* (1981:454) that a defendant's statements to a psychiatrist during a competency evaluation may not be used against the defendant in a capital sentencing proceeding unless, prior to the evaluation, the defendant was "informed of his right to remain silent and the possible use of his statements."

Still, information gathered by a mental health professional may end up being used against a capital defendant in ways that would seem to give the professional much greater—and arguably unethical—involvement in the capital punishment process. An extreme example is where the competency examination has been sought by the prosecutor as a means of gaining discovery, and the evaluating professional is acting largely as an "investigator" for the prosecution. In that case, however, it may not be necessary to reach the issue of nonmalfeasance, since it seems clear that the mental health professional is violating a number of other less debatable ethical and legal proscriptions, e.g., the duty to secure informed consent to any examination.

But even when not merely acting as a prosecution tool, the mental health professional runs the risk that data gathered from the defendant during the competency evaluation will later be used against the defendant, directly or indirectly. For example, information gathered from the defendant in a competency examination might provide leads for the prosecution or other mental health experts to uncover incriminating and/or aggravating evidence that could be used at trial or sentencing. Or another mental health expert might rely upon such information to formulate his or her own opinion regarding aggravating aspects of the defendant's background, personality, or functioning. In such cases, the link between the competency evaluation and the death penalty becomes much less attenuated and thus more ethically objectionable.

At the very least, to minimize the risk of an ethical breach, the examining mental health professional should maintain objectivity at all times, carefully limit his or her inquiry, opinion, and report to the narrow issue of competency, and make every effort to avoid disseminating information that could be used against a capital defendant at other stages of the litigation.

Restoring Competency to Stand Trial

Generally, when a criminal defendant is ruled incompetent to stand trial, he or she is committed to a state facility for treatment aimed at restoring competency. Such treatment will likely include both psychotherapy and the administration of psychotropic medications. The former may be offered by a variety of mental health practitioners, the latter only by a licensed physician. If the treatment is successful, the defendant is returned to court to stand trial.

In this context, the treating professional is not merely acting as a forensic evaluator but functioning in a more traditional healing or therapeutic role—a function much more clearly governed by medical ethics. Is it a violation of ethical standards for a physician or other health care professional to administer medication and/or other treatment aimed at restoring the trial competency of a capital defendant?

Logical extension of Bonnie's argument cited previously would suggest that health care professionals may ethically provide such treatment, for to hold otherwise would call into question their treatment efforts to restore the competency of non-capital defendants—a function generally regarded as ethically acceptable.

On a more positive note, it might also be argued that treating the incompetent capital defendant does actually benefit that defendant. To deny generally efficacious treatment to such a defendant not only may prolong whatever suffering is associated with his/her mental illness but also deny him/her the opportunity to go to trial, present a defense, and possibly be acquitted. This argument seems particularly compelling since in many jurisdictions an incompetent defendant who is not restored to competency may be doomed to spend many years, if not the remainder of his or her life, in a secure psychiatric institution.

Thus, while providing treatment to the capital defendant who is incompetent to stand trial runs the risk of contributing to that defendant's ultimate conviction, sentence, and execution, that risk must be weighed against the potential benefits that might accrue from such treatment.

The one area in which such a cost-benefit analysis might be undermined is where the incompetent capital defendant refuses treatment to restore his or her competency but such treatment is ordered by the court over his or her objection. In that case, providing such treatment would seem to be much less ethically defensible, especially where effective treatment will not simply restore competence but might also alter the defendant's demeanor and presentation in ways that undermine a possible defense (such as insanity) or make the defendant appear less sympathetic to the sentencing authority in the event he or she is convicted.

Here, as with assessing trial competency, ethical considerations seem to dictate professional action that is narrowly calculated to meet the needs of the legal system while avoiding or minimizing any potential for harm to the defendant.

Mitigating and Aggravating Circumstances

In *Lockett v. Ohio* (1978:604), the U.S. Supreme Court held that:

> the Eighth and Fourteenth Amendments require that the sentencer, in all but the rarest kind of capital case, not be precluded from considering, as a mitigating factor, any aspect of the defendant's character or record and any of the circumstances of the offense that the defendant proffers as a basis for a sentence less than death.

As a practical matter, *Lockett* has been viewed as permitting a convicted capital defendant to present to the sentencing authority virtually any evidence that might lead to a sentence short of death.

More recently, in *Atkins v. Virginia* (2002), the U.S. Supreme Court held that imposing the death penalty upon a mentally retarded defendant violates the Eighth Amendment ban on cruel and usual punishment. Whereas under *Lockett*, mental retardation was a mitigating factor sentencing authorities could take into account in deciding whether to impose a sentence of death, the Court in *Atkins* established mental retardation as an absolute barrier to capital punishment. Most death penalty laws also require the sentencer to consider aggravating circumstances—factors that suggest that the death penalty is warranted in any given case. Generally, those aggravating factors are spelled out in the various capital punishment statutes and include, for example, elements such as the heinous nature of the crime, the past criminal record of the defendant, and the defendant's future dangerousness.

Today, in virtually all death penalty prosecutions, the defendant is examined by one or more mental health professionals and, in many cases, the opinions of those professionals are used at sentencing to support aggravation or mitigation. For example, professionals retained by the defense may present mitigating evidence in the form of diagnoses of mental illness or mental retardation and descriptions of the convicted capital defendant's troubled childhood (e.g., history of abuse, neglect, family dysfunction, and other trauma). Mental health professionals called by the prosecution may rebut such mitigating testimony and/or offer aggravating evidence (e.g., testimony that the defendant is sociopathic or dangerous).

There can be little doubt that mental health professionals who provide this kind of testimony—whether for defense or prosecution—are direct participants in the death penalty process. In at least some cases, their testimony has the potential for swaying the sentencing authority to impose a sentence of death or to spare the defendant's life.

Expert mental health testimony for the prosecution at capital sentencing raises serious ethical questions. First, when such testimony deals with the defendant's dangerousness, there is good reason to question the empirical basis for such testimony, since research has consistently cast doubt upon the accuracy of predictions of future dangerousness. Thus, in providing such testimony, mental health professionals may violate their fundamental "ethical obligation to render judgments that rest on a scientific basis" (Ewing 1983:418).

But beyond scientific ethics, medical and mental health professionals who testify regarding aggravating factors engage in conduct that directly contravenes the ethical imperative to do no harm. To put the matter most bluntly, those professionals are assisting the state in securing a warrant to execute the defendant:

> In effect, [they are] telling the sentencing authority that the state has good reason to execute the defendant. The mental health expert, of course, does not have the final say in a legal sense, but the cases leave little doubt that his or her testimony [often] seals the defendant's fate (Ewing 1983:420).

In defense of professionals who testify for the prosecution at capital sentencing, some have raised the "society as patient" argument—the contention that "the healer's responsibility extends beyond the individual patient to society as a whole, and...the healer's true commitment is to improving the health and well-being of both" (Ewing 1983:419). By this reasoning, the health professional who testifies for the prosecution in a capital sentencing hearing might be likened to the "public health physician who his or her medical expertise to help rid the community of a common threat to the health and well-being of its members" (Ewing 1983:419).

This "public health" rationale evaporates, however, upon consideration of the alternatives facing a capital sentencing jury. Their decision is never between death and freedom for the convicted capital defendant. Almost invariably, their options are to sentence the defendant to die or to require him/her to spend the rest of his/her life in prison. Thus, if health professionals chose not to testify for the prosecution in capital sentencing proceedings, the convicted capital murderer would at a minimum be sentenced to life in prison, and might still be sentenced to die. In either event, in keeping with ethical standards, no "harm" would be done by the health professional to either the defendant or society.

But what of the medical or mental health professional who testifies *on behalf of* a convicted capital defendant, e.g., testifies that the defendant is mentally ill, brain damaged and/or the victim of child abuse? Although at first blush such participation in the death penalty process might seem ethical, as Bonnie (1990:77) has observed, that may not be the case:

> In some jurisdictions, if the defense chooses to introduce mental health testimony in mitigation (or exculpation), it thereby opens the door not only to testimony by any experts who were permitted to evaluate the defendant at the behest of the prosecution but also to other mental health evidence that it has obtained. In these juris-

dictions, the expert who is troubled by the possibility that his or her testimony could increase the likelihood of a death sentence may find himself or herself obligated to present highly damaging evidence even though the evaluation was performed for the defense.

Bonnie suggests that this problem may be obviated by precluding the prosecution from using any mental health evaluations conducted for the defense in a capital case. That would be a step in the right direction but far from a solution to the underlying ethical problem. As he points out, defense testimony in mitigation may "open the door" for prosecution testimony or evidence that might otherwise be inadmissible, and thereby enhance rather than reduce the chances of a death sentence.

As long as the testimony of a health professional increases (or has the potential to increase) the likelihood that a capital defendant will be sentenced to die, such testimony must be regarded as arguably unethical. At a minimum, health professionals who consider giving such testimony should be as certain as possible with regard to all the implications (immediate and potential) of their testimony. Additionally, they should strive to minimize if not avoid altogether any possibility of contributing to the likelihood of a death sentence. Finally, when they are uncertain as to the potential implications of their testimony, medical ethics would seem to dictate abstention from the process.

Assessment and Restoration of Competency for Execution

In 1986, in *Ford v. Wainwright*, the U.S. Supreme Court held that the Eighth Amendment Cruel and Unusual Punishment clause would be violated by execution of the "insane," i.e., death row inmates who lack the capacity to understand the nature of the death penalty or why it is being imposed upon them. In so holding, the Court "constitutionalized" what was already the practice in every American jurisdiction with a death penalty law.

The rule banning the execution of the "insane" virtually demands that health care professionals, primarily psychiatrists and psychologists, participate in two ethically questionable roles: (1) the assessment of claims of "insanity" brought on behalf of death row inmates; and (2) the treatment of those death row inmates found to be "insane" and thus not fit for execution.

Assessment of Death Row Inmates

Typically, a panel of mental health professionals is asked to evaluate the competency of a death row inmate who asserts "insanity" as a bar to execution. While the ultimate decision ordinarily rests with a legal rather than clinical decision-maker, the input of the mental health professionals is generally critical if not dispositive.

Although psychologists, psychiatrists, and other mental health professionals are the natural choice to assess a condemned inmate's competence, their participation in this evaluative function raises obvious and serious ethical concerns:

> The ethical objection to such participation seems clear. Psychiatry and clinical psychology are, above all else, healing professions. From the ancient Hippocratic Oath...to the Principles of Medical Ethics...physicians consistently have professed their primary commitment to healing and the preservation of life.... Clinical psychology, though not a branch of medicine, is similarly devoted to healing and the relief of suffering. According to the American Psychological Association, provision of clinical psychological services involves "the application of principles, methods and procedures for understanding, predicting and *alleviating* intellectual, psychological, and behavioral *disability and discomfort.*"
>
> To render a clinical judgment which has the practical effect of authorizing the execution of a convicted capital defendant is clearly contrary to the fundamental ethical commitments of psychology and psychiatry to healing and the relief of human suffering (Ewing 1987:182).

Treatment of Death Row Inmates

When a death row inmate is found to be "insane" and thus incompetent to be executed, he or she will in all likelihood be offered, if not required to accept, psychiatric treatment—generally in the form of anti-psychotic medication—aimed at restoring his or her competency. Although the U.S. Supreme Court has not yet ruled on whether a death row inmate may constitutionally be forcibly medicated for such a purpose, at least one state court has held that medication over objection under such circumstances violates the inmate's due process rights. In *Louisiana v. Perry* (1992), the Louisiana Supreme Court reached this conclusion in part based upon what it viewed as the ethical dilemma imposed when the state orders an inmate medicated to restore his competency to be executed. As the Court explained, as an ethical matter, "drugging for execution" cannot be regarded as "medical treatment":

> The Hippocratic Oath, dating to the fifth century B.C. is the seminal source of the principles of medical ethics and the goals of medical treatment. Under the oath the physician pledges to do no harm and to act only in the best medical interests of his patients. Consequently, medical treatment cannot occur when the state orders a

physician to administer antipsychotic drugs to an insane prisoner in an attempt to render him competent for execution.

Because the physician is required by his oath to alleviate suffering and to do no harm, the state's order forces him to act unethically and contrary to the goals of medical treatment. If any physician administers the drugs forcibly for execution, the doctor knowingly handles the prisoner harmfully and contrary to his ultimate medical interest....

Accordingly, we conclude that a physician's prescription and administration of antipsychotic drugs to a prisoner against his will, pursuant to the order of a state court or other government official, for purpose of carrying out the death penalty, does not constitute medical treatment but forms part of the capital punishment sought to be executed by the state (*State v. Perry* 1992:753).

Although the court's legal reasoning in *Perry* may be followed by other courts confronting the issue of involuntary medication to restore competency for execution, it does not provide a direct answer to the ethical question of voluntary medication for the same purpose.

When a death row inmate is incompetent to be executed as a result of psychosis and is willing to accept antipsychotic medication that would alleviate his or her psychotic symptoms, the physician appears to face a much more difficult dilemma. In fact, however, even in the voluntary context, this dilemma is more apparent than real.

Certainly, all penal inmates have a right to necessary medical care, including psychiatric treatment, and prison physicians have a legal and ethical duty to provide such care. Moreover, denying treatment to the willing psychotic death row inmate may well prolong that inmate's psychopathology and mental distress, thus arguably violating the physician's ethical duty to relieve the suffering of his or her patient.

On the other hand, providing such treatment in this unique context is likely to result in the inmate's death since the state's interest is not in healing the inmate or alleviating psychotic suffering but in restoring sanity so that the inmate may be lawfully executed.

Under those circumstances, the appropriate response seems clear:

[W]here the healing professional's choice is between (a) providing treatment which relieves psychological suffering but results in the death of an otherwise healthy human being and (b) refusing to provide such treatment, there can be little if any doubt that the latter course of (in)action is the ethically proper one (Ewing 1987:184).

Health Care Professionals in the Execution Process

Throughout the modern history of capital punishment in the United States, physicians and other medical personnel have been involved in the execution process. For the most part, their participation has been limited to pronouncing the death of the executed inmate—a function that was, until very recently, thought to be in keeping with medical ethics. In the post-*Furman* era (i.e., since the Supreme Court's 1972 landmark decision in *Furman v. Georgia* striking down all then-existing death penalty laws), however, the potential role of health care professionals has greatly expanded.

The explanation for this expanded medical role lies in the growing use of lethal injection as a means of execution. As the American College of Physicians et al. (1994:9) has explained:

> The death penalty was reinstated in 1976 in a series of Supreme Court decisions. These cases upheld the constitutionality of the death penalty.... The following year, Gary Gilmore was executed by firing squad in Utah. Public outcry over the use of the firing squad generated support for a new method of execution: lethal injection. In 1977, Oklahoma became the first state to approve use of lethal injection, with three other states quickly following suit. The first execution by lethal injection, that of Charles Brooks, took place in Texas in 1982.

Today, in nearly all the states that allow capital punishment, executions may be carried out by lethal injection. In roughly half of those states, lethal injection is the only form of execution permitted. From 1976 through mid-2001, 555 (77%) of the 718 executions carried out in the United States involved lethal injections (Khan and Leventhal 2002). In some jurisdictions, physicians and/or other medical personnel now assist in the preparation and administration of the lethal substances used to terminate the lives of convicted capital defendants.

Pronouncing Death

In 1980, the Council on Ethical and Judicial Affairs of the American Medical Association (AMA) issued the following statement with regard to physician participation in executions:

> A physician, as a member of a profession dedicated to preserving life when there is hope of doing so, should not be a participant in a legally authorized execution. A physician may make a determina-

tion or certification of death as currently provided by law in any situation (AMA Council on Ethical and Judicial Affairs 1980).

Thereafter, similar pronouncements were made by other professional health care organizations including the American College of Physicians (1984), American Public Health Association (1993), and American Nurses Association (1983).

It was not until 1992, however, that the AMA clarified its ruling as to physician participation in executions. One important aspect of that clarification dealt with the distinction between "determining" and "certifying" death, neither of which had previously been classified as "participation" in an execution (AMA Council on Ethical and Judicial Affairs 1993).

This distinction has both practical and ethical implications. "Certifying" death is a legal formality in which a physician simply affirms what has already been determined by another party, i.e., that an individual is dead. "Determining" death, however, requires the physician to make that clinical judgment in the first instance.

The physician who "determines" the death of an executed inmate is clearly a participant in the execution process and acts contrary to medical ethics. As the American College of Physicians et al. (1994:22) has explained: "Inevitably there will be instances where the physician finds that death has not occurred. In these cases, the physician must then signal to the executioner that the procedure must continue or recommence."

Truog and Brennan (1993:1348) cite as an example the case of Alpha Stevens:

> When Alpha Otis Stevens was electrocuted in Georgia in 1984, the first two minute charge of electricity failed to kill him. His body had to cool for six minutes before doctors could examine him, during which time Stevens appeared to be struggling to breathe. After two doctors determined that he was still alive, a fatal charge of electricity was applied.

Not surprisingly, in its 1992 clarification, the AMA Council on Ethical and Judicial Affairs (1993:365) declared that "determining death," i.e., "monitoring the condition of the condemned during the execution and determining the point at which the individual has actually died," constitutes "participation" in an execution and is thus a violation of medical ethics.

Assisting in the Execution Process

With the advent and increased use of lethal injection as the preferred if not sole method of execution, many jurisdictions have attempted to utilize the skills of medical professionals in the actual execution process. For example, physicians have helped prepare protocols for lethal injection, advised corrections personnel regarding specific executions, pronounced death, and even inserted the intravenous catheters used to inject the combination of deadly chemicals.

Such conduct not only violates the Hippocratic Oath but is clearly proscribed by the Ethical and Judicial Affairs Council's 1992 statement of clarification regarding the AMA's earlier ban on "physician participation in capital punishment." The 1992 statement defines participation in an execution to include prescribing or administering tranquilizing drugs to inmates faced with imminent execution; monitoring the vital signs of condemned inmates during the execution process; attending or observing an execution in the role of physician; providing technical advice regarding execution procedures; selecting injection sites or starting intravenous lines for lethal injection; inspecting, testing or maintaining devices used for lethal injection; and consulting with or supervising other personnel in the lethal injection process.

Summary and Conclusion

Prior to the Supreme Court's landmark decision in *Furman v. Georgia* striking down all then-existing death penalty statutes, health care professionals played a rather limited role in the capital punishment process. Traditionally, psychologists and psychiatrists had assessed the competency of capital defendants to stand trial, and conducted forensic mental health examinations related to defenses such as insanity. With few exceptions, general physicians were involved almost exclusively in pronouncing the death of the executed individual.

In the wake of *Furman*, however, many states revised their death penalty laws. Those revised laws which provided for "guided discretion" were subsequently upheld by the Court, and capital punishment was reinstated in 1976. These laws required the sentencing authority (whether judge or jury) to consider both aggravating and mitigating factors. Since many of these factors were psychological in nature, psychologists, psychiatrists, and other mental health professionals began to assume a larger role in the process, often evaluating capital defendants and testifying at the sentencing phase of capital proceedings.

With the post-*Furman* reinstatement of the death penalty and resumption of executions also came a growing demand for more humane methods of capital punishment. Since 1982, the intravenous injection of lethal drugs has become the most widely used means of execution in the United States. As a result, there has been a concomitant demand for medical participation in the actual execution process. In recent years, medical personnel, including physicians, have played an active role in both preparing and administering lethal injections.

While some states and courts have recognized the ethical dilemmas posed for health care professionals by such involvement in the capital punishment process, physicians, psychiatrists, psychologists, and other medical personnel continue to participate at all levels from pre-trial evaluations to the actual execution. Over the past decade or so, most of the major health care professional organizations have taken affirmative stands against at least some of these practices, certainly those most clearly related to the actual execution process.

While the limited participation of some health care professionals in certain aspects of the capital punishment process (e.g., evaluating competency to stand trial and insanity) appears necessary if not inevitable, those who participate in any aspect of this process bear the personal and professional burden of reconciling their participation with the highest principle of their professions: "Above all, do no harm."

References

American College of Physicians (1984) "American College of Physicians Ethics Manual." *Annals of Internal Medicine* 101:263–274.

American College of Physicians, Human Rights Watch, National Coalition to Abolish the Death Penalty, and Physicians for Human Rights (1994) *Breach of Trust: Physician Participation in Executions in the United States*. Philadelphia: American College of Physicians.

American Medical Association (AMA) Council on Ethical and Judicial Affairs (1980) "Report A." Reprinted in *Death Penalty Reporter* 1:8–9.

American Medical Association (AMA) Council on Ethical and Judicial Affairs (1993) "Physician Participation in Capital Punishment." *Journal of the American Medical Association* 270:365–368.

American Nurses Association (1983) *Code for Nurses with Interpretive Statements*. Kansas City: American Nurses Association.

American Public Health Association (1993) *Position Paper No. 8521: Participation of Health Professionals in Capital Punishment*. Washington, D.C.: American Public Health Association.

Atkins v. Virginia (2002) 122 S.Ct. 2242.

Bonnie, R. J. (1990) "Dilemmas in Administering the Death Penalty." *Law and Human Behavior* 14(1):67–90.

Drope v. Missouri (1975) 420 U.S. 162.

Dusky v. United States (1960) 362 U.S. 402.

Estelle v. Smith (1981) 451 U.S. 454.

Ewing, C. P. (1983) "'Dr. Death' and the Case for an Ethical Ban on Psychiatric and Psychological Predictions of Dangerousness in Capital Sentencing Proceedings." *American Journal of Law and Medicine* 8:407–428.

Ewing, C. P. (1987) "Diagnosing and Treating Insanity on Death Row: Legal and Ethical Perspectives." *Behavioral Sciences and the Law* 5:175–185.

Ford v. Wainwright (1986) 477 U.S. 399.

Furman v. Georgia (1972) 408 U.S. 238.

Grisso, T. (1988) *Competency to Stand Trial Evaluations: A Manual for Practice.* Sarasota: Professional Resource Press.

Hippocrates (c. 460–400 B.C.) "Hippocratic Oath" *Steadman's Medical Dictionary, 4th Unabridged Lawyer's Edition* (1976):647.

Khan, A. and R. M. Leventhal (2002) "Medical Aspects of Capital Punishment Executions." *Journal of Forensic Sciences* 47(4): 847–851.

Lockett v. Ohio (1978) 438 U.S. 586.

Pate v. Robinson (1966) 383 U.S. 375.

Perlin, M. L. (1994) *Law and Mental Disability.* Charlottesville: Michie Company.

State v. Perry (1992) 610 So.2d 746 (La.).

Truog, R. D. and T. A. Brennan (1993) "Participation of Physicians in Capital Punishment." *New England Journal of Medicine* 329(18):1341–1350.

Chapter 20

The Impact of the Death Penalty on the Families of Homicide Victims and of Condemned Prisoners

*Margaret Vandiver**

Introduction

Anyone who has attended a capital trial in the United States has observed the families of the accused and the victim sitting in the courtroom, often alone, sometimes with a few friends or supporters. The gulf that separates these families at trial seems immense, even unbridgeable. The observer is likely to feel painful empathy for both families and frustration at how little comfort or assistance the criminal justice system can provide them. Given that the crime cannot be undone, what can the criminal justice system offer to the victim's family? And what kind of sentence can be imposed on a defendant found guilty of first degree murder that is commensurate to the crime, protects society, and yet does not destroy the defendant's family in turn?

If there is one unchanging aspect of capital punishment, it must be the pain that homicides and executions cause the families involved. Much of the trauma and loss caused by the violent death of a loved one is a private experience, largely untouched by the social and legal context in which it occurs. The way in which a society responds to survivors of homicide victims and the way in which it punishes offenders cannot eliminate the pain of either set of families, although it may be able to ease certain aspects of their suffering. Unfortunately,

---
* I am grateful to the editors of this volume for their helpful suggestions and comments on drafts of this chapter. I also would like to thank Susan Cary, Dr. David J. Giacopassi, Gordon Haas, and Rev. Joseph B. Ingle for reading and commenting on the chapter and Dr. Elizabeth Vandiver for her assistance with revisions.

the social and legal response is able to aggravate and prolong families' distress, and add other dimensions of suffering to those which they already experience.

In the years since the *Furman v. Georgia* decision, the victims' rights movement has led to significant changes in the ways victims are viewed and treated by the legal system and American society in general. For many years, the families of homicide victims were largely ignored, except for flurries of media attention at the time of the crime and during the trial. Beginning in the 1970s, researchers, the criminal justice system, and society at large began to pay more attention to these "indirect victims of crime" (Riggs and Kilpatrick 1990). The growing political clout of the victims' rights movement has been amply demonstrated in local, state, and national elections, with politicians making extensive use of victims and their experiences in speeches and campaign advertisements. No corresponding change has occurred for the families of homicide defendants in the last decades. They continue to be nearly invisible. Their experiences have been the subject of very limited research. No politicians mention them in their campaigns, very few advocacy groups are concerned with their needs, and there is little public recognition or concern for their situation.

This chapter examines and discusses the experiences of the families of homicide victims and of condemned prisoners in the context of America's use of the death penalty since *Furman*.[1] First is a brief review of what is known

---

1. I will not attempt to quantify the pain of either set of families, or to conclude who suffers most: the pain of both is immeasurable. Engaging in a contest of suffering is not helpful to anyone. In many ways, victims' families are uniquely able to understand the grief of the defendants' families, and vice versa. Occasionally, the families are able to reach across the many barriers between them and comfort each other, even if they remain divided about the appropriate sentence. Such an experience was described in a letter written to a local newspaper by the mother of a murder victim in Florida after the trial of her daughter's killer:

> Today I met a woman. Not just an ordinary woman, but one with deep faith, love in her heart and sorrow written all over her face. I had watched this woman from a distance for a week as she sat quietly giving strength to her husband and daughter. I know the grief I felt in my heart and could imagine the grief she felt in hers. Today she was waiting for the verdict on her son's future. Almost nine months ago, her son decided the future of my little daughter. Strange as this may sound, this woman has given me more faith and more strength to go on. Just before we went in the courtroom, I walked over and talked with this woman. We really didn't have to say many words to each other...we both knew. We walked into the courtroom holding hands. This woman's name is Mrs. Aubrey Dennis Adams, Sr. Her sorrow is not of her own making. But her faith and love in such a horrible situation is a shining example of what being a Christian is all about. My prayers and the prayers of my family are with her and her family as they face the rest of this ordeal (Thornley 1978:4A).

about the feelings and experiences of the families, focusing on the effects of the criminal processing of the case, and the significance of the penalty imposed. Next is a discussion of the experiences of the families within the legal context of modern capital sentencing. Finally, the chapter discusses the implications of the families' experiences for the use of the death penalty in the future.

Despite the importance of the experiences of these families, until recently the vast literature on capital punishment and violent crime contained little research on the families of homicide victims, and the families of condemned prisoners continue to be nearly ignored by researchers. Even the number of family members affected by homicide and capital punishment has not been definitively established. Redmond (1989:5) did genograms of the families of 300 murder victims and concluded the "average number of mourners for each murder victim includes seven to ten surviving family members." Amick-McMullan, Kilpatrick, and Resnick (1991) took a national sample of 12,500 adults contacted through random digit dialing. Respondents were asked whether a family member had been the victim of homicide at any time during the respondent's lifetime. The authors found that 1.6 percent of the respondents had lost an immediate family member to homicide, 3.7 percent had lost other relatives, and 2.7 percent had lost close friends. In addition, 1.2 percent had lost immediate family members to vehicular homicide. Combining these figures, the authors concluded "9.3% of adults surveyed were survivors of homicide victims" (at 551). The authors used these figures to estimate that in the United States "5 million adults have lost immediate family members to homicide [including vehicular], another 6.6 million have lost other relatives, and yet another 4.8 million have lost close friends, for a total of 16.4 million..." (at 551–552). Another survey of slightly more than 4,000 American women received a positive response from 13.37% of the sample to the question: "Has a close friend or family member of yours ever been deliberately killed or murdered by another person or killed by a drunk driver?" (Resnick et al. 1993:985). The number of people affected by a relative's execution is much smaller. Since 1976 when current death penalty laws were upheld by the U.S. Supreme Court (*Gregg v. Georgia*), 785 people have been executed in America through late July 2002 (Death Penalty Information Center 2002a). As of spring 2002, the death row population stood at 3,711 (NAACP Legal Defense and Educational Fund, Inc. 2002).

Families of Homicide Victims

Case studies, interviews with small numbers of survivors, and autobiographies are a rich source of descriptive accounts of the feelings and experiences of individuals bereaved by homicide.[2] Since the mid 1970s, researchers have shown more interest in homicide victims' survivors, and a growing body of literature explores their experiences. Several studies give an overview of reactions to a family member's murder.[3] Some focus on specific populations, such as children who witness the homicide of one parent by another, or the siblings of homicide victims,[4] while other studies are concerned specifically with therapeutic interventions[5] or the effects of the criminal justice system upon survivors.[6] Several guides have been written to assist victims and those working with them.[7] An increasing number of studies exploring grief and trauma reactions to homicide have used larger samples, comparison groups, and/or statistical analysis.[8] Some recent work has focused on the related area of survivors of war and genocide.[9]

The conclusions of these different studies are strikingly similar. To summarize the most important:

- The loss of a close relative to homicide is a shatteringly traumatic event. The pain, disruption, and trauma caused by homicide cannot be overstated.
- The trauma and difficulty of adjusting to loss by homicide is such that survivors often experience the symptoms of Post Traumatic Stress Dis-

---

2. See Bosco 2001; Brown 1991; Capote 1965; Danto 1982; Geberth 1992; Henry-Jenkins 1993; Hoard 1994; Magee 1983; Molhan 1996; Schlosser 1997; Wilkinson 1993. Some of the best qualitative descriptions of bereavement by homicide come from these works. They are unsatisfactory, however, from a social science perspective, because the cases or small samples are not necessarily representative of any larger population.

3. Amick-McMullan, Kilpatrick, Veronen, and Smith 1989; Amick-McMullan, Kilpatrick, and Veronen 1989; Asaro 2001a; Burgess 1975; Johnson and Young 1992; Rynearson 1984; Rynearson and McCreery 1993; Sprang, McNeil, and Wright 1989.

4. Burman and Allen-Meares 1994; Craig 1999; Freeman, Shaffer, and Smith 1996; Malmquist 1986; Rinear 1988.

5. Asaro 2001b; Getzel and Masters 1984; Jackson 1979; Lyon, Moore, and Lexius 1992; Masters, Friedman, and Getzel 1988; Parkes 1993; Salloum, Avery, and McClain 2001; Temple 1997.

6. Day and Weddington 1996.

7. Jenkins 2001; Redmond 1989; Spungen 1998.

8. Amick-McMullan, Kilpatrick, and Resnick 1991; Murphy, Braun, Tillery, Cain, Johnson, and Beaton 1999; Sprang, McNeil, and Wright 1992–1993; Thompson, Norris, and Ruback 1998; Vargas, Loya, and Hodde-Vargas 1989.

9. Survivors of large scale political violence have faced loss on an unimaginable scale. In addition to the murder of family members—sometimes their entire family—they often have experienced forced expulsion, rape, torture, siege, and the loss of their homes and livelihoods. The recent genocides in Rwanda and Bosnia have produced a number of accounts of survivors' experiences, e.g., Hatzfeld 2000; Hukanovic 1996; Weine 1999.

order (PTSD). Many survivors report losing their sense that there is any justice or safety in the world; many feel that life itself has lost all meaning.

- Survivors can expect to encounter difficulties in many other areas of their lives, including their marriages, relationships with children, friendships, and work.
- The process of recovery takes years, if not decades. Expectations of quick grieving and recovery are unrealistic and damaging.[10] Even after survivors resolve their grief, it is unlikely that their emotional lives will ever be the same as before the crime.
- Survivors often are not helped, and sometimes are further victimized, by the criminal justice system. Both formal and informal supports for homicide victims' survivors are inadequate.
- The experience of isolation is very common—at the time they most need contact and support, families often feel the most isolated. The opposite situation of intrusion is often a problem as well, with unwelcome contacts from the criminal justice system, the media, and curiosity seekers.
- There seems to be much potential for advancing the process of healing through non-judgmental, ongoing, emotionally involved listening, without suggestions as to how the survivors should feel or what they should do.

Experiencing the death of a loved one is always difficult, but violent death "compounds the trauma and shock effects...and these responses are difficult to resolve" (Raphael 1983:29). As Antoinette Bosco, who lost her son and his wife to murder, wrote: "if the death is caused by murder, there is a collapse in the heart and soul that cannot be described. For murder is the entrance of the worst evil imaginable into your home, into all the safe places of your life, forever shattering any illusion you might have had that good can protect you from evil" (2001:13). Two recent studies have documented the particularly devastating effect of homicide on surviving family members. A study of the reactions of parents to children's deaths by accident, suicide, and homicide found "twice as many parents whose children were murdered met PTSD criteria" (Murphy et al. 1999:286). Thompson, Norris, and Ruback (1998:236) compared family members of homicide victims to other trauma victims and to nonvictims, and found that the subjects who had experienced bereavement by homicide were "significantly more distressed" than the other subjects.

---

10. A particularly egregious example of unrealistic expectations in this regard was published by *Newsweek* in an account of the murder of Michael Jordan's father. The article referred to "the normal six- to 12-month grieving process" (Begley 1993:59), a period of time barely sufficient to assimilate the initial shock of the murder, much less to recover from it.

An element common to nearly all homicides is the shock of sudden death. This suddenness makes the loss difficult to believe or to comprehend. A study of nearly 1,200 relatives of homicide victims found that:

> the murder of a loved one leads to repeated eruptions of overwhelming emotional firestorms in the survivor. Victims' relatives told us that often without warning, they experienced in rapid succession: grief, rage, despair, and guilt. Typically, survivors relived again and again some aspect of the murder; for example, the call from the police or the sight of the dead body at the morgue. Some were obsessed with disturbingly vivid ideas of revenge. Most were preoccupied with fantasies of undoing—thoughts of how they might have prevented the murder (Masters, Friedman, and Getzel 1988:113).

Along with overwhelming feelings of grief and longing for the murdered person, bereaved families are likely to feel intense anger, rage, and desire for revenge. Although survivors rarely do resort to violence, it is likely that many have wished that they could take such a course of action (see Hoard 1994 for a personal account and Prejean 1993:138–139 for a description of a father's decision not to attempt such action). Temple reports that adolescents he counseled after their siblings' murders sometimes felt obligated to seek revenge and were urged to do so by their peers (1997:134). Some survivors may be troubled by their desire to get even with the killer, feeling that it conflicts with their ethical and religious beliefs.

Many families find themselves wanting a real expression of apology from the offender.[11] Despite the obvious fact that an apology cannot restore the victim, and the risk that any apology, no matter how abject and heartfelt, risks seeming trivial considering the wrong done, the wish to hear the offender express sincere regret is often voiced by murder victims' relatives. Sister Helen Prejean reported that "Lloyd LeBlanc has told me that he would have been content with imprisonment for Patrick Sonnier. He went to [witness] the execution, he says, not for revenge, but hoping for an apology" (1993:244). The child of a murder victim, reflecting on the execution of the man convicted of the crime, said "I'm never going to hear that son of a bitch say, 'Sorry.' I don't feel free here. I have extreme anger and a desperate, desperate need for [the defendant] to say he was sorry" (Craig 2002).

There are significant differences in survivors' experiences depending on the circumstances of the case.[12] Unsolved murders leave families in continuing un-

---

11. The desire for apology is a little explored aspect of the reactions of homicide victims' families. One author wrote that parents of murdered children may want "not so much the extermination of a killer as an equivalency of feeling: they want their suffering communicated and shared. They want the people who murdered their children to know the torture of their loss" (Brown 1991:74).

12. One author presented a "working typology of grief among homicide survivors." He classified survivors into five groups, based on the type of homicide, and discussed their typical

certainty.[13] Some survivors report that they imagine the murderer everywhere, are suspicious of everyone, and fear that the murderer will return to kill them as well. As reported in one study, the father of a victim said:

> The cops say the fellow who shot Jimmy was about twenty and sort of Scandinavian looking. I walk down the street and find myself hating every twenty-year old I meet. If he's blond and tall, I want to strangle him—some guy who's probably totally innocent. Then too, I get scared. Maybe the guy who killed Jimmy will read about us in the papers. Maybe he'll come to where we live and shoot my other children. I wake up at night and am afraid for my family. We live in a constant fog of fear (Masters, Friedman, and Getzel 1988:116).

If a suspect is found and charged with the homicide, the victim's family may be engaged with several levels of the criminal justice system. The experiences of families in this situation will differ based on several factors. First is whether the suspected murderer is a family member, in which case conflicts of loyalty are likely to greatly complicate the process of grieving. When the suspect is a stranger, treatment of the families may vary according to the way they and the victim are perceived by the criminal justice system and the media. Certain victims are devalued from the first by the media—they are portrayed as criminals themselves, gang members, drug users/dealers, difficult, troublesome, frightening, no great loss. Families may feel that the media's portrayal is false and prejudicial, but there probably is little they can do to counteract it. Even if the allegations of the victim's criminal activities are true, having them publicly aired is difficult and humiliating (Fox 1981:257).

Some victims are given highly disproportionate amounts of media and public attention, although they were unknown before the crime. Their deaths may be viewed as evidence of the decay of moral values and even the collapse of society. They become symbols of lost innocence and their deaths are widely

---

responses. Survivors of "isolated sudden murder" and of serial murder were found to respond with "feelings of unreality, exacerbation of guilt feelings, the need to blame someone for what happened, sense of helplessness, and regrets…" (Key 1992:150–151). Survivors of "drug/alcohol-related murder" and "gang-related murder" often knew of the danger their relative was in and "during this period of anticipation had actually begun the task of mourning…" (at 151). Reactions to "domestic violence homicide," the fifth type, were similar, in that family knew of their relative's ongoing violent relationship.

13. Cases of missing persons where murder is strongly suspected but no body has been found leave the families in a perpetual state of uncertainty. Not having proof that their relative is dead, they continue to hope year after year that eventually the person will return. A mother expressed her feelings nine years after her daughter's disappearance: "You don't sleep; the phone rings, your blood pressure goes up…. For nine years, we've never gone to my mailbox without my stomach feeling sick and nervous, 'Yes, today is the day' " (Ragavan et al. 2001:14).

mourned. These highly regarded victims often are women or children and nearly always are white.

Families whose murdered relatives do not fit the model of the "real victim" may find that criminal justice attention — or lack of it — parallels that of the media. A study of the processing of homicide cases in the Chattahoochee district of Georgia found much evidence of the devaluation of certain victims, following racial lines. When the victims were white, "the DA is solicitous of the family's feelings, often paying them courtesy visits at their homes, and then announcing, at a press conference, that he will be seeking the death penalty in accordance with the family's wishes." When blacks were victims of homicide, their families were often ignored or even abused by the criminal justice system:

> Jimmy Christian was informed by the police in 1988 that his son had been murdered. That was the last he heard from any officials. He was never advised of any court proceedings. When an arrest was made, he heard about it on the street. He was not informed of the trial date or the charges.
>
> Johnny Johnson came home from church in 1984 to find the body of his wife, her throat cut. His one contact with officials occurred when he was briefly jailed on suspicion of her murder. Ultimately, an arrest was made, but Mr. Johnson was not informed either of the arrest or of the trial and sentencing. "They didn't tell me nothing," he testified.
>
> Lola Comer's daughter was murdered in 1981. She heard there was a suspect, and phoned the police to ask if there would be a trial. The case was already resolved, she learned, in a plea bargain, and the perpetrator sentenced to twelve years. No one from the DA's office talked to her at all. "How did it make you feel?" she was asked on the stand. "It made me feel bad. It hurted me real bad."
>
> Gregory Henderson's brother was robbed and murdered in 1987, and his girlfriend shot to death. Mr. Henderson was asked to go to the police station to identify the possible perpetrators. Once there, he was physically assaulted by the police and told he was a suspect in his brother's murder.... He learned later — through the news media — that arrests had been made. No one from the DA's office ever contacted him or his family about the arrests, the plea bargains, or the jail [sic] sentences (Kroll 1991:12–13, footnotes omitted).

If the case goes to trial, the victim's family will have to cope with a number of difficult situations. Family members may be excluded from the courtroom, if they are to be witnesses. Being excluded can cause much distress, as the family is unable to observe the trial and hear the evidence which concerns them so intimately. On the other hand, being inside the courtroom is also terribly diffi-cult. No matter how much the relatives have tried to prepare themselves, it is excruciatingly painful to hear the details of the killing, especially as it is de-scribed in detached medical and legal language. Being in the same room as the defendant, within sight and hearing and almost within reach, but unable to ex-press their feelings either verbally or physically, must call for a degree of self-control very difficult to achieve.

The end of the trial and sentencing may mark an end to the involvement of the victim's family with the legal system. If the defendant is sentenced to life without parole or to a very long term of imprisonment, the sentence will begin immediately, and there should be no reason for the family to have to deal with the defendant again. If the defendant is sentenced to a short term of years, or will be eligible for parole after a short time, or above all, if he[14] is sentenced to death, then the victim's family is likely to face a prolonged engagement with the criminal justice system.

Even "repetitive confrontations with the criminal justice system" through the end of the trial have been found to disrupt the recovery of victims' families (Masters, Friedman, and Getzel 1988:116). If the sentence is death, the fam-ily's involvement with the criminal justice system will continue beyond the trial for three or four years at a minimum, and may go on for as many as 20 or more years. Every hearing in the case, every appellate court decision, every re-quest for commutation, every death warrant, every stay of execution will result in a flurry of interest by the media and the public. Pictures of the victim and the prisoner, footage of the crime scene, graphic descriptions of the murder, and speculations about the ultimate outcome of the case are likely to be aired at every decision point in the appellate process, especially in high profile cases. Under these circumstances, families will find it very difficult to put the murder behind them, or to focus their memories on the victim's life rather than on his or her death. A murder victim's husband said of the appellate process, "Every time [his wife's parents] hear about another appeal, another delay, it throws them into a grave depression.... I think it happens to all of us. We're all thrown back to square one" (Gibbons 1988:64). Helen Prejean described a vic-tim's family as being like "deer paralyzed by headlights in the road. All they can think, all they know, all they want is the death of their child's murderer that the state has promised them.... They wait and wait, reliving their daughter's murder again and again" (1993:137). David Von Drehle wrote of the struggle

---

14. Because the overwhelming majority of defendants in capital cases and of condemned prisoners are men, the masculine pronoun will be used throughout. Of the 785 people executed from 1976 through late July 2002, only nine were women (Death Penalty Information Center 2002b). Male inmates made up 98.54% of the death row population as of Spring 2002 (NAACP Legal Defense and Educational Fund, Inc. 2002).

of Wendy and Dave Nelson to cope with a new sentencing for the man convicted of murdering their daughter Elisa:

> Eight years had passed since Mann's death sentence had been imposed; almost nine since the death of their daughter. Through all those years, Dave and Wendy had waited for the system to deliver on the justice they had been promised. Now they were back to square one....
>
> "If somebody had asked me years ago what I would do if all this happened, I wouldn't have thought I'd still be alive. I am amazed," [Wendy Nelson] said, "to be functioning at whatever level."
>
> "We were aware of all the delays. But I have to say I'm surprised we're this far back—ten years later and we're still at the first step. If things go well for us, it could be another three or four years...." She paused, and the silence in the house was enormous. "The bottom line," she began again: "If they're dead, they can't commit any more crimes. I want a finality, I'm tired of hearings and court proceedings. I want him out of my life, and I really see only one way to do that" (1995:369–370).

Awaiting the execution is also very painful for those victims' families who did not want the death penalty to be imposed.

A number of states allow victims' families to witness the execution of their relative's murderer. One victim's mother who was allowed to watch by private television screen the lethal injection of the man who killed her son and raped her reported, "The execution itself was very satisfying.... [I] know that man is not around anymore and that he can't go out and hurt anyone else" (Barnes 1996:37). No research has been done to learn how witnessing the execution may affect family members, and some have warned that viewing the execution may actually add to the trauma of the survivors (Spiegel 2001:B03; Goodwin 1997).

The effects of executions on homicide victims' families simply are not known. It may be that some families experience a real and lasting sense of peace and closure[15] from the execution of their relative's killer. Statements made by victims' survivors at the time of execution often indicate that they feel

---

15. I use the word "closure" with some hesitation. Although it is frequently mentioned as something desirable for victims' survivors to achieve, it is rarely defined. I take it to mean, at its best, a turning point in the process of grieving beyond which survivors are able to feel more in control of their lives and better able to face the future. It does not mean an end of grief or a return to things as they were before the murder. As a relative of one of Timothy McVeigh's victims said, "The only 'closure' I'm ever going to have is when they close the lid on my coffin" (quoted by Spiegel 2001:B03).

a great sense of relief.[16] No systematic interviews have been done with these families to learn whether the execution does result in long-term improvement in their emotional condition. Some families may find that the execution does not provide them much if any comfort. In fact, losing the object of their anger may leave them feeling empty and unfocused. If they have believed for years that the execution of their relative's killer would bring them substantial emotional relief and it does not, they may even feel worse after the execution.[17]

Regardless of the legal outcome of the case, victims' families will endure a long period of grieving. There can be no quick recovery from the violent death of a loved one. Alec Wilkinson's book, *A Violent Act,* gives a fine por-

---

16. The following quotes are taken from newspaper interviews with victims' families in Florida at the time of the execution of their relatives' killers:

> As Betty Anderson watched a hearse drive away with the body of her husband's slayer, she let out a sigh of relief. "The ordeal is over. It's been a long time coming...It was a relief to know that he is no more—that he's not sitting up there with those evil, evil thoughts of his."... Dottie Luce, Anderson's only sister, said watching the hearse leave the prison grounds "was the most beautiful sight I've ever seen" (Associated Press 1986).
>
> Betti Shupe [daughter of a murder victim]...told reporters, "I can't say I'm happy, but I'm relieved. It's good to be out here. There's no more worry that he's going to get out" (Myer 1986).
>
> "I am relieved. You just can't understand what enormous relief it is that all this is finally over and done with," said Traci Freeman, the older sister of [the victim] (Saul 1989).

But not all victims express these feelings:

> Helen Turman, widow of the man slain 10 years ago by Willie Jasper Darden, calls his stay of execution Thursday "an answer to a prayer." She also hopes his sentence will be reduced to life in prison before another death warrant can be signed.... "Since he got a stay, I've had a burden lifted from my heart.... I know God's going to punish him," she explained. "But that's for God to do, not me. And I feel, by these death warrants, that they are asking some other man to do the very sin that he committed. That's no good" (Anderson 1983:1A, 10A).

Lindi James strongly opposed the execution of Pedro Medina, who was condemned for the murder of her mother. After Medina's execution Ms. James told a journalist, "This is almost impossible for me to talk about anymore.... I am exhausted. I spent years trying to get people to listen" (Shapiro 1997:5).

17. After witnessing the execution of the man convicted of murdering two of her children, the victims' mother said, " 'I'm glad it's done and glad it's over and glad he's off this earth.' She then acknowledged her fear that she and her family may return to the deep depression that followed the murders and the conviction. 'I'm trying to make myself realize that even when I'm back home Saturday morning and this is all over, Mark and Kara are still gone and we still have to live with this. It's with us forever and he's getting out of this. He will have no more pain' " (Quoted in Goodwin 1997:587, notes omitted).

trait of the deep sorrow and slow tentative healing of the widow and young children of a murdered man. He quotes the widow during the second year after the murder:

> You work hard the first year trying to recover, then the second arrives and you realize that with grieving there is no accomplishment; things will never change, nor will they ever again be the same. There is no reward. There's nothing at the end. Your loss is permanent (1993:201).

Families of Condemned Prisoners

Whatever effect executions may have on victims' families, it is certain that they are devastating for the families of defendants. Camus' description of their experiences remains one of the best:

> The relatives of the condemned man then discover an excess of suffering that punishes them beyond all justice. A mother's or a father's long months of waiting, the visiting-room, the artificial conversations filling up the brief moments spent with the condemned man, the visions of the execution are all tortures.... [The death penalty] punishes, in iniquity, their innocence and their misfortune (1961:205).

The families of executed inmates are like murder victims' families in that they have lost a relative to intentional violence, but they differ in several important ways from the families of other victims of violent death.[18]

- The families of condemned prisoners know for years that the state intends to kill their relatives and the method that will be used. They experience a prolonged period of anticipatory grieving, complicated by the hope that some court or governor will grant relief.
- Their relatives' deaths will come about as the result of the actions of dozens of respected and powerful persons. Their deaths will not be caused by a breakdown in social order, but by a highly orchestrated and cooperative effort of authority.
- Their relatives are publicly disgraced and shamed; they have been formally cast out of society and judged to be unworthy to live.

---

18. Family members of capital defendants frequently have been victims of violent crime themselves; indeed, it is not unusual for these families to have lost relatives to homicide. Yet, because of class and racial inequities in sentencing, it is unlikely their relatives' deaths were punished harshly. How ironic for these families that when a relative encounters the criminal justice system as a defendant rather than a victim, the system turns from leniency to severity.

- The deaths of their relatives are not mourned and regretted the way other violent deaths are; rather, the death is condoned, supported and desired by many people, and actively celebrated by some.

There is much less research on the experiences of families of condemned and executed prisoners than on families of homicide victims.[19] Two scholarly studies completed when executions occurred very infrequently addressed the issues presented by having a family member on death row. Radelet, Vandiver, and Berardo published the first of these studies in 1983. They examined the experiences of condemned inmates' family members in Florida in the early 1980s. At that time, adverse court decisions and death warrants setting a specific date of execution were frequently faced by the prisoners and their families, but only one inmate had been executed in the preceding 20 years. The authors found that the families faced tremendous social and emotional difficulties as they tried to cope with their relatives' death sentences. All the families in the study maintained contact with their condemned relatives, often at the cost of much effort, expense, and emotional distress. The families lived in chronic dread of the eventual execution of their relatives, and experienced a prolonged and unresolved period of anticipatory grief.

John Ortiz Smykla (1986; 1987) interviewed 40 relatives of eight inmates on Alabama's death row. Smykla found "prolonged suffering" and "distorted grief reactions" in each family studied (1987:338). These difficulties were compounded by "an unbelievable mixture of other physical, emotional, and social problems" (1987:343). The families' grief reactions included self-accusation, social isolation, and a sense of powerlessness (1987:346). Although these experiences are similar to those of victims' families, the relatives of condemned prisoners are more likely to face mockery and deliberate cruelty because of their situation.

A study of ten families with relatives on death row (Vallejo 1995) found many of the same emotional reactions—"pain, anger, isolation and humiliation" (54)—reported by other researchers. Vallejo's subjects uniformly re-

---

19. In addition to these studies, there is some relevant literature written by the families themselves. Shirley Dicks, whose son died on Tennessee's death row, has written two books about hers and other families' experiences (1990; 1992). Mikal Gilmore (1994) wrote a memoir about his brother Gary, the first person executed in the post-*Furman* era. The sister of a prisoner executed in Alabama wrote an essay describing the effect of the execution on her family (Crawford 1997). Descriptions of condemned inmates' families can be found also in writings by those who have worked with them in various capacities. See Cabana 1996 (warden who supervised executions); Frady 1993 (reporter who wrote article about Arkansas execution); Ingle 1990 (minister serving condemned prisoners); Prejean 1993 (nun working with condemned prisoners and families of victims); Vandiver and Berardo 2000; Vandiver 1989; 1992 (legal assistant for defense attorneys in capital cases).

sponded that there had been no "formal support groups or systems" (50) to assist them during their relatives' trials; after imposition of the death sentence, many found informal support from other families of condemned prisoners. Vallejo found that the relatives she interviewed had all come to think of themselves differently as a result of having a family member on death row; a number of them noted that the experience had made them stronger and increased their faith in God (42–43).

Rachel King and Katherine Norgard (1999) interviewed 28 people with family members who were on death row, had been on death row, or had been executed. Their respondents spoke of feelings and experiences consistent with those found in other studies. The families reported that they received no services or support from the state. They felt stigmatized by their situation and experienced isolation, depression, and chronic grief (1138–1142). Stress related health problems were very common (1127). Quotations from two family members eloquently express their distress. The mother of a condemned prisoner told King and Norgard:

> The family almost ceases.... Death would have been so easy.... This pain, there is no way to describe it. I don't know how to put it into words. The family dies. We went into hibernation, a stand still. Everything is going on but it isn't. Everything shuts down. Everything totally shuts down.... You just got to go through the motions, in a zombie like state (1155–1156).

The younger brother of a man sentenced to death described the effect the death sentence had on him:

> I was eleven years old when I heard the judge pronounce the death sentence on my brother by electrocution until he was "dead, dead, dead."... At that time, I didn't know when it would be carried out. I had an eleven-year-old imagination of electrocution. Those nightmares have haunted me for nineteen years now. I couldn't find anyone to express my feelings to. I was also condemned. My lifelong friends were told they couldn't play with me because I had a brother on death row.... I was always looked at as an outsider. My self-esteem dropped. My anger started growing. The fear that they could take away any person that I loved at any time increased.... I had no belief in anything.... I felt we were outcasts from God. It crushed all my self-esteem and faith. I was lost for a good many years (1159–1160).

Although there is no published research specifically examining the effect on children of having a parent on death row, the emotional and psychological strains placed on children by the incarceration of a parent are well documented (Beatty 1997; Henriques 1982; Johnston 1995; Kampfner 1995; Reed and Reed

1997). Mauer and Huling (1995:22) wrote: "The multiple negative effects of parental arrest and incarceration on children...include traumatic stress, loss of self-confidence, aggression, withdrawal, depression, gang activity, and interpersonal violence." It seems reasonable to assume that a parent's death sentence and eventual execution would have even more severe negative effects on children than would simple incarceration.

Condemned prisoners in modern America generally serve long prison terms before their executions (Crocker 1998). There are inmates who have spent more than twenty years on death row, awaiting the resolution of their cases in the courts. In a sense, condemned inmates now serve both life and death sentences. The length of time prisoners can expect to spend appealing their death sentences means that a significant proportion of their lives may be spent on death row. Confinement on death row is more severe and more stressful than confinement in a maximum security prison (Jackson and Christian 1980; Johnson 1981; Magee 1980). The emotional effect of such harsh confinement, in combination with prolonged dread of execution, constitutes a condition referred to by the European Court of Human Rights as the "death row phenomenon" (Lillich 1991). The impact of the death row phenomenon is also felt by the prisoners' families, who face many years of uncertainty and emotional strain as their relatives' cases work their way through the courts.

The families are nearly helpless to improve conditions of confinement for their relatives, apart from providing them canteen money, filling package permits, and writing and visiting whenever possible. Visiting is especially important as a way to maintain emotional ties and provide support to the prisoners. Visiting can be complicated and difficult, involving considerable effort and expense. The visitor must make arrangements to be away from work and family responsibilities, in many states must travel to rural areas not served by public transportation, and must be sure to comply with prison regulations about identification, dress, and prior approval for visits. These regulations often seem arbitrary to visitors, and may change frequently and without notification. Failure to comply in every detail can result in denial of a visit, even if the visitor has traveled from out of state. Families fear that complaining about prison conditions or about problems with visiting will mark them as troublemakers and cause difficulties for their relatives. Death row visits generally are held under restrictive circumstances, and the prisoner and his family may be separated by a wire or glass barrier. Despite the difficulties and frustrations of visiting, many family members make heroic efforts to visit as frequently as possible (Vandiver 1989:133–134; Vandiver 1992:58).

The family of the death sentenced prisoner must adjust to the rules of the prison and the rulings of the courts, but perhaps most importantly, they have to learn to cope with the changed moral status of their relative:

> To be condemned, expelled from life by one's fellows, makes
> death not a natural event or a misfortune but a stigma of final re-

jection. The knowledge that one has been found too odious to live is bound to produce immense anxiety.... To be singled out as too loathsome, as unfit to live, by the solemn judgment of one's fellow men is the most desolating of rejections (van den Haag 1975:212).

This desolating rejection is felt by the family as well as by the condemned prisoner. Relatives risk ostracism if they acknowledge their relationship to the condemned, as described by family members in the following quotes:

People that really know me have stood by me. It's the strangers who, when they find out that I'm Kenneth's mother, act as if I have something catching. When it first happened, people would stand in groups and talk about Kenneth killing this girl (Dicks 1990:112).

It was not that hard to figure out where she [Gary Gilmore's mother] lived, and sometimes, late at night, about the hours the bars were letting out...she would hear a car pull up outside. She would hear voices, whispers, laughs, profanities, threats. Some people yelled horrible things, some people threw bottles or cans at the trailer. She sat there in the dark, not moving, knowing full well that the world outside her walls was a world of no forgiveness (Gilmore 1994:359).

Probably the most difficult period for the families is the time just before the execution. All the chronic problems of having a relative on death row pale in comparison with the acute crisis of the final death watch. The families' final visits occur while lawyers for the state and defense frantically file last minute motions, while politicians and prosecutors speculate on the likelihood that the execution will occur, and while news reporters keep a countdown to the moment of the execution. Family members try to hide their own distress for the prisoner's sake, as he does for theirs. The final farewells take place in the presence of guards, under rigid time constraints, and conditions of extreme security (see Cabana 1996:176–177 for a description of a mother's last visit with her son). In some states, the prisoner's family members are permitted to witness the execution. The anguish of watching the deliberate killing of a family member while being helpless to intervene is difficult to imagine, but relatives endure the experience in order to offer a last gesture of support and love to the prisoner.

Families of condemned men must bear the additional pain of knowing that their relatives' deaths are actively desired by many people. They can look for almost no sympathy from the public, and the death of their relative is not recognized as a real loss. Indeed, there have been public celebrations outside prisons during executions. The viciousness of some of these displays can hardly be exaggerated. At the execution of James Briley in Virginia in 1985: "[Demonstrators], men and women, sported signs saying, 'Fry Em,' 'Burn Briley Burn,' 'Kill the Negro.' Some waved Confederate flags…and uttered all manner of racial epithets…one white woman carried a sign reading, 'How does it feel to be burned in a chair? Burn—damn you—koon!'" (Dance 1987:135–136, 139–140). The same year, 75 police officers from Jacksonville, Florida, celebrated with champagne and cheering outside the prison as James Raulerson's execution took place. James Reston described the scene outside the prison in North Carolina the night Velma Barfield was executed: "…a clutch of death-penalty boosters egged on the state. 'Hip, hip, hurrah…K-I-L-L.' 'Burn, bitch, burn.' Their delirious, high-pitched cackles floated over the scene…" (Reston 1985:82). The execution of Ted Bundy in Florida in 1989 resembled a "macabre carnival" (Von Drehle 1995:393; see also Paredes and Purdum 1990).

The inmate may be unaware of the celebration outside the prison as he is killed, but his family certainly knows of it, and has to live with the memories. Gary Gilmore's brother Mikal has expressed the enduring alienation resulting from such an experience:

> For the rest of your life, you will have to move around in a world that wanted this death to happen. You will have to walk past people every day who were heartened by the killing of somebody in your family…. You turn on the television, and the journalist tells you how the warden put a black hood over Gary's head and pinned a small, circular cloth target above his chest, and how five men pumped a volley of bullets into him. He tells you how the blood flowed from Gary's devastated heart and down his chest, down his legs, staining his white pants scarlet and dripping to the warehouse floor. He tells you how Gary's arm rose slowly at the moment of the impact, how his fingers seemed to wave as his life left him.
>
> You will have to try to find a way to live with the sorrow that will now always be at the heart of your heart. You will have to try to find a way to live in this world, in this life, and not hate it—and you will have to try despite the impossibility of such a task (Gilmore 1994:349–350).

No systematic research has been done to learn how a relative's execution affects a family in the long term. It seems reasonable to assume that healing from such a traumatic loss would require much time, just as it does for the families of homicide victims. Whether the level of public glee over the inmate's death affects the family's recovery is another important but unexplored question. Perhaps the most important question is the effect on children of losing a parent under such circumstances.

The Legal Context

Much of the aftermath of homicide occurs within a legal context beyond the control of the families concerned. The law as it has developed in the post-*Furman* era does allow both sets of families to play a potentially important role at the sentencing hearing, however. This section of the chapter discusses the relevant cases, their impact on families, and briefly explores some of the issues and problems raised by current practices.

Mitigation Testimony

Post-*Furman* death penalty statutes and Supreme Court decisions attempted to improve the system of capital sentencing in two principal ways. First was the attempt to develop a sentencing system that eliminated arbitrariness, capriciousness, and discrimination in the imposition of the death penalty.[20] The second, which is the element that concerns this chapter, was the emphasis placed on individualized sentencing. The Supreme Court held in the 1978 case of *Lockett v. Ohio* that capital sentencers must "not be precluded from considering as a mitigating factor, any aspect of a defendant's character or record and any of the circumstances of the offense that the defendant proffers as a basis for a sentence less than death" (at 604, footnote omitted).

Ideally, this means that the judge and the jury should hear information about every aspect of the defendant's development, history, and character. Mitigating evidence can include, but is not limited to, any history of mental illness in the family, prenatal care of the defendant, the circumstances of birth and infancy, all childhood illnesses and injuries, school, military, and employment history, and any history of sexual, physical, and emotional abuse (Norton 1992). These details of the defendant's life history should humanize him in the eyes of the judge and jury, and help them to understand the circumstances that shaped and influenced him. The judge and jury can then consider the crime within the total context of the defendant's life.[21]

---

20. A quarter century of increasingly sophisticated research has revealed the continuing failure of the system to provide fair and consistent sentencing in capital cases, or even to reliably distinguish the guilty from the innocent. This reality is gradually being acknowledged by policy makers and the public and has resulted in many recent calls to reform the capital punishment system.

21. All too often mitigating evidence is poorly researched and poorly presented, if indeed, it is presented at all (Coyle, Strasser, and Lavelle 1990; Bright 1994). The judge and jury are likely to receive only fragmentary information about the defendant's family and social history, and thus have an incomplete understanding of the circumstances that led him to his present situation.

The involvement of the defendant's family is essential to properly develop mitigating evidence. Family members are likely to know more about the histories of prior generations of the family, the defendant's prenatal care, and his early childhood experiences than he does himself. They can confirm his memories of childhood events, and can lead investigators to other witnesses, such as neighbors and teachers. They will be able to point investigators in the direction of school reports, medical records, and other important documents.

This opportunity to assist in the defense comes at a price, however. Family members must openly discuss with strangers the most secret, difficult, and often shameful aspects of their family life. They must reveal their own and their relatives' failures and shortcomings. Deeply hidden family secrets may have to be revealed, and the most intimate aspects of their lives held up for public examination. The life histories of most condemned prisoners contain horrifying accounts of emotional, physical, and sexual victimization in childhood, often against a background of severe poverty, racial discrimination, and family and community instability.[22] During the sentencing hearing, the defendant's family is likely to be called upon to testify about these matters in open court, an experience that causes many family members much dread and shame. Undergoing the ordeal of testifying about the most intimate of family secrets is no guarantee that the death sentence will be avoided. A death sentence imposed after such testimony must leave the family wondering if something they said or failed to say might have saved their relative's life.

Victim Impact Statements

Victim impact statements are an important way in which victims can influence the outcome of judicial proceedings. The United States Supreme Court has reversed itself on the issue of victim impact statements in capital cases. The Court's rulings in *Booth v. Maryland* (1987) and *South Carolina v. Gathers* (1989) held that the Eighth Amendment prohibited evidence of the impact of the homicide on the victim's family. These holdings were overruled in *Payne v. Tennessee* (1991). Chief Justice Rehnquist, delivering the opinion of the Court, wrote, "We are now of the view that a State may properly conclude that for the jury to assess meaningfully the defendant's moral culpability and blameworthi-

---

22. There is substantial evidence to support the assertion that the great majority of condemned inmates suffered violent victimization and/or severe neglect in their childhoods. Dorothy Lewis and her colleagues documented the abuse experienced by two groups of death row inmates, one adult and one juvenile, and the resulting psychiatric and neurological impairments (Lewis et al. 1986; Lewis et al. 1988). Anecdotal and case studies of the lives of condemned prisoners give consistent life histories (Miller and Miller 1989; Laughlin 1990). For the best accounts of the meaning and importance of these experiences for mitigation, see Haney (1995, 2003).

ness, it should have before it at the sentencing phase evidence of the specific harm caused by the defendant" (at 825).

Victim impact statements give the survivors of homicide victims the opportunity to tell the judge and jury, and the defendant, about the victim's character and life, and how the murder of their relative has affected them. These statements often include wrenching descriptions of long term loss and grieving after a homicide[23]:

> Consider the effect on the child. My daughter was 22 months old the day she witnessed her mother's murder. Last month she celebrated her fourth birthday, the third one without her mother.... Beginning two days after her mother's burial and for the following week thereafter, Maureen's behavior became so erratic that it was virtually impossible to parent her. She would not eat, and although she had been weaned from her bottle more than four months before, she became reattached to it.... She would not sleep or nap until she was totally exhausted, and then she would constantly lie awake crying for her mother. She would cry hysterically for long periods of time, and no amount of holding or rocking soothed her. One of these jaunts lasted for four and a half hours.... It was 14 months after her mother's death until she would sleep again through the night. She would awaken from three to five times per night screaming, "No, no. Mommy, Mommy." From time to time, she still has nightmares with similar intensity, and to this day, she refuses to go to sleep without a light on.... For almost eight months after her mother's murder, Maureen would make stabbing motions to her chest while simultaneously saying, "Ug, ug, ug.".... Also, for approximately eight months after witnessing her mother's murder, Maureen would poke at your eyes and attempt to choke you while you were holding her. When doing so, she would contort her face and make noises like a growling dog. Even now she refuses to wear constrictive clothing around her neck.... On every birthday and holiday, she notes her mother's absence. This last Christ-

---

23. Several dozen victims and survivors testified at the sentencing hearing of the trial of Timothy McVeigh for the killing of 168 people in the Oklahoma City bombing. Although the judge limited the victim impact testimony, the emotional effect was overwhelming. "Emotional witnesses today painted a horrific picture of the pain the Oklahoma City bombing has caused them, as the government urged an often teary jury to sentence Timothy J. McVeigh to death. In some of the trial's most gruesome and heart-wrenching testimony yet, sobbing mothers spoke of losing children, wives choked back tears describing husbands who perished, and rescue workers struggled for composure recounting the devastation they witnessed on April 19, 1995" (Romano 1997:A01).

mas while visiting my mother-in-law in upstate New York, we were singing Christmas carols together when I noticed Maureen had become silent. Her shoulders were slumped. Her head hung down with her chin on her chest, and she sobbed, "I miss Mommy" (*State v. Moore* 1987).

The opportunity to state publicly their loss, pain, and anger, and to have their statements heard respectfully, may provide an important step toward healing for some families. There are substantial problems with the use of victim impact statements in capital cases, however. Some victims will not have families willing or able to come to court and give statements, and some survivors who do testify may find the pressure of giving such testimony an added burden. All survivors will not make an equally good impression on the judge and jury. If the impact of victim impact testimony correlates with the race of those testifying, the use of these statements could increase the already disproportionate number of death sentences in cases with white victims. It is likely that jurors are emotionally affected by the statements of victims' families[24] (Bandes 1996:393; Luginbuhl and Burkhead 1995), which opens the door to precisely the extralegal influences the current system of capital sentencing was designed to overcome. The use of victim impact statements in capital sentencing also raises the ugly possibility of "creating a contest of weeping families" (Berger 1992:58, note 192). Most troubling of all, perhaps, is the implicit test of the worthiness of victims; if the jury does not return the maximum sentence the prosecutor has requested, the victim's family may feel that the legal system has belittled the victim and their loss (Bandes 2000:1605).

Most of the commentary on the *Payne* ruling has concerned victims' families who wish for a death sentence to be imposed. But some families expressly do not want the death sentence imposed on the defendant. Occasionally their wishes are respected. Reva Griffith wrote of her successful appeal to the judge not to impose death on the killer of her son. The judge explicitly recognized that to "sentence Donald Edward Reese to death in this murder of Christopher Griffith... would do injury to his parents and those who loved him and worked with him with regard to the death penalty and his feelings about violence" (1992:177). Ms. Griffith and her husband responded to the life sentence "as if a door had opened just a crack and let some light into our sadness.... We left the courtroom with a lightness in our hearts we had not felt since Chris's death. We felt the action of the judge was a tribute to Chris and the way he had tried to live" (at 179, 180). In a Tennessee case in which the jury voted for life:

---

24. The potential emotional effect of victim impact testimony is so strong that several scholars have argued that "execution impact evidence" (Logan 1999–2000; Thomas 2000) or "defendant family impact evidence" (King and Norgard 1999) should be admitted as a balancing factor. This would allow members of the defendant's family to tell the jury how the defendant's death sentence and execution would affect them.

Dennis Brooks asked a Henry County jury to give his son's convicted murderer something his son was denied—mercy and compassion. The jury listened, and came back with a sentence of life without parole instead of a death sentence.... Brooks was shot, stabbed, dismembered, sexually mutilated, his heart cut out, then burned inside his truck.... "The agonizing pain I've gone through as a parent, I don't wish on any other parent," Brooks said, his voice quivering and eyes glistening with tears (Taylor 1994).

The desire of a victim's family for a life sentence is not always granted; indeed, the family may not even be allowed to express their preference or the opinion of the victim about capital punishment. SueZann Bosler witnessed her father's murder and was stabbed repeatedly herself. In none of the defendant's three trials was she allowed to testify that her father opposed the death penalty and that she wanted a life sentence for his killer. At the third trial, desperate to let the jury know her wishes, Ms. Bosler identified herself as a beautician and opponent of the death penalty. Astonishingly, the judge threatened to jail her: "'If you violate the order, and I find you in direct criminal contempt, you face six months in a Dade County jail with a $500 fine,' the judge told her." Speaking to the jury after they returned a life sentence, Ms. Bosler "said that the sentence was 'the happiest moment of the last 10 1/2 years for me. Now I can go on with my life.... And I thank you very much for that. God bless you all'" (Zarrella 1997).

Implications for the Future Use of Capital Punishment

The death penalty is undergoing serious reevaluation for the first time in a generation. This reevaluation involves nearly every aspect of the use of capital punishment, from method of execution to fairness of imposition to cost. In this section of the chapter, I will briefly discuss only two points directly relevant to the families involved: wrongful convictions and victims' families' efforts to abolish the death penalty.

Much public attention has been directed to the recent exonerations of a number of prisoners, both on death row and serving long prison terms.[25] An aspect of this issue that has received very little discussion is the effect that the discovery of a wrongful conviction must have on the family of the victim. The victim's family must deal with the fact that the person they believed to be guilty

---

25. According to the Death Penalty Information Center, as of late July 2002, 101 death sentenced prisoners have been formally exonerated since 1973 (Death Penalty Information Center 2002c).

is actually innocent and has been suffering and facing death for something he did not do. Perhaps even more painful, they must cope with the corollary of this discovery: the guilty person has not been identified or punished, is probably still free, and may have hurt others.[26] In this situation, the criminal justice system has profoundly failed both sets of families as well as the defendant and the public. If new cases of wrongful convictions continue to emerge, public confidence in the criminal justice system and support for the death penalty are likely to decline.

A second important development is the new level of activism by victims' family members who oppose the death penalty and the increasing public recognition given to their position. Victims' families sometimes actively seek a life sentence before or at trial or by appealing to the governor for a commutation. Some families may wish for a death sentence at trial, but as time passes, find their feelings changing. Recently Ross Byrd, whose father was killed by white supremacists who dragged him behind a pickup truck, has spoken out against the execution of his father's killers although he strongly supported the death penalty during their trials. " 'When I heard King had exhausted his appeals, I began thinking, 'How can this help me or solve my pain?' and I realized it couldn't,' Byrd said" (Dove 2002:A1).

Family members of the victim might oppose the execution of their relative's killer for a number of reasons besides general opposition to the death penalty. Some victims' families have stated that they feel the memory of their relative would be diminished or belittled by an act of violence. Others may wish to avoid the prolonged contact with the criminal justice system that the death penalty requires, and the public attention it bestows upon the condemned prisoner. If an alternative sentence of life without parole or a very long term of years is available, they may prefer the finality of that sentence and the obscurity into which the defendant will quickly fall to the continued uncertainty and publicity of the death penalty. These considerations seem to have influenced the family of Matthew Shepard, the victim of a vicious hate crime; Shepard's parents supported a plea agreement for a sentence of life without parole because, as Mr. Shepard stated to the killer in court:

> It means no drawn-out appeals process, chance of walking away
> free due to a technicality, and no chance of a lighter sentence due

---

26. In a non-death penalty case in which the defendant was found to be innocent after serving many years in prison, the victim's family expressed sympathy for the defendant and his family. The defendant's uncle met with the victim's family to encourage them to pursue efforts to find the guilty person, instructing them in the ways his own family had worked to free their relative. A member of the victim's family said, "We didn't have any hard feelings toward each other. He gave us some advice on what we need to do and so that we don't have to learn how to do it on our own" (Rice 2000).

to a 'merciful' jury. Best of all, you won't be a symbol. No years of publicity, no chance of commutation, no nothing—just a miserable future and a more miserable end. It works for me ("Excerpts" 1999:A22).

Some families may want the offender to have time to reflect on his deed, and perhaps to feel remorse for it. A few may even hope that in the future there can be some sort of mediation or reconciliation between them and the offender (see Molhan 1996, for a personal account).

Recently a significant number of victims' families have moved beyond trying to influence the outcome of their individual cases and are actively working to abolish the death penalty. Murder Victims' Families for Reconciliation is an anti-death penalty group formed by victims' survivors (including family members of executed inmates) who actively oppose and work against all executions. Members of MVFR engage in much public education and outreach, speaking to audiences around the country, giving interviews to the media, testifying before legislative committees, and calling for clemency when executions are scheduled. In June of 2001, MVFR held a national conference for abolitionist victims' families. The group issued an important report in 2002 documenting ways in which victims' families opposing the death penalty are ignored, marginalized, and denied support and information by victim service providers and prosecutors (Cushing and Sheffer 2002). The activism of these families probably has greater potential to change and elevate the terms of the death penalty debate than the work of any other group. (For a book on members of MVFR, see King 2003; for further examples of victims' families who have rejected the death penalty, see Tabak and Lane 1989:129–131).

Discussion and Conclusion

Supporters of capital punishment frequently argue that the prisoner's death will offer some combination of comfort, closure, and a restored sense of justice to the victim's survivors. In a succinct statement of this position, a columnist wrote:

> There is little enough we can do to ease the pain of grieving survivors, but hanging murderers would help. Many families can find no peace as long as the slayer of their loved one lives. They are filled with rage and despair; they want the killer dead. By seeking the death penalty for willful murderers, society can offer these families a measure of comfort, and assure them that their loss is taken seriously (Jacoby 1996).

Several assumptions underlie these remarks: that the victim's family will benefit from the offender's execution, that the wishes of the victim's family should influence the outcome of the case, that the victim's family wants the death penalty for the offender, and most basically, that one of the functions of criminal sentences should be to ease the suffering of innocent people.

As discussed above, the long-term effects of executions on victims' families are not known, and any claims about the benefits of executions remain speculative. It is clear, however, that the wishes of surviving family members cannot determine the outcome of homicide cases.[27] For example, some victims' relatives feel that imposition of the death sentence is too light a punishment; they want the death of the victim to be duplicated, blow for blow, upon the defendant, although clearly this is a desire our legal system will not fulfill. A system of justice driven largely or entirely by the victims' wishes would be utterly arbitrary and would not meet even the minimum requirements of due process. To further complicate the issue, families of homicide victims differ widely on how they think offenders should be punished, and sometimes members of the same family,[28] or families victimized by the same defendant,[29] may disagree on the proper punishment.

But assume for argument's sake that all victims' families do want the execution of the offenders. To carry out their wishes, the criminal justice system would have to impose a death sentence in response to every homicide, which obviously is a moral, legal, financial, and social impossibility. Every death penalty jurisdiction distinguishes potential death penalty cases from other homicide cases, and in every death penalty jurisdiction, capital punishment is

---

27. Although it is not possible to construct a sentencing system based on victims' wishes, it is important to note two points: no one should be judgmental about what victims want done to offenders, and no one is obliged to agree with them. No outsider, including other victims' families, has the right to belittle families that want vengeance or reconciliation or any other outcome. There is no single correct response to a family member's murder that can be held up as a model for other bereaved families to follow. No one can demand or expect families to forgive; no one has the right to question whether families who do forgive cared less for their relatives than families who want the most severe sanctions.

28. Family members of Victoria Lamm were divided as to the appropriate sentence. At a hearing concerning commutation of the death sentence, Ms. Lamm's husband and daughter wished to speak against execution, but were not allowed to address the Nebraska Board of Pardons and Paroles. Ms. Lamm's sister, who supported the execution, was allowed to address the Board, leading Mr. Lamm and his daughter to file suit claiming discrimination on the grounds of their views. The case was ultimately returned for resentencing on other issues and the prosecution decided not to seek the death penalty again. The district attorney stated in court that he "recognized that the original death sentence had caused damage by creating divisions within the victims' families" ("No Death Sentence" 2001:3).

29. Many of the people who lost family members in the Oklahoma City bombing expressed their desire for Timothy McVeigh to be executed, but "a surprising number of [victims' survivors]...say they oppose death for McVeigh and believe they will heal faster if he is spared" (Pooley 1997:35; see also Welch 1997:36 and 2001, for a personal statement by a victim's father).

imposed in only a small percent of cases. Only by the wholesale dismantling of due process requirements at both the trial and appellate levels, i.e., a return to the pre-*Furman* situation or worse, could the system greatly increase the number of executions without astronomically increasing their cost. This administrative reality means that only a very few victims' families will ever receive the putative benefits of executions. Therefore, even if the death penalty benefits the few families for whose relatives' deaths it is imposed, it does not necessarily follow that the death penalty would be helpful to victims' families in general. The satisfaction a few victims' families might receive from a death sentence and execution would be outweighed by the dissatisfaction of the vast majority of victims' families who see the convicted killer receive a sentence less than death.

A final problem with the argument that executions should be used to comfort victims' families lies in the assumption that the law should be used to ease the suffering of the innocent. If the pain of innocent family members does have a claim, then it must have a claim for the families of the defendants as well as the victims. One cannot base an argument for the death penalty on its presumed benefit for the victims' families without confronting the devastation it imposes on the defendants' families. To argue that families of victims are innocent and families of offenders are somehow guilty violates one of the most fundamental assumptions of our legal system—that only the perpetrators are guilty of the crime, not those who happen to be associated with them through ties of family or friendship. Arguing that one set of families is less deserving than the other is repugnant per se and risks replicating the racial and class divisions so obvious in our death sentencing patterns.

If capital punishment were a deterrent to murder, if it were a better form of incapacitation than life in prison, if it demonstrably benefitted society in any way, it might be possible to weigh the pain of condemned prisoners' families against the benefits provided by executions. But the death penalty fails on every empirical criterion. The moral question retentionists must answer is whether the undemonstrated, questionable, and unevenly distributed benefits of executions for victims' families outweigh the indisputable present anguish and probable long term damage the death penalty inflicts on the prisoners' families.

References

Amick-McMullan, A., D.G. Kilpatrick, and H.S. Resnick (1991) "Homicide as a Risk Factor for PTSD Among Surviving Family Members." *Behavior Modification* 15:545–559.

Amick-McMullan, A., D.G. Kilpatrick, and L.J. Veronen (1989) "Family Survivors of Homicide Victims: A Behavioral Analysis." *The Behavior Therapist* 12 (4):75–79.

Amick-McMullan, A., D.G. Kilpatrick, L.J. Veronen, and S. Smith (1989) "Family Survivors of Homicide Victims: Theoretical Perspectives and an Exploratory Study." *Journal of Traumatic Stress* 2:21–35.

Anderson, M. (1983) "'I Forgive Him'; Darden Victim's Widow Glad Execution Stayed." *The Ledger* (September 3):1A, 10A.

Asaro, M.R. (2001a) "Working with Adult Homicide Survivors, Part I: Impact and Sequelae of Murder." *Perspectives in Psychiatric Care* 37:95–101.

Asaro, M.R. (2001b) "Working with Adult Homicide Survivors, Part II: Helping Family Members Cope with Murder." *Perspectives in Psychiatric Care* 37:115–124, 136.

Associated Press (1986) "Victim's Wife Relieved After Thomas Execution." *Gainesville Sun* (April 17):1B, 3B.

Bandes, S. (2000) "When Victims Seek Closure: Forgiveness, Vengeance, and the Role of Government." *Fordham Urban Law Journal* 27:1599–1606.

Bandes, S. (1996) "Empathy, Narrative, and Victim Impact Statements." *The University of Chicago Law Review* 63:361–412.

Barnes, P.G. (1996) "Final Reckoning: States Allow Victims' Families to Watch Executions." *ABA Journal* (March):36–37.

Beatty, C. (1997) *Parents in Prison: Children in Crisis.* Washington, DC: Child Welfare League of America.

Begley, S., with K. Springen, M. Starr, and C. Kirkpatrick (1993) "'Pouring Salt in My Open Wound.'" *Newsweek* (August 30):59.

Berger, V. (1992) "*Payne* and Suffering: A Personal Reflection and a Victim-Centered Critique." *Florida State University Law Review* 20:21–65.

Booth v. Maryland (1987) 482 U.S. 496.

Bosco, A. (2001) *Choosing Mercy: A Mother of Murder Victims Pleads to End the Death Penalty.* Maryknoll, NY: Orbis Books.

Bright, S. (1994) "Counsel for the Poor: The Death Sentence Not for the Worst Crime but for the Worst Lawyer." *Yale Law Journal* 103:1835–1883.

Brown, C. (1991) "The Unbearable Loss." *Vanity Fair* (August):60, 62, 64, 66, 68, 73–74.

Burgess, A.W. (1975) "Family Reaction to Homicide." *American Journal of Orthopsychiatry* 45:391–398.

Burman, S. and P. Allen-Meares (1994) "Neglected Victims of Murder: Children's Witness to Parental Homicide." *Social Work* 39:28–34.

Cabana, D.A. (1996) *Death at Midnight: The Confession of an Executioner.* Boston: Northeastern University Press.

Camus, A. (1961) "Reflections on the Guillotine." Pp. 175–234, in A. Camus (trans. J. O'Brien), *Resistance, Rebellion, and Death.* New York: Alfred A. Knopf.

Capote, T. (1965) *In Cold Blood.* New York: Random House.

Coyle, M., F. Strasser, and M. Lavelle (1990) "Fatal Defense: Trial and Error in the Nation's Death Belt." *National Law Journal* (June 11):30–31, 38, 41.

Craig, J. (2002) "Grief, Relief Fill Final Day." *The Columbus Dispatch* (February 20): 01A.

Craig, R. J. (1999) "Healing the Wounds of Sibling Survivors of Lethal Violence." Pp. 527–542, in H.V. Hall (ed.), *Lethal Violence: A Sourcebook on Fatal Domestic, Acquaintance, and Stranger Violence.* Boca Raton, FL: CRC Press.

Crawford, P. (1997) "My Brother, Ed Horsley." Pp. 165–177 in C. Whitman and J. Zimmerman (eds.), *Frontiers of Justice: The Death Penalty.* Brunswick, ME: Biddle Publishing Company.

Crocker, D. (1998) "Extended Stays: Does Lengthy Imprisonment on Death Row Undermine the Goals of Capital Punishment?" *The Journal of Gender, Race & Justice* 1:555–574.

Cushing, R.R. and S. Sheffer (2002) "Dignity Denied: The Experience of Murder Victims' Family Members Who Oppose the Death Penalty." Cambridge, MA: Murder Victims' Families for Reconciliation.

Dance, D.C. (1987) *Long Gone: The Mecklenburg Six and the Theme of Escape in Black Folklore.* Knoxville: University of Tennessee Press.

Danto, B.L. (1982) "Survivors of Homicide: The Unseen Victims." Pp. 85–97, in Danto, B.L., J. Bruhns, and A.H. Kutscher (eds.), *The Human Side of Homicide.* New York: Columbia University Press.

Day, L.E. and M.M. Weddington (1996) "Grief and Justice in Families of Homicide Victims: Initial Results from a Study of the Impact of the Criminal Justice System." Paper presented at the meeting of the American Society of Criminology, Chicago, IL.

Death Penalty Information Center (2002a) "Number of Executions by Year Since 1976." Available at http://www.deathpenaltyinfo.org/dpicexec.html (July 23).

Death Penalty Information Center (2002b) "Women and the Death Penalty." Available at http://www.deathpenaltyinfo.org/womenstats.html (July 23).

Death Penalty Information Center (2002c) "Innocence and the Death Penalty." Available at: http://www.deathpenaltyinfo.org/innoc.html (July 23).

Dicks, S. (1992) *They're Going to Kill My Son.* Far Hills, NJ: New Horizon Press.

Dicks, S. (1990) *Death Row: Interviews with Inmates, Their Families and Opponents of Capital Punishment.* Jefferson, NC: McFarland & Company, Inc.

Dove, S. (2002) "Byrd Son Fighting for Life of Killer." *The Houston Chronicle* (July 4):A1.

"Excerpts from Statement by Father" (1999) *The New York Times* (November 5):A22.

Fox, S.S. (1981) "Families in Crisis: Reflections on the Children and Families of the Offender and the Offended." *International Journal of Offender Therapy and Comparative Criminology* 25:254–264.

Frady, M. (1993) "Death in Arkansas." *The New Yorker* (February 22):105–133.

Freeman, L.N., D. Shaffer, and H. Smith (1996) "Neglected Victims of Homicide: The Needs of Young Siblings of Murder Victims." *American Journal of Orthopsychiatry* 66:337–345.

Furman v. Georgia (1972) 408 U.S. 238.

Geberth, V.J. (1992) "Secondary Victims of Homicide." *Law and Order* (September):91–96.

Getzel, G.S. and R. Masters (1984) "Serving Families Who Survive Homicide Victims." *Social Casework: The Journal of Contemporary Social Work*:138–144.

Gibbons, T. (1988) "Victims Again: Survivors Suffer Through Capital Appeals." *ABA Journal* (September 1):64, 66–68.

Gilmore, M. (1994) *Shot in the Heart.* New York: Doubleday.

Goodwin, M.L. (1997) "An Eyeful For an Eye: An Argument Against Allowing the Families of Murder Victims to View Executions." *Brandeis Journal of Family Law* 36:585–608.

Gregg v. Georgia (1976) 428 U.S. 153.

Griffith, R. (1992) *This Song's for You.* Burnsville, NC: Celo Valley Books.

Haney, C. (2003) "Mitigation and the Study of Lives: On the Roots of Violent Criminality and the Nature of Capital Justice." (This volume.)

Haney, C. (1995) "The Social Context of Capital Murder: Social Histories and the Logic of Mitigation." *Santa Clara Law Review* 35:547–609.

Hatzfeld, J. (2000) *Dans le Nu de la Vie: Recits des Marais Rwandais.* Paris: Seuil.

Henriques, Z.W. (1982) *Imprisoned Mothers and Their Children.* Washington, D.C.: University Press of America, Inc.

Henry-Jenkins, W. (1993) *Just Us: Overcoming and Understanding Homicidal Loss and Grief.* Omaha, NE: Centering Corporation.

Hoard, G.R. (1994) *Alone Among the Living.* Athens, GA: The University of Georgia Press.

Hukanovic, R. (1996) *The Tenth Circle of Hell: A Memoir of Life in the Death Camps of Bosnia.* New York: Basic Books.

Ingle, J.B. (1990) *Last Rights: Thirteen Fatal Encounters with the State's Justice.* Nashville: Abingdon Press.

Jackson, A.M. (1979) "The Availability of Mental Health Services for Dependents of Homicide Victims." Pp. 91–100, in H.M. Rose (ed.), *Lethal Aspects of Urban Violence.* Lexington, MA: Lexington Books.

Jackson, B. and D. Christian (1980) *Death Row.* Boston: Beacon Press.

Jacoby, J. (1996) "Twisted View of Compassion." *The Commercial Appeal* (December 16):A9.

Jenkins, B. (2001) *What To Do When the Police Leave: A Guide to the First Days of Traumatic Loss,* 3rd ed. Richmond, VA : WBJ Press.

Johnson, N.C. and S.D. Young (1992) "Survivors' Response to Gang Violence." Pp. 136–146, in R.C. Cervantes (ed.), *Substance Abuse and Gang Violence.* Newbury Park: Sage Publications.

Johnson, R. (1981) *Condemned to Die: Life under Sentence of Death.* New York: Elsevier.

Johnston, D. (1995) "Effects of Parental Incarceration." Pp. 59–88, in K. Gabel and D. Johnston (eds.), *Children of Incarcerated Parents.* New York: Lexington Books.

Kampfner, C.J. (1995) "Post-Traumatic Stress Reactions in Children of Imprisoned Mothers." Pp. 89–100, in K. Gabel and D. Johnston (eds.), *Children of Incarcerated Parents.* New York: Lexington Books.

Key, L.J. (1992) "A Working Typology of Grief Among Homicide Survivors." Pp. 147–159, in R.C. Cervantes (ed.), *Substance Abuse and Gang Violence.* Newbury Park, CA: Sage Publications.

King, R. (2003) *Don't Kill in Our Names: Families of Murder Victims Speak Out Against the Death Penalty.* New Brunswick, NJ: Rutgers University Press.

King, R. and K. Norgard (1999) "What About Our Families? Using the Impact on Death Row Defendants' Family Members as a Mitigating Factor in Death Penalty Sentence Hearings." *Florida State University Law Review* 26:1119–1173.

Kroll, M. (1991) "Chattahoochee Judicial District: Buckle of the Death Belt. The Death Penalty in Microcosm." Washington, D.C.: Death Penalty Information Center. Available at http://essential.org/dpic/dpic.r11.html.

Laughlin, M. (1990) "The Heart of Lucille Broom." *Miami Herald Tropic Magazine* (February 4):6–11.

Lewis, D.O., J.H. Pincus, M. Feldman, L. Jackson, and B. Bard (1986) "Psychiatric Neurological, and Psychoeducational Characteristics of 15 Death Row Inmates in the United States." *American Journal of Psychiatry* 143:838–845.

Lewis, D.O., J. H. Pincus, B. Bard, E. Richardson, L.S. Prichep, M. Feldman, and C. Yeager (1988) "Neuropsychiatric, Psychoeducational, and Family Characteristics of 14 Juveniles Condemned to Death in the United States." *American Journal of Psychiatry* 145:584–589.

Lillich, R.B. (1991) "Notes and Comments: The *Soering* Case." *The American Journal of International Law* 85:128–149.

Lockett v. Ohio (1978) 438 U.S. 586.

Logan, W.A. (1999–2000) "When Balance and Fairness Collide: An Argument for Execution Impact Evidence in Capital Trials." *University of Michigan Journal of Law Reform* 33:1–56.

Luginbuhl, J. and M. Burkhead (1995) "Victim Impact Evidence in a Capital Trial: Encouraging Votes for Death." *American Journal of Criminal Justice* 20:1–16.

Lyon, E., N. Moore, and C. Lexius (1992) "Group Work with Families of Homicide Victims." *Social Work with Groups* 15:19–33.

Magee, D. (1983) *What Murder Leaves Behind: The Victim's Family.* New York: Dodd, Mead.

Magee, D. (1980) *Slow Coming Dark: Interviews on Death Row.* New York: Pilgrim Press.

Malmquist, C.P. (1986) "Children Who Witness Parental Murder: Posttraumatic Aspects." *Journal of American Academy of Child Psychiatry* 25:320–325.

Masters, R., L.N. Friedman, and G. Getzel (1988) "Helping Families of Homicide Victims: A Multidimensional Approach." *Journal of Traumatic Stress* 1:109–125.

Mauer, M. and T. Huling (1995, October) "Young Black Americans and the Criminal Justice System." Available from The Sentencing Project, 918 F. St. NW, Suite 501, Washington, DC 20004.

Miller, K.S. and B.D. Miller (1989) *To Kill and Be Killed: Case Studies from Florida's Death Row.* Pasadena, CA: Hope Publishing Co.

Molhan, S.P. with J. Kavanah (1996) *A Mother's Mission: The Sue Molhan Story.* South Bend, IN: Diamond Communications, Inc.

Murphy, S.A., T. Braun, L. Tillery, K.C. Cain, L.C. Johnson, and R.D. Beaton (1999) "PTSD Among Bereaved Parents Following the Violent Deaths of Their 12- to 28-Year-Old Children: A Longitudinal Prospective Analysis." *Journal of Traumatic Stress* 12:273–291.

Myer, G. (1986) "Vietnam Veteran Executed." *Gainesville Sun* (April 23):1A, 12A.

NAACP Legal Defense and Educational Fund, Inc. (2002, Spring) Death Row, U.S.A. Available at: http://www.deathpenaltyinfo.org/DEATHROWUSArecent.pdf.

"No Death Sentence for Randy Reeves" (2001) *The Voice: Murder Victims' Families for Reconciliation* (Fall/Winter).

Norton, L. (1992) "Capital Cases Mitigation Investigations." *The Champion* (May):43–45.

Paredes, A. and E. Purdum (1990) "'Bye-bye Ted...': Community Response in Florida to the Execution of Theodore Bundy." *Anthropology Today* 6:9–11.

Parkes, C.M. (1993) "Psychiatric Problems Following Bereavement by Murder or Manslaughter." *British Journal of Psychiatry* 162:49–54.

Payne v. Tennessee (1991) 501 U.S. 808.

Pooley, E. (1997) "Death or Life." *Time* (June 16):31–36.

Prejean, H. (1993) *Dead Man Walking: An Eyewitness Account of the Death Penalty in the United States.* New York: Random House.

Radelet, M.L., M. Vandiver, and F.M. Berardo (1983) "Families, Prisons, and Men with Death Sentences: The Human Impact of Structured Uncertainty." *Journal of Family Issues* 4:593–612.

Ragavan, C., M. Schaffer, R. Dotinga, and I. Lobet (2001) "Lost and Found." *U.S. News and World Report* (August 13):12–18.

Raphael, B. (1983) *The Anatomy of Bereavement.* New York: Basic Books.

Redmond, L.M. (1989) *Surviving: When Someone You Love Was Murdered.* Clearwater, FL: Psychological Consultation and Educational Services, Inc.

Reed, D.F. and E.L. Reed (1997) "Children of Incarcerated Parents." *Social Justice* 24:152–169.

Resnick, H.S., D.G. Kilpatrick, B.S. Dansky, B.E. Saunders, and C.L. Best (1993) "Prevalence of Civilian Trauma and Posttraumatic Stress Disorder in a Representative National Sample of Women." *Journal of Consulting and Clinical Psychology* 61:984–991.

Reston, J. (1985) "Invitation to a Poisoning." *Vanity Fair* (February):82–85, 101.

Rice, H. (2000) "Victim's Family Agrees Convict Didn't Kill Girl." *The Houston Chronicle* (August 19):A31.

Riggs, D.S. and D.G. Kilpatrick (1990) "Families and Friends: Indirect Victimization by Crime." Pp. 120–138, in Lurigio, A.J., W.G. Skogan, and R.C. Dairs (eds.), *Victims of Crime: Problems, Policies, and Programs.* Newbury Park, CA: Sage Publications.

Rinear, E.E. (1988) "Psychosocial Aspects of Parental Response Patterns to the Death of a Child by Homicide." *Journal of Traumatic Stress* 1(3):305–322.

Romano, L. (1997) "McVeigh Jurors Sob at Victims' Pain; Penalty Hearing Witnesses Paint Picture of Suffering in Oklahoma Blast." *The Washington Post* (June 5):A01.

Rynearson, E.K. (1984) "Bereavement after Homicide: A Descriptive Study." *American Journal of Psychiatry* 141:1452–1454.

Rynearson, E.K. and J.M. McCreery (1993) "Bereavement after Homicide: A Synergism of Trauma and Loss." *American Journal of Psychiatry* 150:258–261.

Salloum, A., L. Avery, and R.P. McClain (2001) "Group Psychotherapy for Adolescent Survivors of Homicide Victims: A Pilot Study." *Journal of the American Academy of Child and Adolescent Psychiatry* 40:1261–1267.

Saul, T. (1989) "Killer's Sentence Carried Out." *Ocala Star Banner* (May 5):1A, 9A.

Schlosser, E. (1997) "A Grief Like No Other." *The Atlantic Monthly* (September):37–76.

Shapiro, B. (1997) "False Closure." *The Nation* (April 21):5.

Smykla, J.O. (1987) "The Human Impact of Capital Punishment: Interviews With Families of Persons on Death Row." *Journal of Criminal Justice* 15:331–347.

Smykla, J.O. (1986) "The Impact of Capital Punishment on Death Row Inmates' Families." *USA Today*:86–90.

South Carolina v. Gathers (1989) 490 U.S. 805.

Spiegel, D. (2001) "Closure? The Execution Was Just the Start." *The Washington Post* (April 29):B03.

Sprang, M.V., J.S. McNeil, and R. Wright, Jr. (1992–1993) "Grief Among Surviving Family Members of Homicide Victims: A Causal Approach." *Omega* 26:145–160.

Sprang, M.V., J.S. McNeil, and R. Wright, Jr. (1989) "Psychological Changes after the Murder of a Significant Other." *Social Casework: The Journal of Contemporary Social Work*:159–164.

Spungen, D. (1998) *Homicide: The Hidden Victims; A Guide for Professionals.* Thousand Oaks, CA: Sage Publications.

State v. Moore (January 14, 1987) Criminal No. 39769 (Circuit Court for Montgomery County, Maryland).

Tabak, R. and M. Lane (1989) "The Execution of Injustice: A Cost and Lack-of-Benefit Analysis of the Death Penalty." *Loyola of Los Angeles Law Review* 23:59–146.

Taylor, L. (1994) "Harris Draws Life for Murder; Victim's Father Urged Mercy." *The Commercial Appeal* (April 8):1A.

Temple, S. (1997) "Treating Inner-City Families of Homicide Victims: A Contextually Oriented Approach." *Family Process* 36:133–149.

Thomas, T. (2000) "Execution Impact Evidence in Kentucky: It Is Time to Return the Scales to Balance." *Northern Kentucky Law Review* 27:411–429.

Thompson, M.P., F.H. Norris, and R.B. Ruback (1998) "Comparative Distress Levels of Inner-City Family Members of Homicide Victims." *Journal of Traumatic Stress* 11:223–242.

Thornley, A. (1978) "Faith and Strength." *Ocala Star Banner* (October 25):4A.

Vallejo, C.A. (1995) "Death Sentence Experience: The Impact on Family Members of Condemned Inmates." Master's Thesis, California State University, San Bernardino.

van den Haag, E. (1975) *Punishing Criminals: Concerning a Very Old and Painful Question.* New York: Basic Books.

Vandiver, M. and F. Berardo (2000) " 'It's Like Dying Every Day': The Families of Condemned Prisoners." Pp. 339–358 in G.L. Fox and M.L. Benson (eds.) *Families, Crime and Criminal Justice.* Amsterdam: JAI.

Vandiver, M. (1992) "Beyond All Justice: The Death Penalty and Families of the Condemned." *Odyssey* (Spring):56–63.

Vandiver, M. (1989) "Coping with Death: Families of the Terminally Ill, Homicide Victims, and Condemned Prisoners." Pp. 123–138, in M.L. Radelet (ed.), *Facing the Death Penalty.* Philadelphia: Temple University Press.

Vargas, L.A., F. Loya, and J. Hodde-Vargas (1989) "Exploring the Multidimensional Aspects of Grief Reactions." *American Journal of Psychiatry* 146:1484–1488.

Von Drehle, D. (1995) *Among the Lowest of the Dead.* New York: Random House.

Weine, S. M. (1999) *When History is a Nightmare: Lives and Memories of Ethnic Cleansing in Bosnia-Herzegovina.* Piscataway, NJ: Rutgers University Press.

Welch, B. (2001) " 'I Don't Want the Death Penalty for Timothy McVeigh!': A Father's Struggle with the Death Penalty and the Oklahoma City Bombing." *Loyola Journal of Public Interest Law* 2:53–65.

Welch, B. (1997) "A Father's Urge to Forgive." *Time* (June 16):36.
Wilkinson, A. (1993) *A Violent Act*. New York: Alfred A. Knopf.
Zarrella, J. (1997) "Daughter Thanks Jury for Sparing Her Father's Killer." *CNN Interactive* (June 14). Available at http://www-cgi.cnn.com/US/9706/14/eye.for.eye.

Chapter 21

Life under Sentence of Death: Historical and Contemporary Perspectives

Robert Johnson[1]

> The reality of this waiting place for death is difficult to grasp. It's not a ward in a hospital where sick people wait to die. People here wait to be taken out of their cells and killed. This is the United States of America and these are government officials in charge and there's a law sanctioning and upholding what is going on here, so it all must be legitimate and just, or so one compartment of my brain tells me, the part that studied civics in high school, the part that wants to trust that your country would never violate the human rights of its citizens.
>
> The red block letters say "Death Row."
>
> My stomach can read the letters better than my brain.
> > Sister Helen Prejean
> > *Dead Man Walking* (1993:27–28)

> The place was a dungeon, full of men who were as good as dead.
> > Michael Lesy
> > *The Forbidden Zone* (1987:150)

> I fear that death row means a gradual killing of my humanity, which is more painful than any execution can ever be.
> > Death row prisoner

There is something almost timeless about death row, or at least about the plight of those held captive awaiting execution. Sister Helen Prejean's stomach can "read" the words Death Row better than her brain because she is in touch with something very basic. Her anxiety is rooted in a simple human response—a gut feeling of empathy evoked by the helplessness and vulnerabil-

---

1. Portions of this chapter are reprinted with permission from chapter three of *Death Work: A Study of the Modern Execution Process* (2nd ed., Belmont: Wadsworth 1998).

ity of the condemned (see Prejean 1993). My point is not that others in times past would necessarily share Prejean's concern for the condemned; many, even most, probably did not. We know that empathy for the condemned emerged gradually over human history, starting with the more privileged classes and moving across the social spectrum from there. It was not until the nineteenth century that most Europeans and Americans found public torture and execution revolting, and even then many still joined vast crowds to savor the strong sentiments such spectacles would produce. Rather, my point is that, specifics aside, confinement of the condemned has almost always been a warehousing operation, carried out in what amounts to a human dungeon. The condemned have, as a general rule, died psychologically (the modern word is dehumanization) before they were physically put to death (see, e.g., Johnson 1998).

In the middle ages and even through the early modern period, the rich or noble could sometimes secure privileges that would lighten the burden of their pre-execution confinement. We know that some offenders could and did throw lavish parties on the eve of their executions; others could obtain physical comforts and have free access (in their cells) to family and friends. The term, "Monsters Ball," popularized in a recent movie by the same title, in fact refers to an elaborate party, complete with wine, music and dancing, held on the eve of the execution of a man known as the Monster of London.[2] But the historical record suggests that the vast majority of offenders lived in oppressive, isolated, and often squalid conditions of confinement. They faced public executions marked by a level of torture and brutality inconceivable today. Psychological paralysis born of sheer terror was the most common reaction among the condemned. Prisoners routinely approached the scaffold numb with fear—shaking, soiling themselves—in a state of psychological shock (Gatrell 1994). Some offenders would break down completely and have to be carried to their deaths; a few would attempt to flee the scaffold, only to be caught and put to a decidedly ignoble death. Even would-be suicides received no special consideration; they would be dragged to the gallows, with fresh wounds bleeding freely, strapped to a chair or pole and then summarily hanged so that they could be executed before they expired from their own efforts (see, e.g., Speer 1845/1994). The vast majority of those sentenced to public execution, however, were incapable of any kind of resistance. Defeated and demoralized, they would meekly submit to the executioner.[3]

Much of the work on public executions and the demeanor of convicts exposed to such tortures is drawn from European sources. Such evidence as exists on the deportment of the condemned in America bears out these observa-

---

2. See Johnson 1998:17–18

3. Rare exceptions to this observation have received much attention from historians and criminologists and make up a mythology of the brave condemned (Gatrell 1994).

tions. An observer of mid-nineteenth century executions in America provides evidence that suggests that offenders would first deny the import of impending execution, then be overwhelmed by the threat of death as the event approached. Fully nine out of ten condemned, we learn, would forsake religious advice in their cells and instead delude themselves with "vain hopes of pardon," with distracting visits, and with pointless posturing (maintaining a "determined carriage") — until "the eve of the fatal morning," at which point:

> fatigued, weak, and worn out with his efforts, the mind becomes suddenly depressed with disappointment, corresponding to the condition of the body; he then falls into a state of stupor and insensibility, from which it is almost a cruelty to attempt to rouse him, as it is too late now to make any beneficial religious impression on him. The next morning, when brought out of his cell to be pinioned, you behold a man already half dead; — his countenance has fallen, his eyes are fixed, his lips are deadly pale and quivering, while his whole aspect, in anticipation of the reality, gives you the personification of death's counterpart..." (Spear 1845/1994:50).

Today's condemned prisoners, like those in centuries past, give us "the personification of death's counterpart" and go to the executioner "already half dead" and effectively beyond resistance (see Johnson 1998; Christianson, 2000).[4] Variants on a theme of dehumanization — of being alive physically but dead psychologically — would seem to characterize confinement under sentence of death, whatever may be the particulars of the penal regime, the execution process, or, indeed, of the prisoner population.

Though reliable records are hard to come by, it seems clear that offenders in earlier centuries were a particularly motley crew. The list of capital offenses was long; offenders would include the old and the young, the novice and the hardened criminal, the murderer and the forger, a fair selection of women and even a few rich people, including (in Europe) some of the nobility (Gatrell 1994; Linebaugh 1992). Over this century in America, offenders have included murderers, armed robbers, rapists, and even some burglars. (As recently as the 1970s, one could find nighttime home burglars on North Carolina's death row.) Given the explosive nature of violence, some of the murderers sent to death row were first-time felony offenders; as many as a third had never served hard time in a prison before they were condemned to die (see, e.g. Johnson 1989).

---

4. Over 600 executions were carried out at Sing Sing prison between 1891 and 1960. Only one man resisted, and that "incident didn't last over fifteen to twenty seconds before he was strapped in the usual manner..." Apparently this man had been led to believe he would be getting a reprieve. When one failed to materialize, he broke down. See Christianson 2000:127.

There are some indications that today's offenders—those sentenced in the last decade—are a more hardened and experienced lot, but that is simply an impression shared by some researchers (see Donovan 1997). All we can say with certainty is that today, in comparison to centuries past, there is a smaller range of offense types represented on death row. Today, at least, all of the men and women on death row have been sentenced for murder. We can also suppose that today's death row inmates are more likely than their predecessors to in fact be guilty of the crimes for which they have been convicted; though we know there are innocent men and women on today's death rows—over 100 have been released in the last decade or so—it stands to reason that more persons were wrongfully convicted in years past, when legal safeguards were much less strict.[5] For the most part, then, we have on our death rows today actual capital murderers. Yet, from the point of view of character, the population of offenders remains profoundly immature and, as a result, vulnerable. Commenting on the prisoners of Texas' death row, populated by convicted murderers, Donovan reports, "I was continually struck by how raw, dare I say vulnerable, so many seemed to be just below the layers of mistrust, anger, and violence" (Donovan 1997:8). That vulnerability, we must suppose, can be traced to the marginality—economic, social, psychological—that has marked and indeed marred their lives. In the words of condemned prisoner Ronald Spivey, held on Georgia's death row since 1976:

> America is killing the economically deprived, those of the lower socioeconomic strata, killing the insane, killing the retarded, killing illiterates, killing the emotionally crippled, killing the childishly immature and mentally undeveloped, killing the socially disenfranchised and the politically powerless of our society, killing those so criminally abused as children that they never had a chance to develop normally to a well-balanced human being (Arriens 1997:19).

Who can doubt that Spivey is identifying universal characteristics of the condemned over the centuries? Today, as in times past, we are in large measure killing the unfit, "the weaker of the species. We kill our mistakes. The financially strong and socially fortunate survive and the weak perish…just like the jungle animal kingdom" (Arriens 1997:19).

The conditions of confinement for condemned prisoners appear to have been fairly constant over the centuries. Though, as has been noted, the offender population has changed, the essential contingencies—impending execution wrought upon those held utterly helpless in close captivity—have not changed at all. Close custody has been and remains the central characteristic of life under sentence of death, on the enduring assumption that condemned

---

5. See Christianson 2000:24.

prisoners are desperate and hence dangerous because they have nothing to lose. By some indications, as we shall see, the trend is toward increased isolation and control, aided by modern technology.

Modern Death Rows

Sing Sing Prison's death row, as described in the 1920s and 1930s, embodies much of what is essential about the modern death row. Known among prisoners as "the slaughterhouse," Sing Sing's death row was a remarkably secure custodial environment. The prisoners spent all but fifteen minutes of each day locked in their cells. "While locked in the cell, no condemned prisoner [could] see another," though conversation was possible. Prisoners were "dressed in," meaning that, on arrival, they were assigned "clothing...of such quality that it [could not] easily be used to make a rope to be used in an attempt at suicide by hanging." Only one prisoner succeeded in taking his life in Sing Sing's Condemned Cells (Lawes 1937:162–164). Not a single prisoner ever escaped.[6]

"Rules governed every facet of death house operations," notes Christianson (2000:43), creating a world virtually devoid of privacy and autonomy. Correspondence was carefully censored; letters could be returned if the inmate appeared to be "begging for packages or money" or (my favorite) for failure to "stick to your subject." (One can only guess the sanction for a split infinitive.) Visits were closely monitored, with officers not infrequently writing up reports about what they had overheard. News reporters were excluded from this world. The prisoner was alone, at the mercy of an essentially totalitarian regime. It is troubling to note that, "under today's stricter rules of evidence and other legal standards, a large percentage of the prisoners in the Sing Sing Death House probably would not have been sentenced to death" (Christianson, 2000:24).

A concerted effort was made to prevent makeshift weapons from falling into the prisoners' hands. In their cells, prisoners wore felt slippers instead of shoes; during their brief periods of recreation, they wore special shoes with soft insteps, which made them less formidable weapons. Eating without knives and forks, instead using comparatively harmless spoons, prisoners were also denied the use of pepper, which could be used to temporarily blind an officer. The prisoners were shaved and even manicured by the officers. Cells contained "no movable object" but the prisoner, who moved only rarely and not far. "In fact," stated Warden Lawes, "the condemned prisoner [was] in the same position as a rat caught in a wire-caged trap" (Lawes 1937:164).

---

6. "From the time it opened in 1922 to the day it closed in 1969, nobody escaped" (Christianson 2000:88).

Sing Sing was not in any way unusual. Life on San Quentin's death row, for example, followed a virtually identical pattern (see Duffy 1962). The psychology of life in this and other wire-caged traps reflected the desperate situation of the prisoners. The condemned were chronically tense and deeply despondent. Facing reasonably swift and certain execution—the wait then was at most a matter of months—those prisoners were evidently a dangerous and unstable lot, requiring close confinement to hold them safely. In the words of one prisoner:

> The men in death row have nothing to lose except the hope of a commutation. In the mood of despair that gripped us all, tempers were short, nerves frayed. It was enough to put one prisoner within striking distance of another for murder to be done. It was enough to leave a prisoner alone for seconds, if he meant to take his own life. Neither of these possible occurrences was acceptable to the authorities, if only because they implied that a prisoner still held within himself certain liberties they couldn't touch. If you could kill yourself, or the man in the next cell, it meant that you didn't belong to them entirely. And from the moment the gates shut behind you, everything was calculated to give you the opposite impression: that you were their property (Zimmerman 1964:119–120).

That such a regime actively reduces the person to so much state property, to be dispatched in the execution chamber, is a central theme of research on modern death rows.

Current Conditions on Death Row

Conditions on most death rows have changed little since the officials of Sing Sing built their new and improved wire-caged trap. Perhaps this is to be expected. Death rows are located in prisons; prisons have been and remain today painful, depriving environments. Indeed, "one of the striking things about prisons is that we make no bones about the fact that we intend them to be uncomfortable" (Johnson and Toch 1988:13). Death row is not managed like the rest of the prison, and condemned prisoners are not treated like regular inmates. Always, "the condemned live with the barest services, the minimum contact, the slightest concern" (Jackson and Christian 1980:28). As I have observed elsewhere:

> Death row is the most total of total institutions, the penitentiary most demanding of penitence, the prison most debilitating and disabling in its confinement. On death row the allegorical pound of flesh is just the beginning. Here the whole person is consumed. The spirit is captured and gradually worn down, then the body is disposed of. A century ago prisoners were subjected to the disci-

pline of silence. Today on death row, this silence may prove endless (Johnson 1989:121).

For the death row prisoner more than any other category of inmate, being alone—and being lonely, even when in the presence of others—is a central and perhaps even defining fact of existence. "No one really knows what loneliness is until they come to the row," observed one condemned prisoner. "On the row a person feels lost in deep despair. You feel no one will ever be able to help you. All is lost" (Arriens 1997:44). Death row is the extreme case of the pain and deprivation of prison, the prison's prison.

The silence and isolation of death row stem from the empty and ultimately lifeless regimen imposed on the condemned. Those offenders, typically seen as unfit for life in even the prison community, are relegated to this prison within a prison and held—sometimes even today in virtual solitary confinement—for periods measured in years rather than days or months. Typical maximum security prisoners spend about eight to twelve hours a day in their cells; typical death row prisoners spend twenty to twenty-two or twenty-three hours a day alone in theirs. (On death rows in which prisoners are allowed to spend more time out of their cells, they are relegated to day rooms that serve as congregate death row, with nothing meaningful to do.) Death row prisoners typically leave their cells to shower (often handcuffed) and to exercise (in a restricted area, sometimes fittingly called a "recreation cage" or even a "dog run"). If one has visitors, he leaves his cell to receive them, but visits occur under heavy guard, are restricted in frequency and duration, and become increasingly rare as a prisoner's stay on death row continues. There may be an occasional trip from the cell to the law library for the self-proclaimed "writ writer"—an inmate lawyer of sorts. Otherwise, condemned prisoners remain in their cells. They are, with few exceptions, ineligible for prison jobs or correctional programs, or even the usual forms of prison recreation, such as sports and movies. Deemed beyond correction, they typically are denied access to even the meager privileges, amenities, and services available to regular prisoners.

In general, the custodial routine of death row varies little from state to state. A nationwide survey of death row, living conditions conducted in 1979 revealed that:

> most DSIs [death sentence inmates] cannot work at prison jobs, cannot attend education classes, clubs or religious services, have much less opportunity for exercise and recreation and much less adequate facilities and equipment [than regular prison inmates]. DSIs have little human contact.... Many are shackled for trips within the prison. Most eat in their cells and are separated from visitors by barriers.... [T]he lives of DSIs are grim.... Perhaps more important than any single deprivation is the fact that the impact and effect of each restriction is exaggerated because of the

more general deprivation of being kept in cells most of every day and isolated from almost all contact with other human beings (Else, Kudsk, and Meyer 1981:2).

Aside from a smattering of essentially cosmetic reforms in a number of prisons, death rows today are essentially indistinguishable from their counterparts in earlier years (Nesbitt, Howard, and Wallace 1989; Wunder 1994)[7].

Detailed descriptions of individual death rows, whether civilian or military, holding hundreds of prisoners or only a handful, bear out these observations. The death rows of Florida's Starke Prison, a civilian death row with a population surpassing three hundred, and Fort Leavenworth Penitentiary, a military death row with a population of fewer than ten, are virtually indistinguishable. Each is located in the prison's segregation unit, and each conveys the impression that one is "deeply embedded in the prison—lodged, figuratively, in its bowels—shut off from light and liberty" (Johnson 1989:43). The tomblike ambience of the physical setting complements the empty existence of its inhabitants.

> In Florida, each condemned man is housed in a separate 6 X 9 foot cell, from which [three] departures are scheduled each week. Two of these are for showers, when the man is handcuffed and permitted to walk a short distance down the tier to a special shower cell. The third exit is [for] exercise...in an enclosed blacktopped area. No visits to the prison library, chapel, or gymnasium are permitted.... No education or work opportunities are available to the prisoner, and opportunities for counseling are extremely limited.... Most of the day is spent reading, watching television, and talking with one another (Radelet, Vandiver, and Berardo 1983:595–596).

> On death row at Fort Leavenworth the cells were typical segregation cells and in fact were alongside and connected to the maximum security cells. The difference was that in front of these six cells was a steel caged area. This steel cage encompassed all six cells and provided the exercise room for the inmates. Death row inmates never left the confines of the caged-in cells except to shower, and they were placed in leg-irons when so engaged. Once a day for one hour each prisoner was permitted to exit the cell into the caged area to exercise. The rest of the death row inmate's time was spent in his cell (Dumm 1983).[8]

---

7. These reforms include limited access to educational classes; the availability, on paper at least, of mental health counseling; modest increases in out-of-cell time and access to visitors; in a few states, the availability of part-time work. These reforms are cosmetic in the sense that they do not fundamentally change the nature of the death row experience.

8. This personal communication was confirmed in its essentials in 1989 by Major J. Tyler (Tyler 1989).

Those descriptions, drawn from materials available in 1983, remain accurate today—as a general rule, little of consequence changes on those or any other death rows.

Florida's death row has been moved to a new facility, but the regimen remains unchanged. The stated purpose of Florida's new death row is to provide "the maximum level of security and total segregation of these 'worst-of-the-worst' inmates" (Stimpson 1991:159). If such is possible, Florida's death row prisoners today are even more isolated than they ever were before. Maximum security in Florida's contemporary death row means virtually no contact with other prisoners and only the most limited contact with the custodial staff. "While in their cells, inmates will have no visual contact with one another and they will not be able to communicate" with one another, at least not directly (Stimpson 1991:159). (On other death rows in which such isolation of prisoners is sought, the inmates have been able to make some contact with one another through the use of "peepers"—mirror fragments appended to makeshift handles—that afford a limited if distorted form of visual communication (see Rideau and Wikberg 1992:265). "The only people with whom inmates will have contact will be the correctional officers walking the floor" as the officers go about their hourly rounds to maintain a regular count of their captives (Stimpson 1991:159). It is telling that fleeting contact with an officer conducting a count—an impersonal, thoughtless activity, in the main—is seen as providing "death row inmates a greater opportunity to communicate with staff" (Flack 1993:76). Such is the degree of social isolation on death row that the prospect of a nod or wave from a passing officer is taken for a species of human relations. It is perhaps fitting that in Florida (and in Alabama, another solitary confinement death row), steel mesh has been fastened onto the cells in recent years, further isolating the prisoners. In the summer, the reduced air flow as a consequence of these obstructions makes the death row cells like ovens, with temperatures well into the hundreds for days at a time.[9]

In a federal case, the court described in detail the conditions of death row confinement in the state of Tennessee in the mid-1980s. The plaintiff, one Mr. Harries, had lived on death row for a number of years:

> Mr. Harries lives in a six by eight foot cell, which contains a toilet with a wash basin in the toilet well. A bunk bed is provided for his use, which takes up about one-third of the cell. Lighting in the cell consists of one sixty-watt light bulb; additional lighting is available by use of an electrical hook-up, but this must be done at the inmate's expense. There is no window in Mr. Harries' cell and ventilation within his cell consists of blowers drawing out stale air. Ac-

9. For Florida, see "The Living Conditions on Death Row" 2000; Word 2002. For Alabama, see Johnson 2002.

cording to Mr. Harries, the ventilation is so poor that cigarette smoke stains his cell walls and toilet odors frequently make it difficult for him to sleep. Also, fumes from the respondents' [prison officials'] use of oil-based paints [for the walls and such] result in difficulty in normal breathing.... The ventilation problem is exacerbated when the humidity increases due to steam created from the showers of inmates....

Mr. Harries is confined in his cell for twenty-three hours per day. Respondents permit him to exercise during the day for forty to forty-five minutes and to shower daily for ten to fifteen minutes.... The exercise area is too small for running and the number of inmates in the yard restricts them from walking. Moreover, even when the inmates are outside to exercise, the grate that covers the exercise area restricts the sunlight from shining through. While the respondents have provided a set of weights for inmates, many are unable to use them. When the weather does not permit inmates to go into the small exercise area, during the winter or when it rains, no exercise is afforded to inmates. Thus, according to Mr. Harries and other death-row inmates, it is not unusual for inmates not to exercise for a week or more during such times.... At all other times, including the taking of his meals, Mr. Harries remains within his cell. The temperature in Mr. Harries' cell averages, according to the respondents, between eighty and eighty-five degrees Fahrenheit.... A stipulation jointly submitted by counsel for the respondents and Mr. Harries indicates that the temperature within his cell on July 11, 1984 was ninety degrees.... [T]he stipulation indicates that the temperature within Mr. Harries' cell may reach uncomfortable and potentially life threatening limits....

Turning to the area of food service to [death row] inmates, it is undisputed that prior to the commencement of this lawsuit, food served to inmates was cold.... The court...is concerned about the credible assertions of Mr. Harries that he discovered part of a mouse in his food.... [Finally,] inmates receive no religious services or counseling from respondents and the respondents prohibit any such services from outside sources (*Groseclose ex rel. Harries v. Dutton* 1984:959, 960, 961).

Mr. Harries, though a prisoner on death row in the 1980s, might just as well have been held in Warden Lawes's Condemned Cells at Sing Sing during the 1920s.

The court in the *Harries* case concurred in this assessment, finding the conditions of Mr. Harries's confinement to be offensive to contemporary standards of humaneness. As a result of this and subsequent holdings with respect to Mr. Harries' contentions,[10] reforms were put in place on death row. The centerpiece of the reform effort was a three-tiered death row confinement system in which prisoners who avoid disciplinary infractions for specified periods of time are allowed progressively more freedoms within the death row environment, more association with other condemned prisoners, more access to out-of-cell activities including educational programs, religious services, counseling, and even jobs on death row. Tennessee's death row is now housed in a modern facility, so physical conditions have improved considerably.[11] No information is available in the research literature or from official documents of the Tennessee correctional system on the quality of life on this reformed death row. It is therefore impossible to determine if these changes, valuable in themselves, have measurably improved the quality of life and adjustment on Tennessee's death row or in any way helped prisoners come to grips with their impending executions.

Death Row Reforms: The Illusion of Change

Some contemporary death rows are more accommodating than the essentially solitary-confinement based regimes already reviewed, having been liberalized as a result of legal consent decrees developed by reformers and correc-

---

10. Stressing the bleak physical milieu, the long periods of cell time and attendant idleness, and the absence of any type of attention to the unique psychological stresses faced by the condemned, the court in the *Harries* case held Tennessee's death row to be in violation of the Eighth Amendment prohibition of cruel and unusual punishment. However, on appeal the circuit court subsumed *Harries* under *Grubbs v. Bradley* (1982), a prior prison-conditions suit covering the entire Tennessee prison system (*Groseclose v. Dutton* 1987). In *Grubbs,* the court had taken a narrow view of the Eighth Amendment, holding that "the mere fact that inmates may tend to degenerate as a result of incarceration is not actionable." Only "serious physical or psychological deterioration [that] is inevitable" violates the cruel and unusual punishment clause (1124). The presumption is that "core" protections afforded by the Eighth Amendment pertaining to "food, clothing, shelter, sanitation, medical care, and personal safety" would have to be violated to produce serious and inevitable deterioration (1122). In this court's rendering, the Eighth Amendment would seem to require us to preserve the body of the prisoner—which is to be fed, clothed, maintained in clean and hygienic conditions, and held safe from harm—while allowing us to ignore the person. As a result of *Grubbs,* a special master was appointed to oversee reforms on death row and indeed throughout the prison system.

11. See Tennessee Department of Corrections, *Death Row Programming and Management: Policy and Procedures Manual.* Effective September 1, 1992. This policy is still in effect, and almost two-thirds of Tennessee's condemned prisoners are eligible for work, which takes place on the death row unit. They are out of their cells up to eight hours on a work day. The remaining inmates spend twenty-three hours a day in the cell, as is the case on many death rows.

tional administrators (see Johnson and Carroll 1985). A few of those settlements have been quite successful, though they have typically been piecemeal rather than comprehensive efforts. Some reforms have reduced cell time, sometimes also increasing the amount of recreation time prisoners have while out of their cells. Other reforms have expanded prisoners' opportunities for contact visits. The most comprehensive death row reforms were achieved in Texas, and appear to have served as the model for reforms of the Tennessee system discussed above.

On January 3, 1986, Texas initiated a "death row activity plan" that groups death row prisoners into two categories: "work-capable," which at last accounting covered roughly 40 percent of the prisoners; and "death-row segregation," covering roughly 60 percent of the prisoners. (These figures appear to have remained fairly constant over the last ten years; I am aware of no comparable figures for the Tennessee system.) Those deemed capable of working are assigned a meaningful job as prison jobs go, primarily as laborers pulling four-hour shifts in a garment factory located near death row. Moreover, work-capable inmates are afforded a regimen of recreation, work, educational programming, and other out-of-cell activity. Regular death row inmates, though still essentially segregated, also benefit. They are allowed "three hours of out-of-cell time five days a week" and are given access (in their cells) to religious and educational programs as well as psychological counseling. (However, segregated prisoners who are found to pose a danger upon release from the cell may be placed in a "Death Row Segregation—Non Recreation" category.) The frequency and length of visits remain restricted for all of Texas's condemned prisoners, however, and physical contact with visitors is prohibited altogether. When a work-capable inmate receives an execution date, he is immediately segregated until he is executed or his execution date is vacated. If his date is vacated, he can return to work (see Sorensen and Marquart 1989:172).

The reactions of the prisoners are mixed but generally favorable. Though some of Texas's work-capable prisoners compare themselves to slaves in death camps—their labor is unpaid, and they may one day be put to death—others stress that the reforms break up the monotony of the day and offer small but important freedoms (Johnson and Carroll 1985:8, 11–12). And friendships. "Unlike other death-row prisoners, who are isolated in their cells for most of the day, the factory workers form deep friendships. Here, unlike the rest of death row, whites, blacks and Latinos all mix easily together" (Muir 1994). This makes for a more congenial daily regime, but heightens the impact of executions; the "sudden disappearance" of a fellow worker who was known as an individual is made "all the more painful" (Muir 1994). A few prisoners hope that, should their death sentences be commuted, their work experience and solid adjustment will help them make parole (Johnson and Carroll 1985).

In assessing the larger significance of Texas's death row, it is wise to remember that most of the prisoners—60 percent—are not eligible for work (because they are trouble makers) or reject the work option (to avoid troublesome encounters with staff), and hence live constantly under the restrictive conditions generally associated with death row confinement. And though the work regime produces a better social climate on the job for those who avail themselves of the opportunity to work, as well as some meaningful fringe benefits (the prisoners go to visits without being cuffed and can serve their own food and eat in reasonably congenial group conditions), even those prisoners spend most of their time under lock and key in an environment described by one observer as offering "[a] palpable depression [that] clung to everything" and in which both the guards and the inmates were "institutionalized" (Donovan 1997:7).

Some other prisoners on Texas's death row live in maximum security wings, which offer close custody under conditions virtually indistinguishable from Sing Sing's Condemned Cells. Ironically, many are said to choose these settings because of what they perceive as their "honesty"—on these wings it is "us versus them," no friends with one's keepers, no concessions made to staff to secure services or benefits. These high-custody wings tend to draw the younger, tougher, more defiantly violent prisoners, those with a self-described desire for "respect" and who boldly claim they will "engage in physical confrontations with the system to get that respect" (Donovan 1997:11–14). For them, a solitary cell is, if not a castle, at least a haven from interactions with guards who are cast as violent oppressors.

It is fair to say that on Texas's death row, as on other death rows, routine and boredom ultimately prevail, transcending work and whatever small freedoms might be afforded the condemned. This has led one prisoner to describe what might be called the unbearable heaviness of being on death row, and another to frame time itself as a kind of trap that captures the condemned and holds them fast.

> Well, for me personally, when you go through life out there, time is like air to you. You breathe it in and you breathe it out; it passes through you, and you sort of pass through time. But when you're here and it's final...time doesn't go anywhere. It comes and it stops. It builds up inside, and it's actually like a weight after a while. Ten years weighs an awful lot. It just builds up, and there's time in the morning when...you almost literally feel it crushing you when you wake up and you have to look around and see the same things in here and you're in the same cell and doing the same things that you did years ago, and nothing's going to change (Donovan 1997:14).

> You never sit down and say, 'What am I going to do this day, or how am I gonna make it, or what's going to pull me through this day?' You know the routine. You know you're going outside for

three hours, you know you're going to watch TV. Nothing really changes—the atmosphere doesn't really change. It's like you're stuck in time (Donovan 1997:14).

Death row reforms may have a more limited impact than we would like, but the larger point is that even these modest improvements are inherently precarious. Death row has an essentially negative function—to facilitate a smooth execution process. If problems arise, and particularly if these problems come to the public's attention, reforms are likely to be scrapped. This is what happened to Texas's death row. Following a much-publicized escape in 1998, involving five men from the work program (only one of whom actually got out of the prison), the entire death row plan was abolished. All death row inmates were placed in a new prison and held in solitary confinement—twenty-three hours a day alone in the cell, solitary exercise, limited visits, no work. Reforms that had been carefully planned and successfully put in place for years were immediately relegated to the dust bin of prison history.

Death rows, even when reformed, freeze their prisoners in time, holding them captive in a sort of existential limbo until they are either executed or released to the prison world or the free world. Some death rows take their prisoners back in time, recreating through modern technology conditions of confinement that would seem to have an almost timeless currency on death row.

Back to the Future: High-Tech Solitary Confinement on Modern Death Rows

Oklahoma's death row offers a revealing case study of a modern, high-tech human warehouse for the containment and execution of condemned prisoners. Known by the bland name H-Unit, it offers a human existence so lifeless that its nondescript name—a letter in the alphabet, devoid of any intrinsic meaning—somehow seems fitting. H-Unit was expressly built as a thoroughly modern penal establishment, a kind of futuristic rendering of solitary confinement. A planning document for H-Unit notes, "The state of the art design of this unit maximizes security and control, while providing inmates and staff with a safe, modern environment in which to live and work" (Amnesty International 1994:1). For the words security and control, substitute isolation; for the word modern, substitute sterile. H-Unit is nothing if not a solitary and sterile, a cold, oppressive human wasteland in which prisoners are interred—confined underground—in utterly self-contained cell blocks replete with dimly lit and sparely furnished concrete cages. It is telling that in a recent anthology of death row poetry, covering death rows from around the nation, the editor remarks that "The most common image in these poems is of cold—cold

steel, cold cell, cold death." Death row, we learn from the poetry of the condemned, "is like being trapped under ice" (Zimmerman 1995:9). By this reckoning, H-Unit is the quintessential death row.

Located on the grounds of the Oklahoma State Penitentiary, H-Unit serves
as a "super-maximum security" adjunct to the larger prison:

> Constructed of entirely concrete with living accommodations sited
> effectively underground, H-Unit is an electronically controlled fa-
> cility designed to minimize contact between inmates and prison
> staff. Prisoners are confined for 23 or 24 hours a day in windowless
> cells allowing virtually no natural light and no natural air. No
> work, recreational or vocational programs are provided (Amnesty
> International 1994:i–ii).

All male death row prisoners in Oklahoma are held in H-Unit. Other prisoners
are confined there as well, but only for short periods of time. Death row prisoners are the only long-term residents of this facility.

It is both ironic and telling that H-Unit was conceived as a reform institution, meant to be an improvement over an old-fashioned and physically primitive solitary confinement regime. As made clear by an assessment team working under the auspices of Amnesty International (AI), H-Unit represents a
giant step back from the death row conditions it was meant to improve upon.
As the AI report notes, "in some important respects conditions are worse in H-
Unit than they were on the former death row, particularly as regards access to
natural light and air, the exercise facilities and contact with staff and others"
(Amnesty International 1994:2). Indeed, H-Unit is worse than many, perhaps
most death rows. As the AI report notes, "most prisoners under sentence of
death in the USA are held in segregated death rows. However, few appear to
impose restrictions as severe as those in H-Unit and many death row prisoners
have more out-of-cell time and association with fellow inmates; some engage
in prison work or other programs" (Amnesty International 1994:3).

It is a painful irony for the condemned that the cells on this quintessentially
modern death row are today's answer to the medieval dungeon—cramped,
barren, dark and utterly devoid of the human character:

> The cells in the housing area are 7'7" by 15'5" and have two poured
> concrete bunks on either side of an uncovered toilet and sink.
> There is no other furniture in the cells apart from two concrete
> shelves on the back wall which serve as 'tables' and two similar
> shelves above these for TV sets if prisoners can afford to purchase
> them from prison stock. Prisoners are not allowed to pin anything
> on the walls, which are unpainted concrete. The cell doors are solid
> metal, except for the upper part which has a plexiglass window
> with thick bars on the outside.... The only light inside the cells is

provided by two bare light bulbs positioned at eye-level at the back of the cell where the bunks and shelves are situated (Amnesty International 1994:5).

Almost no outside light makes its way into the cell blocks. When the lights in the cells are turned off, even on a sunny day, the cells are enveloped in near total darkness.

As in dungeons of old, life on H-Unit is essentially limited to these impoverished, barren cells:

> Prisoners are confined to [their] cells for 23 hours a day during weekdays and 24 hours a day at weekends. The only out-of-cell time is a 15 minute shower three times a week; an hour's exercise five times a day in an enclosed concrete yard if weather permits; visits (for those who have them); and limited access to the prison's law library. Up to ten inmates at a time may also attend a religious service once a week under makeshift arrangements in a corner of the quad. All meals are eaten in the cells. No work, educational or vocational programs are provided...(Amnesty International 1994:7).

As if to add insult to injury, inmates complain that the food is poor, and the servings small. Often, meals are served cold. Inmates claim they have poor access to medical, dental, and/or psychiatric services—some feel they are treated as if they are terminal pariahs, beyond the reach of medical care or indeed human compassion (Amnesty International 1994:20).

A limited exercise regime is offered in sharply constricted facilities, settings more like dog kennels than recreation yards. "Prisoners exercise in a 23 by 22 foot yard surrounded by 18 foot high solid concrete walls. The roof is constructed of girders covered with wire mesh. There is no view to the outside..." (Amnesty International 1994:11). Little is provided in the way of equipment. There is merely empty, exposed space, lacking even the simple amenity of a drinking fountain or a chair to sit on:

> The H-Unit yards have no facilities apart from a bench press with weights welded to it which all the prisoners interviewed said was difficult or impossible to use. There was no shelter from the rain or heat of the sun in summer and no drinking fountain.... [No] more than five prisoners may exercise on the yard at a time. The only facility available for recreation is a handball court and the yard is so small that, even with only five inmates it is not possible to do anything else if handball is being played. There is nowhere to sit... [which] made the yard almost impossible to use for inmates who

were elderly or suffered from joint diseases and/or were on crutches...(Amnesty International 1994:11–12).

Solitary death rows breed claustrophobic reactions—the feeling that the walls of the cells are closing in, that the very air in cramped cells is in danger of running out. Prisoners on solitary confinement death rows routinely see themselves as "the living dead," their death row worlds as settings that impose "a living death."[12] Modern high-security facilities—sterile, empty, marked by a suffocating routine—do nothing to dispel these sentiments:

> The solid walls of the exercise yard, together with the lack of windows in cells, means that prisoners are virtually confined to a concrete world in which they never see a blade of grass, earth, trees or any part of the natural world. Most prisoners interviewed said this was the most stressful aspect of their confinement.... Several prisoners likened confinement in H-Unit to being locked in a tomb (Amnesty International 1994:13).

Some prisoners became visibly depressed and withdrawn in this unnatural environment. Deeper, long-term reactions of this sort—suggested by prior research (see Johnson 1988; 1989)—were beyond the ken of the Amnesty International team, which was limited to a short visit at the facility.

Physical containment, social isolation, and impersonal control are central objectives of all death row regimes. On Oklahoma's H-Unit, those functions reach absurd and even tragic extremes. The setting, in a nightmare version of a futuristic world, features remote control of convicts caged nearly—and in some cases, literally—around the clock, under the dominion of officers who issue commands that emanate from distant control centers by way of intercoms. The very regime itself bespeaks dehumanization in all its essentials:

> H-Unit was designed to be a 'non-contact' facility, minimizing direct physical contact between prisoners and prison staff, and each quad is managed from a central control room through which guards can operate the unit electronically. Correctional staff do not routinely patrol the cell area, apart from the 'key-men' who open the beanholes [food slots] three times a day to pass food to the prisoners. Most communication between guards and prisoners takes place through the intercom in each cell, which is operated

---

12. Perceptions of death row as a living death and of condemned prisoners as the living dead are widespread and of enduring lineage in America and around the world. See, for example, Johnson 1989 for American prisoners; Vogelman 1989 for South African prisoners; and Hector 1984 for Jamaican prisoners.

from the control room. When prisoners are let out to shower or go to the yard, the cell doors are operated electronically and they are supervised by staff from the other side of the bars (Amnesty International 1994:15).

When contact occurs, it is buffered by the constraining hardware of custody. "On the few occasions when prisoners do have direct contact with guards—for example when being taken to attorney visits, the law library or the medical room—prisoners are placed in handcuffs and leg-irons and are escorted by at least two correctional officers" (Amnesty International 1994:15). The absence of human contact is the norm, extending from the daily cell block regime to visits with loved ones, attorneys, and even to religious services (Amnesty International 1994:17). Given the strain of social isolation on the normal psyche, it is troubling that there was no full-time psychiatrist at H-Unit as recently as 1994, when Amnesty released its report. One former psychiatrist "told Amnesty International that he had little contact with mentally ill prisoners on H-Unit and indicated that they did not receive adequate treatment or monitoring" (Amnesty International 1994:21).

In the original plan, and for a time, H-Unit prisoners were confined one to a cell. With crowding, most cells are now doubled up. Confining two men to a cell "was widely reported to be a source of great stress in the conditions of close confinement on H-Unit. Prisoners described the experience as being permanently locked in a box with someone from whom there was no escape" (Amnesty International 1994:19). And since there are no alarm buttons in the cells, the prisoners are left to their own devices when trouble develops, as has occurred with some regularity according to the prisoners. Privacy concerns are also salient. "The fact that prisoners both showered and exercised with their cell partner increased tensions and some prisoners said they refused exercise—or arranged to exercise on alternate days only—in order to have some brief time and space to themselves" (Amnesty International 1994:19).

Here, as on other death rows, condemned prisoners are treated like desperately dangerous men requiring extreme conditions of confinement. Ironically, death row prisoners, as a general rule, may be less of a security threat than regular maximum security prisoners. In a lawsuit dealing with attorney visits on H-Unit, a U.S. District Judge stated, "Death row inmates pose no greater security risk than any other high-maximum security inmate. Institutional behavior is generally better for death row inmates because such behavior may be used as evidence in mitigation or commutation proceedings" (Amnesty International 1994:24). (Experiences in states like Maryland, which until recently confined condemned prisoners in the general maximum security population, bear out this observation.) This legal holding did nothing to change conditions on H-Unit, which are driven more by deep-seated fears than by rational policy. The

AI report maintains that Oklahoma's death row violates a host of international standards, most notably Article 5 of the United Nations Universal Declaration of Human Rights, as well as a number of prison standards set by the American Correctional Association (Amnesty International 1994:28). Shortly after Amnesty's report was released, Oklahoma officials defended their regime on the grounds that it provided the kind of custodial control necessary for the protection of the staff and the containment of desperate convicts. *Added* restrictions—strip searches before and after *any* exit from a death row cell—were put in place (Hamilton 1994).

Oklahoma's death row gives us a glimpse of solitary confinement in the modern penal dungeon that may well be the death row of the future. New York's death row, housed at Clinton Prison and built in 1995, bears a striking resemblance to H-Unit. Called UCP—Unit for Condemned Prisoners—New York's death row is, in the words of a report of the Correctional Association of New York, "modern and high-tech in design." It is "spotless" and "quiet," and "runs smoothly," with "few grievances and little trouble" (Correctional Association of New York 2002:56). Beneath the surface tranquility, however, we find defeated men, passive and yielding, held in suspended animation by a regime in which the surveillance is constant and unremitting. Prisoners spend at least twenty three hours alone in their cells everyday, with one hour of outdoor recreation, weather permitting, in a fenced area described in one document as a "dog run" (ABCNY 2001). During rare excursions from their cells, the prisoner are handcuffed and manacled. Always and without exception, death row cells are illuminated by overhead flourescent lights; video cameras are always running. There is no privacy. Sleep problems are common. Several of the row's inhabitants "described the constant light and surveillance as maddening" (Correctional Association of New York 2002:56). One man used the term torture. (Note that regimes of torture regularly feature sleep deprivation and the annihilation of privacy.) It is as if, in a perversion of Shakespeare's famous line, we have on New York's Unit for Condemned Prisoners a world in which "All the row's a stage", brightly lit, and the play runs day and night to an unseen and uncaring audience. The prisoner is always exposed, on display, like a specimen in a museum.

The chilling human environments created by Oklahoma's H-Unit and New York's Unit for Condemned Prisoners are reminiscent of the regimen of solitary confinement ruled unconstitutional in the *Medley* case a century ago. Medley was subjected to solitary confinement in a Colorado prison prior to execution. The Supreme Court, drawing on English history, ruled that solitary confinement was unconstitutional because of its severity and because it comprised a second sanction, in addition to that of execution. The court held that in historical terms, solitary confinement had been used as "a further terror and peculiar mark of infamy" that could be added to the death penalty, and hence that such confinement was not merely incidental to the penalty of death but must be considered "an additional punishment of the most important and painful character" (*In re Medley* 1890:170, 171). That character, I have argued, is one of torture (Johnson 1998; 1988). Although today's courts may not be receptive to this argument, there can be little doubt that, from the prisoners' point of view, confinement under sentence of death is a separate and painful punishment that, even more than the method of execution, captures the essence of that which is truly degrading about the modern death penalty.

A Death Row by Any Other Name...

The particulars of death row regimes may vary, but the underlying reality remains the same. Death row is not so much an environment as it is a way of life—and death. As Willie Turner, a long-term resident of Virginia's death row, put it:

> It's the unending, uninterrupted immersion in death that wears on you so much. It's the parade of friends and acquaintances who leave for the death house and never come back, while your own desperate and lonely time drains away. It's the boring routine of claustrophobic confinement, punctuated by eye-opening dates with death that you helplessly hope will be averted. It's watching yourself die over the years in the eyes of family and friends, who, with every lost appeal, add to the emotional scar tissue that protects them...from your death, long before you're gone.... I've spent over 5000 days on death row. Not a single waking hour of any of those days has gone by without me thinking about my date with the executioner. If I don't think of it myself, then something brings it to my mind, like some other prisoner talking about his future, or somebody being executed, or somebody not being executed because of a stay. Dozens of times a day for 5000 days. All that thinking about it [execution] is like a little dying, even if you're on the best death row on earth (*Turner v. Jabe* 1995: para. 22. Declaration of Willie Lloyd Turner).

Nobody fully adapts to the pressures of death row confinement. As Willie Turner has said, reflecting on his many years on death row, "nothing could have prepared me for the despair and the frustration, for the loneliness and the abuse, for the shame and the sorrow, for the hopes raised and dashed, for the dreams and nightmares of my death that my *seventeen years* facing my own advancing demise have served up to me" (*Turner v. Jabe* 1995: para. 22, Declaration of Willie Lloyd Turner). After seventeen years, Turner was known as the Dean of Virginia's death row, in recognition of his long tenure and thoughtful commentary on life under sentence of death. He was executed a few months after giving his affidavit about his experiences on death row.

From the prisoners' point of view, even the most experienced prisoners, *all* death row regimes offer much stress and little hope. All reforms put in place to date are ultimately futile, because they do *nothing* to prepare the prisoners for their fate or to *change* the basic fact that death rows exist to facilitate impersonal, bureaucratic executions. This grim job they do well and with increasing frequency by dehumanizing those—inmate and staff alike—who are a part of the killing routine.

Postscript: Women on Death Row

There are 52 women on death row in America today. Women represent about 2 percent of condemned prisoners in America and about 2 percent of prisoners sentenced to death in any given year. Since 1608, roughly 565 women have been put to death in America; this represents about 3 percent of the roughly 20,000 legal executions that have taken place in America. Nine women have been put to death between the advent of the modern death penalty in 1976 and summer 2002. Seven of these women have been executed since 1998, with three of them drawn from Oklahoma's death row, all executed in 2001 (Death Penalty Information Center 2003; Streib 1995; 1990). Remarkably, Oklahoma's three executions in 2001 is "the highest number in any one year for a single state since Virginia executed six slave women in 1863" (Streib, 2002:2).

Oklahoma's death row for women, temporarily emptied by recent executions, perhaps another first, is a modern facility featuring high security. Condemned women "are housed inside a locked and isolated unit." There they are confined in "single locked cells for 23 out of 24 hours each day" in a setting that, like a typical men's death row, is aptly described as "a prison within a prison." Condemned women are isolated from the regular prison population and from each other. Recreation is allowed for an hour a day, in "a small locked outdoor exercise cage…when weather permits and if correctional officers have the time to escort and observe them." When out of their cells, the women are "handcuffed and shackled." They are not permitted contact visits. When surveyed about their adjustment, the women voiced concerns about "loneliness and isolation" as well as "emptiness and loss." At least one woman used the imagery of "existential death," a variant on the notion of living death so common on death rows for men. On Oklahoma's death rows, then, both men and women would appear to be classed among the dangerous and undeserving, requiring close custody (O'Shea 1993:86).

I am aware of no national survey comparing death rows for men and women. Such literature as exists suggests that Oklahoma's death row for women is in the minority. (Though not alone. California's death row for women is comparable. See Marlette 1992:1, 6.) Nevertheless, it would appear that, in most states, the contrast between men's and women's death rows is quite sharp. More often than not, condemned women are held in settings that are cozy and congenial, more like group homes or even private homes than like prisons or death rows. In those settings, condemned women are not seen as a danger, so a relaxed regime is maintained. "When I visited male death-row inmates in other states," noted a female journalist, "they were separated from me by a glass wall, and sometimes handcuffed to a belt." By contrast, on Alabama's death row for women, she continued "I am locked in the inmates' cells, with the guard coming by only every half hour." The setting was inviting. "On the sunny, plant-rimmed patio, the atmosphere is completely relaxed." Almost. "Except for the screams of a disturbed prisoner from inside the building, we might be spending the afternoon on someone's screen porch" (Rosenberg 1996:122).

In this journalist's experience, "The loose structure of the death row at [Alabama's] Julia Tutwiler Prison is typical of those housing women around the country." So, too, are the pleasant, highly individualized surroundings. "The Florida death row is painted peach. In Texas, for example, in the bungalow containing the state's female death-row population of six, the cells border a day room with area rugs and a small library." Even work takes on the form of a cozy cottage undertaking. "In one cell the women have set up a workshop for making Cabbage Patch-like dolls that sell for $25." The condemned women entertain the writer as though she were a guest in their home. "Neelley offers me a choice of Diet Coke, Coke, or Sprite. I can see the purple sheets on Harris' bed, needlework on the walls, and Neelley's collection of angels above her bed. I am in someone's house" (Rosenberg 1996:122).

All of this may change when and if women are executed with any regularity, as appears to have happened in a few states over the last few years. Women facing a realistic threat of execution may pose—or be seen to pose—a danger. It is perhaps for this reason that women on Texas's death row today describe a regime of intrusive surveillance, including half-hour cell checks throughout the night that make sleep impossible; daily cell searches, often combined with strip searches (not infrequently conducted by male officers); and the termination of in-cell craft work, like knitting, that might give outside observers the notion that this death row was a cottage or bungalow rather than a setting of punitive confinement.[13] There may also be a premium placed on distancing oneself from women on the threshold of execution, so that they may be more efficiently and impersonally put to death. Custody provides distance; cells and bars and deadening routines separate keeper from kept, making an execution

---

13. See "Stop violation of human rights for women on death row within Mountain View Unit, Gatesville, Texas" 2002.

less personal, less compelling. A home, put under heavy guard, becomes a prison. Something like a men's death row regime, already in evidence in some states, may be the norm for condemned women in the coming years.

References

ABCNY (2001) *Dying Twice: Conditions on New York's Death Row*.

Amnesty International (1994) *Conditions of Death Row Prisoners in H-Unit, Oklahoma State Penitentiary*. New York: Amnesty International U.S.A.

Arriens, J. (1997) (ed.) *Welcome to Hell: Letters and Writings from Death Row*. Boston: Northeastern University Press.

Christianson, Scott (2000) *Condemned: Inside the Sing Sing Death House*. New York: New York University Press.

Correctional Association of New York (2002, June) *State of the Prisons: Conditions of Confinement in 25 New York Correctional Facilities*.

Death Penalty Information Center (2003) "Women Executed in the U.S. 1900–2003." Available at http://www.deathpenaltyinfo.org/article.php?scid=24&did=229.

Dumm, P. (1983) Personal communication.

Donovan, S. (1997) "Shadow Figures: A Portrait of Life on The Row." Pp. 7–18, in K. Light, *Texas Death Row*. Oxford, MS: University of Mississippi Press.

Duffy, C. T., with A. Hirshberg (1962) *Eighty-Eight Men and Two Women*. New York: Doubleday.

Else, J. F., E. Kudsk, and J. Meyer (1981) "Living Conditions of Death Sentenced Inmates in the U.S." (Unpublished paper; available from J. F. Else, School of Social Work, University of Iowa, Iowa City, Iowa 52242).

Flack, K. (1993) "In Florida: A Look at Day-to-Day Death Row Operations." *Corrections Today* 55 (4):74–78.

Gatrell, V. A. C. (1994) *The Hanging Tree: Execution and the English People 1770–1868*. Oxford: Oxford University Press.

Groseclose ex rel. Harries v. Dutton (1984) 594 F.Supp. 949 (M.D. Tenn.).

Groseclose v. Dutton (1987) 829 F.2d 581 (6th Cir.).

Grubbs v. Bradley (1982) 552 F.Supp. 1052 (M.D. Tenn.).

Hamilton, A. (1994, August 1) "Oklahoma inmates allege reprisals after critical report." *The Dallas Morning News* :1A, 9A.

Hector, M. (1984) *Death Row*. London: Zed Books.

In re Medley (1890) 134 U.S. 160.

Jackson, B. and D. Christian (1980) *Death Row*. Boston: Beacon Press.

Johnson, B. (2002, Aug. 16) "Lawsuit claims it's too hot on death row." *Associated Press*.

Johnson, R. (1988) "Life Under Sentence of Death." Pp. 129–145, in R. Johnson and H. Toch, *The Pains of Imprisonment*. Prospect Heights, IL: Waveland Press.

Johnson, R. (1989) *Condemned to Die: Life Under Sentence of Death*. Prospect Heights, IL: Waveland Press.

Johnson, R. (1998) *Death Work: A Study of the Modern Execution Process*. 2nd ed. Belmont: Wadsworth.

Johnson, R. and J.L. Carroll (1985) "Litigating Death Row Conditions: The Case for

Reform." Chap. 8, pp. 3–33, in I. Robbins (ed.), *Prisoners and the Law: Prisoner's Rights Sourcebook*. New York: Clark-Boardman.

Johnson, R. and H. Toch (1988) *The Pains of Imprisonment*. Prospect Heights, IL: Waveland Press.

Lawes, L.E. (1937) *Life and Death in Sing Sing*. New York: Sun Dial Press.

Lesy, M. (1987) *The Forbidden Zone*. New York: Farrar, Straus, & Giroux.

Linebaugh, P. (1992) *The London Hanged: Crime and Civil Society in the Eighteenth Century*. Cambridge: Cambridge University Press.

Marlette, M. (1992, Jan.) "Confining the Condemned." *Corrections Compendium* 17 (1):1, 6.

Muir, K. (1994, Feb. 27) "Worked to Death in Texas." *The Observer Magazine*.

Nesbitt, C., R.L. Howard, and S.M. Wallace (1989) *Managing Death-Sentenced Inmates: A Survey of Practices*. Washington, DC: St. Mary's Press. (A publication of The American Correctional Association.)

O'Shea, K. A. (1993) "Women on Death Row." Pp. 75–89, in B. R. Fletcher, L.D. Shaver and D. G. Moon (eds.), *Women Prisoners: A Forgotten Population*. Westport: Praeger.

Prejean, Sister H. (1993) *Dead Man Walking: An Eyewitness Account of the Death Penalty in the United States*. New York: Random House.

Radelet, M. L., M. Vandiver, and F. Berardo (1983) "Families, Prisons, and Men with Death Sentences: The Human Impact of Structured Uncertainty." *Journal of Family Issues* 4 (4):593–612.

Rideau, W. and R. Wikberg (1992) *Life Sentences: Rage and Survival Behind Bars*. New York: Time Books.

Rosenberg, T. (1996, Feb.) "Dead Woman Walking" *Harper's Bazaar* 411:110–122.

Sorensen, J. R. and J.W. Marquart (1989) "Working the Dead." Pp. 169–177, in M.L. Radelet (ed.), *Facing the Death Penalty: Essays on a Cruel and Unusual Punishment*. Philadelphia: Temple University Press.

"Stop violation of human rights for women on death row within Mountain View Unit, Gatesville, Texas" (2002, accessed Aug. 29) Available at http://www.PetitionOnline.com/ECADP3/petition.html.

Streib, V. L. (1990) "Death Penalty for Female Offenders." *University of Cincinnati Law Review* 58:845–880.

Streib, V. L. (1995, July 17) "Capital Punishment for Female Offenders." Unpublished paper.

Streib, V.L. (2002) "Death Penalty for Female Offenders: January 1, 1973, through June 30, 2002." Available at http://www.law.onu.edu/faculty/streib/femdeath.pdf or .htm.

Spear, C. (1845/1994) *Essays on the Punishment of Death*. Littleton, CO: Fred B. Rothman, Co.

Stimpson, W. A. (1991) "A Better Design for Safer Detention on Death Row." *Corrections Today* 53 (4):159–161.

Tennessee Department of Corrections (1992) *Death Row Programming and Management: Policy and Procedures Manual*.

"The Living Conditions on Death Row" (2000, Sept. 25) *The Tampa Tribune* 6.

Turner v. Jabe (1995, April 27) Petition for Writ of Habeas Corpus. Civ. No. (E.D.Va.).

Tyler, J. (1989) Personal communication.

Vogelman, L. (1989) "The Living Dead: Living on Death Row." *South African Journal on Human Rights* 5:183–195.

Word, R. (2002, Aug. 8) "Florida inmates claim they're subjected to 'dungeon-like' conditions on death row." *Associated Press.*

Wunder, A. (1994) "Survey Summary: Living on Death Row." *Corrections Compendium* 19 (12):9–21.

Zimmerman, I., with F. Bond (1964) *Punishment Without Crime.* New York: Clarkson N. Potter.

Zimmerman, J. (ed.) (1995) *Trapped Under Ice: A Death Row Anthology.* Brunswick: Biddle.

Chapter 22

The Evolving Role of Clemency in Capital Cases

*Daniel T. Kobil**

Clemency and the death penalty are intimately bound up with one another. In a sense, they are living fossils: both evolved in the primordial seas of ancient legal systems. They have survived into modern times largely unchanged, their archaic appendages flailing in awkward contrast to the smooth workings of more modern aspects of our justice system.

Moreover, the genesis and continuing survival into the Twenty-First Century of each of these relics is in some measure related to the existence of the other. Without a death penalty, there would be a less compelling need for executive clemency, especially in view of enhanced procedural protections and other refinements of the judicial system that today allow ready review of most judicial determinations. Conversely, a criminal system that imposed capital punishment but did not provide for at least the possibility of executive clemency would be "totally alien" to American notions of justice (*Gregg v. Georgia* 1976:200, n. 50).

Given the symbiotic relationship between capital punishment and clemency, it might be expected that the resurgence of the death penalty in the United States would also have led to an upswing in the use of clemency to mitigate the harshest effects of this irrevocable punishment. This has not been the case. Despite an increasing number of executions and burgeoning population on death row (U.S. Department of Justice 2002), as of 2002 only 48 death sentences had been commuted on humanitarian grounds nationwide since the death penalty was reinstated by the Supreme Court in 1976 (Death Penalty Information Center 2002a). In recent years, the pace nationwide has slowed to about two commutations annually (leaving aside the unprecedented actions of Illinois Governor George Ryan, who made history in 2003 by granting clemency to all 167 persons on death row).

At the same time, the Supreme Court has expressed confidence that clemency fulfills an integral role as a safeguard in our criminal justice system.

---

* I would like to thank David Jackson, Elizabeth Douglas, and Kirsten Bartholomew for their research assistance.

Notwithstanding the increasing rarity of commutations and pardons in capital cases, the Court has characterized clemency as an essential, efficacious means of assuring that the innocent are not executed by the government.

This tension between the idealized role of clemency in the American system of capital punishment and the reality may be to some extent attributable to our longstanding ambivalence toward the death penalty (Death Penalty Information Center 2002b; Haas and Inciardi 1988:11). Such dissonance is also in large measure the result of the clemency power becoming increasingly politicized, a process that has led to the atrophy of clemency at the state and federal levels. A frank assessment of the role actually played by clemency in the past and the present provides a perspective from which it is possible to discern its proper place in the American system of capital punishment.

Clemency Defined

The term "clemency" as it is used in the context of the criminal justice system refers to leniency or mercy in the exercise of authority or power. It is a generic term for actions taken by government, usually the executive branch, that remit the punishment of those who have violated society's laws. "Clemency" includes several specific varieties of leniency recognized under American law. Three of these are relevant to the death penalty: reprieve, commutation, and pardon (Kobil 1991a).

Reprieve is the most limited type of clemency and thus is most apt to be invoked in capital cases. It refers to the temporary postponement of punishment. A reprieve simply stays execution of the death sentence for a specified period of time. Typically, a reprieve is used to give the prisoner an opportunity to complete pending appeals or to allow the Governor to examine last-minute allegations that raise doubt about guilt.

Commutation is a broader form of clemency that consists of the substitution of a milder punishment for the one imposed by the court. Commutations are occasionally granted in capital cases to mitigate the death sentence and impose instead a sentence of life imprisonment, usually without possibility of parole. Sometimes as a condition of receiving a commutation, the condemned must waive his right to a new trial or agree not to make money from selling accounts of his crime.

Finally, pardon is the most expansive form of clemency. A pardon effectively erases both the crime and the punishment originally imposed on the prisoner; if granted, it would allow a capitally sentenced prisoner to walk freely off of death row and back into society. It is often said that a pardon not only eliminates the sentence, it also wipes out the offender's moral guilt as if he were never charged with or convicted of the crime (*Ex parte Garland* 1866). Pardons are almost never granted in capital cases. However, because the term "pardon" is often confused with the generic term "clemency," it is not uncommon for the commutation of a death sentence to be mistakenly referred to as a pardon.

The Development of the Clemency Power in the United States

There are 51 different systems of clemency in the United States: each state and the federal government have adopted distinct variations, usually pursuant to their respective constitutions (National Governor's Association Center for Policy Research 1988). Although it is beyond the scope of this discussion to examine in detail these multifarious approaches to clemency, it is helpful to consider some common trends in the evolution of the clemency power.

Clemency in the States

After declaring their independence from the British monarchy, many of the original colonies were reluctant to repose the clemency power in a chief executive. Eight of the thirteen new states delegated the clemency power either to the legislature, or to the legislature in combination with the governor.

However, our youthful republic's initial confidence in legislative bodies soon waned. The development of state constitutions, and perhaps the influence of the newly ratified federal Constitution, led to the reallocation of the clemency power solely to the executive in a number of states, including most of those newly admitted to the union (Jensen 1922:3–8). Today, the governor retains control of the clemency power in most jurisdictions, although it is not uncommon for specialized administrative boards or panels to assist in making the decision. In some jurisdictions, including several states that frequently impose capital punishment, the governor may not grant clemency unless an administrative body has first recommended it (see, e.g., Arizona Revised Statutes § 31-402(A), 2002; Constitution of the State of Texas: Article IV, Section 11, 2001).

The Federal Clemency Power

In contrast to the "anti-executive" approach initially utilized by most of the original states, the federal Constitution clearly followed the British clemency model. The framers of the United States Constitution made the President the sole repository of the clemency power, after considering and rejecting several suggestions that would have limited the chief executive's power, including a motion that would have allowed the President to grant pardons only with the consent of the Senate (Farrand 1911:419–420). Alexander Hamilton successfully argued in *The Federalist* (No. 74) that such a concentration of the clemency power was desirable because "the sense of responsibility is always strongest in proportion as it is undivided" (Hamilton 1961).

Article II, section 2, of the Constitution, as it was finally ratified, provides that the President "shall have Power to grant Reprieves and Pardons for Offenses against the United States, except in cases of impeachment." The Presidential clemency power set forth in Article II has been interpreted by the judiciary to include the authority to grant commutations, as well as pardons and reprieves (*Biddle v. Perovich* 1927).

The Supreme Court has construed the President's power expansively in other respects as well. The President's clemency power has been held to be comparable to that of the English Crown's broad authority, and consequently the President can condition the granting of a pardon on the recipient's acquiescence to virtually any terms (*Ex parte Wells* 1855). Moreover, as President Ford's pre-conviction pardon of former President Nixon illustrates, the clemency power can be exercised at any time, either before legal proceedings are commenced or after conviction (*Ex parte Garland* 1866). Finally, because the presidential clemency power is constitutionally based, any limitations on it must be found in the Constitution itself (for example, "except in cases of impeachment," Article II, section 2), and cannot be imposed by Congress (*Schick v. Reed* 1974).

It should be noted, however, that the federal clemency power comes into play only when federal law is violated. Because the death penalty has been imposed infrequently at the federal level in recent times, Presidents have rarely had occasion to use clemency in capital cases. One notable exception was President Lincoln, who freely used the clemency power during the Civil War to commute the capital sentences of Confederate spies, or of young Union soldiers who had been sentenced to death by their commanders, often for deserting or for falling asleep while on guard duty (Sandburg 1954:578–592). However, with the current proliferation of federal crimes punishable by death, Presidents once more can expect to be regularly confronted by requests for capital clemency. Indeed, President Clinton in 2001 became the first president in decades to commute a death sentence when he shortened convicted murderer David Ronald Chandler's sentence to life without parole (Goldstein and Schmidt 2001).

Capital Clemency in Practice: A Haphazard "Fail-Safe"

In the context of capital punishment, clemency represents the final deliberative opportunity to consider whether a sentence of death should be imposed by the government, considering all of the circumstances. It might be described as a quintessentially *humane* procedure, one that is intended to provide a last chance for the condemned to plead for mercy with another human being who is charged with the responsibility of considering the plea and vested with the power to do something about it. Because of its inherent flexibility, clemency offers an opportunity to avoid mistakes that may not be corrected through the more rigid procedures that characterize other aspects of our criminal justice system (Bedau and Radelet 1987; Borchard 1932; DiSalle 1965; Yant 1991). It is a necessary check, usually retained by the executive, on overreaching by the judiciary or the legislature. Thus, clemency is sometimes referred to as a necessary "fail safe" in the American legal system (Moore 1989).

A less commonly acknowledged purpose of clemency is dignitary. By permitting another person to consider whether the death penalty is deserved, clemency reinvests the condemned with some of the humanity which may have been impossible to imagine in light of the horrible and violent acts that led to his sentence of execution. Instead of allowing us to continue thinking of the offender as simply an "animal" who has committed unspeakable crimes, clemency properly forces us to confront the fact that we will be executing a person.

Some public officials have used the clemency power in a principled manner consistent with this "fail safe" function, despite the potential unpopularity of their actions. For example, Ohio Governor Mike DiSalle commuted the death sentences of six individuals he concluded deserved clemency and lost his re-election bid partly because of his actions (DiSalle 1965:204).

In January 2003, the country witnessed an especially striking instance of a governor using the clemency power in a courageous manner when Governor George H. Ryan of Illinois, a long-time supporter of capital punishment, made history by issuing clemency to all 167 individuals on death row shortly before leaving office (Possley and Mills 2003). In justifying what are undoubtedly the most extensive remissions of capital punishment by an American governor, Governor Ryan expressed his grave doubts about the soundness of the Illinois system of capital punishment: "the facts I have seen in reviewing each and every one of these cases raised questions not only about the innocence of people on Death Row, but about the fairness of the death penalty system as a whole" (Possley and Mills 2003). Governor Ryan set aside his personal support for capital punishment and acted to remedy what he considered to be the glaring unfairness of an Illinois system that had "the dubious distinction of exonerating more men than we had executed. Thirteen men found innocent, 12 executed" (Ryan 2003). He repeatedly emphasized the inequities of the Illinois system in justifying the blanket clemency grants, explaining that they were warranted "because our three year study has found only more questions about the fairness of the sentencing; because of the spectacular failure to reform the system; because we have seen justice delayed for countless death row inmates with potentially meritorious claims; because the Illinois system is arbitrary and capricious" (*Id.*). Although there has been significant criticism of Ryan and even legal challenges to some of the commutations (Orrick 2003), his actions demonstrate that at least where strong doubts exist regarding the fairness of the system or the validity of a particular conviction, officials may sometimes be persuaded to use the power in principled fashion.

However, perhaps owing to its innate flexibility, as well as its ancient pedigree in the monarch's prerogative of mercy, clemency also retains an air of capriciousness that threatens to undermine its usefulness. In the past, governors and presidents have used the clemency power for a variety of reasons, some of which were suspect. For example, some governors have had a practice of granting "seasonal commutations" around Christmas and Thanksgiving. Scandals involving the sale of pardons and commutations led to the impeachment of Oklahoma Governor J.C. Walton in 1923, and to the indictment and conviction of various members of Tennessee Governor Ray Blanton's administration in the early 1980s (Kobil 1991a). In 1987, the former chairman of the Louisiana Pardon Board pled guilty to charges that he had sold grants of clemency to state prisoners (Hargroder 1987). President Clinton's pardon to indicted expatriate Marc Rich, allegedly as a reward for political contributions, also generated substantial controversy (Fineman 2001).

Fortunately, such uses of clemency are the exception rather than the rule. The greater danger we face in an era when most public officials seem convinced that unstinting retribution is the principal goal of punishment is not that clemency will be exercised too freely, but that it will not be exercised at all in deserving cases. Commentators agree that there has been a sharp decline in grants of clemency in capital cases since 1976 when the Supreme Court reinstituted the death penalty (Banner 2002; Bedau 1990–1991; Palacios 1996; Radelet and Zsembik 1993; Rapaport 2001). Although a few governors have bucked this trend by imposing moratoriums on capital punishment (Grier and Stern 2002), or in the case of Governor Ryan, by granting clemency to everyone on death row (Possley and Mills 2003), the clemency power may well have reached its nadir nationwide. Heightened media scrutiny of capital clemency decisions, coupled with the realization by public officials that a decision to commute a death sentence can be akin to political suicide, may have contributed to this modern atrophy of the clemency power. The intense pressures that conspire to make executive clemency rare are illustrated by the controversy surrounding one of the most significant uses of the clemency power in recent years to commute capital punishment: Ohio Governor Celeste's commutation of the death sentences of eight convicted killers in 1991 (Kobil 1991b).

As his second term as Governor drew to a close in late 1990, Democrat Richard F. Celeste, a lifelong opponent of capital punishment, was asked by the Ohio Public Defender's office to commute the death sentences of all 105 prisoners on the state's death row. Concerned that such a blanket commutation would short-circuit public debate and galvanize support for the death penalty, Celeste chose instead to commute the death sentences of the four men most likely to be executed during the next four years, and the sentences of all four women on death row. Celeste based the commutations of the men on the imminence of their executions, but justified the commutations of the women because of doubts about the fairness of their sentences in light of the fact that all four women were black and three had been sentenced to death in Hamilton County, a mostly white, notoriously conservative jurisdiction (Celeste 2003; *Cleveland Plain Dealer* 1997:12-A). At the time, the eight capital commutations were the most issued by any public official since the death penalty has been reinstated in the United States.

Celeste's actions triggered a firestorm of scathing criticism by politicians, law enforcement officials, and newspapers. Despite Celeste's efforts to make a principled defense of the grants of clemency to the public, eighty-percent of Ohioans disapproved of the commutations.

The incoming Governor, Republican George Voinovich, sought to overturn the grants of clemency on the ground that Celeste had not received a recommendation from Ohio's Adult Parole Authority prior to issuing the commutations. In a lawsuit filed to challenge the commutations, attorneys for the new Governor argued that the courts should invalidate the commutations and limit the scope of the executive clemency authority.

The Ohio Supreme Court, by a single, wavering vote, ultimately decided that Celeste's commutations were valid because of the broad grant of clemency power given to the Governor by the Ohio Constitution (*State ex rel. Mauer v. Sheward* 1994). The court's decision, although plainly in accordance with Ohio law and the express constitutional language, was widely criticized. It sparked a movement to amend the Ohio constitution to limit the Governor's power to commute until there had been an investigation and recommendation made by the Adult Parole Authority. With Governor Voinovich's support, a constitutional amendment curtailing the clemency power passed by a wide margin in 1995. In the aftermath of the commutations, Celeste left public life. Although he contemplated a political comeback, the damage done by the commutations appears to have been irreparable.

The controversy surrounding the Celeste commutations demonstrates why a politician who still aspires to elected office would rarely choose to commute a death sentence, at least absent overwhelming, well-publicized questions about guilt. Indeed, the Ohio saga, which culminated in the irony of a sitting Governor filing a lawsuit designed to limit his own constitutional authority, suggests that clemency is perhaps the only executive power that many public officials are actually anxious to relinquish.

In view of such political pressures, it is hardly surprising that the vast majority of requests for clemency in capital cases are rejected, even when there may be strong reasons for its exercise. In 1990, Louisiana Governor Roemer disregarded a politically unpopular recommendation of the Pardon Board and refused to commute the death sentence of Dalton Prejean, a convicted murderer who was seventeen years old at the time of the offense and who suffered from brain damage caused by physical abuse as a child (*New York Times* 1990:A9). While running for President, then-Governor of Arkansas Bill Clinton denied clemency to Rickey Ray Rector, a murderer who was so brain-damaged from a botched suicide attempt that he suffered from constant hallucinations and even saved the dessert from his final meal "for later" because he could not appreciate that he was being executed (Frady 1993; Olgiati 1993). Former Governor of California Pat Brown was long haunted by his decision, made for admittedly political reasons, to deny clemency to a murderer who had suffered significant brain damage as a child (Brown and Adler 1989). The Utah Board of Pardons—comprised of officials appointed by the Governor—in 1992 allowed William Andrews to be executed notwithstanding the fact that he did not kill anyone, and despite the presentation of strong evidence that his conviction was tainted by blatant racial bias (Palacios 1996). Missouri Governor Mel Carnahan in 1999 denied clemency to Roy Roberts, disregarding extremely compelling evidence that Roberts was innocent of the murder of a prison guard for which he eventually was executed (Bell 1999).

Examples abound of cases where clemency has been summarily denied despite the existence of pervasive doubts about the reliability of the conviction or the presence of substantial mitigating factors. As one commentator has observed, clemency seldom operates properly in the context of capital punishment because decision makers are not adequately insulated from the powerful influence of "strong pro-death penalty public opinion" (Palacios 1996:370). Clemency, far from serving as a reliable safeguard in the justice system, has been relegated to "a freak occurrence" (Banner 2002:291). Nevertheless, the Supreme Court has displayed a deep-rooted faith in the efficacy of clemency as a means of protecting the integrity of the American system of capital punishment, creating a troubling dissonance between the idealized vision of clemency in capital cases and the role it serves in actual practice.

Judicial Interpretations of the Role of Clemency in Capital Cases

Early on, the United States Supreme Court recognized the importance of clemency to our system of justice when it stated that without a meaningful clemency power, our government "would be most imperfect and deficient in its political morality" (*Ex parte Wells* 1855:310). More recently, the Supreme Court has stated that a system of capital punishment that abolished clemency in order to achieve uniformity in capital sentencing "would be totally alien to our notions of criminal justice" (*Gregg v. Georgia* 1976:199, n. 50). Indeed, Justice White considered it "reasonable to expect the [clemency] power to be exercised by the Executive Branch whenever" a person is unjustly convicted and sentenced to death (*Roberts v. Louisiana* 1976:349–350).

The Court, in *Herrera v. Collins* (1993), extensively discussed the role of clemency in the context of capital punishment. In *Herrera*, the Court considered whether a condemned murderer who claimed that he was innocent based on newly discovered evidence had alleged a constitutional violation sufficient to support a federal habeas corpus action to overturn his state death sentence. Several Justices "assumed" that a truly persuasive showing of actual innocence made after trial would render execution of the innocent defendant unconstitutional and warrant ordering a new trial. However, the Court held in a 6 to 3 decision that Herrera's new evidence that someone else had committed the murders was not sufficiently persuasive.

In rejecting Herrera's claim that he deserved a new trial to consider the exculpatory evidence, the majority relied on executive clemency as the proper mechanism for vindicating those who are actually innocent. Although the Court observed that the Constitution does not require states to implement a clemency mechanism, it noted that all 36 of the jurisdictions that then authorized capital punishment also provided for clemency. According to Chief Justice Rehnquist, "executive clemency has provided the 'fail safe' in our criminal justice system" and is "exercised frequently" (*Herrera v. Collins* 1993:415) in cases of actual innocence. Justice Scalia expressed such confidence in the mechanism of clemency that he considered it to be "improbable that evidence of innocence as convincing as today's opinion requires would fail to produce an executive pardon" (428).

Yet the sanguine view of clemency exhibited by the Supreme Court did not seem to comport with the practical realities of the clemency process, something that was frankly acknowledged by lower courts after *Herrera*. In *Graham v. Texas Board of Pardons and Parole* (1996), the Texas Court of Criminal Appeals considered whether the Texas Constitution guaranteed condemned prisoner Gary Graham a fair hearing before the state clemency board. Graham had filed a petition seeking clemency and had sought a hearing before the Board to present evidence of innocence. However, instead of functioning as the "fail-safe" contemplated by the Supreme Court, the Board did not hold a hearing, did not convene as a body, and simply arrived at its "decision" to deny all forms of clemency to Graham when each individual faxed a voting sheet to the Board's headquarters.

Despite these shortcomings, the Texas Court of Appeals refused to order the Board to hold a fair hearing to consider Graham's claims of innocence. It based its decision in part on its doubts about "the efficacy of executive clemency as a 'fail-safe' for death-row prisoners" (*Graham v. Texas Board of Pardon and Paroles* 1996:749). Because of the profound political pressures that affect the clemency process, and the executive's lack of expertise in reexamining criminal convictions, the court suggested that Graham should give up on clemency and pursue his claims of innocence through a judicial action. Thus, the court did not entirely close the door on Graham, but it refused to mandate that the clemency board give any meaningful consideration to Graham's petition.

This approach, while based on a more realistic view of clemency as it is actually practiced, was fundamentally at odds with the Supreme Court's expressed faith in the "fail-safe" function of clemency. The Texas court's solution also appeared to acknowledge that clemency cannot be expected to fulfill its historical role as a check on the judiciary.

In similar fashion, federal courts were unwilling to require that clemency decisions be made in a manner that accorded with due process (*Joubert v. Nebraska Board of Pardons* 1996). For example, the Eighth Circuit Court of Appeals in *Otey v. Stenberg* (1994) held that the Constitution does not impose on states a requirement that death penalty clemency proceedings satisfy due process. Otey had challenged the constitutionality of Nebraska's clemency procedure, which required capital clemency decisions to be made by a three-person board that included the Nebraska Attorney General, despite the fact that two of his subordinates formally opposed Otey's clemency application to the board. The court relied on an earlier Supreme Court decision, *Connecticut Board of Pardons v. Dumschat* (1981), and held that the State was not compelled to provide a condemned prisoner with an impartial clemency decision-making body. It ruled that Otey had no due process right to meaningful consideration of his application, but only a "right to ask for mercy" (*Otey v. Stenberg* 1994:637). In other words, so long as a prisoner was given an opportunity to "ask" for clemency, it did not matter if the decision was ultimately made in a blatantly unfair manner.

Shortly after these cases were decided, a sharply divided Supreme Court in *Woodard v. Ohio Adult Parole Authority* (1998) reasserted its more idealized vision of clemency when it held that state clemency proceedings in capital cases are subject to minimal constitutional protections. Woodard, who was sentenced to death for murder, had argued that new clemency procedures adopted by Ohio violated due process by providing him with inadequate notice prior to his clemency hearing and by preventing his lawyers from participating in that hearing. Five justices (including Justice Stevens in dissent) held that while clemency is ordinarily not the business of the courts, "some *minimal* procedural safeguards apply to clemency proceedings" in capital cases (*Woodard*:289). The Court suggested that "[j]udicial intervention might, for example, be warranted [if] a state official flipped a coin to determine whether to grant clemency, or in a case where the State arbitrarily denied a prisoner any access to its clemency process" (*Woodard*:289). Insofar as the Court rejected the government's assertion that clemency is never limited by constitutional standards, *Woodard* preserved the possibility that courts can prevent states from adopting blatantly unfair capital clemency processes. However, by emphasizing that state procedures need only be "minimal," and by using the example of a coin toss to illustrate the arbitrariness that would warrant judicial action, the Court may have set the standard for constitutionality so low that few, if any, challenges to clemency procedures will succeed.

The Future of Clemency in Capital Cases

Based on *Herrera* and *Woodard*, it appears that the Supreme Court continues to regard executive clemency as an important element of any capital punishment regime. Yet the jury is still out on whether the "minimal" procedural protections that *Woodard* judicially imposes will prove adequate to ensure the integrity of the clemency process in capital cases. Early indications are not encouraging.

Thus far, virtually every challenge to state clemency procedures based on *Woodard* has been summarily rejected by lower courts, despite allegations of serious irregularities. In *Workman v. Bell* (2001), the U.S. Sixth Circuit Court of Appeals held that even if, as the prisoner alleged, government attorneys had fabricated and presented false evidence at the capital clemency hearing, this practice did not violate the "minimal procedural safeguards" standard of *Woodard*. The Eleventh Circuit in *Parker v. State Board of Pardons and Paroles* (2001) rejected a claim of a constitutionally defective process based on bias of the Chairman of the clemency board who had, the court assumed, stated that no one on death row "will ever get clemency as long as [I am] Chairman of the Board." Other allegations of bias by a clemency decisionmaker have likewise been rejected by the courts as not satisfying the *Woodard's* "minimal" standard (see *Anderson v. Davis* 2002; *Bacon v. Lee* 2001; *Duvall v. Keating* 1998; *Roll v. Carnahan* 2000).

However, the most disturbing evidence that the *Woodard* standard is inadequate to protect the viability of state clemency processes comes out of Texas, the nation's most active capital punishment jurisdiction (U.S. Department of Justice 2002). Despite the presence of glaring systemic deficiencies, the Texas capital clemency procedures have been found by federal courts to be constitutionally sufficient under *Woodard*.

Texas is one of a handful of states where clemency cannot be granted unless the Governor has received a favorable recommendation from an administrative body, the Texas Board of Pardons and Paroles (Constitution of the State of Texas: Article IV, Section 11). Notwithstanding the integral role played by the Board, there is no guarantee that applicants for capital clemency receive meaningful consideration of their petitions. In *Faulder v. Texas Board of Pardons and Parole*, the district court noted that Board members "freely admit that they do not consider all of the information" submitted on clemency applications, including evidence calling into doubt the credibility of crucial witnesses in the case (1998:10, n. 5). Moreover, Board members routinely fail to conduct hearings on clemency applications, they make no effort to investigate or verify any evidence provided to them regarding a clemency application, they do not interview clemency applicants, and contrary to Texas law, they do not even keep records of Board actions or provide reasons for their clemency decisions (1998:10–15). One Texas jurist has described as "outlandish" the Board's "refusal to follow the law with apparent impunity" (*Texas Board of Pardons and Paroles v. Williams* 1998:208). The district court in *Faulder* was even harsher in its criticism of the Texas clemency process:

> It is abundantly clear the Texas clemency procedure is extremely poor and certainly minimal. Legislatively, there is a dearth of meaningful procedure. Administratively, the goal is more to protect the secrecy and autonomy of the system rather than carrying out an efficient, legally sound system (1998:16).

Regrettably, the courts have held that the deeply flawed Texas clemency process satisfies the *Woodard* standard. This is because *Woodard* is viewed as requiring states to provide very little in the way of process. As the district court in *Faulder* explained: "[the Texas clemency] process may not meet normal due process standards, but it does meet '*minimal* procedural safeguards'" (*Faulder* 1998:15). The court noted that "Justice O'Connor certainly chose to italicize '*minimal*' for a reason," and that reason was presumably to ensure that courts invalidate only the most outrageous clemency procedures, such as a coin toss (*Id.*). The Fifth Circuit Court of Appeals (without mentioning the troubling aspects of the Texas system described by the district court) affirmed this conclusion (*Faulder v. Texas Board of Pardons and Parole* 1999; *see also Moody v. Rodriguez* 1999).

It remains to be seen whether the Supreme Court will endorse the lower courts' interpretations of the "*minimal* procedural safeguards" standard. If the clemency procedures employed by Texas in capital cases are constitutionally adequate, it is difficult to imagine any state employing a system that could not satisfy the *Woodard* standard. Assuming lower court decisions continue along their current path, it is possible that the Court would eventually be compelled to admit that the *Woodard* standard is really no standard at all. Such an acknowledgment would also call into question the Court's assumption that clemency can be expected to play a meaningful role in America's system of capital punishment. Presumably, the Court would then reevaluate its reliance on clemency as an effective mechanism for ensuring that the innocent are not executed and that the death penalty is administered justly. The Court might find, as did the Texas court in *Graham*, that pleas for remission of punishment based on innocence or mitigating factors are best addressed by the courts directly through existing procedures, rather than by forcing public officials to make "fair" clemency decisions. Indeed, *Atkins v. Virginia* (2002), prohibiting the execution of the mentally retarded, suggests a willingness by some on the Supreme Court to step in and mitigate punishment for reasons that historically have been the province of executive clemency decision makers.

An approach to capital punishment which abandons reliance on executive clemency at least has the advantage of being consistent with the realities of present death penalty systems. However, this course is flawed because it fails to recognize that clemency, properly employed, fulfills a function that is different from simply another layer of judicial review. Clemency is the only mechanism that allows the condemned to tell his or her story fully. It provides an opportunity for the decision-maker to consider all of the evidence and circumstances without the constraint of the legal technicalities that characterize judicial proceedings. Thus, clemency offers not just an additional look at the case, but a fundamentally different perspective—one that, among other things, considers the humanity of the offender and the role that mercy should play in our justice system. It also serves as an important check by the executive on the judiciary, a function that could not be fulfilled merely by additional layer of judicial review.

Another possibility is that the Court may avoid reality by refusing to review any of the cases raising unpleasant truths about how clemency is actually practiced in capital cases. One reason the Court might employ this approach is that clemency challenges in death penalty cases are typically on a fast track that is not conducive to normal, deliberative consideration. Many appeals from denials of clemency occur just prior to execution, making careful judicial review (at least absent a last minute stay of execution) less likely (Silverman 1995). In addition, the apparent desire of some members of the Court to expedite the pace of executions suggests that some justices may not be eager to revisit whether imposition of the death penalty is proper in light of erroneous assumptions about clemency (see *McFarland v. Collins* 1994:35–37 (transcript of oral argument)).

This approach would also be unacceptable. By predicating its defense of capital punishment at least partly on the availability of clemency in deserving cases, the Court has invited greater scrutiny of clemency procedures in jurisdictions using the death penalty. It would be appallingly cynical and morally indefensible for the Court to refuse to acknowledge the flaws that frequently render clemency an ineffective safeguard in capital cases. The Court essentially would be perpetuating a constitutional "bait and switch." On the one hand, the Court would be telling condemned individuals that they have no right to judicial review of claims of innocence because clemency serves that purpose. At the same time, the Court would be turning a blind eye to clemency processes that are fundamentally unfair.

Such a course is unworthy of a Court that historically has been a bastion of liberty and fairness, and is charged with the vital task of interpreting the world's oldest existing constitution. This approach also seems unlikely in light of the increasing number of cases that are calling attention to the perfunctory nature of clemency review.

Yet another possibility for protecting the capital clemency process would be to abandon reliance on the courts entirely and urge decision makers to adopt, of their own volition, fair procedures. No doubt many public officials conscientiously discharge their responsibility in dispensing clemency (DiSalle 1965). Indeed, the recent movement by some governors to impose a moratorium on carrying out capital punishment (Grier and Stern 2002) suggests that executives desire that the death penalty be administered in a scrupulously fair manner. Unfortunately, as the Texas courts have observed, not all jurisdictions are so committed to following procedures that are legally sound. Thus, it is apparent that the courts still have a necessary role to play in overseeing the clemency process.

The most desirable outcome to help ensure that the death penalty is dispensed fairly and humanely (assuming that is possible) would be for the Court to recognize that clemency must be administered in accordance with basic constitutional principles of due process, as opposed to "*minimal*" process. If executive clemency is to function as a meaningful "fail safe," it is unacceptable for states to commit this important decision to overtly biased decision-makers or to employ unreliable procedures for considering clemency applications. The Court would never tolerate in a judicial proceeding the inequities and arbitrariness that often mar executive clemency proceedings.

Just as the Court has seen the need to renovate death penalty procedures to ensure that capital punishment is no longer administered arbitrarily (*Gregg v. Georgia* 1976), it should refine clemency procedures with the same goal in mind. At a minimum, the Court should require clemency proceedings in capital cases to be conducted in a manner that ensures that the defendant receives meaningful consideration of his or her clemency request (Kobil 1993). This is not to say that a prisoner would be entitled to *receive* clemency, but where life is at stake the state at least should be required to take a hard, fair look at whether clemency is deserved. When the Arizona Supreme Court mandated due process protections in clemency proceedings, it observed that basic fairness benefits not merely the individual, but also society, which has an independent interest in seeing that the person who is to be executed has "received his full measure in the struggle against the public will" (*McGee v. Arizona State Board of Pardons and Parole* 1962:781).

Toward Meaningful Procedural Protections and Standards

Due process is a flexible concept that varies in particular circumstances depending on the importance of the individual interests at stake and the objectives that the government is seeking to further (*Matthews v. Eldridge* 1976). In view of the undeniable importance of the defendant's interest in continued life (*Woodard v. Ohio Adult Parole Authority* 1998:288), as well as the state's interest in ensuring that capital punishment is imposed fairly, comprehensive procedures should be employed for making capital clemency determinations. Due process in clemency proceedings ought to include at least the following:

1. An independent, thorough investigation of the circumstances surrounding the clemency application conducted by the clemency authority;
2. The right of the defendant to attend a hearing before an impartial decision-maker, with a provision for recusal where it can be established that the decision-maker is probably biased;
3. The right of the defendant to present evidence and witnesses, secured by some sort of subpoena power;
4. The right of the defendant to challenge evidence and confront witnesses through cross-examination;
5. The right of the defendant to representation by counsel (including the appointment of counsel for indigent defendants) and an adequate opportunity to prepare for the hearing;
6. The right of the defendant to have the hearing transcribed by videotape or a court reporter; and
7. The right of the defendant to receive a written summary of the findings and the decision.

In addition to these procedural protections, it would be desirable for the body or individual charged with making clemency decisions to promulgate relatively detailed standards or guidelines regarding when clemency is properly granted. Such guidelines should not be considered mandatory or exhaustive because to do so would undermine the flexibility of clemency. However, by delineating the circumstances under which clemency is presumed to be appropriate, the clemency authority would call attention to the role of clemency in our justice system and would inevitably begin grappling with the difficult social and philosophical questions raised by each capital clemency decision (Ledewitz and Staples 1993). Possible grounds for granting clemency might include the following:

1. Substantial doubt about the offender's guilt;
2. Diminished mental capacity, which reduces the offender's culpability (this category would take into account brain damage, mental retardation, intoxication, or the minority of the offender);
3. Disparate sentencing of the offender that results in a comparative injustice, as where an accomplice to murder has been sentenced to death while the "triggerman" has received a lesser sentence;
4. Anomalies in sentencing which suggest that the death sentence is based on factors unrelated to culpability, such as the race or gender of the offender or of the victim;

5. Diminished culpability for certain crimes committed out of necessity, coercion, or adherence to moral principles, such as where a religious zealot who believes that abortion is murder kills another to prevent further abortions;

6. Circumstances in which the offender has suffered enough, such as where a murderer has been rendered a quadriplegic by suicide attempt stemming from remorse over the murder; and

7. Official acknowledgment that mercy and forgiveness are necessary components of our system of justice.

Implementation of the safeguards described above would make a major contribution toward protecting clemency as an integral component of capital punishment systems. However, there is no guarantee that even the recognition of due process protections by the judiciary will guarantee fairness in the clemency process, as evidenced by accounts of how clemency is dispensed in Arizona. Arizona was the first state judicially to apply due process protections to clemency proceedings. Moreover, it has statutorily imposed additional safeguards designed to ensure that clemency recommendations are made by a politically independent board. Members of the board are appointed on the basis of broad professional or educational qualifications, and not more than two members may belong to the same profession (Arizona Rev. Stat. §31-401, 2002).

In theory, the Arizona system has much to commend it. However, in practice, it appears flawed. A lawsuit filed with the Arizona Supreme Court in 1997 and dismissed on jurisdictional grounds raised troubling questions about the actual operations of the Executive Clemency Board and the efforts of the Governor, Fife Symington, to influence its decisions (*Greenawalt v. Symington* 1997). Relying on news reports and anecdotal evidence, the lawsuit alleged that Symington and the Attorney General had sought to exert political influence over the Board's decisions, such as when the Governor removed the Chairman of the Board for failing to follow the Governor's directives in clemency cases (Manson and Kwok 1992:B1; Montini 1993; Pitzl 1993).

The lawsuit also contended that despite statutory requirements that the Board be comprised of individuals with diverse occupational backgrounds, six of its seven members were actually law enforcement or corrections personnel. Finally, attorneys who have appeared before the Board in capital cases filed affidavits questioning the Board's fairness and objectivity based on the manner in which clemency hearings had been conducted in the past and were conducted in Greenawalt's case.

These allegations, which ultimately were not considered by the Arizona Supreme Court, call into question the validity of the clemency process in Arizona. The reports of political influence and Board bias suggest that even the most stringent procedural safeguards can be evaded, absent searching judicial scrutiny. Thus, courts undertaking to oversee the integrity of the executive clemency process do not have an easy task.

Conclusion

The institution of clemency represents this country's oldest existing procedure for the remission of punishment. The presence of clemency in every American jurisdiction that imposes capital punishment testifies to its continuing usefulness. Clemency occupies an important place in American death penalty systems since the courts inevitably cannot dispense justice perfectly.

However, because clemency decisions in capital cases have become so highly politicized, the exercise of clemency is often fraught with problems. Thus, it is to be hoped that in the coming years the courts will refine the clemency process to make it fairer—yet preserve its traditional flexibility—so that it can again function as a meaningful check in our criminal justice system. Perhaps then it can one day be said that the American people did not waver in their commitment to fair process, even for those judged to be undeserving of life.

References

Anderson v. Davis (2002) 279 F.3d 674 (9th Cir.).

Arizona Revised Statutes Annotated (2002) Title 31, Chapter 3, Article 1, sec. 31–402 (A).

Atkins v. Virginia (2002) 122 S.Ct. 2242.

Bacon v. Lee (2001) 549 S.E.2d 840 (N.C.).

Banner, S. (2002) *The Death Penalty: An American History.* Cambridge, MA: Harvard University Press.

Bedau, H.A. (1990–1991) "The Decline of Executive Clemency in Capital Cases." *New York University Review of Law and Social Change* 18:255–272.

Bedau, H.A. and M.L. Radelet (1987) "Miscarriages of Justice in Potentially Capital Cases." *Stanford Law Review* 40:21–179.

Bell, K. (1999, March 11) "Inquiry Fails to Shake Guilt; Killer is Executed." *St. Louis Post-Dispatch*, A9.

Biddle v. Perovich (1927) 274 U.S. 480.

Brown, E. and D. Adler (1989) *Public Justice, Private Mercy: A Governor's Education on Death Row.* New York: Weidenfeld and Nicolson.

Borchard, E.M. (1932) *Convicting the Innocent: Errors of Criminal Justice.* New Haven, CT: Yale University Press.

Celeste, R. F. (2003) "Executive Clemency: One Executive's Real Life Decisions." *Capital University Law Review* 31:139–142.

Cleveland Plain Dealer (January 5, 1997) "Celeste at Ease with Commutations."

Connecticut Board of Pardons v. Dumschat (1981) 452 U.S. 458.

Constitution of the State of Texas (2001) Article IV, Section 11.

Death Penalty Information Center (2002a) "Death Penalty Information Center: Facts About Clemency." Retrieved October 11, 2002, from http://www.deathpenalty-info.org/clemency.html.

Death Penalty Information Center (2002b) "Death Penalty Information Center: Summaries of Recent Poll Findings." Retrieved October 11, 2002, from http://www.deathpenaltyinfo.org/Polls.html.

DiSalle, M. (1965) *The Power of Life or Death*. New York: Random House.

Duvall v. Keating (1998) 162 F.3d 1058 (10th Cir.).

Ex parte Garland (1866) 71 U.S. 333.

Ex parte Wells (1855) 59 U.S. 307.

Farrand, M. (ed.) (1911) *The Records of the Federal Convention of 1787* (Vol. 2). New Haven, CT: Yale University Press.

Faulder v. Texas Board of Pardons and Parole (1998), No. A98CA-801SS (U.S. Dist. Ct. W. D.).

Faulder v. Texas Board of Pardons and Parole (1999) 178 F.3d 343 (5th Cir.).

Fineman, H. (2001, February 26) "The Longest Goodbye." *Newsweek,* 26–29.

Frady, M. (1993, February 22) "Death in Arkansas." *The New Yorker,* 105–133.

Goldstein, A. and S. Schmidt (2001, January 21) "Clinton's Last-Day Clemency Benefits 176." *Washington Post,* A-1.

Graham v. Texas Board of Pardons and Parole (1996) 913 S.W.2d 745 (Tex. Ct. Crim. App.).

Greenawalt v. Symington (1997) No. CIV-97-0025-SA (Arizona Sup. Ct.).

Gregg v. Georgia (1976) 428 U.S. 153.

Grier, P. and S. Stern (2002, June 25) "Chipping Away at the Death Penalty" *Christian Science Monitor* Sec. U.S.A., p. 1.

Haas, K.C. and J.A. Inciardi (1988) "Lingering Doubts About a Popular Punishment." Pp. 11–28 in K.C. Haas and J.A. Inciardi (eds.), *Challenging Capital Punishment: Legal and Social Science Approaches*. Newbury Park, CA: Sage.

Hamilton, A. (1961) *The Federalist (No. 74)*. In C. Rossiter (ed.), New York: Mentor Publishing.

Hargroder, C. (1987, October 6) "Sudden Twist in Marsellas Case." *New Orleans Times-Picayune*, Sec. A, p. 11.

Herrera v. Collins (1993) 506 U.S. 390.

Jensen, C. (1922) *The Pardoning Power in the United States*. Chicago, IL: University of Chicago Press.

Joubert v. Nebraska Board of Pardons (1996) 87 F.3d 966 (8th Cir.).

Kobil, D.T. (1991a) "The Quality of Mercy Strained: Wresting the Pardoning Power from the King." *Texas Law Review* 69:569–641.

Kobil, D.T. (1991b) "Do the Paperwork or Die: Clemency, Ohio Style?" *Ohio State Law Review* 52:655–704.

Kobil, D.T. (1993) "Due Process in Death Penalty Commutations: Life, Liberty, and the Pursuit of Clemency." *University of Richmond Law Review* 27:201–226.

Ledewitz, B. and B. Staples (1993) "The Role of Executive Clemency in Modern Death Penalty Cases." *University of Richmond Law Review* 27:227–239.

Manson, P. and A. Kwok (1992, April 30) "Ethics of Woods' Staff Decried in Execution Case." *Arizona Republic*, B-1.

Matthews v. Eldridge (1976) 424 U.S. 319.

McFarland v. Collins (1994) No. 93–6497 (official transcript of oral argument, U.S. Supreme Court), *reversed sub nom.*, *McFarland v. Scott* (1994) 512 U.S. 849.

McGee v. Arizona State Board of Pardons and Parole (1962) 376 P.2d 779 (Ariz.).

Montini, E.J. (1993, August 25) "Fife Waves Magic Wand for His Pals." *Arizona Republic*, B-1.

Moody v. Rodriguez (1999) 164 F.3d 893 (5th Cir.).

Moore, K.D. (1989) *Pardons: Justice, Mercy, and the Public Interest.* New York: Oxford University Press.

National Governor's Association Center for Policy Research (1988) *Guide to Executive Clemency Among the American States.* Washington D.C.: U.S. Department of Justice.

New York Times (1990, May 19) "Louisiana Executes Man Who Killed at Age 17." *New York Times*, A-9.

Olgiati, C. (1993, October 12) "The White House via Death Row." *London Guardian*, p. 18.

Orrick, D. (2003, January 15) "State's Attorney Challenges Clemency Ruling in 10 Cases." *Chicago Daily Herald*, A-1.

Otey v. Stenberg (1994) 34 F.3d 635 (8th Cir.).

Palacios, V.J. (1996) "Faith in Fantasy: The Supreme Court's Reliance on Commutation to Ensure Justice in Death Penalty Cases." *Vanderbilt Law Review* 49:311–372.

Parker v. State Board of Pardons and Paroles (2001) 275 F.3d 1032 (11th Cir.).

Pitzl, M.J. (1993, August 21) "Governor Fires Parole Chief, Claims Insensitivity to Victims." *Arizona Republic*, A-10.

Possley, M. and S. Mills (2003), January 12) "Clemency for All." *Chicago Tribune*, A-1.

Radelet, M.L. and B.A. Zsembik (1993) "Executive Clemency in Post-Furman Capital Cases." *University of Richmond Law Review* 27:289–314.

Rapaport, E. (2001) "Staying Alive: Executive Clemency, Equal Protection and the Politics of Gender in Women's Capital Cases." *Buffalo Criminal Law Review* 4:967–1006.

Roberts v. Louisiana (1976) 428 U.S. 325.

Roll v. Carnahan (2000) 225 F.3d 1016 (8th Cir.).

Ryan, George H. (2003) "Clemency Announcement." Available at http://www.deathpenaltyinfo.org/RyanCommuteSpeech.html.

Sandburg, C. (1954) *Abraham Lincoln: The Prairie Years and the War Years.* New York: Harcourt, Brace.

Schick v. Reed (1974) 419 U.S. 256.

Silverman, S.E. (1995) "There is Nothing Certain Like Death in Texas: State Executive Clemency Boards Turn Deaf Ear to Death Row Inmates' Last Appeals." *Arizona Law Review* 37:375–398.

State ex rel. Mauer v. Sheward (1994) 644 N.E.2d 369 (Ohio).

Texas Board of Pardons and Paroles v. Williams (1998) 976 S.W.2d 207 (Tex. Ct. Crim. App.).

U.S. Department of Justice (2001, December). Capital Punishment 2000. Bureau of Justice Statistics, Bulletin NCJ 190598. Retrieved October 11, 2002, from http://www.ojp.usdoj.gov/bjs/pub/pdf/cp00.pdf.

Woodard v. Ohio Adult Parole Authority (1998) 523 U.S. 272.

Workman v. Bell (2001) 245 F.3d 849 (6th Cir.).
Yant, M. (1991) *Presumed Guilty*. Buffalo, NY: Prometheus Books.

Chapter 23

Lethally Humane?
The Evolution of Execution
Methods in the United States

Deborah W. Denno

Introduction

The history of executions in this country is fraught with paradox about why legislatures change from one execution method to another. This chapter focuses on the most recent versions of this quixotic dilemma—legislative moves from electrocution to lethal injection. Evidence suggests that state patterns of rejecting and retaining execution methods are diagnostic of the status of the death penalty process because they have gauged for more than a century how this country views executions, both literally and symbolically (Denno 2002). Michel Foucault had long observed how methods of punishment and death were vibrant, social and political symbols (Foucault 1977). The symbols have remained, but they have a disturbing modern twist. The death penalty in the United States "has thus been retained more as the symbol of a particular politics than as an instrumental aspect of penal policy" (Garland 1990: 245).

Generally, pro and con debates concerning the death penalty are divisively clear. Such predictability is not the hallmark of reactions to changes in execution methods, however. Oftentimes, friends and foes of the death penalty align both sides of the execution methods debate, despite their different goals. The result is a dangerous and distorted legal "philosophy" of punishment that erodes human rights and constitutional safeguards, most particularly the Eighth Amendment's Cruel and Unusual Punishments Clause (Denno 1994, 1997, 2002).

The core of this execution methods paradox lies, not surprisingly, on whether legal actors want to reject or retain the death penalty and which stance will ensure their success. On the one hand, legislatures and courts have consistently claimed that the change from one method of execution to another provides the condemned the most humane and decent means of death possible given our knowledge of human science. At the same time, however, statutory and judicial behavior contradicts this purported rationale. For example, legislatures typically change an execution method only to stay one step ahead of a looming constitutional challenge to that method because the acceptability of the death penalty process itself therefore becomes jeopardized. Moreover, legislative changes to new execution methods oftentimes have not been retroactive; inmates already on death row when the change occurs must be executed by the older, more problematic method or they are still allowed to "choose" that method (Denno 1997, 2002).

In more recent years, death penalty proponents and opponents have united against lethal injection specifically. For example, some proponents feel that the older, more questionable method, typically electrocution, better represents their retributive sentiments than lethal injection; some opponents believe that lethal injection will increase the number and acceptability of executions because the death penalty will be more palatable. Paradoxically, the two sides also have united by promoting lethal injection because it appears more humane. For this reason, some proponents feel that injection can save the death penalty from abolition while some opponents believe injection can save inmates from torture. Public opinion polls occupy both camps: the public says it wants the death penalty, but it also wants what it believes to be the most humane method of execution. Occasionally, inmates fuel the frenzy by picking for their own death the older, more controversial, execution method if they are in a state that allows such a choice—just to make a point about the barbarity of the death penalty. Of course, the media are allowed, if not required, to record whether the execution process is humane; yet, courts have routinely dismissed the media's accounts of botched executions in cases challenging the constitutionality of execution methods (Denno 2002).

Despite the overwhelming use of lethal injection in this country, many of those individuals who are medically qualified to carry out a proper and humane injection—doctors and nurses—simply do not want to do it. The nineteen percent who do confront opposition by influential medical societies. Legislatures delegate death to prison personnel and executioners who are not qualified to devise a lethal injection protocol, much less carry one out. In an effort to present a medically sterile aura of peace, for example, executioners inject paralyzing drugs that serve no other purpose than to still a prisoner who, in reality, may be experiencing the hideous pains of dying but may not be able to express it. The consequences suggest the most duplicitous irony of all: the very method that seems most appealing in the eyes of the public is also one of the most unjustifiably cruel (Denno 2002, Emanuel & Bienen 2001, Farber et al. 2001). In their all-consuming haste to perpetuate the death penalty, legislatures and courts promote an uncontrolled brutality that should have no place in society or the law. The U.S. stance also starkly contrasts with the approach in the international community, where the number of abolitionist countries increases each year (Denno 1999).

Part I of this chapter describes the current distribution of execution methods in this country as a prelude to discussing the history and modern development of Eighth Amendment standards and an execution methods jurisprudence. This part emphasizes the United States Supreme Court's complete constitutional disregard for how inmates are executed, irrespective of a century-long pattern of horrifying, and entirely preventable, mishaps linked to all execution methods. This part contends that an Eighth Amendment analysis of execution methods requires a simultaneous examination of the behaviors of all three institutional decision makers—legislatures, courts, and prison officials. Even though a legislature may consider a particular method to be the most humane under ideal circumstances, prison officials may, in practice, continually misapply the method. If a pattern of inappropriate application exists, the court should find that method unconstitutional, and the legislature should abandon that punishment.

Part II examines the constitutionality of electrocution using four interrelated criteria derived from the Court's modern Eighth Amendment jurisprudence. These criteria emphasize the importance of pain, the risk of pain, human dignity, and legislative trends reflecting changing execution methods. This part notes that pain is only one of a range of factors for evaluating execution methods, although evidence suggests that even a routine or "properly performed" execution can cause intense pain and a lingering death. When an analysis of electrocution considers other Eighth Amendment factors, such as legislative trends toward lethal injection, there are strong arguments suggesting that electrocution is cruel and unusual.

Part III overviews the origins of lethal injection, the types of lethal injection statutes, the lethal injection procedure, and judicial challenges to injection. Given the problems in all of these areas, this part is a prelude to questioning legislatures' and courts' presumptions that injection meets the Eighth Amendment's standards. Lastly, this part examines case studies in three states (Georgia, Nebraska, and Ohio) that illustrate paradoxical legislative problems with electrocution.

Part IV provides a modern Eighth Amendment analysis of lethal injection relying on the same standards and criteria used to assess electrocution, in addition to a focus on media coverage. Although legislative trends are moving exclusively in the direction of lethal injection, there still are important issues that bear on "evolving standards of decency," most particularly the American Medical Association's prohibition of physicians' participation in lethal injections. This part concludes that there is substantial evidence that lethal injection involves an "unnecessary and wanton infliction of pain," the risk of such pain, and a loss of dignity. These problems seem to be attributed to vague lethal injection statutes, uninformed prison personnel, and missing, skeletal, or inaccurate lethal injection protocols.

Part V discusses the author's study of the most current protocols for lethal injection in all thirty-seven states where anesthesia is used for state executions.

This part first emphasizes the author's difficulty in acquiring protocols or information on incomplete protocols. Of those states with prison officials who agreed to submit a protocol to the author or who had a protocol publicly available (such as through a web site), only a limited number of protocols offered any details on the application of the lethal injection method itself in terms of key criteria, which include the following: (1) the amount of chemicals that are injected into the inmates, since the great majority of states used the standard three-injection chemicals (sodium thiopental, pancuronium bromide, and potassium chloride); (2) the preparation by the execution team for the lethal injection process; (3) the selection, training, and qualifications of the lethal injection team; (4) the involvement of medical personnel; (5) the extent to which guidelines are explicitly enumerated, written down, and made publicly available; (6) the availability of advice if there is a problem or a mistake during the execution procedure (for example, a tube becomes clogged), or instructions on how to revive an inmate if there is a stay in the execution; (7) the allowed or required presence of general witnesses or media witnesses; as well as (8) details on how the procedure is conducted and how much of it witnesses can see. When the protocols do provide details, such as the amount of chemicals that are injected, they oftentimes reveal ignorance and errors that heighten the likelihood that an execution will be botched. Such inaccurate or missing information suggests that states are not capable of executing an inmate humanely.

Part VI analyzes the paradoxical motivations behind legislative changes in execution methods. This part notes that the conflicting goals of death penalty proponents and opponents alike ironically can merge when the topic is a switch in execution methods, particularly the move from electrocution to lethal injection. This part illustrates these tensions and converges in the context of the 2001 federal execution of Timothy McVeigh. McVeigh's execution, which involved the traditional three-chemical lethal injection, was either too painless, humane enough, or too torturous, depending on the political eye and medical education of the observer.

As McVeigh's death indicates, execution procedures often have served as an underlying barometer of social attitudes toward the death penalty in general. Paradoxically, the seemingly serene and medically pristine application of lethal injection satisfies both friends and foes of the death penalty because it fuels the death penalty process for those who want it to continue, but also makes the process seem more humane for those who would like it to end. Perhaps Foucault would have agreed, however, that even though executions have become increasingly hidden from the public and therefore more politically acceptable, they have not become more humane, only more difficult to monitor.

This chapter contends that lethal injection appears to be unconstitutional given the science and faulty application of injections. However, the protocols are so sketchy, and the procedure so covert, that legislatures and courts are able to turn a blind eye toward the consequences. Moreover, prison officials are wrongly delegated a degree of discretion for which they have no training and knowledge.

This chapter does not recommend that prison officials acquire an expertise for killing people. Rather, the goal is threefold—to expose yet one more line of evidence showing the failures of the death penalty process, to provide a possible explanation for why such failures exist, and to detail the difficulties and paradoxes surrounding the attempts to resolve these problems. While death penalty proponents may believe that the increasing refinement of execution methods, irrespective of their humaneness, rightly perpetuates the death penalty, there are no legal or social standards that support this agenda. "The Court has *never* accepted the proposition that notions of deterrence or retribution might legitimately be served through the infliction of pain beyond that which is minimally necessary to terminate an individual's life" (*Glass v. Louisiana* 1985: 1084). Unfortunately, however, it seems that legislatures have accepted this proposition through irresponsible delegation.

I. The Eighth Amendment Execution Jurisprudence

A. Current Methods of Execution and "Choice" States

An analysis of the execution methods paradox requires some perspective on the current distribution of execution methods in this country. Table 1 lists the execution methods currently enacted in the thirty-eight death penalty states. Lethal injection now is the predominant method of execution; it is the sole method of execution in twenty-seven states and one of the two methods in each of the ten choice states. Likewise, lethal injection executions far exceed the numbers of executions conducted by any other method. In contrast, electrocution is the sole method of execution in only one state—Nebraska—and the Nebraska legislature is considering a bill challenging its use (Denno 2002). Electrocution is an option in four of the choice states (Alabama, Florida, South Carolina, and Virginia). Hanging, the firing squad, and lethal gas are no longer the sole method of execution in any state. Although each of these three methods is included as an option in two choice states, the methods are rarely used. The history of their use has been discussed in greater detail elsewhere (Denno 1994, 1997, 2002).

This capsule of the current distribution of execution methods is not the end of the legislative story. The following sections of this chapter discuss the circuitous path that led up to it. The sections will focus first on electrocution because it once was the most widely used execution method and challenges to it have had the strongest impact on legislative developments. Yet, this article examines most closely state uses of lethal injection in an effort to demonstrate how disturbingly errant legislative delegations of death continue to be.

B. The Impact of
Eighth Amendment Standards

A striking oddity of the American death penalty is the Court's complete constitutional disregard for how inmates are executed. While the Court continually recognizes the Eighth Amendment hazards associated with prison conditions (Denno 1997), it has never reviewed evidence on the constitutionality of execution conditions despite repeated, horrifying, and entirely preventable mishaps. Indeed, the Court has recently agreed to hear challenges on the subject twice-involving California (*Gomez v. Fierro* 1996) and Florida (*Bryan v. Moore*, 1999)—only to drop the cases after state legislatures have changed their methods of execution.

Explanations for these circumstances are baffling, yet one result seems clear: by refusing to acknowledge the problems with execution methods, the Court does not question the death penalty process itself. Moreover, states have aided this result through their systematic efforts to change to a new execution method whenever it seems likely that their current method is constitutionally vulnerable. Increasing adoption of lethal injection by the great majority of death penalty states is the most visible evidence of this constitutional sidestepping (Denno 1997).

1. An Historical Intertwining of Courts
and Legislatures

When the United States Constitution was being ratified, the Framers included in the Bill of Rights a prohibition of cruel and unusual punishments that was created expressly to proscribe the kinds of "torturous" and "barbarous" penalties associated with certain methods of execution (*Furman v. Georgia* 1972). To date, however, courts generally have provided only superficial and, at times, inaccurate Eighth Amendment review of the constitutionality of execution methods. Most commonly, courts dismiss the electrocution challenge entirely (often in one sentence) by relying on the century-old precedent of *In re Kemmler* (1890). In *Kemmler*, the Court held that the Eighth Amendment did not apply to the states and deferred to the New York legislature's conclusion that electrocution was not a cruel and unusual punishment under the state's Electrical Execution Act. Courts have mostly relied on *Kemmler* to dismiss challenges to the constitutionality of electrocution, although the case also has been used to bolster challenges to the other four types of execution methods (Denno 1997).

Kemmler's history, however, demonstrates how unique and problematic the case really is. The events surrounding *Kemmler* also suggest that political and financial forces outweighed the purported humanitarian concerns over how death row inmates were executed. For example, the New York Electrocution Act was a direct result of two major legislative events: (1) the Governor of New York's 1885 message to the legislature decrying the barbarity of hanging; and (2) the Governor's appointment of a Commission to investigate "the most humane and practical method known to modern science" of carrying out executions. Compelling evidence suggests that the Commission's ultimate recommendation of electrocution as the most humane method of effecting death was influenced heavily by a financial competition between Thomas Edison and George Westinghouse concerning whose current would dominate the electrical industry: Edison's DC current or Westinghouse's AC current. Edison and his associates would have benefitted by showing that George Westinghouse's AC current was so lethal it could kill someone. If AC current were applied in the electric chair, people would be afraid to use the current in their own homes. Indeed, this Edison-Westinghouse rivalry existed within and throughout the New York Supreme Court's evidentiary hearings. Yet, despite a cross-examination demonstrating Edison's ignorance of the effects of electrical currents on the human body as well as experimental results showing that electrocution did not quickly kill many of the animals tested, Edison's enormous reputation at the time outweighed revelation of his or any other expert's substantive flaws. The New York legislature adopted electrocution and, with time, the medical community recommended AC current in particular (Brandon 1999, Denno 1994, 1997, 2002, *In re Kemmler* 1890, Moran 2002).

2. A Lack of Proper Precedent

For a range of reasons, *Kemmler*'s precedential value has diminished substantially over the last century. First, the *Kemmler* Court never specifically employed the Eighth Amendment's Cruel and Unusual Punishments Clause even though post-incorporation cases have continued mistakenly to cite *Kemmler* as an Eighth Amendment case. Next, the *Kemmler* Court adopted an unusually stringent burden of proof standard that has not been used since in death penalty cases. Moreover, a court reviewing electrocution under the Eighth Amendment would not defer to the state's legislature to the same extent as the *Kemmler* Court. Most critically, because *Kemmler* was decided before anyone had been electrocuted, the Court had limited evidence in reaching its conclusion apart from the law, science, and politics of the time (Denno 1994, 1997, 2002, *In re Kemmler* 1890).

Scientifically, William Kemmler's 1890 electrocution failed. The media reported in graphic detail the confusion and mistakes that surrounded the executioners' attempts to regulate the newly tried electric chair, as well as the physical violence and mutilation that Kemmler experienced. Regardless, Kemmler's mishap was a blight on the memory of state legislatures. Electrocution quickly became a popular means of execution in other states, despite comparable reports of mishaps and botches. It appeared that the desire to perpetuate the death penalty outweighed any humanitarian goal to switch to a new method or to stop executions entirely (Brandon 1999, Denno 1994, 1997, 2002, Moran 2002). Consequently, the Court relied on *Kemmler* decades later in *Malloy v. South Carolina* (1915) and in *Louisiana ex rel. Francis v. Resweber* (1947) to fuel states' uses of electrocution in the face of new kinds of legal challenges.

C. The Modern Development of Eighth Amendment Standards

Since 1962, when the Court held in *Robinson v. California* (1962) that the Eighth Amendment applies to the states, the Court's Eighth Amendment doctrine has emphasized an "evolving standard of decency" of cruel and unusual punishment (*Trop v. Dulles* 1958). This evolution occurs because "[t]ime...brings into existence new conditions and purposes. Therefore, a principle to be vital must be capable of wider application than the mischief which gave it birth" (*Weems v. United States* 1910: 373). For these reasons, the Court has viewed the Eighth Amendment "in a flexible and dynamic manner" (*Gregg v. Georgia* 1976: 171), recognizing that the Clause "draw[s] its meaning from the evolving standards of decency that mark the progress of a maturing society" (*Trop v. Dulles* 1958: 597). Current claims of cruel and unusual punishment must therefore be assessed "in light of contemporary human knowledge" (*Robinson v. California* 1962: 666).

Aspects of *Kemmler* coincide with the "evolving standards of decency" jurisprudence. Although scientific evidence does not support the *Kemmler* Court's factual assumptions regarding the acceptability of electrocution, one of the *Kemmler* Court's legal conclusions remains viable: "Punishments are cruel when they involve torture or a lingering death...something more than the mere extinguishment of life" (*In re Kemmler* 1890: 447).

In conjunction with the "evolving standards of decency" and "torture and lingering death" guideposts, some courts also have considered whether a particular state's execution methods statute is unconstitutionally vague. This approach recognizes that all three levels of decision makers (legislatures, courts, and prison personnel) are simultaneously involved in execution procedures, but that legislatures could play a greater role in either guiding or curtailing prison personnel's discretion in implementing executions (Denno 1997, 2002).

Currently, five states can still apply electrocution (Table 1). Nebraska uses electrocution as its sole method of execution and four states allow the condemned a choice between electrocution and lethal injection (Alabama, Florida, South Carolina, and Virginia). Yet, not one of these five states provides information on the voltage or amperage of the electrical current that should be applied, nor the way that current should be administered. Apart from Nebraska, these states specify nothing more than "death or punishment by electrocution" (Denno 2002: 76).

Overall, the electrocution statutes alone provide insufficient information to assess whether electrocution meets Eighth Amendment standards. For that reason, this chapter focuses more directly on the behavior of prison officials.

The Court's Eighth Amendment jurisprudence suggests four interrelated criteria for determining the constitutionality of an execution method: (1) "the unnecessary and wanton infliction of pain" (*Gregg v. Georgia* 1976: 173, *Louisiana ex rel. Francis v. Resweber* 1947: 463); (2) "nothing less than" human dignity (*Trop v. Dulles* 1958: 100) (for example, "a minimization of physical violence during execution" (*Glass v. Louisiana* 1985: 1085)); (3) the risk of "unnecessary and wanton infliction of pain" (*Farmer v. Brennan* 1994: 842); and (4) "evolving standards of decency" as measured by "objective factors to the maximum extent possible" (*Stanford v. Kentucky* 1989: 369, *Coker v. Georgia* 1977: 592), such as legislation passed by elected representatives or public attitudes (*Atkins v. Virginia* 2002). However, no court has reviewed the constitutionality of electrocution or lethal injection under modern Eighth Amendment standards that consider, as a substantial part of an "evolving standards of decency" analysis, legislative trends and related information, such as public opinion polls and execution protocols. The next part of this chapter briefly attempts such an analysis.

II. A Modern Eighth Amendment Analysis of Electrocution

The Court's modern Eighth Amendment jurisprudence suggests that pain is only one of a range of factors used to evaluate whether an execution method constitutes cruel and unusual punishment. This part discusses the pain and physical violence of electrocution but then focuses on other Eighth Amendment criteria, especially the strong showing of legislative trends away from electrocution. The Court's emphasis on legislative trends in *Atkins v. Virginia* (2002), which supported the Court's holding that the execution of mentally retarded criminals was a cruel and unusual punishment, highlights the importance of the legislative trend criterion.

A. Electrocution Constitutes the "Unnecessary and Wanton Infliction of Pain"

The Court set forth general principles gauging what can be considered proper measures of excessive pain; however, other courts have provided substantially more detail. For example, in an effort to determine if an inmate experienced "unnecessary and wanton infliction of pain" while conscious, the Ninth Circuit has supported consideration of a wide range of evidence, including scientific research and eyewitness accounts of actual executions (*Fierro v. Gomez* 1996).

The most recent research and eyewitness observations suggest that many factors associated with electrocution, such as severe burning, boiling body fluids, asphyxiation, and cardiac arrest, can cause extreme pain when unconsciousness is not instantaneous (Denno 1994, 1997, 2002). Table 4 lists brief summaries of nineteen botched electrocutions following *Gregg v. Georgia* (1976), when the Court ended its moratorium on the death penalty, and up to the end of 2001. These botches provide considerable evidence that prisoners can experience extensive pain and suffering even when the electrocution is routine or "properly performed."

On July 8, 1999, perhaps the most notorious botched electrocution occurred when Allen Lee Davis's execution in Florida's electric chair went terribly awry—an event that garnered worldwide notice and condemnation. The Florida Supreme Court's color photos of the executed Davis (posted on the Internet as part of a case appendix) received so many "hits" from the several millions of interested viewers that the court's computer system crashed and was disabled for months afterwards (Denno 2002).

The photos and witnesses' testimony detailed the horror. Davis suffered deep burns on his head, face, and body, as well as a nosebleed that poured blood down his face and shirt. More troubling was evidence that Davis was partially asphyxiated before and during the electrocution from the five-inch-wide mouth strap that belted him to the chair's head-rest. There also was testimony that, after guards placed the mouth strap on him, Davis's face became red and he tried to get the guards' attention by making sounds—noises described by witnesses as "'screams,' 'yells,' 'moans,' 'high-pitched murmurs,' 'squeals,' or 'groans,' or like 'a scream with someone having something over their—their mouth.'" Execution team members stated that they "ignored" Davis' noises, however, because those kinds of sounds "were not unusual during an electrocution" (Denno 2002: 79, *Provenzano v. Moore* 1999: 433–34). In the post-execution photos taken by Department of Corrections personnel,

> a sponge placed under [Davis's] head-piece obscures the top portion of his head down to his eyebrows; because of the width of the mouth-strap, only a small portion of Davis' face is visible above the mouth-strap and below the sponge, and that portion is bright purple and scrunched tightly upwards; his eyes are clenched shut and his nose is pushed so severely upward that it is barely visible above the mouth-strap.... (*Provenzano v. Moore* 1999: 434).

Thomas Provenzano, who was scheduled to be executed in Florida State Prison the next day, filed a petition with the Florida Supreme Court seeking a stay of execution and argued that the state's electric chair was cruel and un-usual punishment. The Florida Supreme Court remanded Provenzano's case to the circuit court to conduct an evidentiary hearing on the constitutionality of Florida's electric chair. After the hearing, the circuit court held that electrocu-tion in Florida's electric chair "is not unconstitutional" (*Provenzano v. Moore* 1999: 416). In *Provenzano v. Moore*, a 4–3 *per curiam* opinion, a plurality of the Florida Supreme Court affirmed in three pages the circuit court's "finding that the electric chair is not unconstitutional" (*Provenzano v. Moore* 1999: 416). Moreover, the plurality reiterated its previous holding in *Jones v. State* (1997) that had rejected the claim that Florida's use of electrocution violated "evolving standards of decency" (*Provenzano v. Moore* 1999: 415). The court implied there was no need to readdress the "evolving standards of decency" issue.

In *Provenzano*, the Florida Supreme Court's skeletal *per curiam* opinion vir-tually ignored the great bulk of the Court's Eighth Amendment jurisprudence. Therefore, the Florida Supreme Court effectively begged the question of elec-trocution's continued propriety under an "evolving standards of decency" test.

In granting certiorari to review the issue in *Bryan v. Moore* (1999), the Court defied history and expectations. For the first time ever, it seemed willing to consider arguments concerning whether execution by electrocution in any state—in this case Florida—violated the Eighth Amendment's Cruel and Un-usual Punishments Clause. The Court ultimately dismissed its certiorari grant in light of the Florida legislature's decision to switch to lethal injection (*Bryan v. Moore* 2000). Regardless, *Bryan* signifies the beginning of the final end to electrocution.

Because the *Provenzano* court disregarded much of the existing Eighth Amendment jurisprudence, the *Bryan* Court's failure to provide guidance for evaluating execution methods leaves open the possibility that additional factors influenced the Court's decision to grant certiorari. As in *Provenzano*, other courts also have engaged in brief Eighth Amendment reviews that focus pre-dominantly on the amount of pain inflicted while ignoring alternative Eighth Amendment standards (Denno 2002).

B. Electrocution Constitutes "Physical Violence" and Offends "Human Dignity"

Much of the attention directed toward Allen Lee Davis's execution con-cerned not only the pain he might have experienced but, without question, the mutilation that occurred when he and others before him were electrocuted. Evidence of mutilation resulting from electrocution is derived from three sources: (1) post-execution autopsies, which are required in some states; (2) observations provided by experts; and (3) witnesses' descriptions of executions, some of which are detailed in Table 4. The effects of electrocution on the human body include the following: charring of the skin and severe external burning, such as the possible burning away of the ear; exploding of the penis; defecation and micturition, which necessitate that the condemned person wear a diaper; drooling and vomiting; blood flowing from facial orifices; intense muscle spasms and contractions; odors resulting from the burning of the skin and the body; and extensive sweating and swelling of skin tissue (Denno 1994, 1997, 2002).

Similar to Allen Lee Davis's execution, the execution of Wilbert Lee Evans in Virginia also resulted in substantial bleeding; blood poured from Evans's eyes and nose, drenching his shirt. Moreover, the flames witnessed during the 1990 execution of Jesse Joseph Tafero and the 1997 execution of Pedro Medina made the public explicitly aware of how a human body could be burned and distorted during an electrocution (see Table 4).

C. Electrocution Constitutes the Risk of "Unnecessary and Wanton Infliction of Pain"

When legislatures or courts validate the use of electrocution, it is implied that prison officials will perform executions properly and that equipment will not malfunction. A focus on electrocutions in all states and over time, however, reveals the potential for prison personnel to contribute to a risk of unnecessary pain.

In 1990, for example, Jesse Tafero's botched electrocution in Florida suggested there was a substantial likelihood the state's execution procedure could result in severe pain and prolonged agony. Subsequently, a pattern of consecutive malfunctions has been established with the botched Florida electrocutions of Pedro Medina and, now, Allen Lee Davis. Tafero's and Medina's executions shared similar problems (most particularly difficulties with the headset sponge), that created the flames, smoke, smell, and burning in both executions (see Table 4). Notably, both of their executions closely resembled William Kemmler's over a century ago. The new set of problems accompanying Davis's execution suggests that a continuing pattern of botches is highly foreseeable. Indeed, a pattern of consecutive botching also occurred in Virginia even after the state rewired the electric chair due to prior botching. These problems prompted Virginia to allow inmates a choice between electrocution and lethal injection (Denno 1994, 1997, 2002).

D. Electrocution Contravenes "Evolving Standards of Decency"

Legislative trends are an established way to measure "evolving standards of decency." Yet, courts, such as Provenzano (1999), have ignored such trends when they have evaluated the constitutionality of electrocution. A thorough assessment of this aspect of the Court's Eighth Amendment jurisprudence should consider legislative changes in execution methods in all states over the course of the twentieth century, starting with the New York legislature's 1888 selection of electrocution.

1. The Marked Legislative Trends away from Electrocution

Legislative trends from 1888–2001 show three general patterns in the use of the five available execution methods in the United States (Table 2). First, most state legislatures presumably change from one method of execution to another or to a "choice" between a state's old method of execution and lethal injection for humanitarian reasons, most typically because there have been problems with the method. However, other factors, such as cost, also are considered. Second, legislatures demonstrate a fairly consistent pattern of movement from one method of execution to another, suggesting that states take notice of the methods used, and the difficulties encountered, by other states. Third, since 1977, when lethal injection was first introduced, no state has changed to, or included as an additional "choice," any other method of execution but lethal injection. In general, states' changes in execution methods have occurred in the following order: from hanging to electrocution to lethal gas to lethal injection. The firing squad has been used sporadically in only a few states.

In 1853, hanging, the "nearly universal form of execution," was used in forty-eight states and territories (*Campbell v. Wood* 1994: 1119). Nearly four decades later, however, concerns over the barbarity of hanging and the subsequent advent of electrocution prompted states to change their method of execution from hanging to electrocution. Even though the first electrocutions were grotesquely botched, by 1913, a total of thirteen states had changed to electrocution as a result of "a well-grounded belief that electrocution is less painful and more humane than hanging" (*Malloy v. South Carolina* 1915: 185). By 1949, twenty-six states had changed to electrocution, the largest number of states that had ever used electrocution at the same time. Since 1949, however, no state legislature has selected electrocution as its method of execution (Table 2).

It appears that states stopped adopting electrocution initially because of the greater appeal of lethal gas. In 1921, Nevada was the first state to switch from its prior methods (hanging and shooting) to lethal gas in accordance with the state's new Humane Death Bill. By 1955, eleven states were using lethal gas and twenty-two states were using electrocution. By 1973, twelve states were using lethal gas and twenty states were using electrocution. Since 1973, however, no state has selected lethal gas as a method of execution (Denno 1997, 2002).

With each new lethal gas statute came controversy and constitutional challenges, both before and after the Court's moratorium on capital punishment in

Furman v. Georgia (1972). By 1994, there was a "national consensus" concluding that lethal gas was not an acceptable method of execution because of the
cruelty involved. Lethal gas continues to be available for use for executions in
California and Missouri (as Table 1 shows), and it continues to be controversial (Denno 2002).

Research indicates that there is an even more striking national consensus rejecting electrocution. Since 1973, twelve states have abandoned lethal gas as
their exclusive method of execution (Denno 1997, 2002). By contrast, since
1949, twenty-two states have abandoned electrocution as either an exclusive or
choice method of execution. Moreover, eleven (or one-half) of these states
dropped electrocution in the last eight years—starting with Virginia's decision
to become a choice state in 1994 and ending with Alabama's decision to become a choice state in 2002 (Table 2).

These trends suggest that state legislatures may have reached a "sufficient"
degree of national consensus in rejecting both lethal gas and electrocution. Although the Court has never specified how much of a
consensus is considered "sufficient," it has rendered punishments unconstitu-
tional with far less consensus than that shown for lethal gas or electrocution.
In *Atkins v. Virginia* (2002), for example, the Court emphasized the nature and
direction of legislative trends when it ruled that executing mentally retarded
criminals is unconstitutional. The Court explained that when, in 1989, it considered such executions constitutional (*Penry v. Lynaugh* 1989), only two death
penalty states prohibited the punishment for mentally retarded individuals
whereas in 2002, eighteen states prohibited the practice. If the tabulations included the twelve states that no longer allow the death penalty, a total of thirty
states prohibit the execution of mentally retarded individuals. "It is not so
much the number of these states that is significant, but the consistency of the
direction of the change" (p. 315).

The Court's earlier decisions also support a national consensus rejecting
lethal gas and electrocution. In *Enmund v. Florida* (1982), for example, the
Court held the death penalty unconstitutional for some kinds of felony murder, explaining that of the thirty-six death penalty jurisdictions, "only" eight,
"a small minority," allowed capital punishment for such an offense (p. 792).
Furthermore, even if the Court considered, along with these eight states, an
additional nine jurisdictions that allowed the death penalty "for an unintended
felony murder if…aggravating circumstances…outweigh[ed] mitigating circumstances," the Court emphasized that still "*only about a third* of American
jurisdictions" would allow a defendant to be sentenced to death for such offenses (p. 792, emphasis added). The Court noted that even though this trend
was not " 'wholly unanimous among state legislatures'…it nevertheless weighs
on the side of rejecting capital punishment for the crime at issue" (p. 792).
Lastly, in those cases where the Court has rejected Eighth Amendment challenges to a particular punishment, there have been far more states employing

that particular punishment than the number of states employing electrocution (Denno 1997, 2002).

2. The Overwhelming Use of Lethal Injections for Executions

Over time, lethal injection has become the overwhelmingly dominant method of execution, as Table 3 shows. Of those inmates executed by either electrocution or lethal injection between 1978 and 2001, 80% were executed by lethal injection and 20% were executed by electrocution. As the total number of executions from these two methods increased over time (from 1 execution in 1979 to nearly 100 executions in 1999), the percentage of electrocution executions declined, albeit unevenly. The percentage of electrocution executions dropped fairly steadily from 1981 to 1986 (from 100% to 39%), then increased briefly from 1987 to 1991 (up to 50%), then declined steadily thereafter. From 1997 to 2000, electrocutions constituted less than 7% of all executions. In 2001, there were no electrocutions—an unprecedented statistic. Already a rarity, it is likely that electrocution will soon be extinct.

3. Other Evolving Standards of Decency Factors

There are other issues that bear on evolving standards of decency. For example, no country other than the United States uses electrocution. Of the four electrocution states in this country that used electrocution with the most frequency from 1976–2000 (Alabama, Florida, Georgia, and Nebraska), Florida imposed the most electrocution executions. Since 1976, more than half of the electrocutions in this country—and thus in the world—have taken place in Florida (Denno 2002).

Electrocution also is not favored as a method of execution in recent public opinion polls. Polls show that lethal injection is preferred by most, if not the great majority, of respondents. Floridians as a group demonstrated majority support for lethal injection after Davis's execution (Denno 2002).

The Florida Corrections Commission, the body responsible for overseeing Florida's electric chair, also had recommended that Florida change to lethal injection. The Commission's state-wide survey of execution methods revealed that many states had switched from electrocution to lethal injection because injection was perceived as more humane. Lastly, the Humane Society of the United States and the American Veterinarian Medical Association consider electrocution a wholly unacceptable method of euthanasia for animals (Denno 1997, 2002, *Provenzano v. Moore*, 1999).

In *Provenzano* (1999), the Florida Supreme Court failed to address these critical evolving standards of decency factors. Clearly, a modern Eighth Amendment analysis of electrocution reveals the courts unjustified conclusion that electrocution is constitutional. Most perplexing was the *Provenzano* court's failure to consider legislative trends away from electrocution towards lethal injection.

E. Ongoing Legislative Problems with Electrocution: Three Current Case Studies

One of the most disturbing facets of electrocution is the extent to which it has remained a constitutional, legislative, and penal concern. Three cases in three different states illustrate the problems accompanying this persistence: (1) until 2001, the continuing application of electrocution for Georgia death row inmates sentenced before Georgia's enactment of lethal injection (in contrast to Louisiana, which has a similar statute, but declines to use electrocution); (2) the confusion in 2001 accompanying the extent to which the electrocution protocol in Nebraska corresponds with legislative intent; and (3) the difficulties that arise when an inmate unexpectedly decides to choose electrocution when lethal injection is the favored and more predictable choice—a problem Ohio confronted in 2001 (Denno 2002).

1. Georgia (and Louisiana)

In 2000, the Georgia legislature determined that all individuals sentenced to death for capital crimes committed on or after May 1, 2000, should be executed by lethal injection, while all condemned individuals sentenced to death before that date should be executed by electrocution. Previously, electrocution was the only execution method available in Georgia. If this law had stayed in effect, 129 death row men and one woman in Georgia would have been electrocuted.

The Georgia legislature's motivation for devising such a stringent, choice-less bifurcation between execution methods is not unique; other states have recommended this peculiar strategy, eventually switching to a lethal injection-only approach due to the onslaught of litigation over the controversial prior method. The fact that Georgia appeared not to have incorporated the experiences of other states despite the decades-long attacks on electrocution suggests that old methods die hard, along with the punitive philosophies that accompany them. Until *Dawson v. State* (2001) was decided in 2001, no appellate court had found electrocution unconstitutional, although lower courts in Georgia and Nebraska had.

In *Dawson*, the Georgia Supreme Court ruled, 4–3, that the state could no longer use electrocution, explaining that the method's "specter of excruciating pain and its certainty of cooked brains" constitutes cruel and unusual punishment (p. 144). *Dawson* emphasized that the Georgia legislature had, since 2000, been moving in this direction. Similarly, while the *Dawson* court focused on the "purposeless physical violence and needless mutilation" that character-ize electrocution, the court also stressed that "many states" had moved to lethal injection, "clearly" an "important factor" in determining the constitutionality of "an older method" (p. 143).

Georgia's change spotlights the different kinds of relationships that exist between legislatures and prison personnel when the legislature has mandated a controversial execution method. For example, Louisiana's execution method statute is comparable to Georgia's. Louisiana's inmates are to be executed by electrocution if they were sentenced to death before September 15, 1991, and they are to be executed by lethal injection if they were sentenced to death after that date. However, in practice, Louisiana's prison officials have used only lethal injection since the change in statute because they dismantled the electric chair in 1991. Essentially, all judges issue death warrants specifying that lethal injection will be used. No one has ever questioned the fact that Louisiana prison officials do not follow the law, most likely because following it would create so many needless problems (Denno 2002).

2. Nebraska

Two court rulings in 2000 and 2001, respectively, determined that Nebraska's four-jolt method of electrocution violates state law. The first ruling found electrocution to be both illegal and unconstitutional, explaining that the gaps between jolts allow "the potential for the inmate to regain consciousness and experience substantial and unnecessary pain" (Denno 2002: 88). The second ruling upheld the constitutionality of electrocution and the 1980s protocol created for its use; however, the court concluded that the state statute requires that inmates be executed with one continuous jolt and not four separate jolts. As the court explained, "[t]he state 'has the responsibility for following a protocol that will be consistent with the statute.... This is not the case at the present time'" (Denno 2002: 88). On the other hand, the statute is read differently by lawyers with the Nebraska Attorney General's Office and the Director of Nebraska's Department of Correctional Services; they state that there is nothing in the statute's language suggesting one continuous current (Denno 2002).

While both sides continue to wrangle, one issue is clear: the Nebraska legislature's delegation of statutory interpretation to prison officials has caused a crisis over how executions should be carried out. Moreover, by revealing that prison officials may not be operating according to legislative intent, it seems likely that prisoners' Eighth Amendment rights might have been violated. In light of Nebraska's experience with electrocution, the prospect that the Nebraska legislature may ultimately adopt lethal injection indicates that comparable kinds of problems may occur with that method (Denno 2002).

3. Ohio

Ohio presents yet another variation on a theme in terms of the statutory problems associated with electrocution. Until November 2001, under the Ohio statute, condemned inmates were electrocuted unless they affirmatively chose lethal injection. Unlike Georgia's statute, this bifurcation provided all death row inmates the same punishment, and all could choose lethal injection. Unpredictably, however, John Byrd, Jr. wanted to be executed by electrocution. According to Ohio's prison director, who was concerned about the reliability of the state's 104-year-old electric chair, such a choice could have created great emotional stress and technical difficulty, and his staff was not prepared. As a result, in July 2001, prison officials at Ohio's Department of Rehabilitation and Correction asked the Ohio Legislature to abolish the use of electrocution because they were concerned that the electric chair may malfunction. With the support of the state governor, the Ohio legislature enacted an emergency bill eliminating electrocution (Denno 2002).

Such an ironic initiative contradicts the traditional sides that such parties take when the issue concerns the constitutionality of an execution method. The inmate, who does not want to be executed, is requesting the presumably harsher method to make a statement about the cruelty of electrocution and capital punishment. Prison officials clip that gesture entirely and the legislature reinforces them with a change in the statute. In the meantime, legislative change occurs because prison officials concede that they could not properly carry out the punishment that the inmate wanted and the legislature originally prescribed.

Ohio's situation, which is not unique, highlights the paradoxical dilemma when friends and foes of the death penalty align on both sides of the execution method debate, albeit with different purposes in mind. Two state senators, both death penalty proponents, stood on either side of Ohio's debate: one senator argued to get rid of electrocution in order to keep the death penalty, the other argued to keep the chair to show Ohio's law and order bent. Others engaged in the debate—including a non-legislator and opponent of the death penalty—wanted to keep electrocution because lethal injection "sanitizes" and "sugarcoats" killings; "putting someone to death (in any way) is cruel and unusual punishment" (Denno 2002).

The incongruity of this dilemma is all the more pronounced when lethal injection is investigated more thoroughly. The next part contends that lethal injection has just as many, if not more, medical and constitutional problems as electrocution.

III. Questioning Lethal Injection As a Legitimate Alternative for Executions

This part questions legislatures' and courts' presumptions that lethal injection is a constitutional method of execution. Evidence suggests that lethal injection is following a similar constitutional path taken by other execution methods that were initially viewed as humane, but later rendered problematic when there was insurmountable evidence that executions were being botched. The Court's continuing avoidance of the execution method debacle unfortunately ensures that legislatures and courts will confront the problems with lethal injection only after countless numbers of individuals have been executed inhumanely.

This Part first examines lethal injection in the context of the applicable Eighth Amendment standards. It then analyzes some of the problems associated with lethal injection as well as the dubious and limited rationales that courts have offered for finding the method constitutional.

A. The Beginning of Lethal Injection

Lethal injection was considered a potential method of execution as early as 1888. The procedure was briskly rejected, however, predominantly because of the medical profession's belief that the public would begin to link the practice of medicine with death. In 1953, the renowned British Royal Commission on Capital Punishment questioned both the humaneness and practicality of lethal injection because of the problems that could result from the peculiar physical attributes of many inmates (for example, abnormal veins) or the medical ignorance of the executioners. Regardless, the United States commenced a renewed interest in lethal injection in 1976 after *Gregg v. Georgia* (1976), when the country again confronted the dilemma of executing people.

There is a range of opinion concerning the source of the country's interest in lethal injection. Some scholars insist that legislatures at the time seemed to show no preference for a particular execution method. However, others claim that lethal injection became popular along with the conservative shift in the nation's politics. In 1973, for example, then-Governor Ronald Reagan of California recommended the idea of lethal injection for executions when he compared it to animal euthanasia, specifically, the ease of putting a horse to sleep. Still others contend that legislatures favored lethal injection because it appeared more humane and palatable relative to other methods, and it was cheaper (Denno 1997, 2002).

Irrespective of the origins of lethal injection, legislatures embraced the method quickly. In May 1977, Oklahoma became the first state to adopt lethal injection and by 1981, five states had adopted it (Table 2). However, the procedure was not even used until 1982, in the botched lethal injection of Charles Brooks, Jr. (Table 5). The substantial numbers of other botched lethal injections, particularly at the start, did not deter other states from adopting the method with relative confidence and speed.

B. Types of Lethal Injection Statutes

There are six general and overlapping types of lethal injection statutes (Table 6). These types illustrate the complex and peculiar ways in which states have introduced lethal injection as a new method of execution, particularly within the choice states, and how perpetuation of the death penalty appears to be a primary goal. Most striking are the distinctions between states that authorize either retroactive or nonretroactive applications of a new method of execution, depending on whether the amending statute was enacted after the prisoners were sentenced or convicted ("pre-enactment prisoners" or before they were sentenced or convicted ("post-enactment prisoners").

Table 6 shows that twenty-seven states provide no alternative method of execution for prisoners sentenced or convicted after the date the lethal injection statute was enacted or became effective (Type 1). Seven states allow the prisoner to choose between lethal injection and another execution method (Type 2); three states allow someone other than the prisoner (such as the commissioner of corrections) to choose the method of execution (Type 3). Type 3 statutes appear to be partly a function of practicality, in case one method is difficult or unavailable. In turn, five states allow choices between lethal injection and another execution method only to pre-enactment prisoners who were sentenced or convicted prior to the statute's enactment (Type 4).

Table 6's choice statutes (Types 2, 3, and 4) illustrate legislatures' simultaneous efforts to change and retain methods of execution. Yet, such cross purposes result in nonsensical provisions that have no apparent penological or social policy justification. For example, states can allow either the prior method or the new, and purportedly more humane, method to be the default if an inmate refuses to make a choice between methods. Most inmates decline, for whatever reason, to choose a particular method. Consequently, they die by the least humane method in those states that have the least humane method as the default. This least humane default dilemma prompted the California litigation that the Court was going to address before the California legislature changed the default to lethal injection. South Carolina's choice statute is even more perplexing. Both pre-enactment and post-enactment prisoners can choose their method of execution, although the no choice default for the former is electrocution whereas the no choice default for the latter is lethal injection. Predictably, electrocution is the constitutional substitute if lethal injection is rendered unconstitutional (Denno 2002).

The one Type 5 statute for Louisiana is unusual because it does not allow any choice. Rather, it mandates that a pre-enactment prisoner use the method of execution that existed when the prisoner was sentenced to death—electrocution—although post-enactment prisoners receive lethal injection. In *Malloy v. South Carolina* (1915), the Court held that it was not a violation of the Ex Post Facto Clause when a new, purportedly more humane, method of execution was retroactive. Yet, Louisiana has a statute where the new, purportedly more humane, method is not retroactive. What is unique about Louisiana, however, is that the state's statutory "appearances" are deceiving about what happens in practice. Ever since September 15, 1991, when lethal injection was first made available, Louisiana officials have executed all inmates by injection, regardless of what the statute says. Perhaps those officials could foresee that at some point, the use of electrocution would become a source of litigation, similar to what Georgia experienced. Until 2001, Georgia officials executed pre-enactment inmates by electrocution under a statute nearly identical in language to Louisiana's.

The legislative concern for ensuring the continuation of the death penalty process through execution methods, however, is perhaps most clearly illustrated by the constitutional substitute provisions of the eleven states listed in the last category of Table 6 (Type 6). These states have one or more constitutional substitutes in case lethal injection is deemed unconstitutional or invalid. In Oklahoma, for example, if lethal injection is rendered unconstitutional, the death sentence will be carried out by electrocution instead; yet, if both lethal injection and electrocution are rendered unconstitutional, the death sentence "shall be carried out by firing squad" (Okla. Stat. Ann. tit. 22, Sec. 1014 (A-C)). Presumably, the three execution methods are ordered in terms of their relative humaneness; but currently, both constitutional substitutes (electrocution and firing squad) are considered more inhumane or problematic than lethal injection. It appears that the state's interest is not with seeking the method that avoids unnecessary pain, but rather the constancy of the death penalty process itself, with a substitute initially considered to be second or third in a rank ordering of humaneness. States seem to have such a replacement to avoid any possible hiatus that may arise in applying the death penalty should lethal injection prove to be constitutionally troublesome (Denno 1997, 2002).

C. The Lethal Injection Procedure

The constitutional issues concerning lethal injection have as much to do with the substance of the chemicals, as with how they are administered. In line with the paradoxical tale of execution methods generally, the motivation behind the origins of the specific lethal injection procedure that most states follow in this country was linked with improving the humaneness and cost of executions, as well as the palatability of the death penalty. Moreover, it appears that a prominent doctor—Stanley Deutsch—may have had far more influence than he realized.

In 1977, the now-deceased Senator Bill Dawson of Oklahoma asked Dr. Deutsch, then head of Oklahoma Medical School's Anesthesiology Department, to recommend a method for executing prisoners through the administration of drugs intravenously. Senator Dawson was concerned that it would cost the state $62,000 to fix its electric chair and $300,000 to build a gas chamber, and he had been informed that a lethal injection procedure would be substantially cheaper. In his letter of reply to Dawson, Deutsch advised that lethal injection was "[w]ithout question...extremely humane in comparison to" electrocution and lethal gas (Deutsch 1977). As Deutsch explained in a news article, "[f]rom what I had heard of electrocution,...it was pretty grotesque, with eyeballs popping out of their sockets and smoke coming out of the head helmet. It seemed to me a lethal injection would be much more humane. I thought it was a pretty good idea, myself" (Deutsch 1977).

The state adopted lethal injection based in part on Deutsch's recommendation that anesthetizing would be a "rapid[ly] pleasant way of producing unconsciousness" and ensuing death. Indeed, Oklahoma's lethal injection statute, which is representative of other state statutes, repeats nearly verbatim the terminology that Deutsch used in his letter to describe to Dawson the two main types of drugs that Deutsch recommended. According to Deutsch's letter, unconsciousness and then "*death*" would be produced by "[t]he *administration...intravenously...in* [specified] *quantities of...an ultra short acting barbiturate*" (for example, sodium thiopental) in "*combination*" with a "nueormuscular [sic] blocking drug[]" (for example, pancuronium bromide) to create a "long duration of *paralysis*" (Deutsch 1977, emphasis added). According to Oklahoma's statute, "[t]he punishment of death must be inflicted by continuous, *intravenous administration* of a lethal *quantity of an ultrashort-acting barbiturate* in *combination* with a chemical *paralytic* agent until *death* is pronounced by a licensed physician according to accepted standards of medical practice"(Oklahoma Statutes Annotated title 22, sec. 1014 (a)). Deutsch's recommendations of specific drugs also are incorporated in all of the latest lethal injection protocols in those states that identify the chemicals that executioners use (Denno 2002).

The typical lethal injection consists of three chemicals (Table 7), the first two of which were suggested by Deutsch (1977); the origins of the use of the third chemical are not clear. The first chemical is a nonlethal dose of sodium thiopental, commonly known by its trademark name, Sodium Pentothal, a frequently used anesthetic for surgery. This chapter uses the generic name sodium thiopental, unless it is referring to a particular state's protocol, in order to avoid partisanship toward companies that, theoretically, are competing in the same market (Table 7). Like the Oklahoma statute, other lethal injection statutes refer generally to an "ultrashort-acting barbiturate" or an "ultrafast-acting barbiturate," which appropriately characterize the brevity of sodium thiopental's effect (Table 6). Sodium thiopental is supposed to induce a deep sleep and the loss of consciousness, usually in about twenty seconds.

The second chemical is pancuronium bromide, also known as Pavulon, a total muscle relaxant. Given in sufficient dosages, pancuronium bromide stops breathing by paralyzing the diaphragm and lungs (Table 7). Again, this chapter refers to the generic name, pancuronium bromide.

The third and last chemical, potassium chloride—which physicians most frequently use during heart bypass surgery—induces cardiac arrest and stops the inmate's heartbeat permanently (Table 7). Many states now use a saline solution to flush the intravenous line before and after each chemical is administered so that the chemicals do not clog the tubing (Table 8).

It is not clear how or why this chemical combination has persisted, although increasingly, the chemical manufacturers have come under attack for their roles in lethal injections. Sodium thiopental—an "ultra-short" acting drug as Deutsch and the statutes specify—typically wears off very quickly; other similar drugs, such as pentobarbital, endure far longer. The "fast acting" aspect of sodium thiopental can have horrifying effects if the inmate awakens while being administered the other two drugs. Deutsch (1977) recommended a dosage that appears to some doctors sufficient to keep even a drug-resistant individual asleep for an adequately long time period. However, most states do not specify the dosage that the executioners use (Tables 6–9), so that it is unclear whether the amounts are proper. Most importantly, it is totally unnecessary for the barbiturate to be "fast acting" given the availability of longer acting chemicals.

The third drug, potassium chloride, may have been recommended initially for use in lethal injections by two possible sources: (1) advising doctors, some of whom were involved in developing state execution protocols (such as New Jersey's), and/or (2) Fred Leuchter, the highly controversial and later-discredited creator of much, if not most, of the execution equipment in this country, including lethal injection machines. According to Leuchter, the New Jersey doctors agreed with his recommendation that potassium chloride be used as the third chemical in the machine Leuchter created for New Jersey's executions. Because the medical literature did not have articles specifying what dosages of the drugs were adequate to be lethal, Leuchter relied on the information that was available for pigs and estimated accordingly (Denno 2002).

When Deutsch (1977) recommended to Dawson two chemicals rather than three, the second chemical, pancuronium bromide (or a chemical similar to it), was intended to cause death. However, when potassium chloride is used as an additional third chemical, pancuronium bromide serves no real purpose other than to keep the inmate still while potassium chloride kills. Therefore, pancuronium bromide creates the serene appearance that witnesses often describe of a lethal injection execution, because the inmate is totally paralyzed. The calm scene that this paralysis ensures, despite the fact that the inmate may be conscious and suffering, is only one of the many controversial aspects of this drug combination.

As the following sections discuss, from the start, lethal injection was fraught with constitutional challenges that courts regularly have dismissed, despite continuing evidence of egregious mishaps. Such challenges have focused on issues suggesting that lethal injection is cruel and unusual, including, the types of drugs used and their effects, the vagueness of the lethal injection statutes, and the substantial amount of discretion that prison officials have in administering injections.

D. Judicial Challenges to Lethal Injection

Judicial dismissals of lethal injection challenges have resembled those cases dismissing electrocution challenges. However, the variations between the two types of execution methods have introduced some different legal issues as well. Of particular interest in this chapter are challenges concerning the extent to which a state can delegate to prison personnel the discretion and power to punish, a problem of greater relevance in lethal injection cases. In *Ex parte Granviel* (1978), for example, the Texas Court of Criminal Appeals rejected the first Eighth Amendment challenge to lethal injection by emphasizing that courts, such as *In re Kemmler* (1890), had upheld the constitutionality of other execution methods and that injection complied with "evolving standards of decency" (*Ex parte Granviel* 1978: 509). But, the *Granviel* court also countered a wide range of the appellant's additional claims, arguments that would be echoed by other courts over the next quarter century: (1) any possible pain associated with injection-related complications "could be characterized as a possible discomfort or suffering necessary to a method of extinguishing life humanely" (p. 510); (2) the Texas statute's failure to specify the substances to be used in the injection was no less clear than those statutes pertaining to other execution methods, such as electrocution, which no court had declared unconstitutionally vague; and (3) the fact that the Director of the Department of Corrections determined the lethal substance and procedure to be used did not constitute an improper delegation of the state's legislative power.

Using *Granviel* as precedent, courts successfully thwarted two other lethal injection challenges prior to the Court's consideration of a different line of argument in *Heckler v. Chaney* (1985). In *Heckler*, death row inmates claimed that the drugs used for lethal injection had been approved by the Food and Drug Administration (FDA) only for the medical purposes stated on their labels—for example, animal euthanasia—and not for the executions of humans. Given this designation and the likelihood that the drugs would be applied by unknowledgeable prison personnel, "it was also likely that the drugs would not induce the quick and painless death intended" (p. 823). Such practices constituted the "unapproved use of an approved drug" and therefore a violation of the prohibition against "misbranding" under the Federal Food, Drug, and Cosmetic Act (pp. 823–24). Regardless, the Court steadfastly held that the FDA's discretionary authority in refusing to initiate proceedings according to the inmates' demands was not subject to judicial review. One year later, the Fifth Circuit Court of Appeals relied on *Heckler* in *Woolls v. McCotter* (1986) to deny Randy Woolls's claim that Congress failed to provide judicial review for the FDA's refusal to evaluate the use of sodium thiopental as a lethal drug; the court emphasized that the use of such a drug did not constitute cruel and unusual punishment. Six days after his challenge, Woolls's execution was botched (Table 5).

After *Woolls*, courts have rejected a range of additional challenges to lethal injection, including two group actions by inmates. In the first, a class action, Illinois death row inmates contended, among other things, that the State's use of Fred Leuchter's lethal injection machine was unconstitutional because of Leuchter's lack of qualifications and because prison officials administered the wrong drugs (Denno 1997, 2002). Similar arguments condemning lethal injection were raised and dismissed prior to the execution of John W. Gacy. Yet, Gacy's execution was notoriously botched (Table 5). In a second group suit, thirty-six Missouri death row inmates claimed that lethal injection is unconstitutional because of the nature and length of Emmitt Foster's 1995 execution (Table 5). Although a judge granted an order halting all executions in Missouri, the Eighth Circuit Court of Appeals overturned it.

In *Sims v. State* (2000) and a number of preceding cases, the litigation focused again on many of the issues raised in *Ex parte Granviel* (1978). The Supreme Court of Florida discounted Sims's constitutional challenge to lethal injection based upon a range of arguments.

First, Sims was not denied a full and fair evidentiary hearing because of "the State's failure to disclose the execution procedures or the chemicals to be used in administering the lethal injection" (p. 665). According to the court, Sims received a copy of the Florida Department of Corrections' "Execution Day Procedures," which disclosed the chemicals to be used during the execution, and the State presented at the evidentiary hearing three Department of Corrections (DOC) witnesses who gave more specific information about the lethal injection chemicals.

Second, the Florida DOC's execution protocol provided adequate details and procedures for administering lethal injection. The trial court was correct in ruling that lethal injection was neither cruel nor unusual and that "the Department of Corrections is both capable and prepared to carry out executions in a manner consistent with evolving standards of decency" (p. 668). According to the *Sims* court, a comparable kind of challenge to lethal injection was "raised and rejected" by the United States District Court in *LaGrand v. Lewis* (1995), in which the court held that "the written procedures are not constitutionally infirm simply because they fail to specify in explicit detail the execution protocol" (*Sims v. State* 2000: 667). Moreover, in *Sims*, the expert testimony offered by a sociologist documenting lethal injection botches "came from newspaper accounts of the execution and did not come from first-hand, eyewitness accounts or formal findings following a hearing or investigation into the matter" (p. 667 note 19). The *Sims* court also discounted the expert testimony from a neuropharmacologist who provided examples of how a lethal injection execution could be botched if the chemicals were not injected properly or if prison personnel were not fit to administer them (pp. 667–68, 667 note 19). According to the court, the expert "admitted that lethal injection is a simple procedure and that if the lethal substances to be used by DOC are administered in the proper dosages and in the proper sequence at the appropriate time, they will 'bring about the desired effect'" (p. 668 note 19). The expert also stated that "at high dosages of the lethal substances intended [sic] be used by the DOC, death would certainly result quickly and without sensation" (p. 668). As the *Sims* court concluded, "[o]ther than demonstrating a failure to reduce every aspect of the procedure to writing, Sims has not shown that the DOC procedures will subject him to pain or degradation if carried out as planned" (p. 668).

Third, Florida's lethal injection statute does not violate the Separation of Powers Clause in the Florida Constitution due to the improper delegation of legislative power to an administrative agency. Relying on *Granviel*, the *Sims* court explained that the lethal injection statute "clearly defines the punishment to be imposed (i.e., death)" and "makes clear that the legislative purpose is to impose death" (p. 670). While the statute allows the DOC to determine the methodology and chemicals to be used, the court thought that delegation was more preferable than relying on state legislators because the DOC "has personnel better qualified to make such determinations" (p. 670).

The following sections of this chapter point out the weaknesses of the *Sims* court's analyses. The discussion first shows that the precedent the *Sims* court cited is grossly insufficient. For example, *Sims* turns to *Ex parte Granviel*, the first case to challenge lethal injection. However, *Granviel* was decided in 1978, a quarter century ago and four years before lethal injection was ever used in this country. Like *Kemmler* is to electrocution, *Granviel* is to lethal injection — entirely inappropriate scientifically as precedent. The *Sims* court also relied heavily on *LaGrand v. Lewis* (1995). Yet, *Lewis* — a two-page court order that never involved an evidentiary hearing on lethal injection — presents merely a short and diluted look at lethal injection and cites comparably limited reviews of the method.

As this chapter makes clear, an Eighth Amendment analysis of lethal injection also requires that inmates have a public and detailed protocol of the lethal injection procedure far in advance of litigation. The kind of notice the *Sims* court and other courts have found acceptable is out of touch with modern science. The following sections offer a further glimpse of what these courts have lacked.

IV. A Modern Eighth Amendment Analysis of Lethal Injection

A modern Eighth Amendment assessment of lethal injection relies on the same kinds of standards that guide evaluations of electrocution: the "unnecessary and wanton infliction of pain" (*Gregg v. Georgia* 1976: 173, *Louisiana ex rel. Francis v. Resweber* 1947: 463), the "risk" of such pain (*Farmer v. Brennan* 1994: 842), "physical violence" (*Glass v. Louisiana* 1985: 1085), the offense to "human dignity" (*Trop v. Dulles* 1958: 100), and the contravention of "evolving standards of decency" (*Trop v. Dulles* 1958: 101). Granted, there is an ironical dearth of literature available on how to execute people. Much of this chapter's, and the case law's, analysis of the constitutionality of lethal injection relies on the expert opinions of experienced anesthesiologists because their profession is so involved in this country's execution industry.

A. The Significance of Media Coverage of Executions

This chapter's Eighth Amendment analysis of electrocution recognized judicial validation of a diversity of evidence to determine if an inmate experienced "unnecessary and wanton infliction of pain." This evidence included scientific research and eyewitness accounts of actual executions. More recent cases have, once again, emphasized the importance of eyewitness accounts of actual executions, this time in the context of lethal injection executions. Courts have addressed in particular media witnesses who "almost invariably now serve as the public's surrogate" to ensure that "no untoward conduct has occurred" (*California First Amendment Coalition v. Calderon* 1997: 889). The majority of state protocols allow for media witnesses at lethal injection executions (Table 13).

In *California First Amendment Coalition v. Woodford* (2000), the United States District Court for the Northern District of California listed many of the reasons why it considered the media's viewing of executions to be significant: (1) the Eighth Amendment and the First Amendment both mandate the public's presence during the entire execution because the public's perception is needed to determine whether an execution protocol meets evolving standards of decency; (2) courts assessing the constitutionality of execution methods partly rely on eyewitness testimony because it "is crucial to the review of execution protocols which the courts frequently undertake"; (3) the prevailing opinion that lethal injection is the most "humane and painless" available execution method may change with the evolution of technology and society's perceptions; and (4) eyewitness media reports provide the documentation needed for society to make its judgments (p. *9). In a striking statement, the *Woodford* court made clear that "[e]xecution witnesses present by statute [were] entitled to view the entire execution, not just 'the dying'" (p. *9). Therefore, witnesses could observe "the condemned entering the chamber, his placement on the gurney and the installation of the intravenous device" (p. *9).

Given such strong reliance on the presence of the media, the *Sims* court's dismissal of an expert sociologist's organization of newspaper accounts of botched lethal injection executions makes no scientific or legal sense. Granted, the expert did not witness the executions; however, the reporters who wrote the newspaper articles did, often in accordance with statutes and state protocols either requiring or allowing media witnesses. The *Sims* court also contradicts its own conclusions when it quotes for support a portion of *LaGrand v. Lewis* (1995) which refers specifically to "eye-witness reports" of two lethal injections that confirm "the finding that the condemned lose consciousness within seconds, and death occurs with minimal pain within one to two minutes" (*Sims v. State* 2000: 667). The *Sims* court's conclusions regarding newspaper accounts disregard two critical criteria: (1) accepted legal standards concerning the significance of media witnesses, and (2) the court's own evidence for finding lethal injection constitutional.

B. An "Unnecessary and Wanton Infliction of Pain"

The most significant facet of the media case law on executions concerns the extent to which witnesses can see the earlier stages of the lethal injection process—specifically, the point at which the lethal chemicals begin to enter an inmate's body. For example, California now allows witnesses to view the procedure from the point just prior to the inmate "being immobilized," *i.e.*, strapped to the gurney, to the point just after the inmate dies. However, acquiring this range in view was a legal struggle. Prison officials preferred that witnesses see the proceedings only after officials had strapped the inmate to the gurney and had inserted intravenous tubes (*California First Amendment Coalition v. Woodford* 2000; *California First Amendment Coalition v. Calderon* 2000; *California First Amendment Coalition v. Calderon* 1997). Yet, the most serious problems with lethal injection executions oftentimes occur at the start of the procedure, especially when executioners try to find a suitable vein for the first injection (Table 5). Regardless, many execution protocols enforce strict limits on viewing witnesses (Table 13).

In general, executioners strap the inmate to a gurney in the execution chamber, insert a catheter into a vein, and inject a nonlethal solution. After the reading of a death warrant, a lethal mixture is injected by one or more executioners. This entire procedure involves potential Eighth Amendment concerns that have not been sufficiently addressed by courts or legislatures. Moreover, given the breadth and scope of the potential difficulties associated with lethal injection, witnesses for the public should be available to monitor the inmate's last twenty-four hours (with due privacy protections of course)—including the last meal, the walk to the gurney, the tie down, intravenous injections, the pronouncing of death, and the removal of the corpse.

There are many practical reasons for suggesting a wide scope. First, prisoners differ in their physiological constitution as well as their drug tolerance and drug use histories; therefore, some prisoners may need a far higher dosage of sodium thiopental than others "before losing consciousness and sensation." Inmates can experience substantial pain and suffering if they receive an inadequate dosage of sodium thiopental and therefore regain consciousness and sensation while being injected with the second and third chemicals. For example, the procedure initially applied in Illinois required an amount of sodium thiopental that would be insufficient to produce unconsciousness in approximately twenty percent of the population. If the three chemicals are administered out of sequence—for example, pancuronium bromide is administered first—there is a near certainty that the inmate will experience excruciating pain during a lethal injection even without the outside appearance of pain because the pancuronium bromide paralyzes him (Denno 1997, 2002).

Second, the discretion allowed prison officials in administering every procedure enables executioners to ignore each prisoner's physical characteristics (for example, age, body weight, health), even though these factors strongly affect an individual's reaction to the chemicals as well as the condition of their veins. For example, physicians have particular difficulty finding suitable veins among individuals with diabetes, heavily pigmented skin, obesity, or extreme muscularity, as well as the very nervous or drug users. Nearly one quarter of prison inmates' veins may be inaccessible "because they are deep, flat, covered by fat or damaged by drug use" (Denno 1997, 2002).

Third, medically trained people have enough difficulty finding a vein with certain individuals; for untrained executioners, the problems are compounded substantially. Executioners experiencing trouble finding a vein can unnecessarily insert the catheter: (1) into a sensitive area of the body, such as the groin or hand; (2) in the wrong direction so that chemicals flow away from the inmate's heart and therefore hinder their absorption; (3) intramuscularly instead of intravenously. In some cases, executioners must perform a "cutdown," a surgical procedure that exposes the vein if there is difficulty finding one. In addition, if the inmate eats or drinks six-to-eight hours before the execution, he may choke or gag after the injection of sodium thiopental (Denno 1997, 2002).

Finally, lethal injection is considered the most humane method for the euthanasia of animals. However, the Humane Society firmly states that the chemicals must be injected by "well trained and caring personnel"—a sharp contrast to the qualifications available for those executing death row inmates (Denno 2002: 110).

Over time, such difficulties have resulted in a high risk of lethal injection botches, which some experts contend "is the most commonly 'botched' method of execution in the United States"(Sims v. State 2000: 667 note 19). Botches are particularly prevalent in Texas because of the state's frequent and early use of the method. Even Leuchter contends that "about eighty percent" of the lethal injections in Texas "have had one problem or another," although he does not document this estimate (Trombley 1992: 73).

The execution errors in Texas are glaring and repetitive. For example, in 1985, Stephen Peter Morin waited forty minutes while executioners probed both of his arms and legs to find a vein suitable for the injection; in 1988, Raymond Landry also endured forty minutes of needle probing, shortly after which the catheter popped out of his vein and spurted the chemicals toward witnesses two feet across the room; and in 1989, Stephen McCoy's violent physical reaction to the lethal injection drugs was so great (chest heaving, gasping, and choking) that one witness fainted while others gasped (Table 5).

The high percentage of botches in Texas appeared to be partly attributable to the dearth of written procedures provided to the executioners concerning how to perform an execution. Originally, these "procedures" listed little more than the chemicals to be used (in incorrect order of application) and a vague account of the content of the syringes. Moreover, there was no information specifying the nature and extent of the qualifications that executioners should have in order to perform an execution. After Stephen Morin's 1985 botched execution, a prison spokesperson stated that the difficulty caused from inserting the needles "would probably prompt the Texas Department of Corrections to review its procedures for administering the drugs when the condemned person has a history of drug abuse" (Denno 2002: 111). Notably, the Texas Department of Corrections has never changed its procedures to accommodate the special injection problems associated with damaged veins. Indeed, a botched execution attributable to an inmate's unsuitable veins occurred each year following Morin's execution until Landry's botched execution. Texas continues to have difficulties starting intravenous injections in former drug users. These problems also occur in other states (Table 5).

C. "Physical Violence" and Offends "Human Dignity"

Lethal injection does not entail mutilation in the same way as electrocution. Yet, lethal injection does offend an inmate's dignity in light of the accounts of botched lethal injections listed in Table 5 and those discussed in this Part.

D. Evolving Standards and Legislative Trends

Legislative trends are moving exclusively in the direction of lethal injection (Tables 1–2). Regardless, there are significant issues concerning lethal injection that bear on the standards of decency factor. Most predominant is the ongoing stance by the American Medical Association's (AMA) Council on Ethical and

Judicial Affairs, which prohibits physicians' participation in executions. Although the Council's position pertains to all methods of execution, it is particularly applicable to lethal injection, which requires relatively more medical skill and has long been affiliated with the medical profession.

The question of what does and should constitute physician involvement in executions is controversial. The AMA and state medical associations have publicly condemned physician participation in lethal injection executions, stating that a physician's role should be limited to the pronouncement of death. In the past, some states had attempted to solve this dilemma by employing Leuchter's lethal injection machines in which syringes are activated by a mechanical plunger. Yet, Leuchter's reputation has since been destroyed and no state lethal injection protocol that this author studied mentions the use of a machine. In turn, a number of state statutes are extremely vague on the subject of the procedure to be used and the involvement of medical personnel.

This situation is unlikely to change, which raises a number of contentious issues. For example, is it unethical for the medical profession to loan its instruments to the state for the purposes of execution? Is it wrong for physicians to be present at a lethal injection execution even if they could prevent a mishap that could prolong the pain and death of an inmate? While some commentators raise concerns that medical involvement may inappropriately "sanitize or humanize executions," others warn that if physicians relinquish involvement in executions to less trained individuals, there could be far greater inhumanity. A fringe of commentators compare the condemned inmate's situation to that of the terminally ill because neither has a recourse for living. Physicians are responsible for ensuring that the terminally ill die as smoothly and as painlessly as possible. Should inmates have comparable treatment? Would it be cruel and unusual to afford anything less?

Regardless of these kinds of debates and the stance of the medical societies, physicians do participate in lethal injection executions in different ways. Since 1977, for example, physicians have been part of every stage of an execution, "whether preparing for, participating in, or monitoring executions or attempting to harvest prisoners' organs for transplantation" (Emanuel & Bienen 2001: 922). While physicians find some stages more acceptable than others, a substantial minority are involved in every possible stage. In 2001, a cross-sectional survey of 413 practicing physicians showed that forty-one percent of the respondents were willing to perform at least one action involving capital punishment by lethal injection that was disallowed by the American Medical Association. The proportion agreeing to perform a disallowed action ranged from the 19% who were willing to administer the lethal chemicals to the 36% who were willing to determine death (Farber et al. 2001).

The next part of this chapter discusses in greater depth the medical problems with state delegation of death in the context of lethal injection by examining all lethal injection protocols in use in this country in the first half of 2001 (edited portions of these protocols can be found in Denno 2002). The part focuses on the problems that prison officials face in having to enforce a punishment deemed acceptable in theory by legislatures but extremely difficult to apply in practice.

V. State Delegation of Lethal Injection

This part reports the author's study of lethal injection protocols in the thirty-seven states that used lethal injection as an execution method in 2001. Lethal injection protocols or information about them were gathered in at least one of three major ways: (1) by mail, which was forwarded by a prison official; (2) by website, in those states that had them; and (3) by e-mail or phone communication, in those states that had no available protocol or when the protocol that was available had missing information that could not be obtained in any other way except by telephone or e-mail.

As Table 10 shows, about one-half of the 37 lethal injection states have a "complete public protocol," that is, a written protocol that states can provide (for example, on a web site or by mail). A dozen states have a "partially private protocol," because it was necessary to contact these states by phone or e-mail for information that was not in their protocol. Lastly, six states have a "private protocol" because they lacked either a complete public protocol or they failed to provide requested information about their lethal injection procedures. This part concludes that because of the extremely vague nature of lethal injection statutes, prison officials have far too much discretion in administering injections.

A. Missing Protocols and Missing Information

One of the most striking aspects of studying lethal injection protocols concerns the sheer difficulty involved in acquiring them. As Table 7 shows, in four states, prison officials explained by phone or by e-mail that information concerning the types of chemicals used in their lethal injection executions was confidential. Yet, two of these four states—Virginia and South Carolina—ranked high, second and eighth respectively, among those states with the most number of executions since 1976; indeed, Virginia was second only to Texas.

In four other states—Alabama, Kansas, Kentucky, and New Hampshire— officials explained that the information on lethal injection chemicals does not exist. For Kansas and New Hampshire, there is no protocol because there is no prospect of having an execution any time soon. On the surface, such a rationale seems understandable since neither state has executed anyone for decades; yet, such gaps make it impossible to conduct a complete evolving standards of decency analysis of execution methods. If a state is going to have a death penalty with a certain method of execution, the details of that execution method should be provided. In addition, Kentucky does engage in executions with some regularity; there is no reason why the state does not have a protocol (Denno 2002). Alabama provides even more perplexing rationales for its missing protocol. As of this writing, Alabama switched from electrocution to a choice between electrocution and lethal injection only recently (in July 2002). Yet, the legislature failed to appropriate funds to support the kind of research and renovations necessary to create a lethal injection chamber much less the equipment, training regimen, and protocol required to carry out a "proper" execution. Therefore, at the present time, Alabama does not have any execution dates set, perhaps in part because it has no facility, staff, or resources for carrying out its newly chosen execution method (Corbett 2002). In contrast to Kansas and New Hampshire, Alabama does execute with relative regularity. It is disturbing to realize that a legislature can vote in an execution method without any details or concern whatsoever on how that method would operate in practice.

In general, states follow a standard approach to lethal injection. As Table 7 shows, not surprisingly, the great majority (twenty-seven) of the states use the three lethal injection chemicals: sodium thiopental, pancuronium bromide, and potassium chloride. Nineteen, or 70%, of these states also specifically mention the use of a saline solution in their protocol. This is important because, if the lethal injection lines are not properly flushed through with a solution such as saline, "flocculation" (clogging) can occur, as some of the protocols warn. Notably, North Carolina's and New Jersey's decision to use only two—rather than all three—chemicals, can have a bearing on how the execution proceeds. Of particular interest is the fact that although both states use sodium pentothal as their first chemical, they do not use the same second chemical. In North Carolina, where the second chemical is pancuronium bromide, a prisoner would take far longer to die (as much as twenty minutes) because potassium chloride kills so much more quickly. In New Jersey, where the second chemical is potassium chloride, the prisoner may die far more quickly, but the death may not be as still or "serene" as in other states because the prisoner will not be paralyzed. At the same time, there is not the prospect that a prisoner will be paralyzed in pain and unable to scream out—a potential reality in every other state.

A closer look at New Jersey's lethal injection practice suggests, however, that statutes may not reflect the reality of an execution when power is delegated to prison officials. For example, the New Jersey Department of Corrections has stated consistently over the years that it plans to use three drugs when administering a lethal injection, including one to stop breathing. This approach indicates that, contrary to statute, pancuronium bromide or a chemical similar to it will in fact be administered (Denno 2002).

B. Problems with the Quantities of Lethal Injection Chemicals

Tables 8 and 9 show the additional kinds of details that states provide in their protocols beyond simply listing chemicals. For example, only nine states specify the quantity of the lethal injection chemicals that they use. In other words, those states that merely list their chemicals give no indication of whether executioners are injecting sufficient quantities of those chemicals, much less whether they are injecting the chemicals in the correct order. Nor is there any indication that executioners are avoiding flocculation and additional potential problems that witnesses may not be able to detect.

Table 9 lists the nine states that do specify the quantities of chemicals that executioners are supposed to use in lethal injection executions. However, a close examination of Table 9 shows that simply because a state lists the quantities of chemicals that it uses does not mean that it provides such information properly. In order to determine the proper concentration of lethal injection chemicals, chemical quantities should be designated two ways: (1) by weight, which is indicated by grams (gm) or milligrams (mg), and (2) by volume, which is indicated by cubic centimeters (cc) or milliliters (ml). One needs to know both the weight of a chemical and the volume of diluent to determine the chemical's effectiveness. The volume of diluent for chemicals should be (1) at least large enough so that all the chemicals will be dissolved, and (2) sufficiently dilute so that it will not irritate the inmate's vein and cause that inmate pain. For example, 2.5 gm of thiopental sodium is lethal; however, that amount will merely end up as precipitated sludge if there is an attempt to dissolve it in 5 ml. If there is an attempt to dissolve the 2.5 gm of thiopental sodium in 50 ml, the resulting solution will be very irritating to the inmate's veins and therefore painful. However, dissolving 2.5 gm in 100 ml would create an effective concentration.

An examination of California's chemical quantities in Table 9 provides a good illustration of the limited amount of information that state lethal injection protocols offer. The California protocol indicates that the executioner first injects five grams of sodium pentothal (weight) in 20–25 cc of diluent (the diluent is a normal saline solution). This amount of sodium thiopental is more than enough to kill any human being. Thus, the concentration of the injection is "sufficient" at the very least; a twenty percent concentration of sodium thiopental can burn when it goes into the vein. Like most states, California has two additional chemicals to ensure death: pancuronium bromide and potassium chloride. As Table 9 shows, however, there is no designation of weight for either chemical, only volume (cc's). Therefore, it is impossible to know how much California executioners inject.

Similarly, all the chemical designations for Tennessee mention only volume (cc's) and not weight. There is not enough information to determine the adequacy of Tennessee's protocol.

Florida's chemical specifications are accurate, but incomplete, demonstrating a problem that is the converse to California and Tennessee. According to many anesthesiologists, "no less than" two grams of sodium pentothal is enough to put even a very resistant person into a long, deep, sleep; however, Florida's protocol does not mention the volume of fluid used to dissolve the sodium pentothal. Nor does it mention the amount of fluid used to dissolve the pancuronium bromide and potassium chloride. Therefore, in Florida, the concentrations of all three chemicals are unknown.

In contrast to California, Florida, and Tennessee, the weights and volumes for all three lethal injection chemicals in the protocols for Connecticut, Mississippi, New Mexico, and Washington are predictably lethal. Of all the states included in Table 9, however, Connecticut has the most technically sophisticated protocol. The amounts provided are described in a scientific way and the protocol refers both to volume (ml) and to weight (mg), as well as to "mEq" (milliequivalent), a sound technical description. The doses administered in Connecticut are certainly enough to kill even a very resistant person.

For Mississippi, the amounts and descriptions of all three chemicals also seem lethal per syringe. However, the Mississippi protocol's reference to two syringes for pavulon and three syringes for potassium chloride creates considerable confusion regarding how officials actually administer the injection. The Mississippi Department of Corrections representative was unable to elaborate further, making the protocol difficult to evaluate.

The North Carolina protocol specifies the weight for sodium pentothal (typically far more than sufficient). However, the rest of the protocol's description is very confusing. For example, the same protocol provides the unit of liquid for pavulon, but not the weight. The concentration is unknown.

In Montana, the amount of sodium pentothal is not a lethal dose; it is one-fourth or less than that used in other states. Therefore, if the pancuronium bromide is effective while the sodium penothal is wearing off, the inmate would be paralyzed but awake. In turn, the Montana protocol refers only to ampules for the pavulon and the potassium chloride, so that the concentration of either chemical is unknown.

Overall, there is inordinate variation and incompleteness across the states that provide quantities of lethal injection chemicals in Table 9. Note that Table 9 does not list those states where most lethal injection executions have been performed (the "top five" lethal injection states are, in descending order, Texas, Virginia, Missouri, Arkansas, and Oklahoma). Also, Table 9 lists only two states that have had at least five lethal injection executions between 1977–1999

(North Carolina and California). Whereas Montana and Washington have had two and one lethal injection executions, respectively, between 1977–1999, the remaining states listed in Table 15 did not have any (Connecticut, Florida, Mississippi, New Mexico, and Tennessee). Paradoxically, then, those states with the most number of lethal injection executions are the least informative about how they perform those executions. In contrast, those states that have among the fewest lethal injection executions, or that had not lethally injected anyone at all during this time period, are the most informative.

Simply because some states specify the amounts of their chemicals, however, does not mean that their efforts are valid and reliable. Those states that do provide quantities of injection chemicals vary so widely in terms of their doses and instructions, it is not surprising that botched executions result. Furthermore, with rare exceptions, there is no information available on who measures the chemicals or even whether the executioner gives the full amount of chemical quantities that are indicated. For example, even if an execution takes place in a state that appears to have some sophistication in listing its chemicals (such as Connecticut), there is no assurance that the executioner actually injects what the Connecticut protocol lists. The practice in New Jersey suggests that prison officials may not even follow what the state legislature dictates, much less what the lethal injection protocol may describe. As the following section discusses, protocols mention little to nothing about the medical expertise of the executioners (Denno 2002).

C. Executioners and Execution Procedures

The thirty-seven lethal injection states provide minimal information in their protocols on the quality or training of those individuals selected to execute an inmate (Tables 11–12) (details are provided in Denno 2002). Fourteen states, for example, mention "training" or "competency" or "preparation" or "practice" for the executioners. Moreover, even among those states that mention some training, there is little to no indication of what kind of preparation the department of corrections offers. Likewise, only eight states give any direction concerning how an executioner should proceed if there are serious, foreseeable, or unexpected problems with the execution procedure or with the inmate: (1) Florida (if death does not occur initially), (2) Georgia (if a suitable vein cannot be found), (3) Indiana (if an inmate has "extremely small veins"), (4) New Jersey (if a vein cannot be found, warns that medication "must not be rapidly or sporadically injected," and directs that executioners should provide life saving techniques if a stay is called), (5) New Mexico (warns that flocculation can occur if sodium pentothal is not flushed from the line and recommends using the other injection tube), (6) New York (warns that if sodium pentothal is not flushed from the line, flocculation may occur if it mixes with the pavulon), (7) Tennessee (if death does not occur initially), and (8) Washington (notes that the "condemned's file is examined to see if any special instructions may be required") (Table 12).

Ironically, the mere fact that the protocols in eight states warn executioners of problems, suggests that prison officials are aware of the hazards involved if ill-trained individuals administer a lethal injection. An experienced anesthetist would not need such warnings, or surely not in the context of a written protocol to be learned at the time of the execution. Furthermore, the remaining states basically say nothing about preventing problems.

Criteria for selecting or training executioners in these states appear to be nonexistent (Table 12). In eight states, the executioners are anonymous department of corrections staff members, whereas in five states, the warden or commissioner selects executioners without specifying if they are staff members. Five other states simply mention the number of people on an execution team or the mere fact that there is a team. Only Arkansas relies on "unpaid volunteers." In turn, eight states do not provide any information whatsoever. Regardless of such silence about training, state protocols also are lax on giving directions concerning what executioners should do if there is a stay of execution. For example, seventeen states do not indicate whether they have phone lines in effect for the governor or other individuals to call to stop an execution.

In some states, it is unclear who is to pronounce death when the execution goes through, or whether there is any involvement of medical personnel, particularly physicians. Because of the significance of physician contributions, Table 12 examines lethal injection protocols as well as all state statutes specifying the involvement of medical personnel in executions. For most (twenty-seven) states, the protocols overlapped substantively with the statutes. In nine states, however, the statutes offered some additional information. Regardless of the source (protocol or statute), in nine states (including Alabama), there is no mention that medical personnel are to participate in any way, even in pronouncing death. If only protocols are examined for this information and not statutes, this figure would rise to sixteen states. Relying on both protocols and statutes, Table 12 shows that physicians are present to declare or "pronounce" death in thirteen states, a coroner pronounces death in five states, and the warden or deputy commissioner in one state. In South Dakota, there is a required post-mortem exam and report. Only Florida states specifically that a pharmacist prepares the lethal injection. In general, states allow for substantial physician participation, although the roles are limited, at least officially.

There is strikingly little information on the time of the last meal and the time of the execution (Table 11). The length of time between the meal and the execution is important because if the inmate ingests food or drink six-to-eight hours before the execution, the inmate may choke or gag when sodium thiopental is injected. There are six states that provide some information on this time frame: (1) Indiana, five-to-six hour span; (2) New Jersey, not less than eight hours; (3) Ohio, approximately six hours; (4) Oregon, approximately six hours; (5) Texas, approximately two-to-three hours; and (6) Virginia, not less than four hours. Ironically, Texas and Virginia, the states with the highest numbers of lethal injection executions, have the shortest time span between the meal and the execution (of those states that mention any time span), and neither time span even approximates the six-to-eight hour parameter.

The next section examines the extent to which protocols allow or encourage witnesses to view an execution. This issue is particularly significant given the litigation brought by journalists concerning how much of a lethal injection they can watch.

D. General Witnesses and Media Witnesses

Table 13 shows how many states have "general witnesses" for executions—individuals who include anyone from a family member to a physician to a corrections officer—as well as "media witnesses"—individuals who represent one or more of a broad range of media. The great majority of states specify that there should be general witnesses present for the execution, although the types of witnesses vary substantially. Of the eight states that do not provide such specification, six have no protocol at all. Only two states omit any mention of general witnesses from the protocols they do have and one state (Nevada) indicates that the information is confidential. Most states also allow for media witnesses, although eight of the states that provide for general witnesses do not mention explicitly whether they allow for media witnesses as well.

Altogether, fourteen state protocols specified what media witnesses could view during an execution. None of these protocols echoed the liberal scope upheld by the court in *California First Amendment Coalition v. Woodford* (2000), which allowed witnesses to see the entire lethal injection procedure, including the inmate being injected. Rather, all fourteen protocols shield witnesses from the actual injection of the inmate and differ to the extent they cover other parts of the procedure. The protocols can be divided into four general categories (minor differences between them are presented in Denno 2002), ranging from the least restricted (1) to the most restricted (4) viewing:

(1) Witnesses arrive to view the execution before the execution team has inserted intravenous catheters into the inmate's arm. The curtain to the witness room is then closed only to be reopened after the intravenous catheters have been inserted into the inmate. The execution continues and, presumably, death is pronounced (Louisiana and Virginia).

(2) Witnesses arrive to view the execution after the execution team has inserted intravenous catheters into the inmate's arm and they stay to view until the inmate's death is pronounced (Colorado, Georgia, Mississippi, New Mexico, North Carolina, Oregon, South Dakota, and Texas).

(3) Witnesses arrive to view the execution after the execution team has inserted intravenous catheters into the inmate's arm and they stay to view until

all the chemicals have been injected. The curtain is then closed and a physician is called in to pronounce death. After the physician pronounces death, the curtain is raised and there is an official pronouncement of death made to the witnesses (New York, Ohio, and Tennessee).

(4) Witnesses arrive to view the execution after the execution team has inserted intravenous catheters into the inmate's arm and they stay to view until all the chemicals have been injected. The curtain is then closed and the inmate's death is pronounced (Connecticut).

The four categories indicate that the primary distinction among them is whether witnesses are allowed to see the inmate die (categories one and two only). While this distinction may appear to be minor, the practical implications can be significant. Lethal injection botches can occur even if the injection procedure has been hidden from view or has seemingly gone smoothly (for example, the inmate may react to the chemicals).

The following part reviews the preceding sections of this article in the context of the Timothy McVeigh execution which took place on June 11, 2001. From most accounts, the execution appeared quiet and serene except to some of those with a more trained eye.

VI. Discussion: Lethal Injection and Timothy McVeigh

This chapter discusses the paradoxical motivations behind legislative changes from one method of execution to the next. Legislatures and courts have consistently stated that the primary reason states switch execution methods is to ensure greater humaneness and decency for death row inmates. Throughout history, however, it appears that such moves were prompted primarily because the death penalty itself became jeopardized due to a state's particular method — be it hanging, electrocution, or lethal gas. The result has been a warped legal "philosophy" of punishment, at times peculiarly aligning both friends and foes of the death penalty alike. This "death-penalty goal" also has wrongly enabled legislatures to delegate death to uninformed prison personnel.

What frames this paradox are the competing and contradictory efforts by legal actors to abolish or expand the death penalty. Such wrangling has become all the more acute as states increasingly drop electrocution in order to adopt lethal injection. For example, some death penalty proponents feel that electrocution better represents the retributive goal of the death penalty and that lethal injection is far too soft on criminals. This perspective was stunningly represented by Bob Butterworth, the Attorney General of Florida, who stated that Pedro Medina's horrendously botched electrocution would serve as both a means of retribution and as a deterrent. "People who wish to commit murder, they better not do it in the state of Florida because we may have a problem with our electric chair." Yet, Butterworth's pronouncements were consistent with this country's century-long tendency to use execution methods as a punishment device extending well beyond "death," both symbolically and politically (Denno 2002: 125–26).

Other death penalty proponents claim that lethal injection is not cruel enough. As the mother of one crime victim stated in an interview preceding the execution of her daughter's killer, lethal injection "is too quick.... He would need to suffer a little bit more according to what he gave [my daughter], which was a lot of suffering" (Denno 2002: 126). Justice Scalia may have mirrored such views when describing a gruesome case he considered particularly eligible for the death penalty—the rape and murder of an eleven-year-old girl. "How enviable a quiet death by lethal injection compared to that!" (*Callins v. Collins* 1994: 1143). At the same time, legislatures and courts are appealing to such anecdotal accounts from a vengeful minority; the majority of Americans in public opinion polls as well as some prison officials prefer lethal injection because they consider it to be the most humane method. Others view injection as an effective way to perpetuate the death penalty because it makes the process seem less gruesome.

The dialogue surrounding the federal execution of Timothy McVeigh illustrates these tensions. The protocol for federal execution by lethal injection, which is not released to the public without a Freedom of Information Act request, uses the same three chemicals applied in most states. Because McVeigh's death was so rapid, some witnesses complained that it was too painless as compared to that of his victims. "He didn't suffer at all," recounts one witness, but rather "just went to sleep." In general, witnesses appeared to believe that McVeigh's transition from life to death was "subtle"; the relaxing of his eyes and lips was the only indication of his "remarkably uneventful" death (Denno 2002: 126–27).

Other witnesses' observations suggested, however, that McVeigh's death was slightly more difficult. As the first injection occurred, McVeigh's chest moved up and down, his lips puffed air out, his jaw clenched, and his eyes glassed over but remained open. As the next two chemicals were injected, his skin turned pale yellow. The most dramatic account came from a media witness who recalled McVeigh's eyes glassing over to the point of being watery as the injections were administered, a sign to some anesthesiologists that McVeigh may have been tearing due to pain.

The point here is not to invoke sympathy for McVeigh, but rather to scrutinize the process by which he was executed and the inconsistencies surrounding it. On the one hand, the public outrage against McVeigh seemed limitless and death in the form of lethal injection too good for him. On the other hand, the impending execution educated the public about the lethal injection procedure itself and some of the potential hazards associated with it. For these reasons, some death penalty opponents consider lethal injection to be inhumane and not the "deep sleep" it appears to be. Although far less publicized, the events also gave some visibility to those who actually perform the executions and the toll it takes on them emotionally. Regardless of what side the public was on, lethal injection appeared to be a paradox revealing the complexities of the execution process as well as the death penalty itself.

Conclusion

The execution methods debate is played out in terms of legislative decision-makers, who oftentimes turn a blind eye to the concerns of those who actually have to kill. In turn, a considerable portion of doctors, nurses, and other medical personnel willingly participate in executions. Prison officials face the worst of both worlds: they have limited political clout by which to make their choices known, and minimal guidance provided by those who make the choices for them. The process is made all the more perplexing because those who report the problems with the system—media witnesses—have questionable credibility when experts attempt to use their accounts in court. "As a result," in Foucault's words, "justice no longer takes public responsibility for the violence that is bound up with its practice" (Foucault 1977: 9). The system becomes literally and symbolically unobservable. In the context of applying execution methods, when justice becomes unobservable, it ceases to exist.

Acknowledgments

I am most grateful to the following individuals for their contributions to this chapter: Daniel Auld, Stephen Bright, Edward Brunner, Edward Chikofsky, Robert Cowhey, Lawrence Egbert, Juan Fernandez, Bruce Green, Christopher Hale, Rick Halperin, John Hanusz, Roberta Harding, Mark Heath, Hunter Labovitz, Matthew Rubenstein, and Kevin Walsh. I give special thanks to Daniel Auld for creating most of this chapter's tables and for diligently collecting the information on lethal injection protocols. Numerous prison officials and administrators throughout the country graciously gave their time and resources to describe the execution procedures and protocols that this chapter discusses. The names and affiliations of these individuals are listed in Denno 2002. I also appreciate the excellent research assistance provided by Janice Greer and Marianna Politzer, the administrative aid offered by Christian Steriti, as well as the materials made available by the following organizations: the Fair Housing Center (New Jersey), the Georgia Resource Center, the Multicounty Public Defender (Georgia), and the Southern Center for Human Rights (Georgia). Lastly, I thank Fordham Law School for its characteristically generous research support, and the Institute of Advanced Legal Studies, University of London, for its helpful resources.

References

Atkins v. Virginia (2002) 536 U.S. 304.

Brandon, C. (1999) *The Electric Chair: An Unnatural American History* (1999). Jefferson, N.C.: McFarland.

Bryan v. Moore (1999) 528 U.S. 960.

California First Amendment Coalition v. Calderon (1997) 956 F. Supp. 883 (N.D. Cal.).

California First Amendment Coalition v. Calderon (2000) 88 F. Supp. 1083 (N.D. Cal.).

California First Amendment Coalition v. Woodford (2000) No. C-96-1291-VRW, 2000 WL 33173913 (N.D. Cal. July 26, 2000).

Callins v. Collins (1994) 510 U.S. 1141.

Campbell v. Wood (1994) 18 F.3d 662 (9th Cir.) (*en banc*), *cert. denied*, 511 U.S. 1119 (1994).

Coker v. Georgia (1977) 433 U.S. 584 (plurality opinion).

Corbett, J. (2002) Interview (Public Information Office, Alabama Department of Corrections).

Dawson v. State, 554 S.E.2d 137 (Ga. 2001).

Denno, D.W. (2002) "When Legislatures Delegate Death: The Troubling Paradox Behind State Uses of Electrocution and Lethal Injection and What It Says About Us." *Ohio State Law Journal* 63:63–260 (reprinted with permission).

Denno, D.W. (1999) "Capital Punishment and the Human Rights Norm." *Criminal Law Forum* 9:171–187.

Denno, D.W. (1997) "Getting to Death: Are Executions Constitutional?" *Iowa Law Review* 82:319–464 (reprinted with permission).

Denno, D.W. (1994) "Is Electrocution an Unconstitutional Method of Execution? The Engineering of Death Over the Century." *William and Mary Law Review* 35:551–692 (reprinted with permission).

Deutsch, Stanley (1977) Letter to the Honorable Bill Dawson.

Emanuel, L.L. and L.B. Bienen (2001) "Physician Participation in Executions: Time to Eliminate Anonymity Provisions and Protest the Practice." *Annals of Internal Medicine* 135:922–924.

Enmund v. Florida (1982) 458 U.S. 782.

Ex Parte Granviel (1978) 561 S.W.2d 503 (Tex. Crim. App.) (*en banc*).

Farber, N.J., (2001) "Physicians' Willingness to Participate in the Process of Lethal Injection for Capital Punishment." *Annals of Internal Medicine* 135(10):884–888.

Farmer v. Brennan (1994) 511 U.S. 825.

Fierro v. Gomez (1996) 77 F.3d 301 (9th Cir), *vacated on other grounds*, 519 U.S. 918 (remanding for reconsideration in light of changed statute).

Foucault, M. (1977) *Discipline and Punish: The Birth of the Prison.* New York: Pantheon Books (A. Sheridan, trans.).

Furman v. Georgia (1972) 408 U.S. 238 (per curiam).

Garland, D. (1990) *Punishment and Modern Society: A Study in Social Theory.* Chicago: University of Chicago Press.

Glass v. Louisiana (1985) 471 U.S. 1080.

Gomez v. Fierro (1996) 519 U.S. 918 *vacating and remanding* 77 F.3d 301 (9th Cir.).

Gregg v. Georgia, 428 U.S. 153 (plurality opinion).

Heckler v. Chaney (1985) 470 U.S. 821.

In re Kemmler (1890) 136 U.S. 436.

Jones v. State, 701 So.2d 76 (Fla. 1997).

LaGrand v. Lewis (1995) 883 F. Supp. 469 (D. Ariz.).

Louisiana ex rel. *Francis v. Resweber* (1947) 329 U.S. 459 (plurality opinion).

Malloy v. South Carolina (1915) 237 U.S. 180.

Moran, R. (2002) Executioner's Current: Thomas Edison, George Westinghouse, and the Invention of the Electric Chair. New York: Alfred A. Knopf.

Oklahoma Statute Annotated, title 22, section 1014.

Penry v. Lynaugh (1989) 492 U.S. 302.

Provenzano v. Moore (1999) 744 So.2d 413 (Fla.).

Robinson v. California (1962) 370 U.S. 660.

Sims v. State (2000) 754 So.2d 657 (Fla.).

Trop v. Dulles (1958) 356 U.S. 86.

Stanford v. Kentucky (1989) 492 U.S. 361.

Trombley, S. (1992) *The Execution Protocol: Inside America's Capital Punishment Industry.* New York: Crown Publishers.

Weems v. United States (1910) 217 U.S. 349.

Woolls v. McCotter (1986) 798 F.2d 695 (5th Cir.).

Appendix

Table 1
Methods of Execution by State in 2002*

SINGLE METHOD STATES (28)	
LETHAL INJECTION (27)	**ELECTROCUTION (1)**
Arizona • Arkansas • Colorado • Connecticut	Nebraska
Delaware • Georgia • Illinois • Indiana • Kansas	
Kentucky • Louisiana • Maryland • Mississippi	
Montana • Nevada • New Jersey • New Mexico	
New York • North Carolina • Ohio • Oklahoma	
Oregon • Pennsylvania • South Dakota	
Tennessee • Texas • Wyoming	

CHOICE STATES (10)
LETHAL INJECTION OR HANGING (2)
New Hampshire • Washington
LETHAL INJECTION OR FIRING SQUAD (2)
Idaho • Utah
LETHAL INJECTION OR ELECTROCUTION (4)
Alabama • Florida • South Carolina • Virginia
LETHAL INJECTION OR LETHAL GAS (2)
California • Missouri

*Statutory and case law documentation for each state can be found in Denno 1997, 2002; Alabama Code §15-18-82(a) (2002).

Table 2
Changes from Electrocution to Lethal Injection by State, 1888–2002*

YEAR	STATE	HANGING TO ELECTROCUTION	ELECTROCUTION TO LETHAL GAS	ELECTROCUTION TO LETHAL INJECTION
1888	NY	NY	—	—
1896	OH	OH	—	—
1898	MA	MA	—	—
1906	NJ	NJ	—	—
1908	VA	VA	—	—
1909	NC	NC	—	—
1910	KY	KY	—	—
1912	SC	SC	—	—
	VT	VT	—	—
1913	AR	AR	—	—
	IN	IN	—	—
	NE	NE	—	—
	OK	OK	—	—
	PA	PA	—	—
	TN	TN	—	—
1923	AL	AL	—	—
	FL	FL	—	—
	TX	TX	—	—
1924	GA	GA	—	—
1927	IL	IL	—	—
1929	NM	NM	—	—
1935	CT	CT	—	—
	NC		NC	—
1939	SD	SD	—	—
1940	LA	LA	—	—
	MS	MS	—	—
1949	WV	WV	—	—
1951	OK	—	OK	—
1954	MS	—	MS	—
1955	NM	—	NM	—
1965	VT+	—	—	—
	WV+	—	—	—
1977	TX	—	—	TX
1982	MA	—	—	MA++
1983	AR	—	—	AR
	IL	—	—	IL
	NJ	—	—	NJ
1984	MA+	—	—	
	SD	—	—	SD
1990	LA	—	—	LA
	PA	—	—	PA
1993	OH	—	—	OH++
1994	VA	—	—	VA++

— NO CHANGE IN EXECUTION METHOD   ☐ CHANGE IN EXECUTION METHOD

Table 2, *continued*
Changes from Electrocution to Lethal Injection by State, 1888–2002*

YEAR	STATE	HANGING TO ELECTROCUTION	ELECTROCUTION TO LETHAL GAS	ELECTROCUTION TO LETHAL INJECTION
1995	CT	—	—	CT
	IN	—	—	IN
	NY	—	—	NY
	SC	—	—	SC++
1998	KY	—	—	KY
	TN	—	—	TN
2000	FL	—	—	FL++
	GA	—	—	GA
2001	OH++	—	—	OH+++
2002	AL	—	—	AL++

— NO CHANGE IN EXECUTION METHOD   ☐ CHANGE IN EXECUTION METHOD

*Statutory and case law documentation for each state can be found in Denno 1997, 2002; Alabama Code §15-18-82(a) (2002).

+The year these states abolished the death penalty.

++Choice states. For example, if a state (e.g. Massachusetts) changes from one execution method (electrocution) to a choice between that method and a new method (a choice between electrocution and lethal injection in 1982), the new method (lethal injection) only is shown in this table.

+++Formerly a choice state. Ohio is unique in terms of changing from a choice state to a single method state.

Table 3
Numbers and Percentages of Electrocution and Lethal Injection
Executions by Year: 1976–2001*

YEAR	SELECTROCUTION	LETHAL INJECTION	TOTAL
1976	0	0	0
	(0.00)	(0.00)	(0.00)
1977	0	0	0
	(0.00)	(0.00)	(0.00)
1978	0	0	0
	(0.00)	(0.00)	(0.00)
1979	1	0	1
	100%	(0.00)	(100%)
1980	0	0	0
	(0.00)	(0.00)	(0.00)
1981	1	0	1
	100%	(0.00)	(100%)
1982	1	1	2
	50%	50%	(100%)
1983	4	0	4
	100%	(0.00)	(100%)
1984	16	5	21
	76%	24%	(100%)
1985	11	7	18
	61%	39%	(100%)
1986	7	11	18
	39%	61%	(100%)
1987	16	7	23
	70%	30%	(100%)
1988	7	4	11
	64%	36%	(100%)
1989	8	7	15
	53%	47%	(100%)
1990	11	12	23
	48%	52%	(100%)
1991	7	7	14
	50%	50%	(100%)
1992	8	21	29
	28%	72%	(100%)
1993	10	26	36
	28%	72%	(100%)
1994	6	23	29
	21%	79%	(100%)
1995	7	49	56
	13%	87%	(100%)
1996	7	36	43
	16%	84%	(100%)
1997	6	68	74
	8%	92%	(100%)
1998	7	60	67
	10%	90%	(100%)
1999	3	94	97
	3%	97%	(100%)
2000	5	80	85
	6%	94%	(100%)
2001	0	66	66
	(0.00)	100%	(100%)
TOTAL	149	584	733
(1977–2001)	20%	80%	(100%)

*Denno 2002. From 1976 to 2001, executions from other methods (hanging, shooting, and lethal gas) constituted 2.14% of the total number of executions and are excluded from this table.

Table 4
Botched Electrocution Executions Following
Gregg v. Georgia (1976)*

1. **John Spenkelink, May 25, 1979, Florida:** It took three separate jolts of electricity spread over five minutes to kill Spenkelink. After the first jolt, smoke filled the room and a three-inch wound was scorched on his right leg.

2. **Frank J. Coppola, August 10, 1982, Virginia:** After a second jolt of electrical current, the death chamber filled with the smell and sizzle of burning as Coppola's head and leg burst into flames.

3. **John Louis Evans III, April 22, 1983, Alabama:** Three separate jolts over fourteen minutes were required to kill Evans. Flames erupted from the electrode tied to his leg, and smoke was seen coming from his head and leg.

4. **Robert W. Williams, December 14, 1983, Louisiana:** When the electricity was applied, smoke and sparks appeared from Williams's head. Witnesses reported the smell of "burning flesh" and "excessive burning."

5. **Alpha Otis Stephens, December 12, 1984, Georgia:** It took two two-minute jolts of 2,080-volt electricity, eight minutes apart, to kill Stephens. After the first jolt, doctors had to wait six minutes for the body to cool down before examining it. During this time, Stephens took about twenty-three breaths.

6. **William E. Vandiver, October 16, 1985, Indiana:** Indiana's seventy-two-year-old electric chair took over seventeen minutes and five jolts of electricity to kill Vandiver.

7. **Alvin Moore, June 9, 1987, Louisiana:** When examined after his execution, Moore was severely burned on the top of his head and his epidermis was found to be missing in a wide circular pattern.

8. **Wayne Robert Felde, March 15, 1988, Louisiana:** Felde's body evidenced severe third and fourth degree burns. His leg was mutilated, his skin was coming loose, and "chunks of skin" had been "burned off the left side of his head...revealing his skull bone."

9. **Horace F. Dunkins, July 14, 1989, Alabama:** An incorrectly wired chair took nineteen minutes to kill the mentally retarded Dunkins.

10. **Jesse Joseph Tafero, May 4, 1990, Florida:** For four minutes, the executioner applied three 2,000-volt jolts of electricity, causing flames to shoot from Tafero's head. The medical examiner could not determine whether Tafero survived the first two jolts.

11. **Robert T. Boggs, July 19, 1990, Virginia:** Boggs required two fifty-five second applications of 2,500-volts of electricity.

12. **Wilbert Lee Evans, October 17, 1990, Virginia:** During the execution, blood poured from Evans's eyes and nose. Witnesses heard an audible moan, suggesting suffering.

13. **Derick Lynn Peterson, August 22, 1991, Virginia:** Peterson's death occurred after thirteen minutes and two separate jolts of electricity. After the first series of jolts, Peterson's heart appeared to still be beating.

14. **Roger Keith Coleman, May 20, 1992, Virginia:** Executioners applied two 1,700-volt jolts to kill Coleman. A witness spoke of smoke coming from Coleman's leg during the execution.

15. **Gregory Resnover, December 8, 1994, Indiana:** When the electricity was applied, Resnover rose suddenly "from his chair in a giant spasm.... His head jerked back and smoke and spark-like flames came out of the top of his head."

16. **Jerry White, December 4, 1995, Florida:** There were reports that White lunged and screamed during his execution.

17. **Larry Lonchar, November 14, 1996, Georgia:** Lonchar moaned and "seemed to gasp for air" as the executioner applied two jolts of 2,000 volts each to Lonchar's body before he was pronounced dead.

18. Pedro Medina, March 25, 1997, Florida: "Blue and orange flames up to a foot long shot from the right side of Mr. Medina's head and flickered for six to ten seconds, filling the execution chamber with smoke."

19. Allen Lee Davis, July 8, 1999, Florida: After being jolted with 2,300 volts, blood poured from Davis's face, and soaked a large portion of his shirt. Testimony indicated that the strap placed across Davis's mouth hindered his breathing and partially asphyxiated him prior to and during the electrocution.

*Documentation for, and fuller descriptions of, each botched electrocution can be found in Denno 1994, 1997, 2002.

Table 5
Botched Lethal Injection Executions Following
Gregg v. Georgia (1976)*

1. **Charles Brooks, Jr.,** December 7, 1982, Texas: In what was the first execution by lethal injection, an overdose of sodium thiopental took seven minutes to kill Brooks. Witnesses stated that Brooks "had not died easily."

2. **James D. Autry,** March 14, 1984, Texas: Autry took ten minutes to die, complaining of pain throughout. Officials suggested that faulty equipment or inexperienced personnel were to blame.

3. **Thomas Andy Barefoot,** October 30, 1984, Texas: A witness stated that after emitting a "terrible gasp," Barefoot's heart was still beating after the prison medical examiner had declared him dead.

4. **Stephen Peter Morin,** March 13, 1985, Texas: It took technicians over forty minutes to locate a suitable vein to insert the lethal injection needle, and another eleven minutes for Morin to die.

5. **Randy Woolls,** August 20, 1986, Texas: Because of his history of drug addiction, Woolls had to assist execution technicians in finding an adequate vein for insertion.

6. **Elliot Rod Johnson,** June 24, 1987, Texas: Johnson's execution was plagued by repetitive needle punctures and took executioners approximately thirty-five minutes to find a vein.

7. **Raymond Landry,** December 13, 1988, Texas: Two minutes into the execution, after a lengthy search for an adequate vein, the syringe came out of Landry's vein, "spewing deadly chemicals toward startled witnesses."

8. **Stephen McCoy,** May 24, 1989, Texas: In a violent reaction to the drugs, which experts attributed to a weak dosage, McCoy "choked and heaved" during his execution.

9. **George "Tiny" Mercer,** January 6, 1990, Missouri: A medical doctor was required to perform a cutdown on Mercer's groin.

10. **George Gilmore,** August 31, 1990, Missouri: According to a witnessing doctor, force was used to stick the needle into Gilmore's arm.

11. **Charles Troy Coleman,** September 10, 1990, Oklahoma: Technicians had difficulty finding a vein and the execution was delayed by ten minutes.

12. **Charles Walker,** September 12, 1990, Illinois: There was some indication that, while appearing calm on the outside due to the paralyzing drugs, Walker suffered excruciating pain. There were reports of faulty equipment and inexperienced personnel.

13. **Maurice Byrd,** August 23, 1991, Missouri: The machine used to inject the lethal dosage malfunctioned.

14. **Rickey Ray Rector,** January 24, 1992, Arkansas: It took almost an hour for a team of eight to find a suitable vein. Eventually, Rector himself assisted in finding the vein.

15. **Robyn Lee Parks,** March 10, 1992, Oklahoma: There were reports that Parks violently gagged and bucked in his chair after the drugs were administered. One witness said that his death looked "painful and inhumane."

16. **Billy Wayne White,** April 23, 1992, Texas: White's death required forty-seven minutes because executioners had difficulty finding a vein that was not severely damaged from years of heroin abuse.

17. **Justin Lee May,** May 7, 1992, Texas: According to a witness, May gasped and reared against his restraints during his nine-minute death.

18. **John Wayne Gacy,** May 10, 1994, Illinois: Complications caused by a faulty delivery tube resulted in Gacy's execution lasting eighteen minutes.

19. Emmitt Foster, May 3, 1995, Missouri: Foster took twenty-nine minutes to die. The delay was attributed to the difficulty in finding an adequate vein and incorrectly fitted equipment.

20. Ronald Allridge, June 8, 1995, Texas: Allridge's execution was conducted with only one needle, rather than the standard two, because a suitable vein could not be found in his left arm.

21. Richard Townes, Jr., January 23, 1996, Virginia: It took twenty-two minutes for medical personnel to find an adequate vein.

22. Tommie J. Smith, July 18, 1996, Indiana: The execution team required a total of thirty-six minutes to find a vein. Officials acknowledged that they had known beforehand that Smith's unusually small veins might cause problems.

23. Luis M. Mata, August 22, 1996, Arizona: Mata remained strapped to a gurney with the needle in his arm for one hour and ten minutes while his attorneys argued his case. When injected, his head jerked, his face contorted, and his chest and stomach sharply heaved.

24. Scott Dawn Carpenter, May 8, 1997, Oklahoma: Carpenter gasped and shook for three minutes following the injection. He was pronounced dead eight minutes later.

25. Michael Eugene Elkins, June 13, 1997, South Carolina: Liver and spleen problems had caused Elkins's body to swell, requiring executioners to search almost an hour—and seek assistance from Elkins—to find a suitable vein.

26. Joseph Cannon, April 23, 1998, Texas: Cannon's vein collapsed and the needle popped out after the first injection. These events caused him to make a second final statement and be injected a second time behind a closed curtain.

27. Genaro Ruiz Camacho, August 26, 1998, Texas: Camacho's execution was delayed approximately two hours due to last-minute appeals and problems finding suitable veins in Camacho's arms, which had been damaged by his drug problem.

28. Roderick Abeyta, October 5, 1998, Nevada: The execution team took twenty-five minutes to find a vein suitable for the lethal injection.

29. Bennie Demps, June 8, 2000, Florida: The execution team had to forfeit the second injection (Florida protocol demands two injections) after a thirty-three minute search failed to locate a suitable second vein. Demps complained of pain and bleeding in his final statement.

30. Bert Leroy Hunter, June 28, 2000, Missouri: In a violent reaction to the drugs, Hunter lost consciousness and his body convulsed against his restraints during what one witness called "a violent and agonizing death."

31. Joseph Martinez High, November 7, 2001, Georgia: For twenty minutes, prison technicians attempted unsuccessfully to locate a vein in High's arms. Eventually, they inserted a needle in High's chest, after a doctor cut an incision there, while they inserted the other needle in one of High's hands.

---

*Documentation for, and fuller descriptions of, each botched lethal injection can be found in Denno 1997, 2002.

Table 6
Types of Lethal Injection Statutes*

I. LETHAL INJECTION ONLY

These statutes (for twenty-seven states) provide no alternative method of execution for prisoners sentenced or convicted after the date the statute was enacted or became effective. There are three general types of lethal injection-only statutes:

(A) Type A statutes (for eleven states) refer to an injection of a "substance or substances in a quantity sufficient to cause death," or language close to that wording.[1]

(B) Type B statutes (for thirteen states) refer to a "lethal quantity of an ultrashort-acting barbiturate or other similar drug in combination with a chemical paralytic agent until death," or language close to that wording.[2]

(C) Type C statutes (for one state) refer simply to "lethal injection."[3]

Statutes for two states depart slightly from Type A and Type B.[4]

II. LETHAL INJECTION OR OTHER METHOD—PRISONER'S CHOICE

These statutes (for seven states) allow prisoners to choose between lethal injection and another method of execution.[5]

III. LETHAL INJECTION OR OTHER METHOD—ANOTHER'S CHOICE

These statutes (for three states) allow someone other than the prisoner to choose the execution method, or the statute is unclear about who makes this choice.[6]

IV. LETHAL INJECTION AND PRE-ENACTMENT PRISONER'S CHOICE

These statutes (for five states) apply to states that now have a lethal injection-only statute enacted, but provide pre-enactment prisoners a choice between lethal injection and the method that existed when the prisoner was convicted or sentenced to death.[7]

V. LETHAL INJECTION AND NO PRE-ENACTMENT CHOICE

This statute (for Louisiana only) mandates that a pre-enactment prisoner use the method of execution that existed when the prisoner was sentenced to death (electrocution), even though the state has now enacted a lethal-injection only statute. Notably, Louisiana executes all inmates with lethal injection even if they were sentenced before the legislative enactment because prison officials have dismantled the electric chair.

VI. LETHAL INJECTION AND CONSTITUTIONAL SUBSTITUTES

These statutes (for eleven states) provide a constitutional substitute in case lethal injection is held to be unconstitutional or invalid.[8]

---

* Statutory and case law documentation for each state can be found in Denno 1997, 2002; Alabama Code §15-18-82(a) (2002).

1. The eleven states are Arizona, Connecticut, Delaware, Georgia, Indiana, Kansas, Kentucky, Louisiana, New York, Ohio, Texas.

2. There are variations in the wording of the lethal injection statutes, depending on the state. The thirteen states are Arkansas, Illinois, Maryland, Mississippi, Montana, New Jersey, New Mexico, North Carolina, Oklahoma, Oregon, Pennsylvania, South Dakota, Wyoming.

3. The one state is Tennessee.

4. The two states are Colorado and Nevada.

5. The seven states and the other methods they have selected are as follows: *Lethal Injection or Hanging*: Washington. *Lethal Injection or Firing Squad*: Utah. *Lethal Injection or Electrocution*: Alabama, Florida, South Carolina, Virginia. *Lethal Injection or Lethal Gas*: California.

6. *Lethal Injection or Hanging*: New Hampshire. *Lethal Injection or Firing Squad:* Idaho. *Lethal Injection or Lethal Gas:* Missouri.

7. *Lethal Injection or Hanging*: Delaware. *Lethal Injection or Electrocution*: Arkansas, Kentucky, South Carolina. *Lethal Injection or Lethal Gas*: Arizona.

8. Alabama, Arkansas, California, Delaware, Florida, Illinois, New Hampshire, Ohio, Oklahoma, South Carolina, and Wyoming.

Table 7
Types of Lethal Injection Chemical Combinations,
by State for 37 States*

Information Is Confidential (4 States)	
Nevada	Pennsylvania
South Carolina	Virginia**

Information Does Not Exist (4 States)	
Alabama	Kansas
Kentucky	New Hampshire

Sodium Thiopental, Pancuronium Bromide, Potassium Chloride*** (27 States)		
Arizona	Arkansas**	California
Colorado**	Connecticut**	Delaware
Florida**	Georgia**	Idaho
Illinois	Indiana**	Louisiana
Maryland**	Mississippi**	Missouri
Montana**	New Mexico**	New York**
Ohio	Oklahoma**	Oregon
South Dakota**	Tennessee**	Texas**
Utah	Washington**	Wyoming

Sodium Thiopental, Pancuronium Bromide (1 State)
North Carolina**

(Two Trays) 1. Saline and Potassium Chloride, 2. Saline and Sodium Thiopental (1 State)
New Jersey**

* All lethal injection protocols and communications are on file with the author at Fordham University School of Law. The sources for the protocols and communications can be found in Denno 2002.
** The state's lethal injection protocol specifically mentions saline.
*** Sodium thiopental also is known as thiopental sodium or its brand name, sodium pentothol. Pancuronium bromide also is commonly referred to as its brand name, pavulon. States use all of these names in their statutes. This table lists only the generic names of these chemicals.

Table 8
Lethal Injection Chemical Specifications,
by State for 37 States*

States that Specify Quantities of Lethal Injection Chemicals (9)

California	Connecticut	Florida
Mississippi	Montana	New Mexico
North Carolina	Tennessee	Washington

States that do not Specify Quantities of Lethal Injection Chemicals (28)

Alabama**	Arizona	Arkansas	Colorado
Delaware	Georgia	Idaho	Illinois
Indiana	Kansas**	Kentucky**	Louisiana
Maryland	Missouri	Nevada**	New Hampshire**
New Jersey	New York	Ohio	Oklahoma
Oregon	Pennsylvania	S. Carolina**	South Dakota
Texas	Utah	Virginia**	Wyoming

States that Specify Saline in Their Lethal Injection Procedures (19)

Arkansas	Colorado	Connecticut	Florida
Georgia	Indiana	Maryland	Mississippi
Montana	New Jersey	New Mexico	New York
N. Carolina	Oklahoma	South Dakota	Tennessee
Texas	Virginia	Washington	

States that Do Not Specify Saline in Their Lethal Injection Procedures (18)

Alabama**	Arizona	California	Delaware
Idaho	Illinois	Kansas**	Kentucky**
Louisiana	Missouri	Nevada**	New Hampshire**
Ohio	Oregon	Pennsylvania	South Carolina**
Utah	Wyoming		

*All lethal injection protocols and communications are on file with the author at Fordham University School of Law. The sources for the protocols and communications can be found in Denno 2002.
**These states did not provide any information whatsoever.

Table 9
The Quantities of Lethal Injection Chemicals for
the Nine States That Specify Them*

State	Chemicals Specified in State Protocols
California	5.0 g of sodium pentothal in 20–25 cc of diluent. 50 cc of pancuronium bromide. 50 cc of potassium chloride.
Connecticut	2,500 mg thiopental sodium in 50 ml of clear sodium chloride 0.9% solution of an approximate concentration of mg/ml or 5%. 100 mg of pancuronium bromide (contents of ten 5 ml vials of 2 mg/ml concentration) in 50 ml. 120 mEq of potassium chloride (contents of two 30 ml vials of 2 mEq/ml concentration) in 60 ml.
Florida	"No less than" 2 g of sodium pentothal. Next, a saline solution to act as a flushing agent. Next, no less than 50 mg of pancuronium bromide. Then saline, again as a flushing agent. Finally, no less than 150 mEq of potassium chloride.
Mississippi	Sodium pentothal, 2.0 g, 1 syringe. Normal saline, 10–15cc., 2 syringes. Pavulon, 50 mg per 50 cc., 3 syringes. Potassium chloride, 50 mEq per 50 cc., 3 syringes.
Montana	Sodium pentothal, 500 mg w/ diluent. Pavulon, 10 mg ampules. Potassium chloride, 10 mEq ampules. Saline, 1000 C. lidocaine HCL, 2% w/ epinephrine.
New Mexico	Two 50-cc syringes each containing 10–50cc of sterile normal saline. Three 50-cc syringes each containing 50 mEq of potassium chloride in 50-cc. Three 50-cc syringes each containing 50 mg of pavulon in 50-cc. One 50-cc syringe containing 210[sic]g** of sodium pentothal (contents of four 500 mg vials dissolved in the least amount of diluent possible to attain complete, clear suspension). Order of chemicals to be sodium pentothal first, pavulon second, and potassium chloride last.
North Carolina	Three each 1000 ml saline. Four vials of thiopental sodium 5 g, 100 ml each. Twelve vials pavulon 5 ml each.
Tennessee	Sodium pentothal (50 cc). Saline (50 cc). Pancuronium (2) (50 cc). Saline (50 cc). Potassium chloride (2) (50 cc).
Washington	2g/50cc thiopental sodium. 15 cc normal saline. 50 mg/50 cc pancuronium bromide. 15 cc normal saline. 1.50–2.70 mEq/kg potassium chloride (Kcl).

*All lethal injection protocols and communications are on file with the author at Fordham University School of Law. The sources for the protocols and communications can be found in Denno 2002. Much of the wording in this table is taken verbatim from the protocols.
**A typo. The amount should be 2.0 g of sodium pentothal. This corrected amount of sodium pentothal is specified in another section of New Mexico's protocol.

Table 10
A Breakdown of States with Public or
Private Lethal Injection Protocols*

I. STATES WITH COMPLETE PUBLIC PROTOCOLS (19 STATES)

Arizona	Arkansas	California	Colorado
Connecticut	Florida	Georgia	Idaho
Illinois	Montana	New Jersey	New Mexico
New York	North Carolina	Oklahoma	Oregon
South Dakota	Texas	Washington	

II. STATES WITH A PARTIALLY PRIVATE PROTOCOL (12 STATES)
These states were contacted by phone or email for at least some necessary information because that information was not available in the state's protocol.

Delaware	Indiana	Kansas
Louisiana	Maryland	Mississippi
Missouri	New Hampshire	Ohio
Tennessee	Utah	Wyoming

III. STATES WITH A PRIVATE PROTOCOL (6 STATES)
These states did not provide any of the requested information or they provided only a portion of the requested information.

Alabama	Kentucky
Nevada	Pennsylvania
South Carolina	Virginia

* All lethal injection protocols and communications are on file with the author at Fordham University School of Law. The sources for the protocols and communications can be found in Denno 2002.

Table 11
Last Meal and Execution Time Specified in the
Lethal Injection Protocols or Communications of 36 States

State	Time of the Last Meal	Time of the Execution
AZ	Does not specify.	Does not specify.
AR	Will be handled by the warden at the unit.	No information.
CA	At 6:00 p.m. the inmate is moved to the death watch cell and soon the reafter he/she is served his/her last meal.	Does not specify.
CO	Will be served at normal meal time.	No information.
CT	Normal meal time.	As soon after 2:01 a.m. as possible.
DE	No information.	No information.
FL	Does not specify.	Does not specify who or what schedules the execution but the protocol discusses executions being set for different times of day.
GA	Does not specify.	No information.
ID	No information.	No information.
IL	No information.	As determined by the Department of Corrections.
IN	The inmate is escorted to the holding cell at approximately 6:00 p.m. and the meal is served soon thereafter.	Shortly after midnight, the inmate is escorted from the holding cell to begin the execution.
KS	No information.	No information.
KY	No information.	No information.
LA	No information.	Between the hours of 6:00 p.m. and 11:59 p.m.
MD	No information.	No information.
MS	Does not specify.	The new law states by 6:00 p.m.
MO	No information.	No information.
MT	No information.	Anytime after midnight.
NV	The information is confidential.	The information is confidential.
NH	No information.	No information.
NJ	Not less than eight hours prior to the execution.	The Commissioner schedules the time.
NM	No information.	The protocol alludes to a 12:00 a.m. execution time.
NY	Does not specify.	No information.
NC	No information.	No information.
OH	Approximately six hours prior to the execution.	9:00 p.m.
OK	No information.	No information.
OR	6:00 p.m.	As soon after midnight as possible.
PA	Does not specify.	7:00 p.m.
SC	No information.	No information.
SD	The same as the regular feeding time.	The warden selects the exact time which must be between the hours of 12:01 a.m. and 6:00 a.m.
TN	No information.	At 1:00 a.m. the execution begins.
TX	Approximately 3:30–4:00 p.m.	At approximately 6:00 p.m.
UT	No information.	No information.
VA	The meal must be completed no later than four hours prior to the execution.	9:00 p.m.
WA	The same as the regular feeding time.	The superintendent says when to begin.
WY	No information.	No information.

* All lethal injection protocols and communications are on file with the author at Fordham University School of Law. The sources for the protocols and communications can be found in Denno 2002.

Table 12*
Information on Executioners and Execution Procedures Specified in the Lethal Injection Protocols or Communications of 36 States: 2001

State	Information on Executioners Including Number and Qualifications if Mentioned	Problem Prevention or Procedure	Involvement of Medical Personnel
AZ	Thirty-two to thirty-three staff members are required. Training is part of the process.	There is a dedicated phone line to stop the execution.	No information.
AR	Unpaid volunteers.	There is a dedicated phone line to stop the execution.	No information.
CA	Three-member staff unit.	A line is mentioned but it is not specified for what.	A physician is present to declare death. Two physicians serve as witnesses. A coroner pronounces death.
CO	An injection team comprised of two anonymous DOC staff and a strap-down team.	The warden verifies with the governor that it is ok to proceed with the execution.	*A physician shall be present.***
CT	Six primary, six alternates from the correctional staff. A warden designates the correctional executioner(s) who initiate the flow of lethal chemicals. The warden is responsible for screening, selecting, training and conducting drills with the execution team.	A line is mentioned. The warden makes a last minute check for any stays.	Executioners must be properly trained, and be able to properly insert an IV to the satisfaction of a licensed CT physician. A qualified physician is present to certify death.
DE	A voluntary staff executioner.	No information.	No information.
FL	An escort team secures the inmate. An execution team conducts IV procedure and begins the flow of lethal chemicals.	There is an open line to the governor's office. If death doesn't occur after the first administering of lethal chemicals, try a second time and continue until a flat line is indicated on the heart monitor.	A pharmacist prepares the lethal injection. A physician visits the condemned to explain the lethal injection procedure, stands behind the executioner while the injection is being administered, and certifies death. A physician assistant will also certify death. A nurse or medical technician is authorized to attend.
GA	An escort team of six correctional officers secures the inmate. Two members of the IV team are Emergency Medical Technicians.	The protocol describes what to do if a suitable vein cannot be found. If the condemned shows residual life signs after the staff members have	Two staff physicians to determine if death has occurred. One contract physician. A physician's assistant will administer treatment to witnesses

	Three staff volunteers insert the solutions in the IV ports. Security will attend as needed. A designated staff member prepares the lethal injection and delivers it to the chamber.	carried out the execution procedure, they are to repeat the procedure. A line is mentioned but it is not specified for what.	and staff if the need arises. A physician will perform the cut down procedure if necessary.
ID	The Idaho Maximum Security Institution personnel carry out the execution. The warden is the official executioner by statute.	There is a dedicate phone line to stop the execution.	The coroner will pronounce death.
IL	A trained person inserts the catheter.	There is a dedicate phone line to stop the execution.	No information.
IN	An execution team and IV team are mentioned.	There is mention of an execution where an angiocath was required because an inmate had extremely small veins. There is a dedicated phone line to stop the execution.	A physician is present to insert the angiocath. *A physician is present to pronounce death.***
KS	No information.		No information.
KY	No information.		No information. *A physician is present to declare death.***
LA	Escorting officers secure the inmate to the table. An IV technician prepares the inmate. The warden designates a competent person to administer the injection.	No information.	The coroner pronounces death. A physician is present.
MD	The Commissioner of Correction designates an execution commander who supervises the process. A technician inserts a needle into a vein on the inmate's arm. The warden specifies when the drugs are injected into the IV line.	There is a mention of stays but doesn't specify how the executioner is notified of a stay.	No information.
MS	There is a lethal injection team. The executioner advises the superintendent when they are ready to begin.	The superintendent checks for stays before the execution begins.	A physician or coroner pronounce the inmates' death. Two physicians are listed under the witness list.
MO	No information.	No information.	No information.

Table 12*, continued
Information on Executioners and Execution Procedures Specified in the Lethal Injection Protocols or Communications of 36 States: 2001

State	Information on Executioners Including Number and Qualifications if Mentioned	Problem Prevention or Procedure	Involvement of Medical Personnel
MT	The warden: selects an executioner who must be trained; may select alternates; and supervises the execution or designates someone to do so. The executioner need not be a physician, registered nurse, or licensed practical nurse.	There is a dedicated phone line to stop the execution.	The coroner pronounces death.
NV	The information is confidential.	The information is confidential.	The information is confidential. *A competent physician, the county coroner, and a psychiatrist are present.****
NH	No information.	No information.	No information. *A licensed physician pronounces death.****
NJ	The commissioner designates all execution personnel. The medical prep team consists of two physicians, one registered nurse, one certified IV therapist, and two execution technicians.	Provides instructions on what to do if a vein is not found and warns, "The medication must not be rapidly nor sporadically injected." If a stay is called, executioners are to stop the execution and life saving are techniques to be applied if necessary.	A physician is to revive an inmate or pronounce him/her dead. *Prior to the lethal injection, the person shall be sedated by a licensed physician, registered nurse, or other qualified personnel.****
NM	The warden chooses the execution team consisting of two persons and the tie-down team consisting of five persons who must go through practice procedures. There are numerous personnel for security purposes.	Warns that if sodium thiopental is not flushed from the line, flocculation can occur. It recommends using the other injection tube that has already been prepared in the other arm.	The physician pronounces the inmate's death. The medical examiner then takes jurisdiction of the body.
NY	There are eight security staff. The department shall identify two legally qualified individuals proficient in starting and administering the IV.	Warns "if sodium pentothal has not been flushed from the line, mixture with the pavulon may create flocculation." The commissioner checks for a stay before the execution is carried out.	A physician is to revive the inmate if a stay is called or pronounce him/her dead.

NC	Correctional officers.	No information.	The warden pronounces the inmate dead and a physician certifies the death.
OH	At least twelve people, designated by the warden of the Southern Ohio Correctional Facility (SOCF) prepare and test the equipment and carry out pre- and post-execution activities. The execution team will drill and rehearse. A technician, who is a DRC employee, will place the IV into the shunt on each arm.	There are arrangements made in case a stay is called.	Such number of physicians of the institution and medical personnel as the warden or acting warden thinks necessary. Designated personnel examine the body and pronounce death.
OK	Three executioners each administer a different drug.	No information.	No information. *The warden must invite the presence of a physician.***
OR	An assistant superintendent, superintendent, security, special security team leader. Medically-trained individuals are responsible for the insertion of catheters, they connect a heart monitor to the inmate to determine when death has occurred. An assistant superintendent will choose (two) six-person security teams, primary and back-up, and conduct drills with them.	There is a dedicated phone line to stop the execution.	A medical professional is summoned to certify death.
PA	Individuals technically competent by virtue of training or experience carry out the lethal injection procedure.	There is a dedicated phone line to stop the execution.	No information. *Death is pronounced by a coroner.***
SC	No information.	No information.	No information. *The executioner and a physician certify the pronouncement of death.***
SD	No information.	No information.	The prison physician and two other licensed physicians are required to conduct a post-mortem exam and report.

Table 12*, continued

Information on Executioners and Execution Procedures Specified in the Lethal Injection Protocols or Communications of 36 States: 2001

State	Information on Executioners Including Number and Qualifications if Mentioned	Problem Prevention or Procedure	Involvement of Medical Personnel
TN	Those mentioned are the executioner, the IV team and the extraction team.	A line is mentioned but it is not specified for what. If death does not occur after the first administration of the drugs a second administration should be given.	Medical doctor and associate are mentioned but their duties are not. Death must be confirmed by a physician.
TX	A medically-trained individual inserts an intravenous catheter and causes the saline to flow. The designee of the director shall inject the lethal solution.	No information.	A medically-trained individual inserts the catheter and causes the saline to flow.
UT	The person(s) administering the injection must be able to give an IV.	No information.	No information.
VA	The director gives the execution order.	No information.	No information. *A department employed physician or his assistant shall be present.****
WA	The superintendent conducts briefings and rehearsals. The Escort Team secures the inmate in the chamber. An injection team, following word from the superintendent, introduces lethal solutions. The team leader alerts the superintendent when all solutions have been administered.	The condemned's file is examined to prepare for special circumstances.	A physician pronounces death.
WY	No information.	No information.	Two physicians, one being the prison physician, are present.

* All lethal injection protocols and communications are on file with the author at Fordham University School of Law. The sources for the protocols and communications can be found in Denno 2002.

** This table relies on two sources: (1) all lethal injection protocols and (2) all state statutes specifying the involvement of medical personnel in executions. For twenty-seven states, lethal injection protocols overlapped substantively with the statute. *See* ARIZ. REV. STAT. ANN. § 13-705 (West 2000), ARK. CODE ANN. § 16-90-502 (Michie 1999), 2001 Cal. Legis. Serv. 129 (West), CONN. GEN. STAT. ANN. § 54-100 (West Supp. 2001), DEL. CODE ANN. tit. 11, § 4209 (2000), FLA. STAT. ANN. § 922.11 (West 2000), GA. CODE ANN. § 17-10-41 (2000), IDAHO CODE § 19-2716 (Michie 2000), 725 ILL. COMP. STAT. ANN. 5/119-5 (West 2001), IND. CODE ANN. § 35-38-6-1 (West 2001), KAN. STAT. ANN. § 22-4001 (2000), LA. REV. STAT. ANN. § 569 (West 2001), MD. CODE ANN., WITNESSES § 3-907 (2000), MISS. CODE ANN. § 99-19-53 (2000), MO. ANN. STAT. § 546.740 (West Supp. 2001), MONT. CODE ANN. § 46-19-103 (2000), N.M. STAT. ANN § 31-14-15 (Michie Supp. 2000), N.Y. [persons authorized to be present at execution] § 660 (2001), N.C. GEN. STAT. § 15-190 (2000), OHIO REV. CODE ANN. § 2949.25 (West 2001), Or. Laws. (OR. REV. STAT. § 137.463), S.D. CODIFIED LAWS § 34-25-18 (Michie 2001), TENN. CODE ANN. § 40-23-116 (Supp. 2000), TEX. CRIM. PROC. CODE ANN. § 43.14 (Vernon 1999), UTAH CODE ANN. § 77-19-11 (2001), WASH. REV. CODE ANN. § 10.95.185 (West 2001), WYO. STAT. ANN. § 7-13-908 (Michie 2001). For nine states, the statutes provided some additional information. *See* COLO. REV. STAT. § 16-11-404 (2000), KY. REV. STAT. ANN. § 431.220 (Michie 2000), 2001 Nev. Stat. 176.355, N.H. REV. STAT. ANN. § 630:5 (2000), N.J. STAT. ANN. § 2C:49-2 (West 2001), OKLA. STAT. ANN. tit. 22, § 1015 (West 2001), 61 PA. CONS. STAT. ANN. § 3004 (West 2000), 24 S.C. CODE ANN. REGS. 24-3-560 (2000), VA. CODE ANN. § 53.1-234 (Michie 2000).

*** Italics refer to information that was taken from state statutes rather than directly from the state protocols.

Table 13*

Numbers and Types of Witnesses Specified in the Lethal Injection
Protocols or Communications of 36 States

State	General Witnesses	Media Witnesses	Specification of What and When Media Can View
AZ	No information.	No information.	No information.
AR	Six to twelve people chosen by Director of the DOC.	No information.	No information.
CA	Up to fifty people may witness. Specified: warden, attorney general, twelve reputable citizens, two physicians, and, if requested, up to five of the inmate's family or friends, and two spiritual advisors.	Seventeen news media representatives, nine state selected witnesses, four staff escorts.	No information.
CO	A select group usually includes the victim's family, the prosecuting and defense attorneys, an official from the investigating law enforcement agency, and approved media representatives.	Approved media representatives.	Allow for viewing after the team has inserted the intravenous catheters through the injection and the pronouncement of death.
CT	The warden, a number of execution personnel deemed by the warden as necessary, and the following people may be present: the commissioner, a physician, a clergyman at the request of inmate, no more than three adults designated by the inmate, and other persons deemed appropriate by the commissioner.	Nine news media are permitted but may be decreased or increased for specified reasons of space and security.	Allow for viewing after the team has inserted the intravenous catheters through the injection but is closed while death is pronounced.
DE	Ten official witnesses who may include: arresting officers, federal officers, police chiefs or a designee, a representative from the Victims Rights Bureau, and criminal justice professionals.	May be invited depending on security issues and space constraints.	No information.
FL	The warden, the physician's assistant with the DOC, Secretary of the DOC.	No information.	No information.

GA	The warden, [two assistants or more as directed by the warden, two staff physicians; one contract physician as designated by Health Services; an IV Team with two Emergency Medical Team (EMT) members; six correctional officers to serve as a special escort team; three volunteers (staff members); one Chaplain; Security personnel as appropriate. Individuals who MAY BE PRESENT: five witnesses chosen by the condemned; the Commissioner may approve five witnesses and include officials with the Executive, Judicial or Legislative Branch of Government or private Citizens. One witness may be present representing the victim.	Six.	Allow for viewing after the team has inserted the intravenous catheters through the injection and the pronouncement of death.
ID	Does mention witnesses but does not specify who they are or how they are chosen.	No information.	No information.
IL	Does mention witnesses but does not specify who they are or how they are chosen.	No information.	No information.
IN	Mentions witnesses but only specifies two staff members in the room during the process; the offender is allowed up to ten individuals.	No information.	No information.
KS	No information.	No information.	No information.
KY	No information.	No information.	No information.
LA	Warden, coroner of West Feliciana Parish or deputy. A Priest, minister or religious advisor if requested by the inmate. Not less than five, or more than seven, other witnesses are required by law to be present. Victim relationship witnesses are authorized to attend the execution; such witnesses may be limited to two.	Of the number of reporters, between five and seven, three will be news media who agree to act as pool reporters.**	Allow for the entire viewing including the injection and the pronouncement of death.

Table 13*, continued
Numbers and Types of Witnesses Specified in the Lethal Injection Protocols or Communications of 36 States

State	General Witnesses	Media Witnesses	Specification of What and When Media Can View
MD	Must be a citizen of Maryland and at least eighteen years of age; they must also send a letter specifying why they want to witness.	No information.	No information.
MS	Sheriff or deputy of the county of the inmate's conviction; two physicians; up to two members of the clergy as requested by the offender; two members of the offender's family.	Up to eight credentialed members of the media.	Allow for viewing after the team has inserted the intravenous catheters through the injection and the pronouncement of death.
MO	Mentions witnesses but specifies only that the chaplain and psychologist shall be available to counsel witnesses as necessary following the execution.	No information.	No information.
MT	No more than twelve. The condemned may choose three; the family of the victim may choose three; state witnesses shall be selected by the Department Director to be part of the twelve.	News media allowed to choose three.	No information.
NV	Information is confidential.	Information is confidential.	Information is confidential.
NH	No information.	No information.	No information.
NJ	The Commissioner shall select six adult citizens and two alternates who have volunteered to witness the execution. Two clergy, at the request of the condemned, who are not related to the condemned, are permitted to attend. Anyone who is related by blood or marriage to the sentenced person or to the victim is not authorized to be present at the execution.	Eight media from four categories.	No information.

	Witnesses	Media	Curtain procedure
NM	The warden, physician, attorney general of state; at least twelve reputable citizens; two ministers of the gospel named by the condemned; a maximum of five inmate relatives or friends; peace officers chosen by the Warden. Any person currently under supervision Witnesses must be at least eighteen years old.	Those media requested by the Warden.	Allow for viewing after the team has inserted the intravenous catheters through the injection and the pronouncement of death.
NY	Up to fourteen Supreme Court Justice; inmate's attorney; D.A. & Sheriff of the county of conviction; two adult citizens; four friends or relatives chosen by the inmate.	Up to four.	Allow for viewing after the team has inserted the intravenous catheters through the injection but closed while the physician is called to pronounce death. The curtain is reopened for the official pronouncement of death.
NC	Sixteen maximum. This includes prison staff that could mean the warden, or designee. A surgeon or physician, four respectable citizens, two members of the crime victim's family, the district attorney and sheriff of the county of conviction and their choice of two witnesses each. The convicted felon can have counsel and any representatives of the felon, a minister or ministers. The district attorney may fill available seats with his or her designees.	Five who will act as pool reporters to brief other reporters. **	Allow for viewing after the team has inserted the intravenous catheters through the injection and the pronouncement of death.
OH	Three witnesses for the inmate; three witnesses representing the victim; one clergy or spiritual advisor.	Five, three of which are pool reporters.**	Allow for viewing after the team has inserted the intravenous catheters through the injection but closed while the physician is called to pronounce death. The curtain is reopened for the official pronouncement of death.
OK	The warden, a doctor, DA, trial judge, police chief, sheriff; two clergy; five inmate family members; victim family members who request to attend but the number allowed is up to the warden's discretion.	Twelve media representatives.	No information because a protocol was not provided.

Table 13*, *continued*
Numbers and Types of Witnesses Specified in the Lethal Injection
Protocols or Communications of 36 States

State	General Witnesses	Media Witnesses	Specification of What and When Media Can View
OR	One or more physicians; the attorney general; county sheriff and district attorney; one or more of the victim's relatives; no more than five inmate friends or relatives; no more than two religious representatives. Other people, including peace officers, may be invited at the discretion of the superintendent. No one under eighteen is permitted.	Five to act as pool for other media.**	Allow for viewing after the team has inserted the intravenous catheters through the injection and the pronouncement of death.
PA	No information because the protocol was not provided.	No information because a protocol was not provided.	No information because a protocol was not provided.
SC	Three members of the victim's family unless there is more than one victim, then the Corrections' director can limit to one per family; a minister of the gospel; inmate's counsel; chief law enforcement officer or designee; solicitor or assistant solicitor in the county where the offense occurred.	Three representatives: one print, one broadcast, and one from the dominant wire service.	No information because a protocol was not provided.
SD	The warden, attorney general, trial judge, state's attorney, sheriff, and up to ten additional citizens including one media representative. The prison physician and two other licensed physicians of the state. The defendant may choose up to two members of the clergy, and up to five relatives or friends.	At least one media representative from the ten additional citizens.	Allow for viewing after the team has inserted the intravenous catheters through the injection and the pronouncement of death.
TN	Staff authorized in the capital punishment complex are: commissioner or designee, warden, deputy warden, administrative assistant, death watch	Once the sentence has been carried out, the media will be so notified by the designated information officer.	Allow for viewing after the team has inserted the intravenous catheters through the injection but closed while the physician is called to pronounce

	supervisor and assigned officers, chaplain, medical doctor and associate, executioner, IV team, extraction team. The warden or commissioner must approve any exceptions to the above. Immediate family members of the victim are mentioned but the number is not specified.		death. The curtain is reopened for the official pronouncement of death.
TX	Up to five requested by the inmate and five for victim family members.	Five media representatives who must agree to act as pool reporters. **	Allow for viewing after the team has inserted the intravenous catheters through the injection and the pronouncement of death.
UT	The inmate chooses five; government witnesses will be identified; two officers visiting from another state reviewing the execution procedure may be present; two members of Attorney General's office; up to two prosecuting attorneys; two members of the investigative law enforcement agency; two individual with an expertise of the history of execution policy; up to four members of the victim's family; department employees such as the warden may participate as well.	Was nine but now up to the Executive Director to decide the number.	No information because a protocol was not provided.
VA	Those individuals allowed to participate: a member of the clergy; the victim's family; media witnesses; and citizen witnesses.	Are allowed to participate, but the number is not specified.	Allow for the entire viewing including the injection and the pronouncement of death.
WA	One representative from the victim's family; one representative from the inmate's family; the superior court judge who signed the death warrant; the inmate's attorney; a county prosecuting attorney.	A maximum of twelve.	No information.

Table 13*, *continued*
Numbers and Types of Witnesses Specified in the Lethal Injection Protocols or Communications of 36 States

State	General Witnesses	Media Witnesses	Specification of What and When Media Can View
WY	The Director of the DOC and anyone deemed necessary to assist him or her; two physicians, which include the prison physician; the inmate's spiritual advisor; the penitentiary chaplain if not the same as one chosen by the inmate; the sheriff of the county where the inmate was convicted; no more than ten relatives or friends requested by the prisoner.	No information.	No information.

* All lethal injection protocols and communications are on file with the author at Fordham University School of Law. The sources for the protocols and communications can be found in Denno 2002.

** Five states mention a limited number of media witnesses who must agree to act as pool reporters who will report to other media following the witnessing of the execution: Louisiana, North Carolina, Ohio, Oregon, and Texas.

About the Authors

James R. Acker is a Professor at the School of Criminal Justice at the University at Albany. He earned his J.D. at Duke Law School and his Ph.D. (in criminal justice) at the University at Albany. He scholarship in the area of capital punishment has focused on variations in death-penalty legislation and the application of social science research to death-penalty issues. He is co-director, with Charles Lanier, of the Capital Punishment Research Initiative at the University at Albany.

Michael E. Antonio is Associate Research Scientist in the College of Criminal Justice at Northeastern University and the project manager for the Capital Jury Project. He is a Ph.D. candidate in the Law, Policy & Society Program at Northeastern University. Using the data gathered from the Capital Jury Project, his dissertation examines how nonverbal communication inside the courtroom influences jurors' decision-making and trial outcomes.

William C. Bailey is Professor of Sociology and Associate Dean of the Graduate School, Cleveland State University. He received the doctoral degree in Sociology from Washington State University in 1971. His major research interests include crime and deterrence, capital punishment, and the relationship between inequality and various aspects of violent crime.

David C. Baldus is Joseph B. Tye Professor of Law at the University of Iowa College of Law. He received his B.A. from Dartmouth College in 1957, and his L.L.B. from Yale Law School in 1964. He is co-author of numerous articles on the death penalty, and co-author of *Equal Justice and the Death Penalty* (Northeastern University Press, 1990).

Hugo Adam Bedau received his B.A. from the University of Redlands, an A.M. from Boston University and from Harvard, and his Ph.D. from Harvard. He was a Liberal Arts Fellow at Harvard Law School in 1961–62. Prior to joining the Tufts faculty, where he is Austin Fletcher Professor of Philosophy Emeritus, he taught at Dartmouth, Princeton, and Reed. He is the author of *The Courts, the Constitution, and Capital Punishment* (1977) and *Death is Different* (1987), the co-author of *In Spite of Innocence* (1992), and the editor of *The Death Penalty in America* (1964, 1982, 1997), and the co-editor of *Capital Punishment in the United States* (1976). He has frequently testified before state and federal legislative committees on death penalty issues, and has been chairman of the board of directors of the National Coalition to Abolish the Death Penalty.

Robert Blecker, a Professor of Criminal Law at New York Law School, received his B.A. from Tufts University where he rebelled against the abolitionism of Hugo Bedau and was the first to design his own interdisciplinary plan of study. Harvard Law School awarded his thesis "To Root in a Flowing Stream: Game and Sport as a Prototype for Social Solution" its Oberman Prize for the best of the 1974 graduating class (sponsored by Laurence Tribe). After a stint as a Special Assistant Attorney General, prosecuting official corruption in New York City's criminal justice system, he was a Harvard University Fellow in Law and Humanities. Professor at New York Law School since 1975, his courses have included: Criminals and Our Urge to Punish Them; Constitutional History; and the Death Penalty. His antifederalist monologue, 'Vote NO!' premiered in Washington, D.C. at the Kennedy Center, toured in sixteen states and was featured on National Public Radio's "All Things Considered." For 13 years (1986 to 1999) he spent thousands of hours inside Lorton prison system probing the lives of street criminals, mostly convicted murderers. His published essays drawing on that experience include "Haven or Hell?" (42 Stanford LR 1990) and "Among Killers, Searching for the Worst of the Worst" Washington Post (12/3/2000). Next year, Basic Books will publish his book, *Who Deserves to Die*.

Robert M. Bohm is a Professor of Criminal Justice and Legal Studies at the University of Central Florida. He received his Ph.D. in Criminology from Florida State University in 1980. He is the author of *Deathquest: An Introduction to the Theory and Practice of Capital Punishment in the United States*, 2nd edition (Anderson 2003) and the editor of *The Death Penalty in America: Current Research* (Anderson 1991). He has also published nearly two dozen book chapters and journal articles on capital punishment. He served as President of the Academy of Criminal Justice Sciences in 1992–93. He was selected the Outstanding Educator of the Year by the Southern Criminal Justice Association in1989; a Fellow of the Academy of Criminal Justice Sciences in 1999; and was the recipient of the Founder's Award of the Academy of Criminal Justice Sciences in 2001.

William J. Bowers received his Ph.D. in 1966 from Columbia University, and his B.A. in 1957 from Washington and Lee University. He is the Principal Research Scientist in the College of Criminal Justice at Northeastern University. Dr. Bowers has authored two books and numerous articles on capital punishment. He is principal investigator of the Capital Jury Project, a national study underway in fourteen states. He received the August Vollmer award (2000) from the American Society of Criminology for his research on the death penalty.

Stephen B. Bright is the Director of the Southern Center for Human Rights, a public interest legal project based in Atlanta which provides representation to persons facing the death penalty and to prisoners challenging unconstitutional conditions in prisons and jails throughout the South. He has taught courses on capital punishment, criminal procedure, international human rights law, and prisoners' rights at the law schools at Yale, Harvard, Georgetown, Northeastern, Florida State, and St. Mary's universities. He serves on the board of the National Association of Criminal Defense Lawyers. His articles include "Counsel for the Poor: The Death Sentence Not for the Worst Crime, but for the Worst Lawyer," in the *Yale Law Journal*, an article on racial discrimination in the infliction of the death penalty published in the *Santa Clara Law Review*, and articles on the political pressures on elected judges that appeared in the *Boston University Law Review* and the *New York University Law Review*.

Deborah W. Denno is Professor of Law at Fordham University School of Law. She earned her B.A. at the University of Virginia, her M.A. at the University of Toronto, and her Ph.D. and J.D. degrees at the University of Pennsylvania. Her published scholarship on the death penalty includes: "When Legislatures Delegate Death: The Troubling Paradox Behind State Uses of Electrocution and Lethal Injection and What It Says About Us," 63 *Ohio State Law Journal* 63 (2002); "Capital Punishment and the Human Rights Norm," 9 *Criminal Law Forum* 171 (1999) (Review Essay); "Getting to Death: Are Executions Constitutional?" 82 *Iowa Law Review* 319 (1997); "Testing Penry and its Progeny," 22 *American Journal of Criminal Law* 1 (1994); "Is Electrocution an Unconstitutional Method of Execution? The Engineering of Death Over the Century," 35 *William and Mary Law Review* 551 (1994); "'Death is Different' and Other Twists of Fate" (Review Essay), 83 *Journal of Criminal Law and Criminology* 437 (1992); and "The Reimposition of Capital Punishment in New Jersey: The Role of Prosecutorial Discretion," 41 *Rutgers Law Review* 27 (1988) (with L. Bienen, N. Weiner, P. Allison & D. Mills). She served as a Consultant on the New Jersey Death Penalty Project for the Office of the Public Defender, Trenton, New Jersey, and has provided expert testimony on executions involving lethal injection and electrocution.

Charles Patrick Ewing is Professor of Law and Adjunct Professor of Psychology at the State University of New York at Buffalo, where he teaches Criminal Law; Psychology, Psychiatry and Criminal Law; Evidence; and Death Penalty Law and Practice. A forensic psychologist and attorney, he received his Ph.D. from Cornell University and his J.D. from Harvard Law School.

Benjamin Fleury-Steiner is Assistant Professor in the Department of Sociology and Criminal Justice at the University of Delaware. His research interests broadly defined involve the complex relationship between social inequality, law, and social control. Currently, he is a Co-Principal Investigator on the National Science Foundation funded study "The Role of Race in Punishing Criminal Violence," a multi-state study of juror decision-making in capital cases. Both an article, "Narratives of the Death Sentence—the Tale of Racial Inferiority and African-American Resistance: Towards a Theory of Legal Narrativity" (*Law & Society Review*), and a book, *Jurors' Stories of Death: How America's Death Penalty Invests in Inequality* (University of Michigan Press), are forthcoming in 2003. His previous research on the death penalty has appeared in various journals, including the *Law & Society Review*, *Cornell Law Review*, *Criminal Justice Policy Review*, *Pennsylvania Journal of Constitutional Law*, and the *Texas Law Review*.

Eric M. Freedman is a Professor of Law at Hofstra Law School, where his courses include Death Penalty, Constitutional Law, and Legal History. A graduate of Yale College and Yale Law School, with a Master's Degree in History from Victoria University of Wellington, New Zealand, Professor Freedman is an elected member of the American Law Institute and the author of *Habeas Corpus: Rethinking the Great Writ of Liberty* (NYU Press 2001). In addition to writing frequently on capital punishment for scholarly and general publications, Professor Freedman is active as a capital defense litigator and consultant.

Craig Haney received his Ph.D. (in Psychology) and J.D. degrees from Stanford University and is currently Professor of Psychology at the University of California, Santa Cruz. He has conducted research on and written widely about many aspects of the death penalty, including death qualification, attitudes toward capital punishment, capital jury decision-making, and the backgrounds and social histories of capital defendants.

Robert Johnson is a Professor of Justice, Law and Society at The American University in Washington, D.C. He holds a B.A. in Psychology from Fairfield University, and an M.A. and Ph.D. in Criminal Justice from the University at Albany. Dr. Johnson's areas of expertise include the prison and other institutions of confinement, the death penalty, and institutional violence. He has testified or provided expert affidavits before state and federal courts, the U.S. Congress, and the European Commission of Human Rights. Professor Johnson's scholarly works include *Culture and Crisis in Confinement* (1976), *Condemned to Die: Life Under Sentence of Death* (1981; reissued 1989), The Pains of Imprisonment (1982; reissued 1988) (with Hans Toch), *Hard Time: Understanding and Reforming the Prison* (1987; 3rd ed. 2002), *Death Work: A Study of the Modern Execution Process* (1990; 2d ed. 1998), and *Crime and Punishment: Inside Views* (Roxbury, 2000) (with Hans Toch), as well as over 30 articles published in journals and anthologies. Dr. Johnson has received a number of awards for his teaching and scholarship. He is the recipient of The American University Award for Outstanding Scholarship, as well as The American University Award for Scholarship and Teaching. His book, *Death Work*, received the Academy of Criminal Justice Science's Outstanding Book Award.

Daniel T. Kobil is a Professor of Law at Capital University Law School in Columbus, Ohio, where he has taught since 1987. Professor Kobil received his J.D. from the University of Toledo College of Law in 1983, and after graduation clerked for Albert J. Engel, a judge on the United States Court of Appeals for the Sixth Circuit. Professor Kobil has researched and published extensively on the subject of clemency, particularly as it relates to the death penalty. He has testified before Congress regarding the clemency power. Some of his articles, which have been cited by various courts including the United States Supreme Court, are "The Quality of Mercy Strained: Wresting the Pardoning Power from the King," 69 *University of Texas Law Review* 569 (1991), and "Due Process in Death Penalty Commutations: Life, Liberty, and the Pursuit of Clemency," 27 *University of Richmond Law Review* 201 (1993). Professor Kobil has also done pro bono legal work in capital cases on behalf of the ACLU and death sentenced individuals.

Charles S. Lanier is an Assistant Editor of the *Sourcebook of Criminal Justice Statistics*, Hindelang Criminal Justice Research Center, and ABD at the School of Criminal Justice, University at Albany. He is co-developer, co-director (with James R. Acker) of the Capital Punishment Research Initiative (CPRI), at the School of Criminal Justice, University at Albany. He has coauthored a series of *Criminal Law Bulletin* articles (with James R. Acker), analyzing death-penalty statutes in the United States. He also has written numerous articles on incarcerated fathers, including most recently " 'Who's doing the time here, me or my children?': Addressing the Issues Implicated by Mounting Numbers of Fathers in Prison," in *Convict Criminology* (2002). His research interests include capital punishment, capital mitigation, corrections, and serial murder. In 1996, he was awarded the Frank J. Remington Prize for Interdisciplinary Legal Study. Since 1997, he has conducted mitigation investigations in capital cases with CVA Consulting Services, Inc., at both the trial and post-conviction level, in New York and in Georgia.

James W. Marquart, Ph.D. (Texas A&M University, 1983), is a tenured Full Professor of Criminal Justice at Sam Houston State University. He has long-term research and teaching interests in prison organizations, capital punishment, criminal justice policy and research methods. He has also published a number of articles on social control and change in prison settings. His books include *The Rope, The Chair, and The Needle: Patterns of Capital Punishment in Texas, 1923–1990* (1994), *Correctional Contexts: Contemporary and Classic Readings* (1996), *Issues in Corrections* (1998), and *An Appeal to Justice: Litigated Reform of Texas Prisons* (1989). The latter, with Ben M. Crouch, received the Outstanding Book Award from the Academy of Criminal Justice for 1991. He has also published in such journals as *Criminology, Deviant Behavior, Law and Society Review, Crime and Delinquency, Child Abuse and Neglect, Ageing and Society, The Prison Journal*, and *Justice Quarterly*. His current research involves investigating youth advocacy and alcohol policy, and inappropriate staff-inmate relationships in prison settings.

Scott McClelland is a Future Faculty Fellow at Indiana University, where he earned a J.D. in 1999. He is currently working on completing a Ph.D. in criminal justice, also at Indiana University. His major research interests include capital punishment, court systems, and the convergence of social science and legal jurisprudence.

Michael Mello received his J.D. from the University of Virginia in 1982. In 1982–83 he was "death clerk" to Judge Robert S. Vance, U.S. Court of Appeals for the Eleventh Circuit. Between 1983–1987 he was a Florida capital postconviction public defender. Following a brief stint as an associate with Wilmer, Cutler & Pickering in Washington, D.C., he joined the faculty at Vermont Law School in 1988, where he was tenured in 1990 and remains today. Mello has published a number of scholarly articles on the death penalty, and his several death-penalty related books include *Against the Death Penalty: The Relentless Dissents of Justices Brennan and Marshall* (Northeastern University Press 1996); *Dead Wrong: A Death Row Lawyer Speaks Out Against Capital Punishment* (University of Wisconsin Press 1999); *The United States of America Versus Theodore John Kaczynski: Ethics, Power and the Invention of the Unabomber* (Context Publications 1999); and *The Wrong Man: A True Story of Innocence on Death Row* (University of Minnesota Press 2002).

Paul J. Perkins received his B.A. degree from the University of Oregon in 1994 and his J.D. in 1998 from Vermont Law School. He is a practicing attorney in Vermont where he represents defendants in state and federal criminal cases, and also represents individuals and businesses in a variety of civil matters. He resides with his family in South Royalton, Vermont.

Ruth D. Peterson is Professor of Sociology and Director of the Criminal Justice Research Center at Ohio State University. She received the doctoral degree in Sociology from the University of Wisconsin in 1983. Her major research interests include the interrelationships among social disadvantage, race, and crime; legal decision-making and sentencing; and crime and deterrence.

Michael L. Radelet is Professor and Associate Chair, Department of Sociology, University of Colorado. He received his Ph.D. from Purdue University and completed three years of postdoctoral work at the University of Wisconsin and the University of New Hampshire. Included among his death penalty publications are *In Spite of Innocence* (1992) (with Hugo Adam Bedau and Constance Putnam) and *Executing the Mentally Ill* (1993) (with Kent Miller).

Marla Sandys is Associate Professor of Criminal Justice at Indiana University. She received a Ph.D. in social psychology from the University of Kentucky in 1990. Her recent publications have drawn on her work with the Capital Jury Project, focusing on early decision-making, death qualification, and the role of race in the deliberation process of capital cases.

Jon Sorensen (Ph.D. in Criminal Justice, Sam Houston State University, 1990) is an Assistant Professor of Criminal Justice at Fitchburg State College. His research on the death penalty has empirically examined proportionality, racial discrimination, and future dangerousness. He is a co-author of *The Rope, the Chair, and the Needle: Capital Punishment in Texas, 1923–1990* (University of Texas Press, 1994), with James Marquart and Sheldon Ekland-Olson. He is currently using data from Texas to assess the major arguments related to capital punishment.

Carol S. Steiker is Professor of Law at Harvard Law School, where she teaches courses on Criminal Law, Criminal Procedure, and Capital Punishment. A graduate of Harvard-Radcliffe Colleges and Harvard Law School, she served as a law clerk to Judge J. Skelly Wright of the D.C. Circuit Court of Appeals and to Justice Thurgood Marshall of the United States Supreme Court. After working as a staff attorney for the D.C. Public Defender Service, she joined the Harvard Law School faculty in 1992. Professor Steiker is the author of numerous articles about criminal law and procedure in general and the death penalty in particular, including "Capital Punishment and American Exceptionalism," 81 *Oregon Law Review* 97 (2002); "Should Abolitionists Support Legislative 'Reform' of the Death Penalty?" 63 *Ohio State Law Journal* 417 (2002) (with Jordan Steiker); and "Sober Second Thoughts: Reflections on Two Decades of Constitutional Regulation of Capital Punishment," 109 *Harvard Law Review* 355 (1995) (with Jordan Steiker). A frequent consultant and expert witness on issues relating to criminal justice, Professor Steiker testified before the Massachusetts state legislature in May, 1997, regarding former Governor Weld's last attempt to reinstate the death penalty.

Jordan M. Steiker is Cooper K. Ragan Regents Professor of Law at the University of Texas School of Law. He graduated magna cum laude from Harvard Law School in 1988. He subsequently clerked for Honorable Louis Pollak, U.S. District Court (Eastern District of Pennsylvania) and Justice Thurgood Marshall of the United States Supreme Court. He has taught constitutional law, criminal law, and death penalty law at the University of Texas since 1990, and works with the law school's Capital Punishment Clinic. He has written extensively on federal habeas corpus and the death penalty. Some of his recent publications include: "Federal Habeas and the Death Penalty: Reflections on the New Habeas Provisions of the Anti-Terrorism and Effective Death Penalty Act," in *Essential Readings on Political Terrorism* (H. Kushner, ed.) (Gordian Knot Press 2002); "Habeas Exceptionalism," 78 *Texas Law Review* 1703 (2000); and "Restructuring Post-Conviction Review of Federal Constitutional Claims Raised by State Prisoners: Confronting the New Face of Excessive Proceduralism," 1998 *Chicago Legal Forum* 315. Professor Steiker has worked with state legislative committees addressing death penalty issues in Texas, including state habeas reform and the availability of the death penalty for juveniles and persons with mental retardation. In addition, Professor Steiker has worked on numerous death penalty cases (postconviction) in conjunction with lawyers from the former Texas Resource Center.

Victor L. Streib is a Professor of Law at Ohio Northern University and an attorney specializing in murder and the death penalty. As a scholar, his published books include *Death Penalty in a Nutshell* (West 2002), *Capital Punishment Anthology* (Anderson 1993), and *Death Penalty for Juveniles* (Indiana University Press 1987). His recent law review articles include: "Executing Juvenile Offenders," 14 *Stanford Law & Policy Review* ____ (2003, forthcoming); "Adolescence, Mental Retardation, and the Death Penalty," 33 *New Mexico Law Review* ____ (2003, forthcoming); and "Gendering the Death Penalty," 63 *Ohio State Law Journal* 433 (2002). In the practice of law, he has served as appellate counsel in such death penalty cases as *Thompson v. Oklahoma*, 487 U.S. 815 (1988). His current work focuses primarily on the law concerning kids who kill.

Ernest van den Haag passed away in 2002. He served as the John M. Olin Professor of Jurisprudence and Public Policy at Fordham Law School, taught political philosophy at New York University, taught at New York Law School, and lectured at the New School for Social Research. He was the author or co-author of 13 books and numerous scholarly articles. He was a Guggenheim Fellow, a Senior Fellow of the National Endowment for the Humanities, a member of the Council of Foreign Relations, a member of the Mont Pelerin Society, and served as President of the Philadelphia Society, among other accomplishments and activities.

Margaret Vandiver is a Professor in the Department of Criminology and Criminal Justice at the University of Memphis. She holds M.A. and Ph.D. degrees in Criminology from Florida State University. Dr. Vandiver has worked extensively with death row inmates and their families, and has written about the effect of executions on the families of defendants and victims. Her main research interest is state violence, ranging from the use of the death penalty in America to contemporary instances of genocide.

Richard J. Wilson is Professor of Law, Director of the Clinical Program, and founding director of the International Human Rights Law Clinic at American University's Washington College of Law, in Washington, D.C, where he has taught since 1989. He teaches in the law school's summer Human Rights Academy and in the Oxford International Human Rights Law Program. He was the director of the law school's summer study program in Chile in 1995 and 1996. He has been a Visiting Lecturer in law at Daito Bunka University in Tokyo, Japan, and at the Catholic University in Lima, Peru. He was a Fulbright Scholar in the Republic of Colombia in 1987, and served as Legal Advisor to the Consulate of the Republic of Colombia in Washington during 1998. He is a co-author of textbooks on international human rights law and practice and on international criminal law and procedure. His scholarly interests include the globalization of public interest law, the death penalty and international law, the role of the defense in international war crimes trials, and clinical legal education in developing or transitional countries. He has lived or consulted in several Latin American countries and has lectured or consulted in the United States, Eastern and Western Europe, and Asia. Professor Wilson has presented three cases at the Inter-American Court of Human Rights in San Jose, Costa Rica and authored the friend-of-court brief for the European Union in the United States Supreme Court arguing that international law prohibits capital punishment for persons with mental retardation. Professor Wilson taught at CUNY Law School in New York City from 1985–1989. He was a Peace Corps volunteer in the Republic of Panama from 1966–1968, and a 1972 graduate of the University of Illinois College of Law. He began his legal career as a public defender in Illinois, and was director of the Defender Division at the National Legal Aid and Defender Association in Washington from 1980–85.

George Woodworth is Professor of Statistics and Actuarial Science, and Professor of Preventive Medicine at the University of Iowa. He received his B.A. in Mathematics from Carleton College (Minnesota) in 1962, and his Ph.D. in Statistics from the University of Minnesota in 1966. He is co-author of numerous articles on the death penalty, and of *Equal Justice and the Death Penalty* (Northeastern University Press, 1990).

Index

Note: Page numbers with *t* indicate tables; *n* indicates notes.